Another first in P/OM
from Allyn & Bacon...
The Annotated Instructor's Edition

PRODUCTION AND OPERATIONS MANAGEMENT, Second Edition

By Howard J. Weiss and Mark E. Gershon,
both of Temple University

Give your students a true
understanding of the problems
Operations Managers face and
how they solve those problems.

Thoroughly updated to reflect an increased emphasis on

☐ **Quality**

◩ **World Class Operations**

■ **The Just In Time Philosophy**

◩ **Computer Integrated Applications**

The ideal text to help your students understand the managerial applications of POM.

The previous edition of this outstanding text has won praise for its treatment of production and operations management from a managerial viewpoint, for its easy-to-understand presentation of the discipline, and for its appropriateness for non-P/OM majors. In this new edition, the authors made improvements in content and features to better serve the needs of both professors and students.

The text offers these important features:

- Simpler models that help student understanding

- A descriptive writing style with an emphasis on management applications of P/OM

- **NEW** — Accompanying, integrated COMAP and Plant Tour Videos, for more effective, real-world illustrations

- **NEW** — Expanded coverage of corporate strategy as an integral part of operations

- **NEW** — A full chapter on World Class Operations (Ch.2)

- **NEW** — Expanded coverage of QUALITY, including a separate chapter on Total Quality Management (Ch. 16) that addresses both behavioral issues and statistical quality control methods, plus a separate chapter on Quality Control (Ch. 17).

- **NEW** — The most extensive and integrated use of the computer available — found throughout the text and problems.

- **NEW** — An outside accuracy check conducted on all problems and solutions in addition to careful checking by the authors themselves.

- A supplements package that provides the most complete teaching support found anywhere.

- **NEW** — An Annotated Instructor's Edition

791

CURRENT TRENDS TOWARD QUALITY

In many production plants, an adversarial relationship develops between production managers and quality managers. The production manager is judged (to some extent) by the quantity of goods produced. If quality standards slip, it is up to the quality manager to stop production and take corrective action or to have poor products reworked or scrapped. A similar relationship can develop between the production worker and the inspector. Good management practice (in terms of the organizational behavior or personnel management) will prevent these adversarial relationships from developing. Furthermore, not only can the development of these relationships be prevented, but these individuals can be convinced that mutual cooperation will help both production and quality and that these functions are not as distinct as they may seem on the company's organizational charts.

CURRENT TRENDS TOWARD QUALITY

As emphasized in Chapters 2 and 16, a great deal has been written in recent years about the higher quality of Japanese goods. Although the Japanese have set the trend in using modern approaches to quality control, in many cases, the approaches used are not Japanese in origin. U.S. management claims to use the same approaches. If there is a difference between the approaches of Japanese and U.S. managements toward quality, it is one of emphasis. U.S. managers talk about quality, while the Japanese really do something about it every day. We now briefly describe three aspects of quality management that are used by Japanese manufacturers.

japanese attitude

EVALUATION OF QUALITY PLANS: THE QUALITY AUDIT

For higher-level managers, there is little time to be concerned with the details of product design, process control, or inspection plans and procedures. Yet upper management needs to be able to evaluate the performance of the company with respect to quality, just as it needs to have an established set of quality control procedures, outlined in a every firm must have an established set of quality control procedures, outlined in a formal quality control plan. This plan should outline the policies and objectives related to quality, in addition to the detailed procedures.

the quality plan

The quality plan must detail the progression from raw material to final product, specifying the procedures employed at each step that ensure that the product is of high quality. It also must include a system of reviews to ensure that the plan truly is aimed at achieving the company's quality objectives. Finally, it must prescribe a system of audits to ensure that the plan is being followed in Japan in the early 1960s; it is now

The **quality audit** was first implemented in Japan in the early 1960s; it is now used extensively in the United States as well. However, in Japan, the audit done has a broader scope than in the United States, where the business implications of the quality function often are excluded. An excellent guide to developing quality plans and quality audits can be found in *Quality and Reliability Assurance Handbook H50*, under the title, "Evaluation of a Contractor's Quality Program." This guide should be used with MIL-STD-9858A, *Quality Program Requirements*. Both guides are available from the U.S. Government Publications and Printing Office.

Wherever possible, the authors explain through logic and intuition rather than a mathematical formula.

Pedagogy that helps you because it helps your students.

APPLICATIONS OF P/OM

The Transportation Problem at Avis

Have you ever wondered how a car rental agency such as Avis can allow a customer to pick up a car in one city and drop it off in another? How do car (and truck) rental agencies maintain the proper number of cars in each location if the car that you picked up in, say, Orlando winds up in Boston? Doesn't that make Orlando short one car and stick Boston with an extra one? Car and truck rental agencies are able to solve the problems caused by one-way renting by using the transportation model.

Source: For All Practical Purposes (New York: W. H. Freeman, 1988).

COMPUTER CASE STUDY 17.1: GREEN RIVER CHEMICAL COMPANY

Green River Chemical Company has had complaints from its customers regarding the sulfate content of its product. Every customer allows some sulfate content, but theoretically there should be none. The usual customer specification is 90 parts per million (PPM) sulfate.

The quality control department at Green River feels that there is no problem with sulfate content, which has been averaging just over 50 PPM. The production department estimates that a substantial investment would be required to lower the amount of this contaminant in the product. These two departments, after consulting with the marketing department and customers, suggest that a control chart be set up to monitor sulfate content. Five samples will be tested per day and plotted as one point on the chart.

Use the data in Table 17.8 to set up the control limits. Then, after the limits are in place for this process, use Table 17.9 to determine whether or not the process remains in control for the week of April 6–10.

TABLE 17.8 Original Green River Chemical Company data

Date	Sample 1	2	3	4	5	$\bar{X}$	R
March 2	57	54	62	45	36	50.8	26
3	56	54	47	42	62	52.2	20
4	40	70	58	45	44	51.4	30
5	52	58	40	52	46	49.6	18
6	57	42	52	58	59	53.6	17
9	62	49	42	33	55	48.2	29
10	40	39	49	59	48	47.0	20
11	64	50	42	57	50	52.6	22
12	58	53	52	48	50	52.2	10
13	60	50	41	41	50	48.4	19
16	52	47	48	58	40	49.0	18
17	55	40	56	49	45	49.0	16
18	47	48	49	48	48	48.6	3
19	50	50	49	51	51	50.2	2
20	51	50	51	51	62	53.0	12
23	51	49	50	50	50	50.0	2
24	45	47	70	46	36	48.8	34
25	50	35	48	39	47	43.8	15
26	55	70	50	30	51	51.2	40
27	49	38	64	36	47	46.8	28
30	59	62	40	54	64	55.8	24
31	36	33	49	48	56	44.4	23
1	44	67	53	43	40	50.6	27
2	70	52	46	47	44	46.6	8
3	45	50	47	41		50.6	29

The textbook retains all the feature innovations that made the first edition so popular...

Chapter Objectives • Chapter Summaries • Key Terms • Margin Notes • Solved Problems • End-of-Chapter Questions and Problems • Demonstrations using AB:POM Software

...and provides these new features that make the Second Edition even better!

Unique End-of-Chapter Computer Cases — Large size problems provide a real-world type sensitivity analysis. These cases can be found at the end of Chapters 3, 4, 5, 6, 7, 8, 9, 11, 12, 13, 14, 15, and 17, and can be used with any software program.

"Applications of P/OM" boxes — many are related to segments of the "FOR ALL PRACTICAL PURPOSES" video and provide real-world examples to illustrate the importance of P/OM.

Examples include: Modeling at Bell Labs • Capacity Disruptions at American Airlines • The Transportation Problem at Avis • Linear Programming at New England Apple Products • Quality Control at Frito-Lay

Shows your students not only "how" but "when" and "why."

While most texts only tell students "how" to use a particular technique, Weiss and Gershon also point out "when and why." One or more detailed examples follow each technique to illustrate its application. This intuitive confidence-building approach to techniques is one that your students are sure to appreciate.

The Annotated Instructor's Edition — Your Silent Partner.

Pulling together course materials has never been so easy and complete.

PRODUCTION AND OPERATIONS MANAGEMENT, Second Edition is the first P/OM text to offer this unique Annotated Instructor's Edition (AIE). Helping you plan for each class, this truly integrated resource combines the Instructor's Section up front with an annotated text in a single volume. The AIE provides instructors with easy access to answers, solutions, and teaching notes while also serving as a "road map" for using the entire supplements package. And, for additional quality assurance, Allyn & Bacon contracted an outside accuracy check for all problems and solutions so you can be sure that your Annotated Instructor's Edition is completely accurate.

Annotations and the Instructor's Section appear only in the AIE. They do not appear in the student text.

---

714   CHAPTER 15   OPERATIONS SCHEDULING

at different times, the usual goal is to find the schedule that finishes the soonest (minimize the makespan). Consider the following example.

minimize the makespan

Teaching Suggestion 15.5: Order Assumption of Two-Machine Scheduling. See the Instructor's Section for details.

Example 15.4   Three jobs are to be processed on two machines. Each job must be performed first on machine 1 and then on machine 2. The processing times are given in the following table.

Job	Processing Time (in hours)	
	Machine 1	Machine 2
A	4	7
B	7	5
C	6	2

Transparency Master 15.6: Two-Machine Scheduling.

Which schedule finishes sooner: ABC or CBA?
Again, the easiest way to examine the schedules is with a Gantt chart. For this ... each schedule, ... basis. As the ... schedule CBA ■

---

120   CHAPTER 3   CAPACITY PLANNING

5. Graphics Design, Inc. (GDI) makes computer graphics for seminar presentations. Each employee and computer combination produces 2 graphs per week. The company estimates a demand of 500 graphs for the coming year. If employees get 4 weeks annual vacation, and 5 percent of the drawings need to be redone due to customer dissatisfaction, how many new employees should be hired (with 1 machine purchased for each new employee)?

5.48 employees

6. Glenside Word processing (GWP) is a one-woman typing center, owned and operated by Alice Glenside. Alice has a word processor with a printer attached to it. Alice can type at a rate of 120 words per minute, and the printer can operate at 120 characters per second. There are, on average, 5 characters per word.

(a) If the word-processing software allows for simultaneous typing and printing, what is the hourly capacity of GWP?

7,200 words/hour

(b) If the word-processing software does not allow for simultaneous typing and printing, what is GWP's hourly capacity? Assume that the total work for printing is equal to the total work for typing.

6,646 words/hour

7. Kleen Karpet cleaned rugs in 57 houses in September. During that month, Kleen Karpet utilized the following resources.

Labor:	480 hours at $12/hour
Secretary:	80 hours at $5/hour
Rental machine:	20 days at $50/day

What is the productivity measure of Kleen Karpet?

.00796 houses/dollar

8. Suppose that Kleen Karpet cleans 65 rugs in October utilizing the following resources.

Labor:	520 hours at $13/hour
Secretary:	100 hours at $5/hour
Rental machine:	20 days at $50/day

(a) What is the productivity measure?

(b) What is the change in productivity from September (Problem 7)?

(c) What is the difficulty with using this measure?

**.00787 houses/dollar
– 1.13 percent
Lost productivity is due to rise in labor costs.**

9. Chips Away produces microcomputers. The company has annual fixed costs of $275,000. Each computer costs $900 to manufacture and is sold to retailers at an average price of $1,150. What is the company's break-even point?

1,100 units

10. Chips Away is considering raising its wholesale selling price by 20 percent. Will the break-even point fall by less than 20 percent, 20 percent exactly, or more than 20 percent?

more than 20 percent

11. Associated Instruments produces guitars. The company's current fixed costs are $450,000 per year. Each guitar costs $700 to manufacture and sells for $1,200. Members of the Guitar Makers Union are going to receive a raise on July 1. This will increase the company's variable costs by 2 percent. By what percentage must the selling price rise in order for the same break-even point to be maintained?

1.17 percent

12. Lebanon Valley University (LVU) is considering the computerization of its manual registration procedure. The following are the estimated costs of both the computerized process and the manual process.

	Manual	Computerized
Fixed cost	$2,000/registration week	$8,000/registration week
Variable cost	$40/student	$10/student

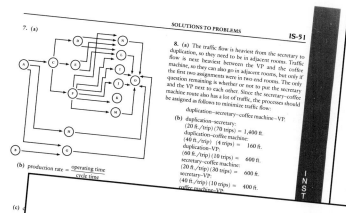

7. (a)

(b) production rate = $\dfrac{\text{operating time}}{\text{cycle time}}$

(c)

(d)

(e)

SOLUTIONS TO PROBLEMS   IS-51

8. (a) The traffic flow is heaviest from the secretary to duplication, so they need to be in adjacent rooms. Traffic flow is next heaviest between the VP and the coffee machine, so they can also go in adjacent rooms. Traffic the first two assignments were in two end rooms. The only question remaining is whether or not to put the secretary and the VP next to each other. Since the secretary–coffee machine route also has a lot of traffic, the processes should be assigned as follows to minimize traffic flow:

duplication–secretary–coffee machine–VP.

(b) duplication–secretary:
(20 ft./trip) (70 trips) = 1,400 ft.
duplication–coffee machine:
(40 ft./trip) (4 trips) =   160 ft.
duplication–VP:
(60 ft./trip) (10 trips) =   600 ft.
secretary–coffee machine:
(20 ft./trip) (30 trips) =   600 ft.
secretary–VP:
(40 ft./trip) (10 trips) =   400 ft.
coffee machine–VP.

I N S T

818   CHAPTER 17   QUALITY CONTROL

APPLICATIONS OF P/OM

Process Control at Frito-Lay

Making potato chips is a carefully controlled process. Actually, it's several processes, all involving human labor and complex machinery. So, how do potato chip manufacturers know when and where they have a problem? In the past, the Frito-Lay company would inspect the product at the end of the process, but that's a little late to find out that something's wrong. There are better ways, including sampling, which allows the manufacturer to check on the process as it's happening. Frito-Lay reduced variability by 50 percent since implementing its statistical process control.

Every fifteen minutes, three batches of Ruffles are sampled for salt content. The batches are ground up, weighed, and placed in an electronic salt meter. The sample mean is plotted on a control chart. Frito-Lay workers know that the process has to be adjusted if any of the following occur.

■ One point is out of control (greater than 3 standard deviations from the mean).
■ Two of three points are more than 2 standard deviations on the same side of the mean.
■ Four of five points are more than 1 standard deviation on the same side of the mean.
■ There is a run of eight points on the same side of the mean.

Source: Against All Odds (New York: W.H. Freeman, 1988).

difference between the largest and smallest reading in each sample. The range is not as easy to use in statistical formulas, but tables of coefficients have been developed for its use in developing $\bar{X}$-charts and R-charts. A small portion of these tables is reproduced in Table 17.7. Using Table 17.7, we can define the control limits for the $\bar{X}$-chart.

$$UCL = \bar{\bar{X}} + A_2\bar{R}$$
$$LCL = \bar{\bar{X}} - A_2\bar{R}$$

The control limits for the R-chart are as follows.

$$LCL = D_3\bar{R}$$
$$UCL = D_4\bar{R}$$

Example 17.7 From the production line, 25 samples of 5 cans each have been selected and tested. $\bar{X}$ is found for each of the 25 samples, and $\bar{\bar{X}} = 18.5$. Similarly, the range for each sample is found, resulting in an $\bar{R}$ of .458. Design the $\bar{X}$-chart and R-chart for this situation.

For the $\bar{X}$-chart, the center line is

$$\bar{\bar{X}} = 18.5,$$

and the control limits are

$$UCL = 18.5 + (.577 \times .458) = 18.764$$

Teaching Suggestion 17.8: Weight Control. See the Instructor's Section for details.

IS-v

Integrated use of the computer throughout the text.

Demonstrations using AB:POM software for the solved problems at the end of each chapter provide detailed instructions for those students who will be using the software.

AB:POM Software

High quality AB:POM Software (Allyn & Bacon Production and Operations Management Software) is a fast, user-friendly program for solving real-world problems.

It requires no previous computer experience, and is written to match the text's terminology. The AB:POM software contains at least one module for every quantitative chapter. The text can be purchased by students separately, or with AB:POM in either 5 1/4" or 3 1/2" IBM compatible format. Documentation for AB:POM is located at the end of each chapter and in Appendix D: Instructions for Use of AB:POM Software.

Data Disk

Free to qualified adopters, this disk includes the files for all the homework problems that can be solved using AB:POM. Adopters are free to make copies for their students.

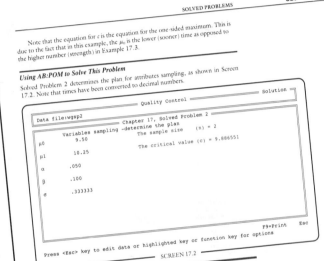

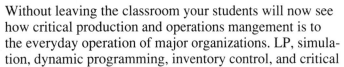

A text-integrated video helps your students experience POM in action!

Without leaving the classroom your students will now see how critical production and operations mangement is to the everyday operation of major organizations. LP, simulation, dynamic programming, inventory control, and critical path analysis all take on added meaning when seen in real-world situations.

APPLICATIONS OF P/OM

Linear Programming at New England Apple Products

Apple-cranberry juice cocktail is one of many VeryFine beverages blended at New England Apple Products. As Steve Rouse, VeryFine's manager of marketing, explains, the company offers consumers plenty of choices.

The juice category includes apple juice, orange juice and grapefruit juice. And also apple-cranberry cocktail and a straight cranberry cocktail. And then we also have a group of fruit drinks that don't contain as large a percentage of pure juice. And these include fruit punch, grape drink, orange drink, pineapple-orange drink, pa-

paya punch, apple-cherry berry drink, lemon-lime drink, tea with lemon, lemonade and a natural energy drink which is an isotonic drink.

How does VeryFine decide which of these products to market and how much of each to make? In other words, how does VeryFine determine the best product mix to make the greatest profit? The answer: linear programming.

Source: For All Practical Purposes (New York: W. H. Freeman, 1988).

The *x*'s represent the *n* **decision variables**, and the object is to determine the values of these *x*'s that optimize (either minimize or maximize) the **objective function**, which is expressed

$$Z = c_1 x_1 + c_2 x_2 + \ldots + c_n x_n.$$

The *c* coefficients represent known cost or profit coefficients.

The optimization is subject to certain restrictions, known as **constraints**. The preceding general problem indicates that there are *m* constraints. The term $\{\leq, = \geq\}$ is used to indicate that exactly one of these three signs appears in each constraint. In Example 11.1, there were two decision variables (x_1 and x_2) and two constraints (material and sewing). There was exactly one sign in each constraint ($\leq$ in constraint 1 and $\leq$ in constraint 2). The coefficients a_{ij} are known as *resource utilization constants*, because they represent the amount of resource *i* used by activity *j*. The values b_1, b_2, . . . , b_m represent the *availabilities* of each of the *m* resources at the manager's disposal. For any specific problem, the coefficients a_{ij}, b_i, c_j are known, and we use linear programming to find the best value of each variable x_j. In the previous example, the profit coefficients were known ($c_1 = 10$, $c_2 = 15$), the resource availability was known ($b_1 = 50$, $b_2 = 36$), and the resource utilization constants were known ($a_{11} = 2$, $a_{12} = 5$, $a_{21} = 4$, $a_{22} = 2$).

GENERAL PROPERTIES OF LINEAR PROGRAMS

The name of the model is *linear* programming because each of the expressions (objective and constraints) is linear. There are three very important properties of this linearity that should be examined.

Property 1: Proportionality. In reviewing Example 11.1, notice that the objective f... the p... Rega...

Insert this side into recorder ▲ Do not touch the tape inside

COMAP Video

Unique videos from COMAP, the Consortium for Mathematics and Its Applications, are now available through an exclusive agreement with Allyn & Bacon. The COMAP video originally appeared on Public Television in the series "For All Practical Purposes," made with major funding from the Annenberg/ CPB Project.

The videos are related to these P/OM in Action boxes:

Modeling at Bell Labs (Ch. 1)

A Clear Specification of Goals Leads to Achievements (Ch. 2)

Capacity Disruptions at American Airlines (Ch. 3)

The Transportation Problem at Avis (Ch. 6)

Queues and Blocking of Phone Calls (Ch. 8)

Apollo II Owes Launch Success to Project Management (Ch. 10)

Linear Programming at New England Apple Products (Ch. 11)

Chinese Postman Problem (Ch. 15)

Deming and "Made in Japan" (Ch. 16)

Quality Control at Frito-Lay (Ch. 17)

Also available...

The Harley Davidson Plant Tour Video — "Making Motorcycles the American Way"
See the next page for details.

The extensive supplements package provides the most complete teaching support found anywhere.

We've answered your request for more support, so you can concentrate on what you do best — teaching. The complete supplements package includes:

Annotated Instructor's Edition

COMAP Video

Harley Davidson Plant Tour Video* — "Making Motorcycles the American Way" — Provides a "walkthrough" plant tour of this leader in quality manufacturing and brings to life the exciting and important applications in American organizations as they compete in a global market.

Test Bank — Provides over 600 multiple choice, true/false, and short answer questions and problems.

Allyn & Bacon Test Manager Plus — a computerized version of the above Test Bank allows you to quickly and easily generate tests using using a microcomputer. Available in 5 1/4" and 3 1/2" IBM format.

Transparency Masters — 100 transparencies have been developed and annotated in the AIE to enhance classroom presentations. Most of these transparencies have been reproduced from the text and the balance have been developed from other sources.

Study Guide — Prepared by O. Felix Offodile of Kent State University, each chapter in the Study Guide contains a summary of the text chapter, notation and formula reviews, questions and problems followed by answers and solutions, as well as worked-out solutions to selected text problems. In addition, computer problem solutions, and analyses are presented.

AB:POM Software — See page *IS-vi* for description.

Data Disk — Free to adopters, the Data Disk includes AB:POM files for all of the end-of-chapter computer problems and cases.

Profiles in Quality: Blueprints for Action from 50 Leading Companies — This unique supplement on quality is available at a reduced price when packaged for students with *Production and Operations Mangement, Second Edition.* This outstanding paperback highlights actual Quality Improvement Programs from well-known companies such as Federal Express, General Electric, Boeing, AT&T, Amana, and Hewlett Packard.

This text can be ordered for students in one of three ways:

Student text only
H33608
ISBN: 0-205-13360-6

Student text w/AB:POM Software
(5 1/4" IBM)
H33632
ISBN: 0-205-13363-0

Student text w/AB:POM Software
(3 1/2" IBM)
H33624
ISBN: 0-205-13362-2

---

* Some restrictions may apply. See your Allyn & Bacon representative for details. All information is acurate as of date of printing. Subject to change without notice.

Allyn and Bacon/Ginn Press

JUST-IN-TIME
PUBLISHING PROGRAM

for Decision Science

More great opportunities.

Using the production and operations management strategy of just-in-time manufacturing, you now have the option of building your own text. By taking advantage of cutting-edge technology, this unique and innovative program allows you to assemble in one book materials selected from a database of several Allyn & Bacon decision science texts including Weiss & Gershon's *Production and Operations Management, Second Edition*, other published sources, and your own materials.

No longer will you be limited to the contents of a single title. Now you can combine the best of Quantitative Analysis, Management Science, and Production and Operations Management in one book using our Just-In-Time publishing program. You select the materials, the length, and even the sequence; then let Allyn & Bacon publish a textbook which exactly fits your course.

The Allyn & Bacon database consists of:

Production and Operations Management, 2/e
by Weiss & Gershon

Production and Operations Management, 2/e
by Heizer & Render

Readings in Production and Operations Management
by Ahmadian, Afifi & Chandler

Profiles in Quality:
Blueprints for Action from 50 Leading Companies

Introduction to Management Science
by Render & Stair

Quantitative Analysis for Management, 4/e
by Render & Stair

Cases and Readings in Management Science, 2/e
by Render, Stair & Greenberg

Call your local Allyn & Bacon Representative for more details.

Annotated Instructor's Edition

**PRODUCTION
AND OPERATIONS
MANAGEMENT**

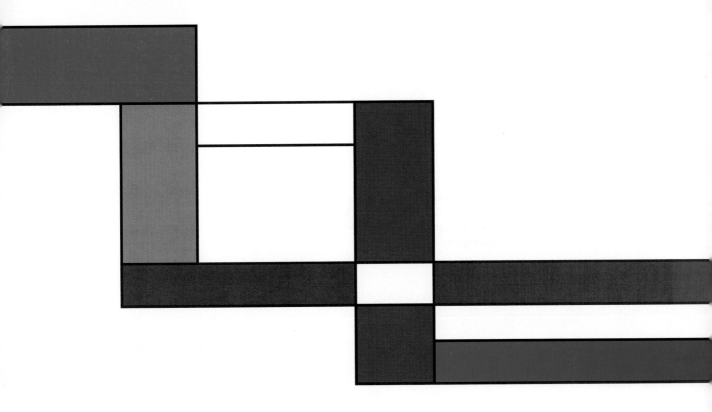

Annotated Instructor's Edition

PRODUCTION AND OPERATIONS MANAGEMENT

Second Edition

HOWARD J. WEISS ▪ MARK E. GERSHON

Temple University

ALLYN AND BACON   BOSTON ▪ LONDON ▪ TORONTO ▪ SYDNEY ▪ TOKYO ▪ SINGAPORE

Executive Editor: Rich Wohl
Senior Editorial Assistant: Cheryl Ten Eick
Cover Administrator: Linda Dickinson
Composition and Manufacturing Buyer: Louise Richardson
Editorial-Production Service: Proof Positive/Farrowlyne Associates, Inc.
Cover Designer: Design Ad Cetera

Copyright © 1993, 1989 by Allyn and Bacon
A division of Simon & Schuster, Inc.
160 Gould Street
Needham Heights, Massachusetts 02194

Printed in the United States of America.

10 9 8 7 6 5 4 3 2 1   96 95 94 93 92 91

ISBN: 0-205-13364-9

BRIEF CONTENTS

Contents of Annotated Instructor's Edition

Contents of Student Text

PREFACE

ABOUT THE ANNOTATED INSTRUCTOR'S EDITION

We are proud to continue our tradition of production and operations management textbook firsts. In the previous edition, we became the first P/OM textbook to include P/OM software with the text. With this edition, we become the first P/OM textbook to have an Annotated Instructor's Edition (AIE). This version of the text, available only to instructors, differs from the student version in two major respects. First, preceding the regular student text in the AIE is a complete instructor's manual. With this Instructor's Section, instructors will have the student text and solutions in front of them at all times, without having to flip back and forth between separate books. In addition, throughout the text, the AIE contains marginal annotations, printed in color, that are designed to help coordinate the use of answers, transparency masters, videos, and teaching suggestions. These annotations do not appear in the student edition.

INSTRUCTOR'S SECTION

The Instructor's Section appears at the beginning of the Annotated Instructor's Edition and can be found by the gray thumb tabs that appear on the outside edges of all pages. The material in this section is organized by chapter. For each chapter, there are teaching notes, teaching suggestions, and answers to Questions. For chapters with quantitative material (the majority of chapters), there are also solutions to Problems.

Teaching Notes: The teaching notes explain our approach and our philosophy toward the material. We briefly discuss the Solved Problems and homework problems, and we identify the Problems that can be solved using the AB:POM software.

Teaching Suggestions: For each chapter, we have written suggestions for making the material more interesting. In some cases, these suggestions point out observations that we do not make in the book; in others, they offer ways to ask the students to apply a concept to their own lives and experiences. Occasionally, we suggest that you have your students prepare something for class. It is important to note that such preparations sometimes must be done well in advance of the lecture.

Answers to Questions: In this section, we present *our* answers to the Questions. You may well have answers of your own. While this section presents what we had in mind, by design, there is room for discussion on many exercises.

Solutions to Problems: In this section, we present our step-by-step solutions to the Problems. In many cases, there may be more than one solution. The answers, however, should agree with ours. Note that many of the answers are given in the annotations in the chapter itself.

TEACHING ANNOTATIONS

Teaching suggestions, transparency masters, and the COMAP videos are keyed to specific passages, figures, tables, and Applications of P/OM boxes through the use of notes that are printed, in color, in the margins. This should help considerably in coordinating the material. Another great help: The answers to many of the Problems also appear in the margin.

ADDITIONAL SUPPLEMENTS FOR INSTRUCTORS

AB:POM SOFTWARE

This text can be ordered with or without the user-friendly AB:POM software. The text references to the software are unobtrusive and easily identified. Almost all of these references appear in the Solved Problems section of the text. Since they are clearly marked, students who are using the book without the software can easily skip these sections.

However, we strongly recommend that students use AB:POM; this integrated and inexpensive program is a very powerful teaching tool. For the past several years, we have had our students use the software to check their regular homework problems and to solve the larger computer cases. Students feel comfortable with the software after a minimal investment of time, and most are very pleased with themselves at being able to comfortably use a computer.

As the following list shows, the AB:POM software contains at least one module for every quantitative chapter of the text.

> Decision Analysis (Chapter 3)
>> Decision Trees
>> Decision Tables
>> Break-even Analysis
> Forecasting (Chapter 4)
>> Time Series (moving averages, exponential smoothing, least squares)
>> Regression (up to six independent variables)
> Location (Chapter 5)
>> Qualitative
>> Quantitative (one- and two-dimensional)
> Transportation (Chapter 6)
> Assembly Line Balancing (Chapter 7)
> Facility Layout (Chapter 7)

Waiting Line Models (Chapter 8)
    $M/M/1$; $M/D/1$; $M/M/s$; $M/M/1$ with Finite Queue
    $M/M/1$ with Finite Population
    $M/G/1$; $M/E_k/1$; $M/M/s$ with Finite Queue
    $M/M/s$ with Finite Population
Reliability (Chapter 9)
Learning Curves (Chapter 9)
PERT/CPM (Chapter 10)
Linear Programming (Chapter 11)
Aggregate Planning (Chapter 12)
Inventory (Chapter 13)
    Economic Order Quantity
    Economic Production Quantity
    EOQ with Shortages
    EPQ with Shortages
    EOQ with Quantity Discount
Materials Requirements Planning (Chapter 14)
Lot Sizing (Chapter 14)
Job Shop Scheduling (Chapter 15)
    One Machine
    Two Machines
Assignment Problem (Chapter 15)
Quality Control (Chapter 17)
    Sampling Plans for Attributes
    Sampling Plans for Variables
    Risks, OC Curve, and AOQ Curves for Attributes Sampling
    p-Charts
    $\overline{X}$-Charts and R-Charts

DATA DISKETTE(S)

Qualified adopters can receive a data disk of Problems from the text that can be solved using the AB:POM software. The file names all begin with WG and contain the chapter and problem number. (For example, WG11-12 is the file for Problem 12 in Chapter 11.)

The data for the computer case studies that appear at the end of each chapter are also included with this disk. You may not wish to make all of the files available to students; in some cases, this will give away the answer. For example, if you want students to develop their own forecasting models, you probably do not want to distribute those files. We recommend that you look at the available files before distributing them to students.

TRANSPARENCY MASTERS

A set of one hundred transparency masters, consisting mostly of figures from the book, is available to qualified adopters. Margin notes indicate the point at which each transparency master should be used.

VIDEOS

Two different videos are available from Allyn and Bacon to qualified adopters of this text. The first, available through an exclusive agreement with the Consortium for Mathematics and Its Applications (COMAP), consists of edited material from the series *For All Practical Purposes,* which was produced for educational television with major funding from the Annenberg/CPB Project. Within the text we have tied a number of the Applications of P/OM boxes to segments of the video.

Modeling (Chapter 1)
A Clear Specification of Goals Leads to Achievements (Chapter 2)
Capacity Disruptions at American Airlines (Chapter 3)
The Transportation Problem at Avis (Chapter 6)
Queues and Blocking of Phone Calls (Chapter 8)
Apollo 11 Owes Launch Success to Project Management (Chapter 10)
Linear Programming at New England Apple Products (Chapter 11)
The Chinese Postman Problem (Chapter 15)
Deming and "Made in Japan" (Chapter 16)
Process Control at Frito-Lay (Chapter 17)

The second video is a plant tour of Harley-Davidson, titled *Making Motorcycles the American Way.* Both videos are designed to bring to life the exciting and important applications of P/OM in organizations of all types.

TEST BANK

A test bank of over six hundred multiple-choice, true-false, and short-answer questions and problems is available as a separate item.

COMPUTERIZED TEST BANK

This test bank is also available to qualified adopters through Allyn and Bacon's computerized testing program, The A&B Test Manager Plus. It is available for IBM and compatible systems in either a 5¼″ or 3½″ format.

VERSIONS OF THIS TEXT AVAILABLE FOR STUDENTS

Production and Operations Management, Second Edition, can be ordered through bookstores in any of five ways:

- Text only
- Text with AB:POM software (5¼″ diskettes)
- Text with AB:POM software (3½″ diskettes)
- Text shrinkwrapped with Personal Storm Version 3.0 (manual and 5¼″ diskettes)
- Text shrinkwrapped with Personal Storm Version 3.0 (manual and 3½″ diskettes)

SUPPLEMENT FOR STUDENTS

STUDY GUIDE

This edition of the *Study Guide* has been prepared by O. Felix Offodile of Kent State University. Each chapter in the *Study Guide* contains a summary of the corresponding text chapter; the notation and formulas from the chapter; questions and problems followed by answers and solutions; as well as worked-out solutions to selected Problems from the text. In addition, computer problems, solutions, and analyses are presented.

Computer Case Studies

Arctic Inc. (Chapter 3)
Human Resources Inc. (Chapter 4)
Consolidated Bottling Inc. (Chapter 5)
Consolidated Bottling Inc. (Chapter 6)
Microfix Incorporated (Chapter 7)
Beer Distributorship (Chapter 7)
Pantry Shopper (Chapter 8)
Cartak's Department Store (Chapter 9)
General Products Inc. (Chapter 11)
Cornwell Glass (Chapter 12)
Rochester Paper Company (Chapter 13)
Brenner Manufacturing (Chapter 14)
Accountfree (Chapter 15)
Green River Chemical Company (Chapter 17)

Applications of P/OM Boxes

Modeling (Chapter 1)
A Clear Specification of Goals Leads to Achievements (Chapter 2)
Capacity Disruptions at American Airlines (Chapter 3)
Monthly Sales Forecasts—Coors Beer Distributorship (Chapter 4)
Low Costs and Weak Dollar Make U.S. Sites Attractive (Chapter 5)
The Transportation Problem at Avis (Chapter 6)
A Faster Path to Finished Steel (Chapter 7)
Queues and Blocking of Phone Calls (Chapter 8)
Apollo 11 Owes Launch Success to Project Management (Chapter 10)
Linear Programming at New England Apple Products (Chapter 11)
Spare Parts Inventory at PennDOT (Chapter 13)
MRP at Uniform Tubes (Chapter 14)
The Chinese Postman Problem (Chapter 15)
Deming and "Made in Japan" (Chapter 16)
Process Control at Frito-Lay (Chapter 17)

1
Introduction

TEACHING NOTES

The goal of this chapter is to introduce the student to the concept of *operations*. We would like students to realize that every organization must provide a product or service and that this provision is the function of operations. One way we have tried to get this point across is by providing two large, categorized lists of organizations (Tables 1.1 and 1.2).

A second goal is to create a framework for understanding operations. We have done this by breaking down operations into five (rather than three) components (see Figure 1.1). We think that delineating inputs and resources as well as outputs and by-products will give students a better understanding and appreciation of operations.

We introduce the concept of time (long, medium, and short range) in this chapter, because students need to realize that managerial decisions vary over time. In addition, we present examples of the types of problems that operations managers face. These examples are developed in greater detail later in the text. The history of operations management is also included to give students some idea of what the field entails. Please note that our history pays homage to James Watt and includes George Westinghouse.

Another goal of the chapter is to indicate the importance of using models to help us make decisions. We emphasize, however, that models, while an important aid in decision making, do not actually make decisions.

Students who are not operations management majors often wonder why operations management is important to their chosen field. At the end of the chapter, we explore the interaction between operations and other business functions, and we point out that the operations function accounts for the majority of costs in many institutions.

When teaching this chapter, try to get students to think about specific organizations and the role of operations in these organizations. The most obvious organization is the university, but we also bring in other organizations with which all of our students are familiar, such as fast-food restaurants, hospitals, and UPS.

We recommend that students, especially MBA students, read *The Official MBA Handbook*. This humorous book explains business, including production, in a light but interesting and relevant vein.

For homework, we strongly suggest that students be assigned the Problems at the end of the chapter in addition to the Questions. The Problems will challenge the better

students to think more closely about some of the issues in operations management.

TEACHING SUGGESTIONS

Teaching Suggestion 1.1: All Jobs Have Operations.
Point out to the non-P/OM majors that their future jobs entail operations in their area.

Teaching Suggestion 1.2: Most Production Companies Have Service Components.
Students typically think of, for example, General Motors as a producer of goods. Point out that retailing, repairing, and financing cars are all services.

Teaching Suggestion 1.3: Make to Order and Just-in-Time.
This is where we introduce our students to the notion of just-in-time. Just-in-time can be viewed as a movement from make to stock toward make to order. Also mention pull system vs. a push system.

Teaching Suggestion 1.4: The 4 M's.
Later, in our chapter on total quality management, we list the 4 M's as the four general inputs to a process: manpower, machines, materials, and methods.

Teaching Suggestion 1.5: Taylor vs. Gilbreth.
Taylor and Gilbreth had opposite outlooks toward assembly line workers. Gilbreth was much more sympathetic toward the workers, while Taylor was more management oriented.

Teaching Suggestion 1.6: Sample Problem.
We like to ask students to apply these six steps to a problem in their everyday lives, such as getting a college degree or deciding on dinner or a restaurant. This provides interesting and, oftentimes, humorous class discussion.

ANSWERS TO QUESTIONS

1. Operations management is the planning and controlling of all activities necessary for the provision of the firm's product or service.

2. inputs, resources, transformation process, direct outputs, by-products

3. See the table on the next page.

4. Among the possible answers are the following: production yields a tangible object, which is ultimately sold after a transformation in form; service facility is closer to the consumer; customer may act as his or her own server in a service facility; in production, transformation (usually) occurs before the demand; production (usually) carries more risk; make to stock versus make to order; work is (usually) less repetitive, job design more difficult in service; demand is more difficult to smooth in service; and quality is more difficult to measure in service.

5. make to stock: items go into inventory because the transformation occurs before the demand; make to order: items produced after the customer has placed an order

6. Many answers are possible.

7. Yes and no; capital is necessary to obtain the other resources that are required for operation, but capital itself cannot physically contribute. (You might mention that capital is a working resource in a casino or bank.)

8. See the table below.

9. example: strategic plan—broaden market base; tactical plan—initiate adult education plan

10. cottage industries

11. Watt: steam engine; Taylor: scientific management; Westinghouse: 5 1/2-day work week

12. formulating the problem, identifying the alternative solutions, testing the alternative solutions, choosing the "best" solution, implementing the chosen solution, and monitoring the system

13. A model is a representation of the system being examined. Its main advantage is that it is easy to manipulate.

14. Iconic models use pictures to represent the real system; analogue models use similarities to represent the real system; and symbolic models use symbols to represent the real system.

15. Many examples are possible.

16. Descriptive models examine the effects of choosing one alternative out of many, while prescriptive models find the best alternative out of many.

17. An optimization technique always finds the best solution to a problem, while a heuristic technique typically finds a very good—but not necessarily the best—solution.

18. satisfying and forecasting long-term demand; satisfying short-term demand (orders); defining and providing feedback on product quality; reducing inventory through sales

19. The integrative nature of organization makes it essential that all managers understand the effect that decisions in their areas will have on the provision of the firm's major asset—its product or service.

SOLUTIONS TO PROBLEMS

1. The primary focus is the need to know how many miles are driven. At $.05 per mile extra for the regular, it will take 60,000 miles to make up the cost difference of $3,000. Other information is needed as well, such as the expected life of each car, the expected usage per year, the salvage value at the end of useful life, and the depreciation used. All of these will complicate and modify the use of the 60,000-mile figure for the decision. Interest rates and other possible uses for the $3,000 that would be saved are also considered. For the purpose of the discussion, we can assume that maintenance and other unpredictable costs have been included in the operating cost figures provided. The goal is to accurately project the total cost of each car.

2. Again, the main concern is the volume of joysticks required. If the volume is large enough to make up the $30,000 setup cost, then the company should produce its

Table for Question 3.

	Barber Shop	**Library**	**Appliance Plant**
Input	Customer	Reader	Steel, electronics
Resources	Chair, scissors, barber, mirror	Catalogs, librarian	Equipment, labor
Transformation	Personal appearance	Educational	Manufacturing (Assembly)
Direct Outputs	Groomed customer	Informed reader	Appliance
By-Products	Satisfaction, hair on floor	Fines	Pollution

Table for Question 8.

	Long Range	**Medium Range**	**Short Range**
Approximate Time	> 18 months	2–18 months	< 2 months
Issues	Broad scope	Acquisition and allocation of resources	Specifics such as scheduling
Managerial Level	Executive	Middle level	First level

own joysticks. Saving $2 per joystick, this would require a usage rate of 15,000 joysticks. Again, time is an important factor; it may not make sense to manufacture joysticks if it takes 4 years to use 15,000. Also, the setup costs will have to be repeated as the equipment wears out.

3. There is a trade-off between the cost of the waiting time in the current situation and the extra cost of the more expensive partsperson. At $4 per hour, the cost per request for 12 requests is $.33. At $7 per hour the cost for 15 requests is $.58 per request. Even at the faster rate, the new person is more expensive. To include the cost of the waiting time—$10 per hour—the time per request is 5 minutes with the current person and 4 minutes with the faster person. The minute saved per request is worth $(1/60)(10) =$ $.17. At 10 requests per hour, $1.70 is saved. The current person is still better in terms of cost.

Note that this analysis never tries to figure how many repairpersons may be in line at a time. This must be done, as explained in Chapter 8.

4. See the table below.

Since the profit on premium is much higher, OCRA should make as much premium as possible, but at least 60 percent must be regular. If 40 percent is premium, we can figure out how many gallons of each per day can be made from the available resources. The total amount of gasoline available is 10,000 gallons, but since each gallon of gasoline requires 1.25 gallons of crude oil, only 8,000 gallons of gasoline can be produced. The 60–40 split yields 4,800 gallons of regular and 3,200 gallons of premium.

This solution uses 4,800 gallons of light crude. Since only 4,000 gallons of light crude is available, we must make less premium and more regular. Trial and error leads us to a solution of producing all regular, or 8,000 gallons of reg-

ular, which uses exactly 6,000 gallons of heavy and 4,000 gallons of light—all that is available.

In Chapter 11, we will solve this problem using linear programming.

5. The goal is to produce in the lowest-cost way. The $8 regular-time cost is the cheapest way, followed by the $12 overtime cost.

Production on regular time for the following month is next at $13 ($8 + $5). In May, 200 should be produced for May. The extra 50, taking May production to 250, should be used in June. Another 250 should be produced in June. With the 50 from May, we are still 50 short. These have to be produced on overtime in May, despite the high ($17) cost. Finally, the demand of 300 in July is met with 250 on regular time and 50 on overtime. This is a trial-and-error approach, but the answer seems to be the best attainable.

6. Our students attempt to solve this problem by using a break-even type of analysis, using the $5 cost, the $4 cost, and the $22 cost. However, they are unable to answer the question, because the $5 cost is not really a recoverable fixed cost. If it were, we could view the $4 cost as being in effect, a savings of $1 per unit. But here the analysis breaks down, because Aman uses 58 gallons per day, and only 22 would break even. We cannot choose the holding cost over the production price; we incur both. As for the reorder point, many of our students correctly state that a three-day supply, or 174 gallons, is the level at which to place an order.

7. Invariably, half of our students answer that the fair thing to do is to paint the houses in the order in which the customers signed the contracts. The others actually decide on their own that shortest processing time is the rule to follow!

Table for Problem 4.

	Revenue	Light Cost	Heavy Cost	Total Cost	Profit
Premium	1.40	.75(1.00)=.75	.5(.90)=.45	1.20	.20
Regular	1.25	.5(1.00)=.50	.75(.90)=.675	1.175	.075

2

World-Class Operations

TEACHING NOTES

Our goal in this chapter is to provide an introduction to current issues in operations. We begin by demonstrating that operations and organizations in general have become globalized. We want students to understand that the markets for goods as well as the production centers are globalized. We also want them to understand that in the past, U.S. firms really did not care about satisfying demands outside of the United States (closed circle economy).

We know that our students are aware of our main competitor, Japan. We also try to make them aware of Germany and of the potential of the Pacific Rim countries, especially South Korea. We show students the factors (imports, productivity) that are symptoms of the problem, after which we discuss the reasons that are typically given for our fall in stature in the world of production. We show that most of the typical reasons, such as lower foreign wage rates, do not really hold true (even though they may have been true twenty years ago). We show that while U.S. firms have tended to have a different approach to quality than foreign firms—relying on marketing—this is now changing.

We indicate that some of the problems are at the governmental level. We show that other governments support domestic industries through trade barriers (a somewhat negative way). We also show the more positive ways governments aid domestic industries, such as with training programs and education and job policies. We try to show that there has been an exaggeration of the differences attributed to culture.

With all of this as background, we lay the groundwork for some general principles. We discuss changes in management–employee relations, changes in attitudes toward quality, and changes in product development approaches, continuous improvement, and flexibility.

This chapter includes a discussion of strategy. We show the different levels of strategy (government, industry, corporate, and functional) and the integration of these levels. We feel that because strategy is a top-down issue, it is not correct to emphasize operations strategy; rather, it is important to discuss the implications of corporate strategy on operations. We use Porter's strategies—strategy 1: provide cost leadership; strategy 2: profit through price; strategy 3: profit through focus—as our model, because we think that this approach best fits operations.

We discuss vertical integration because it fits the strategy discussion and our general picture of the chain of operations, which occurs several times throughout the text. We also discuss joint ventures, since these are becoming more and more common (consider the recent agreement between Apple and IBM).

Recently, an article appeared that emphasizes our point regarding quality versus advertising. Have your students read the article on the Baldridge award from *APICS—The Performance Advantage,* vol. 1, no. 2, August 1991, page 16.

TEACHING SUGGESTIONS

Teaching Suggestion 2.1: World Class Thinks Long Term.
Point out that a major criticism of American business is its focus on short-term profits.

Teaching Suggestion 2.2: Open-Minded Companies.
When Ford, Harley-Davidson, and Xerox were losing market share, they looked to Japan to learn. They quickly discarded the notion that the United States is best, and then set out to try to make it true again.

Teaching Suggestion 2.3: Lack of U.S. Exports.
Why do much smaller countries export more than the United States? Discuss this with students. Mention our lack of interest in other markets as one that needs to change. Also mention geography as a factor that is out of our control.

Teaching Suggestion 2.4: Quality vs. Productivity.
The trade-off usually assumed here is a short-term one. The long-term message of world-class operations is that there is no trade-off: Quality is the way to achieve productivity.

Teaching Suggestion 2.5: Mediocre Quality.
A standard joke about one luxury car manufacturer was that they should sell cars in pairs, so that the owner would still have one to drive when the other was in the shop.

Teaching Suggestion 2.6: Desert Storm Pride.
Recently, U.S. workers demonstrated their pride in such products as the Patriot missile (built by Raytheon) in support of Operation Desert Storm.

Teaching Suggestion 2.7: Fix It Anyway.
Ford Motor Company's Donald Peterson once said, "If it ain't broke, fix it anyway." In total quality management, the saying is, "If you don't see a problem, you haven't looked closely enough."

Teaching Suggestion 2.8: Cost Leadership Through Operations.
Cost leadership was once attained primarily through cheap labor and/or materials. Now, we strive to achieve cost lead-

ership through efficiency, by using such tools and philosophies as JIT to reduce waste and setups.

Teaching Suggestion 2.9: Apple and IBM.
You may want to discuss the implications of the recent IBM-Apple joint venture.

ANSWERS TO QUESTIONS

1. A closed circle economy is one in which producers use parts, equipment, and supplies from companies that are located in the same country. The major causes for the expansion by the United States and other nations beyond a closed circle economy are the improvements in transportation and communication that have occurred in the last twenty years. It is now much easier to move goods from one continent to another.

2. The chapter cites evidence that clearly makes Japan and Germany our major competitors. Competition is arising quickly from the Pacific Rim countries—most notably, Korea.

3. The major evidence is that both imports and exports have increased dramatically for most industrialized countries.

4. There is a great deal of concern among U.S. firms that the Japanese will produce items developed here more inexpensively than the U.S. firms that develop them. An example cited in the chapter is Xerox. To some extent, patent laws protect U.S. firms. If U.S. firms learn to become competitive, the question will be moot.

5. electronic goods, such as cameras and VCRs

6. The major advantage is a lower labor cost. This is the major advantage that Japan began with in the 1950s and used to become dominant. Japan no longer has this advantage.

7. U.S. companies make fewer capital investments than our foreign competitors and are slower to make investment decisions. The result: Japanese and German companies have more up-to-date equipment, which allows them to produce units faster and more inexpensively.

8. A typical response to quality problems is to try to advertise quality into a product.

9. Import quotas and tariffs have been used to restrict U.S. goods from being imported into other countries.

10. A voluntary export restraint is an arrangement whereby one country agrees to limit certain exports to another country. The Japanese have done this with respect to the export of cars into the United States.

11. Technology, although necessary, is ultimately less important than the labor force, because technology cannot operate itself. As long as a company's union workers and management recognize this, the company will flourish. This will benefit both the union and management. Hostile relations allow other companies to produce better products more efficiently.

12. Flexibility refers to several aspects of the operation. Workers must be flexible—that is, prepared to and allowed to perform different tasks. The production system must be flexible in terms of the product line produced and the volume of each product produced.

13. Flexible manufacturing systems are designed to allow individual units of different types to be manufactured with the same equipment.

14. The generic business strategies are cost leadership; performance leadership; and a specialized nook in the marketplace.

15. Research and development is necessary in order to design a production process that can lead to cost leadership or a product that can be differentiated.

16. Vertical integration is when one subsidiary manufactures parts and/or components for another subsidiary. Forward integration is when a company acquires a firm that will use what it manufactures—for example, a lumber producer that buys a newspaper publishing company. Backward integration is when one company buys another company that can supply it with parts—for example, a private college that opens a private high school.

17. A merchant company sells its goods to a variety of customers. A captive producer sells goods only to itself.

18. No; antitrust laws prohibit U.S. automakers from forming joint ventures.

3
Capacity Planning

TEACHING NOTES

We have several different goals in this chapter. First, we wish to introduce students to the notion of capacity. Specifically, they should understand that capacity is a *rate,* that capacity decisions can vary according to time horizon, and that several factors influence capacity. Our second goal for this chapter is getting students to understand that there are different ways to measure capacity, output, and productivity. Students also read about the different long-, medium-, and short-term capacity issues and the options (for example, build a plant or use overtime) available for handling these problems.

This is the first chapter that contains quantitative material. We like to start with easy material so that students can gain confidence. Therefore, the first model that we present is the break-even model. Our treatment of break even differs somewhat from that found in other texts. We are oriented toward production/operations and quickly dismiss the traditional break-even models that contain revenues. We emphasize that break even is used for cost analysis. In addition, we use the break-even models to develop general principles—not just to find numerical answers. We show that higher volume leads to using the option with lower variable costs (make rather than buy). Our feeling is that because students have been introduced to break even in other courses, our focus should be on *cost–volume analysis as it applies to operations management.*

Our second set of quantitative models contains decision tables and decision trees. We have tried to present these topics in the simplest manner possible. Of course, the most difficult aspect of decision tables is filling in the costs—not computing the expected value, maximin, or maximax. This point should be emphasized in the lecture to reinforce the work in the text.

There are two exercises in the Solved Problems section of this chapter. The first deals with capacity definitions; the second is a decision table problem, for which a table must be created. Please note that the latter problem appears again as a one-period inventory problem in Chapter 13.

For homework, we have included some thirty-five problems. The first six deal with computing the capacity of the system; Problem 6 is especially challenging. Problems 7 and 8 (taken together) indicate how to use productivity as a measure. Problems 9 through 20 are break-even problems. We are especially fond of the nontraditional approach taken in Problems 15 and 19 (three processes rather than two), Problem 16 (a bend in the variable cost), and Problem 18 (two types of quantity discounts). Problems 21 through 31 are decision table problems, some of which—Problems 26, 28, 30, and 31—require the student to create the table. Problems 28, 30, and 31 are decision table/inventory problems that can also be approached using single-period inventory methods. Problems 30 and 31 appear again in Chapter 13. (There, minimax and minimin are not used—only expected value.) Problem 25, a break-even analysis of a decision table, requires some thought. Problems 32 through 35 are decision tree problems.

The computer case study for this chapter involves a decision table. No probabilities are given. The main lesson is that students should experiment with different probabilities to draw conclusions and should understand that there is uncertainty in these conclusions; that is, there is no single answer.

The software for this chapter is decision analysis software. It includes submodules on decision tables, decision trees, and break-even analysis. For decision tables, students enter the values in the table and the program identifies the best expected value, maximin, and maximax. The software can be used in two ways: Students can use it to check their work or you can instruct the students to change the probabilities and perform a sensitivity analysis. (Of course, in the latter case, the expected values will change, but the maximin and maximax will not.) For decision trees, students enter the branches, probabilities, and payoffs, and then the expected values and choices are output. For break even, students enter the fixed and variable costs for either two or three options, and the program lists the break-even point(s) and, if desired, draws the graph. The following Problems can be solved using AB:POM: 9–15; 17 and 19 (break even); 21–31 (decision tables)—Problem 25 requires trial and error; and 32–35 (decision trees).

TEACHING SUGGESTIONS

Teaching Suggestion 3.1: Planned vs. Actual.
Not all plans are fully implemented. Conditions often change, which may mean that one part of a plan will be implemented but another part will not. This concept will come up again in aggregate planning, in MRP lot sizing, and in the dynamic notion of job shop scheduling.

Teaching Suggestion 3.2: Marketing–Operations Integration.
Smoothing demand is one area where marketing can be very helpful to operations. Smooth demands lead to lower costs and higher productivity, which are useful to marketing.

Teaching Suggestion 3.3: Rates.
We deal with rates and times throughout operations. It is important that time units are given as part of rates. Students must be comfortable expressing inputs and outputs as rates here in order to handle material in future chapters.

Teaching Suggestion 3.4: Aggregation.
This is our first mention of aggregating across products. Discuss this with the students. Also discuss other aggregations, such as different types of customers in a service organization or different facilities (or, within a facility, different departments) doing the same operation.

Teaching Suggestion 3.5: Global Productivity Data.
To add some perspective to this lecture, use some of the productivity data given in Chapter 2.

Teaching Suggestion 3.6: Demand vs. Forecasted Demand.
Throughout the text, when we speak of demand, we are actually speaking of *forecasted* demand.

Teaching Suggestion 3.7: Controlling Arrivals in Service Through Pricing.
Service facilities try to control arrivals through price discounts—for example, early-bird specials at restaurants. Long-distance telephone companies provide an especially good example of facilities that use this technique for controlling arrivals (phone calls).

Teaching Suggestion 3.8: Capacity Resulting from Preventive Maintenance.
While it is true that preventive maintenance takes equipment out of operation in the short run, world-class manufacturing emphasizes the long run, a period over which preventive maintenance will increase capacity by reducing downtime.

Teaching Suggestion 3.9: Sunk Costs.
Although our discussion omits sunk costs, this is an opportune place to discuss the topic, if desired.

Teaching Suggestion 3.10: Use of Graph.
We ask our students to graph every problem, in order to reinforce the concepts. We find that this builds confidence for students who have difficulty visualizing the equations.

Teaching Suggestion 3.11: Linearity.
This is the first of several places in the text where students encounter the concept of linearity. Be sure that it is well understood.

Teaching Suggestion 3.12: Building Decision Tables.
We emphasize how to analyze decision tables. In practice, the most difficult part is acquiring the data for the tables.

ANSWERS TO QUESTIONS

1. The operation exists to satisfy the demand. If capacity and demand are not matched, one of two general problems will arise. If demand is much larger than capacity, providing goods or services becomes difficult, impossible, or very costly. If capacity is much larger than demand, the efficiency will be lower, thereby increasing the cost of the good or service. In either case, it is important to consider the economies and diseconomies of scale.

2. The system capacity cannot exceed the bottleneck capacity.

3. There are several examples. See Table 3.1 for a partial listing.

4. Failure to take advantage of cost savings due to a higher volume will place the company at a price disadvantage with its higher-volume competitors.

5. As the capacity grows, so do the fixed costs and, therefore, the break-even point. Too much capacity without an increase in demand could move the break-even point above the demand volume, leading to losses.

6. likelihood of the need for a larger facility and comparative cost per unit for a facility of each size

7. Economies of scale are reductions in the cost per unit that result either from spreading the fixed costs over more units or from actually reducing the fixed costs.

8. Using overtime, subcontracting, adding part-time help, modifying capacities of server and/or equipment.

9. Almost every operation has alternative measures of capacity.

10. Design capacity is the maximum production or service rate that can be achieved, without regard to the interactions of products, manpower, machines, and raw materials.

11. Effective capacity is the maximum production or service rate that can be achieved when considering the interactions of products, manpower, machines, and raw materials (and is less than or equal to the design capacity).

12. System efficiency represents the percentage of available capacity that is achieved.

13. Answers will vary.

14. Productivity is a nebulous measure that relates the inputs to the outputs. The productivity number itself is not very meaningful, but changes in the productivity measure are very useful to monitor.

15. Productivity relates output to input; capacity relates output to time.

16. A decrease in quality is accompanied by an increase in the amount of work that needs to be done over or repaired, which reduces the effective capacity.

17. Generally, fixed costs increase as capacity increases. Variable costs decrease to a certain point and then begin to increase as capacity increases (see Figure 3.4).

18. **(a)** As volume increases, more-sophisticated equipment is purchased.

(b) As volume increases, assembly lines (product layout) are implemented.

(c) As volume increases, units are made in-house.

(d) As volume increases, quantity discounts are taken advantage of.

19. Maximax considers only the best outcomes, while maximin considers only worst-case scenarios.

20. Expected value is useful for repeated decisions because it is an averaging process. However, it averages out the extreme outcomes. A rational decision maker is concerned with these extreme outcomes and will incorporate them into the decision-making process.

21. Decision trees are most useful for sequences of decisions under risk.

SOLUTIONS TO PROBLEMS

1. $\left(6 \text{ bays}\right)\left(\dfrac{1 \text{ car}}{.5 \text{ hr.}}\right)\left(\dfrac{8 \text{ hr.}}{\text{day}}\right) = \dfrac{96 \text{ cars}}{\text{day}}$

2. (a) The capacity per technician is

$$\left(\dfrac{1 \text{ X-ray}}{10 \text{ min.}}\right)\left(\dfrac{60 \text{ min.}}{\text{hr.}}\right)\left(\dfrac{40 \text{ hr.}}{\text{wk.}}\right) = \dfrac{240 \text{ X-rays}}{\text{wk.}}$$

The total technician capacity is

$$\left(\dfrac{240 \text{ X-rays}}{\text{wk.}}\right)\left(6 \text{ technicians}\right) = \dfrac{1,440 \text{ X-rays}}{\text{wk.}}$$

The capacity per doctor is

$$\left(\dfrac{1 \text{ X-ray}}{8 \text{ min.}}\right)\left(\dfrac{60 \text{ min.}}{\text{hr.}}\right)\left(\dfrac{40 \text{ hr.}}{\text{wk.}}\right) = \dfrac{300 \text{ X-rays}}{\text{wk.}}$$

The total doctor capacity is

$$\left(\dfrac{300 \text{ X-rays}}{\text{wk.}}\right)\left(3 \text{ doctors}\right) = \dfrac{900 \text{ X-rays}}{\text{wk.}}$$

Therefore, doctors create the bottleneck, and the capacity is 900 X-rays per week.

(b) Since doctors create the bottleneck, hiring an additional technician will not change the capacity of 900 X-rays per week.

(c) One additional doctor will increase the capacity by 4/3. Therefore, the revised capacity will be

$$\left(\dfrac{300 \text{ X-rays}}{\text{wk.}}\right)\left(4 \text{ doctors}\right) = \dfrac{1,200 \text{ X-rays}}{\text{wk.}}$$

This is still the bottleneck, but the system capacity is now 1,200 X-rays per week.

(d) Two doctors will yield a doctor capacity of

$$\left(\dfrac{300 \text{ X-rays}}{\text{wk.}}\right)\left(5 \text{ doctors}\right) = \dfrac{1,500 \text{ X-rays}}{\text{wk.}}$$

Now the 6 technicians create the bottleneck, which is 1,440 X-rays per week. (*Note:* The rooms and machines also represent resources, but these resources are "abundant" compared to the doctors and technicians, so we have not considered the rooms and machines for our computations.)

3. (a) $\dfrac{12 \text{ forms}}{\text{day}} \times 20,000 \text{ employees} \times .90 \text{ reliability}$

$$\times \dfrac{250 \text{ days}}{\text{yr.}} = 54,000,000 \dfrac{\text{forms}}{\text{yr.}}$$

(b) System utilization $= \dfrac{\text{system use}}{\text{system capacity}}$

$$= \dfrac{30,000,000}{54,000,000} = .56, \text{ or } 56\%$$

4. System capacity is 160 games per hour. See the table below.

5. The annual capacity per employee is

$$\left(\dfrac{2 \text{ graphs}}{\text{wk.}}\right)\left[\dfrac{(52-4)\text{wk.}}{\text{yr.}}\right]\left(.95 \text{ reliability}\right)$$

$$= \dfrac{91.2 \text{ graphs}}{\text{yr.}}.$$

The required number of employees is

$$\dfrac{\text{annual demand}}{\text{employees' annual capacity}} = \dfrac{500}{91.2} = 5.48 \text{ employees.}$$

6. (a) The typing capacity is

$$\left(\dfrac{120 \text{ words}}{\text{min.}}\right)\left(\dfrac{60 \text{ min.}}{\text{hr.}}\right) = \dfrac{7,200 \text{ words}}{\text{hr.}}.$$

Table for Problem 4.

Machine	(1) Design Capacity	(2) Number of Machines	(3) Total Capacity $[(1)\times(2)]$	(4) Utilization $\left[\dfrac{\text{bottleneck}}{(3)}\right]$
Board cutter	40/hr	5	200/hr	160/200 = 80%
Plastic producer	30/hr	8	240/hr	160/240 = 67%
Box producer	80/hr	2	160/hr*	160/160 = 100%
Packager	70/hr	3	210/hr	160/210 = 76%

*Bottleneck

The print capacity is

$$\left(\frac{120 \text{ char.}}{\text{sec.}}\right)\left(\frac{3,600 \text{ sec.}}{\text{hr.}}\right)\left(\frac{1 \text{ word}}{5 \text{ char.}}\right) = \frac{86,400 \text{ words}}{\text{hr.}}.$$

Typing is the bottleneck; therefore, the capacity is 7,200 words per hour.

(b) Let p be the percentage of time that Alice spends typing and let $1 - p$ be the percentage of time that Alice waits while the printer is working. The total work done must be equal for both typing and printing.

$$p(7,200) = (1 - p)86,400$$
$$7,200p = 86,400 - 86,400p$$
$$93,600p = 86,400$$
$$p = 86,400/93,600$$
$$p = .9231$$

The capacity equals $p(7,200) = .9231(7,200) = 6,646$ words per hour.

7. Productivity $= \dfrac{\text{output}}{\text{input}}$

$$= \frac{57}{480(\$12) + 80(\$5) + 20(\$50)}$$

$$= \frac{57}{\$7,160} = .00796 \text{ houses per dollar}$$

8. (a) Again, productivity = output/input. For October,

$$\frac{65}{(520)(\$13) + (100)(\$5) + (20)(\$50)}$$

$$= \frac{65}{\$8,260} = .00787 \text{ houses per dollar}$$

(b) productivity ratio $= \dfrac{\text{productivity Oct.}}{\text{productivity Sept.}}$

$$= \frac{.00787}{.00796}$$

$$= .9887, \text{ or } 98.87\%$$

(c) Part of the lost productivity is due to the increased labor costs rather than being "less productive."

9. BEP $= \dfrac{FC}{P - VC} = \dfrac{\$275,000}{\$1,150 - \$900} = 1,100$ units

10. The break-even point will fall by more than 20 percent because Chips Away will be making more money per customer; that is, the contribution margin will increase by more than 20 percent.

Alternatively, the new break-even point is given by

$$\text{BEP} = \frac{FC}{P - VC} = \frac{\$275,000}{\$1,150(1.20) - \$900} = 572.92 \text{ units}$$

11. To maintain the same break-even point, the contribution margin must stay the same.

$$P - VC = \$1,200 - \$700 = \$500$$
$$\$500 = \text{new price} - 1.02(\$700)$$
$$\$1,214 = \text{new price}$$
$$\text{new/old} = 1,214/1,200$$
$$\text{increase} = 14/1,200 = .0117, \text{ or } 1.17\%$$

Note that the selling price does not have to be increased as much as variable cost. Also note that the fixed costs are irrelevant.

12. (a) Total cost (manual) = total cost (automated)

$$FC_M + (VC_M \times Q) = FC_A + VC_A \times Q$$
$$\$2,000 + \$40Q = \$8,000 + \$10Q$$
$$\$30Q = \$6,000$$
$$Q = 200 \text{ students}$$

(b) See the figure.

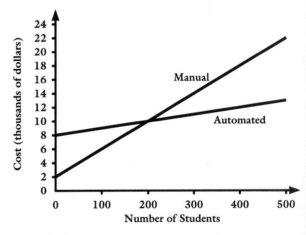

(c) From the graph, use automated for 250 students.

13. Let S = inches of snow.

Total cost (city equip.) = total cost (contract)

$$\$20,000 + \$500S = \$700S$$
$$\$20,000 = \$200S$$
$$S = 100 \text{ in. of snow over 5 years,}$$
$$\text{or 20 in. per year}$$

If the forecast is for less than 20 inches per year, the city should contract for snow removal. Otherwise, the city should purchase the new equipment. See the figure on the next page.

See the figure on the next page.

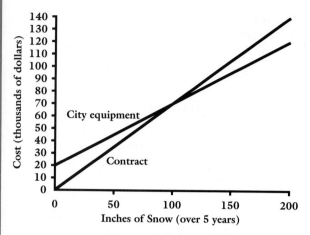

14. Let s = number of soccer balls.

Total cost (process layout) = total cost (product layout)

$$\$20,000 + \$7s = \$30,000 + \$6s$$
$$\$1s = \$10,000$$
$$s = 10,000 \text{ soccer balls}$$

Total revenue = total cost (process layout)

$$\$9.5s = \$20,000 + \$7s$$
$$\$2.5s = \$20,000$$
$$s = 8,000 \text{ soccer balls}$$

If the expected volume is less than 8,000 units, Busko will not break even. If the expected volume is between 8,000 and 10,000 units, Busko should use a process layout. If the expected volume is above 10,000 units, Busko should use a product layout. See the figure.

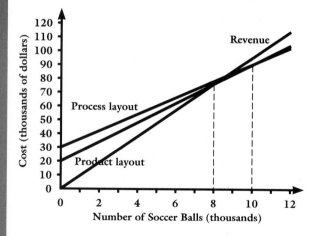

15. (a) See the figure.

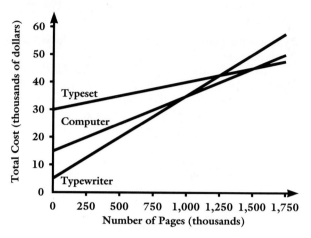

(b) break-even points:

Typewriter	Computer

$$\$5,000 + \$.03x = \$15,000 + \$.02x$$
$$\$.01x = \$10,000$$
$$x = 1,000,000 \text{ pages}$$

Typewriter	Typesetter

$$\$5,000 + \$.03x = \$30,000 + \$.01x$$
$$\$.02x = \$25,000$$
$$x = 1,250,000 \text{ pages}$$

Computer	Typesetter

$$\$15,000 + \$.02x = \$30,000 + \$.01x$$
$$\$.01x = \$15,000$$
$$x = 1,500,000 \text{ pages}$$

Notice that the break-even point between the typewriter and typesetting at 1,250,000 pages is irrelevant, because at that point, the computer is the least costly option. If the volume of pages is less than 1,000,000, the typewriter should be used. If the volume of pages is between 1,000,000 and 1,500,000, the computer should be used. If the volume of pages is above 1,500,000, the typesetter should be used.

16. Regular-time contribution margin = $4 − $2 = $2
Regular-time total contribution = $2(400) = $800
Fixed costs − RT total contribution = $1,000 − $800 = $200 (which must be covered in overtime)
Overtime contribution margin = $4 − $3 = $1

Therefore, 200 bats must be produced during overtime. The break-even point is 400(RT) + 200(OT) = 600 bats. See the figure on the next page.

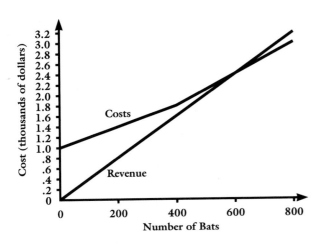

17. See the figure.

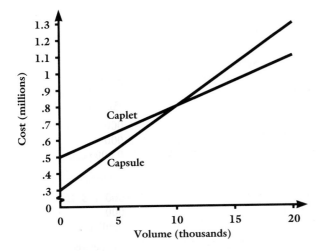

(a) Total cost (capsule) = total cost (caplet)

$$\$300,000 + \$50x = \$500,000 + \$30x$$
$$\$20x = \$200,000$$
$$x = 10,000 \text{ cases}$$

(b) Profit = total revenue − total cost

$$= \text{total revenue}$$
$$\quad - (\text{fixed cost} + \text{total variable cost})$$
$$= \$1,000,000(60)$$
$$\quad - [\$300,000 + \$50(1,000,000)]$$
$$= \$60,000,000 - \$50,300,000$$
$$= \$9,700,000$$

(c)

$$\text{Profit} = \text{total revenue}$$
$$\quad - (\text{fixed cost} + \text{total variable cost})$$
$$\$1,500,000 = \$50x - (\$500,000 + \$30x)$$
$$\$2,000,000 = \$20x$$
$$x = 100,000$$

18. See the figure on the next page.

(a) If tonnage is less than or equal to 40, the costs are as follows: Paper Lion—$1,000 per ton; Plimpton—$1,300 per ton; and Air Drop—$1,100 per ton. Therefore, use Paper Lion. If tonnage is between 40 and 50, the costs are as follows: Paper Lion—$1,000 per ton; Plimpton—($1,300 × 40) + 800(ton − 40); and Air Drop—$1,100 per ton. Therefore, use Paper Lion. If tonnage is greater than 50, the costs are as follows: Paper Lion—$1,000 per ton; Plimpton—($1,300 × 40) + 800(ton − 40); and Air Drop—$950 per ton. Therefore, use Air Drop for up to 133 tons and Plimpton for over 133 tons.

(b) Use Paper Lion for up to 50 tons; use Air Drop Express if over 50 tons.

Plimpton vs. Paper Lion

$$1,300(40) + 800(t - 40) = 1,000t$$
$$52,000 + 800t - 32,000 = 1,000t$$
$$20,000 = 200t$$
$$t = 100 \text{ tons}$$

Plimpton vs. Air Drop

$$1,300(40) + 800(t - 40) = 950t$$
$$52,000 + 800t - 32,000 = 950t$$
$$20,000 = 150t$$
$$t = 20,000/150 = 133 \text{ tons}$$

Paper Lion vs. Air Drop

Break even occurs at 50 tons, where Air Drop price changes. Another break even occurs at 133, where Plimpton becomes less expensive than Air Drop. Use Plimpton for 133 tons or more. (*Note:* For 49 tons, it pays to buy 50 tons from Air Drop at the discounted price. This is true down to 47.5 tons.)

Figure for Problem 18.

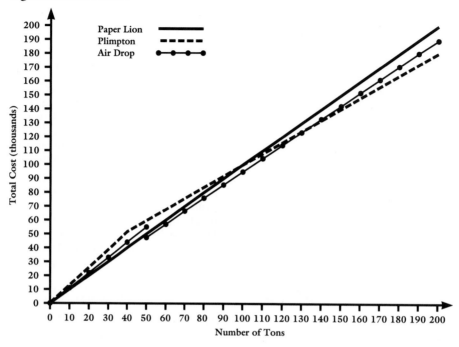

19. (a) See the figure.

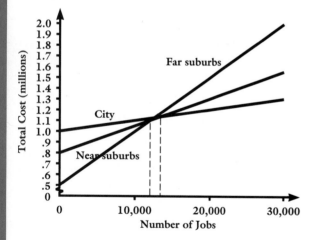

(b) break-even points:

City   *Near Suburbs*

$$\$1,000,000 + 10x = \$800,000 + 25x$$
$$200,000 = 15x$$
$$x = 13,333 \text{ jobs}$$

City   *Far Suburbs*

$$\$1,000,000 + 10x = \$500,000 + 50x$$
$$500,000 = 40x$$
$$x = 12,500 \text{ jobs (irrelevant)}$$

Near Suburbs   *Far Suburbs*

$$\$800,000 + 25x = \$500,000 + 50x$$
$$300,000 = 25x$$
$$x = 12,000 \text{ jobs}$$

20. See the figure for Problem 19.

Number of Jobs		Probability		
5,000	×	.2	=	1,000
10,000	×	.3	=	3,000
15,000	×	.4	=	6,000
20,000	×	.1	=	2,000
				12,000 jobs likely

We are indifferent between the near and far suburbs.

21. $EV(\text{overtime}) = (.4)(5) + (.4)(7) + (.2)(10) = 6.8$

$EV(\text{increase work force}) = (.4)(-5) + (.4)(10) + (.2)(15)$
$$= 5$$

$EV(\text{part-time help}) = (.4)(0) + (.4)(8) + (.2)(12) = 5.6$

$EV(\text{subcontract}) = (.4)(0) + (.4)(9) + (.2)(13) = 6.2$

Therefore, use overtime.

22.

	Minimum (worst)	Maximum (best)
Overtime	5*	10
Increase Work Force	−5	15**
Part-time Help	0	12
Subcontract	0	13

(a) *maximin = 5 by using overtime
(b) **maximax = 15 by increasing work force

23. expected cost:

$$\text{part-time} = .2(0) + .5(35) + .3(100)$$
$$= 0 + 17.5 + 30 = 47.5$$

$$\text{hire} = .2(30) + .5(50) + .3(70)$$
$$= 6 + 25 + 21 = 52$$

Therefore, use part-time help.

24.

	Maximum (worst)	Minimum (best)
Part-time	100	0
Hire	70	30

(a) minimax = 70 through hiring
(b) minimin = 0 through part-time

25. Let p = probability of medium demand and let $.8 - p$ = probability of high demand.

Expected cost of part-time = expected cost of new lawyers

$$.2(0) + p(35) + (.8 - p)(100) = .2(30) + p(50) + (.8 - p)70$$

$$35p + 80 - 100p = 6 + 50p + 56 - 70p$$
$$80 - 65p = 62 - 20p$$
$$18 = 45p$$
$$p = 18/45 = .4$$

Therefore, for any $p > .4$, use part-time help.

26. (a) We will create the decision table as a function of glasses. Note that each glass costs $.10/2 = $.05 and sells for $.25. The numbers in the following table represent the profit if row glasses are made and column glasses are demanded. The profit is

$$\$.25 \text{ (column)} - \$.05 \text{ (row)}.$$

if demand ≤ production. Otherwise, the profit is

$$\$.25 \text{ (row)} - \$.05 \text{ (row)}.$$

	Glasses Sold (demanded)			
Glasses Produced	10 ($p = .2$)	20 ($p = .3$)	30 ($p = .3$)	40 ($p = .2$)
10	2.00	2.00	2.00	2.00
20	1.50	4.00	4.00	4.00
30	1.00	3.50	6.00	6.00
40	.50	3.00	5.50	8.00

(b) The expected profit is computed as follows:

$$E(\text{make } 10) = (.2)(2) + (.3)(2) + (.3)(2) + (.2)(2)$$
$$= \$2.00$$

$$E(\text{make } 20) = (.2)(1.5) + (.3)(4) + (.3)(4) + (.2)(4)$$
$$= \$3.50$$

$$E(\text{make } 30) = (.2)(1) + (.3)(3.5) + (.3)(6) + (.2)(6)$$
$$= \$4.25$$

$$E(\text{make } 40) = (.2)(.5) + (.3)(3) + (.3)(5.5) + (.2)(8)$$
$$= \$4.25$$

The most profitable option is at either 40 glasses or 30 glasses (20 or 15 lemons).

27.

Supply (glasses)	Minimum (worst)	Maximum (best)
10	2.00	2.00
20	1.50	4.00
30	1.00	6.00
40	.50	8.00

(a) The maximin strategy is to produce 10 glasses and have a guaranteed profit of $2.

(b) The maximax strategy is to produce 40 glasses and hope for the large demand and the maximum possible profit of $8.

28. (a) The cost in any cell depends on whether or not the number ordered (the number given in the row) is sufficient to cover the demand (the number given in the column). If supply exceeds demand, cost = $30(number ordered). If demand exceeds supply, cost = $30(number ordered) + $50(pints needed − pints ordered).

(b) Order 150 pints of blood. See the table on the next page.

29.

Pints	Maximum	Minimum
100	8,000	3,000
125	7,500	3,750
150	7,000	4,500
175	6,500	5,250
200	6,000	6,000

(a) The conservative (minimax) strategy is to ensure that there is never a shortage: Order 200 pints with a minimax value of $6,000.

(b) The risky (minimin) strategy is to order as little as possible: Order 100 pints with a minimin value of $3,000.

30. We create the decision table by computing the profit for any given supply and demand combination. The revenue depends on whether supply is greater than or less than demand. The net profit is given by the following: If demand is less than or equal to supply, profit = $1.20(demanded) + $.60(made − demanded) − $1.00(made); if supply is less than or equal to demand, profit = $1.20(made) − $1.00(made) = $.20(made).

The profits are shown in the table below.

(a) Using expected value, the decision is to make 28 dozen.

(b) Using a conservative (maximin) strategy, the decision is to make 26 dozen (as few as possible, so that we will not be stuck with the loss that occurs with leftover doughnuts).

(c) Using an optimistic strategy, the decision is to make as many as possible, 30 dozen, because we are "certain" they will be sold. (*Note:* This is also Problem 22 in Chapter 13. In that chapter, only expected value analysis is considered.)

31. We create the decision table by computing the cost for any given supply and demand combination. The cost depends on whether the number of failures is greater than or less than the number of spares purchased. The net cost is given by the following: If failures do not exceed the number purchased, cost = $800(purchased); and if the number purchased is less than or equal to failures, cost = $800(purchased) + $1,500(failures − purchased).

The profits are shown in the table below.

(a) Using expected value, the decision is to purchase 2 spares.

Table for Problem 28.

Pints Ordered	Pints Needed (Probability)					Expected Value
	100 (.1)	125 (.2)	150 (.3)	175 (.3)	200 (.1)	
100	$3,000	$4,250	$5,500	$6,750	$8,000	$5,625
125	3,750	3,750	5,000	6,250	7,500	5,250
150	4,500	4,500	4,500	5,750	7,000	5,125
175	5,250	5,250	5,250	5,250	6,500	5,375
200	6,000	6,000	6,000	6,000	6,000	6,000

Table for Problem 30.

Dozens Made	Dozens Needed (Probability)					Expected Value	Worst (minimum)
	26 (.1)	27 (.2)	28 (.4)	29 (.2)	30 (.1)		
26	$5.20	$5.20	$5.20	$5.20	$5.20	$5.20	$5.20
27	4.80	5.40	5.40	5.40	5.40	5.34	4.80
28	4.40	5.00	5.60	5.60	5.60	5.36	4.40
29	4.00	4.60	5.20	5.80	5.60	5.14	4.00
30	3.60	4.20	4.80	5.40	6.00	4.80	3.60

Table for Problem 31.

Spares Purchased	Failures (Probability)					Expected Value	Worst (maximum)
	0 (.1)	1 (.3)	2 (.3)	3 (.2)	4 (.1)		
0	$ 0	$1,500	$3,000	$4,500	$6,000	$2,850	$6,000
1	800	800	2,300	3,800	5,300	2,300	5,300
2	1,600	1,600	1,600	3,100	4,600	2,200	4,600
3	2,400	2,400	2,400	2,400	3,900	2,550	3,900
4	3,200	3,200	3,200	3,200	3,200	3,000	3,200

(b) Using a conservative (minimax) strategy, the decision is to purchase 4 spares (as many as possible, so that we will not be stuck with the possibility of having to purchase spares at high prices).

(c) Using an optimistic strategy, we purchase 0 spares and hope for no breakdowns. (*Note:* This is also Problem 24 in Chapter 13. In that chapter, only expected value is considered.)

32. Choose C, yielding a value of $395. See the figure.

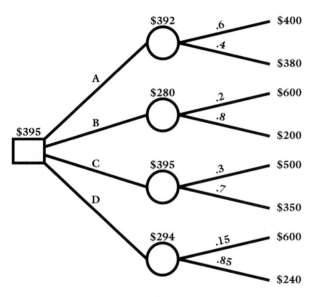

33. Choose B, with a value of 631. See the figure.

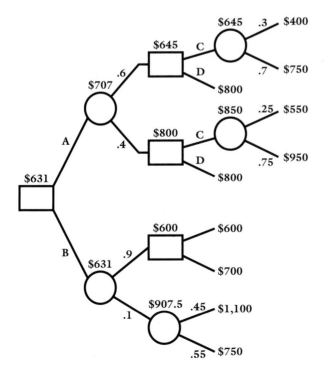

34. Hire part-time help. See the figure.

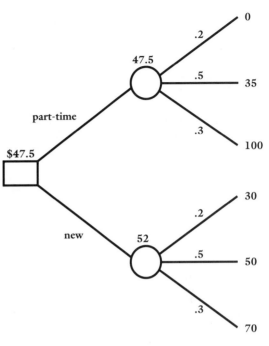

35. Rent small office and expand if the demand becomes higher. See the figure on the next page.

Figure for Problem 35.

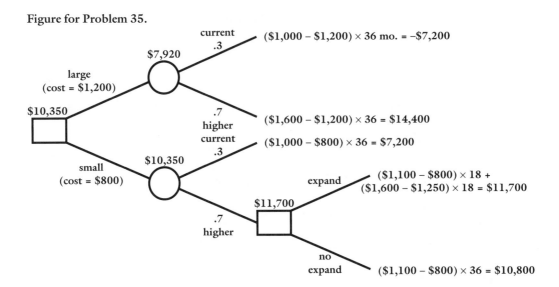

Computer Case Study 3.1

The data on the diskette and the data in the table are identical. No probabilities have been included. As an initial analysis, we expect students to simply load the data and run the program, resulting in a maximin strategy of subcontracting and a maximax strategy of building a new plant. We probably want to keep these two strategies. Further examination of the build a new plant strategy shows a row minimum of −1.63. Clearly, building a new plant can be very good or very bad. Further examination of the row minimums reveals that purchasing can be very risky, with a row minimum of −5.67.

A second analysis would be to determine something about the expected values. Since the probabilities are not known, a first try might be to assign equal probabilities—say, .1666. The best expected value is given by building new, with a value of nearly 2. However, note that this value is not that much greater than the value for expanding the plant. Purchasing has a terrible expected value (.35) and

can be eliminated. Sole sourcing also has a low expected value and can possibly be eliminated from consideration. The question that remains is this: How sensitive are the results to the scenario probabilities? This is where the power of a computer comes in handy. Students can try many different probability combinations and look at the expected values. We are primarily concerned with expanding; building new; subcontracting; and expanding and subcontracting.

Since drop is the worst scenario, we have tried probabilities of .125, .125, and .25 for grow, stable, and drop, respectively. In this case, expand or expand and subcontract are better options. To determine the effects of growth, we have reversed the probabilities. This brings building new to the forefront. *It is impossible to give an exact answer on what option to choose.* The analysis shows that building a new plant can be very profitable, but this strategy can also be very risky. It might be more prudent to focus on the two expansion strategies.

4

Forecasting

TEACHING NOTES

In this chapter, we have tried to indicate that forecasting is a means to an end rather than an end. In other words, this chapter is operational rather than statistical. We explain that different forecasting techniques are available and that the goal is to try to predict demand (or some other variable). We emphasize that, because *all forecasting techniques make errors*, we need to find the technique that minimizes errors.

One way to accomplish this is to gain an understanding of the underlying (demand) process, since different techniques are responsive to different patterns. Another way is to learn to recognize the different time horizons, since qualitative and quantitative techniques vary by time.

Our quantitative emphasis begins with the computation of the errors. (Most texts place this at the end of the forecasting chapter.) Moving this discussion to the beginning of the chapter reinforces the notion that forecasting is an inexact science. In addition, it allows us to indicate that we have a means for comparing forecasting techniques. Included in the error discussion is bias, which is often omitted from P/OM books.

The techniques we cover are moving averages (weighted and unweighted), simple exponential smoothing, and regression. In addition, we have decomposed time series, even though we feel that this is slightly above the level of the students for whom the book is intended. You may wish to skip this section.

This chapter has two exercises in the Solved Problems section. The first is an error analysis of forecasting; the second requires forecasts to be made using four different techniques.

Many of the numerous homework problems use the same data set, requiring students to use different techniques on the same data—notably, Problems 5, 9, and 13; Problems 6, 10, and 14; Problems 7, 11, and 15; and Problems 8, 12, and 16. Problems 1 through 4 deal with error measures; 5 through 8, with moving averages; 9 through 12, with weighted moving averages; 13 through 16, with exponential smoothing; and 17 through 20, with regression. (Problem 20 is tricky: The numbers are given in reverse order.) Problem 21 includes four techniques, Problem 22 uses causal regression, Problem 23 has regression with lag, and Problem 24 uses seasonal factors. Problem 25 *requires thought about seasonality*. Problems 26 and 27 are decomposition problems, while in Problem 28, students use regression to find the trend for the decomposition problems. Problem 29 is regression with seasonal factors, and Problems 30 and 31 deal with tracking signals. Problems 32 and 33, which involve multiple regression, require a computer package.

The software for this chapter is divided into two submodules. The time series submodule will perform moving averages (weighted and unweighted), exponential smoothing, exponential smoothing with trend, and least squares. The regression module will perform multiple regression for up to six independent variables. The standard error is computed for all techniques, and the mean absolute deviation and bias are computed for the smoothing techniques. The same data can easily be used by all of the time series techniques. We have emphasized the error measures, and the software provides an easy means to quickly change n or weights or alpha in order to compute the mean absolute deviation. A reminder: We use n in the denominator of the standard error rather than $n - 1$ or $n - 2$. The following Problems can be solved using AB:POM: 5–25, 28, 29, 32, and 33.

The computer case study for this chapter presents students with a time series of data. Students should begin by plotting the data; they may then experiment with various models. An interesting thing about this data is that multiple regression can be used to model effects of time. The computer case study data diskette contains all of these models. If you want students to develop models themselves, do not distribute the case study data for forecasting.

One more thing: To demonstrate that forecasts are fallible, we have students read W. Coffey's *303 of the World's Worst Predictions* (Tribeca Communications, New York, 1983). This fascinating, easy-to-read book contains many astonishingly inaccurate forecasts made by famous people.

TEACHING SUGGESTIONS

Teaching Suggestion 4.1: Is It Really Guessing?
Since most of the forecasting techniques provide a statistical estimate, the one thing that we know for certain is that they are wrong. However, these techniques are very powerful in that they guarantee a certain closeness. This is what is meant here by an "educated" guess.

Teaching Suggestion 4.2: Plot the Data!
We can't overemphasize to our students the usefulness of plotting the data prior to performing analyses.

Teaching Suggestion 4.3: Group Behavior.
Ask students if they have had similar experiences when working on team projects.

Teaching Suggestion 4.4: Origins of Delphi.

Although the Delphi technique in use today was developed by the Rand Corporation, it has its roots in ancient Greece. The Greeks considered the city of Delphi to be the center of the earth. As the story goes, Zeus released one eagle from the east and another eagle from the west and caused the eagles to fly toward the center. The two eagles met at Delphi. The priestess at Delphi would send messengers to various parts of Greece to collect the opinions of the wise men. The method used today is similar to the method used by the ancient Delphic priestess. The difference is that, now, the information can be gathered and processed much more quickly, making the provision of feedback possible.

Teaching Suggestion 4.5: Benefits to Users.

If users provide good forecasts, the company can provide its goods or services at lower costs. In fact, this accounts, in part, for the emphasis on sole sourcing in JIT and total quality management.

Teaching Suggestion 4.6: Grades: Two Bs vs. A and C.

We ask our students which they would prefer. We then point out that while there is no difference if mean absolute deviation is used, the outcome is not the same if standard error is used.

Teaching Suggestion 4.7: Smoother Is Not Necessarily Better.

It is important to remind students that too smooth might not be responsive enough. This can even be true for a time series dominated by its random component.

Teaching Suggestion 4.8: Unimportant Data.

We sometimes give our students tuition data from the last twenty years and ask for a forecast of next year's tuition. We hope that they will ignore all the data except for that from the last few years, but many students seem to think that they must use all data provided.

Teaching Suggestion 4.9: No Such Thing as Unweighted Moving Average.

Remind students that what they think of as being "unweighted" is actually equally weighted. Furthermore, they tend to forget that, for example, the fourth point in an $n = 3$ moving average is actually still included—it just has a weight of zero.

Teaching Suggestion 4.10: Trends vs. Shift in Data.

The example shows lag due to trend. To show students lag due to a shift, use a time series such as 100, 100, 100, 100, 130, 130, 130, 130.

Teaching Suggestion 4.11: Centered Moving Average.

Be sure to point out that we now use a centered moving average, which differs conceptually from our previous moving average. Also see Figure 4.13.

Teaching Suggestion 4.12: Causal vs. Associative.

Regression is not actually a causal model. It associates variables without distinguishing between cause and effect, if a causal relationship indeed exists. In forecasting, we assume that time is the causal factor.

Teaching Suggestion 4.13: Round-off Error.

This formula is more prone to errors due to rounding than the previous formula.

Teaching Suggestion 4.14: Handling Seasonality.

There are many ways to handle seasonality. We only show one in this section.

Teaching Suggestion 4.15: Importance of Control.

Although it appears last in the chapter for pedagogical reasons, this is the most important subject in application.

ANSWERS TO QUESTIONS

1. Qualitative forecasting techniques are useful for long-range forecasting or in situations where data are not available. Quantitative techniques are useful when an underlying model is known and when data are available—usually the case in short- and medium-range forecasting. Qualitative models are used to supplement quantitative models.

2. A jury of executive opinion collects the forecasts of top-level executives chosen from different business functions so as to represent a wide variety of views within the organization. Each of these executives is given data on, among other things, past sales and profits and is asked to make a forecast. These individual forecasts are then aggregated into one forecast. The major drawback is that the forecast may be unduly influenced by senior executives.

3. The Delphi technique is very similar to the jury of executive opinion except that the Delphi technique maintains anonymity and provides feedback.

4. Bias is used to measure the direction—high or low—of the forecasts; the mean absolute deviation and standard error both measure the amount of the error without regard to direction. If large errors are of concern, standard error is the more appropriate measure; otherwise, the mean absolute deviation is more appropriate.

5. Lag means that the forecasts do not shift as quickly as the data; that is, the forecasts are not responsive. As n gets smaller, lag lessens. A larger n is favorable when the data are expected to be relatively stable—that is, when there is neither trend nor seasonality.

6. The advantage is that fewer data points need to be retained. (The data are retained implicitly with exponential weights.)

7. The significance of α is that it determines the amount of smoothing that will occur. If $\alpha = 0$, the forecasts are perfectly smooth; if $\alpha = 1$, the forecasts are as erratic as the data.

8. Any single piece of data is retained from period to period, but its importance (weight) diminishes each period by a (multiplicative) factor of $1 - \alpha$.

9. Nearly every industry has seasonality. The seasonality must be filtered out for good medium-range planning (of production and inventory).

10. There are several examples. Demand for raw materials or component parts such as steel or tires is a function of demand for goods such as automobiles.

11. Obviously, as we go farther into the future, it becomes more difficult to make forecasts, and we must diminish our reliance on the forecasts.

SOLUTIONS TO PROBLEMS

1.

(1) Month	(2) Forecast	(3) Demand	(4) Error [(3) − (2)]	(5) |Error|	(6) Error^2
June	121	130	9	9	81
July	132	125	−7	7	49
Aug.	129	140	11	11	121
Sept.	136	135	−1	1	1
Oct.	130	132	2	2	4
		Totals	14	30	256
		Averages	2.8	6	51.2

$$bias = 14/5 = 2.8$$

$$MSE = 256/5 = 51.2$$

$$SE = \sigma = \sqrt{MSE} = \sqrt{51.2} = 7.16$$

$$MAD = 30/5 = 6$$

(*Reminder:* Our formula for standard error, σ, uses n rather than $n - 1$ or $n - 2$ in the denominator.)

2. From the normal distribution table (Appendix B), 95% = 1.96σ. Therefore, the interval is

$$F \pm z_\alpha \sigma = 140 \pm 1.96(7.16)$$

$$= 140 \pm 14.0336$$

$$= (125.9664, 154.0336).$$

3.

(1) Year	(2) Sales	(3) Marketing VP's Forecast	(4) Marketing VP's Error [(2) − (3)]	(5) Operations VP's Forecast	(6) Operations VP's Error [(2) − (5)]
1	167,325	170,000	2,675	160,000	7,325
2	175,362	170,000	5,362	165,000	10,362
3	172,536	180,000	7,464	170,000	2,536
4	156,732	180,000	23,268	175,000	18,268
5	176,325	165,000	11,325	165,000	11,325
		Totals	50,094		49,816

$$MAD \text{ (marketing VP)} = 50,094/5 = 10,018.8$$

$$MAD \text{ (operations VP)} = 49,818/5 = 9,963.2$$

Therefore, based on past data, the VP of operations has been presenting better forecasts.

4.

(1) Year	(2) Sales	(3) Marketing VP's Forecast	(4) Percentage Error $[(2) \div (3) - 1]$	(5) Operations VP's Forecast	(6) Percentage Error $[(2) \div (5) - 1]$
1	167,325	170,000	−.016	160,000	.044
2	175,362	170,000	.031	165,000	.059
3	172,536	180,000	−.043	170,000	.015
4	156,732	180,000	.148	175,000	−.117
5	176,325	165,000	.064	165,000	.064
		Totals	−.113		.065

MPE (marketing VP) $= -.113/5 = -.0226 = -.0226$

(On average, he or she is overforecasting by 2.26%.)

$\qquad MPE$ (operations VP) $= .065/5 = .013$

(On average, he or she is underforecasting by 1.3%.)

5. forecast for year 5 $= \dfrac{3.0 + 2.4 + 2.6}{3} = 2.667$ in.

6. (a) $\dfrac{3,700 + 3,800}{2} = 3,750$ mi.

(b)

Year	Mileage	Two-Year Moving Average	Error	|Error|
1	3,000			
2	4,000			
3	3,400	3,500	−100	100
4	3,800	3,700	100	100
5	3,700	3,600	100	100
		Totals	100	300

$\qquad$ bias $= \dfrac{100}{3} = 33.33$

(c) $MAD = \dfrac{300}{3} = 100$

7. (a) $\dfrac{374 + 368 + 381}{3} = 374.33$ pints

(b)

Week of	Pints Used	Three-Week Moving Average	Error	Error^2
Aug. 31	360			
Sept. 7	389			
Sept. 14	410			
Sept. 21	381	386.33	−5.3333	28.4444
Sept. 28	368	393.33	−25.3333	641.7777
Oct. 5	374	386.33	−12.3333	152.1111
			Total	822.3333

$\qquad MSE = 822.33/3 = 274.11$

$\qquad SE = \sqrt{274.11} = 16.55626$

From the normal distribution table, 99-percent confidence occurs for 2.33 standard deviations. (This is one-tailed!) Therefore, the required amount is given by

$$374.33 + 2.33(16.56) = 374.33 + 38.5848$$
$$= 412.9148.$$

8. The computations for both the two- and three-month averages appear in the table; the results appear in the figure below.

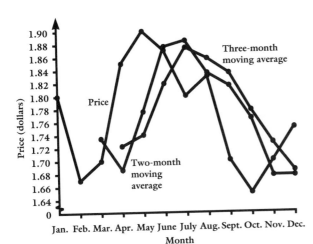

MAD (two-month moving average) $= .750/10 = .075$

MAD (three-month moving average) $= .793/9 = .088$

Therefore, the two-month moving average seems to have performed better.

9. forecast $= .5(3) + .3(2.4) + .2(2.6) = 2.74$ in.

10. (a) forecast $= .6(3,700) + .4(3,800)$
$$= 2,220 + 1,520 = 3,740 \text{ mi.}$$

(b) and **(c)**

Year	Mileage	Weighted Moving Average	Error	|Error|
1	3,000			
2	4,000			
3	3,400	3,600	−200	200
4	3,800	3,640	160	160
5	3,700	3,640	60	60
		Totals	20	420

bias $= 20/3 = 6.67$; $MAD = 420/3 = 140$

11.

Week of	Pints Used	Weighted Moving Average	Error	Error^2
Aug. 31	360			
Sept. 7	389			
Sept. 14	410			
Sept. 21	381	398.7	−17.7	313.29
Sept. 28	368	390.5	−22.5	506.25
Oct. 5	374	376.1	−2.1	4.41
		Forecast 372.9	Total	823.95

$$MSE = 823.95/3 = 274.65$$

$$SE = \sqrt{274.65} = 16.57$$

The amount on hand should be $372.9 + 2.33(16.57)$
$= 372.9 + 38.61 = 411.51$.

Table for Problem 8.

		Forecast		|Error|	
Month	Price per Chip	Two-Month Moving Average	Three-Month Moving Average	Two-Month Moving Average	Three-Month Moving Average
Jan.	$1.80				
Feb.	1.67				
March	1.70	1.735		.035	
April	1.85	1.685	1.723	.165	.127
May	1.90	1.775	1.740	.125	.160
June	1.87	1.875	1.817	.005	.053
July	1.80	1.885	1.873	.085	.073
Aug.	1.83	1.835	1.857	.005	.027
Sept.	1.70	1.815	1.833	.115	.133
Oct.	1.65	1.765	1.777	.115	.127
Nov.	1.70	1.675	1.727	.025	.027
Dec.	1.75	1.675	1.683	.075	.067
			Totals .750		.793

12.

		(.6, .4)		(.7, .3)	
Month	Price per Chip	Forecast	|Error|	Forecast	|Error|
Jan.	$1.80				
Feb.	1.67				
March	1.70	$1.72	$.02	$1.71	$.01
April	1.85	1.69	.16	1.69	.16
May	1.90	1.79	.11	1.81	.09
June	1.87	1.88	.01	1.89	.01
July	1.80	1.88	.08	1.88	.08
Aug.	1.83	1.83	.00	1.82	.01
Sept.	1.70	1.82	.12	1.82	.12
Oct.	1.65	1.75	.10	1.74	.09
Nov.	1.70	1.67	.03	1.67	.04
Dec.	1.75	1.68	.07	1.69	.07
		Totals	$.71		$.68

$MAD(.6, .4) = \$.71/10 = \$.071$

$MAD(.7, .3) = \$.68/10 = \$.068$

The MAD is lower for weights of .7 and .3.

13.

Year	Rain	Forecast	Error	Error × .10	New Forecast
1	2.2	(2.2)	0	0	2.2
2	2.6	2.2	.4	.04	2.24
3	2.4	2.24	.16	.016	2.256
4	3.0	2.256	.744	.0744	2.3304

The forecast is 2.33 in.

14.

Year	Mileage	Forecast	Error	Error × .50	New Forecast
1	3,000	(3,000)	0	0	3,000
2	4,000	3,000	1,000	500	3,500
3	3,400	3,500	−100	−50	3,450
4	3,800	3,450	350	175	3,625
5	3,700	3,625	75	38	3,663
		Total	1,325		

(a) The forecast is 3,663 mi.

(b) bias = 1,325/4 = 331 (Alternatively, one might divide by 5, since there are 5 periods listed; this leads to a bias of 1,325/5 = 265. Note that AB:POM divides by 4.)

(c) $MAD = (1,000 + 100 + 350 + 75)/4$
$= 1,525/4 = 381.25$

15. See the table below.
(a) The forecast is 374.26.
(b) $MSE = 2{,}897.797/5 = 579.560$

(Once again, we remark that we are not including period 1 in our computations, since the forecast was given. Therefore, we divide by 5 rather than 6.)

$$SE = \sqrt{579.5601} = 26.9156$$

(Remember that our formula for standard error uses n in the denominator rather than $n - 1$ or $n - 2$.) From the normal distribution table, 2.33 standard deviations will cover 99 percent of the normal distribution (one-tailed!). Therefore, we need $374.2636 + 2.33(26.92) = 374.2636 + 62.72 = 436$ pints.

16. See the table below.
The MAD is lowest for $\alpha = .5$.

17.

Month	Number of Accidents (y)	x	xy	x^2
Jan.	30	1	30	1
Feb.	40	2	80	4
March	60	3	180	9
April	90	4	360	16
Totals	220	10	650	30
Averages	$\bar{y} = 55$	$\bar{x} = 2.5$		

$$b = \frac{\sum xy - n\bar{x}\bar{y}}{\sum x^2 - n\bar{x}^2} = \frac{650 - 4(2.5)(55)}{30 - 4(2.5)^2} = \frac{650 - 550}{30 - 25}$$

$$= \frac{100}{5} = 20$$

$$a = \bar{y} - b\bar{x}$$

$$= 55 - (20)(2.5)$$

$$= 5$$

The regression line is $y = 5 + 20x$. The forecast for May ($x = 5$) is $y = 5 + 20(5) = 105$.

Table for Problem 15.

Week of	Pints	Forecast	Error	Error × .20	Forecast	Error²
Aug. 31	360	360	0	0	360	0
Sept. 7	389	360	29	5.8	365.8	841.00
Sept. 14	410	365.8	44.2	8.84	374.64	1,953.64
Sept. 21	381	374.64	6.36	1.272	375.912	40.45
Sept. 28	368	375.912	−7.912	−1.5824	374.3296	62.60
Oct. 5	374	374.3296	−.3296	−.06592	374.2636	.11
					Total	2,897.80

Table for Problem 16.

Month	Price per Chip	α = .1 Forecast	|Error|	α = .3 Forecast	|Error|	α = .5 Forecast	|Error|
Jan.	$1.80	$1.80	$.00	$1.80	$.00	$1.80	$.00
Feb.	1.67	1.80	.13	1.80	.13	1.80	.13
March	1.70	1.79	.09	1.76	.06	1.74	.04
April	1.85	1.78	.07	1.74	.11	1.72	.13
May	1.90	1.79	.11	1.77	.13	1.78	.12
June	1.87	1.80	.07	1.81	.06	1.84	.03
July	1.80	1.80	.00	1.83	.03	1.86	.06
Aug.	1.83	1.80	.03	1.82	.01	1.83	.00
Sept.	1.70	1.81	.11	1.82	.12	1.83	.13
Oct.	1.65	1.80	.15	1.79	.14	1.76	.11
Nov.	1.70	1.78	.08	1.75	.05	1.71	.01
Dec.	1.75	1.77	.02	1.73	.02	1.70	.05
Totals			$.86		$.84		$.80
MAD (total/12)			$.078		$.076		$.072

18.

Year (x)	Attendance (y)	xy	x^2
1	77,000	77,000	1
2	80,000	160,000	4
3	93,000	279,000	9
4	90,000	360,000	16
5	98,000	490,000	25
Totals 15	438,000	1,366,000	55
$\bar{x} = 3$	$\bar{y} = 87,600$		

$$b = \frac{\Sigma xy - n\bar{x}\bar{y}}{\Sigma x^2 - n\bar{x}^2}$$

$$= \frac{1,366,000 - 5(3)(87,600)}{55 - 5(3)^2}$$

$$= \frac{1,366,000 - 1,314,000}{55 - 45}$$

$$= 5,200$$

$$a = \bar{y} - b\bar{x}$$

$$= 87,600 - 5,200(3)$$

$$= 87,600 - 15,600$$

$$= 72,000$$

The regression line is $y = 72,000 + 5,200x$. The forecast for next year ($x = 6$) is $72,000 + (6)(5,200) = 72,000 + 31,200 = 103,200$.

19. (a) See the table below.

$$b = \frac{2,880 - 5(3)(180)}{55 - 5(3)^2} = \frac{2,880 - 2,700}{55 - 45}$$

$$= \frac{180}{10} = 18$$

$$a = 180 - 3(18) = 180 - 54 = 126$$

$$y = 126 + 18x$$

For next year ($x = 6$), the number of closings is forecasted as $y = 126 + 18(6) = 126 + 108 = 234$.

(b) $MSE = 160/5 = 32$; $SE = \sqrt{32} = 5.657$

20. (a) (*Note:* We number the days according to real time. This is backward—6 to 1—because the data is given from Sunday backward in time. Alternatively, students may turn the entire table upside down so that the data appear in the proper order.) See the table below.

$$b = \frac{433 - 6(3.5)(21.1667)}{91 - 6(3.5)^2}$$

$$= \frac{433 - 444.5007}{91 - 73.5} = \frac{-11.5007}{17.5} = -.6571$$

$$a = \bar{y} - b\bar{x}$$

$$= 21.17 - (-.6571)(3.5)$$

$$= 21.170 + 2.2999$$

$$= 23.4666$$

Table for Problem 19(a).

Year (x)	Closings (y)	xy	x^2	126 + 18x	Error	Error^2
1	140	140	1	144	−4	16
2	160	320	4	162	−2	4
3	190	570	9	180	10	100
4	200	800	16	198	2	4
5	210	1,050	25	216	−6	36
Totals 15	900	2,880	55			160
$\bar{x} = 3$	$\bar{y} = 180$					

Table for Problem 20(a).

Day	Date	Temperature (y)	x	xy	x^2	23.46 + .6571x	Error^2
Sun.	12/18	20	6	120	36	19.52	.227
Sat.	12/17	21	5	105	25	20.18	.671
Fri.	12/16	18	4	72	16	20.84	8.05
Thurs.	12/15	23	3	69	9	21.50	2.26
Wed.	12/14	22	2	44	4	22.15	.023
Tues.	12/13	23	1	23	1	22.81	.036
	Totals 127		21	433	91		11.28
	$\bar{y} = 21.17$		$\bar{x} = 3.50$				

forecast (Christmas) $= 23.4666 + (-.6571)(13)$

$$= 23.4666 - 8.5423$$

$$= 14.92435$$

forecast (New Year's) $= 23.4666 + (-.6571)(20)$

$$= 23.4666 - 13.142$$

$$= 10.324$$

(b) $MSE = 11.28/6 = 1.88$

$SE = \sqrt{1.88} = 1.371$

Christmas range $= 14.9243 \pm 2.58(1.371)$

$$= 14.9243 \pm 3.537$$

$$= 11.387 \text{ to } 18.461$$

New Year's range $= 10.324 \pm 2.58(1.371)$

$$= 10.324 \pm 3.537$$

$$= 6.787 \text{ to } 13.861$$

21. (a) $\dfrac{3,900 + 3,000 + 2,700}{3} = \dfrac{9,600}{3} = 3,200$

(b) $.75(3,900) + .25(3,000) = 3,675$

(c) $F_5 = F_4 + \alpha(Y_4 - F_4)$

$$= 3,000 + .3(3,000 - 3,000)$$

$$= 3,000$$

$F_6 = F_5 + \alpha(Y_5 - F_5)$

$$= 3,000 + .3(3,900 - 3,000)$$

$$= 3,000 + .3(900)$$

$$= 3,000 + 270$$

$$= 3,270$$

(d)

Year (x)	Sales (y)	xy	x^2
1	2,400	2,400	1
2	3,200	6,400	4
3	2,700	8,100	9
4	3,000	12,000	16
5	3,900	19,500	25
Totals 15	15,200	48,400	55
$\bar{x} = 3$	$\bar{y} = 3,040$		

$$b = \frac{48,400 - 5(3)(3,040)}{55 - 5(3)^2}$$

$$= \frac{48,400 - 45,600}{55 - 45} = \frac{2,800}{10} = 280$$

$a = 3,040 - 280(3) = 3,040 - 840 = 2,200$

The forecast for next year is given by $y = 2,200 + 280(6)$
$= 2,200 + 1,680 = 3,880$.

22. (a)

Year	Rainfall (x)	Harvest (y)	xy	x^2
1	6.4	510	3,264.00	40.96
2	8.0	616	4,928.00	64.00
3	7.2	543	3,909.60	51.84
4	5.2	465	2,418.00	27.04
5	6.8	530	3,604.00	46.24
Totals 33.6		2,664	18,123.60	230.08
$\bar{x} = 6.72$		$\bar{y} = 532.8$		

$$b = \frac{18,123.6 - 5(6.72)(532.8)}{230.08 - 5(6.72)^2}$$

$$= \frac{18,123.6 - 17,902.08}{230.08 - 225.792}$$

$$= \frac{221.52}{4.288}$$

$$= 51.66047$$

$a = 532.8 - 51.66(6.72)$

$$= 532.8 - 347.1552$$

$$= 185.6448$$

$y = 185.6448 + 51.66x$

(b) $y = 185.6448 + 51.66(5.9)$
$= 185.6448 + 304.145 = 489.7898$

23. We begin by reordering the numbers in the table to account for the fact that enrollment lags birth by 5 years. Notice that the table in the problem contains some extraneous information.

Year	Births (x)	Enrollment 5 Years Later (y)	xy	x^2
1	131	148	19,388	17,161
2	192	188	36,098	36,864
3	158	155	24,490	24,964
4	93	110	10,230	8,649
5	107	124	13,268	11,339
Totals 681		725	103,472	99,087
$\bar{x} = 136.2$		$\bar{y} = 145$		

$$b = \frac{103.472 - 5(136.2)(145)}{99,087 - 5(136.2)^2}$$

$$= \frac{103,472 - 98,745}{99,087 - 92,752.2}$$

$$= \frac{4,727}{6,334.8}$$

$$= .746$$

$$a = 145 - .746(136.2)$$
$$= 145 - 101.6052$$
$$= 43.3948$$

We now can use this equation for the next 5 years.

Year	Births 5 Years Earlier	Projected Enrollment (43.3948 + .746x)
11	130	140.3748
12	128	138.8828
13	124	135.8988
14	97	115.7568
15	147	153.0568

24. 1997 is 25 years beyond 1972. Therefore, the quarter numbers are 101 through 104.

(1) Quarter	(2) Quarter Number	(3) Forecast (77 + .43Q)	(4) Seasonal Factor	(5) Adjusted Forecast [(3) × (4)]
Winter	101	120.43	.8	96.344
Spring	102	120.86	1.1	132.946
Summer	103	121.29	1.4	170.558
Fall	104	121.72	.7	85.204

25. (a)

Year	Season	Sales (y)	(x)	(xy)	x^2
1	SS	26,825	1	26,825	1
	FW	5,722	2	11,444	4
2	SS	28,630	3	85,890	9
	FW	7,633	4	30,532	16
3	SS	30,255	5	151,275	25
	FW	8,745	6	52,470	36
	Totals	107,810	21	358,436	91

$$\bar{y} = 17,968.33 \quad \bar{x} = 3.5$$

$$b = \frac{358,436 - 6(3.5)(17,968.33)}{91 - 6(3.5)^2}$$

$$= \frac{358,436 - 377,335}{91 - 73.5}$$

$$= \frac{-18,899}{17.5}$$

$$= -1,080$$

$$a = 17,968.33 - 3.5(-1,080)$$
$$= 17,968.33 + 3,780$$
$$= 21,748.33$$

$$y = 21,748 - 1,080x$$

(b) The problem with this line is that it shows a decreasing trend when sales have been *rising* each year.

(c) Two separate forecast lines should be generated—one for Spring/Summer and one for Fall/Winter—or the analysis can be performed as a multiple regression (see Problem 32).

26. The first step is to reorder the data and compute five-period centered averages, followed by ratios. Then compute average ratios (6). See the table on page IS-27.

27. See the table on page IS-27.

28. We create a regression table, but we use the adjusted forecasts.

Period (x)	Adjusted (y)	xy	x^2
1	89.54	89.543	1
2	90.00	180.000	4
3	90.74	272.235	9
4	93.80	375.198	16
5	96.18	480.907	25
6	98.50	590.985	36
7	100.00	700.000	49
8	102.09	816.705	64
9	104.22	937.996	81
10	105.80	1,057.996	100
11	107.45	1,181.970	121
12	110.00	1,320.000	144
13	113.43	1,474.605	169
14	114.64	1,605.015	196
15	115.42	1,731.267	225
Totals 120	1,531.820	12,814.42	1,240
Averages 8	102.1213		

$$b = \frac{12,814.42 - (15)(8)(102.1213)}{1,240 - 15(8)^2}$$

$$= \frac{12,814.42 - 12,254.56}{1,240 - 960}$$

$$= \frac{559.86}{280}$$

$$= 1.999, \text{ which is the trend}$$

$$a = 102.1213 - 1.999(8)$$
$$= 102.1213 - 15.992$$
$$= 86.1293$$

(b) The trend is obviously 2.

Table for Problem 26.

(1) Week	(2) Day	(3) Demand	(4) Centered Moving Average	(5) Ratio [(3)/(4)]	(7) Seasonal Factor	(8) Adjusted Demand
1	Mon.	100			1.11678	89.54
1	Tues.	90			1.00000	90.00
1	Wed.	80	92	.86957	.88159	90.74
1	Thurs.	90	94	.95745	.95949	93.80
1	Fri.	100	96	1.04167	1.03970	96.18
2	Mon.	110	98	1.12245	1.11678	98.50
2	Tues.	100	100	1.00000	1.00000	100.00
2	Wed.	90	102	.88235	.88159	102.09
2	Thurs.	100	104	.96154	.95949	104.22
2	Fri.	110	106	1.03774	1.03970	105.80
3	Mon.	120	108	1.11111	1.11678	107.45
3	Tues.	110	110	1.00000	1.00000	110.00
3	Wed.	100	112	.89286	.88159	113.43
3	Thurs.	110			.95949	114.64
3	Fri.	120			1.03970	115.42

	Ratio				(6)
Day	Week 1	Week 2	Week 3	Total	Average
Mon.		1.12245	1.11111	2.23356	1.11678
Tues.		1.00000	1.00000	2.00000	1.00000
Wed.	.86957	.88235	.89286	2.64478	.88159
Thurs.	.95745	.96154		1.91899	.95949
Fri.	1.04167	1.03774		2.07940	1.03970

Table for Problem 27.

(1) Week	(2) Day	(3) Demand	(4) Centered Moving Average	(5) Difference [(3) − (4)]	(7) Seasonal Factor	(8) Adjusted Demand
1	Mon.	100			12.00	88
1	Tues.	90			0.00	90
1	Wed.	80	92	−12	−12.00	92
1	Thurs.	90	94	−4	−4.00	94
1	Fri.	100	96	4	4.00	96
2	Mon.	110	98	12	12.00	98
2	Tues.	100	100	0	0.00	100
2	Wed.	90	102	−12	−12.00	102
2	Thurs.	100	104	−4	−4.00	104
2	Fri.	110	106	4	4.00	106
3	Mon.	120	108	12	12.00	108
3	Tues.	110	110	0	0.00	110
3	Wed.	100	112	−12	−12.00	112
3	Thurs.	110			−4.00	114
3	Fri.	120			4.00	116

	Ratio				(6)
Day	Week 1	Week 2	Week 3	Total	Average
Mon.		12	12	24	12.00
Tues.		0	0	0	0.00
Wed.	−12	−12	−12	−36	−12.00
Thurs.	−4	−4		−8	−4.00
Fri.	4	4		8	4.00

29.

(1) Week	(2) Day	(3) Demand (y)	(4) x	(5) xy	(6) x^2	(7) Forecast ($87.714 + 1.78x$)	(8) Ratio [(3)/(7)]	(9) Seasonal	(10) Adjusted Forecast
1	Mon.	100	1	100	1	89.50	1.117	1.118	100.02
1	Tues.	90	2	180	4	91.28	.986	.997	91.03
1	Wed.	80	3	240	9	93.07	.860	.881	82.01
1	Thurs.	90	4	360	16	94.85	.949	.963	91.33
1	Fri.	100	5	500	25	96.64	1.035	1.042	100.66
2	Mon.	110	6	660	36	98.42	1.118	1.118	110.00
2	Tues.	100	7	700	49	100.21	.998	.997	99.93
2	Wed.	90	8	720	64	102.00	.882	.881	89.88
2	Thurs.	100	9	900	81	103.78	.964	.963	99.92
2	Fri.	110	10	1,100	100	105.57	1.042	1.042	109.96
3	Mon.	120	11	1,320	121	107.35	1.118	1.118	119.97
3	Tues.	110	12	1,320	144	109.14	1.008	.997	108.84
3	Wed.	100	13	1,300	169	110.92	.902	.881	97.74
3	Thurs.	110	14	1,540	196	112.71	.976	.963	108.51
3	Fri.	120	15	1,800	225	114.49	1.048	1.042	119.26
	Totals	1,530	120	12,740	1,240				
	Averages	102	8						

$$b = \frac{12{,}740 - (15)(102)(8)}{1{,}240 - 15(8)^2}$$

$$= \frac{12{,}740 - 12{,}240}{1{,}240 - 960}$$

$$= 1.7857$$

$$a = 102 - 8(1.7857)$$

$$= 102 - 14.286$$

$$= 87.714$$

(a) $y = 87.714 + 1.7857x$

(b) seasonals (from ratio column in the table):

Day	Week 1	Week 2	Week 3	Week 4
Mon.	1.117329	1.117604	1.117833	1.117588
Tues.	.985930	.997904	1.007919	.997251
Wed.	.859573	.882395	.901544	.881170
Thurs.	.948821	.963574	.975990	.962795
Fri.	1.034771	1.042008	1.048116	1.041631

(c) forecasts for week 4:

Day	Unadjusted Forecast	Seasonal Factor	Adjusted Forecast
Mon.	116.28	1.118	129.95
Tues.	118.06	.997	117.74
Wed.	119.85	.881	105.61
Thurs.	121.63	.963	117.11
Fri.	123.42	1.042	128.55

30.

marketing vice-president:

Sales	Forecast	Error	RSFE	Two-Year MAD	Tracking Signal
167,325	170,000	−2,675	−2,675		
175,362	170,000	5,362	2,687		
172,536	180,000	−7,464	−4,777	1,343.5	−3.556
156,732	180,000	−23,288	−28,045	1,051.0	−26.684
176,325	165,000	11,325	−16,720	15,366.0	−1.088

operations vice-president:

Sales	Forecast	Error	RSFE	Two-Year MAD	Tracking Signal
167,325	160,000	7,325	−9,395		
175,362	165,000	10,362	967		
172,538	170,000	2,536	3,503	8,843.5	.396
156,732	175,000	−18,268	−14,765	6,449.0	−2.290
176,325	165,000	11,325	3,440	7,866.0	−.437

31. (a)

(1) Month	(2) Price per Chip	(3) Two-Month Moving Average	(4) Error [(2) − (3)]	(5) RSFE ΣErrors	(6) Three-Month MAD	(7) TS [(5)/(6)]
Jan.	$1.80					
Feb.	1.67					
March	1.70	1.735	−.035	−.035		
April	1.85	1.685	.165	.130		
May	1.90	1.775	.125	.255	.1083	2.3538
June	1.87	1.875	−.005	.250	.0983	2.5424
July	1.80	1.885	−.085	.165	.0717	2.3023
Aug.	1.83	1.835	−.005	.160	.0317	5.0526
Sept.	1.70	1.815	−.115	.045	.0683	.6585
Oct.	1.65	1.765	−.115	−.070	.0783	−.8936
Nov.	1.70	1.675	.025	−.045	.0850	−.5294
Dec.	1.75	1.675	.075	.030	.0717	.4186

(b) The tracking signals at the beginning were beyond the two-*MAD* limit, but the process seems to have reversed itself and now is in control.

32. See the screen on page IS-30, which shows the output from AB:POM.

33. See the screen on page IS-30, which shows the output from AB:POM. We have entered the six lines of data and let the season be 1 for Spring/Summer and −1 for Fall/Winter. (This choice was arbitrary; we could have used 0 and 1 or 1 and 2. It does not matter which numbers we choose, as long as we interpret the results correctly.)

The regression equation is that sales have a base of 14,741.8, and Spring/Summer (1) adds 10,601.7 to this base, while Fall/Winter (−1) subtracts 10,601.7 from this base. Furthermore, sales have been increasing at a rate of 1,613.25 per year over the past three years.

The equation enrollment = 58.6172 + .688(births) − 2.47(time), yields the following forecasts.

Births	Time	Enrollment
130	6	133.3036
128	7	129.4508
124	8	124.2205
97	9	103.1488
147	10	135.1113

Screen for Problem 32.

```
 Data file:wg4-32                    Forecasting                        Solution
  Number of past data periods (2-99) 5  Number of independ. variables (1-6)  2
```

```
                          Weiss/Gershon, Chapter 4, Problem 32
  Method-->Least Squares - Simple and Multiple Regression
            B 0      B 1      B 2
  Coef--->  58.6172 .688756 -2.4753
            Enroll   Birth     timeForecast Error    |Error|  Error^2
  Year 1    148.00   131.00   1.00 146.369   1.631    1.631     2.66
  Year 2    188.00   192.00   2.00  185.91 2.09212  2.09212    4.377
  Year 3    155.00   158.00   3.00 160.015 -5.0149  5.01489    25.15
  Year 4    110.00    93.00   4.00 112.770   -2.77  2.77045  7.67538
  Year 5    124.00   107.00   5.00 119.938 4.06225  4.06225  16.5019
  TOTALS                                     0.00     15.57  56.3634
  AVERAGE                                    0.00   3.11413  11.2727
                                          (Bias)    (MAD)    (MSE)


            Regression Line : See summary table
            Correlation coefficient =   0.9921936   Standard error = 3.357481
```

Screen for Problem 33.

```
 Data file:wg4-33                    Forecasting                        Solution
  Number of past data periods (2-99) 6  Number of independ. variables (1-6)  2
```

```
                          Weiss/Gershon, Chapter 4, Problem 33
  Method-->Least Squares - Simple and Multiple Regression
            B 0      B 1      B 2
  Coef--->  14741.8 10601.7 1613.25
            Sales    season    yearForecast Error    |Error|  Error^2
  obs  1    26825.0   1.00    1.00 26956.8 -131.75   131.75   17358.1
  obs  2    5722.00  -1.00    1.00 5753.42 -31.417  31.4165  986.997
  obs  3    28630.0   1.00    2.00 28570.0   60.00    60.00  3600.00
  obs  4    7633.00  -1.00    2.00 7366.67 266.333  266.333  70933.5
  obs  5    30255.0   1.00    3.00 30183.3   71.75    71.75  5148.06
  obs  6    8745.00  -1.00    3.00 8979.92 -234.92  234.916  55185.5
  TOTALS                                   0.00098  796.166   153212
  AVERAGE                                     0.00  132.694  25535.4
                                          (Bias)    (MAD)    (MSE)

        Regression Line = Sales = 14741.8 +10601.67*season  +1613.25*year
                                        Standard error = 195.7116
```

Computer Case Study 4.1

We have provided three different data sets for this problem. One data set can be used for time series analysis; the other two can be used for multiple regression.

The immediate action should be to look at the data. After the time series data (file name = CASE4-1T) has been loaded, any method can be run. (We have it initialized to regression.) After execution, the graph can be plotted, making obvious the increasing trend. Therefore, it would be unwise to use the moving averages options or simple exponential smoothing. Exponential smoothing with trend is available, but as it is not discussed in the text, we do not expect students to use it. When running the regression, the standard error is 8.27 (and the correlation is .84). Of course, this is very good. But we might be able to do better.

Data set CASE4-1M contains the data in a multiple regression form. One independent variable (column X4) consists of the period numbers (as in single regression). In addition, we have one column for three of the four seasons. We do not have a column for period 4, because this would make the columns linearly dependent. The equation is $y = 54.68 + .064(x_1) - 9.62(x_2) - .53(x_3) + 1.24(x_4)$. Stu-

dents should be asked to interpret this line. The correlation coefficient is .89 and the standard error is 7.17.

We make one more try with the data (file = CASE4-1X). We have used multiple regression and put in the data for the previous four seasons as the independent variables. This is a common forecasting "trick." The results are

$$y = 30.5 - .023\,(x_{t-1}) + .089\,(x_{t-2}) + .119(x_{t-3}) + .47(x_{t-4}).$$

This equation yields a standard error of 7.24 and a correlation coefficient of .787.

The third run was not as good as the second, but there is one more model that makes sense. Students can add to the second model a new column (using the ESC-INS key sequence), in which the numbers 1, 2, 3, 4, . . . are placed in order to pick up any trend. The results are

$$y = 75.52 - .21(x_{t-1}) - .14(x_{t-2}) - .13(x_{t-3}) + .29(x_{t-4}) + 1.15\ (\text{trend}),$$

which has a correlation coefficient of .823 and a standard error of 6.67. While our results have improved, they are not as good as the first multiple regression model (CASE4-1M).

5

Facility Location

TEACHING NOTES

In this chapter, we point out the many critical factors within operations that apply to location. We present the current trends in location in order to indicate which factors institutions currently feel are important. We organize our discussion in the traditional way, exploring regional, community, and site factors.

The facility location discussion is one of the few opportunities for providing concrete examples in a P/OM book. In this chapter, we get specific about the advantages and disadvantages of locations within the United States and throughout the world; whenever possible, we use well-known companies for our examples. In addition to the qualitative rating schemes that are included in most texts, *we have also included simple quantitative analysis, a topic that is usually omitted from P/OM books*. We present location on the mean and median for one and two dimensions and explain the difference between the two. We do this for two important reasons. First, this is one of the few places in any course where the median is used instead of the mean. Second, it makes students think about whether the goal

should be to minimize a distance or a distance squared (see Problem 10).

There are three exercises in the Solved Problems section of this chapter. The first involves qualitative location analysis; the second involves two-dimensional siting, and the third involves weighted two-dimensional siting.

Problems 1, 2, and 3 are break-even problems that deal with location. Problems 4 through 7 are factor rating problems. Problems 8 and 9 are location on a line problems. Problem 10 is the same type of problem, although most students will not realize this; in Problem 10, students must decide what the objective is. Problems 11 and 12 are two-dimensional location problems that use the city block (taxi) measure. Problems 13, 14, and 15 are two-dimensional location problems that use air distance.

The software for this chapter solves both the qualitative (Problems 5 and 7) and quantitative (Problems 8, 9, and 11 through 14) location problems. Break-even analysis can be used for Problems 1 and 2.

The computer case study for this chapter is a very straightforward two-dimensional location problem.

TEACHING SUGGESTIONS

Teaching Suggestion 5.1:   Examples of Trends.
For several of the trends discussed, we provide lists of examples. Ask students which local companies could be included in these tables.

Teaching Suggestion 5.2:   Lifestyle Choice.
We always begin our lecture by asking our students where they would like to get a job after graduation. In addition to listing the city, state, and region, students must give the reasons for their choices.

Teaching Suggestion 5.3:   Raw Materials and Components.
We speak here of raw materials in a limited sense. A broader definition would include components and subassemblies provided from other locations.

Teaching Suggestion 5.4:   Lifestyle Choice II.
We use a variation of the exercise described in Teaching Suggestion 5.2, asking students in which neighborhood they would like to live in the Philadelphia area. Once again, the reasons are more important than the choices.

Teaching Suggestion 5.5:   Subjective Numerical Data.
Our students think that any model that uses numbers is an exact quantitative model. We like to stress that this approach includes much subjective information. It also uses numbers to "quantify" opinions or qualitative factors.

Teaching Suggestion 5.6:   Analysis vs. Design.
In some of the quantitative models, we choose from among a fixed set of potential sites, analyzing or describing the costs or distances for each site. Other models are more open-ended in that the location is "designed," or prescribed.

Teaching Suggestion 5.7:   Which Is Better?
As we did with forecast errors in the previous chapter, we ask students if they prefer to make two customers walk three blocks each or to make one customer walk one block and the other walk four blocks.

Teaching Suggestion 5.8:   Midpoint vs. Mean/Median.
We point out that, in a sense, the midpoint of the range of customer locations (the halfway point between the two extremes) is fairest, because it minimizes the maximum distance traveled. We compare this to the minimax criterion used in the decision tables in Chapter 3.

Teaching Suggestion 5.9:   Location/Transportation Method.
Example 6.9 applies the transportation method to site selection in a multi-facility network.

ANSWERS TO QUESTIONS

1. New facilities create jobs and bring in revenue and taxes to a community. Most communities welcome new businesses; many use development authorities to promote their area and to influence companies' facility location decisions.

2. Companies build facilities when capacity is not sufficient, technology changes, market location changes, or labor costs become critical.

3. The advantages of decentralization are that a disruption in one facility may not affect another facility and that shipping costs are lower.

4. The major reason is lower labor costs, but there may also be a market for the firms' products in the foreign country.

5. The major reason is to satisfy the demand for foreign goods in the United States; in addition, U.S. locations allow foreign firms to circumvent quotas and/or tariffs.

6. locating in foreign countries; moving from cities to suburbs; clustering in industrial parks; using single-story buildings; decentralizing; moving to the Sun Belt

7. Industries, companies, and competition have become global. In order to minimize costs and risks, companies today are more prone to using foreign parts and partners.

8. market location; raw material location; transportation facilities; labor supply; labor availability; skill levels; wage rates; labor–management relations; climate

9. managerial preference; living environment; housing; public transportation; facilities (schools, churches, playgrounds, hospitals); attitudes; local government and taxes; site availability

10. Nearly all factors in Questions 8 and 9 are relevant. However, the factors in Question 9 are more relevant.

11. Businesses that must locate near resources—for example, lumber and coal—have little (regional) flexibility, which is also true of businesses that must locate near the market—for example, retail stores. Businesses that use readily available raw materials and produce goods that are distributed over wide areas have a great deal of flexibility.

12. Different weights can be given to different factors.

13. The qualitative approach considers many more factors, but its results are less exact.

14. one dimensional, city block, distance squared, and straight-line

SOLUTIONS TO PROBLEMS

1. See the figure.

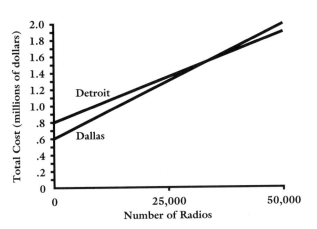

Cost(Dallas) = cost(Detroit)

FC(Dallas) $+ Q \times VC$(Dallas) $= FC$(Detroit) $+$
$$Q \times VC(\text{Detroit})$$
$$\$600,000 + \$28Q = \$800,000 + \$22Q$$
$$\$6Q = \$200,000$$
$$Q = \$200,000/\$6$$
$$Q = 33,333$$

2. See the figure.

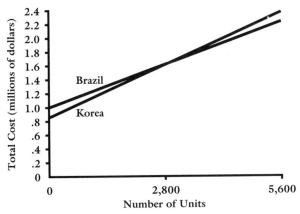

Cost(Brazil) = cost(Korea)
$$FC_B + VC_B(Q) = FC_K + VC_K(Q)$$
$$\$1,000,000 + \$220Q = \$860,000 + \$270Q$$
$$\$140,000 = \$50Q$$
$$Q = \$140,000/\$50$$
$$Q = 2,800$$

3. City profit = revenue − cost
$$= \text{demand} \times \text{price} -$$
$$(\text{fixed cost} +$$
$$\text{variable cost} \times \text{demand})$$
$$= 20,000(\$2) -$$
$$[\$5,000 + \$.60(20,000)]$$
$$= \$40,000 - (\$5,000 + \$12,000)$$
$$= \$40,000 - \$17,000$$
$$= \$23,000$$

Suburbs profit = revenue − cost
$$= \text{demand} \times \text{price} -$$
$$(\text{fixed cost} +$$
$$\text{variable cost} \times \text{demand})$$
$$= 12,000(\$1.80) -$$
$$[\$2,000 + \$.65(12,000)]$$
$$= \$21,600 - (\$2,000 + \$7,800)$$
$$= \$21,600 - \$9,800$$
$$= \$11,800$$

Therefore, Sam should locate in the city.

4.

Factor	Philadelphia (weight × score)	New York (weight × score)
Customer convenience	17.5	20
Bank accessibility	8.0	18
Computer support	17.0	15
Rental costs	13.5	8.25
Labor costs	8.0	5.0
Taxes	9.0	5.0
Totals	73.0	71.25

ISA should locate in Philadelphia.

5. Since Philadelphia violates the discordance level (for bank accessibility) and New York has no violations, choose New York.

6. See the table on page IS-34.
Site B is best.

7. Site B violates the discordance level for zoning laws. Therefore, choose site C.

8. (a) The median is the 2200 block. The distances from 2200 are as follows.

Table for Problem 6.

Factor	Site A (weight × score)	Site B (weight × score)	Site C (weight × score)
Land space	18	21	24
Land costs	10	20	7.5
Traffic density	10	16	12
Neighborhood income	7.5	10.5	6
Zoning laws	8	2	9
Totals	53.5	69.5	58.5

Client Address	Distance
1100	1,100
1500	700
2200	0
3700	1,500
5400	3,200
Total	6,500

The average distance is $6{,}500/5 = 1{,}300$ (13 blocks).

   (b) The mean is $1100 + 1500 + 2200 + 3700 + 5400 = 13900/5 = 2780$. Therefore, CC should locate near 2780 Hightech Road. (This minimizes distance squared.) The distances from 2780 are as follows.

Customer	Distance
1100	1,680
1500	1,280
2200	580
3700	920
5400	2,620
Total	7,080

The average distance is $7{,}080/5 = 1{,}416$ (14.16 blocks).

  9. (a) The median trip is the 22nd trip, which occurs on block 3700. Locate here to minimize the total distance traveled.

The distances from 3700 are shown in the table.

Customer	Distance	Number of Trips	Trips × Distance
1100	2,600	8	20,800
1500	2,200	6	13,200
2200	1,500	6	9,000
3700	0	15	0
5400	1,700	8	13,600
		Total	56,600

The total distance is 566 block-trips.

  (b)

Address	Number of Trips	Address × Number of Trips
1100	8	8800
1500	6	9000
2200	6	13200
3700	15	55500
5400	8	43200
Totals	43	129700

Since the average is $129700/43 = 3016$, CC should locate near 3016 Hightech Road to minimize the distance squared.

   The distances from 3016 are shown in the table below. The total distance is 9,964 block-trips.

Table for Problem 9(b).

Customer	Distance	Distance²	Number of Trips	(Trip × Distance²)/10,000
1100	1,916	3,671,056	8	2,936.844
1500	1,516	2,298,256	6	1,378.953
2200	816	665,856	6	399.514
3700	684	467,856	15	701.784
5400	2,384	5,683,456	8	4,546.764
			Total	9,963.860

10. The median trip is the 105th trip (of 80 + 130 trips). Therefore, to minimize the travel distance, CoLoan should locate the duplicating machine as close as possible to the median (the payment office). This is Room I. However, while this is optimal, the secretaries in the southwest room will be very unhappy. Therefore, it might be better (fairer) to locate in Room G, although it is not better in terms of the distance walked by the secretaries.

11.

Location	Coordinates	
	E-W	N-S
A	20W	50N
B	15E	30N
C	25E	10S
D	10W	40S

E-W median is anywhere between 10W and 15E. N-S median is anywhere between 10S and 30N. Paramedic should locate in the rectangle bordered by 10S, 30N, 10W, and 15E. (*Note:* Rather than a rectangle, AB:POM gives only one answer.)

12.

Location	Trips
A	60
B	40
C	100
D	50
Total	250

The median trip is the 125th (or 126th). Moving from west to east, A is at 20 W (60 trips); D is at 10 W (50 trips − total = 110); and B is at 15 E (40 trips − total = 150). So the E-W coordinate is 15E. Moving from north to south, A is at 50N (60 trips); B is at 30N (40 trips − total = 100); and C is at 10S (100 trips − total = 200). So the N-S coordinate is 10S. Paramedic should locate at 15E, 10S.

13. We simply need to find the average latitude and longitude.

City	Longitude (°W)	Latitude (°N)
Los Angeles	118	34
San Francisco	123	38
Houston	95	30
Dallas	97	33
St. Louis	90	38
Chicago	87	42
Pittsburgh	80	41
Atlanta	84	34
Totals	774	290
Averages	96.75	36.25

The most central location is (96.75°, 36.25°).

14. With regard to the number of trips, we have to find the average weighted latitude and weighted longitude. See the table below.

Now we average the weighted longitude and latitude by 28 trips: longitude = 2,725/28 = 97.32; latitude = 1,003/28 = 35.82. The most central location is (97.32°, 35.82°).

15. First, we will evaluate St. Louis. The St. Louis coordinates are longitude = 90° and latitude = 38°. Therefore, the distance from each of the cities to St. Louis is given by

$$\text{Distance} = \sqrt{(\text{long.} - 90°)^2 + (\text{lat.} - 38°)^2},$$

which we place in column (5) of the table for St. Louis (see page IS-36). For part (b) of the problem, we multiply the distance by the number of trips and place this in column (6).

Now we will evaluate Dallas. The Dallas coordinates are longitude = 97° and latitude = 33°. Therefore, the distance from each of the cities to St. Louis is given by

$$\text{Distance} = \sqrt{(\text{long.} - 97°)^2 + (\text{lat.} - 33°)^2},$$

which we place in column (5) of the table for Dallas.

Table for Problem 14.

(1) City	(2) Number of Trips	(3) Longitude (°W)	(4) Latitude (°N)	(5) Weighted Longitude [(2) × (3)]	(6) Weighted Latitude [(2) × (4)]
Los Angeles	6	118	34	708	204
San Francisco	3	123	38	369	114
Houston	1	95	30	95	30
Dallas	4	97	33	388	132
St. Louis	1	90	38	90	38
Chicago	1	87	42	87	42
Pittsburgh	5	80	41	400	205
Atlanta	7	84	34	588	238
Totals	28	774	290	2,725	1,003

(a) The unweighted distance from St. Louis (101.972) is slightly better than that from Dallas (104.988).

(b) The weighted distance from St. Louis (420) is slightly worse than that for Dallas (416).

Computer Case Study 5.1

Three data sets are included. One data set (CASE5-1P) contains the plant cities and their capacities. Another data set (CASE5-1Q) contains all cities and the capacities. In other words, CASE5-1Q adds to CASE5-1P the cities with a distributorship and sets their capacities to 0. CASE5-1D refers to the distributor cities and their demands.

Running CASE5-1P yields the following: If we will locate anywhere, the center of all plants *unweighted by volume* is at (38.83°, 96.17°), while the center of all plants *weighted by volume* is at (37.75°, 95.6°). Toggling the results yields the best city on the list. Kansas City has the minimum distance weighted or unweighted. CASE5-1Q allows us to locate in any of the cities, including cities that have no plants. Running the program yields coordinates that are irrelevant. However, after toggling, we get the distances weighted or unweighted and find that the best city, once again, is Kansas City. Running CASE5-1D is irrelevant, because this data set contains the demands and we are interested only in plants.

Tables for Problem 15.

St. Louis

(1) City	(2) Number of Trips	(3) Longitude (°W)	(4) Latitude (°N)	(5) Distance	(6) Weighted Distance
Los Angeles	6	118	34	28.284	169.706
San Francisco	3	123	38	33.000	99.000
Houston	1	95	30	9.434	9.434
Dallas	4	97	33	8.602	34.409
St. Louis	1	90	38	0.000	0.000
Chicago	1	87	42	5.000	5.000
Pittsburgh	5	80	41	10.440	52.202
Atlanta	7	84	34	7.211	50.478
			Totals	101.97	420.228

Dallas

(1) City	(2) Number of Trips	(3) Longitude (°W)	(4) Latitude (°N)	(5) Distance	(6) Weighted Distance
Los Angeles	6	118	34	21.024	126.143
San Francisco	3	123	38	26.476	79.429
Houston	1	95	30	3.606	3.606
Dallas	4	97	33	0.000	0.000
St. Louis	1	90	38	8.602	8.602
Chicago	1	87	42	13.454	13.454
Pittsburgh	5	80	41	18.788	93.941
Atlanta	7	84	34	13.038	91.269
			Totals	104.988	416.444

6
The Operations Network

TEACHING NOTES

For a number of reasons, this is a somewhat unusual chapter. First of all, we take a broader view of location here, moving from the relatively simplistic treatment found in the previous chapter (and most other P/OM texts), where each location stood by itself, to a discussion of multiple locations in a network.

We also emphasize distribution as an operation. Most P/OM texts ignore distribution, and many business schools treat distribution as a marketing function—without acknowledging that if distribution really is a marketing function, doing it well becomes an operations function. Stress the obvious overlap between these two business functions. When we use the word *logistics,* we are talking about distribution *and* the related operational concerns.

Any text featuring MRP and JIT concepts, as this one does throughout, cannot discuss distribution without getting into distribution requirements planning. Students should become familiar with the philosophical differences between a pull system and a push system.

We discuss the transportation model and the transportation method in this chapter. We begin by presenting the model and its assumptions. We then state the general iterative algorithm, followed by the specifics for the steps. We present the northwest corner method, but we emphasize that looking at the costs at the beginning of the problem is useful (we call this the minimal cost method). We do not present Vogel's approximation method, because we think it is unnecessary in a P/OM course. If you do choose to show your students this method, however, they probably will think that you are a genius, so we feel that we have done both those who do teach it and those who do not a big favor by omitting it. The same is true of the MODI method, since we have included only the stepping stone method.

You will find a section that addresses concerns such as maximization and unbalanced problems, as well as an Example consisting of an assignment problem. The latter item should prove useful in Chapter 15, since there is no specific assignment software; in other words, the transportation method can be used later to solve assignment problems.

The last section is the most important. In it we show that transportation costs are part of the location decision (as mentioned in Chapter 5), and we present the transportation model for aggregate planning (which we present again in Chapter 12).

This chapter has two exercises in the Solved Problems section. One demonstrates the initialization, and the other demonstrates the solution technique.

The homework problems for this chapter constitute a kind of mixed bag. Problems 1 through 7 deal with different types of networks—they are more like our Questions than our Problems. Problems 8 through 20 use the transportation method. Note that Problems 12 and 13 together demonstrate that a constant can be added to a row without changing the solution. In conjunction with Problem 16, Problem 17 demonstrates that irrelevant (unused) cells do not change the optimal solution. Problem 18 (again in conjunction with Problem 16) demonstrates that an arbitrarily high cost is our way of saying that certain cells cannot be used. Problem 19 applies transportation to location and Problem 20 applies transportation to aggregate planning.

The software for this chapter is, of course, the transportation method. Problems 8 through 20 can be solved using the software.

The computer case study is a straightforward exercise of the transportation method applied to location. The model must be changed and run twelve times.

TEACHING SUGGESTIONS

Teaching Suggestion 6.1: Product Flows.
Figure 6.4 can be very useful for introducing the concepts of push and pull systems. While the arrows in the figure are meant to indicate only the product flow, they also serve as indicators of a push system.

Teaching Suggestion 6.2: Proportionality.
Point out that shipping costs are not proportional to distance.

Teaching Suggestion 6.3: Linearity.
We like to point out that this is the third time (break even, regression, and transportation) that the concept of linearity has come up. It will come up again.

Teaching Suggestion 6.4: Vogel's Approximation Method (VAM).
The key point of VAM is that costs cannot be considered to be high or low until they are related to other costs. Adding a large constant to the row having the smallest cost (in our example, Atlanta) will demonstrate this. We make a similar point with Problems 12 and 13.

Teaching Suggestion 6.5: Reading the Tables.
Be sure to emphasize the importance of distinguishing shipments from costs in the table. We circle the shipments.

Our students often forget to do this and then cannot read their own tables.

Teaching Suggestion 6.6:   Putting the Marginal Cost in the Table.

To minimize confusion, you might want to place an X in any cell with a positive marginal cost, rather than the cost itself.

Teaching Suggestion 6.7:   Alternative Optimal Solutions.

If the optimal set of shipments produces one or more marginal costs of zero, then at least one other set of shipments is equally optimal. This is another special case that is not developed in the text but that is easy to demonstrate in class.

Teaching Suggestion 6.8:   Capacities or Costs May Vary.

Even though the capacities in each time period remain the same in our example, the model does allow for the capacities to vary over time. The same is true of the costs.

Teaching Suggestion 6.9:   Pull System and Make to Stock.

As noted in Chapter 1, the use of this pull system leads to a make-to-stock operating environment. The current JIT trend pushes us in this direction.

ANSWERS TO QUESTIONS

1. land (rail, truck, and pipeline), sea, and air

2. cost, time, and reliability (security and safety) factors

3. arborescent: spreads out from a single source location (such as a factory) to several distribution centers or warehouses and then spreads out from each of these to several locations at the next level(s); coalescent: components and/or raw materials come from several locations and meet at a single location (there can be several levels of this coalescence); series: a combination of the other two, possibly with multiple origins and destinations

4. In a simple distribution network, there is no choice of route. In a complex network, we allow a demand location to be supplied from any of a variety of supply locations and/or a supply location to supply any of a variety of demand locations.

5. plane, train, truck, boat, pipeline/pumps, telecommunications, and satellites

6. a single time period; any destination can be supplied by any source; costs are known, fixed, and proportional; costs are additive; total supply = total demand

7. step 1: find a starting solution; step 2: check to see if the solution is optimal; step 3: improve the solution and return to step 2

8. A feasible solution is any solution that satisfies the supply and demand requirements. An optimal solution is a feasible solution that minimizes costs or maximizes profits.

9. An optimal solution has been reached when all marginal costs (profits) are non-negative (non-positive).

10. Total supply is not equal to total demand in an unbalanced transportation problem. Such a problem can be balanced by adding a dummy row (supply < demand) or column (demand < supply).

11. Negative marginal costs (minimization) indicate that the solution can be improved. Positive marginal profits (maximization) indicate that no solution can be improved.

12. $m + n - 1$ cells

13. No; costs generally rise less than proportionately to distance. However, with trucking and airline deregulation, *anything* is possible with costs.

14. yes (although this is not true if quantity discounts are offered)

15. quantity

16.

Route	Advantage	Disadvantage
Air	Speed	Cost
Rail	Cost	Speed
Road	Flexibility	Cost vis-à-vis rail, water
Waterway	Cost	Speed
Pipeline	Cost	Limited products

17. bulk packing; in-process individual; final product individual

18. uses containers of a common size, which allows loading facilities and vehicles to achieve greater efficiency

19. types of products being stored; whether or not products can be stacked; shelf life; value; temperature; and pressure

20. pull: demands initiate production; push: production occurs and units are allotted to the next level based on needs

SOLUTIONS TO PROBLEMS

1.

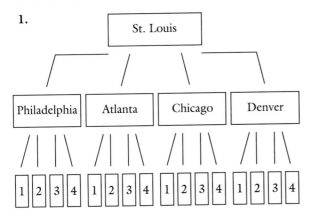

There will be 24 pharmacies for each of the 16 local distributors, yielding 384 pharmacies. This is an arborescent network.

2.

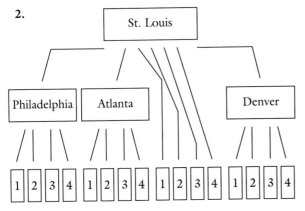

This is still an arborescent network, and it is still a simple network.

3.

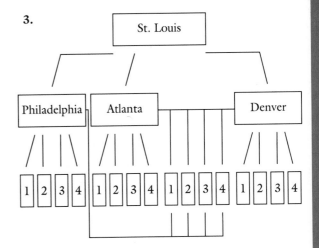

This is now a complex network.

4. This is a coalescent network.

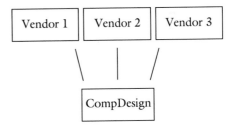

5. See the figure below.

Figure for Problem 5.

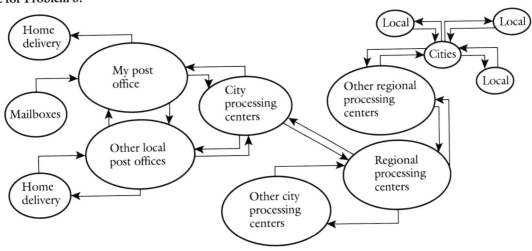

6. There can be many answers. The figure shows one simple attempt.

Branch offices / Central computers at other banks

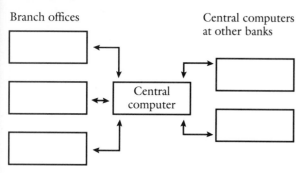

7. Average cost per ton from St. Louis:

$$\frac{\$14 + \$6 + \$11 + \$5}{4} = \frac{\$36}{4} = \$9 \text{ per ton}$$

Average cost per ton from Chicago:

$$\frac{\$8 + \$7 + \$5 + \$10}{4} = \frac{\$30}{4} = \$7.50 \text{ per ton}$$

This yields a savings of $1.50 per ton. Now we need to compute the amount needed to recover the $300,000 fixed costs:

$$\frac{300,000}{1.50} = 200,000$$

So, if 200,000 tons or more are shipped annually, the Chicago warehouse should be kept open.

8. (a)

From	To V	W	X	Y	Z	Supply
A	$61 (60)	$86 (15)	$88	$66	$22	75 ~~15~~
B	$85	$48 (65)	$7 (35)	$82	$36	100 ~~35~~
C	$58	$29	$25 (55)	$99 (20)	$51	75 ~~20~~
D	$31	$49	$44	$55 (20)	$65 (30)	50 ~~30~~
Demand	60	80 ~~65~~	90 ~~55~~	40 ~~20~~	30	

Cost = $61(60) + $86(15) + $48(65) + $7(35) +
 $25(55) + $99(20) + $55(20) + $65(30)
 = $3,660 + $1,290 + $3,120 + $245 +
 $1,375 + $1,980 + $1,100 + $1,950
 = $14,720

(*Note:* This is the initial cost, *not* the optimal cost.)

(b)

From	To V	W	X	Y	Z	Supply
A	$61 (10)	$86	$88	$66 (35)	$22 (30)	75 ~~45~~ 35
B	$85	$48 (5)	$7 (90)	$82 (5)	$36	100 ~~10~~ 5
C	$58	$29 (75)	$25	$99	$51	75
D	$31 (50)	$49	$44	$55	$65	50
Demand	60 ~~10~~	80 ~~5~~	90	40	30	

Cost = $61(10) + $66(35) + $22(30) + $48(5) +
 $7(90) + $82(5) + $29(75) + $31(50)
 = $610 + $2,310 + $660 + $240 +
 $630 + $410 + $2,175 + $1,550
 = $8,585

(*Note:* This is the initial cost, *not* the optimal cost.)

9. total supply = 220 + 300 + 435 = 955
total demand = 160 + 120 + 200 + 230 = 710

Therefore, we first add a dummy destination with a demand of 955 − 710 = 245 and shipping costs of 0.

From	To W	X	Y	Z	Dummy	Supply
A	$132 (160)	$116 (60)	$250	$110	$0	220 60
B	$220	$230 (60)	$180 (200)	$178 (40)	$0	300 240 40
C	$152	$173	$196	$164 (190)	$0 (245)	435 245
Demand	160	120 60	200	230 190	245	

initial cost = $132(160) + $116(60) + $230(60) +
 $180(200) + $178(40) + $164(190)
 = $21,120 + $6,960 + $13,800 +
 $3,600 + $7,120 + $31,160
 = $116,160

10.

From	To Dallas	Denver	Detroit	Supply
Memphis	$17 – (600)	$20 + (100)	$25 + 14	7̶0̶0̶ 1̶0̶0̶
Minneapolis	$20 + 5	$18 – (400)	$9 + (200)	6̶0̶0̶ 2̶0̶0̶
Miami	$12 + – 11	$30 + 4	$17 – (300)	3̶0̶0̶
Demand	6̶0̶0̶	5̶0̶0̶ 4̶0̶0̶	5̶0̶0̶ 3̶0̶0̶	

cost = $26,300

From	To Dallas	Denver	Detroit
Memphis	$17 (300)	$20 (400)	$25 + 14
Minneapolis	$20 + 5	$18 (100)	$9 (500)
Miami	$12 (300)	$30 + 15	$17 + 11

cost = $17(300) + $20(400) + $18(100) +
$9(500) + $12(300)
= $5,100 + $8,000 + $1,800 + $4,500 + $3,600
= $23,000 (optimal)

11.

From	To Dallas	Denver	Detroit	Supply
Memphis	$17 (300)	$20 (400)	$25 + 14	7̶0̶0̶ 4̶0̶0̶
Minneapolis	$20 + 5	$18 (100)	$9 (500)	6̶0̶0̶ 1̶0̶0̶
Miami	$12 (300)	$30 + 15	$17 + 11	3̶0̶0̶
Demand	6̶0̶0̶ 3̶0̶0̶	5̶0̶0̶ 1̶0̶0̶	5̶0̶0̶	

cost = $17(300) + $20(400) + $18(100) +
$9(500) + $12(300)
= $5,100 + $8,000 + $1,800 + $4,500 + $3,600
= $23,000

12. We start with the minimum cost method.

Origin	Destination A	B	C	D	Supply
X	$13 (7)	$14 (12)	$19 (13)	$25 + 10	3̶2̶ 2̶5̶ 1̶3̶
Y	$18 – 4	$20	$28 (2)	$24 (18)	2̶0̶ 2̶
Z	$10 (20)	$17	$18	$28	2̶0̶
Demand	2̶7̶ 7̶	1̶2̶	1̶5̶ 2̶	1̶8̶	

total cost = $1,194

Origin	Destination A	B	C	D
X	$13 (5)	$14 (12)	$19 (15)	$25 + 6
Y	$18 (2)	$20 + 1	$28 + 4	$24 (18)
Z	$10 (20)	$17 + 6	$18 + 2	$28 + 12

total cost = $13(5) + $14(12) + $19(15) + $18(2) +
$24(18) + $10(20)
= $65 + $168 + $285 + $36 +
$432 + $200
= $1,186

13.

Origin	Destination A	B	C	D	Supply
X	$23 – 6	$24	$29 (15)	$35 (17)	3̶2̶ 1̶7̶
Y	$18 (7)	$20 (12)	$28	$24 (1)	2̶0̶ 1̶3̶
Z	$10 (20)	$17	$18	$28	2̶0̶
Demand	2̶7̶ 7̶	1̶2̶	1̶5̶	1̶8̶ 1̶7̶	

cost = $1,620

Origin	Destination A	B	C	D
X	$23 (7)	$24 −7	$29 (15)	$35 (10)
Y	$18 +6	$20 (12)	$28	$24 (8)
Z	$10 (20)	$17	$18	$28

cost = $1,578

Origin	Destination A	B	C	D
X	$23 (7)	$24 (10)	$29 (15)	$35 +7
Y	$18 −1	$20 (2)	$28	$24 (18)
Z	$10 (20)	$17	$18	$28

cost = $1,508

Origin	Destination A	B	C	D	Supply
X	$23 (5)	$24 (12)	$29 (15)	$25 +5	32
Y	$18 (2)	$20 −1	$28 ±0	$24 (18)	20
Z	$10 (20)	$17 +6	$18 +12	$28 +8	20
Demand	27	12	15	18	

total cost = $23(5) + $24(12) + $29(15) + $18(2) + $24(18) + $10(20)
$$= \$115 + \$288 + \$435 + \$36 + \$432 + \$200$$
$$= \$1,506$$

(*Note:* Iterations may differ, but the final result and table will be the same.)

14.

Origin	Destination D	E	F	G	Supply
A	$30 (10)	$15	$50	$25	~~10~~
B	$40 − (5)	$35 + (13)	$40	$15	~~18~~ ~~13~~
C	$55 + 30	$20 (2)	$65 − (10)	$30 (5)	~~17~~ ~~15~~ ~~5~~
Demand	~~15~~ ~~5~~	~~15~~ ~~2~~	~~10~~	~~5~~	

total profit = $1,795

Origin	Destination D	E	F	G
A	$30 − (10)	$15	$50	$25 + +20
B	$40 (3)	$35 (15)	$40	$15
C	$55 + (2)	$20	$65 (10)	$30 − (5)

total profit = $1,855

Origin	Destination D	E	F	G
A	$30 − (5)	$15	$50 + +10	$25 (5)
B	$40 (3)	$35 (15)	$40	$15
C	$55 + (7)	$20	$65 − (10)	$30

total profit = $1,955

Origin	Destination D	E	F	G
A	$30	$15	$50 (5)	$25 (5)
B	$40 (3)	$35 (15)	$40	$15
C	$55 (12)	$20	$65	$30 (5)

total profit = $50(5) + $25(5) + $40(3) + $35(15) + $55(12) + $65(5)

= $250 + $125 + $120 + $525 + $660 + $325

= $2,005 (optimal)

15. We use the maximum profit as a starting method.

Destination

Origin	D	E	F	G	Supply
A	$30	$15 − (5)	$50 + (+20)	$25 (5)	1̶0̶
B	$40 − (8)	$35 + (10)	$40	$15	1̶8̶ 10
C	$55 + (7)	$20	$65 − (10)	$28	1̶7̶ 7
Demand	1̶3̶ 8	1̶3̶ 8	10	5	

total profit = $1,905

Destination

Origin	D	E	F	G
A	$30	$15	$50 (5)	$25 (5)
B	$40 (3)	$35 (15)	$40	$15
C	$55 (12)	$20	$65 (5)	$30

total profit = $50(5) + $25(5) + $40(3) + $35(15) + $55(12) + $65(5)

= $250 + $125 + $120 + $525 + $660 + $325

= $2,005 (optimal, as in Problem 14)

16.

To

From	Dallas	El Paso	Ft. Wth.	Galv.	Houston	Supply
Austin	$20 (35) +20	$48	$10 (65)	$30 +25	$40 +5	1̶0̶0̶ 35
Beaumont	$70 +15	$60 (70)	$55 +10	$90 +50	$70 (10)	8̶0̶ 10
Corpus Christi	$45 (15)	$80 +27	$50 +15	$30 (55)	$60 (80)	1̶5̶0̶ 9̶5̶ 80
Demand	5̶0̶ 1̶5̶	7̶0̶	6̶5̶	5̶5̶	9̶0̶ 1̶0̶	

This is optimal.

total cost = $20(35) + $10(65) + $60(70) + $70(10) + $45(15) + $30(55) + $60(80)

= $700 + $650 + $4,220 + $700 + $675 + $1,650 + $4,800

= $13,375

17. Because the Beaumont to Galveston route is not part of the optimal solution, we do *not* change our shipping plans. The cost remains the same.

18. We start with the minimum cost method.

To

From	Dallas	El Paso	Ft. Wth.	Galv.	Houston	Supply
Austin	$20 (50)	$48 +M	M	$30 (50)	$40 −20	1̶0̶0̶ 50
Beaumont	$70	$60 (70)	$55	$90	$70 (10)	8̶0̶ 10
Corpus Christi	$45	$80	$50 (65)	$30 (5)	$60 (80)	1̶5̶0̶ 9̶5̶ 80
Demand	5̶0̶	7̶0̶	6̶5̶	5̶5̶ 5	9̶0̶ 10	

To

From	Dallas	El Paso	Ft. Worth	Galv.	Houston
Austin	$20 (50)	$48	$10	$30 +20	$40 (50)
Beaumont	$70 +20	$60 (70)	$55 −5	$90	$70 (10)
Corpus Christi	$45	$80	$50 (65)	$30 (55)	$60 (30)

To

From	Dallas	El Paso	Ft. Worth	Galv.	Houston
Austin	$20 (50)	$48 ±0	M M	$30 +20	$40 (50)
Beaumont	$70 +20	$60 (70)	$55 (10)	$90 +55	$70 +5
Corpus Christi	$45 +5	$80 +25	$50 (55)	$30 (55)	$60 (40)

total cost = $20(50) + $40(50) + $60(70) +
$55(10) + $50(55) + $30(55) + $60(40)
= $1,000 + $2,000 + $4,200 + $550 +
$2,750 + $1,650 + $2,400
= $14,550

(*Note:* The change has cost us $14,550 − $13,375 = $1,175.)

19. We need to solve two separate transportation problems. One will include Philadelphia and the other will include Seattle. In either case, we need a dummy destination. For both cases, we begin with the minimal cost method.

Philadelphia

Warehouse

Plant	Pitt.	St. Louis	Denver	Dummy	Supply
Los Angeles	$100 +100	$75 +65	$50 ⑮⓪	$0 +40	1̶5̶0̶
New Orleans	$80 +40	$60 +10	$90 ②②⑤	$0 +0	2̶2̶5̶
Philadelphia	$40 ②⓪⓪	$50 ①⓪⓪	$90 ㉕	$0 ㉕	3̶5̶0̶ 1̶5̶0̶ 5̶0̶ 2̶5̶
Demand	2̶0̶0̶	1̶0̶0̶	4̶0̶0̶ 2̶5̶0̶ 2̶5̶	2̶5̶	

total cost = $50(150) + $90(225) + $40(200) +
$50(100) + $90(25) + $0(25)
= $7,500 + $20,250 + $8,000 + $5,000 +
$2,250 + $0
= $43,000 (A second solution exists; see New Orleans–Dummy.)

Seattle

Warehouse

Plant	Pittsburgh	St. Louis	Denver	Dummy
Los Angeles	$100 ⑦⑤	$75 −5	$50 ⑤⓪	$0 ㉕
New Orleans	$80 ①②⑤	$60 ①⓪⓪	$90	$0
Seattle	$110	$70	$30 ③⑤⓪	$0

Warehouse

Plant	Pittsburgh	St. Louis	Denver	Dummy
Los Angeles	$100 +5	$75 ⑦⑤	$50 ⑤⓪	$0 ㉕
New Orleans	$80 ②⓪⓪	$60 ㉕	$90 +55	$0 +15
Seattle	$110 +35	$70 +15	$30 ③⑤⓪	$0 +20

total cost = $75(75) + $50(50) + $0(25) +
$80(200) + $60(25) + $30(350)
= $5,625 + $2,500 + $0 + $16,000 +
$1,500 + $10,500
= $36,125

Therefore, shipping costs are lower for Seattle.

20. (a) Certain combinations cannot occur. For example, units cannot be produced in August for the previous June. These unfeasible combinations are indicated with an X. Now we may fill in the costs. The cost for regular time in the month with the same demand is $0. For production in one month with use in later months, the cost increases by $8 per month (see June, for example). For overtime, we add $10 to the regular time cost, which yields the following table.

Option	Month June	July	Aug.	Sept.	Capacity
June regular time	$0	$8	$16	$24	125
June overtime	$10	$18	$26	$34	25
July regular time	X	$0	$8	$16	125
July overtime	X	$10	$18	$26	25
August regular time	X	X	$0	$8	125
August overtime	X	X	$10	$18	25
September regular time	X	X	X	$0	125
September overtime	X	X	X	$10	25
Demand	100	140	170	90	100

(b) In order to get a starting solution, we need a dummy column. We will use cells in order of regular-time production in the same month, storage for one month, storage for two months, and so on.

Option	June	July	Aug.	Sept.	Dummy	Capacity
June regular time	$0 ⑩⑩	$8 ⑮	$16 ⑩	$24 +	$0 +	~~125~~ ~~25~~ ~~10~~
June overtime	$10 +	$18 +	$26 +	$34 +	$0 ㉕	~~25~~ ~~10~~
July regular time	X	$0 ⑫⑤	$8 + 0	$16 +	$0 +	125
July overtime	X	$10 + 0	$18 ⑩	$26 +	$0 ⑮	25
August regular time	X	X	$0 ⑫⑤	$8 +	$0 +	125
August overtime	X	X	$10 ⑳	$18 +	$0 +	25
September regular time	X	X	X	$0 ⑨⓪	$0 ㉟	~~125~~ ~~35~~
September overtime	X	X	X	$10 +	$0 ㉕	25
Demand	~~100~~	~~140~~ ~~15~~	~~170~~ ~~45~~ ~~35~~ ~~10~~	~~90~~	~~100~~	

Computer Case Study 6.1

total cost = $710

(*Note:* There are several other optimal solutions.)

The approach to this case is very straightforward. The data set contains an 18-by-18 table. Six of the rows have a 0 for the supply. Students need to replace each 0 first with 130 and then with 180 and solve for the total cost, as shown in the table.

City	Total Cost with 130	Total Cost with 180
Columbus	$3,556	$3,406
Indianapolis	3,405	3,205
Miami	3,674	3,674
Montreal	3,511	3,511
Raleigh	3,779	3,729
San Francisco	3,375	3,175

Clearly, the solution is to add 180 to San Francisco. The new and old routes can be compared from the following output screens. (*Note:* All numbers are in thousands.)

```
═ Data file:case6-1 ═══════════ Transportation ═══════════ Solution ═
  Number of sources (1-99) 18        Number of destinations (1-99)   18
  minimize
═══════════════════ Comp Case 6-1:Consolidated Bottling ═══════════════
  SHIPMENTS
  From       To        Units          From       To        Units

  Albuquerq  Albuquer     24          Denver     Denver       51
  Albuquerq  Los Ange    124          Detroit    Detroit     121
  Baltimore  Baltimor     62          Houston    Houston     123
  Baltimore  Columbus     53          Kansas Ci  Chicago     154
  Baltimore  Detroit      30          Kansas Ci  Indianap     36
  Baltimore  Miami        33          Kansas Ci  Kansas C     50
  Baltimore  Montreal     42          Los Angel  Los Ange    157
  Baltimore  Raleigh      12          Portland   Portland     38
  Boston     Boston       64          Portland   San Fran     71
  Boston     Montreal     79          St. Paul   Indianap     38
  Chicago    Chicago     182          St. Paul   St. Paul     30
  Dallas     Dallas       84
  The minimum total cost =     $4,037 NOTE: alternate optimal solutions exist
```

```
╔═ Data file:B:case6-1 ════════════ Transportation ═══════════════ Solution ═╗
║  Number of sources (2-99) 18          Number of destinations (2-99)    18   ║
║  minimize                                                                   ║
║  ┌══════════════════════ Comp Case 6-1:Consolidated Bottling ════════════┐  ║
║  │ SHIPMENTS                                                             │  ║
║  │ From       To         Units         From        To        Units      │  ║
║  │                                                                       │  ║
║  │ Albuquerq  Albuquer     24           Dallas      Dallas      84       │  ║
║  │ Albuquerq  Los Ange     15           Denver      Denver      51       │  ║
║  │ Baltimore  Baltimor     62           Detroit     Detroit    121       │  ║
║  │ Baltimore  Chicago      38           Houston     Houston    123       │  ║
║  │ Baltimore  Columbus     53           Kansas Ci   Chicago    116       │  ║
║  │ Baltimore  Detroit      30           Kansas Ci   Indianap    74       │  ║
║  │ Baltimore  Miami        33           Kansas Ci   Kansas C    50       │  ║
║  │ Baltimore  Montreal     42           Los Angel   Los Ange   157       │  ║
║  │ Baltimore  Raleigh      12           Portland    Portland    38       │  ║
║  │ Boston     Boston       64           St. Paul    St. Paul    30       │  ║
║  │ Boston     Montreal     79           San Franc   Los Ange   109       │  ║
║  │ Chicago    Chicago     182           San Franc   San Fran    71       │  ║
║  │ The minimum total cost =    $3,175 NOTE: alternate optimal solutions exist │ ║
║  └───────────────────────────────────────────────────────────────────────┘  ║
╚═════════════════════════════════════════════════════════════════════════════╝
```

7

Facility Layout

TEACHING NOTES

Many of the chapters in this text can be considered optional for an introductory P/OM course. This one is mandatory, mostly because of the first three sections.

The first section describes considerations that influence facility design decisions. Every business—from the retail store to the steel mill—has layout problems relating to these considerations.

The second section, on production processes, contains the material that allows us to characterize and classify production processes. No student should leave a P/OM course without knowing the differences between a flow shop and a job shop; between a continuous process and most other production processes; and between large-volume producers and small-batch producers.

The third section takes the characteristics from the previous section and illustrates how different types of layouts are more or less appropriate for particular situations. We return to the process layout in Chapter 8 (waiting lines)

and in Chapter 15 (discussion of job shop scheduling). Chapter 10 (project management) relates to the use of fixed position layouts. Most of the other chapters refer, directly or indirectly, to product layouts (assembly lines).

We follow the section on layout types with a discussion of advanced manufacturing technology. In this section we talk about automation, numerical control, and robotics.

The next two sections (assembly lines and process layouts) take students beyond the general decision about which type of layout is most appropriate to the more detailed decisions about designing the layout. For product layouts, this means learning how to balance an assembly line. After providing some background material on assembly lines, we illustrate a simple line balancing procedure. For process layouts, we provide an informal approach that, while it yields good layouts, can seem somewhat arbitrary at times. The method is useful, but only if taught correctly. When presenting this method, emphasize the trial-and-error process, using the word *design* instead of the word *solution*.

The chapter concludes with a discussion of the principles of materials handling. Handling costs are the major cost difference between alternative layouts. They also lead to work-in-process inventory, as described in Chapter 13.

The two exercises in the Solved Problems section review the only two quantitative techniques presented in the chapter: line balancing and process layout. The sixteen discussion questions emphasize the important concepts of the chapter over hypothetical discussion situations. Although fewer in number than in most other chapters, the thirteen Problems in this chapter provide plenty of variety.

The software for this chapter comes from two modules—assembly line balancing and operations layout. There are several different rules available for assembly line balancing. The software has the capability to determine the cycle time given the demand rate. The layout module requires two tables—one consisting of distances between rooms and one consisting of trips between operations. It is possible for the user to assign a specific room to a specific process. Problems 1 through 7 can be solved with the assembly line balancing module; Problems 8 through 13 can be solved with the layout module.

This chapter is unique in that it has two computer case studies. Both case studies are straightforward. The case study that deals with assembly line balancing makes the point that adding a 41st work hour per week can make the system more efficient. The other case study deals with operations layout.

TEACHING SUGGESTIONS

Teaching Suggestion 7.1: Move Toward Batch or Unit Processing.
JIT attacks the notion that continuous, or assembly line, production is best. Smaller lot sizes provide cost efficiencies and greater flexibility.

Teaching Suggestion 7.2: Marketing Layout.
We have omitted the marketing layout, but this is the time to discuss it.

Teaching Suggestion 7.3: Customized Automation.
The implication here is that more sophistication is best. More sophistication than is needed for a given situation is not desirable; that is, the system should be tailored to the requirements.

Teaching Suggestion 7.4: Machining Operations.
Our descriptions of machining operations are necessarily brief. To add a real operations flavor to the class, it is a good idea to go into more detail on these during the lecture.

Teaching Suggestion 7.5: Interchangeable Parts.
It is always interesting to note that this used to be a basic principle of American manufacturing. It is now coming back as a feature of JIT.

Teaching Suggestion 7.6: Minimum Number of Stations.
There is no formula for determining the actual minimum number of stations. Point out that the theoretical number may be unattainable.

Teaching Suggestion 7.7: Goals of Assembly Line Balancing.
Emphasize that there are two objectives in assembly line balancing: maximizing efficiency and maximizing the production rate.

Teaching Suggestion 7.8: Grouping Constraints.
Point out that, in practice, certain activities cannot be performed at the same station because of physical considerations; perhaps work must be done on both the left and right sides of a product or perhaps there is some climate control requirement. Our discussion assumes that activities can be mixed.

ANSWERS TO QUESTIONS

1. product cost; efficiency of operations; flexibility in changing product or service; quality; and retention of quality employees

2. Facility layout is the physical arrangement of everything needed for the product or service, including machines, personnel, raw materials, and finished goods.

3. materials handling; bottlenecks; machine interference; employee morale and safety; equipment choice; flexibility

4. Answers will vary.

5. In a flow shop, each input to the transformation follows the same path from the beginning to the end. The personnel and machines perform the same type of operation on each input. One example is the assembly line found in many industries. Another example is the processing of paperwork at large institutions (government, insurance, banking, retailing).

6. In a job shop, each input follows a different path through the system. Job shops usually handle one-of-a-kind or low-volume items. In addition to the many examples provided in the chapter, tool-and-die shops and most repair services are job shops.

7. Moving along the spectrum from unit production to batch processing to mass production to continuous production corresponds to a movement from project to job shop to flow shop.

8. Flow shop systems may dictate a product layout, because the processes need to be laid out in order according to the specifications of the products or services. The process layout groups similar equipment in the same location without respect to product flows.

9. For process layouts and product layouts, whether a given characteristic is an advantage or a disadvantage depends on what a particular producer values most—typically, volume or variety of products produced. For example, flexibility and lower setup costs are often cited as advantages of process layouts. However, producers interested in achieving a high rate of production at low cost ordinarily are better served by a product layout, even given the added expense associated with product-specific equipment.

10. Most of the emphasis in layout (and in the chapter) is on physical considerations such as materials handling and bottlenecks. However, in many service organizations, employee morale (and status, prestige, and political power) is of prime importance in the layout decision.

11. smooth work flow; short distances; division of labor; interchangeable parts

12. Overall, the quality of life has improved dramatically due to the increased availability of products made possible by mass production. In many cases, however, the quality of work life and the quality of workmanship has suffered due to mass production.

13. The components are a production (or demand) rate; tasks; precedences for tasks; and times. The goal is to meet the demand using the fewest possible stations (workers).

14. The number of stations is not necessarily the same. The product of cycle time and number of stations is the same. The line design with the larger number of stations costs more but also produces more.

15. The layout problems described in this chapter cannot be solved by an optimization technique. Therefore, we use heuristics, which provide good, though not necessarily optimal, solutions.

16. The required number of trips is typically not fixed. The answer can range from a pure subjective estimate on the interactions to a more scientific collection of data. Also, management may require some departments to be near (or far from) one another for reasons other than the quantity of interactions.

SOLUTIONS TO PROBLEMS

1. (a) cycle time $= \left(\dfrac{40 \text{ hr.}}{4{,}800 \text{ units}}\right)\left(\dfrac{60 \text{ min.}}{\text{hr.}}\right)\left(\dfrac{60 \text{ sec.}}{\text{min.}}\right)$

$= \dfrac{30 \text{ sec.}}{\text{unit}}$

(b) $N = \Sigma t / CT = 120/30 = 4$ stations

(c) The assembly line balance for a cycle time of 30 seconds requires five stations, as shown in the table.

Station	Task	Time (sec.)	Time Left (sec.)	Ready Tasks
				A
1	A	20	10	B, C, D
2	B	30		C, D
3	C	15	15	D, E
	D	15		E
4	E	10	20	F
5	F	30		None

2. (a)

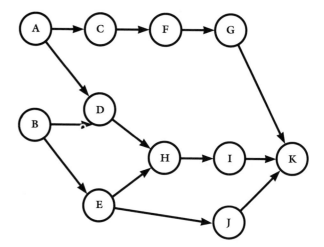

(b) $\left(\dfrac{24 \text{ hr.}}{96 \text{ units}}\right)\left(\dfrac{60 \text{ min.}}{\text{hr.}}\right) = 15 \text{ min.}$

(c) $\left(\dfrac{1 \text{ unit}}{10 \text{ min.}}\right)\left(\dfrac{60 \text{ min.}}{\text{hr.}}\right)\left(\dfrac{24 \text{ hr.}}{\text{day}}\right) = \dfrac{144 \text{ units}}{\text{day}}$

(d) $\dfrac{50 \text{ min./unit}}{10 \text{ min./cycle}} = 5 \text{ stations}$

(e) efficiency $= \dfrac{\text{time needed/unit}}{\text{time allocated/unit}}$

$= \dfrac{\text{total task time}}{(\text{cycle time})(\text{number of stations})}$

$= \dfrac{50}{(10)(6)}$

$= \dfrac{50}{60}$

$= .8333, \text{ or } 83.33\%$

(f) idle time = time allocated/unit
$$- \text{ time needed/unit}$$
$$= 60 - 50$$
$$= 10 \text{ min./cycle}$$

3. (a) We begin by using the precedence graph in Problem 2 to construct a table that shows the number of following tasks.

Task	Following Tasks	Number of Following Tasks
A	C, F, G, K, D, H, I	7
B	D, H, I, K, E, J	6
C	F, G, K	3
D	H, I, K	3
E	H, I, K, J	4
F	G, K	2
G	K	1
H	I, K	2
I	K	1
J	K	1
K		0

Station	Task	Time (sec.)	Time Left (sec.)	Ready Tasks
				A, B
1	A	3	11	B, C
	B	6	5	E, C, D
	E	2	3	C, D, J
2	C	7	7	D, J, F
	D	5	2	J, F, H
3	F	4	10	J, H, G
	H	7	3	J, G, I
	I	1	2	J, G
4	G	5	9	J
	J	6	3	K
5	K	4	10	

(b)

Station	Task	Time (sec.)	Time Left (sec.)	Ready Tasks
				A, B
1	B	6	8	A, E
	A	3	5	E, C, D
	D	5		E, C
2	C	7	7	E, F
	F	4	3	E, G
	E	2	1	G, H, J
3	H	7	7	G, J, I
	J	6	1	G, I
	I	1		G
4	G	5	9	K
	K	4	5	

4. (a)

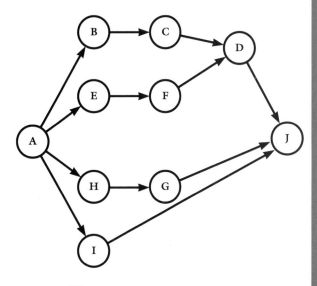

(b) $\dfrac{650}{120} = 5.4167$, which we round *up* to 6.

(c)

Station	Task	Time (sec.)	Time Left (sec.)	Ready Tasks
1	A	120		B, E, H, I
2	E	100	20	B, H, I, F
	F	20		B, H, I
3	H	60	60	B, I, G
	B	50	10	I, G, C
4	G	90	30	I, C
	I	30		C
5	C	40	80	D
	D	80		J
6	J	60	60	None

(d) efficiency $= \dfrac{650}{720} = .903$, or 90.3%

5. (a) $\left(\dfrac{8\ \text{hr.}}{96\ \text{units}}\right)\left(\dfrac{60\ \text{min.}}{\text{hr.}}\right) = 5$ min.

(b) $\dfrac{20}{5} = 4$ stations

(c)

Station	Task	Time (min.)	Time Left (min.)	Ready Tasks
1	A	4	1	B
2	B	5		C
3	C	3	2	D
	D	2		E
4	E	1	4	F
5	F	5		

(d) efficiency $= \dfrac{20}{5 \times 5} = \dfrac{20}{25} = .80$, or 80%

6. (a) cycle time $= \dfrac{8\ \text{hr./day}}{2{,}000\ \text{units/day}}$

$= .004$ hr./unit

$= .24$ min./unit, or 14.4 sec./unit

minimum number of stations $= \dfrac{65}{14.4} = 4.51$, or 5 stations

The line balance is developed as shown in the following table.

Station	Task	Time (sec.)	Time Left (sec.)	Ready Tasks
				A
1	A	7	7.4	B, C
	C	6	1.4	B, F
2	B	10	4.4	D, F, E
3	D	12	2.4	F, E
4	F	8	6.4	E
	E	5	1.4	G, H
5	G	9	5.4	H
	H	5	.4	I
6	I	3	11.4	—

(b) Adding 20 min./day = 100 min./week means that the cycle time can be increased, which will save one station.

cycle time $= \dfrac{500\ \text{min./day}}{2{,}000\ \text{units/day}}$

$= .25$ min./unit, or 15 sec./unit

minimum number of stations $= \dfrac{65}{15} = 4.33$, or 5 stations

The following table shows the line balance for a cycle time of 15 seconds.

Station	Task	Time (sec.)	Time Left (sec.)	Ready Tasks
				A
1	A	7	8	B, C
	C	6	2	B, F
2	B	10	5	D, F, E
	E	5		D, F
3	D	12	3	F
4	F	8	7	G, H
	H	5	2	G
5	G	9	6	I
	I	3	3	None

7. (a)

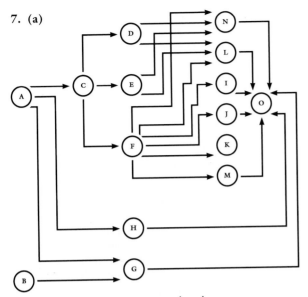

(b) production rate = $\dfrac{\text{operating time}}{\text{cycle time}}$

$$= \dfrac{(40 \text{ hr./wk.}) (60 \text{ min./hr.}) (60 \text{ sec./min.})}{48 \text{ sec./unit}}$$

$= 3,000$ units/wk.

(c) cycle time = $\dfrac{28,800 \text{ sec./day}}{1,200 \text{ units/day}} = 24$ sec.

(d) See the table below.

(e) efficiency = $\dfrac{254}{300} = .8467$, or 84.67%

8. (a) The traffic flow is heaviest from the secretary to duplication, so they need to be in adjacent rooms. Traffic flow is next heaviest between the VP and the coffee machine, so they can also go in adjacent rooms, but only if the first two assignments were in two end rooms. The only question remaining is whether or not to put the secretary and the VP next to each other. Since the secretary–coffee machine route also has a lot of traffic, the processes should be assigned as follows to minimize traffic flow:

duplication–secretary–coffee machine–VP.

(b) duplication–secretary:
(20 ft./trip) (70 trips) = 1,400 ft.
duplication–coffee machine:
(40 ft./trip) (4 trips) =   160 ft.
duplication–VP:
(60 ft./trip) (10 trips) =   600 ft.
secretary–coffee machine:
(20 ft./trip) (30 trips) =   600 ft.
secretary–VP:
(40 ft./trip) (10 trips) =   400 ft.
coffee machine–VP:
(20 ft./trip) (50 trips) = 1,000 ft.
Total movement   4,160 ft.

9. The duplication combination can go in rooms 1 and 2 and the others in rooms 3 and 4. Placing the secretary near the office yields the following: room 1—secretary; room 2—duplication; room 3—coffee machine; room 4—VP.

Table for Problem 7(d).

Station	Task	Time (sec.)	Time Left (sec.)	Ready Tasks
1	B	48	12	A
	A	12		C
2	C	8	52	D, F, E, G, H
	D	18	34	F, E, G, H
	F	15	19	M, E, K, G, J, I, H
	M	15	4	E, K, G, J, I, H
3	E	13	47	N, L, K, G, J, I, H
	N	18	29	L, K, G, J, I, H
	L	14	15	K, G, J, I, H
	K	12	3	G, J, I, H
4	G	8	52	J, I, H
	J	8	44	I, H
	I	7	37	H
	H	6	31	O
5	O	52	8	None

(b) duplication–secretary:
   $(10 \text{ ft.}/\text{trip}) (70 \text{ trips}) =$ 700 ft.
   duplication–coffee machine:
   $(20 \text{ ft.}/\text{trip}) (4 \text{ trips}) =$ 80 ft.
   duplication–VP:
   $(10 \text{ ft.}/\text{trip}) (10 \text{ trips}) =$ 100 ft.
   secretary–coffee machine:
   $(10 \text{ ft.}/\text{trip}) (30 \text{ trips}) =$ 300 ft.
   secretary–VP:
   $(20 \text{ ft.}/\text{trip}) (10 \text{ trips}) =$ 200 ft.
   coffee machine–VP:
   $(10 \text{ ft.}/\text{trip}) (50 \text{ trips}) =$ $\underline{500 \text{ ft.}}$
                                            1,880 ft.

10. The same layout as in Problem 7 would be best. The problems are identical!

11. B and C should be adjacent, because they have the most trips. Traffic is next heaviest between A and D, so they should be adjacent. Continuing in this fashion, F should be adjacent to D and A should be next to F, but the latter two have already been placed. Finally, E should be placed next to F. Thus, we are left with

    B–C–A–D–F–E

or

    A–D–F–E–B–C.

(*Note:* This is *not* the optimal solution.)

12. Using the same logic we used to solve Problem 11, B and C are put in adjacent rooms, as are A and D. F is again placed next to D. Filling in E yields the following: room 1—B; room 2—C; room 3—E; room 4—A; room 5—D; room 6—F. (*Note:* Other combinations may be just as good.)

13. AB:POM yields the following: room 5—A; room 2—B; room 3—C; room 4—D; room 1—E; and room 6—F. The total movement is 35,280.

Computer Case Study 7.1

The initial analysis is very straightforward. The line is balanced using the data exactly as presented in the case study. The theoretical minimum number of stations is 11. However, none of the rules we've looked at thus far leads to 11 stations. The following table shows the answers given by the different rules.

Rule	Number of Stations	Minimum Slack
Longest operation time	13	.16
Most following tasks	13	0
Ranked positional weight	13	.11
Shortest operation time	14	Irrelevant
Fewest following tasks	13	.19

The balance given by fewest following tasks is best, since it has the fewest stations and the cycle time can be reduced by the largest amount of time. An alternative is to see what happens for 41 hours (even though the problem says not to). The following table shows the results.

Rule	Number of Stations	Minimum Slack
Longest operation time	12	Irrelevant
Most following tasks	12	Irrelevant
Ranked positional weight	11	.03
Shortest operation time	12	Irrelevant
Fewest following tasks	13	Irrelevant

Clearly, the ranked positional weight balance leads to the fewest number of stations. Furthermore, the cycle time could be reduced (by .03) or the production rate could be increased by a small amount without changing the number of stations.

Computer Case Study 7.2

This case has three data files. We use the same distance measures for all three files. The distances are measured as right-angle distances from center of room to center of room.

Data set CASE7-2 contains the sales data in the loading dock column. Running this gives the answer that the products should be stored in order of sales; that is, the product with the most sales should be closest to the dock. This is, of course, intuitive; you don't need a computer program to get this result.

Data set CASE7-2T illustrates that the previous answer, while it is intuitive, may be based on the wrong data. This data set uses the number of trips rather than sales.

Data set CASE7-2S uses the sales slips, which give some idea of the interaction between product areas. However, this is not perfect information. For example, if a sales slip contained all seven products, the order would not matter. The imperfection of the data provides an opportunity for discussion about exactly how the question should be answered and what data should be collected.

8
Waiting Line Models

TEACHING NOTES

This chapter presents a managerial approach to waiting lines. We begin by describing where waiting line situations occur. We then describe means for improving these situations, noting that the costs involved need to be analyzed. While we present the queueing results, we emphasize (and provide examples of) the *decision-making uses* of queueing models.

In the course of describing the basic queueing model, with its six parameters, we also mention the models we will not be examining (such as batch arrivals, batch service, queues in series, round robin queues). We do use *Kendall's notation;* we feel that an *M/M/1* queue should be called just that, rather than being called "model 1."

We present the following models: *M/M/1, M/D/1* (for which we present equations), *M/M/s, M/M/1* with finite system size, and *M/M/1* with finite population (for which we present tables to get the answers). (Note that our tables for the *M/M/1* finite population model are much easier to use than the tables in some other textbooks.)

In the last section of the chapter, we detail the steps involved in a queueing study and indicate when simulation may be needed. We have not covered simulation as a separate topic because we do not think that any P/OM text can give simulation its due in only one chapter.

This chapter has three exercises in the Solved Problems section. The first is an *M/M/1* queue, the second is an *M/M/2* queue, and the third incorporates costs into the analysis.

The homework problems include traditional waiting line problems, of course. More interesting are the problems for which decisions must be made—notably, Problems 9 through 15.

The software for this chapter includes the five models in the chapter as well as Erlang and general service times. The model outputs are the standard outputs. It also is possible to perform a cost analysis. Note that the software can charge customer costs against system time or against waiting time. Except for the *M/D/1* model, it is also possible to get the probabilities as output.

TEACHING SUGGESTIONS

Teaching Suggestion 8.1: A Light Introduction.
We like to lighten the discussion by first observing that the word *queue* has four consecutive vowels. We challenge students to come to the next lecture with a list of other words with four consecutive vowels. Some of the findings from past years: onomatopoeia, obsequious, guaiac, and sequoia.

Teaching Suggestion 8.2: We Wait Everywhere.
One lecture before the lecture on queueing, we ask our students to compile a list of every situation in which they have to wait. We then compile a master list of waiting situations in class, and refer to this list as we lecture—something that students appreciate.

Teaching Suggestion 8.3: McDonald's vs. Wendy's.
Figure 8.4(a) depicts the line structure at Wendy's, while Figure 8.4(b) shows it at McDonald's. Point out that if either were superior to the other, one of these companies would change.

Teaching Suggestion 8.4: Queue Structure Trend.
Although the averages are identical, many institutions have changed their line structure so that one line feeds all servers. This is due to fairness (FCFS) and to the fact that it balances waiting times (compare waiting times of two minutes and two minutes with times of one minute and three minutes).

Teaching Suggestion 8.5: Classifying Waiting Situations.
Here, we have the students classify many of their waiting examples (see Teaching Suggestion 8.2) in terms of Kendall's notation.

Teaching Suggestion 8.6: Applicability of Models.
We point out how many of the examples are covered by these three models.

Teaching Suggestion 8.7: Importance of Measures.
We ask our students which measure is most important to them as customers. This leads to a lively discussion on line length vs. time (most students prefer the fast line, even if it is longer). After agreeing that time is the more important measure, W vs. W_q is discussed. Feelings are mixed, but run slightly in favor of W_q, because people are relieved once service begins.

Teaching Suggestion 8.8: Rates.
Rates have been stressed (over times) in all our models. Our students confuse them no matter how much we stress the difference. Stress that λ and μ are rates.

Teaching Suggestion 8.9: Queueing Results Not Linear.
We have pointed out that many relationships in operations are linear. Queueing results, as shown in these examples, are not linear.

Teaching Suggestion 8.10: Total Quality Management (TQM).

A cornerstone of TQM is that the way to improve is to become more consistent, to reduce variation. In this example, service times did not improve. Only consistency changed, yet the waiting times (W_q) were cut in half, thus demonstrating a TQM principle in a different environment.

Teaching Suggestion 8.11:   Alternate Approach.

Our students seem compelled to multiply the cost ($10, in this example) by the time instead of the number waiting. This is an acceptable approach, *provided* that they also multiply the time by the arrival rate. Some students think that 6.81 (L) is the actual number that wait. This is wrong. Since $\lambda = 10$, all 10 had to wait the average waiting time, W. There were 6.81 in the system at any one time, on average.

ANSWERS TO QUESTIONS

1. calling population, arrival process, queue size, queue discipline, number of servers, service time distribution

2. The arrival rate includes all customers who come *to* the door, but the effective arrival rate includes only the customers who come *through* the door (and are served).

3. Essentially, jobs entering a business are customers entering a queue. The jobs enter and wait for service just as customers do. One difference is that job owners (customers) are not present. For example, the auto owner does not wait at the body shop for the work to be done. The implication is that the job owners do not know if someone gets ahead of them in line, while queueing customers typically see this. Therefore, in the job situation, the notion that first come, first serve (FCFS) is fair is less important than in the queueing situation. Other criteria, such as the due date, become more important. (See also Chapter 14.)

4. In the one-line system, the effective arrival and service rates are the same, as are the *average* waiting time, waiting line, system time, and system line. The one-line system has a smaller variance of waiting times (something that is not mentioned in the chapter), but the most important difference is that customers *perceive* the one-line system to have less waiting time. One reason for this perception is that the waiting line moves *n* times faster (but, of course, is *n* times as long). The real advantage of the one-line system is that a customer will not be stuck behind another customer who takes an inordinate amount of time. The advantage of the multiple-line situation is that the customer can pick his or her server.

5. This system is a finite population queueing system with one server (the bulldozer) and four customers (the dump trucks). The queue discipline will be first come, first served. Capacity could be increased in a number of ways, but it depends on who causes the bottleneck—the trucks or the bulldozer. If the bulldozer causes the bottleneck—that is, if the effective arrival rate of the trucks is greater than the service rate of the bulldozer—the capacity could be increased by getting a faster bulldozer or a second bulldozer. If the trucks cause the bottleneck, more trucks or larger trucks will increase the capacity.

6. This is, of course, how most supermarket bakeries operate—FCFS by the use of numbers. This is good, because at the bakery we cannot distinguish long jobs from short ones. (This can be compared with the situation at the checkout counter, where we can estimate job length according to the number of items being purchased by a customer in a particular line.)

7. Having the express lane permits short jobs to get processed quickly. However, if the line is empty and the server is idle, this represents wasted capacity.

8. A restaurant manager certainly wants to give the impression that his or her establishment is busy. A grocery store manager might create a line to encourage impulse buying. A waiting line also will be preferred anytime the cost (server idle time) of reducing the waiting line is larger than the benefit of this reduction.

9. Lines for "ticketed passengers only" restrict the flow of passengers; therefore, they cannot improve the queueing situation. These lines exist to encourage passengers to purchase tickets prior to arriving at the airport.

10. We have stated that space must be allocated for in-process goods. The queueing analysis is one factor in determining the amount of goods and, therefore, space.

11. The answers students give to this question may prove very interesting. Our experience is that students tend to undervalue their time. If a student's response is less than minimum wage, we ask the student to work for us.

12. Answers will vary, but this provides a good discussion question to highlight the description of queues.

13. The major costs traded off are the investment and operating (or labor) costs versus the "costs" of having customers waiting in line. Note that investment and operating costs are on the same side here, whereas they are typically opposed.

14. fairness and the aesthetics of the area in which waiting takes place

15. An assembly line is a system in series, with deterministic service times.

16. Items wait in stock to be demanded by customers. The items are the queueing system customers and the real-world customers are the queueing system servers. Average inventory is analogous to average number of customers in the system.

SOLUTIONS TO PROBLEMS

1. This is an $M/M/1$ queue; $\lambda = 3/$hr.; and $\mu = 5/$hr.

(a) $L_q = \dfrac{\lambda^2}{\mu(\mu - \lambda)} = \dfrac{3^2}{5(5 - 3)} = \dfrac{9}{5(2)} = .9$ persons

(b) $L = \dfrac{\lambda}{\mu - \lambda} = \dfrac{3}{5 - 3} = \dfrac{3}{2} = 1.5$ persons

(c) $W_q = \dfrac{\lambda}{\mu(\mu - \lambda)} = \dfrac{3}{5(5 - 3)} = \dfrac{3}{10}$ hr. $= 18$ min.

(d) $W = \dfrac{1}{\mu - \lambda} = \dfrac{1}{5 - 3} = \dfrac{1}{2}$ hr. $= 30$ min.

(e) $\rho = \dfrac{\lambda}{\mu} = \dfrac{3}{5} = .60,$ or 60%

2. This is an $M/M/1$ queue.

$\lambda = \dfrac{1}{7.3}$ days $= .137/$day

$\mu = \dfrac{1}{2.5}$ days $= .4/$day

(a) $L_q = \dfrac{\lambda^2}{\mu(\mu - \lambda)}$

$= \dfrac{.137^2}{.4(.4 - .137)}$

$= \dfrac{.018769}{.4(.263)}$

$= \dfrac{.018769}{.1052}$

$= .178$ owners

(b) $W = \dfrac{1}{\mu - \lambda} = \dfrac{1}{.4 - .137} = \dfrac{1}{.263} = 3.8$ days

(c) $P_n = (1 - \lambda/\mu)(\lambda/\mu)^n$

$P_0 = (1 - .137/.4)(.137/.4)^0$

$= (1 - .3425)(.3425)^0$

$= (.6575)(1)$

$= .6575$

$P_1 = (1 - .137/.4)(.137/.4)^1$

$= (1 - .3425)(.3425)^1$

$= (.6575)(.3425)$

$= .2252$

$P_2 = (1 - .137/.4)(.137/.4)^2$

$= (1 - .3425)(.3425)^2$

$= (.6575)(.1173)$

$= .0771$

$P_3 = (1 - .137/.4)(.137/.4)^3$

$= (1 - .3425)(.3425)^3$

$= (.6575)(.0402)$

$= .0264$

The probability that three or fewer owners are without appliances is

$$P_0 + P_1 + P_2 + P_3 = .6575 + .2252 + .0771$$
$$+ .0264 = .9862.$$

Therefore, the probability that more than three owners are without working appliances is $1 - .9862 = .0138$.

(d) The probability that more than three are waiting is the probability that more than four are in need of repair (three waiting plus 1 in service).

$P_4 = (1 - .137/.4)(.137/.4)^4$

$= (1 - .3425)(.3425)^4$

$= (.6575)(.0137)$

$= .0090$

Therefore, we subtract .009 from the previous answer, yielding .0048.

(e) $\rho = \dfrac{\lambda}{\mu} = \dfrac{.137}{.4} = .3425,$ or 34.25%

Therefore, the repairperson is idle 65.75 percent of the time.

3. This is an $M/D/1$ queue; $\lambda = 13/$hr.; and $\mu = 20/$hr.

(a) $L_q = \dfrac{\lambda^2}{2\mu(\mu - \lambda)}$

$= \dfrac{13^2}{(2)(20)(20 - 13)}$

$= \dfrac{169}{280} = .604$ cars

(b) $L = L_q + \dfrac{\lambda}{\mu}$

$= .604 + \dfrac{13}{20}$

$= .604 + .65 = 1.254$ cars

(c) $W_q = \dfrac{\lambda}{2\mu(\mu - \lambda)}$

$= \dfrac{13}{(2)(20)(20 - 13)}$

$= \dfrac{13}{280} = .046$ hr., or 2.79 min.

(d) $W = W_q + \dfrac{1}{\mu}$

$\qquad = .046 + \dfrac{1}{20}$

$\qquad = .046 + .050 = .096$ hr., or 5.79 min.

(e) idle $= 1 - \rho$

$\qquad = 1 - \dfrac{\lambda}{\mu}$

$\qquad = 1 - \dfrac{13}{20}$

$\qquad = 1 - .65 = .35$, or 35%

4. This is an $M/D/1$ queue; $\lambda = 2/$min.; and $\mu = 3/$min.

(a) $L_q = \dfrac{\lambda^2}{2\mu(\mu - \lambda)}$

$\qquad = \dfrac{2^2}{(2)(3)(3 - 2)}$

$\qquad = \dfrac{4}{6} = .67$

$L = L_q + \dfrac{\lambda}{\mu}$

$\qquad = .67 + \dfrac{2}{3}$

$\qquad = .67 + .67 = 1.33$ customers

(b) $W_q = \dfrac{\lambda}{2\mu(\mu - \lambda)}$

$\qquad = \dfrac{2}{(2)(3)(3 - 2)}$

$\qquad = \dfrac{2}{6}$ min., or 20 sec.

$W = 20$ sec. $+ 20$ sec. $= 40$ sec.

(c) $\rho = \dfrac{\lambda}{\mu} = \dfrac{2}{3} = .667$, or 66.7%

5. This is an $M/M/s$ system, with $s = 3$; $\lambda = 30/$hr.; $\mu = 15/$hr.; and $\dfrac{\lambda}{\mu} = 2$.

(a) From Appendix C1, we find that $L_q = .889$ shoppers.

(b) $W_q = \dfrac{L_q}{\lambda}$

$\qquad = \dfrac{.889}{30}$

$\qquad = .0296$ hr., or 1.776 min.

$W = 1.776$ min. $+ 4$ min., or 5.776 min.

(c) $\rho = \dfrac{\lambda}{s\mu}$

$\qquad = \dfrac{30}{3(15)}$

$\qquad = \dfrac{30}{45} = .667$, or 66.7%

6. This is an $M/M/s$ system, with $s = 5$; $\lambda = 204/$hr.; $\mu = 60/$hr.; and $\lambda/\mu = 204/60 = 3.4$.

(a) From Appendix C1, we know that $L_q = .737$ customers.

$L = L_q + \dfrac{\lambda}{\mu} = .737 + 3.4 = 4.137$ customers

(b) $W_q = \dfrac{L_q}{\lambda}$

$\qquad = \dfrac{.737}{204}$

$\qquad = .0036$ hr., or .216 min., or 13 sec.

7. This is an $M/M/1$ queue, with a finite system; $\lambda = 14/$hr.; $\mu = 20/$hr.; and $\dfrac{\lambda}{\mu} = .7$.

(a) From Appendix C5, we know that $L = 1.533$ phone lines.

(b) From Appendix C3, we know that the probability that the system is full, P_c, is .057; that is, 5.7 percent of the customers get a busy signal.

8. This is an $M/M/1$ queue; $\lambda = 6/$hr.; and $\mu = 12/$hr.

(a) $L_q = \dfrac{\lambda^2}{\mu(\mu - \lambda)}$

$\qquad = \dfrac{6^2}{12(12 - 6)}$

$\qquad = \dfrac{36}{72} = .5$ people in line

(b) $L = \dfrac{\lambda}{(\mu - \lambda)} = \dfrac{6}{12 - 6} = 1$ person in system

(c) $W_q = \dfrac{\lambda}{\mu(\mu - \lambda)}$

$\qquad = \dfrac{6}{12(12 - 6)}$

$\qquad = \dfrac{6}{72} = .083$ hr., or 5 min.

(d) $W = \dfrac{1}{\mu - \lambda} = \dfrac{1}{12 - 6} = .1667$ hr., or 10 min.

(e) $P_0 = 1 - \dfrac{\lambda}{\mu} = 1 - \dfrac{6}{12} = .5$

9. This is an $M/D/1$ queue; $\lambda = 6/$hr.; and $\mu = 12/$hr.

(a) $L_q = \dfrac{\lambda^2}{2\mu(\mu - \lambda)}$

$= \dfrac{6^2}{(2)(12)(12 - 6)}$

$= \dfrac{36}{144} = .25$ people in line

(b) $L = L_q + \dfrac{\lambda}{\mu}$

$= .25 + \dfrac{6}{12} = .75$ people in system

(c) $W_q = \dfrac{\lambda}{2\mu(\mu - \lambda)}$

$= \dfrac{6}{(2)(12)(12 - 6)}$

$= \dfrac{6}{144} = .0417$ hr., or 2.5 min.

(d) $W = W_q + \dfrac{1}{\mu}$

$= .0417 + \dfrac{1}{12}$

$= .125$ hr., or 7.5 min.

10. This is an $M/M/1$ queue; $\lambda = 25/$hr.; and $\mu = 30/$hr.

(a) $L_q = \dfrac{\lambda^2}{\mu(\mu - \lambda)}$

$= \dfrac{25^2}{30\,(30 - 25)}$

$= \dfrac{625}{150} = 4.1667$ students

(b) $W = \dfrac{1}{\mu - \lambda} = \dfrac{1}{30 - 25} = \dfrac{1}{5}$ hr. $= 12$ min.

(c) $\lambda = 25/$hr.; $\mu = 40/$hr.

$W = \dfrac{1}{\mu - \lambda} = \dfrac{1}{40 - 25} = \dfrac{1}{15}$ hr., or 4 min.

The new time is 4 min., a reduction of 8 min.

(d) This is an $M/M/2$ queue; $\lambda = 25$; $\mu = 30$; and $\lambda/\mu = .833$. From Appendix C1, $L_q = .18$, using $(.84)$.

$L = L_q + \dfrac{\lambda}{\mu} = .18 + .833 = 1.013$

$W = L/\lambda = 1.013/25 = .04$ hr., or 2.43 min.

11. This is an $M/M/1$ queue; $\lambda = 50$ pages/day; and $\mu = 64$ pages/day. (*Note:* 1 day = 8 hr.)

(a) $L_q = \dfrac{\lambda^2}{\mu(\mu - \lambda)}$

$= \dfrac{50^2}{64(64 - 50)}$

$= \dfrac{2,500}{896} = 2.79$ pages waiting

(b) $L = \dfrac{\lambda}{\mu - \lambda} = \dfrac{50}{64 - 50} = \dfrac{50}{14} = 3.57$ pages

(c) $W = \dfrac{1}{\mu - \lambda} = \dfrac{1}{64 - 50} = .0714$ day,
or .5712 hr.

(d) $P_0 = 1 - \dfrac{\lambda}{\mu} = 1 - \dfrac{50}{64} = .22$, or 22%

(e) This is still an $M/M/1$ queue, but now $\lambda = 55$ pages/day and $\mu = 64$ pages/day.

part (a): $L_q = \dfrac{\lambda^2}{\mu(\mu - \lambda)}$

$= \dfrac{55^2}{64(64 - 55)}$

$= \dfrac{3,025}{576} = 5.25$ pages waiting

part (b): $L = \dfrac{\lambda}{\mu - \lambda} = \dfrac{55}{64 - 55} = 6.11$ pages

part (c): $W = \dfrac{1}{\mu - \lambda}$

$= \dfrac{1}{64 - 55} = .111$ day, or .888 hr. in system

part (d): $P_0 = 1 - \dfrac{\lambda}{\mu} = 1 - \dfrac{55}{64} = .14$, or 14%

(f) This is an $M/M/2$ queue, with $\lambda = 50$ pages/day and $\mu = 64$ pages/day.

part (a): $\dfrac{\lambda}{\mu} = \dfrac{50}{64} = .78125$

We look for this number, .78125, in Table 8.3 and find that $L_q = .140$.

part (b): $L = L_q + \dfrac{\lambda}{\mu}$

$= .140 + .78125 = .921$

part (c): $W = W_q + \dfrac{1}{\mu}$

$W_q = \dfrac{L_q}{\lambda} = \dfrac{.140}{50} = .0028$ days, or .0224 hr.

$W = .0028 + \dfrac{1}{64} = .0184$ days, or .1475 hr.

part (d): $= \lambda/2\mu = 50/128$. (Each secretary is busy 39 percent of the time and idle 61 percent of the time.)

12. (a) This is an *M/M/1* queue, with $\lambda = 30$ and $\mu = 60$.

$$P = P_0 + P_1 + P_2 + P_3$$

$$P_n = (1 - \lambda/\mu)(\lambda/\mu)^n$$

$$P_0 = (1 - 30/60)(30/60)^0 = .5$$

$$P_1 = (1 - 30/60)(30/60)^1 = .25$$

$$P_2 = (1 - 30/60)(30/60)^2 = .125$$

$$P_3 = (1 - 30/60)(30/60)^3 = .0625$$

$$1 - (.5 + .25 + .125 + .0625) = .0625$$

The probability that a fire regulation will be violated is 6.25 percent.

(b) This is an *M/M/1* queue, with a finite queue/system. From Table 8.5, we know that 6.7 percent will be lost.

13. current: *M/M/1* queue, with $\lambda = 10$/hr. and $\mu = 12$/hr.

$$L_q = \frac{\lambda^2}{\mu(\mu - \lambda)}$$

$$= \frac{10^2}{12(12 - 10)} = 4.166 \text{ in customers in line}$$

hourly cost = registrar's cost + waiting cost

$$= \$5 + (\$2 \times 4.16)$$

$$= \$5 + \$8.32$$

$$= \$13.32$$

option 1 (computer): *M/D/1* queue, with $\lambda = 10$/hr.; $\mu = 15$/hr.

$$L_q = \frac{\lambda^2}{2\mu(\mu - \lambda)} = \frac{10^2}{(2)(15)(15 - 10)} = \frac{10}{15} = .667$$

hourly cost = computer rental cost + waiting cost

$$= \$7 + (\$2 \times .667)$$

$$= \$7 + \$1.33$$

$$= \$8.33$$

option 2 (new registrar): *M/M/1* queue, with $\lambda = 10$/hr. and $\mu = 20$/hr.

$$L_q = \frac{\lambda^2}{\mu(\mu - \lambda)} = \frac{10^2}{20(20 - 10)} = .5$$

hourly cost = registrar's cost + waiting cost

$$= \$8 + (\$2 \times .5)$$

$$= \$8 + \$1$$

$$= \$9$$

14. current: *M/M/1* queue, with $\lambda = 10$/hr. and $\mu = 12$/hr.

$$L = \frac{\lambda}{\mu - \lambda}$$

$$= \frac{10}{12 - 10} = 5 \text{ customers in line}$$

hourly cost = registrar's cost + waiting cost

$$= \$5 + (\$2 \times 5)$$

$$= \$5 + \$10$$

$$= \$15$$

option 1 (computer): *M/D/1* queue, with $\lambda = 10$/hr. and $\mu = 15$/hr.

$$L_q = \frac{\lambda^2}{2\mu(\mu - \lambda)}$$

$$= \frac{10^2}{(2)(15)(15 - 10)}$$

$$= \frac{10}{15}$$

$$= .667$$

$$L = L_q + \lambda/\mu = .667 + .667 = 1.333$$

hourly cost = computer rental cost + waiting cost

$$= \$7 + (\$2 \times 1.33)$$

$$= \$7 + \$2.66$$

$$= \$9.66$$

option 2 (new registrar): *M/M/1* queue, with $\lambda = 10$/hr. and $\mu = 20$/hr.

$$L = \frac{\lambda}{(\mu - \lambda)} = \frac{10}{(20 - 10)} = 1$$

hourly cost = registrar's cost + waiting cost

$$= \$7 + (\$2 \times 1)$$

$$= \$7 + \$2$$

$$= \$9$$

15. $\lambda = 120$/hr.; $\mu = 60/2 = 30$/hr.; $\dfrac{\lambda}{\mu} = \dfrac{120}{30} = 4$

From Appendix C1, we know that $L_q + \lambda/\mu < 6$. So,

$$L_q + 4 < 6$$

$$L_q < 2$$

Therefore, 6 servers are needed.

Computer Case Study 8.1

Beth wants to get a general idea of the system behavior. She first will need to decide whether she is interested in time waiting or time in system. Some students may use system time, but since most shoppers are relieved when it is their turn, we use waiting time as our measure. For all of our analyses, we use current service times, even though a UPC reader is going to be installed. This means that our waiting times are an upper bound for the new, better system. We also assume memorylessness in the service process (the *M/M/s* model).

We begin with a rough analysis (one that is going to have a very interesting feature, by the way). We assume that there are no express lanes. Then, we want to find the average service time and rate. The time is given by

$$t = .2 \ (2 \text{ min.}) + .8 \ (4 \text{ min.})$$
$$= .4 + 3.2$$
$$= 3.6 \text{ min.}$$

This means that the average service rate is $60/3.6 = 16.67$ customers per hour. Notice that this is not the same as taking 20 percent of the rate of 30 and 80 percent of the rate of 15, which would equal 18 and would be wrong.

Using an arrival rate of 100 and a service rate of 16.67, the minimum number of servers is 6. (This is due to round off.) In reality, the minimum number is 7, and the average waiting time is 2.2 minutes. (This is the data file CASE8-1.) Trying one more server leads to a waiting time of .64 minutes.

Now we separate the express and regular. Assume that all express customers go into the express lane (even though they can go into any lane) and assume that all non-express customers go into the proper lanes (even though we all have seen people with twenty packages get into a ten-items-or-less line).

For the express lane, with an arrival rate of 20 and a service rate of 30, one server yields an average wait of 4 minutes, while two servers yield an average wait of .25 minutes.

For the regular lane, with an arrival rate of 80 and a service rate of 15, 6 servers yield an average wait of 4.28 minutes and 7 servers yield an average wait of .98 minutes.

If Beth uses 7 servers, they will be split this way: 6 in regular lanes and 1 in an express lane. If Beth uses 8 servers, a 6-2 split between regular lanes and express lanes yields an average wait of

$$(.2)(.25) + (.8)(4.28) = .05 + 3.424 = 3.47 \text{ min.}$$

A 7-1 split yields an average wait of

$$(.2)(4) + (.8)(.98) = .8 + .784 = 1.584 \text{ min.},$$

which is better. However, the express lane would be *slower* than the regular lanes!

9
Work Measurement and Design

TEACHING NOTES

Many P/OM texts include a chapter on product design and then turn it into a chapter on reliability analysis. While product design relates to operations, this topic is outside the scope of operations at almost all companies. Instead, the major application of reliability in operations is to the equipment and methods used. For this reason, our chapter on work measurement and job design begins with the topic of work systems (methods and machines) design. The section is divided into discussions both of human factors in design and of reliability. It is easy to generate lively discussions on human factors by talking about items in everyday use, such as the dashboard of a car. The reliability discussion is limited to systems (managerial, or macro) reliability. The use of exponential reliabilities is more detailed and should be left to the reliability engineers.

The rest of the chapter offers a brief introduction to some of the major tools of industrial management engineering. In practice, job design precedes work measurement; we have reversed this order. Work measurement (time and motion study, work sampling) is introduced first, so that students can get a feel for the detailed analysis of work. This is a requirement for the study of job design. Many practical situations are described, again enhancing the operational flavor of the text.

We stress that once job design and work measurement are complete, labor standards are designed to plan for and to control worker output—these standards are the basis of pay systems. We go beyond pay systems in this chapter, discussing incentive systems that attempt to motivate better work both in terms of quality and of quantity. The chapter ends with a discussion of learning curves.

Three Solved Problems are provided—one on reliability, one on time study analysis, and the third on learning curves. The Questions, for the most part, are less discussion-oriented than those of most chapters, instead focusing on the unusually large amount of non-quantitative material found in this chapter.

Nineteen Problems are provided, almost half on reliability. For every topic in this chapter, standard types of problems are provided, as well as problems that require reversing the thinking process from the way these problems are presented in the chapter. Assign some of each.

The software for this chapter comes from two modules. One module solves reliability problems. In some cases, it may be necessary to break up the system into different components and to run the program once for each component in order to get the answer. The second module performs a learning curve analysis. Problems 3, 5, and 7 can be solved with the reliability module, while Problems 18 and 19 can be solved using the learning curve module.

TEACHING SUGGESTIONS

Teaching Suggestion 9.1:   Individualized Examples.
Most of our students are working. We ask them to identify and discuss these six steps for their jobs.

Teaching Suggestion 9.2:   Too Much Time.
Some studies have indicated that errors rise to the right of the mean as well, only more slowly. Ask students why this might be.

Teaching Suggestion 9.3:   Automobile Controls.
Ask students about the pros and cons of different designs for automobile controls. We find that it takes a few minutes for students with the same make of car to agree on exactly where the controls are. A major criticism is clutter on the turn-signal lever on many cars.

Teaching Suggestion 9.4:   Improve Operating Conditions.
While reliability refers to normal operating conditions, it is the never-ending responsibility of management to try to improve the operating conditions, thus improving reliability.

Teaching Suggestion 9.5:   Decimal Accuracy.
Our students ask on the first day of class how many decimal places we want in answers. We answer, "Enough to answer the question," which is usually fewer places than they provide. In this chapter, since reliabilities are often measured between .99 and 1.00, more decimals than usual may be required.

Teaching Suggestion 9.6:   Standardization.
All workers should do the same job in the same way. Not only is this not always the case, but individual efforts aimed at improvement often result in different targets for different workers. If all workers could agree on the best way to perform a job, all would be better off.

ANSWERS TO QUESTIONS

1. Psychophysics studies the human neurological system. As such, it describes the speed with which the worker senses stimuli and the speed with which the worker makes an appropriate response.

2. Anthropometry deals with the measurement of the physical features or characteristics of the body. It relates to workplace design in that it is important that the worker be as comfortable as possible, be able to work at maximum speed, and generally be able to use the equipment provided.

3. Biomechanics relates to the classification of body movements and the human capability to perform them. It tells us the human capacity for repetitive work and describes how much time should be given for various movements.

4. The operations manager can focus on reliability engineering, which includes design improvement and the use of backups as possible alternatives, and on maintenance—keeping the system working.

5. In a series system, unless every component works, the system fails. Therefore, the more components there are, the lower the reliability. In a parallel system, only one component needs to work for the system to work, which means that the more components there are, the higher the reliability.

6. time and motion study; work sampling

7. eliminating unnecessary work; performing the remaining work in the best order; standardizing the proper work methods; establishing accurate time standards for the work

8. Work sampling might be preferred to a time and motion study because it covers a longer period of time or because a more representative sample can be used. Another potential advantage is that the observer can do other work at the same time. Other reasons for using work sampling: It is flexible enough to be expanded or compressed as needed; it provides valuable time-for-activity information; and it is less intrusive on workers.

9. Using snapshot-like observations, work sampling records the state of the worker at a brief moment in time to determine the percentage of time in each state.

10. In ratio delay, the analyst knows the complete list of activities performed; in the occurrence study, this list is built up as the activities are observed. Therefore, ratio delay tends to be used for equipment, while occurrence study tends to be used for workers. More accuracy is required with ratio delay because its results are often used in determining allowance factors for standard settings.

11. system job design philosophy; job conditions; job difficulty; job growth and employee opportunity; job security

12. material, design, sequence, equipment, and method

13. how the operator's performance compares with that of other employees and how the job compares with other operations in terms of difficulty and complexity

14. amount of body used; hand or foot patterns required; weight resistance overcome; directional eye–hand coordination; positional eye–hand coordination; muscular pressure control; muscular tilt control; decisions required; pace

15. starting point; shape; rate of increase; steady state (time to reach steady state)

SOLUTIONS TO PROBLEMS

1. total time: 60 hr.; down time: 2 hr.

$$\text{reliability} = \frac{60 - 2}{60} = \frac{58}{60} = .9667$$

2. failures: 4; successes: 187; sample size: $(4 + 187) = 191$ times

$$\text{reliability} = \frac{187}{191} = .979$$

3. system reliability $= R_1 \times R_2 \times R_3$
$$= (.96)(.98)(.99)$$
$$= .931$$

4. $R_4 = .99$ yields a component reliability of .9975 per burner.

5. system reliability $= 1 - (1 - R_1)(1 - R_2)$
$$= 1 - (1 - .98)(1 - .90)$$
$$= 1 - (.02)(.10)$$
$$= 1 - .002$$
$$= .998$$

6. system reliability $= .99999$
$$= 1 - (1 - .99)^n$$
$$= 1 - .01^n$$

If $n = 1$, $R = 1 - .01^1 = .99$.

If $n = 2$, $R = 1 - .01^2$
$$= 1 - .0001$$
$$= .9999.$$

If $n = 3$, $R = 1 - .01^3$
$$= 1 - .000001$$
$$= .999999.$$

Therefore, 3 fuses should be carried with each device.

7. The system can be drawn in series as

I → II → III → IV,

where

$R_I = .99$

$R_{II} = 1 - (1 - .95)^2 = .9975$

$R_{III} = .98$

$R_{IV} = 1 - (1 - .95)(1 - .98) = .999.$

system reliability $= (R_I)(R_{II})(R_{III})(R_{IV})$
$$= (.99)(.9975)(.98)(.999)$$
$$= .9668$$

8. The system can be drawn in series as

I → II,

where $R_{II} = .99$. R_I requires more steps. Draw R_I as two units, R_A and R_B, in parallel, where

$R_A = R_{A1} \to R_{A2}$ (in series)

$R_B = R_{B1} \to R_{B2} \to R_{B3}$ (in series)

$R_{A1} = .97$

$R_{A2} = 1 - (1 - .95)^2 = .9975$

$R_{B1} = .98$

$R_{B2} = .97$

$R_{B3} = .98$

So, $R_A = (.97)(.9975) = .967575$ and $R_B = (.98)(.97)(.98) = .9316$. From R_A and R_B,

$R_I = 1 - (1 - R_A)(1 - R_B)$
$$= 1 - (1 - .967575)(1 - .9316)$$
$$= 1 - (.0324)(.0684)$$
$$= .99778$$

system reliability $= (R_I)(R_2)$
$$= (.99778)(.99)$$
$$= .9878$$

9. $\bar{x} = 1.6$ min.; $s = .2$ min.; $\alpha = .90$, $z_\alpha = 1.64$; $\beta = .05$

$$n = \frac{(z_\alpha s)^2}{(\beta x)^2}$$
$$= \frac{[(1.64)(.2)]^2}{[(.05)(1.6)]^2}$$
$$= 16.8, \text{ or } 17$$

10. Teller 1: $\bar{x} = .5$ min.; $s = .1$ min.; $\alpha = .95$, $z_\alpha = 1.96$; $\beta = .10$

$$n = \frac{(z_\alpha s)^2}{(\beta x)^2}$$

$$= \frac{[(1.96)(.1)]^2}{[(.10)(.5)]^2}$$

$$= 15.36, \text{ or } 16$$

Teller 2: $\bar{x} = .9$ min.; $s = .2$ min.; $\alpha = .95$, $z_\alpha = 1.96$; $\beta = .10$

$$n = \frac{(z_\alpha s)^2}{(\beta x)^2}$$

$$= \frac{[(1.96)(.2)]^2}{[(.10)(.9)]^2}$$

$$= 18.97, \text{ or } 19$$

11. (a) $OT = \dfrac{\sum x_i}{n}$

$$= \frac{2.1 + 2.2 + 2.2 + 2.0 + 2.2 + 2.3 + 2.1 + 2.0 + 2.1 + 2.2}{10}$$

$$= \frac{21.4}{10} = 2.14 \text{ min.}$$

(b) $NT = PR \times OT = (.95)(2.14) = 2.033$ min.

(c) $ST = AF \times NT = (1.04)(2.033) = 2.114$ min.

12. (a) $OT = \dfrac{\sum x_i}{n}$

$$= \frac{.18 + .16 + .17 + .16 + .16 + .18}{6}$$

$$= \frac{1.01}{6} = .16833$$

(b) $NT = PR \times OT = (1.08)(.16833) = .1818$ min.

(c) $ST = AF \times NT = (1.2)(.1818) = .218$ min.

13. $z_\alpha = \beta \bar{x} \sqrt{n}/s$

$$= (.02)(2.1)\sqrt{10}/.1$$

$$= 1.33$$

The confidence associated with $z_\alpha = 1.33$ is 81.6 percent.

14. $p = .9$; $E = .02$

$$N = \frac{4p(1 - p)}{E^2}$$

$$= \frac{(4)(.9)(1 - .9)}{(.02)^2}$$

$$= \frac{(4)(.9)(.1)}{.0004}$$

$$= \frac{.36}{.0004} = 900 \text{ observations}$$

15. $p = .4$; $E = .05$

$$N = \frac{4p(1 - p)}{E^2}$$

$$= \frac{(4)(.4)(1 - .4)}{(.05)^2}$$

$$= \frac{(4)(.4)(.6)}{.0025}$$

$$= \frac{.96}{.0025} = 384 \text{ observations}$$

16. (a) $N = 147$; occurrences $= 132$

$$p = \frac{132}{147} = .898$$

(b) $E = 2 \sqrt{\dfrac{p(1 - p)}{147}}$

$$= 2 \sqrt{\frac{(.898)(1 - .898)}{147}}$$

$$= .0499$$

percentage: 89.8% $\pm 5\%$

17. (a) $N = 1,200$; occurrences $= 140$

$$p = \frac{140}{1,200} = .11667$$

(b) For 99 percent, the number of standard deviations is 2.58.

$$E = 2.58 \sqrt{\frac{p(1 - p)}{n}}$$

$$= 2.58 \sqrt{\frac{(.11667)(1 - .11667)}{1,200}}$$

$$= .0239$$

percentage: 11.67% $\pm 2.4\%$

18. (a) In order to try to determine the learning curve rate, we first find the ratios of pairs of production times.

(1) Patient Number	(2) Time	(3) Patient Number	(4) Time	(5) Ratio [(2)/(4)]
2	240	1	260	.9231
4	220	2	240	.9167
6	210	3	228	.9211
8	202	4	220	.9182
			Total	3.6791

The average learning rate is 3.6791/4 = .9198, which rounds to .92.

(b) We will compute each doubling as 92 percent of the previous time.

$$\text{patient 16 time} = (.92)(\text{patient 8 time})$$
$$= (.92)(202) = 186 \text{ (rounded)}$$

$$\text{patient 32 time} = (.92)(\text{patient 16 time})$$
$$= (.92)(186) = 171 \text{ (rounded)}$$

$$\text{patient 64 time} = (.92)(\text{patient 32 time})$$
$$= (.92)(171) = 157$$

19.

Unit Number	Time (min.)	Time × .87*
1	126	110
2	110	96
4	96	84
8	84	73
16	73	64
32	64	56
64	56	49
128	49	42
256	42	37
512	37	32

*Rounded to nearest minute

The 500th unit will take between 37 and 42 minutes. The time will be much closer to 37 minutes (the time for unit 512) than 42 minutes (the time for unit 256). (*Note:* More exact numbers can be found with AB:POM.)

Computer Case Study 9.1

This case study does not really require a computer, but it does require some thought. In order for the checking system to fail, the item must be both miscoded and misverified. This means that coding and verification act as parallel (not serial) processes. Data file CASE9-1 has two items in parallel and a total reliability of .99768. Students must add to that a third item (second verifier) with a reliability of .92. This yields an overall reliability of .99981. The net benefit is that reliability will increase by .99981 − .99768 = .00213. In other words, 21 out of 10,000 additional items will be caught by adding the new verifier. It probably is not worth the cost of adding a new verifier, although it may be if the errors themselves are large enough.

In a related vein, if the error is an overcharge, customers might notice and become upset. Many stores do not require customers to pay for items for which they have been overcharged; in effect, the stores use their customers as verifiers. It would also make sense for stores to tell customers that they will not be charged for items for which they have been undercharged.

10
Project Scheduling

TEACHING NOTES

In this chapter, we emphasize the traditional time management of projects. Prior to going into detail on PERT and CPM, we explain the objectives of project management and tell why the production of a project differs from the production of a good or service.

We describe three graphical representations of projects—the Gantt chart, the activity on node (AON) network (traditionally used with CPM), and the activity on arc (AOA) network (traditionally used with PERT). We present the enumeration method and the two-pass method for determining project completion time, after which we describe the three-time-estimate procedure of PERT. We point out the problems associated with using the project standard deviation. (We use the sum of the critical activity variances as the project variance; other books do it differently.)

Other topics covered in this chapter include cost analysis, crashing, and limited resources. We do not emphasize these topics due to the introductory nature of this text.

For homework, we have asked students to read and draw charts (Problems 1, 2, and 13) as well as to analyze projects with activities on nodes (Problems 3 through 7) and activities on arcs (Problems 8 and 10). Problems 9 and 12 use the three-time estimate of PERT; Problems 10 and 11 use standard deviations of activities. Problem 14 requires students to perform a cost analysis. In Problem 15, students must analyze crashing, while in Problem 16, they must perform a cost analysis of crashing. Finally, Problem 17 requires students to perform resource leveling.

The software for this chapter will analyze CPM networks and PERT networks with one or three time estimates. Critical activities can be identified, although the critical path is not explicitly identified. The software can be used to solve Problems 3 through 9; 12; 15; and 17.

TEACHING SUGGESTIONS

Teaching Suggestion 10.1: PERT vs. CPM.
Many people write "PERT/CPM," as if these two network planning techniques were one. Both are critical path methods, but they have a few different options. We include both sets of options and stress that the options from either technique can be used.

Teaching Suggestion 10.2: Risk.
Closely related to estimation difficulty is risk. Projects have more risks than everyday operations. The most obvious risk is associated with project completion time. Also obvious is the risk associated with project cost. Less obvious is the risk of failure. The results of many projects, especially R&D projects, cannot be predicted.

Teaching Suggestion 10.3: Shifting Priorities.
Each major decision made by the project manager takes into account conformance, time, and budget. On large projects, it has been observed that the priorities on these three concerns change over the life of the project. Early on, conformance seems to take top priority. Later, it is cost, until finally, toward the completion of the project, time becomes the top priority.

Teaching Suggestion 10.4: Multiple Starts or Finishes.
Our example has a unique starting activity and a unique ending activity. You may want to provide an example having either multiple starts or multiple finishes.

Teaching Suggestion 10.5: Enumeration Method.
The concept of completing each path sometimes confuses our students, who think that if an activity appears on two or more paths, it is being duplicated. Point out that this is not the case.

Teaching Suggestion 10.6: Criticality.
No project manager can monitor every activity all of the time. While all activities need some attention, the critical activities should get more.

Teaching Suggestion 10.7: Interpretation of Slack.
Point out that while slack is computed for each activity, it is shared by all activities along the same branch. Therefore, if one activity uses up the slack, there is no slack left for the others, as illustrated by activities B and D in our example.

Teaching Suggestion 10.8: Symmetric Times—Shortcut.
If the optimistic and pessimistic times are equidistant from the most likely time, the time estimate is simply the most likely time.

Teaching Suggestion 10.9: Choice of Distribution.
Students are used to seeing the normal distribution and question why the beta is used here. There are two reasons: First, this is a truncated distribution; second, the distribution can take many shapes. The truncation means that the optimistic and pessimistic times are the absolute limits. There should be no chance of going outside them.

Teaching Suggestion 10.10: Bonuses and Penalties.
Contracts for large projects often include bonus and penalty clauses. When this is the case, crashing must be examined. Many times, the extra cost of crashing is due to overtime.

Teaching Suggestion 10.11: Scheduling News at WBZ.
The video accompanying this text shows an example of scheduling news production at WBZ, where the limited resource is the number of VCRs available.

ANSWERS TO QUESTIONS

1. Project management consists of three stages: project definition; project planning; and project execution and control.

2. There are many possible answers.

3. infrequency/uniqueness; estimation difficulty; managerial control problems

4. conformance; time; budget

5. project completion date; identification of critical tasks; identification of slack, or noncritical tasks; actual times to schedule activities; budget conformance during the project; budget–time trade-offs

6. The question could be rephrased, "How do you *forecast* the task times?" If the task has a history, the quantitative forecasting techniques are useful. Otherwise, a subjective estimate is made by the most expert person available. Sometimes, a task can be broken down using MTM methods, as discussed in Chapter 9.

7. It depends on the situation. In general, however, we question the reliability, which is why we use the three-time-estimate method.

8. There are many possible answers.

9. The AON network does not require dummy activities. The AOA network does not require a list of precedence, because the naming convention $a \rightarrow b$ indicates the precedence.

10. Any late start or extension of an activity on the critical path will delay the completion of the project.

11. The path is probably critical in that its expected length is the longest. There is a possibility that a different path will, in fact, be critical.

12. Technically, the formula is based on a beta distribution. Intuitively, standard deviation is based on the fact that $\pm 3\sigma$ takes in the entire probability distribution.

13. pay money to add resources (overtime, extra help)

14. In the planning stages, this assumption is the rule, because it forms the basis for indicating the actual (daily) resource needs. In the execution and control stages, however, it often is not the rule.

15. See the answer to Question 14.

SOLUTIONS TO PROBLEMS

1. (a)

Task	Day Task Begins
A	0
B	0
C	4
D	10
E	0
F	7
G	14
H	21

(b) The project takes 30 days.
(c) days 1–12
(d) A–C–D–G–H (There is no slack.)

2. (a)

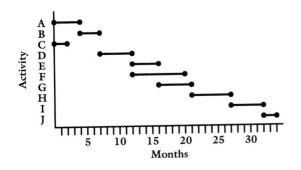

(b)

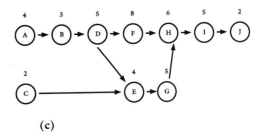

(c)

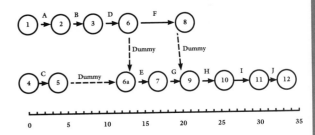

(d)

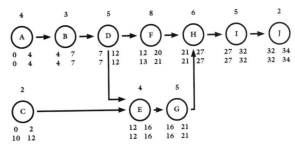

3. (a) from the CPM network:

Path	Time (months)
A–B–D–F–H–I–J	33
A–B–D–E–G–H–I–J	34 (critical path)
C–E–G–H–I–J	24

(b)

critical path: A–B–D–E–G–H–I–J; project length: 34 mo.

(c)

Task	Slack (LS − ES or LF − EF)
A	0
B	0
C	10
D	0
E	0
F	1
G	0
H	0
I	0
J	0

5. (a)

Path	Time (days)
A–B–E–G	21 (critical)
A–B–D–G	20
A–C–D–G	19
A–F–G	17

(b) If C takes 4 days instead of 2, A–C–D–G will become critical at 21, but the project will not be delayed.

6. See the table below.

4.

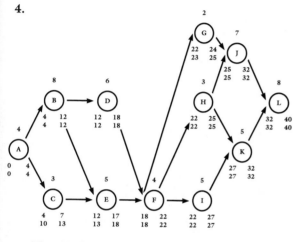

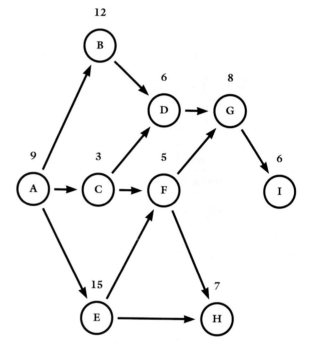

(a) critical paths: A–B–D–F–I–K–L and A–B–D–F–H–J–L; project length: 40

(b) noncritical:

Task	Slack
C	6
E	1
G	1

Table for Problem 6.

Path	Time (days)	
A–B–D–G–I	9 + 12 + 6 + 8 + 6	= 41
A–C–D–G–I	9 + 3 + 6 + 8 + 6	= 32
A–C–F–G–I	9 + 3 + 5 + 8 + 6	= 31
A–C–F–H	9 + 3 + 5 + 7	= 24
A–E–F–G–I	9 + 15 + 5 + 8 + 6	= 43 (critical path)
A–E–H	9 + 15 + 7	= 31

7.

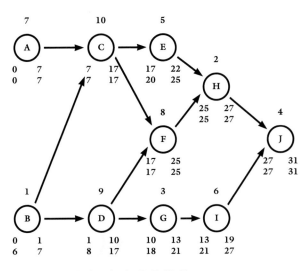

(a) critical path: A–C–F–H–J
(b) project ends in 31 days
(c)

Noncritical Activity	Slack Times
B	6
D	7
E	3
G	8
I	8

8.

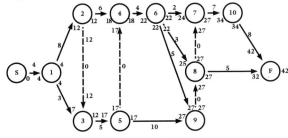

The critical path is S–1–2–4–6–9–8–7–10–F, and the time is 42.

9. See the table below.

10. (a) See the table below.
(b) critical path = S–1–3–6–F; expected length = 25 days

11. (a) 23 days
(b)

Path	z	Probability	
1	$\dfrac{22 - 21}{5} = .2$	.5793	
2	$\dfrac{22 - 23}{2} = -.5$	.3085	$(1 - .6915)$
3	$\dfrac{22 - 20}{1} = 2$	.9772	

probability = $(.5793)(.3085)(.9772) = .1746$

Table for Problem 9.

Activity	t_o	t_m	t_p	$t = \dfrac{t_o + 4t_m + t_p}{6}$	$\sigma = \dfrac{t_p - t_o}{6}$
A	11	15	19	15	1.33
B	27	31	41	32	2.33
C	18	18	18	18	0
D	8	13	19	13.17	1.83
E	17	18	20	18.17	.5
F	16	19	22	19	1

Table for Problem 10(a).

Path	Expected Project Length (days)	σ^2	σ
S–1–3–6–F	$4 + 8 + 7 + 6 = 25$	$1^2 + 3^2 + 2^2 + 1^2 = 15$	3.87
S–1–4–F	$4 + 6 + 10 = 20$	$1^2 + 1.5^2 + 1.5^2 = 5.5$	2.35
S–2–5–F	$10 + 5 + 7 = 22$	$2^2 + .5^2 + 1^2 = 5.25$	2.29

(c)

Path	z	Probability
1	$\dfrac{25-21}{5}=.8$	.7881
2	$\dfrac{25-23}{2}=1$	.8413
3	$\dfrac{25-20}{1}=5$	1.0

The probability that the project will be completed is $(.7881)(.8413)(1.0)=.6630$. Therefore, $1-.663=.337$ is the probability the project will not be completed within 25 days.

12. (a)

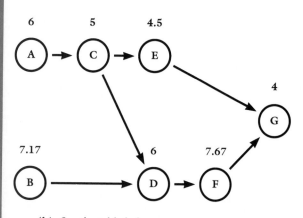

6　　　5　　　4.5

7.17　　　6　　　7.67

(b) See the table below.

Path	Time (weeks)
A–C–E–G	19.5
A–C–D–F–G	28.67 (critical)
B–D–F–G	24.84

(c) 28.7 weeks

(d) using critical path:

$$\text{variance} = \sigma^2 = .67^2 + 1^2 + 0^2 + .67^2 + .33^2$$
$$= .4489 + 1 + 0 + .4489 + .1089$$
$$= 2.0067$$

$$\text{standard deviation} = \sigma = \sqrt{2.0067} = 1.42$$

(e) $z = \dfrac{30 - 28.67}{1.42} = \dfrac{1.33}{1.42} = .94$

Therefore, from Table B2, $p = .8264$.

13.

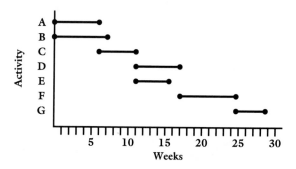

14. (a)

Activity	Start	Cost per Day	Duration	Activity Cost
A	1	$20	5	$100
B	6	17	8	136
C	6	19	3	57
D	9	23	6	138
E	14	25	3	75
F	16	15	5	75
			Total	$581

Table for Problem 12(b).

Activity	t_o	t_m	t_p	$t = \dfrac{t_o + 4t_m + t_p}{6}$	$\sigma = \dfrac{t_p - t_o}{6}$
A	4	6	8	6	.67
B	6	7	9	7.17	.5
C	2	5	8	5	1
D	6	6	6	6	0
E	3	4	8	4.5	.83
F	5	8	9	7.67	.67
G	3	4	5	4	.33

(b) See the table below.

15. The times in the diagram are *after* crashing.

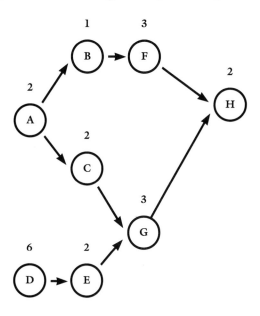

Path	Time (days)
A–B–F–H	8
A–C–G–H	9
D–E–G–H	13 (critical path)

16.

Path	Time (days)
A–B–F–H	14
A–C–G–H	16
D–E–G–H	17

Iteration 1: The cheapest of D–E–G–H is E ($14). The table shows the new times.

Path	Time (days)
A–B–F–H	14
A–C–G–H	16
D–E–G–H	16

Iteration 2: The cheapest option is H ($15).

Path	Time (days)
A–B–F–H	13
A–C–G–H	15
D–E–G–H	15

Iteration 3: The cheapest option is G ($18). Since $18 > $16, stop; any future reductions cost more money than they save.

Table for Problem 14(b).

Day				Daily Cost	Cumulative Cost
1	A(20)			$20	$ 20
2	A(20)			20	40
3	A(20)			20	60
4	A(20)			20	80
5	A(20)			20	100
6		B(17)	C(19)	36	136
7		B(17)	C(19)	36	172
8		B(17)	C(19)	36	208
9		B(17)	D(23)	40	248
10		B(17)	D(23)	40	288
11		B(17)	D(23)	40	328
12		B(17)	D(23)	40	368
13		B(17)	D(23)	40	408
14			D(23)	E(25)	48	456
15				E(25)	25	481
16				E(25) F(15)	40	521
17				F(15)	15	536
18				F(15)	15	551
19				F(15)	15	566
20				F(15)	15	581

17. (a)

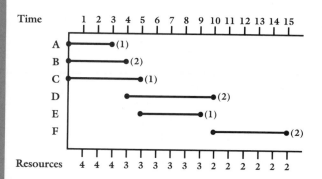

Time

The project length is 15.

(b) The maximum number of resources at any one time is 4.

(c) trial and error:

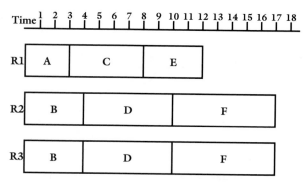

In the preceding figure, the R1 bar represents the schedule for resource 1, the R2 bar represents the schedule for resource 2, and the R3 bar represents the schedule for resource 3.

(d) trial and error:

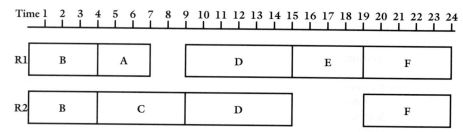

11

Linear Programming

TEACHING NOTES

Perhaps this chapter should have been titled "Applications of Linear Programming in Operations Management." We have not written the typical operations research linear programming chapter; instead, we have written an applied chapter that emphasizes the formulation of linear programs.

We begin with the general linear program and then present formulation examples using product mix/resource allocation, the diet problem, ingredient blending (refinery), personnel scheduling, production planning, and distribution/transportation. Along the way, we point out exactly what is linear in linear programming and demonstrate that there may be more than one way to formulate a problem.

Following the formulation section is our presentation of the graphical analysis of a problem. Note that we do not present the simplex method in this text.

Homework problems are of two types: formulations (Problems 1–10) and graphical analyses (Problems 11–21). Our formulations require students to think. They deal with resource allocation (Problems 1 and 5), definition of ratios (Problem 2), diet (Problems 3 and 4), scheduling

(Problems 6 and 7), and aggregate planning (Problems 8 and 9). Problem 10, a kind of hodgepodge, was included to demonstrate that money is not always the objective.

The software that can be used for this chapter is the simplex method. The LP software, which is extremely easy to use, presents solutions, shadow prices, and graphs. All homework problems in this chapter can be solved with the software, including those problems for which there are formulations but for which students are not asked to find a solution.

The computer case study for this chapter is a very straightforward production planning case. Students must run nine scenarios of the constraints. Of course, as students relax the constraints, they will find that the cost gets lower.

TEACHING SUGGESTIONS

Teaching Suggestion 11.1:   Programming and Planning.
The word *programming* as used here should not be confused with computer programming. Before computers, this word was synonymous with the word *planning*. Linear programming is a technique for using linear models for planning purposes.

Teaching Suggestion 11.2:   Technique vs. Application Area.
We emphasize that all previous chapters are related to some function of operations. This chapter focuses on a technique useful for a wide variety of functions.

Teaching Suggestion 11.3:   Variable Names.
The choice of x_1 and x_2 for our variables here was somewhat arbitrary. We selected x_1 and x_2 primarily because they appear in the general form. Point out that variables can have any name. For example, for obvious reasons, J and S would be good choices here.

Teaching Suggestion 11.4:   Strict Inequalities.
Point out that strict inequalities are not permitted. Presumably, if a resource is available, all of it may be used. Challenge your students to think of a situation in which a strict inequality would make sense.

Teaching Suggestion 11.5:   Integrality Example in Homework.
The solution to Problem 7 is not an integer. While the problem calls only for modeling—not solving—you may want to discuss the implications of a solution that calls for a fractional number of workers.

Teaching Suggestion 11.6:   Applicability of Diet Problem.
This is a very common and valuable application of linear programming. Major food producers solve this problem daily, as prices of ingredients fluctuate on the commodities markets. Ask your students why this cannot be applied to individuals' diets.

Teaching Suggestion 11.7:   Linearity.
Point out that nutrients behave linearly. Two portions pro-

vide twice the nutrients of one portion (an example of proportionality). Eating one portion of Cheerios and one portion of Wheaties gives the sum of the nutrients listed on the packages (an example of additivity). However, taste is not linear. Twice as much salt in a recipe does not necessarily make the recipe taste twice as salty.

Teaching Suggestion 11.8:   Biggest Use of LP.
While Example 11.3 is rather simplistic, it is representative of the more complex problems associated with oil refineries. Oil companies are the biggest users of LP, running their refinery models every day. A major U.S. oil producer purchased a supercomputer dedicated solely to running these models. The chemical refining relationships are indeed linear.

Teaching Suggestion 11.9:   Ratios Are Linear.
This company policy, expressed as a ratio, is easily converted to a linear constraint. The fact that ratios are linear expands the applicability of linear programming.

Teaching Suggestion 11.10:   Schedule Not Complete.
It is important to point out that the solution to Example 11.4 provides the number of nurses for each period but does not provide any further details. Scheduling is a difficult problem that must take into account, among other things, days off and weekend and shift rotations.

Teaching Suggestion 11.11:   Alternate Formulations.
Example 11.5 can be formulated using different variables. It is common to include a variable for inventory. As an alternative, double subscripted variables could be used, where the subscripts refer to the production period and the usage period (in transportation-like fashion).

Teaching Suggestion 11.12:   Transportation Structure.
Point out that the coefficients are all 1 or 0 and that the matrix has a special structure. Any problem with this structure is a transportation problem, whether or not it has anything to do with transportation.

Teaching Suggestion 11.13:   Unbounded Region vs. Unbounded Solution.
Example 11.2 has an unbounded region. Ask your students what would happen if this were a maximization problem.

Teaching Suggestion 11.14:   Shadow Prices.
Finding shadow prices is beyond the scope of this discussion. We introduce shadow prices through the use of software; see our discussion of Solved Problem 2. Have the students solve Solved Problem 2 with the right-hand side of constraint 1 changed to 25 and then to 23.

ANSWERS TO QUESTIONS

1. prescriptive

2. The objective contains the profit or cost information that enables us to determine whether one solution is better than another solution. Our choice of best depends *only* on the objective.

3. Before activity values can be placed into the objective, they must meet the constraints. Notice that the objective function has no minimum-required profit level unless it is included as a constraint.

4. Management can control the parameter b_i most easily. Typically, the a_{ij} coefficients are technological in nature, and the c_j coefficients are determined by markets and the environment.

5. A modification of the a_{ij} coefficients might occur through work improvement or methods analysis by reducing the time (resource) required for an activity. Material (resource) usage for an activity change could occur through engineering design and analysis. The cost/profit coefficients, c_j, could change through changes in purchasing procedures or through changes due to marketing. The right-hand-side coefficients, b_i, could change by changing the capacities or inventories.

6. a_{ij} because we would try to reduce our resource usage

7. Two or more constraints conflict; no solution satisfies all constraints simultaneously.

8. In a profit maximization problem, this means that profit is unbounded. Either you should enter this business or, more likely, a constraint is missing from the model. In a cost-minimization problem (see Figure 11.11), an unbounded feasible region is not a problem, because we want to be near the origin.

9. When there are quantity discounts on raw materials, it is possible that costs per unit diminish as the variable increases.

10. If increases in volume necessitate additional fixed costs, the costs per unit may increase as the variable increases.

11. Additivity overestimates resource usage when there is leftover capacity for an activity. For example, the scraps that are left over when cloth is cut for a suit can be put to some other use.

12. Additivity underestimates resource usage when there are setup times between activities.

13. When the variables take on large values—for example, when they represent the output of U.S. automakers—the solution can be rounded to the nearest integer without much loss.

14. When the variables take on small values—for example, when they represent small fleets of cars—the integrality is critical.

15. As long as the costs do not change, the diet problem always provides the same answer. In other words, the diet is the *same* every day. Unlike animals, people enjoy variety, and variety cannot be included as a linear constraint.

16. The number of feasible solutions is infinite. We only need to consider extreme points—corner points—to find the optimal solution. If we use isoprofit lines, we only examine one corner point to find the optimal solution.

SOLUTIONS TO PROBLEMS

1. Let

H = number of home computers

and let

B = number of business computers.

Maximize $Z = 600H + 1{,}000B$

Subject to

$40H +$	$30B \leq 2{,}400$	(chips)
$2H +$	$3B \leq 200$	(labor)

$H, B \geq 0$

2. $H \geq .70(H + B)$ or $.30H - .70B \geq 0$.

3. Let

C = servings of Corn Sweets

and let

G = servings of Granny's Brannies.

Minimize $.25C + .22G$

Subject to

$80C +$	$60G \geq 100$	(vitamin A)
$20C +$	$40G \geq 100$	(vitamin B)
$70C +$	$30G \geq 100$	(vitamin C)

$C, G \geq 0$

4. Let

P = amount of paste,

S = amount of sauce, and

C = amount of catsup.

Maximize $Z = .80P + 1.90S + 1.20C$

Subject to

$2P + 1.50S + 1C \leq 32{,}000$	(tomatoes)
$1P + 3S + .5C \leq 20{,}000$	(spice)

$P, S, C \geq 0$

5. Let

C = number of custom seats

and let

R = number of regular seats.

Maximize $Z = 300C + 200R$

Subject to

$$3C + 4R \le 36,000 \quad \text{(wood)}$$
$$5C + 4R \le 50,000 \quad \text{(square feet)}$$
$$C, R \ge 0$$

6. Let

W_0 = number of waitresses starting at 2 A.M.;

W_4 = " " 6 A.M.;

W_8 = " " 10 A.M.;

W_{12} = " " 2 P.M.;

W_{16} = " " 6 P.M.; and

W_{20} = " " 10 P.M.

Minimize $Z = W_0 + W_4 + W_8 + W_{12} + W_{16} + W_{20}$

Subject to

$$W_0 \qquad\qquad\qquad + W_{20} \ge 4$$
$$W_0 + W_4 \qquad\qquad\qquad \ge 8$$
$$W_4 + W_8 \qquad\qquad \ge 10$$
$$W_8 + W_{12} \qquad \ge 7$$
$$W_{12} + W_{16} \qquad \ge 12$$
$$W_{16} + W_{20} \ge 4$$
$$W_0, W_4, W_8, W_{12}, W_{16}, W_{20} \ge 0$$

7. Let

F_8 = number of full-time workers starting at 8 A.M.;

F_{12} = " " noon;

F_{16} = " " 4 P.M.;

P_8 = number of part-time workers starting at 8 A.M.;

P_{12} = " " noon;

P_{16} = " " 4 P.M.; and

P_{20} = " " 8 P.M.

Minimize $Z = (6.37)(8)(F_8 + F_{12} + F_{16}) + (5.00)(4)(P_8 + P_{12} + P_{16} + P_{20})$

Subject to

$$F_8 \qquad\qquad + P_8 \qquad\qquad \ge 4$$
$$F_8 + F_{12} \qquad\qquad + P_{12} \qquad \ge 3$$
$$F_{12} + F_{16} \qquad + P_{16} \qquad \ge 7$$
$$F_{16} \qquad\qquad + P_{20} \ge 4$$
$$F_8 \qquad\qquad\qquad \ge 2P_8$$
$$F_8 + F_{12} \qquad\qquad \ge 2P_{12}$$
$$F_{12} + F_{16} \qquad \ge 2P_{16}$$
$$F_{16} \qquad\qquad \ge 2P_{20}$$
$$F_8, F_{12}, F_{16}, P_8, P_{12}, P_{16}, P_{20} \ge 0$$

8. Let

DR = number of bottles in regular time during Dec.;

DT = " " overtime during Dec.;

JR = " " regular time during Jan.;

JT = " " overtime during Jan.;

FR = " " regular time during Feb.; and

FT = " " overtime during Feb.

Minimize

$$Z = 5DR + 7.50DT + 5JR + 7.50JT + 5FR + 7.50FT + .5(DR + DT - 750) + .5(DR + DT + JR + JT - 1,650) + .5(DR + DT + JR + JT + FR + FT - 2,650)$$
$$Z = 6.5DR + 9DT + 6JR + 8.5JT + 5.5FR + 8FT + (-2,525)$$

(The constant gets dropped from the objective function.)

Subject to

$$RT\,capacity \begin{cases} DR \le 700 \\ JR \le 700 \\ FR \le 700 \end{cases}$$

$$demand \begin{cases} DR + DT \ge (800 - 50) \\ DR + DT + JR + JT \ge \\ \quad (800 + 900 - 50) \\ DR + DT + JR + JT + FR + FT \ge \\ \quad (800 + 900 + 1,000 - 50) \end{cases}$$

$$\begin{matrix} production \\ stability \end{matrix} \begin{cases} DR + DT \le (1.15)(900) \\ DR + DT \ge (.85)(900) \\ JR + JT \le 1.15(DR + DT) \\ JR + JT \ge .85(DR + DT) \\ FR + FT \le 1.15(JR + JT) \\ FR + FT \ge .85(JR + JT) \end{cases}$$

$$DR, DT, JR, JT, FR, FT \ge 0$$

(*Note:* If one assumes that total production = total demand, the last demand constraint is unnecessary, as is the last term—line 4—in the objective function.)

9. Let

R_{ij} = number of sofas produced in month i for month j in regular time

and let

O_{ij} = number of sofas produced in month i for month j in overtime.

A regular-time sofa costs $(10 \times 8 \times 3,000 \text{ pesos})/3 = 80,000$ pesos. An overtime sofa costs $(10 \times 8 \times 4,500 \text{ pesos})/3 = 120,000$ pesos.

Minimize $\Sigma\Sigma$ 80,000 R_{ij} + $\Sigma\Sigma$ 120,000 O_{ij} (production costs)

      + 15,000(R_{12} + O_{12} + R_{23} + O_{23} + R_{34} + O_{34})   (items held one period)

      + 30,000(R_{13} + O_{13} + R_{24} + O_{24})   (items held two periods)

      + 45,000(R_{14} + O_{14})   (items held three periods)

Subject to

$$demand \begin{cases} R_{11} + O_{11} = 60 \\ R_{12} + O_{12} + R_{22} + O_{22} = 80 \\ R_{13} + O_{13} + R_{23} + O_{23} + R_{33} + O_{33} = 70 \\ R_{14} + O_{14} + R_{24} + O_{24} + R_{34} + O_{34} + R_{44} + O_{44} = 80 \end{cases}$$

$$regular\text{-}time\ capacity \begin{cases} R_{11} + R_{12} + R_{13} + R_{14} \le (3)(20) \\ R_{22} + R_{23} + R_{24} \le (3)(20) \\ R_{33} + R_{34} \le (3)(20) \\ R_{44} \le (3)(20) \end{cases}$$

10. Let

  T = number of trash trucks;

  R = number of recycling trucks;

  B = number of brooms;

  t = number of trash operators;

  r = number of recycle operators; and

  b = number of broom pushers.

Maximize Z = 200,000T + 2.64(100,000)R + .5B

Subject to 22,000T + 26,000R + 2B + 20,000t + 20,000r + 13,000b $\le$ $1,000,000

$$\begin{array}{rrrll} & t + & r & \ge 29 & (\text{union}) \\ -T & + & t & \ge 0 & (t \ge T) \\ -2R & + & r & \ge 0 & (r \ge 2R) \\ -B & & + b & = 0 & (B = b) \end{array}$$

$$T, R, B, t, r, b \ge 0$$

11.

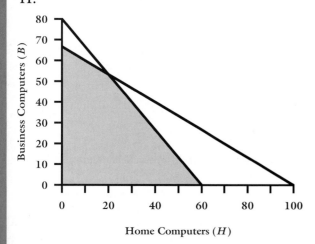

H	B	$600H + 1{,}000B$
0	0	0
60	0	36,000
0	66.667	66,667 (opt.)
20	53.333	65,333

12.

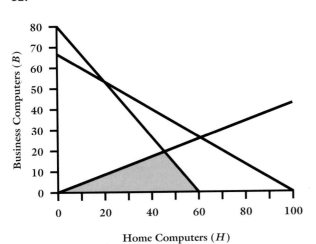

(a)

H	B	600H + 1,000B
0	0	0
60	0	36,000
45.41	19.46	46,703 (opt.)

(b) $66,667 - $46,703 = $19,964

13.

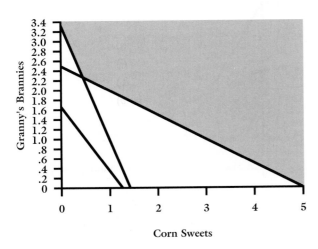

Corn Sweets

C	G	.25C + .22G
5	0	1.25
0	3.33	.7326
.4545	2.27	.613635 (opt.)

14.

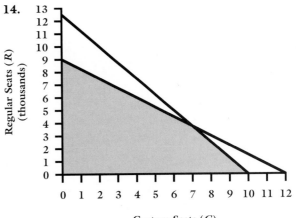

Custom Seats (C)
(thousands)

C	R	300C + 200R
0	0	0
10,000	0	3,000,000 (opt.)
0	9,000	1,800,000
7,000	3,750	2,850,000

15.

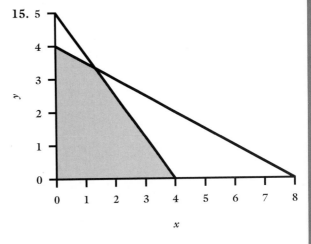

x	y	4x + 6y
0	0	0
4	0	16
0	4	24
1.33	3.33	25.33 (opt.)

16.

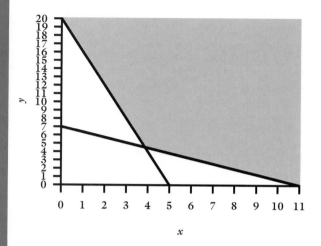

x	y	$24x + 15y$
0	20	300
11	0	264
3.86	4.54	160.86 (opt.)

18.

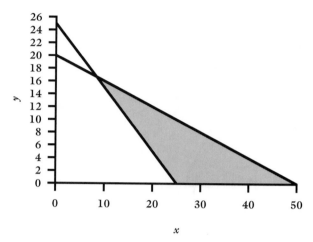

x	y	$8x + 5y$
25	0	200
50	0	400
8.33	16.67	150 (opt.)

17.

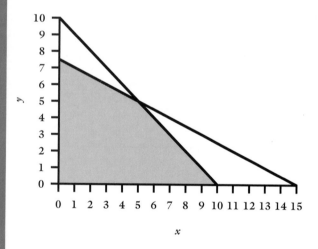

x	y	$x + 4y$
0	7.5	30 (opt.)
10	0	10
5	5	25

19.

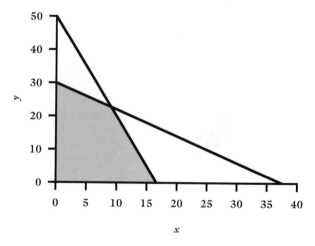

x	y	$6x + 2y$
0	0	0
16.67	0	100 (opt.)
0	30	60
9.09	22.72	100 (opt.)

20.

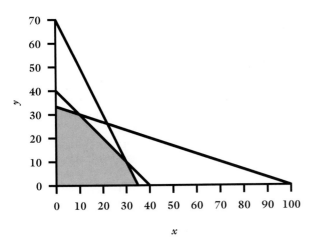

x	y	$5x + 7y$
0	0	0
35	0	175
0	33.33	233.33
10	30	260 (opt.)
30	10	220

21.

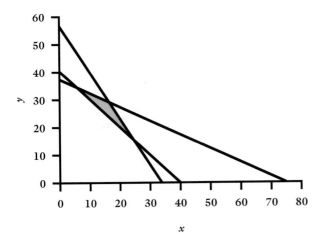

x	y	$10x + 13y$
25	15	445
16.43	29.29	545 (opt.)
5	35	505

Computer Case Study 11.1

In order to answer the question regarding the inventory policy, we must run the system three times—once with a requirement of 10 percent; once with a requirement of 5 percent; and once with a requirement of 0 percent. The original data set is set at 10 percent, so halving the numbers on the right-hand side will change it to 5 percent. Changing the numbers to 0 will change the data set to 0 percent. The original data set has hiring restricted to no more than 999. Changing the hiring to 1 and to 2 yields the following table of costs for the nine runs.

		Hire/Fire	
Inventory	Unlimited	Limited to 2	Limited to 1
10%	$55,706	$55,997	$56,919
5%	53,394	53,701	54,614
0%	51,088	51,668	52,308

Point out that even before we started to solve the problem, we knew that the less restrictive we were (0-percent inventory, unlimited hiring/firing), the better off we would be. The real question was *how much* better off, which is precisely what the costs in the table tell us.

12

Aggregate Planning

TEACHING NOTES

This is a key chapter because aggregate planning figures prominently in the operations manager's (primary) role as planner of operations. The chapter introduces the key concerns that must be taken into consideration when developing aggregate plans. Make sure that students know exactly what constitutes aggregate planning and how it differs from other planning situations.

After you have set the stage, spend some time discussing strategies. In other words, take this opportunity to work on developing the thought process of the operations manager. We have tried to help in this regard by providing an alternative to the quick, quantitative solutions to contrived problems that characterize most presentations of aggregate planning.

Focus on techniques for incorporating the strategies. The trial-and-error approach presented in the text gives students a feel for the difficulty of this task. Have students practice many scenarios, preferably using software so that they learn the importance of implementing strategies quickly.

The aggregate plan for multiple items introduces some real-world complexity. A simple approach to handling it is provided, as is an approach to updating aggregate forecasts—both useful concepts for operations managers that are not included in most texts.

Some operations texts place too much emphasis on the tools of management science, often turning the aggregate planning chapter into a chapter on applying linear programming. Texts that share this text's more operational view often mention the use of these tools for aggregate planning but do not develop and demonstrate them. We present the linear programming formulation here for two reasons: (1) it is frequently used in practice and (2) it represents a payoff to work students did in Chapter 11. We also provide an approach that can be used within the context of the transportation method (presented in Chapter 6) and that can be demonstrated with a spreadsheet.

Matching workforce levels (supply) and demand to determine if production schedules should be expedited or slowed is the topic of the next-to-last section. We end the chapter with a discussion of master production scheduling (treated separately from MRP because it is a planning problem, to which MRP merely responds).

Typically, this chapter's Questions are intended to generate discussion, and its Solved Problems allow students to review the important techniques presented. Homework problems basically follow the chapter sequence. We note that many of the Problems are linked. They can be assigned separately, of course, but they work best when used together, so that students may compare different strategies.

The software for this chapter will perform aggregate planning using trial-and-error methods. The two pure strategies can be implemented directly or users may input production quantities themselves. Problems 1 through 11 can use the aggregate planning module; Problems 12 and 13 can use the transportation module. The solution to Problem 14, a linear programming formulation, can be found by using the linear programming module.

The computer case study for this chapter is an aggregate planning problem. It should be solved by trial and error.

TEACHING SUGGESTIONS

Teaching Suggestion 12.1: Top Management.
Medium-range planning is dependent on production capacities determined by top management in the past. It is also dependent on the number of new products introduced, product changes, and packaging changes, all also previously determined by top management. Poor or inconsistent decisions by top management can make the aggregate planner's job very difficult. The quality of long-term planning will only be evident *now*.

Teaching Suggestion 12.2: Lost Sales vs. Backorders.
Our examples always have backorders. Explain the difference between backorders and lost sales. Also mention that, in either case, the cost is difficult to assess.

Teaching Suggestion 12.3: Other Factors.
It may not be possible to produce 400 units each month due to other factors that affect the capacity. For example, what if the facility has two weeks of downtime planned during this period?

Teaching Suggestion 12.4: Trial-and-Error Approach.
Real aggregate planning involves a lot of trial and error. To demonstrate this, ask students for a fourth plan that is better than the three in the text. We have the whole class work together to complete this exercise, which is greatly facilitated by a computer in the classroom.

Teaching Suggestion 12.5: Fixed Inventory/Labor Cost Ratio.
In the example, the inventory costs are all equal to $4 per labor hour. Ask how students would approach the problem if inventory costs were $4 per unit for each of the three units (A, B, and C).

ANSWERS TO QUESTIONS

1. The aggregate plan interacts with personnel to coordinate work force levels; with marketing to monitor availability or shortages of inventory; and with finance to provide the funds for resources.

2. The aggregate plan is limited by the capacities that have been dictated by long-range capacity planning.

3. The major decisions involve the work force levels; inventory and shortage levels; regular-time, overtime, and part-time help; and subcontracting.

4. Maintain a specified level of customer service; do not exceed some upper limit on inventory investment; maintain a specified level of employment; minimize labor costs; minimize inventory costs; and maximize equipment usage.

5. Maintaining the work force levels can be done only by varying the other factors from period to period. Production planning is performed for a group of products. Because products have different characteristics, the products are typically aggregated by (labor) hours.

6. The key word is planning. Only the first period of a production plan is implemented. Production plans are updated to account for changes in demands and demand forecasts.

7. The three most commonly used options for the aggregate planner are regular-time production, overtime production, and subcontracting.

8. The general objective is to minimize the total cost. The most relevant costs are those associated with the six objectives in Question 4.

9. Turnover ratio = sales/inventory.
Increased sales (a marketing function) can improve the turnover ratio, as can decreased inventory (an operations function).

10. In an ideal situation, production rates never change from month to month. Because demand does vary from month to month, inventory is used to allow production rates to stay the same.

11. A pure strategy is one that varies only one factor—for example, maintain a constant work force level or maintain a constant inventory. Trade-offs are ignored.

12. A mixed strategy attempts to trade off the costs of different factors by allowing all factors to vary. This is more complex than a pure strategy, but it typically yields a better strategy.

13. A negative inventory means that we owe units to our customers, in which case we either lose sales or we make up the demands in future periods (backorder).

14. The just-in-time approach indicates that we use a pure strategy of maintaining no inventory.

15. Just-in-time has no inventory costs but requires production levels to vary from period to period, creating problems and costs involving the appropriate usage of personnel and machines.

16. The operations managers must know exactly what is produced at a given time in terms of the individual products and the individual machines used. The first step is to create the master production schedule, which disaggregates the aggregate plan by product. (The second step of scheduling is discussed in Chapter 15.)

SOLUTIONS TO PROBLEMS

1. The following schedule shows the pure strategy of balancing work force levels, using an average demand of 90,000 per quarter.

Quarter	Production
1	90,000
2	90,000
3	90,000
4	90,000

The following schedule shows the pure strategy of meeting each of the demands exactly in each quarter (minimizing inventory).

Quarter	Production
1	80,000
2	60,000
3	100,000
4	120,000

The strength of the first schedule is the smooth work force level required. Its weakness is that 40,000 units of inventory accumulate by the end of the second quarter. The strength of the second schedule is that no inventories accumulate. Its weakness is that it requires layoffs after the first quarter and then a doubling of the work force by the fourth quarter. Neither schedule results in any shortages.

2. The following schedule illustrates the pure strategy of balancing work force levels, using an average demand of 65,000 per quarter.

Quarter	Production
Fall	65,000
Winter	65,000
Spring	65,000
Summer	65,000

The following schedule illustrates the pure strategy of meeting each of the demands exactly in each quarter (minimizing inventory).

Quarter	Production
Fall	72,000
Winter	87,000
Spring	53,000
Summer	48,000

The strength of the first schedule is the smooth work force level required. Its weakness is the shortages that occur in the first three quarters. The strength of the second schedule is that no shortages occur. The weakness is that it requires layoffs in the last two quarters, after requiring the hiring of additional people earlier. No inventories accumulate in either schedule.

3. Because of the end-of-month inventory policy, it is first necessary to calculate the net demands for each month:

Net demand = demand + ending inventory − beginning inventory.

Month	Beginning Inventory	Demand	Required Ending Inventory	Net Demand
Apr.	300	1,800	260	1,760
May	260	2,600	290	2,630
June	290	2,900	250	2,860
July	250	2,500	270	2,520
Aug.	270	2,700	40	2,470
Sept.	40	400	—	360

The net demand column is the only production schedule that meets the inventory policy. Any other schedule would violate it.

4. (a)

Month	Demand	Cum. Demand	Prod.	Cum. Prod.	Ending Inv.	Shortage	Variation Incr.	Variation Decr.
July	80	80	90	90	10	0	0	0
Aug.	50	130	90	180	50	0	0	0
Sept.	70	200	90	270	70	0	0	0
Oct.	90	290	90	360	70	0	0	0
Nov.	100	390	90	450	60	0	0	0
Dec.	80	470	90	540	70	0	0	0
Jan.	110	580	90	630	50	0	0	0
Feb.	120	700	90	720	20	0	0	0
Mar.	100	800	90	810	10	0	0	0
Apr.	70	870	90	900	30	0	0	0
May	90	960	90	990	30	0	0	0
June	80	1,040	90	1,080	40	0	0	0
					510	0	0	0

(b) no

(c) 40

(d) pure

5. (a)

Month	Demand	Cum. Demand	Prod.	Cum. Prod.	Inventory Excess	Inventory Shortage	Variation Incr.	Variation Decr.
Oct.	600	600	500	500	—	100	—	
Nov.	400	1,000	400	900	—	100	—	100
Dec.	300	1,300	400	1,300	—	—	—	—
Jan.	700	2,000	600	1,900	—	100	200	
Feb.	600	2,600	600	2,500	—	100	—	
Mar.	500	3,100	600	3,100	—	—	—	
					0	400	300	

(b) yes—months 1, 2, 4, and 5
(c) 0
(d) mixed

6. (a)

Month	Demand	Cum. Demand	Prod.	Cum. Prod.	Inventory Excess	Inventory Shortage	Variation Incr.	Variation Decr.
Oct.	600	600	517	517	—	83	—	—
Nov.	400	1,000	517	1,034	34	—	—	—
Dec.	300	1,300	517	1,551	251	—	—	—
Jan.	700	2,000	517	2,068	68	—	—	—
Feb.	600	2,600	517	2,585	—	15	—	—
Mar.	500	3,100	517	3,102	2	—	—	—
					355	98	0	0

(*Note:* AB:POM produces 516 in February and March so that total production equals total demand.)

(b)

Month	Demand	Cum. Demand	Prod.	Cum. Prod.	Inventory Excess	Inventory Shortage	Variation Incr.	Variation Decr.
Oct.	600	600	600	600	—	—	—	—
Nov.	400	1,000	400	1,000	—	—	—	200
Dec.	300	1,300	300	1,300	—	—	—	100
Jan.	700	2,000	700	2,000	—	—	400	—
Feb.	600	2,600	600	2,600	—	—	—	100
Mar.	500	3,100	500	3,100	—	—	—	100
					0	0	400	500

(c) There are several possible answers; one possibility is given.

Month	Demand	Cum. Demand	Prod.	Cum. Prod.	Inventory Excess	Inventory Shortage	Variation Incr.	Variation Decr.
Oct.	600	600	433	433	—	167	—	—
Nov.	400	1,000	433	866	—	134	—	—
Dec.	300	1,300	433	1,299	—	1	—	—
Jan.	700	2,000	600	1,899	—	101	167	—
Feb.	600	2,600	600	2,499	—	101	—	—
Mar.	500	3,100	600	3,099	—	1	—	—
					0	505	167	0

7.   *Schedule 5(a)*

Shortage: 400 × $10 = $4,000

Variation: 300 × $3 = $\underline{900}$

Total cost $4,900

Schedule 6(a)

Excess: 355 × $1.25 = $ 443.75

Shortage: 98 × $10   = $\underline{980.00}$

Total cost $1,423.75

Schedule 6(b)

Variation: 900 × $3 = $\underline{\$2,700}$

Total cost $2,700

Schedule 6(c)

Shortage: 505 × $10 = $5,050

Variation: 167 × $3 = $\underline{501}$

Total cost $5,551

The best schedule is 6(a), but it is possible that another
mixed strategy could be used in 6(c) that would produce a
better strategy.

8. (a)

Month	Demand	Cum. Demand	Prod.	Cum. Prod.	Inventory Excess	Inventory Shortage	Variation Incr.	Variation Decr.
Oct.	600	600	600	600	0	—	—	—
Nov.	400	1,000	500	1,100	100	—	—	100
Dec.	300	1,300	400	1,500	200	—	—	100
Jan.	700	2,000	500	2,000	0	—	100	—
Feb.	600	2,600	600	2,600	0	—	100	—
Mar.	500	3,100	500	3,100	0	—	—	100
					300	0	200	300

(b) Excess: 300 × $1.25 = $ 375.00

Variation: 500 × $3.00 = $\underline{1,500.00}$

Total cost $1,875.00

9.

Schedule 1 *(minimize inventories and shortages)*

Month	Demand	Cum. Demand	Prod.	Cum. Prod.	Inventory Excess	Inventory Shortage	Variation Incr.	Variation Decr.
May	790	790	790	790	—	—	140	—
June	640	1,430	640	1,430	—	—	—	150
July	580	2,010	580	2,010	—	—	—	60
Aug.	430	2,440	430	2,440	—	—	—	150
Sept.	540	2,980	540	2,980	—	—	110	—
Oct.	620	3,600	620	3,600	—	—	80	—
Nov.	730	4,330	730	4,330	—	—	110	—
Dec.	860	5,190	860	5,190	—	—	130	—
Jan.	730	5,920	730	5,920	—	—	—	130
Feb.	630	6,550	630	6,550	—	—	—	100
Mar.	570	7,120	570	7,120	—	—	—	60
Apr.	680	7,800	680	7,800	—	—	110	—
					0	0	680	650

Increases: $680 \times \$2 = \$1,360$

Decreases: $650 \times \$4 = \underline{2,600}$

Total cost $\$3,960$

Schedule 2 *(minimize work force variation)*

Month	Demand	Cum. Demand	Prod.	Cum. Prod.	Inventory Excess	Inventory Shortage	Variation Incr.	Variation Decr.
May	790	790	650	650	—	140	—	—
June	640	1,430	650	1,300	—	130	—	—
July	580	2,010	650	1,950	—	60	—	—
Aug.	430	2,440	650	2,600	160	—	—	—
Sept.	540	2,980	650	3,250	270	—	—	—
Oct.	620	3,600	650	3,900	300	—	—	—
Nov.	730	4,330	650	4,550	220	—	—	—
Dec.	860	5,190	650	5,200	10	—	—	—
Jan.	730	5,920	650	5,850	—	70	—	—
Feb.	630	6,550	650	6,500	—	50	—	—
Mar.	570	7,120	650	7,150	30	—	—	—
Apr.	680	7,800	650	7,800	—	—	—	—
					990	450	0	0

Holding: $990 \times \$1 = \$ \ \ 990$

Shortage: $450 \times \$5 = \underline{2,250}$

Total cost $\$3,240$

The second strategy is better for this problem.

10. The following is one possible solution.

Month	Demand	Cum. Demand	Prod.	Cum. Prod.	Inventory		Variation	
					Excess	Shortage	Incr.	Decr.
May	790	790	790	790	—	—	140	—
June	640	1,430	640	1,430	—	—	—	150
July	580	2,010	580	2,010	—	—	—	60
Aug.	430	2,440	574	2,584	144	—	—	6
Sept.	540	2,980	573	3,157	177	—	—	1
Oct.	620	3,600	573	3,730	130	—	—	—
Nov.	730	4,330	730	4,460	130	—	157	—
Dec.	860	5,190	730	5,190	—	—	—	—
Jan.	730	5,920	730	5,920	—	—	—	—
Feb.	630	6,550	630	6,550	—	—	—	100
Mar.	570	7,120	625	7,175	55	—	—	5
Apr.	680	7,800	625	7,800	—	—	—	—
					636	0	297	322

$$\text{Total cost} = 636(1) + 297(2) + 322(4)$$
$$= 636 + 594 + 1,288$$
$$= 2,518$$

This schedule is better than the previous one.

11.

Month	Demand	Inventory		Prod.	Variation	
		Beg.	End.		Incr.	Decr.
May	790	—	158	948	298	—
June	640	158	138	620	—	328
July	580	138	116	558	—	62
Aug.	430	116	86	400	—	158
Sept.	540	86	108	562	162	—
Oct.	620	108	124	636	74	—
Nov.	730	124	146	752	116	—
Dec.	860	146	172	886	134	—
Jan.	730	172	146	704	—	182
Feb.	630	146	126	610	—	94
Mar.	570	126	114	558	—	52
Apr.	680	114	136	702	144	—
			1,570		928	876

Inventory: $1,570 \times \$1 = \$1,570$

Shortages: $0 \times \$5 = $ 0

Increases: $928 \times \$2 = $ $1,856$

Decreases: $876 \times \$4 = $ $3,504$

Total cost $\$6,930$

This policy is more costly than the policies developed in the previous two problems.

12.

Option	Jan.	Feb.	Mar.	Capacity
Jan. Reg.	$8.00	$9.25	$10.50	700
Jan. OT	$9.50	$10.75	$12.00	100
Feb. Reg.	X	$8.00	$9.25	700
Feb. OT	X	$9.50	$10.75	100
Mar. Reg.	X	X	$8.00	700
Mar. OT	X	X	$9.50	100
Demand	800	600	900	2,300 \ 2,400

(header spanning Jan./Feb./Mar.: **Month**)

13.

	Month				
Option	Jan.	Feb.	Mar.	Dummy	Capacity
Jan. Reg.	$8 / 700	$9.25	$10.50	$0	700
Jan. OT	$9.50 / 100	$10.75	$12	$0	100
Feb. Reg.	$3,000	$8 / 600	$9.25 / 100	$0	700
Feb. OT	$3,000	$9.50	$10.75	$0 / 100	100
Mar. Reg.	$3,000	$3,000	$8 / 700	$0	700
Mar. OT	$3,000	$3,000	$9.50 / 100	$0	100
Demand	800	600	900	100	

700($8) + 100($9.50) + 600($8) + 100($9.25) +
100($0) + 700($8) + 100($9.50) = $18,825

14. Let

JR = number of units in January regular time;
JT =   " January overtime;
FR =   " February regular time;
FT =   " February overtime;
MR =   " March regular time; and
MT =   " March overtime.

Minimize $Z = 8JR + 9.50JT + 8FR + 9.50FT + 8MR + 9.50MT + 1.25(JR + JT - 800) + 1.25[JR + JT + FR + FT - (800 + 600)] + 1.25[JR + JT + FR + FT - (800 + 600 + 900)]$

$Z = 11.75JR + 13.25JT + 10.50FR + 12.00FT + 9.25MR + 10.75MT$

Subject to $JR \leq 700$
$FR \leq 700$
$MR \leq 700$
$JT \leq 100$
$FT \leq 100$
$MT \leq 100$
$JR + JT \geq 800$
$JR + JT + FR + FT \geq 800 + 600$
$JR + JT + FR + FT + MR + MT \geq 800 + 600 + 900$
$JR, JT, FR, FT, MR, MT \geq 0$

Assuming that total demand = total supply, the objective function cost does not include the last term, and the last constraint is either excluded or written as an equality.

15. Note that we must first convert the demands to labor hours.

	Labor Hours Required		
Month	A	B	Total
Feb.	180	420	600
Mar.	255	360	615
Apr.	210	380	590
May	195	480	675
June	180	440	620
July	195	400	595
			3,695

16. Average demand = 3,695/6 = 616 hr./mo.

Month	Hours Required	Regular Hours	Inventory Hours	Overtime Hours
1	600	616	16	—
2	615	616	17	—
3	590	616	43	—
4	675	616	—	16
5	620	616	—	4
6	595	616	20	—
			96	20

Overtime cost: 20 × $10 = $200
Labor inventory: 96 × $1.50* = 144
                 Total cost $344

*The cost of labor inventory is $2.25/1.5 for item A and $3/2 for item B, both of which equal $1.50/labor hr.

17.

Month	Average Usage (tons)	Percent of Usage	Percentage Done
Dec.	50	.23	.23
Jan.	60	.28	.51
Feb.	75	.35	.86
Mar.	30	.14	1.00
	215		

We need to incorporate the data from the current season. Since only 85 tons of salt have been used by the end of the second month, the revised estimate for salt usage is

$$F_{salt} = \frac{85}{.51} = 167.$$

The revised salt requirement is 167 tons for the season.

Computer Case Study 12.1

The data file is given in file CASE12-1. Toggling the pure strategies and trying them yields the following costs.

Plan 1 (smooth production): $849,077

Plan 2 (meet demand exactly): $104,575

Plan 3 (produce 1,900 as base, then use OT and subcontracting): $82,858

At this point, the question is, can we do better with trial and error? A better solution follows.

```
Data file:a:case-ans        Aggregate Planning                Solution
Number of time periods (1-99) 52


                    Computer Case 12-1:Cornwell Glass
METHOD->  User defined
SHORTAGES:Backorders - Carry shortages from period to period
All pds-->   1900      0       0   $0.00   $8.00   $10.0   $0.12   $20.0   $5.63   $15.7
                SCHEDULE                            U N I T S
  Pd  Demnd Regtm Ovrtm Subcn Regtim Ovrtim Subcon Holdng Shortg Incres Decres
Init    73  1900     0     0
A15   1829  1900   250     0   1900    250      0    394      0      0      0
 22   1820  1900   250     0   1900    250      0    724      0      0      0
 29   1887  1900   250     0   1900    250      0    987      0      0      0
M 6   1958  1900   250     0   1900    250      0   1179      0      0      0
 13   2011  1900   250     0   1900    250      0   1318      0      0      0
 20   2063  1900   250     0   1900    250      0   1405      0      0      0
 27   2104  1900   250     0   1900    250      0   1451      0      0      0
J 3   2161  1900   250     0   1900    250      0   1440      0      0      0
 10   2258  1900   250     0   1900    250      0   1332      0      0      0
 17   2307  1900   250     0   1900    250      0   1175      0      0      0
 24   2389  1900   250     0   1900    250      0    936      0      0      0
J 1   2434  1900   250     0   1900    250      0    652      0      0      0
  8   2402  1900   250     0   1900    250      0    400      0      0      0
 15   2385  1900   250     0   1900    250      0    165      0      0      0
 22   2330  1990   250    15   1900    250     15      0      0      0      0
 29   2323  1990   250   173   1900    250    173      0      0      0      0
A 5   2317  1900   250   167   1900    250    167      0      0      0      0
 12   2222  1900   250    72   1900    250     72      0      0      0      0
 19   2134  1900   234     0   1900    234      0      0      0      0      0
 26   2065  1900   165     0   1900    165      0      0      0      0      0
S 2   1973  1900    73     0   1900     73      0      0      0      0      0
  9   1912  1900    12     0   1900     12      0      0      0      0      0
 16   1854  1900     0     0   1900      0      0     46      0      0      0
 23   1763  1900     0     0   1900      0      0    183      0      0      0
 30   1699  1900     0     0   1900      0      0    384      0      0      0
0 7   1620  1900     0     0   1900      0      0    664      0      0      0
 14   1689  1900     0     0   1900      0      0    875      0      0      0
 21   1754  1900     0     0   1900      0      0   1021      0      0      0
 28   1800  1900   207     0   1900    207      0   1328      0      0      0
N 4   1864  1900   250     0   1900    250      0   1614      0      0      0
 11   1989  1900   250     0   1900    250      0   1775      0      0      0
 18   2098  1900   250     0   1900    250      0   1827      0      0      0
 25   2244  1900   250     0   1900    250      0   1733      0      0      0
D 2   2357  1900   250     0   1900    250      0   1526      0      0      0
  9   2368  1900   250     0   1900    250      0   1308      0      0      0
```

16	2387	1900	250	0	1900	250	0	1071	0	0	0
23	2402	1900	250	0	1900	250	0	819	0	0	0
30	2418	1900	250	0	1900	250	0	551	0	0	0
J 6	2417	1900	250	0	1900	250	0	284	0	0	0
13	2324	1900	250	0	1900	250	0	110	0	0	0
20	2204	1900	250	0	1900	250	0	56	0	0	0
27	2188	1900	250	0	1900	250	0	18	0	0	0
F 3	2168	1900	250	0	1900	250	0	0	0	0	0
10	2086	1900	186	0	1900	186	0	0	0	0	0
17	1954	1900	54	0	1900	54	0	0	0	0	0
24	1877	1900	0	0	1900	0	0	23	0	0	0
M 3	1822	1900	0	0	1900	0	0	101	0	0	0
10	1803	1900	0	0	1900	0	0	198	0	0	0
17	1777	1900	0	0	1900	0	0	321	0	0	0
24	1799	1900	0	0	1900	0	0	422	0	0	0
31	1803	1900	0	0	1900	0	0	519	0	0	0
A 7	1805	1900	0	0	1900	0	0	614	0	0	0
TOTL	107544	98800	8931	427	98800	8931	427	32949	0	0	0

```
                SUBTOTAL COSTS->      0 71448  4270 3953.9    0    0    0
                TOTAL COST = 79671.88
```

13
Inventory Management

TEACHING NOTES

As we have done with previous topics, we would like to point out how our treatment of inventory management differs from that found in other texts. First, because of the trend toward fixed order-quantity systems, we omit the topic of fixed order-interval systems. (The way most texts present this topic—for the deterministic case—makes it redundant anyway.) Second, we include the EOQ model with shortages, with an acknowledgment that it is common practice to select a service level instead of using this model. We present the two approaches together in the same chapter to emphasize the close link between service level and shortage cost. Operations managers need to be aware that specifying either one identifies the other implicitly. Finally, our more complete discussion of the implementation of inventory systems also distinguishes this text from most others.

The first section of this chapter is especially important in that it lays out the types of inventory systems that later sections attempt to implement. (The topic of ABC systems is somewhat less important than the other topics in the introductory section.)

We begin our treatment of continuous review by presenting the basic EOQ model. We then go on to look at sensitivity in this model, as well as the model's use with price discounts. Extensions of the EOQ model—the EPQ model and models with shortages—take up the balance of this section. Point out that sensitivity and quantity discounts are concepts that are also applicable to these extensions of the basic EOQ model.

You will not find a section in this chapter labeled "Probabilistic Demand." This is because we treat this topic within the context of its primary operational concern—reorder points. After calculating reorder points for the deterministic case, we look at safety stocks (service levels are the basis here, as they are in practice) and optimal service levels. Only the case of probabilistic demand is considered; that is, we omit a discussion of probabilistic lead times. The single-period model is also addressed as a probabilistic (demand) case.

Three Solved Problems provide a good opportunity for students to review the techniques presented earlier in the chapter. As in the other chapters, the Questions are designed to test general knowledge as well as to provoke class discussion. However, the exercises in this chapter are less discussion oriented, more implementation oriented. The Problems follow the chapter outline, with several exercises of varying degrees of difficulty for each topic. With twenty-five exercises to choose from, there is plenty of variety.

The software for this chapter solves the four basic continuous review models and solves the EOQ with quantity discounts. Problems 3 through 15 can be solved using the software.

The computer case study for this chapter is a sensitivity analysis that demonstrates how a reduction in setups can save money.

TEACHING SUGGESTIONS

Teaching Suggestion 13.1:   The Operations Chain.
We like to constantly remind our students that it takes a chain of operations to provide the goods or service. Inventory (and quality) at one level depends on inventories (and qualities) at other levels.

Teaching Suggestion 13.2:   Determining Holding Costs.
Operations managers do not determine holding costs. This is a function of accounting/finance.

Teaching Suggestion 13.3:   Continuous vs. Periodic.
We ask our students what kind of "inventory system" they use for certain items. For example, most of our students buy gasoline when the tank gets low—a continuous system. Most of them shop for groceries on the same day each week—a periodic system. You can also ask what system students use to maintain their inventories of cash.

Teaching Suggestion 13.4:   Pareto Distribution.
ABC analysis is just one example of Pareto analysis. Other examples: critical jobs in a project and occurrence of quality problems.

Teaching Suggestion 13.5:   Unit Costs.
While our equation for total cost includes PD here, elsewhere it may not, depending on the situation. The equation *must* include PD for quantity discounts, however.

Teaching Suggestion 13.6:   Discount Structure.
Remind students that there are two types of discounts—all units and incremental. This chapter discounts all units. You might point out that, in our example, this leads to a situation where 40 units cost less than 39. The IRS tax structure is incremental; of course, tax increments may be up or down. Examples 3.9 and 3.10 also show the two types of discounts.

Teaching Suggestion 13.7:   Utilization.
Point out that the percentage of time that production is taking place is d/p. Knowing the percentage allows us to identify the utilization but not the run length, T_p. If the utilization is $2/3$, is T_p 4 days of 6 or 2 weeks of 3? T_p provides the answer.

Teaching Suggestion 13.8:   Use of These Models.
We do not advocate using these models in practice. We use them in class to motivate the discussion of service levels. See Example 13.15.

Teaching Suggestion 13.9:   Ease of Execution.
The difficult task is determining Q and R. Executing the policy after that is easy because the policy is so specific—order exactly Q units each time inventory levels are reduced to R units.

Teaching Suggestion 13.10:   Definition of Service Level.
There are alternative measures of service level—most notably, the percentage of items supplied on time. Using the same policy, the service level would be much higher when this alternate definition is used.

Teaching Suggestion 13.11:   Decision Tables.
This decision table is identical in form to those in Chapter 3. In inventory, only expected value is used, not the other rules (maximin, maximax).

ANSWERS TO QUESTIONS

1. a stock of goods that is maintained by a business in anticipation of some future demand.

2. raw materials; in-process goods; finished goods; and supplies and miscellaneous

3. holding cost: capital invested and space required; shortage cost: the cost of lost sales or customers who never return; the cost of lost good will; order cost: the fixed cost associated with ordering, transporting, and receiving the items; unit cost: the actual cost of the item

4. In a continuous review system, the inventory level is monitored at all times, and an order is placed for a fixed quantity when the inventory level reaches the reorder point. In a periodic review system, the inventory level is monitored at regular intervals, and the size of the order depends on the inventory level.

5. The purpose of the ABC system is to identify those items that require more attention due to cost or volume.

6. The EOQ increases as demand increases or as the setup cost increases; it decreases as the holding cost increases. The changes in the EOQ are proportional to the square root of the changes in the parameters.

7. Discount points below the EOQ have higher inventory costs, and the prices are no lower than at the EOQ. Points above the EOQ have higher inventory costs than the corresponding price break point or EOQ at prices that are no lower than either of the price beaks or the EOQ. (It depends on whether or not there exists a discount point above the EOQ.)

8. If the same costs hold, more can be ordered using an EPQ, because the average inventory is less than the corresponding EOQ system.

9. $P(s) = 1 - SL$.
It is difficult to identify a shortage cost, G. But the specification of the service level carries with it an implied shortage cost.

10. A safety stock is an extra stock that is carried to account for the random variation of demands. Its size varies directly with the service level.

11. A few of the many possible examples are newspapers, clothing, perishable foods, and farm products.

12. Most department stores have a computerized cash register system. At the time of purchase, the computer system simultaneously rings up the bill and reduces the inventory level in its records for the products sold.

SOLUTIONS TO PROBLEMS

1.

Class	Item	Usage
A	12	166
	2	154
B	1	123
	14	118
	5	114
	10	72
	6	63
	4	54
C	9	35
	8	32
	7	29
	3	19
	11	4
	13	2

Alternatively, we could group the items as follows.

A: 12, 2

B: 1, 14, 5

C: 10, 6, 4, 9, 8, 7, 3, 11, 13

The items do not break down nicely into the recommended A-B-C split (15-35-50 percent). Using this split yields the following.

A: 12, 2

B: 1, 14, 5, 10, 6

C: 4, 9, 8, 7, 3, 11, 13

It seems preferable to group item 4 (54 used) with item 6 (63 used) rather than with item 9 (only 35 used).

2. We first classify according to volume usage.

Class	Item	Usage
A	5	2,754
	2	1,496
	3	1,223
	14	1,199
B	6	1,112
	15	1,084
	4	1,008
	10	987
	18	941
	19	827
C	1	561
	7	558
	12	523
	8	490
	11	269
	13	248
	16	44
	9	41
	17	9

Next we compute the dollar volume.

(1) Item	(2) Demand	(3) Price (in $)	(4) Dollar Volume [(2) × (3)]
1	561	8.50	$ 4,768.50
2	1,496	1.67	2,498.32
3	1,223	6.58	8,047.34
4	1,008	7.68	7,741.44
5	2,754	9.36	25,777.44
6	1,112	9.94	11,053.28
7	558	6.51	3,632.58
8	490	7.03	3,444.70
9	41	5.81	238.21
10	987	4.46	4,402.02
11	269	.22	59.18
12	523	8.50	4,445.50
13	243	.11	26.73
14	1,199	9.79	11,738.21
15	1,084	6.32	6,850.88
16	44	5.28	232.32
17	9	5.37	48.33
18	941	1.14	1,072.74
19	827	6.23	5,152.21

Finally, we sort by dollar volume. See the table on page IS-90.

3. (a) $Q^* = \sqrt{2DS/H} = \sqrt{(2 \times 2{,}440 \times 35)/2}$
$= 292$ bottles

(b) $n = D/Q = 2{,}440/292 = 8.4$ times per year, or about every 43 days (of a 365-day year)

(c) $TC = HQ/2 + SD/Q$

$= (2 \times 292)/2 + (35 \times 2{,}440)/292$

$= \$292 + \$292 = \$584$, ignoring the price of the cider (not given)

4. (a) $Q^* = \sqrt{2DS/H}$

$= \sqrt{[2 \times 400 \times (12 \times 50)]/5} = 310$ seats

(b) $n = D/Q = (400 \times 12)/310 = 15.5$ times per year

(c) $TC = HQ/2 + SD/Q$

$= (\$5 \times 310)/2 + (\$50 \times 4{,}800)/310$

$= \$775 + \$774 = \$1{,}549$, ignoring price per seat (difference due to rounding)

5. (a) $D = 25/mo.$

$H = \$.50/unit-mo.$

$S = \$25/order$

$L = 10$ days $= 10/25 = .40$ mo.

$Q^* = \sqrt{2DS/H}$

$= \sqrt{(2 \times 25 \times 25)/.50}$

$= 50$ corkscrews

(b) $T^* = Q/D = 50/25 = 2$ mo.

(c) $R = LD = .4$ mo. $\times 25/mo. = 10$ corkscrews

(The store should order 50 corkscrews whenever the supply is down to 10.)

6. $D = 40$ cigarettes/day

$H = \$.01/cigarette-day$

$S = \$5/game$

$Q^* = \sqrt{2DS/H}$

$= \sqrt{(2 \times 40 \times 5)/.01}$

$= 200$ cigarettes

7. (a) *JC Peanut:*

$D = 90{,}000$ peanuts/wk. $= 900$ jars/wk.

$H = \$.01/jar-wk.$

$S = \$32/order$

$P = \$.00333/peanut = \$.333/jar$

$Q^* = \sqrt{2DS/H}$

$= \sqrt{(2 \times 900 \times 32)/.01}$

$= 2{,}400$ jars/order

$TC = PD + HQ/2 + SD/Q$

$= (\$.333 \times 900 + \$.01 \times 2{,}400)/2 +$
$(\$32 \times 900)/2{,}400$

$= \$300 + \$12 + \$12 = \$324$ per wk.

Table for Problem 2.

Class	Item	Demand	Price	Dollar Volume	Percentage of Total Dollar Volume	Cumulative Percentage
A	5	2,754	$9.36	$25,777.44	25.4	25.4
	14	1,199	9.79	11,738.21	11.6	37.0
	6	1,112	9.94	11,053.28	11.0	48.0
B	3	1,223	6.58	8,047.34	7.9	55.9
	4	1,008	7.68	7,741.44	7.6	63.5
	15	1,084	6.32	6,850.88	6.8	70.3
	19	827	6.23	5,152.21	5.1	75.4
	1	561	8.50	4,768.50	4.7	80.1
C	12	523	8.50	4,445.50	4.4	84.5
	10	987	4.46	4,402.02	4.3	88.7
	7	558	6.51	3,632.58	3.6	92.3
	8	490	7.03	3,444.70	3.4	95.7
	2	1,496	1.67	2,498.32	2.5	98.2
	18	941	1.14	1,072.74	1.1	99.3
	9	41	5.81	238.21	.2	99.5
	16	44	5.28	232.32	.2	99.7
	11	269	.22	5.92	<.1	99.7
	17	9	5.37	48.33	<.1	99.7
	13	243	.11	26.73	<.1	99.8

Brother Bill:

$D = 900$ jars/wk.

$H = \$.01/$jar-wk.

$S = \$8.00/$order

$P = \$.50/$jar

$Q^\star = \sqrt{2DS/H}$

$\quad = \sqrt{(2 \times 900 \times 8)/.01}$

$\quad = 1,200$ jars/order

$TC = PD + HQ/2 + SD/Q$

$\quad = (\$.50 \times 900) + (\$.01 \times 1,200)/2 +$
$\quad\quad (\$8 \times 900)/1,200$

$\quad = \$450 + \$6 + \$6 = \$462$ per wk.

Therefore, Panzer should buy from JC Peanut at $324 per week.

(b) $T = Q/D = 2,400/900 = 2.67$ wk.

Panzer will purchase peanuts every 2-2/3 wk.

(c) The cost per jar is $324 per wk./900 jars per wk. = $.36 per jar. This is the inventory cost spread over the units.

(d) Based on an order of 2,400 jars, the maximum inventory is $2,400 \times 100$, or 240,000, peanuts. The new policy should be to order 1,800 jars, still from JC Peanut.

8. (a) $D = 12,000/$yr.

$H = \$.10/$light-yr.

$S = \$50/$setup

$P = \$1.00/$light

$p = 100/$day

$d = \dfrac{12,000/\text{yr.}}{300 \text{ days/yr.}} = 40/$day

$Q^\star = \sqrt{2DS/H} \times \sqrt{p/(p-d)}$

$\quad = \sqrt{(2 \times 12,000 \times 50)/.10}$
$\quad\quad \times \sqrt{100/(100-40)}$

$\quad = 4,472$ lights per run

(b) $\dfrac{HQ}{2} \times \dfrac{p-d}{p} = \dfrac{\$.10 \times 4,472}{2} \times \dfrac{100-40}{100}$

$\quad = \dfrac{\$447.20 \times 60}{2 \times 100}$

$\quad = \dfrac{\$26,832}{200}$

$\quad = \$134.16$

(c) $SD/Q = (50 \times 12,000)/4,472 = \$134.16$

(d) $TC = PD + \$134.16 + \$134.16$

$\quad = (\$1 \times 12,000) + \$134.16 + \$134.16$

$\quad = \$12,268.32$ per yr.

(e) $n = D/Q = 12,000/4,472 = 2.68$ runs per yr.

(f) $T = 1/n = Q/D = 1/2.68 = .373$ yr.

$.373$ yr. $(300$ days/yr.$) = 112$ days

(g) $\$12,268.32/12,000$ nose lights $= \$1.0224$ per nose light

(h) $T_p = Q/P = 4,472/100 = 44.72$ days in production *per cycle*

Since each cycle is 112 days, Rudolf produces nose lights $44.72/112 = .40$, or 40%, of the year.

9. buy cans:

$D = 50,000/$wk.

$H = .03/$can-wk.

$S = \$7.50/$order

$P = \$.15/$can

$Q^\star = \sqrt{2DS/H}$

$\quad = \sqrt{(2 \times 50,000 \times 7.50)/.03}$

$\quad = 5,000$ cans

$TC \text{ (buy cans)} = PD + HQ/2 + SD/Q$

$\quad = \$.15 \times 50,000 + \dfrac{\$.03 \times 5,000}{2}$

$\quad\quad + \dfrac{\$7.50 \times 50,000}{5,000}$

$\quad = \$7,500 + \$75 + \$75$

$\quad = \$7,650/$wk.

produce cans:

$D = 50,000/$wk. (also, $d = 50,000/$wk.)

$H = .03/$can-wk.

$S = \$30/$setup

$P = \$.10/$can

$p = 56,250$ cans/wk.

$Q^\star = \sqrt{2DS/H} \times \sqrt{p/(p-d)}$

$\quad = \sqrt{(2 \times 50,000 \times 30)/.03} \times$
$\quad\quad \sqrt{56,250/(56,250 - 50,000)}$

$\quad = 30,000$ cans

$TC(\text{produce cans})$

$\quad = PD + \left(\dfrac{HQ}{2} \times \dfrac{p-d}{p}\right) + \dfrac{SD}{Q}$

$\quad = \$.10 \times 50,000 +$

$\quad\quad \left(\dfrac{\$.03 \times 30,000}{2} \times \dfrac{1}{9}\right) + \dfrac{\$30 \times 50,000}{30,000}$

$\quad = \$5,000 + \$50 + \$50 = \$5,100/$wk.

Tasty-Host should produce the cans.

10. **(a)** $D = 8,000/\text{yr.}$

$H = \$2/\text{seat/yr.}$

$S = \$50/\text{order}$

$Q^* = \sqrt{2DS/H} = \sqrt{(2 \times 8,000 \times 50)/2}$

$\quad = 632.5$

(b) $HQ/2 = (2 \times 632.5)/2 = \$632.50$ per yr.

(c) $SD/Q = (50 \times 8,000)/632.5 = \$632.50$ per yr.

(d) $Q^* = \sqrt{2DS/H} \times \sqrt{p/(p-d)}$

$\quad = 632.5 \times \sqrt{12,000/(12,000 - 8,000)}$

$\quad = 1,095$

(e) $SD/Q = (50 \times 8,000)/1,095 = \$365.30$ per year

(f) The inventory cost for buying is much higher ($\$1,265$ vs. $\$731$). Note that this ignores the purchase price and the production cost.

11. $D = 20,000/\text{yr.}$

$H = 20$ percent of purchase price per year

$S = \$40/\text{order}$

$P = \$20/\text{tire if fewer than 500 are ordered;}$

$\$18/\text{tire if between 500 and 1,000 are ordered; and}$

$\$17/\text{tire if 1,000 or more are ordered}$

$Q^*_{20} = \sqrt{2DS/H}$

$\quad = \sqrt{(2 \times 20,000 \times 40)/(.2 \times 20)}$

$\quad = 632.5$ (not valid)

$Q^*_{18} = \sqrt{2DS/H}$

$\quad = \sqrt{(2 \times 20,000 \times 40)/(.2 \times 18)}$

$\quad = 666.7$ (valid)

$Q^*_{17} = \sqrt{2DS/H}$

$\quad = \sqrt{(2 \times 20,000 \times 40)/(.2 \times 17)}$

$\quad = 686$ (not valid)

We compare the cost of ordering 667 with the cost of ordering 1,000.

$TC_{667} = PD + HQ/2 + SD/Q$

$\quad = \$18 \times 20,000 + (.2 \times \$18 \times 667)/2 +$
$\quad\quad (\$40 \times 20,000)/667$

$\quad = \$360,000 + \$1,200 + \$1,200$

$\quad = \$362,400$ per year

$TC_{1,000} = PD + HQ/2 + SD/Q$

$\quad = \$17 \times 20,000 + (.2 \times \$17 \times 1,000)/2$
$\quad\quad + (\$40 \times 20,000)/1,000$

$\quad = \$340,000 + \$1,700 + \$800$

$\quad = \$342,500$ per year

Rocky Mountain should order 1,000 tires each time.

12. $D = 5,000 \text{ gross/yr.}$

$H = \$1/\text{gross-yr.}$

$S = \$11/\text{order}$

$P = \$8/\text{gross for less than 500 gross and}$
$\quad \$7.50/\text{gross for 500 gross or more}$

$Q^* = \sqrt{2DS/H}$

$\quad = \sqrt{(2 \times 5,000 \times 11)/1}$

$\quad = 331.7$

Now we need to compare the cost of ordering 332 with the cost of ordering 500.

$TC_{332} = PD + HQ/2 + SD/Q$

$\quad = \$8 \times 5,000 + (\$1 \times 332)/2 +$
$\quad\quad (\$11 \times 5,000)/332$

$\quad = \$40,000 + \$166 + \$166$

$\quad = \$40,332$ per yr.

$TC_{500} = PD + HQ/2 + SD/Q$

$\quad = \$7.50 \times 5,000 + (\$1 \times 500)/2 +$
$\quad\quad (\$11 \times 5,000)/500$

$\quad = \$37,500 + \$250 + \$110$

$\quad = \$37,860$ per yr.

Order quantity should be 500 gross.

13. $D = \$25/\text{mo.}$

$H = \$.50/\text{unit-mo.}$

$S = \$25/\text{order}$

$L = 10 \text{ days} = 10/25 \text{ or } .40 \text{ mo.}$

$G = \$5/\text{unit}$

$Q^* = \sqrt{2DS/H} \times \sqrt{(H + G)/G}$

$\quad = 50\sqrt{(.5 + 5)/5}$

$\quad = 52.44$

Slightly more corkscrews (52.44 vs. 50) are ordered. Maximum backorder, B, is $HQ/(H + G) = [(.5)(52.44)]/5.5 = 4.77$ Reorder point is still 10, but this is 10 above -4.77, or 5.23.

14. **(a)** *JC Peanut:*

$D = 900 \text{ jars/wk.}$

$H = \$.01/\text{jar-wk.}$

$S = \$32/\text{order}$

$p = \$.333/\text{jar}$

$G = \$.01/\text{jar}$

$Q^* = \sqrt{2DS/H} \times \sqrt{(H + G)/G}$

$\quad = 2,400 \sqrt{(.01 + .01)/.01}$

$\quad = 3,394 \text{ jars}$

$$B = Q[G/(H + G)]$$
$$= 3,394[.01/(.01 + .01)]$$
$$= 1,697$$

$$TC = PD + H(Q - B)^2/2Q + SD/Q + GB^2/2Q$$
$$= \$.333 \times 900 +$$
$$[\$.01 \times (3,394 - 1,697)^2/(2 \times 3,394)]$$
$$+ (\$32 \times 900)/3,394 +$$
$$\$.01 \times (1,697)^2/(2 \times 3,394)$$
$$= \$300 + \$4.24 + \$8.48 + \$4.24$$
$$= \$316.96 \text{ per wk.}$$

Brother Bill:

$$D = 900 \text{ jars/wk.}$$
$$H = \$.01 \text{ jar-wk.}$$
$$S = \$8/\text{order}$$
$$P = \$.50/\text{jar}$$
$$G = \$.01$$
$$Q^* = \sqrt{2DS/H} \times \sqrt{(H + G)/G}$$
$$= 1,200 \sqrt{(.01 + .01)/.01}$$
$$= 1,697$$

$$B = QG/(H + G)$$
$$= (1,697 \times .01)/(.01 + .01)$$
$$= 848.5$$

$$TC = PD + H(Q - B)^2/2Q + SD/Q + GB^2/2Q$$
$$= \$.05 \times 900 +$$
$$[\$.01 \times (1,697 - 848.5)^2]/(2 \times 1,697)$$
$$+ (\$8 \times 900)]/1,697 +$$
$$[\$.01 \times (848.5)^2]/(2 \times 1,697)$$
$$= \$450 + \$2.12 + \$4.24 + \$2.12$$
$$= \$458.48/\text{yr.}$$

The same supplier (JC Peanut) is chosen.

(b) More is ordered (less often) and average inventories are lower due to the shortages.

(c) The maximum size of the shortage, *B*, is 1,697 jars.

(d) Panzer's is short exactly half of the time:

$$H/(G + H) = 1/2.$$

15. (a) $D = 12,000/\text{yr.}$
$$H = \$.10/\text{light-yr.}$$
$$S = \$50/\text{setup}$$
$$P = \$1.00/\text{light}$$
$$p = 100/\text{day}$$
$$d = 40/\text{day}$$
$$G = \$.05/\text{light}$$

$$Q^* = \sqrt{2DS/H} \times \sqrt{p/(p - d)} \times \sqrt{(H + G)/G}$$
$$= 4,472\sqrt{(.10 + .05)/.05}$$
$$= 7,746 \text{ lights}$$

(b) $I_{max} = Q\left(\dfrac{p - d}{p}\right) - B$

$$= 7,746\left(\dfrac{100 - 40}{100}\right) - 3,098$$
$$= 1,550 \text{ lights}$$

(c) $B = \dfrac{HQ[(p - d)/p]}{H + G}$

$$= \dfrac{(.1 \times 7,746) \times [(100 - 400)/100]}{.1 + .05}$$
$$= 3,098 \text{ lights}$$

(d) 7,746 lights per run/100 lights per day = 77.46 days per run

(e) $H/(G + H) = .10/(.05 + .10) = .67$
Rudolf is short 67 percent of the time.

16.

Demand	Probability	Cumulative Probability (Service Level)
7	.03	.03
8	.07	.10
9	.10	.20
10	.70	.90
11	.06	.96
12	.04	1.00

We need to use a reorder point of 11 to meet the 95-percent service level (actually achieves 96 percent). Order point of 10 only provides 90-percent confidence.

For safety stock, we use $SS = R - \overline{m}$.

$$\overline{m} = (.03)(7) + (.07)(8) + (.10)(9) + (.70)(10) +$$
$$(.06)(11) + (.04)(12) = 9.81$$

$$SS = 11 - 9.81 = 1.19$$

(b) For a confidence level of 85 percent, use a reorder point of 10.

17. $D = 25/\text{mo.}$
$$H = \$50/\text{unit-mo.}$$
$$G = \$500/\text{unit}$$
$$Q = 50$$

The optimal probability of a shortage, $P(s)$, is

$$P(s) = HQ/GD = (50 \times 50)/(500 \times 25) = .2$$

The optimal service level, then, is

$$1 - P(s) = 1 - .2 = .8, \text{ or } 80\%.$$

For an 80-percent service level, $R = 10$ (actually achieves 90 percent).

$$SS = R - \overline{m} = 10 - 9.81 = .19$$

For a shortage cost of $200, $P(s) = HQ/GD = (50 \times 50)/(200 \times 25) = .5$, so $SL = .5$. The reorder point is still 10. The safety stock is $R - \overline{m} = 10 - 9.81 = .19$. In other words, there is no effect.

18. (a) $P(s) = .05$ for a service level of 95 percent. If $P(s) = HQ/GD$, then

$$G = \frac{HQ}{[P(s)]D}$$

$$= \frac{.5 \times 50}{.05 \times 25}$$

$$= \$20/\text{unit}.$$

(b) For the 85-percent service level, $P(s) = .15$ and

$$G = (.5 \times 50)/(.15 \times 25) = \$6.67/\text{unit}.$$

As the service level increases, the implied shortage cost increases.

19. (a) $R = \overline{m} + SS$

$SS = z_\alpha\sigma$ (one-tailed)

$R = 10 + 1.64(.8) = 11.31$

$SS = 1.31$

(b) $z_{.85} = 1.04$ (one-tailed)

$R = 10 + 1.04(.8)$

$R = 10.83$

$SS = .83$

20. (a) $G = \dfrac{HQ}{[P(s)]D} = \dfrac{.5 \times 50}{.05 \times 25} = \$20/\text{unit}$

The result is the same as that for Problem 18.

(b) (Note that the formula for G does not contain a probability distribution.)

21. optimal service level $= 1 - P(s) = 1 - (HQ/GD)$

$$= 1 - (50 \times 50)/(500 \times 25)$$

$$= .80$$

$R = \overline{m} + z_{.80}\sigma$

$= 10 + (.84 \times .8)$

$= 10.672$

$SS = .672$

The optimal service level is the same, but it results in different operating parameters. The service level is the same because it is independent of the distribution assumed.

22. MP = cost of being short (profit)

$$= 1.20 - 1.00 = .20$$

ML = cost of having excess $= 1.00 - .60 = .40$

$$P \geq \frac{ML}{ML + MP} = \frac{.40}{.4 + .2} = .67$$

Sales (in dozens)	Probability	Probability of Selling
26	.1	1.00
27	.2	.90
28	.4	.70
29	.2	.30
30	.1	.10

Because there is a 70-percent chance of selling the 28th dozen (which is better than the required 67 percent), 28 dozen should be made. (*Note:* This problem is Problem 30 in Chapter 3.)

23. From Problem 22, the optimal probability is still .67. For a 67-percent chance of selling a given amount of doughnuts or more, the cumulative normal table should show a probability of $1 - .67 = .33$. The z-value for .33 is $-.44$. Huachuca should make $\mu + z_\alpha\sigma = 28 - (.44 \times .75) = 27.67$, or 28 dozen. (Since this problem uses a continuous probability distribution to describe an integer number of doughnuts, we feel that 27 is also an acceptable answer.)

24. $MP = 1,500 - 800 = 700$

$ML = 800$

$P \geq 800/(700 + 800) = .5333$

Failures	Probability	Probability of Needing
0	.1	1.00
1	.3	.90
2	.3	.60
3	.2	.30
4	.1	.10

Two compressor spares should be ordered now with the furnace. (*Note:* This problem is Problem 31 in Chapter 3.)

25. From Problem 24, the optimal probability is again .5333. We need a z of .4667, which is $-.085$. Carbon Steel should order $\mu + z_\alpha\sigma = 2 - (.085 \times .7) = 1.94$, or 2, spares. (Again, note that we have used a continuous distribution to describe an integer number of failures.)

Computer Case Study 13.1

This is a very straightforward case study. The production model needs to be used four times in order to get the new costs for the revised system with a setup cost of $52 instead of $70. The costs are as follows:

Color	Inventory Costs
White	$8,615.80
Yellow	$7,923.08

Green	$7,530.60
Blue	$6,649.96
Total	$30,719.44

This represents a net savings of $35,641.87 − $30,719.44 = $4,922. Since the employee costs 20 percent of $12,840, or $2,568, per year for setting up, the change is indeed economical.

14
Materials Requirements Planning and Just-in-Time

TEACHING NOTES

This chapter takes a standard approach to MRP and JIT. We suggest that you emphasize the link between materials management and production scheduling provided by MRP. Also, it is important to stress the differentiating characteristics of the environment that are most conducive to the use of MRP, such as dependent and nonconstant demands. While we have talked about the just-in-time philosophy throughout the text, we treat it most fully here because MRP is the most visible application of JIT (a fact that should be stressed).

The greatest portion of this chapter is given over to a discussion of the basic MRP approach. We carry one example through the development of the various types of bills of materials and the MRP scheduling tables. While the step-by-step approach is easy to follow, the example we use is not trivial. With thirty-eight entries and five levels in the parts explosion, students will have to pay attention to the details. (They will also appreciate the need for MRP software.)

The lot sizing discussion is somewhat unusual in that it includes an EOQ in addition to the lot-for-lot and the part period approach. Purists may argue that this is inappropriate, but it is reasonable to use an EOQ as a heuristic if demands are not too erratic. Our approach also links this chapter and the foregoing chapter.

The section on extensions of MRP does not go into great detail. Instead of showing students how to use these approaches, we provide an overview. The section is aimed primarily at keeping up with current trends. DRP and examples of its application are presented here.

The chapter concludes with a discussion of implementation concerns. These recommendations hold true for any new technology—especially computer based—but we emphasize them for MRP because of the high failure rates experienced by companies who try to adopt this approach.

The Solved Problems follow the MRP sequence from bill of materials to scheduling purchase orders. The Questions are designed to be more thought provoking than those in most of the other chapters. Some exercises link material from this chapter to material covered in previous chapters in ways that may not be obvious. The Problems follow the chapter sequence closely and do not attempt to extend the chapter material. They are fairly straightforward.

The software for this chapter consists of two modules—one is an MRP system and the other performs lot sizing. Problems 5 and 6 and 9 through 12 can use the MRP module, while Problems 13 and 17 can use the lot sizing module.

TEACHING SUGGESTIONS

Teaching Suggestion 14.1:   JIT Analogy.
A standard classroom analogy is that of guiding a boat across a lake that has rocks (problems) on the bottom. The just-in-case approach is to increase the water (inventory) level. The just-in-time approach *lowers* the water level, exposing the rocks (problems) so that they may be removed.

Teaching Suggestion 14.2:   Apparent Contradiction.
In the context of EOQ, JIT would say that $Q = 1$. However, EOQ usually provides a larger Q. In order to reduce Q, JIT suggests reducing setup (fixed) costs to drive Q to 1. See Table 13.4.

Teaching Suggestion 14.3:   Low-Level Coding.
Low-level coding is useful for tracking part numbers. With low-level coding each part appears on one level only—although in reality each part may be at several levels depending on *when* it is needed.

Teaching Suggestion 14.4:   Planned Orders.
As we have seen previously (in Chapters 4 and 11), the orders listed are merely plans. The plan for the first week will be implemented, but it is subject to change after that.

Teaching Suggestion 14.5:   Last Order in EOQ.
Because this is only a plan, we force the last order to complete the forecasted demand (660 rather than 1,200). If you do not do this, the cost analysis is misleading. Obviously, an order for 660 will never be placed.

Teaching Suggestion 14.6:   Push System.
Safety stock is typically pushed to the end user in a distribution network. Consequently, DRP can be used in a push mode. Ask your students what it would mean to push the product through our example.

ANSWERS TO QUESTIONS

1. In MRP, demand is not necessarily constant. Also, in the MRP system, which is used primarily for production, the demand for one item depends on the demand for others—in particular, the end item.

2. MRP is preferable for complex manufacturing. For stocking independent demand items, EOQ, or lot sizes, is preferable.

3. MRP is part of the overall production planning process. Its most important capability is including the timing factor in inventory planning.

4. Time phasing is the means by which the just-in-time philosophy is implemented. Material should arrive when—not before, not after—it is needed.

5. Yes; materials are delivered only when needed. Otherwise, zero inventory is maintained.

6. There are many examples. Almost every manufactured product has a bill-of-materials relationship.

7. A basic underlying assumption of the EOQ is that demand is continuous. The holding costs are very much a function of this assumed continuity. If this is not the case, the EOQ will have inventory when it is not necessary.

8. With JIT, the problem will be fixed. With a safety stock, the demand will be met, but the problem will occur again and again.

9. Lot sizing is applicable for any situation with known, nonconstant demands.

10. The unstructured bill of materials contains the total number of each part. The structured bill of materials provides information in a different way. For each assembly, the number of assemblies is given. The advantage of this structured BOM is that the sequencing is obvious. The disadvantage is that the total number of each part is not obvious (but can be computed).

11. The inventory record file tracks inventory levels. Subtracting inventory from the requirements yields the amount to order. The inventory record file also includes lead time information. The bill of materials gives the relationship among parts, including the number of each part required for each assembly/subassembly. The master production schedule drives the system by giving the production levels for the end item, which creates the needs at the lower levels.

12. The scheduler will try different master production schedules to evaluate the resulting schedules at the lower levels. He or she uses the MRP system as a simulator to design the best schedule. The forecasts generate the end-product requirements to be met.

13. Items with many levels of subassemblies/parts and long lead times have less flexibility (slack) than items with few or no parts.

14. Low-level coding ensures that a single part is always coded at the same level, regardless of its level of usage in different assemblies. This makes it easy to identify the total number of parts required.

15. The orders are planned to be released in time for the desired receipt. The lead time is used to calculate exactly how much sooner the release should be.

16. MRP is a pull system. The demands of the master production schedule pull items through the system as needed.

17. Lot sizing allows for inventory to be carried (which is not just-in-time). However, it is cost-effective to carry inventory to avoid production setups for small quantities of some items.

18. A closed loop system has feedback, while an open loop system does not.

19. ■ Form a task force.
   - ■ Indoctrinate employees in the principles of MRP.
   - ■ Coordinate people and departments.
   - ■ Assign input responsibilities to specific departments.
   - ■ Prepare departments for forthcoming changes.
   - ■ Conduct in-house seminars prior to and simultaneous with initial module implementation.
   - ■ Implement one module at a time in digestible subsections.
   - ■ Develop minor in-house modifications with the vendor, as necessary.

SOLUTIONS TO PROBLEMS

1.

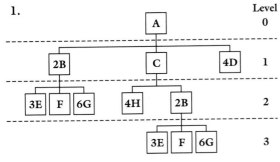

	Level
A	0
2B C 4D	1
3E F 6G 4H 2B	2
3E F 6G	3

2.

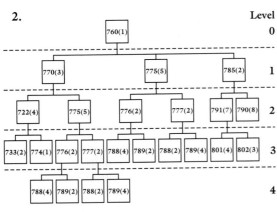

3.

Part	Number Required
A	1
B	2
D	2
H	3
I	1
J	2
E	3
F	5
C	6
B	4
D	2
H	3
I	1
J	2
E	3
F	5
G	2
H	1
I	3

4.

Part	Number Required
1100	1
1110	3
1111	1
1112	1
1113	1
1120	1
1124	1
1127	1
1130	2
1131	6
1134	1
1138	2
1139	1

5.

Part	Total Requirement
760	124
770	$3 \times 124 = 372$
775	$5 \times 124 + 15 \times 124 = 2,480$
785	$2 \times 124 = 248$
722	$12 \times 124 = 1,488$
776	$10 \times 124 + 30 \times 124 = 4,960$
777	$10 \times 124 + 30 \times 124 = 4,960$
791	$14 \times 124 = 1,736$
790	$16 \times 124 = 1,984$
733	$24 \times 124 = 2,976$
774	$12 \times 124 = 1,488$
788	$40 \times 124 + 20 \times 124 + 120 \times 124 + 60 \times 124 = 29,760$
789	$20 \times 124 + 40 \times 124 + 60 \times 124 + 120 \times 124 = 29,760$
801	$56 \times 124 = 6,944$
802	$42 \times 124 = 5,208$

INSTRUCTORS' SECTION

6.

Part	Total Requirement
A	517
B	$2 \times 517 + 24 \times 517 = 13{,}442$
C	$6 \times 517 = 3{,}102$
D	$4 \times 517 + 48 \times 517 = 26{,}884$
E	$6 \times 517 + 72 \times 517 = 40{,}326$
F	$10 \times 517 + 120 \times 517 = 67{,}210$
G	$12 \times 517 = 6{,}204$
H	$12 \times 517 + 144 \times 517 + 12 \times 517 = 86{,}856$
I	$4 \times 517 + 48 \times 517 + 36 \times 517 = 45{,}496$
J	$8 \times 517 + 96 \times 517 = 53{,}768$

8.

Part			Number Required		
A			1		
	B			2	
		E			3
		F			1
		G			6
	C			1	
		H			4
		B			2
			E		3
			F		1
			G		6
	D			4	

7.

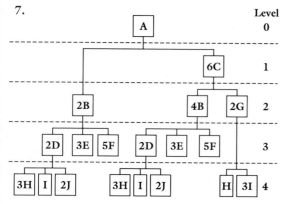

9. (a)

	Week							
	1	2	3	4	5	6	7	8
Tot. Req.						120		
On-hand Inv.								
Net Req.						120		
Ord. Rct.						120		
Ord. Rel.					120			

item A

	Week							
	1	2	3	4	5	6	7	8
Tot. Req.					240			
On-hand Inv.								
Net Req.					240			
Ord. Rct.					240			
Ord. Rel.				240				

item B

	Week							
	1	2	3	4	5	6	7	8
Tot. Req.					360			
On-hand Inv.								
Net Req.					360			
Ord. Rct.					360			
Ord. Rel.				360				

item C

			Week						
	1	2	3	4	5	6	7	8	
Tot. Req.					600				item
On-hand Inv.									D
Net Req.					600				
Ord. Rct.					600				
Ord. Rel.				600					

			Week						
	1	2	3	4	5	6	7	8	
Tot. Req.				240					item
On-hand Inv.									E
Net Req.				240					
Ord. Rct.				240					
Ord. Rel.			240						

			Week						
	1	2	3	4	5	6	7	8	
Tot. Req.				480					item
On-hand Inv.									F
Net Req.				480					
Ord. Rct.				480					
Ord. Rel.			480						

			Week						
	1	2	3	4	5	6	7	8	
Tot. Req.				2,400					item
On-hand Inv.									G
Net Req.				2,400					
Ord. Rct.				2,400					
Ord. Rel.			2,400						

			Week						
	1	2	3	4	5	6	7	8	
Tot. Req.				1,200					item
On-hand Inv.									H
Net Req.				1,200					
Ord. Rct.				1,200					
Ord. Rel.			1,200						

(b)

Part	Release Week	Quantity Ordered
A	5	120
B	4	240
C	4	360
D	4	600
E	3	240
F	3	480
G	3	2,400
H	3	1,200

10.

	Week								
	1	2	3	4	5	6	7	8	
Tot. Req.				150	80	120		175	
On-hand Inv.									item
Net Req.				150	80	120		175	A
Ord. Rct.				150	80	120		175	
Ord. Rel.			150	80	120		175		

	Week								
	1	2	3	4	5	6	7	8	
Tot. Req.			300	160	240		350		
On-hand Inv.									item
Net Req.			300	160	240		350		B
Ord. Rct.			300	160	240		350		
Ord. Rel.		300	160	240		350			

	Week								
	1	2	3	4	5	6	7	8	
Tot. Req.			450	240	360		525		
On-hand Inv.									item
Net Req.			450	240	360		525		C
Ord. Rct.			450	240	360		525		
Ord. Rel.		450	240	360		525			

	Week								
	1	2	3	4	5	6	7	8	
Tot. Req.			750	400	600		875		
On-hand Inv.									item
Net Req.			750	400	600		875		D
Ord. Rct.			750	400	600		875		
Ord. Rel.		750	400	600		875			

	Week								
	1	2	3	4	5	6	7	8	
Tot. Req.		300	160	240		350			
On-hand Inv.									item
Net Req.		300	160	240		350			E
Ord. Rct.		300	160	240		350			
Ord. Rel.	300	160	240		350				

	Week								
	1	2	3	4	5	6	7	8	
Tot. Req.		600	320	480		700			
On-hand Inv.									item
Net Req.		600	320	480		700			F
Ord. Rct.		600	320	480		700			
Ord. Rel.	600	320	480		700				

	Week							
	1	2	3	4	5	6	7	8
Tot. Req.		3,000	1,600	2,400		3,500		
On-hand Inv.								
Net Req.		3,000	1,600	2,400		3,500		
Ord. Rct.		3,000	1,600	2,400		3,500		
Ord. Rel.	3,000	1,600	2,400		3,500			

item G

	Week							
	1	2	3	4	5	6	7	8
Tot. Req.		1,500	800	1,200		1,750		
On-hand Inv.								
Net Req.		1,500	800	1,200		1,750		
Ord. Rct.		1,500	800	1,200		1,750		
Ord. Rel.	1,500	800	1,200		1,750			

item H

The following table shows the planned orders for Problem 10.

Part	Release Week	Quantity Ordered
A	3, 4, 5, 7	150; 80; 120; 175
B	2, 3, 4, 6	300; 160; 240; 350
C	2, 3, 4, 6	450; 240; 360; 525
D	2, 3, 4, 6	750; 400; 600; 875
E	1, 2, 3, 5	300; 160; 240; 350
F	1, 2, 3, 5	600; 320; 480; 700
G	1, 2, 3, 5	3,000; 1,600; 2,400; 3,500
H	1, 2, 3, 5	1,500; 800; 1,200; 1,750

11.

	Week							
	1	2	3	4	5	6	7	8
Tot. Req.								70
On-hand Inv.								
Net Req.								70
Ord. Rct.								70
Ord. Rel.							70	

item A

	Week							
	1	2	3	4	5	6	7	8
Tot. Req.						1,680	140	
On-hand Inv.								
Net Req.						1,680	140	
Ord. Rct.						1,680	140	
Ord. Rel.					1,680	140		

item B

	Week							
	1	2	3	4	5	6	7	8
Tot. Req.							420	
On-hand Inv.								
Net Req.							420	
Ord. Rct.							420	
Ord. Rel.						420		

item C

	Week							
	1	2	3	4	5	6	7	8
Tot. Req.					3,360	280		
On-hand Inv.								
Net Req.					3,360	280		
Ord. Rct.					3,360	280		
Ord. Rel.			3,360	280				

item D

	Week							
	1	2	3	4	5	6	7	8
Tot. Req.					5,040	420		
On-hand Inv.								
Net Req.					5,040	420		
Ord. Rct.					5,040	420		
Ord. Rel.				5,040	420			

item E

	Week							
	1	2	3	4	5	6	7	8
Tot. Req.					8,400	700		
On-hand Inv.								
Net Req.					8,400	700		
Ord. Rct.					8,400	700		
Ord. Rel.				8,400	700			

item F

	Week							
	1	2	3	4	5	6	7	8
Tot. Req.								
On-hand Inv.						840		
Net Req.								
Ord. Rct.						840		
Ord. Rel.					840	840		

item G

	Week							
	1	2	3	4	5	6	7	8
Tot. Req.			10,080	840	840			
On-hand Inv.								
Net Req.			10,080	840	840			
Ord. Rct.			10,080	840	840			
Ord. Rel.	10,080	840	840					

item H

				Week				
	1	2	3	4	5	6	7	8
Tot. Req.			3,360	280	2,520			
On-hand Inv.								
Net Req.			3,360	280	2,520			
Ord. Rct.			3,360	280	2,520			
Ord. Rel.		3,360	280	2,520				

item I

				Week				
	1	2	3	4	5	6	7	8
Tot. Req.			6,720	560				
On-hand Inv.								
Net Req.			6,720	560				
Ord. Rct.			6,720	560				
Ord. Rel.		6,720	560					

item J

The following table shows the planned orders for Problem 11.

Part	Week	Quantity Ordered
A	7	70
B	5, 6	1,680; 140
C	6	420
D	3, 4	3,360; 280
E	4, 5	5,040; 420
F	4, 5	8,400; 700
G	5	840
H	1, 2, 3	10,080; 840; 840
I	2, 3, 4	3,360; 280; 2,520
J	1, 2	6,720; 560

12.

item A

						Week					
	1	2	3	4	5	6	7	8	9	10	11	12
Tot. Req.								70	120	70	120	70
On-hand Inv.												
Net Req.								70	120	70	120	70
Ord. Rct.								70	120	70	120	70
Ord. Rel.							70	120	70	120	70	

item B

						Week					
	1	2	3	4	5	6	7	8	9	10	11
Tot. Req.						1,680	3,020	1,920	3,020	1,920	140
On-hand Inv.											
Net Req.						1,680	3,020	1,920	3,020	1,920	140
Ord. Rct.						1,680	3,020	1,920	3,020	1,920	140
Ord. Rel.					1,680	3,020	1,920	3,020	1,920	140	

item C

	Week										
	1	2	3	4	5	6	7	8	9	10	11
Tot. Req.							420	720	420	720	420
On-hand Inv.											
Net Req.							420	720	420	720	420
Ord. Rct.							420	720	420	720	420
Ord. Rel.						420	720	420	720	420	

item D

	Week										
	1	2	3	4	5	6	7	8	9	10	11
Tot. Req.					3,360	6,040	3,840	6,040	3,840	280	
On-hand Inv.											
Net Req.					3,360	6,040	3,840	6,040	3,840	280	
Ord. Rct.					3,360	6,040	3,840	6,040	3,840	280	
Ord. Rel.			3,360	6,040	3,840	6,040	3,840	280			

item E

	Week										
	1	2	3	4	5	6	7	8	9	10	11
Tot. Req.					5,040	9,060	5,760	9,060	5,760	420	
On-hand Inv.											
Net Req.					5,040	9,060	5,760	9,060	5,760	420	
Ord. Rct.					5,040	9,060	5,760	9,060	5,760	420	
Ord. Rel.				5,040	9,060	5,760	9,060	5,760	420		

item F

	Week										
	1	2	3	4	5	6	7	8	9	10	11
Tot. Req.					8,400	15,100	9,600	15,100	9,600	700	
On-hand Inv.											
Net Req.					8,400	15,100	9,600	15,100	9,600	700	
Ord. Rct.					8,400	15,100	9,600	15,100	9,600	700	
Ord. Rel.				8,400	15,100	9,600	15,100	9,600	700		

item G

	Week										
	1	2	3	4	5	6	7	8	9	10	11
Tot. Req.						840	1,440	840	1,440	840	
On-hand Inv.											
Net Req.						840	1,440	840	1,440	840	
Ord. Rct.						840	1,440	840	1,440	840	
Ord. Rel.					840	1,440	840	1,440	840		

item H

	Week								
	1	2	3	4	5	6	7	8	9
Tot. Req.			10,080	18,120	12,360	19,560	12,360	2,280	840
On-hand Inv.									
Net Req.			10,080	18,120	12,360	19,560	12,360	2,280	840
Ord. Rct.			10,080	18,120	12,360	19,560	12,360	2,280	840
Ord. Rel.	10,080	18,120	12,360	19,560	12,360	2,280	840		

item I

	Week								
	1	2	3	4	5	6	7	8	9
Tot. Req.			3,360	6,040	6,360	10,360	6,360	4,600	2,520
On-hand Inv.									2,520
Net Req.			3,360	6,040	6,360	10,360	6,360	4,600	2,520
Ord. Rct.			3,360	6,040	6,360	10,360	6,360	4,600	
Ord. Rel.		3,360	6,040	6,360	10,360	6,360	4,600	2,520	

item J

	Week								
	1	2	3	4	5	6	7	8	9
Tot. Req.			6,720	12,080	7,680	12,080	7,680	560	
On-hand Inv.									
Net Req.			6,720	12,080	7,680	12,080	7,680	560	
Ord. Rct.			6,720	12,080	7,680	12,080	7,680	560	
Ord. Rel.		6,720	12,080	7,680	12,080	7,680	560		

The following table shows the planned purchase orders for Problem 12.

Part	Week	Quantity Ordered
A	7, 8, 9, 10, 11	70; 120; 70; 120; 70
B	5, 6, 7, 8, 9, 10	1,680; 3,020; 1,920; 3,020; 1,920; 140
C	6, 7, 8, 9, 10	420; 720; 420; 720; 420
D	2, 3, 4, 5, 6, 7	3,360; 6,040; 3,840; 6,040; 3,840; 280
E	4, 5, 6, 7, 8, 9	5,040; 9,060; 5,760; 9,060; 5,760; 420
F	4, 5, 6, 7, 8, 9	8,400; 15,100; 9,600; 15,100; 9,600; 700
G	5, 6, 7, 8, 9	840; 1,440; 840; 1,440; 840
H	1, 2, 3, 4, 5, 6, 7	10,080; 18,120; 12,360; 19,560; 12,360; 19,560; 840
I	2, 3, 4, 5, 6, 7, 8	3,360; 6,040; 6,360; 10,360; 6,360; 4,600; 2,520
J	2, 3, 4, 5, 6, 7	6,720; 12,080; 7,680; 12,080; 7,680; 560

INSTRUCTORS' SECTION

13. $PPV = \dfrac{S}{H} = \dfrac{20}{.02} = 1,000$

					Week					
	1	2	3	4	5	6	7	8	9	10
Planned Order	460	120	370	410	180	350	220	540	410	500
Part Periods	0	120	740	>1,000/0	180	700	660/0	540	810/0	500
Cumulative Part Periods	0	120	860	>1,000/0	180	880	>1,000/0	540	>1,000/0	500
Order	950			940			760		910	

Order	Week	Quantity
1	1	950
2	4	940
3	7	760
4	9	910

14. $PPV = \dfrac{S}{H} = \dfrac{50}{.05} = 1,000$

						Week		
	1	2	3	4	5	6	7	8
Planned Order	170	0	210	30	0	180	210	20
Part Periods	0	0	420	90	0	900/0	210	40
Cumulative Part Periods	0	0	420	510	510	>1,000/0	210	250
Order	410					410		

Order	Week	Quantity
1	1	410
2	6	410

15. average usage =

$$\dfrac{460+120+370+410+180+350+220+540+410+500}{10}$$

$$= \dfrac{3,560}{10} = 356$$

$Q^* = \sqrt{2DS/H}$

$\quad = \sqrt{(2 \times 356 \times 20)/.02} = 844$ per order

Order	Week	Quantity
1	1	844
2	3	844
3	6	844
4	8	844
5	10	184*

*Sum must equal total demand.

Now we need to find the costs. Using the part period approach, the cost of 4 orders is $80. The holding cost is 120($.02) + 370($.04) + 180($.02) + 350($.04) + 540($.02) + 500($.04) = $65.60. So the total cost is $80 + $65.60 = $145.60. Using the lot-for-lot approach, the cost of 10 orders is $200. Using EOQ, the cost of 5 orders is $100. To compute the holding cost, we first must find the sum of the weekly ending inventories.

Week	Starting Inventory	Order Arrival	Demand	Ending Inventory
1	0	844	460	384
2	384		120	264
3	264	844	370	738
4	738		410	328
5	328		180	148
6	148	844	350	642
7	642		220	422
8	422	844	540	726
9	726		410	316
10	316	184	500	0
			Total	3,968

holding cost = 3,968 × $.02/unit-week = $79.36

For EOQ, the total cost is $100 + $79.36 = $179.36. Therefore, part period provides the best results. (*Note:* The Wagner-Whitin solution is 580; 0; 960; 0; 0; 570; 0; 950; 500. It leads to a cost of $130.40.)

16. Using part period, the cost of 2 orders is $100. The holding cost is 210($.10) + 30($.15) + 210($.05) + 20($.10) = $38. So the total cost is $100 + $38 = $138. Using the *lot-for-lot* approach, the cost of 6 orders is $300. For EOQ, we first must find the average usage: 820/8 = 102.5 per week.

$$Q^* = \sqrt{2DS/H} = \sqrt{(2 \times 102.5 \times 50)/.05} = 453$$

Order	Week	Quantity
1	1	454
2	6	366

Using EOQ, the cost of 2 orders is $100.
To compute the holding cost, we first must find the sum of the weekly ending inventories.

Week	Starting Inventory	Order Arrival	Demand	Ending Inventory
1	0	453	170	283
2	284		0	283
3	284		210	73
4	74		30	43
5	44		0	43
6	44	367*	180	230
7	230		210	20
8	20		20	0
			Total	975

*total supply = total demand

holding cost = 975 × $.05 = $48.75

The total cost for EOQ is $100 + $148.75. Therefore, part period is best. (*Note:* The Wagner-Whitin solution is 410; 0; 0; 0; 0; 410; 0; 0, at a total cost of $138.)

17.

	Week									
	1	2	3	4	5	6	7	8	9	10
Order	460	120	370	410	180	350	220	540	410	500
Utilization	1.15	.3	.925	1.025	.45	.875	.55	1.35	1.025	1.25

No; the schedule cannot be met in weeks 1, 4, 8, 9, and 10.

modified schedule 1 (local shifts)

	Week									
	1	2	3	4	5	6	7	8	9	10
Production	400	180	380	400	200	400	400	400	400	400

modified schedule 2 (averaging): produce 356 per week

The modified schedule changes all the lower-level items with requirements generated by part 7510. The higher-level items may also change if, as in week 1, 7510s are delayed. It could also push up production of some higher-level items, but this is not necessary.

18.

Munich

			Month			
	0	1	2	3	4	5
Gross Req.		1,000	1,100	1,200	900	
Avail. Inv.	2,500	2,500	1,500	400	700	1,300
Planned Rct.				1,500	1,500	
Planned Ord.			1,500	1,500		

Dusseldorf

			Month			
	0	1	2	3	4	5
Gross Req.		800	700	900	1,000	
Avail. Inv.	1,100	1,100	300	800	1,100	100
Planned Rct.			1,200	1,200		
Planned Ord.		1,200	1,200			

Krephauser makes shipments of 1,200 cases to Dusseldorf in weeks 1 and 2 and shipments of 1,500 to Munich in weeks 2 and 3.

19.

Munich

			Month			
	0	1	2	3	4	5
Gross Req.		1,000	1,100	1,200	900	
Avail. Inv.	2,500	2,500	1,500	400	200	300
Planned Rct.				1,000	1,000	
Planned Ord.			1,000	1,000		

Dusseldorf

			Month			
	0	1	2	3	4	5
Gross Req.		800	700	900	1,000	
Avail. Inv.	1,100	1,100	300	600	700	700
Planned Rct.			1,000	1,000	1,000	
Planned Ord.		1,000	1,000	1,000		

(a) Only one additional shipment is made in this short time frame, to Dusseldorf (but more are needed to be made over time if shipments are smaller).

(b) Comparing available inventory in periods 2 through 5 (after each demand), Munich has an average of 975 (3,900/4) under the first plan and 600 (2,400/4) under the second. Dusseldorf has an average of 575 (2,300/4) in each case but has a higher ending inventory under the second plan.

20.

Munich

	Month					
	0	1	2	3	4	5
Gross Req.		1,000	1,100	1,200	900	
Avail. Inv.	2,500	2,500	1,500	400		
Planned Rct.				800	900	
Planned Ord.			800	900		

Dusseldorf

	Month					
	0	1	2	3	4	5
Gross Req.		800	700	900	1,000	
Avail. Inv.	1,100	1,100	300			
Planned Rct.			300	900	1,000	
Planned Ord.		300	900	1,000		

This plan has the same number of shipments as the previous one, but in the long run will require more shipments because demands cannot be combined.

21.

center 1

	Week						
	0	1	2	3	4	5	6
Gross Req.		20	30	20	30	40	30
Avail. Inv.	200	200	180	150	130	100	60
Planned Rct.							
Planned Ord.							

center 2

	Week						
	0	1	2	3	4	5	6
Gross Req.		50	40	35	40	50	40
Avail. Inv.	75	75	25	45	10	30	40
Planned Rct.			60		60	60	
Planned Ord.		60		60	60		

center 3

	Week						
	0	1	2	3	4	5	6
Gross Req.		35	40	30	20	50	40
Avail. Inv.	80	80	45	5	35	15	25
Planned Rct.				60		60	60
Planned Ord.			60		60	60	

center 4

	Week						
	0	1	2	3	4	5	6
Gross Req.		40	30	40	40	50	60
Avail. Inv.	110	110	70	40		20	30
Planned Rct.					60	60	60
Planned Ord.				60	60	60	

Atlanta

	Week						
	0	1	2	3	4	5	6
Gross Req.		60	60	120	180	120	
Avail. Inv.	0	0	140	80	160	180	60
Planned Rct.		200		200	200		
Planned Ord.	200		200	200			

Location	Week	Quantity
Atlanta	0, 2, 3	200; 200; 200
center 1	—	—
center 2	1, 3, 4	60; 60; 60
center 3	2, 4, 5	60; 60; 60
center 4	3, 4, 5	60; 60; 60

Computer Case Study 14.1

The data file (CASE14-1.SIZ) has all of the information necessary. Using the EOQ option leads to a total cost of $2,582.44. Using lot for lot leads to a total cost of $2,905, which is worse. Of course, Wagner-Whitin leads to the best cost ($1,553.54). In this instance, the same result is obtained with part period balancing.

15

Operations Scheduling

TEACHING NOTES

In previous chapters, we have noted that there is a relationship between the types of scheduling problems faced and the type of layout that exists. In this chapter, we have organized the scheduling problems along the lines of layout.

We begin with a very brief section on projects (we cover project scheduling in detail in Chapter 10). This is followed by job shop scheduling. Note that we distinguish between lateness and tardiness and that we explain to students the reason for doing this. The one-machine methods presented are shortest processing time, due date scheduling, slack, and slack per operation. In addition, we use Moore's method to minimize the number of tardy jobs. We emphasize that, in general, there are different criteria that might interest the manager in different situations.

For product layout, we introduce the problem of running more than one type of product on a single line or machine. This leads to problems with setups and sequencing and runouts, all of which are discussed in the chapter.

Lastly, we devote an entire section to assignment-type problems. There we cover the assignment problem as well as the bottleneck assignment problem, the machine changeover problem, and the traveling salesman problem.

Problems 1 through 4 are one-machine scheduling problems. Problems 5 through 10 are traditional two-machine problems. Problems 11, 12, 13, and 15 require a more detailed analysis of the schedules. Problem 14 is a three-machine problem. Problems 16 and 17 are machine changeover problems; Problem 18 is a traveling salesman problem; Problems 19, 20, and 21 are aggregate scheduling problems; and Problems 22 through 28 are variations of the assignment problem.

The software for this chapter consists of two modules, one for solving job shop scheduling problems and one for solving assignment problems. Problems 1 through 10 can be solved using the job shop scheduling module, while Problems 22 through 26 can be solved by using the assignment module.

TEACHING SUGGESTIONS

Teaching Suggestion 15.1:   Another Example.
Perhaps the classic job shop is the print shop. Each unique job, in general, must pass through three processes: design and layout, printing, and binding.

Teaching Suggestion 15.2:   Flow Time Assumption.
We note that, for ease of discussion, the examples assume that all jobs enter the shop at time zero. Essentially, for each of our examples and the homework problems, we look at average completion time rather than flow time.

Teaching Suggestion 15.3:   Late vs. Tardy.
We distinguish between *late* and *tardy*. Challenge your students to cite situations in which being early is beneficial (other than the example of contract incentives given in the text).

Teaching Suggestion 15.4:   Due Date Scheduling.
Many people use due date scheduling because they back themselves into a position where they feel that they have to perform the task that is due next. This is a very myopic approach.

Teaching Suggestion 15.5:   Order Assumption of Two-Machine Scheduling.
The assumption that every job must go through the two machines in the same order is not as limiting as our students seem to feel. There are many situations you might cite: for example, drying follows painting, binding follows printing, stapling follows collating, a trial follows an indictment. Furthermore, a method exists to solve the two-machine problem without this assumption.

Teaching Suggestion 15.6:   Drawing Gantt Charts.
We draw our first Gantt chart for two machines according to time because this is the more intuitive approach to explain the job-machine relationships in class. Thereafter, we draw them by machine because it is easier.

Teaching Suggestion 15.7:   Row/Column Order.
We like to point out that the table has no order. Rows could

be examined after columns, in any order, or steps 1 and 2 could be reversed.

Teaching Suggestion 15.8:   Bottleneck Method.
The bottleneck assignment problem is easier to solve than the regular assignment problem presented earlier.

Teaching Suggestion 15.9:   Multiple Traveling Salesman Problem.
Many situations are modeled as traveling salesman problems with more than one salesman: for example, newspaper delivery to stores, school busing, express package delivery, and utility repair/installation.

ANSWERS TO QUESTIONS

1. routing: *where* the work is to be done; scheduling: *when* the work is to be done; dispatching: issuing the order to begin work; control: monitoring the process; expediting: improving the completion time of a job

2. There are many examples. A sample answer is given for schoolwork.
routing: choices of where to study or do homework for each subject, such as library, computer center, home, or bar; scheduling: when exactly to do each piece of homework or studying; dispatching: beginning the homework (always the hardest part); control: during the execution of the schedule, a clock or watch and for the longer-term execution of the schedule, exams to provide feedback; expediting: studying the subject on which you had the lowest midterm grade or, possibly, working as a team on assignments

3. The timing of the individual tasks requires coordination.

4. A static job shop is one in which all jobs that will ever enter the system are known. A dynamic shop is one in which more jobs arrive as current jobs are processed. Most shops are dynamic.

5. In a general job shop, jobs are processed in any sequence, while in a flow shop, all jobs follow the same sequence of operations.

6. The specific service times in a queueing situation are unknown, whereas in a job shop, the times are known (to a large extent). Knowing the times makes scheduling—for example, SPT—worthwhile. Not knowing the times makes fairness—for example, FCFS—worthwhile. Aside from this difference, queueing systems and job shop systems are very similar.

7. A due date may range from a (meaningless) promise to a contractual obligation. It is a target with or without penalties.

8. flow time: the length of time a job is in the system; makespan: the maximum flow time, which is the time at which all jobs are completed; lateness: completion time minus due date; tardiness: either 0 or the lateness

9. SPT minimizes the average flow time, average lateness, and average number of jobs in the system. It maximizes the number of jobs completed at any point. The disadvantage is that long jobs are pushed back in the schedule.

10. One of the many examples would be a print shop, in which items are first printed and then bound.

11. ROT is the length of time until the current inventory of an individual item is depleted. ART is the length of time until the inventory across items is depleted, given one period's worth of processing.

12. The goal of the assignment problem is to minimize the total costs, while the goal of the bottleneck assignment problem is to minimize the largest cost.

13. none

SOLUTIONS TO PROBLEMS

1. (a)

SPT method	602	405	227	312	711	822
Total number of passengers	20	60	120	190	320	530

The average number of passengers handled—the flow time, so to speak—is

$(20 + 60 + 120 + 190 + 320 + 530)/6 = 206.67.$

On average, it takes

206.67 passengers × 1.5 bags/passenger × 4 sec./bag = 1,240 sec. = 20.67 min. to unload each plane.

No schedule can do better than this!

2. (a)

SPT	E	A	C	B	D
Flow	5	12	22	37	57
Due	15	52	30	45	20
Late	−10	−40	−8	−8	37
Tardy	0	0	0	0	37

average flow time = (5 + 12 + 22 + 37 + 57)/5
= 133/5 = 26.6 hr.

average lateness = (−10 − 40 − 8 − 8 + 37)/5
= −29/5 = −5.8 hr.

(On average, jobs are 5.8 hr. *early.*)

average tardiness = (0 + 0 + 0 + 0 + 37)/5 = 7.4 hr.

(b)

EDD	E	D	C	B	A
Flow	5	25	35	50	57
Due	15	20	30	45	52
Late	−10	5	5	5	5
Tardy	0	5	5	5	5

average flow time = (5 + 25 + 35 + 50 + 57)/5
= 172/5 = 34.4 hr.

average lateness = (−10 + 5 + 5 + 5 + 5)/5
= 10/5 = 2 hr.

(On average, jobs are 2 hr. late.)

average tardiness = (0 + 5 + 5 + 5 + 5)/5 = 4 hr.

3. For both parts (a) and (b) the method is SPT.

SPT	A	C	D	B
	0 10 22 40 65			

Job	Flow Time	Due Date	Late Days	Tardy Days
A	10	22	−12	—
B	65	45	20	20
C	22	18	4	4
D	40	30	10	10
	137		22	34

For part (c) the method is due date scheduling.

EDD	C	A	D	B
	0 12 22 40 65			

Job	Flow Time	Due Date	Late Days	Tardy Days
A	22	22	—	—
B	65	45	20	20
C	12	18	−6	—
D	40	30	10	10
	139		24	30

(a) SPT = 137/4 = 34.25 days flow time
(b) SPT = 22/4 = 5.5 days late (not tardy)
(c) due date scheduling; maximum (worst) tardiness = 20

4. (a)

F	A	C	B	D	E

(b)

A	F	B	D	C	E

(c)

(1) Job	(2) Processing Time	(3) Due Date	(4) Slack [(3) − (2)]	(5) Slack/ Operation
A	2	3	1	1/3 = .33
B	4	8	4	4/1 = 4
C	3	12	9	9/2 = 4.5
D	6	11	5	5/1 = 5
E	8	16	8	8/4 = 2
F	1	4	3	3/2 = 1.5

Using the slack column, we have the following schedule.

A	F	B	D	E	C

(d) Using the slack per operation column, we have the following schedule.

A	F	E	B	C	D

(e) For Moore's method, we begin with the slack time schedule.

A	F	B	D	E	C

	A	F	B	D	E	C
Done	2	3	7	13	21	24
Due	3	4	8	11	16	12

The first late job is job D. The longest job of all jobs through D (A, F, B, D) is D. Schedule D last.

	A	F	B	E	C	D
Done	2	3	7	15	18	24
Due	3	4	8	16	12	11

The first late job is job C. The longest job of all jobs through C (A, F, B, E, C) is E. Schedule E last.

	A	F	B	C	D	E
Done	2	3	7	10	16	24
Due	3	4	8	16	11	12

The minimum number of late jobs is 2.

5. (a) Johnson's method:

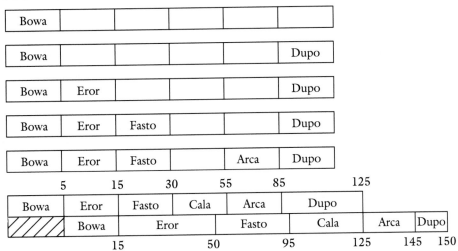

(b) Processing ends at 3:00 P.M. + 150 min. = 5:30 P.M.

6. (a)

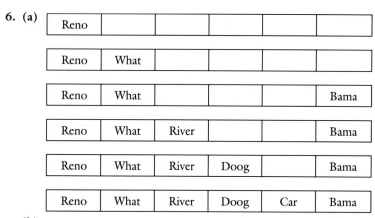

(b)

	16	41	93	156	260	297

Reno	What	River	Doog	Car	Bama

| /// | Reno | What | River | Doog | Car | Bama |

| 16 | 44 | 86 93 | 174 | 246 260 | 460 | 489 |

total hours = 489/60 = 8.15 hr., or 8:09 A.M.

7. (a) Johnson's method:

0	40	160	270	370	420	480	500

| A | G | E | C | F | B | D |

| /// | A | /// | G | /// | E | /// | C | F | B | D |

| 0 | 40 90 | 260 270 | 360 370 | 450 | 490 | 520 530 |

(b) $\dfrac{530 \text{ min.}}{60}$ = 8 hr., 50 min., or 5:50 P.M.

(c) $\dfrac{90 + 260 + 360 + 450 + 490 + 520 + 530}{7}$ = 385.71 min.

8. (a) Johnson's method:

0	10	50	170	270	380	430	450

| B | A | G | C | E | F | D |

| /// | B | /// | A | /// | G | C | /// | E | F | D |

| 10 | 40 50 | 100 | 170 | 270 | 350 380 | 440 | 480 | 490 |

(b) $\dfrac{490}{60}$ min. = 8 hr., 10 min., or 4:10 P.M.

(c) $\dfrac{40 + 100 + 270 + 350 + 440 + 480 + 490}{7}$ = 310 min.

9.

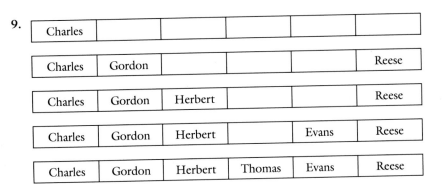

Charles					

Charles	Gordon				Reese

Charles	Gordon	Herbert			Reese

Charles	Gordon	Herbert		Evans	Reese

Charles	Gordon	Herbert	Thomas	Evans	Reese

(a)

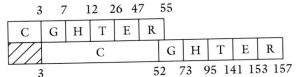

3   7   12   26   47   55

C	G	H	T	E	R

3 ... C ... G H T E R

52 73 95 141 153 157

(b) $157/60 = 2.62$ hr., or 11:37 A.M.

10. **(a)** Johnson's method:

5   15   30   55   85   125

B	E	F	C	A	D

B E F C A D

5   17   62   112   147   167   175

(b) $175/60 = 2.92$ hr., or 10:55 P.M.

(c) SPT rule

B	E	F	C	A	D

11.

6   10   12

A	C	B

$$\frac{\$1{,}000}{(1.01)^6} + \frac{\$400}{(1.01)^{12}} + \frac{\$700}{(1.01)^{10}} = \$942 + \$355 + \$634 = \$1{,}931$$

6   8   12

A	B	C

$$\frac{\$1{,}000}{(1.01)^6} + \frac{\$400}{(1.01)^{8}} + \frac{\$700}{(1.01)^{12}} = \$942 + \$369 + \$621 = \$1{,}932$$

2   8   12

B	A	C

$$\frac{\$1{,}000}{(1.01)^8} + \frac{\$400}{(1.01)^{2}} + \frac{\$700}{(1.01)^{12}} = \$923 + \$392 + \$621 = \$1{,}931$$

```
     2    6    12
   ┌───┬───┬───┐
   │ B │ C │ A │
   └───┴───┴───┘
```

$$\frac{\$1,000}{(1.01)^{12}} + \frac{\$400}{(1.01)^2} + \frac{\$700}{(1.01)^6} = \$887 + \$392 + \$659 = \$1,938$$

```
     4    10   12
   ┌───┬───┬───┐
   │ C │ A │ B │
   └───┴───┴───┘
```

$$\frac{\$1,000}{(1.01)^{10}} + \frac{\$400}{(1.01)^{12}} + \frac{\$700}{(1.01)^4} = \$905 + \$355 + \$673 = \$1,933$$

```
     4    6    12
   ┌───┬───┬───┐
   │ C │ B │ A │
   └───┴───┴───┘
```

$$\frac{\$1,000}{(1.01)^{12}} + \frac{\$400}{(1.01)^6} + \frac{\$700}{(1.01)^4} = \$887 + \$384 + \$673 = \$1,944$$

While there is not much difference among the schedules, C–B–A has the highest present value of payments. (*Note:* The present values have been taken from Table A2 in Appendix A.)

12. Johnson's method solves (a), but we need complete enumeration for (b) and (c).

schedule A–B–C

```
0    3         9         14
┌──────┬─────────┬─────────┐
│  A   │    B    │    C    │
└──────┴─────────┴─────────┘
  ╱╱╱╱╱╱╱╱
0    3  5         9         17       24
```

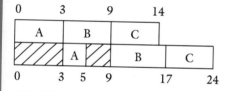

Job	Flow Time	Due Date	Late Days	Penalty
A	5	5	—	— — —
B	17	14	3	3 × \$2 = \$ 6
C	24	12	12	12 × \$8 = 96
	46/3 = 15.33			\$102

schedule A–C–B

```
0    3      8         14
┌──────┬──────┬───────┐
│  A   │  C   │   B   │
└──────┴──────┴───────┘
0    3  5      8         15       23
```

Job	Flow Time	Due Date	Late Days	Penalty
A	5	5	—	— — —
B	23	14	9	9 × \$2 = \$18
C	15	12	3	3 × \$8 = 24
	43/3 = 14.33			\$42

schedule B–A–C

```
0    6      9      14
┌──────┬──────┬──────┐
│  B   │  A   │  C   │
└──────┴──────┴──────┘
0    6         14    16    23
```

Job	Flow Time	Due Date	Late Days	Penalty
A	16	5	11	11 × \$10 = \$110
B	14	14	—	— —
C	23	12	11	11 × \$ 8 = 88
	53/3 = 17.66			\$198

schedule B–C–A

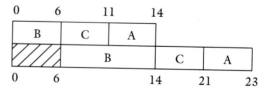

```
0    6    11   14
┌──────┬─────┬─────┐
│  B   │  C  │  A  │
└──────┴─────┴─────┘
0    6         14    21    23
```

Job	Flow Time	Due Date	Late Days	Penalty
A	23	5	18	18 × $10 = $180
B	21	14	7	7 × $2 = 14
C	14	12	2	2 × $8 = 16
	58/3 = 19.33			$210

schedule C–A–B

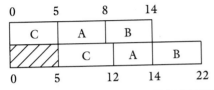

0   5   8   14 (top) — C   A   B; 0   5   12   14   22 (bottom) — C   A   B

Job	Flow Time	Due Date	Late Days	Penalty
A	14	5	9	9 × $10 = $ 90
B	22	14	8	8 × $2 = 16
C	12	12	—	—
	48/3 = 16			$106

schedule C–B–A

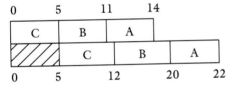

0   5   11   14 (top) — C   B   A; 0   5   12   20   22 (bottom) — C   B   A

Job	Flow Time	Due Date	Late Days	Penalty
A	22	5	17	17 × $10 = $170
B	20	14	6	6 × $2 = 12
C	12	12	—	—
	54/3 = 18			$182

(a) C–B–A; 22 days
(b) A–C–B; $42.00
(c) A–C–B; 14.33 days per job

13. complete enumeration:

schedule A–B–C

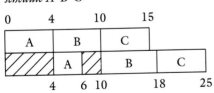

0   4   10   15 (top) — A   B   C; 4   6   10   18   25 (bottom) — A   B   C

Job	Flow Time	Due Date	Late Days	Penalty
A	6	5	1	1 × $5 = $ 5
B	18	14	4	4 × $4 = 16
C	25	12	13	13 × $3 = 39
	49/3 = 16.33			$60

schedule A–C–B

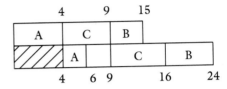

4   9   15 (top) — A   C   B; 4   6   9   16   24 (bottom) — A   C   B

Job	Flow Time	Due Date	Late Days	Penalty
A	6	5	1	1 × $5 = $ 5
B	24	14	10	10 × $4 = 40
C	16	12	4	4 × $3 = 12
	46/3 = 15.33			$57

schedule B–A–C

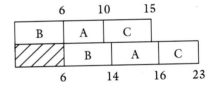

6   10   15 (top) — B   A   C; 6   14   16   23 (bottom) — B   A   C

Job	Flow Time	Due Date	Late Days	Penalty
A	16	5	11	11 × $5 = $55
B	14	14	—	—
C	23	12	11	11 × $3 = 33
	53/3 = 17.66			$88

schedule B–C–A

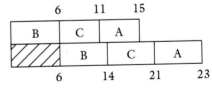

6   11   15 (top) — B   C   A; 6   14   21   23 (bottom) — B   C   A

Job	Flow Time	Due Date	Late Days	Penalty
A	23	5	18	18 × $5 = $ 90
B	14	14	—	— = —
C	21	12	9	9 × $3 = 27
	58/3 = 19.3			$117

schedule C–A–B

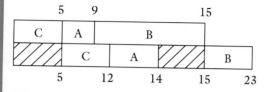

Job	Flow Time	Due Date	Late Days	Penalty
A	14	5	9	$9 \times \$5 = \$45$
B	23	14	9	$9 \times \$4 = 36$
C	$\underline{12}$	12	—	$\underline{—}$
	$49/3 = 16.3$			$\$81$

schedule C–B–A

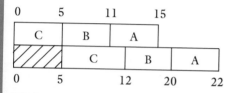

Job	Flow Time	Due Date	Late Days	Penalty
A	22	5	17	$17 \times \$5 = \$85$
B	20	14	6	$6 \times \$4 = —$
C	$\underline{12}$	12	—	$\underline{—}$
	$54/3 = 18$			$\$109$

　(a) A–C–B; $57

　(b) A–C–B; 15.33 hr.

　(c) C–B–A; 22 hr.

14. The minimum on machine 1 is 15, which is greater than the maximum (14) on machine 2. We can use Johnson's method after regrouping the times.

Job	New Machine 1	New Machine 2
A	22 + 8 = 30	8 + 10 = 18
B	18 + 6 = 24	6 + 5 = 11
C	16 + 3 = 19	3 + 3 = 6
D	20 + 12 = 32	12 + 17 = 29
E	15 + 14 = 29	14 + 12 = 26

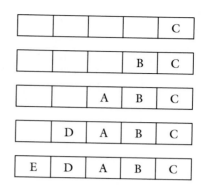

15. *schedule A–B–C*

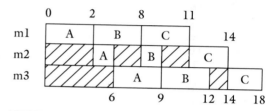

Job	Flow Time	Due Dates	Tardy Days	Early Days	[(2 × tardy) − early]
A	9	16	—	7	
B	12	10	2	—	
C	18	15	$\underline{3}$	$\underline{}$	
			5	7	3

schedule A–C–B

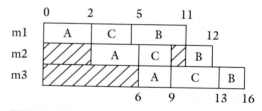

Job	Flow Time	Due Date	Tardy Days	Early Days	[(2 × tardy) − early]
A	9	16	—	7	
B	16	10	6	—	
C	13	15	—	2	
			6	9	3

schedule B–A–C

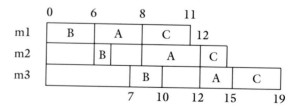

Job	Flow Time	Due Date	Tardy Days	Early Days	[(2 × tardy) − early]
A	15	16	—	1	
B	10	10	—	—	
C	19	15	4	—	
			4	1	7

(a) A–C–B; 16 days
(b) B–A–C; 4 days
(c) A–C–B; 1 job
(d) A–B–C; 3

16. explicit enumeration:

[sky blue → indigo → violet → sky blue]
sky blue → indigo = 80
indigo → violet = 40
violet → sky blue = 55
　　　　　Total   175 min.

[sky blue → violet → indigo → sky blue]
sky blue → violet = 35
violet → indigo = 60
indigo → sky blue = 15
　　　　　Total   110 min., which is better

17. We begin, arbitrarily, with A.

$$A \to D \to F \to B \to E \to C \to A$$
$$\quad 10 \quad 12 \quad 18 \quad 30 \quad 15 \quad 30$$

The total time is 115 min. per cycle.

18. (a) We arbitrarily start at A. Although Alice starts at A, the greedy method could start at any location because it identifies a complete cycle.

$$A \to D \to B \to C \to E \to A$$
$$\quad 15 \quad 5 \quad 10 \quad 10 \quad 20$$

The total is 60.

There is a tie when using the greedy method starting at A. Another possibility is

$$A \to D \to E \to C \to B \to A,$$
$$\quad 15 \quad 5 \quad 10 \quad 10 \quad 25$$

which has a total of 65. The first is better.

(b) 60 min.

19.

(1) Item	(2) Current Inventory	(3) Demand	(4) Runout Time (ROT) [(2) ÷ (3)]
A	3,000	1,000	3
B	1,600	400	4
C	1,200	600	2
D	2,000	2,000	1

The order is $D \to C \to A \to B$.

20. (a)

Item	Inventory	Forecast	ROT
A	10	25	.4
B	35	40	.875
C	15	10	1.5
D	10	20	.5
E	20	15	1.33

$$A \to D \to B \to E \to C$$

(b)

Item	Hours/ unit	Inventory	Inventory Hours	Lot Size	Lot Time
A	.5	10	5	150	75
B	.2	35	7	200	40
C	.1	15	1.5	75	7.5
D	.3	10	3	100	30
E	.4	20	8	50	20
			24.5		172.5

total hours available: $120 + 24.5 = 144.5$

total hours required: 172.5

(*Note:* E and C do not have to be produced, as they have sufficient inventory to cover the demand.)

21.

$$ART = \frac{\text{machine hours inventory} + \text{machine hours/period}}{\text{demand}}$$

demand in hours $= 25(.5) + 40(.2) + 10(.1) + 20(.3) + 15(.4)$

$$= 12.5 + 8 + 1 + 6 + 6$$
$$= 33.5$$

$$ART = 144.5/33.5 = 4.3134$$

Produce units for 4.3134 weeks of demand, as shown in the table.

Item	Forecast	4.3134 per Week Forecast	Inventory	Net Required	Net Hours
A	25	108	10	98	49
B	40	173	35	138	27.6
C	10	43	15	28	2.8
D	20	86	10	76	22.8
E	15	65	20	45	18
					120.2

22.

step 1

10	15	0	5
20	5	0	10
20	0	15	0
15	10	5	0

step 2

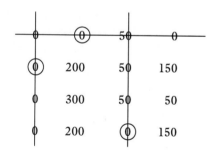

minimum cost = $25 + $10 + $5 + $5 = $45

23.

0	200	100	50
0	400	100	200
0	500	100	100
0	400	50	200

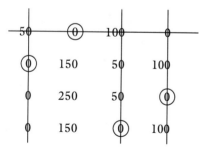

total cost = $2,000

(*Note:* The exact numbers depend on how the lines are drawn. The solution is the same regardless of how the lines are drawn: Assign 2 to Al, 1 to Bill, 4 to Carl, and 3 to Dean.)

24.

6	20	0	3	53	54
86	44	19	72	33	0
61	63	0	52	24	8
79	60	10	21	3	0
0	33	26	15	43	6
48	14	28	49	0	7

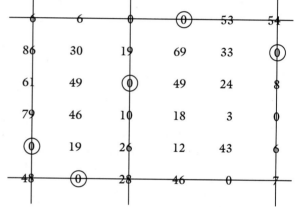

The minimum is 3; therefore, add and subtract 3.

9	6	3	0	53	57
86	27	19	66	30	0
61	46	0	46	21	8
79	43	10	15	0	0
0	16	26	9	40	6
51	0	31	46	0	10

total cost = $157

25.

20	32	0	74	24
22	0	22	25	28
41	56	0	82	41
53	48	7	17	0
57	2	0	19	45

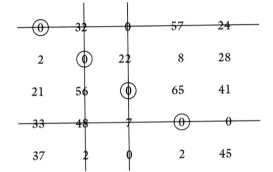

The minimum is 2.

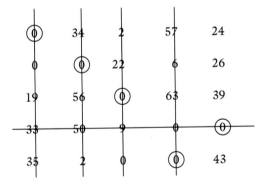

total profit = $387

26.

ⓐ47	97	26	74
45	ⓐ87	26	74
38	82	ⓐ13	62
59	96	37	ⓐ66

bottleneck = 87

47	X	26	ⓐ74
45	X	ⓐ26	74
38	ⓐ82	13	62
ⓐ59	X	37	66

Bottleneck of 82 cannot be improved.
(*Note:* There are multiple solutions.)

27.

ⓐ46	59	24	62	67
47	ⓐ56	32	55	70
44	52	ⓐ19	61	60
47	59	17	ⓐ64	73
43	65	20	60	ⓐ75

bottleneck = 75

46	59	24	62	ⓐ67
47	56	32	ⓐ55	70
44	52	ⓐ19	61	60
47	ⓐ59	17	64	73
ⓐ43	65	20	60	X

bottleneck = 67

46	ⓐ59	24	62	X
47	56	32	ⓐ55	X
44	52	19	61	ⓐ60
47	59	ⓐ17	64	X
ⓐ43	65	20	60	X

The final bottleneck is 60.
(*Note:* There are multiple solutions.)

28. We begin by converting hours to costs (in hundreds of dollars).

414	531	216	558	603
188	224	128	220	280
264	312	114	366	360
329	413	119	448	511
215	325	100	300	375

198	315	0	342	387
60	96	0	92	152
150	198	0	252	246
210	294	0	329	392
115	225	0	200	275

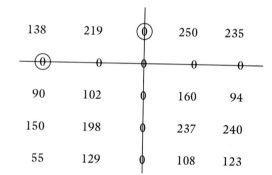

The minimum is 55.

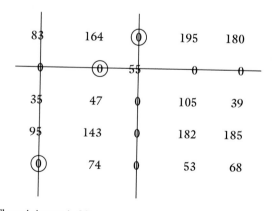

The minimum is 39.

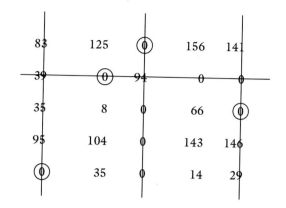

The minimum is 8.

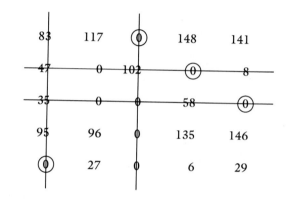

The minimum is 6.

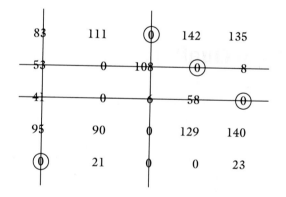

The minimum is 90.

Ⓞ	28	0	59	52
53	Ⓞ	191	0	8
41	0	89	58	Ⓞ
12	7	Ⓞ	46	57
0	21	83	Ⓞ	23

We return to the original table and mark the assignments with asterisks.

*414	531	216	558	603
188	*224	128	220	280
264	312	114	366	*360
329	413	*119	448	511
215	325	100	*300	375

The total cost is $414 + $224 + $360 + $119 + $300 = $1,417.

Computer Case Study 15.1

The data file has translated the due dates to minutes. Thus, for the monthly clients, the due dates are $9 \times 60 = 540$; for the biweekly clients, the due dates are $12 \times 60 = 720$; and for the weekly clients, the due dates are $15 \times 60 = 900$. The table shows the results of running the program under several different processing rules.

Rule	Average Number of Jobs in System	Average Flow Time	Average Lateness
Due Date	20.81	929	194
SPT	12.03	537	135
Slack	22.52	1,005	248
Moore's	15.05	671	142
Critical Ratio	22.82	1,018	273

It can be seen from the table that the rules that seem most intuitive work least well. The two best rules seem to be shortest processing time (with its well-known advantages) and Moore's method (which also minimizes the number of late jobs).

16
Total Quality Management: The Deming Approach

TEACHING NOTES

This chapter serves two purposes. First, through its discussion of the philosophy of continuous improvement, it shows how all of the previous P/OM approaches can be helpful. Second, it leads in to the quality function described in the last chapter. To be more specific, the Deming approach—its philosophy and tools—is discussed.

The major difference from other chapters is that this chapter contains no quantitative material. Even though most of the techniques are quantitative, the philosophy is so much more important that the techniques are left for the next chapter. Here, each technique is described in terms of how it fits into the Deming program and why all the tools are needed together—not in terms of algorithms.

The key concept to get across when teaching this chapter is how the different parts of the Deming approach feed each other and rely on each other. As each part is taught, use examples to show how that part will be of little benefit if the other pieces are not in place. Students never fail to appreciate the beauty and logic of the Deming approach when it is presented in this way.

The first three sections of the chapter deal with philosophy and culture, problem-solving tools, and control charts. The links between these concepts need to be stressed, as TQM requires all three. The fourth section—on the design of experiments—can be discussed separately. (It can be discussed as an advanced portion of the statistical tools.)

Our discussion of the philosophy and culture of total quality management focuses on Deming's "fourteen points." Although the points are discussed and analyzed, little is provided on the behavioral actions required to achieve this culture. (Our students get this in other courses.)

Provide your students with exercises that will require them to use the problem-solving tools discussed here. The importance of these tools to the TQM process will become immediately obvious.

The statistical sections leave all the quantitative details for the next chapter. In fact, how to do design of experiments is beyond the scope of this text. Again, this chapter merely tells students what the tools are and why they are important.

There are no homework problems in this chapter. The Questions will lead to some good class discussion, as will some of the exercises contained in the Teaching Suggestions.

TEACHING SUGGESTIONS

Teaching Suggestion 16.1: TQM in Action.
The majority of our students work. We ask them if they have been exposed recently to any changes in attitudes toward quality at their workplaces. Surprisingly, many of them actually use the term *TQM*.

Teaching Suggestion 16.2: Price vs. Cost.
Price is the cost of purchasing. Cost adds to price the hidden cost of using the material in terms of scrap, rework, time, and so forth. Using cost instead of price, quality is a very important consideration in the purchasing decision.

Teaching Suggestion 16.3: Industrial Revolution.
The Industrial Revolution caused most of the barriers that separate workers from pride in their work. Some now tout TQM as the "third wave" of the Industrial Revolution. Of course, the "second wave" was scientific management.

Teaching Suggestion 16.4: Peanut Butter and Jelly.
Ask your students to create a process flow sheet detailing how to make a peanut-butter-and-jelly sandwich. Figure 16.1 can be used as a model.

Teaching Suggestion 16.5: Coffee.
We ask students to analyze why a cup of coffee may not taste right. We instruct them to use a diagram based on the 4 inputs (4 M's), as in Figure 16.5.

Teaching Suggestion 16.6: Weight Control.
Our students begin tracking their weights about four or five weeks prior to this lecture. We then have them develop and interpret the control chart, citing reasons (often humorous) for any abnormal variations found. Of course, we ignore the auto correlation. An alternative is to have them track mileage driven per day (weekdays only).

Teaching Suggestion 16.7: Full-Factorial Array.
Have students write out the full-factorial array for five factors with two levels each and/or three factors with three levels.

ANSWERS TO QUESTIONS

1. Since the Deming philosophy relates to all aspects of a business, many answers are possible. Here, we provide a few examples.

We have stressed that quantitative techniques are critical to managing operations; Deming emphasizes that statistical support must be provided for all decisions. Just-in-time is a continuous improvement program; so is the Deming philosophy. They work well together. Deming emphasizes statistical (quantitative) models to support all conclusions. We do the same in each chapter of this text. In waiting lines, reducing the variance without speeding up service led to shorter waiting times, a key Deming assumption.

2. "Finding problems" is certainly one of the three. The selection of the other two is not as clear-cut. Many would say "reducing fear" is important, but its purpose is really to find problems. The first point, on getting management to put forth common goals and stick with them—"constancy of purpose"—is our second choice. The third is "methods"—not giving goals without providing the methods to achieve them.

3. It would be reduced through the use of longer contracts with fewer sources.

4. It creates a purchasing system that is easier and less costly to operate, it reduces product variation, and it helps to create a loyal partnership with suppliers that aids in problem solving.

5. If students are fearful, they will not ask questions.

6. To identify the critical problems and separate them from the less important ones.

7. If there is fear, people will not bring up problems. If there is no pride in work, there is no motivation. If management does not lead by example, why should employees care?

8. normal and abnormal

9. Investigate its cause, take corrective action, and take preventive action. First, of course, stop the process if the abnormality is bad.

10. management

11. In the short term, no action is required. Still, the employee should look for ways to reduce the normal variation (improve the system) in the long term.

12. $\overline{X}$, R, p, np, and individuals are five types mentioned.

13. The chart helps us to visualize a normal curve. If the curve is truly representative of the process, all normal variation will be within the 3-sigma limits and a normal pattern will take shape over time. If this does not happen, there must be an abnormality.

14. to optimize parameter settings within a complex process

15. Taguchi describes a loss to society that results from any deviation from target. This loss grows proportionally to the square of the deviation. Where the loss equals the value of the product or service is the place to set the specification limit.

17
Quality Control

TEACHING NOTES

This chapter focuses on quality management, the role of the quality control function in the day-to-day operations of a company. Consequently, the chapter emphasizes inspection, acceptance sampling, and control charts—the three primary tools of quality control.

If Chapter 16 was not covered, the starting point for the discussion here should be the effects of the Industrial Revolution on quality—specifically, the changes in the relationship between the worker and quality. The Deming approach and quality circles should be discussed as ways to overcome the barriers that have been placed between the worker and the completed product.

You may choose to skip the section on inspection, particularly if you have no industrial experience. However, we feel that it is important to bring the material to the level of the decisions made on the factory floor, to discuss the quality characteristics of common consumer goods in terms of which goods to inspect and how to inspect them.

The acceptance sampling discussion provides the first quantitative material encountered in this chapter. Most P/OM texts only provide attributes plans. Given the current trend toward using variables inspection, we thought it important to include this topic, too—in a simplified manner that students should have no trouble using. You will notice that our treatment of OC curves is a little lighter than that found in most books. In practice, most quality control work with OC curves involves interpreting them to determine the suitability of their associated sampling plans; seldom do we calculate OC curves from scratch (and the procedures for doing so are better left for statistics classes anyway). We give published tables a little more emphasis here, due to their widespread use.

We discuss control charts—a hot topic right now—but the only control charts provided are the most commonly used charts. We recommend the use of 3 sigma limits as they really are meant to be used, but also provide examples that relate the topic closer to confidence intervals to enhance the students' quantitative analysis capabilities.

There are three Solved Problems in this chapter. The first is an attributes plan, the second is a variables plan, and the third is a variables control chart. The twenty-two Questions provide ample room for class discussion, especially the first three. The twenty homework problems follow the chapter outline. The first two require the development of attributes plans, while the next two analyze risks on the same topic. Problems 5 and 6 are variables plans. Problems 7 through 12 deal with OC curves and average outgoing quality. Note that Problem 8 can have many shapes, as long as the AQL and LTPD are at the appropriate heights. Problems 13 and 14 are simple applications of MIL-STD-105. The remaining Problems concern control charts. For Problem 20, point out that the mean of a 155 mm shell ideally should be 155 mm. The process for which the data is provided is running high.

The software for this module has several different submodules. It can be used to find attributes sampling plans, variables sampling plans, operating characteristic curves, probabilities of errors given a plan, p-charts, or mean and range control charts. The following Problems can be solved using the software: 1, 2, 5, 6, 17, and 20.

The first part of the computer case study for this chapter is a simple control chart case, for which AB:POM can be used. Additional readings are then given, for which students must compute (by hand) and interpret the means and the ranges.

TEACHING SUGGESTIONS

Teaching Suggestion 17.1: The Operations System.
Have your students draw the operations system (Figure

1.1), linking these four item types to the system components in the figure. Point out that the quality image established by the company is a by-product.

Teaching Suggestion 17.2: The Operations Chain. We draw two systems. The output from one is the input to another. We also list inspections at each. Ask why the second inspects raw materials after the first has inspected its finished product (duplication of inspection). Ask if trust would overcome the duplication. Ask if trust can help operational efficiency.

Teaching Suggestion 17.3: The Quality Plan and Audit. On the first day of class, we have our students develop a quality plan for the course, in which they outline their goals for the course with regard to specific areas such as homework, studying, tests, and attendance. At this point in the course, we have an audit of the plan.

Teaching Suggestion 17.4: 100-percent Inspection. To demonstrate that 100-percent inspection is not 100-percent accurate, we ask our students to count the number of times the letter *f* appears on this page of the book.

Teaching Suggestion 17.5: Consumer's Risk. Point out that what appears to be a consumer's problem in the short term (buying a bad product) will actually cost the producer in the long term. There may also be a short-term cost in terms of warranty obligations or returns.

Teaching Suggestion 17.6: Standard Deviation of Sample Mean. Although it really *shouldn't* be necessary to discuss it in this class, our students seem to have difficulty with the concept of two different standard deviations.

Teaching Suggestion 17.7: Interpretation. For this example, ask students what to do if the next three samples have the following numbers of defectives: 6, 1, and 6; 1, 6, and 6; 7, 4, and 2; 2, 4, and 7; or 1, 0, and 1. (You may wish to supply your own combinations for discussion.)

Teaching Suggestion 17.8: Weight Control. See Teaching Suggestion 16.6. Now the calculation of limits can be completed.

ANSWERS TO QUESTIONS

1. The definition of quality must be tailored to the individual environment in which any product or service will be used.

2. By the time inspection occurs, it is too late to achieve good quality, which means that we have to think about quality before the product is manufactured.

3. When the quality manager rejects production, the production manager often tries to get this decision overturned because it lowers his or her production rate.

4. raw materials: acceptance sampling; equipment: control charts; in-process goods: control charts; finished products: acceptance sampling

5. policy, planning, and administration; product design and design change control; control of purchased material; production quality control; user contact and field performance; corrective action; and employee selection, training, and motivation

6. Quality control includes the areas management can change. Quality assurance includes areas outside of management's authority.

7. Generally speaking, the following elements are quality control functions: policy, planning, and administration; production design and design change control; production quality control; corrective action; and employee selection, training, and motivation. Two elements—control of purchased material and user contact and field performance—are quality assurance functions.

8. The identical philosophy applies. Most defectives can be traced to a small percentage of the quality characteristics. Using an 80/20 rule, about 80 percent of the defectives are caused by 20 percent of the characteristics.

9. The quality audit is just as important to the long-term success of the company, but the financial audit is a more pressing short-term concern. Many companies are (wrongly) oriented toward the short term. Also, financial audits for publicly held companies are required by law.

10. The presence of a manager might inhibit the employees from speaking freely.

11. Anytime a machine is changed over from one operation to another, there is the possibility of a malfunction. Therefore, the first item produced must be inspected. Similarly, for many operations, a wearing-down process takes place. Therefore, it is fairly safe to assume that if the last item is good, the preceding items are also good.

12. In destructive testing, the items cannot be used after they are inspected. In nondestructive testing, the items can be used and/or sold after inspection. Examples of destructive testing include tensile and compressive tests to determine the strength of materials, life tests (for light bulbs, for example), or crash tests (for automobiles, for example). Nondestructive testing includes taking measurements of dimensions, checking for imperfections, and testing for performance (starting a lawn mower, for example).

13. Any characteristic that relates to the performance or desirability of the product for its intended use should be inspected. Some characteristics are not inspected because they do not affect performance or because their inspection might be redundant.

14. If poor material is used, the cost of the operation in which it was used is wasted. Performing the inspection prior to the operation saves this cost.

15. Attributes inspection determines whether or not an item is defective. Variables inspection provides a specific measure of how good or bad the item is.

16. a graph showing the probability of accepting a lot given a certain quality (percentage of defective)

17. type I error: rejecting a good lot; type II error: accepting a bad lot

18. The purpose of acceptance sampling is to determine a course of action (accept or reject) regarding the disposition of a lot without inspecting each item in a lot. Acceptance sampling does not estimate the quality of a lot.

19. The major advantage is that it allows for inspection of fewer items. In fact, use of this plan encourages quality improvement by holding out the reward of less inspection. There is a psychological advantage in that the producer is given a second chance to demonstrate the quality of the lot.

20. As the quality deteriorates, it becomes increasingly easy to identify bad lots.

21. Yes; "out of control" means that the process has changed. If we are doing something "too well," then the process has changed from the norm. We want to find out what we are doing "too well" so that we can do the same thing in the future and for other products.

22. Control charts are designed for specific sample sizes because the sample standard deviation or range is dependent on the sample size. The control charts presented here should not be used if the sample size varies.

SOLUTIONS TO PROBLEMS

1. $AQL = .01$; $LTPD = .03$; $\alpha = .05$; $\beta = .10$

Step 1. ratio = $LTPD/AQL = .03/.01 = 3$
Step 2. The nearest number in Table 17.2 is 2.96.
Step 3. This entry occurs in row $c = 7$.
Step 4. Holding α fixed, $n = 3.981/.01 = 398$.

The sampling plan is to inspect 398 items and accept the lot if 7 or fewer are defective. (*Note:* Playing it safe, you can round up and inspect 399 items. Of course, the difference between 398 and 399 is trivial. Furthermore, any manager would round either answer up to 400.)

2. $AQL = .02$; $LTPD = .05$; $\alpha = .05$; $\beta = .10$

Step 1. ratio = $LTPD/AQL = .05/.02 = 2.5$
Step 2. From Table 17.2, $c = 10$.
Step 3. Holding α fixed, $n = 6.169/.02 = 308$;
holding β fixed, $n = 15.41/.05 = 308$.

The sampling plan is given by $n = 308$, $c = 10$. Alternatively, $n = 309$ is the safe (rounded up) choice. Of course, $n = 300$ is what would likely be used in practice.

3. $n = 100$; $c = 7$; $\alpha = .05$; $\beta = .10$
Since c is 7, the number from the third column is 3.981. Therefore, $AQL = 3.981/100 = .04$. Since c is 7, the number from the last column is 11.77. Therefore, $LTPD = 11.77/100 \approx .12$. Also, $LTPD/AQL \approx .12/.04 = 3$, as in the second column.

4. $n = 100$; $c = 6$; $\alpha = .05$; $\beta = .10$
As in Problem 3,

$$AQL = 3.285/100 \approx 3.3\%$$

and

$$LTPD = 10.53/100 = 10.5\%.$$

$LTPD/AQL = 10.5/3.3 \approx 3.2$, as in column 2. (Alternatively, since $LTPD/AQL = 3.21$, then $LTPD = 3.21 \times \$3.3 = 10.6\%.$) Both the AQL and the LTPD have been reduced. (*Note:* This is the opportunity to declare the AQL and LTPD as fixed—at .04 and .12, respectively, from the previous problem—and state that α increases but β decreases.)

5. $\sigma = 200$; $\mu_1 = 1,200$; $\mu_0 = 1,300$; $\alpha = .025$; $\beta = .05$

$$n = \frac{(z_{1-\alpha} - z_\beta)^2 \sigma^2}{(\mu_1 - \mu_0)^2}$$

$$= \frac{(z_{.975} - z_{.05})^2 \times (200)^2}{(1,200 - 1,300)^2}$$

$$= \frac{[1.96 - (-1.64)]^2 \times (200)^2}{(100)^2}$$

$$= 51.84, \text{ or } 52 \text{ bulbs}$$

$$c = \mu_0 - z_{1-\alpha}\sigma/\sqrt{n}$$

$$= 1,300 - 1.96(200)/\sqrt{52}$$

$$= 1,300 - 392/7.21$$

$$= 1,300 - 54.36$$

$$= 1,246 \text{ hr.}$$

6. $c = \mu_0 - z_{1-\alpha}(\sigma/\sqrt{n})$

$$= 1,300 - 392/10$$

$$= 1,300 - 39$$

$$= 1,261$$

The critical value has gone up (closer to the goal of 1,300). (*Note:* α and β change. They are better because the sample size has increased.)

7. $\alpha = 1 - .9 = .1$; $\beta = .2$

8.

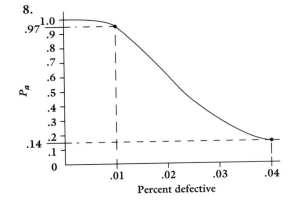

Percent defective

9. the top curve, B

10. $AOQ = pP_a(p)$

$$= .03(.95) = .0285$$

On average, 2.85 percent of the bolts that are sold will be defective if 3 percent of the bolts that are manufactured are defective.

$$AOQ = .06(.45) = .0270$$

On average, a smaller percentage of defective bolts will be sold (2.7 percent) if a larger percentage of defectives (6 percent vs. 3 percent) are manufactured. Of course, more lots are rejected prior to sale because the lots contain more defectives.

11. The probabilities below are subject to interpretation of the curve.

$$p = 0, \quad AOQ = 0$$
$$p = .01, AOQ = (.01)(.99) = .0099$$
$$p = .02, AOQ = (.02)(.98) = .0196$$
$$p = .03, AOQ = (.03)(.95) = .0285$$
$$p = .04, AOQ = (.04)(.85) = .0340$$
$$p = .05, AOQ = (.05)(.70) = .0350*$$
$$p = .06, AOQ = (.06)(.45) = .0270$$
$$p = .07, AOQ = (.07)(.20) = .0140$$
$$p = .08, AOQ = (.08)(.10) = .008$$
$$*AOQL = 3.5\% \text{ at } p = .05$$

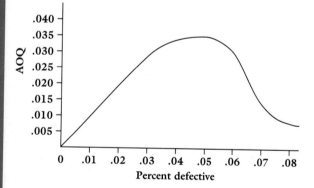

12.

Percent Defective	$P_a(p)$	$\dfrac{pP_a(p) \times (N - n)}{N}$
0	1.00	0
.01	.98	.0085
.02	.95	.0165
.03	.90	.0235
.04	.75	.0261
.05	.40	.0174
.06	.15	.0078
.07	.10	.0061

The AOQL occurs somewhere between .03 and .05 and has a value near 2.6 percent.

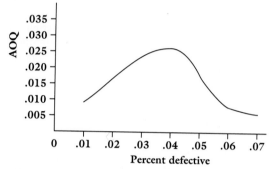

13. For $N = 12,000$ and general inspection level II, Table 17.4 has a code letter of M. Table 17.5 yields $n = 315$, $c = 7$.

14. For $N = 12,000$ and general inspection level III, the code letter in Table 17.4 is N. From Table 17.5, $n = 500$, $c = 10$.

15. $CL = .02$

$$\sigma_p = \sqrt{\frac{.02(.98)}{25}} = \sqrt{.000784} = .028$$

$$UCL = CL + 3\sigma_p = .02 + 3(.028)$$
$$= .02 + .084 = .104$$

$$LCL = CL - 3\sigma_p = .02 - 3(.028) = .02 - .084$$
$$= -.064 = 0$$

16. $p = \dfrac{221}{17,000} = .013$

$$\sigma_p = \sqrt{\frac{.013(.987)}{36}} = \sqrt{.0003564} = .019$$

$$CL = .013$$

$$UCL = CL + 1.96\sigma_p = .013 + 1.96(.019)$$
$$= .013 + .037 = .05$$

$$LCL = CL - 1.96\sigma_p = .013 - 1.96(.019)$$
$$= .013 - .037 = -.024 = 0$$

17. (a) The total number defective is 57.

$$p = 57/1,000 = .057$$

$$\sigma_p = \sqrt{\frac{(.057)(.943)}{100}} = \sqrt{.0005375} = .023$$

$$CL = .057$$

$$UCL = .057 + 3(.023) = .057 + .069 = .126$$

$$LCL = .057 - 3(.023) = .057 - .069$$
$$= -.012 = 0$$

(b) The process is out of control on the third day.

18. $\sigma = \sigma_x/\sqrt{n} = .1/\sqrt{36} = .1/6 = .0167$

$CL = 14$ oz.

$UCL = CL + 3\sigma = 14 + 3(.0167) = 14 + .05$
$= 14.05$ oz.

$LCL = CL - 3\sigma = 14 - 3(.0167) = 14 - .05$
$= 13.95$ oz.

19. To construct the charts, we use Table 17.7, with $n = 5$.

$\overline{X}$-chart for width:

$CL = 36$ in.

$UCL = \overline{\overline{X}} + A_2\overline{R} = 36 + (.577 \times 2.4) = 37.4$ in.

$LCL = \overline{\overline{X}} - A_2\overline{R} = 36 - (.577 \times 2.4) = 34.6$ in.

R-chart for width:

$CL = 2.4$ in.

$UCL = D_4\overline{R} = 2.115(2.4) = 5.076$ in.

$LCL = D_3\overline{R} = 0$

$\overline{X}$-chart for height:

$CL = 60$ in.

$UCL = 60 + (.577 \times 6) = 63.5$ in.

$LCL = 60 - (.577 \times 6) = 56.5$ in.

R-chart for height:

$CL = 6$ in.

$UCL = 2.115(6) = 12.7$ in.

$LCL = 0$

20. $\overline{\overline{X}} = \dfrac{156.9 + 153.2 + 153.6 + 155.5 + 156.6}{5}$

$= 155.16$

$\overline{R} = \dfrac{4.2 + 4.6 + 4.1 + 5.0 + 4.5}{5} = 4.48$ mm

$\overline{X}$-chart:

$CL = \overline{\overline{X}} = 155.16$ mm

$UCL = \overline{\overline{X}} + A_2\overline{R} = 155.16 + (.308 \times 4.48)$
$= 156.54$ mm

$LCL = \overline{\overline{X}} - A_2\overline{R} = 155.16 - (.308 \times 4.48)$
$= 153.78$ mm

R-chart:

$CL = 4.48$ mm

$UCL = D_4\overline{R} = 1.777(4.48) = 7.96$ mm

$LCL = D_3\overline{R} = .223(4.48) = 1.00$ mm

(*Note:* The mean of a process for 155 mm shells should be 155 mm, not 155.16 mm. In addition to the control chart, an investigation should take place to find the discrepancy and correct it.)

Computer Case Study 17.1

This is a very straightforward case. Running the data file will generate the $\overline{X}$-chart as

UCL: 61.13
CL: 49.78
LCL: 38.42

and the range chart as

UCL: 41.62
CL: 19.68
LCL: 0.00.

Next, students need to take the means and ranges for the five additional samples.

Date	Mean	Range
April 6	52	14
7	57	25
8	47	16
9	51.4	22
10	51.6	21

The means and the ranges are all well within the control limits for this week. There is, however, a noticeable change in the original date at time 13, where the range suddenly dropped. It then goes back up at time 16. The data were generated by students in class and changes in the process were made at the aforementioned times. The control chart identifies that these changes took place.

Appendix A
Capital Investment

TEACHING NOTES

Appendix A is essentially a supplementary chapter in which we explain the financial decision-making techniques that are applicable to operations management. In particular, we would like students to be able to deal with buy/lease questions, or questions on the type of equipment to purchase when the equipment will last for a long period of time. The topics covered here are financial/accounting topics, but the emphasis is entirely on operations management decisions.

There are three Solved Problems in Appendix A. The first asks students to find an internal rate of return. The second is a buy/lease problem. The third is a buy/lease problem that is not an annuity. Some of the Problems deal with compound interest and present value simple calculations; some demonstrate the relationship between *IRR, NPV,* and loan payments; and some demonstrate the broad picture and the application of the present value techniques and measures to operations management. There is no software module for this chapter.

TEACHING SUGGESTIONS

Teaching Suggestion A.1: Reality: Student Perceptions. Offer students a choice between receiving $1 today or $20 in one year. Most students will opt for the $1 today. Apparently, students are more concerned with risk than with present value.

Teaching Suggestion A.2: Effects of Compounding. Have students look at Table A.2 to see the effects of compounding. For example, 2% per month for 12 months (1.268) can be compared with 24% per year for 1 year (1.24).

Teaching Suggestion A.3: Closed-Form Annuity Formula.
We have not presented the present value of an annuity in closed form because we rely so heavily on tables. However, the formula is quite simple:

$$PVA = \frac{1 - [1/(1 + i)]^n}{i}.$$

Teaching Suggestion A.4: Annuity Timing.
The annuity tables are for end-of-year computations. In many cases, these tables will be an approximation of reality. For example, in reality, the maintenance costs of Example A.4 would be paid monthly.

Teaching Suggestion A.5: Different Approaches.
For the present value analysis, different students have dif-

ferent intuitive approaches to these problems. Some like to compute taxes; others like to compute tax savings. Students should be encouraged to approach these problems in the way that makes them feel most comfortable. All reasonable approaches will yield the same answer.

ANSWERS TO QUESTIONS

1. a stream of revenues and/or expenditures over time

2. The value of money changes over time, so it is imperative that we know the cash flow rather than just the total.

3. Methods suitable for investments with different life-times are equivalent annual cost and internal rate of return.

4. Depreciation affects taxes, which *are* an outflow of cash.

5. The internal rate of return is the profit expressed as an annual interest rate.

6. equivalent annual cost method and loan payment annualize a total (net present value) at a given interest rate; internal rate of return finds an interest rate

7. Payback is easier to compute but does not consider that the value of money changes over time.

8. Equivalent annual cost makes an equal series of payments out of an unequal series of payments.

9. Straight-line depreciation has equal amounts each year, while the other two methods accelerate the depreciation. The acceleration yields a higher net present value profit, since the higher depreciation leads to lower taxes.

10. inflation and risk

11. In general, leasing is more appropriate for equipment with relatively short lifetimes. Buying is more appropriate for high-volume items. Examples of industries will vary.

SOLUTIONS TO PROBLEMS

1. (a) $FV = PV \times CVSP(i, n)$
   $= 15{,}000 \times CVSP(15\%,4)$ (Table A.2)
   $= 15{,}000 \times 1.749$
   $= 26{,}235$

   (b) $FV = PV \times CVSP(i, n)$
   $= 15{,}000 \times CVSP(15\%,8)$ (Table A.2)
   $= 15{,}000 \times 3.059$
   $= 45{,}885$

2. (a) Find n such that $CVSP(15\%,n) = 2$. From Table A.2, $n = 5$. (At $n = 5$, $CVSP(15\%,5) = 2.011$, which is slightly greater than 2.)

(b) Find n such that $CVSP(10\%,n) = 2$. From Table A.2, $7 < n < 8$ (7 is closer).

$$CVSP(10\%,7) = 1.949$$

(*Note:* A useful rule of thumb is the "rule of 72," which says that money doubles in $n = 72/i$ periods, where i is the interest rate in each period. In the problem, this yields $n = 72/15 = 4.8$ for part (a) and $n = 72/10 = 7.2$ for part (b).

3. $FV = PV \times CVSP(i,n)$

$100,000 = PV \times CVSP(18\%,3)$ (Table A.2)

$100,000 = PV \times 1.643$

$$\frac{100,000}{1.643} = PV$$

$$PV = 60,864$$

4. $FVA = PV \times CVA(i,n)$

$\quad = 2,200 \times CVA(12\%,4)^*$

$\quad = 2,200 \times 4.770$

$\quad = 10,494$

$^*CVA(i,n) = \Sigma CVSP(i,j), j = 0$ to $n - 1$

5. The present value if payments are made at the *end* of the year is

$PVA = A \times PVA(i,n)$

$\quad = 17,000 \times PVA(10\%, 10)$ (Table A.4)

$\quad = 17,000 \times 6.145$

$\quad = 104,465.$

Since payments are made at the *beginning* of the year, we must compound by one year's interest.

$PVAD = PVA \times (1 + i)$

$\quad = 104,465 \times 1.10$

$\quad = 114,912$

6. The second alternative is an annuity due.

$PVAD = PVA \times (1 + i)$

$\quad = A \times PVA(i,n) \times (1 + i),$

where $PVA(i,n)$ is from Table A.4

(a) at 6%: $PVAD = \$100,000 \times 12.783 \times 1.06$
$\quad = \$1,354,998$

(b) at 8%: $PVAD = \$100,000 \times 10.675 \times 1.08$
$\quad = \$1,152,900$

(c) at 10%: $PVAD = \$100,000 \times 9.077 \times 1.10$
$\quad = \$998,470$

Therefore, the decision clearly depends on the anticipated interest rates over the next 25 years.

7. The savings represent an annuity. Therefore, we are looking for i such that

$$11,800 = 5,000 \times PVA(i,n)$$

$$11,800 = 5,000 \times PVA(i,3)$$

$$11,800/5,000 = PVA(i,3)$$

$$PVA(i,3) = 2.361$$

From Table A.4, we know that $i = 13\%$.

$$PVA(i,3) = 2.361$$

8. The savings are *not* an annuity. Therefore, we will use a trial-and-error process. We begin with $i = 13\%$, since the solution to Problem 7 has nearly identical numbers (which have an identical sum).

Year	Savings	$PVSP(13\%,n)$ (Table A.3)	Present Value of Savings
1	$7,000	.885	$ 6,195
2	5,000	.783	3,915
3	3,000	.693	2,079
		Subtotal	$12,189
		Cost	− 11,800
		Total (NPV)	$ 389

The net present value is positive, which means that the IRR is greater than 13 percent. Let us try 18 percent.

Year	Savings	$PVSP(18\%,n)$	Present Value of Savings
1	$7,000	.847	$ 5,929
2	5,000	.718	3,590
3	3,000	.609	1,827
		Subtotal	$11,346
		Cost	− 11,800
		Total (NPV)	$ −454

The net present value is negative, which means that the IRR is less than 18 percent. Let us try 15 percent.

Year	Savings	$PVSP(15\%,n)$	Present Value of Savings
1	$7,000	.870	$ 6,090
2	5,000	.756	3,780
3	3,000	.658	1,974
		Subtotal	$11,844
		Cost	− 11,800
		Total (NPV)	$ 44

The IRR is slightly above 15 percent. (15.2 percent)

9. (a) payment $= \dfrac{\text{loan}}{PVA(i,n)}$

$= \dfrac{\$8,658}{PVA(8\%,5)}$ (Table A.4)

$= \dfrac{\$8,658}{3.993}$

$= \$2,168/\text{yr.}$

(b) total payment $= \$2,168 \times 5$

$= \$10,840$

$\underline{-\ 8,658}$ (loan)

$\$\ 2,182$ (interest)

10. payment $= \dfrac{\text{loan}}{PVA(i,n)}$

$= \dfrac{\$20,000}{PVA(15\%,10)}$ (Table A.4)

$= \dfrac{\$20,000}{5.019}$

$= \$3,985$

11. Since the return is an annuity, we want to find i such that

$\$3,985 \times PVA(i,10) = \$20,000$

$= \dfrac{\$20,000}{\$\ 3,985}$

$= 5.019$

Therefore, from Table A.4, $i = 15\%$. (See Problem 10.)

12. $EAC = \dfrac{NPV}{PVA(i,n)}$

$= \dfrac{\$20,000}{PVA(15\%,10)}$ (Table A.4)

$= \dfrac{\$20,000}{5.019}$

$= \$3,985/\text{yr.}$

(See Problems 10 and 11.)

13. total depreciation $=$ cost $-$ salvage

$= \$10,000 - \$2,000$

$= \$8,000$

(a) straight-line depreciation $= \dfrac{\text{total depreciation}}{n}$

$= \dfrac{\$8,000}{4\ \text{yr.}}$

$= \$2,000/\text{yr.}$

(b) sum of years' digit:

$S = 1 + 2 + 3 + 4 = 10$

(1) Year	(2) Fraction %	(3) Depreciation	(4) Annual Depreciation [(2) × (3)]
1	4/10	$8,000	$3,200
2	3/10	8,000	2,400
3	2/10	8,000	1,600
4	1/10	8,000	800
	10/10 = 1		$8,000

(c) declining balance method at 20%:

Year	Book Value, Beginning of Year	Depreciation (20% × Book Value)	Book Value, End of Year
1	$10,000	$2,000	$8,000
2	8,000	1,600	6,400
3	6,400	1,280	5,120
4	5,120	3,120*	2,000

*The depreciation is taken to force the book value at the end to equal the salvage value.

14. (a) straight-line depreciation $= \dfrac{\text{total depreciation}}{n}$

$= \dfrac{\$12,000 - \$3,000}{6}$

$= \dfrac{\$9,000}{6}$

$= \$1,500$

The tax savings in each year is 35 percent of $1,500, or $525. The total tax savings is $525 × 6 yr. = $3,150.

(b) $S = 1 + 2 + 3 + 4 + 5 + 6 = 21$ (See the table on page IS-133.)

(c) See the table on page IS-133.

15. (a) payback:

investment A $= 2.5$ yr.

investment B $= 1.4$ yr.

investment C $= 15,000/6,000 = 2.5$ yr.

Investment B has the fastest payback.

(b) See the table on page IS-133 for net present value.

16. (a) $EAC = \dfrac{NPV}{PVA(i,n)}$

$= \dfrac{NPV}{PVA(9\%,5)}$

$= \dfrac{NPV}{3.890}$ (Table A.4)

investment A $= EAC = \$6,081/3.89 = \$1,563$

investment B $= EAC = \$7,765/3.89 = \$1,996$

investment C $= EAC = \$8,328/3.89 = \$2,141$

(b) Try 30 percent for investment A.

Year	Income	PVSP(30%,n)	Present Value of Income
1	$4,000	.769	$ 3,076
2	3,000	.592	1,776
3	6,000	.455	2,730
4	1,000	.350	350
5	7,000	.269	1,883
		Subtotal	$ 9,815
		Cost	− 10,000
		Total (NPV)	$ −185

The return is slightly less than 30 percent (29 percent). For investment B, try 30 percent.

Year	Income	PVSP(30%,n)	Present Value of Income
1	$10,000	.769	$ 7,690
2	5,000	.592	2,960
3	3,000	.455	1,365
4	3,000	.350	1,050
5	3,000	.269	807
		Subtotal	$13,872
		Cost	− 12,000
		Total (NPV)	$ 1,872

The NPV is positive, hence the return is greater than 30 percent. The return on investment C is an annuity.

Table for Problem 14(b).

(1) Year	(2) Fraction	(3) Total Depreciation	(4) Annual Depreciation [(2) × (3)]	(5) Tax Savings
1	6/21	$9,000	$2,571.43	$ 900
2	5/21	9,000	2,142.86	750
3	4/21	9,000	1,714.29	600
4	3/21	9,000	1,285.71	450
5	2/21	9,000	857.14	300
6	1/21	9,000	428.57	150
	21/21 = 1		$9,000.00	$3,150

Table for Problem 14(c).

(1) Year	(2) Book Value	(3) Depreciation @ 15 Percent	(4) New Book Value [(2) − (3)]	(5) Tax Benefit
1	$12,000.00	$1,800.00	$10,200.00	$ 630.00
2	10,200.00	1,530.00	8,670.00	535.50
3	8,670.00	1,300.50	7,369.50	455.18
4	7,369.50	1,105.43	6,264.08	386.90
5	6,264.08	939.61	5,324.46	328.86
6	5,324.46	2,324.46*	3,000.00	813.56
		$9,000.00		$3,150.00

*taken to have an ending book value of $3,000

Table for Problem 15(b).

Year	PVSP(9%,n)	A	Present Value of A	B	Present Value of B	C	Present Value of C
1	.917	$4,000	$ 3,668	$10,000	$ 9,170	$6,000	$ 5,502
2	.842	3,000	2,526	5,000	4,210	6,000	5,052
3	.772	6,000	4,632	3,000	2,316	6,000	4,632
4	.708	1,000	708	3,000	2,124	6,000	4,248
5	.650	7,000	4,550	3,000	1,950	6,000	3,900
			$16,084		$19,770		$23,334
			− 10,000		− 12,000		− 15,000
			$ 6,084		$ 7,770		$ 8,334

A 30-percent return would yield an annual return given by

return $= 15,000/PVA(30\%,5)$

$\qquad = 15,000/2.436$

$\qquad = 6,157.$

Hence, the return of $6,000 is slightly less than 30 percent.

17. (a) loan payment $= \dfrac{\text{loan}}{PVA(i,n)}$

$\qquad = \dfrac{\$400,000}{PVA(16\%,5)}$

$\qquad = \dfrac{\$400,000}{3.274}$

$\qquad = \$122,175$

total amount of interest $=$ total of loan payments $-$

$\qquad\qquad\qquad\qquad$ principle

$\qquad = (5 \times \$122,175) - \$400,000$

$\qquad = \$610,875 - \$400,000$

$\qquad = \$210,875$

(b) total depreciation $=$ cost $-$ salvage

$\qquad = \$400,000 - \$100,000$

$\qquad = \$300,000$

$\qquad S = 1 + 2 + 3 + 4 + 5 = 15$

Year	Fraction	Total Depreciation	Annual Depreciation
1	5/15	$300,000	$100,000
2	4/15	300,000	80,000
3	3/15	300,000	60,000
4	2/15	300,000	40,000
5	1/15	300,000	20,000
			$300,000

(c) See the table below.

18. maintenance cost and insurance

$\qquad = \$600 \times PVA(14\%, 8)$

$\qquad = \$600 \times 4.639$

$\qquad = \$2,783$

salvage $= \$1,000 \times PVSP(14\%, 8)$

$\qquad = \$1,000 \times .351$

$\qquad = -\$351$

$NPV =$ purchase cost $+$

$\qquad$ maintenance cost and insurance $-$ salvage

$\qquad = \$11,000 + \$2,783 - \$351$

$\qquad = \$13,432$

Table for Problem 17(c).

(1) Year	(2) Beginning Balance	(3) Interest $[(2) \times .16]$	(4) Loan Payment	(5) Ending Balance $[(2) + (3) - (4)]$	(6) Depreciation
1	$400,000	$ 64,000	$122,175	$341,825	$100,000
2	341,825	54,692	122,175	274,342	80,000
3	274,342	43,895	122,175	196,062	60,000
4	196,062	31,370	122,175	105,257	40,000
5	105,257	16,841	122,175	$-77^\star$	20,000
		$210,798	$610,875		$300,000

(7) Year	(8) Total Deductions $[(3) + (6)]$	(9) Tax Benefit $[.3 \times (8)]$	(10) Annual Cost $[(4) - (9)]$	(11) PVSP @ 16% (Table A.3)	(12) Present Value Cost $[(10) \times (11)]$
1	$164,000	$ 49,200	$ 72,975	.862	$ 62,904
2	134,692	40,408	81,767	.743	60,753
3	103,895	31,168	91,007	.641	58,335
4	71,370	21,411	100,764	.552	55,622
5	36,841	11,052	111,123	.476	52,894
	$510,798	$153,239	$457,636	3.274	$290,508
				Salvage	$-$ 100,000
				Total	$190,508

$\star$This should be 0. The -77 is round-off error.

(a) end of year:

$$\text{payment} = \frac{NPV}{PVA(14\%,8)} = \frac{\$13,432}{4.639} = \$2,895/\text{yr.}$$

(b) At the beginning of the year, *less* needs to be paid (since it is worth more money). Therefore, we discount by one year.

$$\text{payment} = \$2,895 \times PVSP(14\%,1)$$
$$= \$2,895 \times 1/1.14$$
$$= \$2,539$$

19. (a) straight-line depreciation:

$$\text{tax benefit} = (\text{depreciation} +$$
$$\text{maintenance and insurance}) \times \text{tax rate}$$
$$= [(\$10,000/8) + \$600] \times .25$$
$$= (\$1,250 + \$600) \times .25$$
$$= \$1,850 \times .25$$
$$= \$462.50$$

Purchase cost		$11,000.00
Maintenance and insurance [$600 × $PVA(14\%,8)$]	+	2,783.00
Tax benefit [$462.5 × PVA(14\%,8)$]	−	2,145.54
Subtotal		$11,637.46
Salvage [$1,000 × PVSP(14\%,8)$]	−	351.00
		$11,286.46

(b) For the sum of years' digits method, see the table below.

Table for Problem 19(b).

(1) Year	(2) Fraction	(3) Total Depreciation	(4) Annual Depreciation [(2) × (3)]	(5) Insurance Cost	(6) Deductions	(7) Tax Benefit [.25 × (6)]
1	8/36	$10,000	$ 2,222.22	$600	$ 2,822.22	$ 705.56
2	7/36	10,000	1,944.44	600	2,544.44	636.11
3	6/36	10,000	1,666.67	600	2,266.67	566.67
4	5/36	10,000	1,388.89	600	1,988.89	497.22
5	4/36	10,000	1,111.11	600	1,711.11	427.78
6	3/36	10,000	833.33	600	1,433.33	358.33
7	2/36	10,000	555.56	600	1,155.56	288.89
8	1/36	10,000	277.78	600	877.78	219.44
36	36/36		$10,000.00		$14,800.00	$3,700.00

(8) Year	(9) Total Cost [$600 − (7)]	(10) PVSP @ 14% (Table A.2)	(11) Present Value of Cost [(9) × (10)]
1	$ − 105.56	.877	$ − 92.58
2	− 36.11	.769	− 27.79
3	33.33	.675	22.50
4	102.78	.592	60.85
5	172.22	.519	89.45
6	241.67	.456	110.10
7	311.11	.400	124.44
8	380.56	.351	133.41
		4.639	$ 420.38
		Salvage −	351.00
			$ 69.38
		Initial cost +	11,000.00
		Total	$11,069.38

20.

Year	Income	Depreciation	Income	Tax	Net Income After Taxes	PVSP	Present Value of Income
1	$100,000	$100,000	$ 0	$ 0	$100,000	.893	$ 89,286
2	150,000	100,000	50,000	20,000	130,000	.797	103,635
3	300,000	100,000	200,000	80,000	220,000	.712	156,592
4	350,000	100,000	250,000	100,000	250,000	.636	158,880
5	400,000	100,000	300,000	120,000	280,000	.567	158,880
							$667,272
						Initial cost	− 500,000
						Total	$167,272

21. From Problem 20, since the *NPV* is positive, we know that *IRR* > 12%. We simply need to use a trial and error process with the numbers from the "Net Income After Taxes" column. Let us try 20 percent.

Year	Net Income After Taxes	PVSP @ 20%	Present Value of Revenue
1	$100,000	.833	$ 83,333.33
2	130,000	.694	90,227.78
3	220,000	.579	127,314.81
4	250,000	.482	120,563.27
5	280,000	.402	112,525.72
	$980,000	2.991	$534,014.92
		Initial cost	− 500,000.00
		Total	$ 34,014.92

The *NPV* is still positive. Let us try 25 percent.

Year	Net Income After Taxes	PVSP @ 25%	Present Value of Revenue
1	$100,000	.800	$ 80,000.00
2	130,000	.640	83,200.00
3	220,000	.492	108,307.69
4	250,000	.379	94,674.56
5	280,000	.291	81,565.77
	$980,000	2.602	$447,748.02
		Initial cost	− 500,000.00
		Total	− $ 52,251.98

The *NPV* is negative, so 25 percent is too high. Let us try 23 percent.

Year	Net Income After Taxes	PVSP @ 23%	Present Value of Revenue
1	$100,000	.833	$ 81,967.21
2	130,000	.672	87,342.11
3	220,000	.551	121,155.52
4	250,000	.451	112,849.77
5	280,000	.370	103,599.79
	$980,000	2.864	$506,914.40
		Initial cost	− 500,000.00
			$ 6,914.40

This is very close. The *IRR* is very near 23 percent.

22. payment = $1,000/PVA(16\%,4)$

$$= \$1,000/2.798$$

$$= \$357.40$$

total depreciation = $3,500 - $1,500 = $2,000

(1) Year	(2) Balance	(3) Payment	(4) Interest [.16 × (2)]	(5) Fraction	(6) Total Depreciation	(7) Annual Depreciation [(5) × (6)]	(8) Operating Expenses
1	$1,000.00	$ 357.40	$160.00	4/10	$2,000	$800	$80
2	802.60	357.40	128.42	3/10	2,000	600	80
3	573.62	357.40	91.78	2/10	2,000	400	80
4	307.99	357.40	49.28	1/10	2,000	200	80
		$1,429.60					

(9) Year	(10) Income	(11) Deductions [(4) + (7) + (8)]	(12) Taxable Income [(10) − (11)]	(13) Tax [.3 × (12)]	(14) Net Income After Taxes [(10) − (13)]	(15) PVSP(20%)	(16) Present Value of Income After Taxes [(14) × (15)]
1	$1,700	$1,040.00	$ 660.00	$198.00	$1,502.00	.833	$1,251.67
2	1,700	808.42	891.58	267.48	1,432.52	.694	994.81
3	1,700	571.78	1,128.22	338.47	1,361.53	.579	787.92
4	1,700	329.28	1,370.72	411.22	1,288.78	.482	621.52
						Subtotal	$3,655.92
						Initial investment	− 2,500.00
						Total (NVP)	$1,155.92

Since the *NPV* is positive, the *IRR* is greater than 20 percent.

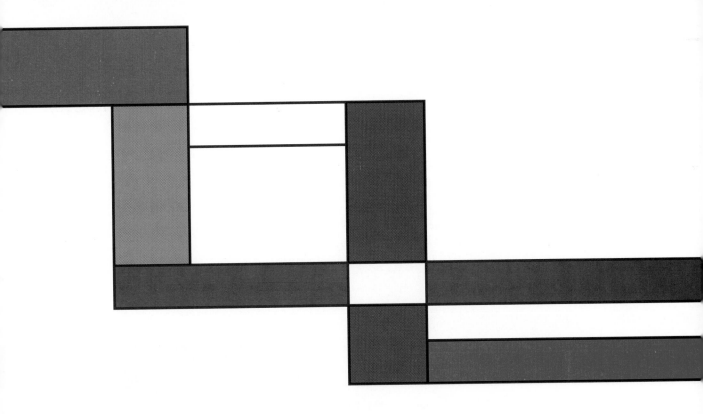

PRODUCTION AND OPERATIONS MANAGEMENT

Second Edition

HOWARD J. WEISS ▪ MARK E. GERSHON

Temple University

ALLYN AND BACON   BOSTON ▪ LONDON ▪ TORONTO ▪ SYDNEY ▪ TOKYO ▪ SINGAPORE

Executive Editor: Rich Wohl
Senior Editorial Assistant: Cheryl Ten Eick
Cover Administrator: Linda Dickinson
Composition and Manufacturing Buyer: Louise Richardson
Editorial-Production Service: Proof Positive/Farrowlyne Associates, Inc.
Cover Designer: Design Ad Cetera

Copyright © 1993, 1989 by Allyn and Bacon
A division of Simon & Schuster, Inc.
160 Gould Street
Needham Heights, Massachusetts 02194

Library of Congress Cataloging-in-Publication Data

Weiss, Howard J.
    Production and operations management / Howard J. Weiss, Mark E.
  Gershon. — 2nd ed.
      p.   cm.
    Includes bibliographical references and index.
    ISBN 0-205-13360-6
      1. Production management.   I. Gershon, Mark E., 1953– .
II. Title.
TS155.W445   1991 <MRCRR>   91-38412
658.5—dc20   CIP

Printed in the United States of America.

10 9 8 7 6 5 4 3 2 1   96 95 94 93 92 91

TO

Lucia
Martin and Rosalie Gershonowitz

QUANTITATIVE METHODS AND APPLIED STATISTICS SERIES

ALLYN AND BACON

Barry Render, Consulting Editor
Roy E. Crummer Graduate School of Business, Rollins College

CONTENTS

v

PREFACE

Over the past three decades, increasing attention has been paid to the operations of production and service systems. Today, it is widely recognized that successfully running an organization requires some exposure to operations. The emphasis within management is shifting from staff areas toward the fundamental business activities—that is, operations. Consequently, all students need to be familiar with production and operations management (P/OM), and, not surprisingly, an increasing number of students choose to concentrate in this area.

This is an introductory text on production and operations management, and the emphasis is on *introductory*. The majority of students who are enrolled in a P/OM course are not P/OM majors. This book was written with these students in mind. As was the case in the first edition, our goal is to acquaint general business students with the concepts, models, techniques, and terminology that are now standard fare for those responsible for the operations of manufacturing and service systems. Again, the book is designed for students who are *not* operations management majors. We have written it to enable these students to understand the general problems encountered by their colleagues in operations and the approaches that are taken toward solving these problems. As we explain in the new chapter "World-Class Manufacturing" (Chapter 2), it has never been more important for managers of other functions to feel comfortable interacting with the person responsible for operations. In fact, the competitiveness of many American companies, especially with respect to their counterparts in Japan and Germany, depends in large part on an understanding of and appreciation for the operations management function by *all* of the company's managers.

OVERVIEW OF THE SECOND EDITION

In today's globally competitive environment, quality and productivity are just as important as pricing and advertising, which means that operations is a major competitive weapon. For this reason, we have added to this edition a new chapter on world-class operations. This chapter is intended to demonstrate to nonmajors the importance of P/OM.

Recent innovations make P/OM a dynamic and exciting field. Some of these innovations, such as just-in-time and total quality management, are philosophical in nature. Because of the widespread acceptance of these philosophies over the last few years, we have greatly increased our coverage of these topics in this edition. We have added a new chapter on total quality management, increased our coverage of just-in-time with respect to materials requirements planning, and integrated just-in-time with other topics throughout the book.

The implementation of the abovementioned innovations and others has resulted in the development of new quantitative and computer methods for improving operations. The development of computers over the past thirty years and the accompanying development of the quantitative methods allows us to routinely solve many complex operations that were previously difficult or impossible to approach—all with standard software packages. With the advent of microcomputers, these problems are being controlled at businesses and institutions of every size. The software that accompanied the first edition of this book has been enhanced, expanded, and renamed AB:POM. Due to the growing importance of software—in general and in the field—we have included more explanations of software usage at the end of the chapters. Sample screens displayed as part of the "Using AB:POM to Solve This Problem" sections following selected Solved Problems should prove handy, especially when sitting at the computer.

LEARNING FEATURES OF THIS BOOK

While retaining from the previous edition several outstanding features that generate interest and make learning the material easier, this edition also incorporates some exciting new features.

- Each chapter begins with a set of objectives that identify the broad concepts that are emphasized in the chapter.
- Each chapter begins descriptively and has a management emphasis. This descriptive, managerial approach provides intuitive motivation for the quantitative techniques that follow.
- The necessity and logic of applying mathematical tools are explained in an intuitive, commonsense manner. Wherever possible, we have presented logic and intuition rather than a mathematical formula.
- For each technique introduced, we present one or more examples illustrating its application. The goal is to build a full appreciation for the various quantitative methods and recognition of the types of problems that can be solved with these methods. Of course, the many detailed examples in each chapter also serve as an aid for mastering the concepts presented.
- To make apparent the integrative nature of production/operations management, many concepts and examples are carried over from chapter to chapter. The way we have structured the text reveals the P/OM function to be much more than a collection of different topics.
- Each chapter contains a summary to reinforce the managerial concepts presented in the chapter.
- Each chapter contains a list of key terms that play a crucial role in enabling nonmajors to be able to communicate with operations people.
- Each chapter has margin notes that identify key concepts.
- Solved Problems at the end of each chapter reinforce an understanding of the models and techniques presented.
- Detailed instructions for using the AB:POM software are included for selected Solved Problems.
- End-of-chapter Questions and Problems (along with answers to selected problems at the back of the book) provide plenty of opportunities for applying the concepts and techniques in the chapter.
- End-of-chapter Computer Case Studies enable students to solve larger problems, allowing for the type of sensitivity analysis encountered in the real world.

- Applications of P/OM boxes, which appear in nearly every chapter, provide real-world examples and illustrate the value of the P/OM topics covered. Many of these applications are taken from the *For All Practical Purposes* video series and include applications at AT&T Labs, American Airlines, NASA, New England Apple, and Frito-Lay.

CONTENT CHANGES FROM THE FIRST EDITION

We have made some rather important structural changes in this edition.

- A new chapter on world-class operations has been added (Chapter 2).
- A new chapter on total quality management has been added (Chapter 16). In combination with a separate chapter on quality control, this represents comprehensive, state-of-the-art coverage of a very important topic.
- Just-in-time coverage has been expanded throughout the text and just-in-time now appears—together with materials requirements planning—as a chapter heading (Chapter 14).
- Distribution requirements planning has been moved to the materials requirements planning chapter.
- The transportation method has been incorporated into the chapter on the operations network.
- The supplement on financial analysis has been moved to the appendix.
- AB:POM software descriptions have been added to the Solved Problems sections.
- Computer Case Studies have been added at the end of most chapters.
- We have expanded our coverage of multiple regression.
- We have expanded our material on learning curves.
- We have simplified our coverage of inventory models with shortages.
- We have simplified our discussion of push systems within DRP.
- We have expanded our coverage of international competition.
- We have included additional Problems.

QUALITY ASSURANCE: TEXT ACCURACY

An extra step has been incorporated into the production of this edition: Our efforts to provide a high-quality text have been aided by an outside accuracy checker. The purpose of this extra step was to ensure complete accuracy in the text and all ancillaries. Thus, quality has received increased attention both in the content of this edition and in its production, which seems entirely appropriate for a text on production and operations management.

SUPPLEMENTS

A comprehensive supplement package accompanies this text.

- *Study Guide.* O. Felix Offodile of Kent State University has prepared a student workbook containing chapter outlines, a summary of notational definitions and formulas, and questions and problems for additional practice.
- *Annotated Instructor's Edition.*
- *AB:POM software in 5¼" or 3½" format.*
- *Data disk.*

- *Videos.* Two videos are available to qualified adopters. The first, available through an exclusive agreement with COMAP (the *Consortium for Mathematics and Its Applications*), consists of edited material from their series *For All Practical Purposes.* That series was produced for educational television with major funding by the Annenberg/CPB Project. The different modules explain the application of management science techniques to operations management. Also available is a plant-tour video entitled *Making Motorcycles the American Way* that takes a look at a Harley-Davidson manufacturing facility.
- *Transparency masters.*
- *Value pack.* This contains Personal Storm Version 3.0 in either a 5¼″ or 3½″ format.

ACKNOWLEDGMENTS

This edition has been reviewed by O. Felix Offodile of Kent State University, Robert M. Saltzman of San Francisco State University, Tom Bramorski of the University of Wisconsin–Whitewater, C. M. Bush of the University of North Carolina–Charlotte, and Frank P. Jozsa of Allentown College. We are extremely grateful for their insightful comments. Special thanks go to Tom Bramorski for providing the accuracy check for this edition. In addition, we would like to thank the following, our colleagues at Temple University who have given us many useful suggestions: Fred Murphy, Ed Rosenthal, Shevy Gunter, Jugoslav Milutinovich, and Tom Tierney.

For their reviews of the first edition, we would once again like to thank Kathy Fitzpatrick, Appalachian State University; Roger C. Schoenfelt, Murray State University; J. Roberta Minifie, Texas Tech University; Michael Umble, Baylor University; Wayne H. J. Cunningham, Bucknell University; Robert S. Boothe, Memphis State University; Jerry L. Geisler, Eastern Illinois University; William H. Turnquist, Eastern Washington University; Douglas A. Elvers, University of North Carolina–Chapel Hill; Steve Kleisath, University of Wisconsin–Platteville; David R. McKenna, Boston College; Walter Warrick, Drake University; Bruce Simmons, University of Akron; Jesse Tartleton, College of William and Mary; K. Ravi Kumar, University of Illinois–Urbana; William Clegg, University of Toledo; Bob Nydick, Villanova University; and Claudia Harris, University of Scranton.

Many students at Temple University have been exposed to this book both in manuscript and text form and we are grateful for all of their comments. In particular, we would like to thank Karen R. Iannuzzi, Nabil Tamimi, Ju Ho Kim, John Aloysius, Zhongxian Wang, and Lawrence Sze for their help, both with the text and with the software.

We are indebted to our secretaries Florence Finnerty and Ruth Urban for all of their help.

Finally, we once again must express a deep amount of gratitude, love, and appreciation to our families. They have sacrificed a great deal of family time as we have worked on this revision. Without their support, it would have been very difficult to finish the task at hand. Thank you, Lucia and Debbie and Lisa, Ernie, Sarah, Toby, and Rona.

PART ONE

OVERVIEW

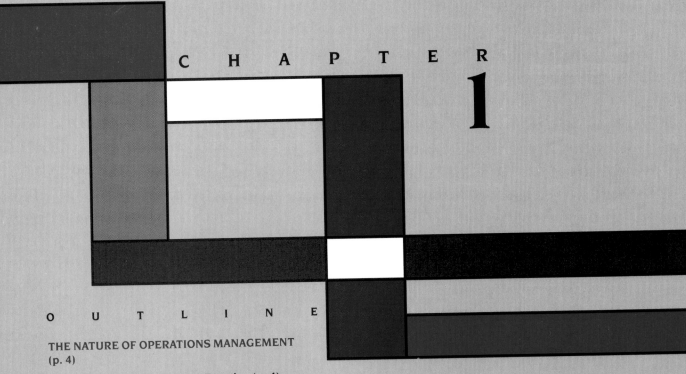

C H A P T E R

1

O U T L I N E

INTRODUCTION

- To explain the operations management function
- To describe the components of the operations function
- To classify organizations along dimensions that are relevant to operations
- To place operations in its historical perspective
- To describe the decision-making methodology and the use of models and solution techniques
- To show the integral nature of organizations and the relationship of operations to other business functions

THE NATURE OF OPERATIONS MANAGEMENT

The typical organization consists of the integration of many different functions. The two most obvious functions are to provide the product or service and to sell the product or service. **Operations management** focuses on the function of providing the product or service. It is concerned with the planning and controlling of all activities necessary for the provision of the firm's product or service.

operations: provide a product or service

The goal of this book is to introduce the activities that are related to operations, the types of problems that arise in these activities, and the methods that exist for approaching those problems. The importance of operations management to those who will be future managers cannot be overstated. It is important even to those who will not actually be operations managers because the integrative nature of organizations makes it essential that managers of other functions (for example, marketing, finance, and engineering) understand the effect that decisions in their areas will have on the provision of the firm's major asset—namely, its product or service.

goal of this book

Teaching Suggestion 1.1: All Jobs Have Operations. See the Instructor's Section for details.

THE OPERATIONS MANAGEMENT FUNCTION

Operations refers to the conversion of input to output. (Economists would use the term *production,* but we will reserve this word for later use.) A general framework for operations is given in Figure 1.1, where we have indicated the five major components of an operation: the **inputs** and the **resources,** which are fed into the **transformation process,** yielding the **direct outputs** and the **by-products.** Before we consider these individual components, let us examine the operations for a system with which we are all familiar—the educational system.

components of an operation

Consider the operations management course in which you are enrolled. The input to the course is the student, and the direct output is a student who is knowledgeable about the operations management function. Resources include books, teachers, classrooms, blackboards, computers, and calculators. The transformation is education. It might not be readily apparent what the by-product is, but one does exist—namely, the grade the student receives for the course. Note that our designation of an educated

Transparency Master 1.1:
The Operations System.

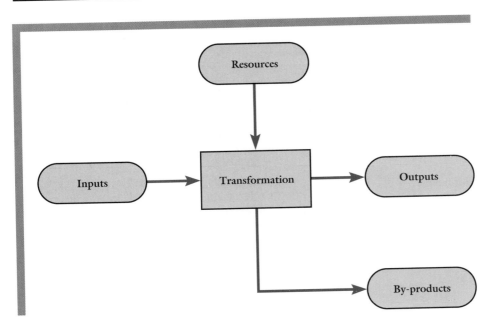

FIGURE 1.1 The operations system

student as a direct output and a grade as a by-product presumes that the goal is to educate the student. If the goal is to receive an A, then the grade becomes the direct output and the educated student becomes the by-product. This role reversal would be quite reasonable if we were discussing courses that prepare students for standard exams (such as SAT, LSAT, GMAT, and GRE) rather than your operations management course. The lesson to be learned is (to modify an old saying), "output is in the eyes of the beholder." We will discuss goals in more detail in the next section, when we talk about planning and control. Let us now consider each of the five components and their place in the operations function.

THE TRANSFORMATION PROCESS

There exist as many different transformations as there do entries in the index of the yellow pages. Therefore, it is useful to classify transformations. One classification scheme is the Standard Industrial Classification (SIC), which is provided by the U.S. Office of Management and Budget and is used by the Census Bureau. This appears in Table 1.1. The table lists eighty-six industry titles that have been aggregated into twelve categories. It is more useful to reorganize the SIC classifications in order to draw attention to the important differences between and similarities among the eighty-six industries.

classification of transformations

One distinguishing feature is whether the transformation is a **production** (goods-producing) transformation or a **service** transformation. Although the SIC has a services category (see industries 72–77), the listing is based on a very limited definition. In fact, most operations managers would consider items 65–86 to be service industries. Our immediate goal is to identify the difference between production and service. There are no hard-and-fast rules about the distinction, but we can make some generalizations.

production vs. service

Teaching Suggestion 1.2: Most Production Companies Have Service Components. See the Instructor's Section for details.

TABLE 1.1 Standard industrial classifications

Industry Number and Title	Industry Number and Title
Agriculture, forestry, and fisheries	39 Metal containers
1 Livestock and livestock products	40 Heating, plumbing, and fabricated structural metal products
2 Other agricultural products	
3 Forestry and fishery products	41 Screw machine products (bolts, nuts, and so on) and metal stampings
4 Agricultural, forestry, and fishery services	
Mining	42 Other fabricated metal products
5 Iron and ferroalloy ores mining	43 Engines and turbines
6 Nonferrous metal ores mining	44 Farm machinery and equipment
7 Coal mining	45 Construction, mining, and oil field machinery and equipment
8 Crude petroleum and natural gas	
9 Stone and clay mining and quarrying	46 Materials handling machinery and equipment
10 Chemical and fertilizer mineral mining	47 Metalworking machinery and equipment
Construction	48 Special industry machinery and equipment
11 New construction	49 General industrial machinery and equipment
12 Maintenance and repair construction	50 Machine shop products
Manufacturing	51 Office, computing, and accounting machines
13 Ordinance and accessories	52 Service industry machines
14 Food and kindred products	53 Electric transmission and distribution equipment and electrical industrial apparatus
15 Tobacco products	
16 Broad and narrow fabrics, yarn and thread mills	
17 Miscellaneous textile goods and floor coverings	54 Household appliances
	55 Electric lighting and wiring equipment
18 Apparel	56 Radio, television, and communication equipment
19 Miscellaneous fabricated textile products	
20 Lumber and wood products, except containers	57 Electronic components and accessories
	58 Miscellaneous electrical machinery, equipment, and supplies
21 Wooden containers	
22 Household furniture	59 Motor vehicles and equipment
23 Other furniture and fixtures	60 Aircraft and parts
24 Paper and allied products, except containers and boxes	61 Other transportation equipment
	62 Professional, scientific and controlling instruments and supplies
25 Paperboard containers and boxes	
26 Printing and publishing	63 Optical, ophthalmic, and photographic equipment and supplies
27 Chemical and selected chemical products	
28 Plastics and synthetic materials	64 Miscellaneous manufacturing
29 Drugs, cleaning, and toilet preparations	**Transportation, communication, electric, gas, and sanitary services**
30 Paints and allied products	
31 Petroleum refining and related industries	65 Transportation and warehousing
32 Rubber and miscellaneous plastics products	66 Communications, except radio and television broadcasting
33 Leather tanning and industrial leather products	
	67 Radio and television broadcasting
34 Footwear and other leather products	68 Electric, gas, water, and sanitary services
35 Glass and glass products	**Wholesale and retail trade**
36 Stone and clay products	69 Wholesale and retail trade
37 Primary iron and steel manufacturing	**Finance, insurance, and real estate**
38 Primary nonferrous metals manufacturing	70 Finance and insurance
	71 Real estate and rental

continued

TABLE 1.1 (Continued)

Industry Number and Title	Industry Number and Title
Services	**Imports**
72 Hotels and lodging places; personal and repair services, except automobile repair	80 Gross imports of goods and services
73 Business services	**Dummy industries**
74 Research and development	81 Business travel, entertainment, and gifts
75 Automobile repair and services	82 Office supplies
76 Amusements	83 Scrap, used and secondhand goods
77 Medical, educational services, and nonprofit organizations	**Special industries**
Government enterprises	84 Government industry
78 Federal government enterprises	85 Rest-of-the-world industry
79 State and local government enterprises	86 Household industry

Source: "The Detailed Input-Output Structure of the U.S. Economy" (U.S. Office of Management and Budget, 1977).

GENERALIZATION 1: A production transformation produces a direct output that

- is a tangible object,
- is ultimately sold, and
- has had a (physical) transformation in form.

As a general rule (which has exceptions), if the output of an organization satisfies the three requirements listed, then that organization falls in the production classification. However, if one or more of the three requirements is not met, the organization is a member of the service industry.

GENERALIZATION 2: The distance between the production operation and the consumer is greater than the distance between the service operation and the consumer.

Consider two operations related to automobiles: manufacturing and repair. The direct output of an automobile plant (production transformation) is a car, something tangible that has been physically transformed and that (after shipping) is sold to the consumer. The direct output of the repair shop (service transformation) is the repaired car itself, which is another tangible good that has been physically transformed but which, obviously, is not sold to the customer. Furthermore, the repair shop is in the customer's neighborhood, while the automobile plant is likely to be hundreds of miles away—perhaps even across an ocean.

To a large extent, there is very little conceptual difference between operating a production organization and operating a service organization. However, there are some differences that should be noted.

In a service system, it is possible for the customer to act as his or her own server. **self-serve** Examples of such systems are self-service gasoline stations, automatic teller machines, food vending machines, salad bars, and automatic toll booths. It is unusual, but not impossible, for a customer to be his or her own server in a production system. An example of a self-service production organization is a picture-framing business where the store provides the materials but the customers make their own frames.

Another way to distinguish between service and production systems involves the timing of the transformation. In some cases, the transformation occurs after the demand, which is termed **make to order**; in other cases, the transformation occurs before the demand, which is termed **make to stock**. As a general rule, service usually is provided after it is demanded (make to order), while products are provided before they are demanded (make to stock). For example, insurance claims are processed after they are submitted, while appliances are manufactured before they are ordered. Of course, there are goods that are manufactured after they are demanded. Any custom-made good (clothing, furniture) is an example of this. In general, however, services are first demanded and then provided, while goods are first provided and then demanded. In Figure 1.2, we present examples of each case for both service and production organizations. The implication of this distinction is that it is more difficult, if not impossible, to carry an inventory of finished "goods" in a service operation. The television manufacturer can carry an inventory of televisions if it produces too many sets. The hotel cannot carry its inventory of empty rooms from one day to the next.

There is yet another difference between service and production: the element of **risk**, which is a major consideration in decision making at all levels of management. As a general rule, a service transformation involves a different type of risk than does a production transformation. The production of an automobile, like most production, takes place without any assurance that someone will buy it. Hence, there is the risk that a product will be produced but not sold. (This risk can be partially offset by putting the item into inventory, but at a cost.) However, the service on the car (the repair) is never performed until the car (the customer) is present. Thus, there is no risk that the service will be performed without a customer to buy the service. Of course, this risk of not selling the product can occur in service institutions. For example, every unsold airline seat or unused hotel room is an unsold "product" from the service sector. Because of this demand-serve relationship, service companies tend to be more flexible in the staffing of their organizations than do production organizations. (The

FIGURE 1.2 Timing of production in relation to demand

	Production Before Demand (Make to Stock)	Demand Before Production (Make to Order)
Production	Most goods Fast-food restaurants	Custom goods (clothes, furniture) Restaurants (ordered meals) House construction Paints (custom colors) Printing (forms, business cards)
Service	Hotel (rooms) Hospital (beds) Airline (seats) Supermarket (groceries) Theatre (Movies, Plays)	Most services

reader has likely been made aware of the flexibility in the educational system either by having had a course canceled or by having been taught by a part-time instructor.)

The distinction between production and service operations may become blurred. Some operations consist both of production and of service. Consider a local restaurant. Within the restaurant, there may be more than one operation. The inputs to the bakery (production) operation at the restaurant are eggs, flour, milk, and other ingredients, which are transformed into the direct output of, for instance, cake, which is sold via the menu. Overall, however, the restaurant is a service process that transforms a hungry customer into a satisfied customer. Of course, because the restaurant is located very close to the customer, we tend to think of such an operation as a service.

Even after transformations are classified as service or production, there are many different types that may be identified in each of the two categories, as Table 1.2 demonstrates. Some transformation examples in the production category are construction (homes, highways), extraction (coal, fishing), and agriculture (cotton, sugar). Within the service category are transformations that relate to health (hospitals, counseling), entertainment (bowling, museums), transportation (warehousing, distribution), and education (vocational training, colleges—including operations management courses). Industries within a subclassification tend to have related problems.

Service or production? Some operations have characteristics of both. (© Richard Sobol/ Stock, Boston)

TABLE 1.2   A classification of some operations by transformation

Production				
Agriculture and forestry	Extraction	Construction	Manufacturing	Personal, personal property, and repair
Wheat	Pine gum	Family homes	Tobacco products	Laundries
Rice	Fishing	Highways and streets	Food products	Garment pressing
Corn	Hunting	Electrical work	Textile products	Linen supply
Cotton	Iron ores	Carpentering	Lumber products	Dry cleaning
Tobacco	Mercury	Plastering	Wood products	Beauty
Sugar	ores	Floor laying	Furniture	Legal
Vegetables	Oil	Bridges	Paper products	Barber
Cattle	Stone	Water well drilling	Newspapers	Shoe repair
Hogs, sheep	Limestone	Roofing	Books	Funeral
Turkeys	Granite	Concrete work	Chemical products	Photography studios
Eggs	Clay		Petroleum	Automobiles
Timber tracts	Rock salt		Leather	Televisions
	Sulphur		Fabricated metal products	Paint shops
	Coal			Electrical repair
	Lead			Car washes
	Aluminum			Parking lots
	Gypsum			Gardening
				Jewelry repair
				Reupholstery
				Refrigeration repair

INPUT

In the course of discussing transformations, we have necessarily referred to the inputs. Among the examples of inputs to the transformation process that we have discussed thus far are component parts for assembling cars; ingredients for baking cakes; people to be served in universities, restaurants, and banks; and automobiles to be repaired. Input to a transformation process can be put into one of three categories:

- raw materials or component parts for processing;
- customer for direct processing; and
- customer-related material, goods, or information for indirect processing.

The first two categories are self-explanatory. For the third category, consider our automobile repair example. Although the car is being repaired, it will not appear in the shop without its owner. Similarly, consider the processing of medical insurance. Papers are what actually are processed, but the papers are submitted on behalf of the patient.

Typically, if the input is a raw material, then the process is a production process. If the input is a customer or is related to a customer, we have a service process.

Services				
Health and social	Entertainment and educational	Business and trade	Transportation, communication, and utilities	Government and nonprofit
Physicians	Elementary schools	Automobiles	Warehousing	Fire protection
Dentists	Secondary schools	Furniture	Railroads	Police
Chiropractors	Colleges	Department stores	Telephone	Armed forces
Nurses	Libraries	Bakeries	Telegraph	Highway repair
Psychiatric hospitals	Data processing schools	Banks	Radio	Postal services
Outpatient care facilities	Vocational training	Credit agencies	Television	Legal system
Fitness centers	Technical training	Real estate agencies	Taxis	Labor unions
Health clubs	Secretarial and business schools	Legal services	Trucking	Religious organizations
Job training	Museums	Insurance agencies	Distribution	Red Cross
Residential care	Art galleries	Investment counseling	Buses	
Vocational rehabilitation	Zoological gardens	Advertising	Air freight	
Child day care	Movies	Stenographers	Airports	
Hospitals	Theaters	Employment agencies	Storage	
Counseling	Restaurants	News syndicates	Ferries	
	Dance halls	Temporary help agencies	Pipelines	
	Bands and orchestras	Detective agencies	Freight forwarding	
	Actors	Protective services	Car rental	
	Billiards and pool	Auditors		
	Bowling alleys	Bookkeepers		
	Amusement parks	Hotels		
	Laboratory research			
	Travel agencies			

OUTPUT

Since input may be classified in one of three categories, it follows that direct output may be similarly identified. The three categories of direct output are as follows:

- finished good to be sold;
- processed customer; and
- processed entity for customer.

Examples that we have already mentioned of each of the three types are, respectively, the baked cake, the educated student, and the repaired car.

RESOURCES

For nearly every operation, necessary resources are of five types:

- labor,
- machines and equipment,
- energy,

Teaching Suggestion 1.4:
The 4 M's. See the Instructor's Section for details.

■ facility, and
■ materials.

The first four items in our list are self-explanatory. By materials, we mean materials that are used during the operation, rather than raw materials. For example, a standard material in manufacturing is lubricating oil, while in the health service operation, a hospital gown is a material. One necessary resource is missing from our list: namely, capital. We omit capital because it is not a direct resource. That is, capital itself does not (physically) contribute to the production or service process. Furthermore, capital itself usually is in the hands of the financial manager rather than the operations manager. Although capital does not appear in our list of resources, it is implicit in the list because we need capital for each of the five resources that are listed.

major emphasis in operations

The specific resource requirements may vary from process to process, but the major emphasis in operations is the same: *Acquire the appropriate amount of each resource at the appropriate time and use the resources in the most efficient manner.* Types of questions to be addressed include the following: Should manpower levels fluctuate over time? Should machines be purchased or leased? Should components be bought from outside or made in-house? Should a new facility be opened? Which job should be run next on the machine?

BY-PRODUCTS

Almost every transformation has by-products. Some are obvious: in manufacturing, by-products typically consist of pollution—chiefly of the water and air—and scrap material. Another by-product is the hole left in the ground by strip mining. Not as obvious (but very important) is the typical by-product of the service operation—namely, customer satisfaction. The auto repair shop should repair the car and, in addition, should do it in a reasonable amount of time. If the repair is not done within a reasonable time frame, then we have, to borrow a phrase from the medical profession, a case of the operation being a success but the patient dying. Another example of a by-product of a service operation occurs at a drive-in bank. Although the object is to serve customers, traffic congestion can be a by-product when the drive-in line extends out into the street.

In Table 1.3, we list the five components for several different types of operations. Because operations management is the planning and control of operations, let us continue by examining the planning function and determining the general types of planning and control associated with each of the five components.

FROM PLANNING THROUGH CONTROL

planning horizons

Generally, managerial planning activities are categorized according to the length of time it takes to accomplish them (see Figure 1.3). Typical time classifications are long-range planning (for more than twelve months in the future), medium-range planning (for one to twelve months) and short-range planning (for current execution). Of course, the times given (one month and twelve months) vary, depending on the specific institution. For example, most mining companies consider any plans up to two years as short range. Some companies actually separate short-range planning from current execution.

Long-range (or strategic) planning typically deals with issues of broad scope, such as product lines, the opening or closing of facilities, and capital equipment replace-

TABLE 1.3 Operations processes

Transformation	Inputs	Resources	Direct Output	By-products
Manufacturing	Raw material	Plant, labor, equipment, energy (electricity)	Finished goods	Refuse, air pollution, water pollution
Distribution	Goods, materials	Warehouse, trucks, fuel, drivers	Delivered product	Air pollution
Mass transit	People	Drivers, buses, fuel, bus and train stops	Delivered people	Air and noise pollution
Retailing	Goods	Store, salespeople, cash registers	Sales	Goodwill
Mining	Earth/rock	Machines, labor	Ore	Pit, waste
Ore refining	Gold ore	Machines, labor	Gold	Waste, hazardous chemicals
Oil refining	Crude oil	Storage tanks, labor, equipment	Petroleum products	Pollution, waste
Health care	Patient	Hospital, doctors, nurses, medical equipment	Healthy patient	Treatment side effects
Education	Student	Books, blackboard, instructor	Learned (degreed) student	Grade
Entertainment	Customer	Facility, equipment, performers	Entertained customer	
Farming	Seeds, water, soil	Labor, equipment, pesticides, fertilizer	Food	Soil erosion
Assembling	Parts	Labor, equipment	Automobiles, machines	Scrap material
Repairing	Broken equipment	Labor, tools	Repaired equipment	Customer satisfaction
Cooking	Vegetables, meats, spices	Chefs, kitchens, cookware	Prepared food	Garbage

ment. Medium-range (or operational) planning deals with general issues regarding, for example, the acquisition of raw materials or the addition or removal of personnel. Short-range planning deals with the specifics of scheduling operations. Examples of questions asked in short-range planning are as follows: Which product is to be run on the machine? Which operator works at the machine? Should overtime be scheduled? Of course, the three time classifications are not entirely distinct: medium-range planning might indicate the need for another production facility (a long-range plan) or the need to subcontract for the next three months (a short-range plan).

LONG-RANGE PLANNING

Typically, long-range plans are classified either as *strategic* or *tactical*. Strategic planning establishes the general corporate goals and objectives. Tactical planning selects the specific methods for carrying out the strategic plan. For example, part of a company's strategic plan might be to build plants in foreign countries, while part of its

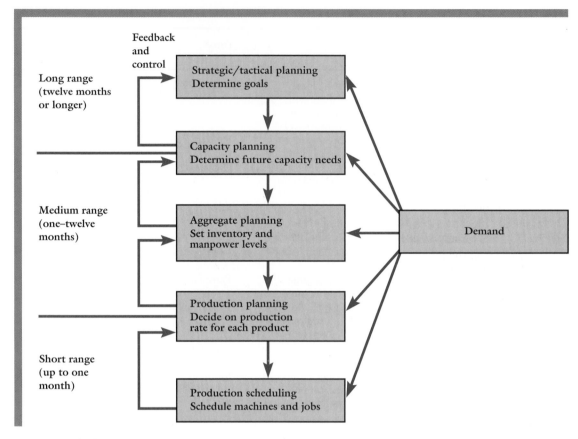

FIGURE 1.3   Categories in operations management planning

**determine company's
direction**

tactical plan might be to build a plant in Brazil. Although tactical plans are long-range plans, they usually are more specific than strategic plans.

    The strategic plans determine the company's direction in respect both to its desired profits and to its role in society. Certain types of questions must be answered in order to formulate an organization's strategic plan: What should be the primary business of the organization? What will allow the company to maintain stability and/or grow? What are the financial objectives (profit and/or return on investment)? What are the strengths and weaknesses of the firm? What is the basic role of the firm in society? What is the responsibility of the firm with regard to ecology, product quality, equal opportunity, and other societal issues? The strategic plan leads to the tactical plan. Of course, both the strategic and the tactical plans deal with the organization as a whole. However, our concern is with strategic and tactical plans as they relate to operations. The strategy–operations relationship is discussed further in Chapter 2.

    One major operations element that affects strategic planning is the long-range **capacity** needs of the company. We have discussed the five resources (labor, equipment, energy, facility, and materials) that are a part of the operations. There is, of course, a great deal of interaction among these resources—laborers, for example, need equipment to accomplish their jobs, and this equipment must be housed in a facility. The long-range capacity decision-making process decides on the amount of these resources that will be available in the distant future. Long-range capacity decisions affect the company at different levels because the methods for modifying capacity vary from short range (working overtime) through medium range (adding a shift) to long range (opening a new plant). Although decisions on resources are made in short- and medium-range planning as well as in long-range planning, long-range plans tend to deal with the addition (or deletion) of large blocks of capacity, such as the construction of a new facility or the purchase of new equipment.

MEDIUM-RANGE PLANNING

The underlying objective of medium-range (or intermediate-range) planning is to meet customer demand. Intermediate-range planning is stressed in this text because it is the type of planning most often performed by the managers who are working in operations. Long-range decisions are often made by the financial, accounting, marketing, or legal personnel within a company. The implementation of those long-range plans then falls on the operations manager.

meet customer demand

Medium-range planning in operations consists of production planning and/or aggregate planning. In production planning, production rates for as far into the future as eighteen months are set. Setting the production rate directly affects plans for the inventory levels both of raw materials and of finished goods; for employment levels; and, hence, for training and compensation costs. Of course, production rates are limited by capacities dictated by the long-range plans.

The types of decisions made in medium-range planning deal both with the acquisition and the use of resources. The effect on capacity of the medium-range plans is not as great as the effect of long-range plans. Decisions regarding the level of the labor force, investment in new machines, the layout of the facility, and the finished goods inventory levels for the coming year are examples of medium-range planning.

SHORT-RANGE PLANNING

The medium-range aggregate plan has to be broken down into specific production plans for each product at each factory, shop, or office. These plans then have to be implemented through the scheduling of the resources (personnel, materials, machines) and the ordering of the raw materials or component parts.

At this level, a foreman or shop manager has responsibility for operations, but he or she must live within the constraints imposed by the longer-term plan for the system. At this level, most of the work consists of *"putting out fires."* In other words, the operations manager responsible for day-to-day operations most often has no time to plan, working in a reactive mode instead of the desirable proactive mode. The complaint most often voiced by operations managers is that they could do their jobs better if only the proper tools (resources) were available to them. Providing these tools is the function of the longer-term planners. In Figure 1.4, we have indicated the types of planning performed in the different ranges.

day-to-day operations

CONTROL

Once plans are made and a business starts operating, the operations manager needs to become involved in the control of operations. Since planning does not stop, the manager often has to handle two responsibilities—planning and control—simultaneously.

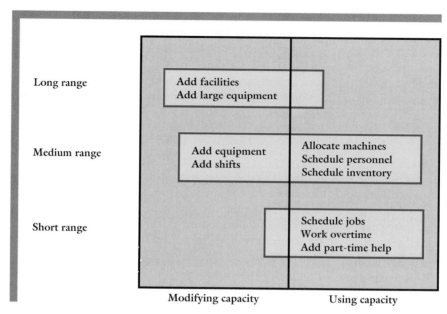

FIGURE 1.4 Types of planning in relation to time horizon

We have already discussed planning. Control is the means by which the manager measures how effectively the plans are being carried out.

    To control operations, something that involves controlling the level and quality of output from each worker and each piece of equipment, the manager must have a way of getting as much useful information as possible as fast as possible. This **management information system** (MIS) takes different forms. It may be a computer system

management information system

FIGURE 1.5 Planning levels in relation to management levels

	Production Companies	Universities	Banks	Hotels	Airlines
Strategic planning	Board of directors	Board of trustees	Board of directors	Board of directors	Board of directors
Tactical planning	Top management	President	President	President	President
	Vice President, operations	Vice President	Vice President, operations	Vice President	Vice President
Medium-range planning	Plant managers	Deans	General managers	Hotel managers	Chief officer, scheduling and operations
Short-range planning	Foremen	Department chairs	Branch managers	Housekeepers	Executive director

providing daily reports to management. Or it may be the manager's spending time with workers to get a feel for how operations are going. A good MIS will include both of these approaches.

The key to control, then, is information. The successful manager focuses on the information that provides the best picture of operations, whether that picture shows success or failure. Thus, it is necessary for managers to have measures that define the success of a business. Profits, revenues, costs, production quantities, customers served, product quality, and return customers are some frequently used measures of success.

information required for control

A PLANNING CONTINUUM

Although we have explained the planning stages separately, they actually reside on a time continuum and, of course, involve a great deal of feedback, because the specific tactics are highly interrelated. Much of this feedback is used in the control function. In Figure 1.3, we provided a general picture of operations management planning and indicated where feedback occurs. We also indicated that demand is a critical input to the decision-making process at all levels.

LEVELS OF MANAGEMENT

An alternative way to classify the types of planning is to view them as belonging to different levels of management as well as to different time horizons (see Figure 1.5). Upper management is considerably less interested in detail than lower management. On the other hand, planning decisions made by upper management are more far-reaching in their effects on the company than are planning decisions made by lower management. Links between upper management and long-range planning, middle management and intermediate-range planning, and lower management and short-

types of decisions: upper, middle, lower management

Hospitals	Mail-Order Companies	Federal Post Office	Federal Government	Construction Companies
Board of directors	President and CEO	Post office board	President of U.S.	President
President	Vice President	Director general	National security advisor	Vice President, operations
Vice President	General sales manager		Secretary of state	
Medical director	Regional sales managers	Regional directors	Under-secretaries	Chief engineers
Head of departments	District sales managers	Head postmasters	Ambassadors	Site engineers

range planning are obvious. However, a strategic decision may be made for short-range reasons. The manager making such a decision has a short-range problem but will not oversee short-range details. In this situation, it is the type of decision to be made, not the length of time involved, that separates planning levels. A strategic decision with a short-term planning horizon may be made when a company is going through a reorganization or has a temporary cash-flow problem. In either case, top management will "watch the numbers" very closely and make plans for the short term to get through the crisis. But top management will only look at aggregate figures. Their decisions must be implemented immediately, but many of the details of the implementation will be left to subordinates.

Our discussion of planning and control has been very general. In order to get a better feel for the tasks of operations management, let us consider some specific problems that might be faced by operations managers.

EXAMPLES OF OPERATIONS PROBLEMS

Every organization—whether public, private, or governmental, whether for profit or not for profit—performs some transformation. Hence, someone (or some group) is responsible for decision making regarding the operation. Whether this person is called the operations manager is irrelevant. The problems he or she faces are common to many industries. Consider the following brief examples, all of which appear in later chapters and all of which are representative of operations management problems. In parentheses we have indicated the location of each Example that is repeated in a later chapter; for those Examples that appear only here, we have indicated the location of the concept(s) illustrated by the problem.

capacity

Example 1.1   Gamma Computers Inc. projects a growth in demand for their microcomputers. Hence, their capacity must grow from its current value of 300 units per (three-shift) day to 900 units per day over the next ten-year period. Should they expand their current facility, or should they plan on building one, two, or more new plants? During the times when capacity is insufficient, should they use overtime, add shifts, or subcontract? (Chapter 3; see Figure 3.1) ■

equipment choice

Example 1.2   Gateway Delivery Service is purchasing a new car to use as a delivery vehicle. The choice has been narrowed down to two cars: one with a regular engine, and one with a diesel engine. The purchase prices are $10,000 for the regular car and $13,000 for the diesel car. The operating costs for the regular car are $.32 per mile, while the operating costs for the diesel car are $.27 per mile. Which car should be purchased? (Example 3.7) ■

buy/make

Example 1.3   Tiara Computer Company produces microcomputer systems for home use. Provided with the system are joysticks. Currently, Tiara purchases the joysticks from Trackit Inc. for $10 per pair. A feasibility study has indicated that Tiara could produce the joysticks itself. The cost to set up the production would be $30,000 and the joysticks could be produced at a cost of $8 per pair. Should Tiara purchase the joysticks or manufacture them? (Example 3.8) ■

Example 1.4 LG Inc. has plants in Phoenix and Philadelphia. Due to an expected increase in sales, the company plans to build a new plant. The two cities being considered as the site of the new plant are Dallas and Chicago. Regardless of its site, the plant will be built with a given capacity. Goods are shipped from the company's plants to warehouses in Vancouver, St. Louis, Miami, and Boston. Which site, Dallas or Chicago, will minimize the total shipping cost of goods from the three plants to the four warehouses? (Chapter 6; see Figure 6.8) ▪

transportation

Example 1.5 Ambler University is a small college that has recently expanded its library. One new wing of the library has three rooms, each of which will house one of the following services: duplication, periodicals, and a lounge. Which process should be in which room in order to minimize the amount of traffic in the hallway? (Example 7.4) ▪

layout

Example 1.6 Warranty Unlimited (WU) repairs home appliances that are still under the manufacturer's warranty. Each of WU's many employees works on one appliance at a time and is paid $10 per hour. When the repairperson needs a part, he or she goes to the parts counter, waits until his or her turn, and then requests the part. Repairpersons tend to arrive at the parts counter at a rate of 10 per hour. The manager of WU has heard complaints from the repairpersons about the time they spend waiting for parts and is considering replacing the current partsperson with a more experienced (and more expensive) one. The current wages for the partsperson are $4 per hour, and the average service time is 5 minutes per request. The replacement would be paid $7 per hour but could service repairpersons in an average of 4 minutes. Should the manager make the change? (Example 8.6) ▪

waiting lines

Example 1.7 Abington Township is planning on building a new township playground. Building the playground requires the coordination of several activities, from the planning (architect's drawings), clearing of the land, excavation, and purchase of the materials to assembly of the equipment, placement and cementing of the equipment, and painting of the equipment. Some activities must precede others. For example, planning must precede all of the other activities. The township has time estimates for each of the activities and is interested in determining the following: If the project starts on February 1, will the playground be completed before the end of the school term (June 21) for use during the summer? If not, which activities need to be accelerated in order for the project to finish on time? (Chapter 10) ▪

project management

Example 1.8 OCRA Industries refines crude oil into gasoline. Two types of crude oil are available: light and heavy. Light crude oil costs $.90 per gallon, and heavy crude oil costs $1 per gallon. The oils are blended into premium and regular gasolines. Premium sells for $1.40 per gallon, while regular sells for $1.25 per gallon. One gallon of premium consists of .75 gallon of heavy crude and .5 gallon of light crude. (There is a refining loss of .25 gallon.) One gallon of regular consists of .5 gallon of heavy oil and .75 gallon of light crude. (Again, there is a refining loss.) Company policy dictates

resource allocation

that at least 60 percent of the gasoline refined be regular. How much of each type of gas should be refined if heavy oil and light oil are available in quantities of 6,000 gallons and 4,000 gallons per day, respectively? (Example 11.3)   ■|

production planning

Example 1.9   Ace Electronics is planning its VCR production for May, June, and July. The projected sales are 200 units in May, 500 units in June, and 300 units in July. The production level at Ace is 250 VCRs per month, with overtime capacity of an additional 150 VCRs per month. The labor cost of production is $8 at regular time and $12 at overtime in each of the three months. However, each VCR that is not sold in the month in which it was produced must be placed in inventory, at a cost of $5 per unit per month. How many VCRs should be produced in each month during regular time and during overtime? (Example 12.4)   ■|

inventory

Example 1.10   The Aman Painting Company consumes 58 gallons of paint per day, at a cost of $5 per gallon. Assuming that the company works 251 days per year, its annual consumption is 14,558 gallons. The holding cost is $4 per gallon per year, and the order cost is $22 per order. Assuming a lead time of three days, how many gallons of paint should be requested at each order, and how low should the inventory of paint fall before new paint is ordered? (Example 13.5)   ■|

job scheduling

Example 1.11   College Prose Painters (CPP) is a team of college students who paint houses during the summer. CPP has lined up six houses for painting. The students will paint one house at a time. The houses take 9, 7, 3, 4, 8, and 6 days to paint, respectively. In which order should the houses be painted? (Example 15.1)   ■|

personnel scheduling

Example 1.12   Four programmers—Bob, Carol, Ted, and Alice—have the capability to write any of programs 1, 2, 3, or 4 that need to be completed. Although they have this capability as a group, their individual capabilities vary, due to the fact that the four programmers have strengths in different programming languages. Hence, the time required for each of the four programs is a function of the programmer. Each programmer is paid $10 per hour. The problem is to assign each programmer to a single program in order to complete all four programs in the minimum amount of time. (Example 15.10)   ■|

quality control

Example 1.13   Allied Can Manufacturing (ACM) produces tin cans. The strength of the cans must be 10 pounds per square inch. ACM has neither the time nor the money to inspect every can it produces, so it takes samples of some of the cans. What sample size will accept 95 percent of the cans that meet the 10-pound requirement and yet reject 90 percent of the cans that do not even meet an eight-pound requirement? (Example 17.3)   ■|

These examples give an indication of the types of problems for which modern operations management can provide either a solution or insight into the solution. The questions that they pose are addressed by the subject of this text and, as previously mentioned, many of these same problems are solved in later chapters.

THE HISTORY OF OPERATIONS MANAGEMENT

We have already indicated that every organization faces operations management problems. This, of course, is true not only of today's organizations but also of those organizations of times past. The major difference between the operations problems of yesteryear and the operations problems faced by the modern operations manager is not one of type, but one of degree.

Several ancient civilizations were very efficient at management in general and at operations management in particular. It would be very interesting to see whether, given the simpler tools available to their ancestors, Egyptians today could manage the magnificent feats of building the pyramids and sphinxes. Could modern Chinese build the Great Wall of China? Or could the Greeks construct the Parthenon today? Notwithstanding these ancient marvels, the need for operations management can be traced to the industrial revolution.

THE INDUSTRIAL REVOLUTION

In 1769, James Watt patented the first practical steam engine. Prior to that time, there were steam-driven devices, but most were not fuel-efficient enough to merit being used. The first steam engine was described by Hero of Alexandria (circa 130 B.C.), the earliest steam engine built is credited to Thomas Savery (1698), and the predecessor to Watt's machine was invented by Thomas Newcomer and John Cawley (1705). It is widely known that Watt's steam engine eventually was put to use in locomotives (1829) and paddle-wheel steamboats (1802). However, the major impact of the steam engine was not on transportation but on the manufacturing system.

James Watt

Prior to the invention of the steam engine, most businesses were family businesses operated at home, or cottage industries. A family would buy a relatively inexpensive and simple machine, such as a loom, and convert raw materials into a finished product. However, machinery driven by steam was too expensive for a single family to purchase and too large to be placed in the home. Thus, the factory system emerged, whereby all machinery was placed in one location and workers traveled to that location to do their work.

cottage industries

One of the earliest problems addressed in operations management was the problem of facility location. The 1800s saw a major development of factories, and a natural question was where to locate these new factories. Much of the early work on this problem was performed in Germany; Johann von Thunen and A. Schaffle (1878) were two pioneers in the facility location field. In 1909, Alfred Weber developed a comprehensive theory on facility location, which has been used extensively since then.

emergence of the factory

SCIENTIFIC MANAGEMENT

It is difficult to give a time for the beginning of operations management as a unified field. Prior to 1911, different areas of operations management were under scrutiny by several people (see Table 1.4). However, in 1911, Frederick Taylor published his classic work, *The Principles of Scientific Management*. Taylor's basic premise was that the management of men and machines should be approached scientifically. Specifically, he advocated the following: defining each job in a single best fashion (job description), developing the appropriate output standards through measurement (time and motion studies), and implementing a differential piece-rate system.

Frederick Taylor

TABLE 1.4 Milestones in operations management

Date	Contribution	Contributor
1700s	Steam engine, factories	James Watt
	The Wealth of Nations, division of labor	Adam Smith
	Interchangeable parts	Eli Whitney
	Plant layout (flow of operations)	James Watt, Matthew Boulton
1800s	Location analysis	Johann von Thunen, A. Schaffle, Alfred Weber
	Division of labor	Charles Babbage
	Shop management	Henry Towne
	Industrial psychology	George Westinghouse
1910s	*The Principles of Scientific Management*	Frederick Taylor
	Motion study	Frank Gilbreth
	Assembly line	Henry Ford
	Scheduling	Henry Gantt
	Inventory analysis	F. W. Harris
1930s	Industrial psychology	Elton Mayo, Lillian Gilbreth
	Quality control	Harold F. Dodge and H. G. Romig
	Work sampling	L. H. C. Tippett
1940s	Computers	Sperry (Unisys) Corporation
	Linear programming	George Dantzig
	Total quality management	W. Edwards Deming
1950s	Project scheduling	Rand Corporation
1960s	Computer simulation	Geoffrey Gordon and others
1970s	*Materials Requirements Planning*	Joseph Orlicky
1980s	Robotics	George C. Devol and others

Teaching Suggestion 1.5: Taylor vs. Gilbreth. See the Instructor's Section for details.

Although Taylor organized these ideas in his famous book, he was not the first person to develop most (if not all) of these ideas. In the 1800s, Matthew Boulton and James Watt developed a factory for manufacturing the steam engine. The factory was laid out according to the flow of operations (an assembly line). The job of each worker was defined and analyzed (job description, time and motion study). Wage payment systems were created to correspond to an expected amount of output. Later in the century, Charles Babbage, who is famous for his contributions to mathematics and computer science, offered his comments on what later became scientific management. Taylor's work began a period that saw an enormous amount of research on operations management. Among the major contributors were Frank and Lillian Gilbreth, Elton Mayo, and L. H. C. Tippett. Frank Gilbreth studied work simplification, while his wife studied industrial psychology (also studied by Mayo). Tippett examined work sampling.

George Westinghouse

Another nineteenth-century contributor to the development of operations management was George Westinghouse, who is typically overlooked in management and operations management texts. Westinghouse is very famous among engineers because he was granted 361 patents, an average of more than five patents per year from his birth in 1846 to his death in 1914. However, besides his major engineering accomplishments, which include the gas meter, the air brake, the air spring (shock absorber), and the electric streetcar, Westinghouse was very concerned with the well-being of his employees. He was a pioneer in the institution of pension plans, medical benefits, and employee recreational and educational programs. However, his most significant contribution was reducing the workweek from six to five and a half days by declaring, in 1881, that Saturday would be a half-day holiday. This is rather significant because, from the time of cottage industries through 1881, the workweek was six days. Of course, this initial reduction from six days led to our current five-day workweek. For his contributions, we have classified Westinghouse as an industrial psychologist, though he predates that field.

reduction of workweek

Parallel with the developments of scientific management were the advances in the quantitative models of operations. The earliest notable model was presented in 1914 by Henry Gantt, who developed the activity chart. This chart is used extensively today, as will be seen in the chapters on project and job scheduling. Although Gantt is famous for his chart, he also studied incentive pay. A second notable achievement was the inventory control model, developed by F. W. Harris in 1917. This model forms the basis for many of the inventory systems used today. In 1931, Harold Dodge and H. G. Romig derived the first quality control tables.

quantitative models

THE COMPUTER REVOLUTION

The development of modern computers began in the 1940s (discounting the machines of Babbage). Although these machines were clumsy and expensive compared with machines today, they greatly enhanced the scope of numerical computations. The arrival of the computer facilitated the development and use of the quantitative models that are standard fare in most operations today.

In the 1940s, George Dantzig presented linear programming, a model used for resource allocation, the transportation of goods, and the assignment of jobs to machines. In the 1950s, critical path methods, as well as many job shop (non-assembly line) scheduling models, were developed. In the 1960s, computer simulation was developed and refined. In the 1970s, materials requirements planning was developed. The 1980s saw the rapid development of higher-level forms of automation, such as robotics and flexible manufacturing systems.

One of the reasons that it is difficult to give a date of origin of the field is that operations management draws on several different areas—notably, finance, industrial engineering, operations research, statistics, computer science and psychology (see Figure 1.6). Furthermore, the field has evolved into its current form—where we speak in terms of a general transformation—from its original form, which relied strictly on the manufacturing transformation. That is, before the term *operations management* came into use, the name of the field was *production management* and, prior to that, was *manufacturing management*. Although the field's original concerns were examined in the context of a factory, production managers realized that service operations had the same or similar problems. Hence, the expansion of the field from factory to all organizations parallels the evolution of our national economy from one based on production to one weighted toward service.

from manufacturing to service

THE OPERATIONS MANAGEMENT DECISION PROCESS

Our explanation of operations management has centered on the long-, medium-, and short-range decision-making responsibilities of management. The examples stated previously lend some insight into the types of problems faced by an operations man-

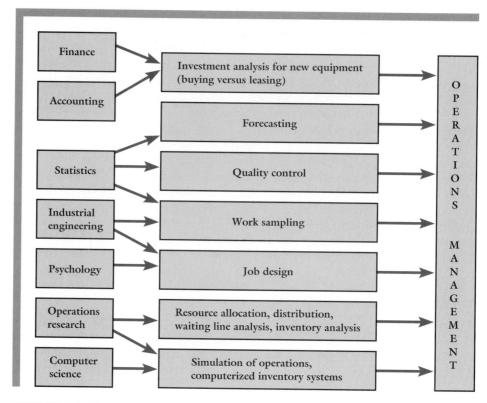

FIGURE 1.6 The interdisciplinary nature of operations management

**management is
situational**

ager. The modern operations manager understands the problems of his or her orga-nization, the general models that have been developed for solving similar types of problems, and the assumptions and implications of these models. Effective manage-ment is situational. All managers, including operations managers, strive for the best possible solutions to problems specific to their company and its situation. Thus, we cannot overemphasize that the *output of these standard models is only an aid to the decision-making process and does not constitute the decision-making process itself.*

As described previously, operations managers are constantly faced with decisions. The problems encountered range from the immediate (for example, whether or not to work overtime today) to the long range (for example, whether or not to build a plant in Taiwan). Many of the decisions, especially for the short-term problems, are made repeatedly. Furthermore, many of the problem types are common to several institutions. Therefore, it is useful to have standard methods for helping us to make these decisions. Ultimately, these standard methods will evolve either into the use of a formula (equation) or into a quantitative procedure for "solving" the problem. It is imperative that the operations manager (and his or her associates) understand the basis for the formula, the assumptions underlying the formula, and the repercussions of using the formula. In order to attain this understanding, it is necessary to understand the general decision-making methodology.

The decision-making process consists of six highly interrelated steps.

1. Formulate the problem.
2. Identify the alternative solutions.

3. Test the alternative solutions.
4. Choose the "best" solution.
5. Implement the chosen solution.
6. Monitor the system.

decision-making methodology

FORMULATING THE PROBLEM AND IDENTIFYING THE ALTERNATIVES

A problem exists whenever the decision maker is faced with a choice of alternatives. Many of the alternatives faced by the operations manager are alternatives in quantity: for example, whether to produce 10 units rather than 15 units, whether to order 100 pounds of raw material rather than 50 pounds, or whether to hire four salespeople rather than three salespeople. Other alternatives are qualitative in nature: whether to locate production in Dallas rather than in Philadelphia, whether to have the second clerk in the supermarket bag for the first clerk rather than open a new cash register, whether to replace a bridge toll collector with a machine, or whether to change the jobs on an assembly line.

Each alternative leads to a different outcome. For example, hiring four salespeople rather than three leads to faster service and higher total wages. An automatic teller machine usually lowers operating costs, but it also reduces the variety of services offered. As these two examples indicate, most decisions involve a **trade-off** among objectives. Therefore, one of the first steps the operations manager must take is the identification of the goals and/or objectives. These objectives may take many forms. For example, an objective might be to satisfy *all* customer demands (never run out of stock) or it might be to *try* to satisfy all customer demands (do not run out of stock more than 1 percent of the time). Only after the goals are identified is it possible to determine how well the competing alternatives meet the various goals.

identification of the goals

TESTING THE ALTERNATIVES

In an ideal system, a manager would be able to test alternatives by actually implementing them in the system. Sometimes this is possible in the real world. For example, if a supermarket manager is undecided between a staff of three checkers and a staff of four checkers, he or she can run the store for one month with three checkers and then hire temporary help for a second month to see what happens with four.

However, there are situations in which the alternatives cannot be implemented in the real system. If we are trying to decide on the location of a new plant, we cannot open a plant in two trial cities. When we cannot implement alternatives, the most common method for testing them is with the use of models. A **model** is a representation of the entity or system being examined. The models are less complicated than the real systems and, hence, are easier to manipulate and examine. There are three types of models.

models

ICONIC MODELS: An icon is a picture or image. Hence, an iconic model is a representation of the system or object that differs from reality only in scale. The iconic model looks like what it is supposed to represent. Familiar examples of iconic models are scale representations of buildings or airplanes, the NASA space shuttle simulator (which never leaves the ground), blueprints and road maps (one inch = one mile), and the famous Macintosh computer icons.

NASA wind tunnel at Ames Research Center: an iconic model. (Edward/Gamma Liaison)

ANALOGUE MODELS: Analogue means *similarity*. An analogue model uses similar properties to represent the real system. For example, a graph is an analogue model, as is a relief map that uses three-dimensional detail to represent height above sea level.

SYMBOLIC MODELS: A symbolic model represents the properties of the entity through the use of symbols. Notes on a musical scale are a symbolic model of the sounds made when these notes are played. The majority of symbolic models employ mathematical symbols. For example, an equation is a symbolic model (while its corresponding graph is an analogue model). The mathematical model is the easiest to manipulate, so it is the most useful for the operations manager. The reader must bear in mind at all times, though, that an equation is a *model,* and not the real system.

Although the use of models is a great help in decision making, the modeling process takes time and money. The better (more accurate) the model is, the more costly

---

APPLICATIONS OF P/OM

Modeling

Ronald Graham is director of the Mathematics Sciences Research Department of AT&T Bell Labs, Murray Hill, New Jersey. In addition to his own research, he supervises some of the country's most distinguished mathematicians as they investigate the puzzles of management science. What follows are some of his comments on models.

> There are several well-known steps in going from a real-world problem to a model of the problem—a model in which you try to capture the essential aspects of the problem, but in a way that can be dealt with mathematically. Once you convert the problem into the world of mathematics, you can say something about all the mathematical possibilities. Then you translate it back to the real-world situation. How well it works depends crucially on how accurate the translation of the model was.

Now, it's always good to check a few of the things that you've predicted are going to happen. If the translation is good and you've captured the essence of the problem, then there is a good chance that you can say something sensible about the thing you've studied. If it isn't, you can get some pretty bizarre conclusions. There are famous examples of this. One that comes to mind is the case where the people who first analyzed how bees fly were able to prove mathematically that bees *couldn't* fly. That didn't bother the bees, of course, and the model was eventually modified to show that bees could fly after all.

Source: S. Garfunkel, ed., *Introduction to Contemporary Mathematics* (New York: W.H. Freeman and Company, 1988), pp. 54–55.

---

it will be. Hence, there is a trade-off that must be controlled. This is exhibited in Figure 1.7. This figure will apply to many different problems presented in this text. The idea of making trade-offs in decision making is a central one in operations management, and understanding the set of underlying factors to be traded off against each other is the key both to understanding the problems and to building models to solve them.

CHOOSING THE "BEST" SOLUTION

The models that are used by operations managers may be described as *descriptive* or *prescriptive*. **Descriptive models** examine the effects of choosing one alternative out of many; **prescriptive models** find the best alternative out of many. When using a descriptive model, one simply uses the same model on different alternatives and then chooses the alternative that best meets the goals. When using a prescriptive model, the goals must be specified first (maximize profit, minimize lateness, or minimize number of employees, for example) and then the best alternative is found.

analyzing alternatives

For the prescriptive models, there are two types of solution techniques. For many problems, techniques have been developed that always find the best (optimal) solution to the problem. These techniques are termed **optimization** methods. For other problems, techniques that are guaranteed to solve the problem optimally have not yet been developed or the optimization technique will not work on large problems. In these situations, we apply techniques that find very good solutions, but that are likely not the best possible solutions. Such methods are called **heuristic** techniques, a term that comes from the Greek, meaning "to point out" (a good solution). Trial-and-error techniques or rules of thumb are examples of heuristic techniques.

finding the solution

IMPLEMENTATION

The last step in the decision-making process is the implementation of the chosen solution. Sometimes this can be simple, such as when an order quantity (of parts) can easily

Transparency Master 1.4:
Cost Trade-offs in
Modeling.

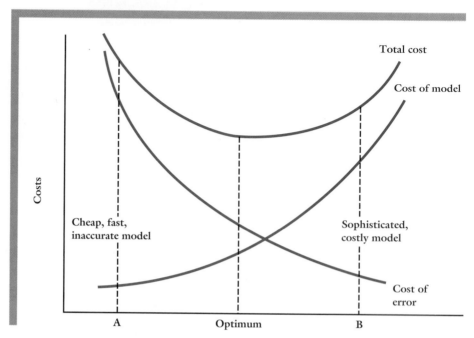

FIGURE 1.7 Cost trade-offs in modeling

be changed from fifty parts per order to one hundred parts per order. At other times, implementation may be difficult, such as the building of a new plant.

MONITORING THE SYSTEM

Transparency Master 1.5:
Decision-Making
Methodology.

We just identified implementation as the last step of the decision-making process, but we have not yet spoken of monitoring the system. Monitoring is not a part of solving any one particular problem; rather, it is an ongoing activity, as is indicated in Figure 1.8.

FIGURE 1.8 Decision-making methodology

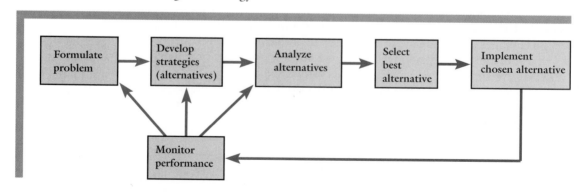

OPERATIONS MANAGEMENT WITHIN THE ORGANIZATION

This text focuses on the functions and tools of operations management; however, operations clearly is not an isolated organization function. Operations necessarily interacts with the entire organization, as we will show throughout the following chapters. Some examples of these relationships follow.

The most basic and essential functions of a business are operations (provide the product or service), marketing (sell the product or service), and finance (provide the money to execute operations and marketing). Obviously, there must be a great deal of coordination among these three functions. The coordination involves implementing several different approaches.

coordination among business functions

MARKETING

1. *Satisfying demand (long term):* In order to plan for production, the operations manager must have a forecast of the future demand. While the operations manager might estimate demand on his or her own, it is usual for the manager to involve the marketing department, which has the information that yields the most accurate forecasts. This is particularly true when the manager is forecasting demand for a new product because there exist no past data on which the manager can rely.
2. *Satisfying demand (short term):* The sales orders provide the information on what needs to be produced immediately. Good communication channels between marketing and operations will avoid problems that can arise when there is a sudden and unexpected order.
3. *Quality:* Although quality of the product or service is determined at both the engineering and production stage, the feedback on quality typically comes through the marketing function.
4. *Inventory control:* Inventory is one of the primary responsibilities in operations management. Both too much and too little inventory are of concern. Sometimes, inventories will be too high, and this will result in high costs. One way to reduce inventory is through aggressive sales. If inventories are too low, customer service may be adversely affected.

FINANCE AND ACCOUNTING

The operations manager may be faced with decisions regarding equipment. Two common decisions are whether to buy or lease equipment and whether one type of equipment is preferable to another.

1. *Provision of money:* Previously, we excluded capital as a resource. We did this because it is the function of finance to provide the money for equipment, for raw materials, or for a new plant.
2. *Analysis:* It is with the tools of finance (present value and so forth) and accounting (taxes and depreciation) that these decisions are analyzed.
3. *Cost data:* The accounting function is responsible for providing the costs of materials, labor, overhead, and so on.

PERSONNEL (HUMAN RESOURCE MANAGEMENT)

Most firms are not run by robots—not yet anyway. The personnel department responds to the operations needs with respect to recruiting labor, training labor, and labor (union) relationships.

RESEARCH AND DEVELOPMENT

New products and new processes are the province of research and development (R&D). However, new products currently under development may eventually be produced by a production facility. The operations people responsible for mass production must be involved in R&D to assure that prototypes are designed in such a way as to facilitate assembly by modern production equipment. The mass production environment is very different from the lab where the prototype is assembled. As a result, many companies have started to include their manufacturing groups in strategic and product development decisions. One such company is S. C. Johnson & Sons, whose manufacturing executives saved the company $250,000 in the mid 1980s simply by suggesting that the bottle for the company's then-new Curel skin lotion be sized to fit existing equipment.

Other operations functions are involved with R&D as well. Project scheduling is required to ensure that the R&D effort is accomplished within time and budget constraints. The inventory problems of R&D are of special interest because of the small inventories maintained. Finally, quality assurance people are involved to assure that the resulting design facilitates inspection, and reliability people are involved to establish standards of product performance.

COMPUTER AND INFORMATION PROCESSING

Very few organizations today function without computers. Computer usage will become even more prevalent in the future; the value of microcomputers to business will increase with decreasing cost and expanded software capabilities and availability. While the computer is useful for mundane data processing tasks, such as payroll, one of its greatest assets is that it can be used to analyze operations management models. In fact, as previously mentioned, one of the reasons for the growth of the field of operations management is the development of the computational capability for analyzing large models provided by computers.

QUANTITATIVE SUPPORT SERVICES

While there are general models available for standard operations problems, each institution will have its own specific problem details. It is the responsibility of the operations manager to ascertain whether the model is representative of the company's specific problem. If it is, then all is well—typically, software exists to solve the problem. If the model is not representative, new or modified models must be developed, and this is generally the responsibility of the firm's quantitative support service. The operations manager must be able to converse with the quantitative people, and vice versa.

The importance of the interaction between operations and other business functions should be clear. Obviously, the non-operations management major will benefit from a complete understanding of this relationship. But anyone who still questions the applicability of an operations management course to other areas of study or interest should consider this: In many institutions, the operations function accounts for the majority of costs, as indicated in Table 1.5. Therefore, the success of all employees in an organization very likely will depend on the efficiency and cost effectiveness of the operations function.

TABLE 1.5 Operations cost as a percentage of total cost

Institution	Cost of operations (%)
Mutual savings banks	.6
Other banks	.1
Savings and loans	1.0
Personal credit institutions	20.8
Life insurers (stock)	45.9
Life insurers (mutual)	33.2
Other insurers	49.7
Agents, brokers, services	19.1
Securities industry	7.8
Real estate developers	25.3
Electric utilities	48.3
Combined utility services	54.1
Supermarkets	78.0
Bars	45.0
Liquor stores	79.5
Apparel and accessory stores	58.7
Furniture and home furnishing stores	62.9
Hardware stores	67.2
Car dealers	87.4
Gas stations	86.3
Auto repair and services	51.6
Airlines	47.7
Hotels	47.6
Movie theaters	35.3
Doctors' offices	8.5
Dentists' offices	15.7
Hospitals	17.4
Nursing homes	22.4
Medical and dental testing labs	30.7
Law firms	7.7
CPA firms	15.2
Advertising agencies	60.6

Source: David Horowitz and Dana Shilling, *The Business of Business* (New York: Harper & Row, 1989).

THE SCOPE AND PLAN OF THIS BOOK

In our discussion of planning and our examples of operations management problems, there was one common denominator: *capacity*. The goal of operations management is to meet demand in the most efficient manner. In fact, in our discussion on resources, we stated that the major emphasis in operations is twofold: Acquire the appropriate amount of each resource at the appropriate time, and use the resources in the most efficient manner. This means that operations management activities can be divided into two types. There are tasks that modify (increase or decrease) the amount of capacity available, and there are tasks that indicate the best way to allocate the available capacity in order to meet demand. This book is organized along these lines.

In Chapter 2, we continue our overview of operations. In Part II of this book, we discuss the basic notion of capacity and general methods for modifying capacity. In addition, we discuss forecasting demand, because forecasts indicate the amount of capacity that will be required. Capacity and demand (forecasting) form the base of operations management.

Part III is devoted to the decisions that actually modify the capacity. These include decisions on opening new facilities, designing the facilities, designing the distribution network, designing jobs, and deciding on the number of workers.

Part IV deals with those activities devoted to the proper allocation of the available resources, many of which are limited by capacity decisions made earlier. These activities include aggregate planning, linear programming, inventory, job scheduling, project scheduling and job and personnel assignment. Part V addresses the quality function as it relates to all operations topics throughout the book.

KEY TERMS

operations management	service	descriptive models
operations	make to order	prescriptive models
inputs	make to stock	optimization
resources	risk	heuristic
transformation process	capacity	
direct outputs	scientific management	
by-products	trade-off	
production	model	

QUESTIONS

1. Define operations management.

2. List the five major components of an operation.

3. Describe the five components in each of the following.

   (a) a barber shop
   (b) a library
   (c) an appliance plant

4. What are the major distinctions between a production organization and a service organization?

5. Explain the difference between make to stock and make to order.

6. Give examples not already given in the chapter of each of the three types of input and their corresponding output.

7. Is capital an operations management resource?

8. Distinguish between long-range, medium-range, and short-range planning.

9. Give an example of a strategic plan for a university and its corresponding tactical plan.

10. What type of industry existed prior to factories?

11. What are the contributions of Watt, Taylor, and Westinghouse to operations management?

12. Name the six steps in decision making.

13. What is a model? What is the advantage of using a model?

14. Describe iconic models, analogue models, and symbolic models.

15. Give an example that is not given in the chapter of each of the three types of models.

16. What is the difference between a descriptive and a prescriptive model?

17. What is the difference between an optimization technique and a heuristic technique?

18. What is the relationship between marketing and operations?

19. Why does a finance major, marketing major, or accounting major need to study operations management?

PROBLEMS

The examples given at the end of "The Nature of Operations Management" (the first section of the chapter) are solved in later chapters. However, for fun and a better understanding of these problems, try to solve the examples listed below. Do not look ahead. The commonsense approach that you take now should pique your interest in the actual techniques developed later.

1. Example 1.2
2. Example 1.3
3. Example 1.6
4. Example 1.8
5. Example 1.9
6. Example 1.10
7. Example 1.11

REFERENCES

Buffa, E. S. *Meeting the Competitive Challenge.* Homewood, Ill.: Dow Jones Irwin, 1984.

Buffa, E. S., and R. Sarin. *Operations Management: The Management of Production Systems.* 8th ed. Santa Barbara, Calif.: Wiley and Sons, Inc., 1987.

Chase, R. B., and N. J. Aquilano. *Production and Operations Management.* 5th ed. Homewood, Ill.: Richard D. Irwin, 1989.

Collier, D. A. *Service Management: Operating Decisions.* Englewood Cliffs, N.J.: Prentice-Hall, 1987.

Fitzsimmons, J. A., and R. S. Sullivan. *Service Operations Management.* New York: McGraw-Hill, 1982.

Fogarty, D. W., J. H. Blackstone, and T. R. Hoffman. *Production and Inventory Management.* 2nd ed. Cincinnati, Ohio: South-Western Publishing Company, 1991.

Hayes, R. M., and S. C. Wheelwright. *Restoring Our Competitive Edge: Competing Through Manufacturing.* New York: John Wiley and Sons, 1984.

Hirshfield, D. S. "From the Shadows," *Interfaces* 13, no. 2 (April 1983): 72–76.

Hodgetts, R. M. *Management: Theory, Process and Practice.* Philadelphia: W. B. Saunders Company, 1982.

Koontz, H., C. O'Donnell, and H. Weihrich. *Management.* 9th ed. New York: McGraw-Hill, 1988.

Mondy, R. W., R. E. Holmes, and E. B. Flippo. *Management: Concepts and Practices.* 4th ed. Boston: Allyn and Bacon, 1988.

Schonberger, R. J. *Japanese Manufacturing Techniques: Nine Hidden Lessons in Simplicity.* New York: The Free Press, 1982.

Skinner, W. *Manufacturing: The Formidable Competitive Weapon.* New York: John Wiley and Sons, 1985.

C H A P T E R

2

O U T L I N E

WORLD-CLASS OPERATIONS

- To explain the international nature of business and how this affects operations management
- To introduce the problems that have caused the general decline in U.S. operations
- To detail the current issues facing operations managers
- To explain the relationship between federal strategy, corporate strategy, and the operations function

INTRODUCTION

production as a competitive weapon

For decades, top management in the United States viewed operations as a cost center. Only recently have we learned that this is the wrong paradigm. Foreign manufacturers, most notably the Japanese, have taught us that production, like marketing and finance, is an asset that can be used to gain a competitive advantage.

For decades, top management in the United States concerned itself primarily with satisfying the demand of consumers in the United States. Two things were assumed: that everyone wanted American-made goods and that there was no such thing as foreign competition. Foreign-made goods were dismissed as being inferior or mere toys. After all, how could one compare a Volkswagon Beetle with a Cadillac? The Beetle began the infestation of our production fields, and its Japanese cousins have created chaos in the auto industry. In fact, prior to World War II 94 percent of the cars sold in the United States were manufactured in the United States. In 1990, 25 percent of the cars sold in this country were made in Japan, and the best-selling car model in the United States was the Honda Accord. We now know that foreign manufacturers must be taken seriously. We now know that operations must respond to a global market. We now know that operations must be world-class.

the global economy

After World War II, the U.S. market was eight times as large as the next largest market. By 1993, when economic and monetary union is expected to be complete, the twelve-nation European Community (Iceland, United Kingdom, Denmark, the Netherlands, Belgium, Germany, France, Luxembourg, Portugal, Spain, Greece, and Italy) will comprise a significantly larger market than the U.S. market. Markets in the Far East and in Eastern Europe are growing more and more significant. The process of finding demand points and building new supply points has become **globalized**. Heinz is attempting to become a market leader in ketchup in Europe. U.S. firms such as Boeing, Caterpillar, Dow, Eastman Kodak, Ford, Hewlett-Packard, Merck, Scott Paper, Sun Microsystems, and 3M all have products for which over one-quarter of total sales is in foreign markets. We no longer have a **closed circle economy** of U.S. firms producing for U.S. consumers.

Any definition of **world-class** manufacturer must include references to quality, inventory, and employee relations. However, achieving world-class operations requires more than improving quality, reducing inventory, and involving workers. World-class manufacturing is a philosophy that recognizes that improvements in transportation and communications have made the world smaller; changes in one country have a far greater effect on other countries than was once the case. The concept of interrelatedness extends to the individual firm as well; changes in one functional area, such as quality, affect other functional areas, such as inventory. World-class operations is about total, long-term commitment, from the top down, in all functional areas. As noted by Harley-Davidson board chairman Vaughn L. Beals, "Ten years ago there was little public knowledge as to how the Japanese were accomplishing their seeming miracles. Today there are no excuses for ignorance." [Vaughn L. Beals, Jr., "The Stark Choice: Become a World Class Manufacturer or Die," *P&IM Review with APICS News* (May 1990), p. 20] The Japanese secured their position with a combination of long-term thinking, persistence, and flexibility. Foreign companies in other newly developed countries are emulating Japan. It is time that we did the same.

World-class ideas will be presented throughout the text, especially in chapters discussing location, inventory, and quality. In our location discussion, we will present the relationship between vendors and users. In our inventory chapters, we will detail the just-in-time philosophy. In our quality control chapters, we will detail total quality management. In this chapter, we present a broad outline of the origins of world-class manufacturing, the current state of world-class manufacturing, and the future of world-class manufacturing. With proper management attitudes, it *is* possible for U.S. companies to recapture lost market shares, as Ford, Harley-Davidson, and Xerox have demonstrated.

> **crossing functional lines**

> Teaching Suggestion 2.1: World Class Thinks Long Term. See the Instructor's Section for details.

> Teaching Suggestion 2.2: Open-Minded Companies. See the Instructor's Section for details.

INTERNATIONAL COMPETITION

In the years following the Civil War, the United States surpassed Great Britain to become the world's dominant producer nation. The work force at the time was not only highly skilled and capable but, during war times certainly—that is, during the Spanish-American War and both world wars—highly motivated as well. Natural resources were abundant. There was a great deal of research and development into new technologies. The United States had economies of scale that could not be matched by any other country. The United States possessed outstanding managers. This country lost its longtime lead in manufacturing only recently—the last few decades. Now, of the 50 largest industrial corporations worldwide (ranked by sales), 19 are U.S. corporations, 21 are European, and 10 are Asian. The United States has abdicated its lead in manufacturing primarily to the Japanese and the Germans. The international Fortune 500 (which excludes U.S. firms) is led by 159 Japanese firms, 74 British firms, 53 West German firms, and 39 French firms. In this section, we will explore some of the reasons for the United States' decline and the advancement of other countries. Especially with the recent upheaval in Eastern Europe and the Soviet Union, the United States has an unprecedented opportunity to make a place for itself in the "New World Order"—if we learn from our mistakes. The competition, however, is only going to get tougher. Of immediate concern is the rapid growth of industry in the **Pacific Rim nations**—Japan, South Korea, China, Taiwan, Hong Kong, Philippines, Vietnam, Thailand, Singapore, New Zealand, and Australia. After Japan, most notable among these countries is Korea, which is home to—among other manufacturers—Hyundai, Samsung, Lucky-Goldstar, and Daewoo.

Light-truck assembly at Nissan's Smyrna, Tennessee, facility. (© Jim Pickerell/Tony Stone Worldwide)

globalization of production

globalization of demand

As a result of globalization, towns like Marysville, Ohio, and Smyrna, Tennessee, are home to foreign automobile manufacturing facilities. These American towns have or will have counterparts in Europe. For example, Nissan, Toyota, and Honda all plan to open facilities in the United Kingdom. Globalization results, not only from matters of production and supply, but also from matters of consumption and demand. World markets are expanding rapidly. For example, East Asia (excluding Japan, Australia, and New Zealand) currently accounts for 3.2 percent of the automobile market, but this is expected to rise to 10 percent.

INDICATIONS OF CONCERN: IMPORTS, EXPORTS, AND THE TRADE DEFICIT

Americans have known for some time that we are failing in our production efforts. We couldn't help but notice; the evidence is overwhelming.

It is widely known that the U.S. trade deficit is growing each year. However, this widely discussed public information does not present a complete picture of what has taken place in the United States over the past three decades or so.

Imports have been growing. On a percentage basis, imports rose from 5.1 percent to 10.7 percent of purchased goods. This observation by itself simply says that U.S. consumer demand is increasingly being satisfied by foreign companies. This trend is pervasive, but certain industries have been hit particularly hard: namely, automobiles, chemicals, commercial aircraft, consumer electronics, machine tools, semiconductors, computers, office equipment, steel, and textiles.

imports are growing

The fact that exports rose from 4.3 percent of manufactured goods in 1965 to 13.5 percent in 1980 also indicates the growth in global markets over the past decades. No longer do U.S. firms simply produce to satisfy U.S. demand. Increased consideration is being given to satisfying world markets.

exports are growing

Figure 2.1 displays the dollar volume of U.S. exports and imports through 1988 (the most recent data available). Figure 2.1 reveals that *imports are growing faster than exports,* indicating a failure of U.S. manufacturing organizations to keep pace with those in the rest of the world. In some cases, foreign competition has virtually forced American companies out of the market. For example, in 1970 there were eighteen manufacturers of television sets in the United States; in 1990, only one—Zenith—was left (and many of its sets are manufactured in Mexico). The same story could be told of manufacturers of radio receivers and duplicating machines. The duplicating machine was invented by a U.S. firm, Xerox, but the Japanese were able to produce units at half the cost of those made in the United States. Fortunately for Xerox, the company was able to learn from its Japanese subsidiary, Fuji Xerox, how to become more efficient and productive.

The United States is still competitive in the manufacture of certain products. Figure 2.2 shows the dollar value in 1988 of imports, exports, and net exports (exports minus imports) of manufactured goods for six major producer nations. The United States is still a major player, but the biggest exporter is Germany, with exports of $323 billion compared to $320 billion for the United States. The biggest net exporter is Japan.

Teaching Suggestion 2.3: Lack of U.S. Exports. See the Instructor's Section for details.

The principal goods manufactured by Japan are given in Figure 2.3. The bar heights represent exports as a percentage of total manufactured goods. Clearly, the bulk of the watches, cameras, cash registers, duplicating machines, and VCRs produced in Japan are exported. In addition, more than half of the cars and microwave ovens produced in Japan are exported.

CAUSES OF DECLINE IN OPERATIONS

As you will see, there is no shortage of explanations for the decline of U.S. operations. Still, reversing the decline has proven to be a difficult task. The United States' fall from its position of leadership seems to have resulted not from a single cause but from a complex of causes.

WAGES

The loss of industry was originally attributed to lower wage rates in foreign countries. If this was ever a satisfactory explanation, it no longer is. Table 2.1 presents the hourly compensation costs (wages and benefits) for 1975 and for 1988 (the most recent data available) for selected nations. In 1975, the wages of the average American production worker were $6.36 per hour, the fourth highest in the world. By 1988, the United

U.S. wages have dropped

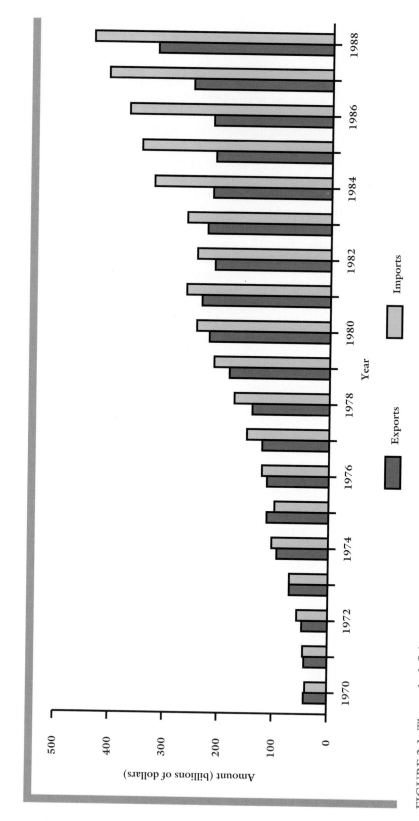

FIGURE 2.1 The trade deficit
Source: U.S. Department of Commerce, *Statistical Abstract of the United States,* 1990, p. 804.

Transparency Master 2.1:
The Trade Deficit.

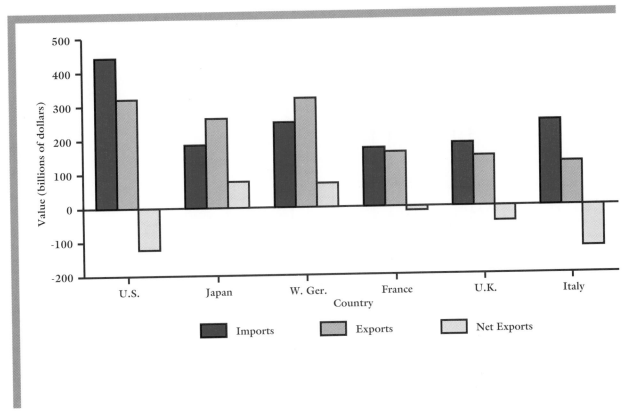

FIGURE 2.2 Foreign trade of selected countries, 1988
Source: U.S. Department of Commerce, *Statistical Abstract of the United States,* 1990, p. 856.

Transparency Master 2.2:
Imports and Exports of
Major Producer Nations.

States had dropped to ninth on the list. Most notably, West Germany, which had similar wages in 1975, had wages that were 30 percent higher ($18.07 compared to $13.90) than those in the United States by 1988. Thus, the lower wage rate explanation does not hold in the case of West Germany's advance over the United States in manufacturing.

Our other major competitor is, of course, Japan. In 1975, the average compensation in Japan was slightly less than half that in the United States—$3.05 compared to $6.35. By 1988, the average wage in Japan was 95 percent of the average wage in the United States. Japan no longer enjoys a wage advantage over the United States.

Lower wage rates in foreign countries would account for the loss of highly labor-intensive industries in the United States. Lower wage rates cannot be the primary reason for this nation's loss of leadership in high technology products, however, as labor costs for these products typically account for less than 10 percent of total costs. Also, many countries that have historically had lower wages than the United States have never been major manufacturing competitors. Brazil, Mexico, and India all have extremely low wage rates, but we are not concerned about competing with these countries. In addition, there is little fear that low labor costs in Eastern Europe will create a threat to U.S. firms.

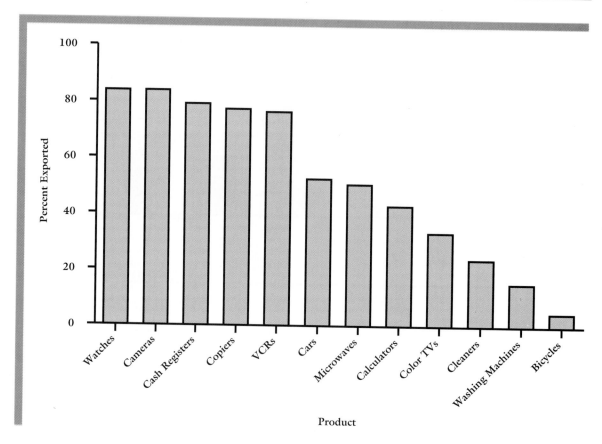

FIGURE 2.3 Japan's principal manufactured products
Source: Japan—An International Comparison (Tokyo, Japan: Keizai Koho Center, Japanese Institute for Social and Economic Affairs, 1990).

If lower wage rates are a factor at all, there is still reason for concern. Although wage rates in Japan and West Germany are on par with those in the United States, other newly emerging industrial countries—in particular, those countries known as Pacific Rim countries—seem to be capable of taking advantage of low wages to cause problems for the United States, Japan, and other higher wage rate nations.

Table 2.2 contains the percentage change in the cost per unit of output that occurred in ten industrial nations between 1955 and 1975 and between 1975 and 1988. Notice that labor costs in virtually every other nation in the table rose faster than they did in the United States—both between 1955 and 1975 and between 1975 and 1988. Notice also that Japan and Germany experienced the highest rates of increase.

productivity

Now let's compare the rate of increase in wages with the rate of increase in output (see Table 2.3). While wages have been going up in these countries, so has the output per hour. If the output per hour increases at the same rate as the wages, then there is no net increase in cost per unit. For example, costs in the United States have increased by 4 percent more than output since 1977. For most countries, costs have increased more than output. Notable exceptions are the Scandinavian countries and Japan.

TABLE 2.1 International wage comparison

Country	Hourly Compensation in U.S. Dollars	
	1975	1988 (except where noted)
United States	$6.36	$13.90
Canada	5.79	13.58
Brazil	.86	1.49 (1987)
Mexico	2.00	1.57 (1987)
Venezuela	2.03	3.78 (1981)
Australia	5.54	11.01
Hong Kong	.76	2.43
India	.19	.42 (1984)
Israel	2.25	6.34 (1987)
Japan	3.05	13.14
Korea	.35	2.46
New Zealand	3.21	6.85 (1987)
Pakistan	.21	.37 (1981)
Singapore	.84	2.67
Sri Lanka	.28	.30 (1987)
Taiwan	.39	2.71
Austria	4.34	13.84
Belgium	6.41	15.68
Denmark	6.28	15.88
Finland	4.60	15.48
France	4.52	12.99
Germany, F.R.	6.35	18.07
Greece	1.69	4.61 (1987)
Ireland	3.01	9.86
Italy	4.65	12.87
Luxembourg	6.35	10.63 (1986)
Netherlands	6.58	16.30
Norway	6.78	19.43
Portugal	1.58	2.73
Spain	2.59	8.75
Sweden	7.18	16.85
Switzerland	6.09	17.94
Turkey	.70	.41 (1984)
United Kingdom	3.32	10.56

Source: U.S. Bureau of Labor Statistics, *Handbook of Labor Statistics,* 1989, p. 572.

Transparency Master 2.3: International Wage Comparison.

STRIKES

Higher wages are commonly attributed to unionization, a topic to which we will return in our discussion of facility location in Chapter 5. Also attributed to unions are inefficient work stoppages. One might guess that part of the U.S. decline in manufacturing is due to strikes. However, the data in Table 2.4 indicates otherwise. Our chief

TABLE 2.2   Unit labor costs for selected
countries, 1955–1988

Country	Increase in Labor Costs	
	1955–1975	1975–1988
United States	291%	155%
Canada	289	169
Denmark	662	195
France	356	176
Germany, F.R.	784	203
Japan	620	217
Italy	510	158
Netherlands	627	151
Sweden	475	158
United Kingdom	570	205

Source: U.S. Bureau of Labor Statistics, *Handbook of Labor Statistics,* 1989, p. 567.

Striking workers in Taejon, South Korea— inefficient work stoppages are not limited to economies in decline. (Reuters/ Bettmann)

TABLE 2.3 Change in cost/output, 1977–1988	
Country	**Change (%)**
United States	+ 4
Canada	+27
Denmark	+49
France	+20
Germany, F.R.	+33
Italy	+ 1
Japan	− 1
Netherlands	− 9
Sweden	−10
United Kingdom	+36

Source: U.S. Bureau of Labor Statistics, *Handbook of Labor Statistics,* 1989, p. 567.

TABLE 2.4 Work stoppages, involving one thousand or more workers, 1988	
Country	**Work Stoppages**
United States	40
Australia	—
Belgium	63
Canada	—
Denmark	157
France	—
Germany, F.R.	—
Italy	1,620
Japan	498
Netherlands	38
New Zealand	—
Norway	—
Sweden	—
Switzerland	4
United Kingdom	725

Source: U.S. Bureau of Labor Statistics, *Handbook of Labor Statistics,* 1989, p. 579.

competitor, Japan, had more than ten times as many work stoppages in 1988 as the United States did. Strikes occur not only in developed countries but also in the newly developing countries, as evidenced by Hyundai's month-long strike in June 1988 in Korea. In addition, strikes have occurred at Motorola, IBM, and Tandy plants in Korea.

THE VALUATION OF THE DOLLAR

We also blamed our lack of competitiveness on the overvalued dollar. The high value of the dollar after World War II made it difficult to sell our products in other countries and made imports extremely cheap in the United States. There is some truth to this argument. However, things have changed in our favor. Table 2.5 gives the value of foreign currency. The value of the dollar has suffered a serious decline compared with our two major competitors. In 1975, one dollar would purchase 297 yen or 2.46 deutschemarks; in 1989, the dollar would buy only 133 yen or 1.89 deutschmarks. Note that the dollar has risen against the other currencies in the table.

PRODUCTIVITY

Are foreign workers more productive than their U.S. counterparts? If so, what part has this fact played in the United States' fall from preeminence? In Chapter 3 we will discuss the measurement of productivity in detail. For now, we will note that there are

TABLE 2.5 Foreign exchange rates, 1975–1989 (currency units per U.S. dollar)

Year	Canadian Dollar	French Franc	Italian Lira	Japanese Yen	British Pound	West German Mark
1975	1.02	4.28	653	297	.45	2.46
1976	0.99	4.78	833	296	.55	2.52
1977	1.06	4.91	882	268	.57	2.32
1978	1.14	4.51	849	210	.52	2.01
1979	1.16	4.26	831	219	.47	1.83
1980	1.17	4.23	856	227	.43	1.81
1981	1.20	5.44	1,138	221	.49	2.26
1982	1.23	6.58	1,354	249	.57	2.43
1983	1.23	7.62	1,519	238	.65	2.55
1984	1.30	8.73	1,756	237	.75	2.84
1985	1.37	8.98	1,908	238	.76	2.94
1986	1.39	6.93	1,491	168	.68	2.17
1987	1.33	6.01	1,297	144	.60	1.80
1988	1.23	5.95	1,302	128	.56	1.76
1989	1.19	6.42	1,384	133	.59	1.89

Source: U.S. Department of Commerce, *Statistical Abstract of the United States,* 1990, p. 858.

recent productivity changes

several ways to measure productivity and that the measures are open to different inter-pretations. For example, one measure of worker productivity is gross domestic prod-uct. Table 2.6 expresses gross domestic product (GDP) per employee in six nations as a percent of GDP per employee in the United States. Using this measure, productivity in the United States improved relative to each of the countries in the table, although both Canada and West Germany maintained an advantage. Interestingly, the table shows the United States as being comfortably ahead of Japan in terms of productivity.

Table 2.7 shows the output per hour for seven countries in 1970 and in 1988 (the most recent data) and the percentage change over the eighteen-year period. In 1970, the United States had the highest output rate and Japan had the lowest. By 1987, the

TABLE 2.6 Per capita gross domestic product, 1982–1986 (percent of U.S. GDP)

Year	Nation					
	Canada	France	Italy	Japan	England	West Germany
1982	112	108	70	82	81	112
1983	111	105	68	81	81	111
1984	108	100	66	80	78	108
1985	109	99	66	81	79	109
1986	109	99	67	81	80	109

Source: U.S. Department of Commerce, *Statistical Abstract of the United States,* 1989, p. 436.

TABLE 2.7 Output per hour (1977 = 100)

Country	1970	1988	Increase (%)
United States	80.8	136.2	69
Japan	64.8	190	193
France	70.0	144.1	106
Canada	75.6	124.3	64
Britain	80.4	154.9	93
West Germany	71.2	135.9	91
Italy	72.7	167.1	130

Source: U.S. Department of Commerce, *Statistical Abstract of the United States,* 1990, p. 850.

situation had almost reversed. Only Canada and West Germany had lower rates than the United States in 1988. In fact, only Canada had a smaller increase between 1970 and 1988 than the United States. Japan experienced a productivity increase two and a half times greater than that of the United States. Unless we make changes, we will fall farther behind.

CAPITAL INVESTMENT IN OPERATIONS

Since 1965, U.S. capital investment as a percentage of manufacturing output has been less than 12 percent; the comparable figure for Japan is greater than 20 percent. In this section we will explore some of the consequences of this disparity.

After World War II, U.S. companies made capital investments because increased prosperity and a baby boom created a need to increase capacity. When the demand for new capacity slowed in the 1970s, most U.S. companies stopped investing in capital equipment. Japanese companies, meanwhile, continued to invest in new plants. When demand once again increased, the Japanese were positioned to handle it, but the U.S. firms were out of capacity. Even U.S. firms that made timely capital investments found themselves at a disadvantage: It takes longer to develop a new plant in the United States than in other parts of the world. For example, in Japan or Korea a new blast furnace can be on line in two or three years, while in the United States the same furnace will take five years to bring on line.

When U.S. firms stopped adding new capacity, they also stopped implementing new technologies. The equipment gap reached its peak around 1970, when U.S. manufacturing equipment was nearly twice as old, on average, as Japanese equipment. This gap has narrowed recently due both to the aging of Japanese equipment and to the installation of new equipment in the United States. Because we understand the age gap, many companies have begun capital investment programs in modern equipment. For example, Firestone Tire & Rubber (which is owned by Japan's Bridgestone Corporation) is investing $350 million to double its capacity and will spend over $1 billion to both improve and expand current facilities. Alcoa, Reynolds, and Alcan (Canada) all are opening new plants for aluminum. Mead Corporation opened a new paperboard plant in Phenix City, Alabama, in 1989—its first new plant in fourteen years. Ford Motor Company is expected to spend $29 billion on capital investments.

equipment gap has narrowed

An example of capital investment in a service industry—Greyhound's state-of-the-art Chicago terminal. (Jacob Bachman)

Oneida, a flatware manufacturer, has recently made more than $26 million worth of capital investments. Capital investment is not limited to production facilities; it also occurs in service industries. Greyhound Lines Inc. has spent $30 million to upgrade its bus terminals. Greyhound also has invested in new fuel-efficient vans to serve rural customers. Ryder Systems Inc., the truck rental giant, has expanded its fleet by adding 10,000 new trucks with special, modern features. In fact, investment in plant and equipment spending for services eclipsed spending for manufacturing in 1986 and has been higher ever since.

TECHNOLOGY

After World War II, the United States had the best manufacturing technology in the world. This technology has now spread throughout the world. Many countries have technologies in place that are equal to or better than ours. Since, as a rule, U.S. firms are slower to implement new technology than most foreign firms and since technology is changing so rapidly, U.S. firms must be less hesitant and must become more aggressive in using Advanced Manufacturing Technologies (AMT). We will explore this topic in Chapter 8.

QUALITY

In a complete turnaround from the 1950s, the phrase *Made in Japan* is now regarded by most Americans as synonymous with *quality*. This accounts for things such as the sales advantage the Mitsubishi Eclipse enjoys over the Plymouth Laser—identical cars (except for the name plate) manufactured *in the same U.S. plant* by Diamond Star, a Chrysler–Mitsubishi joint venture.

In large part because of stiff competition from the Japanese, U.S. manufacturers discovered quality in the 1980s—at least their marketing departments and advertising agencies did. Ford, in fact, made quality "Job One." As the following advertising slogans from the pages of *Fortune* magazine show, Ford was not alone.

Company	Slogan
Xerox	At Xerox our dedication to quality is well documented.
IBM	October is National Quality Month. At IBM, we're working on 11 more just like it.
Moore	When you're serious about quality, nothing stands in your way.
AT&T	Our commitment to quality goes back a long way. And ahead even further.
Westinghouse	Quality is its own reward.
Baldor	The result of a 'Quality Policy' that puts customer requirements and expectations first.
Texas Instruments	Quality is a way of life for more than 75,000 Texas Instruments employees around the world.
AMP	In technology, quality is the language of manufacturer/supplier relationships.
ODI	In the race to quality, there is no finish line. But there are front-runners.

Of course, to remain competitive, American businesses must do more than *advertise* quality into their products; they must also *build* it in.

We will delay a detailed discussion of quality until the last two chapters of this text. For now, we will briefly explore the transformation in attitudes toward quality in this country. For years, quality in operations meant conformance to standards. Operations experts paid a great deal of attention to finding defective products. Today, quality is considered to be built, rather than inspected, into a product. The definition has been expanded to include performance, features, reliability, durability, serviceability, aesthetics, and perceived quality—as well as conformance.

productivity vs. quality

Until fairly recently, it was believed that quality reduced productivity: You are not adding value to the product during inspection. (In other words, people felt about quality the way they do about materials handling: You don't add any value to a product when you move it from one place to another.) The current philosophy is that *productivity and quality do not compete.* Even though it takes time to perform a process properly or to make an inspection, this is not time wasted but, rather, time invested. By examining for quality, future mistakes can be arrested before they occur. Early inspection will lead to a reduction in waste later on. There is now widespread agreement that *quality must be an integral part of a company's mission.*

Teaching Suggestion 2.4: Quality vs. Productivity. See the Instructor's Section for details.

Until recently, quality had *not* been very important to many American companies. In 1988, the U.S. Department of Commerce instituted an annual National Quality Awards competition to recognize companies that emphasize quality. The first year, ten thousand application forms were distributed, but only sixty-six were returned. The judges from the National Institute of Standards & Technology (formerly, the National Bureau of Standards) sent experts to thirteen of the respondents but were able to award only three of the six available awards (to Motorola, Westinghouse Electric's Commercial Nuclear Fuel Division, and Globe Metallurgical). There seems to have been more interest in this award—and in quality—since 1988. Winners in 1989 included Xerox and Milliken. Cadillac, Federal Express, IBM, and Wallace Company won in 1990.

customers expect quality

Teaching Suggestion 2.5: Mediocre Quality. See the Instructor's Section for details.

Customers expect quality. Providing a defect-free product or service merely gives an organization a chance to compete in the marketplace. Success will be dictated by other factors. Japan now gives priority not to quality but to cost reduction and flexibility. It is not that Japan no longer expects quality. Rather, since quality is *expected* of every person and product, attention has shifted to other factors that can be controlled to boost profitability. Almost universal conformance to standards, even to rising standards, guarantees that competitors will seek out new fields on which to do battle.

Quality spreads quickly throughout the production chain. For example, due to Japanese competition—that is, consumer demand for high quality—the Big Three automobile manufacturers began to demand higher-quality components. This caused quality upgrades at the provider level. At the same time, auto manufacturers demanded price cuts from their suppliers, which forced productivity improvements at the lower levels.

emphasis on quality employees

We should mention one last thing about quality: High-quality products and services begin with high-quality employees. Educated, trained, and dedicated employees are essential for quality operation.

GOVERNMENT POLICIES

The policy of the U.S. government toward industry is essentially laissez-faire. The governments of many countries, however, take a proactive stand toward domestic business. In some cases, it takes the form of financial assistance in the development of a company or product. For example, a desire by firms in Britain, France, and Germany to penetrate the commercial aircraft market led the governments in those countries to back an aircraft manufacturing consortium— Airbus Industrie. In other cases, a proactive stand takes the form of trade barriers, which foreign firms often find unfair.

trade barriers

The major trade barriers are **tariffs** and **quotas**. Tariffs are taxes imposed on goods entering a country. The purpose of tariffs is to provide a price advantage to domestic manufacturers. Quotas are limits on the quantity of a particular type of good allowed into a country. A new type of quota is a **voluntary export restraint** (VER). With VERs, the producing country "voluntarily" agrees to limit its exports of a product to a certain country. For example, Japan has agreed to a limit on automobile exports and voluntary restraint arrangements limit steel imports to 20 percent of the U.S. market. Such agreements typically come about amidst threats by the importing country to impose involuntary quotas. (Notice that VERs provide an incentive for Japanese automakers to open plants in the United States—Japanese cars produced and sold in the United States do not count toward the voluntary export restraint.) Table 2.8 lists some of the trade barriers imposed against U.S. goods and companies.

TABLE 2.8 Trade barriers for U.S. firms

Product	Countries	Barrier
Grain	European Community	Price supports, variable duties
Soybeans	European Community	Price supports
Rice	Japan	Ban
Beef	European Community	Ban on hormones in livestock
Aircraft	Britain and others	Subsidies to Airbus Industrie
Telecommunications	EC and S. Korea	Standards stacked against imports
Satellites	Japan	Ban on imports
Pharmaceuticals	Argentina, Brazil	No patent protection
Videocassettes	Brazil	Requires subsidies of local films
Software	Thailand	Poor patent protection

Source: Rahul Jacob, "Export Barriers the U.S. Hates Most," *Fortune* (February 27, 1989), pp. 88–89.

Despite barriers such as these, the trend is toward opening national boundaries. We have already mentioned the removal of trade restrictions between member nations of the European Community. Similarly, a free-trade agreement between the United States and Canada and discussions between the United States and Mexico may result in a unified North American market. A notable holdout in this era of crumbling barriers is Japan. U.S. firms frequently complain about how difficult it is for them to get access to the Japanese market. (Meanwhile, the Japanese are stymied by European import quotas; their 11-percent share of the European market could easily double if such restrictions were eased.)

CULTURAL DIFFERENCES

Many of the differences in Japanese and U.S. management styles, some of which we have already mentioned, are cultural in nature. Does this difference in management style account for Japan's success? Japanese managers must interact with employees; Japanese workers must regulate themselves. Japanese workers are hired *for life* after they finish their schooling, and they receive a great deal of training. Employment is guaranteed; workers do not have to fear being displaced by someone from a different company. There is seniority-based promotion. All employees believe they are part of a family. The needs of management and labor are met before those of stockholders. Management is not evaluated on current results and can concentrate on the long term. Job rotation is used for generalist training and to eliminate "turf" problems. Overtime is typically not compensated.

Contrary to popular belief, pride in their work must be instilled in Japanese workers—just as it must in American workers. For example, prior to 1985, Japan Air Lines (JAL) performed its airplane maintenance procedures in the same way that U.S. airlines do. After a JAL Boeing 747 crashed into a mountain in August 1985, killing 520 people, JAL instituted new maintenance procedures. Since the crash, JAL has assigned fifteen-person teams of mechanics who are responsible for specific planes. Team mem-

Teaching Suggestion 2.6: Desert Storm Pride. See the Instructor's Section for details.

bers sign their names on a plaque on the airplane, and the team leader flies the plane after maintenance. Having the repair team "own" the planes it works on instills a great deal of pride and improves quality.

EDUCATION AND TRAINING

American attitudes toward education may have had as much to do with the decline of U.S. manufacturing as direct governmental intervention or subtle cultural differences. We have stated that high-quality products begin with high-quality workers. Unfortunately, it appears that the U.S. educational system is increasingly unable to supply such workers in large numbers. Some place the bulk of the blame on ill-prepared teachers; others cite an inadequate or irrelevant curriculum. The length of time students spend in the classroom in this country also has been receiving a lot of attention lately. Japanese students spend an average of thirty-three hours per week in class, compared with twenty-six hours per week for their counterparts in the United States. Furthermore, Japanese schools operate 220 days per year, compared with 178 days in the United States. Those who are troubled by this disparity have called for lengthening the school year—a proposal that historically has been viewed with suspicion by parents and students, if not dismissed outright.

Transparency Master 2.4: Comparison of Annual School Days for Selected Countries.

> The standard American response to proposals for a longer school year is to argue that Americans should learn to more efficiently use the current 180 days before they worry about adding more days. Such a response is to get the whole problem backwards. Instead of starting with what is easy to do—work longer and harder—Americans start with what is very difficult to do—work smarter. The argument is also a form of implicit American arrogance. Americans think that they can learn in 180 days what the rest of the world takes 200 to 240 days to learn. It also forgets that the rest of the world is trying to use its 220 or 240 days more efficiently. (Lester Thurow, quoted in Michael J. Barrett, "The Case for More School Days," *Atlantic Monthly* (November 1990), p. 100)

Not only are American workers poorly educated, they are also poorly trained—especially relative to workers in Germany and Japan. In Japan, firms guarantee employment for life, which means that Japanese workers often receive better training than their counterparts in the United States (they are a much safer investment for the firms that hire them) and that what training they do receive is not wasted. In Germany, meanwhile, a highly structured system of apprenticeships and technical institutes ensures that that nation is well supplied with capable production workers.

WORLD-CLASS MANAGEMENT FOR THE FUTURE

Few would argue against the need for a change in the general management of U.S. corporations and in the management of the production facilities of these corporations. U.S. firms can no longer rely on nearly century-old scientific management methods. Managers must be concerned with long-term goals rather than short-term profits. In general, human-resource and flexibility issues must become far more important to manufacturing than short-term profits. Specifically, outmoded management styles must be overcome by improving employee–management relations, by integrating product design into the production process, by making continuous improvements in products and the production process, and by learning to adapt to change.

EMPLOYEE–MANAGEMENT RELATIONS

An adversarial relationship between management and labor is no longer acceptable. Decisions must be made from the top down *and from the bottom up*. Management can dictate the long-term strategic goals, but the day-to-day operations are known best by the employees. Tom Barrett, the chairman, president, and CEO of Goodyear Tire and Rubber Company, recently offered managers a six-step program for improving operations by strengthening the bonds between them and their employees.

need for cooperation

- Provide a safe working environment for your employees;
- Provide a clean and comfortable working environment for your employees;
- Reduce the physical exertion required to do a given job;
- Share with your employees, giving them a sense of belonging;
- Empower your employees, through training, to handle the responsibilities of their assignments;
- Create an environment of continuous improvement for all employees in all operations. (Tom H. Barrett, "World Class Manufacturing: Can America Compete?" *P&IM Review with APICS News* (November 1990), p. 22.)

emphasis on human side of operations

In Fremont, California, the New United Motor Manufacturing Inc. (NUMMI), a joint venture between General Motors and Toyota, has created a new atmosphere of teamwork, pride, and quality, where before there might have been hostility between the management team and the workers, all members of the United Automobile Workers Union (UAW). The plant is unionized, but now there is a sense of harmony, in which employees and their bosses work together to enforce the plant's strict drug and alcohol policy and employees willingly submit to drug and alcohol tests. Quality defects have been reduced from an average of five to ten per car to one every five to ten cars.

Big steel has joined Detroit in moving toward increased cooperation. In its West Mifflin, Pennsylvania, facility, USX Corporation has an excellence program that involves teams of hourly and salaried employees in several meetings per month to discuss problems with quality. A similar program is in operation at the USX plant in Gary, Indiana, where seminars also have been held for all employees. In Lorain, Ohio, more than thirty USX quality control teams meet daily. In Pittsburg, California, management began intensive technical training of union employees.

A.O. Smith Corporation, a Milwaukee manufacturer of automotive works, has successfully implemented workers into the decision-making process. **Quality circles** (discussed in Chapter 17) have been added, joint management–union problem solving committees have been established, work teams have been set up, and unions have been directly involved in managerial decision making. The employee involvement plan has increased productivity and decreased defect rates.

Quality circles and employee participation programs are not limited to production facilities. The Price Chopper chain of supermarkets in upstate New York has used quality circles to reduce problems such as absenteeism, damage, and shrinkage. The Kroger supermarket chain has also used quality circles in its retail outlets. The reason for this is simple:

When management recognizes that most workers know their own jobs better than anyone else and, given the chance, will gladly accept the responsibility of managing their own work, the specific systems a manufacturer wishes to impose can be implemented with relative ease. (H. J. Shapiro and T. Cosenza, *Reviving Industry in America* (Cambridge, Mass.: Ballinger, 1987), p. 27)

workers know jobs best

There is a natural incentive for workers to cooperate with management. If the company succeeds, then workers maintain their jobs. In order to emphasize the workers' contributions, it is worthwhile for management to consider some form of incentive pay system. American Express added productivity incentives upwards of $7,000 annually for employees who increase their efficiency. Another type of incentive program gives employees a share of the company's profits. One study estimates that productivity increases by 5 percent to 10 percent in companies with **profit sharing**.

PRODUCTS DEVELOPED IN CONJUNCTION WITH THE PROCESS

For years, product design was the research and development laboratory's responsibility, completely separate from the operations function. New-product engineers would come up with ideas and prototype models, paying attention to material and labor costs but not to manufacturing details. We now realize the extent to which product design influences the product's costs. Products must be designed for ease of manufacturing, and standardization of components will help, by allowing the firm to use fewer vendors and to use the same components in different products. Manufacturing and marketing must work closely with the product engineering teams. Product engineers must be aware of the manufacturing technology the company is using.

The Japanese have **product development teams**, whose multiple goals include quality goals and production goals. These teams also assist in determining marketing and design features of the new product. U.S. firms, however, all too often have an initial team for design, a second team for engineering design, and a third team for process design. This is not economical. The production process must be considered at the outset, in the earliest stages of new product development.

CONTINUOUS IMPROVEMENT

Product design, including reliability and quality, does not have to change in jumps. There can be continuous improvements in the production process and in the product itself. Progress is the sum of major breakthroughs and minor improvements. The American philosophy about the manufacturing process or the product seems to have been, "If it ain't broke, don't fix it." U.S. firms would be better off imitating the Japanese, whose philosophy (known as *kaizen*) is that even minor changes may help improve the product or the production process.

Teaching Suggestion 2.7: Fix It Anyway. See the Instructor's Section for details.

FLEXIBILITY

We must accept that the world changes more quickly now than in the past and that these changes involve attitudes as well as technology. Management must be willing to make changes in managerial style, product design, and process design. The key to success in the next century will be flexibility, the ability to make changes quickly.

New products have shorter **life cycles**. One reason that the United States lost much of the textile market is because foreign companies were better prepared to make production changes as styles changed. Recently, American fabric manufacturers have come to realize the value and necessity of flexibility. For example, Milliken has reduced its production lot sizes. The new focus on flexibility extends to other industries as well. Boeing now designs its airplanes so that the company can easily develop and produce new products using existing components and equipment. Westvaco Corporation has invested $175 million in order to be able to quickly change from coated paper to uncoated paper.

Evidence that U.S. automakers have recognized the problems associated with entrenched, inflexible bureaucracies and are trying to change management style includes new car projects such as Saturn (GM), Liberty (Chrysler), and Alpha (Ford) and joint ventures with foreign manufacturers. Flexibility at the automobile manufacturing plant leads to flexibility at the suppliers' plants. Recently, auto parts manufacturers have cut the size of their production runs nearly in half. The operations goal must be to maximize adaptability in order to be long-term competitive rather than short-term profitable.

Flexibility should be both a long-term and a short-term objective. In order to be competitive, it must be possible to quickly deliver custom orders. General Electric can deliver a custom-made circuit breaker box in three days, whereas it used to take three weeks. Motorola produces electronic pagers in less than three hours rather than the formerly typical three weeks. This kind of short-term flexibility has been made possible by flexible manufacturing systems (FMS), the name given to a group of machines that are linked by automated materials handling systems and controlled by computer to enable assorted products to be manufactured by the same equipment with a minimum of changeover.

One more remark about flexibility: There must be flexibility in work design. Workers must be trained to handle several different tasks—and permitted by union rules to do so. However, as the notion of flexible workers runs contrary to the tradition of skilled tradesmen, this change may prove especially slow in coming.

OPERATIONS AND STRATEGY

> Every firm competing in an industry has a competitive strategy, whether explicit or implicit. This strategy may have been developed explicitly through a planning process or it may have evolved implicitly through the activities of the various functional departments of the firm. Left to its own devices, each functional department will inevitably pursue approaches dictated by its professional orientation and the incentives of those in charge. However, the sum of these departmental approaches rarely equals the best strategy. (Michael F. Porter, *Competitive Strategy: Techniques for Analyzing Industries and Competitors* (New York: Free Press, 1980), p. xiii.)

These are the opening words of a classic book for managers of all organizations. There are two major lessons in this short paragraph. The first lesson is that if a firm has existed for some time, it must have been doing something right over that period of time. More precisely, it must have been doing something better than its competitors. The firm may have been designed for this (as a result of "a planning process") or this advantage may have developed by accident ("evolved implicitly"). Prior to the 1980s, it was quite likely that this advantage came about by accident rather than by design. For example, Henry Ford produced only black Model T cars. It is not clear whether this was a **strategy** or simply a pattern of behavior and production. Today, we realize that to be successful and to be able to compete in the new global market, our competitive strategy must be explicitly designed; we cannot wait for one to evolve.

The second lesson from Porter's introduction is that an organization is the integration of many different functions. The traditional business functions do not operate in isolation but are intimately related to one another. If each function has its own strategy and goals, then the organization will not be as effective as it should be. Again, "the sum of departmental approaches rarely equals the best strategy."

The way that an organization will operate in the year 2000 and beyond is determined by decisions—on, among other things, capital investment and quality—made today. These decisions must be coherent; they also must be based on the same strategy—a carefully mapped-out strategy for the future.

THE ORGANIZATION OF STRATEGY

levels of strategy

Figure 2.4 presents the different levels of strategy. Strategy goes on at the broadest governmental and industry levels and at the lowest functional levels. In particular, we are interested in the production/operations strategy and the interaction between higher-level strategies and the production/operations function. Each lower-level strategy is a function of the strategies at the levels above. The functional strategy is dictated by the business-level strategy. In the term *business-level strategy, business* refers to a stand-alone business. A corporation may have many stand-alone business units. The business-level strategy is dictated by the strategy of the corporation. Choices made at the corporate level include the types of businesses in which a corporation wishes to operate and the allocation of corporate resources to those businesses. Corporate strategy is to some extent dictated by government "strategy" and industry strategy. The government "strategy" is implemented through tax laws, which encourage or discourage investment; trade barriers such as import quotas; cost of capital; safety standards; and monopoly regulations and patent policies, which encourage or discourage research and development. In developing a strategy, a company must concern itself with other external factors, such as the growth rate of the industry or industries in which they are involved; the competition within a given industry; and societal factors such as shifting demographics and changing patterns of work and leisure.

Although we are concerned primarily with the functional level, we will begin our discussion of competitive strategy with a look at the governmental level. In other words, we will begin at the top and work our way down—just as individual strategies do.

STRATEGIES FOR GOVERNMENT

countering the U.S. decline

A major study was commissioned recently to determine the causes of the decline in U.S. manufacturing and to outline the steps the federal government could take to reverse the slide. The following general strategies emerged, many of which we have already discussed.

■ The federal government should pursue macroeconomic policies that reduce the cost of capital for private investment. This will require measures to increase private savings and reduce the federal budget deficit.

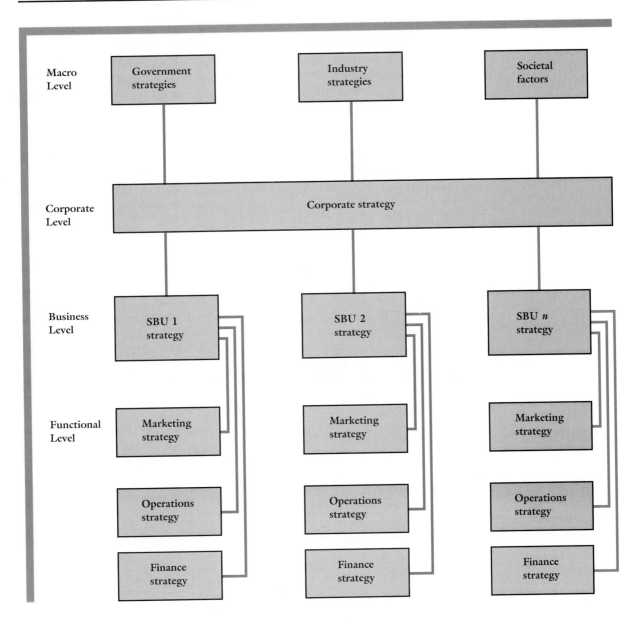

FIGURE 2.4 Types and levels of strategies

- The federal government should continue to press for removal of trade restrictions and for equal access for U.S. firms and products to foreign markets.
- The federal government should adopt programs for K–12 education that will lead to greater technological literacy. This will enable a larger fraction of citizens to participate in and benefit from more productive working careers.
- The government should encourage continuous education and training for the U.S. work force, with special attention to the increased participation of women, blacks, and Spanish-speaking Americans.

Transparency Master 2.5:
Types and Levels of
Strategies.

- The federal government should continue investing in basic research and should provide adequate support for operations, equipment, and modern facilities.
- The federal government's support of research and development should be extended to include a greater emphasis on policies to encourage the downstream phases of product and process engineering and to clear any current obstacles to innovation.
- The government should encourage the establishment of a national information infrastructure.
- The federal government should heed the many voices calling for greater efficiency in military research and development and military procurement to minimize the financial and human resources required to meet national security needs. (M. L. Dertouzos, R. K. Lester, and R. M. Solow, *Made in America* (New York: HarperCollins, 1989), pp. 152–155)

STRATEGIES FOR INDUSTRY

When we talk about industry we are actually talking about management and labor. Our decline can be arrested only by having management and labor make strategic changes. What follows are the steps management and labor must take, according to the MIT Commission on Industrial Productivity, to make America competitive.

- Focus on the production process, with the objective of improving long-term productive performance.
- Adopt as an explicit objective of the production process the delivery of high-quality products to market in a timely fashion at competitive prices.
- Develop techniques to measure and improve the efficiency and quality of the production process, and identify opportunities for progressive improvements in its performance.
- Emphasize product variety and manufacturing flexibility in the development of production systems.

making U.S. industries competitive
- Cultivate a more involved, less specialized, continuously learning work force.
- Flatten organizational hierarchies to give employees greater responsibility and broader experience.
- Integrate and (where feasible) perform concurrently the functions of research and development, product design, and process design to achieve greater efficiency and a shorter time to market.
- Cooperate with suppliers rather than treating them as adversaries.
- Insist that key employees have an adequate understanding of foreign cultures.
- Adopt the best practices of world industry to improve productivity and quality in the manufacturing process.
- In the area of labor-management relations, support diffusion of cooperative industrial relations by accepting labor representatives as legitimate and valued partners in the innovation process.
- Encourage union leaders to champion cooperative and innovative industrial-relations practices and to develop a new generation of leaders skilled in using these new practices to promote the long-run interests of their members and the firms that employ them. (Dertouzos, Lester, and Solow, pp. 148–150)

APPLICATIONS OF P/OM

A Clear Specification of Goals Leads to Achievements

Those who were watching live television that July night in 1969 will never forget the spectacle of seeing the first man walk on the moon. The element of danger and uncertainty, heightened by a history of trial and error, added to the suspense of the lunar landing. Before the 1960s, no one really knew if rockets would ever be able to carry humans into space.

Neil Armstrong's first step onto the moon's surface was a triumph for American science and technology and the culmination of a national quest that had begun in the office of President John F. Kennedy. It was Kennedy's goal to put a man on the moon before the decade was out, a goal realized in the Nixon administration.

In the eight years from 1961 to 1969, we moved from a president's vision to the reality of a lunar landing. Most of us think of this achievement in terms of the tremendous scientific advances it represented—in physics, engineering, chemistry, and associated technologies. But there was another side to this far-reaching project. Someone had to set the objectives, commission the work, suffer the setbacks, overcome unforeseen obstacles, and tie together a project with thousands of disparate components. This is the job of operations management.

Source: S. Garfunkel, ed., *Introduction to Contemporary Mathematics* (New York: W.H. Freeman and Company, 1988), pp. 1–2.

CORPORATE STRATEGIES

Corporate strategies include decisions about which businesses a company wants to be involved in, which countries a firm wants to operate in, what the target markets are, and what the profit and market share goals are. Some of the strategy choices at this level have a direct bearing on operations. For instance, it is at this level that the corporation must determine whether the markets for a product are internal (within the corporation), external, or both.

quantity vs. quality

The corporate strategies of American firms have generally been directed at maximizing short-term profits. This has resulted in quantity-based, rather than quality-based, measures of operations success. We now know that myopic companies will fail; U.S. firms must follow the Japanese model if they are to achieve market share and long-term competitiveness. Managers of U.S. firms must get over their fascination with financial issues such as mergers and acquisitions and get about the business of improving competitiveness—stressing flexibility, proper use of technology, and a good understanding of the human factor in production.

Two corporate strategies that are directly related to operations are vertical integration and joint ventures. These topics are discussed in a later section of this chapter.

BUSINESS-LEVEL STRATEGIES—GAINING A COMPETITIVE ADVANTAGE

An organization succeeds because it outperforms its competitors. A firm must have some competitive advantage in order to distinguish itself from competing firms. The competitive advantage that a firm seeks (or seeks to maintain) will dictate its strategy.

The first type of competitive advantage directly involves the profit equation. We can define profit as the difference between price and cost. Therefore, in order to maximize profit, a company must either minimize cost or maximize price.

BUSINESS-LEVEL STRATEGY 1: Provide cost leadership.

Implicit in providing cost leadership are several operational strategies. The company must be on the cutting edge of technology—that is, must have the most cost-efficient equipment—in order to keep costs down. The company must be providing a large volume of output in order to recover the fixed costs of the new equipment and to take advantage of economies of scale. In order to minimize time-consuming start-up procedures, the company must keep its product line small and, where possible, introduce standardized components. Distribution and transportation costs must be kept down. Heinz is using the strategy of cost leadership in its attempt to become a major player in the European ketchup game. The means to achieving this leadership include plant modernization, the development of regional production centers, the acquisition of related businesses (vertical integration), and, of course, marketing. Windmere is also using cost leadership as a strategy, using inexpensive (thirty cents per hour) Chinese labor to produce hair dryers.

Note the importance of research and development to the success of this strategy. New cost-efficient processes will be examined by R&D, and then the processes and products will be designed in such a way as to be easy and inexpensive to manufacture.

Teaching Suggestion 2.8: Cost Leadership Through Operations. See the Instructor's Section for details.

BUSINESS-LEVEL STRATEGY 2: Profit through price.

In order to profit through high prices, the company must provide goods or services for which customers are willing to pass up lower-cost alternatives. In other words, the company must provide product or service differentiation. For example, the company might produce only luxury items or only the highest standards of service or only custom services. As a general rule, this strategy has a greater impact on marketing than on operations. Marketing must sell consumers on the differentiation.

Four Seasons Hotels is using this strategy to become a major player in the hospitality industry. The chain aims to pamper its guests at any cost and, therefore, often charges the highest rate in each of its markets. The underlying rationale is that executives expect certain amenities when they must travel for business, especially when the hotel tab will end up as a reimbursed company expense.

BUSINESS-LEVEL STRATEGY 3: Profit through focus.

A company might opt for a single focus. This focus might be the set of customers it serves or the company's product line. Many Japanese companies have succeeded with a geographic focus. Other Japanese companies concentrated on large-volume, low-price items when attacking U.S. competitors. Their initial advantage was price. After succeeding with this focus, they tended to move the focus to upscale items. The advantage at this level was quality. In attacking upscale items first, German companies have simply used a variation of the same strategy.

FROM BUSINESS LEVEL TO FUNCTIONAL LEVEL

Different competitive strategies relate to operations, marketing, and finance differently—in part because they require different arsenals. As we have already indicated, the strategy is directly related to the production process being used and to the product or service line being provided.

A company whose focus is on high-quality goods, for example, may need to become more automated. The degree of automation begins at no automation. In the unautomated company, a human performs the operations manually using simple tools. This lack of mechanization would not be unusual for a company seeking to differentiate itself geographically. At the next level of automation, some form of mechanical assistance is provided to the operator. This, of course, helps to speed up the work and to reduce costs, but usually not to such an extent that a company would be tempted to use the cost differentiation strategy. The next level involves fixed-program machinery. These machines perform a sequence of operations that cannot be changed and is ideal for producing one type of product or service. Hence, we would expect to find these machines at companies using the cost differentiation strategy. The highest level of automation is marked by the use of the programmable machine. Programmable machines perform different tasks in the manufacture of different products.

We have stated that the strategy and the product line are also linked. Cost differentiation strategies, for instance, lead to producing a limited line of relatively simple final products. Examples of companies that employ the cost differentiation strategy include McDonald's, whose expanded menu is still far shorter than that of a full-service restaurant, and Hyundai, whose automobiles are considerably less complex to manufacture than, say, a Mercedes-Benz.

CHAIN OF OPERATIONS

Figure 2.5 presents a picture of the material–product flow in a manufacturing organization. The transformation of raw materials into finished goods can be thought of as a chain of operations. At the raw-material end of the chain is the extractor, a company that extracts raw materials from the earth. Examples include companies involved in logging, ore mining, and fishing. Next to the extractor is the basic producer—that is, the company that converts natural resources for use. An example is a company that takes iron ore and transforms it into ingots. This is followed by the converter, who converts the material for specific industrial use. For example, iron is converted into sheet metal or petroleum is converted into plastic or wood pulp is converted into paper. The products at this stage are simple in form, not end products. The last manufacturer in the chain is the assembler/fabricator, who turns various components into finished goods. The final level is the retail operation. In between all levels are the transportation activities required for moving the materials from one process to another.

the operations chain

VERTICAL INTEGRATION

A simple corporation operates at only one level in the diagram. A more complex organization will have companies operating at more than one level. This is termed **vertical integration**. Vertical integration involves an extension—upward or downward in the chain—of the stage(s) of production and distribution in which the firm operates. A tire company that acquires or merges with a rubber producer illustrates backward integration because the movement is "against" the flow in the production chain; a tire company that acquires or merges with a tire distributor illustrates forward integration.

direction of integration

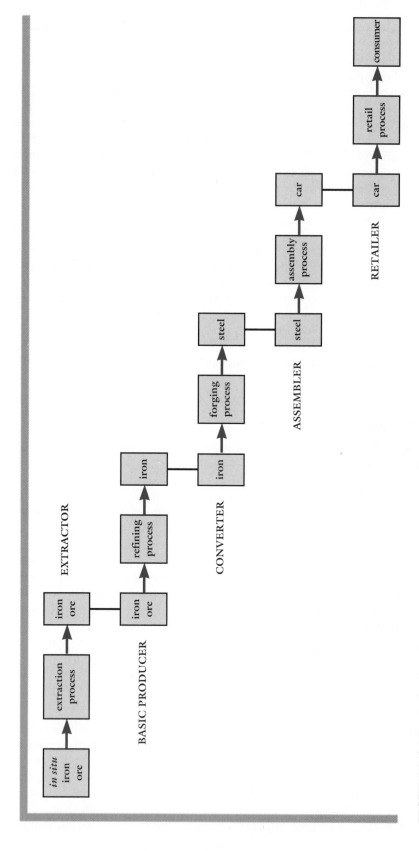

FIGURE 2.5 The production chain

Transparency Master 2.6:
The Manufacturing Chain.

62

Vertical integration in any industry can take place at different levels of the production chain. The paper industry provides a good example. Weyerhauser, International Paper, Container Corporation, Appleton, and Procter & Gamble all operate in this industry, and all have some degree of vertical integration. But these five companies have different types of vertical integration, as shown by Figure 2.6.

Weyerhauser, which produces paper and lumber products, can adjust its product mix according to the demands and returns in different product arenas. International Paper has vast holdings of timber lands. These timber lands are used to supply the paper mills, not to provide the highest return on the timber. Container Corporation manufactures containers. This is their prime goal and market, even though they, too, have timber lands and pulp mills. Appleton is a specialty paper product manufacturer. Procter & Gamble is a consumer products company. (The preceding discussion was suggested by pages 307 and 308 of *The Strategy Process*, by J. B. Quinn, H. Mintzberg, and R. M. James; see the References section at the end of this chapter for the complete citation.)

FIGURE 2.6 Vertical integration: from lumber to consumer products

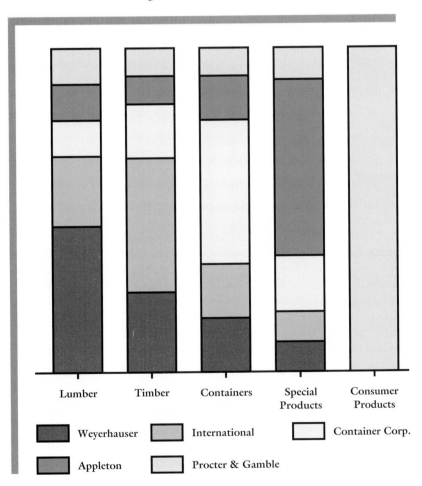

Associated with vertical integration is the notion of **merchant companies** or **captive producers**. A merchant company makes products for use by others; a captive producer makes products only for itself. For example, IBM is a captive producer, manufacturing chips only for itself; Japanese firms are merchant companies, producing more chips than they need and selling the excess on the open market.

JOINT VENTURES

Teaching Suggestion 2.9: Apple and IBM. See the Instructor's Section for details.

Another competitive strategy that is directly related to production is formation of a joint venture. The most significant joint ventures are those that cross cultures—for example, joint ventures involving Japanese and U.S. firms. Many of these ventures have been highly successful in bringing Japanese management and cultural attitudes to U.S. workers and managers. The prime example of such ventures is the General Motors–Toyota venture, NUMMI, in Fremont, California. Corning Glass Works has twenty-three joint ventures, including fifteen ventures with foreign companies. Texas Instruments is involved in a joint venture with Hitachi of Japan (a company, interestingly, that TI had previously sued). Ford Motor Company has joined Nissan and Volkswagen. Mitsubishi and Chrysler have a joint venture. Fuji and Isuzu have a joint venture. Suzuki and GM of Canada are involved in a joint venture. General Electric has alliances with companies in Europe, Japan, and South Korea. Nynex (one of the "Baby Bells" created when AT&T agreed to divest local operating companies) has ventures with companies in Asia and Europe. Nippon Steel and Inland Steel are jointly constructing a plant in Indiana. Armco Inc. and Kawasaki Steel are involved in a joint venture, as are National Steel (Pittsburgh) and Nippon Kokan.

SUMMARY

U.S. firms, which for decades led the world in manufacturing, felt that they could continue to do so indefinitely without making major changes at the factory level. Top management emphasized finance and marketing; the operations emphasis was on quantity rather than quality. While U.S. firms focused outside the factory, foreign firms—particularly Japanese and German firms—increased their market shares. With U.S. firms concentrating almost exclusively on short-term profits, foreign firms easily made demand beachheads on U.S. shores.

Foreign firms excelled at producing quality products at low cost. Some firms had a head start due to low wage rates and more modern equipment. However, foreign firms continue to lead the way, even though discrepancies in wage rates and equipment age have become less pronounced. These firms lead the way by using *world-class* management techniques.

The new management considers quality a given. The *starting point* for success in the market is a product or service that conforms to standards. World-class management recognizes that even minimum standards for competitiveness in today's global market cannot be achieved when there is hostility between management and workers. World-class management also recognizes the dynamic state of the world, building flexibility into the product and the production process.

Very important to maintaining competitiveness is strategy. There are several different levels of strategies, which form a top-down structure from government to industry to corporation to business to business function. Coordination among all strategic participants is crucial in order to ensure that everyone is trying to achieve the same goals. Two corporate strategies that greatly influence operations are *vertical integration* and *joint ventures*. At the business level, we can identify three generic strategies: provide cost leadership, profit through price, and profit through focus.

KEY TERMS

globalized	quotas	life cycles
closed circle economy	voluntary export restraint	strategy
world-class	quality circles	vertical integration
Pacific Rim nations	profit sharing	merchant companies
productivity	product development teams	captive producers
quality	*kaizen*	
tariffs		

QUESTIONS

1. Define the term *closed circle economy*. What factors have caused the U.S. economy to expand beyond the closed circle?

2. Which countries are currently our major competitors? Which countries are emerging as new competitors?

3. Cite examples of the globalization that has occurred in the past few decades.

4. Discuss the following statement: It no longer pays to perform research and development because foreign countries can produce items developed in the United States.

5. What products are under attack in Japan?

6. What advantage do many Pacific Rim countries have over the United States and Japan?

7. Explain the relationship between capital investment and the decline of U.S. manufacturing.

8. How have U.S. manufacturers typically responded to quality concerns?

9. What foreign government policies have hurt U.S. manufacturers?

10. What is a voluntary export restraint?

11. Explain how the relationship between unions and management affects manufacturing.

12. Explain the various aspects of flexibility.

13. What are flexible manufacturing systems?

14. What are the three main generic types of business-level strategies?

15. How are research and development related to cost leadership and product differentiation?

16. What is vertical integration? forward integration? backward integration?

17. What is a merchant company? What is a captive producer?

18. Is it possible for two U.S. auto manufacturers to become involved in a joint venture?

REFERENCES

Dertouzos, M. L., R. K. Lester, and R. M. Solow. *Made in America*. New York: HarperCollins, 1989.

Eckstein, O., C. Caton, R. Brinner, and P. Duprey. *The DRI Report on U.S. Manufacturing Industries*. New York: McGraw-Hill, 1984.

Ettlie, J. E. *Taking Charge of Manufacturing*. San Francisco: Jossey-Bass, 1988.

Gunn, T. G. *Manufacturing for Competitive Advantage*. Cambridge, Mass.: Ballinger Publishing Co., 1987.

Hax, A. C. and N. S. Majluf. *Strategic Management: An Integrative Perspective*. Englewood Cliffs, N.J.: Prentice-Hall, 1984.

Hayes, R. F., S. C. Wheelwright, and K. B. Clark. *Dynamic Manufacturing: Creating the Learning Organization*. New York: The Free Press, 1988.

Kotha, S. and D. Orne. "Generic Manufacturing Strategies: A Conceptual Synthesis," *Strategic Management Journal,* vol. 10 (1989), pp. 211–231.

Manufacturing Studies Board. *Toward a New Era in U.S. Manufacturing*. Washington, D.C.: National Academy Press, 1986.

Quinn, J. B., H. Mintzberg, and R. M. James. *The Strategy Process*. Englewood Cliffs, N.J.: Prentice-Hall, 1988.

Shapiro, H. J. and T. Cosenza. *Reviving Industry in America*. Cambridge, Mass.: Ballinger, 1987.

PART TWO

CAPACITY: SUPPLY AND DEMAND

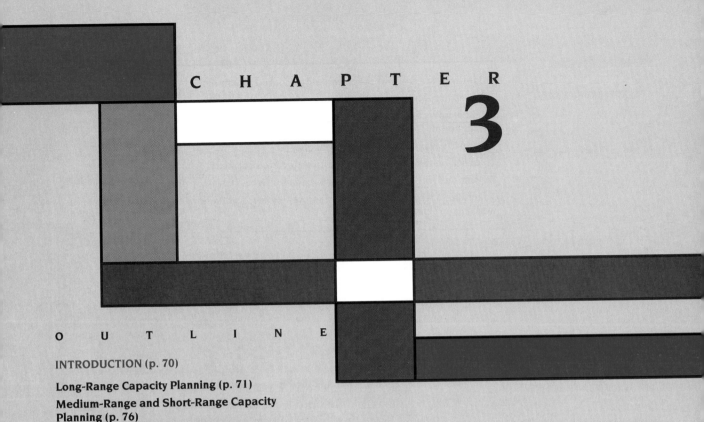

C H A P T E R

3

O U T L I N E

CAPACITY PLANNING

- To define capacity and other concepts related to volume
- To illustrate the importance of capacity planning
- To show how capacity decisions relate to other operational decisions in operations management
- To provide ways of measuring capacity
- To describe the factors that help to determine capacity
- To demonstrate a variety of approaches for determining appropriate capacity levels
- To outline a framework for decision making for application to capacity problems as well as more general decisions

INTRODUCTION

goal of operations management

We introduced operations management as the planning and controlling of all activities necessary for the provision of a firm's product or service. We will begin to clarify this somewhat vague definition in this chapter. A firm uses resources to take a product or service to market. Rather than defining operations management as the provision of a product or service, let us state that the goal of operations management is to provide the product or service *in the amounts required by the market and of the quality required by the market*. A major determinant of the amount that *can* be provided is the **capacity** of the system. In the next section, we will present different definitions of capacity. Loosely speaking, however, the capacity of a productive system is the maximum production or service rate that the system can achieve and sustain. Before delving into more specific definitions, let us consider an example that helps to explain the factors that affect capacity.

Consider a supermarket checkout system. Clearly, the system's capacity is limited by several factors. Among these are the number of checkout cash registers; the type of cash register system (universal price code readers read prices faster than can cashiers); the number of employees, which may be fewer, equal to, or greater than the number of registers; the speed and quality of the employees, and the arrangement of the employees (for instance, if two persons are working, each could be at a separate register or they could work together, with one checking and one bagging groceries).

several factors affect capacity

In this supermarket example, we see that capacity is affected by the quantity of resources (the number of cash registers and the number of employees), the quality of the resources (the service rates and accuracy of the cash register/price reader and the cashier), and the arrangement of the resources (cashier alone versus cashier and bagger per register). One more factor must be noted. We are interested, not only in the number of customers who *can* be served, but also in the number of customers who actually are served. Obviously, one of the factors affecting the number of shoppers checked out is the number of shoppers who arrive at the checkout lines. Hence, demand for the product or service is also a critical element in our analysis.

Although the types of capacity questions that an institution faces vary according to its product or service, we can draw a distinction between short-term capacity prob-

Capacity is affected by several factors. Planning requires design of space and labor utilization against likely flows of traffic. (© Jonathan Kirn/Picture Group)

lems, medium-range capacity problems, and long-term capacity problems that is generally applicable across industries. As mentioned in Chapter 1, the lengths of time of short-, medium-, and long-range planning vary according to the industry, but, as a general rule, short-range refers to over the next month, medium-range is from one month to one year, and long-range is beyond one year. Even though we separate the time ranges, long-, medium-, and short-range capacity planning are intimately related, as will be shown in the following section.

LONG-RANGE CAPACITY PLANNING

The long-term problem is typified by Figure 3.1. The figure indicates a company that is currently operating at 80 percent of its one-shift capacity of 100 units per day. The demand is expected to grow to a rate of 900 units per day over the next ten years. Companies in this position today typically are high technology firms, such as the manufacturers of microcomputers. It is obvious from the figure that, if the projected demand is accurate, the company needs to build one or more plants over the next ten years. For ease of discussion, assume that the choice is between building one additional

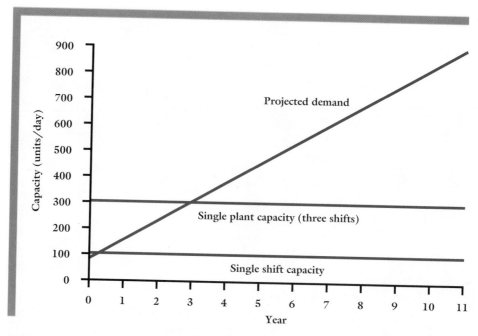

FIGURE 3.1 Long-term capacity planning

plant with a three-shift capacity of 600 units per day or building two additional plants, each with a three-shift capacity of 300 units per day.

In part (a) of Figure 3.2, we have represented the capacity under both the one large plant option, and in part (b), we have developed the two smaller plants option. **advantages of small plants** An examination of the two options reveals several advantages to the option of two smaller plants. In either case, a new plant must be operational within three years. One advantage of the two smaller plants is that, presumably, they are at least as likely as the larger plant to be operational within the three-year time limit. As Figure 3.2 indicates, there is more excess capacity (i.e., available capacity minus projected demand) between years three and seven with one large plant than with the two smaller plants. There is a third critical advantage of the two smaller plants option. When dealing with any long-range plans, only the parts of the plan that can be instituted immediately are certain to be implemented. Suppose that the expected high demand does not materialize. With the large capacity option, we are committed to creating a total capacity of 900 units per day. However, with the small plants option, we are committed only to creating a total capacity of 600 units per day, because in the future we can decide not to build the second small plant. Another advantage of having a number of small plants is that each plant can specialize. With one large plant, the production line must be modified each time there is a change in product. Borden has put this decentralization into practice. The company has fourteen plants in the United States to manufacture pasta. Rather than shutting down production to convert the lines to specialty shapes, Borden has four plants that produce the odd shapes exclusively. The last major advantage of the small plants option is that the plants can be built in different locations, which could lead to lower shipping costs.

According to our discussion thus far, the option of building two smaller plants is clearly superior to the large plant option. There is, however, one very important factor that may lead to the building of the large plant: namely, **economies of scale.** We separate economies of scale into two types—construction and operating.

Teaching Suggestion 3.1: Planned vs. Actual. See the Instructor's Section for details.

CONSTRUCTION ECONOMIES OF SCALE

Assume that we need a total of 20,000 square feet for our sample company. The two options are one plant 20,000 square feet in size or two smaller plants, each 10,000 square feet in size. Two possible designs are represented in Figure 3.3. If we assume

advantages of large plants

FIGURE 3.2 Capacity of one large plant versus capacity of two smaller plants

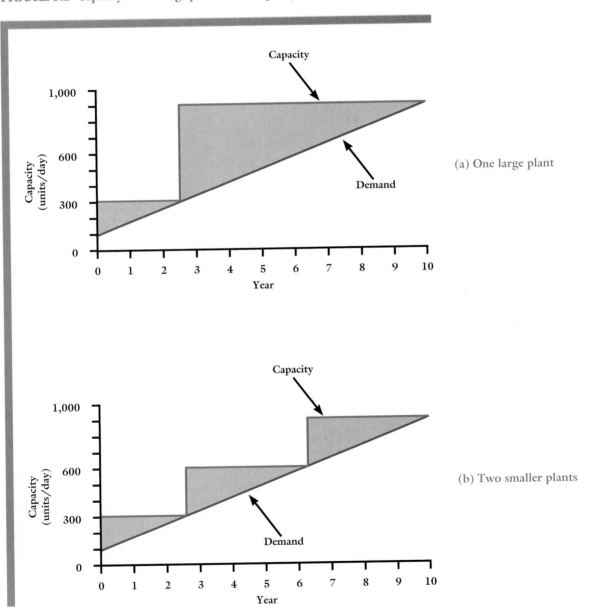

(a) One large plant

(b) Two smaller plants

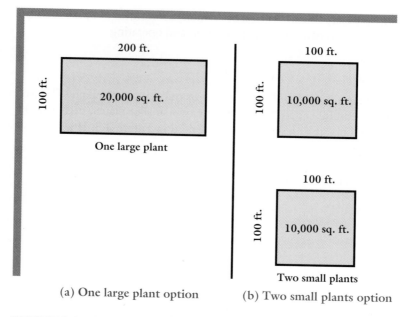

(a) One large plant option   (b) Two small plants option

FIGURE 3.3   Plant designs: perimeters and areas

(as is usually the case) that land costs are based on a per square foot charge, then the total land costs are the same for each option because each option has a total of 20,000 square feet. Next, consider the cost of constructing the frame of the plant. Assume (as is usually the case) that the construction costs are proportional to the perimeter of the buildings. The two-plant option has a total perimeter of 800 (linear) feet, while the large plant has a perimeter of 600 (linear) feet. Therefore, the larger plant will be less costly to construct. More important, the construction economy of scale is that construction costs rise less than proportionately to building size. Because of this economy of scale, the cost of the large building, which involves 600 linear feet, is less than three-fourths of the cost of the two smaller buildings, which total 800 linear feet. In effect, then, the costs are not proportional to size. They increase less than linearly.

OPERATING ECONOMIES OF SCALE

Consider the fact that the two plants will require a duplication of resources, whereas one large plant may not. This is the operating economy of scale. Each of the two smaller plants will require a plant manager, whereas the one large plant may require one plant manager and a (lower salaried) assistant plant manager. Each of the two plants may have a cafeteria, whereas the larger plant would require one with fewer than twice as many employees as either of the two smaller ones. Similar statements can be made about equipment and the inventory of raw materials or component parts. The operating economies of scale are also known as "spreading the overhead costs." Figure 3.4 illustrates the effect of economies of scale on operating costs. It shows that, for any given facility size, there is an optimal operating level that minimizes the cost per unit. For example, in the automobile industry the best level is 100,000 to 200,000 vehicles per year per plant.

Our discussions of construction and operating economies of scale have dealt only with the facility itself. However, there are other types of economies of scale, as will be seen in our discussion of machines later in the chapter.

ADDING SHIFTS

Let us return to our example presented in Figure 3.1. From the figure, it is clear that prior to opening a new facility the company could add capacity by adding a new shift. Each shift increases the capacity by 100 units per day. Notice that either option, adding a shift or building a plant, increases the capacity in large chunks of units. This is a standard feature of long-term capacity options.

In our example, extra capacity (more than 100 units per day) will be required in slightly more than three months. However, rather than adding a new shift at this time, a different, less costly option is available; namely, using overtime. The question that must be addressed is when should we change from overtime to adding the second shift. The cost–volume analysis presented later in this chapter offers a means to approach this question. We note that while we typically think of overtime as a short-term option, it is obvious from our discussion of this example that overtime also is part of the long-term plan. Similarly, adding or removing a shift can be a medium-term option.

We note that while our example is optimistic in that the demand is growing, institutions with declining capacity requirements face similar problems. Examples of insti-

FIGURE 3.4 Effect of economies of scale on operating costs

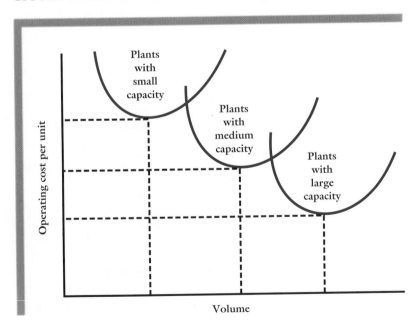

tutions with reduced capacity are school districts that experience declines in enrollments. The typical response of school districts is to close a school and sell the building. Oil refineries that have been closed because of the decreasing demand for oil are another example. A third example is the U.S. steel industry, which closed mills in large part because of a worldwide overcapacity of production and foreign competition.

MEDIUM-RANGE AND SHORT-RANGE CAPACITY PLANNING

The medium-range capacity planning problem is somewhat different than the long-range problem. If demand were constant, then capacity planning would pose no problem. For example, if demand for beer is 1,000 kegs per day, every day, then the brewery manager simply needs to produce 1,000 kegs per day throughout the year. Unfortunately, both short-term demand (such as hamburgers ordered during the day at a fast-food restaurant) and medium-term demand (such as toys purchased per month) tend to vary, making the capacity planning considerably more complex. Trade-offs must be made between having too much capacity during some periods and having too little during others.

medium-range demand is cyclical

The picture of the medium-range problem is given in Figure 3.5. Annual (or monthly or daily) demand is cyclical; in some months, the demand is above the capacity, while it is below the capacity in other months. Options available during peak demand periods include working overtime, hiring part-time help, or subcontracting units. Producing units when demand is lower and storing them until the peak demand period is another option. Notice that these options add capacities in very small amounts—as opposed to the large amounts generated by adding a plant or shift. The

FIGURE 3.5 Medium-range capacity planning: the cyclical nature of demand

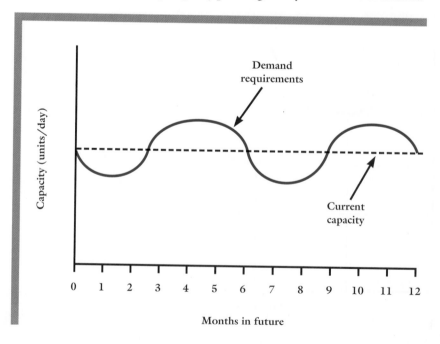

Capacity Disruptions at American Airlines

Most of us have had our travel plans altered by Mother Nature. A slow-moving band of thunderstorms or heavy snow can cause delays that frequently turn into lengthy delays and, sometimes, into flight cancellations. The airline passenger views a cancelled or delayed flight as an inconvenience. As Director of Operations at American Airlines, Thomas Cook views the effects of adverse weather conditions somewhat differently—as a disruption in capacity. His description of the challenges posed by a sudden, weather-related change in an airline's capacity estimates follows.

If we get a major weather disruption at one of the hubs, such as Dallas or Chicago, then a lot of flights may get canceled, which means we have a lot of crews and airplanes in the wrong places. What we need is a way to put that whole operation back together again, so that the crews and airplanes are in the right places. That way we minimize the cost of the disruption and minimize the passenger inconvenience.

Source: S. Garfunkel, ed., *Introduction to Contemporary Mathematics* (New York: W.H. Freeman and Company, 1988), p. 82.

method for trading off the costs of these options, production planning, will be explored in more detail in Chapter 12.

One more medium-range option that must be discussed is that of developing a product with a cycle that is completely opposite to the current product. For example, a company might manufacture both lawn mowers and snowblowers. In Figure 3.6, we indicate that the combined demand for lawn mowers and snowblowers is smoother than the demand for either the snowblower or lawn mower individually. Toro smooths the demand not only with the obvious lawn mower/snowblower combination but also

combining demands

FIGURE 3.6 Products with offsetting demand cycles

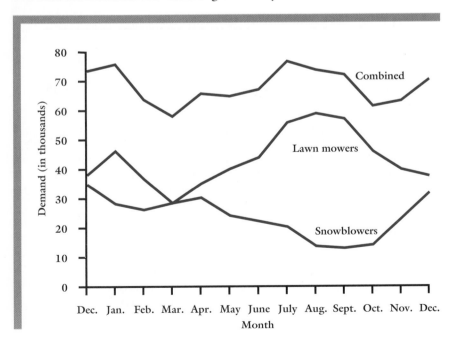

Transparency Master 3.2: Medium-Range Capacity Planning.

with sprinkler systems for golf courses and decorative lighting. Combining products can be useful in the service sector also. For example, Walt Disney World tries to lure conventions in low-demand months in order to smooth out the visitor demand pattern. Other products with offsetting cycles are heating oil and gasoline.

Short-term capacity problems are very different from long- or medium-term capacity problems. Both long- and medium-term capacity plans are based on *estimates* of future requirements. The short-term plans are based on known needs due to customer orders. Although the medium-range plan of a company might not include overtime, the sudden arrival of a large order might force the company to invest in some unplanned overtime. A typical example at a university is an overbooked class section. At many institutions, an additional instructor is found, the original class is split into two on the first day of classes (very short term), and two sections are offered rather than only the one that was originally scheduled. The converse, of course, is when a class is canceled.

Note from our discussion that capacity planning is related to subjects we plan to discuss in other chapters, such as facility location, facility layout, waiting line models, and production planning. These relationships are indicated in Table 3.1.

CONCEPTS RELATED TO VOLUME

In this section, we present the concepts and terminology that relate to the volume of operations. As indicated by our previous discussion in this chapter, both potential output, as given by the capacity, and actual output are critical.

TABLE 3.1 Options for increasing capacity

Capacity	Tool	Chapter
Short term		
Use overtime	Cost–volume analysis	3
Subcontract	Cost–volume analysis	3
Increase server capacity	Waiting line models, job design, scheduling	8, 9, 15
Medium term		
Use overtime, subcontract, or increase labor force size	Production planning, transportation	12, 6
Add machine(s)	Capital investment	A
Restructure facility	Layout and waiting line models, project management	7, 8, 10
Add shift(s)	Cost–volume analysis	3
Resource allocation	Linear programming	11
Restructure job definition	Methods analysis	9
Long term		
Build new facility (or annex)	Decision analysis	3
	Location (which also implies layout, transportation, financial analysis, queueing, and project management)	5

CAPACITY

In order to define the capacity of a system, we must begin by exploring the different types of subsystems. Figure 3.7 is a schematic representation of the checkout system at a typical supermarket. The checkout system consists of a set of subsystems, where each subsystem is an open checkout line. Each checkout line subsystem consists of two (sub-) subsystems: the subsystem of ringing up the prices and the subsystem of bagging the groceries. The subsystem of ringing up the prices consists of two separate resources with different capacities: the cashier and the cash register.

Beginning at the lowest level, we note that the cashier and the cash register work simultaneously. Therefore, the cashier and the cash register represent a **system in unison.** Suppose that the cashier is capable of punching in 50 items per minute and that the cash register is capable of receiving 700 items per minute. Then, because the cashier and cash register must work in unison, the capacity of this subsystem is limited by the cashier and is 50 items per minute. The general rule is this: When a system or subsystem has operations occurring in unison, the capacity of that system is limited by the slowest subsystem.

systems in unison

Now consider the next level subsystem, the individual line. This consists of ringing up the prices, followed by bagging. Since one operation follows another, we call this a **series system.** Suppose that the capacity of the bagger is 35 items per minute. The single-line subsystem is limited by the bagger because he or she is slower than the

systems in series

FIGURE 3.7 Supermarket subsystem configuration

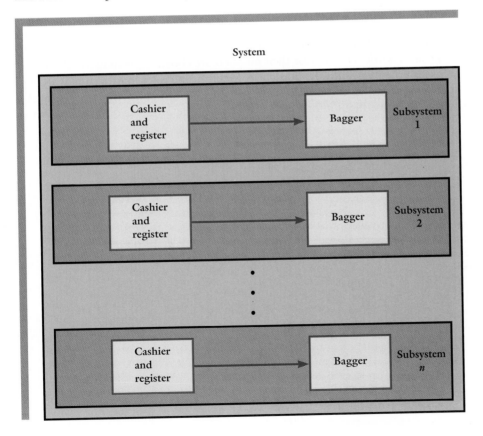

checker. The general rule for series systems is the same as for systems in unison: The capacity of a series system is limited by the slowest subsystem.

systems in parallel

Teaching Suggestion 3.3: Rates. See the Instructor's Section for details.

Lastly, consider the large system. Suppose that the supermarket has five lines, each as described above. A customer needs to go through only one of the five lines. We say that the lines are operating in parallel or are **parallel systems.** The capacity of the system is 35 items per minute for each line. The five lines yield a total capacity of 175 items per minute. When systems are operating in parallel, the total system capacity is the sum of the individual subsystem capacities.

We previously stated that capacity is the maximum sustainable production or service *rate.* We emphasize that capacity is a rate, such as units per week, customers per hour, and so forth. We also have stated that capacity is limited by one of the resources. This makes the computation of some capacities trivial. For example, while there are many resources in a typical hospital (doctors, nurses, orderlies, X-ray machines, stretchers), there is essentially one main resource that limits the number of inpatients who can be served daily. This resource is the number of hospital beds. Hence, the capacity of the inpatient service at a hospital is given by its number of beds (per day). Obviously, the other resources could be limiting, but typically they are not. For example, a hospital with 1,000 beds but only one doctor clearly (hopefully) does not have a capacity of 1,000 patients per day. The identification of the "bottleneck" resource, or simply, **bottleneck,** is a key to where the operations manager should place the emphasis of any long-range capacity studies.

bottlenecks

The reason that it is easy to identify the capacity of a hospital, nursing home, or prison is that the bottleneck resource is clearly identified and each customer requires the same amount of this resource (one bed per patient or inmate per day). A slightly more complex example is airline capacity.

Many resources are required to operate an airline. Among these are the number of airplanes, pilots, flight attendants, and ground attendants. These resources typically do not create a bottleneck because their numbers are chosen according to the requirements of the schedule. Thus the bottleneck for an airline is given by a combination of the seating capacities of the airplanes and the schedule of flights. Consider DelawAir, a small airline whose flight information is given in Table 3.2. One obvious measure of

TABLE 3.2 Daily flight schedule for DelawAir

Flight Number	Miles	Capacity (seats)		Ticket Price	
		First Class	Tourist	First Class	Tourist
405	750	20	100	$225	$150
103	900	50	250	300	200
722	300	—	75	—	100
611	600	20	100	200	120
309	750	—	75	—	150
473	2,000	50	250	500	400
		140	850		

990

TABLE 3.3 Passenger mile capacity of DelawAir

Flight Number	(1) Miles	(2) Capacity (total seating)	(3) Passenger Miles [(1) × (2)]
405	750	120	90,000
103	900	300	270,000
722	300	75	22,500
611	600	120	72,000
309	750	75	56,250
473	2,000	300	600,000
			1,110,750

capacity is the total number of seats available per day, or 990 passengers per day. This measure does not reflect the fact that different passengers use a different amount (miles) of the service.

A second, more useful measure is passenger miles per day. Table 3.3 shows how passenger miles per day are computed for DelawAir. The seating capacity of each flight is multiplied by the number of miles of each flight to arrive at passenger miles per flight. These are summed across the six flights, yielding 1,110,750 passenger miles per day.

capacity measures

Although this is a better measure, it does not reflect the fact that there are two types of passengers. A third measure is the dollar volume capacity. (This, in fact, is a standard capacity measure in many industries.) Table 3.4 shows how dollar volume capacity is computed for DelawAir. The capacity for each type of passenger is multiplied by the ticket cost. These figures are then added together, yielding a dollar volume capacity of $195,750 + $48,500 = $244,250 per day.

There is only one measure of capacity for a hospital. For an airline, however, there are three measures, all of which are routinely used. The Federal Aviation Administra-

TABLE 3.4 Dollar volume capacity of DelawAir

Flight Number	First Class			Tourist		
	(1) Seats	(2) Price	(3) Dollar Volume [(1) × (2)]	(4) Seats	(5) Price	(6) Dollar Volume [(4) × (5)]
405	20	$255	$ 4,500	100	$150	$ 15,000
103	50	$300	15,000	250	$200	50,000
722	—	—	—	75	$100	7,500
611	20	$200	4,000	100	$120	12,000
309	—	—	—	75	$150	11,250
473	50	$500	25,000	250	$400	100,000
			$48,500			$195,750

tion uses seats per day as its measure of airline capacity usage; the Department of Transportation uses passenger miles as its measure of airline safety (that is, deaths per passenger mile by car, train, and plane); and airline company accounting departments use dollar volume as their measure of revenue capacity.

In our hospital and airline examples, it has been relatively easy to define the capacity measures. Unfortunately, there are many situations in which the capacity is not so easily defined. Consider the following situation.

The Wershon Company produces sport jackets and slacks. The company has one seamstress, who works 36 hours per week. She can sew a jacket in 4 hours and a pair of pants in 2 hours. Each jacket requires 2 square yards of material and each pair of pants requires 5 square yards of material. There are 50 square yards of material available weekly. The information is expressed in the following table.

Resource	Product Jacket	Pants	Resources Available
Time	4 hours	2 hours	36 hours
Material	2 square yards	5 square yards	50 square yards

multiple bottlenecks

If the seamstress only produces jackets, then she has enough time to produce 9 jackets per week (36 hours ÷ 4 hours per jacket) and enough material to produce 25 jackets per week (50 yards ÷ 2 yards per jacket). Clearly, time is the bottleneck resource, and the jacket capacity is 9 per week. If she only sews pants, then she has enough time to make 18 pairs of pants (36 ÷ 2) but only enough material for 10 pairs of pants (50 ÷ 5). In this case, the bottleneck resource is material, and the pants capacity is 10 pairs per week.

However, since the seamstress produces both jackets and pants, it is unreasonable to use a single number as a measure of capacity. Two options exist: The capacity may be given as 9 jackets, 10 pairs of pants per week, or it may be given as the amount of resources—36 hours, 50 square yards. Of course, a major question is how to best use this capacity (the resources). For this particular example, linear programming (see Chapter 11) can be used to solve for the optimal use of resources. It turns out that if profit is nearly equal for pants and jackets, then 5 jackets and 8 pants should be made each week (every 36 hours) for optimal use of the resources.

In Table 3.5, we present several standard measures of capacity. The computations of these measures are very straightforward. For the hospital (or prison), the annual capacity is 365 times the number of beds. The airline capacity is the total of the number of seats on each flight to arrive at passengers per year or the total of the number of seats on each flight multiplied by the mileage of the flight to arrive at passenger miles per year. With respect to automobile manufacturing, you may be wondering whether this category doesn't mix apples and oranges or, more precisely, Luminas and Caprices. However, the typical manufacturer produces only one type of car at each plant. Hence, automobiles per day represents the capacity at a particular plant, rather than across all plants.

design capacity

What we have referred to so far is the capacity of the system. In order to determine this, we begin with a more focused view of capacity, termed **design capacity**. Design

Teaching Suggestion 3.4: Aggregation. See the Instructor's Section for details.

TABLE 3.5 Standard capacity measures

System	Standard Measure of Capacity
Hospital or prison	Patient days or inmate days/year
Airline	Passengers/year, passenger miles/year, or dollar volume/year
Oil refinery	Barrels of oil/day
Automobile manufacturing	Automobiles/day
Bank	Transactions/day
Gas station	Gallons/day
Restaurant	Meals/week
Truck	Cubic yards (volume) or tonnage (weight)/day
Computer	Computations/second
Production line	Units/shift
Storage silo	Tons/week
Reservoir	Gallons/day

Transparency Master 3.4:
Standard Capacity
Measures.

capacity usually refers to a specific type of resource and is the maximum production or service rate that can be achieved by this type of resource *without regard to the interactions of products, manpower, machines, and raw materials.* Typically, the design capacity is based on specifications provided by the manufacturer of the machine.

| **Example 3.1** Arro Airlines has just purchased a Ribon 474 airplane. The plane has 150 seats, and Ribon claims that the plane flies at a speed of 400 miles per hour. What is the daily design capacity of the airplane?

The design capacity is given by

150 passengers $\times$ 400 mi./hr. $\times$ 24 hr./day = 1,440,000 passenger mi./day. ∎

This, of course, is unrealistic in that the calculation assumes that the plane is in flight for twenty-four hours each day. In a moment, we will present a second definition of capacity that will correct for this assumption.

If machines are operating in parallel—that is, if any one of the machines can perform the same task—then, as indicated before, the design capacity of the subsystem is simply the design capacity of the individual machines multiplied by the number of machines. For example, if a paint manufacturer has 10 machines for mixing the paint and each has as a design capacity of 250 gallons per hour, then the design capacity of the paint mixing subsystem is 250(10) = 2,500 gallons/hour.

parallel machines

Now take into account that each mixer can be used for different colors, and we run into a problem. Each mixing machine has an individual capacity of 250 gallons per hour if it is operating for the full hour. However, the machine must be stopped and cleaned to prepare for each new color. In effect, each machine might have its capacity reduced to 200 gallons per hour. We term this capacity the **effective capacity**. The effective capacity is the maximum production or service rate that can be achieved *when considering the interactions of products, manpower, machines, and raw materials.* The interactions that would cause the effective capacity to be less than the design capacity

effective capacity

include setups (as in the paint example or airplane refueling), interruptions of production due to the demand process (self-service gas stations, automatic teller machines, and so forth), scheduling conflicts, planned machine maintenance, or bottlenecks. Notice that the effective capacity is a more realistic number than the design capacity in terms of denoting the potential service or production rate. An analogous situation is the system of car mileage ratings as given by the Environmental Protection Agency. These mileage figures are applicable only under ideal situations. As such, they represent design capacities and are somewhat unrealistic. If the figures for different cars are unrealistic to the same extent and with the same (upward) bias, however, then the mileage estimates are very useful for making comparisons across cars. Because the effective capacity is a more realistic representation of the system than the design capacity, we define the **system capacity** as the effective capacity. That is, system capacity and effective capacity are synonymous.

system capacity

EFFICIENCY

Capacity represents the possible output rate under the best of circumstances. The actual production rate and the capacity usually differ, however. The reasons for the difference can vary: Machines break down, workers have unexpected days off, raw material does not arrive on time. There is a formula for determining the **efficiency** of a system:

$$\text{System efficiency} = \frac{\text{actual output}}{\text{system capacity}}.$$

utilization

Another name for system efficiency is **utilization**, or capacity utilization.

Example 3.2 The bottleneck in a certain university's undergraduate business program happens to be the operations management course. Five faculty members are available to teach the course, and each can teach up to 6 sections per year with a limit of 30 students in each class section. However, the faculty members like to teach an assortment of courses and, therefore, although each professor can teach up to 6 sections of operations management per year, no one is scheduled for more than 4 sections per year. (The other 2 sections are different courses.) The number of graduates last year was 500. Find the design capacity, system (or effective) capacity, and system efficiency.

First, the design capacity is found as follows:

$$\text{Design capacity} = 5 \times 6 \times 30 = 900 \text{ students/year.}$$

However, because only four sections are scheduled, the system capacity is considerably lower:

$$\text{System capacity} = 5 \times 4 \times 30 = 600 \text{ students/year.}$$

Note that the system refers to the entire school. The operations management course is the bottleneck. Now let's compute the efficiency.

$$\text{System efficiency} = \frac{\text{actual output}}{\text{system capacity}} = \frac{500}{600} = 83.3\% \qquad \blacksquare$$

Capacity utilization varies by industry and depends upon the economic health of the industry. Table 3.6 presents some sample utilization rates.

Example 3.3   Last year, the production manager recommended the purchase of a new piece of production equipment that could produce 1 part per second, thereby replacing 2 older machines that were experiencing frequent breakdowns. This recommendation was accepted, but now top management wants to evaluate the performance of the new equipment. It is found that the equipment has produced 40 parts per minute over the last few months. What is the efficiency of the equipment?

As the example is stated, the efficiency is

$$\frac{40}{60} = .667, \text{ or } 66.7\%.$$

Suppose now that the production manager points out that, due to age, the machines prior to and immediately after this one in the production line have been turned down to cycle at 50 parts per minute and, therefore, have become the bottlenecks. For this reason, the new machine also has been cycled at 50 per minute. This means that its system efficiency is really

$$\frac{40}{50} = .80, \text{ or } 80\%.$$

The design capacity is 60 parts per minute, but its effective capacity is only 50 parts per minute because of where it is used. To differentiate between these two measures, some define *efficiency* in terms of effective capacity and *utilization* in terms of design capacity. Because there are other measures of efficiency, this distinction is not made here. $\qquad \blacksquare$

TABLE 3.6 **Capacity utilization for selected industries**

Industry	Utilization Rate (%)
Paper	94.8
Primary metals	92.4
Chemicals	89.1
Textiles	87.7
Rubber and plastics	87.3
Aerospace	85.9
Motor vehicles	85.4
All Manufacturing	84.5

Source: Business Week (December 26, 1988), p. 55.

PRODUCTIVITY

One more concept is closely related to capacity and efficiency. This is **productivity,** which we discussed loosely in the last chapter but define somewhat more explicitly now. Productivity is defined as follows:

$$\text{Productivity} = \frac{\text{actual output}}{\text{input}}.$$

Teaching Suggestion 3.5: Global Productivity Data. See the Instructor's Section for details.

Our definition here is a very general one. We have shown that there may be several definitions of output, such as passengers, passenger miles, or dollar volume. In addition, there are several different types of input, such as raw materials, labor, or machines. Typically, the input value in the denominator is the aggregate dollar value of all the inputs.

changes in productivity   Because our definition of productivity is very general, it is not productivity itself but *change in productivity* that is useful to monitor. Consider the following example.

Example 3.4   Albert and Alice Lipps own a landscaping service, Two Lipps, Inc. The following table contains their productivity information for June and July. Find the change in productivity that occurred between June and July.

	June	July
Customers serviced	50	70
Costs		
Lawn mower maintenance	$ 30	$ 40
Plants, flowers, bushes	100	50
Gasoline	75	100
Wages	200	250
Total costs	$405	$440

The productivity (PR) for either month is given by the ratio of customers (output) to total dollar costs (input). Therefore,

$$\text{PR}_{\text{June}} = \frac{50}{405} = .123$$

and

$$\text{PR}_{\text{July}} = \frac{70}{440} = .159.$$

The numbers .123 and .159 do not tell us much on their own. However, let us compute the ratio of July and June productivity.

$$\frac{\text{PR}_{\text{July}}}{\text{PR}_{\text{June}}} = \frac{.159}{.123} = 1.293$$

This tells us that there has been a 29.3-percent increase in productivity between June and July. ∎

An assumption made in the preceding analysis is that the true measure of output is the number of customers served. The implication is that the income from each customer served is the same. A more careful look at the cost figures brings this assumption into question. It appears that more work went into landscaping (plants, flowers, bushes) early in the summer (June), while more routine lawn cutting was performed later on (July). Because customers usually pay more for the type of work performed in June, our answer of 29.3-percent increase in productivity may be misleading.

A further examination of the records of Two Lipps, Inc. shows that income rose from $700 in June to $800 in July. Using income as the output, the productivities are

$$PR_{June} = \frac{700}{405} = 1.73$$

and

$$PR_{July} = \frac{800}{440} = 1.82.$$

By this measure of productivity, there is only a 5-percent increase from June to July ($1.82 \div 1.73 = 1.05$, rounded to the nearest hundredth).

Both measures (and others) are valid for productivity. Which is best depends on the strategic goals of management. For example, if the strategic goal is expressed only in terms of income, using the second measure provides more pertinent data. However, in our example, servicing one large and profitable client (as opposed to many smaller clients) may take all of the company's efforts, and this may be risky. Having more customers lowers this risk. Thus, using some combination of the two measures may actually be practiced.

There are many different productivity measures that may be used. Some will have labor, some capital, and some energy as input. Some will have customers as output, while others will have sales. The most common measure is units of output per employee but Table 3.7 offers several examples of different productivity measures.

productivity measures

TABLE 3.7 Examples of productivity measures

Organization	Productivity Measures
Business	Sales/employee, market share/employee, or completed projects/employee
Education	Enrollment/faculty, or tuition/administrative costs
Health care	Patients/doctor or patients/bed
Airlines	Flights/airplane or passenger miles/pilot
Hotels	Occupants/room or occupants/employee
Banks	Customers/teller or number of bank accounts/administrative costs
Broadcasting	Viewers/administrative costs or market share/employee
Bus transport	Passenger miles/driver or buses/passenger
Manufacturing	Units produced/employee
Construction	Engineers/construction site, projects completed/engineer, or revenues/construction costs

Notice that the productivity measures listed in Table 3.7 closely resemble the volume measures given in Table 3.5. The difference is that the volume measures are given with respect to time (in the denominator), while the productivity measures are given with respect to input (in the denominator).

CAPACITY DETERMINANTS

In this section, we consider the factors that determine capacity. We briefly explain how these factors may be modified to change capacity and, furthermore, specify the later chapters that deal with these factors in more detail.

DEMAND

Teaching Suggestion 3.6: Demand vs. Forecasted Demand. See the Instructor's Section for details.

If demands were constant, such as 100 units per week exactly, then we could rearrange the basic formula for capacity this way:

$$\text{System capacity} = \frac{\text{desired output}}{\text{system efficiency}}.$$

That is, there would be enough capacity built into the organization to allow for the fact that the firm does not operate at 100-percent efficiency. Unfortunately, demand typically follows an unstable pattern. For example, it might be that the demand in the next four quarters is forecast as 1,000 units, 1,500 units, 500 units, and 1,000 units, respectively. Several options exist for handling the varying demands. If the system capacity is set at 1,500 units (assume that the firm can be 100 percent efficient), then demands are all met easily, but efficiency in the four months will be 67 percent, 100 percent, 33 percent, and 67 percent. If the capacity is set at 1,000 (which is the average demand), then the efficiency is much better (100 percent, 100 percent, 50 percent, 100 percent), but the firm is short 500 units, which must be made up through overtime, subcontracting, or lost sales. If the capacity is given, then the planning of production—including overtime, subcontracting, and inventory— is a production planning problem. However, it is in the long-range planning stages that capacity must be determined for use in later medium- and short-range production planning.

Capacity planning decides what resources to make available for production. These decisions are based on the cost and capability of each resource, and, of course, anticipated demand has a key impact on what is decided. One important consideration is plant and plant size. There are four other areas that must be considered. These are machines, raw materials or component parts, labor, and storage. The capacity of each must be carefully coordinated with the capacity of the others because one of these will be the bottleneck that determines the system capacity.

MACHINES

In many cases, there may be more than one type of machine available to perform a task. There are several important factors to be considered when choosing a machine.

Some of the factors are economic, such as purchase cost, operating cost, and salvage value. Some factors relate to the quality of the machine, such as the average length of time the machine will operate before it fails (mean time to failure), the average length of time it will take to bring the failed machine back into service (mean time to repair), and the service on the machine by its manufacturer. The remaining factor is the design (or effective) capacity. These factors are all interrelated because more reliable machines or faster machines cost more money. For example, although a 9,600 baud modem is eight times as fast as a 1,200 baud modem, it also is more costly. One issue that must be addressed is the trade-off between the purchase cost and the operating cost of the machine. For our modems, the 9,600 baud modem is more expensive but, because it is faster, it reduces telephone (operating) costs. Cost–volume analysis, which we discuss later in this chapter, can be used to analyze this type of problem. For more complex situations, financial analysis, including present value analysis, may be used.

Just as there are economies of scale with respect to plants, there are also economies of scale with respect to machines. Consider, for example, transformations that process liquids such as pharmaceuticals, chemicals, or oil. These liquids are maintained in cylinders, with the cost of the cylinder being proportional to its surface area (rather than to its volume). Similar to our construction economy of scale for plant design, the relationship between volume and surface area is nonlinear. In fact, to double the volume of a cylinder, one needs only to increase the surface area by less than a factor of 2. For example, depending on the design, a cylinder with a surface area of 167 square feet may hold twice the volume of a cylinder with a surface area of 100 square feet.

economies of scale

The second type of economy of scale is that one large machine involves lower total operating costs than do two smaller machines. For example, it is less costly (requires less fuel, fewer personnel) to fly one 200-seat plane than two 100-seat planes. The advantage in having two different flights is that the planes can leave at different times.

Operating economies of scale also may be achieved because larger equipment can reduce costs by facilitating the job. Consider a moving company. A larger truck is easier to load than a smaller truck, which means that less time and wages are spent on loading when a larger, rather than a smaller, truck is used.

To some extent, we have already addressed the issue of the number of machines. If the effective capacity of a machine is 100 units per hour and we desire 250 units per hour, then we need three machines. This assumes that machines are constantly running when they should be (allowing for setups). In the production environment, this is a good assumption. In the service environment, machines such as cash registers are operated only when customers are present, and there is no inventory of cash register services. The models for determining the number of machines in these cases are termed *waiting line models* and are presented in Chapter 8.

INPUTS

Typically, productive capacity cannot be used if inputs are not available to work with *at the right time*. In the production sense, the meaning of "at the right time" is that enough raw material is stocked so that the products may be processed. Means for ensuring the appropriate inventory levels are presented in Chapter 13 (inventory) and Chapter 14 (materials requirements planning).

In fact, one of the major current issues in operations management is the just-in-time concept (JIT). The JIT concept goes beyond finding ways to make material avail-

just-in-time concept

able at the right time. The JIT concept involves attempting to ensure that the material is available as close to the time it is needed as possible. While this may yield greater efficiency, there is an increased risk that the material will not become available at the right time.

In the service industries, the input is not raw material; rather, it is typically the person being served, such as the patient in the hospital or the patron at the restaurant. For this reason, it is impossible to guarantee that the input will arrive at the facility at the right time, because arrivals cannot be predetermined and usually are random. Therefore, while hospital labor rooms often sit empty, sometimes the rooms are full. In order to determine the appropriate number of labor beds and associated costs, waiting line models (see Chapter 8) are used. Of course, it is a much more serious problem when the hospital runs out of capacity than when the restaurant cannot seat another patron. For this reason, the capacity design analysis must consider the "cost" of not having enough capacity.

In addition to the timing associated with the necessary materials, the type of material itself serves as a determinant of capacity. For example, a lathe may work at different rates depending on the hardness of the material being shaped. In effect, the same lathe has different capacities for the different materials. In a service industry, a similar factor exists: namely, the time to service a customer. The same hospital can serve more patients if each stays for a shorter rather than a longer time, even though the same number of beds (same capacity) is involved. We see this principle at work all the time in the supermarket. The checker at the express line serves more customers than do the other checkers, yet there is no more physical capacity at this line than at the others.

HUMAN FACTORS

Just as machines cannot be used if inputs are not available, many machines cannot be used if operators are not available. Hence, the size of the labor force, wages, worker morale, and job descriptions are important factors to be considered when determining capacity.

The study of human factors includes observation of the interaction between machines and humans. Of specific interest to our discussion of capacity is how different machine designs affect the capacity of the operator to perform an operation repeatedly and consistently, to respond rapidly to signals from a machine, and to control multiple processes at the same time. For example, the operator may be sitting at a control panel where numerical displays provide the temperatures in sixteen furnaces. The operator possesses some capacity to effectively monitor the sixteen different temperatures. A redesign of the control panel to make the displays green if the temperatures are normal and red if they are abnormal will increase the capacity of a single operator. An audible alarm would not be as effective (although it would help), because it would not identify which furnace is out of control. This brief discussion relates to the topic of job design, which is the subject of Chapter 9.

There is a great deal of interest at present in the efficiency of work teams. It had previously been assumed that the assembly-line (one worker per job) system was the most efficient and productive. However, current results at many locations indicate that perhaps work-team systems lead to the greatest productivity, quality, and capacity. The idea is being explored by the Big Three automakers. The teamwork idea is not limited to production, however. Companies offering financial and insurance services are con-

[margin notes:]

Teaching Suggestion 3.7: Controlling Arrivals in Service Through Pricing. See the Instructor's Section for details.

type of material

work teams

sidering implementing work teams as well. Of course, in many situations, the concept of teamwork not only requires the impetus of management but also the cooperation of the labor union.

Finally, quality circles or employee suggestions can improve capacity. For example, at General Motors' AC-Rochester Division plants in Flint, Michigan, employee suggestions on redesigning the production line allowed the company to increase capacity and decrease the number of employees simultaneously.

FACILITY LAYOUT

We previously discussed the design of a facility with respect to economies of scale. However, other design factors have a major influence on capacity. Recall that, given design capacities for various functions, the effective system capacity depends on the interactions between these functions.

One type of interaction is the flow of the product or customer from process to process. Clearly, as we place machines further and further apart, it is likely that we are reducing the system capacity. In general, we distinguish between two types of layout. **types of layout** *Product layout* refers to the case in which products go through the process in the same manner (assembly line). *Process layout* refers to a situation in which each job (or batch of jobs) is different and machines are grouped by function. Layout is one of the most basic elements of a facility, and the perceptive student will see which type is being used when he or she walks into a business operation.

Process and product layouts, as well as other types, will be explained in more detail in Chapter 7. We note here, however, that there is a trade-off between the costs of setting up and operating an assembly line and the costs of setting up and running a process layout, or job shop, as it is also commonly called. This trade-off will be examined later in this chapter, when we discuss cost–volume analysis.

QUALITY

We began this chapter by noting that the goal of operations management is to provide the product in the amounts required and of the quality required. Our concern at this stage is not with quality in general but, instead, with the effect of quality on the system capacity. In the event that a product is not manufactured properly or a customer is not processed properly, additional work must be performed. The time for doing the additional work is taken from normal operations time. Hence, the capacity is reduced. Consider the following example.

Example 3.5 Pictprint is a laboratory that produces prints from negatives. The laboratory uses a developer, which the manufacturer states has a (design) capacity of 500 prints per hour. Pictprint has found that 2 percent of the prints do not develop properly and, therefore, must be run through the developer again. What is the system's effective capacity?

The system's effective capacity is not the developer's effective capacity of 500 prints per hour. Rather, it is 98 percent of 500 prints per hour, or 490 prints per hour. ∎

Teaching Suggestion 3.8:
Capacity Resulting from
Preventive Maintenance.
See the Instructor's Sec-
tion for details.

Related to quality is the notion of preventive maintenance. The more preventive maintenance performed, the less the capacity. For example, airlines regularly schedule aircraft to overnight maintenance stations, limiting the scheduling of overnight flights to avoid reducing daytime capacity.

Our discussion about capacity is complete. As we have noted, more specific models will be presented throughout the text to address different capacity issues. At this point, we move on to examine some models and techniques that will help us to consider general questions regarding capacity and/or volume. We remind the reader that the models themselves do not make decisions, but they aid the manager in making decisions. The models are very useful for demonstrating properties of standard decisions or problems.

COST–VOLUME ANALYSIS

One of the methods appropriate for examining factors relating to production volume is **cost–volume analysis.** This technique is useful for relating a firm's costs and/or revenues to its volume of operation. Costs are defined as being of two types: **fixed costs** and **variable costs**. More detailed descriptions can be found in accounting texts, but we briefly define the terms.

FIXED COSTS: This category consists of those costs that are independent of volume (see Table 3.8). For example, it is standard practice to charge the cost of equipment as a fixed cost because this cost is paid whether the equipment is used to produce one unit or one hundred units. Similarly, the plant is bought (or leased), and its cost is

TABLE 3.8 Cost classification

Cost	Fixed	Variable
Management salaries	X	
Building (including depreciation)	X	
Land	X	
Machinery	X	
Building insurance	X	
Taxes	X	
Equipment rental	X	
Water, sewer	X	X
Fuel, electricity	X	X
Labor	X	X
Quality control	X	X
Raw materials		X
Overtime		X
Freight		X
Operating supplies		X
Packaging materials		X

independent of the volume of operations. While the cost is fixed with respect to the number of units, fixed costs vary according to time. The cost of leasing a building is always classified as a fixed cost, but with the understanding that the lease is a one-year lease. Obviously, total leasing costs are dependent on the number of months or years of the lease, not on the number of units.

Teaching Suggestion 3.9: Sunk Costs. See the Instructor's Section for details.

VARIABLE COSTS: This category consists of those costs that increase in proportion to the volume of production. For example, material costs increase as more units are produced. This is true of packaging costs, also.

As indicated in Table 3.8, some costs are both fixed and variable. For example, energy costs have both fixed and variable components. The energy costs of lighting a hospital are fixed, but the energy costs of operating X-ray machines increase as a function of the number of X-rays. And as we have seen, when distinguishing between fixed and variable costs, time is also a factor.

costs may be both fixed and variable

THE BASIC BREAK-EVEN MODEL

The most basic cost–volume model is the break-even model, which consists of three factors: a fixed cost (FC); a variable cost (VC), which is given in dollars per unit; and a selling price (P), which also is given in dollars per unit. Given these three factors, if we denote the volume by Q, then the firm's profit is given by

$$
\begin{aligned}
\text{Profit} &= \text{total revenue} - \text{total costs} \\
&= \text{total revenue} - (\text{fixed cost} + \text{total variable costs}) \\
&= P \times Q - (FC + VC \times Q).
\end{aligned}
$$

The goal is to determine the volume at which the firm breaks even, which we denote as the break-even point. The break-even point is the number of units the company needs to produce (and sell) in order to have no profit and no loss (to break even). Thus, when we conduct a **break-even analysis,** we wish to find the volume at which

break-even point

$$\text{Total revenue} - \text{total costs} = 0,$$

or

$$\text{Total revenue} = \text{total costs}.$$

Consider the following example.

Example 3.6   A company has (annual) fixed costs of $20,000. Variable costs are $12 per unit, and the selling price of the item is $20 per unit. Find the break-even point.

As already stated, the break-even point is given by the volume at which there is neither a profit nor a loss. In other words, it is the point at which the total revenue equals the total cost. Let Q represent this volume. Then it follows that we need to find Q such that

$$\text{Total revenue} = \text{total costs,}$$

or

$$P \times Q = FC + VC \times Q.$$
$$\$20Q = \$20,000 + \$12Q$$
$$\$20Q - \$12Q = \$20,000$$
$$\$8Q = \$20,000$$
$$Q = 2,500 \text{ units}$$

Thus, the break-even volume is 2,500 units. Alternatively, this can be expressed in dollar terms—at 2,500 units both the total revenue and the total cost are $50,000. ◼

graphical analysis

Teaching Suggestion 3.10: Use of Graph. See the Instructor's Section for details.

Figure 3.8 presents a graphical picture of this example. From zero to the break-even point of 2,500 units, the firm suffers losses, because the revenue line is below the total cost line. Beyond 2,500 units, the firm nets a profit, as given by the difference between the revenue line and the total cost line.

For this basic problem, the break-even point (BEP) can be calculated according to the formula

FIGURE 3.8 Break-even analysis (Example 3.6)

Transparency Master 3.5: Break-even Analysis.

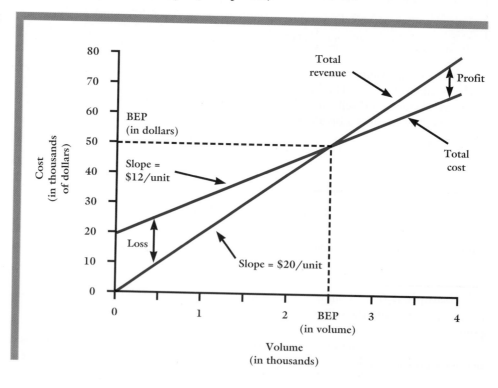

$$\text{BEP} = \frac{\text{fixed costs}}{\text{selling price} - \text{variable cost}} = \frac{FC}{P - VC}.$$

The denominator in this formula is termed the **contribution margin**, because the difference between the selling price and the variable cost is the contribution toward recovering the fixed costs for units produced below the break-even point and, ultimately, toward profit after the break-even volume has been achieved.

contribution margin

The basic model has two assumptions that must be noted. The first assumption is that all units that are made will be sold. The second assumption in that both the total revenue and the total cost are linear in terms of the volume. In Example 3.6, the variable cost of the first unit is $12 and the variable cost of the one-thousandth is still $12. This is often true, but there are also many cases of nonlinearity. For example, if this is the first year that the company is manufacturing this product, the company may learn how to operate more efficiently as more units are produced, thereby reducing the variable cost to $11 per unit in the second year. (This subject of learning curves is discussed in detail in Chapter 9.) Also, it is possible that the company will pay less per unit for 2,500 units of raw material than for 1,000 units; that is, a quantity discount may be given. We cannot always rely on the basic model. For this reason, we will consider more general applications of cost–volume analysis.

model assumptions

Teaching Suggestion 3.11: Linearity. See the Instructor's Section for details.

There is another reason for considering other cost–volume models. The break-even model contains the selling price as one of the factors. This selling price is a function of marketing rather than operations. As a rule, the operations function is concerned with production costs, not company profits. (The two, of course, are related.) Therefore, the types of cost–volume analysis that are useful in production involve cost models that do not include any revenue. Some major decisions faced by an operations manager are which equipment type to choose, which general facility layout to implement, whether to buy component parts or make them in-house, and how to handle quantity discounts on raw material prices.

major cost–volume applications

EQUIPMENT CHOICE

One of the standard problems in operations is determining which type of machine to purchase. Of two machines, one typically has higher purchase (fixed) cost. This higher purchase cost usually is due to the machine's offering more features, and these features lead to greater efficiency, which, in turn, lowers the variable cost. The following example illustrates this situation.

Example 3.7   Gateway Delivery Service is purchasing a new delivery vehicle. Of the two under consideration, one has a gasoline engine and the other has a diesel engine. The purchase prices are $10,000 for the regular car and $13,000 for the diesel car. The operating costs for the regular car are $.32 per mile, while the operating costs for the diesel car are $.27 per mile. Find the break-even point.

In this case , the break-even point is the volume (expressed in miles) at which the total cost of the regular car is equal to the total cost of the diesel car. Letting m represent miles driven, we are looking for the value of m that satisfies the equation

$$\text{Total cost (regular)} = \text{total cost (diesel)}.$$
$$10{,}000 + .32m = 13{,}000 + .27m$$
$$.05m = 3{,}000$$
$$m = 60{,}000$$

The graph for this example is shown in Figure 3.9. From the graph, it should be clear that the regular car should be purchased if the expected mileage over the lifetime of the cars is less than 60,000. However, if the expected mileage is above 60,000, the diesel car is the appropriate choice.   ◼◗

This is a very simple model in that we have not considered interest, taxes, depreciation, or salvage value. If the vehicle is to be used over a period of several years, then it may be better to use financial analysis (present value) methods. However, it is safe to assume that the break-even point is still around 60,000 miles even when using more sophisticated techniques.

CHOICE OF PROCESS

types of production processes

Closely related to the problem of equipment choice is the problem of designing the production process for the system. We distinguish between two common types of pro-

FIGURE 3.9   Cost analysis for Gateway Delivery Service (Example 3.7)

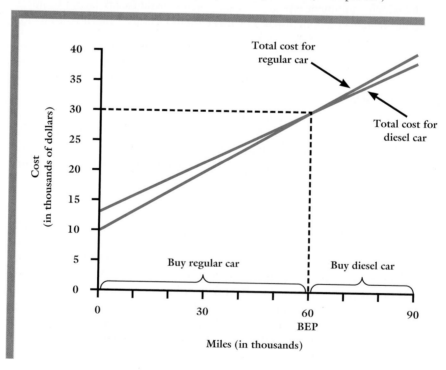

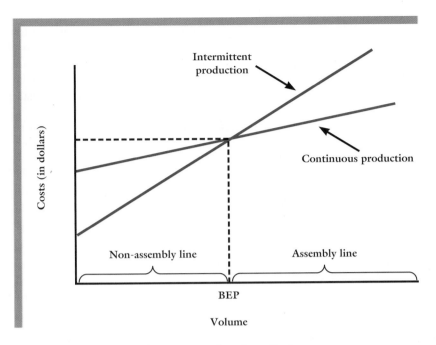

FIGURE 3.10 Choice of process as a function of volume

duction processes: *continuous production* and *intermittent production*. Essentially, a continuous production system is an assembly line, while an intermittent system refers to a job shop—that is, a system where the individual jobs vary from one to another. An example of a job shop is an automobile repair station. One difference between continuous and intermittent production is the type of machinery each uses. In a job shop, general-purpose machinery is required, but on an assembly line, special-purpose machinery is used. The special-purpose machinery costs more to purchase, but it also operates more efficiently. Hence, the variable cost of units produced on the special machinery is less. In addition, it is more costly (in terms of fixed cost) to set up an assembly line, but an efficient assembly line reduces variable cost. The general picture is given in Figure 3.10, where we indicate the higher fixed cost of the assembly line and its lower associated variable cost. The analysis in Figure 3.10 indicates a well-known fact: Assembly lines are cost-effective only if there is sufficient volume.

MAKE/BUY DECISIONS

Another typical operations decision is a **make/buy decision**. Suppose a company manufactures a product that consists of several components. Some of these components can be manufactured by the company itself or purchased from a supplier. The advantage of manufacturing the components is that the variable cost is lower than the purchase price, because it does not include the supplier's profit. The disadvantage is that there is a fixed cost incurred to set up the production. Consider the following example.

Example 3.8   Tiara Computer Company produces microcomputer systems for home use. Provided with the system are joysticks. Currently, Tiara purchases the joysticks from Trackit Inc. for $10 per pair. A feasibility study has indicated that Tiara could produce the joysticks itself. The cost to set up the production would be $30,000, and the joysticks could be produced at a cost of $8 per pair. Find the break-even volume.

Again, it is necessary to set two costs equal to one another. That is, we want to find the volume at which the total cost of producing joysticks is equal to the total cost of purchasing them. We let j represent the number of pairs of joysticks.

$$\text{Total cost (make)} = \text{total cost (buy)}$$
$$30{,}000 + 8j = 10j$$
$$30{,}000 = 2j$$
$$j = 15{,}000$$

Figure 3.11 indicates that the joysticks should be purchased from Trackit if the number of computers produced is less than 15,000 units. However, if the number of computers produced is greater than 15,000, the joysticks should be manufactured by Tiara. ◼◢

Incidentally, this is a typical situation. As the demand for a company's product grows, the company begins to manufacture more and more of the subcomponents necessary for production. For example, when a publisher begins business, the editing is given to professional consultants (freelance editors), and the printing is done by a private press. As the volume increases, in-house editors are hired, and a printing press is purchased.

FIGURE 3.11   Tiara Computer Company make/buy decision (Example 3.8)

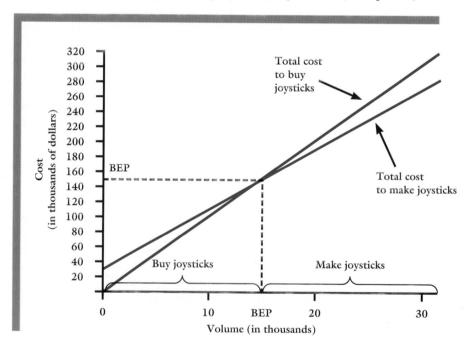

QUANTITY DISCOUNTS

It was mentioned before that when a greater quantity of raw material is purchased, it is more likely that quantity discounts will be offered. The topic of quantity discounts will also be discussed in Chapter 13 (inventory), but its relevance to cost–volume analysis is exemplified by the following two examples.

Example 3.9 Through its intelligence forces, Trackit Inc. has learned that Tiara is considering manufacturing its own joysticks. In order not to lose Tiara as a customer, Trackit is going to offer Tiara a quantity discount. The price for the joysticks will be $10 for the first 10,000 pairs purchased, but $9 for each unit above 10,000. Find the new break-even volume at which Tiara will stop buying from Trackit and instead manufacture its own.

Again, the two costs must be equated. However, this time, the purchase price changes. In fact, the total cost line of purchasing has a bend in it (see Figure 3.12).

$$\text{Total purchase cost} = \begin{cases} 10j \text{ if } j \le 10,000 \\ 100,000 + 9(j - 10,000) \text{ if } j \ge 10,000 \end{cases}$$

FIGURE 3.12 Tiara Computer Company: the effect of a quantity discount (Example 3.9)

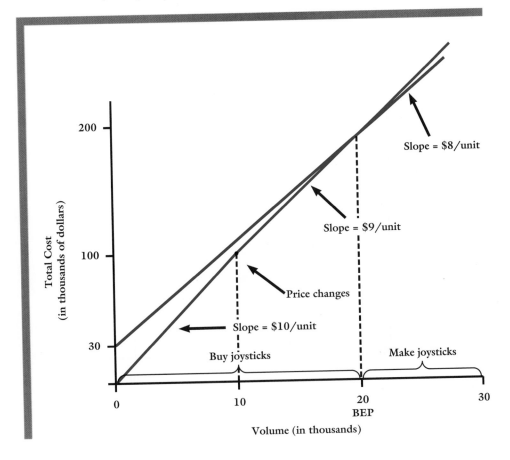

From Figure 3.12, it can be seen that the break-even point is above 10,000, which means that we solve for j as follows.

$$\text{Total cost (buy)} = \text{total cost (make)}$$
$$100,000 + 9(j - 10,000) = 30,000 + 8j$$
$$100,000 + 9j - 90,000 = 30,000 + 8j$$
$$j = 20,000$$

The effect of this quantity discount has been to raise the break-even point from 15,000 pairs of joysticks to 20,000 pairs of joysticks. This, of course, makes purchasing the units more attractive to Tiara. However, consider a second type of quantity discount. ∎

Example 3.10   Trackit Inc. is not sure that it has made its price as attractive as it should. Therefore, Trackit is going to offer Tiara its best quantity discount. The price will be set at $10 per pair if fewer than 10,000 pairs are purchased but $9 per pair if 10,000 or more units are purchased. Although the prices ($10 and $9) are the same, this is a much better discount than in the previous example because even the first 10,000 units are discounted if more than 10,000 units are purchased.

The revised purchase price means that the total price appears in segments of two straight lines (see Figure 3.13). If the quantity is less than 10,000, the $10 per unit

FIGURE 3.13   Tiara Computer Company: the effect of a better quantity discount (Example 3.10)

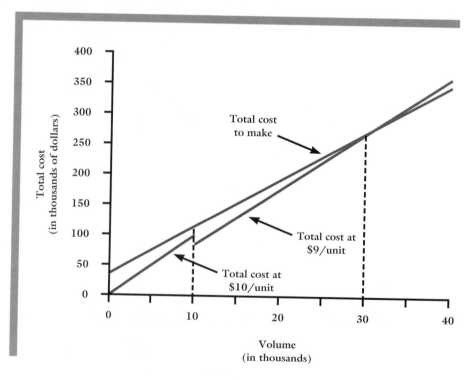

line is the appropriate line, but if the quantity is 10,000 or more, the $9 per unit line is used. As you can see, the break-even point is past the price break on the Trackit line.

$$\text{Total cost (purchase)} = \text{total cost (make)}$$

$$9j = 30,000 + 8j$$

$$j = 30,000$$

The break-even point is now twice its original value.   ■⌋

These last two examples indicate that the total cost is not necessarily a straight line. We will see a different type of analysis involving quantity discounts in the discussion of inventory management in Chapter 13.

DECISION MAKING

We have seen that demand is a critical component both of capacity planning and of cost–volume analysis. Often, the demand is not known exactly, and estimates of the possible demands are given along with the probabilities that these estimates will be correct. In this section, we consider such situations. Although the discussion is limited to capacity decision making, the methods presented are applicable to a much wider class of decision problems. Decision making, in the sense discussed here, is a major function of operations management (perhaps all management). As the reader will soon realize, many of the techniques described throughout the text are really approaches to the general topics of decision making and problem solving.

major function of operations management

In general, the decision problem is stated as one of choosing among a set of possible decisions (alternatives) when the future "state of nature" (scenario) is not known with certainty. If probabilities are associated with the possible scenarios, it is *decision making under risk,* and the **risk** associated with a decision can be measured. If no information is available concerning probabilities, it is *decision making under uncertainty.* **Uncertainty** refers to the fact that we do not know how likely one outcome is relative to other outcomes. The next three sections (on expected value, decision tables, and decision trees) contain discussions pertaining to the case of risk. The case of uncertainty is presented in the last section.

EXPECTED VALUE

Suppose the demand estimates for a product are given as follows.

Demand	Probability
100,000	.3
200,000	.5
300,000	.2

Then the expected value of the demand or expected demand is given as the weighted average of the demand possibilities. The formula for **expected value** is

$$EV = \sum (\text{probability of outcome } i)(\text{value of outcome } i).$$

So, for the product under consideration,

$$\text{Expected demand} = 100,000(.3) + 200,000(.5) + 300,000(.2)$$

$$= 30,000 + 100,000 + 60,000$$

$$= 190,000.$$

assumption of expected value

It is important to note that expected value represents an average if the process is repeated over and over. In the long run, 30 percent of the time, the demand will be 100,000; 50 percent of the time, the demand will be 200,000; and 20 percent of the time, the demand will be 300,000, which yields an average of 190,000. Because the decision will be made only once in actuality, the expected demand of 190,000 will never occur. It is used only as a reasonable basis for reaching a decision.

Consider the application of expected value to cost–volume analysis.

Example 3.11   Homeway Restaurant is considering purchasing one of two ovens. The ovens differ in purchase cost and energy usage.

	Oven A	Oven B
Purchasing cost	$100,000	$60,000
Operating cost	$20/hour	$35/hour

Usage depends on the number of patrons and the amount of food the patrons order. Estimates of usage over the coming year are given as follows.

Cooking Hours	Probability
2,000	.2
2,500	.4
3,000	.3
3,500	.1

Using expected cooking hours, which oven should be selected?

We first compute the expected cooking hours.

$$\text{Expected hours} = 2,000(.2) + 2,500(.4) + 3,000(.3) + 3,500(.1)$$

$$= 400 + 1,000 + 900 + 350$$

$$= 2,650$$

In Figure 3.14, we present the cost–volume chart for this example. It can be seen that 2,650 lies on the part of the chart that indicates that oven B is cheaper. It also should be noted that 2,650 is very close to the break-even point of 2,667. Therefore, a small change in the probability estimates would change the decision. What the answer really tells us is that we are indifferent between the two ovens if our probability estimates are close to being correct. The indifference would have to be resolved based on other factors, possibly using criteria presented in the following sections.

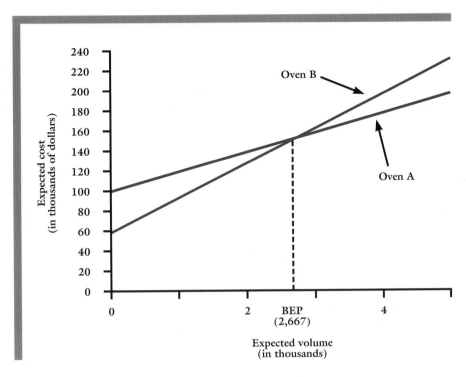

FIGURE 3.14 Expected values in cost–volume analysis (Example 3.11)

DECISION TABLES

A **decision table** is a way of presenting the outcomes of different decisions under different scenarios. The table contains the probability of each scenario and the profit or loss for each decision under each scenario. Given a decision table, we will consider three different strategies for making a decision. These strategies are expected value, maximin, and maximax. Consider the following example.

planning for different scenarios

Teaching Suggestion 3.12: Building Decision Tables. See the Instructor's Section for details.

Example 3.12 Admiral Manufacturing Company is reconsidering its capacity. In the future, demand will either be low, average, or high. These three scenarios have probabilities of 25 percent, 40 percent, and 35 percent, respectively. The company has three different alternatives for increasing its capacity. These options are to use overtime, to increase the size of the work force, or to add an entire shift. In general, overtime is the easiest and least costly option; adding a complete shift is the most expensive option. However, a second shift doubles the capacity, while overtime limits the capacity change to a more modest 25-percent increase (two hours overtime per eight-hour shift). Hiring additional workers is an option that falls between overtime and adding a shift, both in terms of cost and capacity increase.

These comments on the cost and capacity of the three options are reflected by the nine profits listed in the following table. Notice that, regardless of which option is chosen, a larger demand leads to larger profits. However, also notice that adding a shift is best suited to high demand, while overtime is best suited to low demand.

Option	Scenario		
	Low Demand ($p = .25$)	Average Demand ($p = .40$)	High Demand ($p = .35$)
Use overtime	50*	70	90
Increase work force	30	50	100
Add shift	0	20	200

*Profits in millions of dollars

As we've mentioned, there are three strategies available for examining the decision table. The first strategy—expected value—we have already seen. Let us compute the expected value for each of the three possible actions of overtime (OT), increasing the work force (W), and adding a shift (S). We use EV to denote the expected value.

$$EV(\text{OT}) = 50(.25) + 70(.40) + 90(.35)$$
$$= 12.5 + 28 + 31.5$$
$$= 72$$
$$EV(\text{W}) = 30(.25) + 50(.40) + 100(.35)$$
$$= 7.5 + 20 + 35$$
$$= 62.5$$
$$EV(\text{S}) = 0(.25) + 20(.40) + 200(.35)$$
$$= 0 + 8 + 70$$
$$= 78$$

Therefore, based on expected value, the best decision is to add a complete shift.   ■⌡

MAXIMIN

The second decision strategy is termed **maximin**. Using this method, we examine the worst (minimum profit or maximum cost) that can happen if we make any decision and then take the best (maximum for profit, minimum for cost) of these worst outcomes. This procedure is highly conservative and is often referred to as "the pessimist's strategy." The method consists of two steps.

the pessimist's strategy

> **Step 1.** For each option (action, decision, alternative), find the lowest profit among the scenarios that could occur. (This is the worst-case scenario for that decision.)
>
> **Step 2.** From the list of lowest profits, choose the option that yields the highest profit.

This yields the maximum (max) of the minima (min), which is why the strategy is termed *maximin*. In the case of costs, we take the lowest (min) of the highest (max), and term the procedure the *minimax*. In either case, we are taking the best of the worst-case scenarios. We continue with the same capacity example. Following is the extended table, which includes the worst-case analysis.

best of the worst

	Scenario			Worst
Option	Low	Average	High	
Use overtime	50*	70	90	50
Increase work force	30	50	100	30
Add shift	0	20	200	0

*Profits in millions of dollars

The column on the far right indicates the worst (minimum) profit for each of the three options. In this example, the lowest profit is always associated with the same scenario (low demand). This will not always be the case. Step 2 is to pick the largest of these. Therefore, the maximin in this example is the profit of 50, given by using the overtime option.

Notice that when using a maximin criterion, the probabilities are not included in the analysis. For example, even if in our example there were a 98-percent chance of a high demand and a 1-percent chance for both low demand and average demand, the maximin would still be overtime. This would, of course, be a very conservative (and bad) choice.

assumption of maximin

MAXIMAX

Maximax, the third strategy, is precisely the opposite of maximin. It is optimistic and possibly risky—the opposite of conservative— and is used only in desperate situations. The procedure is simple: Find the highest possible profit in the table and choose the alternative that leads to this profit. In the example, the largest profit is 200, which is generated by adding a shift. Notice that, again, the probabilities have not been used for maximax.

the optimist's strategy

best of best

In general, maximax is a very risky strategy and is used only when the decision maker is very desperate or very optimistic. Examples of good uses of maximax can be found in sports (which is a form of operation). These examples include pulling the goalie at the end of a hockey game, throwing a Hail Mary pass at the end of a football game, and fouling the opponent deliberately at the end of a basketball game. In business, those who have gambled all for an idea (Rockefeller at Standard Oil, Jobs at Apple Computer) and were successful are considered heroes. However, there is a much larger group that followed this risky approach and ended up in bankruptcy.

When the decision table contains costs instead of profits, the expected value strategy is to select the option that yields the lowest cost instead of the highest. The maximin becomes minimax (still best of worst), and the maximax becomes the minimin (still best of best).

cost problems

DECISION TREES

Another tool that proves useful in making decisions is the **decision tree**, a pictorial model that represents the structure of the decision problem. One advantage it has over the decision table is that people often find a pictorial model easier to work with than a

sequence of decisions

table of numbers. A more important advantage associated with the decision trees is that they are easily applied to the analysis of sequences of decisions. This application can be somewhat awkward with a decision table.

We will first look at the problem that we just solved using a decision table (Example 3.12). The structure of the problem is such that one decision must be made (there is no sequence of decisions to analyze). A decision tree starts with a decision point. From the decision point, we draw branches indicating each of the alternative decisions that can be made. This has been done in Figure 3.15 for the three alternatives: use overtime, increase work force, and add shift.

decision point

state of nature point

Once the decision is made to follow one of these branches, the return depends upon future demand. Our notation to represent a state of nature point is a circle. More branching occurs from the state of nature point, but this is outside of the control of the decision maker. A probability is associated with each branch from a state of nature point. Thus, the decision tree is useful for decision making under risk. It uses the expected value criterion. The complete tree for the problem is shown in Figure 3.16.

Notice that the returns associated with each branch are placed at the end of the tree. Each branch at the tree's end represents a possible outcome resulting from the decision. Multiplying each return by the probability associated with that outcome and then adding together the products yields the expected value for a state of nature point. Working backward, we take the expected value for all state of nature points. When a decision point is reached, no expected value needs to be taken. The three alternatives yield expected values of 72, 62.5, and 78. We choose the decision (add a shift) that has the highest expected value (78), and the "value" of the tree is 78.

choose best

To summarize, the decision tree is started by branching from a single point to each of its alternatives. If there is a guaranteed outcome associated with any alternative, there is no further branching along that path. Usually, however, a decision is followed by more branching in accordance with the possible states of nature. Once all possible outcomes have been identified, expected values are taken back toward the start of the tree until the value of each alternative is known. At any decision point, the best decision is chosen.

Now let's look at an example in which, rather than one decision, a series of decisions must be made. Again, a decision tree will prove helpful.

Example 3.13 The owner of a small business decides to purchase a computer to keep track of his billing, payroll, inventory, and client records. He needs a small system now, but growth of the business could make a small system inadequate in a few years. After hearing one too many sales pitches, the businessman narrows his choices

FIGURE 3.15
Decision point and
alternatives (Example
3.12)

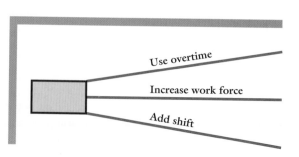

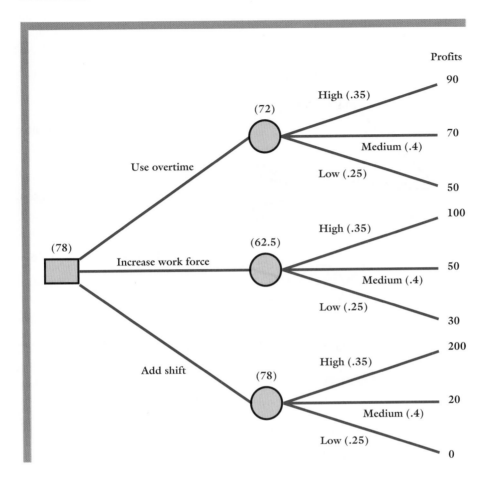

FIGURE 3.16 Complete decision tree (Example 3.12)

down to buying a small system with no expansion capabilities, a small system that can be expanded, or a larger system. The systems cost $4,000, $6,000, and $9,000, respectively. In three years, he can trade in either smaller system for a larger one at a cost of $7,500 or expand the expandable small system at a cost of $4,000. He puts the likelihood of needing the larger system in three years at 80 percent. Ignoring the time value of the funds, which computer should be purchased?

The decision tree for this example is shown in Figure 3.17(a). At the start, there are three decisions: large, expandable, or small. Each of these decisions is affected by two possible states of nature: requiring the large system in three years or needing the small system in the future. Once the large system is purchased, no further actions need to be considered. If the expandable system is purchased and demand increases in the future, a decision can then be made either to expand the system or trade it in. If the small system is purchased and a large system is needed later, the small system must be traded in for a larger system. If either the expandable or the small system is purchased and only the small system is required, no further action is considered.

The tree is developed now, but, as Figure 3.17(a) shows, there is one additional piece of information to be included: the cost of reaching each ending branch. The cost

Transparency Master 3.6:
Decision Trees.

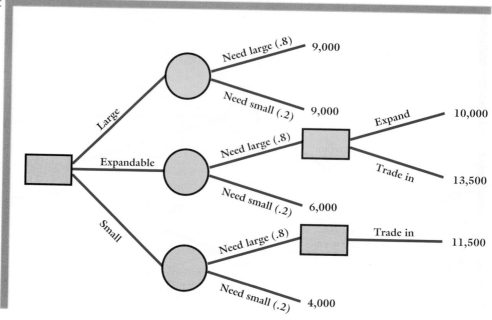

(a) Developing the decision tree

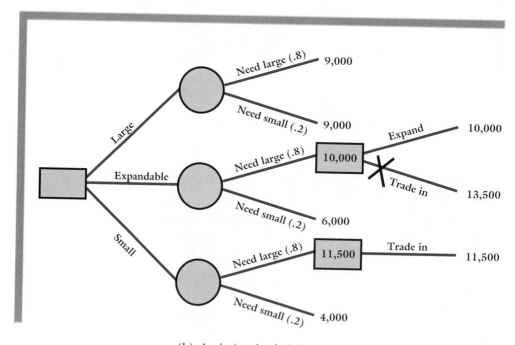

(b) Analyzing the decision tree

FIGURE 3.17   Decision tree from development through solution (Example 3.13)

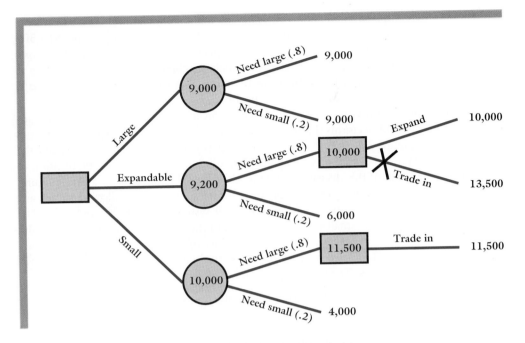

(c) Evaluating expected values in the decision tree

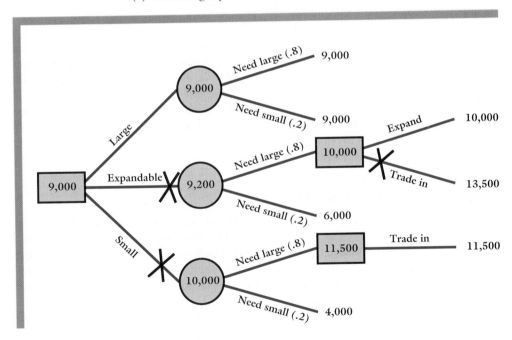

(d) Choosing the best decision

of the large computer is $9,000, regardless of the state of nature. The expandable system costs $6,000 as is, $10,000 ($6,000 + $4,000) if expanded, and $13,500 ($6,000 + $7,500) if traded in. The small system costs $4,000 and, if traded in, costs $11,500 ($4,000 + $7,500). Alternative labeling schemes are to put the costs at either the decision branch or the state of nature branch where they are actually incurred, but neither is necessary for the problem.

The analysis of the tree, conducted from right to left (backward in time), begins with the analysis of decisions that need to be made three years from now. This analysis is shown in Figure 3.17(b). If a large computer is needed, we decide to expand the expandable system because it is cheaper than trading it in. The cost of the decision to expand (the value of this decision point) is $10,000, which is indicated in the figure. The branch for trade-in is crossed off because it will never be followed under any circumstance. For this same situation, the small system can only be traded in. The decision to trade in the small system (lower part of the figure), has a value of $11,500.

The next step is to evaluate the expected values of the three state of nature nodes, as shown in Figure 3.17(c). The first one (along the "large" branch) is $9,000, regardless of the probabilities. The second ("expandable" branch) is

$$.8(\$10,000) + .2(\$6,000) = \$9,200.$$

The third ("small" branch) is

$$.8(\$11,500) + .2(\$4,000) = \$10,000.$$

These values are again indicated by the appropriate nodes in the figure.

The final step is to choose the best decision from among the three alternatives branching from the original decision node. Because the expected cost of $9,000 for the large computer is the least, this is the decision to choose. As shown in Figure 3.17(d), the value of the decision tree is $9,000, and the other two branches are crossed out.

Figure 3.17(d) provides the complete solution to this example. Be sure to notice that the other two decision nodes are never reached, so these decisions do not have to be made, even though they have been analyzed.   ■」

DECISIONS UNDER UNCERTAINTY

no information

Because probabilities are not used for the maximin or maximax strategies, it should be obvious that these strategies are more applicable when the probabilities of each scenario are not known, which occurs when no information is available concerning the probabilities. Examples have been provided to show how these strategies are used. Because the probabilities were ignored in those examples, the same procedures apply when no probabilities are available.

model assumption

It may seem, however, that the expected value strategy cannot be used in the case of uncertainty. It turns out that, although the strategy is not as powerful a tool as it is when the probabilities are known, it can still be applied. Complete uncertainty means not only that the probabilities are unknown, but also that whether there is a greater chance of high demand than lower demand (or vice versa) is unknown as well. Because no information is available to say that one outcome is more or less likely than any other outcome, the expected value strategy can be used with the assumption that all outcomes are equally likely.

To apply this strategy to Example 3.12, we must compute the expected values.

$$EV(OT) = (50)(.33) + (70)(.33) + (90)(.33) = 70$$

$$EV(W) = (30)(.33) + (50)(.33) + (100)(.33) = 60$$

$$EV(S) = (0)(.33) \quad + (20)(.33) + (200)(.33) = 73.3$$

Again, the choice is to add a complete second shift. But notice that, in this case, the choice is not as clear. The difference between this choice and the use of overtime is only 3.3 (73.3 − 70), whereas the previous probabilities yielded a difference of 6 (78 − 72).

SUMMARY

This chapter has been concerned with volume. The underlying capability of the firm's production volume is a rate. There are different measures of this rate—the *design capacity*, which is the ideal rate, or, a more realistic rate, the *effective capacity* (also called the *system capacity*). In many instances, it may be very difficult to measure capacity. The actual output rate in comparison (ratio) with the design capacity yields the *system efficiency*, while actual output in comparison with the resources yields the *productivity*. Productivity itself is a nebulous measure, but changes in productivity are very useful measures.

The capacity is dictated by resources—manpower, machines—and also by demand. Of course, resource changes require capital. To analyze choices that affect the capacity, we use *cost–volume* methods. Such methods encompass the concepts of *break-even analysis, make/buy decisions,* and *equipment choice decisions* and the effects of *quantity discounts*.

Sometimes, decisions are made based on different assessments of what the future may bring. The criterion may be *expected value, maximin,* or *maximax*. Expected value represents a long-run average, while maximin is a conservative (pessimistic) strategy and maximax is a risky (optimistic) strategy.

KEY TERMS

capacity	efficiency	risk
economies of scale	utilization	uncertainty
systems in unison	productivity	expected value
series systems	cost–volume analysis	decision table
parallel systems	fixed costs	maximin
bottleneck	variable costs	maximax
design capacity	break-even analysis	decision tree
effective capacity	contribution margin	
system capacity	make/buy decision	

S O L V E D
P R O B L E M S

1. Galactico Deliveries has a package processing center in Memphis, Tennessee. The center has 30 employees who unload packages from the forty-foot trailers that are used to transport the packages from city to city. Another 20 employees then sort the packages for local delivery, and 40 more employees then load the vans that are used for local deliveries. Unloaders work at a rate of 12 packages per minute, sorters work at a rate of 15 packages per minute, and loaders take approximately 10 seconds to load each package.

    (a) What is the system capacity?
    (b) What is the utilization of each of the three resources if the system operates at its system capacity?

Solution

(a) In order to solve this problem, we need to find the capacities of the three individual subsystems of unloading, sorting, and loading. The capacities for each of these three subsystems are given by the number of employees multiplied by the rate of work, because the employees work in parallel. First, we note that because loaders take 10 seconds per package, their rate is 6 packages per minute. The following table identifies the capacities.

Subsystem	(1) Rate	(2) Number of Employees	(3) Capacity [(1) × (2)]
Unloaders	12/minute	30	360/minute
Sorters	15/minute	20	300/minute
Loaders	6/minute	40	240/minute

Because the three subsystems operate in series, the system capacity is the minimum of the subsystem capacities, or 240 packages per minute. (Note that the capacity is a rate.)

(b) The utilization of each subsystem is the ratio of the output (actual system capacity) to subsystem capacity. For the three subsystems, the utilization is given as follows.

Subsystem	Subsystem Capacity	System Capacity	Utilization
Unloaders	360	240	.67
Sorters	300	240	.80
Loaders	240	240	1.00

2. Chip's Chocolate Chips sells fresh-baked cookies at the main terminal of the Tri-County Airport. Daily demand is distributed as follows.

Dozens Sold	Probability
24	.05
25	.10
26	.20
27	.25
28	.25
29	.10
30	.05

The cookies cost $1.10 per dozen to prepare, and they sell for $2 per dozen. There is no salvage value for day-old cookies.

  (a) Create the decision table.
  (b) Find the maximin strategy.
  (c) Find the maximax strategy.
  (d) Find the strategy that maximizes the expected profits.

Solution

(a) We begin this problem by developing the payoff table. The table will have seven strategies and seven outcomes, each given by the numbers 24 through 30.

Strategy: Dozens Produced	Scenario: Demand (Probability)						
	24 (.05)	25 (.10)	26 (.20)	27 (.25)	28 (.25)	29 (.10)	30 (.05)
24							
25							
26							
27							
28							
29							
30							

Next, we must fill in the profits for each cell. The profit for each cell depends on whether the supply is less than the demand, equals the demand, or is greater than the demand. Let us begin with a situation in which demand equals supply. In this case, each dozen nets a profit of $2.00 - $1.10 = $.90, so the total profit is the number sold (which equals both the demand and the supply) times $.90. The partially completed table appears as follows.

Strategy: Dozens Produced	Scenario: Demand (Probability)						
	24 (.05)	25 (.10)	26 (.20)	27 (.25)	28 (.25)	29 (.10)	30 (.05)
24	21.60						
25		22.50					
26			23.40				
27				24.30			
28					25.20		
29						26.10	
30							27.00

Now consider what happens when supply is greater than demand. In this case, the profit is $.90 per dozen for each dozen sold (which equals the demand), but there is a loss of $1.10 per dozen for each dozen supplied and not sold. For example, if the supply is 30 and the demand is 25, the profit is

$$25 \times \$.90 + (30 - 25) \times (-\$1.10) = \$17.$$

Filling in the entries where supply is greater than demand yields the following.

Strategy: Dozens Produced	Scenario: Demand (Probability)						
	24 (.05)	25 (.10)	26 (.20)	27 (.25)	28 (.25)	29 (.10)	30 (.05)
24	21.60						
25	20.50	22.50					
26	19.40	21.40	23.40				
27	18.30	20.30	22.30	24.30			
28	17.20	19.20	21.20	23.20	25.20		
29	16.10	18.10	20.10	22.10	24.10	26.10	
30	15.00	17.00	19.00	21.00	23.00	25.00	27.00

Finally, we need to consider what happens when demand is greater than supply. In this case, everything that is produced is sold, and a profit of $.90 per dozen is made. (We assume that there is no cost to not meeting the demand.) For example, if we produce 25 dozen, but the demand is for 30 dozen, then we sell 25 dozen and have a total profit of $22.50. Now we can present the final table.

Strategy: Dozens Produced	Scenario: Demand (Probability)						
	24 (.05)	25 (.10)	26 (.20)	27 (.25)	28 (.25)	29 (.10)	30 (.05)
24	21.60	21.60	21.60	21.60	21.60	21.60	21.60
25	20.50	22.50	22.50	22.50	22.50	22.50	22.50
26	19.40	21.40	23.40	23.40	23.40	23.40	23.40
27	18.30	20.30	22.30	24.30	24.30	24.30	24.30
28	17.20	19.20	21.20	23.20	25.20	25.20	25.20
29	16.10	18.10	20.10	22.10	24.10	26.10	26.10
30	15.00	17.00	19.00	21.00	23.00	25.00	27.00

Now that we have the table, we can provide the answers to the questions on strategy.

(b) To find the maximin strategy, we must append to the right-hand side of the table a column that contains the worst (minimum) outcome for each strategy.

Strategy: Dozens Produced	Scenario: Demand (Probability)							Worst Outcome
	24 (.05)	25 (.10)	26 (.20)	27 (.25)	28 (.25)	29 (.10)	30 (.05)	
24	21.60	21.60	21.60	21.60	21.60	21.60	21.60	21.60
25	20.50	22.50	22.50	22.50	22.50	22.50	22.50	20.50
26	19.40	21.40	23.40	23.40	23.40	23.40	23.40	19.40
27	18.30	20.30	22.30	24.30	24.30	24.30	24.30	18.30
28	17.20	19.20	21.20	23.20	25.20	25.20	25.20	17.20
29	16.10	18.10	20.10	22.10	24.10	26.10	26.10	16.10
30	15.00	17.00	19.00	21.00	23.00	25.00	27.00	15.00

The maximin strategy is to pick the best (maximum) of the worst cases. Therefore, the choice is to produce 24 dozen, which will guarantee a profit of $21.60, regardless of the demand. Note that this guarantee is both good and bad. It guarantees that we will not do worse than a profit of $21.60, but because all outcomes are $21.60, it also guarantees that we will not do better than a profit of $21.60.

(c) The maximax strategy is found by taking the best outcome in the table and using the strategy that generates this outcome. In this problem, the best outcome is a profit of $27. Therefore, the maximax strategy is to produce 30 dozen. Note that the maximax strategy disregards the probabilities. The dangers of employing this strategy are apparent: There is only a 5-percent chance that demand will be 30 dozen.

(d) To find the strategy that maximizes the expected profit, we must multiply the value of the outcome for each strategy and the probability, then add together the products in order to find the expected value.

$$EV(24) = (.05 \times 21.60) + (.10 \times 21.60) + (.20 \times 21.60) +$$
$$(.25 \times 21.60) + (.25 \times 21.60) + (.10 \times 21.60) +$$
$$(.05 \times 21.60) = 21.60$$

$$EV(25) = (.05 \times 20.50) + (.10 \times 22.50) + (.20 \times 22.50) +$$
$$(.25 \times 22.50) + (.25 \times 22.50) + (.10 \times 22.50) +$$
$$(.05 \times 22.50) = 22.40$$

Continuing in the same fashion, we find the expected values as given in the last column of the accompanying table. Therefore, according to expected value, the best strategy is to compromise, to produce 27 dozen (the strategy that yields the highest expected value—23.20), rather than the 24 dozen suggested by the conservative strategy (maximin) or the 30 dozen suggested by the risky strategy (maximax).

| | Scenario: Demand (Probability) | | | | | | | |
Strategy: Dozens Produced	24 (.05)	25 (.10)	26 (.20)	27 (.25)	28 (.25)	29 (.10)	30 (.05)	Expected Value
24	21.60	21.60	21.60	21.60	21.60	21.60	21.60	21.60
25	20.50	22.50	22.50	22.50	22.50	22.50	22.50	22.40
26	19.40	21.40	23.40	23.40	23.40	23.40	23.40	23.00
27	18.30	20.30	22.30	24.30	24.30	24.30	24.30	23.20
28	17.20	19.20	21.20	23.20	25.20	25.20	25.20	22.90
29	16.10	18.10	20.10	22.10	24.10	26.10	26.10	22.10
30	15.00	17.00	19.00	21.00	23.00	25.00	27.00	21.10

Using AB:POM to Solve This Problem

Following selected Solved Problems you will find step-by-step directions for generating the solution using AB:POM, the software package that is available with this text. For an overview of AB:POM, see Appendix D.

The decision tables module of AB:POM will examine profit or cost decision tables containing as many as ten alternatives and eight states of nature. After beginning, you must choose either to maximize profits or to minimize costs. Then the program will request at the top of the screen the number of alternatives and the number of states of nature. After these numbers have been given, AB:POM will generate a blank table of the appropriate dimensions. At the time, it will be necessary to fill in the appropriate costs or profits. In Screen 3.1, we present the data screen for Solved Problem 2. The program will not generate the decision table costs, but after the costs have been entered, the program will find the expected values, maximin, and minimin. The alternatives and states have default names, but these can be changed. In the example, we have given appropriate names to both.

To find the solution values, either press the **F10** key or the **Escape (ESC)** key, followed by the letter **R**. The solution screen for this problem is shown in Screen 3.2. If the problem is small—in other words, if it has five or fewer states of nature—the

```
 = Data file:c:wgsp2-2 ============ Decision Tables ========= Data Screen =
   Number of alternatives (1—10) 7            Number of nature states (1—8)   7
   Profits      - maximize profits

 ======================== Chapter 3, Solved Problem 2 =======================
   Probability->     0.050   0.100   0.200   0.250   0.250   0.100   0.050
                    demnd24 demnd25 demnd26 demnd27 demnd28 demnd29 demnd30
   make24            21.60   21.60   21.60   21.60   21.60   21.60   21.60
   make25            20.50   22.50   22.50   22.50   22.50   22.50   22.50
   make26            19.40   21.40   23.40   23.40   23.40   23.40   23.40
   make27            18.30   20.30   22.30   24.30   24.30   24.30   24.30
   make28            17.20   19.20   21.20   23.20   25.20   25.20   25.20
   make29            16.10   18.10   20.10   22.10   24.10   26.10   26.10
   make30            15.00   17.00   19.00   21.00   23.00   25.00   27.00




                                                                        Esc
   Enter the cost/profit for this alternative under this state of nature
```

SCREEN 3.1

```
 = Data file:c:wgsp2-2 ============ Decision Tables ========== Solution =
   Number of alternatives (1—10) 7            Number of nature states (1—8)   7
   Profits      - maximize profits

 ======================== Chapter 3, Solved Problem 2 =======================
                     EMV    Row Min   Row Max
   make24           21.60   21.60    21.60
   make25           22.40   20.50    22.50
   make26           23.00   19.40    23.40
   make27           23.20   18.30    24.30
   make28           22.90   17.20    25.20
   make29           22.10   16.10    26.10
   make30           21.10   15.00    27.00
   column maximum—>  23.20   21.60    27.00
   The maximum expected monetary value is      23.20 given by make27
   The maximin is     21.60 given by make24
   The maximax is     27.00 given by make30




   F1=Display Perfect Information               F9= Print      Esc
   Press <Esc> key to edit data or highlighted key or function key for options
```

SCREEN 3.2

data will remain on the screen with the solution. Because our problem has seven states of nature, the original data disappears and only the answers are given. The first column of answers gives the expected monetary values or expected values for each of the potential decisions. Since this is a profit problem, the maximum expected value of 23.20 is displayed at the bottom of the column. The second column gives the worst-case (row minimum) analysis, with the best of the worst cases (maximin)—21.60—appearing at the bottom of the column. The last column (row maximum) gives the best case for the alternatives; the highest value—27—once again appears at the bottom of the column. The last three lines summarize the solution by giving the best values and the strategies that lead to the best values for the expected value, maximin, and maximax.

QUESTIONS

1. A basic tenet of this text is that the capacity to provide a product or service should be matched with the anticipated demand for that product or service. Why is this basic to operations?

2. What is the relationship between the capacity of a system and the bottleneck of that system?

3. Give examples of each of the following.
(a) a long-range capacity decision
(b) an intermediate-range capacity decision
(c) a short-range capacity decision

4. How could having too little capacity bankrupt a company?

5. How could having too much capacity bankrupt a company?

6. What should be considered when deciding between a large facility and a small facility that can be expanded later, if necessary?

7. What are economies of scale?

8. How can a manager change capacities on a short-term basis?

9. List three situations in which there are alternative measures of capacity.

10. What is design capacity?

11. What is effective capacity?

12. What is system efficiency or utilization?

13. For three different systems, describe the design capacity, the effective capacity, and the efficiency.

14. What is productivity?

15. How does productivity relate to capacity?

16. How does quality affect capacity?

17. In cost–volume analysis, does capacity affect fixed costs, variable costs, or both? Describe how these costs are affected.

18. Describe how volume is important in the economic analysis of each of the following.

(a) equipment choice problems
(b) choice of processes
(c) make/buy decisions
(d) quantity discounts

19. Why are the maximax and maximin strategies considered to be optimistic and pessimistic, respectively?

20. The expected value criterion is considered to be the rational criterion on which to base a decision. Is this really true? Is it rational to consider risk?

21. When are decision trees most useful?

P R O B L E M S

1. Quiet Muffler installs exhaust systems on automobiles. Quiet has 6 work bays. If it takes .5 hour to install a muffler, what is the daily (8-hour) capacity of Quiet Muffler?

96 cars/day

2. Allendale Radiological Associates (ARA) performs radiology tests (X-rays). The facility has 10 rooms with X-ray machines, 6 technicians who operate the machines (which move from room to room), and 3 doctors who read the X-rays. Technicians take approximately 10 minutes to shoot and develop each X-ray, and doctors take approximately 8 minutes to read each X-ray.

(a) What is the weekly (40-hour) capacity of ARA?
(b) What will be the capacity if 1 additional technician is hired?
(c) What will be the capacity if 1 additional doctor is hired?
(d) What will be the capacity if 2 additional doctors are hired?

900 X-rays/week
900 X-rays/week
1,200 X-rays/week
1,440 X-rays/week

3. The External Receipt Corporation (ERCO) performs tax accounting. ERCO has 20,000 employees, each capable of processing 12 forms per day. However, the average employee errs on 1 in 10 forms, and each incorrect form must be reprocessed. ERCO notes that they (correctly) processed 30 million forms last year (250 working days).

(a) What is the system capacity?
(b) What is the system utilization?

54,000,000 forms/year
56 percent

4. Funtime Inc. produces a board game entitled "Chasem-Catchem." The company has 5 machines for producing the game boards, 8 machines for producing the plastic game pieces, 2 machines for producing the cardboard outer boxes, and 3 packaging machines (which put the boards and pieces into the boxes and wrap the boxes in plastic). The design capacities of the individual machines are as follows.

Machine	Design Capacity (games/hour)
Board cutter	40
Plastic producer	30
Box producer	80
Packager	70

(a) What is the system capacity?
(b) If the system is operated at capacity, what is the utilization of each of the machines?

160
80%, 67%, 100%, 76%

5.48 employees

5. Graphics Design, Inc. (GDI) makes computer graphics for seminar presentations. Each employee and computer combination produces 2 graphs per week. The company estimates a demand of 500 graphs for the coming year. If employees get 4 weeks annual vacation, and 5 percent of the drawings need to be redone due to customer dissatisfaction, how many new employees should be hired (with 1 machine purchased for each new employee)?

6. Glenside Word processing (GWP) is a one-woman typing center, owned and operated by Alice Glenside. Alice has a word processor with a printer attached to it. Alice can type at a rate of 120 words per minute, and the printer can operate at 120 characters per second. There are, on average, 5 characters per word.

7,200 words/hour

6,646 words/hour

(a) If the word-processing software allows for simultaneous typing and printing, what is the hourly capacity of GWP?
(b) If the word-processing software does not allow for simultaneous typing and printing, what is GWP's hourly capacity? Assume that the total work for printing is equal to the total work for typing.

7. Kleen Karpet cleaned rugs in 57 houses in September. During that month, Kleen Karpet utilized the following resources.

Labor:	480 hours at $12/hour
Secretary:	80 hours at $5/hour
Rental machine:	20 days at $50/day

.00796 houses/dollar

What is the productivity measure of Kleen Karpet?

8. Suppose that Kleen Karpet cleans 65 rugs in October utilizing the following resources.

Labor:	520 hours at $13/hour
Secretary:	100 hours at $5/hour
Rental machine:	20 days at $50/day

.00787 houses/dollar
−1.13 percent
Lost productivity is due to rise in labor costs.

(a) What is the productivity measure?
(b) What is the change in productivity from September (Problem 7)?
(c) What is the difficulty with using this measure?

1,100 units

9. Chips Away produces microcomputers. The company has annual fixed costs of $275,000. Each computer costs $900 to manufacture and is sold to retailers at an average price of $1,150. What is the company's break-even point?

more than 20 percent

10. Chips Away is considering raising its wholesale selling price by 20 percent. Will the break-even point fall by less than 20 percent, 20 percent exactly, or more than 20 percent?

1.17 percent

11. Associated Instruments produces guitars. The company's current fixed costs are $450,000 per year. Each guitar costs $700 to manufacture and sells for $1,200. Members of the Guitar Makers Union are going to receive a raise on July 1. This will increase the company's variable costs by 2 percent. By what percentage must the selling price rise in order for the same break-even point to be maintained?

12. Lebanon Valley University (LVU) is considering the computerization of its manual registration procedure. The following are the estimated costs of both the computerized process and the manual process.

	Manual	Computerized
Fixed cost	$2,000/registration week	$8,000/registration week
Variable cost	$40/student	$10/student

(a) Find the break-even point.
(b) Draw the break-even graph.
(c) If 250 students are enrolled at the university, should LVU use the manual or the computerized system?

13. The city of Ambler, New Jersey, is concerned about the low quality of its snow removal operations. The mayor has presented two options: purchasing more snow removal equipment or hiring outside contractors for snow removal. The city auditor has estimated that snow removal costs $500 per inch of depth of snow using city equipment and $700 per inch of depth using outside contractors. The new equipment would cost $20,000 and would be useful for 5 years, at which time the equipment would be scrapped (that is, it would have no salvage value). The city manager has been asked to cooperate with the city meteorologists and present a break-even analysis. Find the break-even point.

14. Busko Corporation is deciding on the type of plant layout for their new soccer ball factory. The fixed cost of a process layout is $20,000, and the variable cost using a process layout is $7 per soccer ball. The fixed cost of a product layout is $30,000, and the variable cost using a product layout is $6 per soccer ball. A soccer ball sells for $9.50. What decision rule should be used regarding the layout decision?

15. Black Publishers is a new company just beginning operation. They are unsure of which type of process to use to produce their publications. The costs are as follows.

	Typewriter	Computer	Typesetter
Fixed costs	$5,000	$15,000	$30,000
Variable costs/page	.03	.02	.01

(a) Draw the break-even graph.
(b) Find the break-even points.

16. Ash Products Incorporated produces baseball bats for one particular National League baseball team. The company can produce 400 bats using a one-shift operation. Each bat costs $2 to manufacture. If the company produces more than 400 bats, the cost for the additional bats (over 400) is $3 apiece, because overtime wages must be paid. Each bat sells for $4. What is the break-even point (in volume) if fixed costs are $1,000?

17. TLH has recently developed a cure for the common cold. The cure can be produced as a capsule or a caplet. (TLH will not produce both.) The anticipated costs are as follows.

	Capsule	Caplet
Annual fixed costs	$300,000	$500,000
Product cost	$25/case	$25/case
Capsule cost	$10/case	
Packaging (tamper-proof)	$15/case	$5/case

(a) What is the break-even point in volume?
(b) If the demand will be 1 million cases per year, what would be the profit for the capsule if the wholesale price is $60/case?
(c) If a profit of $1.5 million is desired for the caplets, and the price is $50/case, what volume must be achieved?

See graph in Instructor's
Section.

tons ≤ 40: Paper Lion; 40
≤ tons ≤ 50: still Paper
Lion; 50 ≤ tons ≤ 133:
Air Drop; tons ≥ 133:
Plimpton

18. The government of a Middle Eastern country has requested bids for shipments of arms to a second country. Three air freight companies have submitted bids. Paper Lion has proposed a flat shipping rate of $1,000 per ton. Plimpton Shipping has proposed a rate structure of $1,300 per ton for the first 40 tons, but $800 per ton for each ton above the first 40. Air Drop Express has proposed a rate structure of $1,100 per ton if the tonnage is less than 50 tons, but $950 per ton if the tonnage is 50 tons or more.

(a) Draw the break-even graph.
(b) Identify the appropriate means of shipping as a function of total tonnage.

19. Rica Express is setting up a delivery service near or in Philadelphia. Rica must decide whether to locate in the city, in the near suburbs, or in the far suburbs. The city requires higher rent (fixed cost) but lower transportation expenses (variable costs). The costs are as follows.

See graph in Instructor's
Section.
BEP (city vs. near) =
13,333 jobs;
BEP (city vs. far) =
12,500 jobs (irrelevant);
BEP (near vs. far) =
12,000 jobs

	City	Near Suburbs	Far Suburbs
Fixed cost	$1,000,000	$800,000	$500,000
Variable cost/job	$10	$25	$50

(a) Draw the break-even graph.
(b) Find the break-even point.

20. Rica (see previous problem) is unsure of its number of jobs for the coming years but estimates the distribution as follows.

Number of Jobs	Probability
5,000	.2
10,000	.3
15,000	.4
20,000	.1

near or far suburbs

Which of the locations presented in Problem 19 should be chosen?

21. California High-Tech Integrated Processing Systems is anticipating a possible growth in demand. To meet this growth, the firm has four options available: using overtime, hiring additional employees, adding part-time employees, or subcontracting. The following table indicates the profit under three different demand scenarios.

Option	Demand		
	Low ($p = .4$)	Medium ($p = .4$)	High ($p = .2$)
Using overtime	5*	7	10
Increasing work force	−5	10	15
Using part-time help	0	8	12
Subcontracting	0	9	13

*Profit in millions

EV (overtime) = 6.8

Compute the best decision using expected value.

22. Use the data in Problem 21.

maximin = 5 (given by
overtime)

(a) Find the maximin strategy.

(b) Find the maximax strategy.

maximax = 15 (given by increasing work force)

23. Public Legal Services provides free legal services and is undecided on whether to increase its capacity by using part-time legal help or by hiring more full-time lawyers. The following lists the anticipated *costs* of the two options for different demand patterns.

| | Demand | | |
Options	Low ($p = .2$)	Medium ($p = .5$)	High ($p = .3$)
Use part-time help	0	35	100
Hire new lawyers	30	50	70

Based on expected value, what should the agency do?

24. Use the data in Problem 23.

(a) Find the minimax strategy.
(b) Find the minimin strategy.

EV (part time) = 47.5
minimax = 70 (given by hiring)
minimin = 0 (given by part-time help)

25. In Problem 23, suppose that we know that the probability of low demand is .2 but are unsure of the probability of medium and high demand. Find the break-even probability where we will be indifferent between the choices of using part-time help and hiring new lawyers.

$p = .4$

26. Joe Hill is a six-year-old who runs a lemonade stand. Joe must tell his mom how many lemons to purchase each week in the summer. Mrs. Hill buys the lemons on Saturday night and they cannot be stored for longer than a week. Each lemon costs a dime and can be used in 2 glasses of lemonade. Each glass of lemonade sells for a quarter. Mrs. Hill thinks that the distribution of the number of glasses that Joe will sell in a week is given as follows.

Number of Glasses	Probability
10	.2
20	.3
30	.3
40	.2

(a) Create the decision table for Joe.
(b) How many lemons should Joe order each week based on expected profit?

See Instructor's Section.
20 or 15

27. Use the data in Problem 26.

(a) Find the maximin strategy.
(b) Find the maximax strategy.

maximin = $2 at 10 glasses
maximax = $8 at 40 glasses

28. A hospital purchases blood every 21 days from a blood bank at $30 per pint. Any blood not used must be discarded after 21 days. In the event that the hospital runs out of blood during the period of 21 days, it makes an emergency purchase of blood at a cost of $50 per pint. Demands for blood have been estimated as follows.

Number of Pints (per 21 days)	Probability
100	.1
125	.2
150	.3
175	.3
200	.1

See Instructor's Section.
150 pints

(a) Create the decision table for the hospital.
(b) Find the decision that minimizes the expected cost.

29. Use the data in Problem 28.

minimax = 6,000 at 200
pints
minimin = 3,000 at 100
pints

(a) Find the minimax strategy.
(b) Find the minimin strategy.

30. The Huachuca Doughnut Shop makes its doughnuts fresh daily. Any doughnuts not sold on the day they are made are sold at half-price to an outlet store for day-old baked goods. The popular powdered doughnut costs $1 per dozen to make, and the selling price is $1.20 per dozen. The probability distribution for sales is given in the following table.

Sales (in dozens)	Probability
26	.1
27	.2
28	.4
29	.2
30	.1

How many dozen powdered doughnuts should be made each day, using the indicated strategy?

28 dozen
26 dozen
30 dozen

(a) expected value
(b) maximin
(c) maximax

31. The Carbon Steel Corporation is purchasing a new furnace for its aging Ferrite Hill plant. The manufacturer of the furnace sells spare compressor units for $800 each with the purchase of a furnace. The retailer sells these compressors for $1,500. The probability distribution for failed compressor units is given in the following table.

Failures	Probability
0	.1
1	.3
2	.3
3	.2
4	.1

Using the method indicated, tell how many spare compressors should be purchased.

2 spares
4 spares
0 spares

(a) expected value
(b) minimax
(c) minimin

C; $395

32. Evaluate the following decision tree, where the numbers at the end of each branch are the profits associated with that outcome. What decision is made? What is the value of the tree?

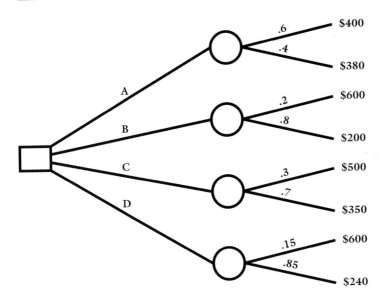

33. Evaluate the following decision tree, where the numbers at the end of each branch are the costs associated with that outcome. What decision is made at each decision point?

B; $631; see Instructor's Section

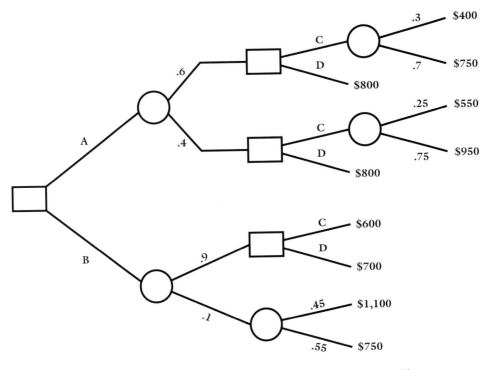

34. For the data given in Problem 23, draw the decision tree and solve the problem.

35. Marktech Systems needs to open a branch office in Denver. Two suites are available, one satisfactory for their current needs, and a larger one capable of satisfying any increase in the demand for their services. The cost of the larger office is $1,200 per month with a three-year lease. The smaller office is available at $800 per month for three years, but its lease offers an

See Instructor's Section for decision tree; hire part-time help.

option to move to a larger suite after eighteen months. The cost of the larger suite would then be $1,250 per month. Expected revenues are as follows.

Smaller office, current demand:	$1,000 per month
Smaller office, higher demand:	$1,100 per month
Larger office, current demand:	$1,000 per month
Larger office, higher demand:	$1,600 per month

smaller office (expand if demand is higher)

The chance of having the current demand for the three years is estimated to be 30 percent, and there is an estimated 70-percent chance of having the higher demand. Determine which office should be chosen for the three-year period. Use a decision tree.

COMPUTER CASE STUDY 3.1: ARCTIC INC.

Arctic Incorporated produces large, glass-door refrigeration units for supermarkets and convenience stores. Arctic Inc. has been experiencing a steady rise in demand for its products over the last ten years. Much of this rise is attributed to the increase in the number of convenience stores over the period. Arctic Inc. sees no decrease in the convenience store business and is concerned about its capacity.

The company currently manufactures only some of the parts that are used for assembly, purchasing the balance. Arctic is particularly concerned about its capacity to manufacture the compressors that are assembled into the refrigeration units.

Arctic has been producing compressors itself since it began operating. Now, with compressor capacity being stretched to its limit, Arctic is considering expansion plans. There is a great deal of concern about what projects should be selected and what resources should be acquired for these projects. While there is much optimism among company officials and employees, Arctic faces a great deal of uncertainty—both with the type of compressor to be used in the future and with the amount of demand for the refrigeration units.

Arctic has several major options with regard to compressor capacity, some of which could be combined into a single plan. The options under consideration are the following.

1. Expand the current plant capacity.
2. Build a new plant.
3. Subcontract among several vendors.
4. Contract with one vendor to provide the needed compressors ("sole sourcing").
5. Purchase a company that provides the needed compressors.
6. Employ some combination of expansion and manufacturing.

Each plan has advantages and disadvantages related to costs and other factors.

The first two plans maintain production control within Arctic, while Plans 3 and 4 relinquish control to other companies. Plan 5 is a compromise with respect to control, since compressor manufacturing would occur in a different strategic business unit (SBU) within the larger corporation.

Both building a new plant and buying a compressor manufacturer would be rather risky, as they would require a large amount of capital input (fixed costs) up front. Plans 2 and 5 would keep the variable costs low, however.

Subcontracting, Plans 3 and 4, would have no fixed costs. The major advantage of sole sourcing is this: By guaranteeing one subcontractor all of the volume, the cost per compressor would be minimized. The major disadvantage should be obvious: If the production is disrupted at the sole-source factory, Arctic will have to shut down its assembly operation. Another concern with the sole-source option is that, in essence, Arctic will be creating a monopoly and will be at the mercy of this company.

In order to evaluate its options, Arctic is considering different scenarios with respect to demand for the product and the future technology. These demand scenarios are as follows.

- Demand grows at a steady rate.
- Demand stabilizes at the current rate.
- Demand drops.

The technology scenarios are the following.

- The technology remains the same.
- The technology changes.

Combining demand and technology scenarios, there are six (3 × 2) different scenarios that Arctic has evaluated. The company has performed a preliminary cost/revenue analysis and the table below presents the net present value of profits over the next ten years for each option evaluated under each scenario.

Option	Demand with Same Technology			Demand with Different Technology		
	Grow	Stable	Drop	Grow	Stable	Drop
Expand	3.14	2.65	1.12	2.43	2.23	.23
Build new	2.98	2.12	.11	5.23	3.14	− 1.63
Subcontract	1.45	1.67	1.34	1.76	1.32	1.88
Sole source	1.89	1.72	1.13	1.34	1.11	.25
Purchase	3.78	1.98	− 2.45	3.21	1.25	− 5.67
Expand/subcontract	2.25	2.27	1.22	2.34	1.89	1.12

As uncertain as the profits in the table are, the probabilities of each of the possible scenarios are even more uncertain. Evaluate the options available to Arctic Refrigeration. Should any of the options be eliminated? Is one option truly outstanding, an obvious choice? Should some options be considered for further analysis? The discussion implies some things concerning the probabilities of the demand scenarios. How does this affect the decision?

REFERENCES

Chen, G. K. C., and R. E. McGarrah. *Productivity Management Text and Cases*. Chicago: The Dryden Press, 1982.

Hayes, R. H., and S. C. Wheelwright. *Restoring Our Competitive Edge: Competing Through Manufacturing*. New York: John Wiley and Sons, 1984.

Monks, J. G. *Operations Management: Theory and Problems*. 3rd ed. New York: McGraw-Hill, 1987.

Moski, B. A. *Manufacturing Management and Engineering Handbook*. Englewood Cliffs, N.J.: Prentice-Hall, 1977.

Sink, D. S. *Productivity Management: Planning, Evaluation, Control and Improvement*. New York: John Wiley and Sons, 1985.

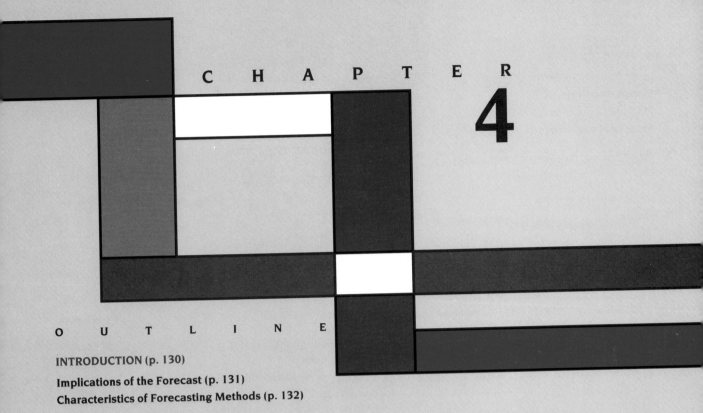

C H A P T E R

4

O U T L I N E

FORECASTING

OBJECTIVES

- ■ To explain the difference between qualitative and quantitative forecasting methods
- ■ To point out that all forecasts have errors and that the measurement of the errors is critical
- ■ To demonstrate techniques that rely on past data and the differences among the smoothing and regression techniques
- ■ To exemplify different approaches for identifying the seasonal nature of demand

---

INTRODUCTION

Many of the operations decisions that are made in any facility are decisions relating to future operating plans. Examples that appear later in this book include decisions regarding plant expansion or relocation, production planning (for example, the number of units to produce), service design, and staffing (for instance, the number of cash registers and/or cashiers in a supermarket) and management of projects. Because all of these decisions involve future activities, it is necessary for decision makers to somehow predict the future and to predict it with some degree of accuracy. Forecasting is simply the scientific name for guessing (in an educated fashion) what the future will bring.

Teaching Suggestion 4.1: Is It Really Guessing? See the Instructor's Section for details.

There are many standard forecasting techniques, each with its own assumptions, benefits, and pitfalls. Some of the techniques rely on examining past data to predict the future. Typically, such techniques are **quantitative.** For example, in production planning, past sales are usually a good indicator of future sales. (Of course, use of this indicator assumes that pricing or marketing strategy will continue as in the past.) However, there are cases where using the quantitative techniques is not appropriate. **Qualitative** techniques are used when the past is not indicative of the future, either because data are not available or are irrelevant. In Chapter 1, we indicated that monitoring performance is an integral part of the decision-making methodology (see Figure 1.8). Control is especially important in forecasting because forecasting is so inexact. This chapter will present several forecasting methods and discuss the differences

130

among them. We note that it is not enough simply to choose a forecasting technique; the chosen technique must be carefully monitored to ascertain how well it is performing. If the performance trails off, the technique should be modified or a new technique should be chosen. Before discussing specific techniques, let us consider the use of the forecast.

IMPLICATIONS OF THE FORECAST

As previously indicated, although many items are forecasted, the area where forecasting is most widely used is demand. The demand (sales) forecast has direct repercussions in many different areas of the company. Figure 4.1 indicates the manner in which sales forecasts affect both the operations and the marketing functions and the budgets for each.

Transparency Master 4.1: The Impact of the Sales Forecast on the Master Budget.

FIGURE 4.1 The impact of the sales forecast on the master budget

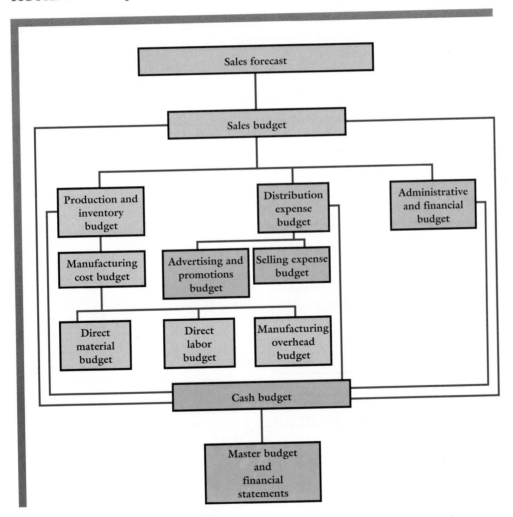

Source: Aly Maascreni, "Use of the Sales Forecast by Management," in *The Management of Forecasting,* ed. John J. Clark (St. John's University Press, 1969).

Because our concern here is with operations, Figure 4.2 contains a more detailed picture of the relationship between forecasting and operations. From our discussion of capacity planning, the importance of the decision to open (or close) additional facilities is well known. The long-range forecast of sales is one of the most critical inputs to this decision. Similarly, when considering the purchase of capital equipment, several factors must be forecast, including maintenance costs, expected lifetime of the equipment, and salvage value. Demand is also a critical component, because, as a general rule, a company is able to purchase more expensive equipment only if its product is in great demand. The layout of the facility, which we know is a function of the type of transformation process, is influenced by demand. In other words, a high (forecasted) demand is generally required before a company implements an assembly line.

Later in the text, we will discuss production scheduling to meet the (forecasted) demand. Production schedules indicate our resource needs and the levels of inventory that we will carry. Of course, all of these factors are input to the financial decisions that determine the capital requirements of the production/operations function.

Current moves toward using just-in-time systems make the forecasting function even more critical. Orders are based on forecasted needs; if additional needs arise, it will not be possible to meet them. JIT also requires that accurate forecasts be provided farther into the future, so that all suppliers can plan their operations efficiently.

CHARACTERISTICS OF FORECASTING METHODS

We may classify forecasting techniques according to several characteristics. Knowledge of these characteristics helps the decision maker choose the most useful forecasting technique given the particular circumstances.

FIGURE 4.2 The relationship between forecasting and operations

Transparency Master 4.2:
The Relationship Between
Forecasting and
Operations.

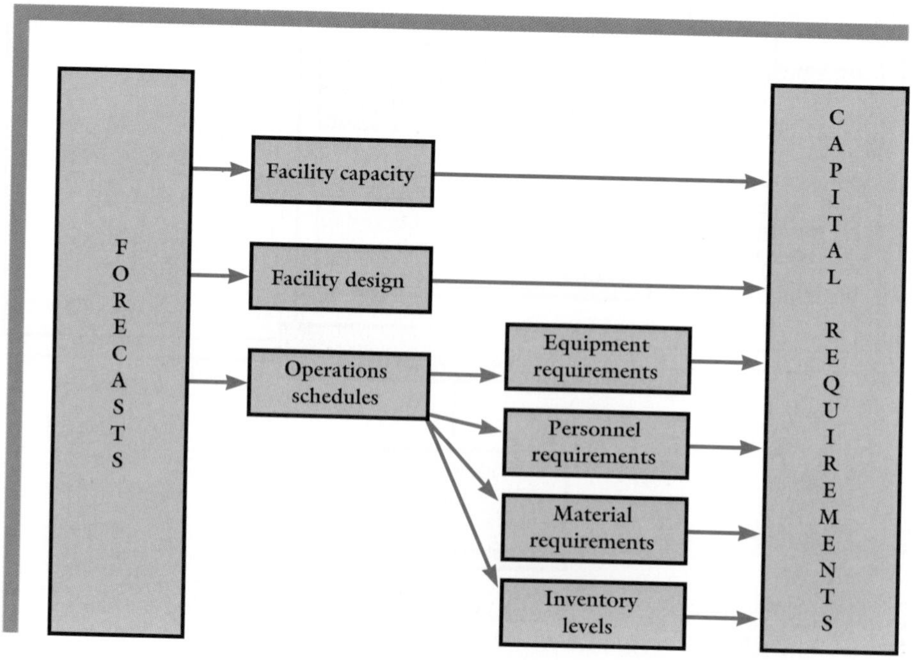

APPLICATIONS OF P/OM

Monthly Sales Forecasts—Coors Beer Distributorship

The Coors beer distributorship in Tucson, Arizona, developed a computer program to forecast the monthly demands for its various beer products. After careful analysis of historical data and interviews with management to get expert opinion regarding future sales, the following conclusions were reached.

- Sales were showing an upward trend.
- The upward trend was expected to continue.
- A cyclical (seasonal) component exists for the demands for beer.

Based on these conclusions, it was decided to use an exponential smoothing approach that would incorporate both the trend and the seasonal components. This approach was programmed for use with the Coors system.

After installation, the program was tested, again using historical data. The results were excellent for nine months of every year. For May, July, and September, however, the results were generally low. The reason for the error, quickly apparent to all, was that each of these three months has a holiday—a big beer-drinking holiday. So the basic model was maintained as developed, but an extra factor was added for these three months to account for the increased demand. This factor, developed using the increased demand in these months as a separate time series, worked well in subsequent tests.

THE UNDERLYING MODEL

As mentioned previously, there are both quantitative and qualitative forecasting methods. The quantitative methods may be grouped according to two types. The first type **quantitative models** assumes that the past data are indicative of the future. For example, sales can be projected into the future based solely on past sales. These models are often called **extrapolative, time series,** or **projective models.** The models that we will examine within this category are smoothing techniques, decomposition techniques, and a special case of linear regression. The second type of quantitative model is called a **causal model,** which assumes that the item being forecasted, such as sales, is a function of some other variable or variables. Classical models of this type are regression and econometric models. Typically, econometric models are very complex and are used to predict factors such as the GNP, and so we will not include them in this chapter.

Qualitative, or **subjective, models** generally are used when we have no quanti- **qualitative models** tative models that seem to be appropriate. This is often the case in long-term forecasting, since predicting far into the future is rather difficult, especially quantitatively. These qualitative models also are used to supplement or replace quantitative forecasts, especially when changes in the demand pattern are anticipated, or when any other nonquantitative information is relevant and available.

THE TIME HORIZON

In Chapters 1, 2, and 3, we referred to short-, medium-, and long-range planning and noted that we encounter different types of problems depending on where we are in the planning horizon. It should not be surprising that we refer to forecasting techniques in the same way. In general, when we speak of long-term forecasting, we are concerned with identifying the long-term trend. Intermediate-term forecasting is useful for incorporating seasonal factors, and short-term forecasting is necessary for scheduling the work and inventory levels.

**accuracy–time
relationship**

The longer the horizon, the more difficult it is to forecast accurately. Thus, many of the long-term techniques are qualitative, using expert opinion rather than some "scientific" method. On the other hand, short-term forecasting is well suited for quantitative analysis. Some of the quantitative techniques are useful for medium-term forecasting, and others are not. As a general rule, long-term models are qualitative, medium-term models are causal or projective, and short-term models are projective.

THE PATTERN OF DATA

Teaching Suggestion 4.2:
Plot the Data! See the
Instructor's Section for
details.

The first step in analyzing past data is to plot the data and try to discern any patterns. In Figure 4.3, we demonstrate four different patterns that might arise. Two of these plots seem to have no long-range direction (trend), while the other two do; two seem to cycle up and down, while two do not. (We leave it to you to note which is which.)

The different forecasting methods vary in their abilities to spot trends or cycles. Therefore, it is critical that the forecaster know the underlying pattern when choosing a technique.

COSTS

Several types of costs are involved in forecasting. The major costs are the fixed costs of developing and/or procuring and operationalizing the technique, the variable (computer and manpower) costs of running the technique, and the costs due to the inaccuracy of the technique. As a general rule, there is an inverse relationship between the forecasting system set up plus execution costs and the inaccuracy costs. Hence, the total cost might appear as in Figure 4.4. Notice that the most appropriate technique for a given situation is not necessarily the most accurate technique, since this is generally the most expensive technique to develop and use.

cost trade-off

UNDERSTANDABILITY

A general rule of management is that managers do not use techniques that they cannot understand. A very sophisticated technique is not necessarily preferred to a less sophisticated, less reliable technique. In fact, Smith (1978) argues that the major criterion for a forecasting technique is its understandability and has developed a method, called *focus forecasting,* based on this premise. In Figure 4.5, we have generalized the characteristics of the three types of techniques.

SUBJECTIVE FORECASTING

If past data are available, reliable, and appropriate, then the quantitative forecasting methods that begin in the section on smoothing techniques later in this chapter are extremely useful. However, often the past cannot be used to predict the future. For example, if the product is new, then there are no records of past sales (although there may be records of past sales of similar products). If a supplier of raw materials changes, then past prices may not be relevant to predict future prices of raw materials. If a competitor opens a store nearby, then past sales may exaggerate future sales. As these examples suggest, there are many situations that call for a qualitative approach to forecasting.

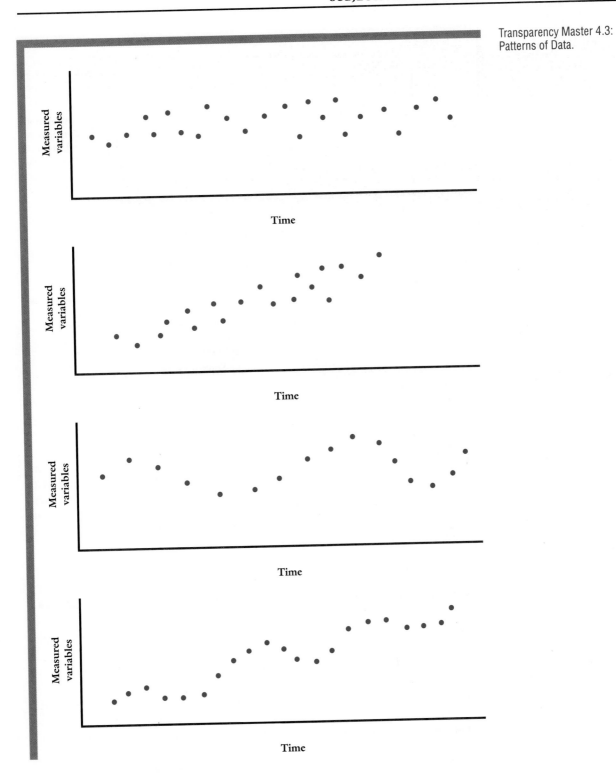

Transparency Master 4.3:
Patterns of Data.

FIGURE 4.3 Patterns of data

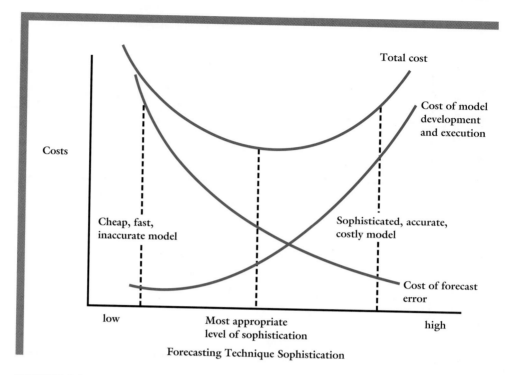

FIGURE 4.4 Forecasting costs

JURY OF EXECUTIVE OPINION

A method of forecasting that is simple and easy to use collects the forecasts (opinions, guesses) of a number of top-level executives. The process is represented in Figure 4.6. Typically, the executives are chosen from different business functions so as to represent a wide variety of views within the organization. Each of these executives is given data on past sales, profits, and so forth in order to form his or her individual forecast. These individual forecasts are then aggregated into one forecast.

FIGURE 4.5 Characteristics of forecasting techniques

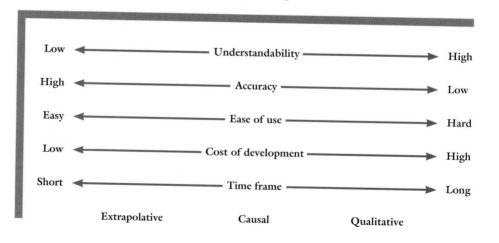

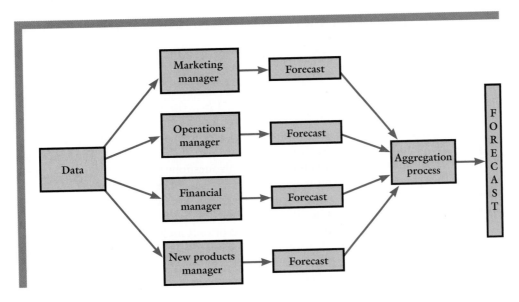

FIGURE 4.6 Jury of executive opinion process

The manner in which the individual forecasts are aggregated will vary from company to company. The individual forecasts may be presented either in written reports or orally in a group meeting. Two goals of the aggregation process are (1) to avoid having extreme forecasts greatly affect the overall forecast and (2) to avoid allowing the forecast of any one manager to dominate the overall forecast. (Note that if one manager is especially good at forecasting, there is no reason to be using the jury: Simply consult the great soothsayer-manager!) An easy means of aggregating the forecasts is to average the forecasts of the individual managers. The average may be unweighted (each manager's forecast counts the same) or weighted toward those more knowledgeable about sales (for example, the marketing manager).

goals of aggregation

Two concerns involving the implementation of this approach are the order of presenting the forecasts and the assignment of weight to each opinion. Often, individuals who are younger or in a lower position in an organization are influenced by the opinions of those with more experience or a higher rank. This influence may be due to intimidation (possibly self-inflicted), respect, or the desire to gain (approval, success, or whatever) by agreeing with one's superiors. To overcome this, the voicing of opinions should start with the youngest or least powerful team member and proceed to the most influential. To correlate with the weights assigned to each forecast, the voicing of opinion may start with the member whose opinion will have the lowest weight and proceed to the member whose forecast will have the highest weight.

implementation concerns

Teaching Suggestion 4.3: Group Behavior. See the Instructor's Section for details.

One approach to assigning the weights to the individual jurors is to let each member of the jury team assign weights to every member except him- or herself. This allows for an impartial consensus on the weights. Often, a second iteration is used to allow jurors to change their opinions after seeing the results. In no event, however, should the weights be assigned after the forecasts are made known. This would bias both the weights and the forecasts.

Finally, because each manager's forecast is simply a guess (however good) about the future, the overall forecast also is a guess. Therefore, it is imperative that the last step of the process be a review of the combined forecast generated by the jury of executive opinion technique.

THE DELPHI TECHNIQUE

anonymity and feedback

The **Delphi technique** is a second method for aggregating the opinions of experts. The Delphi technique differs from the jury of executive opinion with respect to two properties: anonymity and feedback. To ensure that each expert will give his or her best forecast, the forecasts are compiled through questionnaires, as opposed to a meeting, or jury, of executive opinion; individual responses are kept anonymous. Results of the questionnaires are tabulated, and the aggregation is presented to the experts. Then the experts are asked to revise their answers if they so desire. Furthermore, if an expert's forecast is in either the top 25 percent or bottom 25 percent of the forecasts, he or she is asked to justify that forecast. Thus, each participant either revises his or her forecast or justifies the "deviant" forecast. The revised forecasts are again aggregated, returned to the participants, and the process continues. In the majority of cases, the Delphi technique will converge to within a small range of forecasts in a reasonable number of iterations.

Teaching Suggestion 4.4: Origins of Delphi. See the Instructor's Section for details.

applications of the Delphi technique

Since its development, the Delphi method has been used extensively. One of its earliest applications was in the prediction of horse races. Gambling aside, most of the applications have been toward forecasting long-range technological changes or market changes. For example, McDonnell Douglas Corporation has used the Delphi technique to forecast the long-range future of commercial air transportation.

The Delphi technique also has been used to forecast the following specific events (Fusfeld and Foster, 1971):

- the year in which there will be a single building code;
- the year in which polymers will be created by molecular tailoring, with service temperature ranges in excess of 1,000°F;
- the year in which SST aircraft will be in regular service over land areas;
- the year in which a hydrocarbon/air fuel cell will be commercially available; and
- the year in which a source of transplant organs for humans will be developed through selective breeding of animals that are tissue compatible. (p. 65)

criticism

Even though it has been and continues to be widely used, there is a great deal of criticism of the Delphi technique. The critics maintain that the long-range questions for which the technique is used may be ambiguous; the selection of the experts who participate in the process is somewhat random and, often, experts drop out of Delphi panels; what's more, even if a consensus is reached, it may be a false one.

SALES FORCE COMPOSITE

Rather than surveying top executives, it may be more appropriate to ask the salespeople in the field for their opinions. This is called a **sales force composite** or the **grass roots method**. Presumably, salespeople have a good feel for which products will or will not sell and for the quantity of sales for various products because they interact directly with consumers. The flow and aggregation of the forecasts is indicated in Figure 4.7, a classic pyramidlike organization chart in which information flows upward.

Sales information drives the demand forecast at a J. C. Penney distribution center.
(© John Blaustein/Woodfin Camp & Associates)

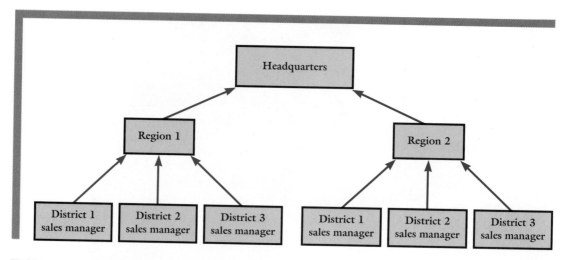

FIGURE 4.7   Flow of forecasts in sales force composite

**tendencies of
salespeople**

The salespeople supply their forecasts to the district manager, who aggregates these forecasts into one that he or she provides to the regional manager. The regional manager, in turn, aggregates the district forecasts into a regional forecast, which can be aggregated with other regional forecasts at the corporate headquarters.

The advantage of using the salespeople's forecasts is that (in theory) salespeople are most qualified to explain the demand for products, especially in their own territories. The disadvantage is that salespeople may tend to be optimistic in their estimates if they believe that a low estimate might lead to the unemployment line. The reverse may be a tendency as well. Many companies assign quotas to their salespeople and award bonuses when the quotas are met. In this case, it is to the salesperson's advantage to offer a pessimistic forecast in order to receive a low quota. Of course, one way to discourage self-serving forecasts is to offer a bonus for good forecasts or a penalty for poor forecasts.

USER EXPECTATIONS

Teaching Suggestion 4.5:
Benefits to Users. See the
Instructor's Section for
details.

An approach that is similar to the sales force composite is to get forecasts of future orders directly from the customers. This approach is called **user expectations.** One example of this method is a survey used by market research. The information received from the customer does not, of course, constitute a contract or commitment to buy the product. Therefore, the forecasts remain guesses. However, the errors may tend to negate one another because one consumer may ultimately purchase more than estimated, while another consumer may purchase less than expected.

Ordinarily, user expectations provide better forecasts than the (optimistic) sales force composite. Unfortunately, it is typically easier and less costly to obtain the sales force composite than it is to obtain the user expectations. However, if the market is not fragmented, the user expectations method may be feasible both in terms of time and of money.

Very fortunate is the company that can get orders—rather than forecasts—from its customers many weeks in advance. Such a company has customer commitments to buy in hand prior to production, making production scheduling less dependent on forecasts. This is commonly the case in high technology fields, such as the computer and aerospace industries.

MEASURING THE FORECASTING ERROR

Because we do not expect whatever forecasting technique we use to make perfectly accurate predictions, we need measurement techniques that determine the accuracy of a forecasting technique. Of course, whatever goodness measure we use will indicate only the usefulness of the technique on past data. This may or may not indicate the accuracy of the technique's predictions for the future. Different measurements of goodness are necessary because we must measure both the direction of the forecasting error (too low versus too high) and the extent of the forecasting error. The measurement both of demand and of forecast variation and errors is critical when setting inventory safety stock levels.

accuracy of forecasting

BIAS

One measure of the value of a forecasting technique is **bias,** the average error of the technique when used. Bias is a measure of the *direction* of the forecast error; it tells us whether we tend to make our forecasts too high or too low. The formula for bias is the following:

$$\text{Bias} = \frac{\sum_{i=1}^{n}(Y_i - F_i)}{n} = \frac{\sum_{i=1}^{n} \text{forecast error in period } i}{n},$$

where

n is the number of (past) time periods used;

Y_i is the actual demand in time period i; and

F_i is the forecast for period i.

The following example demonstrates the computation of bias.

Example 4.1   Given in column (2) of Table 4.1 are the sales of swimsuits for the last seven years for Caribbean Swimwear. The forecasts that the company has been using appear in column (3). Compute the bias.

Column (4) contains the errors that occurred in each year—that is, the actual sales minus the forecast. Figure 4.8 shows the sales and forecasts given in Table 4.1. Notice that some of the errors in column (4) are positive, indicating that the sales were higher than the forecasts, and some errors are negative, indicating just the opposite. The bias (average error) is 24,000/7—the sum of the errors divided by the seven periods for which there is both a forecast and an actual demand. This indicates that, on average, the forecast has underestimated actual sales by 3,429 units. The implication is that if the same technique is used to forecast sales for next year (year 8), then 3,429 should be added to the forecast because previous forecasts with this technique have tended to be, on average, 3,429 units below actual sales.   ■

TABLE 4.1 Caribbean Swimwear computation of error measurements (Example 4.1)

(1) Year	(2) Actual Sales	(3) Forecasted Sales	(4) Forecast Error $[(2) - (3)]$	(5) Squared Error	(6) Absolute Value of Error	(7) Percentage Error $[(4) \div (2)]$
1	27,000	23,000	4,000	16,000,000	4,000	+.148
2	35,000	25,000	10,000	100,000,000	10,000	+.286
3	29,000	31,000	− 2,000	4,000,000	2,000	−.069
4	33,000	30,000	3,000	9,000,000	3,000	+.091
5	37,000	32,000	5,000	25,000,000	5,000	+.135
6	41,000	34,000	7,000	49,000,000	7,000	+.171
7	35,000	38,000	− 3,000	9,000,000	3,000	−.086
			24,000	212,000,000	34,000	.676

$$\text{Bias} = \frac{\Sigma \text{ error}}{n} = \frac{24,000}{7} = 3,429$$

$$\text{Mean squared error} = \frac{\Sigma(\text{error})^2}{n} = \frac{212,000,000}{7} = 30,285,714$$

$$\text{Standard error} = \sqrt{\text{mean squared error}} = \sqrt{30,285,714} = 5,503$$

$$\text{Mean absolute deviation} = \frac{\Sigma|\text{error}|}{n} = \frac{34,000}{7} = 4,857$$

$$\text{Mean percentage error} = \frac{\sum \frac{\text{error}}{\text{actual}}}{n} = \frac{.676}{7} = .097 = 9.7\%$$

bias allows offsetting errors

The difficulty with using bias as a measure of forecast error is that mistakes of underforecasting are offset by mistakes of overforecasting. For example, if the forecasting errors for the last four periods are $+100$, -100, $+50$, and -50, then the bias is zero! The average error is nonexistent, even though the forecasts are always wrong. Because this might lead to a misunderstanding of the effectiveness and accuracy of the forecasting technique, it is necessary to ensure that overforecasting and underforecasting do not offset one another. We do this by allowing only positive terms in the error summation, which can be accomplished in two ways, yielding the standard error and the mean absolute deviation.

STANDARD ERROR

In order to keep all error terms nonnegative, we can square each term. Hence, we define the **mean squared error** (*MSE*) as follows:

mean squared error

$$MSE = \frac{\sum_{i=1}^{n} (Y_i - F_i)^2}{n} = \frac{\sum_{i=1}^{n} (\text{forecast error in period } i)^2}{n}.$$

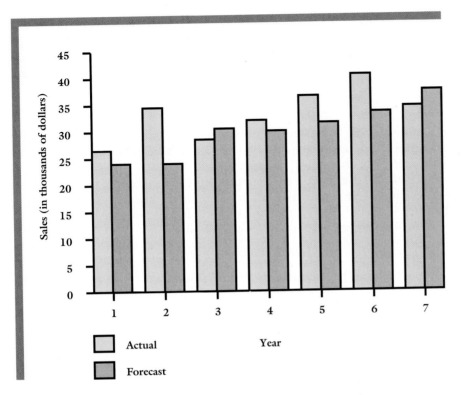

FIGURE 4.8 Caribbean Swimwear: forecast errors (Example 4.1)

Furthermore, we define the **standard error** (*SE*) or root mean square (*RMS*) as

$$SE = \sqrt{MSE}. \ast$$

standard error

We will use the data given in the previous example and compute the standard error.

Example 4.2 In Table 4.1, we have computed the mean squared error and the standard error for Caribbean. The individual errors are squared in column (5), which results in all positive terms. The sum of the errors is 212 million, which we divide by 7 to find a mean squared error of 30,285,714. The standard error is found to be 5,503 by taking the square root of the mean squared error. ∎

Standard error sometimes is called the **consistency,** and typically is used with the regression techniques. The formula for standard error is strikingly similar to the formula for (population) standard deviation:

standard error is a standard deviation

$$\sigma = \sqrt{\dfrac{\sum\limits_{i=1}^{N} (Y_i - \bar{Y})^2}{N}}.$$

*Some forecasters prefer *n* − 1 to *n* in the denominator of the standard error. Others prefer *n* − 2. If *n* is large, then the difference between using *n*, *n* − 1, and *n* − 2 is very small.

Standard deviation uses the square of the difference between the data and the mean, while standard error uses the square of the difference between the data and the forecast. Because of their similarity in nature, the standard error is used as a standard deviation. The following example will demonstrate a major application of the standard error.

Example 4.3   By using the same technique that generated the forecasts in Table 4.1, the forecast for sales in year 8 (F_8) is found to be 37,000. Give a 95-percent confidence interval for sales.

From the normal distribution table (Appendix B1) 95 percent of the normal distribution lies within 1.96 standard deviations of the mean. The confidence interval is given by $F_8 \pm 1.96\sigma$, where F_8 is the forecast for year 8 and σ is the standard error. Hence, we are 95-percent certain that sales will fall within

$$1.96(5,503) = 10,786$$

of the 37,000 forecast. The interval is (26,214, 47,786). ∎

MEAN ABSOLUTE DEVIATION

absolute values

An alternative method for generating all nonnegative terms is to take the absolute value of each forecast error rather than squaring these terms. Note that it is somewhat easier to take an absolute value rather than a square. We define the **mean absolute deviation** (*MAD*) as follows:

mean absolute deviation

$$MAD = \frac{\sum_{i=1}^{n}|Y_i - F_i|}{n} = \frac{\sum_{i=1}^{n}|\text{forecast error in period } i|}{n}.$$

In the next example, we will again use the same data presented in previous examples, but this time we will compute the mean absolute deviation.

Example 4.4   In Table 4.1, we have computed the mean absolute deviation for the Caribbean data. Column (6) contains the absolute values of the individual errors, and the *MAD* is 4,857. ∎

A general rule of thumb is that

MAD–SE relationship

$$1 \; MAD = .8 \text{ standard errors.}$$

Thus, in the example, since the standard error (consistency) is 5,503, the mean absolute deviation is approximated by .8(5,503) = 4,402, which is not far from the actual *MAD* of 4,857 (an error of 9 percent), given that the example has a small number of time periods (7).

PERCENTAGE ERRORS

The three errors presented to this point are all based on the difference between the actual value and the forecast. However, an error of 200 units when sales are 1,000 is different from an error of 200 units when sales are 100,000. To take this into consideration, we define one additional term that averages the percentage errors rather than the actual errors. We use a **mean percentage error** (*MPE*) to correspond to the bias. This percentage error is given by the following formula:

$$MPE = \frac{\sum_i \frac{(Y_i - F_i)}{Y_i}}{n} .$$

mean percentage error

In Table 4.1, we have computed the mean percentage error for the data presented in Example 4.1. Column (7) contains the error divided by the actual sales in each year. Notice that plus and minus signs are included. The average percentage error is 9.7 percent.

CHOICE OF MEASURE

Four measures (bias, standard error, mean absolute deviation, and mean percentage error) have been introduced to evaluate error associated with forecasting. A legitimate question is which of the four should be implemented in a given forecasting environment.

First, let us look at how the measures differ from one another. Bias, mean absolute deviation, and mean percentage error use the actual deviations, and standard error uses the square of the actual deviations. The next example considers bias, mean absolute deviation, and standard error to show the effect of this difference.

Example 4.5   The following data provide the actual occurrence of demand for the past three months, along with the forecasts provided by three different techniques for Williams Ltd.

| Month | Actual | Forecast | | |
		A	B	C
1	14	16	12	14
2	17	19	15	17
3	15	17	17	19

In Table 4.2, we have computed the errors for each of the three forecasting methods. The four error measures for each forecast technique are summarized from Table 4.2 as follows.

Forecast	Bias	Mean Absolute Deviation	Standard Error	Mean Percentage Error
A	−2	2	2	−.131
B	2/3	2	2	.042
C	−4/3	4/3	2.3	−.088

According to the bias measure, technique B is the best. However, remember that when we use the bias as our measure of accuracy, large errors in opposite directions cancel each other. The same is true for the mean percentage error.

Let us then focus on the other two measures, both of which use only nonnegative deviations. The mean absolute deviation indicates that technique C is the best, while the standard error indicates that both techniques A and B are better than technique C. Further analysis shows us that technique C is right on target $(14 = 14, 17 = 17)$

TABLE 4.2 Williams Ltd. comparison of errors (Example 4.5)

Month	Actual Sales	Forecast Sales	Error	Absolute Error	Error Squared	Percentage Error	
1	14	16	−2	2	4	−.14	
2	17	19	−2	2	4	−.12	Method
3	15	17	−2	2	4	−.13	A
		Total	−6	6	12	−.39	
		Average	−2	2	4	−.13	
				Square root	2		

Month	Actual Sales	Forecast Sales	Error	Absolute Error	Error Squared	Percentage Error	
1	14	12	2	2	4	.14	
2	17	15	2	2	4	.12	Method
3	15	17	−2	2	4	−.13	B
		Total	2	6	12	.13	
		Average	.67	2	4	.04	
				Square root	2		

Month	Actual Sales	Forecast Sales	Error	Absolute Error	Error Squared	Percentage Error	
1	14	14	0	0	0	.00	
2	17	17	0	0	0	.00	Method
3	15	19	−4	4	16	−.27	C
		Total	−4	4	16	−.27	
		Average	−1.33	1.33	5.33	−.09	
				Square root	2.31		

for the first two months. However, it is off by 4 (19 − 15) for the third month. Techniques A and B are always off by 2. ∎

Which technique is "best" depends in part upon the tolerance for error. The squared term in the standard error places a heavy emphasis on the largest deviations. The mean absolute deviation, bias, and mean percentage error measures give equal emphasis to all deviations, regardless of size. This is the key. We must ask ourselves if one large error is better or worse than many smaller errors. If it is better, mean absolute deviation is best. If no large error can be tolerated, even at the price of better accuracy in the rest of the forecast, standard error is best.

> **standard error emphasizes large deviations**

> Teaching Suggestion 4.6: Grades: Two Bs vs. A and C. See the Instructor's Section for details.

One note of caution at this point: In practice, most users apply whichever measure is provided with their computer output. Usually, the use of mean absolute deviation is associated with smoothing techniques (presented in the following section), while standard error is used in association with regression techniques (presented later in this chapter).

SMOOTHING TECHNIQUES

Now that we have techniques to measure the goodness of the forecasts (based on past data), we can examine particular forecasting methods. We begin by considering quantitative forecasting methods that are useful when predicting the future of an item based only on its past history. When looking at data that are ordered according to time, we term the data a *time series*. For example, we might predict the future price of gasoline based solely on past prices and not consider other indicators, such as the consumer price index, world politics, and so forth. If there are other indicators that are relevant, then one of the appropriate techniques is multiple regression (to be discussed later).

> **past history**

There are two important goals that a forecasting method aims to achieve. First, it must be responsive to changes in the data. However, some of the fluctuation in the data is due to random fluctuation rather than the presence of a trend or shift in the item being forecasted. For this reason, it is undesirable to be "too responsive" to shifts in the data. This second goal allows for responsivity only after the trend has been established, leading to a problem called *lag*, which will be discussed later in this chapter. The methods discussed in this section are smoothing techniques that attempt to minimize the lag.

> **responsiveness**

The underlying principle of the smoothing techniques is that, although demand does vary, some of the variation is due to randomness that should be taken out of the underlying demand pattern. For example, examine Figure 4.9. In this figure, the past sales of Caribbean, as presented in Table 4.1, are plotted. The points are connected by straight lines to make the graph more readable. It is clear from the graph that the overall trend is increasing. Also clear from the graph is that the peak in year 2 appears excessively high and the drop in year 7 is lower than what might be expected. These sharp increases and decreases might be explained by exogenous factors. For example, the weather in year 2 might have been unusually warm, which led to greater swimsuit sales, or the economy in year 7 was depressed, which led to lower sales. These weather and economy effects are what need to be smoothed out of the data, because Caribbean can neither control nor predict these factors for the coming years.

> **randomness**

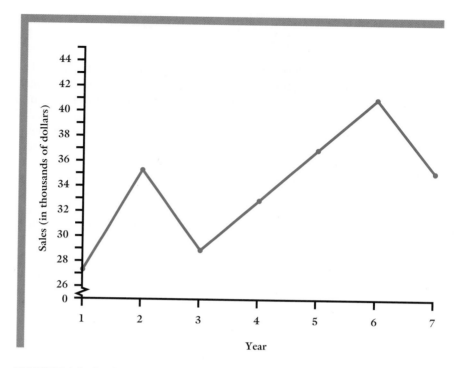

FIGURE 4.9 Caribbean Swimwear: past sales

MOVING AVERAGES

Given a time series of data where there is no trend, the easiest way to smooth the data for forecasting is to average all of the past data and use this average as the forecast. There are two problems with this approach. First, it requires keeping all of the past data, no matter how long the time series records are kept. Second, it will become weighted too much toward data in the distant past (be too smooth) and fail to be responsive to any changes in recent data.

A way to achieve a compromise between the smoothing and responsiveness goals is to use the forecasting method called the **n period moving average.** Only the data for the previous n periods are kept, and the forecast is the average of these n periods of data. Less data are maintained, and the amount is kept constant by dropping off the oldest piece of data every time a new one is made available. By using an average, a smoothing effect is still seen, but, because a smaller amount of data is averaged, the method will be more responsive to changes in the data.

selecting n

Beyond having an understanding of how to use this approach, it is necessary to decide how large n should be (how much data should be averaged). A common approach is to try various choices of n, forecast against the past data for each n, and compute the mean absolute deviation for each. The n yielding the lowest *MAD* (or *MSE*) provides the best "fit" to that particular time series.

large n = smooth; small n = responsive

It is perhaps more important, though, to understand the meaning of n in terms of the goals of smoothness and responsiveness. As n increases, the approach leads to a forecast that is more smooth and less responsive. In other words, to be more responsive to changes, choose a smaller n.

Teaching Suggestion 4.7: Smoother Is Not Necessarily Better. See the Instructor's Section for details.

In general, when given a set of data, one of the first steps should be to plot the data and examine it visually. Consider the following example.

Example 4.6   Given in Table 4.3 is the number of admissions at Merci General Hospital over the past ten weeks. The administration would like to predict the number of admissions for the coming week.

The data are plotted in Figure 4.10. Overall, the admissions pattern seems to be increasing, but there have been weeks when admissions did drop. Notice that the average over the ten weeks is 30.7. There are times when the average of all of the data may be a reasonable forecast, but, in this case, it appears that the more recent data are well above the overall average. Therefore, a reasonable method for forecasting is to use only the more recent data. This minimizes the lag. By "more recent," we mean either last week's data alone, or the data from only the last two weeks, or the data from the past three or four weeks. The general procedure is to average the data from the last n weeks (or months or years). For example, the following forecasts would be made for n ranging from 1 to 5.

Teaching Suggestion 4.8: Unimportant Data. See the Instructor's Section for details.

n	Forecast
1	37
2	$(37 + 41)/2 = 78/2 = 39$
3	$(37 + 41 + 37)/3 = 115/3 = 38.33$
4	$(37 + 41 + 37 + 33)/4 = 148/4 = 37$
5	$(37 + 41 + 37 + 33 + 29)/5 = 177/5 = 35.4$

Of course, if $n = 1$, the method simply uses the data of one week to predict admissions for the next, while the overall average is the predictor in this example if $n = 10$ (because we have ten weeks' worth of data).   ▪

Table 4.4 uses the three-week moving average to present forecasts for all of the data. Note that the computations cannot begin until week 4, because three weeks of data are needed for forecasting.

TABLE 4.3 Merci General Hospital admissions (Example 4.6)

Week Number	Admissions
1	22
2	21
3	25
4	27
5	35
6	29
7	33
8	37
9	41
10	37
	307

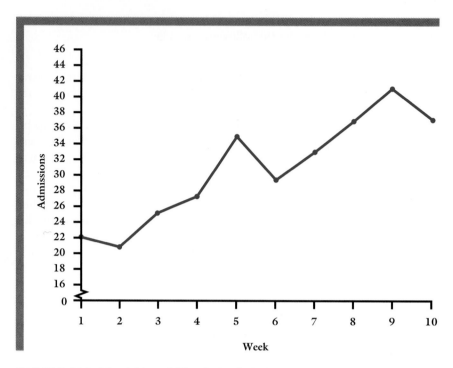

FIGURE 4.10 Merci General Hospital: admissions (Example 4.6)

These averages are plotted in Figure 4.11. Notice that the three-week moving averages have a smoother curve than do the actual data. One problem remains at this point: how to find the appropriate value of n. That is, it must be determined whether or not a two-week moving average is better than a three-week moving average, a four-week moving average, or moving averages of longer periods. These comparisons typically are made by computing the mean absolute deviation for different values of n. The

TABLE 4.4   Computation of three-week moving average for Merci General Hospital data (Example 4.6)

Week	Actual Admissions	Forecast of Admissions Using Three-Week Moving Average
1	22	
2	21	
3	25	
4	27	$(22 + 21 + 25)/3 = 68/3 = 22.67$
5	35	$(21 + 25 + 27)/3 = 73/3 = 24.33$
6	29	$(25 + 27 + 35)/3 = 87/3 = 29$
7	33	$(27 + 35 + 29)/3 = 91/3 = 30.33$
8	37	$(35 + 29 + 33)/3 = 97/3 = 32.33$
9	41	$(29 + 33 + 37)/3 = 99/3 = 33$
10	37	$(33 + 37 + 41)/3 = 111/3 = 37$
11	?	$(37 + 41 + 37)/3 = 115/3 = 38.33$

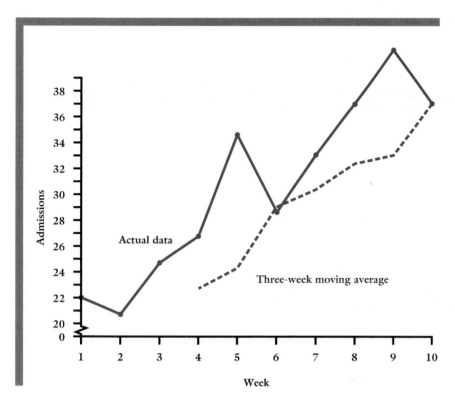

FIGURE 4.11   Merci General Hospital: three-week moving average

n that yields the lowest *MAD* is chosen as the appropriate averaging period for the given series of data. The following example demonstrates the process by which *n* may be chosen.

Example 4.7   Merci Hospital is undecided between a two-week moving average and a three-week moving average. Which has had less error (mean absolute deviation) in the past?

The mean absolute deviation for the three-week moving average is computed directly from Table 4.4 as the average of the absolute differences.

$$
\begin{aligned}
MAD &= (|27 - 22.67| + |35 - 24.33| + |29 - 29| + |33 - 30.33| + \\
&\quad |37 - 32.33| + |41 - 33| + |37 - 37|)/7 \\
&= (4.33 + 10.67 + 0 + 2.67 + 4.67 + 8 + 0)/7 \\
&= 30.33/7 \\
&= 4.33
\end{aligned}
$$

Table 4.5 presents the computations for the two-week moving average and shows a mean absolute deviation of 4.19. Hence, in this example, the two-week moving average is preferred over the three-week moving average. Also, note that the two-week moving average has a bias of 3.1875. That is, on average, this technique is underforecasting admissions by 3.19 persons each week.   ◼◢

WEIGHTED MOVING AVERAGES

In the example of the three-week moving average, the forecast for week 11 is given by
$(37 + 41 + 37)/3$. Note that this is the same as taking the admissions for each of the
last three weeks, multiplying each by a weight of one-third, and adding the products—
$37(1/3) + 41(1/3) + 37(1/3)$. There is no reason that the admissions data must be
multiplied by the same weight. In fact, it is quite reasonable to weight the data from
last week more than the data from two weeks ago. The **n period weighted moving
average** does just this. Different weights are assigned for the different periods. The
weights assigned should add to 1. For example, if the hospital has decided that the
weights to be used are .5, .3, and .2, then the forecast for week 11 is given by

$$.5(\text{last week's admissions}) + .3(\text{admissions two weeks ago})$$

$$+ .2(\text{admissions three weeks ago})$$

$$= .5(37) + .3(41) + .2(37)$$

$$= 18.5 + 12.3 + 7.4$$

$$= 38.2.$$

**largest weight is on
most recent datum**

It should be clear that the largest weight is usually for the most recent datum.
Table 4.6 presents the three-week weighted moving averages which use weights of .5,
.3, and .2, and the absolute deviations. The sum of the absolute deviations is 30.6;
hence, the mean absolute deviation is $30.6/7 = 4.37$. Based on past data, the weights
.5, .3, and .2 are worse than the equal weights of one-third in this case because they
produce a greater mean absolute deviation. Of course, other weighting schemes could

TABLE 4.5 Two-week moving average for
Merci General Hospital data (Example 4.7)

Week	Actual Admissions	Two-Week Moving Average	Error (Actual − Forecast)	Absolute Error
1	22			
2	21			
3	25	$(22 + 21)/2 = 21.5$	3.5	3.5
4	27	$(21 + 25)/2 = 23$	4	4
5	35	$(25 + 27)/2 = 26$	9	9
6	29	$(27 + 35)/2 = 31$	−2	2
7	33	$(35 + 29)/2 = 32$	1	1
8	37	$(29 + 33)/2 = 31$	6	6
9	41	$(33 + 37)/2 = 35$	6	6
10	37	$(37 + 41)/2 = 39$	−2	2
			25.5	33.5

$$\text{Bias} = \frac{25.5}{8} = 3.1875$$

$$MAD = \frac{33.5}{8} = 4.1875$$

TABLE 4.6 Three-week weighted moving average for Merci General
Hospital data (Example 4.7)

Week	Actual Admissions	Three-Week Weighted Moving Average	Absolute Deviation
1	22		
2	21		
3	25		
4	27	.5(25) + .3(21) + .2(22) = 23.2	3.8
5	35	.5(27) + .3(25) + .2(21) = 25.2	9.8
6	29	.5(35) + .3(27) + .2(25) = 30.6	1.6
7	33	.5(29) + .3(35) + .2(27) = 30.4	2.6
8	37	.5(33) + .3(29) + .2(35) = 32.2	4.8
9	41	.5(37) + .3(33) + .2(29) = 34.2	6.8
10	37	.5(41) + .3(37) + .2(33) = 38.2	1.2
11	?	.5(37) + .3(41) + .2(37) = 38.2	
			30.6

be tried, as could a change in the number of weeks used. The assignment of weights is up to the forecaster, provided they are positive and sum to 1. As with all forecasting techniques, the mean absolute deviation can be applied here to help the forecaster decide on the best weighting system.

EXPONENTIAL SMOOTHING

Exponential smoothing is a technique that is similar to weighted moving averages but that requires the retention of less information. For a fifty-two week moving average, the data for the last fifty-two weeks must be stored. Exponential smoothing requires only the storage of the forecast and data from the previous week, while implicitly using the data from all preceding weeks. The method is given by this formula:

$$F_{t+1} = F_t + \alpha(Y_t - F_t),$$

where

F_t = the forecast for period t;

Y_t = the actual data for period t; and

α = a given constant (between 0 and 1).

When using exponential smoothing, an initial forecast is required before forecasts can be made for each subsequent period. For example, for the hospital admissions data presented in the preceding examples, suppose that the given forecast for week 1 is 25 and α is set at .5. Using our exponential smoothing equation, we may make the following forecasts.

Period	Forecast
Week 2	$25 \quad + .5(22 - 25) \quad = 23.50$
Week 3	$23.50 + .5(21 - 23.50) = 22.25$
Week 4	$22.25 + .5(25 - 22.25) = 23.63$
Week 5	$23.63 + .5(27 - 23.63) = 25.32$
Week 6	$25.32 + .5(35 - 25.32) = 30.16$
Week 7	$30.16 + .5(29 - 30.16) = 29.58$
Week 8	$29.58 + .5(33 - 29.58) = 31.29$
Week 9	$31.29 + .5(37 - 31.29) = 34.15$
Week 10	$34.15 + .5(41 - 34.15) = 37.58$
Week 11	$37.58 + .5(37 - 37.58) = 37.29$

For this example, the weekly deviations from the actual data are $-3, -2.5, 2.75,$ $3.37, 9.68, -1.16, 3.42, 5.71, 6.85,$ and $-.58$. The total absolute deviation is 39.02, and the mean absolute deviation is $39.02/10 = 3.902$. Hence, the exponential smoothing technique gives more accurate results than the other methods we have used (using the old data as a basis). However, we point out that only one value of α has been tried (.5). It is quite possible that $\alpha = .4$ or $\alpha = .6$ will perform even better. The only way to find out is to try these values and others and compare the mean absolute deviations. A larger α yields a more responsive forecast.

selecting α

small α **= smooth;**
large α **= responsive**

If $\alpha = 1$, the smoothing equation yields a moving average with $n = 1$. That is,

$$\text{New forecast = previous week's data.}$$

If $\alpha = 0$, the smoothing equation reduces to a nonsensical (but very smooth) result:

$$\text{New forecast = original forecast.}$$

The importance of any data diminishes exponentially as time goes by—hence the name *exponential smoothing*. The following will illustrate this. We have that

$$F_{t+1} = F_t + \alpha(Y_t - F_t).$$

We can rewrite this as $F_{t+1} = (1 - \alpha)F_t + \alpha Y_t$. Now, $F_2 = (1 - \alpha)F_1 + \alpha Y_1$ and $F_3 = (1 - \alpha)F_2 + \alpha Y_2$. Substitution for F_2 yields

$$F_3 = (1 - \alpha)[(1 - \alpha)F_1 + \alpha Y_1] + \alpha Y_2$$
$$= (1 - \alpha)^2 F_1 + (1 - \alpha)\alpha Y_1 + \alpha Y_2.$$

The importance of Y_1 is $(1 - \alpha)\alpha$ in week 3 and α (which is larger) in week 2. Notice that the larger the value of α, the shorter the memory of the smoother.

SMOOTHING DIFFICULTIES

lag

One of the drawbacks to using smoothing techniques in forecasting is a problem mentioned earlier—**lag.** Consider the following data.

Month	Sales	Forecast by Two-Week Moving Average
January	10	
February	20	
March	30	15
April	40	25
May	50	35

Sales are increasing at a rate of 10 per month. Similarly, the two-week moving average is increasing at a rate of 10 per month. Unfortunately, the two-week moving average is always 15 units behind the actual sales. The same problem occurs with exponential smoothing. A method termed *exponential smoothing with trend* overcomes this problem, but it is beyond the scope of this book.

Teaching Suggestion 4.10: Trends vs. Shift in Data. See the Instructor's Section for details.

A second drawback is that, without modifications, the smoothing methods cannot easily predict more than one period into the future. For example, in the case of Merci Hospital, if we are interested in forecasting admissions for week 15, then both the moving averages and exponential smoothing techniques require data from week 14, which means that the prediction could not be made prior to knowing the number of admissions during week 14. The later section on regression presents a technique that does not have either the drawback of lag or the restriction to one period. Prior to our discussion of regression, however, we examine time series analysis.

DECOMPOSITION OF TIME SERIES

Decomposition is the name applied to methods that are based on factoring the demand according to four components: a **trend factor** T_t, a **cyclical factor** C_t, a **seasonal factor** S_t, and a random factor R_t. The two simplest time series models are multiplicative and additive. The multiplicative model is expressed as

four components

$$Y_t = T_t \times S_t \times C_t \times R_t$$

and the additive model is expressed as

$$Y_t = T_t + S_t + C_t + R_t.$$

In the time series models, we assume that there is some underlying trend for period t, which is given by T_t. However, variations due to the season of the year require that demand be modified by a factor S_t. Note that season is a general term that may refer to month of the year, day of the week, or even hour of the day. The demand is further modified by a business cycle factor, C_t. The last factor of randomness, R_t, is used to account for unexplained errors. The smoothing techniques presented in the previous section were actually time series models that concentrated only on this random factor. No trend, seasonal, or cyclical factors were included in those special cases. Because the business cycle is difficult to define—it has no fixed time period—we will concentrate on the seasonal factors that are seen in many practical situations. Therefore, the formula we will use for the multiplicative model is the following:

$$Y_t = T_t \times S_t.$$

For the additive model, we will use this formula:

$$Y_t = T_t + S_t.$$

Our goal is to decompose the data in order to identify (isolate) the trend and the seasonal effects.

THE MULTIPLICATIVE MODEL

We begin with the multiplicative model. Consider the data given in columns (1), (2), and (3) of Table 4.7 and plotted in Figure 4.12. The data show the past sales of corn

TABLE 4.7 Time series analysis with multiplicative model (Tornado Inc.)*

(1) Year	(2) Quarter	(3) Sales	(4) Moving Average	(5) Ratio [(3) ÷ (4)]	(6) Index	(7) Deseasonalized Sales [(3) ÷ (6)]
1	Winter	3,773			.96	3,930
	Spring	4,100			1.01	4,061
	Summer	4,431	4,110	1.08	1.07	4,149
	Fall	4,023	4,140	.97	.97	4,158
2	Winter	4,002	4,146	.97	.96	4,166
	Spring	4,107	4,147	.99	1.01	4,068
	Summer	4,476	4,135	1.08	1.07	4,192
	Fall	3,985	4,144	.96	.97	4,118
3	Winter	3,942	4,162	.95	.96	4,104
	Spring	4,237	4,188	1.01	1.01	4,197
	Summer	4,489	4,253	1.06	1.07	4,204
	Fall	4,183	4,325	.97	.97	4,323
4	Winter	4,262	4,396	.97	.96	4,437
	Spring	4,495	4,470	1.01	1.01	4,452
	Summer	4,796	4,528	1.06	1.07	4,491
	Fall	4,470	4,584	.98	.97	4,620
5	Winter	4,439	4,647	.96	.96	4,621
	Spring	4,763	4,694	1.01	1.01	4,718
	Summer	5,039	4,736	1.06	1.07	4,719
	Fall	4,601	4,781	.96	.97	4,755
6	Winter	4,640	4,805	.97	.96	4,831
	Spring	4,928	4,804	1.03	1.01	4,881
	Summer	5,064			1.07	4,742
	Fall	4,564			.97	4,705

(8) Year	(9) Winter	(10) Spring	(11) Summer	(12) Fall
1			1.08	.97
2	.97	.99	1.08	.96
3	.95	1.01	1.06	.97
4	.97	1.01	1.06	.98
5	.96	1.01	1.06	.96
6	.97	1.03		
Total	4.80	5.05	5.34	4.84
Average	.96	1.01	1.07	.97

*Some numbers have error due to rounding off. All errors are less than .17%.

by Tornado Inc. From the plot, it is obvious that, overall, the sales are increasing and, in addition, that the sales seem to vary according to the quarter. That is, in general, the fall and winter quarters of each year seem to have the lowest sales, while the spring and summer quarters seem to have the highest.

remove seasonal effect Because the sales seem to vary by season, the first thing that we wish to do is to remove the seasonal effect. We will use a moving average to do this. Because there are four quarters in a year, the length of the moving average will be four quarters. The

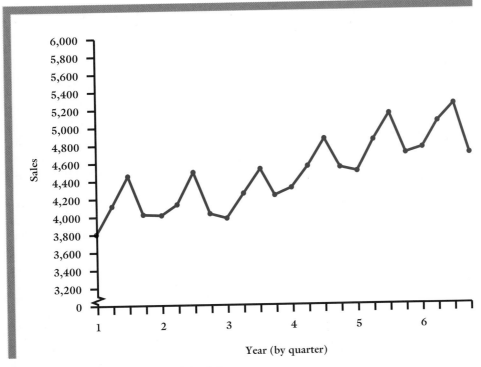

FIGURE 4.12 Tornado, Inc.: original data

number of terms in the moving average is chosen to be equal to the number of seasons in the period. Furthermore, we will be taking a moving average around a quarter rather than using the moving average to forecast a quarter. (This is slightly different than what we did before.) We do not have enough data to start with the winter or spring of year 1, so we begin with summer of year 1.

The sales during this quarter are 4,431. However, we have already noted that summer quarter sales are typically higher than average. Let us consider the average sales for the year surrounding the summer of year 1. We encounter a slight difficulty because a year has an even number of quarters. Look at Figure 4.13. The figure breaks down the data by quarter. Our current concern is with the summer quarter of year 1. The midpoint of this quarter is August 15. We want data for the year surrounding this quarter—namely, six months prior to August 15 and six months past August 15. The figure indicates that our concern is with February 15 of year 1 through February 15 of year 2. That is, we want to include half of each of the winter quarters in years 1 and 2. Therefore, the average sales is given by one-half of quarter 1, all of quarters 2, 3, and 4, and one-half of the fifth quarter. Hence, the average to the nearest integer is

Teaching Suggestion 4.11: Centered Moving Average. See the Instructor's Section for details.

$$\frac{(1/2)(3,773) + 4,100 + 4,431 + 4,023 + (1/2)(4,002)}{4} = 4,110.$$

The average of 4,110 appears in column (4) for the summer of year 1. We continue in this fashion and compute the remaining moving averages in column (4). For example, for spring of year 4 we add the following amounts from column (3) of Table 4.7.

One-half of fall of year 3[(1/2)(4,183)]	2,091.5
Winter of year 4	4,262
Spring of year 4	4,495
Summer of year 4	4,796
One-half of fall of year 4[(1/2)(4,470)]	2,235
	17,879.5

Dividing the total by 4 to average the answer, we get 4,469.875, which we have rounded and put in the table as 4,470. The interpretation of this figure is that, during the one-year period from November 15 of year 3 to November 15 of year 4, the demand averaged 4,470 per quarter. Notice that the midpoint of this one-year period is May 15 of year 4, or the spring of year 4, which is where we have placed this average in Table 4.7.

The moving average column—column (4)—presents the smoothed data. By taking one-year moving averages, we have eliminated the seasonal effect. That is, each number in this column represents the average over a complete year, which means that seasonality is not present.

measuring seasonality   Our next goal is to use the smoothed data in column (4) and the original sales data in column (3) to determine exactly what the seasonal effects have been. Therefore, we compute the ratios of the sales to the moving averages. These are given in column (5). The 1.08 in column (5) for summer of year 1 indicates that summer sales in year 1 were 8 percent above the average for the year surrounding that summer. Now, in column (5), we have the ratio of sales in a quarter to average sales in the year surrounding that quarter. At this point, we need to separate the ratios in column (5) and analyze the information on a quarter-by-quarter basis. At the bottom of Table 4.7, the same numbers that appear in column (5) are sorted on a quarter-by-quarter basis in columns (8)–(12). For example, column (9) contains the five ratios that appear in the winter rows of column (5). The average of the winter ratios is .96. This means that winter sales have averaged 96 percent of the annual sales, with "annual" meaning from August 15 to August 15. Similarly, the summer average is 1.07. Hence, summer sales have been, on average, 7 percent above annual sales, with "annual" meaning from February 15 to February 15. The definition of annual "moves" because we have been using a moving average. The averages at the bottom of the tables are termed the **seasonal indices.**

FIGURE 4.13 Centering the moving average

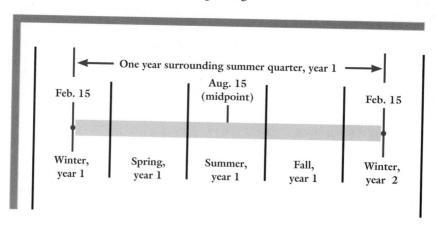

From our plot of the original data, we knew that sales were lower in the fall and winter and higher in the spring and summer. Now we have a more precise notion of what "higher" and "lower" mean.

Finally, we can use these seasonal indices to extract the seasonality from the original data. We take the seasonal indices and put them into the table in column (6). Consider winter of year 1. The actual sales were 3,773. However, we just determined that the winter seasonal index is .96. Our underlying equation is

extracting seasonality

$$Y_t = T_t \times S_t.$$

We know that $Y_t = 3,773$ and $S_t = .96$. Hence the deseasonalized sales T_t are given by the following:

$$T_t = Y_t/S_t$$
$$= 3,773/.96$$
$$= 3,930.$$

That is, the underlying sales rate during this time was 3,930, but only 96 percent of this has been achieved on average. The number 3,930 has been placed in column (7) of our table. The numbers in column (7) are computed as the actual sales divided by the seasonal index. The deseasonalized sales in column (7) represent what sales would have been had seasonality not come into play. Figure 4.14 contains a plot of the original data and the deseasonalized data. Notice that the plot of the deseasonalized data

FIGURE 4.14 Tornado, Inc.: multiplicative model of deseasonalized data

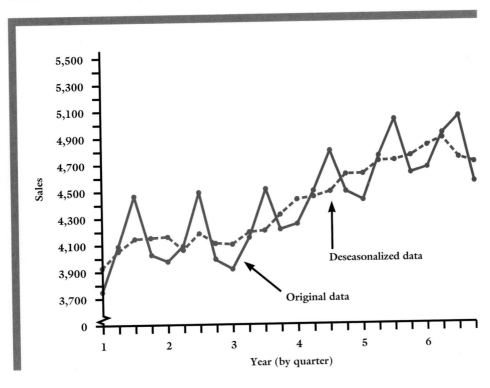

is smoother than the plot of the original data because we have taken out the seasonal bias. We can use the deseasonalized data to compute the overall trend. This is done using the regression techniques that we will discuss later.

THE ADDITIVE MODEL

The additive model is very similar to the multiplicative model. We begin by computing the one-year moving average exactly as we did in the multiplicative model. These results appear in column (4) of Table 4.8. At this point, our concern is with the difference between (rather than the ratio of) the actual sales and the moving average. For example, sales in the summer of year 1 were 321 units above the average annual sales of 4,110. This difference of 321 appears in column (5), as do all of the differences given by subtracting the moving average in column (4) from actual sales in column (3).

Again, we want to examine the differences on a quarter-by-quarter basis. At the bottom of Table 4.8, in columns (8)–(12), we have listed the differences from column (5). The differences are sorted by quarter. For the winter quarter, the average difference is − 174.2, which indicates that, on average, sales in the winter quarter were 174 units below the average annual sales. The four averages at the bottom of the table represent the seasonal indices for the model.

We place these indices in column (6) of our table. As before, we want to deseasonalize the data, this time using the model

$$Y_t = T_t + S_t.$$

Since we know Y_t and S_t, we rewrite the equation as follows:

$$T_t = Y_t - S_t.$$

To deseasonalize the data, we subtract the seasonal index from the actual sales. The results of this appear in column (7) and in Figure 4.15.

REGRESSION

advantages

Teaching Suggestion 4.12: Causal vs. Associative. See the Instructor's Section for details.

Regression is a technique that can be applied both to time series data and to causal data. It has several advantages. Among these are that it identifies the overall trend, it does not have a lag problem, and it can be used for projecting more than one period in advance. The technique is very simple and widespread in use—as evidenced by the fact that regression is a function on most business calculators and is a function on some spreadsheet software.

LEAST SQUARES

Refer back to Figure 4.10. It appears that the admissions pattern at Merci General Hospital is very nearly a straight line, with a couple of deviations. Therefore, we can assume that admissions are in fact linear with respect to time, attributing the variations

TABLE 4.8 Time series analysis with additive model (Tornado, Inc.)

(1) Year	(2) Quarter	(3) Sales	(4) Moving Average	(5) Ratio [(3) − (4)]	(6) Index	(7) Deseasonalized Sales [(3) − (6)]
1	Winter	3,773			− 174	3,947
	Spring	4,100			45	4,055
	Summer	4,431	4,110	321	294	4,137
	Fall	4,023	4,140	− 117	− 142	4,165
2	Winter	4,002	4,146	− 144	− 174	4,176
	Spring	4,107	4,147	− 40	45	4,062
	Summer	4,476	4,135	341	294	4,182
	Fall	3,985	4,144	− 159	− 142	4,127
3	Winter	3,942	4,162	− 220	− 174	4,116
	Spring	4,237	4,188	49	45	4,192
	Summer	4,489	4,253	236	294	4,195
	Fall	4,183	4,325	− 142	− 142	4,325
4	Winter	4,262	4,396	− 134	− 174	4,436
	Spring	4,495	4,470	25	45	4,450
	Summer	4,796	4,528	268	294	4,502
	Fall	4,470	4,584	− 114	− 142	4,612
5	Winter	4,439	4,647	− 208	− 174	4,613
	Spring	4,763	4,694	69	45	4,718
	Summer	5,039	4,736	303	294	4,745
	Fall	4,601	4,781	− 180	− 142	4,743
6	Winter	4,640	4,805	− 165	− 174	4,814
	Spring	4,928	4,804	124	45	4,883
	Summer	5,064			294	4,770
	Fall	4,564			− 142	4,706

(8) Year	(9) Winter	(10) Spring	(11) Summer	(12) Fall
1			321	− 117
2	− 144	− 40	341	− 159
3	− 220	49	236	− 142
4	− 134	25	268	− 114
5	− 208	69	303	− 180
6	− 165	124		
Total	− 871	227	1,469	− 712
Average	− 174.2	45.4	293.8	− 142.4

to randomness. In Figure 4.16, an arbitrary line is drawn through the data. The line is given by the equation

$$y = 20 + 2x,$$

where y = admissions, x = week number, and y is a function of x. The bars in the figure indicate the deviations of the actual data from this particular line.

For technical reasons, rather than using the absolute deviation from the data (as with mean absolute deviation), let us use the deviation squared (as with standard error)

linearity assumption

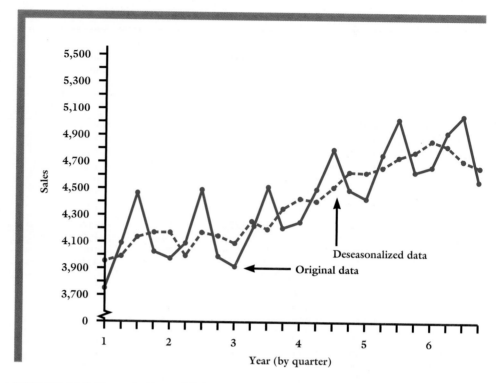

FIGURE 4.15 Tornado, Inc.: additive model of deseasonalized data

FIGURE 4.16 Merci General Hospital: admissions with arbitrary line $y = 20 + 2x$

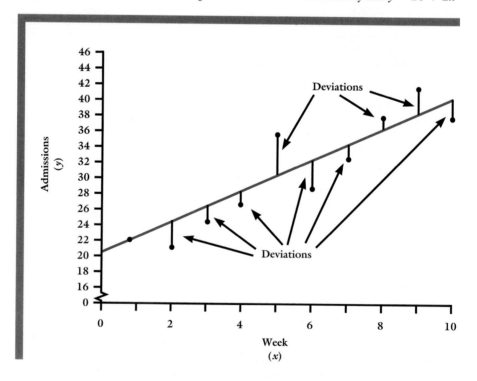

to measure the goodness of this line. Notice that this still prevents us from negating overforecasts and underforecasts. Now, there exists an infinite number of lines that could be chosen, all of the form

$$y = a + bx,$$

where a is the intercept and b is the slope of the line. Our interest is in determining which line minimizes the sum of the errors squared. Fortunately, the best line can be found easily (through calculus). It is given by using the following equations:

$$b = \frac{\Sigma xy - n\bar{x}\bar{y}}{\Sigma x^2 - n(\bar{x})^2}$$

slope

and

$$a = \bar{y} - b\bar{x},$$

intercept

where

$$\bar{y} = \sum_{i=1}^{n} \frac{y_i}{n} \text{ and}$$

$$\bar{x} = \sum_{i=1}^{n} \frac{x_i}{n}.$$

For this example, the computations are performed and presented in Table 4.9. The least squares line is given by

$$Y = 19.15 + 2.10x.$$

Using this line, the forecast for week 11 is given by

$$Y = 19.15 + 2.10(11) = 42.25.$$

There is one major advantage that the least squares method of forecasting has over moving averages and exponential smoothing. Forecasts may easily be made for more than one period in advance. For example, if a forecast is desired for week 13, then we cannot use the simple averaging or exponential smoothing methods because these methods require knowing the number of admissions during week 12. However, with the least squares method, the forecast may be determined by substituting $x = 13$ into the least squares line:

$$Y = 19.15 + 2.10(13) = 46.45.$$

The farther into the future a prediction is made, the less confidence can be associated with the prediction. A confidence interval can be calculated for each future time period through the use of the standard error.

confidence interval

Example 4.8 Perform a least squares analysis for the Caribbean data given in Table 4.1 and find the bias and the standard error.

TABLE 4.9 Linear regression for Merci General Hospital data

Week (x)	Admissions (y)	xy	x^2
1	22	22	1
2	21	42	4
3	25	75	9
4	27	108	16
5	35	175	25
6	29	174	36
7	33	231	49
8	37	296	64
9	41	369	81
10	37	370	100
55	307	1,862	385

$$\bar{x} = \frac{55}{10} = 5.5$$

$$\bar{y} = \frac{307}{10} = 30.7$$

$$b = \frac{\Sigma xy - n\bar{x}\bar{y}}{\Sigma x^2 - n\bar{x}^2} = \frac{1,862 - 10(5.5)(30.7)}{385 - 10(5.5)^2} = \frac{1,862 - 1,688.5}{385 - 302.5} = \frac{173.5}{82.5} = 2.10$$

$$a = \bar{y} - b\bar{x} = 30.7 - 2.1(5.5) = 19.15$$

linear regression is unbiased

The computations are performed in Table 4.10. Of course, if we want to forecast for year 10, we simply use $x = 10$. Also, notice that the bias is 0. Linear regression is an unbiased technique; it always generates a zero bias. The effects of overforecasting and underforecasting always negate each other. The standard error has been computed as follows:

$$SE = \sqrt{\frac{\Sigma(y - Y)^2}{n}}.$$

When using least squares, there is an alternative formula for computing the standard error:

alternate formula for standard error

$$SE = \sqrt{\frac{\Sigma y^2 - a\Sigma y - b\Sigma xy}{n}}.$$

This formula is easier to use when doing computations by hand or with a calculator (as opposed to with a computer).

We present one more example. In the previous section on time series analysis, we factored out the seasonal factors and were left with deseasonalized data. We can use regression in order to find the long-term trend of the deseasonalized data. In Table 4.11, we present the computations for the data given in Table 4.7.

Teaching Suggestion 4.13: Round-off Error. See the Instructor's Section for details.

TABLE 4.10   Least squares analysis for Caribbean swimwear (Example 4.8)

Year (x)	Sales* (y)	xy	x^2	Forecast* (Y = 27.57 + 1.57x)	Error (y − Y)	Error Squared [(y − Y)²]
1	27	27	1	29.14	−2.14	4.5796
2	35	70	4	30.71	4.29	18.4041
3	29	87	9	32.28	−3.28	10.7584
4	33	132	16	33.85	− .85	.7225
5	37	185	25	35.42	1.58	2.4964
6	41	246	36	37.00	4.00	16.0000
7	35	245	49	38.57	−3.57	12.7449
28	237	992	140		0	65.7059

$$\bar{x} = \frac{28}{7} = 4$$

$$\bar{y} = \frac{237}{7} = 33.86$$

$$SE = \sqrt{\frac{65.7059}{7}} = \sqrt{9.387} = 3.06$$

$$b = \frac{\Sigma xy - n\bar{x}\bar{y}}{\Sigma x^2 - n\bar{x}^2} = \frac{992 - 7(4)(33.86)}{140 - 7(4)^2} = \frac{44}{28} = 1.57$$

$$a = 33.86 - 1.57(4) = 27.57$$

$$Y = 27.57 + 1.57x*$$

*In thousands

CAUSAL MODELS

A second advantage when using linear regression is that data other than time-related data can be regressed using the same general model, $Y = a + bx$. That is, x does not need to refer to time in order to generate forecasts. Consider the next example.

> **Example 4.9**   The following data relate the sales of snow shovels to the inches of snow over the past four years. Perform a linear regression that relates sales to snow (rather than to time).

Year	Snow	Sales
1	16 inches	330
2	12 inches	270
3	18 inches	380
4	14 inches	300

The analysis is performed in Table 4.12. The forecasting equation is found to be

$$Y = 50 + 18x,$$

where x is the number of inches of snow. Hence, if the forecast is for 20 inches of snow, then the sales forecast is $50 + 18(20) = 410$ shovels. Notice that each inch of snow accounts for 18 additional sales of shovels.   ▪⌐

condition for use

Although we now have an equation that relates the sales to the snowfall, we are not better off than without the equation because, at this point, we still must forecast the snowfall. In order to use a causal model, the dependent variable, Y, must lag behind the independent (or leading) variable, X. For example, demand for plumbing fixtures usually lags behind new housing starts by approximately three months. A causal regression can be used for plumbing fixtures because housing starts are known in advance.

TABLE 4.11 Trend for time series analysis (Tornado Inc.)

Year	Quarter	Sales (y)	x	xy	x^2
1	Winter	3,930	1	3,930	1
	Spring	4,061	2	8,122	4
	Summer	4,149	3	12,447	9
	Fall	4,158	4	16,632	16
2	Winter	4,166	5	20,830	25
	Spring	4,068	6	24,408	36
	Summer	4,192	7	29,344	49
	Fall	4,118	8	32,944	64
3	Winter	4,104	9	36,936	81
	Spring	4,197	10	41,970	100
	Summer	4,204	11	46,244	121
	Fall	4,323	12	51,876	144
4	Winter	4,437	13	57,681	169
	Spring	4,452	14	62,328	196
	Summer	4,491	15	67,365	225
	Fall	4,620	16	73,920	256
5	Winter	4,621	17	78,557	289
	Spring	4,718	18	84,924	324
	Summer	4,719	19	89,661	361
	Fall	4,755	20	95,100	400
6	Winter	4,831	21	101,451	441
	Spring	4,881	22	107,382	484
	Summer	4,742	23	109,066	529
	Fall	4,705	24	113,208	576
	Total	105,652	300	1,366,324	4,900
	Average	4,402.166	12.5		

$$b^\star = 39.71652$$
$$a^\star = 3,905.710$$

TABLE 4.12 Demand for snow shovels as a
            function of snow (Example 4.9)

x	y	xy	x^2
16	330	5,280	256
12	270	3,240	144
18	380	6,840	324
14	300	4,200	196
60	1,280	19,560	920

$$\bar{x} = \frac{60}{4} = 15$$

$$\bar{y} = \frac{1,280}{4} = 320$$

$$b = \frac{\Sigma xy - n\bar{x}\bar{y}}{\Sigma x^2 - n\bar{x}^2} = \frac{19,560 - 4(15)(320)}{920 - 4(15)^2} = \frac{360}{20} = 18$$

$$a = \bar{y} - b\bar{x} = 320 - 18(15) = 50$$

$$Y = 50 + 18x$$

MULTIPLE REGRESSION

When using regression, we are not limited to having the dependent variable, Y, be a function of only one independent variable, X. We may extend the model as follows:

$$Y = a + b_1X_1 + b_2X_2 + b_3X_3 + \ldots + b_nX_n.$$

For example, in the case of the snow shovels, we could model sales as

$$Y = b_0 + b_1X_1 + b_2X_2,$$

where X_1 refers to time and X_2 refers to inches of snow.

The computations are a little too complex to be presented here, but standard software packages (SPSS, BMDP, SAS) will perform the computations to determine the values of b_0, b_1, and b_2. Figure 4.17 presents the analysis of the snow shovel example as displayed by AB:POM. The regression coefficients appear under the method. The multiple regression equation is

$$Y = 45 + 18X_1 + 2X_2.$$

Sales are given by a base of 45 and increase by 18 for each inch of snow and by 2 per year. The standard error of this multiple regression is 5, which is better than the standard error of 7.75 obtained by the single regression equation (it did not include time as the second variable). The equation can be displayed by pressing the **F1** key.

Prior to using any software package, one should become familiar with the assumptions of multiple regression. This will avert misuse, because the programs will perform the same calculations with faulty or inadequate data as they will with good data.

```
┌─ Data file:wgsp4-2 ══════════════ Forecasting ═══════════════ Solution ═
│  Number of past data periods (2-99) 4      Number of independ. variables (1-6) 2
├──────────────────────── Example 4.9 ════════════════════════════════════
│  Method-->Least Squares - Simple and Multiple Regression
│           B 0     B 1     B 2
│  Coef--->  45.00   18.00   2.00
│           Sales   Snow    Year Forecast Error  |Error| Error^2
│  Year 1   330.00  16.00   1.00  335.00  -5.00    5.00   25.00
│  Year 2   270.00  12.00   2.00  265.00   5.00    5.00   25.00
│  Year 3   380.00  18.00   3.00  375.00   5.00    5.00   25.00
│  Year 4   300.00  14.00   4.00  305.00  -5.00    5.00   25.00
│  TOTALS                                  0.00   20.00  100.00
│  AVERAGE                                  0.00    5.00   25.00
│                                         (Bias)  (MAD)  (MSE)
│
│           Regression line : See summary table
│           Correlation coefficient =      0.9923953   Standard error =      5.00
│
└──────────────────────────────────────────────────────────────────────────
 F1=Summary Table
 Press <Esc> key to edit data or highlighted key or function key for options
                                                      F9=Print    Esc
```

FIGURE 4.17   AB:POM analysis of Example 4.9

Although these programs are valuable tools, they are probably the most misused programs on the market.

SEASONAL COMPONENTS

Previously, we stated that one of our objectives is to filter out as many effects in the data as possible. One common effect is seasonality, and this can be easily filtered out.

Teaching Suggestion 4.14: Handling Seasonality. See the Instructor's Section for details.

Example 4.10   The following are sales of toys over the last twelve quarters. Use linear regression to forecast the sales for the next year and determine how well this line has fit the past data *on a quarter-by-quarter basis.*

| | | Year | |
Quarter	1	2	3
Winter	90	130	190
Spring	130	190	220
Summer	200	250	310
Fall	170	220	300

TABLE 4.13 Seasonal factors with regression (Example 4.10)

(1) Year	(2) Quarter	(3) Actual Sales Data (y)	(4) x	(5) xy	(6) x^2	(7) Y = a + bx	(8) Ratio (Sales ÷ Forecast)
1	Winter	90	1	90	1	113.4615	.793220
	Spring	130	2	260	4	129.1958	1.006224
	Summer	200	3	600	9	144.9300	1.379975
	Fall	170	4	680	16	160.6643	1.058106
2	Winter	130	5	650	25	176.3986	.736967
	Spring	190	6	1,140	36	192.1328	.988898
	Summer	250	7	1,750	49	207.8671	1.202691
	Fall	220	8	1,760	64	223.6013	.983893
3	Winter	190	9	1,710	81	239.3356	.793864
	Spring	220	10	2,200	100	255.0699	.862508
	Summer	310	11	3,410	121	270.8041	1.144738
	Fall	300	12	3,600	144	286.5384	1.046979
	Total	2,400	78	17,850	650		
	Average	200	6.5				

$$b^* = 15.73426$$
$$a^* = 97.72727$$

(9) Year	(10) Winter	(11) Spring	(12) Summer	(13) Fall
1	.793220	1.006224	1.379975	1.058106
2	.736967	.988898	1.202691	.983893
3	.793864	.862508	1.144738	1.046979
Total	2.324051	2.857632	3.737405	3.088980
Average	.774683	.952544	1.242468	1.029660

The regression appears in Table 4.13. According to the equation, these are the forecasts for the next four periods (year 4):

Winter	97.73 + 15.73(13) = 302.22
Spring	97.73 + 15.73(14) = 317.95
Summer	97.73 + 15.73(15) = 333.68
Fall	97.73 + 15.73(16) = 349.71

We will compute the seasonal factors in a fashion similar to the time series analysis. Column (7) contains the forecast for past periods according to the regression line. Column (8) contains the ratio of the actual sales to the forecast. These ratios are regrouped by season at the bottom of the table, where the average seasonal ratios are computed. In winter, sales have been, on average, 77 percent of the forecast. Thus, we revise our forecasts as follows.

(1) Year 4	(2) Forecast	(3) Seasonal Index	(4) Revised Forecast [(2) × (3)]
Winter	302.22	.77	232.71
Spring	317.95	.95	302.05
Summer	333.68	1.24	413.76
Fall	349.41	1.03	359.89

CONTROL OF THE FORECASTING PROCESS

Teaching Suggestion 4.15: Importance of Control. See the Instructor's Section for details.

Forecasting is an ongoing process, which means that it is not sufficient to simply pick a technique and then continuously use that technique. Control must be exercised in order to ensure that the technique is working. If it is not, either the technique must be adjusted or a new technique must be used. In order to monitor the forecasts, we use **tracking signals.** Prior to considering specific tracking signals, it is useful to briefly describe the concepts of control charts. More detail on these charts is presented in Chapters 16 and 17 (quality control).

control chart

A sample control chart is presented in Figure 4.18. On the **control chart,** we plot the value of the variable being controlled (which, in this case, is the tracking signal) versus time. Also on the chart are three horizontal lines. The middle line represents the mean of the variable. This is the expected value of the variable. The top and bottom lines are control limits. These lines are set so that, if the value is above the upper

FIGURE 4.18 Blank control chart

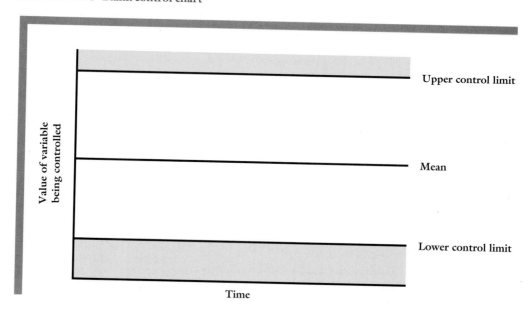

control limit or below the lower control limit, there is cause for alarm. This alarm is in a probabilistic sense. For example, there might be a 2.5-percent probability that, even though the process is in control, we are below the lower control limit simply by chance. After plotting the values of the variable controlled, we expect the picture to appear as shown in Figure 4.19. We will use a control chart to monitor the forecasts.   **monitor the forecasts**

We begin by considering the cumulative forecast error over time through time period t, or the *running sum of forecast errors*. The formula for the running sum of forecast errors is as follows:

$$RSFE(t) = \sum_{i=1}^{t} (Y_i - F_i) = \sum_{i=1}^{t} error_i.$$

Consider the data presented in Example 4.1. In Table 4.14, we give the actual sales in column (2), the forecasts in column (3), the errors in column (4), and the cumulative errors in column (5). If the error in a given period is positive, then the running sum of forecast errors will increase; if the error is negative, the running sum of forecast errors will decrease (for example, see years 2 and 3). In general, $RSFE$ may be positive or negative and, if the forecasting technique is unbiased, it will be near 0.

What if $RSFE$ is not near 0? How far away from 0 (either positive or negative) should $RSFE$ be before we become alarmed? Because an error of 100 in 1,000 differs from an error of 100 in 100,000, we need a base to which we can compare the running sum of forecast errors. The base we use is a moving mean absolute deviation. First, we fix the time period over which the MAD will be computed. For example, we might use a mean absolute deviation based only on the three most recent periods. We then denote by $MAD(t)$ the mean absolute deviation evaluated for the three most recent

FIGURE 4.19 Plotted control chart

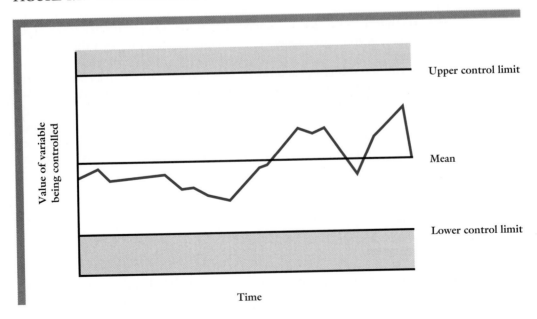

TABLE 4.14 Tracking signal computation (Example 4.1)

(1) Year	(2) Actual Sales	(3) Forecasted Sales	(4) Error	(5) RSFE(t)	(6) MAD(t) (n = 3)	(7) RSFE(t)/MAD(t)
1	27,000	23,000	4,000	4,000		
2	35,000	25,000	10,000	14,000		
3	29,000	31,000	−2,000	12,000	5,333	2.250
4	33,000	30,000	3,000	15,000	5,000	3.000
5	37,000	32,000	5,000	20,000	3,333	6.000
6	41,000	34,000	7,000	27,000	5,000	5.400
7	35,000	38,000	−3,000	24,000	5,000	4.800

time periods ending at time t. In column (6) of our table, we have computed the three-period mean absolute deviation for years 3 through 7.

Lastly, we define the tracking signal, $TS(t)$, as follows:

$$TS(t) = \frac{RSFE(t)}{MAD(t)},$$

where

$TS(t)$ = the tracking signal at time t;

$RSFE(t)$ = the running sum of forecast errors through time t; and

$MAD(t)$ = the mean absolute deviation through time t (using the most recent n periods to compute MAD).

Column (7) of Table 4.14 presents the computation for the data in Example 4.1. If the forecasting system is working well, the tracking signal should hover near 0, in either direction (positive or negative). Notice that, in our example, this is not the case. The tracking signal is above the upper control limit, which means that the forecasts are out of control.

In order to use a tracking signal properly, it is necessary to set up a control chart similar to that given in Figure 4.8. The control chart in Figure 4.20 represents a 95-percent control chart because we are using 2.45 MADs. (Since 1 MAD = .8 standard deviations, this is equivalent to 1.96 standard deviations.) If one of the plots is above the upper limit or below the lower limit, this indicates that there is a problem and the forecast errors are out of control. In our example, the forecasting process is very much out of control.

S U M M A R Y

Forecasts of future demands and costs are a major input in all aspects of operations decision making as well as in marketing and financial decision making. The two general types of forecasting techniques are *qualitative,* or *subjective,* techniques, which use

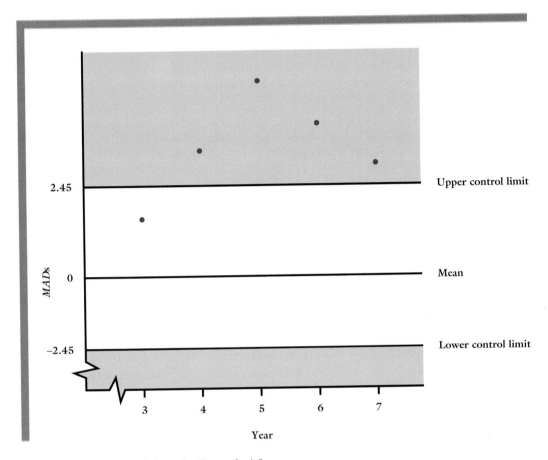

FIGURE 4.20 Control chart for Example 4.1

either experts, salespeople, or customers to make the forecasts, and *quantitative* techniques, most of which rely on past data to make the forecasts. The quantitative techniques may be further subdivided into *time series, extrapolative,* or *projective methods* and *causal methods.* The quantitative techniques are more appropriate for short-range and medium-range forecasting, while the qualitative techniques are most useful for making long-range forecasts. For any of these techniques, there are development costs, execution costs, and error costs that must be evaluated in order to determine which technique is the most economical to use.

Because the future cannot be foretold perfectly, it is necessary to be able to measure the errors of any technique. The *bias* and the *mean percentage error* indicate whether forecasts are, on average, too high or too low. The *standard error,* or *consistency,* and the *mean absolute deviation* indicate the degree of the error and may be used to yield a forecasting range rather than a single point. The *tracking signal* is used to keep track of the forecast errors and indicates when it is time to adjust or change the technique.

In examining time series data, one goal is to take out the fluctuations that are due to chance. The techniques of *moving averages* and *exponential smoothing* do this by smoothing the past data. *Time series decomposition,* however, explicitly creates seasonal factors. The *regression* technique smoothes the data by regressing them onto a straight line and identifies the trend. Regression also can be used for causal models, but it is applicable only when the variable to be forecast lags behind the causal variable. *Multiple regression* can be used when there is more than one independent variable.

We know that forecasting is an inexact process and that errors are unavoidable. However, regardless of what technique is chosen, one must exercise care. We repeat here the incident of an avoidable error that was reported by Barnett (1982).

> A manufacturing firm, wanting to estimate the sales of one of its products, asked a sample of retailers to pick two days per month at random and record the number sold on those days. The two-day totals were then multiplied by 15 to yield monthly sales estimates. It took years before someone pointed out that this procedure was generating inflated statistics, given that stores typically sell more on days they are open than on those they are closed. (p. 47)

KEY TERMS

quantitative	grass roots method	exponential smoothing
qualitative	user expectations	lag
extrapolative models	bias	trend factor
time series models	mean squared error	cyclical factor
projective models	standard error	seasonal factor
causal model	consistency	seasonal indices
qualitative models	mean absolute deviation	regression
subjective models	mean percentage error	tracking signals
jury of executive opinion	*n* period moving average	control chart
Delphi technique	*n* period weighted moving average	
sales force composite		

SOLVED PROBLEMS

1. The sales and the forecasts of sales for five months are given.

Month	Sales	Forecast
November	6,239	6,000
December	7,483	6,200
January	6,923	7,000
February	6,321	7,000
March	6,189	6,500

Compute the bias, mean squared error, and mean absolute deviation for this information.

Solution

We need to build a table in order to compute the bias, mean squared error, and mean absolute deviation. The table must have a column that includes the error for each year (error = sales − forecast), a column that has the absolute value of the error, and a column that has the square of the error.

Month	Sales	Forecast	Error	Absolute Error	Squared Error
November	6,239	6,000	239	239	57,121
December	7,483	6,200	1,283	1,283	1,646,089
January	6,923	7,000	−77	77	5,929
February	6,321	7,000	−679	679	461,041
March	6,189	6,500	−311	311	96,721
		Total	455	2,589	2,266,901
		Average	91	517.8	453,380.2

Therefore, the bias is 91. That is, on average, there has been a tendency to underforecast sales by 91 units per month. *MAD* is 517.8, and *MSE* is 453,380.2, which means that the standard error is given by its square root, or 673. Note that the mean absolute deviation is 76 percent of the standard error, which is near the approximate value of 80 percent.

2. Given below is data on the number of fires in Springfield township over the past four quarters.

Quarter	Fires
1	28
2	36
3	33
4	43

(a) Forecast the number of fires for the next quarter using a two-month moving average.

(b) Forecast the number of fires for the next quarter using a three-month weighted moving average (.45, .35, .2).

(c) Forecast the number of fires for the next quarter using exponential smoothing with an initial forecast for quarter 1 of 30 and a smoothing constant of .2.

(d) Forecast the number of fires for the next two quarters using linear regression.

Solution

(a) To forecast the number of fires for the next quarter using a two-month moving average, simply calculate the average of the most recent two periods as follows:

$$F_5 = (33 + 43)/2 = 38.0.$$

(b) To forecast the number of fires for the next quarter using a three-month weighted moving average (.45, .35, .2), calculate the product of the most recent data with the appropriate weights as follows:

$$F_5 = (.45 \times 43) + (.35 \times 33) + (.2 \times 36) = 38.1.$$

(c) To forecast the number of fires for the next quarter using exponential smoothing with an initial forecast for quarter 1 of 30 and a smoothing constant of .2, we must begin with the forecast for quarter 2 and use the exponential smoothing formula:

$$F_{t+1} = F_t + \alpha(Y_t - F_t).$$

$$F_2 = F_1 + .2(Y_1 - F_1)$$

$$= 30 + .2(28 - 30)$$

$$= 30 + (-.4)$$

$$= 29.6$$

$$F_3 = 29.6 + .2(36 - 29.6)$$

$$= 29.6 + 1.28$$

$$= 30.88$$

$$F_4 = 30.88 + .2(33 - 30.88)$$

$$= 30.88 + .424$$

$$= 31.304$$

$$F_5 = 31.304 + .2(43 - 31.304)$$

$$= 31.304 + 2.3392$$

$$= 33.6432$$

(d) To forecast the number of fires for the next two quarters using linear regression, we begin by building a four-column table and then use the formulas for the intercept and slope.

	Quarter (x)	Fires (y)	x^2	xy
	1	28	1	28
	2	36	4	72
	3	33	9	99
	4	43	16	172
Total	10	140	30	371
Average	2.5	35		

We insert the information in the table into the formula for the slope:

$$b = \frac{\Sigma xy - n\bar{x}\bar{y}}{\Sigma x^2 - n\bar{x}^2}$$

$$= \frac{371 - (4 \times 2.5 \times 35)}{30 - (4 \times 2.5^2)}$$

$$= 21/5$$

$$= 4.2.$$

Next, we find the intercept, a.

$$a = \bar{y} - b\bar{x}$$

$$= 35 - (4.2 \times 2.5)$$

$$= 35 - 10.5$$

$$= 24.5$$

The line that fits this data best is given by

$$Y = 24.5 + 4.2x,$$

where y = fires, x = the quarter, and the rate of increase in fires is 4.2 per quarter. The forecasts for the next two quarters are given by

$$Y_5 = 24.5 + 4.2(5) = 45.5$$

and

$$Y_6 = 24.5 + 4.2(6) = 49.7.$$

Using AB:POM to Solve This Problem

The forecasting module can do different types of forecasting and can do regression in two different ways. After beginning each new problem, you will be given the option of choosing either time series analysis or multiple regression. Time series analysis includes moving averages, weighted moving averages, exponential smoothing, and least squares/linear regression with one independent variable. Multiple regression does regression for up to six independent variables.

The program will request the number of past periods of data when time series analysis is chosen. In Solved Problem 2, there are four past periods. The program then will set up the data screen and begin by showing the time series methods that are available and the user will be asked to choose one. (The method can easily be changed later.) Screen 4.1 shows the data and solution for Solved Problem 2, part (a). The initial question asked for a simple two-period moving average. The line "n pds-->" is used to enter the number of periods to be used in the moving average—in this case, 2. The data for years 1–4 have been entered in the "Demand(y)" column. (This column can be renamed, if desired.)

The remaining numbers have been computed by AB:POM. Under the data column, the total demand (140) and average demand (35) are displayed. A column labeled "Forecast" has been created and the moving forecasts appear in this column. The final moving forecast (38) appears at the bottom of the column. The last three columns are used for the error analysis. The actual error (Demand − Forecast), the absolute value of the error, and the squared error are displayed. The sum and average

```
┌─Data file:wgsp4-2 ═══════════════════Forecasting ═══════════════════Solution ═
║ Number of past data periods (2-99) 4
║
║                          ══════════════Solved Problem 2(a) ═══════════
║  Method-->Moving averages (Unweighted)
║  n pds-->          2
║
║               Demand(y)        Forecast    Error     |Error|    Error^2
║  qtr 1          28.00
║  qtr 2          36.00
║  qtr 3          33.00           32.00       1.00      1.00       1.00
║  qtr 4          43.00           34.50       8.50      8.50      72.25
║  TOTALS        140.00                       9.50      9.50      73.25
║  AVERAGE        35.00                       4.75      4.75      36.625
║                                            (Bias)    (MAD)      (MSE)
║            Next period forecast=    38.00   Standard error =    6.05
║
║
║
║
║ F1=Summary Table    F3=Graph                      F9=Print      Esc
║ Press <Esc> key to edit data or highlighted key or function key for options
```

SCREEN 4.1

of these columns are presented at the bottom of the columns. The average error (4.75) is the bias, the average absolute error (4.75) is the *MAD*, and the average squared error (36.625) is the mean squared error. The standard error (6.05) is given and is computed as the square root of the *MSE*.

Pressing the **F1** key or the **S** key causes a summary table to appear. Pressing the **F3** key or the **G** key causes a graph to appear.

Screen 4.2 has been created by returning to the top row of the data screen and changing the method to a weighted moving average, which results in a prompt that asks first for the number of periods and then for the weights to be used. We have used a three-period moving average with weights of .45, .35, and .20. The weight on the left, .45, will be applied to the most recent data. The solution format for the weighted moving averages is the same as for the unweighted moving averages.

Part (c) of Solved Problem 2 involves exponential smoothing. Once again, we have gone back to the top to change the method, as seen in Screen 4.3. Selecting exponential smoothing results in a prompt that asks for the smoothing constant, α. In this case, $\alpha = .2$. In addition, we have moved to the "Forecast" column and set the original forecast equal to 30. Once again, the output format is the same as for the previous two methods.

Part (d) of Solved Problem 2 involves linear regression. Screen 4.4 shows that the method has been changed at the top; with regression, there is no need to enter additional information, such as the smoothing constant or the number of periods. In a new column, the periods (x) are numbered 1–4. It is possible to change these numbers, but in most cases it will not be necessary. The output display for regression differs somewhat from that for the other methods in that columns showing x^2 ($x\char`^2$) and $x*y$ have been added. These columns aid the computation of the intercept, *a*, and the

```
┌──Data file:wgsp4-2 ════════════════Forecasting ═══════════════════Solution ═┐
│  Number of past data periods (2-99) 4                                        │
│ ┌═════════════════════════════Solved Problem 2(b) ═══════════════════════════┐
│ │ Method-->Weighted moving averages                                          │
│ │ n pds-->        3                                                          │
│ │ Weights->    0.45      0.35      0.20                                      │
│ │          Demand(y)           Forecast    Error      |Error|     Error^2    │
│ │ qtr 1      28.00                                                           │
│ │ qtr 2      36.00                                                           │
│ │ qtr 3      33.00                                                           │
│ │ qtr 4      43.00              33.05      9.95000    9.95000     99.0024     │
│ │ TOTALS    140.00                         9.95000    9.95000     99.0024     │
│ │ AVERAGE    35.00                         9.95000    9.95000     99.0024     │
│ │                                          (Bias)      (MAD)       (MSE)      │
│ │          Next period forecast=   38.10    Standard error =   9.95000       │
│ │                                                                            │
│ └────────────────────────────────────────────────────────────────────────────┘
│  F1=Summary Table    F3=Graph                        F9=Print     Esc         │
│  Press <Esc> key to edit data or highlighted key or function key for options  │
└──────────────────────────────────────────────────────────────────────────────┘
```

—— SCREEN 4.2 ——

```
┌──Data file:wgsp4-2 ════════════════Forecasting ═══════════════════Solution ═┐
│  Number of past data periods (2-99) 4                                        │
│ ┌═════════════════════════════Solved Problem 2(c) ═══════════════════════════┐
│ │ Method-->Exponential Smoothing                                             │
│ │ alpha(α)  0.200                                                            │
│ │                                                                            │
│ │          Demand(y)           Forecast    Error       Error      Error^2    │
│ │ qtr 1      28.00              30.00                                        │
│ │ qtr 2      36.00              29.60       6.40        6.40       40.96      │
│ │ qtr 3      33.00              30.08       2.12        2.12       4.49440    │
│ │ qtr 4      43.00              31.304      11.696      11.696     136.796    │
│ │ TOTALS    140.00                          20.216      20.216     182.25     │
│ │ AVERAGE    35.00                          6.73867     6.73867    60.7503    │
│ │                                           (Bias)      (MAD)       (MSE)     │
│ │          Next period forecast=  33.6432    Standard error =   7.79425      │
│ │                                                                            │
│ └────────────────────────────────────────────────────────────────────────────┘
│  F1=Summary Table    F3=Graph                        F9=Print     Esc         │
│  Press <Esc> key to edit data or highlighted key or function key for options  │
└──────────────────────────────────────────────────────────────────────────────┘
```

—— SCREEN 4.3 ——

```
┌─Data file:wgsp4-2 ═══════════════Forecasting ═══════════════════Solution ═┐
│ Number of past data periods (2-99) 4                                       │
│  ┌══════════════════════════════Solved Problem 2(d) ════════════════════┐  │
│  │ Method-->Linear Regression/least squares                             │  │
│  │                                                                      │  │
│  │                                                                      │  │
│  │          Demand(y) Period(x)  x^2       x * y      Forecast   Error^2│  │
│  │ qtr 1      28.00       1      1.00       28.00      28.70     .490001 │  │
│  │ qtr 2      36.00       2      4.00       72.00      32.90    9.60999  │  │
│  │ qtr 3      33.00       3      9.00       99.00      37.10     16.81   │  │
│  │ qtr 4      43.00       4     16.00      172.00      41.30      2.89   │  │
│  │ TOTALS    140.00     10.00   30.00      371.00              29.8000   │  │
│  │ AVERAGE    35.00      2.50                                  7.45000   │  │
│  │                                                              (MSE)    │  │
│  │                        Next period forecast=     45.50               │  │
│  │          Regression line = : Y =    24.50 +     4.20 * X             │  │
│  │          Correlation coefficient =     0.8645563  Standard error = 2.729468│  │
│  │                                                                      │  │
│  └──────────────────────────────────────────────────────────────────────┘  │
│                                                                            │
│  F1=Summary Table    F3=Graph                         F9=Print     Esc      │
│  Press <Esc> key to edit data or highlighted key or function key for options│
└────────────────────────────── SCREEN 4.4 ──────────────────────────────────┘
```

slope, b. The totals and averages of the four columns—demand, period, x^2, and $x*y$—
are used in computing the regression line. The line $(24.5 + 4.2x)$ is given at the
bottom, along with the correlation coefficient $(.86)$ and the standard error (2.729).
The *MAD* and bias are not shown but can be seen in the summary table. Remember,
linear regression always generates a bias of 0. It also is possible to use the multiple
regression option rather than the time series to perform the regression. ▬▬▬▬

QUESTIONS

1. Contrast qualitative and quantitative forecasting.

2. Describe the forecasting method of jury of executive opinion. What is its major drawback?

3. Describe the Delphi technique and compare it to the jury of executive opinion technique.

4. Explain the differences between bias, mean absolute deviation, and standard error. In what
cases would mean absolute deviation be a better measure of error than standard error? In what
cases would standard error be better than mean absolute deviation?

5. Explain the concept of lag. In moving averages, how would a larger n versus a smaller n
affect lag? When would a larger n be more favorable than a smaller n?

6. What is the major benefit gained by using exponential smoothing rather than weighted
moving averages?

7. Explain the significance of α in exponential smoothing. What does it mean when α is 0? 1?

8. Explain how exponential smoothing is actually a weighted moving average technique.

9. Give examples of industries that are affected by seasonality. Why would these businesses want to filter out seasonality?

10. Give examples of industries where demand forecasting is dependent on the demand for other products.

11. What happens to our ability to forecast as we forecast for periods farther into the future?

PROBLEMS

1. Logistics Corporation (LoCo) has been using a certain forecasting technique to estimate demand for service. The demands for the past five months and the forecasts that were made prior to each of the five months are as follows.

Month	Forecast	Demand
June	121	130
July	132	125
August	129	140
September	136	135
October	130	132

Compute the bias, standard error, and mean absolute deviation for these data.

bias $= 2.8$; $MSE = 51.2$; $SE = 7.16$; $MAD = 6$

2. Given the data in Problem 1, if the forecast for November is 140, give a 95-percent confidence interval for the forecast.

125.9664 to 154.0336

3. Sam Spade is the president of Garden Products Limited. Over the last five years, he has asked both his vice-president of marketing and his vice-president of operations to provide sales forecasts. The actual sales and the forecasts are given below. Which vice-president is better at forecasting?

Year	Sales	VP, Marketing	VP, Operations
1	167,325	170,000	160,000
2	175,362	170,000	165,000
3	172,536	180,000	170,000
4	156,732	180,000	175,000
5	176,325	165,000	165,000

Operations VP

4. Compute the mean percentage error for the forecasts given by both vice-presidents in Problem 3.

Marketing VP $MPE = -2.26\%$; Operations VP $MPE = 1.30\%$

5. In the last four years, the number of inches of rain in May has been 2.2 (year 1), 2.6 (year 2), 2.4 (year 3), and 3.0 (year 4). Predict the number of inches of rain for the next May (year 5), using a three-year moving average.

2.667 inches

6. The Undergraduate Hospital is considering the purchase of a new ambulance. The decision will rest partly on the anticipated mileage to be driven next year. The miles driven during the past five years are as follows.

Year	Mileage
1	3,000
2	4,000
3	3,400
4	3,800
5	3,700

3,750 miles
bias = 33.33
MAD = 100

(a) Forecast the mileage for next year using a two-year moving average.
(b) Using a two-year moving average on all of the data, find the bias.
(c) Using a two-year moving average on all of the data, find the mean absolute deviation.

7. The following gives the number of pints of Type A blood used at Woodlawn Hospital in the past six weeks.

Week of	Pints Used
August 31	360
September 7	389
September 14	410
September 21	381
September 28	368
October 5	374

374.33 pints
412.9148 pints

(a) Forecast the demand for the week of October 12 using a three-week moving average.
(b) How much blood should the hospital have in stock to be 99-percent confident that it has enough available during the week of October 12?

8. TRS, Inc. uses an X63 chip in its computers. The prices for the chip during the last twelve months have been as shown.

Month	Price per Chip
January	$1.80
February	1.67
March	1.70
April	1.85
May	1.90
June	1.87
July	1.80
August	1.83
September	1.70
October	1.65
November	1.70
December	1.75

See graph in Instructor's Section.
See graph in Instructor's Section.
two-month average

(a) Use a two-month moving average on all of the data and plot the averages and the prices.
(b) Use a three-month moving average and add the three-month plot to the graph created in part (a).
(c) Which is better (using the mean absolute deviation): the two-month average or the three-month average?

2.74 inches

9. For the data in Problem 5, compute the forecast for next May using a three-year weighted moving average with weights of .5, .3, .2.

10. For the data in Problem 6, use a two-year weighted moving average with weights of .6 and .4 and compute the following.

(a) the forecast for year 6
(b) the bias
(c) the mean absolute deviation

3,740 miles
bias = 6.67
MAD = 140

11. For the data in Problem 7, use a three-week weighted moving average with weights of .6, .3, and .1 and compute the following.

(a) the forecast for the week of October 12
(b) the amount of blood that the hospital should have available to be 99-percent confident that it has enough on hand during the week of October 12

372.9 pints
411.51 pints

12. For the data in Problem 8, compute the forecasts for each month using a two-month weighted moving average with weights (.6, .4) and a two-month weighted moving average with weights (.7, .3). Which set of weights is better using mean absolute deviation?

(.7, .3)

13. For the data in Problem 5, compute the forecast for next May using exponential smoothing with $F_{year1} = 2.2$ and $\alpha = .1$.

2.33 inches

14. For the data in Problem 6, do the following.

(a) Compute the forecast for year 6 using exponential smoothing with $F_1 = 3,000$ and $\alpha = .5$.
(b) Compute the bias using the forecasts made in part (a).
(c) Compute the mean absolute deviation using the forecasts made in part (a).

3,663 miles
bias = 331
MAD = 381.25

15. Use the data in Problem 7 for the following.

(a) Compute the forecast for the week of October 12 using exponential smoothing with $F_{8/31} = 360$ and $\alpha = .2$.
(b) How much blood should the hospital have in stock to be 99-percent confident that it has enough available during the week of October 12?

374.26 pints

436 pints

16. For the data in Problem 8, compute the forecasts for each month using $F_{January} = \$1.80$ and $\alpha = .1, \alpha = .3$, and $\alpha = .5$. Which α is the best using mean absolute deviation?

$\alpha = .5$

17. The following gives the number of accidents that have occurred on a state's throughway during the last four months.

Month	Number of Accidents
January	30
February	40
March	60
April	90

Forecast the number of accidents that will occur in May, using linear regression.

105 accidents

18. Attendance at the past five Army vs. Navy football games is given as follows. Forecast next year's attendance, using linear regression.

Year	Attendance
1	77,000
2	80,000
3	93,000
4	90,000
5	98,000

103,200

19. The following gives the number of plant closings in the Northeast during the past five years.

Year	Closings
1	140
2	160
3	190
4	200
5	210

234 closings
SE = 5.657

(a) Forecast the number of plant closings for next year, using linear regression.
(b) Compute the standard error when using linear regression.

20. The temperatures for the last six days, measured at midnight at City Hall, are as follows.

Day	Date	Temperature
Sunday	12/18	20°
Saturday	12/17	21°
Friday	12/16	18°
Thursday	12/15	23°
Wednesday	12/14	22°
Tuesday	12/13	23°

Christmas: 14.92; New Year's: 10.32
Christmas: (11.387, 18.461); New Year's: (6.787, 13.861)

(a) Forecast the temperatures for Christmas and New Year's days, using linear regression.
(b) To be reasonably (99-percent) confident, allow a 2.58 standard error of estimate and predict the lower and upper limits on temperatures for Christmas and New Year's days.

21. Pear Computer, Inc. is a manufacturer of microcomputers. The sales of the Pear 88 computer over the last five years are as follows.

Year	Sales
1	2,400
2	3,200
3	2,700
4	3,000
5	3,900

Forecast next year's sales, using the method indicated.

3,200
3,675
3,270
3,880

(a) three-year moving average
(b) two-year weighted moving average (.75, .25)
(c) exponential smoothing (forecast for year 4 = 3,000, α = .3)
(d) linear regression

22. The following presents the data for the most recent five years for spring rainfall (in inches) and fall harvests of corn (in bushels per acre).

Year	Rainfall	Harvest
1	6.4	510
2	8.0	616
3	7.2	543
4	5.2	465
5	6.8	530

(a) Compute the linear equation for the fall harvest as a function of spring rainfall.

(b) If the spring rainfall in year 6 is 5.9 inches, what can we expect the size of the fall harvest to be?

$Y = 185.6448 + 51.66X$

489.79 bushels/acre

23. Moreland School District is trying to forecast its needs for kindergarten teachers for the next five years. The district has data on births and kindergarten enrollments for the past ten years. The enrollments lag the births by five years. Forecast kindergarten enrollments for the next five years, given the following data from the past ten years.

Year	Births	Enrollments
1	131	161
2	192	127
3	158	134
4	93	141
5	107	112
6	130	148
7	128	188
8	124	155
9	97	110
10	147	124

year 11: 140.3748 students; year 12: 138.8828 students; year 13: 135.8988 students; year 14: 115.7568 students; year 15: 153.0568

24. Central States Electric Company estimates its demand trend line (in millions of kilowatt hours) to be

$$D = 77 + 0.43Q,$$

where Q refers to the sequential quarter number and $Q = 1$ for the winter of 1972. In addition, the multiplicative seasonal factors are as follows.

Quarter	Factor
Winter	.8
Spring	1.1
Summer	1.4
Fall	.7

Forecast energy use for the four quarters of 1997, beginning with winter.

winter: 96.344; spring: 132.946; summer: 170.558; fall: 85.204

25. The sales of Gemini lawn mowers for the last three years are given by season as follows.

Year	Season	Sales
1	Spring/Summer	26,825
	Fall/Winter	5,722
2	Spring/Summer	28,630
	Fall/Winter	7,633
3	Spring/Summer	30,255
	Fall/Winter	8,745

$Y = 21,748 - 1,080X$
Trend coefficient $(-1,080)$ is negative, but sales are increasing.
Use two separate regressions or multiple regression.

(a) Use linear regression to find the best fit line.

(b) What is wrong with this line?

(c) How should forecasts be made for year 4?

26. Perform a time series analysis for the following sales data. Use the multiplicative model.

	Day				
Week	Mon.	Tue.	Wed.	Thur.	Fri.
1	100	90	80	90	100
2	110	100	90	100	110
3	120	110	100	110	120

See Instructor's Section.

See Instructor's Section.

$Y = 86.1293 + 1.992X$
$Y = 88 + 2X$

$Y = 87.714 + 1.7857X$
See Instructor's Section.
See Instructor's Section.

See Instructor's Section.
2.3538, 2.5424, 2.3023,
5.0526, .6585, − .8936,
− .5294, .4186
process in control

year 11: 133 students; year
12: 129; year 13: 124; year
14: 103; year 15: 135

$Y = 14,742 +$
1,613 × year
{ + 10,602 if spring/
summer
− 10,602 if fall/
winter}

27. For the data in Problem 26, perform a time series analysis using the additive model.

28. Use the model indicated to find the trend for the data in Problem 26.

(a) multiplicative model
(b) additive model

29. Use the raw (unadjusted) data in Problem 26.

(a) Find the least squares line.
(b) Find the seasonal factors.
(c) Forecast demand for next week.

30. For the data given in Problem 3, compute the tracking signals using a two-year *MAD* for both vice-presidents.

31. Use the two-month forecasts found in Problem 8.

(a) Compute the tracking signals, using a three-month *MAD*.
(b) Using limits of 2 *MAD*s, determine if the forecasting process is in control.

32. Use a multiple regression software package to solve Problem 23. Include time as an independent variable.

33. Use a multiple regression software package for the data given in Problem 25, with season and year as the two independent variables, to find the regression line. Interpret the results.

COMPUTER CASE STUDY 4.1: HUMAN RESOURCES INC.

Human Resources Incorporated (HR Inc.) is a small company that conducts seminars on productivity issues for corporate executives. HR Inc. focuses on improving the quality of work and the attitude of workers in service organizations. The company tries to provide seminar participants with the tools essential for dealing with issues and parameters that are hard to measure. Originally, HR's seminars were geared toward hospital administration—specifically, topics included how to motivate nursing staffs and how to provide quality care for patients. Over the years, the demand for seminars has grown—as has the company's client base. The client base now includes insurance executives who want to improve the quality and productivity of their claims recorders, travel agency directors who want to improve the service of their agencies, and managers of secretarial pools who wish to improve the attitudes in their offices.

HR Inc. has offered one seminar in each season since 1983. Each seminar lasts for one week and is typically given at a resort or spa. The location has varied over the years, but the winter seminars have tended to be in Florida, the spring seminars have been given in Chicago, the summer seminars have been given in the Carolinas and the fall seminars have been given in the Northeast corridor (between Washington and Boston).

The table shows the number of persons attending seminars since their inception.

Year	Quarter	Participants
1983	Winter	35
	Spring	44
	Summer	54
	Fall	49
1984	Winter	68
	Spring	61
	Summer	61
	Fall	75
1985	Winter	70
	Spring	62
	Summer	70
	Fall	74
1986	Winter	64
	Spring	72
	Summer	76
	Fall	72
1987	Winter	73
	Spring	62
	Summer	85
	Fall	72
1988	Winter	89
	Spring	66
	Summer	82
	Fall	92
1989	Winter	96
	Spring	78
	Summer	95
	Fall	94
1990	Winter	93
	Spring	80
	Summer	88
	Fall	101
1991	Winter	95
	Spring	82
	Summer	89
	Fall	87

HR Inc. is considering a major expansion program. Before committing to this expansion program, however, the company would like to be able to forecast its success and the size of the programs in the four regions. HR is interested in determining if they should expand in all four seasons/regions or if they should concentrate on one. They would like to know if the growth has been even in all four regions or not. Find a forecasting model that best suits HR Inc.'s goals.

REFERENCES

Bails, D. G., and L. C. Peppers. *Business Fluctuations: Forecasting Techniques and Applications.* Englewood Cliffs, N.J.: Prentice-Hall, 1982.

Barnett, A. "Misapplications Reviews: An Introduction," *Interfaces* 12, no. 5 (October 1982):47–49.

Chambers, J. C., S. K. Mullick, and D. D. Smith. "How to Choose the Right Forecasting Method," *Harvard Business Review* (July–August 1971):45–74.

Clark, J. J., ed. *The Management of Forecasts.* New York: St. John's University Press, 1969.

Freund, J. E., and F. J. Williams. *Elementary Business Statistics: The Modern Approach.* 4th ed. Englewood Cliffs, N.J.: Prentice-Hall, 1982.

Fusfeld, A. R., and R. N. Foster. "The Delphi Technique: Survey and Comment," *Business Horizons* 14, no. 3 (June 1971).

Murray, T. J. "Delphi Methodologies: A Review and Critique," *Urban Systems* 4 (1979):153–158.

Sackman, H. *Delphi Critique.* Lexington, Mass.: Lexington Books, D. C. Heath, 1975.

Smith, B. T. *Focus Forecasting: Computer Techniques for Inventory Control.* Boston: CBI Publishing Co. Inc., 1978.

Wheelwright, S. C., and S. Makridakis. *Forecasting Methods for Management.* 4th ed. New York: John Wiley and Sons, 1985.

P A R T
T H R E E

MODIFYING CAPACITY

C H A P T E R

5

O U T L I N E

FACILITY LOCATION

- To introduce the factors on which location should be based
- To enumerate the current trends in location
- To provide specific methods for analyzing the location decision

INTRODUCTION

Of all the decisions made by management, none will have more serious ramifications than those regarding where to locate the facility and how to design the facility. Both the location and the design require large capital investments in land, buildings, and machinery. Such decisions are long term, and the firm must be willing to live with them. To give an idea of the decisions' long-term nature, when General Foods consolidated its Jello operations by closing four plants and opening one new plant, its cost analysis indicated a payback period of over ten years—that is, the move would not show a profit until more than ten years in the future (see Whitman and Schmidt, 1966). It is of extreme importance for decision makers to exercise a great deal of care when choosing a new location or designing a new facility. The penalty for bad choices can be much greater than the reward for good choices.

Recent changes in world politics have made location an even more important and difficult decision. For one thing, there are more new location possibilities today than there were ten or fifteen years ago, when it would have been unthinkable for a foreign company to consider building a facility in China, the Soviet Union, or Eastern Europe. With Chevron, RJR Nabisco, Eastman Kodak, and Johnson & Johnson, among others, considering ventures in the Soviet Union, it may not be long before citizens there find Ritz crackers, Winston cigarettes, and the like filling their once nearly empty store shelves. Already, Muscovites can enjoy McDonald's hamburgers or bottles of Pepsi-Cola, and residents of Beijing can dine at that city's Kentucky Fried Chicken restaurant, the largest in the world.

Political change is not synonymous with expanding markets or location possibilities, however. The Chinese government's handling of student protests in Beijing's Tiananmen Square in the spring of 1989 suddenly made locating in China much less attractive to foreign companies. Uncertainty in the Soviet Union has had a similarly chilling effect on foreign investment there, although the failed coup attempt by Communist party hard-liners in August 1991 clarified somewhat the nation's economic and political future. Despite an improving political situation in South Africa, there is still pressure on American firms not to do business in South Africa until apartheid is completely dismantled and racial equality is assured.

We must remember that in today's global economy, the United States, too, is viewed as a prime new location by many foreign firms. For example, eight Japanese automakers now have plants or joint ventures in the United States, producing 2.1 million automobiles per year. And the Sony Corporation has manufacturing facilities from coast to coast: San Diego, California, and New Stanton, Pennsylvania (picture tubes); Terre Haute, Indiana (compact discs); Delano, Pennsylvania, and Fort Lauderdale, Florida (audio equipment); and Dothan, Alabama (floppy disks).

THE LOCATION DECISION

There are several scenarios that would necessitate the building of a new plant or facility. If the company is initiating a new product or service, then there are, of course, no existing production or service facilities, and some location must be found. If a company decides to manufacture a new product, and its current facilities do not have the technology to make the product, the company must find another location. If the technology to manufacture a product changes, then either the existing plant should be redesigned to accommodate the new technology or, as might be better, the manufacturing should be relocated. General Motors realized that a car (Saturn) whose assembly would make maximum use of robotics and automation could not be built at an existing plant. Similarly, for a new or old product, it is possible that current capacity is insufficient to accommodate an increase in demand. It is also possible for the market for a product to change, necessitating a change in location. Similarly, the location of the raw materials may change. Witness the lumber industry, which has gradually shifted from the Northeast (Maine) to the Northwest (Oregon and Washington). If labor costs in a region are too high, then a company might find a location change to be advantageous economically.

reasons for location decisions

The scenarios we have described are listed in Table 5.1, along with the different options that are available in each case. Although building a new facility is always a possibility, other solutions may be feasible as well. The choice among these options can be made with the help of the analytical approaches provided in Chapter 3, especially break-even analysis.

One common problem is insufficient capacity. An obvious way to increase capacity is to build a new facility. In fact, a distinct advantage of a new facility is that it can be built in a different city, which may reduce shipping costs to customers. However, other options do exist and must be explored before the decision to build a new facility is made.

expand capacity

If an operation is operating less than full time—that is, less than twenty-four hours per day or less than seven days per week—then the first two options are obvious and

TABLE 5.1 Scenarios requiring a facility decision

Scenario	Problem	Possible solutions
New company	No existing facility	Build, rent, or buy
New product	No existing technology	Redesign layout, build, or expand
New or old product	Insufficient capacity	Build, expand, subcontract, work overtime, or add shift
Old product	Reduction in market demand	Redesign layout, close, or lower wages
Old product	Change in market location	Close or move
Old product	Increase in labor and/or technology costs	Move or union concessions

relatively simple to implement. As was noted in Chapter 3, the capacity may be increased by either of the following:

- working overtime or
- adding shifts.

If the plant is operating at capacity, then at least two options other than adding a new facility exist:

- subcontracting work or
- expanding facility.

Expansion in the same location is a typical method for community services. For example, many schools have annexes, many hospitals have new wings, and many governmental buildings expand. However, it would be unusual for the Philadelphia city government to build a second city office building across the river in Camden, New Jersey, even though it would be less costly than building on a site in the center of Philadelphia.

The cost analysis of the options of working overtime, adding a shift, and subcontracting typically is performed using the cost–volume analysis tools developed in Chapter 3. The analysis of expansion versus new location involves the assessment of capital investments and requires the financial analysis presented in Appendix A. Furthermore, building a new facility, expanding an existing facility, or redesigning an existing facility are all long-term projects that require the careful coordination of all planning and construction tasks to be performed. This coordination requires project scheduling analysis, which is presented in Chapter 10. Of course, all location and layout decisions are functions of the forecasted demands (Chapter 4) as well as the costs and nonquantitative factors that are discussed later in this chapter.

CURRENT TRENDS IN LOCATION

Teaching Suggestion 5.1: Examples of Trends. See the Instructor's Section for details.

Before examining the factors that are relevant to the location decision, let us consider some of the current trends in plant location.

LOCATION IN FOREIGN COUNTRIES

Recently, many companies have located their plants in foreign countries, as can be seen in Table 5.2, Table 5.3, and Table 5.4. With respect to the United States, this international locating has gone in both directions: Foreign companies, such as Volkswagen, have located plants in the United States, while U.S. companies, such as Ford and IBM, have located plants outside the United States. There are three primary reasons for a company to locate in a foreign country. One is to meet the objective of being near the **market proximity** market, or achieving **market proximity,** which is especially important in service industries. For example, McDonald's cannot sell many hamburgers in Munich if the nearest branch is in Pittsburgh. A second major factor that typically leads U.S. companies to **labor costs** locate plants outside of the United States, is labor costs (see Table 5.5 on page 199). For example, in the early 1980s, a large appliance manufacturer closed a plant in California that manufactured metal irons but opened three plants in foreign countries to produce plastic irons. Product design was the reason given by the manufacturer, but we note that foreign labor costs are less than half of labor costs in California. As discussed in Chapter 2, a third major factor in locating a plant in a particular country is **gain access to markets** **market access,** the ability to gain access to markets that may be closed by import limits or that may be limited by high tariffs. Japanese auto manufacturers have done this very successfully by building plants in the United States.

TABLE 5.2 U.S. companies located in foreign countries

Company	Location(s)
Abbott Laboratories	Sweden, Switzerland, and Mexico
Avon	Ireland, Portugal, and Brazil
Black & Decker	Italy, Great Britain, and New Zealand
Bristol-Myers Company	South Africa and Spain
Chrysler Corporation	Canada and Mexico
Control Data Corporation	Belgium, Great Britain, and Germany
Dow Chemical Company	Canada, Hong Kong, and Australia
E. I. DuPont De Nemours Company	France and Luxembourg
Eastman Kodak	Algeria, Argentina, and Austria
Exxon Corporation	Germany, Netherlands, and Japan
Ford Motor Company	Australia, Belgium, and Brazil
General Electric Company	Canada
General Mills, Inc.	Canada and France
General Motors Corporation	Canada, Brazil, and Spain
Gillette Company	Canada and Philippines
Goodyear Tire	Thailand and Taiwan
Hewlett Packard Company	Mexico
IBM	Mexico
International Telegraph & Telephone	Argentina, Australia, and Canada
Johnson & Johnson	Belgium, Mexico, and Puerto Rico
McDonald's Corporation	France, Australia, and Great Britain
Monsanto	Mexico, Brazil, and Canada
NCR Corporation	Mexico
Nike Inc.	South Korea and China
Owens-Corning Fiberglass Corporation	Belgium, Brazil, and France
Quaker Oats Company	Italy, Germany, and Great Britain
Readers Digest	Hong Kong and Australia
R. J. Reynolds Industries, Inc.	Mexico, Canada, and Great Britain
Revlon Inc.	Australia, Japan, Great Britain, and Canada
Rohm & Haas Company	Argentina, Brazil, Canada, and Spain
Swift & Company	Mexico and Canada
United Technologies Corporation	Canada, Spain, and Great Britain
Wang Laboratories	Great Britain (including Scotland and Ireland)
Whirlpool Corporation	Brazil and Canada
Xerox Corporation	Canada and Mexico

Source: Directory of Corporate Affiliations 1990/91 (Wilmette, Ill.: National Register Publishing Co., Inc., June, 1990).

TABLE 5.3 Foreign companies located in the United States

Company	State	Nation of Origin
Adidas	Pennsylvania, New Jersey	West Germany
Allied Breweries Ltd.	Maryland	Great Britain
BASF	Virginia, New Jersey	West Germany
Babcock & Wilcox Ltd.	New Jersey	West Germany
Bayer AG	Illinois	West Germany
Bridgestone Tire Company	Tennessee	Japan
British Petroleum	Alaska	Great Britain
Cadillac Fairview Corporation Ltd.	California	Canada
Capitol Records, Inc.	Virginia	Great Britain
Ciba-Geigy Ltd.	New York	Sweden
Coats Patons Ltd.	Virginia, South Carolina	Scotland
DeLaval	Missouri	Sweden
Distillers Company, Ltd.	New Jersey	Scotland
Dunlop Company, Ltd.	Alabama	Great Britain
Fiat SpA	Wisconsin	Italy
Frankona American	Missouri	West Germany
Grinstead Products Inc.	Missouri, Kansas	Denmark
Hitachi Ltd.	Georgia	Japan
Honda Motor Company	Ohio	Japan
J. Lyons (Baskin Robbins)	California	Hong Kong
Jardine, Matheson, & Company, Ltd.	Illinois	Great Britain
Kawasaki Jukogyo KK	Nevada	Japan
Kiwi International Company, Ltd.	Pennsylvania	Australia
Mazda	Missouri	Japan
Mitsubishi	Washington, California	Japan
Nestle, SA	Ohio	Switzerland
Nippon Electric Corporation	California	Japan
Nippon Kokan	Michigan	Japan
Nissan Motor Company	Tennessee, Illinois	Japan
Rolls Royce, Ltd.	Virginia	Great Britain
S Persons & Son Ltd.	Florida	Great Britain
SKF AB	Florida, Pennsylvania	Sweden
SAAB-Scania AB	Arizona	Sweden
Sanyo Electric Company, Ltd.	Texas, Pennsylvania	Great Britain
Shell Transport & Trading Company	Missouri	Great Britain
Shubrooks Inc.	North Carolina	Sweden
Sony	Missouri, New Jersey	Japan
Toyota	California	Japan
United Bisquits	Pennsylvania, Illinois	Great Britain
Volvo	New Jersey	Sweden

Sources: Directory of Corporate Affiliations 1990/91 (Wilmette, Ill.: National Register Publishing Co., Inc., 1990) and *International Directory of Corporate Affiliations 1987/1988* (Wilmette, Ill.: National Register Publishing Co., Inc., 1987).

TABLE 5.4 Foreign companies located in other foreign countries

Company	Nationality	Location
Alcan Aluminum Ltd.	Canada	Guinea, India, and Jamaica
Alfa-Lavai AB	Sweden	Netherlands, Norway, and Spain
BASF	West Germany	Canada, Belgium, and Brazil
British Petroleum	Great Britain	Canada
Chloride Group PLC	Great Britain	Denmark, India, and Singapore
Ciba-Geigy, Ltd.	Sweden	Argentina, Austria, and Brazil
Coats Patons, PLC	Scotland	Canada
Cycles Peugeot	France	West Germany, Spain, and Italy
Fijitsu Fanuc Ltd.	Japan	Luxembourg and Great Britain
General Electric Company, PLC	Great Britain	Hong Kong, India, and Bangladesh
Heineken NV	Netherlands	Zaire, Italy, and Singapore
Honda Motor Company	Japan	Belgium
I. P. Sharp Associates, Ltd.	Canada	Australia, Ireland, and Japan
Japan Victor Company	Japan	West Germany
Krauss Maffei	West Germany	Austria, Italy, and France
Nestle S.A.	Switzerland	Norway, West Germany, and Spain
Nippon Electric Corporation	Japan	Taiwan, Korea, and Singapore
SAAB-Scania AB	Sweden	Finland and France
Samsung Electronics	Japan	Mexico, Great Britain, and Spain
Sony	Japan	Great Britain and Switzerland
Swedish Match AB	Sweden	Argentina, Belgium, and Brazil
TDK Electronics Ltd.	Japan	Korea, Brazil, and West Germany
Toyota	Japan	Australia
Unilever	Great Britain	Netherlands and Argentina
United Bisquits	United Kingdom	France, Spain, and Belgium
Volvo	Sweden	Netherlands and Belgium
Yuasa Battery Company	Japan	Wales

SUBURBAN LOCATIONS

Years ago, many plants were located near the centers of major cities. The primary reason for this was that the transportation facilities that were essential for the plants' operations were located in or near the city. In particular, waterways and the railroads joined cities together and allowed for efficient trade. Moreover, transportation from the suburb to the city was a major effort. Now, however, most regions have transportation systems and/or highway networks that allow for quick, easy, and inexpensive transportation through and/or around a city. Because transportation in the suburbs is no longer a problem, the cities have no hold on companies' location decisions. In fact, quite the contrary is true because, when compared with their suburbs, cities tend to have more transportation congestion, higher taxes for both the companies and their employees, higher crime rates, more physical deterioration, and a smaller quantity of

---

APPLICATIONS OF P/OM

Low Costs and Weak Dollar Make U.S. Sites Attractive

The United States has quietly become one of the world's low-cost producers. This is due partly to the return of the dollar to competitive levels and partly to sweeping and painful structural changes in the U.S. economy. For many firms, U.S. sites are looking more and more attractive.

Illinois Tools, based in Glenview, Illinois, recently scrapped its plans to build another nail factory in Germany. It now costs the company about 20 percent more to make a nail in Germany than in the United States. It also costs twice as much to add capacity in Germany. Not only are the bricks and mortar more expensive there, but companies are required to take on more commitments in benefits and job guarantees for their workers. "We can produce nails here with less overhead and fewer social costs," says W. James Farrell, an executive vice-president of Illinois Tools.

Osram, a subsidiary of Siemens, the German electronics giant, recently poured $3 million into a plant in Maybrook, New York, that makes light bulbs and auto headlamps. Osram expects to ship about one-fifth of its production to European and Asian automakers. "From an efficiency standpoint, we stack up very well to our German counterparts, sometimes to their surprise," says Paul Caramagna, vice-president of Osram.

Source: New York Times, April 21, 1991.

---

more expensive land for development. The problems in cities are viewed by some as indicative of a cycle of never-ending deterioration. As more companies flee the cities for the suburbs, the cities become less attractive locales for new or existing companies. This causes even more companies to consider moving to the suburbs. We note that, although there has been much movement of manufacturing companies to the suburbs, the void left by their departure has been filled partially by service and governmental industries, spurring revitalization that is improving some inner cities.

INDUSTRIAL PARKS

In order to separate industrial plants from residences yet still attract companies, many suburbs have built or supported **industrial parks.** Industrial parks are large tracts of land that are zoned for, built for, and dedicated exclusively to industries. The major advantage to companies is that, because plants are located in the same general area, raw materials for one plant may well be produced in a nearby plant, which takes advantage of the just-in-time philosophy. Furthermore, community attitudes toward a plant typically are much more hospitable when the plant is isolated from residential areas, yet still contributes to the community's tax base.

just-in-time philosophy

SINGLE-STORY BUILDINGS

Another advantage to suburban industrial parks is that they make a great deal more land available at a lower cost, enabling companies to build single-story buildings rather than the multi-story buildings found in urban centers. This greatly facilitates materials handling—in particular, by eliminating the need for freight elevators. Furthermore, it is useful to locate heavy machinery on the ground floor rather than on upper floors, where support for this machinery is more difficult—and, thus, more expensive—to

TABLE 5.5 Hourly compensation costs for manufacturing production workers in countries with costs below U.S. minimum wage

Country	Hourly Wage*
Brazil	$1.49
Mexico	1.57
Venezuela	3.78
Hong Kong	2.43
Korea	2.46
Singapore	2.67
Taiwan	2.71
Portugal	2.73
Turkey	.41

Source: Handbook of Labor Statistics (Washington, D.C.: U.S. Department of Labor, Bureau of Labor Statistics, August 1989).

provide. As is the case with suburban locations, the advantage of single-story buildings is realized almost exclusively by manufacturing industries. This is another factor that contributes to the recent concentration of service industries in the high-rise buildings of our cities.

DECENTRALIZATION

In order to serve markets that are widely disbursed and to minimize shipping costs, many companies use a technique called **decentralization.** To put it another way, they invest in multiple locations. A second benefit of having multiple locations is that a local strike at one plant will not necessarily close the operations of the other plants. A third advantage is the increased product visibility achieved by being viewed as a "local" product in more than one community.

LOCATING IN THE SUNBELT

During the past two decades, there have been many articles written regarding the movement of companies to the South and Southwest. Therefore, one may be forgiven for thinking that this trend is recent; however, it began shortly after World War II, as evidenced by McLaughlin and Robock in *Why Industry Moves South,* written in 1949. The dominating factor is that the wage rate in the South is (on average) lower than the wage rate in the Northeast and Midwest. For example, in 1991, the average hourly wage for manufacturing in Flint was $18.37, while in San Antonio it was $8.12 (see Table 5.6). Energy costs and availability are also major factors in the move south, as cited by General Motors when it located its Saturn plant in Spring Hill, Tennessee. A

Transparency Master 5.1: Wage Rates.

TABLE 5.6 Wage levels in manufacturing for selected areas, 1991

Area	Average Hourly Earnings
Flint, Michigan	$18.37
Rochester, New York	13.09
St. Louis, Missouri	12.93
Philadelphia, Pennsylvania	12.28
Cleveland, Ohio	12.24
Milwaukee, Wisconsin	12.11
Pittsburgh, Pennsylvania	11.53
Anchorage, Alaska	11.25
Duluth, Minnesota	11.19
Lincoln, Nebraska	10.87
Atlanta, Georgia	10.86
Portland, Maine	10.48
Salem, Oregon	10.09
Knoxville, Tennessee	9.77
Jackson, Mississippi	9.63
Binghamton, New York	9.51
Asheville, North Carolina	8.95
San Antonio, Texas	8.12
Fayetteville, Arkansas	7.82
Miami, Florida	7.58
San Juan, Puerto Rico	6.29

Source: Employment and Earnings, vol. 38, no. 5 (Washington, D.C.: U.S. Department of Labor, Bureau of Labor Statistics, May 1991).

perceived better lifestyle and lower cost of living are other concerns for companies striving to attract and retain qualified employees. Table 5.7 presents a regional comparison of the changes in manufacturing employment that took place during the 1980s.

TAKEOVER OF OLD FACILITIES

The general decline in manufacturing since the 1970s has led to a great number of plant closings. Often, when a plant closes, it is taken over by a different company in the same or similar industry. Some examples of such plant takeovers are presented in Table 5.8. Due to the rapid expansion of service industries, many of the older factories that were closed have been converted to office buildings or shops for use by service industries. One of the earliest and most famous examples of such conversions is the Ghirardelli Square shopping complex in San Francisco, which is on the site of the former Ghirardelli Chocolate factory. The replacement of one service facility by another service facility is actually the most common occurrence of this phenomenon. We recognize the architecture of many corner stores of all kinds as being that of former gas stations. Many of the W. T. Grant stores that closed became Woolworths and now are K-Mart, Target, Wal-Mart, or other similar stores. Another frequently encoun-

TABLE 5.7 Regional comparison of changes in population and manufacturing

Region	Population Change (1980–1989)	Manufacturing Employment Change (1980–1988)
New England (Maine, New Hampshire, Vermont, Massachusetts, Rhode Island, Connecticut)	+5.7%	−11.4%
Middle Atlantic (New York, New Jersey, Pennsylvania)	+2.6%	−6.5%
East North Central (Ohio, Indiana, Illinois, Michigan, Wisconsin)	+1.5%	−10.8%
South Atlantic (Delaware, Maryland, District of Columbia, Virginia, North Carolina, South Carolina, Georgia, Florida)	+16.7%	+4.4%
East South Central (West Virginia, Kentucky, Tennessee, Alabama, Mississippi)	+5.0%	+2.6%
West South Central (Arkansas, Louisiana, Oklahoma, Texas)	+13.7%	−8.5%
Mountain (Montana, Idaho, Wyoming, Colorado, New Mexico, Arizona, Utah, Nevada)	+18.8%	+11.9%
Pacific (Washington, Oregon, California, Alaska, Hawaii)	+20.4%	+7.0%

Sources: Statistical Abstract of the United States, 1990 (Washington, D.C.: U.S. Department of Commerce, Bureau of the Census) and *Handbook of Labor Statistics* (Washington, D.C.: U.S. Department of Labor, Bureau of Labor Statistics, January 1990).

tered facility takeover occurs at airports, when one airline takes over the gates formerly used by another.

LOCATION OF SUPPLIERS CLOSE TO USERS

One of the reasons that governors were so anxious to have GM's Saturn plant located in their state is that, not only would GM build a plant there, but the suppliers of components to GM also would build plants there. This is due to the just-in-time production philosophy that is pervading industries. Manufacturers do not want the raw materials or component parts delivered much sooner than they are needed. The proper timing of deliveries is much easier to accomplish if the suppliers are located next door to the users. We will discuss how this just-in-time philosophy is used in the planning of shipments when we present information about distribution networks in Chapter 6 and when we deal with materials requirements planning in Chapter 14.

just-in-time and location

LOCATIONAL FACTORS

We presented several important locational factors in our discussion of the history of facility location. In this section, we present, in order, regional factors, community factors, and site factors. Regional, community, and site factors are not independent, how-

TABLE 5.8   Selected plant takeovers

Name	Product	Former Owner	Location
Monfort of Colorado, Inc.	Meat processing	Swift & Company	Shenyant City, China
Sanyo Electric Company	Televisions	N. V. Phillips	Grand Lake, Nebraska
Bridgestone Tire Ltd.	Tires	Firestone	LaVergne, Tennessee
Devon Apparel	Sportswear	Nicholson File Company	Philadelphia, Pennsylvania
Adidas	Shoes	Brierwood Shoe Corporation	Kutztown, Pennsylvania
Toyota Motor Corporation	Cars	General Motors	Fremont, California
Nippon Kokan	Steel	Ford Motor Company	Dearborn, Michigan
Manville Corporation	Forest products	Crown Zellerbach Corporation	Joyce, Louisiana
Volkswagen	Autos	Chrysler	New Stanton, Pennsylvania
Sony	Picture tubes	Volkswagen	New Stanton, Pennsylvania

ever. We present them in this order because that is how they typically are considered in the plant location decision-making process. That is, first we decide on the region in which to locate, then we choose the community within that region, and finally we choose the site within the community.

REGIONAL FACTORS

Teaching Suggestion 5.2: Lifestyle Choice. See the Instructor's Section for details.

The term *region* has several meanings, depending on the type of company that is analyzing the location problem. For an international corporation, region typically means a continent or country. For a national corporation, region usually indicates a section of the country or state or province. For a local concern (such as banking), region may mean a county or city.

MARKET LOCATION

primary location factor (service)

It may be of utmost importance to locate the operation near the customers. In service industries, market location usually is the primary location factor. In manufacturing industries, the problems associated with transporting the finished goods to the customers make market location important. Such problems may be of several types. For example, in general, the greater the distance an item is shipped, the more it costs to ship the item. However, since airline deregulation, the price per flight is not proportional to the distance per flight. Today, it frequently is less expensive to ship (or fly) from city A to city B than from city A to city C, even though the distance between city A and city B is greater than the distance between city A and city C.

fragile or perishable products

Aside from the cost of shipping, there are other shipping factors that necessitate locating operations close to the market. If the finished product is fragile, then transporting the goods a greater distance increases the risk of damaging or destroying them. If the product is perishable, then the company cannot afford the long shipment time. This is precisely why bakeries and dairies have local plants. Other products that tend to be near their markets are those that require ubiquitous (readily available) resources and increase in bulk during production. For example, the production of bottled or canned soft drinks requires syrup and water, mostly water. Because water is available everywhere, most cities have local bottling plants. It would be foolish to bottle Coca-Cola in Atlanta for sales in Los Angeles, paying for shipment of water from Atlanta to Los Angeles. In addition, glass (as opposed to cans or plastic) is fragile; to avoid breakage, products in glass bottles or jars may need to be packaged near the market.

Locating near the market usually is important when the company is a service company, such as a hospital, gas station, restaurant, hotel, or company that produces custom-made goods. In fact, as we noted in Chapter 1, location is one of the primary distinctions between service and manufacturing companies. A service company almost always is located near the market, while a production company usually needs to consider many other factors in its location decisions.

Lastly, as we have already noted, suppliers locate near users to facilitate the timing of deliveries. This is becoming more common as the trend toward the use of the just-in-time production continues.

RAW MATERIAL LOCATION

The importance of the location of raw materials was one of the first factors introduced in location analysis. Some reasons why companies locate near the raw materials relate to the reasons they locate near their markets. Products for which there is a **reduction in bulk** during production typically are located near the raw materials. It makes little sense to ship a tree from Washington or Oregon to Pennsylvania and then to trim its branches. Hence, lumber mills tend to be located near timber resources. Once the timber resource is depleted, the company must move to a new location. In general, the lumber industry has moved gradually from the Northeast to the upper Midwest to the far Northwest. Reseeding in depleted areas will necessitate a move back to these areas in future years. Mining is another operation that, obviously, must be located near the raw material. However, in this industry, there is no restoration of the raw materials. Other typical items that reduce in bulk during production are some dairy products (cheese and butter) and paper products (again, from wood).

Perishability was discussed as a reason for locating near the markets. There also are products that perish *before* production and, hence, must be located near their raw materials. An example of this is frozen seafood. The fish may perish before they are frozen, but once frozen the fish are nonperishable (as long as they remain frozen).

reduction in bulk

Teaching Suggestion 5.3: Raw Materials and Components. See the Instructor's Section for details.

perishable raw materials

TRANSPORTATION FACILITIES

Prior to the 1950s, regional transportation was of great concern in the plant location problem. The concern has since lessened, due to improvement in air transport (in terms both of accessibility and of cost) and improvement in the interstate highway system. It is interesting, though, to examine the history of transportation.

Ships constituted the first major form of transportation (hence the term *shipping*). Because of the need for water to transport goods and people, all major cities developed near some waterway. Later, railroads were constructed, and these served to unify the country. Companies could ship from virtually any point in the United States to any other location in the United States much more quickly by rail than by water. Even greater shipping speed and flexibility were realized with trucks and the highway system.

In the most recent development, airlines began to be used for transporting goods. The truck/airline combination leads to a transportation network that covers virtually the entire globe. In chronological order, we have sea, rail, highway, and air—which also happens to be the order according to cost. In other words, it is still cheapest to ship by sea. Hence, bulky products that do not perish tend to be shipped by barge whenever possible. Examples include ore, grain, and crude oil. Air shipments are both the most expensive and the quickest. Thus, perishable products such as flowers, live Maine lobsters, or fresh San Francisco sourdough bread are shipped long distances by air. Some industrial service companies have one central location and ship repair crews by air as the need arises. For example, a chemical company might have its headquarters in St. Louis and plants in several other cities. Because the company does not know which plant will require repair next, it maintains the repair crew in St. Louis, which is centrally located in the United States. When necessary, the repair crew flies out on the next commercial plane. This is less costly and less redundant than staffing repair crews in each plant.

LABOR SUPPLY

availability of labor

Crucial to the operation of a business is its labor force. Although many factors relating to labor are essential, the primary factor with respect to location decisions is the availability of labor in the region. Typically, a company wants to see a high ratio between the number of potential employees and the number of jobs available. The reason for this is twofold. First, this gives the company a large pool of applicants to screen, allowing the company to be selective in hiring those it feels will best fit its needs; this leads to a productive work force. In addition, if there is competition for the positions due to the large labor pool, there will be less chance of the company's losing workers. Second, a company typically does not want a region to be dependent on it. If most workers in the region depend on Company X and the company then moves or goes out of business, the entire region will be affected adversely, which reflects poorly on the company. This has occurred in Kenosha, Wisconsin (which relied heavily on the production of cars), company mining towns throughout the West, and in towns such as Bethlehem, Pennsylvania, and Youngstown, Ohio, which were each dominated by a single steel company bearing the name of the town.

labor skills

A second component of the labor supply is the level of skill required of the employees. Some companies require workers with certain skills, other companies require semiskilled labor, and still others can use unskilled labor. For example, one factor in the relocation of furniture companies to the South was the large pool of workers who had acquired woodworking skills in high school.

wage rates

The facts that wage rates are lower in the South and that there are fewer unions in the South also encourage companies to locate there. If labor is a large part of the cost of the finished good, then, typically, wage rate is a primary factor in terms of plant location. Table 5.9 indicates two of the primary reasons companies have moved from the Northeast and Midwest to the South. In addition, we note that wage rates in all regions of the United States are higher than those in many foreign countries (see Table 5.5). This is a prime reason for a U.S. manufacturer to locate a plant overseas. We caution, however, that low wage rates may not be as good as they sound; they may simply be a reflection of low skills or low productivity.

TABLE 5.9 State-by-state comparison of unionization and wages

State	Percentage of Unionization, 1988	Average Hourly Earnings, 1990
Alabama	15.3	9.48
Alaska	25.5	11.51
Arizona	3.8	10.33
Arkansas	12.0	8.57
California	22.6	11.51
Colorado	10.0	11.15
Connecticut	15.6	11.46
Delaware	20.5	12.52
Florida	8.9	9.06
Georgia	11.9	9.22
Hawaii	41.4	10.90
Idaho	8.6	10.37
Illinois	33.3	11.45
Indiana	37.6	10.45
Iowa	20.8	11.19
Kansas	11.4	10.86
Kentucky	23.0	10.67
Louisiana	20.4	11.57
Maine	18.7	10.43
Maryland	30.0	11.68
Massachusetts	19.9	11.30
Michigan	53.6	13.79
Minnesota	18.1	11.17
Mississippi	8.1	8.37
Missouri	32.4	10.79
Montana	25.0	11.32
Nebraska	9.9	9.59
Nevada	6.2	11.30
New Hampshire	6.7	10.72
New Jersey	24.8	11.66
New Mexico	10.4	8.81
New York	48.2	11.07
North Carolina	4.6	8.81
North Dakota	10.4	8.91
Ohio	40.9	12.69
Oklahoma	17.1	10.77
Oregon	21.4	10.96
Pennsylvania	40.7	11.03
Rhode Island	11.1	9.41
South Carolina	3.1	8.92
South Dakota	2.7	8.33
Tennessee	13.5	9.54
Texas	15.1	10.55
Utah	5.0	10.41
Vermont	8.3	10.47
Virginia	12.2	10.12
Washington	28.2	12.69
West Virginia	29.8	11.58
Wisconsin	24.3	10.97
Wyoming	15.9	10.83

Source: Statistical Abstract of the United States, 1990 (Washington, D.C.: U.S. Department of Commerce, Bureau of the Census) and *Employment and Earnings* (Washington, D.C.: U.S. Department of Labor, Bureau of Labor Statistics, October 1990).

labor–management relations

Associated with the wage rate in a region are the general labor–management relations. Some companies look for a nonunion shop. Some companies accept unions and try to work with them, as was noted in Chapter 2. Of course, forecasting labor–management relations in a region is a rather formidable task. Table 5.9 also presents the percent of unionization on a state-by-state basis. States having right-to-work laws, such as Tennessee and North Carolina, offer advantages to most employers, but companies that are highly unionized will be pressured to avoid locating new facilities in these states.

CLIMATE

energy costs

Regional climate is, in most location decisions, of secondary interest. However, the increase in energy costs has increased the importance of climate in the facility location decision-making process. Figure 5.1 indicates heating and cooling degree days throughout the United States.

The total energy cost is a function not only of the climate but also the regional (per unit) energy costs. As Table 5.10 indicates, regional energy costs vary greatly. Common to all areas during the 1980s, however, were rising energy costs.

COMMUNITY FACTORS

managerial preference

After choosing the region, the next step is to determine the community within the chosen region. Before there was scientific analysis of plant location, the community typically was chosen according to the preference of the manager. In fact, headquarters (as opposed to plants or warehouses) often are still chosen in accordance with managerial preference. During the consolidation of Army bases in the mid-1970s, for example, rumor had it that Picatinny Arsenal in New Jersey was kept open and elevated to a command headquarters because of its golf course, a game favored by the general. Similarly, Anaconda Minerals built its research center, since closed, in Tucson, Arizona, to satisfy the desires of the research director the company wanted to run the center. There are, however, several more important factors that should be considered when determining the community.

Teaching Suggestion 5.4: Lifestyle Choice II. See the Instructor's Section for details.

facilities

attitudes

Because one goal of operations is to maintain a stable work force, it is useful to choose a community that will benefit the employees. Therefore, community facilities should be examined. These include housing, public transportation, schools, churches, playgrounds, hospitals, and stores. Second, community attitudes are important. Although attitudes may be difficult to quantify, they often are obvious. Many times, a community objects to a plant before the company is even sure it wishes to locate in that area. Typical objections include a fear of pollution or fear about the influx of a new type of labor force in the community. Of course, if the labor force is to be found in the community, rather than brought in from other areas, objections usually fade away very quickly. Given the economic situation today, businesses do not need to locate in any community that is less than hospitable.

government

Local government and taxes are two more community considerations. New zoning may be required before the plant can be built, or new zoning may be required in the future for plant expansion. Thus, the company should look for a community government that has a demonstrated history of acting favorably on industrial zoning requests. Furthermore, it is the community government that will respond to com-

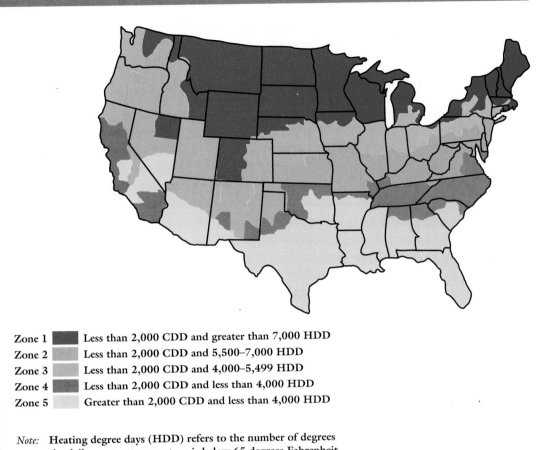

Zone 1 ▮ Less than 2,000 CDD and greater than 7,000 HDD
Zone 2 ▮ Less than 2,000 CDD and 5,500–7,000 HDD
Zone 3 ▮ Less than 2,000 CDD and 4,000–5,499 HDD
Zone 4 ▮ Less than 2,000 CDD and less than 4,000 HDD
Zone 5 ▮ Greater than 2,000 CDD and less than 4,000 HDD

Note: Heating degree days (HDD) refers to the number of degrees
the daily average temperature is below 65 degrees Fahrenheit.

Cooling degree days (CDD) refers to the number of degrees
the daily average temperature is above 65 degrees Fahrenheit.

Source: Chart prepared by U.S. Bureau of the Census.

FIGURE 5.1   U.S. weather zone map of heating degree days (HDD) and cooling degree
days (CDD)

Transparency Master 5.2:
Energy Requirements.

plaints about the plant—in particular, complaints about pollution. The government
should be one with which the manufacturer can work well when problems arise.

The analysis of corporate taxes will be part of the general financial analysis in terms   **taxes**
of plant location, but personal taxes must also be included. If a company is to be competitive when hiring employees, it must compensate for any wage taxes levied in the
community under consideration. This is especially true if no wage tax exists in neigh-
boring communities. This, of course, is one reason why companies have fled cities with
wage taxes, such as New York, Philadelphia, and St. Louis, for the suburbs of those
cities.

The federal government has a program to develop **enterprise zones** in inner-city
areas. Incentives for companies that locate in these zones include a hiring credit, a
construction credit, a credit for training disadvantaged workers, an individual income

Transparency Master 5.2:
Energy Requirements.

TABLE 5.10 Industrial electricity costs for selected cities, 1980 and 1988

City	Industrial Electricity Cost (cents per kilowatt-hour)	
	1980	1988
Boston	18.21	19.96
Chicago	11.82	15.14
Detroit	13.18	15.94
Los Angeles	16.04	20.15
Miami	11.65	15.56
Minneapolis	11.22	12.31
Newark	16.96	19.83
Philadelphia	12.87	16.18
St. Louis	11.21	14.44
Seattle	2.26	7.68

Source: U.S. Energy Information Administration.

Note: Industrial consumption based on 200,000 kilowatt-hours at 500 kilowatt demand.

tax credit, and tax-exempt bonds. Local governments often put together attractive bid packages to lure plants to their cities. They promise zoning changes and tax incentives in advance of the location decision. Table 5.11 lists the **investment incentives** that governments may offer.

site availability

Finally, one major community factor is site availability. The site may be land or it may be a vacant building that fits the needs of the company. For example, Adidas (of Germany) decided to locate nearer the U.S. market and chose a site in Reading, Pennsylvania, where there was a vacant shoe factory that Adidas could easily convert for the production of athletic footwear.

SITE FACTORS

engineering

If the site being chosen is a new site, in contrast with the Adidas example, then most of the site considerations are of the engineering type. That is, is there sufficient land on which to build and expand? Is water drainage sufficient? Is the soil able to bear the load of heavy equipment? Are utilities (water, gas, electricity) readily available? Is waste disposal sufficient? And, finally, is the transportation system appropriate both for loading and unloading and for employees? Site factors appear in Table 5.12.

traffic

Although many of the site factors just mentioned apply both to manufacturing and service industries, most are aimed specifically at the manufacturing sector. The service sector has a set of site location factors of its own. Let us begin with retail businesses. The key factor here is to find a location that has a lot of traffic. Because every individual that passes the site is a potential customer, it helps to have heavy traffic passing the business. Some types of businesses, such as small food stands or small specialty shops, require that this traffic be pedestrian traffic, which leads them to locate

TABLE 5.11 Possible investment incentives available from a state, county, or city

Financial Help	Tax Programs
Industrial revenue bonds	Corporate tax exemption
General obligation bonds	Excise tax exemption
Private development credit	Moratorium or exemption on goods in transit (free port)
Loans for building construction	
Loans for machinery and equipment	Moratorium or exemption on land and capital improvements
Incentives for investments in areas with high unemployment	Exemption on manufacturer's inventories
Plant expansion assistance	Stabilization agreements for specified industries
Guarantees for machinery and equipment loans	Exemption on raw materials used in manufacturing
Guarantees for building construction loans	Accelerated depreciation for pollution control and other equipment
Free land for industry	
State matching funds for local industrial financing programs	Tax credits for the use of specified state products
	Sales/use exemption on new equipment, particularly equipment for pollution control
State-, city-, county-owned industrial parks	Credits against corporate income tax for pollution control facilities
University R&D available to industry	
Employee training/retraining programs	Personal income tax exemption

Source: U.S. Department of Commerce.

on busy city streets and in shopping malls. Others, such as movies or restaurants, are more often on busy auto routes, because most people do not just walk in to these establishments on the spur of the moment. Gas stations, where one may stop on the spur of the moment, are found on auto routes for obvious reasons, but they are even more prevalent at the intersection of two busy routes.

Another factor in site selection for retail businesses relates to the idea of complementary businesses. A shopping center usually is built around a large department store and/or a large supermarket. These businesses will attract the most customers, as people can meet most of their needs by going to one or the other. The smaller businesses in the shopping center or mall depend on the traffic provided by these bigger stores.

Site factors for service businesses other than retail vary by the type of business, so it is difficult to deal with them in a general way. Specialized consulting firms can locate anywhere, with no ill effects on their business from the decision to locate away from their customers because they offer a unique service. Computer software developers often locate in the same building with their time-sharing vendor (where the computer is) so as to avoid large phone bills.

FACTOR IMPORTANCE

In the preceding sections, we have discussed the factors affecting location. Surveys of corporations have been performed to ascertain the relative importance of each of these factors. The survey results were different and are open to interpretation (as is true with any survey results). However, obvious common concerns are community attitudes, labor costs, transportation both of raw materials and of finished goods, and state or

TABLE 5.12 Criteria for evaluation of a specific site

Access
    Immediate vicinity
        Street width
        Traffic volume and characteristics
        Turning movements and signalization
        Parking and other traffic controls
        Public transportation
        Possible access points to site
        Known plans for improvements
    Regional (employee- and customer-oriented)
        Driving time to population centers
        Road capacity and future highway improvements
        Availability of public transportation
Utilities
    Availability and capacity to serve the site
        Water supply
        Storm sewers
        Electricity
        Communications
        Sanitary sewers
        Gas
        Heating
    Estimated cost and timing for providing the above
Site Development Factors
    Size
    Topography
    Drainage
    Natural features, vegetation, conservation factors, views, appearance
    Zoning of site
    Condition, utilization of existing buildings
    Shape of property
    Soils
    Tree coverage
    Space for expansion
Neighborhood Development Factors
    Existing development patterns/trends in the immediate area and district
    Zoning of the surrounding area
    Relationship to community's master plan
    Community and neighborhood factors
    Availability of supporting commercial and industrial activities
    Availability of supporting educational, cultural, and recreational activities
    Housing
Legal and Other Impediments
    Deed restrictions
    Easements
    Other government programs and restrictions affecting the site
    Need for zoning changes

Source: Kenneth H. Ripnen, *Office Space Administration* (New York: McGraw-Hill, 1974), p. 174.

local taxes. Noticeable in the later surveys, after the oil shortage and increase in fuel prices, was that energy rose to the top of the list. Given world politics of recent years, energy is obviously still a major concern in location decision making. **energy**

A fixed ranking of location factors in order of importance cannot be provided, because different types of businesses have different rankings. Instead, it is most useful to be aware of which classes of businesses focus on which types of factors.

Manufacturing companies very often are dependent on one or more particular raw materials. Locating near the source of these materials is a highly ranked factor for these businesses, although it is of little importance to most other businesses. The steel industry is one example; it needs to locate near iron ore and coal sources. Processing industries, such as the food industry, provide another example: Pillsbury and General Mills are located in Minneapolis to be near their agricultural sources. **raw materials**

These same types of industries rank locating near good transportation facilities very highly. To use the example of the steel industry again, almost all steel mills are located on water transportation routes. This is also true of chemical and oil refineries. For these industries, factors such as wage rates and taxes are considered only after the raw materials and transportation criteria are satisfied. Regional concerns are much more important than community or siting factors. **transportation**

An oil refinery—access to waterways is critical in many industries. (© Jean Gaumy/ Magnum Photos, Inc.)

labor

Many service industries are very labor intensive and depend on a large pool of unskilled or semiskilled workers. For obvious reasons, these businesses look at wage rates first. The textile industry, light manufacturing, and even data entry tasks in the data processing industry fall into this category, and many of these businesses have located facilities in Asia or the Caribbean to take advantage of lower wage rates. These industries, too, look at regional concerns before community or siting concerns.

Community factors are of primary concern to service businesses. A doctor, for example, will locate his or her office in a community where there are few doctors of the same specialty and where there is a large pool of potential patients (demographic groupings). For service businesses, siting factors are less important, and regional factors are generally outside the scope of their location decisions.

Siting factors are most important to retail businesses that require locations to provide maximum visibility to potential customers. To this type of business, community factors are less important and regional factors are the least important.

GENERAL APPROACHES TO FACILITY LOCATION

As we have just indicated, there are many factors affecting plant location. Some of the factors, such as shipping costs and labor, are quantitative. Other factors, such as labor–management relations and legal considerations, are rather qualitative. In order to address the location problem, two approaches have been taken. One is to ignore the qualitative factors and concentrate only on those factors with costs that are readily determined. The other approach is to include the qualitative factors by applying a quantitative scale.

The approach that includes qualitative factors is presented first, because it attempts to take all factors into account. To take all factors into account, it is necessary to collect a great deal of data. If one location factor is more important than the other factors and if this factor is easily quantifiable, it may be wise to use a purely quantitative approach. The examples that follow choose cost, time, or distance as the quantifiable factor, but cost is a consideration for all of them.

Two additional approaches to making location decisions are available. The transportation method is used to select one location to add to a network of facilities. We will look at an example of this in the next chapter. To locate many sites simultaneously—that is, to design an optimal grid of locations—linear programming (see Chapter 11) is used. Both of these approaches are quantitative and are more useful for making more complex decisions, which is why they are explained later in the text. The problem presented in this section involves selecting one location, and there is no interaction between the location selected and other similar facilities located elsewhere.

QUALITATIVE MODELS

As we mentioned earlier, plant location factors are both quantitative and qualitative. The quantitative approaches to location decision making ignore the qualitative factors. They also ignore the fact that, even if all of the factors were quantitative, the factors still may not be quantified in the same kinds of units. For example, for a given location, we cannot directly compare the investment required (where units are dollars) with market size (where units are numbers of people). Although some may wish to convert all factors to dollar units, this practice is inadvisable.

An approach is needed that finds the solution that provides the greatest overall benefit in terms of all of the factors. Fortunately, a number of such techniques have been developed. A simple **weighting approach** uses the following steps:

weighting approach

1. List the factors that are considered to be important.
2. Assign a weight (relative importance) to each factor.
3. Evaluate (score) each of the alternative sites in terms of each factor.
4. Multiply each score by the weight for its factor.
5. Add the scores for each alternative.
6. Select the location with the highest score.

Teaching Suggestion 5.5: Subjective Numerical Data. See the Instructor's Section for details.

An example demonstrates the use of these steps.

Example 5.1 A Japanese automaker desires to locate a plant in the United States. Although proximity to market is one motivation, the automaker's primary motivation is to circumvent any current or future U.S. import limits on automobiles. After a preliminary analysis, four states are chosen for further consideration: Pennsylvania, Tennessee, California, and Texas.

Four factors are considered to be most relevant in making the choice among these finalists:

- availability (quantity and quality) of labor;
- taxes and incentives;
- raw materials availability; and
- proximity to markets.

The weights assigned to these factors by management are 2, 1.5, 1, and .5, respectively.

Each site has been evaluated and scored on a scale of 0 to 10, with 10 being the best.

Transparency Master 5.3: Qualitative Model.

Factor	Weight	State			
		Pennsylvania	Tennessee	California	Texas
Labor	2.0	8	6	7	5
Taxes	1.5	4	8	4	9
Raw materials	1.0	7	4	7	6
Markets	0.5	8	5	9	6

Multiplying each row by its weight yields the following.

	State			
Factor	Pennsylvania	Tennessee	California	Texas
Labor	16	12	14	10
Taxes	6	12	6	13.5
Raw materials	7	4	7	6
Markets	4	2.5	4.5	3
Total	33	30.5	31.5	32.5

The total scores are Pennsylvania: 33; Tennessee: 30.5; California: 31.5; and Texas: 32.5. The numbers 33, 30.5, 31.5, and 32.5 have no real meaning; they are used for comparative purposes only. Since Pennsylvania has the highest total score, it is chosen, but with Texas a particularly close second, further evaluation of the top two choices may be necessary. ■⌐

Sometimes, simply adding the scores may be inappropriate. This occurs when one of the choices is the best overall (by adding the scores), but is unsatisfactory with respect to one important factor. To consider an extreme case, let us say that the World Health Organization is considering ways to eliminate a disease that only occurs in human beings. Five factors are being used to measure how well each plan will perform with respect to eliminating the disease, and a sixth factor measures the risk to the human population associated with the plan. Someone suggests that one plan would be to eliminate the entire human population. This plan is ideal for all of the factors (it does eliminate the disease) except the sixth one, and, when the scores are added, it has the highest score of all the alternatives. This is, of course, an unacceptable result. To avoid such a situation, a cutoff, or **discordance level,** is introduced. The cutoff is the minimum score that would be accepted on any of the criteria. One discordance level could be used for the entire problem, or a different level could be used for each of the factors.

discordance level

| Example 5.2   Assume that a cutoff of 5 is used for all factors in Example 5.1. Which site should be chosen?

Pennsylvania is unacceptable because it only has a score of 4 on taxes. Tennessee and California also fail to meet this cutoff. Only Texas has scores of 5 or higher on all its factors, so it should be chosen. ■⌐

QUANTITATIVE MODELS

Depending on the situation, different quantitative methods may be used to evaluate the location problem. We consider descriptive methods for evaluating potential sites. The most common methods use cost–volume analyses or the use of distance and/or frequency analyses. We also examine prescriptive methods that determine exactly where a facility should be located based on distance (or cost or time) and/or frequency. These methods are used in a single dimension (along a line) and in two dimensions (on a plane).

Teaching Suggestion 5.6: Analysis vs. Design. See the Instructor's Section for details.

COST–VOLUME ANALYSIS

The anticipated costs of locating a plant in one city versus the anticipated costs of locating it in another city are given in the following table.

descriptive methods

Cost	Philadelphia	St. Paul
Fixed	$1,000,000	$800,000
Variable	$73/unit	$112/unit

The costs are broken down into fixed costs and variable costs, which, of course, implies that a cost–volume analysis is useful. Figure 5.2 contains the break-even analysis for this example, and which city is better can be determined easily once the demand is assessed. This suggests that St. Paul would be the choice until volume exceeds 5,128 units.

One of the factors in the break-even model is freight. In order to determine shipping costs, several models might be employed. One model is the transportation model, which will be presented in Chapter 6. Essentially, the transportation model is most applicable to the shipping of finished goods from various factories to warehouses or

FIGURE 5.2 Break-even analysis

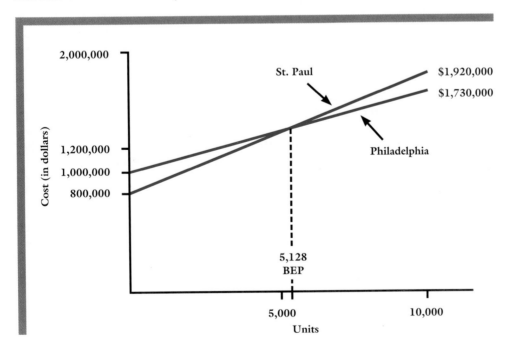

distributors. Note that the potential sites are given. Our analysis of the location problem will look first at how to evaluate and compare alternative locations with respect to shipping costs. Later, we will design the optimal location.

DISTANCE/FREQUENCY ANALYSIS

To analyze alternative locations, we need a way to compare them. Comparing the shipping costs related to the use of each location has been suggested already. Many times, though, it is easier to use shipping distances—if they are proportional to costs. Shipping times also may be used. In each case, the location resulting in the minimum cost (or time or distance) is the best. Consider the following example, which shows how to use travel distance as a location criterion.

Example 5.3   Advanced Data Systems (ADS) maintains a staff of service engineers to repair and maintain its computers. Four new clients have just purchased computers, and a new service office will be opened and dedicated to these four clients. Two locations have been suggested for the office. The distances from each location to each of the customers are as follows.

	Customer			
Office Location	A	B	C	D
1	7 miles	4 miles	12 miles	14 miles
2	11 miles	10 miles	7 miles	5 miles

Which site should be selected?

Assuming that putting the office closest to each of the clients is the best, the distances simply can be added. For location 1, the total distance is 7 + 4 + 12 + 14 = 37 miles. For location 2, the total distance is 11 + 10 + 7 + 5 = 33 miles. Therefore, location 2 is preferred.   ∎

total distance criterion   Using the total distance, as in the previous example, will result in the selection of the most central of the location alternatives. This certainly is a desirable result, but it does not account for frequency of service calls. That is, it would be more desirable to locate near the client that will require the most visits. The distances used should be weighted in favor of the client(s) with the greatest needs. The next example takes this into account.

Example 5.4   Each of the four ADS clients has purchased a different model ADS computer. From past sales and service records, ADS has estimated the number of maintenance and repair visits per month to each client.

Customer	Number of Visits
A	9
B	7
C	3
D	6

In terms of the total distance to be traveled per month, which office location should be selected?

The total distance traveled per month is now the basis for the selection. This distance is the product of the number of trips and the distance per trip. Using the distances given in Example 5.3, the analysis for location 1 is

$$(9 \times 7) + (7 \times 4) + (3 \times 12) + (6 \times 14) = 211 \text{ miles.}$$

For location 2, the analysis is

$$(9 \times 11) + (7 \times 10) + (3 \times 7) + (6 \times 5) = 220 \text{ miles.}$$

In this case, location 1 is preferred. This result was expected because customers A and B, both of which are located closer to location 1 than to location 2, will require more trips.

Of the two methods presented in the preceding examples, the method used in Example 5.4 provides a better basis on which to make the location decision. Of course, the additional information that it requires must be available.

In the preceding two examples, the distances (in miles) were given. In many cases, however, the distance must be determined. In addition, we were restricted to picking from a small set of potential locations in the preceding examples. In many cases, we may locate almost anywhere on a two-dimensional map. In the following sections, we will relax both of the assumptions under which we have been operating.

In either one or two dimensions, our main concern typically is with finding a "central location." In other words, more often than not, we are interested in finding the location that minimizes the total distance from the central location to all other points. We note that distances can vary, however, and that there are times when minimizing total distance is not completely satisfactory.

Whenever possible, it is better to pick the best site from among all possible sites, rather than from among a small set of alternative sites. The examples that follow illustrate how this is accomplished. First, we look at one-dimensional problems because these illustrate the key points more simply. Then we proceed to the true location problem, that of two dimensions. **prescriptive methods**

ONE-DIMENSIONAL SITING

In one dimension, the distance from one point to another is defined as the absolute value of the difference between the coordinates of the two locations. For example, the distance between companies located on floors 3 and 47 of an office tower is $|47 - 3| = |3 - 47| = 44$ floors. The distance between companies located on the 1000 and 2000 blocks of a street is $|2000 - 1000| = 1000$, and since blocks are usually numbered by hundreds, this translates to $1000/100 = 10$ blocks. There is a very simple rule, the **median rule,** for finding the location that minimizes the total distance.

To minimize total distance in one dimension, locate at the median.   **median rule**

The median is the middle number in a group of *ordered* numbers. For example, the median of the numbers 10, 70, 80, 90, 20 is 70 , which is easy to see when the numbers are reordered as 10, 20, 70, 80, 90. Now let's consider a location example using one-dimensional siting.

Example 5.5   El Camino, a copying service, plans to open a new office. Five of El Camino's clients are located at the following addresses on East Esperanza Boulevard.

Client	Address
Appelbaum	1000
Berman	7000
Carto	8000
Dulles	9000
Eskan	2000

Where should the new office be located?

To find the location that minimizes the total distance traveled, we use the median rule. We begin by writing the locations in order: 1000, 2000, 7000, 8000, 9000. The solution is to locate at the median, which is 7000 East Esperanza Boulevard.   ▪

We have shown that, using the median rule, the most central address in Example 5.5 is 7000 East Esperanza Boulevard. The distance computations for this result are as follows.

Transparency Master 5.4:
One-Dimensional Location.

Client	Address	Distance from 7000
Appelbaum	1000	6,000
Berman	7000	0
Carto	8000	1,000
Dulles	9000	2,000
Eskan	2000	5,000
	Total	14,000

Using the median rule, no location has a lower total distance than 14,000, which equals 140 blocks. Also, no location has a lower average distance than $140/5 = 28$ blocks.

minimize distance

As we have seen, to minimize the total travel distance in one dimension, we apply the median rule, which provides us with the location such that half the trips go in one direction and half the trips go in the opposite direction. Notice that we have introduced the term *trips*. The median rule applies for any number of trips to the different locations. In Example 5.5, we did not include the number of trips. This is the same as assuming an equal number of trips per client.

Example 5.6   Consider the number of trips per month to each of the five addresses in Example 5.5.

Client	Address	Number of Trips
Appelbaum	1000	18
Berman	7000	12
Carto	8000	8
Dulles	9000	10
Eskan	2000	15
	Total	63

Where should the office be located to minimize the total distance of all trips made?

The total number of trips is 63, which means that the median trip is the 32nd trip. We will reorganize the data from the 1000 block to the 9000 block and label the trips.

Block	Number of Trips	Trip Numbers
1000	18	1–18
2000	15	19–33
7000	12	34–45
8000	8	46–53
9000	10	54–63

The 32nd trip is at the 2000 block, which has trips 19–33. Therefore, we should locate at the 2000 block. The total trip distance is computed as follows.

(1) Client	(2) Block	(3) Distance from 2000	(4) Blocks from 2000 [(3) ÷ 100]	(5) Number of Trips	(6) Total [(4) × (5)]
Appelbaum	1000	1000	10	18	180
Berman	7000	5000	50	12	600
Carto	8000	6000	60	8	480
Dulles	9000	7000	70	10	700
Eskan	2000	0	0	15	0
				Total	1,960

No location will have a total less than 1,960 blocks. ▪

While we have used the median as a measure of centrality, another common measure is the mean. In fact, the mean location is very useful because the mean minimizes the sum of the squared distances. This is of utmost interest when a main concern of the company is the longer trips (response times). To apply the **mean rule,** we use the following equation for finding the optimal location, L^*: **minimize distance squared**

$$L^* = \frac{\sum_{i=1}^{n} X_i}{n},$$

Teaching Suggestion 5.7:
Which Is Better? See the
Instructor's Section for
details.

where

X_i = the distance that client i is situated from some zero point and

n = the number of client locations.

The zero point in our example can be the cross street from which the addresses start—that is, 0 East Esperanza Boulevard.

Example 5.7   Use the equation to calculate the location that minimizes the sum of the distances squared for the problem presented in Example 5.5.

$$L^* = \frac{1,000 + 7,000 + 8,000 + 9,000 + 2,000}{5} = \frac{27,000}{5} = 5,400$$

Using this criterion, the new office should be located at 5400 East Esperanza Boulevard.   ◼〗

To weight the distances using the number of trips required to each location, we use the equation

$$L^* = \frac{\sum_{i=1}^{n} (NT_i)(X_i)}{NT},$$

where

NT_i = the number of trips to client i and

NT = the total number of trips to all clients.

In the previous equation, we assumed that $NT_i = 1$ for each client, or, more generally, that the number of trips to each client was the same.

Example 5.8   Consider the data presented in Examples 5.5 and 5.6. Where should the office be located to minimize the sum of the distances squared?
In this case, the total number of trips is 63, and the location is

$$L^* = \frac{(18 \times 1,000) + (12 \times 7,000) + (8 \times 8,000) + (10 \times 9,000) + (15 \times 2,000)}{63}$$

$$= \frac{286,000}{63} = 4,540.$$

The office should be at 4540 East Esperanza Boulevard, if such a number exists. If not, it should be about four-tenths of the way up the 4500 block.   ◼〗

This answer could have been anticipated. Notice that more trips are made east of the 2000 block than west of it and that these trips are longer (the higher the number of the address on East Esperanza, the farther east the building is). It is only logical to place the office in this direction from the center.

Teaching Suggestion 5.8: Midpoint vs. Mean/ Median. See the Instructor's Section for details.

TWO-DIMENSIONAL SITING

In one dimension, distance measurement is relatively straightforward ($d = |x_1 - x_2|$). However, this is not the case in two dimensions. Consider the four points shown in Figure 5.3. Suppose we are interested in determining the distance between any two of these points—for example, between A and B. *The actual distance depends on how we travel.*

CITY BLOCK MODEL   If Figure 5.3 represents a city, then we have to travel along city blocks at right angles. In order to get from A to B, we must travel eastward from 20 (the east–west coordinate of A) to 50 (the east–west coordinate of B), or a distance of $|20 - 50| = 30$. We also must travel downward from 70 to 20, a distance of 50. The total distance traveled is simply the sum of the one-dimensional distances—in this case, $30 + 50 = 80$. Distance between (x_i, y_i) and (x_j, y_j) in a city block model is given by the following general equation:

$$d = |x_i - x_j| + |y_i - y_j|.$$

FIGURE 5.3 Minimum shipping costs for two-dimensional location

Transparency Master 5.5: Two-Dimensional Location.

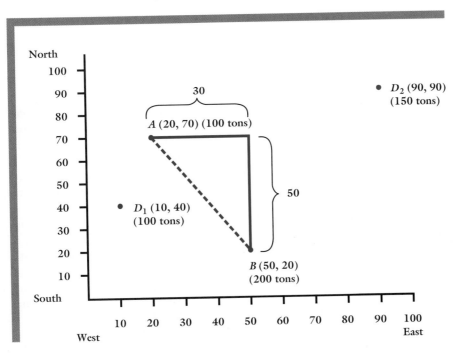

When a number of trips or a weight (NT_{ij}) is associated with the amount of traffic between two points, we simply multiply the distance by the weight. For example, if 127 trips occur between A and B, the weighted distance is $127 \times 80 = 10{,}160$.

Having determined that the city block model consists of two one-dimensional models, we arrive at an easy rule for linking distances with the city block model:

> To minimize total distance in two dimensions using the city block measure of distance, locate at the medians of the two coordinates.

Consider the following example.

Example 5.9 Consider the two-dimensional problem indicated in Figure 5.3. In order to make a product, two raw materials (A and B) are required. These raw materials come from plants located at points A and B, respectively. The distributors are located at points D_1 and D_2, respectively, and the goal is to minimize the total freight cost (raw materials and finished goods are functions of the weight of the shipment and the distance shipped). The following tables contain the appropriate information.

Raw Material	Weight
A	100 tons
B	200 tons

Distributor	Demand
D_1	100 tons
D_2	150 tons

city distance–median rule

First, we find the median amount of goods shipped, as in the one-dimensional case. Because the total tonnage shipped is 550 tons (300 into the plant and 250 out of the plant), the median amount is 275 tons. (Technically, the median is 275.5.) To find the x-coordinate and the y-coordinate for the new plant, we examine Figure 5.3. The x-coordinate is chosen so that one-half of the shipments will move east and one-half will move west. Thus, if we examine the graph from the origin eastward, we find that the first facility is D_1, with a shipment of 100. Continuing eastward, we find A, with a shipment of 100 for a total of 200. Further eastward, we have B, with a shipment of 200 for a total of 400. Thus, the x-coordinate should be 50 because half of the shipments move east and half move west. (From B, 125 of the tons move east a distance of 0 and 75 tons move west a distance of 0.) The y-coordinate is found in an identical fashion. Starting at the origin and moving north, we first find B (200 tons) and then D_1 (100 tons). Thus, the y-coordinate is 40, because, again, half of the shipments move north and half move south. Hence, the plant should be located at (50, 40). The shipping cost is computed in the following table.

(1) Facility	(2) Location (x, y)	(3) Distance from Plant at (50, 40) $(\lvert 50 - x \rvert + \lvert 40 - y \rvert)$	(4) Tonnage	(5) Ton-Miles $[(3) \times (4)]$
A	(20,70)	$\lvert 50 - 20 \rvert + \lvert 40 - 70 \rvert = 60$	100	6,000
B	(50,20)	$\lvert 50 - 50 \rvert + \lvert 40 - 20 \rvert = 20$	200	4,000
D_1	(10,40)	$\lvert 50 - 10 \rvert + \lvert 40 - 40 \rvert = 40$	100	4,000
D_2	(90,90)	$\lvert 50 - 90 \rvert + \lvert 40 - 90 \rvert = 90$	150	13,500
				27,500

STRAIGHT-LINE MODEL   If we can get from one location to another in a straight line, then the distance is measured differently than in the city block model. Typically, distances between cities are termed *straight-line*, or *air*, *distances*. Look again at Figure 5.3, but, this time, assume that we are talking about air distances. The figure contains a right triangle with the two sides represented by solid lines and the hypotenuse represented by the dashed line. It is the distance represented by the hypotenuse that concerns us. Recall that the Pythagorean theorem states that for a right triangle, $a^2 + b^2 = c^2$, where a and b are the two sides and c is the hypotenuse. Thus, between A and B, we know that the distance squared is $30^2 + 50^2 = 900 + 2,500 = 3,400$. So the distance is $\sqrt{3,400} = 58.30$. Thus, the distance measure between two points is

$$d = \sqrt{(x_i - x_j)^2 + (y_i - y_j)^2} \,.$$

If there is a weight attached, we simply multiply the distance by the weight.

Now we may state a general rule for the straight-line model:

To minimize total distance in two dimensions using the straight-line measure of distance, locate at the means of the two coordinates.

In equation form, the solution is given by setting x and y as follows:

$$x = \frac{\sum_{i=1}^{n}(NT_i)x_i}{NT} \text{ and}$$

$$y = \frac{\sum_{i=1}^{n}(NT_i)y_i}{NT} \,.$$

Consider the following example.

Example 5.10   Use the data in Example 5.9 and solve it using air distance.

For the example, we have the following:

$$\sum NT_i = 100 + 200 + 100 + 150 = 550$$

$$\sum NT_ix_i = 100(20) + 200(50) + 100(10) + 150(90)$$

$$= 2,000 + 10,000 + 1,000 + 13,500 = 26,500$$

$$\sum NT_iy_i = 100(70) + 200(20) + 100(40) + 150(90)$$

$$= 7,000 + 4,000 + 4,000 + 13,500 = 28,500$$

Hence,

$$x = \frac{26,500}{550} = 48$$

and

$$y = \frac{28,500}{550} = 52.$$

Note that the difference in the two locations is due to the manner by which the distances are measured—air mileage versus city block mileage. ■

Teaching Suggestion 5.9:
Location/Transportation
Method. See the Instructor's Section for details.

The following table recaps the material presented in Examples 5.5–5.10.

	Model		
	One-Dimensional	Two-Dimensional (City Block)	Two-Dimensional (Air Distance)
Points	x_1, x_2	(x_1, y_1) and (x_2, y_2)	(x_1, y_1) and (x_2, y_2)
Distance	$\lvert x_1 - x_2 \rvert$	$\lvert x_1 - x_2 \rvert + \lvert y_1 - y_2 \rvert$	$\sqrt{(x_1 - x_2)^2 + (y_1 - y_2)^2}$
To Minimize Total Distance	median (Example 5.5)	median x, median y	mean x, mean y
To Minimize Total Weighted Distance	weighted median (Example 5.6)	weighted x median, weighted y median (Example 5.9)	weighted x mean, weighted y mean (Example 5.10)
To Minimize Total Squares of Distances	mean (Example 5.7)	_____	_____

S U M M A R Y

Opening a new facility is one of the most costly operations decisions a company faces. Some of the issues involved with such a decision are political, as noted in Chapter 2. Some of the costs are related to capacity issues, as was indicated in Chapter 3. Many other costs are related to where the new facility is to be located.

Two of the major costs are the shipping costs of raw materials and the shipping costs of finished goods. For certain industries, such as bottling or dairy products, it is most cost effective to be near the market. For other industries, such as lumber, it is cost effective to locate near the raw materials. In many other cases, markets and raw materials are not as important as other factors. These other factors include the labor supply, labor skills, wage rates, climate, and regional transportation.

The community in which the facility locates should be more than hospitable toward the new facility. There are a wide variety of incentive programs that a community, city, or state can offer to a new facility. The site chosen should meet the engineering requirements of the facility.

Several trends in locating new facilities are apparent. Companies have fled urban areas in the Northeast and Midwest for foreign countries, the Sunbelt, and suburban areas. Often the new plants are single-story facilities located in industrial parks.

Both qualitative and quantitative methods are available for the evaluation of different locations. The qualitative methods identify the important factors, weight these factors, score selected areas on these factors, and generate weighted scores for the possible locations. The quantitative methods minimize the total shipping costs.

In this chapter, we have not considered the interaction between facilities. That is, we have not discussed the case of a company that currently has facilities and wishes to add another. This will be covered in the next chapter.

KEY TERMS

market proximity	reduction in bulk	discordance level
market access	enterprise zones	median rule
industrial parks	investment incentives	mean rule
decentralization	weighting approach	

SOLVED PROBLEMS

1. Bill Badwell owns a professional basketball team. He wishes to move the team out of the Midwest and into either Baltimore or Albuquerque. The following gives the factors that Mr. Badwell considers important, their weights, and the scores of Baltimore and Albuquerque on these factors. Based on this information, which site should be chosen?

Factor	Weight	Baltimore	Albuquerque
Population	.4	80	60
Nearest competitor	.3	20	50
Weather	.2	40	90
Support for other sports	.1	70	30

Solution

In order to determine the overall rating, we simply take the sum of the factor ratings times the factor weight.

$$\text{Baltimore} = .4(80) + .3(20) + .2(40) + .1(70) = 53$$

$$\text{Albuquerque} = .4(60) + .3(50) + .2(90) + .1(30) = 60$$

Based on these factors and weights, the team should move to Albuquerque.

Using AB:POM to Solve This Problem

The plant location module has three models: the qualitative/subjective/factor weighting model; the one-dimensional location model; and the two-dimensional location model.

Screen 5.1 shows the input and solution for Solved Problem 1. After the weighting model has been selected, the program asks for the number of factors and the number of locations—in this case, 4 and 2, respectively. The table is set up to input weights for the factors and scores for each site on each factor. The factors can be named, as can the sites. The program multiplies each score by the weight and sums over the site, with the sum presented at the bottom of each site's column. The bottom line contains a summary of the results.

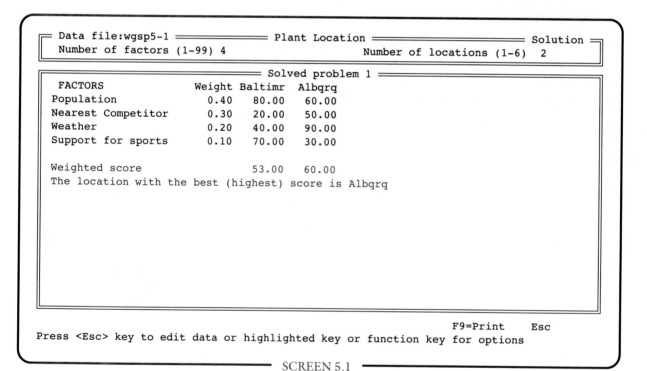

```
 ┌ Data file:wgsp5-1 ══════════ Plant Location ══════════ Solution ═
 │ Number of factors (1-99) 4                Number of locations (1-6)  2
 ╞══════════════════════════ Solved problem 1 ══════════════════════
    FACTORS              Weight Baltimr  Albqrq
   Population             0.40   80.00   60.00
   Nearest Competitor     0.30   20.00   50.00
   Weather                0.20   40.00   90.00
   Support for sports     0.10   70.00   30.00

   Weighted score                53.00   60.00
   The location with the best (highest) score is Albqrq




                                            F9=Print    Esc
   Press <Esc> key to edit data or highlighted key or function key for options
```

SCREEN 5.1

2. Mackey Shirt Service is going to open a plant to launder shirts for six different laundries located in the same city. What is the most central location for the Mackey cleaning plant if the laundries have the following locations?

Customer	Location
A	10E, 30N
B	20W, 20N
C	50E, 20S
D	30E, 30S
E	30E, 40N
F	40W, 10N

Solution

In order to find the central location, we must find the median coordinates for the east–west coordinates and for the north–south coordinates. Because the east–west coordinates are, from east to west, 50E, 30E, 30E, 10E, 20W, and 40W, the median is in the center of this list. That is, the median is anywhere between 30E and 10E. The north–south coordinates are 40N, 30N, 20N, 10N, 20S, and 30S. The median is anywhere between 20N and 10N.

Using AB:POM to Solve This Problem

Screen 5.2 shows the input and solution for Solved Problem 2. The model chosen is the two-dimensional model. The beginning information is simply the number of sites, which in this example is 6. The program sets up a table that allows the user to enter the number of trips or weight carried, the x-coordinate, and the y-coordinate. These numbers are entered for the example. We have used negative numbers for west and south coordinates.

The output contains two additional columns. These are the weights multiplied by the coordinates. In this example, since all of the weights are 1, the last two columns correspond to the original coordinates. The bottom two lines are the total and aver-

```
 ═ Data file:D:wgsp5-2 ═════════ Plant Location ═══════════ Solution ═
   Number of sites (1-99) 6

 ══════════════════════ Solved problem 2 ═══════════════
                                                    Weighted Coordinates
       SITES      Weight/trips    x coord    y coord    X-coord     Y-coord
   A                   1.00        10.00      30.00      10.00       30.00
   B                   1.00       -20.00      20.00     -20.00       20.00
   C                   1.00        50.00     -20.00      50.00      -20.00
   D                   1.00        30.00     -30.00      30.00      -30.00
   E                   1.00        30.00      40.00      30.00       40.00
   F                   1.00       -40.00      10.00     -40.00       10.00
   TOTAL               6.00        60.00      50.00      60.00       50.00
   AVERAGE                         10.00     8.33333     10.00      8.33333
   The unweighted center of gravity is x =   10  y =   8.333333
   The   weighted center of gravity is x =   10  y =   8.333333
   The median trip is trip/weight  3  and occurs at x =  8.333333  y =  10



 F1=Table of distances                              F9=Print    Esc
 Press <Esc> key to edit data or highlighted key or function key for options
```

SCREEN 5.2

ages for the columns. The first two averages give the answers for unweighted problems; the last two give the answers for weighted problems. In this example, these answers (10, 8.33) are the same, but in the next example they will be different because different weights will be used. The center of gravity solves the air distance model. The city block model is solved by the median. In this case, the median is not unique because the number of locations is even. The program has chosen the coordinates, but there are other answers as well, as noted previously. ▬▬▬

3. Suppose that Mackey Shirt Service (from Solved Problem 2) knows that the demands for service from the six laundries are as follows. Find the central location.

Store	Demand (pounds/week)
A	80
B	20
C	60
D	40
E	10
F	30

Solution

We now must find the central location according to demand (pounds/week). The first step is to find the total number of pounds per week, which is 240. The median pound is pound 120. (Technically, it is any pound between pound 120 and pound 121, but let us not quibble.)

Next, we must find pound 120 in each direction. Again, we must sort from east to west and from north to south. First, we sort from east to west. In order, the stores are C, D, E, A, B, F. Adding the pounds in that order, we look for the pound 120.

$$C = 60 \text{ pounds}$$
$$C + D = 100 \text{ pounds}$$
$$C + D + E = 110 \text{ pounds}$$
$$C + D + E + A = 190 \text{ pounds}$$

Therefore, the median east–west coordinate occurs at store A, or 10E.

We repeat the process for the north–south coordinates. The north–south order of stores is E, A, B, F, C, D. Again, we present the partial sums to find pound 120.

$$E = 10 \text{ pounds}$$
$$E + A = 90 \text{ pounds}$$
$$E + A + B = 110 \text{ pounds}$$
$$E + A + B + F = 140 \text{ pounds}$$

The north–south coordinate for the new plant is given by the median north–south coordinate, which occurs at store F, at 10N.

The central location, weighted by demand, is 10E, 10N.

Using AB:POM to Solve This Problem

The screen for Solved Problem 3 is given in Screen 5.3. The screen format is the same as for Solved Problem 2. However, this time, the weighted columns differ from the

Data file:D:wgsp5-3 ========= Plant Location ========= Solution

Number of sites (1-99) 6

====================== Solved problem 3 ======================

				Weighted Coordinates	
SITES	Weight/trips	x coord	y coord	X-coord	Y-coord
A	80.00	10.00	30.00	800.00	2400.00
B	20.00	-20.00	20.00	-400.00	400.00
C	60.00	50.00	-20.00	3000.00	-1200.00
D	40.00	30.00	-30.00	1200.00	-1200.00
E	10.00	30.00	40.00	300.00	400.00
F	30.00	-40.00	10.00	-1200.00	300.00
TOTAL	240.00	60.00	50.00	3700.00	1100.00
AVERAGE		10.00	8.33333	15.4167	4.58333

The unweighted mean is x = 10 y = 8.333333

The   weighted mean is x = 15.41667 y = 4.583333

The median trip is trip/weight 120 and occurs at x = 10 y= 10

F1=Table of distances (air)   F9=Print   Esc

Press <Esc> key to edit data or highlighted key or function key for options

---------------------- SCREEN 5.3 ----------------------

Date file:D:wgsp5-3 ========= Plant Location ========= Solution

Number of sites (1-99) 6

====================== Solved problem 3 ======================

				AIR DISTANCE	
SITES	Weight/trips	x coord	y coord	Distance	Weighted
A	80.00	10.00	30.00	235.11	8843.31
B	20.00	-20.00	20.00	259.168	11404.9
C	60.00	50.00	-20.00	325.128	11107.9
D	40.00	30.00	-30.00	306.940	10934.2
E	10.00	30.00	40.00	285.616	11745.4
F	30.00	-40.00	10.00	327.861	14433.9
TOTAL	240.00	60.00	50.00	3700.00	1100.00
AVERAGE		10.00	8.33333	15.4167	4.58333

The unweighted mean is x = 10 y = 8.333333

The   weighted mean is x = 15.41667 y = 4.583333

The median trip is trip/weight 120 and occurs at x = 10 y = 10

Distances are from row site to all other sites

First column is distance, second is weighted by trips

F1=Table of distances (city)   F9=Print   Esc

Press <Esc> key to edit data or highlighted key or function key for options

---------------------- SCREEN 5.4 ----------------------

unweighted columns. The answers differ also. As you know, if all six sites are weighted equally, the best location is (10, 8.33). If this is not the case, the best solution is (15.42, 4.58).

Pressing **F1** or the **T** key causes a table of distances, as seen in Screen 5.4, to appear. The numbers represent the distances and weighted distances from every city to the city on the given line. For example, the distance from A to all other cities is 235, while the distance to all other cities multiplied by the appropriate number of trips is 8,843. In fact, if you must locate at A, B, C, D, E, or F, then, based on the distance column (or the weighted distance column), A is most central; the other five cities have larger distances.

QUESTIONS

1. Many communities have industrial development authorities who lobby companies to locate new facilities in their communities. Why?

2. Why do companies build new facilities?

3. Why are new facilities built on sites that are far away from the companies' present sites?

4. Why do so many U.S. firms build facilities in other countries?

5. Why do so many foreign companies build facilities in the United States?

6. List four current trends in location.

7. Chrysler sells cars that are made in Japan, the Japanese sell cars made in the United States, and the Chevy Nova, for example, is a mixture of components from all over the world. What trends contribute to these practices?

8. Make a list of regional factors affecting a company's location decision.

9. Make a list of community factors affecting a company's location decision.

10. Compare the lists created in Questions 8 and 9 with a list of factors on where you would like to live and work.

11. Name some types of businesses that have a lot of flexibility and some that have very little flexibility in their location choices.

12. How does factor weighting incorporate personal preference in location choices?

13. What are the advantages and disadvantages of a qualitative (as opposed to a quantitative) approach to location decision making?

14. What measures of distance are used for quantitative location analysis?

PROBLEMS

1. Car Stereo Inc. supplies car radios to auto manufacturers and is going to open a new plant. The company is undecided between Detroit and Dallas as the site. The fixed costs in Dallas are lower due to cheaper land costs, but the variable costs in Dallas are higher, because shipping distances would increase. Given the following costs, perform the break-even analysis.

	Dallas	Detroit
Fixed costs	$600,000	$800,000
Variable costs	$28/radio	$22/radio

BEP = 33,333 units

2. Given below are the costs involved in opening a computer plant in two foreign countries. Perform the break-even analysis.

	Brazil	Korea
Fixed costs	$1,000,000	$860,000
Labor costs/unit	$100	$80
Material costs/unit	$40	$20
Transportation costs/unit	$30	$90
Foreign taxes/unit	$50	$80

BEP = 2,800 units

3. Sam Which has just bought a lunch truck. Sam is undecided about whether to run his lunch truck in the city or in the suburbs. Given the following costs and demands, where should Sam locate?

	City	Suburbs
Annual rental for space	$5,000	$2,000
Average variable cost/sandwich	$.60	$.65
Expected annual demand	20,000	12,000
Average price/sandwich	$2.00	$1.80

city

4. Insurance Company of South America (ISA) is considering opening an office in the United States. The two cities under consideration are Philadelphia and New York. The factor ratings (higher scores are better) for the two cities are given in the following table. In which city should ISA locate?

Factor	Weight	Philadelphia	New York
Customer convenience	.25	70	80
Bank accessibility	.20	40	90
Computer support	.20	85	75
Rental costs	.15	90	55
Labor costs	.10	80	50
Taxes	.10	90	50

Philadelphia

5. Suppose that ISA (see Problem 4) has a discordance level of 50 for all factors. Which site should be chosen and why?

New York

6. Holiday Health Homes is opening a new spa. Three locations in the suburbs are being considered. The following table gives the factors for each site. At which site should Holiday open the new spa?

site B

Factor	Weight	Site A	Site B	Site C
Land space	.30	60	70	80
Land costs	.25	40	80	30
Traffic density	.20	50	80	60
Neighborhood income	.15	50	70	40
Zoning laws	.10	80	20	90

7. Suppose that Holiday Health Homes (see Problem 6) has discordance levels of 50 for land space, 30 for land costs, 40 for traffic density, 30 for neighborhood income, and 30 for zoning laws. Which site should be chosen?

site C

8. Computer Consultants (CC) has clients in the 1100, 1500, 2200, 3700, and 5400 blocks of Hightech Road. Using the method indicated, find the block of Hightech Road on which CC should locate its facilities. Give the average distance from each client to this central location.

2200 block; 13 blocks
2780 block; 14.16 blocks

(a) median
(b) mean

9. From past records, CC (see Problem 8) has determined the average number of weekly trips to their five clients. This information is given in the following list.

Client Address	Number of Trips
1100	8
1500	6
2200	6
3700	15
5400	8

3700 block; 566 blocks
3016 block; 10,974 blocks

(a) Which block minimizes the total distance traveled and what is the total distance?
(b) Which block minimizes the total squared distance traveled and what is the total squared distance?

10. Consumer Loan Company (COLoan) is designing the office layout for its new suite. The suite is L-shaped, as indicated in the figure on the next page, with the two corner rooms allocated to secretarial pools. The estimated number of trips to the duplicating machine is 80 trips per week from the applications secretaries in the southwest corner and 130 trips per week from the secretaries in the payment office at the northeast corner of the suite. Two rooms, G and I, are available. Which room should house the duplicating machine?

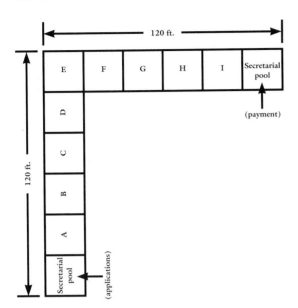

Room I minimizes total movement; room G is more fair.

11. Paramedic Transport serves four hospitals within the city. The hospitals' locations are given in the figure below.

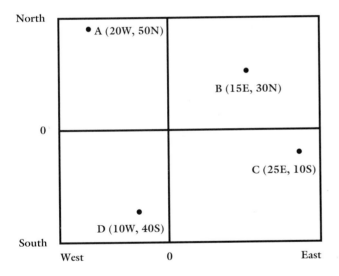

Where should Paramedic set up its offices in order to be centrally located?

between 10W and 15E and between 10S and 30N

12. The average number of trips Paramedic (see Problem 11) makes to each hospital are A(60), B(40), C(100), and D(50). Where should Paramedic locate?

15E, 10S

13. Mountain Chemicals has plants located in Los Angeles, San Francisco, Houston, Dallas, St. Louis, Chicago, Pittsburgh, and Atlanta. They use one central repair crew for plant breakdowns. The crew flies out on commercial airlines. Assume that the cost of airfare is proportional to the distance traveled. Using the table on the next page, tell what longitude and latitude are most central to the eight plants.

City	Longitude	Latitude
Los Angeles	118°	34°
San Francisco	123°	38°
Houston	95°	30°
Dallas	97°	33°
St. Louis	90°	38°
Chicago	87°	42°
Pittsburgh	80°	41°
Atlanta	84°	34°

longitude: 96.75°; latitude: 36.25°

14. Consider the data given in Problem 13. Assuming the following average number of trips to each plant, what longitude and latitude are most central to the eight plants?

City	Monthly Trips
Los Angeles	6
San Francisco	3
Houston	1
Dallas	4
St. Louis	1
Chicago	1
Pittsburgh	5
Atlanta	7

longitude: 97.32°; latitude: 35.82°

15. Consider the data given in Problems 13 and 14. Which location is a better site to house the repair crew if the choice is restricted to either Dallas or St. Louis, under the following conditions?

St. Louis
Dallas

(a) without regard to the number of trips
(b) with regard to the number of trips

COMPUTER CASE STUDY 5.1: CONSOLIDATED BOTTLING INC.

Consolidated Bottling Incorporated bottles spring water. Consolidated began its operations with one small plant in Baltimore and still maintains its corporate headquarters in Baltimore. Over the years, the company has grown; it now has bottling operations in or near twelve cities in the United States and distributors in or near eighteen cities in North America (including the twelve bottling plants).

The following table presents the plant capacities in the twelve cities.

Plant	Monthly Capacity (in thousands of cases)
Albuquerque	250
Baltimore	270
Boston	143
Chicago	182
Dallas	265
Denver	183
Detroit	121
Houston	265
Kansas City	240
Los Angeles	157
Portland	121
St. Paul	105

The monthly demand of the eighteen distributorships is reflected in the following table.

Plant	Monthly Usage (in thousands of cases)
Albuquerque	24
Baltimore	62
Boston	64
Chicago	336
Columbus	53
Dallas	84
Denver	51
Detroit	151
Houston	123
Indianapolis	74
Kansas City	50
Los Angeles	281
Miami	33
Montreal	121
Portland	38
Raleigh	12
St. Paul	30
San Francisco	71

Consolidated is about to embark on a large total quality management program. A new functional group is being created to bring new quality techniques to the operations. The group will visit each plant in an effort to improve the quality of the bottling operations there.

Because the new quality team will be spending so much time traveling, Consolidated feels that it is best to locate it central to the company's facilities rather than in Baltimore. Consolidated has developed a table of the coordinates of each of its facilities.

City	Type	Latitude	Longitude
Albuquerque	P/D	35°	107°
Baltimore	P/D	39°	77°
Boston	P/D	42°	71°
Chicago	P/D	42°	88°
Columbus	D	40°	83°
Dallas	P/D	33°	97°
Denver	P/D	40°	105°
Detroit	P/D	42°	83°
Houston	P/D	30°	95°
Indianapolis	D	39°	86°
Kansas City	P/D	39°	95°
Los Angeles	P/D	34°	119°
Miami	D	26°	81°
Montreal	D	46°	74°
Portland	P/D	45°	123°
Raleigh	D	36°	79°
St. Paul	P/D	45°	94°
San Francisco	D	38°	122°

Examine the information and present a set of plans for centrally locating the total quality management team. Suppose that Consolidated wishes to place its team in a city in which the company has a plant. Which city is best? Suppose that Consolidated wants to put its team into any city in which it has either a plant or a distributor. Which city is best? Suppose that Consolidated does not restrict itself to a city in which it currently operates. Where in the United States should the team be located?

REFERENCES

Amrine, H. T., J. A. Ritchey, and C. L. Moodie. *Manufacturing Organization and Management.* 5th ed. Englewood Cliffs, N.J.: Prentice-Hall, 1987.

Facility Location Decisions. New York: Fortune, 1977.

Hamer, A. M. *Industrial Exodus from Central City: Public Policy and the Comparative Costs of Location.* Lexington, Mass.: Lexington Books, 1973.

Hamilton, F. E. I., ed. *Spatial Perspectives on Industrial Organization and Decision Making.* London: John Wiley and Sons, 1974.

Isard, W. *Methods of Regional Analysis: An Introduction to Regional Science.* Cambridge, Mass.: The M.I.T. Press, 1960.

Mandell, L. *Industrial Location Decisions.* New York: Praeger Publishers, 1975.

McLaughlin, G. E. and S. Robock. *Why Industry Moves South,* National Planning Association, Committee of the South, Report no. 3, Washington, D.C., 1949.

Miller, E. W. *Manufacturing: A Study of Industrial Location.* University Park, Penn.: The Pennsylvania State University Press, 1977.

Whitman, E. S., and W. J. Schmidt. *Plant Relocation.* New York: American Management Association, 1966.

THE OPERATIONS NETWORK

■ To introduce the network of operations that exists for providing the product or service to the consumer

■ To explain the different types of networks and the relationship of the networks to the overall product or service cost

■ To present the model for shipping from multiple origins to multiple destinations

■ To present the various means of transportation and their advantages and disadvantages

■ To enumerate the concerns of shipping

■ To differentiate between production and distribution strategies that are driven by demand and production and distribution strategies that are driven by supply

INTRODUCTION

In the previous chapter, we discussed the critical factors to be considered when deciding where to open or close a facility. Most of that chapter implied that location decisions are made independently, without reference to the existence of any other sites already in operation. The assumption was that any new location operated in its own **site interactions** environment with little or no interaction from these other sites. In fact, both the quantitative and qualitative methods presented in Chapter 5 did not account for the fact that we might be locating our second, third, or tenth facility. A more detailed analysis is necessary to account for the fact that a facility is but one part of a much larger network of operations.

Our original description of the components of operations management was given in Chapter 1, and this description is illustrated in Figure 6.1. However, this diagram really applies to only one particular aspect or specific operation of the organization. A more global picture of the operations process, as described in Chapter 2, is given in Figure 6.2. This expanded diagram indicates that organizations consist of flows of **flows of** transformations and that the output of one transformation is the input to the next **transformations** transformation. In the figure, the first transformation represents a plant that produces an output that is used in the third transformation; the third transformation is shown to produce an output that is sold at the retail outlet, represented by the fifth transformation. The second and fourth transformations represent the shipping of the component part and the finished goods, respectively. In some cases, all five transformations will belong to the same company; in other cases, they may belong to up to five different companies.

Figure 6.2 shows only one type of flow. In this chapter, we will describe the different types of networks. Obviously the location of a new facility depends on its relationship to the larger operations network. Furthermore, a great deal of money is saved when a network is structured and operated properly. The operation of the network is termed *distribution management,* and its importance will be detailed in this chapter.

Distribution management involves the design and utilization of a network of available channels for the movement of raw materials, component parts, and finished products. Many complex logistics problems are encountered in distribution management and, as we shall see, a technique known as the transportation method is most useful in solving these problems. But, first, let us describe some distribution systems and how they link the analyses of other operations problems.

In many businesses, the primary operation is distribution. Certainly, our electric, gas, telephone, and water utilities fall into this category. Yet these businesses differ in operation and in location of facilities. The gas and water that reaches our homes, schools, and offices most often follows a fixed route. The distribution system is static. The electric utility and the telephone utility, however, often are linked to a national or regional grid that adds flexibility to the distribution system and introduces a dynamic element to it. For these utilities, location decisions are technical ones, the problem being how to keep up the required pressures (or voltages) for every customer while minimizing the number of locations (pumps, transformers, switches). The distribution system is designed to meet a specified capacity (see Chapter 3), and this design capacity is defined by forecasts (see Chapter 4) of peak demand usage (not average demand).

In other businesses, distribution is not the main operation but represents a support function to the primary operations. Sometimes, as in many service operations, the distribution function contributes as much or more to company costs (seldom does it contribute to profits) than do the primary operations themselves. A supermarket chain provides a good example, because the cost of storing goods in warehouses and shipping them to the stores may cost as much as the operation of the stores themselves. If we view the two primary operations of a mining company as extraction and processing, then this is another good example, because most of the operating cost at a mine involves the transportation between the point of extraction and the processing plant.

(margin notes) **distribution management**

distribution is primary operation

distribution is a link

FIGURE 6.1 Basic components of operations management

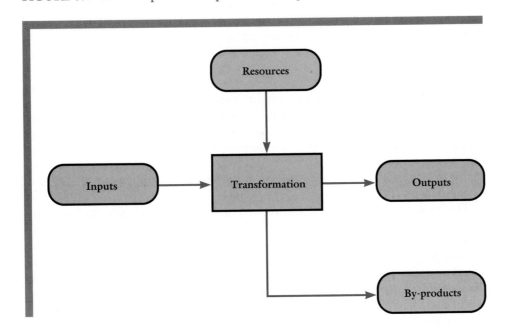

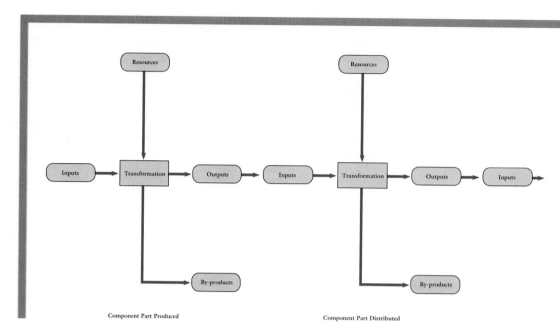

Component Part Produced   Component Part Distributed

Transparency Master 6.1:   **FIGURE 6.2 Sequence of operations**
Sequence of Operations.

distribution is sole product

A third group of businesses specializes in distribution; that is, distribution is the primary operation (transformation) of these companies. Examples include postal and package delivery services (primarily, the Postal Service, Federal Express, and UPS), trucking companies and moving companies (Allied, Mayflower, North American, and others), and transportation companies (Amtrak, Greyhound, United Airlines, among others). For the latter group, location of facilities in their transportation networks is critical, in terms both of cost and of competitive position. Also, the "commodity" being shipped or distributed usually is people. These distribution companies differ from the first group (utilities) because that group must both produce and distribute a product (electricity, gas, water, telephone), whereas these companies' "product" is simply distribution.

description of network

In general, the operations (or multifacility) network consists of (1) a set of locations that ship, receive, or store material or customers and (2) the set of routes or means available to connect them. These locations may include factories, regional warehouses, parts suppliers, local distributors, or consumer outlets. For a given shipment, they can be classified as either supply locations or demand locations. Because all locations are storage points, they also have inventory problems. The concern about inventory has led a great number of companies to locate near their suppliers (as we discussed in Chapters 2 and 5).

The routes available for distribution are, traditionally, land, sea, and air. The options for sea and air routes are obvious. Land route options are rail, truck, and pipeline. Recently, however, a new form of distribution has been made available for the "shipping" of information. Today, data are shipped between computers and offices by satellite or cable on a regular basis, and this route should not be overlooked. Which option or combination of options should be used? Between them, the discussions of cost analysis in Chapter 3 and Appendix A provide a means for answering this question; usually, the lower cost option is selected. However, it is not purely a financial

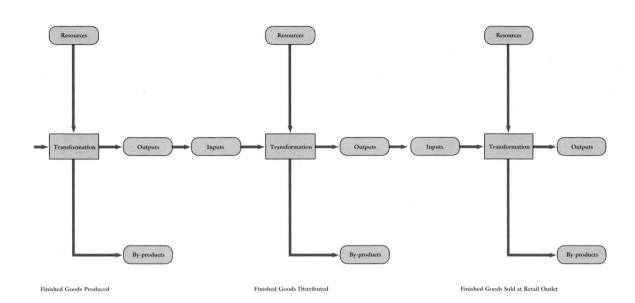

Finished Goods Produced   Finished Goods Distributed   Finished Goods Sold at Retail Outlet

decision, because time factors (speed of delivery) and reliability factors (security, safety) also may affect the decision.

Teaching Suggestion 6.1: Product Flows. See the Instructor's Section for details.

SIMPLE DISTRIBUTION NETWORKS

A simple distribution network has only one initial source of supply, one final repository of demand, or both, as shown in Figure 6.3. Locations and routes are fixed, so there is little or no flexibility. The major decisions are when to order, how much to order, and when to ship. These decisions are based on purchasing and the related inventory considerations. There are three types of simple networks:

major decisions

- arborescent,
- coalescent, and
- series.

The **arborescent network** (it spreads out like a tree; see Figure 6.4) illustrates the case of pure distribution. The term *pure distribution* refers to the case where no operations are done on the material except for shipping and storing it. What a factory produces supplies a series of regional warehouses, which ship the product to local distributors, who ship it to retail outlets. A local distributor may obtain supplies only from its regional supplier, so the system is very rigid. However, the location decisions that were made when setting up the system should have tried to minimize the distribution costs. The arborescent network shown in Figure 6.4 applies to most of our consumer goods. A supermarket chain is an especially good example of a company that has much leverage over the locations, because the large chains usually own all the levels of the distribution network.

arborescent network

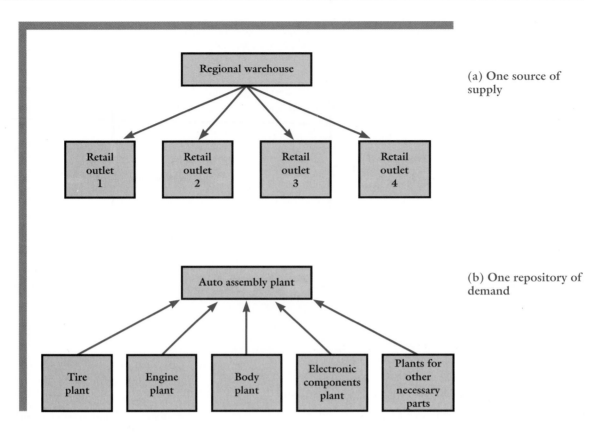

(a) One source of supply

(b) One repository of demand

FIGURE 6.3 Simple distribution networks

FIGURE 6.4 Arborescent network

Transparency Master 6.2:
Arborescent Network.

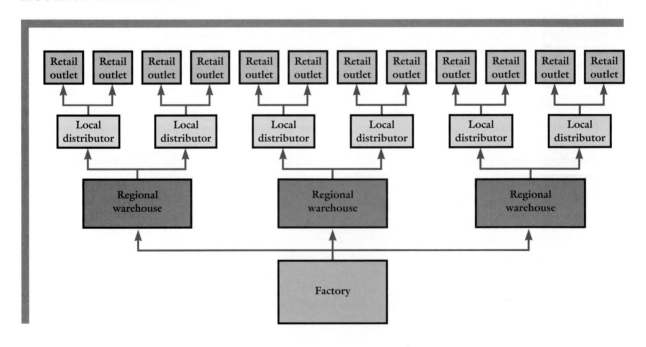

The flow in a **coalescent network** is exactly the opposite from that in an arborescent network. The coalescent network is seen in the large-scale production of complex products assembled from many subcomponents. The automobile industry (see Figure 6.5) is a prime example: Raw materials are shipped to the companies that produce gaskets, tires, radiators, and so forth, and all of these items are shipped to the plant, where the next higher-level assembly is performed. Finally, the auto assembly plant receives all of these items and assembles (coalesces) them into a final product (the car).

coalescent network

FIGURE 6.5 Coalescent network for auto assembly

Transparency Master 6.3: Coalescent Network.

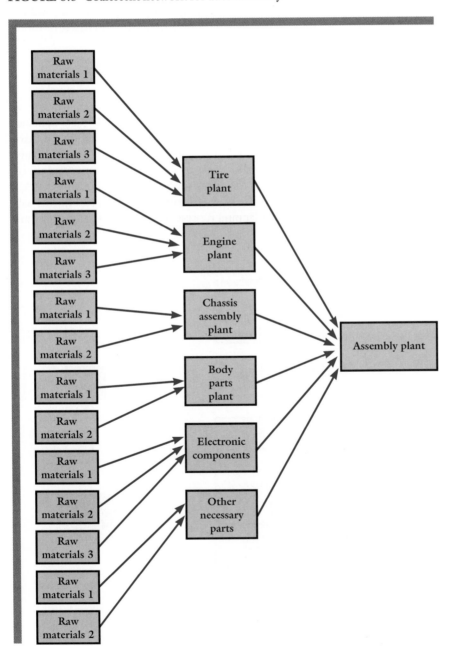

series network

The **series network** is neither arborescent nor coalescent, but is a combination of the two. It is a distribution system where a product is shipped from one location to another for further processing, such as may occur in the mining industry or the lumber industry. Figure 6.6 shows a series network.

Another example of a series system is the line balancing problem, which will be described in the next chapter. In this case, the "shipping" is from one machine to the next in a production facility. Locations can be areas of a production plant just as easily as they can be cities hundreds or thousands of miles away from the plant. The internal type of distribution network is known as a materials handling system. Its design is crucial to the success of any complex operation, and it usually consists of series of conveyors, storage racks, forklifts, pallets, and even the people who move a product from one workstation to another. Materials handling systems are discussed in more detail in the next chapter.

internal distribution

COMPLEX DISTRIBUTION NETWORKS

choice of route

In the simple arborescent network shown in part (a) of Figure 6.3, each demand point is supplied by only one supplier; in the simple coalescent network shown in part (b) of Figure 6.3, each supply point supplies only one demand point. However, many distribution networks allow for a demand location to be supplied from a variety of supply locations and for a supply location to supply several different demand points. In Figures 6.3, 6.4, 6.5, and 6.6, no arcs are drawn across any other arcs, but this will occur in the **complex network.** The overlapping represents choices. One type of com-

FIGURE 6.6 Series
distribution network
for a copper mine

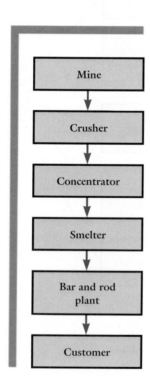

Chi-Chi Restaurants, Inc.

Chi-Chi Restaurants, Inc., the leader in the Mexican full service segment, has been in business for fifteen years. There are 260 Chi-Chi's throughout the United States, Canada, and Europe, as well as one in Kuwait. Their long range strategic planning recognizes a need to continually keep pace and evolve with industry and customers needs. They place considerable emphasis on service and cleanliness, while presenting a positive, caring attitude for their customers.

The restaurant is a service process that transforms the hungry customer into the satisfied customer. At Chi-Chi's, the goal is to serve the guests' orders within 16 minutes of it being placed.

Chi-Chi's hires 5 vice-presidents, 32 area supervisors, 1250 managers and over 24,000 employees. As a service company they must be flexible in their staffing and able to anticipate customer demand so that adequate staffing patterns are maintained. Here, a manager is training an employee in the proper procedures for clearing and cleaning tables.

(Photographs courtesy of Chi-Chi Restaurants Inc.)

High Quality standards are always important to maintain. Here a manager is performing the regular duty of checking the quality of the ground beef. All Chi-Chi restaurants prepare food items daily and expect management to monitor quality standards.

By providing salad bars, or in this instance a luncheon buffet, the food service industry can take advantage of an opportunity to turn the customer into his/her own server.

Inventory analysis is one way of satisfying the crucial goal of providing the appropriate resource at the appropriate time and using those resources in the most efficient manner possible.

The scheduling of operations is more difficult in a service operation than in manufacturing, yet just as important. This manager observes a strict schedule assuring the successful continuation of their customer oriented process. In this instance he is performing the 10:30 a.m. Line Test.

Short range planning includes coping with the specifics of schedules, as well as putting out fires. Problem solving measures, such as having food servers make a final check on food quality before presentation to the customer, helps to reduce stress and improve overall performance.

No step of the process is unimportant, everything must flow smoothly despite any unexpected challenges. In the kitchen, a dish machine operator inspects every pot, pan and dish for cleanliness.

To remain competitive Chi-Chi's must constantly revise its tactical planning. This year the Chi-Chi's restaurant chain embarked upon "Operation Restage", a medium range plan intended to revise the design of entryways, waiting areas and main dining rooms. In addition they are testing a new plan for putting "fresh made" tortilla machines in the highly visible areas of the restaurants.

The by-product of the service industry is customer satisfaction, sometimes difficult to estimate. Chi-Chi's attempts to please its customers by providing them with well-trained servers; by providing their servers with the benefits and support services they need; and by asking their managers to be receptive to the complaints and compliments of all parties involved.

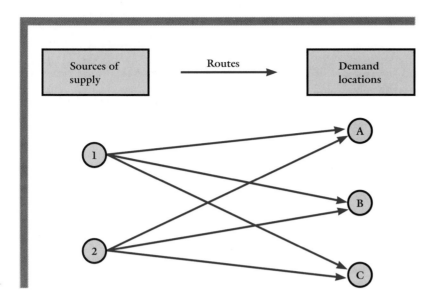

FIGURE 6.7 Complex network for transportation problem

plex system is the transportation problem discussed in the next section. A diagram representing a complex network is presented as Figure 6.7.

The distribution network illustrated in Figure 6.7 is complex because material from either source may be shipped to any of the three demand locations. This allows for the use of six possible routes of shipment.

There is another difference between complex and simple systems. In the simple networks shown previously, all routes (branches) are used. In this complex network, it is not necessary to use all six routes. A minimum of three would be required to service the demand locations. The technique used to decide which routes to use in any given situation is a topic of the next section. (It turns out that the number of routes necessary will be less than the total number of locations.)

Another, more complex distribution network is described by the transshipment problem. In this problem, all of the complexities of the transportation problem are present, plus there is the added feature that each location may serve as both a supply and a demand point. This allows for shipping from one city to a second by way of a third, which is an option that is used in many practical distribution systems (see Figure 6.8). Anyone who has flown recognizes that the airlines handle their passenger routes in this way. Although the transportation method described in the next section can solve the transshipment problem, the procedure for doing so is beyond the scope of this text.

transshipment

THE TRANSPORTATION PROBLEM

The classic transportation problem concerns the transportation of a single product from several sources, typically plants or factories, to many destinations, typically warehouses or distributors (as, for example, in Figure 6.7). Each source has a limited capac-

transportation model assumptions

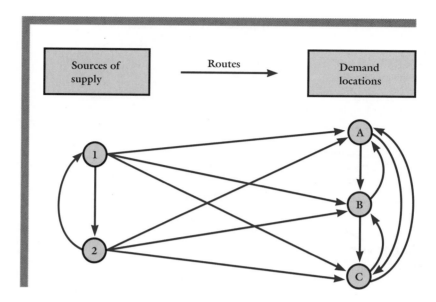

FIGURE 6.8 Complex network for transshipment problem

ity to manufacture the product, and each destination has certain requirements regarding the demand for the product. The only concern is the cost of shipping, which depends primarily on the distance between any source and any destination, the means of transportation, and the quantity shipped from source to destination. The goal is to minimize the total transportation cost that accrues between all sources and destinations *subject to* meeting the supply (capacity) and demand restrictions for the product.

The transportation model was developed independently in the 1930s and 1940s by three different researchers—Leonid Kantorovich, Tjallings Koopmans, and Frank Hitchcock. The transportation model is important for two reasons. The first reason is obvious. Many firms face the problem of shipping units from several origins to several destinations and have various ways to do this. These companies wish to find the way that minimizes the total cost. The transportation model is also important because it was the first model of a more general type known as linear programming. As we noted in Chapter 1, the major early developments in linear programming occurred in the late 1940s and are attributed to George Dantzig. Linear programming and transportation formed the foundation for what is now commonly known as Management Science or Operations Research. In recognition of this, Kantorovich and Koopmans were awarded the 1975 Nobel Memorial Prize in Economics for their pioneering work on the transportation problem.

Even though the problem is called a transportation problem, its model also is used for solving problems not related to transportation. The same solution technique may be utilized for an array of problems, such as those related to production planning (discussed in Chapter 12), job or machine assignment (explained in Chapter 15), and plant location, which we present later in this chapter.

optimal solution   The algorithm provided for this problem is guaranteed to find the **optimal solution** to any transportation problem. Thus, it is one of a group of **optimization** techniques. For any problem, the best of all possible solutions is found.

The Transportation Problem at Avis

Have you ever wondered how a car rental agency such as Avis can allow a customer to pick up a car in one city and drop it off in another? How do car (and truck) rental agencies maintain the proper number of cars in each location if the car that you picked up in, say, Orlando winds up in Boston? Doesn't that make Orlando short one car and stick Boston with an extra one? Car and truck rental agencies are able to solve the problems caused by one-way renting by using the transportation model.

Source: For All Practical Purposes (New York: W. H. Freeman, 1988).

This is the first such technique presented in this text. Others presented later, such as linear programming (in Chapter 11) and the assignment method (in Chapter 15), use similar approaches. It is necessary, however, to put each of these tools of management science into their proper perspective within the world of operations management. The problem itself, be it distribution or any of the other topics in this text, is an integral part of operations management. These solution techniques belong to the field of management science. Consequently, in this context, one may view management science as providing support, aids, or tools that enable the operations manager to make better decisions.

The transportation problem involves the routing of shipments from a set of supply points (sources) to a set of demand points (destinations). The general problem is described as having m sources and n destinations. Each source has a known available supply to ship, and each destination has a known demand requirement.

The first, implicit assumption of the model (often not recognized) is that the shipments must all occur during the same time period. That is, one time period or planning period is assumed, during which all shipments must be carried out. The planning period might be one day, one month, or one year. Each route, if used, is used only once, and no duplication of effort or reuse of resources or equipment is allowed. Of course, the same routes may be reused during a future planning period.

one time period

A second assumption is that every source can supply each destination and that each destination can be supplied from any or all of the sources. That is, for a case in which there are 6 sources and 14 destinations, there are $6 \times 14 = 84$ (or $m \times n$) possible routes that could be used. Because our solution method requires that all of these routes be available, we need to be aware that practical considerations present in any such problem may prohibit the use of one or more routes. What should be done in such a case? Rather than abandon the technique, the assignment of a ridiculously high cost to the use of that route, while allowing its use, will yield the desired result. The route with such a high shipping cost will not be used. An example of this is presented at the end of our section on special cases.

$m \times n$ routes

A third assumption is that the cost of shipping along each route is known and fixed and that this cost is **proportional** to the amount being shipped. Proportionality is the assumption that is most often brought into question because of discounts provided by most rail and trucking companies to larger-volume users. It is necessary to check whether this assumption holds; in the event that it does not, the effect of the lack of proportionality on the resulting decisions must be determined. If a lack of

Teaching Suggestion 6.2: Proportionality. See the Instructor's Section for details.

cost is known, fixed, proportional, and additive

Teaching Suggestion 6.3: Linearity. See the Instructor's Section for details.
total supply = total demand

information required

proportionality on the costs will significantly affect the decisions, then the approach described here is not suitable.

A fourth assumption is that the costs of shipping are **additive.** That is, if we ship one unit from St. Louis to Indianapolis and one unit from St. Louis to Dayton, the cost is the sum of the two individual shipping costs (from St. Louis to Dayton and from St. Louis to Indianapolis), even though Indianapolis is en route to Dayton from St. Louis. When costs are both additive and proportional, we term them **linear.**

A fifth assumption crucial to the working of the algorithm is that the total of the supplies from all sources is exactly equal to the total of all of the demand requirements. Practically, this is seldom the case. We show how to correct for this inequality later in the chapter.

The prototype problem presented next assumes that all of the model's assumptions hold true. Keep these assumptions in mind while reading the problem in order to judge which, if any, assumption may be questionable. Example 6.1 demonstrates the standard transportation model. Although we will solve the example later, our immediate concern is indicating what information is required for a transportation problem and how that information should be structured.

> **Example 6.1**   Supercola Incorporated bottles cola in three plants located in Chicago, Atlanta, and Seattle. These plants have annual capacities of 8, 12, and 16 million cases of cola, respectively. The cola is shipped from these three plants to four major distributors located in Newark, Pittsburgh, Detroit, and Boston. The annual demands of the four distributors are 7, 9, 11, and 9 million cases, respectively. Notice that the total supply and the total demand both equal 36 million cases. The cost of shipping the cola from each plant to each distributor, as well as the supplies and demands, are given in Table 6.1. (Note: The costs in Table 6.1 are in thousands of dollars per million cases shipped. For example, the cost of shipping a million cases from Chicago to Newark is $22,000.) As there are three plants and four distributors, there are $3 \times 4 = 12$ routes available for use, but it is not necessary to use all the routes. The question is, Which plants(s) should supply which distributor(s) in order to minimize the total shipping cost?   ∎

TABLE 6.1 Supercola transportation parameters (Example 6.1)

		To			
From	Newark	Pittsburgh	Detroit	Boston	**Supply**
Chicago	$22	$18	$16	$28	8
Atlanta	$14	$12	$19	$23	12
Seattle	$37	$35	$30	$40	16
Demand	7	9	11	9	36

Note: Supply and demand in millions of cases; costs in thousands per one million cases shipped

In the next section, we will present the solution method for answering the question posed in Example 6.1. For now, note that the problem's costs are linear; in other words, they satisfy the properties of proportionality and additivity. By proportionality, we mean that because the cost of shipping one million cases from Chicago to Newark is $22,000, the cost of shipping two million cases from Chicago to Newark is 2 × $22,000 = $44,000. By additivity, we mean that the cost of shipping one million cases from Chicago to Newark and one million cases from Chicago to Boston is $22,000 + $28,000 = $50,000. There is no quantity discount, nor is there any reduction in cost due to the relative proximity of Newark to Boston.

The method for solving the transportation problem is an algorithm. That is, it is a step-by-step procedure for solving a problem. The algorithm consists of three steps, two of which may be repeated several times. The first step is determining a feasible starting solution. A feasible starting solution is a solution that satisfies the supply and demand requirements. The second step is performing an optimality test to determine whether the current solution is optimal, in which case the procedure should stop. The third step improves the current solution if it is not optimal. The algorithm is presented in Figure 6.9.

THE SOLUTION PROCEDURE

The solution method, termed appropriately, the transportation method, is presented in this section. As we just mentioned, there are three basic steps:

Step 1. Find a starting solution.

Step 2. Check to see if the solution is optimal.

Step 3. Improve the solution and return to step 2.

The first step is performed once, and it may utilize one of several available techniques. The second step is performed on the starting solution and all subsequent solutions. The algorithm always terminates after step 2 (but not necessarily the first time that step 2 is performed). The third step is implemented only if the solution is not optimal. Each new solution is better than the previous one. Thus, the approach is to find a series of continually improving solutions until the optimal solution is found. The iterative portion of the algorithm (steps 2 and 3) is referred to as the stepping stone method.

The easiest method for finding a starting solution is termed the **northwest corner method** and is presented shortly. An alternative starting method, the **minimal cost method,** is presented later. The minimal cost method does not replace the entire algorithm—it is just another way to accomplish the first step of the procedure. Generally, the minimal cost method provides better starting solutions than does the northwest corner method, without requiring that much more work. This reduction in work is important if the problem is solved by hand.

THE NORTHWEST CORNER METHOD

The first step in solving a transportation problem is, as we have noted, to obtain a starting solution. There are different methods that provide feasible starting solutions. The better the starting solution is, the fewer the number of improvements that are

Transparency Master 6.4:
The Transportation
Algorithm.

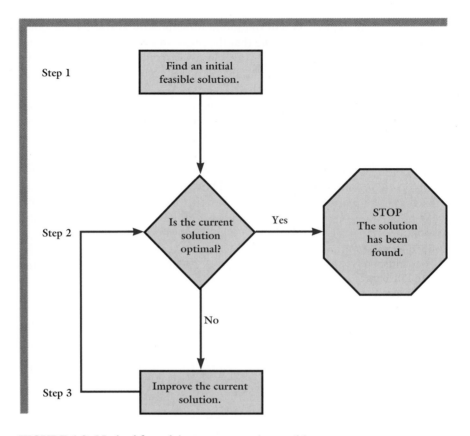

FIGURE 6.9 **Method for solving transportation problem**

required to reach the optimal solution. If one begins with a "bad" starting point, much more computational time and much greater effort are spent than if one begins with a good starting point. There is a trade-off between the amount of work invested in the starting solution and the time invested in improving the solution to optimality. This trade-off is shown in Figure 6.10.

Teaching Suggestion 6.4:
Vogel's Approximation
Method (VAM). See the
Instructor's Section for
details.

In this section, we first present the easiest starting solution method: the northwest corner method. Later, we provide a better method, which is almost as easy. A third method, Vogel's approximation method (VAM), is available, but we do not present it because its benefits are only marginal. (It is available in AB:POM, however.)

The reason the northwest corner method is the easiest method for finding a starting solution is that it does not consider the transportation costs. In this method, we begin in the upper left-hand corner of the table (the northwest corner) and proceed to the lower right-hand corner, moving either down or to the right, always satisfying a demand or depleting a supply at each step.

ship as many as possible in each chosen cell

Let us return to Example 6.1, this time omitting the millions for the sake of convenience. In the example, the starting point is the Chicago to Newark cell (see part (a) in Table 6.2). The supply at Chicago is 8 and the demand at Newark is 7. Therefore, we schedule for shipment 7 units from Chicago to Newark. This satisfies the demand at Newark, and leaves 1 unit (8 − 7) at Chicago. The demand at Newark is satisfied, so we proceed to the next distributor, which is one column to the right (see part (b) in Table 6.2). Pittsburgh has a demand of 9 units, but Chicago now has a supply of 1 unit. Therefore, we schedule for shipment 1 unit from Chicago to Pittsburgh. This reduces the demand at Pittsburgh from 9 to 8 units and depletes the supply at Chicago, so we proceed to the next supply point, which is one row down (see part (c) of Table 6.2). Atlanta has a supply of 12 units. Pittsburgh needs 8 more units to meet its demand, hence 8 units are scheduled for shipment from Atlanta to Pittsburgh. We continue in this fashion, with the remaining steps as given in Table 6.2. Note that part (f) of Table 6.2 represents a complete shipping schedule.

total shipping cost

Given a shipping schedule, computing the total shipping cost is a simple matter. The total cost of any shipping schedule is simply the sum of the cost of each scheduled shipment. For our example, we have the following.

Shipment	Shipment Cost (Units × $/Unit)
Chicago to Newark	7 × $22 = $154
Chicago to Pittsburgh	1 × $18 = $ 18
Atlanta to Pittsburgh	8 × $12 = $ 96
Atlanta to Detroit	4 × $19 = $ 76
Seattle to Detroit	7 × $30 = $210
Seattle to Boston	9 × $40 = $360
	$914

Again, note that we have omitted 000s in our dollar figures.

FIGURE 6.10 The trade-off between step 1 and steps 2 and 3

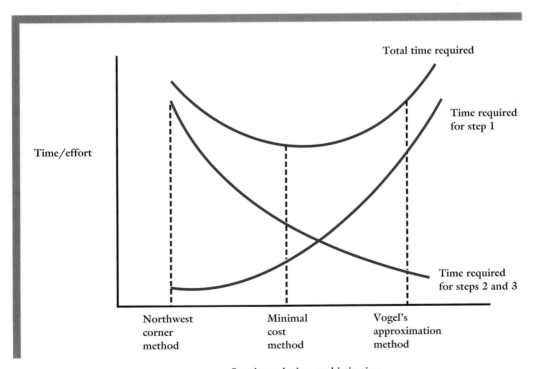

TABLE 6.2 Supercola northwest corner method (Example 6.1)

From	To Newark	Pittsburgh	Detroit	Boston	Supply	
Chicago	7				8̸ 1	(a)
Atlanta					12	
Seattle					16	
Demand	7̸	9	11	9	36	

From	To Newark	Pittsburgh	Detroit	Boston	Supply	
Chicago	7	1			8̸ 1̸	(b)
Atlanta					12	
Seattle					16	
Demand	7̸	9̸ / 8	11	9	36	

From	To Newark	Pittsburgh	Detroit	Boston	Supply	
Chicago	7	1			8̸ 1̸	(c)
Atlanta		8			1̸2 4	
Seattle					16	
Demand	7̸	9̸ / 8̸	11	9	36	

From	To Newark	Pittsburgh	Detroit	Boston	Supply	
Chicago	7	1			8̸ 1̸	(d)
Atlanta		8	4		1̸2 4̸	
Seattle					16	
Demand	7̸	9̸ / 8̸	1̸1 / 7	9	36	

continued

TABLE 6.2 (Continued)

	To				
From	Newark	Pittsburgh	Detroit	Boston	Supply
Chicago	7	1			~~8~~ ~~1~~
Atlanta		8	4		~~12~~ ~~4~~ (e)
Seattle			7		~~16~~ 9
Demand	~~7~~	~~9~~ ~~8~~	~~11~~ ~~7~~	9	36

	To				
From	Newark	Pittsburgh	Detroit	Boston	Supply
Chicago	7	1			~~8~~ ~~1~~
Atlanta		8	4		~~12~~ ~~4~~ (f)
Seattle			7	9	~~16~~ ~~9~~
Demand	~~7~~	~~9~~ ~~8~~	~~11~~ ~~7~~	~~9~~	

Note: Shipments in millions of cases

At this point, we have no idea whether $914,000 is a high or a low total shipping cost, but our schedule does satisfy the supply and demand requirements of the plants and distributors. Thus, we see that the northwest corner method is simple and easy to apply. However, as mentioned before, the method typically does not give a good starting solution because it does not consider the shipping costs when assigning the shipments. Also, when assigning shipments to cells, one may be inquisitive and ask why it is not possible to start from the northeast, southwest, or southeast corners. As a matter of fact, any corner is permissible, and there is no way to tell which corner provides the best starting point.

There is one important fact that we should point out because it is a basis for the improvement of the solution that is presented next. Because the example has three supply points and four demand points, there are $3 \times 4 = 12$ origin–destination pairs, each of which is represented by a cell in the 3×4 table. However, the solution we generated by the northwest corner method did not use all twelve cells; instead, it used only six. The following is the rule that we follow for determining the number of stepping stones in the solution of transportation problems.

All solutions (shipping schedules) must use exactly $m + n - 1$ cells, where m represents the number of supply (origin) points and n represents the number of demand (destination) points.

rule for number of stepping stones

Thus, because our example has $m = 3$ rows and $n = 4$ columns, any solution to our problem must use exactly $3 + 4 - 1 = 6$ cells. In a problem that is 10×100, the number of cells must be $10 + 100 - 1 = 109$ exactly.

SOLUTION EVALUATION

Once a starting solution has been found, the next step is to evaluate that solution. That is, we want to determine whether the current solution is optimal or if it needs to be improved. The way that we determine the optimality of the solution is to ask the following question: Would it pay—that is, reduce costs or increase profits—to assign a shipment to any one of the empty cells? If the answer is yes, it is necessary both to assign the shipment and to provide a mechanism to maintain feasibility by not violating the supply or demand requirements. However, if the answer is no (in which case all empty cells should remain empty), then this indicates that an optimal solution has been reached and no further improvements are possible.

Teaching Suggestion 6.5: Reading the Tables. See the Instructor's Section for details.

boxed number is shipping cost

circled number is shipment

Transparency Master 6.5: The Initial Solution.

STEPPING STONE METHOD: Table 6.3 presents the starting solution that was found by using the northwest corner method. Notice that the table contains both per unit shipping costs and cell allocations. It will be necessary to place different types of numbers in each cell. Therefore, we will maintain the following conventions: In the upper left-hand corner of each cell we will place a box, inside which will be the cost of shipping one unit. For any given problem, these numbers will never change. The allocations will be represented by circled numbers. Uncircled numbers inside a cell will refer to **marginal cost,** a concept that we now develop.

Our concern now is with the six empty cells in Table 6.3. Could we reduce the shipping cost if we shipped units from Chicago to Detroit or Boston, from Atlanta to

TABLE 6.3 Supercola northwest corner method

From	Newark (N)	Pittsburgh (P)	Detroit (D)	Boston (B)	Supply
Chicago (C)	$22 ⑦	$18 ①	$16	$28	8
Atlanta (A)	$14	$12 ⑧	$19 ④	$23	12
Seattle (S)	$37	$35	$30 ⑦	$40 ⑨	16
Demand	7	9	11	9	36

Note: Shipments in millions of cases; costs in thousands per one million cases shipped

Newark or Boston, or from Seattle to Newark or Pittsburgh? If none of these six combinations can reduce the cost, then the current solution is optimal.

Let us begin by examining the cell from Chicago to Detroit, which we denote as cell (C–D). We want to determine what will happen if we ship some number of units from Chicago to Detroit. Let us pick the smallest number of units possible—namely, one unit. (Remember, a unit is one million cases.)

In part (a) of Table 6.4 we have listed the current solution and, in addition, placed a +1 in cell (C–D) to indicate that we want to ship one unit from Chicago to Detroit. (This +1 is not a marginal cost. Only the sign will be used in future tables.) This one unit causes two problems. The total amount shipped out of Chicago is one unit too many and the total amount shipped into Detroit is one unit too many. Let us take care of the Chicago problem first.

creating a loop of +1s and −1s

Because there is now one unit too many in the Chicago row, we must subtract one unit from one of the cells in the Chicago row. Of course, we cannot subtract a unit from Chicago–Boston cell because it currently has no units. The choice is between cell (C–N) and cell (C–P). We choose cell (C–P) for reasons that will soon be clear. The subtraction is represented in part (b) of Table 6.4. Notice that, rather than actually subtracting one unit from our circled allocation, we place −1 in the cell instead.

We now have an additional problem: Because we took one unit from cell (C–P), too few units are being shipped into Pittsburgh. Therefore, we must add one unit either to cell (A–P) or to cell (S–P). We choose cell (A–P), because there is a shipment in that cell already. The +1 appears in part (c) of Table 6.4.

Adding the unit in cell (A–P) means that one unit too many is being shipped from Atlanta. We must subtract a unit from a cell that has a shipment. The only cell available is cell (A–D), so we subtract one unit from that shipment. The −1 is given in part (d) of Table 6.4. Notice that by subtracting one from cell (A–D), we have balanced not only Atlanta but also Detroit. Thus, part (d) in Table 6.4 contains two +1s and two −1s, which cancel each other out and preserve the original supply and demand requirements.

The next question is, If we make the changes indicated by the +1s and −1s, how will these changes affect the cost? Examining the costs given in the table, we see that adding one unit from Chicago to Detroit will *increase* the cost by $16, subtracting one unit from Chicago to Pittsburgh will *decrease* the cost by $18, adding one unit from Atlanta to Pittsburgh will *increase* the cost by $12, and subtracting one unit from Atlanta to Detroit will *decrease* the cost by $19. The net effect, then, is $16 − $18 + $12 − $19 = −$9, which means that the total shipping cost will *decrease* by $9. Therefore, the current solution is not optimal and the next step (step 3 of the algorithm) is to make the changes in the shipping schedule that are necessary to reduce the total cost. Before we actually make the changes, let us present the rules for generating the +1s and −1s and examine some of the other empty cells for practice. First the rules.

computing the marginal cost

1. Begin at the empty cell that is to be evaluated. Place a + in this cell.
2. Balance the row by placing a − in the same row where the + was just placed *in a cell that already has an allocation.*
3. Balance the column by placing a + in the same column where the − was just placed *in a cell that already has an allocation.*
4. Repeat steps 2 and 3 until all rows and columns are balanced—that is, either each row and column has no +s or −s or it has exactly one + and one −.

Teaching Suggestion 6.6: Putting the Marginal Cost in the Table. See the Instructor's Section for details.

Before looking at the other empty cells, we should note that all cells that are part of a chain of $+$s and $-$s must already have an allocation, except for the very first cell. We should also note that there is one and only one possible chain that can be constructed from one empty cell. Therefore, if the rules are followed, it is impossible to pick a wrong chain. To demonstrate this, let us again consider the empty cell (C–D). Suppose that after placing a $+1$ in (C–D) we chose to put the -1 in cell (C–N) rather than (C–P), as we had done before. It would then be impossible to balance the New-

only one chain is possible

TABLE 6.4 Supercola evaluation of Chicago–Detroit cell

From	Newark (N)	Pittsburgh (P)	Detroit (D)	Boston (B)	Supply	
Chicago (C)	$22 ⑦	$18 ①	$16 +1	$28	8	
Atlanta (A)	$14	$12 ⑧	$19 ④	$23	12	(a)
Seattle (S)	$37	$35	$30 ⑦	$40 ⑨	16	
Demand	7	9	11	9	36	

From	Newark (N)	Pittsburgh (P)	Detroit (D)	Boston (B)	Supply	
Chicago (C)	$22 ⑦	$18 ① -1	$16 +1	$28	8	
Atlanta (A)	$14	$12 ⑧	$19 ④	$23	12	(b)
Seattle (S)	$37	$35	$30 ⑦	$40 ⑨	16	
Demand	7	9	11	9	36	

continued

TABLE 6.4 (Continued)

	To				
From	Newark (N)	Pittsburgh (P)	Detroit (D)	Boston (B)	**Supply**
Chicago (C)	$22 ⑦	$18 ① −1	$16 +1	$28	8
Atlanta (A)	$14	$12 ⑧ +1	$19 ④	$23	12 (c)
Seattle (S)	$37	$35	$30 ⑦	$40 ⑨	16
Demand	7	9	11	9	36

	To				
From	Newark (N)	Pittsburgh (P)	Detroit (D)	Boston (B)	**Supply**
Chicago (C)	$22 ⑦	$18 ① −1	$16 +1	$28	8
Atlanta (A)	$14	$12 ⑧ +1	$19 ④ −1	$23	12 (d)
Seattle (S)	$37	$35	$30 ⑦	$40 ⑨	16
Demand	7	9	11	9	36

Note: Shipments in millions of cases; costs in thousands per one million cases shipped

ark column because neither cell (A–N) nor (S–N) has an allocation, and rules 2 and 3 state that we must only use cells with allocations.

In Table 6.5, we present the chains for each of the six empty cells. Notice that the chains appear as squares in parts (a), (c), (d), and (f) of the table, while, in parts (b) and (e) of the table, the chains are not square in shape. In these two cases, the chains use six cells rather than four cells (as used by chains that appear as squares). In all cases, the number of cells in the chain must be even, because there must be an equal number

TABLE 6.5 Supercola chain identification

Chicago–Detroit loop

From	To			
	Newark	Pittsburgh	Detroit	Boston
Chicago	7	1		
Atlanta		8	4	
Seattle			7	9

(a)

Chicago–Boston loop

From	To			
	Newark	Pittsburgh	Detroit	Boston
Chicago	7	1		
Atlanta		8	4	
Seattle			7	9

(b)

Atlanta–Newark loop

From	To			
	Newark	Pittsburgh	Detroit	Boston
Chicago	7	1		
Atlanta		8	4	
Seattle			7	9

(c)

Atlanta–Boston loop

From	To			
	Newark	Pittsburgh	Detroit	Boston
Chicago	7	1		
Atlanta		8	4	
Seattle			7	9

(d)

continued

TABLE 6.5 (Continued)

From	To			
	Newark	Pittsburgh	Detroit	Boston
Chicago	⑦ −	+ ①		
Atlanta		− ⑧	+ ④	
Seattle	+		⑦ −	⑨

(e)   **Seattle–Newark loop**

From	To			
	Newark	Pittsburgh	Detroit	Boston
Chicago	⑦	①		
Atlanta		⑧ −	+ ④	
Seattle		+	⑦ −	⑨

(f)   **Seattle–Pittsburgh loop**

Note: Shipments in millions of cases

---

of +s and −s. The method of finding these chains is termed the **stepping stone method,** because the picture of the chains reminds us of stones on which one steps so as not to get wet when crossing a stream.

Given the chains for each of the empty cells, we could compute the changes in cost that would occur and use the cell with the most negative marginal cost. However, we are *not* going to do this. The easiest way to solve a transportation problem is to change the shipping schedule as soon as it is found that using an empty cell will reduce the cost. Therefore, in terms of our example, we have found that cell (C–D) will improve the cost, so we now wish to include this cell in our shipping schedule.

change shipments if marginal cost is negative

SOLUTION IMPROVEMENT

We are going to add units to cell (C–D). Furthermore, whatever number of units we add to cell (C–D) must be subtracted from cell (C–P), added to cell (A–P), and subtracted from (A–D) in order to maintain a balance in the supply and demand. If we add one unit, our cost will decrease by $9. If we add two units, our cost will decrease by 2 × $9 = $18, because the costs are proportional. Therefore, we wish to add as many units as possible to cell (C–D), because the more units we add, the greater will be our savings. The only limit to the number of units that can be added to cells (C–D) and (A–P) is the number of units that can come from cells (C–P) and (A–D). As shown in

move as many units as possible

find smallest shipment in the cells with minuses

part (a) of Table 6.6, there are four units in cell (A–D), so it is impossible to subtract more than four units from that cell. More restrictive, though, is that there is only one unit in cell (C–P). Because the number added and subtracted to the four cells must be the same, our decision has to be to use the number 1. In general, the number added and subtracted is the smallest shipment in the cells with minuses. Therefore, our new solution is generated by adding one unit to cell (C–D), subtracting one unit from cell (C–P), adding one unit to cell (A–P), and subtracting one unit from cell (A–D). The

TABLE 6.6 Supercola stepping stone method

(a) Initial solution (cost = $914; savings = $9 × 1 = $9)

include Chicago–Detroit

From	To			
	Newark	Pittsburgh	Detroit	Boston
Chicago	$22	$18	$16	$28
	⑦	− ①	+ −9	
Atlanta	$14	$12	$19	$23
		+ ⑧	− ④	
Seattle	$37	$35	$30	$40
			⑦	⑨

(b) Solution 2 (cost = $905; savings = $11 × 3 = $33)

include Atlanta–Newark

From	To			
	Newark	Pittsburgh	Detroit	Boston
Chicago	$22	$18	$16	$28
	− ⑦		+ ①	
Atlanta	$14	$12	$19	$23
	+ −11	⑨	− ③	
Seattle	$37	$35	$30	$40
			⑦	⑨

continued

TABLE 6.6 (Continued)

(c) Solution 3 (cost = $872; savings = $2 × 4 = $8)

From	To			
	Newark	Pittsburgh	Detroit	Boston
Chicago	$22 — ④	$18 + −2	$16 ④	$28
Atlanta	$14 + ③	$12 − ⑨	$19	$23
Seattle	$37	$35	$30 ⑦	$40 ⑨

include Chicago–Pittsburgh

(d) Solution 4 (final cost = $864)

From	To			
	Newark	Pittsburgh	Detroit	Boston
Chicago	$22 2	$18 ④	$16 ④	$28 2
Atlanta	$14 ⑦	$12 ⑤	$19 9	$23 3
Seattle	$37 3	$35 3	$30 ⑦	$40 ⑨

optimal solution: shipments and marginal costs

Note: Shipments in millions of cases; costs in thousands per one million cases shipped

new solution appears as solution 2 in part (b) of Table 6.6. Because cell (C–P) now has zero units, we leave it blank and, hence, our new solution has the required six cells with allocations. (Recall that all solutions must have $m + n - 1$ cells with allocations.) Note that it is not necessary to compute the shipment costs between each pair of cities to determine the total cost of the improved solution. Since our previous total was $914 and we saved $9, we know that our new total will be $905 (which the following computations confirm).

Shipment	Shipment Cost (Units × \$/Unit)
Chicago to Newark	7 × \$22 = \$154
Chicago to Detroit	1 × \$16 = \$ 16
Atlanta to Pittsburgh	9 × \$12 = \$108
Atlanta to Detroit	3 × \$19 = \$ 57
Seattle to Detroit	7 × \$30 = \$210
Seattle to Boston	9 × \$40 = \$360
	\$905

At this point, we are in the same position as before. That is, we have a solution, but we do not know if this solution is optimal. We again must evaluate the empty cells and make changes if so indicated by the marginal costs of the empty cells. The remainder of the process is given in pairs (c) and (d) of Table 6.6, where we see that the minimum cost is \$864 and all marginal costs are positive.

MINIMAL COST METHOD

The northwest corner method generally provides a rather poor initial solution, as we have indicated. The minimal cost method is presented now as an alternative means of obtaining a better initial solution.

The minimal cost method uses the shipping costs to decide which cell receives the next shipping allocation. At each step, the cell with the lowest cost is chosen, and as many units as possible are allocated to that cell.

alternative starting method

Based on the data in Example 6.1, the cell with the lowest cost is Atlanta to Pittsburgh, which has a per unit cost of \$12. Because the supply at Atlanta is 12 and the demand at Pittsburgh is 9, the demand at Pittsburgh is satisfied by our scheduling a shipment of 9 units from Atlanta to Pittsburgh, which leaves 3 units at Atlanta (see part (a) of Table 6.7). The cell with the next lowest cost is Atlanta to Newark, which has a per unit cost of \$14. We schedule 3 units for shipment to Newark, because that is all that remains at Atlanta. Newark still requires 4 more units (see part (b) of Table 6.7). We continue in this fashion until we generate the schedule given in part (d) of Table 6.7. The total cost is $(8 \times \$16) + (3 \times \$14) + (9 \times \$12) + (4 \times \$37) + (3 \times \$30) + (9 \times \$40) = \$876$, which is (not surprisingly) better than the \$914 generated by the northwest corner method but is *not* optimal.

solution is not optimal

We note again that there exists another starting solution method, which is better than the minimum cost method. This better method is Vogel's approximation method. However, for problems solved by hand, it is not so much better that it warrants presentation in this text. (If you are interested in learning more about Vogel's approximation method, consult the References section at the end of this chapter.)

SPECIAL CASES

To this point, we have limited our examination to the standard transportation problem. That is, the only problem we've looked at has total supply equal to total demand, and all $m \times n$ routes are available. Our solution minimized cost and had $m + n - 1$ cells, as required. We now examine situations that differ from the standard problem. We begin with the maximization of profit (as opposed to the minimization of cost).

TABLE 6.7 Supercola minimal cost method

From	Newark	Pittsburgh	Detroit	Boston	Supply
Chicago	$22	$18	$16	$28	8
Atlanta	$14	$12 ⑨	$19	$23	~~12~~ 3 (a)
Seattle	$37	$35	$30	$40	16
Demand	7	~~9~~	11	9	36

start with
Atlanta–Pittsburgh

From	Newark	Pittsburgh	Detroit	Boston	Supply
Chicago	$22	$18	$16	$28	8
Atlanta	$14 ③	$12 ⑨	$19	$23	~~12~~ ~~3~~ (b)
Seattle	$37	$35	$30	$40	16
Demand	~~7~~ 4	~~9~~	11	9	36

Atlanta–Newark

continued

TABLE 6.7 (Continued)

Chicago–Detroit

From	To				Supply
	Newark	Pittsburgh	Detroit	Boston	
Chicago	$22	$18	$16 ⑧	$28	8̶
Atlanta	$14 ③	$12 ⑨	$19	$23	1̶2̶ 3̶ (c)
Seattle	$37	$35	$30	$40	16
Demand	7̶ / 4	9̶	1̶1̶ / 3	9	36

put remainder in Seattle row

From	To				Supply
	Newark	Pittsburgh	Detroit	Boston	
Chicago	$22	$18	$16 ⑧	$28	8̶
Atlanta	$14 ③	$12 ⑨	$19	$23	1̶2̶ 3̶ (d)
Seattle	$37 ④	$35	$30 ③	$40 ⑨	1̶6̶
Demand	7̶ / 4̶	9̶	1̶1̶ / 3̶	9̶	36

Note: Shipments in millions of cases; costs in thousands per one million cases shipped

MAXIMIZATION PROBLEMS

The example problem and solution method presented in the previous section dealt with a situation in which the goal was to minimize the cost. However, the transportation method may be used for maximization problems as well as for minimization problems. In fact, the method is identical, although the way we interpret the marginal costs is different because now they represent marginal profits. Consider the following example.

Example 6.2 Florenzo Foods has a contract to provide bull feed for five bull breeders. The five breeders require 1,200; 1,600; 1,000; 2,600; and 2,000 pounds of bull feed per week, respectively. Florenzo has two plants that manufacture the bull feed, and the plants have capacities of 4,800 and 3,600 pounds per week. The bull feed sells for $20 per pound, and the manufacturing costs are $2 per pound at plant 1 and $3 per pound at plant 2. Transportation costs are given by the following table.

Plant	Breeder				
	A	B	C	D	E
1	$6	$7	$1	$6	$3
2	$5	$4	$3	$1	$5

Which plant should provide each breeder in order to maximize the profit?

The first step in the solution process is to develop a profit for each cell. The profit is $20 less the production cost less the shipping cost. Hence, the profit matrix is given by the following.

Plant	Breeder				
	A	B	C	D	E
1	$20 − $2 − $6	$20 − $2 − $7	$20 − $2 − $1	$20 − $2 − $6	$20 − $2 − $3
2	$20 − $3 − $5	$20 − $3 − $4	$20 − $3 − $3	$20 − $3 − $1	$20 − $3 − $5

We can present the profit matrix in simpler form as follows.

Plant	Breeder				
	A	B	C	D	E
1	$12	$11	$17	$12	$15
2	$12	$13	$14	$16	$12

TABLE 6.8 Florenzo profit maximization (Example 6.2)

(a) Initial solution

Plant	A	B	C	D	E	Supply
Breeder						
1	$12	$11	$17	$12	$15	4,800
	(1,200)	(600)	(1,000)		(2,000)	
2	$12	$13	$14	$16	$12	3,600
		(1,000)		(2,600)		
Demand	1,200	1,600	1,000	2,600	2,000	8,400

(b) Evaluation of cell (1–D)

Plant	A	B	C	D	E	Supply
Breeder						
1	$12	$11 −	$17	$12 +	$15	4,800
	(1,200)	(600)	(1,000)		(2,000)	
2	$12	$13 +	$14	$16 −	$12	3,600
		(1,000)		(2,600)		
Demand	1,200	1,600	1,000	2,600	2,000	8,400

To generate the initial solution, we want to use the minimal cost method, because it is better than the northwest corner method. However, because we wish to maximize the profit rather than minimize the cost, we pick the highest number (because it represents profit) and fill its cell. Thus, cell (1–C), which shows a profit of $17, is our first choice. Continuing in this manner of picking highest profits, our initial solution is as given in part (a) of Table 6.8. Note that $m + n - 1$ cells are filled.

Now let us examine cell (1–D). The chain is as given in part (b) of Table 6.8. The profit difference is $12 − $11 + $13 − $16 = −$2. In a minimization problem, this marginal value would indicate the need for a change. However, because this is a maximization problem, the −2 means a reduction in profit by $2. Therefore, the cell should not be included.

TABLE 6.9 D&B shipping costs per unit (Example 6.3)

	Distributor			
Plant	Wilmington	Xenia	Youngstown	Zanesville
Akron	$8	$6	$10	$12
Bowling Green	$3	$7	$6	$9
Cincinnati	$7	$4	$2	$6

In this example, each of the empty cells has a negative marginal profit; hence, the solution given in part (a) of Table 6.8 is the optimal solution. ◼️

You may have noticed that total revenue in this example is fixed at 8,400 units $\times$ $20 = $168,000 and that total production cost is fixed at ($2 $\times$ 4,800 units) + ($3 $\times$ 3,600 units) = $9,600 + $10,800 = $20,400. Hence, maximizing profit is identical to minimizing total transportation costs.

UNBALANCED PROBLEMS

So far in this chapter we have discussed only balanced problems, or problems in which total supply is equal to total demand. In real-life situations, however, transportation problems may have greater supply than demand or greater demand than supply. The former situation is best illustrated by the company whose production capability is greater than the demand for its product, and the latter situation may occur when a company's market requirement exceeds its production capacity. When an unbalanced situation occurs, it is necessary to introduce a new, artificial supply or demand that absorbs the difference between total supply and demand. When demand is greater than supply, a dummy source is established to "supply" the difference between what is needed and what is available. The transportation cost from the dummy source to any destination is zero, because the artificial source does not really exist. Similarly, the transportation cost from any source to a dummy destination is zero. With this simple modification, an unbalanced transportation problem may be converted into a balanced one. Let us consider two examples.

use of dummy location

Example 6.3   D&B manufactures garden tools. D&B plants in Akron, Bowling Green, and Cincinnati have capacities of 8 million, 3 million, and 6 million tools per year, respectively. The company has four distributors, located in Wilmington, Xenia, Youngstown, and Zanesville, with demands of 4 million, 2 million, 5 million, and 5 million units per year, respectively. The shipping costs per unit are given in Table 6.9. Find the shipping allocation that minimizes the total cost.

supply greater than demand

Because the total supply is 17 million and the total demand is 16 million, the first step is to balance the supply and the demand. We do this by adding a dummy (nonexistent) destination with a demand of one million, which accounts for the difference between total supply and total demand. Because this destination does not exist, the shipping costs to it are $0 per unit from any origin. We use Table 6.10 to solve the

TABLE 6.10   D&B with dummy destination (Example 6.3)

| Plant | Distributor | | | | | Supply |
	Wilmington (W)	Xenia (X)	Youngstown (Y)	Zanesville (Z)	Dummy (D)	
Akron (A)	$8	$6	$10	$12	$0	8
Bowling Green (B)	$3	$7	$6	$9	$0	3
Cincinnati (C)	$7	$4	$2	$6	$0	6
Demand	4	2	5	5	1	17

Note: Shipments in millions of units; costs in dollars per unit

problem. This table represents a balanced transportation problem, and we use our usual methods to solve it. We emphasize that the dummy cells are treated as if they were regular cells. (For our purposes, they are regular cells.)

We generate the initial solution with the minimum cost method. The smallest cost is zero, and we arbitrarily choose cell (A–D) over cells (B–D) or (C–D). The next smallest cost is $2/unit at cell (C–Y), followed by $3/unit at cell (B–W), and $4/unit at cell (C–X). At this point, only row A is available, so we put the remaining demands in row A. The initial solution is given in Table 6.11. Notice that we use 5 + 3 − 1 = 7 allocations, as is our rule.

TABLE 6.11   D&B initial solution and marginal costs (Example 6.3)

| Plant | Distributor | | | | | Supply |
	Wilmington (W)	Xenia (X)	Youngstown (Y)	Zanesville (Z)	Dummy (D)	
Akron (A)	$8 (1)	$6 (1)	$10 6	$12 (5)	$0 (1)	8
Bowling Green (B)	$3 (3)	$7 6	$6 7	$9 2	$0 5	3
Cincinnati (C)	$7 1	$4 (1)	$2 (5)	$6 −4	$0 2	6
Demand	4	2	5	5	1	17

Note: Shipments in millions of units; costs in dollars per unit

TABLE 6.12 Optimal solution and marginal costs (Example 6.3)

	Distributor				
Plant	Wilmington	Xenia	Youngstown	Zanesville	Dummy
Akron	$8 ①	$6 ②	$10 2	$12 ④	$0 ①
Bowling Green	$3 ③	$7 6	$6 7	$9 2	$0 5
Cincinnati	$7 5	$4 4	$2 ⑤	$6 ①	$0 6

Note: Shipments in millions of units; costs in dollars per unit

Our next step is to evaluate each of the empty cells, including cells (B–D) and (C–D). Because cell (C–Z) has a marginal cost given by -4, we need to change the table. We add and subtract one unit to the cells on the loop (C–Z), (A–Z), (A–X), and (C–X), generating the shipments shown in Table 6.12. The new marginal costs, indicated in Table 6.12, are all positive and so the problem is solved. The total shipping cost is $93 million rather than the $97 million of the initial solution. ◾

The approach to handling unbalanced problems that have a total demand larger than total supply is analogous to the previous example, where supply was greater than demand. Again, a dummy needs to be added, but, this time, a dummy supply point (warehouse) rather than a dummy destination is added.

Example 6.4 Chunky Cheese manufactures mousetraps in Anaheim, Boca Raton, and Chicago. Each of its plants is identical, and each has a capacity of 12,000 traps per month. The traps are shipped to distribution centers in Denver, Evanston, Fort Worth, and Glenside (Pennsylvania) that have demands of 9,000; 10,000; 11,000; and 12,000 traps, respectively. The shipping costs (per 1,000) are given by the following table. Find the optimal shipping schedule and cost.

demand greater than supply

	Warehouse			
Factory	Denver (D)	Evanston (E)	Fort Worth (F)	Glenside (G)
Anaheim (A)	$30	$40	$35	$60
Boca Raton (B)	$50	$70	$25	$35
Chicago (C)	$20	$5	$40	$40

The total supply is 36,000, and the total demand is 42,000. Thus, the first step is to add a dummy origin with 42,000 − 36,000 = 6,000 traps. The initial table appears in part (a) of Table 6.13. Notice that the costs from the dummy destination are each zero, because these are nonexistent units that will not get shipped. We now treat the balanced problem as given by part (a) in Table 6.13 as a regular transportation problem.

ignore zeroes

We begin by finding an initial solution, and we will use the minimum cost method (with a minor variation). The lowest cost is $0. However, that lowest cost appears four times, and, essentially, we are indifferent about which of these four zeroes to choose. Our variation, then, is to ignore the zeroes and to start with the lowest positive cost, which is the $5 in cell (C–E). Therefore, we schedule 10 units for shipment from Chicago to Evanston. This is followed by scheduling shipments of 2 units from Chicago to Denver; 11 units from Boca Raton to Fort Worth; and 7 units from Anaheim to Denver. The remainder all go to Glenside, because this is the only column still available. The initial solution appears in part (b) of Table 6.13. Notice that the number of shipments is 7 (4 + 4 − 1).

Next, we need to evaluate all of the empty cells. Our evaluation must include the three empty cells in the dummy row. Examining cell (A–F), we see that the marginal cost is $35 − $60 + $35 − $25 = −$15. Therefore, we need to move units around the loop (A–F), (B–F), (B–G), (A–G). The number of units to move is 5, and the new solution appears in part (c) of Table 6.13. The marginal costs are given in the empty cells, and this solution is the optimal solution. The total cost is computed as follows (with shipments in thousands of units and costs in dollars per thousand units shipped).

Shipment	Shipping Costs (Shipment × Unit Cost)
A–D	7 × $30 = $210
A–F	5 × $35 = $175
B–F	6 × $25 = $150
B–G	6 × $35 = $210
C–D	2 × $20 = $ 40
C–E	10 × $5 = $ 50
D–G	6 × $0 = $ 0
	$835

implications of dummy rows and columns

Although the procedure for solving the transportation problem is the same whether demand exceeds supply or supply exceeds demand, the implications of the two situations are different. The usual situation is for supply to exceed demand. That is, the capacity is designed to more than meet the demand. In our last example, Chunky Cheese has indeed minimized its shipping costs, but, each month, Glenside is shipped 6,000 fewer units than it requires. Thus, although we can minimize shipping costs for the case of larger demand than supply, this situation is a symptom of a problem in the production or capacity planning stages. In other words, when the supply does not meet the demand, the major problem for the operations manager is not a shipping problem; rather, it is a problem of increasing capacity or productivity so that the demand can be met.

THE ASSIGNMENT PROBLEM

In this section, we examine a very special case of the transportation problem. This is the case where the number of supply points is equal to the number of destination

TABLE 6.13   Chunky Cheese balanced problem with dummy origin (Example 6.4)

(a)

From	To				Supply
	D	E	F	G	
A	$30	$40	$35	$60	12
B	$50	$70	$25	$35	12
C	$20	$5	$40	$40	12
Dummy	$0	$0	$0	$0	6
Demand	9	10	11	12	42

(b)

From	To				Supply
	D	E	F	G	
A	$30 (7)	$40	$35	$60 (5)	~~12~~ 5
B	$50	$70	$25 (11)	$35 (1)	~~12~~ 1
C	$20 (2)	$5 (10)	$40	$40	~~12~~ 2
Dummy	$0	$0	$0	$0 (6)	~~6~~
Demand	~~9~~ 7	~~10~~	~~11~~	~~12~~	

continued

TABLE 6.13 (Continued)

	To			
From	D	E	F	G
A	$30 (7)	$40 25	$35 (5)	$60 15
B	$50 30	$70 65	$25 (6)	$35 (6)
C	$20 (2)	$5 (10)	$40 15	$40 5
Dummy	$0 15	$0 30	$0 10	$0 (6)

(c)

Note: Shipments in thousands of units; costs in dollars per one thousand units shipped

points (that is, $m = n$), and each supply and each demand is exactly one. Such a problem is termed an **assignment problem.** Consider the following example.

> **Example 6.5** Four programmers, Bob, Carol, Ted, and Alice, are capable of writing any one of programs 1, 2, 3, or 4. Their individual capabilities vary, because each programmer has different strengths. The following presents the cost of assigning any one of the programmers to any one of the programs.

Programmer	Program			
	1	2	3	4
Bob	$80	$120	$125	$140
Carol	$20	$115	$145	$ 60
Ted	$40	$100	$ 85	$ 45
Alice	$65	$ 35	$ 25	$ 75

The task is to assign each programmer to a single program (and each program to a single programmer) so that all four programs are completed at minimum cost.

In transportation terms, each programmer can be supplied (the supply equals one at Bob, one at Carol, one at Ted, and one at Alice) and each program needs one programmer (the demand equals one at each program 1, 2, 3, and 4). The total supply and the total demand are each four. Hence, this assignment problem may be solved by using the transportation method. There is, however, an easier solution method (which we will present in Chapter 15), so we will not solve Example 6.5's problem at this time. Furthermore, there are certain difficulties with this problem, which we address next. ▪

One solution to the assignment problem in Example 6.5 is to assign Bob, Carol, Ted, and Alice to programs, 1, 2, 3, and 4, respectively. This solution is represented in Table 6.14. Notice that only four assignments have been made, which violates our rules about $m + n - 1$, or $4 + 4 - 1 = 7$, allocations needing to be made. Such a solution is termed a **degenerate solution.** Using Table 6.14, it is impossible to find loops for the empty cells because we need seven cells with allocations and we have only four. This is actually a minor problem, as we now demonstrate.

DEGENERATE SOLUTIONS

If a solution to a transportation problem has fewer than $m + n - 1$ cells with allocations, the solution is a degenerate solution. Degenerate solutions may occur at the beginning of the problem (step 1), as exemplified by the assignment problem in Exam-

TABLE 6.14 The assignment problem (Example 6.5)

Programmer	Program 1	2	3	4	Supply
Bob	$80 ①	$120	$125	$140	1
Carol	$20	$115 ①	$145	$60	1
Ted	$40	$100	$85 ①	$45	1
Alice	$65	$35	$25	$75 ①	1
Demand	1	1	1	1	4

ple 6.5, or in the middle of the algorithm (step 3), as we will demonstrate soon. In order for each empty cell to have a chain, it is necessary for exactly $m + n - 1$ cells to have allocations. Therefore, to handle degenerate solutions, we must treat some of the empty cells as if they were filled. For example, in the assignment example, we must treat three of the empty cells as if they were filled so that the total number of allocations will be 7, the required number.

DEGENERACY AT INITIALIZATION: We first look at a problem where degeneracy arises at the initialization step.

Example 6.6   A company ships goods from locations A, B, and C to locations D, E, and F. The shipping costs, supplies, and demands are given in the following table. Find the optimal schedule and the minimum shipping cost.

Source	**Destination**			Supply
	D	E	F	
A	$14	$18	$22	10
B	$22	$19	$18	15
C	$17	$23	$14	8
Demand	13	12	8	

We will use the northwest corner method to begin our solution. First, we put 10 units in cell (A–D), cross off the 10 in the supply column, row A, and reduce the demand in column D to 3 (see part (a) of Table 6.15 on page 276). Notice that we crossed off only one supply (and zero demands). We continue by placing 3 units in cell (B–D), crossing off the demand of 3 in column D and reducing the supply in row B to 12 (see part (b) of Table 6.15). Notice that, this time, we crossed off only one demand (and zero supplies).

At this point, we put 12 units into cell (B–E). We are tempted to cross off both the supply of 12 in row B and the demand of 12 in column E. However, if we do this, we will end up with a degenerate solution (try it). The rule that we will follow is to cross off the supply but not the demand. Instead, we change the demand to zero and treat the zero as a legitimate number (see part (c) of Table 6.15). Because we have not crossed off column E, we stay in the column and move down to cell (C–E). The number of units that we place in this cell is zero! We now cross off the zero demand in column E (see part (d) of Table 6.15). We complete the initialization by placing 8 units in cell (C–F). The initial solution is given by the following.

Destination

Source	D	E	F
A	$14 (10)	$18	$22
B	$22 (3)	$19 (12)	$18
C	$17	$23 (0)	$14 (8)

We have the required $m + n - 1 = 5$ cells with allocations (even though one allocation is zero).

From this point on, we treat the problem in the regular fashion. In particular, we treat the zero in cell (C–E) in the same manner we would any positive number. For example, consider the evaluation of cell (C–D). The loop is (C–D), (C–E), (B–E), and (B–D). The marginal cost is $17 - $23 + $19 - $22 = -$9. The number of units we move is the smaller of the three in (B–D) and the zero in (C–E). Therefore, we move zero units, generating the following solution.

Destination

Source	D	E	F
A	$14 (10)	$18	$22
B	$22 (3)	$19 (12)	$18
C	$17 (0)	$23	$14 (8)

The total cost does not change, but the move must be made because the marginal cost of (C–D) was negative.

We continue by examining cell (B–F). The loop is (B–F), (B–D), (C–D), and (C–F), and the marginal cost is $18 - $22 + $17 - $14 = -$1. Therefore, we move three units around this loop for the following solution.

Source	Destination		
	D	E	F
A	$14 (10)	$18	$22
B	$22	$19 (12)	$18 (3)
C	$17 (3)	$23	$14 (5)

This is the optimal solution, with a minimum shipping cost of $593, and what is interesting to note is that it is *not* degenerate. It is possible, as this example demonstrates, to go from a degenerate solution to a nondegenerate solution. The following

TABLE 6.15 Degeneracy at initialization (Example 6.6)

Source	Destination			Supply	
	D	E	F		
A	(10)			~~10~~	
B				15	(a)
C				8	
Demand	~~10~~ 3	12	8		

Source	Destination			Supply	
	D	E	F		
A	(10)			~~10~~	
B	(3)			~~15~~ 12	(b)
C				8	
Demand	~~10~~ ~~3~~	12	8		

continued

TABLE 6.15 (Continued)

Source	Destination			Supply		
	D	E	F			
A	⑩			~~10~~		
B	③	⑫		~~15~~ ~~12~~		(c)
C				8		
Demand	~~15~~	~~12~~	8			
	~~3~~	0				

Source	Destination			Supply		
	D	E	F			
A	⑩			~~10~~		
B	③	⑫		~~15~~ ~~12~~		(d)
C		⓪		8		
Demand	~~15~~	~~12~~	8			
	~~3~~	~~0~~				

will illustrate that it also is possible to go from a nondegenerate solution to a degenerate solution.

DEGENERACY AT STEP 3: Now we present an example showing degeneracy at step 3 of the algorithm.

Example 6.7 Transformer Inc. has been using the following shipping schedule for the last five years.

From	To		
	X	Y	Z
A	10	15	
B		10	9

The shipping costs along route (B–X) have been reduced to encourage use of a new trucking company. The costs are as follows.

	To		
From	X	Y	Z
A	$63	$60	$90
B	$64	$65	$52

Should Transformer Inc. change its shipments?

We can combine the Transformer Inc. information into one table.

	To		
From	X	Y	Z
A	$63 (10)	$60 (15)	$90
B	$64	$65 (10)	$52 (9)

The loop for cell (B–X) is (B–X), (B–Y), (A–Y), and (A–X), with a marginal cost of $64 − $65 + $60 − $63 = − $4. Therefore, we want to add and subtract 10 units around the loop. However, if we do this, *two* cells will go to zero simultaneously. If we allow both to be blank, we will have a degenerate solution. To avoid this, we will use the following rule: If more than one cell goes to zero, let one cell be blank and use zero as the shipment allocation in each of the remaining cells. With this rule, our solution becomes the following.

	To		
From	X	Y	Z
A	$63	$60 (25)	$90
B	$64 (10)	$65 (0)	$52 (9)

This is the optimal solution, which indicates that Transformer Inc. should change its shipments. ∎

PROBLEMS WITH UNAVAILABLE ROUTES

In all of our examples, all $m \times n$ routes (cells) have been available for use. In some cases, it may not be possible to use a route. This is a very simple problem to overcome. We simply put an extremely high cost in the unavailable cell and then solve the problem in the normal fashion. The extremely high cost will guarantee that the cell does not appear in the ultimate solution. When solving a problem by hand, the cost used can be denoted by ∞, with the understanding that ∞ minus some number is still ∞. When solving the problem on a computer, a symbol such as ∞ cannot be used, so we put in a very large number, such as one million.

Example 6.8 Given below is the information for a transportation problem. Find the optimal solution.

	To		
From	W1	W2	**Supply**
P1	N/A	$10	100
P2	$12	$18	300
P3	$ 5	$93	200
Demand	350	250	

The initial solution is given as follows, using the northwest corner method.

The marginal cost of cell (P1–W2) is $10 − \$\infty + \$12 − \$18 = −\$\infty$, so we move 50 units around the loop, as shown in the following table.

From	To		
	W1		W2
P1	∞	(50)	$10	(50)
P2	$12	(300)	$18	
P3	$5		$93	(200)

The marginal cost of cell (P3–W1) is $5 − $\infty + $10 − $93 = −$\infty$, so we move another 50 units around the loop.

From	To		
	W1		W2
P1	∞		$10	(100)
P2	$12	(300)	$18	
P3	$5	(50)	$93	(150)

Teaching Suggestion 6.7: Alternative Optimal Solutions. See the Instructor's Section for details.

This is the final solution, and route (P1–W1) is not used due to its high (∞) cost. ◼

APPLICATIONS OF THE TRANSPORTATION MODEL

We indicated at the beginning of this chapter that the transportation model is useful in other areas of operations. Some of the examples have demonstrated this. In this section, we present examples related to plant location and capacity planning.

THE MULTIFACILITY LOCATION DECISION

At the beginning of this chapter, we stated that the problem of locating a second, third, or fourth facility differs from that of locating the first facility. There are many factors to consider when locating the newest facility. In Chapter 3, we described the

TABLE 6.16 Plant location (Example 6.9)

| Source | Destination | | | | Capacity |
	Vancouver	St. Louis	Miami	Boston	
Phoenix	$10	$70	$65	$95	18
Philadelphia	$90	$40	$60	$20	22
Chicago	$40	$30	$80	$50	25
Dallas	$60	$50	$60	$70	25
Demand	17	19	18	11	65

issues of economy of scale in designing plants. We also indicated, in Chapter 5, that the current trend is away from having a small number of large plants to having a large number of small plants. One of the advantages of having many plants is that a disruption at one plant will not disrupt production at the remaining plants. A second advantage of having several decentralized plants is that shipping costs can be reduced. Although facility location is a qualitative decision, shipping costs are quantitative, and this aspect of the decision can be solved by using the transportation method.

Example 6.9 LG Inc. has plants in Phoenix and Philadelphia. Due to an expected increase in sales, the company is going to build a new plant. The two cities being considered by the company are Dallas and Chicago. Either plant will be built with a capacity of 25,000 units per year. Table 6.16 contains the remaining information, including the demands at the four warehouses and the shipping costs from all four cities (Phoenix, Philadelphia, Dallas, and Chicago) to the four warehouses. Only one of the plants can be built. Which will lead to lower total shipping costs and what is the cost difference?

In order to determine the costs, we need to solve two separate problems—one for Chicago and one for Dallas, as illustrated in Figure 6.11. Table 6.17 presents the Chicago problem and the initial solution is generated by the minimum cost method. This solution is optimal, and the total cost is given as follows:

Shipment	Shipment Costs (Shipment × Unit Cost)
Phoenix–Vancouver	17 × $10 = $ 170
Phoenix–Miami	1 × $65 = $ 65
Philadelphia–Miami	11 × $60 = $ 660
Philadelphia–Boston	11 × $20 = $ 220
Chicago–St. Louis	19 × $30 = $ 570
Chicago–Miami	6 × $80 = $ 480
	$2,165

For the Dallas problem, Table 6.18 presents the initial solution, which, again, is optimal. The total cost is $2,315. Hence, from the standpoint of transportation costs, Chicago would be $150 less expensive than Dallas. ∎

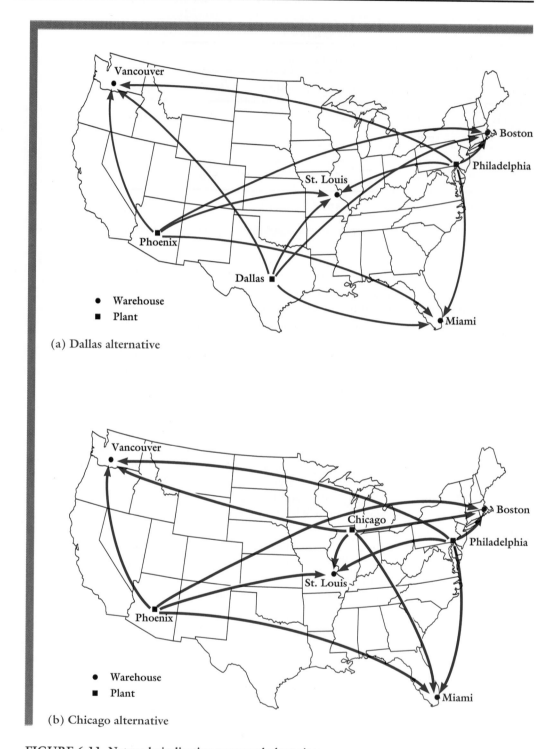

(a) Dallas alternative

(b) Chicago alternative

FIGURE 6.11 Networks indicating proposed plant sites

TABLE 6.17 Location in Chicago (Example 6.9)

Source	Destination			
	Vancouver	St. Louis	Miami	Boston
Phoenix	$10 ⟨17⟩	$70 55	$65 ⟨1⟩	$95 70
Philadelphia	$90 85	$40 30	$60 11	$20 ⟨11⟩
Chicago	$40 15	$30 ⟨19⟩	$80 ⟨6⟩	$50 10

TABLE 6.18 Location in Dallas (Example 6.9)

Source	Destination			
	Vancouver	St. Louis	Miami	Boston
Phoenix	$10 ⟨17⟩	$70 155	$65 ⟨1⟩	$95 60
Philadelphia	$90 95	$40 ⟨11⟩	$60 10	$20 ⟨11⟩
Dallas	$60 55	$50 ⟨8⟩	$60 ⟨17⟩	$70 40

PRODUCTION PLANNING

One of the standard problems in operations is production planning. This will be discussed in detail in Chapter 12, but now we present a special case that can be modeled as a transportation problem.

Example 6.10 Cycles Unlimited is planning its production for the next four quarters, using the following expected demands.

Quarter	Demand
Fall	1,000
Winter	500
Spring	3,000
Summer	2,000

The company has a regular-time capacity of 1,200 bikes per quarter. The regular-time cost is $100 per bike. Overtime may be used for up to 800 bikes per quarter, but bikes produced during overtime cost $110 apiece due to extra labor costs. Bikes can be produced in any quarter for delivery in a later quarter, but there is an inventory cost of $25 per quarter for each bike held. What plan minimizes the total production and storage costs?

In Table 6.19, we list the options available for the company in a form similar to that used in the transportation method. An **X** indicates that an option is not available. For example, the company cannot produce bikes in the summer for delivery during the previous winter. To have a complete transportation table, we need to fill in the costs and add a dummy destination to account for the 1,500 unit difference between capacity (8,000 units) and demand (6,500 units). We term this dummy destination *excess capacity* and note that (as usual) all costs in its column are zero. The costs are given by the production cost (either $100 or $110) plus the storage costs ($25 per quarter). Hence, the transportation table appears as in Table 6.20.

Teaching Suggestion 6.8: Capacities or Costs May Vary. See the Instructor's Section for details.

TABLE 6.19 Cycles Unlimited production planning option (Example 6.10)

	Quarter				
Option	Fall	Winter	Spring	Summer	**Capacity**
Fall regular time					1,200
Fall overtime					800
Winter regular time	X				1,200
Winter overtime	X				800
Spring regular time	X	X			1,200
Spring overtime	X	X			800
Summer regular time	X	X	X		1,200
Summer overtime	X	X	X		800
Demand	1,000	500	3,000	2,000	

TABLE 6.20 Cycles Unlimited production planning costs computations (Example 6.10)

					Quarter			
Option	Fall	Winter	Spring		Summer		Excess Capacity	Capacity
Fall regular time	$100	$100 + $25	$100 + $25 + $25		$100 + $25 + $25 + $25		$0	1,200
Fall overtime	$110	$110 + $25	$110 + $25 + $25		$110 + $25 + $25 + $25		$0	800
Winter regular time	X	$100	$100 + $25		$100 + $25 + $25		$0	1,200
Winter overtime	X	$110	$110 + $25		$110 + $25 + $25		$0	800
Spring regular time	X	X	$100		$100 + $25		$0	1,200
Spring overtime	X	X	$110		$110 + $25		$0	800
Summer regular time	X	X	X		$100		$0	1,200
Summer overtime	X	X	X		$110		$0	800
Demand	1,000	500	3,000		2,000		1,500	8,000

A solution (there is more than one) is given in Table 6.21. Notice that the number of allocations is $8 + 5 - 1 = 12$, as required.

Transparency Master 6.6: Aggregate Planning

LOGISTICS

In describing a distribution network, we have stated that it is basically a system or a set of locations that ship, receive, or store material plus the routes that connect these locations. Whether the network is spread over some geographic region or is within a single facility, the definition remains the same. Implicit in this definition, however, is that both the locations and the transportation between these locations must be considered in any decisions regarding the design of the operation of the overall network. The link to the location analysis discussed in the previous chapter is obvious.

To many, the distribution management function encompasses much more than merely the design and operation of the distribution network. It includes many of the decisions concerning specific requirements at each location and along each route. For example, how the product should be shipped will need to be decided. This question may be refined even further. We may be concerned with

- the appropriate means of transportation,
- the form of packing for shipment, and
- the size (or frequency) of shipments.

Each of these concerns relates to the way in which the product is moved. Other considerations are the design of each location or each route as well as the operation of the individual storage locations. These concerns include

- the capacity of the facility;
- the capacity of the routes;
- the storage mechanism;
- the appropriate amount to store; and
- the appropriate route to choose.

TABLE 6.21 Cycles Unlimited production planning optimal schedule (Example 6.10)

| Option | Quarter | | | | | Capacity |
	Fall	Winter	Spring	Summer	Excess Capacity	
Fall regular time	$100 (1,000)	$125	$150	$175	$0 (200)	1,200
Fall overtime	$110	$135	$160	$185	$0 (800)	800
Winter regular time	X	$100 (500)	$125 (700)	$150	$0	1,200
Winter overtime	X	$110	$135 (300)	$160	$0 (500)	800
Spring regular time	X	X	$100 (1,200)	$125	$0	1,200
Spring overtime	X	X	$110 (800)	$135	$0	800
Summer regular time	X	X	X	$100 (1,200)	$0	1,200
Summer overtime	X	X	X	$110 (800)	$0 (0)	800
Demand	1,000	500	3,000	2,000	1,500	8,000

The decisions addressing both kinds of concerns are interrelated. Many are considered in other chapters, but all relate to the topic of logistics. (In the military, definitions of the terms *operations* and *logistics* are closely related.) Each of these topics is discussed briefly here. Let us now look at some of the options available to the operations manager who must make these decisions.

APPROPRIATE MEANS OF TRANSPORTATION

Between sites, the distribution network consists of some combination of the following seven ways to transport a product.

Material	
Route	Means
Air	Plane
Rail	Train
Road	Truck
Waterway	Boat
Pipeline	Pump
Information	
Route	Means
Cable	Telecommunications
Airwaves	Satellites and relays

Some of these ways may overlap. For example, a cable can be considered to be a special kind of a pipeline. However, the first five ways form a distinct set. These five are means of **physical distribution.** That is, they are ways of shipping items that have some bulk or weight. The last two are ways to ship information, which is becoming an increasing percentage of the total value of shipments. In order to better understand the distribution network and, consequently, to become better able to make decisions regarding the design and operation of a distribution network, one should be aware of the advantages and disadvantages of each of these ways to transport products.

AIR

The major advantage of air transport is speed. Otherwise, air transport has only drawbacks—and it has many of these. First, air transport is very expensive. Its high cost limits its use to items of very high value, usually smaller items such as specialized instrumentation. Items that must arrive very soon after shipment, such as perishable products, also tend to move by air. Another drawback of air transport is accessibility: The plane cannot be loaded at the plant. In fact, three shipments are required: plant

air transport is fast, expensive

to airport A by truck, airport A to airport B by plane, and airport B to destination by truck. Air transport, of course, is used only for long-distance transport.

RAIL

rail's advantage: flexibility

Rail transport is an inexpensive form of long-haul transport. Although it cannot compare with air travel for speed, it is generally as fast as trucks over long distances and is faster than water transport. It is used most extensively for the transportation of bulk products, for which it is ideally suited. However, another strength is its easy adoption, through the design of specialized cars, to the needs of specific commodities. For example, every freight train has special railroad cars for liquids (tankers), gases (tankers), automobiles (three-level ramps), and perishable goods (refrigerated cars). The use of **piggybacking** has improved the accessibility of rail transport. In piggybacking, a truck trailer is loaded at the origination site of the shipment, secured onto a flatbed rail car, shipped to the destination rail terminal, and driven to the final destination. Other terms for this practice include trailer on flat car (TOFC) and container on flat car (COFC).

ROAD

trucking's advantage: accessibility

Trucking (or using a motor carrier) is more expensive than rail or water transport, but is less costly than air transport. For speed, it is comparable or slightly better than rail over long distances and much better than rail over short distances. Today, it is the dominant means of transport in the United States both in terms of number of shipments and total tonnage. The reasons for this should be clear. Trucking has a monopoly on the short-haul market because none of the other means of transport can handle short hauls at a reasonable price. Also, for short distances, trucking is the fastest. Because a truck can be driven to and loaded at virtually any location, it is by far the most accessible means of transport. Trucking is not as widely used, however, as either water or rail when the measure used is ton-miles (tons times miles shipped).

WATERWAY

water transport is inexpensive, slow

The major advantage and the major disadvantage of water transport are just the opposites of those for air transport. That is, water transport is the least expensive means of transport, but it also is the slowest. It is used for heavy bulk products over long-distance routes. In terms of accessibility, it is the worst means of transport, because it is accessible only in coastal areas and major inland waterways. However, the increasing use of container ships, itself a form of piggybacking, has improved water transport's accessibility. In container ships, the containers for which the ship is designed often are rail freight cars or truck trailers. Such ships present exciting possibilities in the practice of logistics management. It is possible for a truck to be loaded with grain in Parsons, Kansas, driven to a rail terminal in St. Joseph, Missouri, piggybacked on a train to St. Louis, New Orleans, or Galveston, loaded onto a container ship bound for a port anywhere in the world, transferred to a train, and then driven to a mill or a bakery. All of this can be done with no intermediate loading and unloading (if so allowed by union contracts), because the same trailer can be used all the way!

PIPELINE

Pipelines are actually less expensive (in most cases) than water transport, but they are very limited in terms of the kinds of products that can be shipped through them. Only liquids or gases can be shipped through a pipeline. Much research is now being conducted to develop coal slurries (a liquefied coal, or coal mixed with water) and coal-to-gas conversion facilities, so as to reduce the high cost of shipping coal. The end result of these two avenues of research would be a series of coal slurry or coal gas pipelines to service our electric utilities. In fact, the first coal slurry pipelines are now in operation. Because coal is one of the major commodities shipped in the United States and Canada, the successful development of either of these types of processes has the potential to significantly increase the share of total shipping handled by pipelines. Although pipelines are very slow, this should not be considered a drawback, because

The distribution network—moving goods from truck to ship. Note packing and use of pallets. (© J. P. Laffont/Sygma)

the types of products shipped through them do not require high-speed shipment. Instead, the products require a continuous flow, and pipelines are successful in achieving this. Pipelines also have limited accessibility, but, again, this is not really that much of a problem because they are designed to give access only to the limited customer base that needs them. There is one drawback to pipelines that has not been addressed for the other means of transport: maintenance. Pipelines require pumps at regular intervals along their routes, and these pumps can be damaged by internal or external factors. Furthermore, every inch of pipeline must be checked periodically for damage, either by ultrasonic or eddy current inspection. This is especially true for the Alaska oil pipeline, where a leak of the hot oil would cause great devastation to the permafrost.

a drawback of pipelines: maintenance costs

PLANNING THE TRANSPORTATION MEANS

The selection of a means of transportation is crucial in both long-term and short-term planning. For long-term planning, the relationship to location analysis already has been stated and cannot be overemphasized. Industries that rely on the shipment of bulk raw materials are most often located on rivers. The steel industry, with its reliance on iron ore, coal, and limestone, is an excellent example. Similarly, mines that cannot locate near waterways always build rail lines close to their operations. Once the route for a coal slurry pipeline is chosen, any slurry plants built will be located along that route.

For short-term planning, the relationship is not so obvious. Consider, however, that some shipment is sent via air to meet a deadline. The originator of the shipment had no choice and was willing to pay a premium to meet the schedule. The efficient use of a just-in-time or materials requirements planning system, as discussed in Chapter 14, would eliminate, or at least reduce, the need for emergency shipments. A reduction in shipping costs, then, can result from successful planning and scheduling. Job shop scheduling (see Chapter 15) also can reduce the need for emergency shipments and thereby save in shipping costs.

planning reduces costs

The reverse situation can occur also. In Chapter 13 the use of safety stocks of inventory is discussed. Although the use of safety stocks can reduce the need for emergency shipment, many low-use, high-cost items, such as machine replacement parts, are too expensive to keep in inventory for long periods of time. The use of air transport, although expensive, can be very economical in this case, if it results in a significant reduction of inventory costs.

The subject of transporting materials within a site is considered further in the next section on materials handling.

FORM OF PACKING

Most packing for shipment takes one of three forms:

- bulk,
- in-process individual packing, or
- final product individual packing.

The level of packing that is chosen depends on the level of protection needed by the product during shipment as well as the use of the product when it arrives at its destination.

Bulk packing is used for products such as coal or other minerals. In the case of coal and oil, no actual packaging is used. The products are just loaded into freight cars or tankers and shipped. Trains, ships, or pipelines can handle this type of packing. Many other types of products are bulk packed in boxes. Gardening tools, hardware, lumber, clothes such as gloves or socks, and produce are among the articles that usually are placed in a box in an orderly fashion but are not individually packaged. We might think of this kind of packing as a more organized form of bulk packing.

Most products, however, cannot be packed in bulk, due to the damage they would suffer during shipment. In bulk packing, products could rub against one another, causing scratches on shiny surfaces, or the weight of many parts together could break fragile components.

If the product being shipped will be used to make another product, its individual packing is of a protective nature only. This **in-process individual packing** is the second level of packing. Computer components are packed in styrofoam protection, but in such a way that the styrofoam is the only container. Items simply requiring protection from scratching usually are separated in the box by inserts made of some grade of corrugated board (cardboard). The thickness of the corrugated board used is determined by the amount of protection required.

Final-product individual packing must meet all of the packing requirements of the in-process packing and more. The additional requirements stem from the fact that this is the packing that will eventually be seen by the customer. Whereas the in-process packing looks somewhat crude, the final product packaging must look very professional. Many kinds of labeling information must be on it, and it must be appealing to the eye or must attract attention. Final packing is performed by the operations function, but the design of the package is performed by operations, engineering, and marketing.

Proper logistics management can reduce packing costs by reducing the number of times an item is packed and repacked. More important, the packaging decisions made at each branch of the distribution network can influence costs of packing, costs of shipping, costs of handling, and costs due to damaged or lost products.

SIZE OR FREQUENCY OF SHIPMENTS

A major consideration in the operation of the distribution system is how often shipments should be made. A shipment may be made for every order, or orders may be combined into larger, less frequent shipments. The analysis of the size of a shipment is, essentially, the economic order quantity problem of inventory control, which is discussed in Chapter 13. However, there are considerations other than those presented in Chapter 13 that affect order size. Priority levels assigned to different orders will affect the frequency of shipping, as will the due dates of these orders. In addition, the distance between the origin and destination will affect the size and frequency of shipments. With proper coordination, the grouping of orders can be planned to reduce costs.

To a large extent, the coordination of orders falls into the category of just-in-time inventory. The JIT concept requires an increase in the frequency of orders but a decrease in the size of orders. This will be discussed in more detail in later chapters on inventory and materials requirements planning.

Another consideration is the possibility of **transshipment.** Transshipment is the shipping of goods to one or more intermediate destinations prior to their arrival at the final destination. The ability to transship opens additional opportunities for combining orders, if the distribution network is so structured. Transshipment is a common practice in industry. Very often, when a customer calls to learn why the product he or she ordered is late, the customer is told that it has been sent, but is going "by way of" another city.

Combining orders to make larger shipments is done, of course, to reduce costs. It is a form of strategy known as the **unit load concept,** which attempts to attain a common, or unit-size, load for all shipments. This strategy has led to a practice called **containerization,** which allows loading facilities and vehicles to achieve greater efficiency by using common-size containers. Containerization is used in cargo ships especially and is a major contributor to the efficiency of piggybacking.

ADDITIONAL LOGISTICS CONCERNS

CAPACITY OF THE FACILITY

The capacity of the facility, as we explained in Chapter 3, becomes a factor only when the facility becomes a bottleneck within the network. Proper facility size, in terms of the physical design of the facility, is a long-term decision. This decision must determine the capacity to store material as well as the capacity to process or load material. For instance, having four loading docks instead of two doubles the capacity to load the material, but does not affect the size of the facility (storage capacity). Short-term capacity decisions deal with modifying the capacity of the facility by either increasing or decreasing the work force (see Chapter 12 on production planning) or by acquiring better equipment for internal materials handling (see the next section).

CAPACITY OF THE ROUTES AND VEHICLES

The capacity of the routes should be designed to work most efficiently with the capacity of the facilities and the size of shipments in order to reduce costs. Defined literally, route capacities are not critical in road, rail, or air transport. These routes could carry more trucks, train cars, or flights. Mostly, it is the choice of vehicle size that limits road, rail, and air transport. However, in the literal sense, capacity design is most significant for pipeline or telecommunications relays. Capacity of water routes is limited by the size of the waterway, which limits the size of the ships that traverse it. Vehicle capacity also limits the total distribution system capacity. Truck size is, in some states, limited by law. Airplane size is limited by, for example, runway length.

STORAGE MECHANISM

Decisions regarding the storage mechanism usually are obvious. They depend directly on the type of product to be stored. Many products are simply stacked, while others require elaborate shelving. Some products have a specific shelf life, so that the warehouse manager must not only keep track of where it is, but also must know how long it has been there. The value of the product will determine the level of security built into and maintained at the storage facility. The final consideration in the selection of a storage mechanism is climate. Some liquids must be heated during storage; some gases must be kept in environments with extremely low temperatures, and others must be stored under pressure. Perishable items must be refrigerated. Of course, the least expensive product to store is one that can be warehoused in a facility with no heating or cooling.

AMOUNT TO STORE

Yet another concern is the appropriate amount of inventory to maintain at each point in the distribution network. More specifically, the consideration is the levels of safety stocks required. In our presentation of distribution requirements planning later in this chapter, we will show that safety stock, to the extent possible, should be maintained at the location that is closest (among the set of facilities in the distribution network) to the customer. This maximizes the effect of the safety stock with regard to the service level and, of course, keeps the marketing division happy. This service level, the major measure of customer service, is the ultimate goal of the logistics network. The trade-off in a logistics decision usually is between cost and customer service level. These concepts are expanded in the later chapter on inventory management.

goal of logistics

ROUTE TO CHOOSE

In a complex distribution system, there are always alternative routes that can be taken, especially when transshipment is used. There may even be the possibility of choosing among alternative means of shipment. Algorithms have been developed for a variety of network optimization problems, such as

- the optimal set of routes;
- the shortest route (time or distance) through a network between any two points; and
- the maximum flow through a (fixed) network.

Although operations managers do not need to know the details of these techniques, they are wise to know that such techniques for routing within a network exist.

When a series of deliveries must be made on one trip, the delivery truck is required to follow some loop through the network, reaching a predetermined set of nodes on one trip. Many small and large businesses need deliveries (or repairs) to be made in this way. The problem is to select the best loop, or the best sequence of visiting the customers. This general problem is called the traveling salesman problem, and many efficient procedures have been developed to solve it. The problem is identical to a certain machine scheduling problem, one approach to which is provided in Chapter 15.

The preceding material summarizes most of the decisions that must be made in logistics management. The importance of logistics management may be better understood when we consider that fully 20 percent of the U.S. gross national product comes from the cost of distributing products through distribution networks from production site (factory, mine, farm) to consumption site (retail store, factory). Clearly, this is an area where an alert manager can introduce beneficial cost-saving suggestions and improvements.

impact of logistics

DISTRIBUTION REQUIREMENTS PLANNING

Distribution requirements planning (DRP) focuses on the material needs (in terms of timing, quantity, and location) within the distribution network. The purpose of the entire distribution function, as we have seen, is to meet those material needs in a timely and cost-effective manner. Therefore, DRP is central to the operation of the system.

Prior to commencing a specific discussion of DRP, some strategies for the management of materials within a distribution system should be discussed. The primary decision to be made in selecting an appropriate DRP system is the level of centralization in the planning. A **push system** is used in conjunction with centralized planning. In this approach, the central warehouse or the factory "pushes" material through the system as it becomes ready. A **pull system** is used when each local facility sets its own ordering policy. In this approach, a shipment is made only if there is a specific need for the material. These descriptions of the push system and the pull system are expanded in the sections that follow. To most practitioners, DRP is a pull system, and a push system is a different approach. However, because both are used for the purpose of distribution requirements planning, we will consider them together here.

Alternative systems to DRP, which have fallen out of favor in recent years, include base stock systems and reorder point systems. The base stock system is used in (and is still highly recommended for) situations in which orders are very infrequent. It is also known as a "sell one–buy one" system because the goal is to stay at some minimal level of inventory. Each time an item is sold, an order is placed for one unit to replace it in stock. Furniture stores, appliance stores, electronics stores, and heavy-equipment dealers may all use this type of system.

The reorder point system works in a similar way, but involves orders of larger quantities. The goal of this system is to bring stock levels up to some level that is considered to be a full stock. For this reason, it is called a *replenishment* policy. The stock is replenished each time it gets down to some minimal level, or reorder point. As we shall see in our study of inventory management, there is a closely related alternative approach. In this approach, the stock is filled at regularly timed intervals. The approach does not use a reorder point, but, in terms of distribution requirements planning, it is identical to the reorder point system. For each, the underlying philosophy is to give all the local outlets or distributors the freedom to implement their own ordering policies. Thus, these systems are pull systems.

level of centralization

base stock system

reorder point system

A PULL SYSTEM

The standard DRP is a pull system. That is, orders are initiated, as required, at the lowest level of the distribution network. This is where the product is finally sold. The retail store initiates the order, which forces the product to be "pulled" through the network from the factory, through the various levels of distribution centers, to the store. Mattell is an example of a company that lets demand pull shipments, rather than flooding stores with too many items. The traditional way of planning material needs has always been to respond to the lowest-level needs (decentralized planning). So, in this sense, the pull system described here introduces better order and better planning into the process, without significantly changing operating strategy. Second, the approach is very similar to that of materials requirements planning (MRP). Many advanced MRP commercial software packages possess a DRP capability. Those DRP capabilities are always pull systems, as you will see in Chapter 14.

Teaching Suggestion 6.9: Pull System and Make to Stock. See the Instructor's Section for details.

A PUSH SYSTEM

In a push system, the same concept of overall planning and coordination between plant, warehouse, and store is used, but the plant initiates all shipments. The stores and warehouses do not order supplies; the plant manufactures the products and then "pushes" them through the distribution network.

There are three factors that motivate the use of a push system over the use of a pull system. First, analysis of effective safety stock levels in distribution systems shows that the effective safety stock is highest when it is kept closest to the customer level. Thus, no stock should be held at the factory or the warehouse; instead, it should be pushed through the network as soon as possible. Second, all pull systems are based on some lot sizing concept, such as order quantities.

However, lot sizes are not always applicable in the various levels of a distribution network. This is because lot sizes usually are based on some trade-off between ordering costs and holding costs. However, the company incurs the same holding cost at each location in the network. As long as the inventory is still held within the same company, the inventory balance sheet is unchanged. Finally, the third factor concerns the trade-off between production costs and inventory costs at the store level. A pull system dictates production schedules without considering the costs of fluctuating production levels from one time period to the next. Because these costs are usually higher than the inventory costs incurred at other levels of the distribution network, it is helpful first to perform some organized production planning analysis and then to push the production through the distribution network.

motivating factors for using a push system

benefits of push systems

S U M M A R Y

Any individual facility must fit into a larger, more complex network of operations. The problems of designing a distribution network are closely related to those of location choice and design, except that they are more complex because the network involves both the location and coordination of multiple facilities. Distribution management deals with the design and movement of products, customers, or information from the source, provider, or producer to the final destination, or the consumer. The way in which a business distributes products, customers, or information requires a great deal of analysis. This chapter has provided an overview of the relevant concerns, instilling in the reader a concern for an area that is most often viewed as peripheral to the more pressing problems of business. Objectives are not only financial in nature; they also include service level, timing, and customer satisfaction.

The chapter explained the factors that a company considers when designing and implementing a distribution network. Types of distribution networks, modes of transportation, packaging, and shipping costs are some of these factors. Methods for scheduling shipments and allocation of inventories in a distribution network were provided, also. Two types of approaches are push systems and pull systems. Both systems fall into a larger category known as distribution requirements planning.

The transportation model was explained in detail. Its assumptions as well as its solution and application to other operations problems were discussed.

KEY TERMS

distribution management

arborescent network

coalescent network

series network

complex network

optimal solution

optimization

proportional cost

additive cost

linear cost

northwest corner method

minimal cost method

marginal cost

stepping stone method

assignment problem

degenerate solution

logistics

physical distribution

piggybacking

bulk packing

in-process individual packing

final-product individual packing

transshipment

unit load concept

containerization

distribution requirements planning

push system

pull system

SOLVED PROBLEMS

1. For the following transportation problem, find a starting solution using the method indicated.

(a) the northwest corner method

(b) the minimal cost method

From	To			Supply
	X	Y	Z	
A	$10	$18	$12	100
B	$17	$13	$ 9	50
C	$20	$18	$14	75
Demand	40	90	70	

Solution

The first step in solving a transportation problem is to be sure that the total demand equals the total supply. In this problem, the total supply is 225, and the total demand is 200. Therefore, we must begin by adding a dummy demand point with a demand of 225 − 200 = 25. The shipping cost for each added entry is zero. The new table appears as follows.

From	To				Supply
	X	Y	Z	Dummy	
A	$10	$18	$12	$0	100
B	$17	$13	$ 9	$0	50
C	$20	$18	$14	$0	75
Demand	40	90	70	25	225

(a) To use the northwest corner method, we begin in the upper left-hand corner (the northwest corner) and work our way to the lower right-hand corner. At each cell, we always put in as many units as possible. The number of units is limited by the supply in the row and the demand in the column.

Beginning with cell (A–X), insert 40 units, which meets the demand, but leaves 60 units in row A. We move on to cell (A–Y) and insert 60 units here. This depletes row A, but leaves 30 units in column Y. Our next cell, (B–Y), is in the same column, but one row down. We place the 30 units from row B in this cell, reducing the number available in the row to 20, and move to cell (B–Z). We allocate the available 20 units in row B to this cell, depleting row B and reducing the column Z demand to 50. We move to the bottom row, where we put 50 of the units in cell (C–Z) and the remaining 25 units in cell (C–Dummy). This gives us our final allocation.

From	To				Supply
	X	Y	Z	Dummy	
A	40	60			100
B		30	20		50
C			50	25	75
Demand	40	90	70	25	225

Notice that the number of cells with allocations is given by 3 + 4 − 1 = 6.

(b) Using the minimal cost method, we begin by finding the cell that has the minimum shipping cost. In this case, because of the dummy destination, three cells have the same minimum cost of $0. Let us begin with the minimum cost above zero, which occurs in cell (B–Z). We want to load cell (B–Z) with as many units as possible—50. This exhausts row B supply but leaves 20 in column Z.

From	To				Supply
	X	Y	Z	Dummy	
A	$10	$18	$12	$0	100
B	$17	$13	$9 (50)	$0	5̶0̶
C	$20	$18	$14	$0	75
Demand	40	90	7̶0̶ 20	25	225

The next lowest shipping cost is $10, in cell (A–X). We are limited by the demand of 40, which we place in cell (A–X) and subtract from row A and column X, thereby depleting column X and reducing row A from 100 to 60.

From	To				Supply
	X	Y	Z	Dummy	
A	$10 (40)	$18	$12	$0	1̶0̶0̶ 60
B	$17	$13	$9 (50)	$0	50
C	$20	$18	$14	$0	75
Demand	4̶0̶	90	7̶0̶ 20	25	225

The next cheapest shipping cost is $12, in cell (A–Z). We place the 20 in this cell to finish the column Z demand and reduce row A supply from 60 to 40.

From	To				Supply
	X	Y	Z	Dummy	
A	$10 ⑩(40)	$18	$12 (20)	$0	~~100~~ ~~60~~ 40
B	$17	$13	$9 (50)	$0	~~50~~
C	$20	$18	$14	$0	75
Demand	~~40~~	90	~~70~~ 20	25	225

The next lowest cost occurs in cell (B–Y), but we cannot use this cell because row B supply has been depleted. We find that the lowest remaining cost in row A or row C is the $18 in cell (A–Y). We put 40 in this cell, finish with row A, and leave 50 in column Y.

From	To				Supply
	X	Y	Z	Dummy	
A	$10 (40)	$18 (40)	$12 (20)	$0	~~100~~ ~~60~~ ~~40~~
B	$17	$13	$9 (50)	$0	~~50~~
C	$20	$18	$14	$0	75
Demand	~~40~~	~~90~~ 50	~~70~~ 20	25	225

At this point, the only remaining row is row C, so the remaining demands must enter row C.

From	To X	Y	Z	Dummy	Supply
A	$10 (40)	$18 (40)	$12 (20)	$0	~~100~~ ~~60~~ ~~40~~
B	$17	$13	$9 (50)	$0	~~50~~
C	$20	$18 (50)	$14	$0 (25)	~~75~~
Demand	~~40~~	~~90~~ ~~50~~	~~70~~ ~~20~~	25	225

Notice again that the number of cells in the solution is $3 + 4 - 1 = 6$.

Using AB:POM to Solve This Problem

The first of many options in the transportation module is whether to minimize costs or maximize profits. After making this decision, you enter the number of sources (rows) and the number of destinations (columns) to set up the data table. On top of the data table are three toggle switches. The first toggle switch is used to set the transportation initialization method. The methods available are "NO steps" (in which case the computer performs the initialization), the northwest corner method, Vogel's approximation method, or the minimal cost method. If you are interested in the final answer only, then choose "NO steps." The other three choices ("Northwst," "Vogel," and "Mincost") will solve the problem more slowly, one step at a time. If you want to see the intermediate tables, then you must choose one of these three as the starting method.

Screen 6.1 contains the costs for Solved Problem 1. The rows and columns have been named and the costs of the problem and the supplies and demands are filled in. Notice that the option at the top is the "Northwst" option.

Pressing the **F10** key gives the first of the solution screens, as shown in Screen 6.2. The information in the table on the screen is of two types. Numbers that are not accompanied by a + or − represent the shipments. So we know to ship 40, 60, 30, 20, and 50 units. These are actually the answers to the solved problems. Numbers with a sign represent the marginal costs of the cells without shipments. You can press any key (except the **Esc** key) to continue iterating.

Screen 6.3 presents the initial minimal cost solution. The solution on the screen differs from that above because AB:POM began in the Dummy section (A–Dummy)

```
╔══════════════════════════════════════════════════════════════════════════╗
║ ═ Data file:D:wgsp6 ═══════════ Transportation ═══════════ Data Screen ═  ║
║   Number of sources (2-99) 3              Number of destinations (2-99)  3  ║
║   minimize                                                                 ║
║ ╔════════════════════════ Solved problem 1(a) ════════════════════════╗   ║
║ ║ Options→ Northwst Comptr  PrntOFF                                    ║   ║
║ ║                                                                      ║   ║
║ ║                X        Y        Z    Supply                         ║   ║
║ ║                                                                      ║   ║
║ ║  A             10       18       12      100                         ║   ║
║ ║                                                                      ║   ║
║ ║  B             17       13        9       50                         ║   ║
║ ║                                                                      ║   ║
║ ║  C             20       18       14       75                         ║   ║
║ ║                                                                      ║   ║
║ ║  Demand        40       90       70                                  ║   ║
║ ║                                                                      ║   ║
║ ╚══════════════════════════════════════════════════════════════════════╝   ║
║                                                                            ║
║ F1=Help F2=New  F3=Load F4=Main F5=Util F6=Quit F7=Save F9=Prnt F10=Run  Esc║
║ Press space bar to toggle who selects entering cell or RETURN for menu     ║
╚══════════════════════════════════════════════════════════════════════════╝
```

SCREEN 6.1

```
╔══════════════════════════════════════════════════════════════════════════╗
║ ═ Data file:D:wgsp6 ═══════════ Transportation ═══════════ Solution ═     ║
║   Number of sources (2-99) 3              Number of destinations (2-99)  3  ║
║   minimize                                                                 ║
║ ╔════════════════════════Solved problem 1(a)════════════════════════╗     ║
║ ║ Options→ Northwst Comptr  PrntOFF                                  ║     ║
║ ║                                                                    ║     ║
║ ║                X        Y        Z    Dummy                        ║     ║
║ ║                                                                    ║     ║
║ ║  A             40       60       -2      +0                        ║     ║
║ ║                                                                    ║     ║
║ ║  B            +12       30       20      +5                        ║     ║
║ ║                                                                    ║     ║
║ ║  C            +10       +0       50      25                        ║     ║
║ ║                                                                    ║     ║
║ ║                                                                    ║     ║
║ ║  The total cost is       $2,750                                    ║     ║
║ ║  NOTE: Dummy column has been added                                 ║     ║
║ ╚════════════════════════════════════════════════════════════════════╝     ║
║                                                                            ║
║ Press <Esc> key to end computations  Press <Esc> key when done iterating   ║
║ Press any key to iterate or ESC to stop                                    ║
╚══════════════════════════════════════════════════════════════════════════╝
```

SCREEN 6.2

```
╔═ Data file:D:wgsp6 ═════════════ Transportation ══════════════ Solution ═╗
║  Number of sources (2-99) 3                    Number of destinations (2-99)  3 ║
║  minimize                                                                       ║
╠════════════════════════════ Solved problem 1(b) ═══════════════════════════╣
║  Options→ Mincost  Comptr  PrntOFF                                              ║
║                                                                                 ║
║                  X        Y        Z   Dummy                                    ║
║                                                                                 ║
║  A              40   .   15       20      25                                    ║
║                                                                                 ║
║  B             +10       -2       50      +3                                    ║
║                                                                                 ║
║  C             +10       75       +2      +0                                    ║
║                                                                                 ║
║                                                                                 ║
║                                                                                 ║
║                                                                                 ║
║  The total cost is          $2,710                                              ║
║  NOTE: Dummy column has been added                                              ║
╚════════════════════════════════════════════════════════════════════════════╝
   Press <Esc> key to end computations  Press <Esc> key when done iterating
   Press any key to iterate or ESC to stop
```

SCREEN 6.3

and we did not. Once again, you can keep pressing keys until the solution screen states that the final solution has been found. ■

2. Find the optimal solution for Solved Problem 1 using the initial solution generated by the minimal cost method.

Solution

We need to examine the marginal costs for each of the empty cells. If all of the costs are nonnegative (zero or more), then we are done. Otherwise, we will have to change some shipments. We begin with cell (A–Dummy).

The loop for this cell is (A–Dummy), (A–Y), (C–Y), and (C–Dummy). The costs in these cells yield a marginal cost of

$$\$0 - \$18 + \$18 - \$0 = \$0.$$

Next, we try cell (B–X), which has a loop of (B–X), (B–Z), (A–Z), and (A–X) and a marginal cost of $\$17 - \$9 + \$12 - \$10 = \$10$.

Next, we try cell (B–Y), which has a loop of (B–Y), (B–Z), (A–Z), and (A–Y) and a marginal cost of $\$13 - \$9 + \$12 - \$18 = -\$2$. This cell can help us, so we immediately move units around its loop. The number of units in the cells from which we are subtracting—cells (B–Z) and (A–Y)—are 40 and 50, so we choose the minimum of these two numbers and move 40 units around the loop, yielding the following new solution.

	To				
From	X	Y	Z	Dummy	**Supply**
A	$10 ⑩(40)	$18	$12 (60)	$0	100
B	$17	$13 (40)	$9 (10)	$0	50
C	$20	$18 (50)	$14	$0 (25)	75
Demand	40	90	70	25	225

Again, we must check every empty cell. We continue with cell (B–Dummy), which has a loop of (B–Dummy), (B–Y), (C–Y), and (C–Dummy) and a marginal cost of $0 − $13 + $18 − $0 = $5.

We next try cell (C–X), which has a slightly more complex loop of (C–X), (C–Y), (B–Y), (B–Z), (A–Z), and (A–X) and a marginal cost of $20 − $18 + $13 − $9 + $12 − $10 = $8.

The loop for cell (C–Z) is (C–Z), (B–Z), (B–Y), and (C–Y); the marginal cost is $14 − $9 + $13 − $18 = $0.

The loop for cell (A–Y) is (A–Y), (A–Z), (B–Z), and (B–Y); the marginal cost is $18 − $12 + $9 − $13 = $2.

The loop for cell (A–Dummy) is somewhat complex and is given by (A–Dummy), (A–Z), (B–Z), (B–Y), (C–Y), and (C–Dummy); the marginal cost is $0 − $12 + $9 − $13 + $18 − $0 = $2.

The loop for cell (B–X) is (B–X), (B–Z), (A–Z), and (A–X); the marginal cost is $17 − $9 + $12 − $10 = $10.

All empty cells have been examined, proving our solution to be optimal. The minimum cost is given by

($10 × 40) + ($12 × 60) + ($13 × 40) + ($9 × 10) + ($18 × 50) + ($0 × 25)

$$= \$400 + \$720 + \$520 + \$90 + \$900 + \$0 = \$2,630.$$

Using AB:POM to Solve This Problem

As you know, choosing "NO steps" bypasses the starting or intermediate solutions, arriving at the final, optimal solution. Screen 6.4 shows the results of the NO steps option for Solved Problem 2. The optimal shipments are in the table, and the total cost is given below the table.

To display the marginal costs, you must press the **F1** key or the **T** key, as shown in Screen 6.5. Notice that the word in the upper left of the table has changed from "SHIPMENTS" to "Marginals." Further, notice that the numbers have signs (+) next to them.

```
┌─ Data file:D:wgsp6 ══════════ Transportation ══════════════ Solution ═
│  Number of sources (2-99) 3              Number of destinations (2-99)  3
│  minimize
│
│  ┌══════════════════════════ Solved problem 2 ══════════════════════
│  │ Options→ NO steps  Comptr  PrntOFF
│  │
│  │ SHIPMENTS        X        Y        Z   Supply
│  │
│  │ A                40               60     100
│  │
│  │ B                         50             50
│  │
│  │ C                         40       10     75
│  │
│  │ Demand           40       90       70
│  │
│  │ The minimum total cost =        $2,630
│  │
│  │
│  │ NOTE:Dummy column has been added      NOTE: alternate optimal solutions exist
│
│  F1=Toggle SHIPMENTS/marginal costs                      F9=Print    Esc
│  Press <Esc> key to edit data or highlighted key or function key for options
```

SCREEN 6.4

```
┌─ Data file:D:wgsp6 ══════════ Transportation ══════════════ Solution ═
│  Number of sources (2-99) 3              Number of destinations (2-99)  3
│  minimize
│
│  ┌══════════════════════════ Solved problem 2 ══════════════════════
│  │ Options→ NO steps Comptr  PrntOFF
│  │
│  │ Marginals        X        Y        Z   Supply
│  │
│  │ A                         +2             100
│  │
│  │ B               +10               +0      50
│  │
│  │ C               +8                        75
│  │
│  │ Demand           40       90       70
│  │
│  │ The minimum total cost =        $2,630
│  │
│  │
│  │ NOTE:Dummy column has been added      NOTE: alternate optimal solutions exist
│
│  F1=Toggle SHIPMENTS/marginal costs                      F9=Print    Esc
│  Press <Esc> key to edit data or highlighted key or function key for options
```

SCREEN 6.5

One more press of **F1** will generate a table that contains both shipments and marginal costs, as shown in Screen 6.6.

```
┌══ Data file:D:wgsp6 ═════════════ Transportation ═══════════════ Solution ═┐
│  Number of sources (2-99) 3                    Number of destinations (2-99)  3 │
│  minimize                                                                       │
├─────────────────────────────── Solved problem 2 ══════════════════════════┤
│  Options→ NO steps Comptr   PrntOFF                                             │
│                                                                                 │
│  Both              X       Y       Z   Supply                                   │
│                                                                                 │
│  A                40      +2      60     100                                     │
│                                                                                 │
│  B               +10      50      +0      50                                     │
│                                                                                 │
│  C                +8      40      10      75                                     │
│                                                                                 │
│  Demand           40      90      70                                            │
│                                                                                 │
│  The minimum total cost =        $2,630                                         │
│                                                                                 │
│                                                                                 │
│  NOTE:Dummy column has been added        NOTE: alternate optimal solutions exist│
└─────────────────────────────────────────────────────────────────────────────┘
  F1=Toggle SHIPMENTS/marginal costs                           F9=Print   Esc
  Press <Esc> key to edit data or highlighted key or function key for options
```

SCREEN 6.6

QUESTIONS

1. What are the traditional routes available for distribution?

2. What factors should be considered when choosing a specific distribution route?

3. Describe the three types of simple distribution networks.

4. What is the difference between a simple and a complex distribution network?

5. What are the seven means of transporting a product?

6. What are the five basic assumptions of the transportation method?

7. What are the three steps required to solve the transportation problem?

8. What is the difference between a feasible solution and an optimal one?

9. How do you know when an optimal solution has been reached?

10. What is meant by an unbalanced transportation problem, and how would you balance it?

11. What is the difference in marginal cost interpretation between a maximization problem and a minimization problem?

12. How many cells must all solutions use?

13. Are shipping costs usually proportional to shipping distances?

14. Are shipping costs usually proportional to the quantities shipped?

15. Which proportionality assumption (distance or quantity) is critical to the transportation method?

16. Identify the advantages and disadvantages of each of the five physical distribution transportation routes.

17. What are the three forms of packing?

18. Explain the practice of containerization.

19. What considerations should be taken into account when selecting a storage mechanism?

20. Briefly contrast the pull and push systems.

PROBLEMS

1. First-Aid Drugstores (FAD) maintains a national distribution center in St. Louis, where all of the products for its pharmacies are procured. From the St. Louis warehouse complex, four regional warehouses (in Philadelphia, Atlanta, Chicago, and Denver) are supplied. Each of these regional warehouses, in turn, supplies four local distribution centers, each of which supplies twenty-four pharmacies. Draw the simple distribution network from the national warehouses to the local distributors. Do not include the pharmacies on your chart, because there are too many. How many pharmacies are there? What type of network is this?

See Instructor's Section for diagram; 384 pharmacies; arborescent.

2. FAD (see Problem 1) is considering closing its Chicago regional warehouse and telling the local distributors in that region to obtain products directly from the St. Louis center. Draw the distribution network that would result from this change. What type of network is this?

See Instructor's Section for diagram; simple arborescent.

3. FAD (see Problem 1) also is considering closing the Chicago regional warehouse and telling the local distributors to obtain products from *any* of the three remaining regional warehouses. Draw the resulting distribution network. What type of network is this?

See Instructor's Section for diagram; complex.

4. CompDesign (CD) designs and assembles computer systems for small businesses to their individual configurations. CD uses two hardware vendors and one software distributor. Vendor 1 provides the main circuit boards and the CRTs. Vendor 2 provides the disk drives, printers, and cables. Draw the network that describes the flow of components in support of the CD operations. What type of network is this?

See Instructor's Section for diagram; coalescent.

5. Draw a network representing the complex distribution of mail through the U.S. postal system.

See Instructor's Section for diagram.

6. Draw a network representing the check-clearing system of U.S. banks.

See Instructor's Section for diagram.

7. The costs (in Problem 1) of shipping from St. Louis to the four local centers in the Chicago region are $14, $6, $11, and $5 per ton, respectively. The costs of shipping from Chicago are $8, $7, $5, and $10 per ton, respectively. Closing the Chicago warehouse will save $300,000 in fixed costs. How many tons must be shipped annually to justify keeping the Chicago warehouse open? Use a break-even analysis and assume that all four centers require the same quantity of material.

200,000 or more tons

8. For the following transportation problem, find the starting solution and cost using the indicated method.

(a) the northwest corner method
(b) the minimal cost method

A–V: 60; A–W: 15; B–W: 65; B–X: 35; C–X: 55; C–Y: 20; D–Y: 20; D–Z: 30; total cost = $14,720

A–V: 10; A–Y: 35; A–Z: 30; B–W: 5; B–X: 90; B–Y: 5; C–W: 75; D–V: 50; total cost = $8,585

From	To					Supply
	V	W	X	Y	Z	
A	$61	$86	$88	$66	$22	75
B	$85	$48	$7	$82	$36	100
C	$58	$29	$25	$99	$51	75
D	$31	$49	$44	$55	$65	50
Demand	60	80	90	40	30	

9. For the following transportation problem, find the starting solution and initial cost using the northwest corner method.

From	To				Supply
	W	X	Y	Z	
A	$132	$116	$250	$110	220
B	$220	$230	$180	$178	300
C	$152	$173	$196	$164	435
Demand	160	120	200	230	

A–W: 160; A–X: 60; B–X: 60; B–Y: 200; B–Z: 40; C–Z: 190; C–Dummy: 245; total cost = $116,160

10. Solve the following transportation problem, starting with the northwest corner method. What is the minimum cost?

From	To			Supply
	Dallas	Denver	Detroit	
Memphis	$17	$20	$25	700
Minneapolis	$20	$18	$9	600
Miami	$12	$30	$17	300
Demand	600	500	500	

Memphis–Dallas: 300; Memphis–Denver: 400; Minneapolis–Denver: 100; Minneapolis–Detroit: 500; Miami–Dallas: 300; total cost = $23,000

11. Solve Problem 10 by starting with the minimal cost method.

See answer to Problem 10.

12. Solve the following minimum cost transportation problem.

Origin	Destination				Supply
	A	B	C	D	
X	$13	$14	$19	$25	32
Y	$18	$20	$28	$24	20
Z	$10	$17	$18	$28	20
Demand	27	12	15	18	

X–A: 5; X–B: 12; X–C: 15;
Y–A: 2; Y–D: 18; Z–A: 20;
total cost = $1,186

13. Solve the following minimum cost transportation problem. (Note the similarity to Problem 12.)

Origin	Destination				Supply
	A	B	C	D	
X	$23	$24	$29	$35	32
Y	$18	$20	$28	$24	20
Z	$10	$17	$18	$28	20
Demand	27	12	15	18	

X–A: 5; X–B: 12; X–C: 15;
Y–A: 2; Y–D: 18; Z–A: 20;
total cost = $1,506

14. Solve the following *maximization* of profit transportation problem. Start with the northwest corner method.

Origin	Destination				Supply
	D	E	F	G	
A	$30	$15	$50	$25	10
B	$40	$35	$40	$15	18
C	$55	$20	$65	$30	17
Demand	15	15	10	5	

A–F = 5
A–G = 5
B–D = 3
B–E = 15
C–D = 12
C–F = 5
total profit = $2,005

15. Solve Problem 14 by starting with the minimal cost method. (Remember: This is a *maximization* problem.)

See answer to Problem 14.

16. Solve the following minimum cost transportation problem.

From	Dallas	El Paso	Fort Worth	Galveston	Houston	Supply
			To			
Austin	$20	$48	$10	$30	$40	100
Beaumont	$70	$60	$55	$90	$70	80
Corpus Christi	$45	$80	$50	$30	$60	150
Demand	50	70	65	55	90	

Austin–Dallas: 35; Austin–Ft. Worth: 65; Beaumont–El Paso: 70; Beaumont–Houston: 10; Corpus Christi–Dallas: 15; Corpus Christi–Galveston: 55; Corpus Christi–Houston: 80; total cost = $13,375

17. In Problem 16, suppose that it is impossible to ship from Beaumont to Galveston. What is the optimal shipping plan and cost?

See answer to Problem 16.

18. In Problem 16, suppose that it is impossible to ship from Austin to Fort Worth. What is the optimal shipping plan and cost?

See Instructor's Section; total cost = $14,550.

19. Captain Hook manufactures fishing equipment. Currently, the company has a plant in Los Angeles and a plant in New Orleans. The company is deciding where to build a new plant—Philadelphia or Seattle. Use the following table to find the total shipping costs for each potential site.

Plant	Pittsburgh	St. Louis	Denver	Capacity
		Warehouse		
Los Angeles	$100	$75	$50	150
New Orleans	$80	$60	$90	225
Philadelphia	$40	$50	$90	350
Seattle	$110	$70	$30	350
Demand	200	100	400	

Philadelphia.
LA–Denver: 150; New Orleans–Denver: 225; Philadelphia–Pittsburgh: 200; Philadelphia–St. Louis: 100; Philadelphia–Denver: 25; Philadelphia–Dummy: 25; total cost = $43,000 (An alternative solution exists.)

Seattle.
LA–St. Louis: 75; LA–Denver: 50; LA–Dummy: 25; New Orleans–Pittsburgh: 200; New Orleans–St. Louis: 25; Seattle–Denver: 350; total cost = $36,125

20. Suncool Inc. produces suntan lotion. Suncool is planning its production for the next four months. The demands are 100 cases for June, 140 cases for July, 170 cases for August, and 90 cases for September. Regular-time production is limited to 125 cases per month. Overtime production is limited to 25 cases per month. Cases produced in overtime cost $10 more than cases produced during regular time. Cases are stored at a cost of $8 per case per month.

(a) Formulate this into a transportation table.
(b) Find the optimal production schedule.

See Instructor's Section.
See Instructor's Section.

COMPUTER CASE STUDY 6.1: CONSOLIDATED BOTTLING INC.

Consolidated Bottling Incorporated (also see Computer Case Study 5.1) bottles spring water. The company has bottling operations in or near twelve cities in the United States and distributors in or near eighteen North American cities, including the twelve cities with bottling plants. Recently, Consolidated has encountered some problems at two of its plants: The level of chemicals in the bottled water coming from these plants is too high.

After a great deal of thought, management decides that it is time to reevaluate the entire shipping plan to determine if it is worthwhile to upgrade either or both of these plants or if new plants should be built in different locations. Especially attractive as potential sites for new facilities are the six cities that already have distributorships. The analysis that is to be done is large; it includes the evaluation of many location factors. For example, the (fixed) costs associated with revamping the old plants must be weighed against those associated with building new plants. There are also labor-related factors to consider.

The major concern in this chapter is shipping costs. The following table lists the plant capacities in the twelve cities with bottling plants and demand for Consolidated bottled water at each of the eighteen distribution sites.

Plant	Monthly Capacity (in thousands)	Monthly Usage (in thousands of cases)
Albuquerque	250	24
Baltimore	270	62
Boston	143	64
Chicago	182	336
Columbus	—	53
Dallas	265	84
Denver	183	51
Detroit	121	151
Houston	265	123
Indianapolis	—	74
Kansas City	240	50
Los Angeles	157	281
Miami	—	33
Montreal	—	121
Portland	121	38
Raleigh	—	12
St. Paul	105	30
San Francisco	—	71

The shipping costs depend on several factors. Different truck lines carry the products on different routes. Since this is a rough analysis, it is sufficient to assume that the intercity shipping costs are proportional to the intercity distances. The distances between all pairs of cities are given in the following table (in rounded hundreds of miles between cities).

Plant	Distributor																	
	AL	BA	BO	CH	CO	DA	DEN	DET	HO	IN	KC	LA	MI	MON	PO	RA	SP	SF
Albuquerque	0	18	22	13	14	6	4	15	8	13	7	8	19	21	13	17	12	11
Baltimore	18	0	4	7	4	14	16	5	14	6	10	26	11	5	27	3	11	28
Boston	22	4	0	10	7	17	19	7	18	9	10	25	14	4	26	6	9	27
Chicago	13	7	10	0	3	9	10	3	11	2	6	22	11	8	23	5	7	24
Columbus	14	4	7	3	0	10	12	2	11	2	7	22	12	7	24	5	7	24
Dallas	6	14	17	9	10	0	8	11	2	9	5	14	13	17	20	12	9	17
Denver	4	16	19	10	12	8	0	13	10	11	6	11	20	18	12	17	8	12
Detroit	15	5	7	3	2	11	13	0	13	3	7	23	13	6	23	7	7	24
Houston	8	14	18	11	11	2	10	13	0	10	7	15	12	18	22	12	12	19
Indianapolis	13	6	9	2	2	9	11	3	10	0	5	20	11	8	22	6	6	23
Kansas City	7	10	10	6	7	5	6	7	7	5	0	16	14	13	18	11	4	18
Los Angeles	8	26	25	22	22	14	11	23	15	20	16	0	27	29	10	25	19	4
Miami	19	11	14	11	12	13	20	13	12	11	14	27	0	17	33	8	17	30
Montreal	21	5	4	8	7	17	18	6	18	8	13	29	17	0	28	8	12	30
Portland	13	27	26	23	24	20	12	23	22	22	18	10	33	28	0	28	17	6
Raleigh	17	3	6	5	5	12	17	7	12	6	11	25	8	8	28	0	12	29
St. Paul	12	11	9	7	7	9	8	7	12	6	4	19	17	12	17	12	0	19
San Francisco	11	28	27	24	24	17	12	24	19	23	18	4	30	30	6	29	19	0

A new plant would have a capacity anywhere between 130 thousand cases per year and 180 thousand cases per year. If a new plant is to be built in one of the six cities that serves as a distributorship but currently does not have a plant, which city should be chosen? How large should the plant be? How much would be saved in shipping miles (money) each year? How will the shipping routes be affected by the opening of a new plant?

REFERENCES

Ammer, D. S. *Materials Management and Purchasing.* Homewood, Ill.: Irwin Publishers, 1980.

Ballou, R. H. *Basic Business Logistics.* 2nd ed. Englewood Cliffs, N.J.: Prentice-Hall, 1987.

Blumenfeld, A., et al. "Reducing Logistics Costs at General Motors," *Interfaces* 17, no. 1 (1987): 26–47.

Brown, R. G. "The New Push for DRP," *Inventories & Production Magazine* (July 1981): 25–27.

Cooper, L., and D. Steinberg. *Methods and Applications of Linear Programming.* Philadelphia: Saunders, 1974.

Hillier, F. S., and G. J. Lieberman. *Introduction to Operations Research.* 5th ed. New York: McGraw-Hill, 1990.

Lev, B., and H. J. Weiss. *Introduction to Mathematical Programming.* New York: North Holland Publishing Co., 1982.

Magee, J., W. Capacino, and D. Rosenfield. *Modern Logistics Management.* New York: John Wiley and Sons, 1985.

Perry, W. "The Principles of Distribution Requirements Planning (DRP)," *P & IM Review* (December 1982): 19–33.

Schonberger, R. J. *World Class Manufacturing Casebook: Implementing JIT and TQC.* New York: Free Press, 1987.

Winston, W. L. *Operations Research: Applications and Algorithms.* Boston: Duxbury, 1987.

Zenz, G., and G. Thompson. *Purchasing and the Management of Materials.* 6th ed. New York: John Wiley and Sons, 1988.

C H A P T E R

7

O U T L I N E

FACILITY LAYOUT

OBJECTIVES

- To explain the objectives of facility design
- To describe the characteristics of production and service processing
- To evaluate the different types of layouts
- To illustrate the principles of assembly lines
- To present the basic concepts of materials handling

INTRODUCTION

As we mentioned in Chapter 5, both facility location and facility layout decisions are extremely important because of their long-term implications. It is very costly to redesign a building, which means that it is of the utmost importance that the original design be done well. Facility design, or redesign, becomes necessary for essentially the same reasons that the location of a new facility must be chosen. A change in demand may require a change in the capacity. (As you know, the capacity of any operation, in a long-term sense, is determined by facility size; layout fixes capacity further.) The product may be redesigned, or a product may be added to or deleted from the product line. There may be a change in the technology for making the product.

The necessity for good facility design is mandated by five of the major management concerns for any business:

- product/service cost;
- efficiency of operations;
- flexibility in changing product or service;
- quality; and
- retention of quality employees.

how layout affects operations

Product cost is increased if the layout requires more inventory (added overhead), prohibits keeping enough inventory (causing shutdowns of operations), or increases

314

the movement of material (slowing the operation). Layout affects efficiency by its impact on how time, materials, and (most of all) space are used. Flexibility refers to the ability to modify, if the need arises, the method of operation, the design of a product, or the quantity or variety of products or services offered. Different layouts may improve the quality of the end product by providing for more consistent and accurate work and, also, better accountability for the work performed. The latter is especially important in service operations, where face-to-face contact with the customer is influenced by the facility layout. Finally, employees want to do their jobs in a pleasant environment that is free from distractions and safe from hazards. The layout must take into account these factors as well as the propensity for employees to become bored performing repetitive tasks.

We begin this chapter with a brief presentation of the major considerations that influence the choice of facility design. As one might expect, these considerations relate to the management concerns just mentioned. We then discuss the characteristics of how jobs are processed and the standard types of layouts that are available. Next, we provide approaches for designing the best of two different types of layout: product layout (assembly line balancing) and process layout. Finally, we explore the close connection between materials handling and facility layout.

Facility layout is the physical arrangement of everything needed for the product or service, including machines, personnel, raw materials, and finished goods. The criteria for a good layout necessarily relate to people (personnel and customers), materials (raw, finished, and in process), machines, and their interactions. Therefore, we begin by discussing the general objectives of facility design. Later, we will consider standard types of layouts and how these layouts meet the objectives.

physical arrangement

FACILITY DESIGN CONSIDERATIONS

The general objective is to design a facility so that operations may be carried out as inexpensively as possible. Several factors—some direct, some indirect—contribute to processing costs (as opposed to material costs). These factors are of prime concern in the layout decision-making process. Table 7.1 shows different areas of concern in the facility design process. More specifically, we will concentrate on the following:

- movement of materials;
- bottlenecks;
- machine interference;
- employee morale and safety;
- equipment choice; and
- flexibility.

MOVEMENT OF MATERIALS

In a typical production system, materials are moved from operation to operation through the entire production process, from the receipt of raw materials to the delivery of finished goods. Similarly, in a service operation, customers (or forms) are moved from process to process through the system. The movement of the materials or customers has no benefit. That is, no value is added during movement, and, actually, the movement is very costly. The most obvious cost is the salary paid to the person who—

Transparency Master 7.1:
Layout Factors.

TABLE 7.1   Factors in selecting layouts

Potential Criterion	Explanation
1. Ease of future expansion or contraction	Will it be simple to increase or decrease the space employed?
2. Adaptability and versatility	Will the planned layout easily accommodate changes in the type and/or variety of items produced without rearrangement?
3. Flexibility of layout	How easy will it be to physically rearrange the layout to accommodate changes?
4. Flow or movement effectiveness	How effective will be the sequence of working operations or steps of materials, paperwork, or people?
5. Materials handling effectiveness	Will the handling system, equipment, and containers be easy and simple to manage?
6. Storage effectiveness	What will be the effectivenesss of holding required stock?
7. Space utilization	To what degree will floor area and cubic feet be used?
8. Effectiveness of supporting service integration	Will supporting areas be arranged to best serve the operating areas?
9. Impact on safety and house-keeping	What will be the effect of the layout on accidents and general cleanliness?
10. Impact on working conditions and employee satisfaction	To what extent will the layout contribute to making the area a pleasant place to work?
11. Ease of supervision and control	Will the layout help supervisors to direct and control operations?
12. Promotional value of appearance for public or community relations	Will the layout have engaging or attractive features that will aid the company's reputation?
13. Impact on quality of product or material	To what extent will the layout affect product quality?
14. Impact on maintenance	To what extent will the layout help or hurt maintenance?
15. Fit with organizational structure	To what degree will the layout match the desired organizational structure?
16. Equipment utilization	To what extent will operating and service equipment be used?
17. Impact on security	How will the layout contribute to controlling theft and pilferage?
18. Utilization of natural conditions	To what extent will the layout take advantage of the natural conditions of the site?
19. Ability to meet capacity	How well will the layout meet output needs?
20. Compatibility with long-range plans	To what extent will the layout fit with the long-range plan?

Note: For a more detailed discussion of each criterion, see R. Muther, *Systematic Layout Planning* (Boston: Cahners Books, 1973), appendix IV.

or the expense of running the machine that—moves the material; less movement means a lower direct cost of movement. Also, the more materials or customers are moved, the greater the chance of an accident, which would incur more cost. More movement makes breakage, damage, or spoilage of goods more likely and even increases the likelihood that papers will be lost (a customer may be represented by papers). In addition to breakage or misplacement, there is the possibility of injury to an employee. Another problem that can arise with poor materials handling is the buildup of inventories and the cost associated with maintaining inventories. Lastly, slow materials handling at the distribution center can result in dissatisfied customers and lost sales. In Table 7.2, we present principles of materials handling. This subject is discussed in more detail later in the chapter.

BOTTLENECKS

As we noted in Chapter 3, a bottleneck is a stage in the production or service process at which the production rate is slowed down. A bottleneck typically occurs because one process has less capacity than the other processes. To some extent, the lower capacity can be overcome by increasing the number of machines or workers employed at that stage. In some cases, bottlenecks also may be reduced by locating the slower processes closer to the center of the production process. As with inefficient materials handling, a bottleneck causes both a reduction in overall output and an increase in inventory at the bottleneck. Being the slowest in a sequence of processes, the bottleneck is the weak link in the chain, serving to limit the maximum capacity of the operation.

MACHINE INTERFERENCE

Machines tend to produce noise, heat, dust, vibrations, and fumes. At a low level, these factors may not disrupt the operations process. However, at high levels, these factors may indeed slow down production. Thus, it is useful to isolate machines that cause interference. However, this may be contrary to the objectives of minimizing materials handling and avoiding bottlenecks. Therefore, the trade-off between a decrease in interference and an increase in speed of operations must be considered. Interference can be a major cause of poor product quality in addition to having a detrimental effect on efficiency.

EMPLOYEE MORALE AND SAFETY

The impact of employee morale on productivity is well known: The better the morale, the more productive the employees. Therefore, layout should be designed in a way that boosts morale. Some ways layout design can increase morale are obvious, such as providing for light-colored walls, windows, and space. In Sweden, uniformity of office size is often a factor in layout design. The rationale can be expressed with the following equation: Equal floor space = equal commitment. Other ways of building morale are less obvious and are not directly related to the production process. Some examples are including a cafeteria or even a gymnasium in the facility design. Companies that pro-

TABLE 7.2 Principles of materials handling

1. Eliminate wasteful methods by:
   a. Reducing to a minimum the number of handlings of materials.
   b. Eliminating unnecessary mixing and subsequent sorting.
   c. Using mechanical aids to eliminate the use of hand labor in movement of materials.
   d. Avoiding the unnecessary transfer of materials from floor to workplace or from container to container.
   e. Increasing the speed of handling.
   f. Utilizing containers and unit loads.
   g. Utilizing gravity as a moving force wherever practicable.
   h. Introducing automation into the materials handling plan.

2. In laying out the plant:
   a. Plan a system for materials flow and combine handling with processing wherever possible.
   b. Provide for continuous or appropriate intermittent flow of materials.
   c. Provide for the optimal flow of materials between operations and with a minimum of retrograde movement.
   d. Plan the layout of the workstation area for a minimum of handling of the product.
   e. Maximize the quantity and size of weight handled.
   f. Coordinate the overall materials handling throughout the entire plant.
   g. Provide for safe handling and safe equipment and integrate with the management information and control system.
   h. Plan for adequate receiving, storage, and shipping facilities.
   i. Make optimum use of building cubage.
   j. Design adequate aisle and access areas.

3. In the selection and application of materials handling equipment:
   a. Plan activities and analyze equipment needs before considering the purchase of new equipment.
   b. Insure that the existing equipment is being used effectively.
   c. Use the simplest equipment that is adaptable to the problem; avoid the use of complicated mechanisms and controls.
   d. Adopt standard equipment if possible; insure that the purchase of special equipment is economically justified.
   e. Select equipment that is flexible in its application.
   f. Select equipment that will minimize the ratio of mobile equipment deadweights to pay loads.
   g. Determine comparative costs of equipment before purchasing.
   h. Recognize the need for different equipment for different jobs.
   i. Recognize the need to provide suitable building conditions for the equipment.
   j. Provide for alternative methods for use in emergencies.
   k. Give consideration to the maintenance of the equipment.
   l. Replace obsolete methods and equipment with more efficient ones.

Source: H. T. Amrine, A. Ritchey and C. L. Moodie, *Manufacturing Organization and Management,* Fifth Edition, © 1987, pp. 164–165. Reprinted by permission of Prentice-Hall, Inc., Englewood Cliffs, N.J.

vide fitness centers include Lands' End (the mail-order catalog company), Pepsi-Cola, Saatchi & Saatchi Advertising (New York), and Tenneco. Many companies that are precluded from building elaborate fitness centers nevertheless run exercise programs for employees. Examples include AT&T and Chevron. Money spent on space and programs designed for wellness is returned in the form of reduced medical benefit programs, reduced absenteeism, and increased morale. Again, however, there are costs to be traded off. For example, does the increase in morale due to a cafeteria increase productivity to the extent that the increased productivity covers the cost of building and staffing the cafeteria? Another trade-off is made when extra space is allocated to a work area, thereby increasing materials handling.

One key component of employee morale is safety. Safety is aided by the use of ventilation systems, guard rails, and other protective devices. Of course, much of the safety-related aspects of design is dictated by OSHA.

EQUIPMENT CHOICE

The type of layout and the type of equipment chosen are highly correlated. In an assembly line, special-purpose equipment may be warranted. While such equipment typically costs more than a general-purpose machine, it usually has a higher production capacity, which leads to a lower cost per unit. General-purpose machinery allows for the manufacturing of a wider assortment of products, adds greater flexibility in case of product changes, and, usually, is easier and less expensive to repair. Break-even analysis provides the basis for this choice (see Chapter 3).

FLEXIBILITY

No matter how well a facility has been designed, no matter how many steps the original designer took to avoid the enormous expense involved in redesign, there is always the possibility that a redesign will be necessary. Therefore, any design should be flexible. Methods for building in flexibility are detailed in Table 7.3. **Flexible manufacturing systems**, now gaining in popularity, also address this need.

Flexible manufacturing systems most often are highly automated facilities having intermediate-volume production of a variety of products. Their goal is to minimize changeover or setup times for producing the different products, while still achieving close to assembly line (single-product) production rates.

The use of numerical control (NC) equipment and computer-aided manufacturing (CAM) also increases the flexibility of production equipment. In each case, the equipment can be programmed to perform a variety of tasks or a given task to a variety of specifications. The latest phase in this trend is the increased use of robotics.

In the service sector, the major innovation in recent years has been the adoption of modular office systems, or "offices without walls." In these setups, workers are separated only by temporary partitions, making it convenient to change the layout whenever necessary. These partitions also may improve morale by providing each employee with his or her own "office."

TABLE 7.3 Planned production flexibility

Five steps in the study of flexibility requirements	*Four areas in which this method of flexibility planning is used*
1. Define probable areas of change—volume, process, raw materials, or product.	1. Building design—Keep the original layout as free as possible from fixed, permanent, or special features.
2. Estimate the maximum and minimum impact of these changes on personnel and facilities.	2. Plant services—Place services (electricity, compressed air, steam, gasses, oils, waters, etc.) just beneath the floor or below the ceilings and try to use plug-in connections.
3. Determine how flexibility adequate to meet these changes can be provided.	3. Equipment selection—Maintain a wide variety of materials handling equipment that automatically provides flexibility.
4. Evaluate the cost of providing flexibility against the probability of future changes, using both monetary and intangible comparisons.	4. Planned expansion—To increase the space for individual functions, absorb storage or warehouse space. Also locate nonmanufacturing areas on floors above or below manufacturing. Utilize building construction that permits quick and inexpensive changes. Plan each phased expansion so that the next change involves minimal effort. Plan expansion geographically (for example, in the center of a building lot rather than along a highway).
5. Design into the facility those desired flexibility provisions that were determined in the previous steps.	

Source: R. Craig, J. Moore, and W. Turner, "Planned Production Flexibility," *Industrial Engineering 7,* no. 10 (1975), pp. 33–37. Reprinted from the Journal of Industrial Engineering, October, 1975. Copyright Institute of Industrial Engineers, 25 Technology Park/Atlanta, Norcross, GA.

PRODUCTION PROCESSES

two-dimensional classification

In Chapter 3, we briefly described two different production processes—continuous and intermittent production. We now classify these transformations in more detail. Essentially, our classification is two-dimensional, including the arrangement of the operations and the repetitiveness of the operations. The two dimensions are interrelated.

FLOW CHARACTERISTICS

identical operations

In a **flow shop,** each input to the transformation follows the same path from the beginning to the end. The personnel and machines perform the same type of operation on each input. In some cases, the operations are not simply of the same type, they are identical. Such cases include mass production (for example, the production of automobiles and personal computers) and some service businesses (such as Jiffy Lube). In other cases, the sequence of activities is the same, but specific activities or activity times may vary. A hospital emergency room is an example of a flow shop in which the activities are not precisely the same. The flow for all hospital patients is registration, examination, and billing, but the actual activities in these three processes vary according to patient needs. Similarly, hamburger production at Burger King is a flow shop in which the end products vary—a fact the company touted in its "Have it your way" advertising campaign.

In a **job shop,** each input follows a different path through the system. Examples of job shops are (custom) furniture factories, hospitals, print shops, and universities. Job shops usually handle one-of-a-kind or low-volume items.

A special case of the job shop type of flow is the **project.** A project is a one-time job that is very complex and may consist of many activities. Its complexity warrants the assignment of a special project manager to see to it that all parts of the project are done on time and that the components of the job shop that are needed will be available on schedule. Project management is discussed in detail in Chapter 10.

REPETITIVENESS OF THE OPERATIONS

We also classify transformations according to the repetitiveness of the operations. At one end of the classification is **continuous production.** This includes the set of transformations that are running continuously. Examples of such systems are chemical and pharmaceutical processing, oil drilling and refining, and paint production. Industries with continuous production are termed **process industries.** The next level down is assembly line production, or **mass production.** Examples of mass-produced items include automobiles, pens, light bulbs, and screws. The next level is **batch processing,** where products are made in batches or lots. Examples of such systems are airplanes, classes at a university, or the cooking of food at McDonald's. The last type is **unit production,** where units are processed one at a time. Examples of such systems include a hospital operation, the building of a plant, or development of a new product.

Teaching Suggestion 7.1: Move Toward Batch or Unit Processing. See the Instructor's Section for details.

This classification relates to the previous one in the following way: As we go along the spectrum from continuous production to unit production, we increase the odds of using a job shop over a flow shop. Unit production may mean production of one-of-a-kind items, where each unit will follow a different path of operations. In this case, a job shop would be used, possibly the special case known as a project.

STANDARD LAYOUT TYPES

We have just spoken about the types of production processes. We distinguished between the job shops and flow shops. Associated with these two types of systems are two types of layouts—**process layout** and **product layout,** respectively.

PROCESS LAYOUT

When the production process is a job shop, the completion of each item requires a different set of operations. Examples of such processes include automobile repair shops (cars require different operations for repair), universities (students often take different courses for a degree), hospitals (patients require different services for diagnosis/cure), fast-food operations (customers require different items for their orders), custom-order shops (customers often have different specifications for their orders). In these cases, the machines and/or operations are grouped together by function. For

---

APPLICATIONS OF P/OM

A Faster Path to Finished Steel

I/N Tek, a joint venture between Inland Steel and Nippon Steel, will produce finished steel using a new process that cuts manufacturing time to less than one hour from about twelve days. The new plant changes the cold mill steel-making process from the traditional batch process to a continuous process.

Traditionally, the batch process involved physically moving the steel coils from one site to another, requiring almost two weeks and five hundred employees.

The new plant has two hundred employees. "The I/N Tek facility is clearly a leader in technology," says John Jacobson, an analyst with AUS Consultants. "It will save production costs because you don't have to start and stop the process, like in a conventional processing plant. There is no waste of energy and labor."

Source: New York Times (April 7, 1991).

---

example, in an auto repair shop, all tire repair equipment is kept in the same location; in a university, all economics courses are taught in a central location; in a hospital, all X-ray machines are kept in the same department. The item or person being processed is moved from process location to process location according to the individual needs of that item or person.

advantages of process layout

Given the variety of operations that use a process layout, it may not be apparent why and when this type of layout should be used. One reason for using a process layout is flexibility—much needed when a company provides a variety of products or services. In fact, businesses with job shop production processes often are selling their expertise in their process rather than selling a particular product. The fact that they are experts in that process should mean that they provide higher quality—whatever the product. A process layout also has cost advantages because the equipment it requires may cost less than product-specific equipment. The reliability and availability (see Chapter 9) of the equipment are better. It is easier to repair more standard types of equipment, and it is easier to schedule preventive maintenance on the equipment in a process layout, because other equipment of the same type is located at the same place. Similarly, if one machine breaks down, others are available to continue the work.

PRODUCT LAYOUT

In contrast to job shops, flow shops may dictate a product layout. As we indicated in Chapter 3, volume must be high enough to warrant a product layout because it is more costly to set up. The processes are laid out in order according to the specifications of the products and/or services. Essentially, a product layout (sometimes called *straight line layout*) is synonymous with an assembly line. The difference between the two types of layouts is illustrated in Figure 7.1.

The figure shows each layout and two products, A and B. The process layout shows six different processing centers, each available for use in servicing any of a variety of products. The products require the following order of processing.

$$A \rightarrow 1 \rightarrow 4 \rightarrow 2$$

$$B \rightarrow 3 \rightarrow 4 \rightarrow 3$$

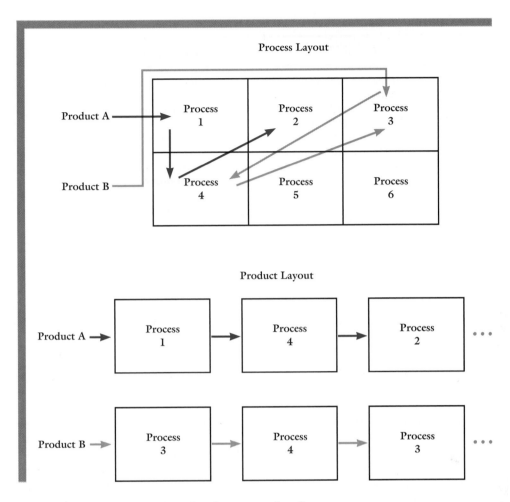

FIGURE 7.1 Process versus product layout: product flow

In the process layout, the products or customers move from center to center, as required. In the product layout, however, movement is very different. Notice that processes 5 and 6 are not even part of the production process for products A and B. These two products do not require these processes. Also, notice that processes 3 and 4 each appear in two places. What has happened is that all of the capacity of the processing centers (process layout) is divided up and located exactly where needed in the product layout. The product movement between processes is minimized in this way, thereby maximizing the speed of operation.

Transparency Master 7.2: Process and Product Layout.

There are many reasons for selecting product layout. The most obvious reason is that it allows for the fastest production rate. Another reason is that the product layout is easier to manage, because the flows of material are built into the layout. Finally, the reduced materials handling reduces costs in terms of efficient utilization of time, space, material, and labor.

advantages of product layout

In Table 7.4, we offer a comparison of the advantages and disadvantages of the two types of layouts with respect to how each performs in terms of management cri-

TABLE 7.4 Performance of product and process layouts on management concerns

Management Concern	Process Layout	Product Layout
Materials handling	Slow movement from process to process	Continuous movement
Bottlenecks	Problem occurs if different jobs require the same process	Problem occurs if machine breaks down
Machine interference	Machines can be isolated	No isolation of machines
Morale/safety	Morale enhanced by better job variety	Movement of goods can create hazards
Product flexibility	Major goal of process layout	New product requires change in layout
Equipment choice	General purpose	Special purpose
Equipment cost	Typically cheaper	More costly, but also more efficient
Production	High cost, low rate	Low cost, high rate
Job scheduling	Continual	None or in batches
Inventory	High levels	Minimal
Quality	Improves through process expertise	Improves through repetition
Equipment reliability	Backup available; facilitates preventive maintenance	No backup, requires more preventive maintenance
Response to design changes	Ideal	May require new layout

Transparency Master 7.3: Layout Comparison.

teria. It can be seen from this table that each type of layout has its own advantages and disadvantages. There is no one reason why one type of layout should be used over the other. Typically, the choice is a function of the variety of products manufactured and volume. In general, setup costs for production are higher for product layout, but variable costs of production are lower. This leads to the situation depicted by the break-even chart of Figure 7.2. Low-volume products cannot justify the high costs of setting up an assembly line.

planning concerns

The two types of layouts lead to different types of planning problems. The product layout leads to the problem of designing the assembly line and determining batch size. The process layout leads to two problems: locating each process and scheduling each process. Determining which process to schedule first is the topic of Chapter 15. The planning problems associated with each of these two layouts and the approaches for solving these problems will be discussed later in this chapter.

FIXED POSITION LAYOUT

There is a third type of layout—**fixed position layout**. In this type of layout, the production process goes to the product; the product does not move through a product or process layout. Examples of fixed position layouts include building or repairing a ship, a road, or a bridge. This layout is used by necessity, so no trade-offs need be considered.

The types of jobs that most often use fixed position layout are projects. Because the production process, by necessity, is moved to the job, many problems of schedul-

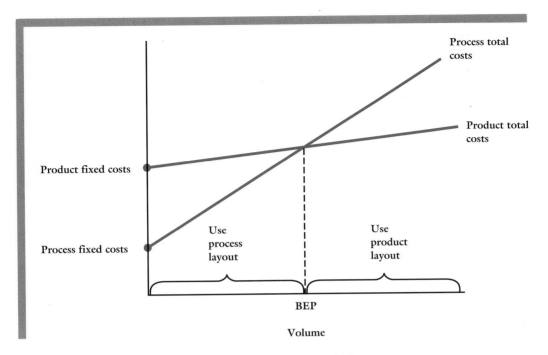

FIGURE 7.2 Process versus product layout: break-even analysis

Transparency Master 7.4: Automation and Mass Production.

Teaching Suggestion 7.2: Marketing Layout. See the Instructor's Section for details.

ing and resource availability may arise. Such problems are bound to arise if the project requires that many different processes be performed. Controlling the schedule becomes just as critical as planning the schedule, because delicate scheduling balances must be maintained. Chapter 10 is devoted to the topic of scheduling projects.

WORKER SKILL REQUIREMENTS

A worker does the same job over and over again on the same product if a product layout (assembly line) is used. This high degree of work task specialization produces benefits and problems when compared to the worker skill requirements of a process layout. For a comparable job, the product layout can utilize workers possessing lower skill levels. The worker in a production line does not really have to understand the operation in general. The worker only needs to understand the task performed on that one product at that stage of the operation. For example, consider the data entry function in a DP (data processing) department. In a product layout, all that is required of the worker is the ability to type the correct character in the correct spaces. In a process layout, however, the worker needs to be prepared for any set of data input for any program, and so a more thorough knowledge of the subject is required. Where a skilled worker usually is required in a process layout, a semiskilled worker often will be able to do the job in a product layout, reducing the company's labor costs and training costs.

work specialization

Some problems that are associated with the product layout in terms of worker skills are closely related to the general problems related to the use of this type of layout.

For example, there is less flexibility of worker skills if the product or method of operation changes. However, there also are some unique employee problems on the assembly line. Boredom is a major problem. Possibly related, absenteeism and turnover are higher when product layout is used. Recognizing that such problems can result in a high rate of defects, Volvo decided to assemble its 740 series automobiles using teams of workers rather than an assembly line. Workers at Volvo's Uddevalla, Sweden, plant are trained to handle different assembly jobs and they do not repeat a task for approximately three hours, greatly reducing the likelihood that they will become bored.

It should be apparent that the first generations of robots now available are most useful in the product layout. In fact, various business operations, from assembly lines to automated cafeterias, are using them. The design of robots for use in process layouts is still in the future.

ADVANCED MANUFACTURING TECHNOLOGY

Advanced manufacturing technology is the term used for the many new technological developments in use in the production process today. In this section we will briefly describe these modern techniques and explain their applications. First, however, let us talk more generally about automation.

AUTOMATION

Automation is any technique, system, or device that controls an operation through mechanical or electrical means. (The term *mechanization* is restricted to mechanical devices.) Automated systems are found in production industries (robots) and service industries (automatic teller machines, automatic toll booths, vending machines).

The type of automation can vary in sophistication. Older forms of automation were fixed systems. These systems had a processing sequence that could not be changed. Next came programmable automation, in which the sequence of operations could be changed. The most recent development is flexible automation, which is an extension of programmable automation made possible in part by computer technology. Automated systems that use computers for control are termed **computer integrated manufacturing** (CIM) systems. With flexible automation, different products can be manufactured with little or no setup time. Each type of system obviously requires a different amount of capital investment and each is not without its advantages.

There are a number of reasons to consider automating.

- Higher production rates. Automated systems are typically faster than non-automated systems. This does not mean, however, that they are always more productive. It is true that output will increase, but this will be accompanied by an increase in (capital) input.
- Reduction in labor costs. Automation typically means that some jobs can be eliminated, since they will be performed by machines rather than humans.
- Automation is a substitute for labor. While we in the United States are very concerned about unemployment, other countries—notably, West Germany—have faced labor shortages in the past. Automation can reduce the labor requirement.

Teaching Suggestion 7.3: Customized Automation. See the Instructor's Section for details.

- Reduced inventories.
- Reduced lead times.
- Competitors are automating.

There are five areas within manufacturing that can be automated.

- Processing (transforming raw material).
- Assembly (joining two or more components together).
- Materials handling (moving and storing material between processes).
- Inspection and testing (quality control).
- Control (tracking, routing, sequencing).

NUMERICAL CONTROL

Numerical control (NC) equipment transmits a set of operating instructions to the machinery. The first demonstration of a numerically controlled machine occurred in 1952 at MIT. Originally, NC controllers were (hard-wired) electrical units that could not be reprogrammed. Today, numerical control is computerized.

The set of instructions in a numerical control system might include instructions to move a drill two inches to the left or to move a piece on a platform two inches to the right. The major applications of numerical control are to five basic machining operations:

- turning;
- drilling;
- milling;
- shaping; and
- grinding.

Teaching Suggestion 7.4: Machining Operations. See the Instructor's Section for details.

Advantages of NC machines include less wasted time, smaller lead times (important for JIT), greater flexibility, and improved accuracy. They are particularly advantageous when running small batches—that is, quantities of fifty or less.

Groover (1987) states that NC machines should be used for jobs with certain characteristics.

- Parts are processed frequently and in small to medium lot sizes.
- Part geometry is complex.
- Close tolerances must be held on the workpart.
- Many operations must be performed on the part being processed.
- Much metal needs to be removed (for machining applications).
- Engineering design changes are likely.
- Parts are expensive, making mistakes in processing costly.
- Parts require 100 percent inspection. (p. 225)

ENHANCEMENTS TO NUMERICAL CONTROL

Direct numerical control (DNC) allows one computer to control several NC machines. As the price of computers has fallen, use of direct numerical control has risen. The increased accessibility of computer technology also has made possible computer numerical control (CNC), in which one computer controls one machine. Yet another improvement in numerical control is adaptive control, which has the capability to measure variables and to compensate for problems.

ROBOTICS

A robot is a general-purpose programmable machine. Note that we could use the same definition for an NC machine. However, there is a difference between an NC machine and a robot: A robot possesses some human-like feature. Many times, this feature is an arm-like device. Robots contain joints similar to the joints in the human body. The joint allows the robot (arm) to move in one direction. (Three joints at right angles give the robot full 360° flexibility.)

The end of the robot arm often has a tool—typically, a welding gun, spray painter, screwdriver, cutting tool, or drill. The robot controls both the position of the part and the tool.

Robots are extremely useful when, for example, the work is hazardous, repetitive, or difficult. They are also useful when the work is done over an extended period or has

A robot automated assembly line for Renault. (© Magnum Photos, Inc.)

infrequent changeovers. Robots allow for the necessary flexibility discussed in Chapter 2. At the Nissan Sentra plant in Zama, Japan, approximately fifty robots are used for body production. It is possible to program the robots to produce a sedan and then follow that car, in less than one minute, with a hatchback or a station wagon. Robotics are a major aid in increasing the flexibility of a company's product line because the flexibility in production allows Nissan to tailor each day's production to the current demand. Robots permit Matsushita Electric Industrial Co., which produces Panasonic bicycles, to offer its customers eighteen models (with different pedals, tires, and logos) in nearly two-hundred colors.

Table 7.5 indicates the number of robots that were in use at the end of 1988 in selected countries. It should come as no surprise that Japan led the way, with more than five times as many robots in use as in the United States.

THE ASSEMBLY LINE

Henry Ford is given credit as the designer of the assembly line because he introduced the first automobile assembly line in 1913. The moving assembly line reduced the production time of the Model T chassis from over twelve hours to slightly more than one and one-half hours. Although Ford gets the credit, the assembly line is the result of a collection of concepts. We discuss these concepts next, and then we outline problems with assembly lines.

PRINCIPLES OF MASS PRODUCTION

By mass production, we mean the manufacturing of products in large quantities. There are different methods for increasing the quantity (capacity). One method is to hire more workers and/or purchase more machines. Although this is not the typical

TABLE 7.5 Leading users of robotics, 1988

Country	Number of Robots
Japan	175,000
United States	33,600
Germany	17,700
Italy	8,300
France	7,930
United Kingdom	5,034
Sweden	3,042
Spain	1,382
Belgium	1,231
Canada	1,032
Netherlands	845

Source: Japan—An International Comparison (Tokyo, Japan: Keizai Koho Center, Japanese Institute for Social and Economic Affairs, 1990).

solution we seek, it is a possible solution. In fact, this is what the Phoenicians of 600 B.C. did to manufacture bricks in large quantities. Until very recently, this approach was used in less-developed countries with large populations, such as China.

Today, mass production typically refers to the assembly line. There are several principles involved in setting up an assembly line, and these principles are what we consider now.

SMOOTH WORK FLOW

A major advantage of the assembly line is that it provides for a smooth flow of materials and semifinished goods. The product moves one machine or process to the next at regularly timed intervals. There is no uncertainty as to the timing of operations or, as in the case of job shop, the scheduling of different processes. The well-timed flow means that, if the system is working well, we need to have in the system only the semifinished goods that are about to be processed. Thus, the amount of inventory in the form of work-in-progress is minimized. In addition to minimizing inventory, the goal of easing management attention to routing and scheduling also is achieved.

The disadvantage to the assembly line flow is that a breakdown of one process precludes work at following processes. Therefore, many times, a buffer stock of semi-finished goods is maintained at intermediate processes.

SHORT DISTANCES

Not only is the flow on the assembly line smooth, but the distances that the goods are moved are minimal. Hence, the assembly line achieves the objective of minimizing the amount of materials handling. Furthermore, the movement is predictable; we know where each process occurs. Thus, assembly lines follow fixed routing, meaning that materials handling equipment, such as conveyors, can be put into place. The short distances on fixed routes assure that the goal of maximum quantities produced at minimum cost is met.

DIVISION OF LABOR

Division of labor is useful in its own right, but it is critical on an assembly line. Each worker performs a specific set of tasks. One obvious advantage is that the workers become very skilled at their tasks. A major drawback is the possibility of worker boredom on the assembly line. Boredom can be minimized through good design, a topic to which we return in Chapter 9.

INTERCHANGEABLE PARTS

Teaching Suggestion 7.5: Interchangeable Parts. See the Instructor's Section for details.

Some assembly lines are set up to manufacture only one product; others are used for a small variety of products. In order to manufacture a variety of products, it is essential that the components of the final products be interchangeable, so that the same equipment can be used to manufacture the different parts. Credit for interchangeable parts goes to Eli Whitney, who used the principle to manufacture weapons. An excellent example of this concept at work is the cafeteria line: The menu offered differs each day, but the system handles each menu in a similar manner. Table 7.6 presents the development of mass production principles.

TABLE 7.6 Stages in the development of flow production

1260	Division of labor in Venice commented on by Dante and Marco Polo.
1438	Flow line at Venice arsenal described.
1496	Mass production of needles by Leonardo da Vinci.
1617	Use of automatic straight-line process in Spanish mint.
1717	Unsuccessful attempt to manufacture guns using interchangeable parts in France.
1731	Manufacture of buttons and pins on flow line in Moscow.
1746	Description of flow-line production of pins in England.
1785	Oliver Evans designs "automatic" flour mill.
1785	Production in France of interchangeable parts for muskets.
1793	Outbreak of war between France and England.
1796	Outbreak of war between Spain and England.
1798	Eli Whitney's first contract for 10,000 guns (he later used interchangeable parts in production).
1799	Government contract for gun manufacture to Simeon North (who later used interchangeable parts).
1803–1815	Napoleonic wars.
1804	Manufacture of ships' biscuits on flow line in England.
1809	Mass production of ships' blocks in England.
1830	"Pennypress" launched.
1830	Manufacture of brass clocks with interchangeable parts by Chauncey Jerome in the United States.
1837	Assembly-line layout principle used at Bridgewater foundry in England.
1839	Use of flow-line principle at Chorlton Mills, England.
1845–1848	U.S. war with Mexico.
1846	Use of interchangeable parts in manufacturing of sewing machines.
1847	Use of interchangeable parts in production of farm machinery in the United States.
1848	Use of interchangeable parts in manufacture of watches in the United States.
1851	Crystal Palace Exhibition, where interchangeable parts were demonstrated.
1854–1856	Crimean War.
1855	Enfield and B.S.A. arms factories modeled on Colt systems.
1861	Flow-line production in meat processing in Chicago.
1861–1865	U.S. Civil War.
1891	Manufacture of freight cars on flow line.
1899	Design of "low-cost" Oldsmobile in the United States.
1906	Oldsmobile and Cadillac cars made in large quantities in the United States.
1908	First Model T Ford made in the United States.
1913	Use of first assembly line at Ford plant in the United States.
1922	Use of transfer line at A.O. Smith Corporation in the United States.
1923	Use of hand transfer line at Morris Engines in England.
1924	Use of automatic transfer line at Morris Engines in England.

Source: R. Wild, *Mass Production Management* (London: John Wiley and Sons, Ltd., 1972), p. 42.

ASSEMBLY LINE BALANCING

Assembly line balancing is the procedure for designing the assembly line so that production will be as smooth as possible, as inexpensive as possible, and able to achieve a rate that meets the demand requirements.

Consider the "assembly line" we all know as "I'll wash, you dry." We can think of this job as having four tasks:

1. Wash dishes.
2. Dry dishes.

3. Stack dishes.
4. Shelve dishes.

One person can do all of the tasks, but this would be slow. To increase the "production" rate (or decrease the time per dish), the principle of division of labor is used. To achieve the fastest possible rate of production, four people can be used.

It would seem to most people, though, that using four people is inefficient. A better balance between production and use of resources usually is achieved by using two people. This is due in large part to the fact that the four-person assembly line is not balanced. That is, the task of washing a dish takes longer than the other tasks. The dish washer works continually, while the others get to rest between each dish. As it turns out, there usually is enough slack time for one person to handle the latter three jobs (dry, stack, and shelve) while the other person washes, thereby providing a better balance of work along the line.

This scenario explains the problem of assembly line balancing and suggests the trade-offs to be considered in favoring one line design over another. The example that follows illustrates the use of actual task times, more formally defines the considerations, and shows the procedure for accomplishing the task of designing production lines through line balancing.

Example 7.1   Given in Table 7.7 are the steps (tasks, operations, or jobs) necessary for final assembly of an electronic organ. Listed for each step are both the length of time needed to perform that step and the operations that must be done prior to that step. These rules governing the order in which steps must be performed are termed *precedences* and are comprehended more easily through the use of a graph rather than the table. The **precedence graph** for the organ assembly appears in Figure 7.3. (We note that precedence graphs will be used again when we discuss project management

TABLE 7.7   Precedence table (Example 7.1)

Task	Time (in seconds)	Predecessors
A	40	None
B	55	None
C	75	None
D	40	A
E	30	A, B
F	35	B
G	45	D, E
H	70	F
I	15	G, H
J	65	I
K	40	C, J
	510	

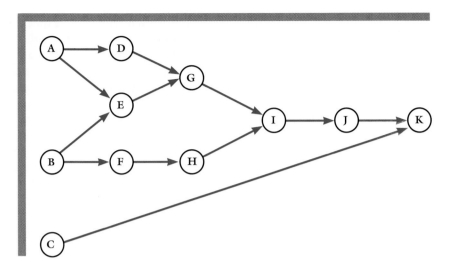

Transparency Master 7.5:
A Precedence Graph.

FIGURE 7.3 Precedence graph for organ assembly (Example 7.1)

in Chapter 10.) Notice that the precedences are transitive. In other words, because task H follows task F and task F follows task B, on any organ task H cannot be performed until task B is completed. The column labeled "Predecessors" in Table 7.7 provides the key to drawing the precedence graph.

The table indicates that the sum of the task times is 510 seconds. If one person were to perform all of the operations, it would take that person 510 seconds to assemble one organ. Because the workday is eight hours long, it follows that one person working alone could assemble

$$\frac{8 \text{ hours/day} \times 60 \text{ minutes/hour} \times 60 \text{ seconds/minute}}{510 \text{ seconds/organ}} = 56.47 \text{ organs/day.}$$

In this case, the labor cost per organ with a wage rate of $10 per hour is

$$\frac{8 \text{ hours/day} \times \$10/\text{hour}}{56.47 \text{ organs/day}} = \$1.42 \text{ per organ.}$$

One person working alone is an extreme case. Consider the other extreme. Suppose that there are eleven persons working on the assembly line, each one of whom is assigned one of the eleven tasks. Furthermore, assume that a bell rings every 75 seconds and that, between bells, each worker performs his or her task exactly once. In this case, because each task is being performed every 75 seconds, organs roll off the assembly line at a rate of one every 75 seconds, or

$$\frac{8 \text{ hours/day} \times 60 \text{ minutes/hour} \times 60 \text{ seconds/minute}}{75 \text{ seconds/organ}} = 384 \text{ organs/day.}$$

The eleven-worker assembly line has a higher production rate than the one-worker assembly line, but the labor cost is higher. (Verify that the labor cost is $2.30 per organ.) Assembly line balancing is a technique that trades off production rate and cost. ∎⌐

The interval of 75 seconds in Example 7.1 was not chosen randomly. A quick glance at Table 7.7 shows that the 75 seconds required for task C happens to be the longest of the task times. If an interval longer than 75 seconds were chosen, then all eleven workers would have idle time between tasks. On the other hand, if an interval shorter than 75 seconds were chosen, then the third worker on the line (the one doing task C) would fall behind, creating a bottleneck. It turns out that 75 seconds is the fastest that the organs can be produced on a single assembly line (without providing more capacity for task C).

LINE BALANCING PROCEDURE

In a typical assembly line balancing problem, one usually begins with the precedence table or graph and the desired production rate. Given the production rate goal and the time to make one unit, the first step is to determine the largest possible cycle time that will achieve the production goal.

Cycle time is the length of time between units finished on the assembly line. For its minimum, we choose the largest task time because it is the bottleneck in the process. It yields the fastest production, often exceeding the production rate desired. For a slower rate, choose a higher cycle time. In Example 7.1, the cycle time for the one-worker line was 510 seconds, while, for the eleven-worker line, the cycle time was 75 seconds. These times represent the extremes for that example. We use the following **cycle time calculation** method for determining the maximum cycle time: Convert the given production rate (units/week, units/month, or whatever unit to time period ratio is appropriate) into a time per unit basis (seconds/unit, minutes/unit, and so forth).

Example 7.2   Reconsider the data presented in Example 7.1. Suppose that the production goal is 200 organs per day. What is the largest possible cycle time?

To answer this question, simply invert 200 organs per day, yielding one two-hundredth of a day per organ, or

$$\frac{1 \text{ day}}{200 \text{ organs}} \times \frac{8 \text{ hours}}{\text{day}} \times \frac{60 \text{ minutes}}{\text{hour}} \times \frac{60 \text{ seconds}}{\text{minute}} = \frac{144 \text{ seconds}}{\text{organ}}.$$

That is, if organs are completed in no longer than 144 seconds, then the production goal of 200 organs per day will be met. We will allocate 144 seconds to each organ. ■

The second step of the line balancing procedure is to find the theoretical minimum number of stations necessary when using the given cycle time. A **station** is a grouping of tasks performed within one cycle. In practice, the workstation is where a worker performs one or more tasks. This step is determined by the formula

---

number of stations

Teaching Suggestion 7.6: Minimum Number of Stations. See the Instructor's Section for details.

$$\text{Theoretical minimum number of stations} = \frac{\text{time to produce one unit}}{\text{cycle time}},$$

---

with the answer always rounded to the next highest whole number. The time to produce one unit is the sum of all of the task times.

Example 7.3   Find the theoretical minimum number of stations for the organ assembly, using a cycle time of 144 seconds.

Using our formula, the minimum number of stations is given by

$$\frac{510 \text{ seconds per organ}}{144 \text{ seconds per organ per station}} = 3.54,$$

which, once rounded up, tells us that four stations are necessary.   ◾

always round up

Even if the answer had been 3.04, we would have had to round up to 4. Rounding 3.04 up to 4 is logical because the required production rate cannot be achieved by three stations. This adjustment, however, will reduce efficiency to about 75 percent, because four stations are more than are needed. In addition to the decrease in the utilization of the workstations, the rounding up incurs a possibly large investment in the fourth station. For these two reasons, most managers will wish to explore options such as overtime or subcontracting when faced with this situation. The cost trade-offs probably would favor the other options in this (admittedly extreme) situation.

To this point, we have determined that, in order to meet the production goal, the cycle time must be no longer than 144 seconds and, furthermore, that at least four workstations are required. There is, however, no guarantee that the tasks can be grouped in such a way that they can be accomplished at four stations using a cycle time of 144 seconds. Trying to fit the required tasks into a given number of stations is assembly line balancing and is a function both of the task times and of the precedence constraints.

Unfortunately, there is no method available that is guaranteed to balance the assembly line in the best way possible. Therefore, the methods that are used are heuristic methods, which is simply a fancy way of saying that they employ trial and error, educated guesses, or rules of thumb. Table 7.8 contains the completed heuristic assembly line balancing for the organ example, which we now explain.

In order to balance the assembly line, we proceed station by station. That is, we allocate 144 seconds to each station and fill in the tasks one by one without violating the precedences. In the beginning, our choice is between the three tasks A, B, and C, because these are the only tasks that have no preceding tasks. For the purpose of this example, we decide among the competing tasks by choosing the one that requires the most time (but still fits into the remaining time at the station). This is termed the *longest task time rule*. Applying this rule at the beginning, we choose C as the first task, because C takes longer than A or B. Task C is inserted in the table at station 1; the operation time is 75 seconds, which means that 144 − 75 = 69 seconds still remain available at station 1. Of the remaining tasks, only A and B can be performed. We schedule B at station 1, because it requires more time than task A. Task B is listed in the table, and its time of 55 seconds is subtracted from the remaining time of 69 seconds, yielding a remaining time at station 1 of 14 seconds. Now, because task B has been completed, the precedence graph (see Figure 7.3) indicates that task F is available. Note that task E is not available, even though B has been completed, because A has not yet been done. Because both A and F take longer than the 14 seconds remaining at station 1, we begin station 2 with a fresh 144 seconds. The remainder of the table is generated in the same way. Using longest operation time, five stations are required—not four, as had been the goal.

Because we did not accomplish the goal of grouping the tasks into four stations, two possibilities exist. One possibility is that it simply cannot be done, while the sec-

task priority rule 1

TABLE 7.8 Assembly line balance using longest task time rule

Station	Task	Time	Time Remaining	Ready Tasks
				A, B, C
1	C	75	69	A, B
	B	55	14	A, F
		130		
2	A	40	104	F,D,E
	D	40	64	F,E
	F	35	29	E,H
		115		
3	H	70	74	E
	E	30	44	G
		100		
4	G	45	99	I
	I	15	84	J
	J	65	19	K
		125		
5	K	40	104	None

Design cycle time = 144 seconds
Achieved cycle time = 130 seconds

task priority rule 2

ond possibility is that a rule other than longest task time will generate a four-station balance. Let us try a second common rule—the *most following tasks rule*.

Examining the precedence graph, we count the number of tasks that follow each task.

Task	Following Tasks	Number of Following Tasks
A	D, E, G, I, J, K	6
B	E, F, G, H, I, J, K	7
C	K	1
D	G, I, J, K	4
E	G, I, J, K	4
F	H, I, J, K	4
G	I, J, K	3
H	I, J, K	3
I	J, K	2
J	K	1
K	None	0

In choosing among the ready tasks, we pick the task that has the most followers. (In case of a tie, we choose the one with the longest operation time.) The balance using the most following tasks rule is given in Table 7.9. The first task chosen at station 1 is B, because more tasks follow it than either A or C. Continuing with the different decision rule yields a four-station balance. The cycle time is the same in each of the two balances, so the balance that requires fewer stations—the second—is chosen. Furthermore, there is no need to continue because the minimum theoretical number of stations is four. In other words, we knew in advance of balancing that it is impossible to balance in fewer than four stations.

We have presented only two priority rules. There are others—most notably, ranked positional weight. All priority rules are heuristics, however. You should keep in mind that none is guaranteed to give the optimal solution.

EFFICIENCY

Consider the balance given in Table 7.9. Four stations are used, and the cycle time is 144 seconds. Hence, 576 seconds (144 seconds × 4 stations) are available for work in each cycle. However, although one unit is completed every cycle, one unit requires only 510 seconds of work. The difference, 576 − 510 = 66 seconds, must be idle time. This idle time may be seen in the table as 9 seconds of idle time per cycle at each

TABLE 7.9 Assembly line balance using most following tasks rule

Station	Task	Time	Time Remaining	Ready Tasks
				A, B, C
1	B	55	89	A, C, F
	A	40	49	C, F, D, E
	D	40	9	C, F, E
		135		
2	F	35	109	C, E, H
	E	30	79	C, H, G
	H	70	9	C, G
		135		
3	G	45	99	C, I
	I	15	84	C
	C	75	9	J
		135		
4	J	65	79	K
	K	40	39	None
		105		

Design cycle time = 144 seconds
Achieved cycle time = 135 seconds

of stations 1, 2, and 3 and 39 seconds of idle time per cycle at station 4: $9 + 9 + 9 + 39 = 66$ seconds. The efficiency of the balance is a function of the idle time and is measured as follows:

balance efficiency

$$\text{Efficiency} = \frac{\text{time to produce one unit}}{\text{time allocated per cycle}},$$

where

$$\text{Time allocated per cycle} = \text{cycle time} \times \text{number of stations.}$$

In this example, the efficiency is given by the following:

$$\text{Efficiency} = \frac{510}{144 \times 4} = \frac{510}{576} = 88.5\%.$$

Because the maximum time used at any station is 135 seconds, instead of 144, the cycle time clearly can be reduced by 9 seconds and the efficiency recalculated.

$$\text{Efficiency} = \frac{510}{135 \times 4} = \frac{510}{540} = 94.4\%$$

It should be clear that, in theory, the smallest possible cycle time is given by the formula

$$\text{Theoretical minimum cycle time} = \frac{\text{time to produce one unit}}{\text{number of stations}},$$

which, in this example, is 510 seconds/4 stations = 127.5 seconds per station. This cycle time allows for no idle time at any station, and, of course, there is no guarantee that a four-station balance could be achieved using the theoretical minimum cycle time. It is not a coincidence that the ideal (theoretical minimum) cycle time divided by the achieved cycle time matches the efficiency:

$$\frac{\text{Ideal}}{\text{Achieved}} = \frac{127.5}{135} = 94.4\%.$$

Teaching Suggestion 7.7:
Goals of Assembly Line
Balancing. See the Instructor's Section for details.

Teaching Suggestion 7.8:
Grouping Constraints. See
the Instructor's Section for
details.

The general relationship between productivity and efficiency is shown in Figure 7.4. As the cycle time decreases (to the left in the figure) the efficiency increases (as, for example, occurred when we dropped the cycle time from 144 to 135 seconds). When the cycle time reaches a certain point, it cannot drop any further without necessitating an increase in the number of stations, thereby causing an increase in the time allocated per cycle and, thus, a decrease in efficiency. Figure 7.5 shows this general relationship for the specific case of our example.

PROCESS LAYOUT

As we mentioned previously, the primary goal in layout design for a process layout is to minimize the amount of movement (materials handling, walking) required. It is important to recognize that different layouts will require different amounts of movement, that this movement can be calculated, and that, on average, some layouts will be better than others.

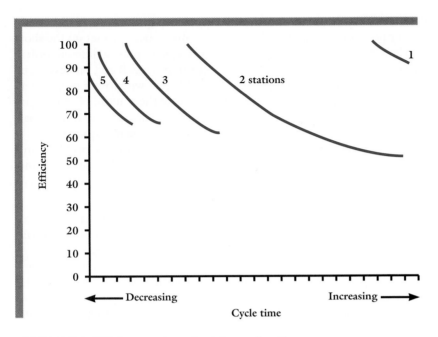

FIGURE 7.4 Efficiency and productivity trade-offs

FIGURE 7.5 Efficiency and productivity trade-offs (Example 7.1)

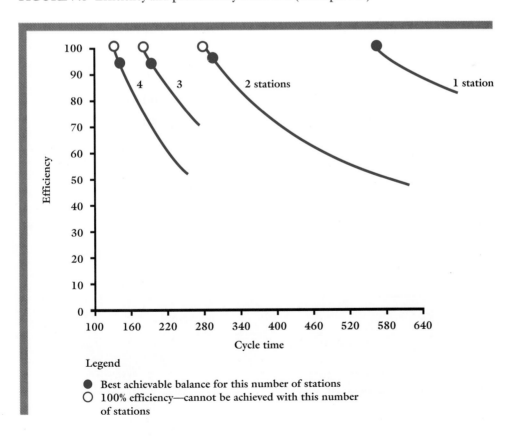

Consider a machine shop with four types of machines (processes). If all jobs go through the four processes in the same order, it is probably better to set up the shop as an assembly line. But if, as is most often the case, each job requires a different order, the process layout is preferred. Now, if most jobs go to process B and process C (in either order) without any intervening process, it would seem wise to put processes B and C as close together as possible. This tends to minimize the amount of movement required. Bear in mind, though, that if the mix of customers changes over time, it may be necessary to modify the layout to keep down the total movement required.

The example that follows demonstrates the framework of a specific problem, the application of process layouts in a service organization, and a procedure for designing a layout that will be efficient.

Example 7.4   Ambler University is a small college that recently has expanded its library facilities. One new wing of the library has three rooms, each of which will house one of the following services: duplication, periodicals, and a lounge. Figure 7.6 depicts the wing and the three rooms (A1, A2, and A3). The distances between rooms are given in Table 7.10 as well as in the figure. The head librarian has gathered data on the movement of the students, and this is presented in Table 7.11. The question is, Which service should be in which room so as to minimize the total distance students must walk?

In this particular example, there are six possible ways to assign the functions of the room. Let us consider one of these assignments: duplication in A1, periodicals in A2, and lounge in A3. Using this assignment, the total distance traveled is given by the sum of the number of trips between the two rooms times the distance between those two rooms.

$$
\begin{array}{llll}
\text{A1 to A2} & (70 \text{ trips} & \times\ 10 \text{ feet/trip}) = & 700 \text{ feet} \\
\text{A1 to A3} & (15 \text{ trips} & \times\ 15 \text{ feet/trip}) = & 225 \text{ feet} \\
\text{A2 to A1} & (100 \text{ trips} & \times\ 10 \text{ feet/trip}) = & 1{,}000 \text{ feet} \\
\text{A2 to A3} & (20 \text{ trips} & \times\ 5 \text{ feet/trip}) = & 100 \text{ feet} \\
\text{A3 to A1} & (90 \text{ trips} & \times\ 15 \text{ feet/trip}) = & 1{,}350 \text{ feet} \\
\text{A3 to A2} & (20 \text{ trips} & \times\ 5 \text{ feet/trip}) = & \underline{100 \text{ feet}} \\
& & \text{Total} & 3{,}475 \text{ feet}
\end{array}
$$

FIGURE 7.6 New wing of Ambler University library (Example 7.4)

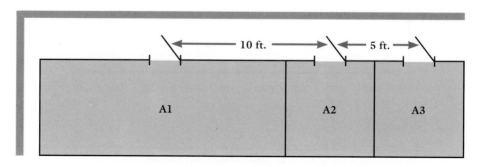

TABLE 7.10 Distances between rooms in Ambler
University library (Example 7.4)

	To		
From	A1	A2	A3
A1		10	15
A2	10		5
A3	15	5	

TABLE 7.11 Usage pattern of rooms in Ambler
University library (Example 7.4)

	To		
From	Duplication	Periodicals	Lounge
Duplication		70	15
Periodicals	100		20
Lounge	90	20	

Transparency Master 7.6:
Process Layout.

Table 7.12 contains the computations for the remaining five layouts, and it can be seen that the best assignment is duplication in A2, periodicals in A3, and lounge in A1.   ◾

In Example 7.4, we see the possible consequences of assigning the library services to the wrong rooms. The six possible assignments vary in the total travel distance they will require from 2,500 feet to 3,800 feet. Choice of the worst layout instead of the best would have resulted in a more than 50-percent increase in distance traveled! Even the second best layout represents a 7.5-percent increase. The increased costs due to

TABLE 7.12 Evaluation of all six layouts (Example 7.4)

Assignment			
Duplication	Periodicals	Lounge	**Total Distance Traveled (in feet)**
A1	A2	A3	3,475
A1	A3	A2	$(170 \times 15) + (105 \times 10) + (40 \times 5) = 3,800$
A2	A1	A3	$(170 \times 10) + (105 \times 5) + (40 \times 15) = 2,825$
A2	A3	A1	$(170 \times 5) + (105 \times 10) + (40 \times 15) = 2,500$
A3	A1	A2	$(170 \times 15) + (105 \times 5) + (40 \times 10) = 3,475$
A3	A2	A1	$(170 \times 5) + (105 \times 15) + (40 \times 10) = 2,875$

the use of an improper layout could place a difficult burden on a business right from the start.

The focus of our discussion of process layout thus far has been one of analysis . In a more complex problem, we could not be expected to analyze every possible layout, as we did in Table 7.12, and choose the best one. We must design the best one from scratch. Unfortunately, there is no available technique for designing the best layout. Again, we are forced to use a heuristic method.

Our heuristic method may be summed up in one sentence:

most interaction, closest together

> Locate the processes that have the most interaction with each other closest together!

This may sound like common sense, but, as a method, it may be difficult to implement as stated. The following example illustrates the application of the heuristic method.

Example 7.5   Use the heuristic method to design a good layout for the Ambler University library (refer to the data presented in Example 7.4).

Step 1: The number of trips between each of the pairs of services are as follows.

Service Pair	Trips
Duplication–periodicals	170 (100 + 70)
Duplication–lounge	105 (90 + 15)
Periodicals–lounge	40 (20 + 20)

We select duplication and periodicals.

Step 2: The distances between rooms A1, A2, and A3 are given in Table 7.10. We select rooms A2 and A3 because they are the closest.

Step 3: Now, we may assign the services either as

    Periodicals–A2

    Duplication–A3

or as

    Duplication–A2

    Periodicals–A3.

Either assignment follows our rule, but we arbitrarily choose the latter assignment.

Step 4: There is only one empty room, so the lounge goes there. That the complete assignment of

    Lounge–A1

    Duplication–A2

    Periodicals–A3

is the best possible solution is proven in Table 7.12.   ∎

You may have wondered what the difference would have been in Example 7.5 if, at step 3, we had chosen the other possible assignment. Our assignment then would have been the last layout evaluated in Table 7.12, which was one of the better layouts. This heuristic provides good layouts, but not necessarily the best ones. When using the heuristic, it is recommended that you make a note of each step at which an arbitrary decision is made. Then go back and design a new layout using the alternative decision(s). In this way, a number of good layouts are designed and only these need to be evaluated to find the best of them.

MATERIALS HANDLING

The movement of materials or customers in any business has been cited as a key factor to be considered in designing facility layout. The study of how this movement is accomplished is known as **materials handling.** Materials handling systems usually are designed by industrial engineers.

Materials handling costs are closely related to location, but within an office, a warehouse, or a factory, the costs really are related to layout. In this section, we provide some insight into the factors that contribute to materials handling costs and that must therefore be considered in facility design and layout decision making.

MATERIALS HANDLING FACTORS

Although not pertaining directly to materials handling, there is one overriding rule that should always be considered when making layout decisions:

Never handle (ship, pack, and so forth) materials unless absolutely necessary.

layout decision-making rule

use of rule

The implications of this rule are clear. It is better to perform multiple steps at a single location than to have to handle the material between steps. This may involve locating the appropriate equipment at one workstation; it may even involve redesign of the manufacturing sequence or the product itself to try to eliminate handling steps. A subrule is to avoid storage whenever possible as well. Another subrule is that travel distances should be minimized when handling material. A key point to remember is that the rule cannot be mandated during actual operations because, by then, it will be too late. The rule must be considered during the design stage to gain a maximum reduction in handling costs.

Handling costs are, as are logistics or distribution costs, a function of the efficiency of the shipments. Once the distances (routes) are known, savings are achieved by using these routes most wisely. For example, it is desirable to achieve the highest possible utilization of equipment. This implies that partial loads should not be a regular practice. Combining small amounts of material into a full load for the handling equipment—the **unit load concept**—increases its utilization and, consequently, the efficiency of the operation. In shipping, application of the unit load concept has led to the practice of containerization; in materials handling, it has led to the use of **palletization.** A pallet is a flat wooden support on which material is stacked. It is built in such a way that a forklift can easily pick it up and transport it to the next operation or the shipping dock.

The accumulation of material to make unit loads requires that this material be stored temporarily, which is undesirable. It is better to move materials one at a time so that no stock is waiting to be moved. This is known as the **piece-by-piece concept.**

Minimizing delays in pickups and deliveries is another consideration. Such delays are especially prevalent and costly with a materials handling system. Even with a conveyorized production line, accumulations of materials awaiting processing at the next operation contribute to a very large amount of in-process inventory. How to address this problem of delays is discussed more fully in the section on waiting line models in Chapter 8.

Not surprisingly, savings can be achieved within a materials handling system by knowing what material is available and by keeping track of where it is at all times. This seems an obvious part of inventory management. However, most companies have trouble keeping track of their material inventories, which leads to increased handling of materials. We have already seen that it is easier to minimize handling of materials with a product layout than with a process layout.

One might think that an operations goal should be to mechanize wherever possible. It is true that mechanized systems are more efficient. But such systems also cost a lot in terms of initial investment. Mechanization should not be used simply to have the most modern facility. Instead, it should be used to reduce costs and to make the operation more manageable. Thus, the mechanization choice should be based, in large part, on a break-even analysis (see Chapter 3). The more efficient mechanized equipment must lower the unit cost enough to make up for the investment, given a known level of usage.

rule of mechanization

An often overlooked option to mechanization is the use of gravity. Often, gravity can accomplish the same task for which energy-devouring mechanized systems are used. Of course, using gravity can yield significant savings in energy cost and usage. Consider an example familiar to everyone: the distribution of water to our homes. Water distribution requires a constant pressure in the system that most often is provided by a series of pumps. Now consider the dominant feature of the skylines (if that term is appropriate) of most small American towns. Other than church steeples, the dominant structures are water towers. A water tower, using gravity, provides the pressure for the town's water system. Many factories have similar structures to utilize gravity.

gravity systems

In materials handling, gravity is employed in many ways. The most common use is with a roller conveyor built at a slight downward angle. Multistory structures often have chutes and, less commonly, dumbwaiters. Ramps of various kinds are used in many situations. A slightly different use of gravity produces savings in the wear and tear on mechanized trucks. A good facility is designed so that, if necessary, trucks can travel downhill when fully loaded and uphill when empty. Again, the use of gravity in facility design and layout requires advance planning.

We have briefly laid out the fundamental considerations of materials handling. Now we will discuss some of the mechanisms for accomplishing the movement of materials. We will elaborate on a few manual situations before giving some of the options for mechanized materials handling.

MANUAL HANDLING SYSTEMS

The most basic handling system would be for each worker to carry each piece of production directly to the next operation when he or she is finished with it. Although this is not done in practice, many companies, especially smaller ones, operate very close to this level. In one such system, the job of "carrier" is created to facilitate the process. The carrier responds to the verbal ("hey, you") and hand signals of the workers to supply the needed materials. Often used is a more complex system, where the carrier moves bins of materials from place to place according to a sophisticated set of color-coded cards that are placed on the lines. This system is similar in practice to the Japanese system of *Kanban,* which is discussed later in the text.

The bins just mentioned are examples of the equipment used in a manual materials handling system. Hand trucks and dollies are the most commonly used equipment. Various types of carts are also used. A common example is the supermarket cart.

An example of a manual system that requires more of an initial investment, but no energy power, is the roller conveyor mentioned earlier. To transfer a product from one workstation to the next, a worker merely gives it a slight push along the conveyor. When it reaches the end, it falls into the input bin at the next workstation.

MECHANIZED HANDLING SYSTEMS

Mechanized equipment is classified as one of the following two types:

- **fixed path** and
- **variable path.**

As its name implies, fixed-path equipment is installed to transfer material from one point to another point along a designed path. It can be viewed as a single-purpose materials handling system. The roller conveyor and the automated conveyor are examples of fixed-path equipment.

The dominant form of the mechanized fixed-path handling system is the conveyor. A completely automated production line usually consists of a set of conveyors and feeders and the production equipment. After having been processed on one machine, the production part is placed on a conveyor and transported to a bin to await processing at the next machine. The feeder bin may use gravity to feed the part, or a vibrating feeder may be used to position the part as required by the production machine. Conveyors come in many varieties. A common example is the baggage handling system used at larger airports.

Variable-path equipment can take a path from any point to any of a variety of other points. The manual systems, of course, are variable path. Humans have variable-path capability, which is difficult to build into a machine. Any kind of truck, forklift, or tractor, all of which are driven manually, also has variable-path capability. Generally, more automated equipment has less flexibility as to paths.

A production line at a Paul Masson winery. (© Joel Gordon Photography)

ROBOTICS AND MECHANIZED HANDLING SYSTEMS

Since the advent of the mechanized conveyors, engineers have sought ways to provide these automated systems with variable path capabilities. The simplest way to do this with conveyors is to put a bar code on each item that will go on the conveyor. A scanner reads the code and transfers it to the proper sequence of conveyors. Other computerized versions of this approach that do not utilize bar codes have been implemented. When a part reaches its proper destination, a robotic arm picks it up and places it in the proper position for processing. This is the simplest of robots. More advanced robots, using optical scanners to "see" the part, can distinguish among types of parts and handle each type accordingly.

In many factories, trucks and forklifts have been automated. Again, using bar codes, scanners, or some other input device, the vehicle follows the route selected for the given material and takes it to its proper destination. If a truck is used, the handling system is closely related to a conveyor system. However, the newer systems utilize floor sensors to guide the vehicles.

SUMMARY

Facility layout must be considered very carefully because we do not want to constantly redesign the facility. Some of the goals in designing the facility are to ensure a minimum amount of materials handling, to avoid bottlenecks, to minimize machine interference, to ensure high employee morale and safety, and to ensure flexibility. Essentially, there are two distinct types of layout. *Product layout* is synonymous with *assembly line* and is oriented toward the products that are being made. *Process layout* is oriented around the processes that are used to make the products. Generally, product layout is applicable for high-volume repetitive operations, while process layout is applicable for low-volume, custom-made goods.

Choosing production layout leads to the problem of *assembly line balancing*—that is, spreading the tasks among workstations so that a specified *cycle time* can be achieved with a minimum number of workers. The choice of process layout leads to arranging the processes so that there will be a minimum amount of materials handling. In addition, each layout incurs different types of scheduling problems, which are discussed in Chapter 15.

KEY TERMS

facility layout	unit production	cycle time
flexible manufacturing systems	process layout	station
flow shop	product layout	materials handling
job shop	fixed position layout	unit load concept
project	automation	palletization
continuous production	computer integrated manufacturing	piece-by-piece concept
process industries	numerical control	fixed path
mass production	assembly line balancing	variable path
batch processing	precedence graph	

SOLVED PROBLEMS

1. A product coming off an assembly line requires ten separate operations. The times for each of these ten tasks and their precedence relationships are as follows.

Task	Time (in minutes)	Predecessors	Task	Time (in minutes)	Predecessors
A	.6	None	F	.3	E
B	.8	A	G	.4	None
C	.2	B, E	H	.1	G
D	.7	None	I	.3	C, F
E	.9	D	J	.6	F, H

Production quotas require that 300 completed units be assembled in an eight-hour shift. A productive time per shift of 450 minutes is used for planning purposes.

Using the longest task time rule, develop a production line that will achieve the goals with a minimum number of workstations.

Solution

The first step is to draw the precedence diagram.

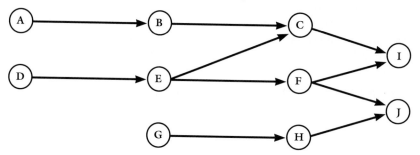

Next, the required cycle time must be calculated.

$$\text{Cycle time} = \frac{450 \text{ minutes/day}}{300 \text{ units/day}} = 1.5 \text{ minutes/unit}$$

The theoretical minimum number of stations is

$$\text{Number of stations} = \frac{\text{total processing time}}{\text{cycle time}} = \frac{4.9}{1.5} = 3+,$$

which means that at least four stations are required.

We will build a table one task at a time. We begin by noting that tasks A, D, and G are ready (they have no predecessors). Because D is the longest, we choose D and insert it into the table. This leaves .8 minutes at workstation 1, and the ready tasks now are A, G, and E. The longest task time is .9 (for E), but this will not fit. Therefore, we choose A, with a time of .6 (which is longer than G's time of .4). Task A is added to the table, leaving .2 minutes at workstation 1. Now tasks G, E, and B are ready. Because none of these three tasks fits with the remaining time at station 1, we begin a new station.

The task we begin station 2 with is E, because it takes the longest of G, E, and B. This leaves .6 minutes at station 2, and F is now ready (but C is not). Task B will not fit, so we place task G in the station, which leaves .2 minutes and adds H to the ready list. Tasks B and F will not fit, but H will, so we add H to station 2 and start a new station.

Station 3 begins with B, and so C becomes ready. Because task F is longer than task C, it is added to the list. Task J now becomes ready. Task J is longer than C but will not fit, so we add C, thereby adding I to the ready list. Neither J nor I fits, so we open station 4.

Because task J takes longer, we choose J before we choose task I. Now we are finished. We have managed to balance the system in our goal of four stations.

Cycle Time = 1.5

Station	Task	Time	Time Left	Ready Tasks
				A, D, G
1	D	.7	.8	A, G, E
	A	.6	.2	G, E, B
2	E	.9	.6	G, B, F
	G	.4	.2	B, F, H
	H	.1	.1	B, F
3	B	.8	.7	F, C
	F	.3	.4	C, J
	C	.2	.2	J, I
4	J	.6	.9	I
	I	.3	.6	C

Using AB:POM to Solve This Problem

The assembly line balancing module has five methods for balancing and two methods for determining the cycle time. Screen 7.1 contains the information from Solved Problem 1. The initial screen asks for the number of tasks. After this number is entered, a table is set up. The top line of the table contains the toggle for the method. The next two lines contain the information necessary for the cycle time. The problem states that the production rate is to be 300 units per 450-minute day; this is entered on line 2. This line contains three pieces of input. The first is the number of units (300), the second is the length of time (450), and the third is a toggle for the time unit (minutes). In other problems, the cycle time can be entered directly on line 3. The main body of the table contains the task names, the times, and the names of the predecessors. (Uppercase and lowercase letters are treated the same. For example, there is no difference between task A and task a.) The top of the time column is a toggle to change the time unit, which in this example is minutes.

In the assembly line balancing modules, the solution screen (Screen 7.2) erases the data screen. The top left lists the rule that was used (longest operation time), while the top right lists the cycle time. The main body of information is the balancing procedure, which includes the stations, the tasks at each station, the time used, the remaining time, and the tasks that are ready. Underneath the main table, the minimum theoretical number of stations, the idle time, and the efficiency are presented.

```
═══════════════════ Balancing, Assembly line ═══════════════ Data Screen ═
 Number of tasks (1-99) 10
 ════════════════════════════ Solved problem 1 ════════════════════
 Rule          Longest operation time
 Demand rate      300 units per  450.00 minutes
 Cycle Time      0.00
 Task        minutes  Predecessors
 A            0.60     —      —      —      —      —      —
 B            0.80     A      —      —      —      —      —
 C            0.20     B      E      —      —      —      —
 D            0.70     —      —      —      —      —      —
 E            0.90     D      —      —      —      —      —
 F            0.30     E      —      —      —      —      —
 G            0.40     —      —      —      —      —      —
 H            0.10     G      —      —      —      —      —
 I            0.30     C      —      —      —      —      —
 J            0.60     F      —      —      —      —      —

F1=Help F2=New F3=Load F4=Main F5=Util F6=Quit F7=Save F9=Prnt F10=Run    Esc
Enter a predecessor for this task
```

SCREEN 7.1

```
═══════════════════ Balancing, Assembly line ═══════════════ Solution ═
 Number of tasks (1-99) 10
 ════════════════════════════ Solved problem 1 ════════════════════
 Longest operation time                Cycle time = 1.5 minutes
 Station      task        Time    Time left ready tasks
                                            A,D,G
 1           D          0.70      0.80 A,G,E
             A          0.60      0.20 G,E,B
 2           E          0.90      0.60 G,B,F
             G          0.40      0.20 B,F,H
             H          0.10      0.10 B,F
 3           B          0.80      0.70 F,C
             F          0.30      0.40 C,J
             C          0.20      0.20 J,I
 4           J          0.60      0.90 I
             I          0.30      0.60
 Time allocated (cyc*sta)=   6.00;   Min (theoretical) # of stations = 4
 Time needed    (sum task)=   4.90;   EFFICIENCY= 81.67%;
 Idle time (alloc-needed)=   1.10 minutes per cycle

                                        F9=Print    Esc
Press <Esc> key to edit data or highlighted key or function key for options
```

SCREEN 7.2

2. Geomax Inc., a consulting group, has six departments: (1) software development; (2) consulting; (3) software design; (4) R&D; (5) user support; and (6) administration. Their new offices have the following layout.

A	B	C
D	E	F

The adjacent rooms are located an equal distance from each other, contiguous diagonal rooms are farther apart, and noncontiguous rooms are the farthest apart.

The interaction requirements between the groups have been evaluated and rated on a scale of 1 to 10, with 10 being the highest.

			To			
From	1	2	3	4	5	6
1		4	8	3	10	2
2			4	3	7	3
3				9	3	2
4					4	3
5						4
6						

In which room should each of the departments be placed?

Solution

Groups 1 and 5 (software development and user support) have the highest interaction requirement, so they need to be closest together. Because many pairs of rooms are equally close together, the fact that these two groups also seem to have more interaction with all the other groups leads us to place them centrally in rooms B and E.

A	B 1	C
D	E 5	F

Groups 3 and 4 have the next greatest amount of interaction. We will place them in rooms A and D. Which one goes in A depends on a slightly deeper analysis to determine which group needs to be closer to 1 and which needs to be closer to 5. Group 4 does not need to be closer to groups 1 or 5, but group 3 should be very close to group 1, having an interaction requirement of 8.

A		B		C	
	3		1		
D		E		F	
	4		5		

The next greatest interaction requirement is 7, between groups 2 and 5. Placing 2 in room F next to group 5 leaves only room C vacant. By placing group 6 there, the layout is complete.

A		B		C	
	3		1		6
D		E		F	
	4		5		2

Using AB:POM to Solve This Problem

Screen 7.3 presents the data and solution for Solved Problem 2. The input consists of two tables. One table contains the number of trips from department to department. For example, there are 10 "trips" between software development and users. The sec-

```
┌─ Data file:D:wgsp7-2 ═══════════ Operations Layout ═══════════ Solution ═┐
│  Number of departments (3-8) 6                                            │
│ ┌═══════════════════════════ Solved problem 2 ═══════════════════════════┐│
│ │                            Flow matrix                                 ││
│ │        1-deve  2-cons  3-desi  4-R&D  5-user  6-admn    Department in Room
│ │ 1-deve    0       4       8      3      10      2       1-deve in      B  ││
│ │ 2-cons    0       0       4      3       7      3       2-cons in      A  ││
│ │ 3-desi    0       0       0      9       3      2       3-desi in      C  ││
│ │ 4-R&D     0       0       0      0       4      3       4-R&D in       F  ││
│ │ 5-user    0       0       0      0       0      4       5-user in      E  ││
│ │ 6-admn    0       0       0      0       0      0       6-admn in      D  ││
│ │                          Distance Matrix                               ││
│ │         A       B       C       D       E       F                      ││
│ │ A       0       1       2       1       3       4                      ││
│ │ B       1       0       1       3       1       3                      ││
│ │ C       2       1       0       4       3       1                      ││
│ │ D       1       3       4       0       1       2                      ││
│ │ E       3       1       3       1       0       1                      ││
│ │ F       4       3       1       2       1       0                      ││
│ │ The total movement is 121                                              ││
│ └════════════════════════════════════════════════════════════════════════┘│
│                                                 F9=Print      Esc          │
│ Press <Esc> key to edit data or highlighted key or function key for options│
└──────────────────────────── SCREEN 7.3 ────────────────────────────────────┘
```

```
┌─ Data file:D:wgsp7-2 ════════ Operations Layout ═══════════ Solution ─┐
│  Number of departments (3-8) 6                                        │
├──────────────────────── Solved problem 2 ════════════════════════────┤
│                        Flow matrix                                    │
│            1-B    2-F    3-A    4-D    5-E    6-C  Department in Room   │
│   1-B       0      4      8      3     10      2  1-B in         1-B    │
│   2-F       0      0      4      3      7      3  2-F in         2-F    │
│   3-A       0      0      0      9      3      2  3-A in         3-A    │
│   4-D       0      0      0      0      4      3  4-D in         4-D    │
│   5-E       0      0      0      0      0      4  5-E in         5-E    │
│   6-C       0      0      0      0      0      0  6-C in         6-C    │
│                       Distance Matrix                                 │
│            3-A    1-B    6-C    4-D    5-E    2-F                       │
│   3-A       0      1      2      1      3      4                        │
│   1-B       1      0      1      3      1      3                        │
│   6-C       2      1      0      4      3      1                        │
│   4-D       1      3      4      0      1      2                        │
│   5-E       3      1      3      1      0      1                        │
│   2-F       4      3      1      2      1      0                        │
│                                                                       │
│  The total movement is 123                                            │
├───────────────────────────────────────────────────────────────────── │
│  F9=Print    Esc                                                      │
│  Press <Esc> key to edit data or highlighted key or function key for options │
└───────────────────────────────────────────────────────────────────────┘
```

SCREEN 7.4

ond table contains the distance from room to room. The problem gives relative distances, so we have input the distances of 1–4. The solution is listed starting at the top right.

It is possible to assign a department to a particular room by giving the room and the department the same name. For example, if the name "1-deve" is changed to "1-B" in the example and room B is changed to room 1-B then software development (now renamed "1-B") will be in room B (which has the same name). By assigning names to all departments, a specific layout can be examined for its total movement. Screen 7.4 shows the solution given above. Notice that its total movement, 123, is greater than the 121 previously found. ▬▬▬▬▬▬▬▬▬

QUESTIONS

1. What are the five major managerial concerns that necessitate good facility design?

2. Define facility layout.

3. List the facility design considerations described in this chapter.

4. Relate the facility design considerations to your home.

5. Describe a flow shop and give two examples.

6. Describe a job shop and give two examples.

7. What is the relationship between flow and repetitiveness?

8. Describe process and product layouts.

9. Contrast the advantages and disadvantages of product and process layouts.

10. A large law firm assigns offices to lawyers by seniority. If a senior person retires, approximately fifty lawyers change offices. Comment on this situation.

11. List the major principles of mass production.

12. What have been some effects (both good and bad) of the use of mass production on our daily lives?

13. Describe the components and goals of the assembly line balancing problem.

14. Two different line designs for the same product have the same efficiency. Do they necessarily have the same number of stations? Why might one line design be better than the other?

15. Comment on the use of heuristic rules for solving layout problems.

16. How can the required number of trips between different processes in a process layout be determined?

PROBLEMS

1. The Tample Toy Company has decided to manufacture a new toy, the production of which is broken into six steps.

Task	Performance Time (in seconds)	Predecessors
A	20	None
B	30	A
C	15	A
D	15	A
E	10	B, C
F	30	D, E

30 seconds/unit

4 stations

1–A; 2–B; 3–C, D; 4–E; 5–F

(a) If the required output is 4,800 toys per 40-hour week, what is the cycle time required in order to meet the production goal?

(b) Using the answer to part (a), what is the *theoretical* minimum number of stations necessary?

(c) Balance the assembly line using the longest operation time rule.

2. The following presents an assembly table for a product.

Task	Time (in minutes)	Predecessors
A	3	None
B	6	None
C	7	A
D	5	A, B
E	2	B
F	4	C
G	5	F
H	7	D, E
I	1	H
J	6	E
K	4	G, I, J
	50	

(a) Draw the precedence diagram.

(b) If the daily (twenty-four hour) production rate is 96 units, what is the greatest possible cycle time?

(c) If the cycle time is given as 10 minutes, what is the daily (twenty-four hour) production rate?

(d) If the cycle time is given as 10 minutes, what is the theoretical minimum number of stations with which the line can be balanced?

(e) If the cycle time is given as 10 minutes and the number of stations is given as 6, what is the efficiency?

(f) What is the total idle time per cycle if the cycle time is given as 10 minutes and the number of stations is given as 6?

See Instructor's Section.

15 minutes/unit

144 units/day

5 stations

83.33 percent

10 minutes/cycle

3. For the data in Problem 2, use a cycle time of 14 minutes and the rule indicated to balance the assembly line.

(a) the most following tasks rule

(b) the longest operation time rule

See Instructor's Section.
See Instructor's Section.

4. An assembly line must be established to include the following ten tasks.

Task	Time (in seconds)	Predecessors
A	120	None
B	50	A
C	40	B
D	80	C, F
E	100	A
F	20	E
G	90	H
H	60	A
I	30	A
J	60	D, G, I

See Instructor's Section.
6 stations
See Instructor's Section.
90.3 percent

(a) Draw a precedence diagram.
(b) If the cycle time is 120 seconds, what is the theoretical minimum number of stations?
(c) Use the longest task time rule to balance the line with a cycle of 120 seconds.
(d) What is the efficiency of the balance done in part (c)?

5. Demand for a certain subassembly in a toy manufacturing facility is 96 items per eight-hour shift. The following six tasks must be done to produce one subassembly.

Task	Time (in minutes)	Predecessors
A	4	None
B	5	A
C	3	A
D	2	B
E	1	B, C
F	5	D, E

5 minutes
4 stations
1–A; 2–B; 3–C, D; 4–E;
5–F
80 percent

(a) What is the maximum possible cycle time?
(b) What is the theoretical minimum number of stations?
(c) Balance the assembly line using the longest task time rule.
(d) What is the efficiency of the balance done in part (c)?

6. The following is the assembly chart for a doohickey.

Task	Time (in seconds)	Predecessors
A	7	None
B	10	A
C	6	A
D	12	B
E	5	B, C
F	8	C
G	9	D, E
H	5	D, E, F
I	3	G, H

See Instructor's Section.
Yes; it allows using one
less station.

(a) Balance the assembly line as efficiently as possible, with as few stations as possible, while meeting the demand of 10,000 doohickeys per week. (Assume 5 eight-hour days.)
(b) Is there any benefit to adding 20 minutes of overtime per day?

7. Consider the following precedence table.

Task	Time (in seconds)	Predecessors
A	12	None
B	48	None
C	8	A
D	18	C
E	13	C
F	15	C
G	8	B, C
H	6	C
I	7	F
J	8	F
K	12	F
L	14	D, E, F
M	15	F
N	18	D, E, F
O	52	G, H, I, J, L, M, N

(a) Draw the precedence diagram.
(b) If the cycle time is 48 seconds, what is the weekly production rate (assuming a forty-hour week)?
(c) If the daily production rate is 1,200 units per eight-hour day, what is the largest possible cycle time?
(d) Balance the assembly line using a cycle time of 60 seconds and the longest task time rule.
(e) State the efficiency of the balance done in part (d).

See Instructor's Section.

3,000 units/week

24 seconds/unit
See Instructor's Section.
84.67 percent

8. An office corridor is to be laid out in an arrangement of four rooms by one hallway. Each room is 20 feet from adjacent rooms. The weekly traffic flow is shown in the table.

(a) Which process should be assigned to which room?
(b) What is the total movement?

duplication–secretary–
coffee–VP
4,160 trip-feet

	To			
From	Secretary	Vice President	Coffee Machine	Duplication
Secretary		10	30	70
Vice President			50	10
Coffee Machine				4
Duplication				

9. Suppose the office presented in Problem 8 is laid out in a 2 × 2 area with distances as follows.

(a) What layout minimizes the traffic (as measured by trips × distance)?
(b) What is the total movement?

room 1–secretary
room 2–duplication
room 3–coffee
room 4–vice president
(*Note:* Other solutions exist.)
1,880 trip-feet

	To			
From	1	2	3	4
1		10	10	20
2			20	10
3				10
4				

10. Suppose that the office presented in Problem 8 is laid out in a ring, as given by the following figure. What layout minimizes the traffic flow?

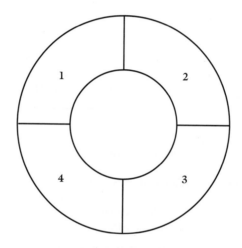

room 1–secretary
room 2–duplication
room 3–coffee
room 4–vice president
(*Note:* Other solutions
exist.)

11. Six processes are to be laid out in a 6 × 1 pattern. The distance between adjacent work centers is 40 feet. The amount of traffic from work center to work center is given in the following table. Use the heuristic to assign the processes to the rooms in a way that minimizes the total traffic flow.

	To					
From	A	B	C	D	E	F
A		18	25	73	12	54
B			96	23	31	45
C				41	22	20
D					19	57
E						48
F						

B–C–D–A–F–E or A–D–F–
E–B–C

1–B, 2–C, 3–E, 4–A, 5–D,
6–F

12. Suppose that the work centers in Problem 11 are laid out in a 2 × 3 grid, with distances as given in the following table. Use the heuristic to assign the processes to rooms.

	To					
From	1	2	3	4	5	6
1		40	80	40	70	105
2	40		40	70	40	70
3	80	40		105	70	40
4	40	70	105		40	80
5	70	40	70	40		40
6	105	70	40	80	40	

A–5; B–2; C–3; D–4; E–1;
F–6; total = 35,280

13. Solve Problem 12 using a software package.

COMPUTER CASE STUDY 7.1: MICROFIX INCORPORATED

Microfix Inc. has been manufacturing peripherals for microcomputers for the past decade. Their operations began shortly after the first Apple II came off of the assembly line, and the company has experienced substantial growth since. While Microfix originally geared its product line toward the Apple II, the company's current line encompasses products for the Apple II line of computers and Macintosh computers, as well as IBM-compatible microcomputers. Over the years, Microfix's mainstay has been hard (fixed) disk drives.

Because of a recent slump in sales, Microfix has decided to expand its product line. After much deliberation among executives, engineers, production personnel, and marketing personnel, a decision was made to produce tape backup systems for the IBM PS/2 line of computers. Microfix intends to convert its hard disk expertise to tape expertise and to become the cost leader for this one type of product for this one series of machines.

The marketing department has performed a major analysis of machines and backup systems and feels that after one year 60,000 units per year is a reasonable sales goal. The feeling among upper management, however, is that this might be overly optimistic; the number preferred by management is 1,000 units per week. Current operations use a standard forty-hour week, and the operations vice-president insists that this be maintained for the new product.

Developing the steps involved in producing the tape system has been a project in itself. Engineers, production managers, and assembly line workers collaborated in order to create a precedence graph and table. The collaboration entailed several steps. First, some twenty-five different steps involved in production were identified. Then careful thought was given to the precedences for each task. At this point, the line workers developed the task times, using known task times for tasks that are identical to current tasks, estimates for tasks that are similar to current tasks, and, for some tasks, conjecture. After all of this effort, the following assembly line table was developed.

Task	Time (in minutes)	Predecessors
A	1.00	None
B	.40	A
C	.45	A
D	1.10	A
E	.36	A
F	.05	None
G	1.32	B, C
H	.49	C, D
I	.54	E
J	1.54	E
K	.35	F
L	2.10	G
M	.30	H, I
N	1.82	I
O	.89	J
P	1.20	L, M, N
Q	1.30	N, O
R	.62	O
S	1.30	K
T	1.20	P, Q, R, S
U	1.80	S
V	.30	T
W	.87	U
X	1.20	U
Y	1.90	V, W, X

The managers still have much work to do. They must begin by determining the appropriate balance that operations should strive for. They must consider that some of the time estimates may be off by as much as 10 percent, and they must consider that the demand will change over time. Find their initial balance and determine how sensitive this balance is to all of these factors.

COMPUTER CASE STUDY 7.2: BEER DISTRIBUTORSHIP

Three recent college graduates have decided to open a beer distributorship together to serve their neighborhood. After a long series of discussions, they decide to attempt to reach an exclusive arrangement with one of the major beer producers. The successful conclusion of this strategy means that once in business they will only sell one brand of beer but will control that brand in their small geographic area. The partners have worked with business consultants to obtain financing, develop an accounting system, and prepare marketing plans.

One of their early decisions was the selection of a building to rent. The building, which measures 120 ft. by 220 ft., is separated into a 50 ft. by 70 ft. office area and a warehouse. The decision is made to maintain a 20-foot-wide aisle up the middle and to provide for seven storage areas along the aisle, each of which will measure 50 ft. by 50 ft. The last 20 feet on the opposite side of the building from the office is devoted to loading the beer onto trucks at the loading dock. (See the accompanying floor plan.)

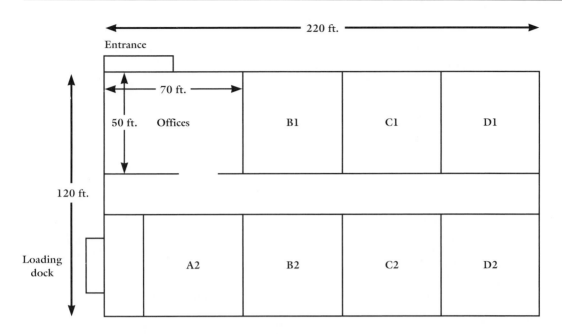

Each of the seven products the partners plan to sell will be stored in its own area. In the absence of any knowledge of inventory analysis, they will keep only the amount of inventory that will fit into each storage area, regardless of differing levels of sales and different product size (space) requirements.

By establishing dedicated product storage areas, the three partners hope to

1. Systematize order storing and picking;
2. Reduce damage and spoilage; and
3. Facilitate inventory checking.

An important fourth goal, one which to this point they have ignored, is reducing the materials handling requirements. By assigning the seven products to certain storage areas, they can increase or decrease the materials handling requirements. The following shows the estimated monthly sales of the seven products.

Product	Sales
Kegs	341
Cans (six-packs)	1,421
Cans (twelve-packs)	277
Lite (cans)	148
Bottles (six-packs)	137
Bottles (other)	97
Quarts	76

Which product should be stored in which storage area?

Now suppose that the three partners decide to make the number of trips to each area from the loading dock, not sales, the measure for reducing materials handling requirements. After all, each keg sold requires one trip, but as many as twelve six-packs can be carried in one trip—even more if bought by the case. As a rule, different products are not picked up on the same trip into the warehouse.

The estimated monthly trips into the warehouse for each product are as follows.

Product	Trips
Kegs	341
Cans (six-packs)	178
Cans (twelve-packs)	55
Lite (cans)	19
Bottles (six-packs)	34
Bottles (other)	32
Quarts	25

Does this affect your layout in any way?

Upon further thought, the partners realize that they have been very shortsighted. They have only considered the trips that they make when they unload the trucks. One of the partners suggests that they should minimize the amount of walking and carrying done when they pick up orders. In order to get an idea of the customer flow, they look at past records and make a table that shows the number of times that two items appear on the same sales slip.

	Kegs	Cans (six-packs)	Cans (twelve-packs)	Lite (cans)	Bottles (six-packs)	Bottles (other)	Quarts
Kegs		12	15	100	29	48	3
Cans (six-packs)				273	421	98	7
Cans (twelve-packs)				351	162	130	99
Lite (cans)					265	88	25
Bottles (six-packs)						54	8
Bottles (other)							1
Quarts							

(For example, on twelve of the sales slips, a person had ordered kegs and six-pack cans. Keep in mind that any of the sales slips with a keg and a six-pack of cans could also have listed other items.) Given this information, how should the warehouse be laid out?

REFERENCES

Armine, H. T., J. A. Ritchey, and C. L. Moodie. *Manufacturing Organization and Management.* 5th ed. Englewood Cliffs, N.J.: Prentice-Hall, 1987.

Craig, R., J. Moore, and W. Turner. "Planned Production Flexibility," *Industrial Engineering 7,* no. 10 (1975): 33–37.

Groover, M. P. *Automation, Production Systems, and Computer-Integrated Manufacturing.* Englewood Cliffs, N.J.: Prentice-Hall, 1987.

Konz, S. *Facility Design.* New York: John Wiley and Sons, 1985.

Muther, R. *Systematic Layout Planning.* Boston: Cahners Books, 1973.

Smith, H. T., W. H. Baker, M. Sumner, and A. J. Bate. *Automated Office Systems Management,* New York: John Wiley and Sons, 1985.

Wild, R. *Mass-Production Management.* London: John Wiley and Sons, 1972.

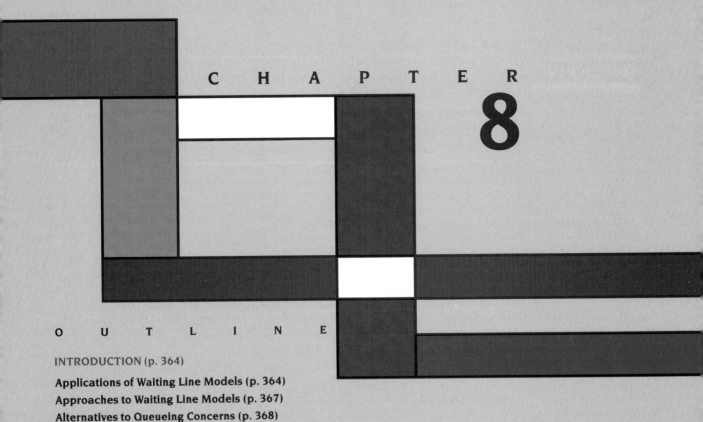

C H A P T E R

8

WAITING LINE MODELS

- To explain the different types of waiting line, or queueing, systems
- To illustrate the managerial options available for improving queueing systems
- To present the means for analyzing and measuring the performance of waiting lines
- To provide the tools for comparing options for operating queueing systems
- To demonstrate the cost analysis of queueing system operations

INTRODUCTION

Teaching Suggestion 8.1: A Light Introduction. See the Instructor's Section for details.

Waiting in line is an irritating situation that one faces continually. A typical day might include waiting for the use of the bathroom, waiting at an expressway entrance for an opening in traffic, waiting in a parking lot for a parking space, waiting for the elevator to the office, waiting while being put on hold on the telephone, waiting in the cafeteria for lunch, waiting at the supermarket on the trip home, and, finally, waiting to use the tennis courts to relax from all of the waiting. Most of these situations can be improved. For example, one can add another bathroom to the house, another elevator in the office building, more parking spaces in the parking lot, or more cashiers in the super-

relationship to capacity

market. Each of these options represents an addition to capacity (discussed in Chapter 3). However, the costs these additions would incur may not be worth the reduced waiting time that would result from the improvements. This cost–benefit trade-off requires analysis. The necessary analytical tools come under the title of *waiting line*

queueing

models, or **queueing** models.

APPLICATIONS OF WAITING LINE MODELS

Listed in Table 8.1 are several different examples of waiting lines. These situations involve different types of concerns, which we broadly categorize as *capacity concerns* and *policy concerns.*

CAPACITY

In Chapter 3, we noted that the capacity of a system is dictated by several factors. Recall that among these factors are the number of employees and/or machines, the speed of the employees and/or machines, and the arrangement of the employees and/or machines. Queueing analysis enables us to look at customer waiting time and other measures as a function of the system capacity. There are a variety of questions that queueing analysis will answer for us.

maximum number of servers

We begin with the most basic question—namely, What is the maximum number of servers that the system should operate? For most of the examples listed in Table 8.1, this question must be answered at the time the system is built or redesigned. For example, the number of barber chairs in a barber shop, gasoline pumps at a gas station, toll

TABLE 8.1 Examples of waiting lines

Situation/Location	Customer	Server
Barber shop	Patron	Barber
Gasoline station	Motorist	Island/gas pump
Intersection	Car	Traffic light
Toll booth	Car	Toll collector/machine
Restaurant	Patron	Table and waiter and cook
Bank	Customer	Teller
Library	Borrower	Book(s)
Airport	Plane	Runway
Office building	Rider	Elevator
Computer	Job	CPU/IO device
Cafeteria equipment	Vending machine	Repairperson
Hospital emergency room	Patient	Doctor
Historical site	Tourist	Tour guide
Duplicating room	Secretary	Duplicating machine
Telephone (installation)	Homeowner	Installer
Telephone (calls)	Caller	Phone line(s)
Police	Victim	Police officer
Parking lot	Car	Parking space
Mass transportation	Commuter	Bus, train
Grocery store	Customer	Cashier
Loading dock	Truck	Crew and dock

Teaching Suggestion 8.2: We Wait Everywhere. See the Instructor's Section for details.

Transparency Master 8.1: Examples of Queues.

booths at an interchange, tables in a restaurant, elevators in a building, phone lines at a business, or cash registers at a grocery store must be determined at the design or redesign stage. We say "maximum number of servers" because, in many instances, not all of the capacity will be used. For example, a supermarket may decide (through queueing analysis) that twenty cash registers are necessary to meet the peak load, but not all twenty registers are used throughout the rest of the week.

design for peak load

We note that one misallocation of queueing space has been the topic of countless newspaper articles and has been at the center of a public debate. The much-publicized arrest of a woman for using the men's restroom at a concert in Texas—the line for the women's restroom had spilled out into the corridor—focused attention on a queueing problem frequently encountered outside of women's restrooms at crowded events. Several state legislatures began to investigate ways of eliminating or reducing these long lines. The Washington state Department of Transportation found that women need, on average, 79 seconds of "stall time," compared to 49 seconds for men. Since architects often devote no more area to women's restrooms than they do to men's, the predictable result is long lines outside of women's restrooms. In Washington state, the Department of Transportation believes that this queueing concern can be addressed by requiring a ratio of toilets of 3:2 for women's and men's restrooms.

This brings us to a second, similar question: What staffing levels should be maintained throughout the week? A bank probably would perform a different queueing analysis for each day of the week, because the demand at a bank varies by day of the week. These analyses would indicate the number of tellers that should be on duty throughout the week.

staffing levels

use customer as server

One way to increase the number of servers without incurring extra wages is to use the customer as server. Examples of such systems are self-service gasoline pumps, automatic teller machines, cafeterias or vending machines, exact change machines on tollways and bridges, and self-service beverage dispensers or salad bars.

We know that capacity is affected by the speed of the resources; we can use queueing analysis to determine the effects. For example, we can compare computers (or line printers or modems) that operate at different rates.

resource arrangement

The last question relating to capacity is, How should resources be arranged? Queueing models can be used in a comparison of, say, a system where one employee rings up prices and one employee bags groceries and another system where two employees each perform both tasks. Similarly, queueing models can be used to examine the effects of having two express lanes in a supermarket instead of one.

There is one capacity feature that is unique to queueing situations—the waiting line itself. Customers wait for service, and we must be sure that there is sufficient room for the customers to wait. For example, if a restaurant asks diners to wait in the bar until a table is available, the bar should be designed to accommodate all of the waiting customers. Similarly, the lanes at a drive-through bank window must be designed in such a way that lines of waiting cars do not block a street or parking lot. The queueing models enable us to determine the number of customers waiting, which, in turn, enables us to compute the waiting space required.

POLICY EFFECTS

After the system is designed, there may be no question as to the number of servers, but there will be questions on how the servers are best used. Consider an intersection with a traffic light. There is only one light; the operating problem is to determine the cycle of the lengths of time that the light is green, then yellow, then red. A similar problem arises at a bank. Bank tellers perform functions that do not require interaction with a customer. As the waiting line grows, at what point should a teller open his or her window for customer service? The dispatching of elevators is a matter of queueing policy. Suppose that an elevator is sitting idle on the fourth floor of a building, another is sitting idle on the eighth floor of the building, and a customer on the sixth floor presses the "up" button. Which elevator should be sent is a matter of queueing policy, and a very difficult question to answer. As further examples of how queueing theory may be applied to answer policy questions, consider a library that must decide on the length of time books may be borrowed or a duplicating facility that must set a limit on the number of pages that a customer will be allowed to duplicate.

Some companies have designed policies to offset the waiting line problem. For example, the now-defunct Zayre department store chain maintained a policy whereby another checkout lane would be opened if more than three people were waiting in line at a checkout lane. Many airlines use expediters, employees whose job it is to make certain that passengers are in the right line, to inform some passengers that they can check in at the gate rather than waiting in line in the terminal, and to move passengers to the front of the line if their flight times are nearing. Chemical Bank has installed a program in some of its busy Manhattan branch locations that calls for giving customers five dollars if they wait more than seven minutes in line. Burger King has installed a division-of-labor process in many of its outlets: One cashier takes the order and the money, while a second processes the order.

American Airlines gets more complaints about the length of time it takes for baggage to arrive at the baggage claim area in Dallas than in Los Angeles. In Dallas, it is a

APPLICATIONS OF P/OM

Queues and Blocking Phone Calls

Rich Wetmore is district manager of AT&T's Communications Network Operations Center in Bedminster, New Jersey. As the following remarks about long distance phone service make clear, general queueing models are applicable to more situations than the familiar clerk–customer model on which we have concentrated thus far.

> When a customer places a call, it's our job to see that it goes through. We monitor the performance of our AT&T network by displaying data collected from all over the country on a special wallboard. The wallboard is configured to tell us if a customer's call is not going through because the network doesn't have enough capacity to handle it.
>
> That's when we step in and take control to correct the problem. The typical control we use is to reroute the call. Instead of sending the customer's call directly to its

destination, we'll route it via a third city—to someplace else in the country that has the capacity to complete the call. When we put the reroute through, people's calls are completed and everyone is happy.

Our fundamental principle is that no matter where you live, you receive equitable treatment in terms of the way the network performs and in terms of the blocking level you get. The traditional guideline we use is that whether you live in Chicago or Horseheads, New York (where I'm from), you should get an average of zero blocking throughout the day. And we try to build just enough capacity both to Chicago and to Horseheads so that you don't get blocked.

Source: S. Garfunkel, ed., *Introduction to Contemporary Mathematics* (New York: W.H. Freeman and Company, 1988), pp. 33–34.

relatively short walk from the gate to the baggage claim area; in Los Angeles, the walk is longer, which means that passengers spend less time standing by the baggage carousel. The fact that customers tend to equate standing around with a lack of progress accounts for the long snake-like lines found at banks, airline ticket counters, and amusement parks.

APPROACHES TO WAITING LINE MODELS

The analysis of waiting lines, or queues, began in the early 1900s by A. K. Erlang, whose major interest was telephone traffic engineering (that is, phone calls waiting for a line). Since then, a great deal of research has been accomplished in the area. Much of the early work was descriptive, such as determining the effect of having two toll booths rather than three. Much of the recent work is prescriptive, in that the models determine how the service facility can be controlled to improve the general waiting situation. The emphasis in this chapter is on the descriptive models, because these models tend to be both more general and more applicable. For the interested reader, a bibliography of queueing control models has been developed by Crabill, Gross, and Magazine (1977).

descriptive models

Refer again to our examples in Table 8.1. Although each example represents a different situation, clearly there are similarities between several of the examples. For instance, some of the systems have human customers, while others have inanimate customers. Some of the systems serve one customer at a time, while others serve batches of customers at one time. The general goal is to develop a broad classification of queueing systems that includes as many different situations as possible. Then, using this classification scheme, we find the effects of different operating plans, such as varying the number of servers. The effects would be measured in terms of average waiting time or average number of customers in the system, which can be traded off against the costs of additional servers or other operating plans.

ALTERNATIVES TO QUEUEING CONCERNS

Our goal in this chapter is to present models that enable us to compare the waiting lines of different systems. Sometimes the system is fixed, and the waiting lines cannot be reduced. In these instances, rather than reducing the time that a customer spends in the system, we might instead make the waiting time more pleasant. This can be done by providing magazines in waiting rooms, mirrors outside of elevators, or a waiting bar at a restaurant (preferably with free hors d'oeuvres).

make waiting a pleasant experience

waiting lines are not all bad

We make one final remark before presenting the queueing models: Waiting lines are not all bad. Many consumers will not enter a restaurant or supermarket if they observe no waiting lines. These customers feel that there is a high correlation between the quality of food or service and the waiting time. Also, supermarket managers like customers to wait a short while so that they will buy the impulse items that are located at the waiting areas. By planning the length of the waiting lines, the manager also can increase the utilization of the servers.

A GENERAL QUEUEING FRAMEWORK

A diagram of the general waiting system appears in Figure 8.1. A customer leaves the general population, enters the queueing system, and then exits. Of course, there may be many variations to the picture; in particular, many different figures may represent the queueing system itself. The goal is to describe the system with a minimum number of parameters.

THE SYSTEM PARAMETERS

The most basic queueing systems are described by six critical parameters—the calling population, the arrival process, the maximum queue size, the queue discipline, the number of servers, and the service process. We now describe these parameters in detail.

CALLING, OR SOURCE, POPULATION

finite or infinite

With respect to Figure 8.1, the first parameter is the **calling,** or **source, population**—the larger set from which the smaller set of customers arrive. In particular, it will be of major concern whether this set of potential customers is finite or infinite. More often than not, the calling population is very large compared to the system size and so may be considered infinite. For example, the number of persons who might arrive at the local bank is equal to the neighborhood population, which will be considerably larger than the number of people working at the bank. On the other hand, suppose that a computer rental company has leased six computers to other companies. When one breaks down (crashes), the rental company sends its lone repairperson. Obviously, the ratio of six potential customers to one service person is not infinite. This distinction between finite and infinite is important because it tells us the likelihood that more

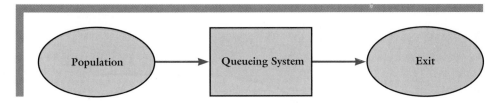

FIGURE 8.1 General queueing system

customers will enter a system. That is, in the case of finite population, if customers are already in the system, there is less chance that additional customers will enter the system. On the other hand, in the case of the bank, if six neighborhood people are in the bank, there still is a good chance that other customers will enter because the population is so large. More often than not, the source population is infinite, and this is reflected by the fact that most queueing models assume an infinite source population. Making this assumption also simplifies the analysis.

ARRIVAL PROCESS

The next consideration is the **arrival process**—that is, how customers leave the source population and enter the queueing system. The major concern is with the arrival pattern, as given by the probability distribution of the times between arrivals. Typically, the time between arrivals is random rather than constant (unless one is observing the arrival process on an assembly line or in rush-hour traffic). That is, there might be five minutes between the arrival times of customer 1 and customer 2, three minutes between the arrival times of customer 2 and customer 3, eight minutes between the arrival times of customer 3 and customer 4, and so forth. If the interarrival times are random, then it is necessary to specify their probability distribution. The most common interarrival time distribution is given by the exponential distribution (also called the negative exponential distribution). Figure 8.2 contains a graph of the exponential distribution function. **probabilistic interarrival times**

If the interarrival times have an exponential distribution, then the number of arrivals during a period of length t has a Poisson distribution, as given by

$$P(N_t = k) = \frac{e^{-\lambda t}(\lambda t)^k}{k!} \text{ for } k = 0, 1, 2, \ldots$$

where N_t is the number of arrivals during the period of length t. Notice that λ represents the mean **arrival rate.** For example, if $\lambda = 4$ arrivals per hour, then the mean time between arrivals is $1/4$ hours, or 15 minutes. It has been demonstrated that, when many customers act independently and converge at the same spot, they tend to generate a **Poisson arrival process.** For example, the reason that one person goes food shopping on Saturday is not because the person's neighbor does. Each makes this decision independently. Hence, arrivals at a supermarket typically follow a Poisson process. (The interarrival times are exponential.) However, arrivals to the company parking lot at 8:00 A.M. are not independent of one another, which implies that it is unlikely that this process is well represented by a Poisson distribution. **rate vs. time**

A second concern relating to the arrival process is the distinction between single and batch arrivals. All of the models in this chapter assume that each arrival represents **single arrivals vs. batch arrivals**

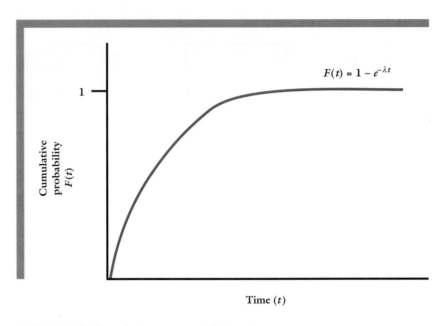

FIGURE 8.2 Cumulative exponential distribution

a single customer. We exclude systems where one arrival might bring more than one customer. For example, the airport limousine arrives at the airport with a batch of travelers, each requiring separate treatment. This differs from a family of four arriving at a restaurant and being seated together, which is a single, not a batch, arrival.

customer behavior

The last concern with respect to the arrival process relates to customer behavior. There is the distinct possibility that a customer may arrive at the system but not enter the system because the line is too long. This is termed **balking,** and we will not consider it directly. Nor will we consider **reneging**—the act of entering the system, waiting in line, and then leaving the system *before* being serviced. We consider all customers to be patient in that they neither balk nor renege.

PHASES

In some systems, a customer requires only one service; in others, a customer requires more than one service (in consecutive order). For example, at a drive-in bank, the customer sits in his or her car, waits in line, drives up for service, and then exits. However, in a hospital radiology department, the patient typically waits in line to register, registers, waits in line for a changing room, changes clothing, waits in line for the X-ray machine, is X-rayed, waits to change clothing, gets dressed, and then leaves the hospital. The two types of systems are represented in Figure 8.3. Each queue/service

single vs. multiple phase

combination is termed a **phase,** and an important distinction is made between single-phase systems, such as the drive-in bank, and multiple-phase systems, such as the radiology department. Also, when there are multiple phases, we refer to them as **queues in series.** In general, few analytical approaches have been developed for multiple-phase systems. (We use simulation for such models.) All of the models we will examine in this text are single-phase models.

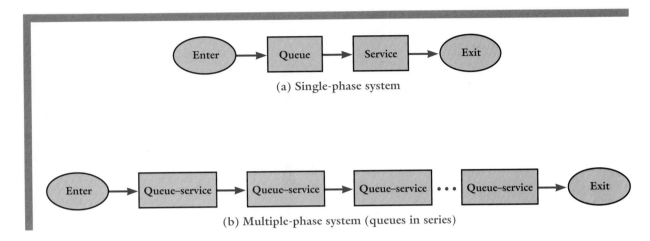

FIGURE 8.3 Service phases

QUEUE SIZE

As with the calling population, a distinction must be made as to the number of persons allowed to wait in the queue at one time. Typically, this number is unlimited. It would be rather unusual for the store manager to ask a customer not to enter the store because there are too many customers inside. Note that a finite queue produces the same effect as balking: The customer arrives at the system, but does not enter. The difference is that the customer who balks could have entered if he or she so desired, but chose not to. However, if the queue is limited, the customer simply cannot enter the system when the system is full. Although limited queues are not common, a typical example is a parking lot that is full and has a gate that restricts entrance when the lot is full. Notice that, if the queue size is finite, then the system size is finite also and is equal to the queue size plus the number of servers. A second and more common example of a finite queue is a telephone system. When the system is full, the caller hears a busy signal and knows that all lines are busy.

Transparency Master 8.2: Special Queues: Phases and Feedback.

finite vs. infinite

QUEUE STRUCTURE AND DISCIPLINE

If there is only one server, then, typically, there is only one line leading to the server. However, if there are multiple servers (in parallel, not in series), then there may be either one line for each server or one line for all servers (see Figure 8.4). If there is one line feeding all servers, then the **queue discipline** is, typically, **first come, first served** (FCFS). If there is one line feeding each server, then service typically will be first come, first served within any one line but not for the entire system. (It is common knowledge that every line moves faster than the one we are standing in.) There is no difference between the two types of lines, in terms of the system averages, as long as customers shift lines so that a server is never idle while a customer is waiting. Observing customers switching lines is commonplace in a bank or supermarket but not at a drive-in bank with multiple lanes. Hence, a supermarket with five cashiers and one line will have the same average waiting time as a supermarket with five cashiers and five lines. (The amount that the individual waiting times vary will change.) In fact, even if service is on a **last come, first served** (LCFS) basis, the system averages will be the same. (With

Teaching Suggestion 8.3: McDonald's vs. Wendy's. See the Instructor's Section for details.

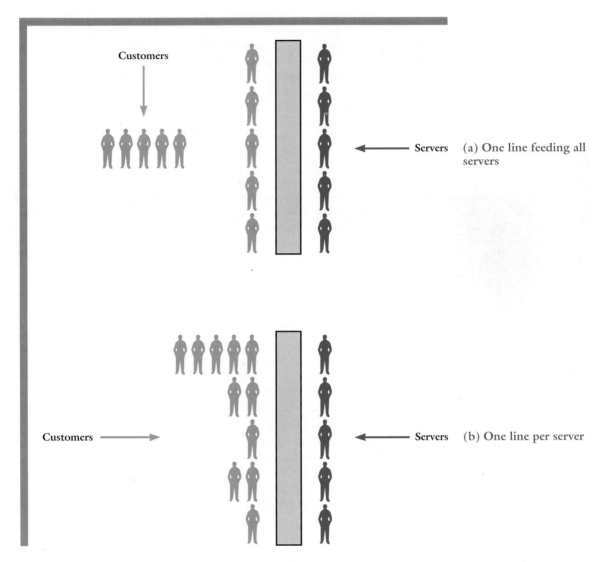

FIGURE 8.4 Queue structure when servers are parallel

respect to averages, the system does not care who the customers are!) Other queue disciplines are priority service, as in a hospital emergency room, and **service in random order** (SIRO), where the next customer is chosen randomly. Typically, LCFS and SIRO are used only if the customers are not persons. With human customers, FCFS is the most common queue discipline, primarily because it indicates some sense of fairness. However, again note that, on the average, FCFS does not perform any better than LCFS, SIRO, or priority service.

THE SERVICE PROCESS

Two parameters are of prime importance with respect to service. The first is the number of servers, also called **channels,** and the second is the length of time required to perform the service. As with the interarrival times, the service time in most cases is

One line feeding all servers at a Boston unemployment office. (© Rob Crandall/Picture Group)

random and, thus, is represented by a probability distribution. Again, a common assumption is that the service times have an exponential distribution where $1/\mu$ is the average service time and μ is the rate at which the server works when he or she is busy.

One of the features of the exponential distribution is that it is memoryless. This means it assumes that, even though the server may already have been occupied with one customer for, say, three minutes, the probability that service takes another five minutes is the same as if the server just began with that customer. This property is appropriate for some systems but not for others. For example, suppose that a supermarket cashier has checked all but one of a customer's items; that last item might require a price check, the customer might need to have a check approved, or—what everyone has experienced—the customer might go back to an aisle for one item that was forgotten, and so more time will be required before service ends.

memoryless

The exponential and Poisson distributions are intimately related. The exponential distribution describes *time* (either interarrival or service), while the Poisson distribution describes the *rate* (of arrivals or service). Both refer to an underlying process that is termed *Poisson*. The relationship is this: If the arrival distribution is Poisson with a rate of λ, then the interarrival times have an exponential distribution with a mean time between arrivals of $1/\lambda$. Similarly, if the service times have an exponential distribution with a mean of $1/\mu$, then the server can serve customers according to a Poisson distribution with a mean service rate of μ.

relationship of Poisson and exponential distributions

It is not critical that service times follow an exponential distribution, because results also exist for queueing models with general service distributions. Essentially, all that is required is that the mean and variance of the service times be known.

Note that, if there are s servers, each one serving with a rate of μ, then the system service rate is $s\mu$ at best, if all servers are busy. Furthermore, if the system service rate

system service rate

One line in front of each server at a passport checkpoint in Madrid, Spain. (© Peter Menzel/Stock, Boston)

$s\mu$ is less than or equal to the system arrival rate λ, then customers are arriving faster than they are leaving, which means that the queue and the system are growing continually. A typical example of this is traffic at a stoplight during rush hour. Cars keep backing up until the arrival rate begins to slow down. Systems with an arrival rate larger than their service rate, or with a variable arrival rate (like traffic), are not considered here.

batch service

One last service feature that we note is the case of servers with the capability of serving customers in batches. Typically, this occurs in mass transportation; a bus or an airplane is an obvious batch server. Other examples of batch servers are a tour guide, a ceramic oven, and an elevator. All models in this chapter exclude the possibility of batch service because of the complex calculations involved.

THE EXIT PROCESS

In most cases, the exit process is very simple: After a customer is served, he or she exits. However, there are many queueing systems in which the customer might not leave directly. These are called **queues with feedback,** or **round robin queues** (see Figure 8.5). One example of this structure is the radiology department in a hospital. After the X-ray is taken, the patient waits until the film is developed. If the picture is clear, the patient leaves; however, if the film is not acceptable, the patient returns to the queue to wait for another X-ray. The systems examined in this chapter have no feedback.

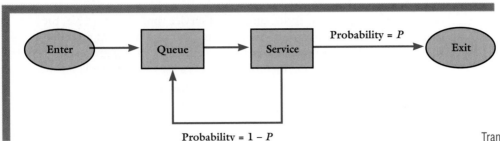

FIGURE 8.5 Queue with feedback

STANDARD NOTATION

Figure 8.6 contains a detailed picture of the systems examined in this chapter and our six parameters of interest.

In 1953, D. G. Kendall proposed a standard notation in order to unify queueing models. Kendall's notation has since been universally accepted. In Kendall's notation, the first character stands for the type of arrival process, the second character stands for the type of service process, and the third character stands for the number of servers— that is, Kendall's notation takes the form

Arrival Process/Service Process/Number of Servers.

Knowledge of these three factors—the arrival process, the service process, and the number of servers—provides most of the important information needed to describe a waiting line situation. We use the following abbreviations for three standard types of arrival and service processes.

M stands for a *memoryless* distribution. As was explained in the discussion on the service process, one of the features of the exponential or Poisson distribution is

FIGURE 8.6 General queueing system and its parameters

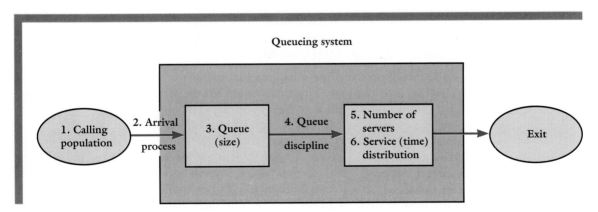

that it is memoryless. This means that the amount of service time that has already elapsed will not affect the future amount of service time. For example, the fact that there have been no arrivals in the past ten minutes does not make for a sooner arrival. Memorylessness can apply to either the arrival process or the service process or both. In fact, memoryless queues are the most basic queues.

D stands for *deterministic* times. This is the symbol that we use when either the times between arrivals or the service times are always the same—as is true of an automated process. For example, the times between arrivals would be the same for a product on an assembly line, while the service times would be the same for a car wash or a vending machine.

G stands for *general.* This is the symbol we use when we are not dealing with Poisson (memoryless) arrivals or exponential (memoryless) service times or constant interarrival or service times.

Three of the six parameters that were mentioned previously are not part of the notation. These are the population size, the queue size, and the service discipline. Unless specified otherwise, we assume that the population size is infinite, the queue size is infinite, and the service discipline is first come, first served (or that it does not matter because the queue discipline does not affect the system averages).

We will primarily base our analyses on just three models of a queueing system. A brief description of each model is given below:

The M/M/1 model—The M/M/1 model (pronounced "em em one") is used for the most basic queueing system. The first *M* refers to the arrival process (memoryless). Therefore, we have a Poisson arrival process: people acting independently but converging at the same spot. The second *M* refers to the memoryless (exponential) service times. The 1 refers to the fact that there is only one server. Because we have not mentioned the other three parameters, we assume an infinite population, an infinite queue size, and FCFS service. Typical examples of such a queueing system are an automatic teller machine, a bakery with one server, or a single duplication machine.

The M/M/s model—This model is identical to the basic M/M/1 model except that we allow for more than one server. We use the notation *s* to refer to the number of servers in the system. This system still has Poisson arrivals, exponential service times, an infinite population, an infinite queue size, and FCFS service. The checkout lines at many retail outlets are M/M/s systems.

The M/D/1 model—This model differs from the basic M/M/1 model in that the service times are deterministic (constant). Examples of M/D/1 systems are car washes, instant photo booths, and vending machines. The other parameters are identical to the basic M/M/1 model.

Teaching Suggestion 8.6: Applicability of Models. See the Instructor's Section for details.

Again, we remark that the standard notation for the arrival rate is λ (interarrival times average $1/\lambda$) and the standard notation for the service time is $1/\mu$ (a service rate of μ). If the service time is neither exponential nor constant, then we must specify not only the mean ($1/\mu$) but also the standard deviation (σ).

Furthermore, at times, we need to distinguish between the arrival rate and the **effective arrival rate**, as well as distinguish between the service rate and the **effective service rate**. Suppose that the arrival rate, λ, is given by 10 per hour, and the service rate for a single-server system is given by $\mu = 20$ per hour. It is obvious that the server does not serve at a rate of 20 per hour because there are only 10 customers per hour to serve. The effective service rate (μ_{eff}) is, therefore, 10 customers per hour. The following formula is used to find the effective service rate:

$$\mu_{eff} = \mu \times \text{percentage of time server is busy.}$$

effective service rate

The effective arrival rate and the arrival rate will be the same whenever all customers who arrive at the system do indeed enter the system. However, if the system size is finite, then there is the possibility that customers will arrive, find the system full, and, therefore, not enter. Thus, the effective arrival rate, which is the rate of those who not only arrive but actually enter the system, is given by this formula:

$$\lambda_{eff} = \lambda \times \text{percentage of time the system is } \textit{not} \text{ full.}$$

effective arrival rate

Finally, because the number of customers who enter must equal the number of customers who leave, it must be true that

$$\lambda_{eff} = \mu_{eff}.$$

The practical use of the effective arrival and service rates is seen in terms of system capacity. If the effective arrival rate is different from the arrival rate that would be in effect if customers were not turned away, then it is possible to evaluate the effect of the two system design capacities that lead to these cases. The two systems may be compared in terms of cost, utilization, number of customers served, and profit, as well as the other system performance measures discussed next. A similar analysis may be performed on the effective service rate. A design service rate that is much higher than the service rate (than the effective arrival rate) results in underutilization of the facility of servers. The trade-off is that, as this utilization increases (as the service rate is lowered), the length of the waiting line grows.

In our discussion of queue disciplines earlier in the chapter, we stated that the averages of the system measures are not affected by the queue discipline (FCFS, SIRO, and the others). The effective arrival and service rates help us to understand this phenomenon. For example, λ_{eff} is affected by limiting the system size, but, as long as no customers are turned away, it is unaffected by the queue discipline. Similarly, μ_{eff} is equal to the effective arrival rate, regardless of the order in which the customers are served.

MEASURES OF PERFORMANCE

key questions

There are several questions that a manager might have regarding the operation of a queueing system. These questions would center around the percentage of time the servers are busy; the length of time a customer waits in line, or the length of time a customer is in the system (waiting time plus service time); and the average number of customers waiting, or the average number of customers in the system (those waiting plus those being served). Standard steady state results exist for many models. By **steady state,** we mean long-run operation. The queue length one minute after a store has opened is not indicative of queue length the rest of the day. Steady state results imply that the system has been operating for some time already.

Teaching Suggestion 8.7:
Importance of Measures.
See the Instructor's Section for details.

The standard notation for the measures of performance for a system is as follows:

ρ = $\lambda/s\mu$ is the utilization, or the average percentage of time that each of the servers is busy (s is the number of servers);

L_q = the average number of customers in the queue;

L = the average number of customers in the system;

W_q = the average length of time a customer is in the queue; and

W = the average length of time a customer is in the system.

It should be obvious that the time a customer spends in the system (W) is equal to the time spent in line (W_q) plus the service time ($1/\mu$). That is,

$$W = W_q + 1/\mu$$

for all queueing systems. Less obvious are three other fundamental relationships:

fundamental relationships for all queueing systems

$$L = \lambda W;$$
$$L_q = \lambda W_q; \text{ and}$$
$$L = L_q + \lambda/\mu.$$

The four equations relating L, L_q, W, and W_q are important because they imply that, if one of the four is known, then the other three may be computed. For example, suppose that we have a queueing system with an arrival rate of $\lambda = 10$ customers per hour and a service rate of $\mu = 20$ customers per hour and we know that the average queue size (L_q) is 5 customers. (Notice that we have not indicated the number of servers or the distributions of arrival or service times.) From the fundamental relationships just presented, it follows that the average number of customers in the system is given by

$$L = L_q + \lambda/\mu = 5 + 10/20 = 5.5 \text{ customers.}$$

The average length of time a customer waits in line is

$$W_q = L_q/\lambda = 5/10 = .5 \text{ hours,}$$

and the average time a customer spends in the system is

$$W = L/\lambda = 5.5/10 = .55 \text{ hours.}$$

probability equals percentage of time

One more measure of interest is P_n, which is the probability that exactly n customers are in the system. Note that P_0 is the percentage of time that exactly zero customers are in the system—that is, the percentage of time the system is empty.

RESULTS, APPLICATIONS, AND PRINCIPLES

At the beginning of the chapter, we noted the types of questions that can be answered with the use of queueing models. In this section, we will demonstrate the application of queueing models by means of several examples. Some of the results that we will use are from formulas, and others are from tables. In either case, the four fundamental formulas that relate L, L_q, W, and W_q can be used because they hold true for any queueing system. The first type of queueing system that we will examine is the *M/M/1* queue. The formulas for the *M/M/1* queue as well as other systems are given in Table 8.2.

Prior to applying the relationships provided in Table 8.2, let us repeat the interpretation of the two primary inputs to the model, λ and μ. Both represent rates of occurrences: arrivals per time period and services per time period, respectively. If an arrival or service is expressed in terms of time, it is necessary to convert the time to a

Teaching Suggestion 8.8: Rates. See the Instructor's Section for details.

Transparency Master 8.5: Queueing Models and Results.

TABLE 8.2 Standard notations and formulas for queueing models*

M/M/1 Model	*M/D/1* Model	*M/M/s* Model (multiple servers)	*M/M/1* Model with Finite Queue (system size, C)	*M/M/1* Model with Finite Population (population size, N)
$L_q = \dfrac{\lambda^2}{\mu(\mu - \lambda)}$	$L_q = \dfrac{\lambda^2}{2\mu(\mu - \lambda)}$	L_q (Table 8.3)	$L_q = L - \dfrac{\lambda_{eff}}{\mu}$	$L_q = L - \dfrac{\lambda_{eff}}{\mu}$
$L = \dfrac{\lambda}{\mu - \lambda}$	$L = L_q + \dfrac{\lambda}{\mu}$	$L = L_q + \dfrac{\lambda}{\mu}$	L (Table 8.6)	L (Table 8.7)
$W_q = \dfrac{\lambda}{\mu(\mu - \lambda)}$	$W_q = \dfrac{\lambda}{2\mu(\mu - \lambda)}$	$W_q = \dfrac{L_q}{\lambda}$	$W_q = \dfrac{L_q}{\lambda_{eff}}$	$W_q = \dfrac{L_q}{\lambda_{eff}}$
$W = \dfrac{1}{\mu - \lambda}$	$W = W_q + \dfrac{1}{\mu}$	$W = W_q + \dfrac{1}{\mu}$	$W = W_q + \dfrac{1}{\mu}$	$W = W_q + \dfrac{1}{\mu}$
		or	or	or
		$W = \dfrac{L}{\lambda}$	$W = \dfrac{L}{\lambda_{eff}}$	$W = \dfrac{L}{\lambda_{eff}}$
$\rho = \dfrac{\lambda}{\mu}$	$\rho = \dfrac{\lambda}{\mu}$	$\rho = \dfrac{\lambda}{s\mu}$	$\rho = \dfrac{\lambda_{eff}}{\mu}$	$\rho = \dfrac{\lambda_{eff}}{\mu}$
$P_n = \left(1 - \dfrac{\lambda}{\mu}\right)\left(\dfrac{\lambda}{\mu}\right)^n$			P_0 (Table 8.4)	$\lambda_{eff} = \lambda(N - L)$
			P_c (Table 8.5) $\lambda_{eff} = \lambda(1 - P_c)$ $= \mu(1 - P_0)$	

λ = arrival rate

μ = service rate

    (*Note:* λ and μ are rates and have the same time unit.)

L_q = average number of customers in the *queue*

L = average number of customers in the *system*

W_q = average time spent waiting for service

W = average time spent in the system

ρ = utilization (percentage of time each server is busy)

P_n = the probability that *exactly* n customers are in the *system*

*Appendix C contains more complete queueing tables.

rate. For example, if we are told that the average service time is 2 minutes, then the effective rate is 30 per hour (if hour is the standard time period being used) or 1/2 per minute (if minute is the time period being used). Be sure that all rates λ and μ are expressed in terms of the same time period.

DESCRIPTIVE EXAMPLES

We begin with examples that describe the effects of service speed, number of servers, variance in service, and allocation of servers.

SPEED OF SERVICE

One way to reduce waiting time in a queueing system is to have a faster server. But what is the relative effect of having a faster server? If server speed doubles, is the waiting time cut in half? Consider the following example.

Example 8.1 Students arrive at the single duplicating machine in the university's library at a rate of 40 per hour in a memoryless fashion (that is, according to a Poisson process). The length of time that students spend duplicating papers has an exponential distribution (that is, memoryless) with a mean time of 1 minute. The library is considering replacing the current machine with a faster machine. The new machine would reduce the average duplication time to 40 seconds. Contrast the two systems.

This is an *M/M/1* queueing system: Arrivals are memoryless, service times are memoryless, there is 1 machine, the service order is FCFS (the students are polite), the calling population (set of students) is very large (infinite), and there is no limit to the number of students who can wait. For either the old machine or the new machine, the arrival rate, λ, is 40 per hour. For the current system, the service *time* is 1 minute, which means that the service *rate*, μ, is 60 per hour. For the proposed machine, the service time is 40 seconds, which means that the service rate, μ, is 90 per hour. The new machine has a service time that is 2/3 the time of the current machine. This means that the new machine can serve 3/2 the number of students per hour. For both cases, the appropriate formulas appear in Table 8.2.

CURRENT MACHINE: $\lambda = 40, \mu = 60$

(a) $\rho = \dfrac{\lambda}{\mu} = \dfrac{40}{60} = \dfrac{2}{3}$

The duplicating machine is busy 67 percent of the time and idle 33 percent of the time.

M/M/1
$\mu = 60$

(b) $L_q = \dfrac{\lambda^2}{\mu(\mu - \lambda)} = \dfrac{(40)^2}{60(60 - 40)} = \dfrac{4}{3}$ students

On the average, 1-1/3 persons are waiting to use the machine. Note that because this is an average, it is quite permissible to have a "fractional" person.

(c) $L = \dfrac{\lambda}{\mu - \lambda} = \dfrac{40}{60 - 40} = 2$ students

On average, 2 people are in the system. This average includes both the students in line and the student who is using the machine.

(d) $W_q = \dfrac{\lambda}{\mu(\mu - \lambda)} = \dfrac{40}{60(60 - 40)} = .033$ hours $= 2$ minutes

The average time spent waiting to use the machine is 2 minutes.

(e) $W = \dfrac{1}{\mu - \lambda} = \dfrac{1}{60 - 40} = \dfrac{1}{20}$ hour $= 3$ minutes

On average, the time between entering the line and completing the duplication is 3 minutes.

PROPOSED MACHINE: $\lambda = 40, \mu = 60$

(a) $\rho = \dfrac{\lambda}{\mu} = \dfrac{40}{90} = .44$

M/M/1
$\mu = 90$

The duplicating machine is now busy 44 percent of the time.

(b) $L_q = \dfrac{\lambda^2}{\mu(\mu - \lambda)} = \dfrac{(40)^2}{90(90 - 40)} = .356$ students

The average waiting line is less than 4/10 of a student. The 50-percent increase in service rate has greatly reduced the waiting line.

(c) $L = \dfrac{\lambda}{\mu - \lambda} = \dfrac{40}{90 - 40} = .8$ students

On the average, there is less than 1 person in the system.

(d) $W_q = \dfrac{\lambda}{\mu(\mu - \lambda)} = \dfrac{40}{90(90 - 40)} = .0089$ hours $= .533$ minutes
$= 32$ seconds

The average time in line is 32 seconds.

(e) $W = \dfrac{1}{\mu - \lambda} = \dfrac{1}{90 - 40} = \dfrac{1}{50}$ hour $= 1.2$ minutes

The average time spent in the system is 1.2 minutes, or 72 seconds.

The results for the two systems are summarized in the following table. Notice that we did not need to double the service rate in order to cut the waiting times and lines in half.

Teaching Suggestion 8.9: Queueing Results Not Linear. See the Instructor's Section for details.

	Current Machine	Proposed Machine
Server utilization	67%	44%
Average number in line, L_q	1.33 students	.356 students
Average number in system, L	2 students	.8 students
Average time in line, W_q	2 minutes	.533 minutes
Average time in system, W	3 minutes	1.2 minutes

INCREASING THE NUMBER OF SERVERS

A second way to improve service is to increase the number of servers. Let us consider the effects of this. The multiple-server results (*M/M/s* model) are in Appendix C1, a portion of which is reproduced in Table 8.3.

> **Example 8.2**   A second option the university has is to buy another duplicating machine that is exactly the same as the current machine. Contrast the system characteristics of the two-machine system with that of the current one-machine system.

M/M/2

(a) $\rho = \dfrac{\lambda}{s\mu} = \dfrac{40}{2 \times 60} = \dfrac{1}{3}$

Each machine is busy, on average, 33 percent of the time.

(b) Table 8.3 contains the average number of customers waiting in line, L_q, for different numbers of servers and different values of λ/μ. Since $\lambda = 40$ and $\mu = 60$, $\lambda/\mu = 2/3$. The nearest entry is for $\lambda/\mu = .66$. Examining column 2 (there are two servers), we find that $L_q = .081$ students.

(c) $L = L_q + \dfrac{\lambda}{\mu} = .081 + .667$

      $= .748$ students

(d) $W_q = L_q/\lambda = .081/40 = .002$ hours $= .1215$ minutes

      $= 7.3$ seconds

(e) $W = W_q + \dfrac{1}{\mu} = .002 + \dfrac{1}{60} = .0187$ hours $= 1.12$ minutes

      $= 67.3$ seconds

■⌋

MORE CONSISTENT SERVERS

It is obvious that adding servers or increasing the speed of the servers will reduce the waiting time in a queueing system. There is a less obvious way to reduce the waiting time: improve the consistency of the server. We demonstrate this now.

> **Example 8.3**   The Walt Whitman Bridge is a toll bridge that crosses the Delaware River. Currently, there are 7 toll booths staffed by employees. The Delaware River Port Authority is considering replacing the employees with machines. Many factors must be considered, because the employees are unionized. However, one of the port authority's concerns is the effect that replacing the employees with machines will have on the times that drivers spend in the system. Customers arrive to any one toll booth at a rate of 10 per minute. In the exact change lanes with employees, the service time is essentially constant at 5 seconds for each driver. With machines, the average service time would still be 5 seconds, but it would be exponential rather than constant, because it takes time for the coins to rattle around in the machine. Contrast the two systems for a single lane.

TABLE 8.3 System with multiple servers:
average number of customers in line (L_q)

λ/μ	Number of Servers				
	1	2	3	4	5
.020	.000				
.040	.002				
.060	.004				
.080	.007				
.100	.011				
.120	.016				
.140	.023	.001			
.160	.030	.001			
.180	.040	.001			
.200	.050	.002			
.220	.062	.003			
.240	.076	.004			
.260	.091	.004			
.280	.109	.006			
.300	.129	.007			
.320	.151	.008	.001		
.340	.175	.010	.001		
.360	.203	.012	.001		
.380	.233	.014	.001		
.400	.267	.017	.001		
.420	.304	.019	.002		
.440	.346	.022	.002		
.460	.392	.026	.002		
.480	.443	.029	.003		
.500	.500	.033	.003		
.520	.563	.038	.004		
.540	.634	.042	.004		
.560	.713	.048	.005		
.580	.801	.053	.005	.001	
.600	.900	.059	.006	.001	
.620	1.012	.066	.007	.001	
.640	1.138	.073	.008	.001	
.660	1.281	.081	.009	.001	
.680	1.445	.089	.010	.001	
.700	1.633	.098	.011	.001	
.720	1.851	.107	.013	.001	
.740	2.106	.117	.014	.002	
.760	2.407	.128	.015	.002	
.780	2.765	.140	.017	.002	
.800	3.200	.152	.019	.002	
.820	3.736	.166	.021	.003	
.840	4.410	.180	.023	.003	
.860	5.283	.195	.025	.003	
.880	6.453	.211	.027	.004	
.900	8.100	.229	.030	.004	.001
.920	10.580	.247	.033	.005	.001
.940	14.727	.267	.036	.005	.001
.960	23.040	.287	.039	.006	.001
.980	48.020	.310	.042	.006	.001
1.000	∞	.333	.045	.007	.001

EMPLOYEE SYSTEM: The current system is an *M/D/1* system, because service times are constant or deterministic. The formulas for the *M/D/1* system appear in Table 8.2.

(a) $\rho = \dfrac{\lambda}{\mu} = \dfrac{10}{12} = .83$

The toll collector is busy 83 percent of the time.

(b) $L_q = \dfrac{\lambda^2}{2\mu(\mu - \lambda)} = \dfrac{100}{2(12)(12 - 10)} = \dfrac{100}{48} = 2.08$ drivers

The average number of drivers waiting to pay the toll is 2.08.

M/D/1

(c) $L = L_q + \dfrac{\lambda}{\mu} = 2.08 + .83 = 2.91$ drivers

The average number of drivers at any one toll booth is 2.91.

(d) $W_q = \dfrac{\lambda}{2\mu(\mu - \lambda)} = \dfrac{10}{2(12)(12 - 10)} = \dfrac{10}{48} = .208$ minutes
$= 12.5$ seconds

The average time drivers spend waiting is 12.5 seconds.

(e) W = waiting time + service time = 12.5 seconds + 5 seconds
$= 17.5$ seconds

AUTOMATED SYSTEM: The proposed system is an *M/M/1* system. Again, the formulas are from Table 8.2.

(a) $\rho = \dfrac{\lambda}{\mu} = \dfrac{10}{12} = .83$

The utilization of the new system is the same as that of the old system.

(b) $L_q = \dfrac{\lambda^2}{\mu(\mu - \lambda)} = \dfrac{100}{12(12 - 10)} = \dfrac{100}{24} = 4.16$ drivers

Twice as many drivers are in line under the new, automated system.

M/M/1

(c) $L = L_q + \dfrac{\lambda}{\mu} = 5$ drivers

On average, 5 customers are in the system, which is 67-percent more customers than the current system allows.

(d) $W_q = \dfrac{\lambda}{\mu(\mu - \lambda)} = \dfrac{10}{12(12 - 10)} = \dfrac{10}{24} = .417$ minutes = 25 seconds

The waiting time will double with the new system.

Teaching Suggestion 8.10:
Total Quality Management
(TQM). See the Instructor's
Section for details.

(e) $W = W_q + \dfrac{1}{\mu} = 30$ seconds

The time in the system will rise by 67 percent.   ◼⌐

reduce the variance

One conclusion can be drawn from this example. One method for reducing the average waiting time and queue length is to reduce the variance in the service operation. If all other things are equal, constant service time cuts both waiting time and the **reduce waiting time** waiting line in half when compared with exponential service times.

There is one additional property of queueing systems that we wish to demonstrate at this point.

Example 8.4 Consider again the data on the university duplicating machine presented in Examples 8.1 and 8.2. As opposed to doubling the number of machines, as in Example 8.2, the university can replace the old machine with a new one that is twice as fast. Examine this option, and contrast it with the option in Example 8.2.

This model is, again, the *M/M/1* model. The duplicating time of 30 seconds means that the service rate, μ, is 120 per hour.

(a) $\rho = \dfrac{\lambda}{\mu} = \dfrac{40}{120} = \dfrac{1}{3}$

In this example and in Example 8.2, the system service rate is the same.

(b) $L_q = \dfrac{\lambda^2}{\mu(\mu - \lambda)} = \dfrac{40^2}{120(120 - 40)} = \dfrac{1}{6} = .167$ students

The average number of customers waiting in line is twice as large as the average **M/M/1** number (.081) found in Example 8.2. **$\mu = 120$**

(c) $L = \dfrac{\lambda}{\mu - \lambda} = \dfrac{40}{120 - 40} = \dfrac{1}{2}$ students

On the average, the number of students in the system is 1/2, rather than the 3/4 (.748) found in Example 8.2.

(d) $W_q = \dfrac{\lambda}{\mu(\mu - \lambda)} = \dfrac{40}{120(120 - 40)} = \dfrac{1}{240}$ hour $= \dfrac{1}{4}$ minutes $= 15$ seconds

(e) $W = \dfrac{1}{\mu - \lambda} = \dfrac{1}{120 - 40} = \dfrac{1}{80}$ hour $= \dfrac{3}{4}$ minutes $= 45$ seconds

Thus, average time spent in the system is 15 seconds waiting plus 30 seconds service. The 45 seconds calculated here is less than the 67.3 seconds found in Example 8.2. ◼

Notice that, even though each system has an overall service rate of 120 per hour, the two systems have different operating characteristics. However, the most important measure is that the single server with rate 120 gets customers in and out of the system faster than does two servers with individual rates of 60. This will always be true: If the **a general principle** overall service rate ($s\mu$) is fixed, then the fewer the number of servers needed to achieve this rate, the less time the customers will spend in the system!

We now consider a different type of system—one where the queue is limited to a finite size.

Example 8.5 When too many students are waiting in line, there is a great deal of noise. For this reason, the head librarian is considering adopting a rule that states that no more than 5 customers may be in the system at one time. Hence, if 1 person is

TABLE 8.4 Limited queue size model: probability system is empty (P_0)

λ/μ	Maximum System Capacity (C)									
	1	2	3	4	5	6	7	8	9	10
.1	.909	.901	.900	.900	.900	.900	.900	.900	.900	.900
.2	.833	.806	.801	.800	.800	.800	.800	.800	.800	.800
.3	.769	.719	.706	.702	.701	.700	.700	.700	.700	.700
.4	.714	.641	.616	.606	.602	.601	.600	.600	.600	.600
.5	.667	.571	.533	.516	.508	.504	.502	.501	.500	.500
.6	.625	.510	.459	.434	.420	.412	.407	.404	.402	.401
.7	.588	.457	.395	.361	.340	.327	.318	.313	.309	.306
.8	.556	.410	.339	.297	.271	.253	.240	.231	.224	.219
.9	.526	.369	.291	.244	.213	.192	.176	.163	.154	.146

M/M/1 with a finite queue

duplicating (on the original 60-second machine) and 4 persons are waiting to use the machine, then an arrival (another student) would not be permitted to enter. How many customers would be lost due to the proposed rule?

This represents the *M/M/1* queueing system with a finite queue. The first consideration is how often the system is full. Appendixes C2 and C3 contain the probabilities that a system is empty or full. Portions of these tables are reproduced in Table 8.4 (giving the probability that the system is empty) and Table 8.5 (giving the probability that it is full).

From Table 8.5, we calculate that, with a limit of 5 customers and $\lambda/\mu = .67$, the probability the system is full is .049 (we have interpolated between .033 and .057). Thus, 4.9 percent of the time, a customer will arrive and not enter the system. Business is lost at a rate of $.049\lambda = .049 \times 40 = 1.96$ customers per hour. Alternatively, the effective arrival rate is given by

$$\lambda_{eff} = \lambda P(\text{system not full})$$
$$= \lambda \times [1 - P(\text{system full})]$$
$$= \lambda \times (1 - P_5)$$
$$= 40 \times (1 - .049)$$
$$= 38.04 \text{ customers per hour.}$$

From Table 8.4, we interpolate that the probability the system is empty is .366. Now, $(1 - P_0)$, or .634, is the percentage of time the machine is busy. Hence, the effective service rate is given by

$$\mu_{eff} = \mu(1 - P_0) = 60 \times .634 = 38.04 \text{ customers per hour,}$$

which also is the effective arrival rate. Again, in all queueing systems the effective arrival rate and the effective service rate must be equal, or the system is not in balance. ■

In this example we have only asked for the rate at which customers are lost. In general, we might be interested in the usual system parameters (L, L_q, W, and W_q). To

TABLE 8.5 Limited queue size model: probability system is full (P_c)

λ/μ	Maximum System Capacity (C)									
	1	2	3	4	5	6	7	8	9	10
.1	.091	.009	.000	.000	.000	.000	.000	.000	.000	.000
.2	.167	.032	.006	.001	.000	.000	.000	.000	.000	.000
.3	.231	.065	.019	.006	.002	.000	.000	.000	.000	.000
.4	.286	.103	.039	.016	.006	.002	.001	.000	.000	.000
.5	.333	.143	.067	.032	.016	.009	.004	.002	.001	.000
.6	.375	.184	.099	.056	.033	.019	.011	.007	.004	.002
.7	.412	.224	.135	.087	.057	.038	.026	.018	.012	.009
.8	.444	.262	.173	.122	.089	.066	.050	.039	.030	.023
.9	.474	.299	.212	.160	.126	.102	.084	.070	.059	.050

make the computations easier, we present the computations for the average number of customers in the system (L) as a function of the system size and λ/μ in Appendix C4, a portion of which is reproduced in Table 8.6. The other three parameters are determined by L and the four fundamental equations.

EXAMPLES WITH COSTS

The previous examples have all been descriptive. If a manager wishes to choose one of many options, then he or she simply lists the queueing characteristics and chooses the most appealing one. An alternative approach is incorporating costs into the models and then finding the least costly option. Essentially, two types of costs are incurred in queueing systems. The first is the cost of providing service, which is relatively easy to assess. It may be the wages paid if an extra worker is hired or the cost of building extra parking spaces or the cost of replacing a slow elevator with a faster model. The second

TABLE 8.6 Limited queue size model: average number of customers in the system (L)

λ/μ	Maximum System Capacity (C)									
	1	2	3	4	5	6	7	8	9	10
.1	.091	.108	.111	.111	.111	.111	.111	.111	.111	.111
.2	.167	.226	.244	.248	.250	.250	.250	.250	.250	.250
.3	.231	.345	.396	.416	.424	.427	.428	.428	.429	.429
.4	.286	.462	.562	.615	.642	.655	.661	.664	.666	.666
.5	.333	.571	.733	.839	.905	.945	.969	.982	.990	.995
.6	.375	.673	.904	1.078	1.206	1.298	1.363	1.408	1.439	1.460
.7	.412	.767	1.069	1.323	1.533	1.705	1.844	1.955	2.043	2.111
.8	.444	.852	1.225	1.563	1.868	2.142	2.387	2.605	2.797	2.966
.9	.474	.930	1.369	1.790	2.195	2.582	2.953	3.308	3.647	3.969

type of cost is more difficult to determine. It is the cost of keeping customers waiting and must include lost profit for customers who balk or renege, lost good will for customers who may never return, and/or lost productivity if the customers are employees who would be performing other tasks if they were not standing in line. These waiting costs cannot be measured exactly, but, in some instances, they may be measured with some degree of accuracy.

In order to demonstrate this cost concept, our next example will use a queue with a finite source population. To make the computations easy, we present the average number of customers in the system as a function of the population size, N, and λ/μ in Appendix C5, a portion of which is reproduced in Table 8.7. Again, the other three parameters are determined by L, and the four fundamental equations.

WAITING COSTS

Example 8.6 Warranty Unlimited (WU) repairs home appliances that are still under the manufacturer's warranty. WU has 8 repairpersons. Each repairperson works on 1 appliance at a time and is paid $10 per hour. When the repairperson needs a part, he or she goes to the parts counter, waits until his or her turn, and then requests the part. Each repairperson tends to arrive at the parts counter at a rate of 2 times per hour (in a Poisson process). The manager of WU has heard complaints from the repairpersons about the amount of time they spend waiting for parts and is considering replacing the current partsperson with a more experienced (and expensive) partsperson. The current wage for the partsperson is $4 an hour, and the current average service time is 5 minutes per request (distributed exponentially). The replacement would be paid $7 per hour and would take 4 minutes per request (distributed exponentially). Should the manager make the change?

_M/M/I_ queue with a finite population

Teaching Suggestion 8.11: Alternate Approach. See the Instructor's Section for details.

Either case requires the analysis of an $M/M/1$ system with a finite population. In either case, the individual arrival rate, λ, is 2. The current partsperson has $\mu = 12$, while the new one would have $\mu = 15$. In both cases, the interest is the hourly cost of the idle time for the repairpersons. In order to find the number in the system for the $M/M/1$ model with a finite population we use Table 8.7. To use the table, we need to know both λ/μ and the population size. In the current system, $\rho = 2/12 = .167$ and the population is 8. From Table 8.7 we find that $L = 2.60$ (row .16, column 8). In other words, on average, 2.60 persons are at the parts window rather than repairing an appliance. We may now compute the total cost per hour.

$$\begin{array}{ll} 2.60 \times \$10/\text{hr.} & \text{for the repairpersons} \\ +\quad\ \underline{\$\ 4/\text{hr.}} & \text{for the partsperson} \\ \$30.00/\text{hour} & \end{array}$$

For the proposed partsperson ($\lambda/\mu = 2/15$) the table yields (row .14, column 8)

$$L = 2.19.$$

The total cost then is

$$\begin{array}{ll} 2.19 \times \$10/\text{hr.} & \text{for the repairpersons} \\ +\quad\ \underline{\$\ 7/\text{hr.}} & \text{for the partsperson} \end{array}$$

or $28.90/hr. The difference is $1.10.

TABLE 8.7 *M/M/1* queue with a finite source population: expected number in the system (L)

λ/μ	Population Size, N									
	1	2	3	4	5	6	7	8	9	10
.02	.02	.04	.06	.08	.11	.13	.15	.18	.21	.24
.04	.04	.08	.12	.17	.22	.28	.34	.41	.48	.56
.06	.06	.12	.19	.27	.35	.45	.56	.68	.83	.99
.08	.07	.16	.25	.36	.49	.64	.81	1.01	1.25	1.52
.10	.09	.20	.32	.47	.64	.85	1.09	1.38	1.73	2.15
.12	.11	.23	.39	.57	.79	1.06	1.39	1.78	2.25	2.81
.14	.12	.27	.45	.68	.95	1.29	1.70	2.19	2.78	3.46
.16	.14	.31	.52	.78	1.11	1.51	2.01	2.60	3.29	4.07
.18	.15	.34	.58	.89	1.27	1.74	2.31	2.99	3.76	4.61
.20	.17	.38	.65	.99	1.42	1.96	2.60	3.35	4.19	5.09
.22	.18	.41	.71	1.09	1.58	2.17	2.88	3.68	4.57	5.50
.24	.19	.45	.77	1.19	1.72	2.37	3.13	3.98	4.90	5.86
.26	.21	.48	.83	1.29	1.87	2.56	3.37	4.25	5.20	6.17
.28	.22	.51	.89	1.38	2.00	2.74	3.58	4.50	5.45	6.44
.30	.23	.54	.95	1.48	2.13	2.91	3.78	4.71	5.68	6.67
.32	.24	.57	1.00	1.56	2.25	3.06	3.96	4.91	5.89	6.88
.34	.25	.60	1.06	1.65	2.37	3.20	4.12	5.08	6.07	7.06
.36	.26	.63	1.11	1.73	2.48	3.34	4.27	5.24	6.23	7.22
.38	.28	.65	1.16	1.80	2.58	3.46	4.40	5.38	6.37	7.37
.40	.29	.68	1.21	1.87	2.67	3.57	4.52	5.51	6.50	7.50
.42	.30	.70	1.25	1.94	2.76	3.68	4.64	5.62	6.62	7.62
.44	.31	.73	1.30	2.01	2.85	3.77	4.74	5.73	6.73	7.73
.46	.32	.75	1.34	2.07	2.93	3.86	4.84	5.83	6.83	7.83
.48	.32	.78	1.38	2.13	3.00	3.95	4.93	5.92	6.92	7.92
.50	.33	.80	1.42	2.19	3.07	4.02	5.01	6.00	7.00	8.00
.52	.34	.82	1.46	2.24	3.14	4.10	5.08	6.08	7.08	8.08
.54	.35	.84	1.50	2.30	3.20	4.16	5.15	6.15	7.15	8.15
.56	.36	.86	1.53	2.35	3.26	4.23	5.22	6.22	7.21	8.21
.58	.37	.88	1.57	2.39	3.32	4.29	5.28	6.28	7.28	8.28
.60	.38	.90	1.60	2.44	3.37	4.34	5.34	6.33	7.33	8.33
.62	.38	.92	1.63	2.48	3.42	4.39	5.39	6.39	7.39	8.39
.64	.39	.94	1.66	2.52	3.46	4.44	5.44	6.44	7.44	8.44
.66	.40	.96	1.69	2.56	3.51	4.49	5.49	6.49	7.48	8.48
.68	.40	.98	1.72	2.60	3.55	4.53	5.53	6.53	7.53	8.53
.70	.41	.99	1.75	2.63	3.59	4.58	5.57	6.57	7.57	8.57
.72	.42	1.01	1.77	2.67	3.63	4.61	5.61	6.61	7.61	8.61
.74	.43	1.03	1.80	2.70	3.66	4.65	5.65	6.65	7.65	8.65
.76	.43	1.04	1.82	2.73	3.70	4.69	5.68	6.68	7.68	8.68
.78	.44	1.06	1.85	2.76	3.73	4.72	5.72	6.72	7.72	8.72
.80	.44	1.07	1.87	2.79	3.76	4.75	5.75	6.75	7.75	8.75
.82	.45	1.09	1.89	2.81	3.79	4.78	5.78	6.78	7.78	8.78
.84	.46	1.10	1.91	2.84	3.82	4.81	5.81	6.81	7.81	8.81
.86	.46	1.11	1.94	2.87	3.84	4.84	5.84	6.84	7.84	8.84
.88	.47	1.13	1.96	2.89	3.87	4.86	5.86	6.86	7.86	8.86
.90	.47	1.14	1.97	2.91	3.89	4.89	5.89	6.89	7.89	8.89
.92	.48	1.15	1.99	2.93	3.92	4.91	5.91	6.91	7.91	8.91
.94	.48	1.17	2.01	2.96	3.94	4.94	5.94	6.94	7.94	8.94
.96	.49	1.18	2.03	2.98	3.96	4.96	5.96	6.96	7.96	8.96
.98	.49	1.19	2.05	3.00	3.98	4.98	5.98	6.98	7.98	8.98
1.00	.50	1.20	2.06	3.02	4.00	5.00	6.00	7.00	8.00	9.00

Since the cost in this example is the cost per hour of the idle repair people, it would seem logical that W be the parameter of interest, rather than L. This would give us the expected waiting time for each option, from which the cost comparison could be made. Of course, this approach is equally valid, but by finding L—the average number of idle repair people—the calculations are simplified. ∎

Example 8.7   For the current WU repair system, find the overall rate at which the repairpersons arrive at the parts counter.

While each repairperson arrives 10 times per hour on the average, because of waiting at the parts desk, each repairperson is not working for the full hour. Therefore, the overall arrival rate is not 8 repairpersons times 10 arrivals per hour. Instead, as we see in Table 8.2, the effective arrival rate is found by the formula

$$\lambda_{eff} = \lambda(N - L),$$

where N is the population size and L is the average number in the queueing system as found from Table 8.7. For this problem, then, we have the following.

$$\lambda_{eff} = 2(8 - 2.60)$$

$$\lambda_{eff} = 10.8 \text{ customers per hour}$$

∎

LOST BUSINESS COST

A second important cost application would be to assess the cost of lost business due to a limited system size. For this reason, consider again the system presented in Examples 8.1, 8.2, and 8.4. Assume the system size is limited by the fire code.

Example 8.8   The library manager will lose some money due to the 5-person limit and is considering changing the limit from 5 to 6. The library is open daily from 11 A.M. to 9 P.M., and the profit per student averages \$1.20. What is the difference in profits between the limits of 5 and 6 students?

The item of interest is the additional number of customers that would be served if the limit were 6 rather than 5. In order to determine this, it is necessary to find the effective service rate for the $M/M/1$ finite system with a limit of 6 customers. As before, $\mu_{eff} = \mu(1 - P_0)$, where P_0 is found in Table 8.4. From the table, we interpolate that $P_0 = .354$. The formula for effective service rate yields

$$\mu_{eff} = 60(1 - .354) = 60(.646) = 38.76,$$

which means that the increase in service would be

$$\mu_{eff}^{(6)} - \mu_{eff}^{(5)} = 38.76 - 38.08 \quad \text{(from Example 8.5)}$$

$$= .68 \text{ customers/hour.}$$

Customers per week would be

$$.68(10 \text{ hours/day} \times 7 \text{ days/week}) = 47.6 \text{ customers/week,}$$

and weekly lost profits would be

$$47.6 \times \$1.20/\text{customer} = \$57.12/\text{week.}$$

∎

Note that Example 8.8 assumes that the arrival pattern at the library is constant throughout the day and throughout the week. In practice, each day of the week would be broken down into periods for which this constant arrival pattern assumption would hold.

THE TYPICAL QUEUEING STUDY

Given the picture of the general queueing model in Figure 8.6, it is now possible to outline a framework of the steps necessary for queueing analysis. This analysis appears in Figure 8.7.

Step 1. Analyze the behavior of the queueing system. Start by determining whether or not the queueing system fits the general models developed earlier in the chapter. If it does, then continue the analysis using these models. If not, there are several options.

> **system model**

First, you might decide that an approximation is sufficient. For example, a system that has two servers with a rate of 30/hour each might be approximated by a model that has one server with a rate of 60/hour. The results might not be exact, but they would be easy to find and, in some cases, might be reasonably close.

Second, you should keep in mind that we have presented formulas for only a small number of the queueing models that have been analyzed. Therefore, it is possible—in fact, it is likely—that formulas for the system at hand appear in the literature. A review of the material listed in this chapter's references might lead to the appropriate model and results.

Finally, if all else fails, the system can be simulated. Although simulation is an excellent tool for the analysis of complex systems for which analytical results (formulas) are not available, we do not cover it here because it cannot be adequately covered in a text devoted to operations management.

Step 2. Identify the appropriate system parameters. Regardless of the results of step 1, it is necessary to input to the queueing model or simulation the parameters we identified earlier. Some will, in all likelihood, be obvious, such as the population size, system size, queue discipline, and number of servers. Others must be determined by observation and sampling.

> **system parameters**

In particular, the parameters of arrival and service distributions must be determined. In general, one must observe the interarrival times and the service times; compute the mean of each, yielding $1/\lambda$ and $1/\mu$; and determine whether or not these distributions are exponential. In order to determine this, it is useful to plot the histogram of interarrival and/or service times and see if this plot resembles the exponential distribution shown in Figure 8.2. (You can also test the fit of the data to an exponential distribution using a statistical test, such as the χ^2/goodness of fit test or the Kolmogorov-Smirnov goodness of fit test.) If the service times are not exponential, this does not pose much of a problem, because results for the $M/G/1$ queue (general service times) are readily available. If the interarrival times do not appear to have an exponential distribution, however, the analysis is back at step 1, because the system does not fit the models.

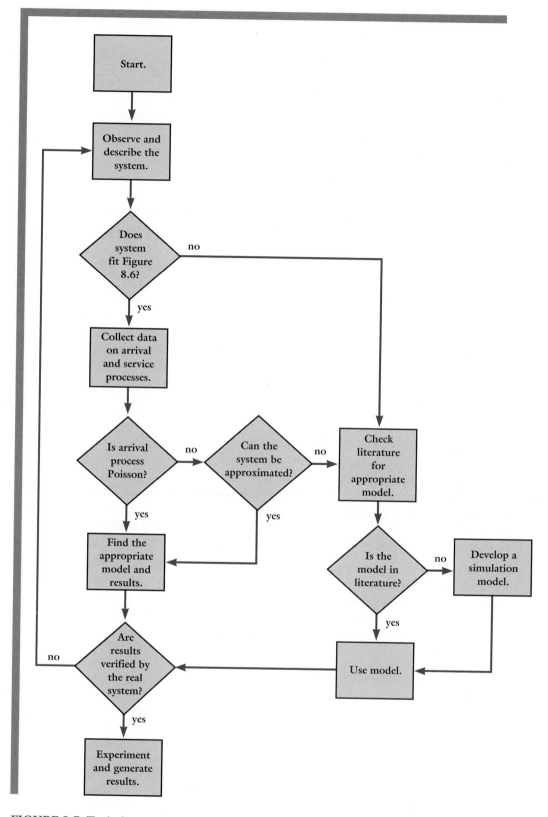

FIGURE 8.7 Typical queueing study

Step 3. Verify the model. At this point, one can determine the results for the appropriate model by using the λ, μ, and other parameters found in step 2. If the model is appropriate, then the output of the model (L, L_q, W, W_q, and ρ, for example) should be very close to the real system values of the same statistics. That is, if the model results in $W = 10$ minutes, our observation of customers waiting should confirm that the actual waiting time averages approximately 10 minutes.

test model

Step 4. Experiment with the model. The previous step should have convinced us that the model is appropriate. At this point, we can experiment with the model by changing the parameters and seeing how the results are affected by the change. Changing the arrival rate, service rate, numbers of servers, or other parameters is merely making a change in an equation, table entry, or input to a computer program, such as the one that accompanies this book.

system design analysis

SUMMARY

Waiting lines pervade our lives and, for the most part, can be improved. However, improvement always involves an explicit or implicit cost trade-off: Reduced waiting costs will necessitate increased service costs. The key parameters in queueing systems are the *calling population*, the *arrival process*, which includes the *arrival rate;* the *queue structure*, which takes into account the number of waiting lines; and the *queue discipline*. Additional parameters are the *service process*, which includes the *service time distribution*, and the *number of servers*, or *channels*.

By using these parameters as input to the queueing model, it is possible to determine such characteristics as the server *utilization, average queue length, average system size, average time spent in line*, and *average time spent in the system*.

Other models that have been mentioned, but not explicitly covered in this chapter, include *multiple service phase models*, models with *batch arrivals* or *batch services*, and *prescriptive* queueing *control* models, which are different from the *descriptive* models found here.

KEY TERMS

queueing

calling, or source, population

arrival process

arrival rate

Poisson arrival process

balking

reneging

phase

queues in series

queue discipline

first come, first served

last come, first served

service in random order

channels

queues with feedback

round robin queues

effective arrival rate

effective service rate

steady state

1. Top Dog Hot Dogs is a small fast-food restaurant that serves hot dogs and nothing else. There is only one line for service. During lunchtime, customer arrivals to this line form a Poisson process with a rate of 3 customers per minute. The time to be served a hot dog is exponentially distributed and averages 15 seconds. Use this information about Top Dog's service to find the following.

(a) the average time a customer is in line
(b) the average time a customer is in the system
(c) the average number of customers in line
(d) the average number of customers in the system
(e) the percentage of time that the server is idle

Solution

This is an *M/M/1* queue, and we have formulas for each of the five factors. To use the formulas, we must know the arrival rate and the service rate. The arrival rate, λ, is given explicitly as 3 customers/minute. The service time is given as 15 seconds, which means that the service rate, μ, is given as $60/15 = 4$.

(a) $W_q = \dfrac{\lambda}{\mu(\mu - \lambda)} = \dfrac{3}{4(4 - 3)} = \dfrac{3}{4}$ minutes = 45 seconds

The average time a customer spends waiting before being served is 45 seconds.

(b) $W = \dfrac{1}{(\mu - \lambda)} = \dfrac{1}{(4 - 3)} = \dfrac{1}{1}$ minutes

On average, customers are in the system for 1 minute. Notice that each customer averages 45 seconds waiting plus 15 seconds service, for a total of $45 + 15 = 60$ seconds, or 1 minute, in the system.

(c) $L_q = \dfrac{\lambda^2}{\mu(\mu - \lambda)} = \dfrac{3^2}{4(4 - 3)} = \dfrac{9}{4} = 2.25$ customers

On average, there are 2.25 customers waiting in line. (This does not include the person who might be being served.)

(d) $L = \dfrac{\lambda}{(\mu - \lambda)} = \dfrac{3}{4 - 3} = 3$ customers

The average number of customers in the system, including the customer being served, is 3.

(e) $\rho = \dfrac{\lambda}{\mu} = \dfrac{3}{4} = 75\%$

Therefore, the server is not utilized (is idle) for 25 percent of the time.

Using AB:POM to Solve This Problem

When beginning the waiting line module, you must first decide which model to use. After choosing the model, the input data is standard queueing input. Screen 8.1 shows the data for Solved Problem 1. The arrival rate is 4, the service rate is 3, and there is 1 server. The output is displayed on the right.

Screen 8.1 illustrates that pressing the **F1** key multiplies the times by 60. Obviously, this is useful for converting hours to minutes or minutes to seconds.

The **F2** key can be used to find the probability that a certain number of persons will be in the system, as illustrated in Screen 8.2. The first probability column is the probability of having *exactly* n persons in the system, the second column is the probability of having n or fewer persons in the system, and the last column is the probability of having *strictly* more than n persons in the system.

```
 ══ Data file:wgsp1 ══════════ Waiting Line Models ═══════════ Solution ═
    M/M/1

 ═══════════════════════ Chapter 8, Solved Problem 1 ═══════════════════
   arrival rate(lambda)      3.00    Average server utilization      0.7500

   service rate(mu)          4.00    Average number in the queue(Lq) 2.2500

   number of servers            1    Average number in the system(L) 3.0000

                                     Average time in the queue(Wq)   0.7500

                                     Average time in the system(W)   1.0000




 F1=Multiply wait and sys times by 60  F2=Display Probabilities  F9=Print    Esc
 Press <Esc> key to edit data or highlighted key or function key for options
```

SCREEN 8.1

```
┌─ Data file:wgsp1 ══════════ Waiting Line Models ═══════════ Solution ─┐
│  M/M/1                                                                  │
├──────────────────── Chapter 8, Solved Problem 1 ══════════════════════┤
│                              Number in    Probability   Cumulative      Decum    │
│                              system, k      P(n=k)       P(n≤k)        P(n>k)   │
│  arrival rate(lambda)   3.00      0          .2500       0.2500        0.7500   │
│                                   1          .1875       0.4375        0.5625   │
│  service rate(mu)       4.00      2          .1406       0.5781        0.4219   │
│                                   3          .1055       0.6836        0.3164   │
│  number of servers       1        4          .0791       0.7627        0.2373   │
│                                   5          .0593       0.8220        0.1780   │
│                                   6          .0445       0.8665        0.1335   │
│                                   7          .0334       0.8999        0.1001   │
│                                   8          .0250       0.9249        0.0751   │
│                                   9          .0188       0.9437        0.0563   │
│                                  10          .0141       0.9578        0.0422   │
│                                  11          .0106       0.9683        0.0317   │
│                                  12          .0079       0.9762        0.0238   │
│                                  13          .0059       0.9822        0.0178   │
│                                  14          .0045       0.9866        0.0134   │
│                                  15          .0033       0.9900        0.0100   │
│                                                              F9= Print   Esc    │
└──────────────────────────────────────────────────────────────────────┘
 Press <Esc> key to edit data or highlighted key or function key for options
```

SCREEN 8.2

2. Consider the data presented in Solved Problem 1. How would the five factors be affected if an additional server were added?

Solution

We solve the multiple-server problem in a somewhat different fashion. Our starting point for the solution is the determination, through the table listing of L (see Table 8.3), of the average number of customers in the queue. In order to use the table, we need to know the utilization and the number of servers. The ratio is $3/4 = .75$, and the number of servers is 2. The value interpolated from the table (row .76 rather than .75) is .123. (We already have computed the one-server case and found a value of 2.25. Notice that 2.25 agrees with the table—see rows .74 and .76—for the single-server case.) Next, we must use our general-purpose queueing formulas to answer parts (a) through (d).

(a) $W_q = L_q/\lambda = .123/3 = .041$ minutes
   The average time spent waiting is .041 minutes, or 2.46 seconds.
(b) $W = W_q + 1/\mu = .041 + .25 = .291$ minutes $= 17.46$ seconds
(c) $L_q = .123$ customers
(d) $L = L_q + \lambda/\mu = .123 + .75 = .873$ customers
(e) Utilization $= \lambda/s\mu = 3/8$

Therefore, each server is idle 5/8 of the time, on average.

Using AB:POM to Solve This Problem

Results for the multiple-server model are found much more easily by using the software rather than the tables in the book. Screen 8.3 presents the results for the two-server system.

```
╔═══════════════════════════════════════════════════════════════════════════╗
║ ═ Data file:wgsp2 ════════════ Waiting Line Models ═══════════ Solution ═  ║
║    M/M/s                                                                    ║
║    ┌──────────────────────── Chapter 8, Solved Problem 2 ═══════════════┐   ║
║    │  arrival rate(lambda)      3.00    Average server utilization   0.3750 │
║    │                                                                   │   ║
║    │  service rate(mu)          4.00    Average number in the queue(Lq) .1227273 │
║    │                                                                   │   ║
║    │  number of servers          2      Average number in the system(L) .8727273 │
║    │                                                                   │   ║
║    │                                    Average time in the queue(Wq)  0.040909 │
║    │                                                                   │   ║
║    │                                    Average time in the system(W)  .2909091 │
║    │                                                                   │   ║
║    └───────────────────────────────────────────────────────────────────┘   ║
║  F1=Multiply wait and sys times by 60  F2=Display Probabilities  F9=Print   Esc ║
║  Press <Esc> key to edit data or highlighted key or function key for options ║
╚═══════════════════════════════════════════════════════════════════════════╝
```

──────── SCREEN 8.3 ────────

3. Suppose that the restaurant's servers are paid $4 per hour and that Top Dog values its customers' time spent in the system at $10 per hour. What are the system costs for (a) one server and (b) two servers?

Solution

The hourly cost consists of the wage rate plus the (average) number of customers in the system multiplied by the waiting cost.

(a) The system cost for one person is

$$\$4 + (3 \times \$10) = \$34.00/\text{hour}.$$

(b) The system cost for two servers is

$$(2 \times \$4) + (.873 \times \$10) = \$16.73/\text{hour}.$$

Using AB:POM to Solve This Problem

Screen 8.4 illustrates Solved Problem 3. This problem is a cost model. The extra inputs are the labor cost, the waiting cost, and a toggle on whether to charge the waiting cost against the entire time a customer is in the system or only against the waiting time.

The two-server model can be computed simply by changing the number of servers.

```
┌──────────────────────────────────────────────────────────────────────────┐
│ ┌─ Data file:wgsp3 ══════════ Waiting Line Models ══════════ Solution ═┐   │
│ │  M/M/s with costs                                                    │   │
│ └──────────────────────────────────────────────────────────────────────┘  │
│ ┌──────────────────── Chapter 8, Solved Problem 3 ═════════════════════┐   │
│ │  arrival rate(lambda)    3.00      Average server utilization    0.7500  │
│ │                                                                       │   │
│ │  service rate(mu)        4.00      Average number in the queue(Lq)   2.2500 │
│ │                                                                       │   │
│ │  number of servers          1      Average number in the system(L)  3.0000 │
│ │                                                                       │   │
│ │  Labor cost $/time       4.00      Average time in the queue(Wq)    0.7500 │
│ │                                                                       │   │
│ │  Waiting cost $/time    10.00      Average time in the system(W)    1.0000 │
│ │                                                                       │   │
│ │  Charge against     system time    Average cost                    34.0000 │
│ │                                                                       │   │
│ └──────────────────────────────────────────────────────────────────────┘  │
│  F1=Multiply wait and sys times by 60  F2=Display Probabilities  F9=Print   Esc │
│  Press <Esc> key to edit data or highlighted key or function key for options │
└──────────────────────────────────────────────────────────────────────────┘
```

──────────── SCREEN 8.4 ────────────

QUESTIONS

1. List the six queueing system parameters.

2. Distinguish between the arrival rate and the effective arrival rate.

3. Many different jobs come into a business, and sometimes the jobs get backed up. Compare this situation with the waiting line systems studied in this chapter. What are the similarities and differences? What are the implications for scheduling the jobs?

4. Most banks have changed from having a line in front of each teller to having one line feeding all of the tellers. Is this better? If so, why?

5. A bulldozer loads a fleet of four trucks that dump the material and return for more. Describe the waiting line system. How could its capacity be increased?

6. Is it good or bad to operate a supermarket bakery system on a strict first come, first serve basis? Why?

7. What is the effect of having an express lane in a supermarket?

8. Cite an example where a manager actually *wants* to have a waiting line. Why would the manager want this?

9. What is the effect of "ticketed passengers only" lines at an airport?

10. How does queueing affect plant layout?

11. What dollar value ($/hour) do you place on yourself when waiting in line?

12. List the last five places you have waited and explain whether or not each of these five queues fits the general model presented in this chapter (as given by Figure 8.6).

13. When designing a waiting line system, what cost trade-offs need to be considered?

14. When designing a waiting line system, what qualitative concerns need to be considered?

15. Describe an assembly line in terms of a waiting line system.

16. Describe an inventory system in terms of a waiting line system.

PROBLEMS

1. Customers arrive at Joe's Barber Shop at a rate of 3 per hour, distributed in a Poisson fashion. Joe can perform haircuts at a rate of 5 per hour, distributed exponentially.

(a) Find the average number of customers waiting for haircuts.   .9 customers
(b) Find the average number of customers in the shop.   1.5 customers
(c) Find the average time a customer waits until it is his turn.   18 minutes
(d) Find the average time a customer spends in the shop.   30 minutes
(e) Find the percentage of time that Joe is busy.   60 percent

2. There are 14 million people in the United States who own Diamond appliances and only 1 lonely Diamond repairperson. The calls for service follow a Poisson pattern, and, on average, there is a call for service every 7.3 days (including weekends and holidays). Repair times have an exponential distribution and average 2.5 days.

(a) Find the average number of appliance owners waiting for the Diamond repairperson.   .178 owners
(b) Find the average time an appliance owner waits before his or her appliance is back in working condition.   3.8 days
(c) What is the probability that more than three appliance owners are without working appliances?   .0138
(d) What is the probability that more than three appliance owners are waiting for the repairperson?   .0048
(e) What percentage of the time is the repairperson idle?   65.75 percent

3. On Saturdays, cars arrive at Alfie's Car Wash at the rate of 13 per hour, distributed in a Poisson fashion. The car wash takes exactly 3 minutes.

(a) Find the average number of cars in line for a wash.   .604 cars
(b) Find the average number of cars at the car wash.   1.254 cars
(c) Find the average time that a car waits before it enters the car wash.   2.79 minutes
(d) Find the average time that cars spend at the car wash.   5.79 minutes
(e) Find the percentage of time that the car wash is idle.   35 percent

4. The coffee vending machine at the local parking garage dispenses a cup of coffee in exactly 20 seconds. Customer arrivals to the machine are according to a Poisson process, and the average time between arrivals is 30 seconds.

1.33 customers
40 seconds
66.7 percent

(a) Find the average number of customers gathered at the machine.
(b) Find the average time a customer spends getting his or her coffee.
(c) Find the percentage of time that the coffee machine is in use.

5. During weekday morning hours, customers at Limekiln Supermarket arrive at the rate of 30 per hour, distributed according to a Poisson process. There are 3 checkout lanes open, and the service times average 4 minutes, distributed according to an exponential process.

.889 shoppers
5.776 minutes
66.7 percent

(a) Find the average number of shoppers waiting in line.
(b) Find the average time shoppers spend between entering the line and leaving the store.
(c) Find the average utilization of each server.

6. Tourists arrive at the ticket booths of Rockytop Amusement Park at a rate of 204 per hour (Poisson fashion). There are 5 ticket booths, and each ticket agent can serve, on average, 1 customer per minute (exponential distribution).

4.137 tourists
13 seconds

(a) Find the average number of tourists in line at the ticket booths.
(b) Find the average time a tourist waits in line for a ticket.

7. Commuter Air, Inc. (CAI), a local airline, has a phone reservation system. The telephone system has 5 lines answered by 1 agent. That is, 4 customers can be placed on hold while 1 is being served. If all 5 lines are in use, any new callers will get a busy signal. Travelers place phone calls to CAI at a rate of 14 per hour (Poisson fashion). The average phone call lasts 3 minutes (exponential distribution).

1.533 phone lines
5.7 percent

(a) What is the average number of phone lines in use?
(b) What is the percentage of phone calls that receive a busy signal?

8. Most arrivals to a hospital emergency room are not considered emergencies in that the patients can wait to see a doctor until they complete the proper forms. At Macomb Hospital, emergency patients arrive at a rate of 6 per hour. This arrival process is, to no one's surprise, a Poisson process. It takes the admission clerk approximately 5 minutes to fill out the patient's form. The length of time is not exact and, in fact, has an exponential distribution. As soon as the form is filled out, the patient is examined. Because this is an *emergency* room, Dr. Brakit, the chief of staff, is concerned about the quality of operations and would like to know the current system values.

.5 people
1 person
5 minutes
10 minutes
50 percent

(a) What is the average number of persons in the queue?
(b) What is the average number of persons in the system?
(c) What is the average waiting time in the queue?
(d) What is the average waiting time in the system?
(e) What is the probability that the system is empty?

8(a): .25 people; 8(b): .75
people; 8(c): 2.5 minutes;
8(d): 7.5 minutes

9. Dr. Brakit (see Problem 8) is considering the computerization of the registration process. This will not reduce the 5 minute service time, but it will make it constant. How will this affect the answers to Problem 8, parts (a) through (d)?

10. Data have been collected at the student grill. It has been found that, between 5:00 P.M. and 7:00 P.M., students arrive at the grill at a rate of 25 per hour (Poisson fashion) and service time takes an average of 2 minutes (exponential distribution). There is only 1 server, who can work on only 1 order at a time.

4.1667 students
12 minutes

would reduce time by 8
minutes, to 4 minutes

(a) What is the average number of students in line?
(b) What is the average time a student is in the grill area?
(c) Suppose that a second server can be added to team up with the first. This would reduce the service time to 90 seconds. How would this affect the average time a student is in the grill area?

(d) Suppose a second server is added and the 2 servers act independently. What would be the average time a student is in the system?

2.43 minutes

11. The management department has 10 faculty members who share 1 secretary. On average, each faculty member brings 5 pages' worth of typing every (8-hour) day. The secretary can type 8 pages per hour.

(a) What is the average number of pages waiting to be typed?
(b) What is the average number of pages in the system?
(c) What is the average time between a page's entering the system and leaving it?
(d) What is the percentage of time that the secretary can devote to tasks other than typing?
(e) If the management department hires another faculty member, how do the answers to parts (a) through (d) change?
(f) If the management department hires a second secretary with the same typing rate as the first secretary's, how do the answers to parts (a) through (d) change?

2.79 pages
3.57 pages
.5712 hours
22 percent
(a): 5.25 pages; (b): 6.11 pages; (c): .888 hours; (d): 14 percent
(a): .14 pages; (b): .921 pages; (c): .1475 hours; (d): 61 percent

12. Customers arrive at the Do-Nut Bakery at the rate of 30 customers per hour. On average, it takes 1 minute to serve a customer his or her coffee and pastry. The arrival process is (you guessed it) Poisson, and the service times are (right again) exponential. Customers take numbers and are served according to these numbers. The owner of the bakery wishes to figure out whether he violates a fire regulation that states that no more than 3 customers can be in the store at any one time. (It's a very small store.)

(a) What is the probability that the fire regulation is violated?
(b) Suppose the owner does not allow the fourth customer to enter. What percentage of his business will be lost?

.0625

6.7 percent

13. At Parkville Community College, one person, the registrar, registers students for classes. Students arrive at a rate of 10 per hour (Poisson) and the registration process takes 5 minutes on the average (exponential). The registrar is paid $5 per hour, and the cost of keeping students waiting is estimated to be $2 for each student for each hour waited (not including service time). Two options are available to improve service. One option is that service can be computerized, resulting in a service time of exactly 4 minutes. The computer rental cost is $7 per hour. The second option is hiring a more efficient registrar. Service time could be reduced to an average of 3 minutes (exponential), and the new registrar would be paid $8 per hour. What are the hourly costs for each of the three systems?

current: $13.32 per hour; option 1: $8.33 per hour; option 2: $9 per hour

14. What are the hourly costs for each of the three systems in Problem 13 if the $2 per hour student cost includes the service time?

current: $15 per hour; option 1: $9.66 per hour; option 2: $10 per hour

15. Richard Gilliam has decided to open a frozen yogurt stand on Three Mile Island. He figures that, during the summer months, tourists would want to cool down and would arrive at his stand at the rate of 2 per minute (a Poisson process). On average, it takes 2 minutes for 1 server to serve a customer (exponential). What is the minimum number of servers that must be hired so that the average number of customers at the stand (waiting and service) is not greater than 6?

6 servers

COMPUTER CASE STUDY 8.1: PANTRY SHOPPER

Pantry Shopper is a supermarket in suburban Philadelphia, where competition among supermarkets is fierce. Pantry Shopper management feels that because prices are so competitive, shoppers will choose one supermarket over another due to the services that are offered. For this reason,

Pantry Shopper prides itself on its in-store bakery; its deli counter, which the store claims offers more varieties of meats, cheeses, and salads than any competitor; and its meat counter, which allows the store to provide custom cuts of meat or poultry.

The store has been in business in the same location since 1953. Over the years, the store has had different owners and different managers, each with his or her own ideas on the management and design of the store. The new manager, Beth Smith-Danton, is no exception. Beth felt that by providing shoppers with faster, more efficient service, she might be able to improve the store's competitive position and market share. To this end, she has already moved check approval from the main desk to the cash register. She has increased the limit on cash back from checks from $20 above the purchase amount to $50 above the purchase amount. She has instituted a delivery service to make shopping more convenient, especially for senior citizens.

To this point, however, Beth has not changed the checkout system itself. The last major remodeling of the checkout system occurred in 1982. Since then, the demand at the store has increased and the technology of the cash registers has changed. Beth needs to use her square footage efficiently when the checkout system is redesigned. She knows that she has to design the system for peak usage but does not want to overdesign the system—that is, install too many cash registers and lanes. It's not that Beth is concerned about the unnecessary expenses involved— the registers, scanners, and conveyors represent a fixed cost that would be spread over many shoppers. Wasted space is a far greater concern.

Planning for a major redesign, Beth collected data at her store on several consecutive Saturday mornings. She noticed that customers arrived at the checkout at a rate of approximately 100 per hour. Fully 20 percent of the customers had 10 items or less. Those people took about 2 minutes to serve on average, while customers with more than 10 items took about 4 minutes to process. Beth expects service time to improve when universal price code readers are installed in the new design. Help Beth with her design for the system.

REFERENCES

Bunday, B. D. *Basic Queueing Theory.* London: Edward Arnold Publishers Ltd., 1986.

Cooper, R. B. *Introduction to Queueing Theory.* 2nd ed. New York: North Holland, 1981.

Crabill, T., D. B. Gross, and M. J. Magazine. "A Classified Bibliography of Research on Optimal Design and Control of Queues," *Operations Research* 25, no. 2 (March/April 1977): 219–232.

Foote, B. L. "A Queueing Case Study of Drive-In Banking," *Interfaces* 6, no. 4 (August 1976): 31–37.

Hillier, F. S., and G. J. Lieberman. *Introduction to Operations Research.* 4th ed. San Francisco: Holden-Day, 1986.

Jones, M. T., A. M. O'Berski, and G. Tom. "Quickening the Queue in Grocery Stores," *Interfaces* 10, no. 3 (June 1980): 90–92.

Kendall, D. G. "Stochastic Processes Occurring in the Theory of Queues and Their Analysis by Means of the Imbedded Markov Chain," *Annals of Mathematical Statistics* 2, no. 24, (1953): 338–354.

Lee, A. *Applied Queuing Theory.* Macmillan: New York, 1966.

Taha, H. A. *Operations Research: An Introduction.* 4th ed. New York: Macmillan, 1987.

Weiss, H. J. "The Computation of Optimal Control Limits for a Queue with Batch Services," *Management Science* 25, no. 4 (April 1979): 320–328.

Weisselberg, R. C., and J. G. Cowley. "Quicken the Queue," *Journal of Systems Management* 20 (October 1969): 30–35. Also appears in *The Executive Strategist: An Armchair Guide to Scientific Decision-Making.* New York: McGraw-Hill, 1969.

C H A P T E R

9

O U T L I N E

WORK MEASUREMENT AND JOB DESIGN

- To explain the man–machine relationship in the organization
- To discuss the physical factors that affect job performance
- To develop measures of machine availability
- To describe considerations in job design
- To present methods to control job performance

INTRODUCTION

macro vs. micro

Thus far in the text, we have tended to describe the management of operations from a macro rather than micro point of view. Taken as a group, decisions relating to capacity, location, and layout reflect the larger considerations and the larger investment expenditures of a business. These macro-oriented decisions also have a common time frame; they are, for the most part, long-term decisions. Making these decisions is the major part of setting up the organizational infrastructure of the operation. Now it is time to look at how operations are conducted within this infrastructure.

The conducting of operations implies that some job—or many jobs—needs to be performed. This is true whether we are speaking of a service job or a production job. For every job that needs to be performed, certain tasks must be done.

1. The time and effort required to do the job must be assessed.
2. The appropriate number of people must be assigned to that job.
3. A workstation must be designed.
4. Methods for training those who will perform the job must be devised.
5. The value of the work must be assessed.
6. Compensation systems must be developed in line with the value of the job.

Teaching Suggestion 9.1: Individualized Examples. See the Instructor's Section for details.

job design

Of course, other tasks are involved. For example, the entire field of automation and robotics is ignored in this list. Certainly, a major decision in job design is making the choice between labor and automated equipment. Reference to this decision has been omitted for two reasons. First, that choice often is based on financial considerations, which might be subjected to a break-even analysis. Second, at some level, a human being is always responsible for the operation of the equipment. The overriding concern in this chapter is the interaction of person and machine—in other words, **man–machine systems.** Regardless of the complexity of the equipment, the principles outlined in this chapter should apply equally well to all people who are responsible for the operation of equipment.

There is more to designing the system of jobs than analyzing man–machine systems, however. An assumption behind the six considerations listed previously is that the work to be performed as part of the job has been defined. In our discussion of line balancing in Chapter 7, we saw one way in which various tasks may be grouped together and performed at one workstation—the cycle time criterion. However useful in line balancing, though, the cycle time criterion often fails in implementation. Many times, the types of equipment required to do the different tasks prohibit the grouping of certain tasks. The mix of skills required for each task also may be prohibitive. In addition to grouping tasks by cycle time, it is helpful (and often mandatory) to group them by skills and equipment required.

All of the considerations just mentioned are part of job design. Work measurement is a useful tool in the process of job design and in the design of the compensation scheme. Job design and work measurement are the subjects of this chapter. Within each section, we will provide some tools and information that are useful for, and sometimes required by, the manager who must develop a system of job functions and workstations that is efficient in terms of quantity, quality, and safety.

work measurement

WORK SYSTEMS DESIGN

One of the most complex workstations, and therefore the most widely studied, is the cockpit of a jet fighter plane. In this workstation, the operator (the pilot) is pushed to the limits of human performance. Therefore, the cockpit must be designed in a way that allows the pilot to perform the required procedures in the necessary time. Otherwise, the consequences can be fatal. The cockpit is the ultimate setting for the design of man–machine systems, and the pilot's characteristics and needs are the **human factors** in the design. These human factors are one topic of this section.

Beyond the man–machine system, job performance is affected by the reliability of the equipment itself. When any production or service system is put into place, the major nonhuman measure of system performance is equipment reliability. Performance measures are the subject of the second part of this section, which covers work systems design.

HUMAN FACTORS

The field of human factors, as it applies to the design of the workplace, may be divided into three main areas:

1. **psychophysics,** the study of human sensory responses;
2. **anthropometry,** the measurement of the human body; and
3. **biomechanics,** the study of body motion.

The study of human factors is an interdisciplinary field, calling on the skills of the psychologist, engineer, biologist, and physicist, among others. It is not the role of any operations management text to teach these fields in detail. However, this section attempts to make the aspiring manager aware of their role in the workplace. Let us briefly look at each of these areas.

PSYCHOPHYSICS

Loosely defined, psychophysics is the study of the operation of the human neurological system. It includes the study of the human sensory processes and information input processes. In practice, the field is concerned with the speed with which the worker will

human sensory processes

The control room of an aluminum plant shows a complex system of display mechanisms.
(© Doug Wilson/Black Star)

sense something (by sight, sound, touch, smell, or movement) and the speed with which the brain can process the sensory information and signal an appropriate response. In addition to response times, the field also investigates our capacity for processing information. A faster response time will increase the number of signals that can be accommodated in a given time; however, it is imperative that the worker not be overloaded with too many signals at once.

One lesson that we learn from studying psychophysics in the work environment concerns the timing of jobs. We will study this in more detail in our discussion of work measurement later in the chapter. For now, we ask this question: What happens to the performance of a worker (in terms of errors made) when the worker is required to work at different speeds? Figure 9.1 shows the relationship between the number of errors made and the time given to complete the job. The "peak" time is the absolute fastest that the job can be performed. This is in the overload region. The other times listed result from the calculation of a mean and standard deviation from actual performance times for the job to be performed. The number of errors are found by requiring—say, through the setting of the speed on a conveyer—that the job be completed in each of the given times. The lesson of Figure 9.1 should be clear:

speed vs. accuracy

Never rush the worker.

The usual time allotted for a job is just below the mean, allowing the worker to produce at the best combination of speed and quality. Although the optimal job time may

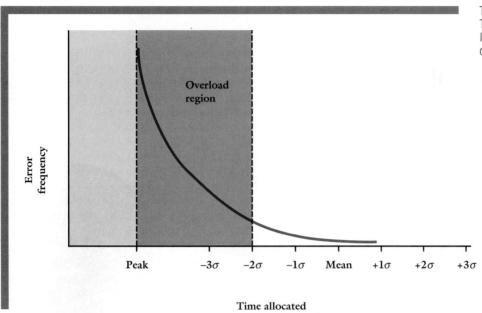

Teaching Suggestion 9.2:
Too Much Time. See the
Instructor's Section for
details.

FIGURE 9.1 Relationship between time allocated for job and errors

change according to the nature of the job and the outside pressures for quality, the principles of this lesson always apply.

A second lesson we learn from psychophysics concerns the design of display mechanisms. There are three major types of display mechanisms:

- visual,
- auditory, and
- tactual.

In visual display, the most common type of display mechanism, a response is elicited by means of a signal that is seen. A clock, for example, is a visual display. As you know, there are many different clock faces. Which face is *best* depends on the purpose for which the display is used. Figure 9.2 shows three faces for a clock (a digital clock is not shown because it is a different type of display mechanism). Part (a) in Figure 9.2 shows the clock face that provides the most information, but takes the longest to read. The face in part (b) in Figure 9.2 provides less information, but can be read faster. The face in part (c) of the figure provides only an approximation of the time and, although it may be adequate for certain purposes, it is not seen very often. We can read the time from the face in part (c) only because we are thoroughly familiar with more complete displays, such as the one in part (a). Many visual displays do take advantage of our familiarity with them. The elimination of unnecessary reading aids frees the senses of the worker who is familiar with the display to respond to other signals. In general, a display should provide the minimum amount of information required to elicit the appropriate responses from the worker. Such simplicity provides for greater accuracy and faster response times.

**minimum amount of
information**

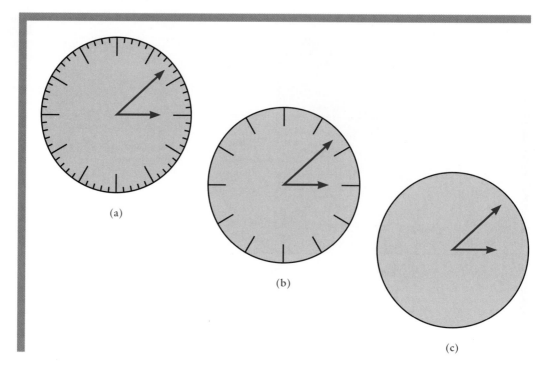

FIGURE 9.2 Clock displays

color coding

The layout of the visual display also should be designed to minimize the effort required to read the display. For example, a display providing the temperature reading inside a nuclear reactor can be enhanced by adding color: green for a safe temperature and red for one indicating danger. This color coding saves the monitoring employee the small amount of time he or she might need to decide whether or not the reading is safe, thereby minimizing the employee's response time. Usually, a warning color (possibly amber) would be added for a "near danger" range to alert the operator to pay closer attention.

reflect the actual layout
In addition, the display's layout should be designed to reflect the actual physical layout of the system. For example, if the operator is responsible for monitoring the temperature in twelve boilers, they should not merely be labeled from one to twelve. Instead, the display's layout should mimic the layout of the boilers. Figure 9.3 shows these two options. Part (b) in Figure 9.3 allows for a faster determination as to which boiler is overheated and where it is located, even though part (a) in the figure shows a more orderly layout. This orderly layout is not what one would find in a tour of the shop floor.

An item in daily use that very often has a poor display is the top of the kitchen stove. The four burners usually are laid out in a square pattern. Yet, as indicated in part (a) of Figure 9.4, the four control dials are most often arranged in a straight line, thereby ensuring maximum confusion concerning which dial is to be used for which burner. Part (b) in Figure 9.4 shows the preferred display, a rectangular layout that clearly indicates the control dial that goes with each burner.

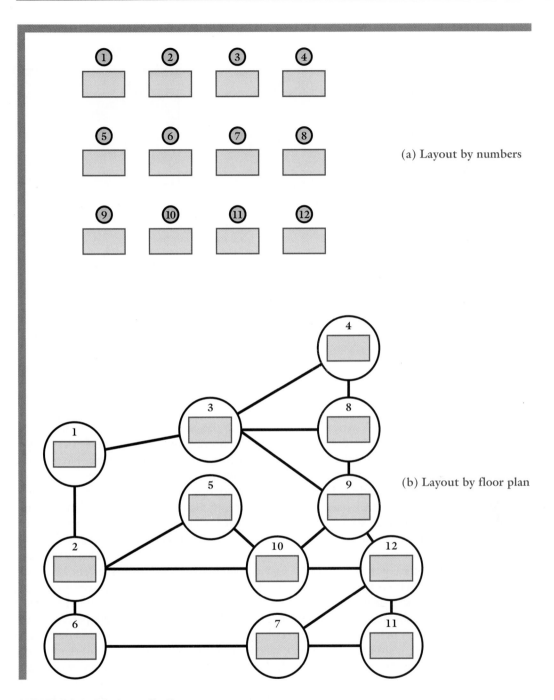

(a) Layout by numbers

(b) Layout by floor plan

FIGURE 9.3 Displays of boiler temperature gauges

Transparency Master 9.1:
Proper Console Display.

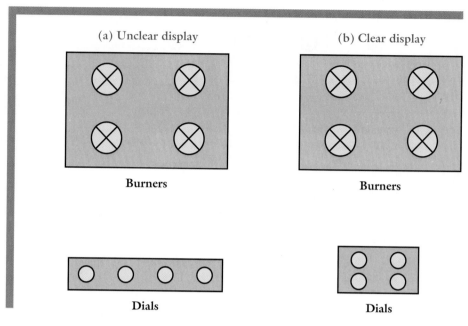

FIGURE 9.4   Stove layouts and dial displays

ANTHROPOMETRY

Anthropometry deals with the measurement of the physical features or characteristics of the body (usually not to be considered in motion). It relates to the workplace design because it is important that the worker be as comfortable as possible, be able to work at maximum speed, and be able to use the equipment provided.

physical characteristics of people

Because workstations and equipment are not designed to the specification of each individual worker, they must be designed for some standard-size person. The dimensions of the average-size person can be used for many things, as long as the level of discomfort associated with a person who is larger than average is the same as the level of discomfort associated with a person who is smaller than average. This is the case with the design of the height of the cashier's counter at the supermarket, the height of a conveyor belt on an assembly line, or the height of a dining table or writing desk. It certainly is not true where access to an area (through a door, for example) is required. In this case, the design is generally made according to the 95th or 99th percentile on the dimension of interest. As an everyday example, consider the door to a house. The average male is about 69 inches tall, but this is not the standard height of doors. The door is usually 84 inches (7 feet) high. Actually, this represents a deliberate overdesign (and an added construction cost), because the 95th percentile is about 73 inches. It seems that we want to make sure that we never make anyone bend to enter our houses (a custom that dates back to a time when this was considered an insult—the host should always bow first to the guest). For another example, consider the height and weight restrictions on military recruits. By limiting the range of allowable heights and weights, the military can standardize the design of its equipment. The access holes on a submarine, to cite an example having strict limits, are designed with a seaman of specific size in mind. For this reason, no tall seaman (such as David Robinson) ever receives a submarine assignment. Much of the data used in anthropomorphic studies, in fact, come from the military.

The design of seating (many people work sitting in seats or on stools of some sort) is a science in itself. While bucket seats are most suitable for driving, a high stool is best for jobs where one must perform reaching motions. It is known that 98 percent of us are within 3 inches of the average height when seated. This is why being able to adjust seat height allows for a high degree of standardization within each type of chair.

The ability of the worker to perform a task quickly and accurately diminishes with the distance the worker is required to reach in order to perform the task. The ideal height of operational mechanisms (levers, knobs, dials, switches) should be between 10 inches below and 40 inches above seat level. Toward the limits of this range (5 inches or more below the seat level or 30 inches or more above it), controls must be *recessed* (placed closer to the worker). Any mechanism placed at seat level or below cannot be in front of the operator if it requires hand operation (foot operation would be feasible). This is why the seat adjustment lever in the car is on the seat, not below the dashboard, where the lever could not be reached. All controls under the dashboard are accessed with the feet.

Teaching Suggestion 9.3: Automobile Controls. See the Instructor's Section for details.

ability diminishes with distance

BIOMECHANICS

Almost all jobs require movement on the part of the worker. Most often, these movements are repetitive. The time and motion studies discussed later in the chapter ana-

The workstation must be designed for comfort and efficiency. (© Sepp Seitz/Woodfin Camp & Associates)

lyze these movements. Biomechanics relates to the classification of these movements and to the human capability to perform them

- over time (both speed and duration) and
- under stress of weight.

Biomechanics has a rich lexicon. Consider the following very specific descriptions of body movement.

body movements

- *flexion:* bending, or decreasing the angle between parts of the body
- *extension:* straightening, or increasing the angle between parts of the body
- *adduction:* moving toward the midline of the body
- *abduction:* moving away from the midline of the body
- *medial rotation:* turning toward the midline of the body
- *lateral rotation:* turning away from the midline of the body
- *pronation:* rotating the forearm so that the palm faces downward
- *supination:* rotating the forearm so that the palm faces upward

Movements can be classified in more operational terms for the work environment.

- *positioning:* moving a body member, such as the hand or foot, from one position to another, as in reaching for a switch
- *continuous:* making continuous control adjustments on the basis of changing stimuli associated with the task, such as the guiding of a piece of material through a jigsaw
- *manipulation:* movement that involves the use or handling of parts, tools, control switches, and the like
- *repetitive:* repeating the same movement; such as in sawing or hammering
- *sequential:* when a specific sequence of independent movements is involved, such as in starting a car, typing, or using a calculator or cash register
- *static:* exerting force to maintain a given position for a period of time (not really a movement)

workload design

The study of biomechanics provides some key rules for the design of work systems by specifying the workload they put on individuals. First, the study of biomechanics tells us that work that causes the expenditure of more than 4 or 5 kilocalories (kc) of energy per minute usually cannot be continued for a full shift without rest. As a frame of reference, consider that sawing a board requires about 7 kc per minute; repairing electric appliances, about 2.5 kc per minute; and laying bricks, about 4 kc per minute.

reaction time

Second, studying biomechanics also allows us to build reaction time into the design of work systems. Simple reaction time is, generally, about .2 seconds. Reaction time, as should be expected, increases as reaction alternatives from which to choose increase. Unexpected signals also increase reaction time. Reaction time that includes movement time to activate controls may take a full second or more (hence, the critical nature of cockpit design).

Finally, some recommendations concerning how to design and group tasks may be garnered from the study of biomechanics. For example, movements may have an economy of scale: Long movements take proportionately less time than short movements. Many tasks require the cessation of activity in response to some visual cue that enough work has been done. In these cases, time can be saved by using a mechanical device to terminate the movement.

Investigation of the three areas of workplace design that involve human factors—psychophysics, anthropometry, and biomechanics—provides an overview of how the worker functions and how the work requirements and workstations may be designed to best utilize the worker's efforts. We have seen how we react to stimuli, how we process information, and how our bodies function in the work environment. In the next section, we look at how to design the work equipment to assure overall system reliability.

WORK SYSTEM MEASURES: RELIABILITY, AVAILABILITY, AND MAINTAINABILITY

The study of **reliability, availability,** and **maintainability** (RAM) is conducted formally in some workplaces and informally in others. We usually think of these measures in terms of their application to the performance of some system. How this system is defined is crucial. The system could refer to

- a business,
- a factory,
- an individual worker,
- a complex piece of equipment,
- one component of the equipment,
- a man–machine system, or
- many other possible definitions within this range.

The ultimate performance measure is availability, because it measures whether or not the system in question is ready to be used in an operating order. We can achieve a high rate of availability by concentrating on two separate components:

- reliability and
- maintainability.

In operations management, the term *reliability* refers to a measure of the capability of a system or subsystem (such as a machine, part, person, or product) to perform its function properly under normal operating conditions. The general definition is vague; we need to decide what we mean by "capability" and "normal operating conditions." In considering the reliability of any individual system, we typically put precise specifications on these terms. Capability is the easier of the terms to specify. The typical definition of capability is probability. That is, reliability measures the probability that a system or subsystem will operate properly under normal operating conditions. The interpretation of the term *probability* is percentage of time or percentage of operations. The term *properly* means that the task is performed according to certain specifications. **work specifications** The specifications might be of the form right versus wrong. The typical measurement of the quality of a typist, for example, is twofold. The first measurement is the speed at which the typist types, which is measured in words per minute. (This is the production rate.) The second measure is the percentage of errors the typist makes. This could be measured as characters typed incorrectly, but it is more common to measure it as the percentage of words typed incorrectly. The reliability of the typist is the percentage of words that the typist types correctly. As exhibited previously, there is an inverse relationship between production rate and error rate. The faster the typist types, the more mistakes he or she is likely to make. Although the production rate (typing speed) and reliability (percentage of correct words typed) are two separate measures, it is common for typing exams to have one score—the adjusted typing rate as given by correct words per minute. It is also possible for a range of values to constitute "proper operation."

By "normal operating conditions," we mean under the circumstances that are routine. For example, the accuracy of the typist obviously will be affected by the room temperature, noise, and other operating conditions. Reliability is measured under the normal operating conditions. In some instances, normal might be a loud office; in others, normal might be a quiet environment.

Maintainability refers to the probability of being able to keep the machines operating over a period of time through the combination of both preventive and corrective maintenance.

Reliability is the best quantitative measure of the integrity of a designed system. Given a failure in the system, maintainability provides the best quantitative measure of the ability to repair the malfunction and bring it back to a functioning status. Maintainability also indicates how fast repair can be accomplished.

The two functions that the operations manager has at ready disposal to improve reliability and maintainability are

■ reliability engineering and
■ maintenance.

Teaching Suggestion 9.4: Improve Operating Conditions. See the Instructor's Section for details.

reliability engineering

maintenance

Reliability engineering provides the theoretical and practical tools for predicting, designing, testing, and demonstrating the probability and capability of parts, components, equipment, subsystems, and systems to perform their required functions without failure for desired periods in specified environments (that is, their desired optimized reliability) as well as their desired and optimized maintainability, availability, safety, and quality levels. Maintenance is any action that retains working systems in a satisfactory operational condition and, if a failure occurs, restores the failed system to a satisfactory operational condition.

Reliability has been defined as the probability of successful performance, which is conditional upon the environment in which the work is performed. Given that

N = number of repetitions;
S = number of successes; and
F = number of errors, or failures,

the reliability, R, is found with the formula

reliability = percentage of successes

$$R = \frac{S}{N},$$

which calculates the percentage of successes. In the same way, the **failure rate,** FR (sometimes called *unreliability*), is the percentage of failures:

failure rate

$$FR = \frac{F}{N},$$

where the failure rate is the probability that the performance is not successful. Of course, the reliability and the unreliability must sum to 1. That is,

$$FR + R = 1.$$

Consequently, another way to compute the reliability is

$$R = 1 - FR.$$

Example 9.1 Two workstations have been designed to accomplish the same job. A group of 10 workers, each using each of the 2 workstations, performed the job 100 times. Use of the first station resulted in 22 errors, and use of the second resulted in 51 errors. Which is the better workstation (man–machine system) and what is the reliability of each?

First, it is obvious that the first workstation is the better of the two, because its use resulted in fewer errors from the same number of trials. Remember, though, that it is only "better" in terms of reliability. We have ignored speed, productivity, and safety—all important concerns. The performance characteristics may be measured in terms of failure rate or reliability. Both measurements are provided here.

FAILURE RATE ANALYSIS

WORKSTATION 1:

$$N = 1,000$$
$$F = 22$$
$$FR = \frac{22}{1,000} = .022$$
$$R = 1 - FR = 1 - .022 = .978$$

WORKSTATION 2:

$$N = 1,000$$
$$F = 51$$
$$FR = \frac{51}{1,000} = .051$$
$$R = 1 - FR = 1 - .051 = .949$$

An alternative approach follows.

RELIABILITY ANALYSIS

WORKSTATION 1:

$$N = 1,000$$
$$S = 1,000 - 22 = 978$$
$$R = \frac{978}{1,000} = .978$$

WORKSTATION 2:

$$N = 1,000$$
$$S = 1,000 - 51 = 949$$
$$R = \frac{949}{1,000} = .949$$

The reliabilities of the two workstations are as follows.

> Workstation 1 = 97.8%
>
> Workstation 2 = 94.9%   ◼

The reliabilities calculated to this point treat each workstation separately. When two or more workstations are used together, each workstation is an individual component of the larger system. The remainder of this section looks at the reliability of component systems.

The reliability of a complex system is not simple to calculate. We will see how to calculate the reliabilities of the following two kinds of systems from their component reliabilities:

- series systems and
- parallel systems.

These systems are shown in parts (a) and (b) of Figure 9.5, respectively. Next, we will see how to calculate the reliabilities of systems having both series and parallel components.

SERIES SYSTEMS

The successful completion of most jobs is dependent upon the successful completion of many smaller tasks. If one of these tasks is not performed successfully (on time, or within quality specifications), then the entire job is considered to be a failure. Because such systems are described by a series of tasks performed in sequence, they are called **series systems.** A common example of a series system (an electrical system, not a system of jobs) that has frustrated many people is a string of Christmas lights. The lights are wired in series, as is proven by what happens every time one of the bulbs on the string fails: They all go out; even the good bulbs fail to light.

We want to be able to predict the system reliability, given the reliability of each of the components. Assume that

$$R_{ss} = \text{reliability of a system in series}$$

and that

$$R_i = \text{reliability of the } i\text{th component.}$$

Then the general formula for the system reliability of n components in series is

series reliability

$$R_{ss} = R_1 \times R_2 \times R_3 \times \ldots \times R_n.$$

Suppose a job consists of a series of 3 tasks. Further, suppose that task 1 is performed correctly 98 percent of the time, task 2 is performed correctly 99 percent of the time, and task 3 is performed correctly 96 percent of the time. The reliability of this job is

$$R_{ss} = (.98)(.99)(.96) = .9304, \text{ or } 93.04\%.$$

It should be obvious that designing a system in series can lead to low system reliabilities, even if all of the individual tasks are performed very well. Table 9.1 shows this effect. For example, as the table shows, if 100 tasks must be done, each of which is 99-

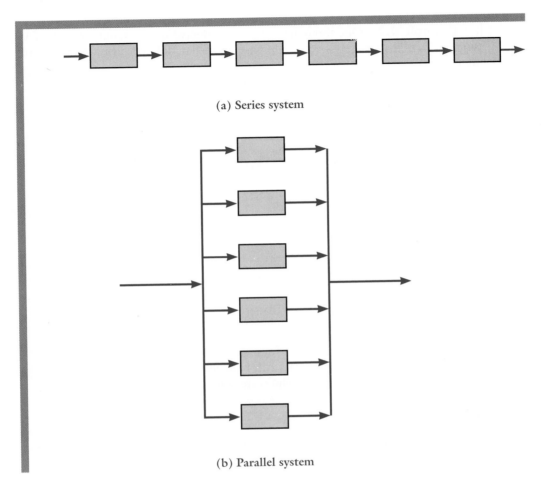

(a) Series system

(b) Parallel system

FIGURE 9.5 Series and parallel systems

percent reliable, the system reliability is only 36.6 percent—unacceptable for any system. The result may be checked using the preceding equation for R_{ss}.

Transparency Master 9.2: System Reliability.

major assumption

A major assumption is being made in this analysis. Recall that we can multiply probabilities in this way only if the failure rate on any one task is *independent* of the failure rate of each of the other tasks. Usually, this assumption holds. In general, there is no reason to believe that one machine or one person will make more errors just because another machine or person does.

However, there will be situations in the workplace where this assumption does not hold. For example, a disruption in the power supply may cause multiple machine failures. The environment in which a job is done can also increase machine failure rates plantwide. On a day when the temperature is much hotter or colder than usual, errors may proliferate across the entire workplace. Morale problems and boredom also can lead to the proliferation of errors. A common tool of management in a workplace where tedious, repetitive tasks are performed is to play music, which has the effect of keeping workers alert, thereby increasing both productivity and quality.

Example 9.2   One thousand tests are conducted on the results of each of 15 different tasks that are required to complete a job. The following numbers of errors are found.

Task	Errors
1	1
2	6
3	4
4	2
5	3
6	1
7	0
8	2
9	1
10	2
11	1
12	1
13	0
14	2
15	3
	29

If these tasks are done in series, what is the reliability of the job?

The resulting component reliabilities are as follows.

Task	Reliability
1	.999
2	.994
3	.996
4	.998
5	.997
6	.999
7	1.000
8	.998
9	.999
10	.998
11	.999
12	.999
13	1.000
14	.998
15	.997

The system reliability is

$$R_{ss} = R_1 \times R_2 \times R_3 \times R_4 \times R_5 \times R_6 \times R_7 \times R_8 \times R_9 \times R_{10} \times R_{11} \times R_{12} \times R_{13} \times R_{14} \times R_{15}$$

$$= .999 \times .994 \times .996 \times .998 \times .997 \times .999 \times 1 \times .998 \times .999 \times .998 \times .999 \times .999 \times 1 \times .998 \times .997$$

$$= .971, \text{ or } 97.1\%.$$

TABLE 9.1 System reliability as a function of the number of steps in series and the reliability of the individual components

Steps in Sequence	Component Reliability					
	.999	.995	.99	.95	.9	.8
1	.9990	.9950	.9900	.9500	.9000	.8000
2	.9980	.9900	.9801	.9025	.8100	.6400
5	.9950	.9752	.9510	.7738	.5905	.3277
10	.9900	.9511	.9044	.5987	.3487	.1074
25	.9753	.8822	.7778	.2774	.0718	.0038
50	.9512	.7783	.6050	.0769	.0052	.0000
100	.9048	.6058	.3660	.0059	.0000	.0000

Transparency Master 9.4: Effect of System Size on Reliability.

PARALLEL SYSTEMS

In the workplace, **parallel systems** are used more for meeting production rates (quantity measurement of reliability) than for improving product quality. If two workers are doing the same job (in parallel), then twice as many units are produced, but unit quality is not necessarily improved. In our presentation of line balancing, we ignored the idea of parallel workstations. All calculations were done on a single series system. To calculate for two or more workstations doing the same job, we simply combine their capabilities into one quantity figure and proceed as with the series system.

> **Example 9.3** A workstation can perform a task once every 4 seconds. What is the production rate to be used for line balancing if 2 of these stations are used?
>
> 1 workstation performs 15 tasks/minute
>
> 2 workstations perform $2 \times 15 = 30$ tasks/minute ∎

A more common use of the parallel system, at least for purposes of determining system reliability, is in providing additional capacity to perform a task (some would use the term *backup*) in case of equipment failure.

We have seen how the reliability of a series system can be predicted from its component reliabilities, and now we will see how it is possible to predict the reliability of a parallel system from its component reliabilities. As before, we have

$$R_{ps} = \text{reliability of a system in parallel}$$

and

$$R_i = \text{reliability of the } i\text{th component.}$$

The general formula for the system reliability of n components in parallel is

$$R_{ps} = 1 - (1 - R_1) \times (1 - R_2) \times (1 - R_3) \times \ldots \times (1 - R_n).$$

parallel reliability

Thus, if a piece of equipment works 80 percent of the time, and two identical pieces of equipment are used in parallel, then their reliability together is

$$R_{ps} = 1 - (1 - .8) \times (1 - .8)$$
$$= 1 - (.2) \times (.2)$$
$$= .96.$$

trade-off in system design

Neither of these components is very reliable, yet when they are used to support each other in parallel, the system reliability is quite good. The trade-off in system design with backup units is the cost of the additional units versus the cost of the additional failures incurred without the backups. An alternative concern, one outside of management design (but one of engineering design), is the trade-off between designing these low reliability units versus designing a more expensive unit with a higher reliability. In this case, the technical feasibility of attaining the required reliability must be considered in addition to cost. Table 9.2 shows the dramatic effects of adding backups on reliability.

Example 9.4   The piece of equipment in Example 9.3 is 80-percent reliable. It has been determined that no more than 1 failure per 1,000 jobs can be tolerated. How many of the pieces of equipment are needed to achieve this goal?

The desired failure rate is .001 or better. So the reliability desired is

$$R_{ps} = 1 - FR$$
$$= 1 - .001 = .999.$$

The equation for finding the reliability of a parallel system is

$$R_{ps} = 1 - (1 - R_1) \times (1 - R_2) \times \ldots \times (1 - R_n).$$

Teaching Suggestion 9.5: Decimal Accuracy. See the Instructor's Section for details.

However, because the reliability of each component is $R_i = .8$, the equation can be written

$$R_{ps} = 1 - (1 - .8)^n,$$

and because R_{ps} is predefined at .999, it is necessary to find n, the number of pieces of equipment that yields

$$.999 = 1 - (1 - .8)^n.$$

To solve the equation

$$.2^n = 1 - .999 = .001,$$

we can try increasing values of n, or we can examine Table 9.2.

n	R_{ps}
1	.8
2	.96
3	.992
4	.9984
5	.99968

To achieve the required goal, five units are needed.   ■」

TABLE 9.2 System reliability as a function of the number of backups (parallel steps) and the reliability of the individual components

Number of Backups	Component Reliability					
	.999	.995	.99	.95	.9	.8
1	.999000	.995000	.990000	.950000	.900000	.800000
2	.999999	.999975	.999900	.997500	.990000	.960000
3	1.000000	1.000000	.999999	.999875	.999000	.992000
4	1.000000	1.000000	1.000000	.999994	.999900	.998400
5	1.000000	1.000000	1.000000	1.000000	.999990	.999680
6	1.000000	1.000000	1.000000	1.000000	.999999	.999936
7	1.000000	1.000000	1.000000	1.000000	1.000000	.999987

COMPLEX SYSTEMS

In actuality, systems are designed with a mixture both of series and parallel functions. The series portion follows the required sequence of tasks, and the parallel portion is used to increase the production rate or the reliability of those series components that cannot meet the goals of management in these areas alone. Systems that contain both parallel and series components are called **complex systems.** Fortunately, as is the case in determining capacity (see Chapter 3), the most complex system can be analyzed by breaking it down into its parallel and series subsystems and analyzing each of these separately. The goal of the analysis is to reduce the complex system to a simple series system in a sequence of steps. Let us see how this can be done.

Transparency Master 9.4: Effect of System Size on Reliability.

Example 9.5 Consider the system shown in Figure 9.6. Nine components are connected in a network, and their individual reliabilities are given. The reliability of the overall system is not given, and it is a complex system, so a series or parallel analysis will not be sufficient to determine the overall system reliability.

The analysis aimed at determining the reliability of this complex system is illustrated in Figure 9.7. First, we divide the system into a series system, as shown in part (a) of Figure 9.7. Notice that this complex system may be viewed as a system of 6 subsystems in series.

After determining the reliabilities of each of these subsystems, we can find the system reliability by multiplying together the subsystem reliabilities connected in series. The subsystem reliabilities are determined as follows.

Subsystem	System type	Reliability
I	Single component	.95
II	Single component	.99
III	Three components in parallel	$1 - (1 - .8)^3 = .992$
IV	Single component	.99
V	Two components in parallel	$1 - (1 - .9)^2 = .99$
VI	Single component	.98

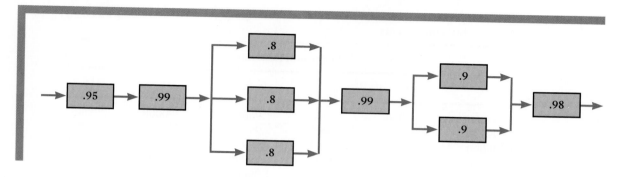

FIGURE 9.6 Complex system (Example 9.5)

These reliabilities are provided in part (b) of Figure 9.7, which shows a series system. Therefore, the system reliability is

$$R_{ss} = .95 \times .99 \times .992 \times .99 \times .99 \times .98$$
$$= .896.$$

Thus, this complex system is 89.6-percent reliable. ∎

Consider a second complex system.

Example 9.6 A student uses a calculator and a pencil for an examination. The probability that the battery in the calculator will fail is 1 percent, while the probability that the point on the pencil will break is 2 percent. If the student brings 1 backup battery and 3 pencils, what is the reliability of the exam system?

Again, we divide the complex system into its two series parts. The reliability of the calculator is given by

$$R_{calc} = 1 - (1 - .99)^2 = .9999 \text{ (also see Table 9.2)},$$

and the reliability of the pencils is given by

$$R_{pencil} = 1 - (1 - .98)^3 = .999998.$$

Therefore, the exam system reliability is given by

$$R_{calc} \times R_{pencil} = .9999 \times .999998 = .9998 \text{ (rounded off)}. ∎$$

WORK MEASUREMENT

Our discussion thus far has centered on the analysis of the capacity to accomplish work. The physical and mental limitations of human operators and the limitations of the equipment are linked with the actual job design (described later), but job design requires knowledge not only of the capacity for work, but also of the amount of work that must be done. Just as in any other operations problem, job design relies on match-

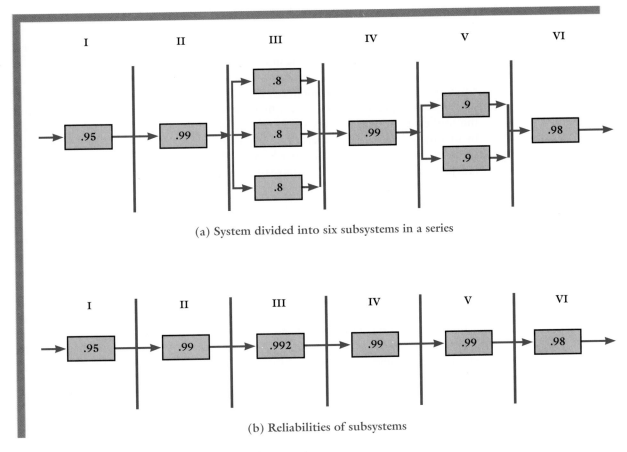

(a) System divided into six subsystems in a series

(b) Reliabilities of subsystems

FIGURE 9.7   Analysis of complex system (Example 9.5)

ing the capacity with the demand. In this case, the work to be accomplished is the demand, and the ability to do the work is the capacity.

Transparency Master 9.3: Reliability Analysis.

Work measurement is the field of study that attempts to quantify, in terms of time required, the amount of work necessary to perform a task. The most important technique used in work measurement is the **time and motion study.** The other technique used in work measurement, very often to complement the time study results, is **work sampling.** These are the subjects of this section.

TIME AND MOTION STUDY

Time and motion study, in principle, was developed as part of the early work in scientific management by Frederick Taylor. In practice, the specific techniques now in use can be traced to the techniques developed by Frank Gilbreth early in this century. Time and motion techniques were instrumental in creating order and efficiency in the workplace during heavy industry's "golden age." In this sense, time and motion study played a large role in creating the high standard of living enjoyed today by industrialized societies.

With the rise of the union movement in the first half of this century, time and motion study took on a central role in labor negotiations. Using these techniques, the setting of job standards and pay scales, as we will see later in this chapter, could be based on neutral scientific evidence. This helped to reduce labor–management tensions from the previous level, where management viewed labor as underworked and the workers felt that they were overworked. Of course, time study experts employed by unions and time study experts employed by management often disagree, but they share scientifically developed standards. A good labor arbitrator usually will employ an independent expert to verify the time study results.

Today, in what many are calling the postindustrial age, the role of time and motion study, rather than diminishing, is expanding. The notion of who is a worker has been expanded in three ways. First, anyone performing some task or set of tasks (some operation) is now considered to be the worker or the operator. The definition of *worker* need not be limited to the industrial environment. Any job, whether in service or production, qualifies. The phenomenal growth of the service sector of our economy has created the same need to establish order and efficiency in providing services as has existed all along in the manufacturing sector.

The definition of the word *worker* has been expanded to include every employee within an operation. Every job, from office clerk to company president, has certain functions that must be accomplished. The measures may be less clear in certain types of jobs than in others, but a study of the required procedures and how they relate to job goals is always helpful.

The third expansion of the notion of the worker shifts the emphasis from the individual to the system of workers and machines. The same techniques that have been used so effectively in the past to measure and to improve individual performance are now being applied to what links the individuals in a system. These links, rather than the system itself, are analyzed because the analytical methods aim to conduct a micro-level study of individual work components in order to improve work methods. Consider the following real-world example, where communication was the missing link in the system.

labor–management relations

define the worker

Example 9.7   One author of this text was involved in developing a series of procedures for the Tucson, Arizona, fire department. A portion of the project involved the printing and mailing of response forms to businesses and the subsequent analysis of the data in the responses. As happens in any large organization, certain required functions could not be done by the fire department. Specifically, due to the cost benefits involved for the city, the printing of the forms had to be done by the city printing office.

In the existing procedure, the forms were printed and sent to the fire department. There, a team of clerks folded them and inserted them into envelopes for mailing. However, because we were redesigning the response forms, we visited the city printing office to discuss the effect of our changes. In our brief tour of the printing shop, we noticed something interesting. After being printed, forms for another department went automatically into another machine that folded them and then into a third machine that stuffed them into envelopes!

When we asked why the forms for the fire department were not processed beyond the printer, we were told, "The fire department only requested that their forms be *printed*." Further conversation showed that there was nothing to prevent the printing office from folding and stuffing our forms, too. Back at the fire department, we learned that they were not aware the printing shop possessed these capabilities.

No one from the fire department had seen the print shop, and no one from the print shop knew how the forms were being used. Although each office may have been operating efficiently, the manner in which they were linked together created inefficiencies. A review of the operations led to this discovery. ∎

Now that we have discussed some of the motivation for using time and motion study and provided an overview of places where it is applied, it is time to describe it more fully. Motion and time study is the use of systematic procedures for the analysis of work in order to

1. eliminate unnecessary work;
2. perform the remaining work in the best order;
3. standardize the proper work methods; and
4. establish accurate time standards for the work.

goals of time and motion study

Operationally, it examines, in detail, every motion required to perform a task.

The first two goals fall under the general heading of **work simplification.** They are used as guiding principles of motion economy. The second two goals are considered to be **work standardization.** Let us look at some examples of each.

ELIMINATE UNNECESSARY WORK

This may be the most important goal. The reader may think that Example 9.7 eliminated unnecessary work, but, actually, it did not. The result of that example led to the design of a better *work method,* a subject addressed in the next section. Recall that time and motion study involves the examination of each motion involved in a task. We examine these motions to see if any can be eliminated. A pure example of eliminating unnecessary motion is the advice that every batting coach in baseball gives to every hitter: "Get that hitch out of your swing." For another example, consider the following.

Example 9.8   The Big Bird Pencil Company sells pencil boxes that are long enough to hold pencils that are 8 inches long. Six pencils fit in each box, and the pencils can be between 7.9 and 8 inches long to be considered of acceptable length. The current inspection procedure is

1. produce pencils;
2. inspect pencils for length (too long);
3. inspect pencils for length (too short); and
4. place six pencils in each box.

Upon review of this procedure, one of the machine operators noted that the pencils will not fit in the box if they are too long. Thus, placing them in the box unsuccessfully means that the inspection for maximum length is not necessary. The second step, then, can be eliminated from the procedure. ∎

PERFORM WORK IN THE BEST ORDER

Many problems presented in this text require an ordering of jobs or tasks. We have already discussed the ordering of tasks on an assembly line (line balancing), and soon we will see how to order jobs in a large project (Chapter 10) and in a job shop (Chapter 15). Although we present no prescriptive procedures to order the work here, we emphasize the general point that *different orders can lead to different completion times.* Production rates and per unit costs can be improved as a result of better completion times.

> **Example 9.9**   A secretary is asked to collate and staple three copies of a paper. The secretary can follow one of the two following orders of tasks.
>
> **Task Order 1**
> Extract the first copy (all three pages).
> Staple it.
> Extract the second copy (all pages).
> Staple it.
> Extract the third copy (all pages.)
> Staple it.
>
> **Task Order 2**
> Sort the three copies (by page).
> Collate the pages (take one page from each sorted pile).
> Staple all three copies.

Which order of the tasks is preferred?

The best way to determine the answer to this question is to try the two methods. Having tried them, you will find that the second sequence collates and staples the pages faster. This second sequence often increases accuracy as well.   ▪◩

Teaching Suggestion 9.6: Standardization. See the Instructor's Section for details.

STANDARDIZE THE PROPER WORK METHODS

Once it has been determined how to eliminate all unnecessary motion from a job and how to set up work to accomplish it in the best order, each worker performing that particular job must be taught the techniques that accomplish these goals. It is this standardization of procedures across the entire work force that produces the large cost savings that have so often been associated with successful time and motion studies. Because these studies usually evaluate many small motions, the individual time and cost savings are, for the most part, small. However, when the evaluated task is performed a few thousand times per day, the cost savings can add up very fast if the changes can be incorporated effectively across the workplace. For a suggestion that saved only .3 cents per part produced, an author of this text was credited with, and rewarded for, savings valued at $604,000 for a three-year period!

small time savings lead to large dollar savings

ESTABLISH ACCURATE TIME STANDARDS

Establishing accurate time standards is the task most people associate with time studies. We have all seen the media's caricature of the "efficiency expert," who runs around the office with a stopwatch, timing everyone's work and driving everyone up a wall. However, the setting of time standards is the one part of motion and time study that is truly scientific, because it is based on realistic experimental measurement. Whereas the first three steps require a perceptiveness on the part of the individual conducting the study, setting time standards relies on methodology, not an individual.

The methodology employed is, essentially, the scientific method. A series of experiments are run, the outcome is observed, and conclusions are drawn. Let us look first at the series of experiments. Each experiment consists of the performance of the task or job under study. In practice, the job is performed, not once, but repeatedly. For this reason and for the reason that a larger sample size is needed to assure confidence in the experiment, the number of cycles of the task (sample size) used in the test must be determined. To determine an appropriate sample size, the manager needs to estimate two parameters, **determine sample size**

- the sample mean ($\bar{x}$) and
- the sample standard deviation (s),

and to specify two other parameters,

- the desired confidence (α) and
- the desired accuracy (β).

Given these parameters, the appropriate sample size, n, is found by using the formula

$$n = \left(\frac{z_\alpha s}{\beta \bar{x}} \right)^2,$$

sample size

where z_α is the standard normal variable obtained from Appendix B1 for confidence level α. The sample size will need to be greater if the standard deviation is larger and if higher confidence and lower maximum errors are required.

In practice, the operations manager may run into a formula for sample size that uses an error parameter specified as an amount rather than as a percentage. This approach is less desirable. Standard practice is to work with percentages, both here and in the allowance factors that often are added to the standard times.

Example 9.10 Applied Data Processing needs to establish time standards for the work that its keypunchers will be performing on a major contract. The cycle observed will consist of entering one line of data into a computer terminal. Initial estimates for the two parameters that can be identified are as follows:

Mean time = .4 seconds and

Standard deviation = .15 seconds.

Management has specified that it must have 95-percent confidence in the results and that the maximum allowable error is 10 percent. How many lines of data (cycles) must be observed to achieve these results?

The number of cycles, n, is given as

$$n = \left(\frac{z_\alpha s}{\beta \bar{x}} \right)^2,$$

where

$s = 15;$

$\bar{x} = .4;$

$z_\alpha = z_{.95} = 1.96;$ and

$\beta = .10.$

Thus,

$$n = \left(\frac{1.96 \times .15}{.10 \times .4}\right)^2 = 54.0225.$$

Theoretically, this number always should be rounded upward to assure that the desired confidences are achieved. In this case, because 54.0225 is so close to 54, an n of 54 is appropriate. ◾

collect data

Now that we know how many cycles to observe, the second step is to actually make the observation. As mentioned previously in regard to the efficiency expert, this consists of using a stopwatch to measure the length of time associated with each task.

Once the sample times have been collected, the times that need to be determined are

- the **observed time** (OT),
- the **normal time** (NT), and
- the **standard time** (ST).

The observed time is the average time, obtained in the experiment, to complete one cycle. Its formula is

observed time

$$OT = \frac{\Sigma x_i}{n},$$

where

x_i = the ith observed time and

n = the number of observations.

Although the observed time, OT, reflects actual data, it is not the measure that is actually used. Two modifications are made to it to find, first, the normal time and, second, the standard time.

The normal time, NT, adjusts the observed time to take into account the performance of the operator. This performance is measured by the **performance rating, PR**. The standard value of PR is 1.0, with a higher rating (say, 1.05) indicating that a faster than normal pace is occurring and a lower rating (say, .95) indicating the opposite. The normal time is found by multiplying the observed time by the performance rating:

normal time

$$NT = OT \times PR.$$

To find the standard time, the actual measure used, it is again necessary to modify the normal time. With this modification, however, there is no possibility that the time will be lowered, as there was in going from the observed time to the normal time. Here, we wish to increase the time by an **allowance factor** (AF) to reflect the delays and interruptions that occur during the course of the normal workday. Such delays may include scheduled breaks, disruptions due to equipment failure or unavailability of materials, and many other smaller interruptions to the work. To obtain the standard time from the normal time, we define a **job time percent allowance** to account for delays and interruptions. This provides us with an allowance factor, which is multiplied

allowing for interruptions

by the normal time to yield the standard time. If the percent allowance is 12 percent, then the resulting allowance factor is 1.12. The simple formula for the standard time is

$$ST = NT \times AF.$$ **standard time**

To obtain the standard time directly from the observed time, we use this formula:

$$ST = OT \times PR \times AF.$$

Example 9.11   A time study was done on the keypunch operation presented in Example 9.10. (That is, the mean time is .4 seconds, and the standard deviation is .15 seconds.) Only twelve measurements were taken in this initial study, and the β level had to remain at 10 percent. The following measurements were found.

Observation	Time (in minutes)
1	.331
2	.243
3	.422
4	.521
5	.511
6	.342
7	.468
8	.766
9	.489
10	.391
11	.413
12	.484

A performance rating of .90 is assigned, along with a percent allowance of 6 percent.

(a) What confidence is obtained using $n = 12$?

(b) Determine the observed time, the normal time, and the standard time.

(a) $$n = \left(\frac{z_\alpha s}{\beta \bar{x}}\right)^2$$

First, we need to solve for z_α.

$$z_\alpha = \beta \bar{x} \sqrt{n}/s$$
$$= (.10)(.4) \sqrt{12}/.15$$
$$= .924$$

Then, from the standard normal table provided in Appendix B1, we find that

$$\alpha = .64.$$

The confidence level attained when $n = 12$ is 64 percent, as opposed to 95 percent when $n = 54$.

(b) $OT = \dfrac{\Sigma x_i}{n}$

$= \dfrac{.331 + .243 + .422 + .521 + .511 + .342 + .468 + .766 + .489 + .391 + .413 + .484}{12}$

$= .4484$ minutes

$$N = OT \times PR$$
$$= .4484 \times .90 = .4036 \text{ minutes}$$

As should be expected, this is close to the initial $\bar{x}$, which was estimated to be .4. Lastly,

$$ST = NT \times AF$$
$$= .4036 \times 1.06 = .428 \text{ minutes.}$$ ∎

use of standard times

In addition to the method of timing the actual work to derive the standard times, the times also can be obtained from standard data in one of two ways. First, **standard elemental times,** derived from past history, may be used. Although there may be reasons to modify these times for a new project, they form a solid foundation for deriving new times and can save a great deal of effort with the stopwatch. A second method, now readily available on microcomputers, uses **methods time measurement** (MTM). MTM tables provide standard elemental times for virtually any motion, over any given distance and under a wide variety of conditions, allowing the user to develop time standards from scratch by observing, but not timing, the motions required for each job. If standard data are used on many motions and added for the total time on a task, it is always wise to confirm the resulting times with some actual timed cycles.

WORK SAMPLING

sample work times

Time and motion studies are very accurate, but conducting them requires a great deal of manpower, and the work is, generally, of a very tedious nature. Another approach to calculating job times is to take random samples and estimate the times on this basis, thereby eliminating the need for constant observation. Work sampling is the term by which this technique is known. It can be used in place of time study, but its major application is in the area of nonrepetitive work, where time study is most difficult. Because work sampling is used for nonrepetitive jobs, this is the tool of work measurement that is applied most often to the job performance of managers.

The jobs of managerial personnel and those performing professional services, such as doctors, lawyers, and consultants, represent situations where the application of time studies is unlikely to be successful. Work sampling, though, is more than just a fallback approach for such situations. It has been used in classic time study situations to provide equally good results with much less effort and expense. Beyond actually measuring work, work sampling provides a quality check on job performance by all individuals in an organization.

Many in the field of work sampling would include in it the techniques of statistical quality control, which are presented in a separate chapter. The "inspection" of job performance here is just as important as the inspection of product quality, where quality control is more commonly used.

There are two major approaches to work sampling:

- the occurrence study and
- the ratio delay technique.

We will briefly discuss and compare the two approaches, but we will present the detailed implementation of only one of them—the occurrence study.

Because both approaches are work sampling techniques, they are very similar. Both use random samples in the form of quick "snapshot" observations as their bases. Both record the "state" of the worker (that is, busy or idle) at the time of the observation. Finally, both seek to determine the percentage of time the worker is in each of the possible states.

There are, however, important differences between these two approaches. When the ratio delay technique is used, the analyst knows the complete list of activities performed by the worker. This is not true in an occurrence study, where the list of activities is built up from observation. Generally, the ratio delay technique is used for machinery (states are operating, idle, or down for repair), whereas the occurrence study is used in dealings with human beings, where greater care is required in the setup and running of the study.

The purpose for which each approach is used also differs in most instances. Ratio delay attempts to measure machine availabilities for use in the determination of allowance factors. Because these measurements are used in time standard determination, the study must have a high degree of accuracy. Less accuracy is required of the results of the occurrence study because this study is used more for methods analysis (see the next section) than for standard setting.

To best illustrate how a work sampling is conducted, we now outline a step-by-step procedure for an occurrence study and give an example of its application. The example concerns the time required for various activities by the sales managers in a department store. These sales managers supervise the salespeople in a number of departments located in one section of the store.

the occurrence study

Step 1: *Goal determination.* There is a need to study the relationship of the sales managers to the salespeople. The longer-range goal is to use this study to define more precisely the job functions and time allocations of the sales managers.

Step 2: *Select areas of study.* In a small operation, all managers may be studied. However, if there are enough managers, the study can gain accuracy if a group that has something in common is chosen. Those managers whose departments primarily serve women shoppers are chosen for this study.

Step 3: *Select individuals.* Again, it is a luxury if we can be selective, allowing us to refine the study further. As a general rule, no more than twenty people are included in an occurrence study. The choice of individuals can be aimed either at obtaining a broad overview or at studying a particular phenomenon; in the latter case, subjects might be people who have registered complaints about work load, people in charge of bottleneck departments, or people in charge of departments that seem to have poor (or unusually good) human relations. For this study, a broad selection is made in order to achieve an overview. A specific list of individuals involved in the study is made, and each person selected is briefed on the nature of the study.

Step 4: *Observe work.* Become familiar with the work by observing the individuals being studied and by discussing with them just how they view their activities.

Step 5: *Compile a list of activities.* This list should be developed from the observation of the work. The list of activities performed by the sales managers is provided in Figure 9.8.

Step 6: *Design an observation form.* The observation form differs from study to study. For this study, the form shown in Figure 9.8 is used. Each column represents a different time period, because it is felt that management activity changes according to the level of customer activity in the store. There are three time periods per day, and observations are made over six days. It is always better to begin with a finer breakdown (and then aggregate results, if necessary) than to use a gross breakdown at the start.

Step 7: *Determine the number of required observations.* Random observations are made of the activity patterns of the managers. The number of observations depends on the amount of error (E) that can be tolerated and the confidence level desired. The amount of error (E) is expressed as a percentage of the estimate. For example, $E = .10$ means that a plus or minus 10-percent error will be tolerated. General practice is to use a 95-percent confidence level (2 sigma limits), as opposed to the 99.7-percent level (3 sigma limits) used in applications such as quality control charts. The reason this confidence level is used is that the extra sampling required to achieve the higher confidence for the value of the better information is not worthwhile in this case. Given these considerations, the formula to use for finding N, the number of observations to take, is

number of required observations for 95% confidence

$$N = \frac{4p(1 - p)}{E^2},$$

where

   4 = the square of the number of standard deviations (2) used;

   p = the estimate of the percent of time spent on an activity; and

   E = the amount of error allowable.

This formula is based on the use of the binomial distribution for the occurrences. While two standard deviations are most often used in practice, z_α can be used in place of the number of standard deviations.

   For our study, it seems that the sales managers spend approximately 20 percent of their time handling returns. If we desire to limit the error on this estimate to plus or minus 3 percent, the required number of observations is

$$N = \frac{4(.2)(.8)}{(.03)^2} = 711 \text{ observations.}$$

If our goal had been to study one particular manager, then 711 observations would have to be taken on each manager in the group. Because our goal is to study the group, we take a total of 711 observations, spread evenly across all of the managers in the study.

| | Week beginning: November 2 | | Service Mgr.: Mr. Williams |
| Floor: 4th | | Dept.: Men's Wear |

Duties	Mon.	Tues.	Wed.	Thurs.	Fri.	Sat.	Total
Handling returns	/ //	/	/	//		/	8
Active supervision		/ // /		//		/	7
Passive supervision	/	/	/	/			4
Handling adjustment		/		/			2
Talking with customer		/ //				/	4
Daily report of salespeople							
Return stock							
Work orders							
Wait on customer							
Exchanges		/				/	2
Distribute service notes							
Charge without plate			/				1
Personal time	/		/				2
Lunch	□		□	□			③
Telephone	/			/		/	3
Sign shoppers' passes		/		/			2
Talk to superintendent						/	1
O.K. bank checks			/				1
Total	1 5 4	3 4 1	1 3 3	2 3 1		1 4 1	37

FIGURE 9.8 Work observation form

Source: G. Nadler, *Motion and Time Study.* New York: McGraw-Hill, 1970.

Step 8: *Take the observations.* This is the data collection phase. Three rules are applied to assure that nothing is done during the actual observations to bias the results.

1. The time between observations must be random.
2. The order of the observations on the people involved must be random.
3. The observations must be instantaneous.

Step 9: *Compile the data.* The data are now summarized and analyzed using the following three steps.

1. Determine the total number of observations.
2. Determine the total number of observations in each category.
3. Divide the number in each category by the total number to obtain the percentage of time spent on each activity.

Of the 711 observations taken, 136 showed the sales managers handling returns. Thus, the percentage of time spent handling returns is

$$\frac{136}{711} = 19.1\%.$$

In an eight-hour shift, then, the sales manager spends approximately

$$480 \text{ minutes} \times .191 = 91.68 \text{ minutes}$$

(or about an hour and a half) handling returns.

Step 10: *Assess errors.* The formula given in step 7 also can be used to assess the resulting error, E, given the number of observations, N, as

creating a range

$$E = 2\sqrt{\frac{p(1 - p)}{N}}.$$

For our estimate of 19.1 percent of the time spent in handling returns, the error is

$$E = 2\sqrt{\frac{.191 \times .809}{711}} = .0295, \text{ or } 2.95\%.$$

This error is to be interpreted as *plus or minus* 2.95 percent. So the appropriate percentage of time spent handling returns is

$$19.1\% \pm 2.95\%.$$

Another interpretation is that we are 95-percent confident that the percentage of time managers handle returns is between 16.15 percent and 22.05 percent.

This ends the work sampling project (occurrence study). We now summarize the advantage of using an occurrence study over using the ratio delay technique.

advantages of occurrence study

1. A longer period of time and a more representative sample may be used.
2. The observer can do other work while taking the observations.
3. It is flexible enough to be expanded or compressed as needed.
4. It provides valuable information on time spent on an activity.
5. It is less intrusive on the workers than are time and motion studies.

JOB DESIGN

major tool

Our discussion of time and motion study has already touched on the major tool of job design: **methods analysis.** But job design encompasses much more than methods analysis. The other factors of job design are reviewed in the first part of this section, followed by a more formal presentation of methods analysis.

JOB DESIGN FACTORS

The design of a job as an amount of work to be done by an individual, a machine, or a man–machine system is a complex task. At the foundation is the procedure describing exactly how the job is done—that is, the method, which we will discuss in more detail in the following section. The factors considered briefly here, all of which contribute to the success or failure of the operation, are

- system job design philosophy,
- job environment,
- job difficulty,
- job growth and employee opportunity, and
- job security.

SYSTEM JOB DESIGN PHILOSOPHY

The philosophy of system job design is to relate the strategic decisions regarding plant capacity and layout to the daily job activity, defining the way in which workers are used. The key consideration here is the degree of **specialization** desired. A high-speed assembly line requires the most extreme use of specialization, each worker or machine repeating the same job all day long. This type of work is boring, provides little job satisfaction, and often leads to lower workforce morale and high rates of absenteeism. As the production manager at a plant in Wisconsin once put it, "When I asked one of the workers why he never showed up on Monday or Friday, he answered that he made enough money in three days." Although to earn money is the major reason most people work, proper job design can motivate the worker and satisfy other human needs as well. Maslow's *hierarchy of needs* is the most famous description of what satisfies us as workers.

degree of specialization

The obvious alternative to specialization is to let each worker complete an entire product or service, or at least larger parts of one. Although this alternative may sacrifice efficiency, it improves the quality of the work and reduces the tedium. In service jobs, this alternative is even more desirable, especially when the service is performed directly for an individual, because quality of service leads to repeat customers and business growth. An assembly line at the hair stylist, although practical from an efficiency viewpoint, would never be accepted by customers. Assembly lines work quite well, though, at the dry cleaners.

specialization relates to quality

To motivate workers in an assembly line environment, a variety of behavioral approaches are used. The simplest is **job rotation,** where workers are moved from one job to another. Besides adding some variety to the job, rotation benefits the business by allowing the workers to see how each job fits into the whole and by creating a more flexible workforce. A second approach is **job enlargement,** where workers are given increased responsibility over more jobs at their same skill level. Although its effects are very similar to those of job rotation, the job growth is on a permanent basis.

behavioral approaches

The other strategic consideration regarding job design is the degree of automation to be used. Most new business operations strive to achieve the highest possible degree of automation, but there are limits to how much is really desirable. Where extremely tight tolerance on machinery is required, numerical control (NC) machines are really the only choice, achieving accuracies of less than one ten-thousandth of an inch. A general rule is that a more repetitive task is more amenable to automation. This is ideal for the human factors as well, because it means that the most boring jobs will be automated.

JOB ENVIRONMENT

The work environment affects the worker's ability to do a job, both directly and indirectly. A primary factor with direct effects is the quality of the equipment made available to the workers. Secondary factors directly affecting job performance are light, heat, and noise. Indirect factors relate to the quality of work life. Company picnics, social clubs, and athletic leagues all add to the quality of work life. A less specific factor is the company's ability to instill a shared organizational mission in each of its employees. The Japanese are most noted for success in this area, although in the United States "IBMers" always seem to be proud of that title.

JOB DIFFICULTY

Job difficulty refers to work load and skill level. Every manager wants to get the maximum amount of work from employees, but work errors increase dramatically as work load exceeds the limits of the individual. In time and motion terminology, the work load is a function of the movement required, the load moved, and the number of repetitions. The basic measure of elemental moves is the *therblig,* which is *Gilbreth* (after Frank Gilbreth, a pioneer in work measurement) spelled backward.

match job skills with employee skills

The skill level required for a job also helps to measure job difficulty. With regard to skill level, the goal in job design is to try to design the job in such a way that the minimum skill level is required. Once skill levels for each task have been determined, the skill levels of employees must be matched with the skill requirements of the job. If required skill levels are too high, errors will again increase; if required skills are beneath the skill level of the individual, boredom and job dissatisfaction will result.

JOB GROWTH AND EMPLOYEE OPPORTUNITY

Every worker must have the opportunity to grow in a job. **Job enrichment** is the term most often used for this, where workers take on increasing responsibilities as their skill levels increase. Management needs to provide at least one of two avenues for growth—technical and/or professional. Employment counselors preach this regularly to their clients. The time to change jobs is when avenues for gaining new skills and for promotion are closed. As long as at least one of these avenues is open, remaining in the job is worthwhile to the worker. We should note that, traditionally, union workers in the United States have been contractually barred from taking on additional responsibilities. However, a growing number of U.S. firms, including General Motors, National Steel, and Motorola are moving away from strict, union-imposed job classification schemes. In an effort to increase quality, efficiency, and productivity, workers at these and other firms are being trained to perform more than one job.

JOB SECURITY

Just as they have in the area of job conditions, the Japanese have set the standard in providing job security. A typical hiring letter from a U.S. company lists a starting date and salary, but seldom mentions a length of employment. Either the company or the worker may terminate the relationship at any time. Although there is much to be learned from Japan, lifetime job security is a concept that most probably would not work in the U.S. business environment.

The operations manager is interested in designing jobs in such a way that workers feel their jobs are secure into the foreseeable future (which, in a sense, is a definition of job security in the United States). The manager can instill this feeling of security by assuring each worker a responsibility that is his or hers alone. The goal here is to make each worker feel that he or she has staked out a "territory" that is vital to the interest of the business and necessitates his or her presence.

METHODS ANALYSIS

Methods analysis is the design of how a job should be done, how the operation should be carried out. Ideally, methods analysis designs a method for a job that has not been done before, a new job. Very often, however, methods analysis is used for jobs that are being performed already. For such cases, the goal of methods analysis is **job improvement,** rather than job design, and this improvement may be either short range or long range. Short-range improvements are aimed at overcoming bottleneck operations in the overall process or at high-cost operations. Although the solution to such problems can be short range, the analysis very often leads to long-range solutions that call for the purchase of different equipment or the redesign of workplace layouts.

Methods analysis identifies the following key items affecting work:

1. material,
2. design,
3. sequence,
4. equipment, and
5. method.

items affecting work

The relationship between these five items is shown in Figure 9.9. The five items affecting work are used to develop the following five strategies that are investigated in a methods analysis.

1. Change the material being used or contemplated for use to help meet the goal for the operation being studied.
2. Change the present or contemplated design of the product to help meet the goal for the operation being studied.
3. Change the present or contemplated sequence of work on the material or product to help meet the goal for the operation being studied.
4. Change the equipment being used or contemplated for use in the operation to help meet the goal for the operation being studied.
5. Change the method or hand pattern being used or contemplated for use in the operation to help meet the goal for the operation being studied.

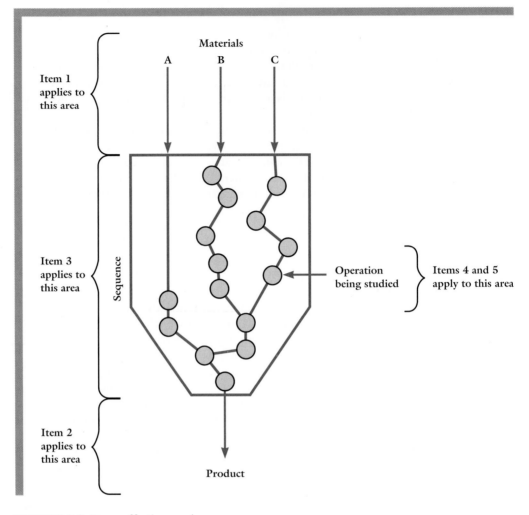

FIGURE 9.9   Items affecting work

In each of these strategies, the word *change* is used. In each case, the aim of the change is really elimination—the elimination of unnecessary work. For any operation, we must ask if we can

eliminate unnecessary work

- eliminate,
- combine,
- simplify, or
- rearrange

each of the items that affect work. In addition, for any task, we must ask certain questions:

- Is it necessary?
- Who does it?
- Where is it done?

- When is it done?
- How is it done?

For any suggestion that seems promising, a study is conducted to see if the desired improvement really can be achieved. If the material is to be changed, an engineering study is in order. If the locations of tools and parts are to be changed, then a time and motion study is in order. In any case, the new method must be tested thoroughly prior to its adoption.

An informal source of many methods improvements is the workers who do the operations. Many companies have adopted high-visibility suggestion programs or value engineering programs to encourage employees to contribute toward increasing the efficiency and quality of their work. In companies where management is not responsive to employee suggestions, employees often make changes without management's knowledge. The employees make operating changes that they know will be beneficial because the changes will make their work easier.

The most successful use of employee knowledge for methods improvement has been achieved through the use of the **quality circle.** The quality circle involves meetings between employees and management to discuss ways of improving the quality of work. We discuss the quality circle concept in more detail in Chapter 16. We mention it here, though, because a side effect of the quality circle has proven to be of greater benefit than its contribution to improved quality: improved *methods,* which can generate millions of dollars' worth of savings.

employee involvement

LABOR STANDARDS AND INCENTIVES

In this section, we see how a job can be evaluated in terms of its worth to the business. This setting of labor standards is used as a basis for all wage scales. In addition to setting wage scales based on the value of the job, management seeks to compensate for work done beyond the standards. By providing incentives, management provides a mechanism whereby labor that exceeds production quotas or quality targets will be rewarded with increased compensation of some sort.

LABOR STANDARDS

Labor standards are used to establish work loads. Because the handling of a work load over any period of time is dependent on the method used and the detailed analysis of that method, standard setting is closely related both to time and motion study and to methods analysis. As such, it is the final step in the logical progression of the job design function. All methods must be finalized prior to standard setting.

final step of job design

Formally, standards setting is the determination of the *time* that an operation performed by a given method, under given job conditions should take

- when it is worked on by an operator who has the necessary skill and has been given sufficient training to perform the operation properly;
- when the operator working on it is working at a pace that is maintainable throughout the day, which is specified as equivalent to the work necessary to earn base pay; and
- when all of the operator's needs are provided for.

This time is known as the standard time, which we mentioned already in our discussion of time and motion study. Recall that the standard time does not actually reflect the stopwatch readings. Allowances to these readings have been made to reach an agreed-upon standard, after normalization of the time.

normalization factors

The normalization process was mentioned briefly earlier, but at the time we did not tell how the normalization factor is selected. This normalization factor is found through two analyses:

- a pace comparison and
- a difficulty comparison.

We have, then, two criteria for selecting the normalization factor.

1. How does the operator's performance compare to that of other employees of the business?
2. How does the job performed by the operator compare, in terms of difficulty or complexity, with the other operations of the business?

pace comparison

The pace comparison often is referred to as the *rating,* or *factor X.*

The normalization factor itself is difficult to define. In fact, many time study practitioners claim that its definition is an unnecessary step. Selection of the proper operator for the study, they say, eliminates the need to normalize the observed times. The general feeling, though, is that no "standard" operator exists and that the normalization factor should measure the causes of operator variation. These causes are summed up in the following three groups:

- psychological,
- physiological, and
- sociological.

Three types of measuring techniques have been used in pace comparisons. One type is overall evaluation. This is the commonsense approach, and it was the first approach developed for this purpose. The analysis assigns a value of 100 percent to some "normal" time and bases the judgment of operators on this value. For example, a worker rated at 120 percent might be classified as "excellent"; a worker rated at 110 percent, "good"; and so on, down to 80 percent. These ratings are used to set standards of expected performance. A similar approach, known as skill and effort, judges workers on two scales (skill and effort) to reach a normalized time.

Example 9.12   The airline agent at the gate handles seat assignments for all passengers after they have been ticketed and have checked their luggage. The 100-percent time used per passenger for seat assignment is 50 seconds. The agent at gate B4 today is rated "good" (110 percent). What average time should we expect this agent to achieve?

Because the rating for this agent is 110 percent, the time should be about 10 percent faster than the 100-percent values, or

$$\frac{50 \text{ seconds}}{1.10} = 45.45 \text{ seconds.}$$

Making seat assignments should take the agent at gate B4 today about 45 seconds per passenger.   ■◧

The second and third types of procedures used in pace comparison are more complex, and we will provide only brief descriptions of them. The second type is statistical manipulation of the time study data. This procedure attempts to eliminate the judgmental characterizations required in the overall evaluation method. The third type is speed evaluation. Because speed is the only really measurable work characteristic, workers are judged according to speed; it is assumed that the measurements will include all of the factors that lead to the proper normalization if enough observations are taken.

The difficulty comparison is more straightforward because it rates the job rather than the operator. The following items are to be considered in assigning a difficulty rating. **difficulty comparison**

1. amount of body used
2. hand or foot patterns required
3. weight resistance overcome
4. directional eye–hand coordination
5. positional eye–hand coordination
6. muscular pressure control
7. muscular tilt control
8. decisions required

One additional factor is applied to the difficulty rating determined from the preceding list of factors: pace. The pace at which the operator works, or is required to work, has a direct effect on job difficulty. Obviously, a faster pace makes the operation more difficult.

In practice, normalization factors are usually in the range of 5 to 10 percent from the observed time.

The final step in standard setting is the addition of the allowances to the normalized times, yielding the standard time. The categories of allowances, mentioned briefly in our earlier discussion of time and motion study, are described more fully here. **allowance factors**

PERSONAL TIME

Some amount of time must be allowed for workers' personal needs, such as thirst or other physical requirements. The amount allowed is very much dependent on working conditions. For example, an office worker will require less personal time than a construction worker. Table 9.3 provides some typical allowances for personal needs.

TABLE 9.3 Allowances for personal needs

Working Conditions	Minutes per 8-hour Day
Comfortable year-round	20
Warm or chilly	30
Wide variations in temperature or noise level	40
Presence of items that cause some breathing difficulties (such as dust or paint) if not properly ventilated	55
Special categories	As needed

IRREGULAR OCCURRENCES

Time also must be allotted for activities that are part of the job but not necessarily part of every regular cycle. Activities such as cleaning tools or the work area, lubricating machinery, or picking up another batch of material are included in this category. Time spent on such activities is determined most often by a work sampling study.

UNAVOIDABLE DELAYS

Delays resulting from unexpected events that are not part of the job but that prevent the operator from performing the job function take time, too. Such delays are attributable to management rather than to the workers and are caused by poor scheduling of various subassemblies or material delivery, poor plant layout, or poor equipment maintenance. Again, work sampling is used to derive this allowance.

MACHINE CONTROL AND INTERFERENCE

In today's highly automated environment, machines control parts of many work cycles. Therefore, allowances must be made to the worker for machine downtime or for time needed to coordinate the work of more than one machine. This allowance is obtained either from a work sampling or, more often, directly from a time and motion study via a complex set of equations.

FATIGUE

The average pace maintained by an operator is not constant over the course of a day, necessitating another allowance. Sometimes, fatigue is included in the normalization factor, but we include it as an allowance, which is the more common practice. This allowance usually is determined from a time study.

INCENTIVES

The reward that the operator receives for work performed is called *compensation*. Compensation most often means wages, but it also can include benefits such as insurance and pension plans, bonuses, and even the satisfaction one can obtain from management's recognition of excellent job performance.

An operator can be assigned a wage based on the standard amount of work expected. This wage also should be related to the value, in terms of profits, that this standard amount of work contributes to the business. Use of this wage assignment approach can lead to a situation where worker compensation does not vary, regardless of whether the workers exceed or fail to achieve their standard rate. The way to get around this problem is to use incentives.

base pay rates   In an incentive system, base pay rates are set, not on the standard rate, but on a lesser figure—usually 80 percent of standard. This pay is guaranteed to all workers, regardless of the amount of work they accomplish. Production records are kept for each worker, and if the 80-percent standard is exceeded, the worker is eligible for additional pay.

A **piece rate** system pays the worker on a per unit basis, but usually is modified as just described to provide a minimum pay base. A piece rate system can be applied either to an individual or to a group. When applied to the individual, that individual is paid based entirely on his or her own performance. In practice, however, an operator is rarely independent of other workers. In these cases, the incentive payments are made to all members of a group that provide input toward the output of an operation. One such group is the crew that performs a job together. A less obvious group is the assembly line that has been designed using a line-balancing technique. Here, the output of the line determines the pay of each individual, encouraging the workers to push each other and even to help each other if a bottleneck occurs. The group also may become competitive with other production lines.

Related to piece rates are company **profit-sharing plans.** If more output is produced, then there will be more profits to share among the workers. One company, Avis, implemented this philosophy in everyday operations by requiring every employee to own part of the company. This requirement encouraged each employee to treat customers well, because, if the customer decided not to rent from Avis again, that loss of business affected the employee. This approach has worked very well for Avis.

profit sharing

Another form of incentive is tied less directly to output. Bonuses, financial or otherwise, often are awarded to outstanding workers. These bonuses vary—from extra pay to extra vacation time to a trip to a resort. The suggestion programs mentioned in our discussion of methods analysis, in which the individual making the suggestion receives a share of the savings, are also a form of incentive plan.

LEARNING CURVES

A standard for a particular operation may be 100 cycles per hour, or 36 seconds per cycle. However, it is not reasonable to expect a newly hired employee to achieve 100 cycles per hour on his or her first day. The actual work rate over the first week may look more like the following.

Day	Cycles/hour	Seconds/cycle
1	30	120
2	55	65
3	75	48
4	88	41
5	93	39

This improvement over time is illustrated by the **learning curve,** or training curve. For this example, the curve is shown in Figure 9.10. The curve usually has this shape, where the time is decreasing (productivity is increasing) along with the rate of learning (productivity increase). This effect of diminishing learning (over time) continues until the curve flattens out, at which point the worker is trained and there is no more learning. Another shape, occurring less often, is shown in Figure 9.11. This is known as the S-shaped learning curve and is characterized by a learning process that is slow at first, followed by a period of faster increases and, finally, by a leveling when the standard is reached.

The concept of the learning curve also is applied to equipment, in terms of reliability or availability. When applied to equipment, the curve is known as a **failure rate curve** because it measures how fast the failure rate of a new piece of equipment can be brought down to the levels guaranteed by the manufacturer.

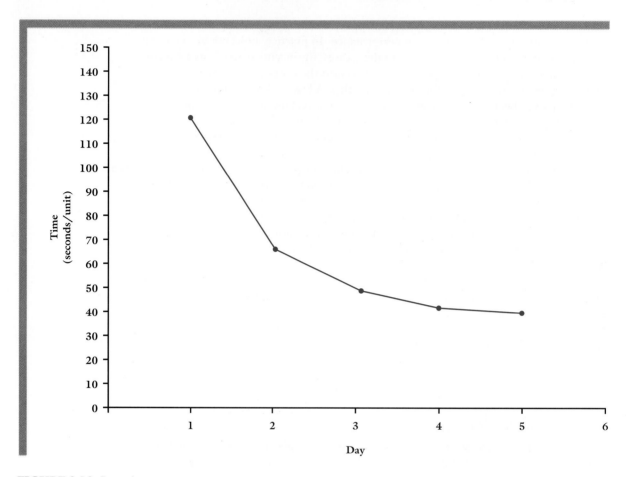

FIGURE 9.10 Learning curve

There are four parameters for learning curves about which the manager is concerned.

1. starting point
2. shape of curve
3. rate of increase
4. steady state

STARTING POINT.   The starting point on the curve is the initial time achieved. In the previous example, the initial time was 120, so this was the starting point for the curve. Figure 9.12 illustrates the effect of the starting point on the curve. As one should expect, the figure shows that, during the training time, a better starting point yields better performance—that is, lower training costs. Most often, the worker having the lower starting point will reach the steady state faster, again reducing training costs. We cannot make a general statement about the level of steady state reached; a worker with a higher starting point may, in fact, reach a lower steady state.

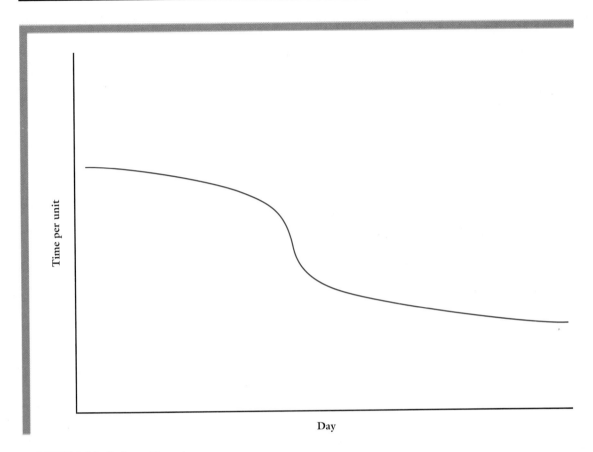

FIGURE 9.11 S-shaped learning curve

SHAPE OF CURVE: Generally, the shape of the curve, which represents the learning process, is either that of the curve in Figure 9.10 or that of the curve in Figure 9.11. In rare cases, the rate of learning is linear (a straight-line learning curve). It is necessary to know the shape of the curve to be able to predict the standard rates for operators in training. The shape of the curve is a function of the specific job, rather than of the individual worker.

RATE OF INCREASE: We all learn at different rates for different jobs. The effect of these different learning rates is shown in Figure 9.13. As they are with the lower starting point, training costs are reduced by employing a faster learner.

STEADY STATE: The minimum time, which appears on the right on each of the learning curves, represents the time when the training is completed, or when the worker reaches his or her steady state rate. The worker with the lowest steady state time is producing the most work and so is the most desirable worker.

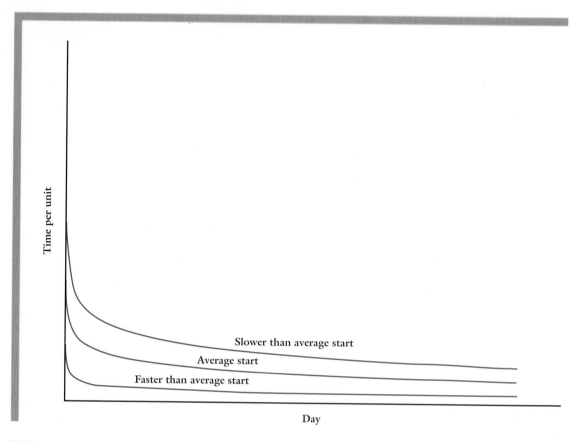

FIGURE 9.12 Effect of starting point on learning curve

Transparency Master 9.6:
Learning Curves.

You may be wondering why another parameter—the time to reach the steady state—is missing. We have omitted this important consideration because it is an outgrowth of the four parameters that we have cited.

Managers are concerned with these parameters when they are hiring new employees. Many companies give aptitude tests to applicants to predict which will be the best workers and which can be "brought down the learning curve" the fastest.

The typical assumption about learning is that a given amount of learning occurs with the doubling of the number of units. For example, a learning rate of 90 percent means that the second unit takes 90 percent of the time it took to complete the first unit, the fourth unit takes 90 percent of the time required for the second unit, the sixth takes 90 percent of the time required for the third, and so on.

Example 9.13 The service times for a new tax processor have been measured and recorded.

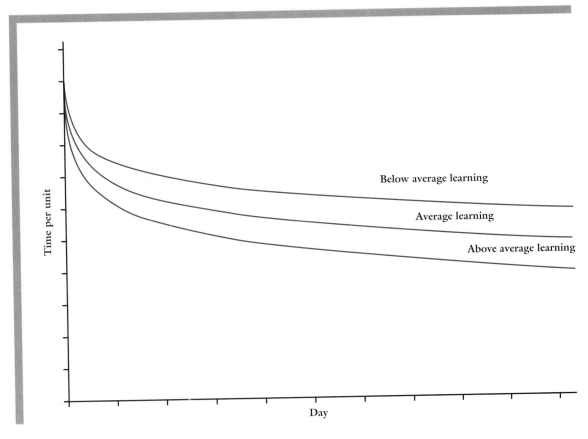

FIGURE 9.13 Effect of rate of learning on early stages of learning curve

Return	Time (in minutes)
1	66
2	56
3	53
4	49
5	47
6	45
7	44
8	42

What is the learning curve rate based on this information?

In order to estimate the learning curve rate, we take the ratios of the units that have doubled.

$$\text{return 2/return 1} = 56/66 = .848$$
$$\text{return 4/return 2} = 49/56 = .860$$
$$\text{return 6/return 3} = 45/53 = .849$$
$$\text{return 8/return 4} = 42/49 = .857$$

The learning curve rates are not identical for each paired comparison, but since they are in the range of 84 percent to 86 percent, we can safely use 85 percent.   ◼️

Given a learning curve rate and the time to produce the first unit, we can compute the time to produce future units. This is critical within the context of job design and time allocation.

⌐ **Example 9.14**   Using an 85-percent learning curve rate and the times in Example 9.13, estimate the length of time to complete the 50th unit.

Since the 6th unit took 45 seconds, the 12th unit should take 85 percent of 45 seconds, or 38.25 seconds. Multiplying again by 85 percent yields a time of 32.5 seconds for the 24th unit. One more multiplication yields a time of 27.6 seconds for the 48th unit. Therefore, we can assume that the 50th unit will take slightly less than the 27.6 seconds computed for the 48th. An exact answer can be found using the AB:POM software.   ◼️

▬▬▬

S U M M A R Y

In this chapter, the many and varied concerns related to the design and analysis of work have been presented. The individual's capacity for work is affected by several *human factors*. For equipment, work capacity is affected by *reliability* and *availability*. The analysis of work, or *work measurement*, includes the study of the time and the motion required to do a job. An alternative technique, better suited to nonrepetitive work, is *work sampling*. The actual design of the job focuses on the method to be used to accomplish the required work. *Methods analysis* allows us to look at various ways to do a job and provides us with formal ways to analyze a job in order to improve the work method. Once the method is finalized, work measurement techniques, especially *time and motion study*, are used to set the standards for each job. Measurement techniques take observations to determine an average or *observed time*, which can be manipulated to yield the *normal time;* allowances can be added to yield a *standard time*. The standard time for each job is used in the scheduling of operations and the setting of wage scales. The use of *incentives* encourages employees to beat the standards, while the use of the *learning curve* sets standards for job training programs.

▬▬▬

K E Y   T E R M S

man–machine systems	availability	work measurement
human factors	maintainability	time and motion study
psychophysics	failure rate	work sampling
anthropometry	series systems	work simplification
biomechanics	parallel systems	work standardization
reliability	complex systems	observed time

normal time	methods analysis	incentives
standard time	specialization	piece rate
performance rating	job rotation	profit-sharing plans
allowance factor	job enlargement	learning curve
job time percent allowance	job enrichment	failure rate curve
standard elemental times	job improvement	
methods time measurement	quality circle	

S O L V E D
P R O B L E M S

1. Four critical inspections have yet to be done on an automotive radiator. If any of these inspections does not find an existing defect, the radiator will malfunction, and the automobile engine will be damaged. The inspections that have been designed have reliabilities of .96, .99, .93, and .90, respectively, where reliability is the percentage of defects found. To increase the reliability of each inspection, duplication is inserted in the work flow. The first inspection is done 3 times, the second is done twice, the third is done 3 times, and the fourth is done 4 times. Draw the reliability diagram and analyze the overall reliability of the testing. Does this reliability represent the probability of producing a good radiator?

Solution

The inspections are linked in series because the failure of any one of them causes the entire inspection to fail. For each inspection, the repetitions are treated as parallel connections, because any one that catches the problem satisfies the criterion of success.

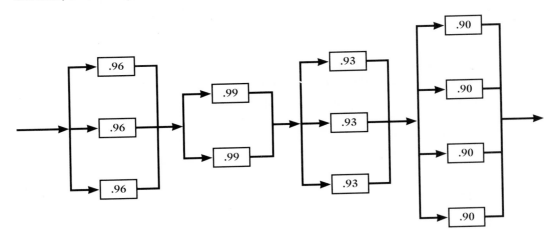

This diagram, because it combines series and parallel components, is considered to be a complex reliability diagram. To assess its reliability, it is necessary to break it down into its series components and then assess each component separately.

There are 4 inspections in series, each of which can be evaluated as a simple parallel reliability. The equation for the reliability of n identical components in parallel is

$$R_{ps} = 1 - (1 - R)^n.$$

For the 4 systems in our diagram, the reliabilities are as follows.

Inspection	Equation	Reliability
1	$1 - (1 - .96)^3$	.999936
2	$1 - (1 - .99)^2$	.999900
3	$1 - (1 - .93)^3$	.999657
4	$1 - (1 - .90)^4$	.999900

It seems that the number of redundant inspections for each test was chosen in order to achieve a target reliability of approximately .9999.

Once this analysis is complete, the reliability diagram can be simplified.

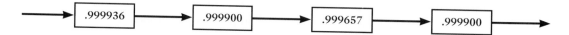

Now we have a series system, the reliability of which is easily determined.

$$R_{ss} = R_1 \times R_2 \times R_3 \times R_4$$
$$= .999936 \times .999900 \times .999657 \times .999900$$
$$= .9994$$

The reliability of this inspection is 99.94 percent.

The answer to the last question is no. This reliability does not represent the reliability of the radiator, which is a function of how well they are produced. This reliability is the reliability of the test. It represents the probability that a bad radiator will be identified as defective by the inspection system.

Using AB:POM to Solve This Problem

AB:POM can be used to find the reliability of systems. The initial input is the number of systems that appear in series and the maximum number of parallel systems within any single system. In Solved Problem 1 there are 4 systems in series with 3, 2, 3, and 4 parallel components. Therefore, the initial entries are 4 and 4. This creates a four-by-four table of entries, in which each column represents one set of parallel components (see Screen 9.1). Then the reliabilities are entered. (Note that zeros are eliminated when computations are performed.)

```
┌─ Data file:wgsp1 ══════════════ Reliability ═══════════════ Solution ─┐
│ Number of systems in series (1–10) 4Max # of parallel components (1-12) 4 │
├══════════════════════ Chapter 9, Solved Problem 1 ══════════════════════┤
│  Parll  Parll  Parll  Parll                                             │
│  Sys 1  Sys 2  Sys 3  Sys 4                                             │
│                                                                          │
│  0.9600 0.9900 0.9300 0.9000                                             │
│                                                                          │
│  0.9600 0.9900 0.9300 0.9000                                             │
│                                                                          │
│  0.9600        0.9300 0.9000                                             │
│                                                                          │
│                       0.9000                                             │
│                                                                          │
│   .99994 0.9999 .99966 0.9999                                            │
│                                                                          │
│  System reliability = .99939                                             │
│                                                                          │
│                                                         F9=Print    Esc  │
│ Press <Esc> key to edit data or highlighted key or function key for options │
└──────────────────────────── SCREEN 9.1 ────────────────────────────────┘
```

The output consists both of the reliabilities of the individual parallel systems (second to last line) and the overall system reliability, which in this case is .99939. ▬▬▬▬

2. The following observations have been taken in a time study experiment.

Observation	Time (in minutes)
1	.11
2	.10
3	.11
4	.10
5	.14
6	.10
7	.10
8	.09
9	.12
10	.09
11	.12
12	.11
13	.10
14	.12
15	.14
16	.09

Determine (a) the observed time, (b) the normal time, and (c) the standard time, using a performance rating of .95 and a percent allowance of 8 percent.

Solution

(a) The observed time is

$$OT = \frac{\Sigma x_i}{n}$$

$$= \frac{.11 + .10 + .11 + .10 + .14 + .10 + .10 + .09 + .12 + .09 + .12 + .11 + .10 + .12 + .14 + .09}{16}$$

= .10875 minutes, or 6.525 seconds.

(b) The normal time is

$$NT = OT \times PR$$
$$= .10875 \times .95$$
$$= .10331 \text{ minutes, or } 6.2 \text{ seconds.}$$

(c) The standard time is

$$ST = NT \times AF$$
$$= .10331 \times 1.08$$
$$= .11158 \text{ minutes, or } 6.7 \text{ seconds.}$$

3. ABC Delivery Company recently hired a new driver. It took the driver 9 hours and 23 minutes to service his route on the first day. Past experience indicates that new drivers have a learning rate of 90 percent and that by the beginning of the fourth week (day 16), the driver should fully learn his route. How long should the route take after the driver learns it?

Since day 1 took 563 minutes, it follows that (rounded to the nearest minute)

day   2 = .9 × 563 = 507 minutes;
day   4 = .9 × 507 = 456 minutes;
day   8 = .9 × 456 = 410 minutes; and
day 16 = .9 × 410 = 369 minutes.

Using AB:POM to Solve This Problem

Screen 9.2 contains the input and output for Solved Problem 3. The input consists of the time for the first unit, the unit number of the last unit, and the learning curve rate. The program computes the time to make all of the intermediate units and displays both the time per unit and the cumulative time for all units. It is also possible to display the learning curve graph.

```
┌─Data file: wgsp3 ═══════ Experience (learning) Curves ═══════ Solution ─┐
│                                                                          │
│ ═══════════════════════ Chapter 9, Solved Problem 3 ════════════════     │
│                              Unit        Production     Cumulative       │
│                              Number      Time           Time            │
│                                1          563.000         563.000       │
│                                2          506.700        1069.700       │
│                                3          476.4139       1546.114       │
│  Labor time for first unit,Y1  563.000   4   456.030     2002.144       │
│                                6*         428.7726       2859.689       │
│  Unit number of last unit,N       16      7   418.8426   3278.531       │
│                                8          410.427        3688.958       │
│  Learning coefficient          0.900      9   403.1443   4092.103       │
│                                11*        391.0331       4874.169       │
│                                12         385.8953       5260.064       │
│                                13         381.2286       5641.293       │
│                                14         376.9583       6018.251       │
│                                16*        369.3843       6757.020       │
│                                                                          │
│  * unit numbers have been skipped                                        │
│                                                                          │
│  F1=Display graph F2=Other graph                    F9=Print      Esc   │
│  Press <Esc> key to edit data or highlighted key or function key for options │
└──────────────────────── SCREEN 9.2 ────────────────────────────────────┘
```

QUESTIONS

1. Describe briefly how the study of psychophysics is related to work system design.

2. Define anthropometry, and discuss how it is related to workplace design.

3. Why is biomechanics an important concept in relation to work system design?

4. What can the operations manager do to improve reliability?

5. Distinguish between series and parallel systems with respect to reliability.

6. What are the two main techniques that are used in work measurement?

7. Briefly explain the main goals of time and motion study.

8. Why is work sampling sometimes preferred to a time and motion study?

9. What is the goal of work sampling?

10. What are the differences between the occurrence study and ratio delay technique?

11. What are the factors that may contribute to the success or failure of a job design?

12. List the five key items affecting work that methods analysis identifies.

13. What criteria are used in selecting the normalization factor?

14. What factors are considered when assigning the difficulty rating?

15. A manager would be concerned about certain parameters of learning curves. Describe these parameters.

PROBLEMS

1. The airline counter representative who checks tickets and baggage can serve departing passengers only if the computerized passenger reservation system is working. This week, the computer system was not working for 2 out of the 60 hours when the counter was open. What is the reliability of the reservation system?

.9667

2. A manufacturing operation requires the continuous use of a drill bit for a one-hour period. In the last month, the equipment failed while performing this operation 4 times and successfully completed the operation 187 times. What is the reliability associated with the operation?

.979

3. In order for a car to start, the starter, battery, and spark plugs all must work. If they have reliabilities of .96, .98, and .99, respectively, what is the system reliability?

.931

4. A kitchen range is defined as working if all four burners operate successfully. KA Inc. wants its ranges to be 99-percent reliable. What should be the reliability level of each burner (assuming each has the same reliability) to achieve this 99-percent range reliability?

.9975 per burner

5. A machining process is critical because the part that is being machined is very expensive. This part must be scrapped if machining has started, the machine breaks, and the work is not resumed within a minute. The only way to avoid losing the part (repair always takes more than a minute) is to purchase a backup machine. The primary machine has a reliability of .98, and the backup (a less-expensive version) has a reliability of .90. What is the overall reliability of the machining process with the two machines?

.998

6. An explosive device that requires one fuse is being tested, and the reliability of the device must be at least .99999. If any fuse is 99-percent reliable, how many fuses should be carried with each device to achieve the specified overall reliability?

3 fuses

7. Evaluate the reliability of the following complex system.

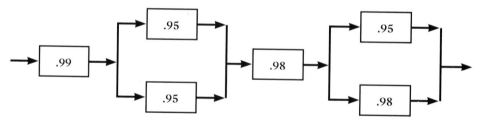

.9668

8. Evaluate the reliability of the following complex system.

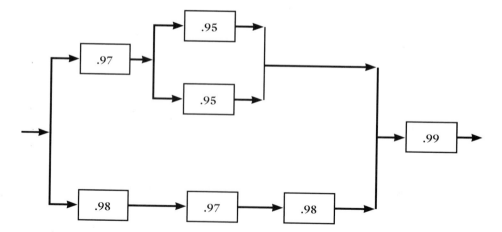

.9878

9. How many time study observations should be taken for the following process?

Mean time = 1.6 minutes
Standard deviation = .2 minutes
Desired confidence = 90 percent
Maximum error = 5 percent

$n = 17$

10. A university's check-cashing service employs two tellers to cash checks. A waiting line analysis has shown that the waiting time in line to cash a check is unacceptably long. One teller, it is discovered, cashes many more checks than the other. Design a time study (number of cycles observed) to achieve a confidence of 95 percent and a maximum error of 10 percent. The mean time and standard deviation per check are as follows.

	Teller 1	Teller 2
Mean time	.5 min	.9 min
Standard deviation	.1 min	.2 min

teller 1: $n = 16$;
teller 2: $n = 19$

How many check cashings should be observed for each teller?

11. A time study finds the following observations.

Observation	Time (in minutes)
1	2.1
2	2.2
3	2.2
4	2.0
5	2.2
6	2.3
7	2.1
8	2.0
9	2.1
10	2.2

(a) What is the observed time?
(b) Using a performance rating of .95, what is the normal time?
(c) Using an allowance factor of 1.04, what is the standard time?

2.14 minutes
2.033 minutes
2.114 minutes

12. A time study yields the following observations.

Observation	Time (in minutes)
1	.18
2	.16
3	.17
4	.16
5	.16
6	.18

(a) What is the observed time?
(b) Using a performance rating of 1.08, what is the normal time?
(c) Using an allowance factor of 1.2, what is the standard time?

.16833 minutes
.1818 minutes
.218 minutes

13. Keeping the maximum error to 2 percent, what confidence level is achieved by using the sample size of 10 in Problem 11? Assume a mean of 2.1 minutes and a standard deviation of .1.

81.6 percent

14. Determine the number of observations that should be taken for a work sampling program if the estimate of p is .90 and the allowable error is plus or minus 2 percent. Assume that 2 standard deviations are used.

900 observations

15. Determine the number of observations that should be taken for a work sampling program if the expected percentage of occurrences is 40 percent and the allowable error is plus or minus 5 percent. Assume that 2 standard deviations are used.

384 observations

16. A work sampling program consists of 147 random observations, during which 132 occurrences were observed.

.898
89.8% ± 4%

(a) What is the probability that the sought-after occurrence was observed?
(b) What error range (using 2 standard deviations) can you place on the estimate?

17. A work sampling program consists of 1,200 random observations, during which the sought-after occurrence was observed 140 times.

p = .11667
11.67% ± 2.4%

(a) What percentage of time does the occurrence take place?
(b) Give a 99-percent confidence estimate for the error range.

18. A new registration clerk in the X-ray department of a hospital had the following times for registering his first eight patients.

Patient	Time (in seconds)
1	260
2	240
3	228
4	220
5	213
6	210
7	205
8	202

.92
157 seconds

(a) Estimate the learning curve factor.
(b) Using the learning curve factor, estimate how long the 64th patient will take.

19. A production process will begin operation next week. From past experience, the industrial engineering department has determined that it takes approximately 500 units to reach steady state and that the learning curve factor is approximately 87 percent. The amount of time for the 500th unit will be used to balance the assembly line and to schedule personnel. How long can we expect the 500th unit to take if the first unit is expected to take 126 minutes?

36.15 minutes (or slightly longer)

COMPUTER CASE STUDY 9.1: CARTAK'S DEPARTMENT STORE

Cartak's Department Store uses a universal price code (UPC) reader to ring up customers' purchases. The item prices are maintained in the store's computer; when the code for a particular item is scanned, the appropriate price is displayed and used in computing the customer's bill. The UPC reader has many benefits. One major benefit is that the checkout time has been reduced from an average of 4.2 minutes to an average of 3.9 minutes. (The store studied the times before and after implementation of the new system.) A second major benefit is that the

UPC scanning has virtually eliminated the mistakes that were made at the cash register by cashiers. Formerly, cashiers made mistakes on an average of 1 out of 300 items entered into the cash register. This meant that approximately 1 in 60 customers had an incorrect bill. Some of the charges were too high; some were too low. Many mistakes were for less than $1 and went unnoticed. Occasionally however, especially when there was an overcharge, the customer reported the mistake.

While the UPC reader has virtually eliminated mistakes at the cash register, it has magnified the value of any mistake made at the computer. For example, if a price of $.98 is entered into the data base, rather than the actual price of $1.98, every customer who buys the item will be undercharged $1. For this reason, the store has one person act as a verifier of the prices when the prices are entered into the computer. The key operator who enters the prices for Cartak is very good, but no one is perfect. Her accuracy rate is approximately 97.1 percent. In other words, on average, out of 1,000 prices entered, 971 prices will be entered correctly. The verifier has an accuracy rate of 92 percent. On average, she catches 92 of every 100 mistakes made. What is the overall accuracy rate of Cartak's price inputting system? By how much would the accuracy rate improve if a second, equally accurate verifier were used?

REFERENCES

Asfahl, C. R. *Robots and Manufacturing Automation.* New York: John Wiley and Sons, 1985.

Barnes, R. M. *Motion and Time Study: Design and Management of Work.* 7th ed. New York: John Wiley and Sons, 1980.

Enrick, N. L. *Quality Control and Reliability.* New York: Industrial Press, 1977.

Herzog, D. R. *Industrial Engineering Methods and Controls.* Reston, Va.: Reston Publishing Company, 1985.

Kececioglu, D. "Reliability Testing." Course materials from the Annual Reliability Testing Institute. Tucson: University of Arizona, 1987.

Kopelman, R. E. *Managing Productivity in Organizations: A Practical People-Oriented Perspective.* New York: McGraw-Hill, 1986.

McCormick, E. J. *Human Factors Engineering.* 6th ed. New York: McGraw-Hill, 1987.

Nadler, G. *Work Design: A Systems Concept.* New York: McGraw-Hill, 1970.

Niebel, B. W. *Motion and Time Study.* 8th ed. Homewood, Illinois: Irwin, 1988.

Taylor, F. W. *Scientific Management.* New York: Harper, 1911.

P A R T
F O U R

USE OF CAPACITY RESOURCES

C H A P T E R

10

O U T L I N E

PROJECT SCHEDULING

■ To describe the nature and management of projects
■ To illustrate the methods for drawing activity relationships
■ To present methods for analyzing project durations and critical tasks
■ To develop cost analyses of projects
■ To discuss the management of resources for a project

INTRODUCTION

In previous chapters, we have indicated that there is a need for the planning and control of large, time-consuming projects. Specific examples that have been presented already are the development of new products, the construction of new plants, and the implementation of new facility layouts. In this chapter, we present general models for just such projects. Generally speaking, the techniques presented here are termed *network planning techniques,* because they are useful for projects that can be represented graphically as a sequence of tasks, forming a picture similar to that of a highway (or electrical) network. The two most widely used network techniques are the **program evaluation and review technique (PERT)** and the **critical path method (CPM).**

PERT and CPM were developed simultaneously but independently for the same purpose: to allow better planning and control of large projects. PERT was developed in the late 1950s by the Department of Defense for the purpose of planning the development of the Polaris missile (the first nuclear missile launched by submarine). The planning included research and development, construction, testing, and implementation. CPM was developed, also in the late 1950s, at Remington-Rand and Du Pont for application in the chemical industry. Since their development, the techniques have been applied extensively, as Table 10.1 indicates. We note that although PERT and CPM are particularly well suited to large, time-consuming projects, the techniques also can be applied to short-term projects.

Teaching Suggestion 10.1: PERT vs. CPM. See the Instructor's Section for details.

PERT and CPM

PROJECT CHARACTERISTICS

Table 10.1 presents a partial listing of the applications of project management. We now identify the characteristics of the items on this list that differentiate projects from the more standard methods of providing a good or service. We note that the characteristics we present are generalizations; as with any generalization, exceptions can be found.

Projects often require temporary resources, such as these registrars at a convention in Baltimore. (© Sue Klemenz/UNIPHOTO)

INFREQUENCY

The first thing to be noticed about the examples in Table 10.1 is that projects are not performed frequently. In fact, many projects are unique, performed only once. Examples of such projects are the development of a new weapons system, the construction of a new building, or the creation of a marketing survey for a new product. Although some might consider the installation of a computer system a standard operation for a computer company, each installation has different requirements, making it—and similar projects—unique.

projects are unique

ESTIMATION DIFFICULTY

Because each project is a new project, it is usually difficult to accurately estimate either the length of time the project will take or the amount of resources—especially fund-

TABLE 10.1 Sample applications of network planning

Auditing
Research and development
Monthly financial closing
Plant construction
New product planning
Shop loading and sequencing
Weapons systems
Personnel planning
Piping installation
Pool construction
Refining systems
Market research
Computer programming
Budget preparation

Teaching Suggestion 10.2: Risk. See the Instructor's Section for details.

ing—it will require. In fact, a major reason for the development of PERT was the need to have a method that addressed uncertainty with respect to time.

CONTROL

The majority of projects with which we are concerned can be decomposed into smaller tasks. Typically, responsibility for each task may be accorded to different divisions, managers, or contractors. Because the employees responsible for a given project task may not be under the project manager's direct supervision, it may prove difficult to exercise firm control over the employees. It may not be possible to offer incentives for good (on time, on budget) performance or to hand out penalties for bad performance. Students who have worked in groups and encountered difficulties in controlling the efforts of their fellow group members will recognize the problem.

PROJECT MANAGEMENT

The project management process consists of three stages, as indicated in Figure 10.1. The first stage is to define the project—that is, to create a description of the goals and the specifications of the final outcome (or output) of the project. The second stage is the planning process. This includes the identification of the tasks involved, the resources and times required for each task, and the timing of the tasks. It is at this **work breakdown structure** (WBS) stage that the network planning techniques of PERT and CPM are most useful. The last stage is the execution and control of the project. The time–cost trade-offs of PERT and CPM are useful at this stage.

work breakdown

The success or failure of a project is measured along three dimensions: conformance, time, and money. We now discuss these dimensions in some detail.

CONFORMANCE

The first stage of the project details the goals of the project. Usually, it is not until the end of the project that we know whether or not the goals have been achieved. Because projects are unique, unforeseen difficulties may arise. There are numerous examples of road construction and nuclear reactor projects that were planned and started, yet not completed due to the objections of the communities or neighborhoods affected. The problems of project control can lead to conformance difficulties, because there may be poor communication between project manager and task manager or even between client and contractor. Most students have had similar experiences; what the client (professor) orders is not always what students (the contractors) deliver.

TIME

The major goal of this chapter is to examine the time component of projects. Our analysis will indicate which tasks are most critical to the timely completion of the project. Even when the critical tasks are known, innumerable problems still could arise and delay the project. To begin with, because each project is unique, the project tasks are often unique, which means that estimating times for the tasks can be an uncertain process. Even if the estimates are "correct," they typically do not account for any unforeseen problems that may arise. In construction, for example, adverse weather conditions and strikes are two common unforeseen problems. It also is possible that

Compiling the evening news—a recurring project. (© John de Visser/Black Star)

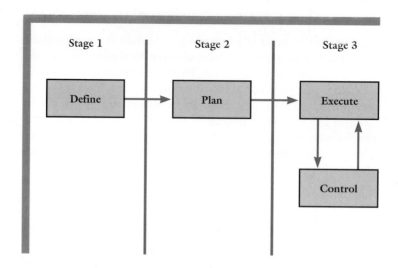

FIGURE 10.1 Project management process

the right resources will not be available at the scheduled time or (especially in government work) that funding will be delayed, thus delaying the project.

BUDGET

Teaching Suggestion 10.3: Shifting Priorities. See the Instructor's Section for details.

The planning stage includes the planning, not only of the time required for the project, but also of the budget requirements for each task and the total project budget. Project uniqueness makes the budget estimation, like the time estimation, very difficult. In addition, budget and time are related. Due to inflation, as the project grows in length of time to completion, it also grows in budget. One other problem might arise: If the tasks are to be subcontracted and the awarding of tasks is through competitive bidding, the winning bid may understate the true cost. Without going into the details of bidding strategies, making a lower bid enhances one's chances of winning the contract, and bidding lower than cost is a not uncommon practice.

In light of our performance dimensions of conformance, time, and budget, the areas we address through PERT and CPM are intended to answer the following basic questions:

1. If each of the activities goes according to plan, when will the project be completed?
2. Which tasks are most critical to ensure the timely completion of the project?
3. Which tasks can be delayed if necessary, without delaying project completion, and by how much can each be delayed?
4. More specifically, at what times should each activity begin and end?
5. At any given time during the project, what is the range of dollars that should have been spent?
6. Is it worthwhile to incur extra costs in order to accelerate some of the activities?

basic questions

The first four questions are the most important; each relates to time, which is our major concern. The last two questions deal with the notion that we can usually trade off time for money.

APPLICATIONS OF P/OM

Apollo 11 Owes Launch Success to Project Management

In 1969 Captain Robert F. Freitag headed the team responsible for landing the Apollo 11 safely on the moon. The success of the lunar mission can be traced to techniques that ensured that thousands of small tasks would come together to meet a single giant objective. Freitag shares his feelings about that historic event:

> I think the feeling most of us in NASA shared was "My gosh, now we really have to do it." When you think that the enterprise we were about to undertake was ten times larger than any that had ever been undertaken, including the Manhattan Project, it was a pretty awesome event. But we knew it was the kind of thing that could be broken down into manageable pieces, and that if we could get the right people and the right arrangement of these people, it would be possible.
>
> In the case of the Apollo program, it was very important that we take a comprehensive system engineering approach. We had to analyze in a very strict sense exactly what the mission was going to be, what each piece of equipment needed was and how it would perform, and all the elements of the system from the concept on through to the execution of the mission, to its recovery back on earth.
>
> We started out in a very logical way, by having a space station in earth orbit. It turned out that this approach was risky, so with the analyses we made, we shifted our whole operation to building a rocket that would go all the way to the moon after it took off from Cape Canaveral.
>
> That was a very comprehensive analysis job. It was probably more deep-seated than the kind of job one would do for building an airplane or a dam because there

were so many variables involved. What you do is break it down into pieces: the launch site, the launch vehicles, the space craft, the lunar module, and world-wide tracking networks, for example. Then, once these pieces are broken down, you assign them to one organization or another. They, in turn, take those small pieces, like the rocket, and break it down into engines or structures or guidance equipment. And this breakdown, or "tree," is the really tough part about managing.

> In the Apollo program it was decided that three NASA centers, one in Huntsville, one in Houston and one in Cape Canaveral, would do the work. Those three centers were pieces, and they could break their pieces down into about 10 or 20 major industrial contractors who would build pieces of the rocket. And then each of those industrial contractors would break them down into maybe 20 to 30 or 50 subcontractors—and they, in turn, would break them down into perhaps 300,000 or 400,000 pieces, each of which would end up being the job of one person. But you need to be sure that the pieces come together at the right time, and that they work when put together. Project management helps with that. The total number of people who worked on the Apollo was about 400,000 to 500,000, all working toward a single objective. But that objective was clear when President Kennedy said, "I want to land a man on the moon and have him safely returned to the earth, and to do so within the decade." Of course, Congress set aside $20 billion. So you had cost, performance and schedule, and you knew what the job was in one simple sentence.

Source: S. Garfunkel, ed., *Introduction to Contemporary Mathematics* (New York: W. H. Freeman and Company, 1988), pp. 2–3.

DIAGRAMMING PROJECTS

There are many ways to represent a project pictorially. The most common methods are **Gantt charts** and **network diagrams.**

GANTT CHARTS

In our discussion of the history of operations management in Chapter 1, we introduced Henry Gantt, who developed a simple but clever method of representing the timing of activities on a bar chart. The Gantt chart is extremely useful for project scheduling, our subject here, and for job scheduling, which is discussed in Chapter 15.

TABLE 10.2 Precedence table for township playground activities

Code	Activity	Description	Time (in days)	Immediate Predecessor(s)
A	Planning	Find location; determine resource requirements	20	None
B	Purchasing	Requisition lumber and sand	60	Planning
C	Excavation	Dig and grade	100	Planning
D	Sawing	Saw lumber into appropriate sizes	30	Purchasing
E	Placement	Position lumber in correct locations	20	Sawing, excavation
F	Assembly	Nail lumber together	10	Placement
G	Infill	Put sand in and under equipment	20	Assembly
H	Outfill	Put dirt and grass around equipment	10	Assembly
I	Decoration	Landscape, paint	30	Infill, outfill

Transparency Master 10.1: Project Management Example.

Table 10.2 describes the steps necessary for designing and building a township playground. Each activity that is part of the project is listed along with its expected length of time to perform and its prerequisite activities. For example, placement of the equipment (activity E) cannot be performed prior to the purchase of the equipment (activity B).

developing the Gantt chart

The Gantt chart for this activity is presented in Figure 10.2. Each activity is represented by a bar, the length of which represents the activity time. We look now at how a Gantt chart is created. We begin with planning (A), which starts at day 0 and ends at day 20. Next, we draw purchasing (B), which starts at day 20 because it cannot begin until the planning is completed. Purchasing takes 60 days, so we end the bar at $20 + 60 = 80$ days. The next activity we chart is excavation, which also begins at 20 days because excavation also occurs after planning. Notice that, according to the Gantt chart, purchasing and excavation occur simultaneously. In creating the chart, we

model assumption

assume there are resources available to perform the two activities at the same time. (Most of the models in this chapter will, in fact, make the assumption that we can perform as many activities as needed at any given time. If the activities are subcontracted, this assumption does not pose a problem.) The next activity in the list is sawing (D). This begins at 80 days (when purchasing is completed) and ends at 110 days. Next on the list is placement (E), which cannot begin until both sawing and excavation are completed. Because we end sawing at 110 days and excavation at 120 days, we begin the bar for placement at the latter of the two—namely, at 120 days. We continue in this fashion until the Gantt chart is completed.

The Gantt chart has just answered one of the questions that was posed in the last section. According to the Gantt chart, decoration (and, hence, the project) will be completed at 200 days.

The Gantt chart in Figure 10.2 is a **scheduling chart.** There are other types of

Gantt charts, the most common of which—the **load chart**—we will discuss in the later section on extensions to basic models and also in Chapter 15.

The Gantt chart we just developed is a "prestart" Gantt chart. That is, the chart represents the schedule of activities as planned prior to starting work. Over the course of a project, Gantt charts are used continually to monitor actual progress. In this way, the project manager can see both actual progress and planned progress on the same chart, increasing his or her ability to identify discrepancies at the earliest possible time. Once actual progress fails to match planned progress, action can be taken to revise the remaining schedule and to bring it in line with the project goals.

charts can be used for control

NETWORK DIAGRAMS

Although Gantt charts are useful for demonstrating the tasks, network diagrams or precedence diagrams better represent the relationships between the activities and are easier to use. We can draw two similar types of networks. An **activity on node (AON) network** places the activities on the nodes of the network; an **activity on arc (AOA) network** places the activities on the arcs. Traditionally, CPM uses the AON network, while PERT uses the AOA network. It is slightly easier to draw an AON network, so we begin with the network used by CPM. Because both networks can be used to represent the same project, each individual is advised to select the one that seems more sensible from his or her perspective and to use this representation for both CPM and PERT.

Transparency Master 10.2: The Gantt Chart.

FIGURE 10.2 **Gantt chart for playground construction**

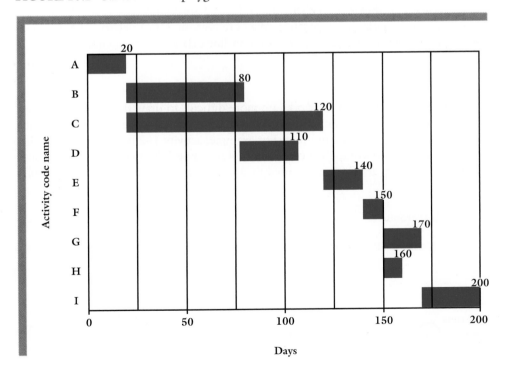

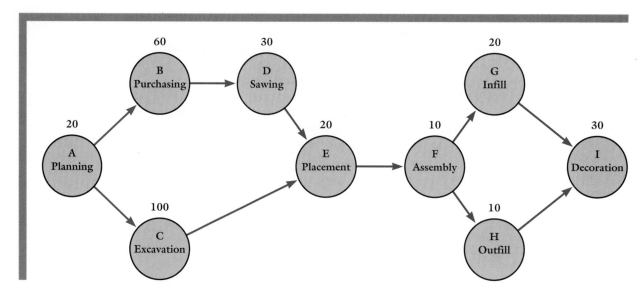

FIGURE 10.3 CPM network for playground construction

CPM (AON) NETWORKS

In Figure 10.3 we present the CPM network for our playground example. The network consists of nodes, which represent the activities, and arrows (arcs), which represent the precedences between the activities. No activity can begin until all of the activities that have an arrow going into that activity have been completed. For example, decoration cannot begin until both infill and outfill are completed because both activities have arrows going to decoration. We note that this CPM network is the type of network that we used earlier to draw assembly line balancing precedence diagrams.

PERT (AOA) NETWORKS

We have stated that PERT networks are more difficult to draw than CPM networks, and this is borne out in Figure 10.4. In this figure, each arrow represents an activity, while each node represents an event. For example, activity 1–2 is planning, event 1 is "project start," and event 2 is "completion of planning." Notice that the figure also contains one extra activity, represented by a broken arrow. This activity is a **dummy**

dummy activity

FIGURE 10.4 PERT network for playground construction

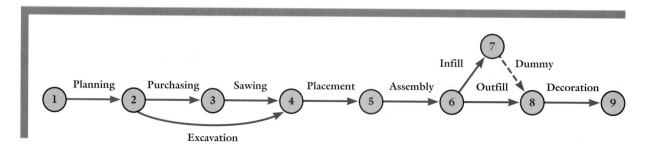

activity, which requires no time to complete and is inserted simply to maintain the appropriate precedence relationships. Without this dummy activity, outfill and infill would both have the same code (6–7). Dummy activities are what make PERT graphs more difficult to develop than CPM charts. There are some advantages to an AOA network (for example, it may be more intuitive to represent activities as arrows, as they represent action) but, on the whole, the advantages of the PERT network do not outweigh the advantages of the CPM (AON) structure.

PERT networks are more difficult to draw

Let's look more closely at the use of dummy activities. In part (a) of Figure 10.5, we have represented a four-activity CPM network. In part (b), we show two incorrect

FIGURE 10.5 Use of dummy activities

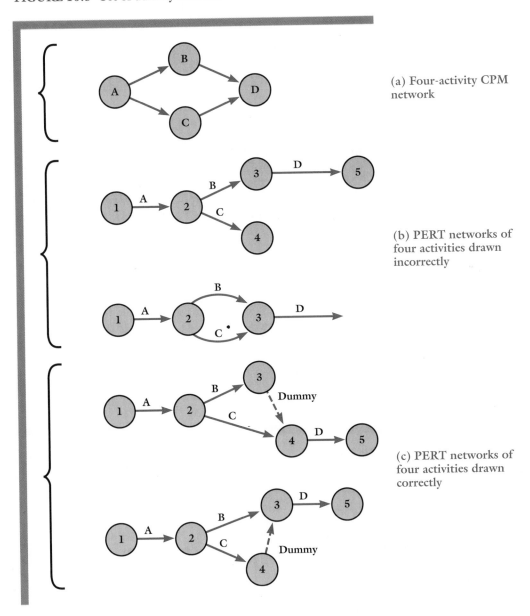

(a) Four-activity CPM network

(b) PERT networks of four activities drawn incorrectly

(c) PERT networks of four activities drawn correctly

ways to draw this project using the PERT network. The first drawing is not permissible because in it D does not follow C; the second gives both activities B and C the same code (2–3). To avoid these problems, we must include a dummy activity that takes no time but does influence the precedences. The dummy activity can be included in either of the two ways indicated in part (c) of the figure.

PERT–TIME NETWORKS

Although networks are drawn for the purpose of indicating precedences, we can include the times required for activities by scaling the arrows so that the length of each arrow is proportional to the length of time of its task. This increases the visual information provided. It also aids in scheduling; notice the similarity between a PERT–time network and a Gantt chart. For our example, the network is shown in Figure 10.6. Because CPM networks have the activities on the nodes, activity times cannot be shown on them in the same way.

CRITICAL PATH ANALYSIS

Previously, we drew a Gantt chart and a PERT–time diagram to determine when a project would be completed, which tasks were most critical, how much each activity might be delayed without affecting project completion time, and when each task should begin and end. Now we present the network methods, which have two distinct advantages: They are simpler to use, and we can extrapolate from them to answer other questions. The methods for analyzing PERT and CPM networks are identical. We begin with CPM.

THE CPM NETWORK

The first question we wish to answer for our playground example is, When will the playground be completed? There are two methods we can use to answer this basic question—the enumeration method and the two-pass method.

FIGURE 10.6 PERT–time network

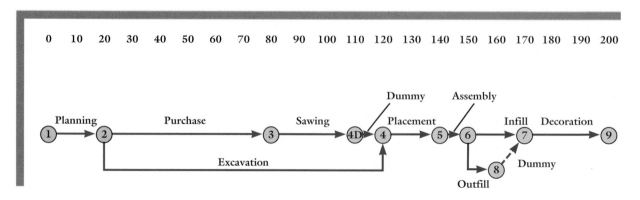

ENUMERATION METHOD

The enumeration method is the easier of the two methods for determining project completion time. However, its use is limited to small problems. The enumeration method consists of the following three steps.

> **Step 1.** Identify all paths from beginning to end in the network. (**A path** is any sequence of activities connecting a start and finish of the project.)
>
> **Step 2.** For each path, add the task times for all tasks on that path.
>
> **Step 3.** Find the *maximum* path time. This is the length of time needed to complete the project.

Teaching Suggestion 10.4: Multiple Starts or Finishes. See the Instructor's Section for details.

Teaching Suggestion 10.5: Enumeration Method. See the Instructor's Section for details.

In the playground example, there are four paths from start to finish (see Figure 10.7): A–B–D–E–F–G–I, A–B–D–E–F–H–I, A–C–E–F–G–I, and A–C–E–F–H–I. The length of time to complete any path is simply the sum of the task times along the path. These times are given in Table 10.3. In order to finish the project, each path must be traversed. Of course, any task that is on more than one path needs to be done only once. The path that takes longest is A–C–E–F–G–I, which means that the playground requires 200 days from start to finish.

The enumeration method not only defines the length of time to finish the project; it also provides the reason for the name *critical path method*. The path A–C–E–F–G–I is critical in the sense that the entire project will be delayed if any task along that path is delayed. For example, if excavation requires 120 days rather than 100 days, then the playground will be completed 20 days late. Each activity on the critical path is a critical activity in that it must start and finish on time or the entire project will be delayed. The noncritical paths contain some critical activities and some noncritical activities. For example, the path A–B–D–E–F–G–I has critical activities A, E, F, G, and I but

FIGURE 10.7 Computation of early start and early finish times

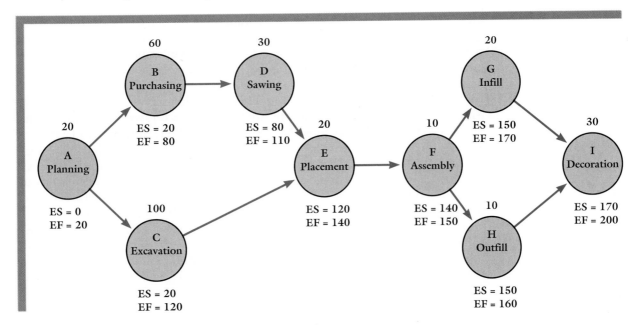

TABLE 10.3 CPM path analysis for playground activities

Path	Task Times (in days)	Total
A–B–D–E–F–G–I	20 + 60 + 30 + 20 + 10 + 20 + 30	190
A–B–D–E–F–H–I	20 + 60 + 30 + 20 + 10 + 10 + 30	180
A–C–E–F–G–I	20 + 100 + 20 + 10 + 20 + 30	200
A–C–E–F–H–I	20 + 100 + 20 + 10 + 10 + 30	190

Teaching Suggestion 10.6: Criticality. See the Instructor's Section for details.

also has noncritical activities B and D. This means that B or D can be delayed (to some extent) without delaying the project. For example, if buying the lumber and sand requires 65 days rather than 60 days, the project still will take 200 days to complete. However, if buying the materials requires 80 days rather than 60 days, then A–B–D–E–F–G–I will require 210 days for completion (the project will be 10 days late). If this happens, A–B–D–E–F–G–I becomes the critical path.

TWO-PASS METHOD

The second method for identifying the time and path is more useful for complex problems, where it may be difficult to enumerate all paths. We begin by computing the times when each activity will begin and finish if all activities are done at their earliest possible time. The completion of the last activity is the project completion time.

forward pass

Figure 10.7 contains all of the information required. It differs from Figure 10.3 only in that the start and finish times are denoted. These start and finish times are termed **early start** and **early finish,** so we represent them by ES and EF on the network. The earliest start time for any activity is the latest finish time of all activities that precede it. For example, the earliest that placement can begin is when both the land is excavated and the lumber is sawed. The sawing will not finish for 110 days, while the excavation will not finish for 120 days. Because both activities must be finished before placement can begin, 120 days is the earliest start time for placement. Finally, the earliest finish time for the decoration is 200 days; hence, this is when the project will be completed.

backward pass

At this point, we know when the project will end, but we do not know the critical path. In order to find the critical path, we must make a backward pass through the network computing the **late finish** and **late start** times for each activity. By late finish, we mean the latest an activity may end without delaying the starting times of all succeeding activities. These times are shown in Figure 10.8. Obviously, the latest finish time for decoration is 200 days, and, because decoration takes 30 days, the latest it can start is 170 days. This implies that the latest finish for both outfill and infill is 170 days. Because outfill takes 10 days, the latest it can start is at $170 - 10 = 160$ days. Because infill takes 20 days, the latest it can start is $170 - 20 = 150$ days. Notice that the early and late starts for infill are both 150 days. This means that infill is on the critical path, because it must begin on time. However, the early start for outfill is 150 days and the late start is 160 days. Hence, outfill has a **slack time** of 10 days and, for this reason, is not on the critical path. The remaining computations are done in a similar fashion.

Teaching Suggestion 10.7: Interpretation of Slack. See the Instructor's Section for details.

The difference between the enumeration method and the two-pass method is that with the forward and backward pass, we find, not only the project completion time

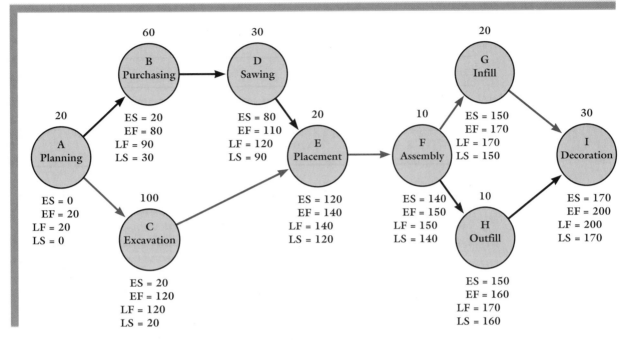

FIGURE 10.8 Computation of late start and late finish times

Transparency Master 10.3: Two-Pass Method.

and the critical path, but also the slack time for each noncritical activity (see Table 10.4), where slack is defined as follows:

$$\text{Slack} = \text{late start} - \text{early start}.$$

slack time

THE PERT NETWORK

When using PERT, the analysis of the playground problem follows the same procedures the CPM analysis utilized. We start the analysis by using path enumeration. The

TABLE 10.4 Computation of slack times

Label	Activity	Early Start	Late Start	Slack (LS − ES)
A	Planning	0	0	0
B	Purchasing	20	30	10
C	Excavation	20	20	0
D	Sawing	80	90	10
E	Placement	120	120	0
F	Assembly	140	140	0
G	Infill	150	150	0
H	Outfill	150	160	10
I	Decoration	170	170	0

following table lists all the paths through the network (see Figure 10.9) and the time for each path.

Path	Task times (in days)	Total
1–2–3–4–5–6–7–8–9	20 + 60 + 30 + 20 + 10 + 20 + 0 + 30	190
1–2–3–4–5–6–8–9	20 + 60 + 30 + 20 + 10 + 10 + 30	180
1–2–4–5–6–7–8–9	20 + 100 + 20 + 10 + 20 + 0 + 30	200
1–2–4–5–6–8–9	20 + 100 + 20 + 10 + 10 + 30	190

The longest path is 1–2–4–5–6–7–8–9; hence, this is the critical path, and the project will end after 200 days. Notice that there is a one-to-one correspondence between the CPM paths listed in Table 10.3 and the PERT paths listed in the preceding table. Only tradition and the difference in network representation differentiate PERT and CPM.

As with CPM, the second analysis makes the forward and backward passes. Figure 10.9 contains the early start and early finish times for each activity as well as their late start and late finish times. The times were computed here exactly as they were in the CPM analysis. The earliest start for any task is the latest finish of all preceding tasks. The latest finish is the earliest start time for all following tasks.

The evaluation of this project is now complete. Earlier in this chapter, we listed questions concerning the scheduling and analysis of projects. Let us see how our tools of CPM and PERT have been useful in answering the first four of these questions.

1. *When will the project be completed?* The analysis showed that the project will require 200 days to complete.
2. *Which tasks are most critical to ensure the timely completion of the project?* Tasks A, C, E, F, G, and I form the critical path, so the timely completion of each is critical to ensure timely project completion (within 200 days).

FIGURE 10.9 Analysis of PERT network

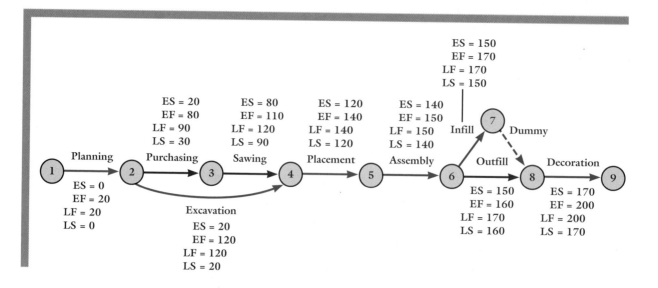

3. *Which tasks can be delayed if necessary, and by how much, without delaying project completion?* Tasks B, D, and H can be delayed if necessary. The amount by which each can be delayed is

> B—10 days;
> D—10 days; and
> H—10 days.

No other task can be delayed at all, because all other tasks are critical. Notice that if B is delayed by 10 days, path A–B–D–E–F–G–I will take 200 days, making it critical. Thus, if B is delayed by 10 days, D becomes a critical task and can no longer be delayed.

4. *When should each activity begin, and when should it end?* The activities should be timed as follows.

Task	Begin Day	End Day
A	0	20
B	20 to 30	80 to 90
C	20	120
D	80 to 90	110 to 120
E	120	140
F	140	150
G	150	170
H	150 to 160	160 to 170
I	170	200

CHOOSING THE TASK TIMES

In the previous section, we assumed that the task times are known. However, it is quite possible that the actual time needed to perform any or each task is not known. The task time for a task that has never been performed before cannot be given with certainty. For a task with a past history, past data might be used to effectively estimate the task time. However, because a great deal of uncertainty is associated with the task time of a task that has not been performed before, we need to incorporate uncertainty into the network models. The ability to incorporate uncertainty was one of the features designed into PERT.

uncertainty

EXPECTED ACTIVITY TIME

The PERT method for assigning task times begins with three estimates for every task in the network. One is an estimate of the most likely time needed to complete the task. Another is an optimistic estimate of the task time—that is, the length of time the task will take if all goes well. The last is a pessimistic estimate, or the length of time needed for the activity if things do not run smoothly. These three estimates are combined into an estimate of the task time according to a weighted average given by

three time estimates

Teaching Suggestion 10.8: Symmetric Times—Shortcut. See the Instructor's Section for details.

$$t = \frac{t_o + 4t_m + t_p}{6},$$

combination into a single time estimate

where t is the time estimate to be used in the PERT (or CPM) analysis, t_o is the **optimistic time** estimate, t_m is the **most likely time** estimate, and t_p is the **pessimistic time** estimate. (The weighted average is based on a beta probability distribution, but that is not particularly relevant to our discussion.) For example, it might be that the excavation times in our playground example are given by a most likely time of 90 days, an optimistic time of 60 days (if, for example, no tree roots are encountered during the excavation), and a pessimistic time of 180 days (if many tree roots are encountered). The time estimate to be used in the analysis is

$$t = \frac{60 + 4(90) + 180}{6} = \frac{600}{6} = 100 \text{ days.}$$

advantages of making three estimates

There are some practical reasons why this method of assigning task times is used. First, it recognizes that the exact amount of time required to complete any task is not known with certainty. A second and perhaps more important advantage is related to political and psychological factors. Usually, the project foreman or the project manager is responsible for creating the time estimates. This individual will be very hesitant about providing firm dates in answer to the question, How long will each task require? However, if he or she is permitted to answer that question by providing best-case and worst-case estimates in addition to a most likely time, the foreman or manager will feel much more comfortable. This added flexibility is desirable from an organizational perspective and, as we shall see, from a quantitative perspective, due to the additional information it provides.

The most likely time should be chosen based on normal circumstances. It should be the manager's best and most honest guess of the time the task will take. As everything must go right to achieve the optimistic time, the time chosen for this measure should be unbeatable. The pessimistic time chosen should account for *all* of the problems that may occur. Usually, many more things can go wrong than right. Thus, the most likely time will usually be closer to the optimistic than to the pessimistic time. This results from the nature of individuals to be conservative—that is, to use the pessimistic time to cover all eventualities. It also matches nicely with observed distributions of times required to complete individual tasks.

Teaching Suggestion 10.9: Choice of Distribution. See the Instructor's Section for details.

The implication of using this method is that the amount of time to excavate is random, with a mean of 100 days. In Table 10.5 we have given optimistic, most likely, and pessimistic values for each of the task times. The expected value for each is computed according to the preceding formula for weighted average. These expected times are the times cited in the previous section. (In fact, this is how those times were derived, but it was not necessary to mention that fact before now.)

Because these numbers are the same as before, the previous analysis still holds, which means that the project completion time is still 200 days. However, now we view that number as an expected value rather than as a fixed time. In other words, because the task times are random, the project completion time must be random also. Because this completion time is random, we would like to be able to answer questions such as, What is the probability that the playground will be completed within 240 days? or How much time must be allowed in order to guarantee that there is a 90-percent chance that the playground will be completed in 240 days? In order to answer these types of questions, we need to know the standard deviation of the project completion time.

TABLE 10.5 Time estimates for playground activities

	Time Estimates (in days)			
Activity	Optimistic (t_o)	Most Likely (t_m)	Pessimistic (t_p)	Mean $\left(\dfrac{t_o + 4t_m + t_p}{6}\right)$
Planning	10	20	30	20
Purchasing	20	65	80	60
Excavation	60	90	180	100
Sawing	25	30	35	30
Placement	15	20	25	20
Assembly	10	10	10	10
Infill	10	15	50	20
Outfill	8	10	12	10
Decoration	20	25	60	30

VARIANCE OF PROJECT TIME

To compute the variance of the project completion time, we use the variances of the paths through the network. In order to compute these variances, we must first compute the variances of the activities along the paths.

ACTIVITY TIME VARIANCE

The formula for computing activity time standard deviation is

$$\sigma = \frac{t_p - t_o}{6}.$$

activity standard deviation

Thus, for the excavation of the playground, the standard deviation is

$$\sigma = \frac{180 - 60}{6} = \frac{120}{6} = 20 \text{ days.}$$

The activity variance is, of course, the square of the standard deviation. When using this formula for σ, the underlying assumption is that activity time has a beta distribution and that the beginning (t_o) of the distribution to the end (t_p) covers approximately 6 standard deviations. The beta distribution is appropriate because it is defined only between a lower boundary and an upper boundary. The use of 6 standard deviations as the range approximates the case of the normal distribution, where only about 3 in 1,000 samples will exceed these limits. The activity standard deviations are given in Table 10.6.

TABLE 10.6 Expected times and standard deviations for playground activities

	Time Estimates and Standard Deviations (in days)				
Activity	Optimistic (t_o)	Most Likely (t_m)	Pessimistic (t_p)	Mean $\left(\dfrac{t_o + 4t_m + t_p}{6}\right)$	Standard Deviation $\left(\dfrac{t_p - t_o}{6}\right)$
Planning	10	20	30	20	3.33
Purchasing	20	65	80	60	10
Excavation	60	90	180	100	20
Sawing	25	30	35	30	1.67
Placement	15	20	25	20	1.67
Assembly	10	10	10	10	0
Infill	10	15	50	20	6.67
Outfill	8	10	12	10	.67
Decoration	20	25	60	30	6.67

PATH VARIANCE

add variances along path

We begin our computations for path variances by referring to a simpler network, as given by Figure 10.10. In this figure, both an expected time and a variance are given for each task. The expected completion time is $15 + 10 = 25$. Recall from statistics that we add variances, not standard deviations. That is, if X and Y are independent, then $Var(X + Y) = Var(X) + Var(Y)$. Therefore, because the time of activity 1–2 and the time of activity 2–3 are independent, the variance of this path is $5 + 4 = 9$. The standard deviation is $\sqrt{9} = 3$. In summary, computing the variance of any path is very straightforward: simply add the variances of the activity times along that path.

Let us use this information to answer the following question: What is the probability that the project in Figure 10.10 is completed within 30 days? In order to answer this, we use the standardized z value for a normal distribution (see Figure 10.11). That is, we compute

$$z = \frac{x - \mu}{\sigma} = \frac{30 - 25}{3} = 1.67.$$

From the normal distribution table (see Appendix B2) we find that, for $z = 1.67$, the probability is 95.25 percent.

In order to demonstrate one of the difficulties with using path variances, consider a slightly more complex example, as given by Figure 10.12. The top path is identical to the path in Figure 10.10. Therefore, the expected completion time for the top path

FIGURE 10.10 Two-activity example

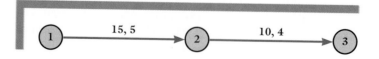

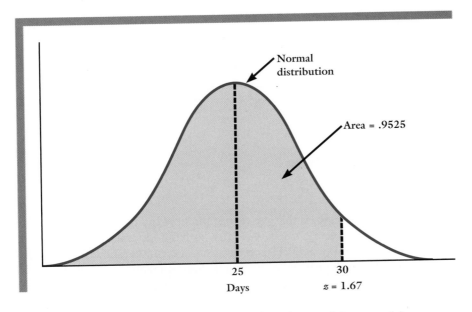

FIGURE 10.11 Distribution of completion times (two-activity example)

is given by 25, with a variance of 9. The expected completion time of the bottom path is given by 28, with a variance of 4. The bottom path is the critical path. Let us address the same question as before—namely, What is the probability that the project will be completed within 30 days? We already know that the top path has a probability of .9525. We compute the bottom path as follows:

$$z = \frac{x - \mu}{\sigma} = \frac{30 - 28}{2} = 1.$$

From the normal distribution table, we find that the probability is .8413. Because the two paths are independent, the probability of completing the project within 30 days is given by the probability that both paths are completed within 30 days, or the product of the probabilities: $p = .9525 \times .8413 = .8013$. **independent paths**

Let us continue with one more brief example, as given by Figure 10.13. The time and variance of the top path on this chart are 25 and 9, respectively, just as in the previous example. The time and variance of the bottom path are 28 and 4, also as

FIGURE 10.12 Independent paths

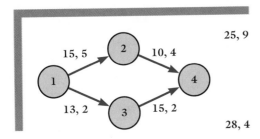

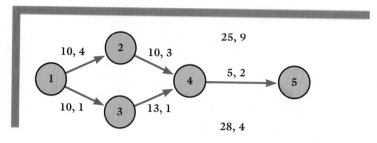

FIGURE 10.13 Paths with common arc

before. The difficulty, though, is that we cannot multiply the two probabilities: The paths here are not independent! Activity 4–5 is on both the top and the bottom paths. If we use our previous answer of 80.13 percent, we will be underestimating the probability. If we use either path probability, we will be overestimating the answer. That is, we know that the answer is between 80.13 percent and 84.13 percent (from the bottom path). In general, finding the exact answer is too difficult. Therefore, we use only the variance of the critical path as the project variance.

Now, to compute the variance of the critical path, we (somewhat arbitrarily) disregard the noncritical activities and use

project variance

$$\sigma_{cp}^2 = \sum_{\text{activities on critical path}} \sigma_{activity}^2.$$

Transparency Master 10.5:
Using Three Time
Estimates.

The variance of the project completion time, then, is the sum of the variances of all activities on the critical path. Table 10.7 contains the standard deviations and variances

TABLE 10.7 Variances and standard deviations for playground activities

	Time Estimates and Variances					
Activity	Optimistic (t_o)	Most Likely (t_m)	Pessimistic (t_p)	Mean $\left(\dfrac{t_o + 4t_m + t_p}{6}\right)$	Standard Deviation $\left(\dfrac{t_p - t_o}{6}\right)$	Variance $\dfrac{(t_p - t_o)^2}{36}$
Planning	10	20	30	20	3.33	11.11*
Purchasing	20	65	80	60	10	100
Excavation	60	90	180	100	20	400*
Sawing	25	30	35	30	1.67	2.78
Placement	15	20	25	20	1.67	2.78*
Assembly	10	10	10	10	0	0*
Infill	10	15	50	20	6.67	44.44*
Outfill	8	10	12	10	.67	.44
Decoration	20	25	60	30	6.67	44.44*

*Variances along critical path

of the activities. Summing only those variances along the critical path, we find that the project completion time variance is $11.11 + 400 + 2.78 + 0 + 44.44 + 44.44 = 502.77$. This means that the project completion time standard deviation is $\sqrt{502.77}$, or 22.4, which we use with the normal distribution table to answer probabilistic questions about the completion time. The examples that follow demonstrate the use of the probabilistic analysis in support of critical management questions.

Example 10.1 What is the probability that building the playground will require more than 240 days?

First, we need to find the z value of 240 days:

$$z = \frac{240 - \mu}{\sigma} = \frac{240 - 200}{22.4} = \frac{40}{22.4} = 1.8,$$

where μ = the mean time of the critical path.

Using the cumulative normal distribution table, we find that 96.4 percent of the distribution lies to the left of 1.8 standard deviations. Hence, there is a $100 - 96.4 = 3.6$-percent chance that it will take more than 240 days to build the playground. ◼

Example 10.2 How much time should be allowed for building the playground if we want to be 90-percent sure of completing it within this amount of time?

Note that the answer obviously is greater than 200 days, because we are 50-percent sure of this amount of time, and less than 240 days, because we are 96.4-percent sure of that amount of time. In order to find the exact time, we again use the normal distribution table, which tells us that 90 percent of the area lies to the left of 1.29 standard deviations. Hence, we must allow $1.29 \times 22.4 = 29$ days beyond the mean time of 200 days, or 229 days, to be 90-percent sure of finishing the playground on time. ◼

COST ANALYSIS

The original goal of network planning was to provide decision makers with the ability to plan and control the completion of projects by providing them with an understanding of the task times. The original models did not include the possibility of controlling project costs. Ultimately, however, **cost control** may be more important than time control. In fact, typically, the major reason that controlling the project timing is so important is because time relates to money. In 1962, the U.S. government, through the Department of Defense and NASA, developed PERT/cost, and, by 1963, many government defense and space contractors were required to use PERT/cost for cost control.

Typically, accounting in a corporation looks at the total cost per department; costs within a department are not isolated by project. The network costing models require knowledge of the cost of each activity (in a department) for each project. Hence, it is possible to isolate cost overruns as a function of an *activity* in a particular project, not just as a function of one of the firm's departments. This, of course, assumes that individual accounting cost centers are responsible for particular project activities and that there is no overlap between cost centers for any activity.

Essentially, two types of cost analyses may be used. One, cost control, is passive in the sense that it compares actual project costs through a certain time period with anticipated project costs. The other method, **cost planning,** evaluates the savings in time that result from performing critical activities faster (at some cost, of course).

COST CONTROL

Table 10.8 contains the description of building our playground with the (anticipated) costs for each of the activities, which have been broken down into average cost rates per day per activity. It is clear that the total cost is $12,300 and that, after 200 days, this should be the outlay.

Note that, on a day-to-day basis, the money laid out can vary, depending on when the noncritical activities begin. Figure 10.14 contains the activity plan—a Gantt chart—assuming that all activities begin as early as possible (at the early start times determined previously). Also noted in the figure are the cumulative project costs on a day-to-day basis.

Similar computations are shown in Figure 10.15, where we have drawn the Gantt chart, computed cumulative costs, and plotted these costs, assuming that all jobs begin as late as possible (at the late start times computed previously).

Finally, in Figure 10.16, we have combined the two graphs, with the result showing all possible budgets that vary as the (noncritical) task start times vary. Any budget between the two curves on the graph is feasible. The figure also may be used to determine cost overruns. For example, if $5,000 has been paid after 60 days, then something is wrong. In addition, too little money spent after this period of time is a bad signal also, because it implies that the project is falling behind schedule.

cost ranges

CRASHING ACTIVITIES

expedite

It is possible that the project completion time as determined by network planning may be unsatisfactory in that it is too long. In such cases, it may be possible to expedite

TABLE 10.8 Township playground costs

Activity	Time (in days)	Immediate Predecessor(s)	Cost (in dollars)	Cost per Day (in dollars)
Planning (A)	20	None	300	15
Purchasing (B)	60	Planning	2,100	35
Excavation (C)	100	Planning	4,000	40
Sawing (D)	30	Purchasing	2,850	95
Placement (E)	20	Excavation, sawing	500	25
Assembly (F)	10	Placement	200	20
Infill (G)	20	Assembly	400	20
Outfill (H)	10	Assembly	600	60
Decoration (I)	30	Infill, outfill	1,350	45
			12,300	

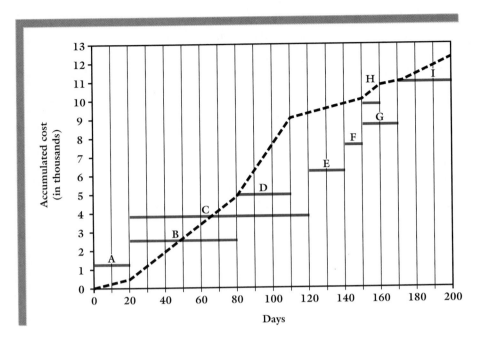

FIGURE 10.14 Early start cost network

FIGURE 10.15 Latest start cost network

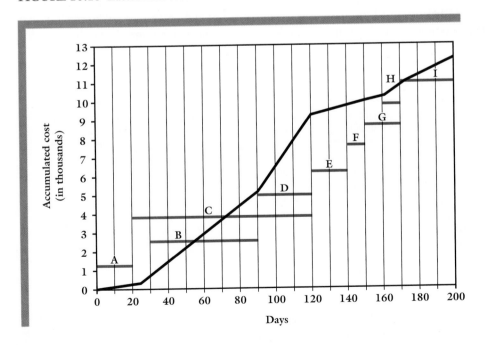

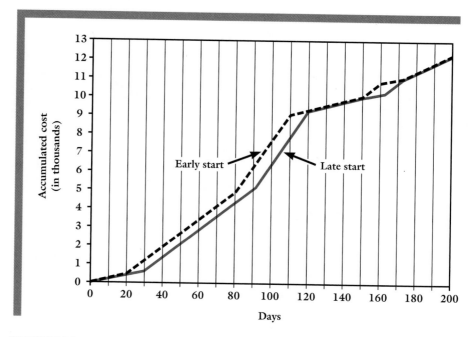

FIGURE 10.16 Combined chart to show all possible budgets

some or all of the activities. Reducing the completion time for an activity is known as **crashing.** Crashing is rarely accomplished without some cost. For example, overtime can be used to get the job done faster, but it is expensive. One goal of project planning is to be able to determine this time–cost trade-off.

Table 10.9 contains the normal times and costs for our playground example, as given before. In addition, it contains **crash times** and **crash costs.** The crash time is the minimum possible time required to perform the activity, and the crash cost is the

TABLE 10.9 Normal and crash times and costs for playground activities

Activity	Normal Time (in days)	Normal Cost (in dollars)	Crash Time (in days)	Crash Cost (in dollars)	Crash Cost per Day (in dollars)
Planning (A)	20	300	15	450	30
Purchasing (B)	60	2,100	50	2,140	4
Excavation (C)	100	4,000	75	4,500	20
Sawing (D)	30	2,850	20	3,000	15
Placement (E)	20	500	*	*	*
Assembly (F)	10	200	*	*	*
Infill (G)	20	400	*	*	*
Outfill (H)	10	600	*	*	*
Decoration (I)	30	1,350	*	*	*
		12,300			

* Not possible to crash

cost of performing the activity in its crash time. Assume that the cost per day of crashing is linear in the number of days the project is crashed (this may or may not be true). Then, the cost per day of crashing, which is in the last column of Table 10.9, is given by

assumption

$$\text{Daily crash cost} = \frac{\text{cost increase due to crashing}}{\text{time decrease due to crashing}}$$

$$= \frac{\text{crash cost} - \text{normal cost}}{\text{normal time} - \text{crash time}}.$$

computing daily crash costs

Now, using the information given in Table 10.9 and the knowledge that the critical path is A–C–E–F–G–I, we can analyze the time–cost trade-off. Suppose that our goal is to reduce the project time by 25 days, to a length of 175 days. It does not pay to crash an activity that is not critical, because this will not shorten the project. Hence, the only activities we consider crashing are planning and excavation, because shortening either one will shorten the project completion time. Because excavation is less expensive to crash, we crash this activity as much as is reasonable. This means that we crash the activity until some currently noncritical activity becomes critical. Therefore, we reduce the activity time by 10 days (at a cost of $20 per day), at which point there are two critical paths: A–C–E–F–G–I and A–B–D–E–F–G–I. At this point, we must crash both of these paths in order to reduce the project completion time. In order to reduce A–B–D–E–F–G–I, we can crash planning, purchasing, or sawing. Because purchasing is less costly to crash than either sawing or planning, we reduce purchasing. In order to reduce A–C–E–F–G–I, we choose excavation, since it is less expensive to crash than planning. We are limited to reducing purchasing by 10 days. Hence, we have a completion time of 180 days, with the last 10 days costing $20 + $4 per day. At this point, we again have to reduce both paths to reduce both critical paths at the same time. One way to do this is to reduce both excavation and sawing at the same time (at a cost of $20 + $15 per day). We reduce both for 5 days, at which point the excavation crash time is reached and our 175-day goal is also reached. Putting these computations together yields the data presented in part (a) of Table 10.10.

crash only critical activities

TABLE 10.10   Time–cost trade-offs

Length of Project (in days)	Cost (in dollars)	Activity Crashed	
200	12,300	None	
190	12,500	Excavation	(a)
180	12,740	Purchasing, excavation	
175	12,915	Sawing, excavation	

Length of Project (in days)	Cost (in dollars)	Activity Crashed	
200	12,300	None	
190	12,500	Excavation	(b)
180	12,740	Purchasing, excavation	
175	12,890	Planning	

Teaching Suggestion 10.10:
Bonuses and Penalties.
See the Instructor's Sec-
tion for details.

**minimum cost project
schedule**

You may have spotted another crashing possibility. If we crash the planning activity, it will reduce the length of both critical paths simultaneously because it is on both paths. Although it is expensive to crash planning ($30 per day), this approach is still cheaper than choosing the cheapest activity to crash on each path, as we have just done. If planning time is reduced, $5 per day will be saved, but only for 5 days, because that is its limit. Having crashed planning, we proceed as before. The result of this approach is shown in part (b) of Table 10.10.

Another common way crashing is used is to find the minimum cost project schedule. For our example, if the daily fixed cost is $25, then it pays to crash to 190 days, because $25 is gained per day at a cost of $20. It also pays to continue to crash until 180 days, because $25 is gained per day at a cost of $24 per day. However, any further crashing can be done only by raising the total project cost. Thus, the minimum cost project schedule is 180 days. We would consider crashing below 180 days only if we had additional reasons (possibly contract incentives) for doing so.

EXTENSIONS TO THE BASIC MODELS

The cost extensions of the previous section have been applied universally. There are, however, other extensions that have been used to approach problems involving network planning. Due to limited resources, it may not always be possible to start all activities when their precedences have been met. Also, the network structure may change due to changes in plans during project execution. We present the extensions for these two network planning problems next.

LIMITED RESOURCES

Teaching Suggestion 10.11:
Scheduling News at WBZ.
See the Instructor's Sec-
tion for details.

To this point, we have assumed that the only reason a task is not begun is because all of its precedence tasks have not been met. For example, if the early stages of a project appeared as in Figure 10.17, we would assume that the m tasks all can be started at

FIGURE 10.17 Multiple tasks starting simultaneously

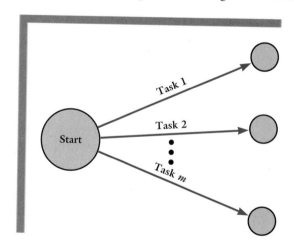

TABLE 10.11 Precedence table for project with limited resources

Task	Time (in days)	Crew Size	Immediate Predecessor(s)
A	2	3	None
B	4	1	A
C	2	3	A
D	1	3	A
E	4	4	B
F	4	3	C
G	7	1	D
H	10	3	E, F
I	2	2	G, H

the inception of the project. However, it is possible that, in some cases, the same resource may be used for different tasks and that this resource may be limited.

Table 10.11 contains the precedence table for a project, including the work crew size required for each task. Disregarding the crew size, the time to complete the project is 22 days. In Figure 10.18, the project is represented as a PERT diagram along a time scale. Also given in this figure is the manpower usage per day for each task. Now suppose that the total availability of manpower is limited to 5 workers per day. Then, obviously, the schedule depicted in Figure 10.18 is not feasible, because it violates this manpower constraint. For example, observe that, although tasks B, C, and D have no technological restrictions, all three tasks cannot be started after day 2 because of manpower restrictions. The object is to find the schedule that minimizes the project completion time without violating either technological or resource constraints. Resource usage is shown in a load chart. Figure 10.19 contains two load charts for our example. Part (a) shows the amount of resources needed for each day; part (b) is more specific, showing the assignments of resources (people) to tasks on each day. Pictorially, the goal is to balance, or flatten out, the load chart.

goal: balance load chart

Unfortunately, there is no general method for doing this. Therefore, we proceed on an intuitive basis and generate a heuristic method for getting a good—although

FIGURE 10.18 Unlimited resources

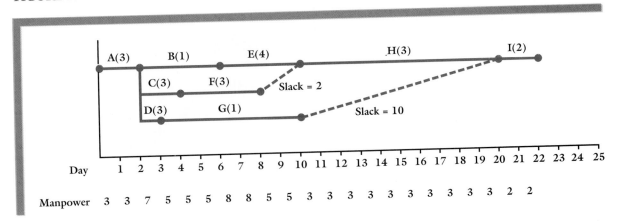

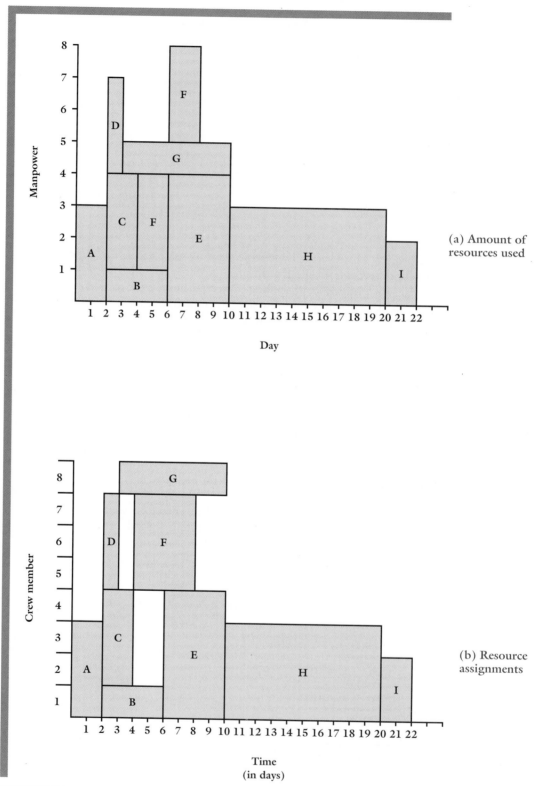

(a) Amount of resources used

(b) Resource assignments

FIGURE 10.19 Load charts

not necessarily optimal—solution. The method is rather simple and requires only a forward pass through the network, scheduling the tasks as resources become available. The only question to be answered is which task to choose when several are competing for the same resources. Standard rules for choosing one task among several possible tasks are to select the task with

■ the least amount of slack,
■ the longest processing time,
■ the shortest processing time,
■ the most following tasks, and
■ the least following tasks.

priority rules

There is a great deal of similarity between these rules and those of assembly line balancing (Chapter 7) and job shop scheduling (Chapter 15). We have "solved" the example problem using the least slack rule, and the results can be seen in Figure 10.20.

The first task we schedule is, of course, task A, which lasts for 2 days. Next, we choose B, because it has the least slack, and C because it has less slack than D (step 2 in Figure 10.20). We see from step 2 that C finishes at day 4 and that it is possible to schedule another activity. F has 2 days' slack, and D now has 8 days' slack (2 days were used up), so F is scheduled, resulting in step 3. In step 3, we see that B's resource is freed after day 6, but, although E and D are technologically ready, each requires more resources than are available. Hence, the next opportunity to schedule is when F finishes. Task E has less slack, so we schedule it, yielding step 4. At this point, both H and D have no slack, but only one can be scheduled. We choose D. Finally, G, H, and I are scheduled (with I last, due to technological restrictions), and the final schedule generated appears in step 5. The load chart for this schedule appears in Figure 10.21.

FIGURE 10.20 The problem of limited resources solved with least slack rule

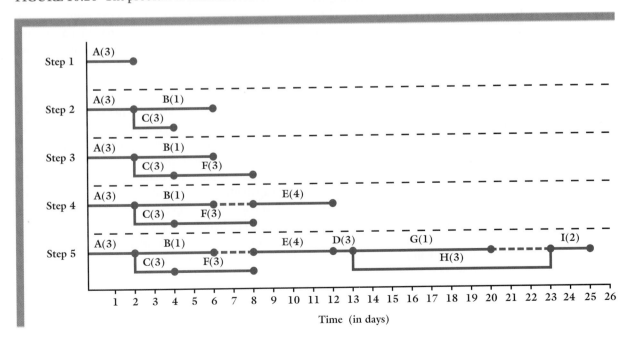

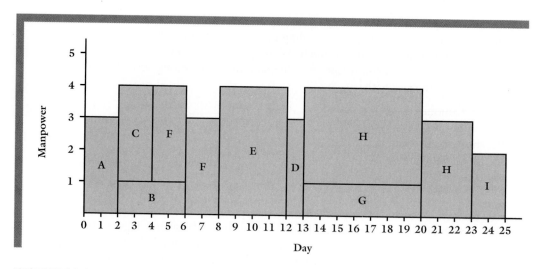

FIGURE 10.21   Improved schedule (twenty-five days) for limited resources problem

Notice that it is much flatter than the unconstrained load chart in part (a) of Figure 10.19. Of course, the schedule is extended by 3 days. It is obvious from this example that limited resources pose a rather difficult problem. In practice, a computer program would be used to generate several different schedules using the preceding rules and others.

BRANCHING ALTERNATIVES

In the previous discussions, we have assumed that the precedences are known. There is the possibility that, due either to choice or to chance, the order in the network is not known. The standard notation for the representation of "or" is a triangle (Δ), rather than the circle or rectangle used in the previous graphs. Figure 10.22 contains two different types of networks. In part (a), the decision maker can choose either C or D after B, while in part (b), either C or D, with probabilities of .6 and .4, respectively, is chosen by chance. The interpretation of the network in part (a) is that the decision maker has equally viable alternatives (make or buy), while in the network in part (b), chance events exist (obtaining a contract or not). Although further discussion of this special case is beyond the scope of this text, we note that a procedure known as GERT (graphical evaluation review technique) is available to handle it.

GERT

The best way to describe GERT without going into detail is to compare it with PERT or CPM in terms of its general capabilities. First, GERT's approach is different. Rather than a calculation of the shortest (optimal) completion time, GERT is a simulation, using decision trees (see Chapter 3) to handle the probabilistic branching just described. The probabilistic branching capability, a significant advance, provides for flexibility in node realization. PERT or CPM allows no such flexibility. Another situation that occurs very often, especially in projects where some sort of test must be passed at various stages, is that an activity must be repeated. GERT allows this, and the others do not.

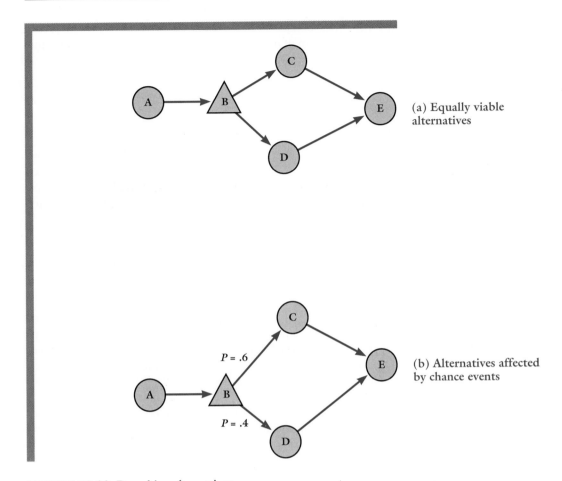

FIGURE 10.22 Branching alternatives

The arcs in PERT (and the nodes in CPM) represent time. In fact, time is PERT's only variable of concern, and cost or resource usage analysis must be done separately. GERT allows the arcs to represent cost, reliability, or almost any variable of interest. Finally, PERT always uses the beta distribution for its probabilistic analysis. GERT uses any distribution. This last advantage is minor, however, because anyone with a good statistics background should be able to use other distributions for activity times while staying within the PERT framework.

The main disadvantage to GERT is that it is difficult to use. Our main objective in using these tools for project management is to be able to *control* large projects. PERT and CPM have proven to be excellent control tools. GERT, although useful in more complex situations, is difficult to use as a control tool, limiting its value.

CRITICISM OF NETWORK PLANNING

PERT and CPM analyses are based entirely on the precedence graph. Either diagram contains only two types of information—the task times and the task precedences.

Hence, it is not surprising that, because network planning is so sensitive to the precedence graph, much of the criticism of network planning has focused on the times and the precedences.

THE TIME ESTIMATES

The PERT method (t_o, t_m, t_p) touches on the fact that, typically, task times are unknown. The problem, however, is that, not only is t unknown, but so are the three estimates—t_o, t_m, and t_p. It must be acknowledged that the data used are not perfect. However, the procedures used are the best way to proceed with the best available information. This is the most that can be asked of us as managers.

THE PRECEDENCE RELATIONS

We assume that the precedences are hard and fast and cannot be violated. Yet, oftentimes, the precedences are merely a good idea, not a requirement. (This is similar to many course prerequisites.) New model development is needed to analyze soft precedence relationships. Our suggestion is to analyze the situation first, disregarding these soft relationships. This will provide the best schedule. Then, if the schedule violates any of the soft precedences, include them and perform the analysis again. This will allow an evaluation of the cost, both in time and money, of requiring the soft precedences. A decision can then be made as to whether or not inclusion of the soft precedences is worth the cost.

S U M M A R Y

Project scheduling refers to the analysis and planning of complex projects, where the project is defined as a set of tasks or activities that must all be completed in order for the entire job, or project, to be completed. Some of these activities may take place simultaneously, and the interdependencies of the activities require close control and coordination by management. In general, we measure project success according to conformance to time, budget, and specifications.

Six key questions need to be answered when planning projects. Four of these reflect operations scheduling concerns, and two reflect budgeting concerns:

1. If each of the activities goes according to plan, when will the project be completed?
2. Which tasks are most critical to ensure the timely completion of the project?
3. Which tasks can be delayed, if necessary, without delaying project completion, and by how much can each be delayed?

4. More specifically, at what times should each activity begin and end?
5. At any given time during the project, what is the range of dollars that should have been spent?
6. Is it worthwhile to incur extra costs in order to accelerate some of the activities?

Project scheduling is examined through the use of network planning techniques, *PERT* and *CPM*, which in their basic forms identify the critical activities that form the project's *critical path*, the *slack time* associated with those tasks that are not on the critical path, and the project completion time. Extensions allow for a probabilistic time estimate by using *optimistic, pessimistic,* and *most likely time* estimates. *Crash times* and *crash costs* refer to speeding up the project completion at some cost.

KEY TERMS

program evaluation and review technique (PERT)

critical path method (CPM)

work breakdown structure

Gantt chart

network diagram

scheduling chart

load chart

activity on node (AON) network

activity on arc (AOA) network

dummy activity

path

early start

early finish

late finish

late start

slack time

optimistic time

most likely time

pessimistic time

cost control

cost planning

crashing

crash time

crash cost

SOLVED PROBLEMS

1. Given below is a table of data that includes the tasks, times, and precedences for a project.

- **(a)** Draw the CPM network for this project.
- **(b)** Find the expected project completion time and the critical path.
- **(c)** Find the amount of slack for each activity.

Task	Time (in days)	Immediate Predecessors
A	18	—
B	22	A
C	14	A
D	19	A
E	12	B, C
F	17	B, C, D
G	16	E, F

- **(a)** We begin by considering the tasks that have no preceding tasks. In this problem, the only task with no predecessor is task A. We draw a node (circle) and place the label A in the node and the task time of 18 on top of the node, as shown in part (a) of Figure 10.23. Next, we add to the diagram all of the activities that have only A as a precedent. These are activities B, C, and D. For each of these activities we draw an arc from A to a new node with the appropriate label and place the time on top of the node. Part (b) contains our partially finished CPM network. We now add all nodes that require only A through D, which have already been drawn, as precedences. The new tasks are E and F. We draw a node for E and a node for F to the right of C, D, and E. Next, we connect node E with a line from both B and C, and we connect node F with a line from B, C, and D and place the task times on top of each of these two circles (see part (c) of Figure 10.23). Finally, we complete the network by adding node G and connecting it with lines from both E and F. The final CPM network is given in part (d) of Figure 10.23.
- **(b)** There are two ways to find the critical path. In this problem, we choose to identify and evaluate each path. (In the next problem, we will use the two-pass method of finding early and late starts and finishes.)

    The paths in this network are given as A–B–E–G, A–B–F–G, A–C–E–G, A–C–F–G, and A–D–F–G. The times for each path are simply the sums of the times of the activities along these paths, as shown in the accompanying table.

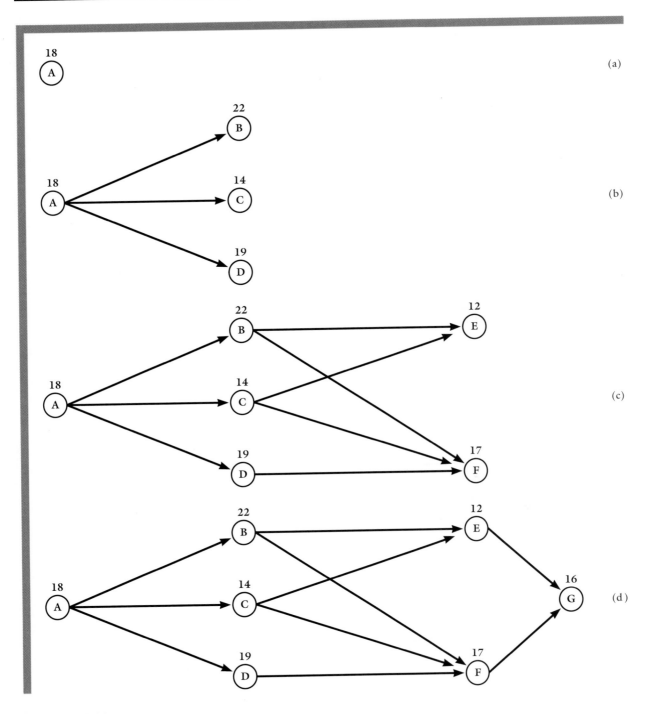

FIGURE 10.23

Path	Times	Sum
A–B–E–G	18, 22, 12, 16	68
A–B–F–G	18, 22, 17, 16	73
A–C–E–G	18, 14, 12, 16	60
A–C–F–G	18, 14, 17, 16	65
A–D–F–G	18, 19, 17, 16	70

The path taking the longest—A–B–F–G—is the critical path. The project will take the length of time given by the critical path—in this case, 73 days.

(c) The slack for the critical activities (A, B, F, and G) is 0. Our concern is with the slack for activities C, D, and E. The most critical (longest) path for C is A–C–F–G, with a time of 65. Therefore, the slack for activity C is $73 - 65 = 8$. The most critical path for activity D takes 70 days, meaning that D has a slack of 3 days. The most critical path for activity E takes 68 days, yielding a slack of 5 for activity E.

Using AB:POM to Solve This Problem

AB:POM can be used both for CPM (activity on node) and for PERT (activity on arc) networks; in either case, there can be either one or three time estimates. The initial question is which of the four models should be chosen. For Solved Problem 1, we have chosen the one-time-estimate CPM network with seven activities, as indicated in Screen 10.1. The input is the standard input of times and predecessors.

```
=== Data file:wgsp2 ======== CPM/PERT Project Scheduling ========= Data Screen =
   Number of activities (1-99) 7

========================= Chapter 10, Solved problem 1 =========================

   Task    Time        Predecessors
   A          18    --    --    --    --    --    --    --
   B          22    A     --    --    --    --    --    --
   C          14    A     --    --    --    --    --    --
   D          19    A     --    --    --    --    --    --
   E          12    B     C     --    --    --    --    --
   F          17    B     C     D     --    --    --    --
   G          16    E     F     --    --    --    --    --




F1=Help F2=New F3=Load F4=Main F5=Util F6=Quit F7=Save F9=Prnt F10=Run      Esc
Enter a predecessor for this task
```

SCREEN 10.1

When the solution screen is displayed, the predecessors are erased, as indicated in Screen 10.2. For each activity, the early start, early finish, late start, late finish, and slack are displayed. The project completion time—73, for this problem—appears at the top of the screen.

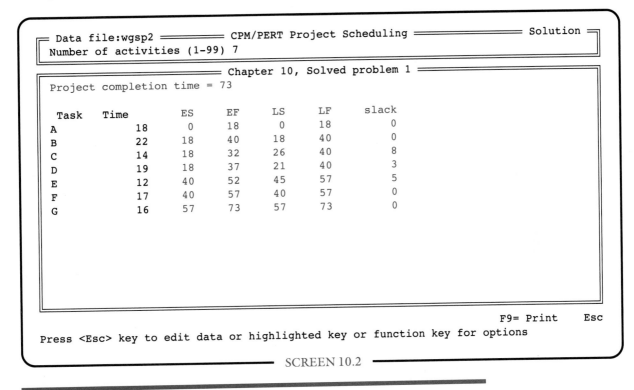

```
┌─ Data file:wgsp2 ════════════ CPM/PERT Project Scheduling ══════════ Solution ─┐
│  Number of activities (1-99) 7                                                  │
│ ┌══════════════════════════ Chapter 10, Solved problem 1 ════════════════════┐ │
│ │ Project completion time = 73                                               │ │
│ │                                                                            │ │
│ │   Task    Time        ES     EF     LS     LF      slack                   │ │
│ │   A          18        0     18      0     18        0                      │ │
│ │   B          22       18     40     18     40        0                      │ │
│ │   C          14       18     32     26     40        8                      │ │
│ │   D          19       18     37     21     40        3                      │ │
│ │   E          12       40     52     45     57        5                      │ │
│ │   F          17       40     57     40     57        0                      │ │
│ │   G          16       57     73     57     73        0                      │ │
│ │                                                                            │ │
│ │                                                             F9= Print   Esc │ │
│ └────────────────────────────────────────────────────────────────────────────┘ │
│   Press <Esc> key to edit data or highlighted key or function key for options   │
└────────────────────────────────── SCREEN 10.2 ────────────────────────────────┘
```

2. Given in Figure 10.24 are the optimistic, most likely, and pessimistic times for the activities in a project.

(a) Compute the mean and standard deviation for each activity time.
(b) Compute the mean and standard deviation for each path in the project.
(c) Find the probability that the project is completed within 70 days.

FIGURE 10.24

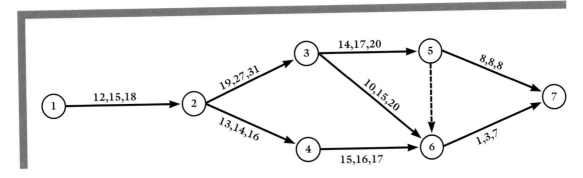

Solution

(a) The mean of each activity is given by the formula

$$t = \frac{t_o + 4t_m + t_p}{6},$$

and the standard deviation for each activity is given by the formula

$$\sigma = \frac{t_p - t_o}{6}.$$

The following table contains the computations for each activity.

Task	t_o	t_m	t_p	t	σ	σ^2
1–2	12	15	18	15	1	1
2–3	19	27	31	26.33	2	4
2–4	13	14	16	14.17	.5	.25
3–5	14	17	20	17	1	1
3–6	10	15	20	15	1.67	2.79
4–6	15	16	17	16	.33	.11
5–6	0	0	0	0	0	0
5–7	8	8	8	8	0	0
6–7	1	3	7	3.33	1	1

(b) The mean for each path is given by the sum of the activity times along that path. The standard deviation is not quite so easy to calculate. The variance of each path is the sum of the variances along the path, and the standard deviation is the square root of this variance. The computations appear in the following table.

Path	Activity Times	Mean	Activity Variances	Path Variance	Path σ
1–2–3–5–7	15, 26.33, 17, 8	66.33	1, 4, 1, 0	6	2.45
1–2–3–5–6–7	15, 26.33, 17, 0, 3.33	61.67	1, 4, 1, 0, 1	7	2.65
1–2–3–6–7	15, 26.33, 15, 3.33	59.67	1, 4, 2.79, 1	8.79	2.96
1–2–4–6–7	15, 14.17, 16, 3.33	48.50	1, .25, .11, 1	2.36	1.54

(c) To determine the probability that the project will be completed within 70 days, we use only the mean and standard deviation along the critical path. The z-value used to go to the normal distribution table is given by the formula

$$z = \frac{\text{Time of interest} - \text{expected path completion time}}{\text{standard deviation of path}}.$$

In this example, our *z*-score is given by

$$z = \frac{70 - 66.33}{2.45} = \frac{3.67}{2.45} = 1.498.$$

Going to the one-tailed normal distribution table, we find that 93.32 percent of the curve lies to the left of 1.498 standard distributions. Therefore, the probability that the project will be completed within 70 days is .9332.

Using AB:POM to Solve This Problem

Solved Problem 2 is a three-time-estimate PERT network. The data and solution are shown in Screens 10.3 and 10.4.

```
 Data file:wgsp3 ========= CPM/PERT Project Scheduling ========= Data Screen
 Number of activities (1-99) 9

========================= Chapter 10, Solved problem 2 =========================
 StartEnd  Opt. LikelPess.
 Node Node Time Time Time
     1    2   12   15   18
     2    3   19   27   31
     2    4   13   14   16
     3    5   14   17   20
     3    6   10   15   20
     4    6   15   16   17
     5    6    0    0    0
     5    7    8    8    8
     6    7    1    3    7




F1=Help F2= New F3=Load F4=Main F5=Util F6=Quit F7=Save F9=Prnt F10=Run      Esc
Enter the pessimistic time estimate for this activity
```

SCREEN 10.3

```
╔═ Data file:wgsp3 ═════════ CPM/PERT Project Scheduling ══════════ Solution ═╗
║  Number of activities (1-99) 9                                              ║
║ ┌══════════════════════════ Chapter 10, Solved problem 2 ═════════════════┐ ║
║ │ Project completion time =  66.33334   Project standard deviation = 2.44949│ ║
║ │StartEnd  Opt. LikelPess.                                                 │ ║
║ │Node Node Time Time Time    Time    ES      EF      LS      LF   slack sd ( σ)│ ║
║ │   1    2   12   15   18     15     0      15       0      15      0      1 │ ║
║ │   2    3   19   27   31 26.333    15 41.333      15 41.333      0      2 │ ║
║ │   2    4   13   14   16 14.167    15 29.167 32.833      47 17.833    0.5 │ ║
║ │   3    5   14   17   20     17 41.333 58.333 41.333 58.333      0      1 │ ║
║ │   3    6   10   15   20     15 41.333 56.333      48      63 6.6667 1.6667│ ║
║ │   4    6   15   16   17     16 29.167 45.167      47      63 17.833 .33333│ ║
║ │   5    6    0    0    0      0 58.333 58.333      63      63 4.6667      0 │ ║
║ │   5    7    8    8    8      8 58.333 66.333 58.333 66.333      0      0 │ ║
║ │   6    7    1    3    7 3.3333 58.333 61.667      63 66.333 4.6667      1 │ ║
║ │                                                                          │ ║
║ └──────────────────────────────────────────────────────────────────────────┘ ║
║                                                           F9=Print    Esc   ║
║  Press <Esc> key to edit data or highlighted key or function key for options║
╚═════════════════════════════ SCREEN 10.4 ═══════════════════════════════════╝
```

QUESTIONS

1. Describe project management.

2. Give an example of a situation where project management is needed.

3. What are three characteristics of projects?

4. What are the three measures of project success?

5. What are the six major concerns with using network planning techniques?

6. If by definition a project is something that is not performed on a regular basis, how should one estimate the task times?

7. How much reliability can be attributed to the estimated task times?

8. Give two examples where Gantt charts or network diagrams can be used in our activities.

9. What are the advantages and disadvantages of the AON network versus the AOA network?

10. What is the significance of the critical path?

11. How does the probabilistic assumption of PERT affect the definition of the critical path?

12. On what is the formula for the activity time standard deviation based?

13. What would a project manager have to do to crash an activity?

14. Do you think that the assumption of unlimited resources is the rule or the exception? Why?

15. Is the analysis of limited resources more useful in the decision-making stage or in the implementation stage?

PROBLEMS

1. The Gantt chart that follows shows a schedule for a planned project. For each task (A through H), the number of days required also is given.

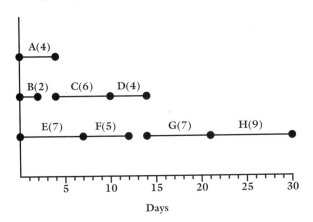

(a) When does each task begin?

(b) How long does it take to complete the project?

(c) On how many days is more than one activity going on simultaneously?

(d) Which tasks appear to form the critical path?

A:0; B:0; C:4; D:10; E:0;
F:7; G:14; and H:21

30 days

days 1–12

A–C–D–G–H

2. The following tasks are required to complete a software development project.

Task	Time (in months)	Immediate Predecessors
A	4	None
B	3	A
C	2	None
D	5	B
E	4	C, D
F	8	D
G	5	E
H	6	F, G
I	5	H
J	2	I

(a) Draw a Gantt chart for this project.

(b) Draw the CPM network for this project.

(c) Draw the PERT network for this project.

(d) Draw the PERT–time network for this project.

See Instructor's Section.
See Instructor's Section.
See Instructor's Section.
See Instructor's Section.

3. Use the data presented in Problem 2 for the following.

(a) Find the critical path and the project length using the enumeration method.

(b) Find the critical path and the project length using the two-pass method.

(c) Find the slack times associated with each task.

A–B–D–E–G–H–I–J; 34 mo.
A–B–D–E–G–H–I–J; 34 mo.
C:10; F:1; all others:0

4. Use the following diagram to find

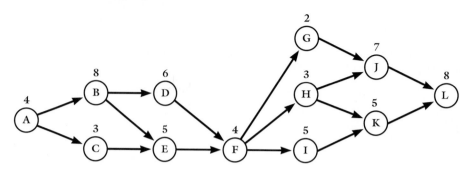

A–B–D–F–I–K–L and
A–B–D–F–H–J–L; 40
C:6; E:1; G:1; all others: 0

(a) the critical path and the project length.
(b) the slack times for each task in this project.

5. For the following network,

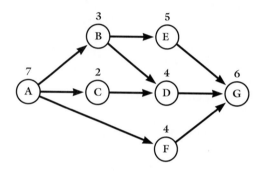

A–B–E–G; 21 days
no

(a) find the critical path and the project completion time.
(b) tell whether the project will be delayed if task C takes 4 days rather than 2 days.

6. Find the critical path and the project completion time for the following data.

Task	Time (in days)	Immediate Predecessors
A	9	None
B	12	A
C	3	A
D	6	B, C
E	15	A
F	5	C, E
G	8	D, F
H	7	E, F
I	6	G

A–E–F–G–I; 43 days

A–C–F–H–J
31 days
B:6; D:7; E:3; G:8; I:8; all others:0

7. Use the network at the top of the following page to find the

(a) critical path.
(b) project completion time.
(c) activity slack times.

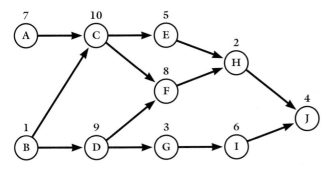

8. Given the following PERT network, find the critical path and the project completion time.

start–1–2–4–6–9–8–7–
10–finish; 42

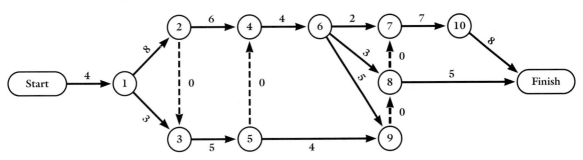

9. For the following estimates of t_o, t_m, and t_p, calculate the expected time and the standard deviation for each activity.

Activity	t_o	t_m	t_p
A	11	15	19
B	27	31	41
C	18	18	18
D	8	13	19
E	17	18	20
F	16	19	22

A:15, 1.33;
B:32, 2.33;
C:18, 0;
D:13.17, 1.83;
E:18.17, .5;
F:19, 1

10. The following PERT network has the expected activity times followed by the standard deviations for each activity.

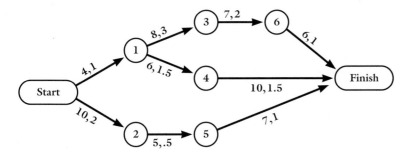

(a) For each path, what is the expected path length and the standard deviation of the path?
(b) What is the expected project length and the critical path?

S–1–3–6–F:25, 3.87;
S–1–4–F:20, 2.35; and
S–2–5–F:22, 2.29
start–1–3–6–finish; 25

11. A project diagram has three independent paths from start to finish. The expected times and standard deviations for each path are as follows.

Path	Expected Time (in days)	Standard Deviation
1	21	5
2	23	2
3	20	1

23 days
.1746
.337

(a) What is the expected project length?
(b) What is the probability of completing the project within 22 days?
(c) What is the probability of failing to complete the project within 25 days?

12. Task time estimates for a production line setup project are as follows.

Activity	t_o	t_m	t_p	Immediate Predecessors
A	4	6	8	None
B	6	7	9	None
C	2	5	8	A
D	6	6	6	B, C
E	3	4	8	C
F	5	8	9	D
G	3	4	5	E, F

Time (in weeks) appears as a spanning header over t_o, t_m, t_p.

See Instructor's Section.
A–C–D–F–G
28.67 weeks
2.0067
.8264

(a) Draw the project precedence diagram.
(b) Identify the critical path.
(c) What is the expected project length?
(d) What is the variance of the project length?
(e) What is the probability of completing the project within 30 weeks?

See Instructor's Section.

13. Based on the expected times, draw the Gantt chart for the project defined in Problem 12.

14. A project schedule has been established, with the following activity start times, costs per day, and lengths.

Activity	Start Day	Cost per Day (in dollars)	Activity Duration (in days)
A	1	20	5
B	6	17	8
C	6	19	3
D	9	23	6
E	14	25	3
F	16	15	5

(a) Prepare a project budget listing the total cost of the project and the cost of each activity.
(b) Calculate the cost on a daily basis and on a cumulative basis for the entire project.

A:$100; B:$136; C:$57;
D:$138; E:$75; F:$75; total
= $581
See Instructor's Section.

15. Consider the following CPM network, which defines a project requiring 17 days.

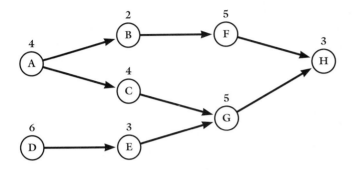

If B, E, and H can be crashed by 1 day, and all other activities except D can be crashed by 2 days, what is the minimum attainable length of the project? *(Note:* D cannot be reduced at all.) 13 days

16. For the project defined in Problem 15, the cost associated with crashing each activity is as follows.

	Crash Cost	
Activity	Day 1	Day 2
A	7	10
B	10	—
C	12	15
D	—	—
E	14	—
F	12	18
G	18	20
H	15	—

The fixed daily charge to the project is $16. What is the optimal length of the project from a cost standpoint? 15 days

17. Consider the following CPM network, which shows times and required resources.

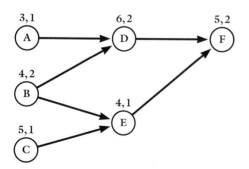

15

4

17 (by trial and error)

24 (by trial and error)

(a) Based on a CPM analysis and disregarding resource availability, what is the length of the project?

(b) What is the maximum number of resources in use at any one time using an early start schedule?

(c) What schedule can be achieved if only three resources are available?

(d) What schedule can be achieved if only two resources are available?

REFERENCES

Cleland, D. I., and W. R. King. *Project Management Handbook.* New York: Van Nostrand Reinhold Company, 1983.

Gido, J. *An Introduction to Project Planning.* 2nd ed. New York: Industrial Press, Inc., 1985.

Gilbreath, R. D. *Winning at Project Management.* New York: John Wiley and Sons, 1986.

M. Karkowski. "PERT and Parkinson's Law," *Interfaces* 5, no. 1 (November 1974): 35–40.

Levine, H. A. *Project Management Using Microcomputers.* Berkeley, Calif.: Osborne/McGraw-Hill, 1986.

Meredith, J. R., and S. J. Mantel, Jr. *Project Management: A Managerial Approach.* 2nd ed. New York: John Wiley and Sons, 1989.

Moder, J. J., C. R. Phillips, and E. W. Davis. *Project Management with CPM, PERT and Precedence Diagramming.* 3rd ed. New York: Van Nostrand Reinhold Company, 1983.

Rosenau, M. D., Jr. *Successful Project Management.* New York: Van Nostrand Reinhold Company, 1981.

Stepman, K. *The 1986 Buyer's Guide to Project Management Software.* Tallahassee, Fla.: New Issues Inc., 1986.

Weist, J. D., and F. K. Levy. *A Management Guide to PERT/ CPM.* 2nd ed. Englewood Cliffs, N.J.: Prentice-Hall, 1977.

C H A P T E R

11

O U T L I N E

LINEAR PROGRAMMING

- To illustrate the usefulness of, and the need for, linear programming as a technique in operations management
- To provide a framework for the modeling of operations problems as linear programs
- To demonstrate the development of a variety of common linear programs
- To solve small linear programs by a graphical procedure to illustrate what takes place as a linear program is solved

INTRODUCTION

limited resources

resource allocation

Teaching Suggestion 11.1: Programming and Planning. See the Instructor's Section for details.

Teaching Suggestion 11.2: Technique vs. Application Area. See the Instructor's Section for details.

The proper allocation of resources is a problem that operations managers face day in and day out. The good operations manager must decide which activities can be pursued without violating the limited resources and (as is always the goal) while obtaining as much reward as possible.

The resource allocation problem is modeled, under certain conditions, as a linear program and is solved by a technique called *linear programming*. The conditions are discussed in detail in the next section; for now, suffice it to say that the relationships between the activities must be linear. Luckily, this is very often the case, and so this chapter will deal with the use of linear programming as a general tool for resource allocation.

Linear programming is a technique for determining the most efficient method for allocating resources. The model was developed in the late 1940s by George Dantzig. It has been widely used since then due to the simplicity and efficiency of the solution method and to the fact that linear programming can be used by virtually any business. For example, economists, chemical engineers, and firemen, as well as operations managers, all face problems that can be solved by the linear programming technique. Computer programs and packages for linear programming are available for almost every computer system.

It is most important that anyone trying to allocate resources efficiently be able to recognize whether a problem can be represented as a linear program. If the problem is a linear program, then solution is immediate. The next sections present the formulation of sample problems into their corresponding linear programming models. These examples also serve to demonstrate the wide applicability of linear programming. In practice, most computer software for linear programming is based on an algebraic method known as the *simplex method*, which is beyond the scope of this text.

FORMULATION OF THE LINEAR PROGRAM

In this section, the building of linear programs (linear models) is explained. Once the model is built, a computer can solve it (no one solves these by hand in practice), so the model formulation is the key. Unfortunately, there is no clear set of rules for building

Linear programming is widely used for resource allocation. (© Bruce Davidson/ Magnum Photos, Inc.)

the model. This must be learned through examples and by practice. We first use a prototype to build the general structure of a linear program, and then we give several examples of linear program formulations.

A PROTOTYPE EXAMPLE—RESOURCE ALLOCATION

The following example demonstrates the formulation process of linear programming.

Example 11.1   Wershon Suit Company produces sport jackets and slacks. The profit on each jacket is $10, and the profit on each pair of slacks is $15. Each jacket requires 2 square yards of material and 4 manhours of sewing, while each pair of slacks requires 5 square yards of material and 2 manhours of sewing. If Wershon has 50 square yards of material and 36 hours of work available each week, how many jackets and how many pairs of slacks should be produced? (Assume that all goods produced are indeed sold.)

The goal is to put the problem in algebraic form. After this is accomplished, the problem may be solved by standard methods, which will be done later in this chapter. We begin by defining the variables that represent the decisions we must make. Let

x_1 = number of jackets produced per week

Teaching Suggestion 11.3: Variable Names. See the Instructor's Section for details.

and let

$$x_2 = \text{number of slacks produced per week.}$$

With a profit of \$10 per jacket and \$15 per pair of slacks, the profit on the jackets is $10x_1$, the profit on the slacks is $15x_2$, and the total profit is $10x_1 + 15x_2$. Therefore, our objective is to

$$\text{Maximize } Z = 10x_1 + 15x_2.$$

We cannot calculate the total profit until the actual number of jackets and number of slacks produced per week (x_1 and x_2) have been determined. Finding the best levels for x_1 and x_2 is the object of solving the model.

There are two constraining factors in this example. The first restriction is the limit of 50 square yards of material. If x_1 jackets are produced, then $2x_1$ yards of material are needed for jackets; if x_2 slacks are produced, then $5x_2$ yards of material are needed for slacks. Thus, the total material required for x_1 jackets and x_2 slacks is $2x_1 + 5x_2$, and this cannot exceed 50 square yards. This is expressed as

$$2x_1 + 5x_2 \leq 50.$$

Similarly, for the sewing hours, $4x_1$ is the number of hours spent sewing jackets, $2x_2$ is the number of hours spent sewing slacks, and 36 hours is the maximum amount of time available. This is expressed as

$$4x_1 + 2x_2 \leq 36.$$

Finally, it does not make sense to produce a negative number of jackets or slacks, so we add another restriction, a **nonnegativity restriction:**

$$x_1, x_2 \geq 0.$$

linear programming model

Combining our objective and our three restrictions gives us the linear programming model.

Maximize	$Z = 10x_1 + 15x_2$ (Profit)
Subject to	$2x_1 + 5x_2 \leq 50$ (Material)
	$4x_1 + 2x_2 \leq 36$ (Sewing)
	$x_1, x_2 \geq 0$ ∎

In general, all linear programs can be expressed in the following form.

general structure of linear program

Transparency Master 11.1: The General Structure of the Linear Program.

Optimize	$Z = c_1x_1 + c_2x_2 + \cdots + c_nx_n$
Subject to	$a_{11}x_1 + a_{12}x_2 + \cdots + a_{1n}x_n \quad \{\leq, =, \geq\}b_1$
	$a_{21}x_1 + a_{22}x_2 + \cdots + a_{2n}x_n \quad \{\leq, =, \geq\}b_2$
	$\vdots \qquad\qquad \vdots$
	$a_{m1}x_1 + a_{m2}x_2 + \cdots + a_{mn}x_n \quad \{\leq, =, \geq\}b_m$
	$x_1, x_2, \ldots, x_n \geq 0$

APPLICATIONS OF P/OM

Linear Programming at New England Apple Products

Apple-cranberry juice cocktail is one of many VeryFine beverages blended at New England Apple Products. As Steve Rouse, VeryFine's manager of marketing, explains, the company offers consumers plenty of choices.

> The juice category includes apple juice, orange juice and grapefruit juice. And also apple-cranberry cocktail and a straight cranberry cocktail. And then we also have a group of fruit drinks that don't contain as large a percentage of pure juice. And these include fruit punch, grape drink, orange drink, pineapple-orange drink, pa-

paya punch, apple-cherry berry drink, lemon-lime drink, tea with lemon, lemonade and a natural energy drink which is an isotonic drink.

How does VeryFine decide which of these products to market and how much of each to make? In other words, how does VeryFine determine the best product mix to make the greatest profit? The answer: linear programming.

Source: For All Practical Purposes (New York: W. H. Freeman, 1988).

The x's represent the n **decision variables,** and the object is to determine the values of these x's that optimize (either minimize or maximize) the **objective function,** which is expressed

$$Z = c_1 x_1 + c_2 x_2 + \cdots + c_n x_n.$$

The c coefficients represent known cost or profit coefficients.

The optimization is subject to certain restrictions, known as **constraints.** The preceding general problem indicates that there are m constraints. The term $\{\leq, =, \geq\}$ is used to indicate that exactly one of these three signs appears in each constraint. In Example 11.1, there were two decision variables (x_1 and x_2) and two constraints (material and sewing). There was exactly one sign in each constraint ($\leq$ in constraint 1 and $\leq$ in constraint 2). The coefficients a_{ij} are known as *resource utilization constants,* because they represent the amount of resource i used by activity j. The values b_1, $b_2, \ldots, b_m$ represent the *availabilities* of each of the m resources at the manager's disposal. For any specific problem, the coefficients a_{ij}, b_i, c_j are known, and we use linear programming to find the best value of each variable x_j. In the previous example, the profit coefficients were known ($c_1 = 10$, $c_2 = 15$), the resource availability was known ($b_1 = 50$, $b_2 = 36$), and the resource utilization constants were known ($a_{11} = 2$, $a_{12} = 5$, $a_{21} = 4$, $a_{22} = 2$).

Teaching Suggestion 11.4: Strict Inequalities. See the Instructor's Section for details.

GENERAL PROPERTIES OF LINEAR PROGRAMS

The name of the model is *linear* programming because each of the expressions (objective and constraints) is linear. There are three very important properties of this linearity that should be examined.

Property 1: Proportionality. In reviewing Example 11.1, notice that the objective function contains the term $10x_1$. This implies that the total contribution to the profit of jackets is directly proportional to the number of jackets produced. Regardless of the value of x_1, the value of c_1 is always 10. Thus, there can be no quantity discount in a linear programming model. Similarly, consider the term $2x_2$ from constraint 2. The total time needed to produce slacks is directly proportional to the number of slacks produced. The first pair takes two hours to produce, and the twentieth pair (if one exists) also takes two hours to produce. Thus, there also can be no learning effect in a linear programming model.

Property 2: Additivity. The profit function $10x_1 + 15x_2$ has the property that if $x_1 = 1$ and $x_2 = 1$, the profit is simply $10 + 15$. The linear programming model does not allow for the possibility that there might be added profit resulting from combining a jacket and a pair of slacks to form a suit, which might have a profit higher or lower than 25.

Property 3: Integrality. The way the problem is formulated, the answer can be any set of numbers (levels of activity) that meet the constraints, including fractions. In Example 11.1, the possibility of a fractional answer does not pose a problem; if the solution is 2.5 jackets, this simply implies that two jackets are made one week and three jackets are made the next. However, there are cases where a fractional answer might not be permitted for some variables. In these instances, we formulate the problem in the same way and note the integrality requirement after stating the nonnegativity restrictions. Formulating the integer problem is straightforward. Solution of the integer problem is much more complex than the solution of the general linear programming problem and is not covered in this text.

Teaching Suggestion 11.5: Integrality Example in Homework. See the Instructor's Section for details.

SUMMARY OF FORMULATION STEPS

For the most part, every linear programming problem is different. However, there are certain steps that should be followed when formulating a linear programming model.

define the variables

The first step is to define the variables. In our example, we have been very specific in defining the units—that is, $x_1 = $ *number of* jackets per week. Every variable has a dimension associated with it, such as gallons, number of, inches, and so forth. The variable name can be anything. In the general form, we use x_j, but using mnemonics can be helpful, as will be seen in the examples that follow.

identify the objective function

The second step is to identify the objective function. Is the problem a maximization or minimization problem? Remember, each variable has exactly one cost or profit (c_j) associated with it.

express the constraints

The last step is to express the constraints. In any given problem, there may be some constraints that are easy to identify and some that are more challenging. A general rule is to start by placing the available resource on the right-hand side of the constraint. If this number represents a true availability, then we cannot use more than this amount, so the sign "$\leq$" can be added. As will be seen in the next section, any given problem may have constraints that require the signs "$\geq$" or "$=$."

On the left-hand side of the constraint equations, the variables are listed. These are multiplied by the resource utilization coefficients. The left-hand side then represents the amount of the resource used (utilization per unit times the number of units), while the right-hand side provides the amount of resource available. A quick check should always be made to ensure that the units are the same on each side of the equation. For Example 11.1, a units analysis for the sewing hours constraint shows that

check units

[(Sewing hours/jacket) × jackets/week] + [(sewing hours/pants) × pants/week] = sewing hours/week. The jackets term and the pants term cancel out, leaving

Sewing hours/week + sewing hours/week = sewing hours/week,

as should be the case.

Figure 11.1 summarizes the structure of the linear programming model for Example 11.1, but the points made in the figure apply to the general model presented earlier as well. Let us now look at some specific applications, all of which are problems that confront the operations manager.

LINEAR PROGRAMMING APPLICATIONS

As was mentioned in the introduction of this chapter, linear programming is useful for a wide variety of problems. In this section, we will present several different applications. This will allow you both to grasp the usefulness of linear programming as a tool in operations management and to see more examples on how practical problems are formulated into the linear programming model. All of these sample problems are currently used on a regular basis in industry.

THE DIET PROBLEM

As we indicated in Chapters 1 and 7, there are several different types of production processes, such as assembly and refining. One such process for which linear program-

FIGURE 11.1 Structure of the linear model

Maximize $Z = 10x_1 + 15x_2$
Subject to $2x_1 + 5x_2 \le 50$
$4x_1 + 2x_2 \le 36$
$x_1, x_2 \ge 0$ (a) Placement of cost (or profit) coefficients

Maximize $Z = 10x_1 + 15x_2$
Subject to $2x_1 + 5x_2 \le 50$
$4x_1 + 2x_2 \le 36$
$x_1, x_2 \ge 0$ (b) Placement of resource availabilities

Maximize $Z = 10x_1 + 15x_2$
Subject to $2x_1 + 5x_2 \le 50$
$4x_1 + 2x_2 \le 36$
$x_1, x_2 \ge 0$ (c) Placement of resource utilizations

ming is useful is the blending of ingredients. The next two examples demonstrate the application of linear programming to the blending process.

> **Example 11.2**   Farmer Spanky raises pigs and needs to mix a pig feed from alfalfa and buckwheat. The cost of each of these grains differs, and each grain has different amounts of vitamins. These costs and vitamin quantities are listed in Table 11.1, as are the minimum daily vitamin requirements for pigs. Farmer Spanky wishes to find the least costly mix that satisfies the vitamin requirements.
>
> The first step is to define the variables. Therefore, let

A = pounds of alfalfa to be used in the mix

and let

B = pounds of buckwheat to be used in the mix.

Notice that our variable names are not x_1 and x_2. We may name variables anything we choose, and using a letter that has some connotation can be helpful. In this example, we are more likely to remember that A, rather than x_1, is alfalfa. Also notice that the variables have a dimension. That is, A stands, not for alfalfa, but for *pounds of* alfalfa.

The second step is to identify the objective. In this example, the objective is to minimize the total cost. The cost of alfalfa is $7 per pound. Therefore, the total cost of the alfalfa used in the mix is $7A$. Notice that there is no quantity discount and that the one-hundredth pound costs the same $7 that the first pound costs. The cost for buckwheat is $9B$. The objective function is given by

Teaching Suggestion 11.6: Applicability of Diet Problem. See the Instructor's Section for details.

$$\text{Minimize } 7A + 9B.$$

The next step is to identify the constraints. As in the previous example, there are three similar constraints. Each of these constraints requires that we have the appropriate amount of each vitamin. "Appropriate" means at least the minimum amount; therefore, the sign in each constraint is $\geq$. The constraints are

Teaching Suggestion 11.7: Linearity. See the Instructor's Section for details.

$$3A + 5B \geq 15 \quad (\text{Vitamin A});$$
$$8A + 8B \geq 32 \quad (\text{Vitamin C}); \text{ and}$$
$$7A + 2B \geq 14 \quad (\text{Vitamin E}).$$

TABLE 11.1 The diet problem parameters (Example 11.2)

Vitamin	Amount per Grain (in units/lb.)		Minimum Daily Requirement
	Alfalfa	Buckwheat	
A	3	5	15
C	8	8	32
E	7	2	14
Cost (in dollars/lb.)	7	9	

Last, we add the nonnegativity restriction, which says that the amount of each grain used cannot be negative.

$$A, B \geq 0$$

Now we can write the complete problem in the appropriate form.

Minimize	$7A + 9B$
Subject to	$3A + 5B \geq 15$
	$8A + 8B \geq 32$
	$7A + 2B \geq 14$
	$A, B \geq 0$

diet problem formulation

■| Transparency Master 11.2: Diet Problem and Minimization.

Written in this form, the problem can be solved by a standard software package. It also can be solved by a graphical procedure, as will be demonstrated later in the chapter.

INGREDIENT BLENDING

The diet problem is not the only type of blending problem for which linear programming is useful. Consider the following refining problem, faced in continuous production.

Teaching Suggestion 11.8: Biggest Use of LP. See the Instructor's Section for details.

Example 11.3 OCRA Industries refines crude oil into gasoline. Two types of crude oil, light and heavy, are available. Light crude oil costs $.90 per gallon, and heavy crude oil costs $1 per gallon. The oils are blended into premium and regular gasolines. Premium sells for $1.40 per gallon, while regular sells for $1.25 per gallon. One gallon of premium consists of .75 gallon of heavy crude and .5 gallon of light crude. (There is a refining loss of .25 gallon.) One gallon of regular consists of .5 gallon of heavy crude and .75 gallon of light crude. (Again, there is a refining loss.) Company policy dictates that at least 60 percent of the gasoline refined be regular. How much of each grade of gas should be refined to maximize profit if heavy oil and light oil are available in quantities of 6,000 gallons and 4,000 gallons per day, respectively?

Although the process here is a blending process, the problem is a resource allocation, or product mix, problem. The resources are light and heavy crude oil, while the products are premium and regular gasoline. As usual, the first step is to identify the variables. Let

P = gallons per day of premium gasoline

and let

R = gallons per day of regular gasoline.

The next step is to identify the objective function. In this example, the objective is to maximize the daily profit. However, unlike our first two examples, the profit is not given directly in the problem. We must compute it. The profit for each gasoline is the selling price less the cost. Therefore, the profit for premium is

$$\$1.40 - [(.75 \times \$1.00) + (.5 \times \$.90)] = \$1.40 - (\$.75 + \$.45)$$
$$= \$1.40 - \$1.20 = \$.20,$$

and the profit for regular is

$$\$1.25 - [(.5 \times \$1.00) + (.75 \times \$.90)] = \$1.25 - (\$.50 + \$.675)$$
$$= \$1.25 - \$1.175 = \$.075.$$

The objective function is given by

$$\text{Maximize } \$.20P + \$.075R.$$

The next step is to identify the constraints. The first two constraints must guarantee that the amount of each oil used does not exceed the supply.

$$.75P + .5R \leq 6,000 \quad \text{(Heavy crude oil)}$$
$$.5P + .75R \leq 4,000 \quad \text{(Light crude oil)}$$

Teaching Suggestion 11.9: Ratios Are Linear. See the Instructor's Section for details.

The last constraint is to satisfy the company policy, which we write as

$$R \geq .6(P + R)$$

and read as, "Regular gasoline must be at least 60 percent of the total gasoline." To get this last constraint in proper form, we subtract $.6(P + R)$ from both the left-hand and the right-hand sides of the inequality, yielding

$$R - .6R - .6P \geq 0.$$

Now we combine terms to obtain

$$-.6P + .4R \geq 0.$$

After adding nonnegativity restrictions, we may now write the complete problem.

OCRA Industries formulation

Transparency Master 11.3: OCRA Blending and Redundancy.

$$
\begin{aligned}
\text{Maximize} \quad & .20P + .075R \\
\text{Subject to} \quad & .75P + .5R \leq 6,000 \\
& .5P + .75R \leq 4,000 \\
& -.6P + .4R \geq 0 \\
& P, R \geq 0
\end{aligned}
$$

Often, there are alternative ways to express a given problem in terms of a linear model. For example, we could express the ingredient blending problem differently—letting, say,

P = gallons per day of premium gasoline;
R = gallons per day of regular gasoline;
L = gallons per day of light crude oil; and
H = gallons per day of heavy crude oil.

These changes produce a quite different-looking model.

Maximize $\quad 1.4P + 1.25R - .90L - H$

Subject to $\qquad\qquad\qquad L \qquad\leq 4,000$

$\qquad\qquad\qquad\qquad\quad H \leq 6,000$

$\qquad .5P + .75R - \quad L \quad= 0$

$\qquad .75P + .5R - \qquad H = 0$

$\qquad -.6P + .4R \qquad\qquad \geq 0$

$\qquad\qquad\quad P, R, L, H \geq 0$

**OCRA Industries:
alternative formulation**

You may wonder which model is better. Each will yield the same solution, so the trade-off is between ease of understanding and solution efficiency. The second formulation is larger and more difficult to solve, but is easier to understand, because it clearly

Linear programming is also widely used in the refining and blending of chemicals, minerals, and petroleum. (© Burt Glinn/Magnum Photos, Inc.)

defines the amounts of each type of gasoline to produce, the amounts of each ingredient required, and the selling prices of gasoline and the costs of crude oil. The first formulation contains the same information, but the amount of each ingredient used and the prices and costs are included only implicitly.

PERSONNEL SCHEDULING

There has been a great deal of work in the area of designing personnel schedules, especially for law enforcement officers and nurses. Much of this work requires a technique that is more sophisticated than linear programming. However, we next present an example that uses linear programming to determine staffing levels for a cyclical operation.

Example 11.4   The emergency room at Niceview Hospital has monitored the arrival of patients over the last year. Based on these data, the director of emergency operations has decided that the minimum number of emergency room nurses should be as given in Table 11.2. The table gives requirements over four-hour time periods. Nurses' shifts last eight hours and can start at any four-hour interval during the day. What is the minimum number of nurses that must be hired?

Again, we begin by defining the variables. Let

n_0 = the number of nurses who begin an eight-hour shift at midnight;

n_4 = the number of nurses who begin an eight-hour shift at 4:00 A.M.;

n_8 = the number of nurses who begin an eight-hour shift at 8:00 A.M.;

n_{12} = the number of nurses who begin an eight-hour shift at noon;

n_{16} = the number of nurses who begin an eight-hour shift at 4:00 P.M.; and

n_{20} = the number of nurses who begin an eight-hour shift at 8:00 P.M.

The objective function is to minimize the total number of nurses and, therefore, is given by

$$\text{Minimize} \quad n_0 + n_4 + n_8 + n_{12} + n_{16} + n_{20}.$$

TABLE 11.2 Minimum number of emergency room nurses

Time Period	Minimum Number of Nurses
Midnight to 4:00 A.M.	10
4:00 A.M. to 8:00 A.M.	8
8:00 A.M. to noon	3
Noon to 4:00 P.M.	7
4:00 P.M. to 8:00 P.M.	5
8:00 P.M. to midnight	12

There are six constraints, each guaranteeing the proper number of nurses during a four-hour time period. The nurses who are working from midnight to 4:00 A.M. are those on the midnight to 8:00 A.M. shift (which we have defined as n_0) and those on the 8:00 P.M. to 4:00 A.M. shift (which we have defined as n_{20}). Therefore, the first constraint is given by

$$n_0 + n_{20} \geq 10.$$

The second constraint is that there must be at least eight nurses working between 4:00 A.M. and 8:00 A.M. The nurses working during these hours are those on the midnight to 8:00 A.M. shift (n_0) and those on the 4:00 A.M. to noon shift (n_4). Therefore, the second constraint is given by

$$n_0 + n_4 \geq 8.$$

In similar fashion, we can determine the remaining constraints and write the complete problem.

$$
\begin{aligned}
\text{Minimize}\quad & n_0 + n_4 + n_8 + n_{12} + n_{16} + n_{20} \\
\text{Subject to}\quad & n_0 \qquad\qquad\qquad\qquad\quad + n_{20} \geq 10 \\
& n_0 + n_4 \qquad\qquad\qquad\qquad \geq 8 \\
& \quad\;\; n_4 + n_8 \qquad\qquad\qquad \geq 3 \\
& \qquad\quad\; n_8 + n_{12} \qquad\qquad \geq 7 \\
& \qquad\qquad\quad n_{12} + n_{16} \qquad \geq 5 \\
& \qquad\qquad\qquad\quad\; n_{16} + n_{20} \geq 12 \\
& n_0, n_4, n_8, n_{12}, n_{16}, n_{20} \geq 0
\end{aligned}
$$

nurse scheduling formulation

Teaching Suggestion 11.10: Schedule Not Complete. See the Instructor's Section for details.

PRODUCTION PLANNING

Another widespread use of linear programming is in the area of production planning—that is, deciding how many units of each product to manufacture during the medium-range time horizon. The topic is discussed in detail in the next chapter, but an example is presented here.

Example 11.5 The Horsehide Company has the following estimates of the demand for baseballs for the next four quarters.

Quarter	Baseballs (in dozens)
Summer	300
Fall	800
Winter	500
Spring	1,000

Horsehide's regular-time operation has the capacity to produce 600 dozen balls per quarter; the company's overtime capacity is 75 dozen balls per quarter. Balls produced during overtime cost an extra $2 per dozen. The storage cost is $1.50 per dozen per quarter. What is the least costly production pattern?

Again, we begin with variable definitions. Let R and O be designated as regular time and overtime, respectively. Let the quarters be denoted by S for summer, F for fall, W for winter, and P for spring. This gives us eight variables: FR = fall regular-time production, FO = fall overtime, and so on. The cost consists of two parts. The first is the overtime cost, which is given by

$$2SO + 2FO + 2WO + 2PO.$$

The second is the storage cost. In order to compute this, we must know how many dozens remain unsold after each quarter. For the summer, this computation is very straightforward. The total number of balls produced is $SR + SO$, and the number shipped is 300. Therefore, the amount leftover is $SR + SO - 300$. For the fall, the computation is not quite as simple. Now we are interested in the total number produced *through* the fall—in other words, the number of baseballs produced in the summer and fall, or $SR + SO + FR + FO$. Through the fall, the number shipped is 800 + 300, which means that the number leftover is $(SR + SO + FR + FO) - 1,100$. The holding costs are given by

$$1.50[(SR + SO) - 300]$$
$$+ 1.50[(SR + SO + FR + FO) - (300 + 800)]$$
$$+ 1.50[(SR + SO + FR + FO + WR + WO) - (300 + 800 + 500)]$$
$$+ 1.50[(SR + SO + FR + FO + WR + WO + PR + PO)$$
$$- (300 + 800 + 500 + 1,000)].$$

After collecting terms, this becomes

$$(6SR + 6SO + 4.5FR + 4.5FO + 3WR + 3WO + 1.5PR + 1.5PO)$$
$$- (1.5 \times 5,600).$$

Because objective functions do not contain constants, we drop the last term. Adding the $2 overtime cost yields the objective function

Minimize $6SR + 8SO + 4.5FR + 6.5FO + 3WR + 5WO + 1.5PR + 3.5PO$.

The first set of constraints guarantees that we meet our production requirements. Their formulation is similar to the development of the holding cost.

$$SR + SO \geq 300$$
$$SR + SO + FR + FO \geq 1,100 \qquad \text{(that is, 300 + 800)}$$
$$SR + SO + FR + FO + WR + WO \geq 1,600 \qquad \text{(300 + 800 + 500)}$$
$$SR + SO + FR + FO + WR$$
$$+ WO + PR + PO \geq 2,600 \qquad \text{(300 + 800 + 500 + 1,000)}$$

Teaching Suggestion 11.11: Alternate Formulations. See the Instructor's Section for details.

The second set of constraints guarantees that we do not exceed our capacity. The first four are for regular time; the last four are for overtime.

$$SR \leq 600$$
$$FR \leq 600$$
$$WR \leq 600$$
$$PR \leq 600$$
$$SO \leq 75$$
$$FO \leq 75$$
$$WO \leq 75$$
$$PO \leq 75$$

∎

DISTRIBUTION

In this section, we show that the transportation problem, introduced in Chapter 6, is a special form of the linear programming problem.

Example 11.6 Consider the transportation problem as given by Table 11.3. Define the variables as AC, AD, AE, BC, BD, and BE, where the meaning of each variable is the number of units shipped from and to the appropriate cities. The problem is to minimize the shipping costs, subject to the supply and demand restrictions.

Minimize $25AC + 60AD + 65AE + 45BC + 30BD + 50BE$

Subject to

$$AC + AD + AE \qquad\qquad = 100$$
$$BC + BD + BE = 400$$
$$AC \qquad + BC \qquad = 200$$
$$AD \qquad + BD \qquad = 150$$
$$AE \qquad + BE = 150$$
$$AC, AD, AE, BC, BD, BE \geq 0$$

transportation formulation

Teaching Suggestion 11.12: Transportation Structure. See the Instructor's Section for details. ∎

Now that we have seen some examples, we can look at the solution techniques.

TABLE 11.3 The transportation problem (Example 11.6)

From	To			
	Cheyenne	Detroit	Evansville	**Supply**
Anchorage, Alaska	$25/unit	$60/unit	$65/unit	100
Bangor, Maine	$45/unit	$30/unit	$50/unit	400
Demand	200	150	150	500

GRAPHICAL SOLUTION OF THE LINEAR PROGRAM

limited to two variables

For the most part, this chapter has dealt with how to *develop* a linear programming model from a real-world problem encountered in operations management. In this section, we provide a graphical procedure for *solving* the linear program. Although the procedure is limited to the solution of problems with only two decision variables, it provides the primary points needed to understand how any linear programming solution procedure works.

MAXIMIZATION EXAMPLES

Let us continue with the problem presented in Example 11.1; for notational ease, we change the decision variables from x_1 and x_2 to x and y, respectively. The problem now is

$$\begin{aligned}
\text{Maximize} \quad & Z = 10x + 15y & \text{(Profit)} \\
\text{Subject to} \quad & 2x + 5y \leq 50 & \text{(Material)} \\
& 4x + 2y \leq 36 & \text{(Sewing)} \\
& x, y \geq 0,
\end{aligned}$$

where x = the number of jackets produced per week and y = the number of slacks produced per week. Because there are only two variables, it is possible to graph this problem. The activity space for the problem is the set of all possible values that the variables x and y might take, without regard to the constraints or the nonnegativity restrictions. As indicated in Figure 11.2, the activity space in this example is the set of all points in two-dimensional space.

The constraints and the nonnegativity restrictions define the set of values that the variables are allowed to take. This set is termed the **feasible region** and is graphed one constraint at a time. Because we have the nonnegativity restrictions, we can restrict our attention to the upper right-hand quadrant.

MATERIAL RESTRICTION: The constraint on raw material is expressed as $2x + 5y \leq 50$. We can use the equation $2x + 5y = 50$ to find the points at which the line intersects the x and y axes by setting first x, then y equal to 0.

For $x = 0$	For $y = 0$
$2(0) + 5y = 50$	$2x + 5(0) = 50$
$5y = 50$	$2x = 50$
$y = 10$	$x = 25$

Thus, the two intersection points are $(0, 10)$ and $(25, 0)$.

The equation $2x + 5y = 50$ is represented in Figure 11.3 as a straight line through the points $(0, 10)$ and $(25, 0)$. Because this is a straight line, any point on the line has a value of 50. For example, we know that the point $(10, 6)$ is on the line because it satisfies the equation: $(2 \times 10) + (5 \times 6) = 50$. Notice that the line in

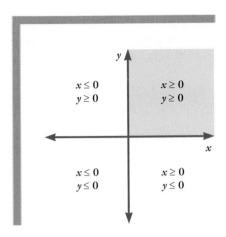

FIGURE 11.2 Two-dimensional space

Figure 11.3 separates the two-dimensional activity space into those points above the line and those points on or below the line (as represented by the shaded region). This is important because the original constraint was an inequality, not an equality, and means that any point that is not in the shaded area does not satisfy the original constraint and, therefore, cannot be a solution to the problem. (Note that points on the line do satisfy the inequality.)

FIGURE 11.3 Material restriction

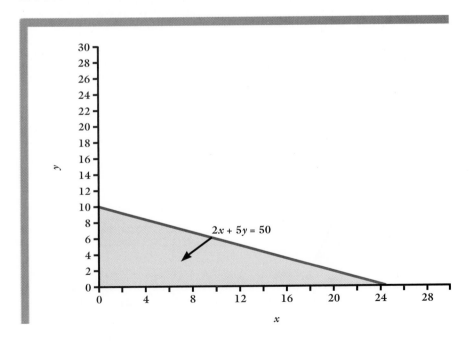

SEWING RESTRICTION: The sewing hours restriction is analyzed in a fashion analogous to the material restriction analysis. We begin by converting the inequality to the equation $4x + 2y = 36$. The two intercepts are determined as before.

For $x = 0$	For $y = 0$
$4(0) + 2y = 36$	$4x + 2(0) = 36$
$2y = 36$	$4x = 36$
$y = 18$	$x = 9$

Hence, the line $4x + 2y = 36$ passes through the points $(0, 18)$ and $(9, 0)$, as shown in Figure 11.4. As before, because the original constraint was an inequality, we are concerned with one of the two regions bounded by the line. The arrow in Figure 11.4 indicates those points that satisfy the constraint $4x + 2y \leq 36$. In general, in order to determine in which direction to point the arrow, see if the origin is feasible. If it is, point the arrow toward the origin; if it is not feasible, point the arrow away from the origin. If the origin is *on* the constraint line, choose another point, say $(1, 1)$, and follow the same procedure.

In Figure 11.5, both constraints—sewing time and material—have been drawn. The arrows indicate those points that satisfy the constraints and the nonnegativity restrictions. The nonnegativity restrictions mean that for a solution to be feasible, it must be in the upper right-hand quadrant—on or above the *x* axis and on or to the

FIGURE 11.4 Time restriction

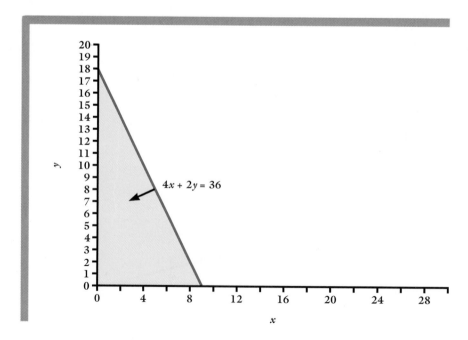

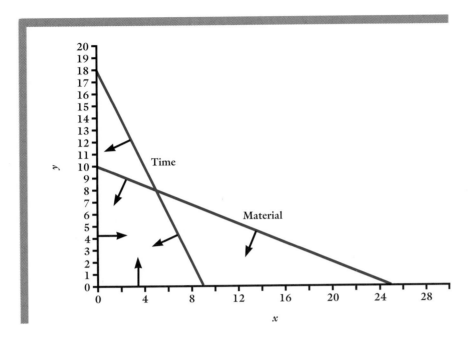

FIGURE 11.5 Time and material restrictions

right of the y axis. In summary, for a point to satisfy all constraints and nonnegativity restrictions, it must be on the proper side of each of the lines (where "proper" is indicated by an arrow). The set of points that meet these requirements—that is, the feasible region—is indicated in Figure 11.6.

Until now, the objective function has not been considered. Now that the feasible region has been determined, the objective function can be incorporated. Notice that the feasible region has four corner points. These points are termed **extreme points,** and a key theorem of linear programming is that the optimal solution occurs at an extreme point. Hence, finding the optimal solution is simply a matter of finding the values of x and y at the extreme points, substituting these values into the objective function $10x + 15y$, and choosing the pair that yields the highest profit.

optimal solution is at a corner

Three of the corner points can be taken directly from the figure—$(0, 0)$, $(0, 10)$, and $(9, 0)$. The last corner point is the point at which the two constraints intersect. The intersection point is determined by solving the two simultaneous equations.

$$2x + 5y = 50$$
$$4x + 2y = 36$$

To solve for y, we can multiply the first equation by 2 and subtract the second equation from the first.

$$4x + 10y = 100$$
$$\underline{-4x + 2y = 36}$$
$$8y = 64$$
$$y = 8$$

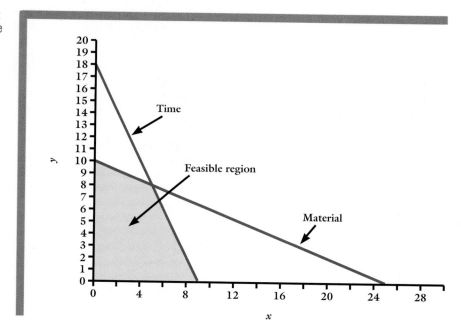

FIGURE 11.6 Feasible region

To find *x*, we substitute $y = 8$ into the first equation.

$$2x + 5(8) = 50$$
$$2x = 50 - 40$$
$$2x = 10$$
$$x = 5$$

This fourth corner point, then, is the point $(5, 8)$.

compute the profit associated with each extreme point   Because all of the corner points have been determined, we can now compute the profit associated with each extreme point.

x	*y*	$10x + 15y$
0	0	$0 + 0 = 0$
0	10	$0 + 150 = 150$
9	0	$90 + 0 = 90$
5	8	$50 + 120 = 170$

Clearly, the solution is to produce 5 jackets and 8 pairs of slacks per week to earn a weekly profit of $170. (In Chapter 3 we asked what the capacity is for this system. At the time, we stated that it was difficult to express because it depended on two resources rather than just one. We now can express the capacity as $170 per week.)

The preceding example had only four extreme points and, therefore, it was relatively easy to evaluate the objective function at all four of them. It is possible, however, to have problems containing many more extreme points. When the number of extreme points is large, it becomes impractical to determine the coordinates of all of the extreme points and the value of the objective function at each extreme point. Fortunately, there is a much simpler alternative method for cases that involve many extreme points. The objective function is $Z = 10x + 15y$. Suppose we want to have exactly \$30 profit. We then set $Z = 30$, and any point (x, y) satisfying $30 = 10x + 15y$ will result in exactly \$30 profit. This line is called the **isoprofit** (same profit) **line** and is shown in Figure 11.7. We can repeat the same process, this time for a profit of, say, \$60. The isoprofit line is $60 = 10x + 15y$. If we plot the two isoprofit lines, we notice that they are parallel to one another and that the profit increases as we move away from the origin. What we shall do, then, is attempt to move as far away from the origin as possible. This is done by moving the isoprofit line parallel to itself until we reach the last contact point in the feasible region. This last contact point is the optimal solution. This procedure is shown in Figure 11.7.

alternative method

last contact point is the optimal solution

Let us consider a second example. We will use the OCRA blending problem, which was presented in Example 11.3. This problem has three constraints, one of which runs through the origin.

The problem has been formulated as

Maximize	$.20P + .075R$	
Subject to	$.75P + .5R \leq 6,000$	(Heavy crude)
	$.5P + .75R \leq 4,000$	(Light crude)
	$-.6P + .4R \geq 0$	(Company policy)
	$P, R \geq 0.$	

FIGURE 11.7 Isoprofit lines

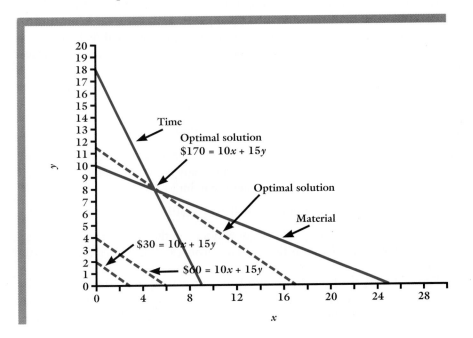

As in our solution to Example 11.1, we need to identify the feasible region by drawing the constraint lines. The first two constraints are drawn as in the previous solution. In other words, we find the points at which the heavy crude constraints intersect the x and y axes.

For $P = 0$	For $R = 0$
$.75(0) + .5R = 6,000$	$.75P + .5(0) = 6,000$
$.5R = 6,000$	$.75P = 6,000$
$R = 12,000$	$P = 8,000$

The heavy crude constraint line is the line that connects the points $(0, 12,000)$ and $(8,000, 0)$.

We follow the same procedure for the light crude.

For $P = 0$	For $R = 0$
$.5(0) + .75R = 4,000$	$.5P + .75(0) = 4,000$
$.75R = 4,000$	$.5P = 4,000$
$R = 5,333$	$P = 8,000$

The light crude constraint is given by the line connecting points $(0, 5,333)$ and $(8,000, 0)$. The constraint lines are shown in Figure 11.8, with the arrows drawn toward the origin because the constraints are $\leq$ constraints.

Now consider the company policy constraint, which is given by $-.6P + .4R = 0$. If we set $P = 0$, we find that $R = 0$. The origin is one point on the line, and we need a second. We cannot set $R = 0$, because this will simply tell us that $P = 0$. Therefore, we must set R to any number other than zero. Let us set $R = 6,000$. Now we have

$$-.6P + .4(6,000) = 0$$
$$-.6P = -2,400$$
$$P = 4,000.$$

The second point is $(4,000, 6,000)$. The line is drawn in Figure 11.9. Next, we must decide which side of the line we are on. We can test any point not on the line to see if it meets the constraint. For example, consider the point $(4,000, 0)$:

$$-.6(4,000) + .4(0) = -2,400.$$

Because $-2,400 < 0$, the point $(4,000, 0)$ does not meet the $\geq$ constraint. Therefore, the feasible side of the constraint is the side away from $(4,000, 0)$, as indicated by the arrow in Figure 11.9.

In Figure 11.10, we have drawn all of the constraints and shaded the feasible region. The feasible region is given by a triangle with corners at $(0, 0)$, $(0, 5,333)$, and a point that is the intersection of the light crude constraint and the policy constraint

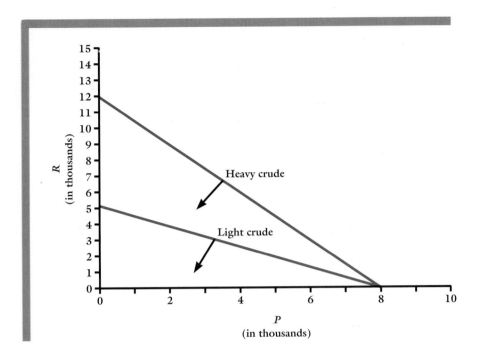

FIGURE 11.8 Heavy and light crude constraints

FIGURE 11.9 Company policy constraint

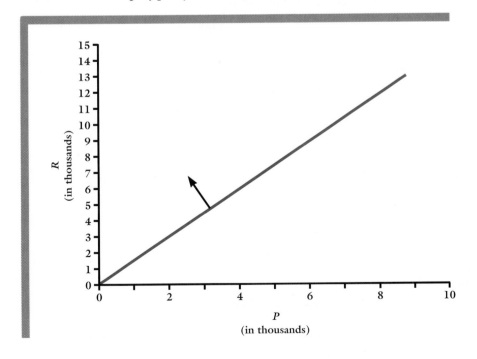

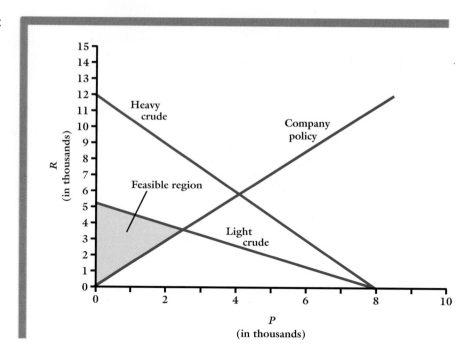

FIGURE 11.10   Feasible region for OCRA blending problem (Example 11.3)

redundant constraint

(which we have yet to determine). Notice from the graph that the heavy crude constraint does not affect the feasible region; therefore, it is a **redundant constraint.**
   The third point solves the simultaneous equations

$$.5P + .75R = 4,000 \text{ and}$$
$$-.6P + .4R = 0.$$

From the second equation, $R = (6/4)P$. Using this in the first equation, we find

$$.5P + .75(3/2)P = 4,000$$
$$.5P + 1.125P = 4,000$$
$$1.625P = 4,000$$
$$P = 2,462.$$

Because $R = (3/2)P$, $R = 3,693$. Thus, we can now complete our table of solutions.

P	R	.20P + .075R
0	0	0 + 0 = 0
0	5,333	0 + 400 = 400
2,462	3,693	492 + 277 = 769

Therefore, the optimal solution is to make 2,462 gallons of premium and 3,693 gallons of regular gasoline at a profit of $769.

A MINIMIZATION EXAMPLE

The solution procedure for a minimization problem is nearly identical to the solution procedure for a maximization problem. We return now to the minimization problem in Example 11.2.

$$\begin{array}{ll} \text{Minimize} & 7A + 9B \\ \text{Subject to} & 3A + 5B \geq 15 \\ & 8A + 8B \geq 32 \\ & 7A + 2B \geq 14 \\ & A, B \geq 0 \end{array}$$

As for a maximization problem, our first step must be to identify the feasible region. We draw each constraint line and use arrows to indicate which side of the line is feasible. The intercepts are

constraint 1: $(5, 0)$ and $(0, 3)$;

constraint 2: $(4, 0)$ and $(0, 4)$;

constraint 3: $(2, 0)$ and $(0, 7)$.

The constraint lines are graphed in Figure 11.11, and the arrows are drawn away from the origin because the constraints are $\geq$ constraints. The feasible region is the shaded area; notice that it is unbounded (it goes forever upward and rightward). Even though the feasible region is unbounded, the solution still occurs at a corner point. Two of the corner points are obvious from the graph; the other two come from the intersection of a pair of constraints.

FIGURE 11.11   Feasible region for diet problem (Example 11.2)

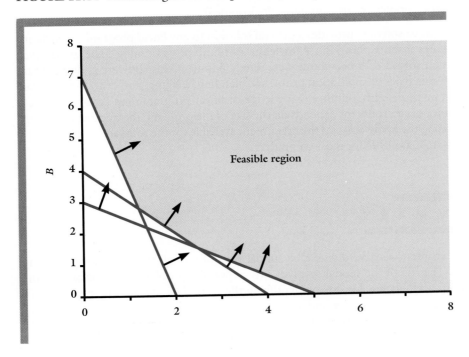

Transparency Master 11.2:
Diet Problem and
Minimization.

Teaching Suggestion 11.13: Unbounded Region vs. Unbounded Solution. See the Instructor's Section for details.

A	B	7A + 9B
5	0	35 + 0 = 35
0	7	0 + 63 = 63
2.5	1.5	17.5 + 13.5 = 31
1.2	2.8	8.4 + 25.2 = 33.6

Because we are minimizing costs, we pick the smallest value. The solution is 2.5 pounds of alfalfa and 1.5 pounds of buckwheat, which yields a total cost of $31.

LINEAR PROGRAMMING IN PRACTICE

No sane person would ever solve a problem modeled as a linear program by hand, unless required to do so in a course such as this one. Requiring you to solve linear programs by hand now permits you to be able to better understand the solution as provided by the computer program you will use on the job. Although all the details of interpreting the various types of data are more appropriately placed in a book on linear programming, there are some things that the operations manager needs to know in order to incorporate the technique into the workplace.

First, there must be someone on-site who knows how to model linear programs. A consultant may be used to help develop the complete model, but someone on-site must know the assumptions built into it.

Second, someone must select the computer software to solve the problem. There are two major decisions to make here:

- Technique software versus application software and
- Microcomputer versus mainframe environment.

Teaching Suggestion 11.14: Shadow Prices. See the Instructor's Section for details.

The technique software provides a general solution to any linear program. As such, its use requires a more thorough knowledge of linear programming. The alternative, application software, is becoming increasingly popular. This software is designed to solve specific types of application problems (blending, refining, and others) and so can be used by those with a limited knowledge of linear programming (the technique). The choice of environment depends on the size of the problem, the number of departments using the hardware, and the investment available for the software. A wide variety of software is available for most computers.

SUMMARY

In this chapter, we have discussed a special type of model, the linear programming model. The use of the model involves two steps—the problem formulation and the solution. Formulation consists of identifying the variables and using these variables to create the *objective function* and *constraints*. Both the objective function and constraints are linear, which means they are *proportional* and *additive*. The sample applications we examined included resource allocation, product mix, product blending, the diet problem, distribution, and production planning.

The graphical solution method was presented for demonstration purposes and to provide a basis for understanding the more complex solution procedures. In this method, the *feasible region* is identified and the optimal solution is calculated as the *extreme point* with the best value.

KEY TERMS

nonnegativity restriction	proportionality	extreme points
decision variables	additivity	isoprofit line
objective function	integrality	redundant constraint
constraints	feasible region	

SOLVED PROBLEMS

1. Formulate (do not solve) the following as a linear programming problem: A manufacturer of floppy diskettes for computers and microcomputers produces three-inch, five-inch, and eight-inch diskettes using one type of machine. Each three-inch diskette requires 1 ounce of diskette material and 2 ounces of plastic for the jacket. The five-inch diskette requires 1.2 ounces of diskette material and 1.2 ounces of plastic. The eight-inch diskette requires 2 ounces of diskette material and 1.6 ounces of plastic for the jacket. The production rates for the three-inch, five-inch, and eight-inch diskettes are 15, 20, and 10 diskettes per minute, respectively. The profits per unit are $.25, $.15, and $.40 for the three-, five- and eight-inch diskettes, respectively. The number of pounds of diskette material available daily is 100, the number of pounds of plastic available daily is 180, and the machine time available is 37 hours. Find the product mix that maximizes the profit.

Solution

The first step is to identify the variables.

T = the number of three-inch diskettes produced

F = the number of five-inch diskettes produced

E = the number of eight-inch diskettes produced

First, we write the profit equation.

$$\text{Maximize} \quad Z = .25T + .15F + .40E$$

Next, we write the constraints. Notice that we need to convert pounds to ounces (or vice versa) and hours to minutes (or vice versa). In addition, we have to change the production rates to production times (by inverting them).

$$T + 1.2F + 2E \leq 100 \times 16 \quad \text{(Diskette material)}$$
$$2T + 1.2F + 1.6E \leq 180 \times 16 \quad \text{(Plastic)}$$
$$(1/15)T + (1/20)F + (1/10)E \leq 60 \times 37 \quad \text{(Production time)}$$

We complete the problem with the nonnegativity restrictions.

$$T, F, E \geq 0$$

2. Solve the following linear program using the graphical solution method.

$$\text{Maximize} \quad Z = 4x + 6y$$
$$\text{Subject to} \quad 6x + 4y \leq 24$$
$$3x + 6y \leq 30$$
$$x, y > 0$$

Solution

We first draw the constraints, then we identify the feasible region and its corner points, and then we determine the feasible corner point that has the greatest value.

The constraints are drawn by finding two points on the line and connecting the line. For the first constraint, if we set $x = 0$, then $y = 6$; if we set $y = 0$, then $x = 4$. Therefore, to draw the first constraint, we connect the two points $(4, 0)$ and $(0, 6)$ with a straight line (see the figure). For the second constraint, setting x and y equal to 0 yields the points $(10, 0)$ and $(0, 5)$, which we also connect with a straight line.

In the figure, the feasible region is shaded. Three of the four corner points are obvious. The fourth is determined by finding the intersection of the two constraint lines, which we find by solving two simultaneous linear equations.

$$6x + 4y = 24$$
$$3x + 6y = 30$$

To solve for y, we multiply the second equation by 2 and subtract it from the first equation.

$$6x + 12y = 60$$
$$\underline{-6x + 4y = 24}$$
$$8y = 36$$
$$y = 4.5$$

Substituting $y = 4.5$ into the first constraint equation allows us to solve for x.

$$6x + 4(4.5) = 24$$
$$6x + 18 = 24$$
$$6x = 6$$
$$x = 1$$

Therefore, the fourth corner point is $(1, 4.5)$. We now check the objective function at the four corner points.

x	y	4x	6y	4x + 6y
0	0	0	0	0
4	0	16	0	16
0	5	0	30	30
1	4.5	4	27	31

The solution to this problem, then, is $x = 1$ and $y = 4.5$.

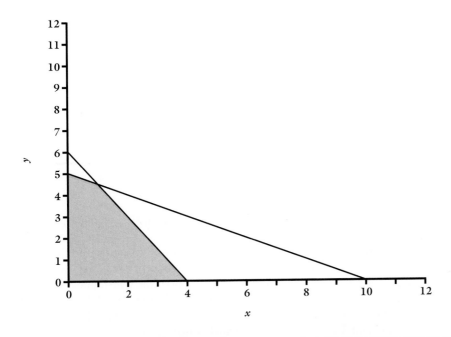

Using AB:POM to Solve This Problem

The linear programming module has many options. First, the program will ask whether the problem is a minimization or a maximization problem. Then it will ask the usual questions concerning the number of constraints (rows) and the number of variables (columns). After these numbers are entered, the data table is set up. Three toggle switches appear above the data table. The first toggle switch is used to set the stepping option: NO STEPS (in which case the computer displays the final solution) or STEP (in which case the iterations can be displayed one tableau at a time). If you are interested in the final answer *only*, choose NO STEPS. If you want to see the intermediate tables, you must choose STEP. (Note: On large problems, the step option is not available.) The other two options that can be chosen will be discussed later.

We continue now with Solved Problem 2. Screen 11.1 contains the input and output for this problem. The columns have been named and the profits (4 and 6),

```
┌─ Data file:wgsp2 ═══════════════ Linear Programming ══════════════ Solution ═┐
│   Number of constraints (2-99) 2              Number of variables (2-99)   2  │
│   maximize                                                                     │
│  ┌══════════════════════════ Chapter 11, Solved Problem 2 ═══════════════════┐│
│  │ Options-> NO step Cmputr PrtOFF                                           ││
│  │                                                                           ││
│  │              x       y          RHS                                       ││
│  │                                                                           ││
│  │   maximize    4       6                   Shadow                          ││
│  │                                                                           ││
│  │   const 1     6       4    ≤      24.00    0.25                           ││
│  │                                                                           ││
│  │   const 2     3       6    ≤      30.00   .833333                         ││
│  │                                                                           ││
│  │   Values -> 1.00    4.50          $31.00                                  ││
│  │                                                                           ││
│  │                                                                           ││
│  │                            Phase  2   Iteration 3     0.06 seconds        ││
│  │                                                                           ││
│  └═══════════════════════════════════════════════════════════════════════════┘│
│                                                                               │
│  F1=Display solution table F3=Graph                        F9=Print    Esc    │
│  Press <Esc> key to edit data or highlighted key or function key for options  │
└───────────────────────────────────────────────────────────────────────────────┘
```

SCREEN 11.1

Transparency Master 11.6: Computer Output (Including Shadow Prices).

shadow prices

resource usages (6, 4, 3, and 6), and resource limits (24 and 30) are filled in. The solutions appear under the columns.

In addition to the values for x and y, there is a column on the far right of the problem that is labeled "Shadow." We briefly present the concept of the shadow price here. The solution for this problem (1, 4.5) will use up all of the constraints. That is, after substituting $x = 1$ and $y = 4.5$ into constraint 1, we find a value of 24, precisely what we expect from looking at the right-hand side of the screen. Similarly, we find a value of 30 for constraint 2 after substitution, which, once again, is equal to the right-hand side. In other words, we are using up all of the resources as represented by the two constraints. A natural question at this point is, How much would we pay for an additional unit of resource 1? One method for finding this out is to solve the problem again, this time substituting 25 in the right-hand side of constraint 1, rather than 24. However, the shadow price will give us this answer directly. In this example, one more unit of resource 1 would add a profit of $.25 to the problem, while one more unit of resource 2 would add a profit of $.83. The numbers $.25 and $.83 are the shadow prices and are computed automatically by any linear programming software.

Assume for the moment that one more unit of resource 1 will pay us an extra quarter. Will a second unit of resource 1 give us a second quarter? In other words, just how many units can be added, leaving the marginal profit contribution of $.25 unchanged? The answer to this second question can be found by examining the table that is available by pressing the **F1** key twice. The table that appears is given in Screen 11.2.

```
┌──────────────────────────────────────────────────────────────────────────┐
│ ┌── Data file:wgsp2 ═══════════ Linear Programming ═══════════ Solution ═┐│
│ │   Number of constraints (2-99) 2          Number of variables (2-99)  2││
│ │   maximize                                                             ││
│ │══════════════════════ Chapter 11, Solved Problem 2 ════════════════════││
│ │  Solution value = 31                                                   ││
│ │                Shadow      Slack or    Original    Lower    Upper      ││
│ │                Prices      Surplus     RHS         Limit    Limit      ││
│ │                                                                        ││
│ │   const 1        0.25        0.00      24.00       20.00    48.00      ││
│ │   const 2      .8333333      0.00      30.00       12.00    60.00      ││
│ │                                                                        ││
│ │                                                                        ││
│ │                                                                        ││
│ │                                                                        ││
│ │                                                                        ││
│ │                                                                        ││
│ │                                                                        ││
│ │                                                                        ││
│ │                                                                        ││
│ │  F1=Display solution table                              F9=Print   Esc ││
│ │  Press <Esc> key to edit data or highlighted key or function key for options│
│ └────────────────────────────────────────────────────────────────────────┘│
└──────────────────────────── SCREEN 11.2 ──────────────────────────────────┘
```

The table has two rows, one for each constraint. The shadow prices are listed in the first column. The second column lists the slack—that is, the amount of the resource left over. Since we are using all 24 of the 24 available units, there is no slack. This is also true for constraint 2, where we use all 30 available units. The next three columns represent the ranges over which the shadow prices hold. So, if the right-hand side is between 20 and 48, the shadow price, or marginal cost, is $.25 per unit. For example, by changing the right-hand side from 24 to 34, we add $2.50 in profit. Similarly, by lowering the right-hand side from 24 to 20, we lose $4 \times \$.25$, or $1, in profit. The range for constraint two is 12–60 units. If we go outside of these ranges, the solution will change enough that these shadow prices no longer hold. ■

QUESTIONS

1. Is linear programming prescriptive or descriptive?

2. Under what circumstances is the objective more important than the constraints in a linear programming model?

3. Under what circumstances are the constraints more important than the objective in a linear programming model?

4. Of the parameters a_{ij}, b_i, and c_j in the linear model, which can be controlled most easily by management?

5. Discuss the implications of modifying the a, b, or c parameters in the context of the organizational environment.

6. Which parameter (a, b, or c) would be the focus of a conservation effort?

7. What would be the interpretation of finding no feasible region?

8. What would be the interpretation of finding an infinitely large (unbounded) feasible region?

9. Provide an example showing that the proportionality property does not hold because the use of $c_j x_j$ would overestimate the cost as x_j increases.

10. Provide an example showing that the proportionality property does not hold because the use of $c_j x_j$ would underestimate the cost as x_j increases.

11. Provide an example showing that the additivity assumption overestimates resource usage.

12. Provide an example showing that the additivity assumption underestimates resource usage.

13. Provide an example showing that linear programming sometimes can be used when the integrality assumption is not valid.

14. Provide an example showing that linear programming is sometimes eliminated as a solution tool when the integrality assumption is not valid.

15. Why is the diet problem, in practice, applicable for animals but not for people?

16. How many feasible solutions are there in a linear program? Which ones do we need to examine to find the optimal solution?

PROBLEMS

Formulate (do not solve) Problems 1–10 as linear programming problems.

1. The Cynwyd Computer Company produces home computers and business computers. The profit on the home computers is $600 per computer, while the profit on the business computers is $1,000 per computer. Each home computer requires 2 hours of labor, while each business computer requires 3 hours of labor. Home computers require 40 chips each, while business computers require 30 chips apiece. If 200 labor hours and 2,400 chips are available weekly, what is the optimal production mix of computers?

See Instructor's Section.

2. The marketing department at Cynwyd Computer Company (see Problem 1) has decided to emphasize home computers. Therefore, the department is demanding that at least 70 percent of the computers produced by the company be home computers. Write the constraint to express the department's demand.

See Instructor's Section.

3. Jack Spratt, who has taken an operations management course, is interested in determining a least-cost breakfast that supplies 100 percent of the daily requirements for vitamins A, B, and C. Given the following information, how should Jack mix his cereals?

Vitamin	Amount per Cereal*	
	Corn Sweets	Granny's Brannies
A	80	60
B	20	40
C	70	30
Cost per Serving	$.25	$.22

*Numbers represent the percent of the minimum daily requirement.

See Instructor's Section.

4. Spectre Incorporated produces tomato paste, tomato sauce, and catsup. The following table contains the requirements for each product.

Product	Requirements			Profit
	Tomatoes	Water	Spice	
Paste	2 oz.	.1 oz.	1 tsp.	$ .80
Sauce	1.5 oz.	3 oz.	3 tsp.	$1.90
Catsup	1 oz.	7 oz.	.5 tsp.	$1.20

The supplier provides 2,000 pounds of tomatoes each week and 1,000 cups of spices (1 cup = 20 teaspoons); the water supply is unlimited. How many containers of each product should Spectre manufacture weekly?

See Instructor's Section.

5. Two types of seats can be installed in a new stadium—custom seats or regular seats. Custom seats are a little wider, which means they take up more space. In addition, the custom seats use more padding and require less wood. Regular seats require 4 board-feet of wood and take up 4 square feet of space. Custom seats require 3 board-feet of wood and take up 5 square feet of space. A total of 36,000 board-feet of wood is available, and the capacity for seating is 50,000 square feet. Each custom seat brings in revenue of $300 per season, while each regular seat brings in revenue of $200 per season. What is the optimal mix of seats?

See Instructor's Section.

6. For a cafeteria that is open twenty-four hours a day, the following minimum number of waitresses is required.

Time of Day	Minimum Number of Waitresses
2 A.M. to 6 A.M.	4
6 A.M. to 10 A.M.	8
10 A.M. to 2 P.M.	10
2 P.M. to 6 P.M.	7
6 P.M. to 10 P.M.	12
10 P.M. to 2 A.M.	4

See Instructor's Section.

Each waitress works eight consecutive hours per day. All waitresses are paid the same; hence, the objective is to find the smallest number required to comply with the requirements.

7. The University Computing Center is open from 8 A.M. to midnight. Sam Spade, the director of the center, has established that the following number of consultants are required during the specified hours.

Hours	Minimum Number of Consultants
8 A.M. to noon	4
Noon to 4 P.M.	3
4 P.M. to 8 P.M.	7
8 P.M. to midnight	4

See Instructor's Section.

Consultants may be either full-time workers or part-time workers. Full-time consultants work eight consecutive hours and are paid $6.37/hour (including fringe benefits). Part-time workers work four consecutive hours and are paid $5.00/hour (they receive no fringe benefits). Furthermore, at any given time, there must be on duty at least two full-time consultants for each part-time consultant. What schedule of work minimizes the total cost of consulting?

8. Ragean Manufacturing produces a line of hair tonic. The cost per bottle is $5 during regular time and $7.50 during overtime. Bottles produced during one month but carried forward to satisfy future demands cost $.50 each per month for storage. The inventory on hand December 1 is 50 units. Demand during the months of December, January, and February is 800, 900, and 1,000 units, respectively. Regular-time capacity in any month is 700 bottles. Overtime capacity in any month is (for all intents and purposes) unlimited. Production cannot vary by more than 15 percent from month to month. What are the monthly regular-time and overtime production amounts for December, January, and February? (Production in November was 900 units.)

See Instructor's Section.

9. Hacienda Furniture is a corporation that produces sofas. The company's forecasting department has indicated that demand for sofas in the next four months will be 60, 80, 70, and 80, respectively. Hacienda's 10 laborers can produce 3 sofas per eight-hour day working as a team. Each worker is paid 3,000 pesos per hour for regular time and 4,500 pesos per hour for overtime. The demands for all four months must be met. If more sofas are on hand at the end of the month than are needed, there is a storage cost of 15,000 pesos per sofa per month. How many sofas should be produced in each month? (A month has 20 working days.)

See Instructor's Section.

10. The budget for Springtown's sanitation department is $1 million for the upcoming fiscal year. This money can be used to pay wages or to lease equipment. The three types of equipment used are trash trucks, recycling trucks, and brooms. (Trash and recyclables are collected separately in Springtown.) Each trash truck costs $22,000/year and can pick up 200,000 tons of trash per year. Each recycling truck costs $26,000/year and can pick up 100,000 tons of recyclables per year. Each broom costs $2 and picks up half a ton of trash per year. Each trash truck requires at least one operator, while each recycling truck requires at least two operators. Operators are paid $20,000/year. Broom pushers are paid $13,000/year. The mayor has promised the local trash and broom union that she will hire at least 29 truck operators. If the long-term value of disposing of recyclable trash is 2.64 times per ton the value of disposing of (regular) trash (as determined by a government study), how should the sanitation department spend its budget?

See Instructor's Section.

$H = 0$; $B = 66.67$;
$Z = \$66,667$

11. Solve Problem 1 graphically.

12. Use Problem 2 for the following.

(a) Solve the problem graphically.

(b) What is the cost of the decision by the marketing department to emphasize home computers?

$H = 45.41; B = 19.46;$
$Z = \$46,702$

$\$19,965$

13. Solve Problem 3 graphically.

$C = .4545; G = 2.27;$
$Z = .613635$

14. Solve Problem 5 graphically.

$C = 10,000; R = 0;$
$Z = 3,000,000$

15. Solve the following problem.

$$\text{Maximize} \quad 4x + 6y$$
$$\text{Subject to} \quad x + 2y \leq 8$$
$$5x + 4y \leq 20$$
$$x, y \geq 0$$

$x = 1.33; y = 3.33;$
$Z = 25.33$

16. Solve the following problem.

$$\text{Minimize} \quad 24x + 15y$$
$$\text{Subject to} \quad 7x + 11y \geq 77$$
$$16x + 4y \geq 80$$
$$x, y \geq 0$$

$x = 3.86; y = 4.54;$
$Z = 160.86$

17. Solve the following problem.

$$\text{Minimize} \quad x + 4y$$
$$\text{Subject to} \quad x + y \leq 10$$
$$2x + 4y \leq 30$$
$$x, y \geq 0$$

$x = 0; y = 7.5; Z = 30$

18. Solve the following problem.

$$\text{Minimize} \quad 8x + 5y$$
$$\text{Subject to} \quad 2x + 5y \leq 100$$
$$x + y \geq 25$$
$$x, y \geq 0$$

$x = 8.33; y = 16.67;$
$Z = 150$

19. Solve the following problem.

$$\text{Maximize} \quad 6x + 2y$$
$$\text{Subject to} \quad 12x + 4y \leq 200$$
$$4x + 5y \leq 150$$
$$x, y \geq 0$$

$x = 16.67; y = 0;$
$Z = 100$ or $x = 9.09;$
$y = 22.72; Z = 100$

20. Solve the following problem.

$$\text{Maximize} \quad 5x + 7y$$
$$\text{Subject to} \quad x + y \leq 40$$
$$2x + y \leq 70$$
$$x + 3y \leq 100$$
$$x, y \geq 0$$

$x = 10; y = 30; Z = 260$

21. Solve the following problem.

$$\text{Maximize} \quad 10x + 13y$$
$$\text{Subject to} \quad 2x + 2y \geq 80$$
$$2x + 4y \leq 150$$
$$5x + 3y \leq 170$$
$$x, y \geq 0$$

$x = 16.43; y = 29.29;$
$Z = 545$

COMPUTER CASE STUDY 11.1: GENERAL PRODUCTS INC.

General Products Inc. (GPI) is a mail-order marketer of cosmetics. The following table gives the company's average demand per month for the past three years.

Month	Demand
October	653
November	847
December	952
January	1,325
February	1,106
March	862
April	531
May	753
June	1,246
July	1,306
August	1,057
September	721

It is obvious from the table that there is a great deal of seasonality/cyclicality in the demand pattern. In fact, GPI has found that each year contains two cycles. For this reason, GPI wishes to determine a production plan for the coming six months that will meet the demand without causing too many problems, which the company identifies as having to hire or lay off employees; running out of the product; or having inventory on hand at the end of any month. The holding cost is known to be $7 per unit per month. However, GPI does not know how costly the other problems are or what should be done to remedy them.

GPI wants to improve its inventory policy. In the past, GPI has used a policy that required the planned end-of-month inventory to be 10 percent of the demand for that month. GPI's management wants to know how much, if any, planned inventory is costing them. What would happen if GPI implemented a zero-inventory system? What would happen if GPI changed to a 5-percent policy? (Currently, there are 86 units in inventory.)

Each worker at GPI currently works approximately 170 hours per month and manufactures 100 units each month. The company currently costs out each hire as $234 per worker (based on training costs and production rates per worker) and each layoff as $537 per worker (based on unemployment compensation and loss of good will). Under consideration is a policy that would require some degree of production stability from month to month. One proposal would not allow production to vary from month to month by more than 200 units (which represents the production rate of 2 workers). In other words, management would limit hires or fires to at most 2 per month. What would happen if the company restricted hiring/firing to 1 person per month? 2 persons per month? (GPI currently employs 9 workers—an initial capacity of 900 units.)

One formulation for this problem that takes into account the questions we have just asked is given in Figure 11.12 (in the form of output from AB:POM). There are five types of variables; each variable exists for six months, yielding a total of 30 variables. There are six types of constraints; each type exists for six months, yielding a total of 36 constraints.

FIGURE 11.12 AB:POM output for Computer Case Study 11.1

```
Data file:case11-1              Linear Programming              Data Screen
Number of constraints (2-99) 36        Number of variables (2-99)  30
minimize
minimize + 8cap10 + 8cap11 + 8cap12 + 8cap1 + 8cap2 + 8cap3 + 234hire10
   + 234hire11 + 234hire12 + 234hire1 + 234hire2 + 234hire3 + 537fire10
   + 537fire11 + 537fire12 + 537fire1 + 537fire2 + 537fire3 + 7inv10 + 7inv11
   + 7inv12 + 7inv1 + 7inv2 + 7inv3 <
Oct inv10%:+ 1inv10 > 65
Nov:+ 1inv11 > 85
Dec:+ 1inv12 > 95
Jan:+ 1inv1 > 132
Feb:+ 1inv2 > 110
Mar:+ 1inv3 > 86
Oct-capact:+ 1cap10 - 100hire10 + 100fire10 = 900
Nov:- 1cap10 + 1cap11 - 100hire11 + 100fire11 = 0
Dec:- 1cap11 + 1cap12 - 100hire12 + 100fire12 = 0
Jan:- 1cap12 + 1cap1 - 100hire1 + 100fire1 = 0
Feb:- 1cap1 + 1cap2 - 100hire2 + 100fire2 = 0
Mar:- 1cap2 + 1cap3 - 100hire3 + 100fire3 = 0
Oct  hire:+ 1hire10 < 999
Nov  limit:+ 1hire11 < 999
Dec:+ 1hire12 < 999
Jan:+ 1hire1 < 999
Feb:+ 1hire2 < 999
Mar:+ 1hire3 < 999
Oct fire:+ 1fire10 < 999
Nov limits:+ 1fire11 < 999
Dec:+ 1fire12 < 999
Jan:+ 1fire1 < 999
Feb:+ 1fire2 < 999
Mar:+ 1fire3 < 999
Oct-caplim:- 1cap10 + 1prod10 < 0
Nov:- 1cap11 + 1prod11 < 0
Dec:- 1cap12 + 1prod12 < 0
Jan:- 1cap1 + 1prod1 < 0
Feb:- 1cap2 + 1prod2 < 0
Mar:- 1cap3 + 1prod3 < 0
Oct-Inv:+ 1prod10 - 1inv10 = 567
Nov:+ 1prod11 + 1inv10 - 1inv11 = 847
Dec:+ 1prod12 + 1inv11 - 1inv12 = 952
Jan:+ 1prod1 + 1inv12 - 1inv1 = 1325
Feb:+ 1prod2 + 1inv1 - 1inv2 = 1106
Mar:+ 1prod3 + 1inv2 - 1inv3 = 862
```

The first six constraints represent the current policy of requiring inventory to be 10 percent of the demand for the month. The second six constraints are used to generate the production capacity for each month, as given by

$$\text{month } j + 1 \text{ capacity} = \text{month } j \text{ capacity} + 100h - 100f,$$

where h = number of hires and f = number of fires. The third set of constraints is used to restrict the number of hires in each month. Currently, hires are unrestricted (999). The fourth set of constraints does the same for the number of persons fired. The fifth set of constraints guarantees that the amount produced in a month is less than the capacity for that month. The last six constraints contain the inventory balance equations for each month, as given by

$$\text{month } j \text{ inventory} = \text{month } j - 1 \text{ inventory} + \text{month } j \text{ production} - \text{month } j \text{ demand}.$$

Find the production schedule that GPI should follow under the various assumptions and policies. Detail the differences among these schedules and give the advantages and disadvantages of each.

REFERENCES

Gass, S. *Linear Programming*. 5th ed. New York: McGraw-Hill, 1985.

Hillier, F., and G. Lieberman. *Introduction to Operations Research*. 5th ed. New York: McGraw-Hill, 1990.

Lee, S., L. J. Moore, and B. W. Taylor. *Management Science*. 3rd ed. Boston: Allyn and Bacon, 1990.

Schrage, L. *Linear Programming Models with LINDO*. 3rd ed. Palo Alto, Calif.: The Scientific Press, 1986.

Thie, P. R. *An Introduction to Linear Programming and Game Theory*. New York: John Wiley and Sons, 1988.

Winston, W. L. *Operations Research: Applications and Algorithms*. Boston: Duxbury, 1987.

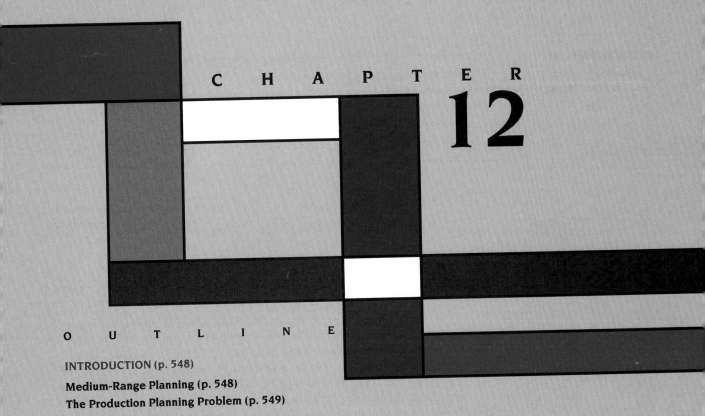

C H A P T E R

12

O U T L I N E

AGGREGATE PLANNING

- To explain medium-range operations planning
- To enumerate the options available for meeting the demand
- To illustrate pure and mixed production strategies
- To analyze the costs for various strategies
- To demonstrate the application of linear programming to medium-range planning

INTRODUCTION

Teaching Suggestion 12.1: Top Management. See the Instructor's Section for details.

In Chapter 3, we classified capacity planning according to three time frames: long range, medium range and short range. We have examined long-range problems, and we have seen that decisions relating to long-range planning, such as location, layout, or equipment purchase decisions, typically take a long time to implement—and, for that matter, a long time to undo. The problem of aggregate planning is one of medium-range planning. It is important to keep in mind that decisions relating to aggregate planning—such as gross production or operating schedules—are developed within the restrictions imposed by the long-term capacities that are already in place.

MEDIUM-RANGE PLANNING

Medium-range planning involves decision making and actions that cannot be done overnight and yet do not take as long to implement as do long-range plans. Medium-range decisions involve the planning of such things as the size of the work force, the amount of inventory, additional tooling, and the use of overtime and/or subcontracting. Fogarty and Hoffman (1983) define three major medium-range operations tasks.

medium-range tasks

- Planning aggregate inventory and production levels to attain a desired level of customer service and to have the sum of the costs of carrying inventory and the costs of changing production rates approach a minimum. This is called the **aggregate planning** problem.
- **Disaggregation,** or planning the production rates and inventory levels for the different product groups. The sum of these values must be equal to the aggregate values.
- Planning the *allocation* of the different product resources among the product groups to be produced.

In Figure 12.1, these tasks are indicated as part of the overall planning process. The figure illustrates operations activities from long range through medium range to short range. Although the ranges are indicated separately, they are closely related through the feedback process. For example, the capacity dictates the amount that can be produced. However, in planning the capacity, the production plan must be considered, as we discussed in Chapter 3.

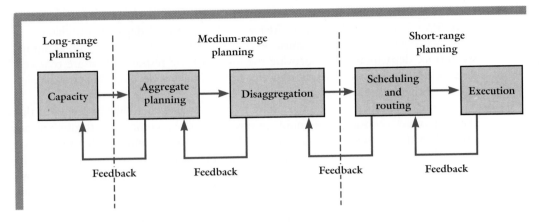

FIGURE 12.1 Planning for operation: from long-range planning to execution

Aggregate planning is the topic of much of the remainder of this chapter. Disaggregation, or master production scheduling, also is covered in this chapter. Scheduling topics are covered in Chapter 15 and inventory concepts are covered in Chapters 13 and 14.

Transparency Master 12.1: The Planning Process.

THE PRODUCTION PLANNING PROBLEM

Production planning is the process of formulating a general medium-range schedule for meeting the demand for a single product or product group. The production plan also is called an *aggregate plan* because it refers to the collection (aggregation) of products across a family of products. The production plan is a function of many parameters, but a key parameter is the expected demand over the coming months. For example, if the production plan calls for producing 200 units for each of the next twelve months, we can presume that the total demand over the next twelve months will be approximately $200 \times 12 = 2,400$ units. Although the demand will be 2,400 units over the next twelve months, it is unlikely to be evenly distributed at a rate of 200 per month. Uneven demand leads to the setting of a major goal of production planning: to keep the production levels as smooth as possible, even when the demand varies from month to month. The benefits of a constant production rate are that hiring and/or laying off employees will not be necessary and the amount of raw materials inventory required each month will not vary. The disadvantage is that, because sales vary on a month-to-month basis, the inventory of finished goods also will vary—at times being too high and at other times not being sufficient to meet the demand. The major task facing the production planner is to find the best trade-off between the costs of work force variation; inventory and shortages; and overtime and subcontracting.

goal: keep production levels smooth

goal: maintain low inventory

trade-off

It must be emphasized that the production plan is simply that—a plan. For example, if the plan developed in June calls for the production of 200 units in December, this does not mean that production in December actually will be 200 units. Demands change, and the aggregate plan is updated to account for these changes. The plan for the first month must be implemented through the use of scheduling techniques, which will be discussed in chapters to follow.

only implement beginning of plan

coordinate plan with other business functions

The aggregate plan interacts with functions other than operations. Changes in work force levels must be coordinated with the personnel department; changes in inventory, especially shortages, must be coordinated with marketing; and, as always, the finance department must provide the funds for the resources that are required. Because of these interactions, the aggregate plan usually is developed in coordination with the other business functions.

product grouping

sales promotion

Before discussing aggregate planning techniques, we would like to point out that the goal to keep production as smooth as possible can be accomplished through means other than those detailed in this chapter. For example, a company that produces a seasonal product can smooth production by producing a similar product with opposite seasonal demands. Two examples of such **product grouping** are lawn mowers/snow-blowers and gasoline/heating oil. Another option is to try to smooth the demand through the use of off-season sales promotions. This is routinely done for air conditioners, which are put on sale during the winter, and for ski equipment, which is put on sale during the summer.

PARAMETERS OF THE PLANNING PROBLEM

basic inputs

Figure 12.2 represents the general production planning model. The basic inputs to the model are the *capacities*, because these limit production rates; the *costs*, because these affect choices between carrying excess inventory, incurring shortages, and acquiring extra resources; and, of course, the forecasted *demands*, because the goal is to have production meet demand. The demand forecasts provide information concerning the requirements that the production schedule must fulfill. The capacities outline and focus the options and resources available to meet the demands. Finally, the costs associated with any production plan allow for an economic evaluation of that plan, leading to the comparison of plans and the selection of the most efficient plan. Let us further consider these factors.

DEMAND FORECASTS

The most important input to the planning process is the estimate of the future demand. The continued presence of a demand is the primary motivation for operations. The forecasts are based on the factors discussed in Chapter 4, so there is no need to mention the details of forecasting here. However, one feature of forecasts, particularly applicable here, is worth mentioning: forecast error. Usually, the forecast is an estimate, and the actual demand is not known. (However, there may be times when the forecast is based on actual sales orders.) Two practices are common in production scheduling. First, although the production plan is developed for a year or two into the future, it is revised on a monthly basis as more data become available concerning forecast accuracy. Second, a safety stock of additional inventory is maintained as a hedge against shortages. This safety stock will be discussed in detail in the chapter on inventory management.

Transparency Master
12.1: The Planning
Process.

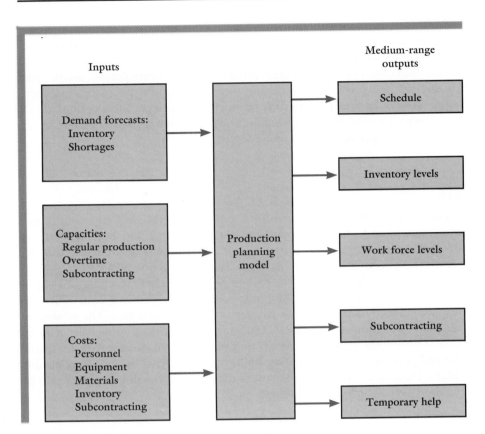

FIGURE 12.2 General production planning model

CAPACITIES

Once the need for production or service has been identified, the means to meet that need must be identified. In the manufacturing environment, a variety of means are available. The three most commonly used are regular production, overtime production, and subcontracting. The operations manager uses these options to obtain flexibility in meeting demands, especially demands that are erratic from month to month. In the service environment, the most commonly used means are overtime, part-time help, or temporary help. For example, retailers often hire temporary employees during the Christmas season and supermarkets often hire part-time employees to assist on weekends. In the airline industry, there are schedule changes in May and November to reflect the north–south orientation of winter travel and the east–west orientation of summer travel.

flexibility is required to meet changing demand

An examination of these options may shed some more light on the nature of the aggregate scheduling problem. Options such as adding equipment or new facilities are not considered because the lead times to implement them place them in the realm of long-term planning. Remember, long-term planning defines the capacities. Therefore, the aggregate planner must work within the defined capacities. Subcontracting, part-time help, and temporary help enable the planner to increase capacities to some extent, but even these means are limited by the capacities of the additional help, the company's ability to inspect the subcontractors' work (an additional task), and company policy regarding subcontracting and the hiring of part-time and temporary help.

short-range options

Other managerial options not considered by the aggregate planner are the temporary shifting of workers, switching the tooling of various pieces of equipment, adjusting lot sizes, and rearranging daily production schedules. These options are at a level too detailed for this stage of planning. The production manager or a foreman, as opposed to the production planner, exercises these options.

COSTS

Any option that the manager uses results in some cost. If the work force is increased to raise capacity and increase production, then recruiting and training costs are incurred. If the work force is decreased, layoff costs and less quantifiable costs that may result from sagging morale are incurred. If the production plan differs from the demand in any month, then either inventory will accumulate, resulting in carrying costs, or shortages will occur, resulting in lost sales or backordering costs. These are the major costs used to evaluate the economics of a production plan. The production manager aims at minimizing the total cost, usually by achieving some balance in the schedule. Other costs, such as overhead, are not considered because they are usually determined prior to aggregate planning and do not vary between competing production plans. Detailed costs, such as the cost of material movement in the plant, are left for the short-term schedulers to consider.

Teaching Suggestion 12.2: Lost Sales vs. Backorders. See the Instructor's Section for details.

A marketing effort used to increase the turnover ratio. (© Barbara Filet/Tony Stone Worldwide)

An alternative, or supplement, to using costs to evaluate a production plan is to use the **turnover ratio:**

Turnover ratio = average sales/average inventory.

This ratio provides a measure of performance and is especially useful in aggregating the performance of production schedules for multiple items. Of course, a higher turnover ratio (commonly called the number of "turns") is desirable.

In order to increase the turnover ratio, either the sales must increase (which is in the domain of marketing, not operations management) or the inventory must be decreased (which is in the domain of operations). Decreasing average inventory is desirable up to the point where inventories are too low to provide good customer service. The industry standards usually suggest what this service level is. The following table contains sample industry ratios, as reported in *Production and Inventory Management Review* (June 1991, p. 17).

Industry	Monthly Sales/Inventory*
Food	1.20
Petroleum	1.16
Paper	.81
Chemicals	.74
Building Materials	.68
Rubber and Plastics	.66
Fabricated Metals	.62
Textiles	.62
Primary Metals	.53
Electrical Machinery	.53
Nonelectrical Machinery	.49
Transportation Equipment	.43
Instruments	.39

*Average from July 1989 through June 1990

PLANNING STRATEGIES

The objective of the planning process is to develop a production schedule that both minimizes the controllable production costs and, possibly more important, can be implemented and controlled with a minimum amount of effort. This latter point implies that the plan must be balanced in terms of costs, use of the production options, levels of inventory maintained, and amount of shortages tolerated. Sharp fluctuations of any of these items are to be avoided.

In terms of capacities, the options that are available to the manager are as mentioned in the previous section. However, one "source" of capacity (not a true source of capacity) provides the manager with the most flexibility. This source is inventory;

Seasonal demand affects production schedules. (© Richard Howard/Black Star)

balancing agent

by reducing or increasing inventory, the manager can modify (within the limits of storage capacity) the overall capacity to meet demands. Inventory, therefore, acts as a balancing agent in the production plan (at a cost, of course).

The use of inventory as a source of capacity is founded on one basic relationship—namely,

inventory equation

Inventory at the end of the period = inventory at the beginning of the period
+ production during the period
− demand (shipments) during the period.

With this relationship in mind, we can examine the strategies considered in aggregate planning. Essentially, the manager will vary (increase or decrease)

- the inventory levels and
- the production levels.

The primary component in changing production levels is the work force level, or utilization.

When the forecasted demands are identical (constant), production planning is rather straightforward. For example, if the demand forecast is 400 units in each of April, May, June, and July, then, presumably, the production plan is to produce 400 units in each of these four months. Production planning is more difficult (and, therefore, more interesting) when the demands vary from month to month. For example, production planning analysis is needed if the forecasted demands are 100, 500, 300, and 700 units for the months of April, May, June, and July, respectively.

Teaching Suggestion 12.3: Other Factors. See the Instructor's Section for details.

INVENTORY

Given a production plan, we can determine the inventory of raw materials required to meet this plan and the inventory of finished goods. The question of meeting the raw material requirements is not typically a part of the production planning problem, although it clearly is related. These models are presented in the following two chapters. On the other hand, finished goods inventory is a major factor in aggregate planning. Consider the following two production plans (A and B) for the varying demands above.

Month	Demand	Production Plan A	Production Plan B	Cumulative Excess, Plan B
April	100	100	400	300
May	500	500	400	200
June	300	300	400	300
July	700	700	400	0
	1,600	1,600	1,600	0

Plan A is developed to meet the demand exactly in each of the four months. Hence, no finished goods remain in inventory at the end of each month. Plan B meets the total demand, but on a uniform production basis of 400 units per month. Because production is uniform but demand is not, there will be leftover stock at the end of April, May, and June. This inventory costs money; hence, from an inventory standpoint, plan A is preferable. The typical assumption is that inventory costs are proportional to the amount of inventory on hand.

Shortages (negative inventory) can occur with a schedule such as plan B. For example, if the demand for April is 700 and the demand for July is 100, there will be a shortage of 300 units in April, 400 units in May (assuming that the April demand is still met), and 300 in June. No inventory will ever build up in this case. Shortage costs also are considered to be proportional to the amount of the shortage, but this may not always be true. Frequent shortages may lead customers to go elsewhere, reducing demand. When this happens, the cost per unit increases as the amount or frequency of the shortage increases.

shortages

PRODUCTION LEVELS

The difficulty with plan A is that varying labor hours must be used each month to meet varying demands. Hence, either some months will require overtime (or subcontracting) and others will require shortened work hours or there will be a need for layoffs during April and June and hirings during May and July. Plan B, however, requires no changes in the level of production activity from month to month. Consequently, in an industry where there is a high cost of changing the work force levels, plan B is clearly superior. (Remember, though, that plan B stores more inventory than does plan A.) In other industries, notably farming, there is no cost for changing work force levels.

just-in-time

Plan A is the production plan that would result from the use of the just-in-time philosophy. If we accept that the smoothing of a production schedule is the primary goal, then we begin to see a major weakness of the just-in-time approach. It requires frequent adjustments to work force levels, which lead to the problems discussed previously. It also requires extremely close managerial attention to controlling operations.

scheduling strategies

Aggregate planning is concerned primarily with the trade-offs between the inventory level and the work force level. Any strategy aimed entirely at cutting one of these costs, such as plan A or plan B, is called a **pure strategy.** Most plans try to reach a trade-off between costs, and these are called **mixed strategies.** We now go into more detail on the development of pure and mixed strategies.

PLANNING TECHNIQUES

There is no unique method for creating the aggregate plan. One reason for this is that different companies have different objectives, some of which we mention below.

planning objectives

- Maintain a specified level of customer service (that is, timely satisfaction of demand).
- Do not exceed some upper limit on inventory investment.
- Maintain a specified level of employment.
- Minimize labor costs.
- Minimize inventory costs.
- Maximize equipment usage.

Clearly, these objectives conflict with one another, and the choice of specific objectives is critical to the aggregate plan. Let us consider different methods of aggregate planning.

TRIAL AND ERROR

It may surprise you to learn that trial and error is perhaps the most common method of aggregate planning. This is not to say that the procedure is random or arbitrary, however. Logic and common sense must be applied during the development and revision of a plan. Consider the following example.

> **Example 12.1**   Given in the following table are the forecasted demands for the next twelve months.

Month	Demand Forecast	Cumulative Forecast
January	4,500	4,500
February	3,100	7,600
March	4,000	11,600
April	5,500	17,100
May	6,600	23,700
June	5,000	28,700
July	4,000	32,700
August	3,000	35,700
September	4,700	40,400
October	6,500	46,900
November	7,000	53,900
December	6,100	60,000
	60,000	

Transparency Master 12.2: Constant Production.

For the sake of simplicity, we assume that there is no inventory at the beginning of January. The material cost is $50 per unit. The cost of excess inventory at the end of a month is 1 percent of the material cost ($.50 per unit per month). The cost of training a new employee is $600 and is charged in the month that the employee is hired. The cost of laying off an employee is $300, which also is charged in the month in which it occurs. Each employee has the capacity to make 200 units per month, and overtime is not permitted. The current number of employees is 25.

Two production plans that result from the use of pure strategies are obvious. One plan is to spread the total demand of 60,000 units evenly over the twelve months and to produce 60,000/12 = 5,000 units per month (balance production). This plan is illustrated in Figure 12.3. In Figure 12.3, we have drawn a chart in which the heights of the bars represent the monthly demands. The production level of 5,000 units per month is represented by the horizontal line. In six of the months, the production exceeds the demand; during these months, there will be a buildup of inventory. In five of the months, the demand exceeds the production; during these months, units will be drawn from inventory. An alternative plan, then, is to meet the demand in each month exactly (eliminate inventory).

In order to understand the effects of the buildup and drawdown, we must create a picture that represents these cumulative effects over the twelve months. In Figure 12.4, the cumulative production is represented by the straight line showing constant production of 5,000 units per month. Plotting the cumulative forecasts results in the curve that represents the cumulative demand. Notice that, in this example, the production always exceeds the demand. The difference between cumulative production and cumulative demand (the shaded area) represents the inventory.

inventory = cumulative production − cumulative demand

Prior to conducting a formal cost analysis, let us informally consider the two plans. At one extreme, we have a plan that is aimed at eliminating costs due to work force size variations; at the other extreme, we have a plan that seeks to eliminate inventory and shortage costs. Of course, each plan performs poorly on the criterion it does not address. The first plan performs poorly with respect to inventory, and the second performs poorly with respect to work force level variations. The cost of the excess inventory is given as $.50 per unit. The cost of hiring ($600) or laying off ($300), in per unit terms, is well over the $.50 inventory costs because each employee produces 200

two pure strategies

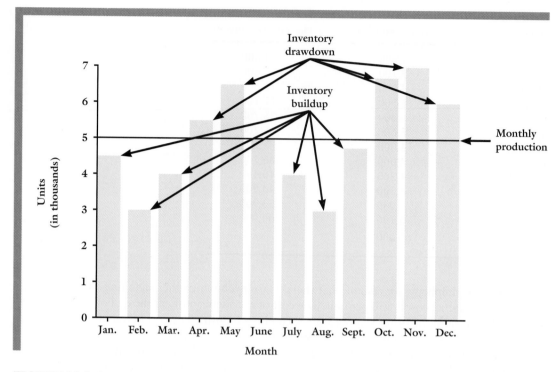

FIGURE 12.3 Month-to-month demand versus production (Example 12.1)

FIGURE 12.4 Cumulative production versus cumulative demand (Example 12.1)

Transparency Master 12.2:
Constant Production.

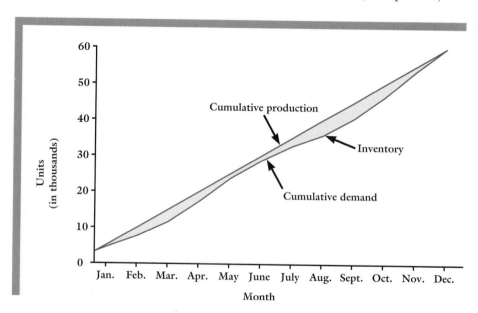

units per month. Clearly, since the inventory costs are less (and no shortages are incurred), the first plan is superior. That is, the smooth production plan is less costly than the plan that produces exactly the monthly amount demanded. ◼

It would be wonderful to be able to generalize from the preceding example. Unfortunately, this is impossible. The choice between two (or more) strategies depends on the relative costs involved. A formal comparison of the plans usually is required. The preceding analysis was not exact and could be used only for plans that are clearly far apart in terms of the costs. We begin with an analysis of the first plan in Example 12.1—equal production in each month. Henceforth we will refer to this plan as plan I.

The information required for evaluating our smooth production plan is exhibited in Table 12.1. Any production plan must include the production levels, which are shown in column (3) and the forecasted demands, which are shown in column (4). We need to compute the inventory in each month, and this is given by the relationship presented previously. That is, the ending inventory in column (5) is given by the beginning inventory—column (2)—plus the amount produced—column (3)—minus the demand—column (4). For example, the ending inventory in January is given by 0 + 5,000 − 4,500 = 500 units. The 500 units become the beginning inventory for February, and the computations are continued until columns (2) and (5) are completed. Because the cost of holding units is $.50 for each unit that is held one month, the cost in January is 500 × $.50 = $250, as seen in column (6). (We have chosen to charge the inventory at the end of the month. Alternatively, we could charge against the average inventory during the month.) The remainder of column (6) is computed in this fashion, and we find that the total inventory cost is $13,600. In order to keep

Transparency Master 12.3: Constant Production Costs.

TABLE 12.1 Aggregate planning: plan I—constant production rate (Example 12.1)

(1) Month	(2) Beginning Inventory	(3) Production	(4) Demand	(5) Ending Inventory	(6) Inventory Cost*	(7) Labor Size	(8) Change in Labor Size	(9) Hiring Cost*	(10) Layoff Cost*
January	0	5,000	4,500	500	250	25			
February	500	5,000	3,100	2,400	1,200	25			
March	2,400	5,000	4,000	3,400	1,700	25			
April	3,400	5,000	5,500	2,900	1,450	25			
May	2,900	5,000	6,600	1,300	650	25			
June	1,300	5,000	5,000	1,300	650	25			
July	1,300	5,000	4,000	2,300	1,150	25			
August	2,300	5,000	3,000	4,300	2,150	25			
September	4,300	5,000	4,700	4,600	2,300	25			
October	4,600	5,000	6,500	3,100	1,550	25			
November	3,100	5,000	7,000	1,100	550	25			
December	1,100	5,000	6,100	0	0	25			
		60,000	60,000		13,600				

* All costs in dollars

our tables consistent, we have included columns relating to manpower changes in this table. However, this production plan maintains a steady work force of 25, so there are no work force variation costs involved. The total cost of this plan is the $13,600 incurred due to holding inventory.

Let us now consider the costs of producing exactly to demand, which we will call plan II. The analysis is contained in Table 12.2. This time, because we are producing to demand, there are no inventory costs. Column (7) contains the size of the work force, which is determined by dividing the amount produced in that month by the regular-time capacity of 200 units per month for each worker (and rounding up to the next integer, if necessary). For example, the number of workers required in January is $4,500/200 = 22.5$, which means that we need 23 workers. Column (8) shows the change in the size of the work force for one month to the next. Because we started with 25 workers, the change in the work force for January is $23 - 25 = -2$. In the months where the number in column (8) is negative, such as January, there has been a work force reduction. Hence, the cost is given by $300 times the number of workers laid off and placed in column (10). In the months where the number is positive, it represents hiring, so we multiply the number by $600 and place the result in column (9). In our example, the total hiring cost is $22,200. The total layoff cost is $9,300. This means that the total cost for plan II is $31,500. As expected, the first plan costs less than the second plan ($13,600 versus $31,500). The wide disparity between the costs of the two plans serves to emphasize the import of aggregate planning decisions.

a compromise plan

We have seen the two extreme plans. Now let us consider a third plan that is a compromise between the two (a mixed strategy). Notice from the cumulative forecasts given in Example 12.1 that demand over the first six months is 28,700 units, while demand over the last six months is 31,300 units. Under the compromise, plan III, we produce 4,800 units per month for the first six months and 5,200 units per month for the last six months. The detailed cost analysis for this schedule is computed as

Transparency Master 12.4: Produce to Demand Costs.

TABLE 12.2 Aggregate planning: plan II—meeting demand exactly (Example 12.1)

(1) Month	(2) Beginning Inventory	(3) Production	(4) Demand	(5) Ending Inventory	(6) Inventory Cost*	(7) Labor Size	(8) Change in Labor Size	(9) Hiring Cost*	(10) Layoff Cost*
January	0	4,500	4,500	0		23	−2		600
February	0	3,100	3,100	0		16	−7		2,100
March	0	4,000	4,000	0		20	+4	2,400	
April	0	5,500	5,500	0		28	+8	4,800	
May	0	6,600	6,600	0		33	+5	3,000	
June	0	5,000	5,000	0		25	−8		2,400
July	0	4,000	4,000	0		20	−5		1,500
August	0	3,000	3,000	0		15	−5		1,500
September	0	4,700	4,700	0		24	+9	5,400	
October	0	6,500	6,500	0		33	+9	5,400	
November	0	7,000	7,000	0		35	+2	1,200	
December	0	6,100	6,100	0		31	−4		1,200
		60,000	60,000					22,200	9,300

* All costs in dollars

described for the first two plans and is provided in Table 12.3 and shown in Figure 12.5.

The results of the three plans are summarized as follows.

Plan	Inventory Cost	Labor Cost	Total
I	$13,600	$0	$13,600
II	$0	$31,500	$31,500
III	$10,000	$1,500	$11,500

Clearly, plan III is the best of the three plans. However, there are other plans that could and should be considered. For example, the production rate could change on a quarterly basis rather than on the semiannual basis of plan III.

We have deliberately kept this example simple. Missing from the example are possible factors of overtime, idle time, subcontracting, and part-time employees. If the costs and capacities of these factors are known, then they, too, enter into the production planning.

We note that the introduction of inexpensive, easy-to-use, spreadsheet software in the business environment has increased the ability of managers to perform cost analysis of plans. The effect of changing the schedule or any of the costs can be evaluated quickly and accurately, and the entire evaluation does not have to be done repeatedly as we did in Tables 12.1, 12.2, and 12.3. In fact, it was the aggravation that resulted from having to repeat these calculations from scratch each time one number changed that motivated an MBA student to develop the first successful microcomputer spreadsheet program (VisiCalc).

trial and error of other plans

Teaching Suggestion 12.4: Trial and Error Approach. See the Instructor's Section for details.

Transparency Master 12.5: Mixed Strategy Costs.

TABLE 12.3 Aggregate planning: plan III—mixed strategy (Example 12.1)

(1) Month	(2) Beginning Inventory	(3) Production	(4) Demand	(5) Ending Inventory	(6) Inventory Cost*	(7) Labor Size	(8) Change in Labor Size	(9) Hiring Cost*	(10) Layoff Cost*
January	0	4,800	4,500	300	150	24	−1		300
February	300	4,800	3,100	2,000	1,000	24	0		
March	2,000	4,800	4,000	2,800	1,400	24	0		
April	2,800	4,800	5,500	2,100	1,050	24	0		
May	2,100	4,800	6,600	300	150	24	0		
June	300	4,800	5,000	100	50	24	0		
July	100	5,200	4,000	1,300	650	26	+2	1,200	
August	1,300	5,200	3,000	3,500	1,750	26	0		
September	3,500	5,200	4,700	4,000	2,000	26	0		
October	4,000	5,200	6,500	2,700	1,350	26	0		
November	2,700	5,200	7,000	900	450	26	0		
December	900	5,200	6,100	0	0	26	0		
		60,000	60,000		10,000			1,200	300

* All costs in dollars

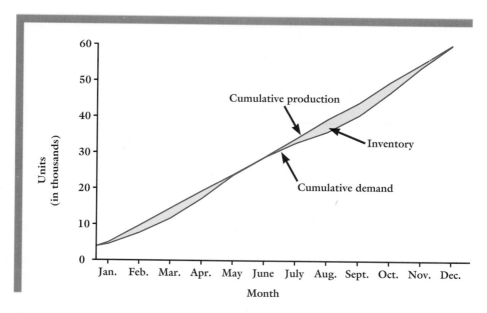

FIGURE 12.5 Cumulative production versus cumulative demand (plan III)

THE AGGREGATE PLAN FOR MULTIPLE ITEMS

Until now, our example has dealt with the scheduling of only one item. Scheduling is much more difficult when shared resources are required for production. The amount of sharing of the critical resources, such as labor and equipment, determines the accuracy of aggregating the items for planning purposes. For example, in the case of a company that produces both snowblowers and lawn mowers, the aggregation of the two products is very useful. It makes the overall planning problem much easier to address because it levels the aggregate product demand throughout the year, overcoming the seasonal demand for each individual item. For this example, the same techniques provided earlier in this chapter apply, with the single item demand being the sum of the demands for the snowblowers and the lawn mowers.

Multiple items may also be aggregated with little loss of detail when the demand for a particular item automatically generates demands for each of the many components that make up that item. Because the demand for this one item automatically specifies the exact need for all of the other items, these items should be grouped in resource and production planning. Again, the technique described earlier in the chapter may be applied to the single item after aggregating, not only the demands, but the various costs as well. This type of demand relationship is the basis for much of the discussion of materials requirements planning in Chapter 14.

This brings us to the situation where a production schedule must be developed for two or more items that are produced at the same time. Again, the same techniques apply, but they become more complicated. The size of the transportation matrix or the linear programming problem (discussed later in this chapter) is multiplied by the number of items produced. The effort needed to perform the trial and error method is multiplied, too.

There is no need to work out an example here. When we treat each item individually, the level of analysis becomes too detailed for the aggregate stage of planning. The planning for each individual item should be left to the short-term scheduler. At this stage, the multiple items should be aggregated.

The best way to aggregate the multiple items is to convert the demands for each item into their individual labor, inventory, and shortage costs. Many companies will not have this information by item; they will only have it aggregated by plant or division within the company. If the costs can be determined on an across-the-board basis, the schedule can be designed to meet the demand, stated in terms of labor hours instead of units. Of course, inventory also must be converted to inventory of labor hours.

common denominator: labor hours

Example 12.2   Table 12.4 gives the monthly demands for three items (A, B, and C) over the next year. The inventory costs are $2, $8, and $12, respectively, per unit held from one month to the next. The labor hours required for each product are .5, 2, and 3, respectively. The work force is to be held constant, with 1,400 hours of labor available each month (8 workers at 175 hours per month). No shortages are allowed, so overtime is the option provided for varying the work force; its cost is $6 per overtime hour. No layoffs are allowed, but idle time is assumed to cost the company $8 per hour. Use the trial and error method to design a production schedule.

Because there are only three items (still a very small number for practical purposes), it is conceivable that one might schedule each item separately. However, the amount of overtime that will be required or the amount of idle time that will occur depends on the levels of production of all of the items. So even for this small problem, aggregation is needed.

TABLE 12.4 Monthly demands (Example 12.2)

Month	Item A	Item B	Item C
	A	B	C
1	500	100	200
2	600	140	250
3	700	120	300
4	600	100	350
5	800	110	400
6	600	80	450
7	500	200	500
8	400	110	450
9	600	100	400
10	800	100	350
11	600	80	300
12	500	90	250
Total	7,200	1,230	4,200
Average	600	102.5	350

First, demands must be converted to labor hours. This is shown in Table 12.5. On average, 1,555 total labor hours are required per month, which is more than the 1,400 hours available per month. Because no shortages are allowed, the simplest schedule to evaluate is the one that results in no shortages and no inventory—that is, the one that calls for producing exactly the amount required each month. For this example, then, we will produce exactly the amounts shown in Table 12.4, resulting in the labor requirements of Table 12.5. Table 12.6 analyzes the aggregate production schedule costs.

The idle time costs are

$$680 \text{ hours} \times \$8/\text{hour} = \$5,440,$$

and the overtime costs are

$$2,540 \text{ hours} \times \$6/\text{hour} = \$15,240,$$

for a total cost of $20,680.

Idle hours cost more than overtime hours ($8 versus $6), so it would seem that a better schedule would be to use the full capacity each month and carry some inventory. However, this can be done for the last two months only if the demands continue into the next year. For this year only, an improved schedule may be to produce at 1,400 hours per month until overtime is needed. The cost analysis for this schedule is given in Table 12.7.

The idle time costs are

$$260 \text{ hours} \times \$8/\text{hour} = \$2,080.$$

The overtime costs are

$$2,120 \text{ hours} \times \$6/\text{hour} = \$12,720.$$

Transparency Master 12.6: Aggregating Across Products.

TABLE 12.5 Monthly labor requirements in hours (Example 12.2)

Month	Item A	Item B	Item C	Total
1	250	200	600	1,050
2	300	280	750	1,330
3	350	240	900	1,490
4	300	200	1,050	1,550
5	400	220	1,200	1,820
6	300	160	1,350	1,810
7	250	200	1,500	1,950
8	200	220	1,350	1,770
9	300	200	1,200	1,700
10	400	200	1,050	1,650
11	300	160	900	1,360
12	250	180	750	1,180
Total	3,600	2,460	12,600	18,660
Average	300	205	1,050	1,555

TABLE 12.6 Costs of first production schedule (Example 12.2)

Month	Regular Labor Hours	Idle Hours	Overtime Hours	Shortage	Inventory
1	1,400	350		0	0
2	1,400	70		0	0
3	1,400		90	0	0
4	1,400		150	0	0
5	1,400		420	0	0
6	1,400		410	0	0
7	1,400		550	0	0
8	1,400		370	0	0
9	1,400		300	0	0
10	1,400		250	0	0
11	1,400	40		0	0
12	1,400	220		0	0
		680	2,540	0	0

It is difficult to evaluate the inventory costs because we do not know which items are held in inventory. For this reason, it is standard practice in aggregate planning to express inventory costs as a percentage of the value of the inventory, thereby avoiding the need to know which items actually are in the inventory. For this problem, the given inventory costs are $4 per labor hour for each product. This translates into $2 for item A ($4 × .5 hour), $8 for item B ($4 × 2 hour), and $12 for item C ($4 × 3 hours), as given in the problem statement.

Teaching Suggestion 12.5: Fixed Inventory/Labor Cost Ratio. See the Instructor's Section for details.

TABLE 12.7 Costs of improved schedule (Example 12.2)

Month	Regular Labor Hours	Idle Hours	Overtime Hours	Shortage	Inventory
1	1,400			0	350
2	1,400			0	420
3	1,400			0	330
4	1,400			0	180
5	1,400		240	0	0
6	1,400		410	0	0
7	1,400		550	0	0
8	1,400		370	0	0
9	1,400		300	0	0
10	1,400		250	0	0
11	1,400	40		0	0
12	1,400	220		0	0
		260	2,120	0	1,280

The resulting inventory costs are

$$1,280 \text{ hours} \times \$4/\text{hour} = \$5,120,$$

which allows us to compute the total cost.

Idle time	$ 2,080
Overtime	12,720
Inventory	5,120
	$19,920

Although this is an improvement over the cost of our first schedule, it is not a significant improvement. Another option, not provided in the problem statement, is to hire an extra worker, bringing the regular production hours up to 1,575 per month. Since this is a trial and error process, many other schedules can be evaluated.

THE PERCENTAGE DONE METHOD

When production planning is to be performed for one product or multiple products having seasonal demand, the planning problem is tied very closely to the forecasting problem. Also, the time frame for the production planning is much closer to short term. The **percentage done method** has been developed to estimate the increase to or decrease from planned production that will be required during the remainder of the current season. This method usually assumes that multiple items are from the same product line or group and that an increased demand for one item will imply an increased demand for the other(s).

The best example of when this method is used in the United States is the annual Christmas season. Producers carefully watch the sales figures week by week, beginning as early as October, to pick up trends before it is too late for them to respond by changing their production rates for the rest of the season. The automotive industry provides another example. Each model year is a season, and seasonal production rates are updated constantly based on early-season sales. A third example may be found in the fashion industry. An example of a seasonal industry where this method would not apply is agriculture, where all production (planting) levels must be decided prior to the start of the season.

assumption　　The percentage done method assumes that the same percentage of seasonal demand is encountered at any given point in the season for each item and that this percentage is known from the demand experienced in previous seasons. It consists of a very simple three-step procedure.

procedure

Step 1. For past data, determine the percentage of cumulative demand for each time period, averaged over the group.

Step 2. At any point in the current season, use the demands to that point and the expected demand to that point (the percentage done estimate) to predict the demand for the remainder of the year.

Step 3. Modify the production schedule to meet the revised demands.

The following example demonstrates the use of the percentage done method.

Example 12.3 Fashion Plate Company produces clothes for its chain of women's clothing stores. Units produced are transported from the factory to the stores in one month, and each season lasts six months. Last year's sales for three items that have been classified as a group (vests, sweaters, and turtlenecks) are given in Table 12.8. The plan is to produce according to the data in Table 12.8—that is, based on last year's sales. Initial inventory at the start of the current season was 50 of each item. At the end of April of the current year, sales have been 120, 140, and 100 units for vests, sweaters, and turtlenecks, respectively. How should the schedule be revised?

The first step is to determine the percentage done—that is, the percentage of demand accounted for through each month. We begin by finding the aggregate monthly demands, or the total demand in each month of vests plus sweaters plus turtlenecks. Table 12.9 contains the original data in columns (2), (3), and (4) and the month-by-month sums in column (5). The total demand for the six months is the sum of the figures in column (5), which is 1,800. In column (6), we compute the monthly percentage of demand as the monthly demand given in column (5) divided by the total demand of 1,800. Lastly, in column (7) we derive the percentage done as the running sum of column (6). For example, 56.11 percent of the demand occurs between March and June.

Step 2 is to incorporate the data from the current season. The sales of vests at the end of April have been 120. According to Table 12.9, this should represent 18.33 percent of the six-month sales. Therefore, the revised estimate of the six-month demand for vests is given by

$$F_{vests} = \frac{120}{.1833} = 655,$$

rather than the original estimate of 550 vests given in Table 12.8. Similarly, the revised estimates for sweaters and turtlenecks are

$$F_{sweaters} = \frac{140}{.1833} = 764$$

and

$$F_{turtlenecks} = \frac{100}{.1833} = 546.$$

TABLE 12.8 **Fashion Plate Company's demands for previous year (Example 12.3)**

Month	Vests	Sweaters	Turtlenecks
		Item	
March	40	30	50
April	60	70	80
May	90	100	120
June	110	120	140
July	120	120	150
August	130	120	150
	550	560	690

TABLE 12.9 Fashion Plate Company: percentage done method (Example 12.3)*

(1) Month	(2) Vests	(3) Sweaters	(4) Turtlenecks	(5) Aggregate Monthly Demand [(2) + (3) + (4)]	(6) Aggregate Monthly Percentage [(5)/1,800]	(7) Percentage Done [Cumulative Sum of (6)]
March	40	30	50	120	.0667	.0667
April	60	70	80	210	.1167	.1833
May	90	100	120	310	.1722	.3556
June	110	120	140	370	.2056	.5611
July	120	120	150	390	.2167	.7778
August	130	120	150	400	.2222	1.0000
	550	560	690	1,800	1.0000	

* Table contains some roundoff error.

Transparency Master 12.7: Percentage Done Method.

Because the initial inventory at the start of the season was 50 of each item, the seasonal requirements are

$$R_{vests} = 655 - 50 = 605;$$

$$R_{sweaters} = 764 - 50 = 714; \text{ and}$$

$$R_{turtlenecks} = 546 - 50 = 496.$$

These needs can be used to increase the production of vests and sweaters and to decrease the production of turtlenecks accordingly, keeping in mind that it is already too late to adjust for the third month of sales. (This lag between production and sales is one motivation for the initial inventory, which acts as a hedge against shortages.) ■⌡

MATHEMATICAL PROGRAMMING

Mathematical programming is used extensively for the production planning problem, especially when the situation is complex, requiring too many calculations and the evaluation of too many alternatives for the trial and error approach to be used. Our first application uses the transportation model. Our second, more general model uses linear programming.

USE OF THE TRANSPORTATION MODEL

Under certain conditions—namely, when the relationships among variables are linear—the transportation model may be used to generate the production plan. In many cases, the relationships are linear. In transportation models, the sources available for production are considered to be the supply points, and the demands (times) are used as the destination points. Consider the following example.

Example 12.4 Ace Electronics is planning its VCR production for May, June, and July. Sales are expected to be 200 for May, increasing to 500 for June, and decreasing to 300 for July. The production level at Ace is 250 VCRs per month, with overtime capacity of an additional 150 VCRs per month. The (labor) cost of production is $8 at regular time and $12 at overtime in each of the three months. However, each VCR that is not sold in the same month in which it is produced results in an inventory cost of an additional $5 for each month that it is held. The decisions to be made include the production level at regular time and overtime for each of the three months, and the objective is to minimize the total production and inventory cost while satisfying the demand.

The problem is shown in Table 12.10. A VCR that is produced in May during regular time costs $8. If a VCR is produced in the overtime period, its cost is $12. If VCRs produced in regular time and overtime in May are stocked at the warehouse and sold during June, there is a holding cost of $5 for each of them, increasing their costs to $8 + $5 = $13 and $12 + $5 = $17, respectively. Furthermore, if the VCRs produced in May are held until July, there would be an additional holding cost of $5 for each VCR, which would further increase each VCR's cost—to $18 and $22, respectively. VCRs produced and sold in June cost either $8 or $12 (depending on whether they are produced in regular time or in overtime), which is identical to the costs for VCRs produced in May. However, VCRs manufactured during June and stocked until July each cost an additional $5 due to inventory charges. The option to produce in June for May is not available, so it is denoted by an X. Similarly, because it is impossible to produce in July and sell in the preceding May or June, these options are each marked with an X. The July costs are simply $8 and $12.

The total production capacity is 1,200 VCRs, while demand is set at 200 + 500 + 300 = 1,000 VCRs. This means that there is a need for a dummy destination that absorbs the difference between the supply of 1,200 VCRs and the demand for 1,000 VCRs. Therefore, let the dummy have a demand of 200. The cost of selling to the dummy destination is zero, regardless of the month or the factors of regular time or

TABLE 12.10 Ace Electronics: production planning as a transportation problem (Example 12.4)

Supply Points	Demand Points				Supply (Capacity)
	May	June	July	Dummy	
May regular time	$8	$8 + $5	$8 + $5 + $5	$0	250
May overtime	$12	$12 + $5	$12 + $5 + $5	$0	150
June regular time	X	$8	$8 + $5	$0	250
June overtime	X	$12	$12 + $5	$0	150
July regular time	X	X	$8	$0	250
July overtime	X	X	$12	$0	150
Demand	200	500	300	200	1,200

overtime, because this destination does not exist. Using the transportation method (see Chapter 6) the solution (the production planning schedule) is as follows.

Number of VCRs	Time Produced	Month Sold
200	May regular time	May
50	May regular time	June
50	May overtime	June
250	June regular time	June
150	June overtime	June
250	July regular time	July
50	July overtime	July

The total cost is

$$Z = (\$8 \times 200) + (\$13 \times 50) + (\$17 \times 50) + (\$8 \times 250) + (\$12 \times 150)$$
$$+ (\$8 \times 250) + (\$12 \times 50) = \$9,500.$$

(This numerical example has alternative optimal solutions.)   ■」

LINEAR PROGRAMMING

The transportation method is a special form of linear programming; linear programming is more general and can be applied to a wider class of aggregate planning problems. In the following example, linear programming is applicable, but the transportation model is not.

Example 12.5   Baker Publishing Company sells only one book, *How to Enter Medical School*. Baker has orders from New Jersey University to deliver 750 copies for the winter quarter (beginning January 1), 900 copies for the spring quarter (beginning April 1), and 500 copies for the summer session (beginning July 1). Books can be produced before January at a cost of $7 each, but because binding costs will rise in January, the cost for books produced after January will be $8 apiece. In addition, the shipping contract expires in May, so books are shipped at $.80 per book for the summer session but at only $.60 per book for the winter and spring quarters.

In order to keep production somewhat steady, it has been decided that production in any given quarter cannot vary from production in the previous quarter by more than 20 percent. This restriction applies to the production for the winter session, which must be within 20 percent of the fall production of 700. (This is the restriction that cannot be fit into the transportation model, primarily because it, in effect, allows variable capacities.) Finally, any books produced but not shipped are held in storage at a rate of $.70 per book per quarter (three months). How many books should be produced in each of the three quarters in order to minimize the total cost? (There is no starting inventory.)

Let x_{ij} = the number of books produced in quarter i for shipment during quarter j. Because there are three quarters, there are, at most, nine variables. However, as in the previous examples, production for times that have already passed is not allowed, so x_{21}, x_{31}, and x_{32} need not be considered. This leads to the six decision variables given by the following table.

Production Dates	Delivery Dates		
	January 1	April 1	July 1
October 1–December 31	x_{11}	x_{12}	x_{13}
January 1–March 31		x_{22}	x_{23}
April 1–June 30			x_{33}

The objective is to minimize the total cost. The following table shows the cost associated with each production decision variable, based on the timing of production and shipping.

Transparency Master 12.9: Linear Programming.

Variable	Quarter Produced	Quarter Shipped	Production Cost	Inventory Cost	Shipping Cost	Total Cost
x_{11}	1	1	7.00	0	.60	7.60
x_{12}	1	2	7.00	.70	.60	8.30
x_{13}	1	3	7.00	1.40	.80	9.20
x_{22}	2	2	8.00	0	.60	8.60
x_{23}	2	3	8.00	.70	.80	9.50
x_{33}	3	3	8.00	0	.80	8.80

Note: All costs are in dollars.

The objective function that results is

Minimize $\quad 7.60x_{11} + 8.30x_{12} + 9.20x_{13} + 8.60x_{22} + 9.50x_{23} + 8.80x_{33}.$

The constraints for this problem fall into the following two groups:

- Demand must be met by production; and
- Production cannot fluctuate by more than 20 percent on a quarter-by-quarter basis.

The demand constraints (assuming no initial inventory on hand) are

$$x_{11} \geq 750;$$

$$x_{12} + x_{22} \geq 900; \text{ and}$$

$$x_{13} + x_{23} + x_{33} \geq 500.$$

The constraints on the production levels are, first, that the production levels for the first quarter cannot vary by more than 20 percent from the 700 books produced in the previous quarter.

$$x_{11} + x_{12} + x_{13} \leq 840$$

$$x_{11} + x_{12} + x_{13} \geq 560$$

There are also constraints on the variation between production levels of the first and the second quarters.

$$x_{22} + x_{23} \leq 1.20(x_{11} + x_{12} + x_{13})$$

$$x_{22} + x_{23} \geq .80(x_{11} + x_{12} + x_{13})$$

Finally, there are constraints on the variation between production levels of the second and the third quarters.

$$x_{33} \leq 1.20(x_{22} + x_{23})$$

$$x_{33} \geq .80(x_{22} + x_{23})$$

The complete linear model, then, contains six variables and nine constraints and is written as follows.

Transparency Master 12.9:
Linear Programming.

$$
\begin{aligned}
\text{Minimize} \quad & 7.6x_{11} + 8.3x_{12} + 9.2x_{13} + 8.6x_{22} + 9.5x_{23} + 8.8x_{33} \\
\text{Subject to} \quad & x_{11} && \geq 750 \\
& x_{12} + x_{22} && \geq 900 \\
& x_{13} + x_{23} + x_{33} && \geq 500 \\
& x_{11} + x_{12} + x_{13} && \leq 840 \\
& x_{11} + x_{12} + x_{13} && \geq 560 \\
& -1.2x_{11} - 1.2x_{12} - 1.2x_{13} + x_{22} + x_{23} && \leq 0 \\
& -8x_{11} - .8x_{12} - .8x_{13} + x_{22} + x_{23} && \geq 0 \\
& -1.2x_{22} - 1.2x_{23} + x_{33} && \leq 0 \\
& -.8x_{22} - .8x_{23} + x_{33} && \geq 0
\end{aligned}
$$

We have used AB:POM to find the following solution.

$$x_{11} = 750$$

$$x_{12} = 90$$

$$x_{13} = 0$$

$$x_{22} = 810$$

$$x_{23} = 0$$

$$x_{33} = 648$$

The total cost is $19,115.40.   ▪〗

In the preceding example, notice that the total production in the first quarter is at the maximum allowable limit (840). This is necessary to take advantage of the $7 cost, which rises to $8 in later quarters. However, more than the required 500 books are produced for the third quarter (648). This is because the demand in this quarter drops by much more than the allowable production variation. The only way to get around this would be to reduce the production in the second quarter, but reduction is not possible because demand must be met.

model generalizations

The production manager has a few options available at this point. First, the schedule can be accepted as suitable, with the extra books carried as inventory into the following quarter. If carrying the extra books as inventory is not possible, the model must be altered and run again to obtain a new production schedule. Based on the results, a likely model change would be to allow for shortages and specify a shortage cost. Then, suitable changes in the constraints would allow the model to trade off the extra costs of shortages in the first two quarters against the extra cost of producing more units in the last quarter. A simpler change, if allowable, would be to permit a production variation of more than 20 percent. This adjustment would require no changes in the constraints, except that the values 540 and 860 and the coefficients 1.2 and .8 would have to be modified. (For example, the coefficients would be 1.3 and .7 for 30-percent variation.)

This example, its model development, its solution, and the analysis of that solution show how linear programming can be useful in production planning and how the production planner can use the results of the linear programming model to further analyze the assumptions of the planning environment. Although the linear model in Example 12.5 is the largest example (9×6) presented in this text, it is still overly simplistic. No overtime is allowed, no shortages are allowed, and no subcontracting is allowed. Outside of the variation from one quarter to the next, no limit on production capacity is considered, and only three time periods are considered. Obviously, a more realistic example would yield a much larger linear programming problem. Fortunately, linear programming can be used to solve problems with thousands of constraints or variables.

WORK FORCE DECISION FRAMEWORK

needs vs. capacity

The work force decision framework for aggregate planning attempts to provide the operations manager with a simpler, more intuitive basis for making decisions. This basis is a measure of the degree of balance achieved between needs and capacities, both in the present and in the future. These needs and capacities are expressed in terms of labor needs. By using both time frames, medium-term and short-term planning are linked.

The measures of the degree of balance are the **current period ratio** (*CPR*) and the **planning period ratio** (*PPR*). The current period ratio is the ratio of current labor needs to current labor capacities. The current labor needs are the labor required to achieve current production minus the labor equivalence of any inventory on hand. Essentially, current labor capacities represent the present work force. Thus, the current period ratio is

$$CPR = \frac{\text{current period production labor needs} - \text{labor equivalence of inventory on hand}}{\text{current period production regular-time labor force}}.$$

Similarly, the planning period ratio is

$$PPR = \frac{\text{average production labor requirements for the planning period}}{\text{average regular-time labor capacity}},$$

where the planning period does not include the current period.

interpretation of ratios   Ideally, the production system is in balance if $CPR \simeq$ (is approximately equal to) 1 *and* $PPR \simeq 1$. If either is less than 1, then the labor needs are less than the labor capacity, meaning that there is excess capacity. An appropriate course of action when there is excess capacity is either to reduce the labor force or to produce more than is needed now and store it for a later period. If $CPR > 1$ or if $PPR > 1$, the labor force will need to be increased in some way.

The planner can simultaneously evaluate these two ratios at any time as an aid in choosing the proper course of action to ensure that future production activity is smooth. The planner can face nine scenarios when using the current period ratio with the planning period ratio, as shown in Table 12.11. Only one scenario requires no corrective action.

> **Example 12.6**   Let us reexamine the data presented in Example 12.2 (see Table 12.5). The total labor hours required in each month as well as the labor hours available (1,400) are known. Apply the work force decision framework to this problem.
>
> Using the first month as the current period and the remaining eleven months as the planning period will yield a first direction for the planning strategy. The current period ratio is the labor hour demand in month 1 divided by the labor hours available in month 1, or

$$CPR = \frac{1,050}{1,400}.$$

Since $CPR < 1$, we know that too much production capacity is available in month 1. The planning period ratio is total labor hour demand in months 2–12 (17,610) divided by the total labor hours available ($11 \times 1,400$), or

$$PPR = \frac{17,610}{15,400}.$$

Since $PPR > 1$, we know that not enough production capacity is available. The initial recommendation is to use all of the capacity of the first month to help to balance these

TABLE 12.11 Work force decision framework: planning scenarios

	$CPR < 1$	$CPR \simeq 1$	$CPR > 1$
$PPR > 1$	Lower PPR and raise CPR	Lower PPR	Lower both ratios
$PPR \simeq 1$	Raise CPR	No action	Lower CPR
$PPR < 1$	Raise both ratios	Raise PPR	Raise PPR

TABLE 12.12 Production plan (based on Example 12.1, plan III)

	May	June	July
Production		4,800	5,200
Forecast		5,000	4,000
Ending inventory	300	100	1,300

ratios. This is the recommendation that was followed in developing the production schedule presented in Table 12.7. ◼◞

MASTER PRODUCTION SCHEDULING

Earlier in this chapter, we noted that the aggregate plan represents production across a family or product line that uses the same resources. The aggregate plan must be broken down on a product-by-product basis into what is termed a **master production schedule** (MPS). We use the term *schedule,* but the MPS is actually a plan. After the MPS is created, it must be broken down into a schedule that can be implemented. The aggregate plan contains the aggregate levels of resources required and inventory that will be on hand. The master production schedule specifies resource and inventory factors for each product. These factors must coincide with the aggregate levels.

Table 12.12 contains the production plan for June and July from Example 12.1's plan III. Suppose that the plan is for three units in a family of units. The master production schedule might appear as in Table 12.13. In this schedule, our weekly production levels are equal, regardless of the product, which means that we have assumed that the production of each product requires the same amount of time. We also have indicated that June has fewer weeks than July (since June 1 is a Saturday). Even though we have increased production for July due to the nature of the calendar, the capacity in July is still underutilized. Even this simple example of a master production schedule reveals the transformation that takes place when one goes from the aggregate plan to the more detailed master production schedule.

TABLE 12.13 Master production schedule

Product	June Week 1	Week 2	Week 3	Week 4	Total	July Week 1	Week 2	Week 3	Week 4	Week 5	Total
1	1,200	800			2,000	1,200	800				2,000
2		400	1,100		1,500		400	1,200	100		1,700
3			100	1,200	1,300				1,100	400	1,500
Total	1,200	1,200	1,200	1,200	4,800	1,200	1,200	1,200	1,200	400	5,200

SUMMARY

The aggregate planning problem is one of scheduling production for medium-range planning. The options, with their capacities, are known; the problem is to choose among these options at various levels of capacity to meet the demands on production. The options include the variation of the work force by hiring, laying off, or using overtime; the accrual of inventory; or the allowance of shortages. Each of these options incurs some cost, and the strategy is to combine the options in such a way that the costs are minimized. Techniques based on trial and error, mathematical programming, and work force levels have been discussed. The aggregation of individual items into groups for planning purposes has been emphasized to differentiate this phase from the detailed short-term planning.

KEY TERMS

aggregate planning

disaggregation

production planning

product grouping

turnover ratio

pure strategy

mixed strategies

percentage done method

current period ratio

planning period ratio

master production schedule

SOLVED PROBLEMS

1. Forecasted demand over the coming year is as follows.

Month	Demand
January	500
February	600
March	600
April	700
May	700
June	800
July	900
August	900
September	800
October	700
November	600
December	600

The backorder (shortage) cost is $10 per unit per period, and the inventory carrying cost is $3 per unit per period. The present work force can produce 700 units per month. The cost of production is $70 per unit, and this cost is increased by $5 per unit for each unit over the 700th produced in any month. If less than 700 units are produced, the per unit cost for each unit under 700 is $12.

Using a pure strategy of minimizing work force variations, develop a production schedule and analyze its costs.

Solution

The total production required over the year is 8,400 units, or 700 per month. Thus, the schedule is to produce 700 per month and have no costs associated with work force variation. The only costs incurred will be the monthly production cost, the inventory cost, and the shortage cost.

The costs are calculated as follows.

Month	Beginning Inventory	Production	Production Cost	Demand	Ending Inventory	Shortage	Inventory Cost	Shortage Cost
January	0	700	$ 49,000	500	200	0	$ 600	$ 0
February	200	700	49,000	600	300	0	900	0
March	300	700	49,000	600	400	0	1,200	0
April	400	700	49,000	700	400	0	1,200	0
May	400	700	49,000	700	400	0	1,200	0
June	400	700	49,000	800	300	0	900	0
July	300	700	49,000	900	100	0	300	0
August	100	700	49,000	900	0	100	0	1,000
September	0	700	49,000	800	0	200	0	2,000
October	0	700	49,000	700	0	200	0	2,000
November	0	700	49,000	600	0	100	0	1,000
December	0	700	49,000	600	0	0	0	0
		8,400	$588,000	8,400	2,100	600	$6,300	$6,000

The total cost of this plan is the sum of the three costs, or $600,300.

Using AB:POM to Solve This Problem

The aggregate planning module is another module that allows for several options. The initial input is the number of time periods. The methods for doing the planning are created by using the top two lines, which represent toggles. The first toggle is shown in Screen 12.1. There are four major methods available in AB:POM. The first method is to have production be as smooth as possible. The second is to allow production to follow the demand pattern as much as possible. The third is to have a constant amount of regular-time production and then to use overtime and/or subcontracting. The last option is to enter the production amounts directly. The second toggle activates whether shortages are lost sales or backordered.

Screen 12.2 contains the costs and capacities for Solved Problem 1. The regular-time capacity is 700 units. This capacity must be set high enough to cover the average demand (700 units). The costs used are $5 per unit for overtime, $3 to hold a unit one month, and $10 per unit for a shortage of one month. (Shortages are backordered, not lost sales.) These costs can be entered at the top of the columns and AB:POM will copy them throughout the columns. Alternatively, they can be modified on a line-by-line basis. That is, it is possible to change any of these costs over the different time periods.

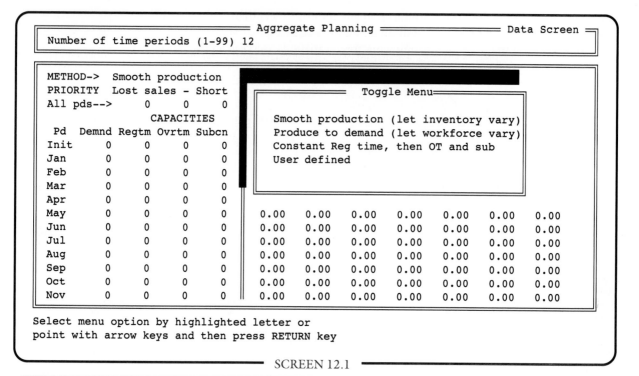

```
================== Aggregate Planning ================== Data Screen ==
 Number of time periods (1-99) 12

 METHOD->   Smooth production
 PRIORITY   Lost sales - Short
 All pds-->      0      0      0
                 CAPACITIES              ========= Toggle Menu=========
  Pd  Demnd Regtm Ovrtm Subcn
 Init    0     0     0     0     Smooth production (let inventory vary)
 Jan     0     0     0     0     Produce to demand (let workforce vary)
 Feb     0     0     0     0     Constant Reg time, then OT and sub
 Mar     0     0     0     0     User defined
 Apr     0     0     0     0
 May     0     0     0     0   0.00  0.00  0.00  0.00  0.00  0.00  0.00
 Jun     0     0     0     0   0.00  0.00  0.00  0.00  0.00  0.00  0.00
 Jul     0     0     0     0   0.00  0.00  0.00  0.00  0.00  0.00  0.00
 Aug     0     0     0     0   0.00  0.00  0.00  0.00  0.00  0.00  0.00
 Sep     0     0     0     0   0.00  0.00  0.00  0.00  0.00  0.00  0.00
 Oct     0     0     0     0   0.00  0.00  0.00  0.00  0.00  0.00  0.00
 Nov     0     0     0     0   0.00  0.00  0.00  0.00  0.00  0.00  0.00

 Select menu option by highlighted letter or
 point with arrow keys and then press RETURN key
```

SCREEN 12.1

```
= Data file:wgsp1 ============= Aggregate Planning ============= Data Screen =
 Number of time periods (1-99) 12

 METHOD->   Smooth production (let inventory vary)
 PRIORITY   Backorders - Carry shortages from period to period
 All pds-->    700     0     0   $70.0 $0.00 $0.00 $3.00 $10.0 $0.00 $0.00
                 CAPACITIES                        C O S T S
  Pd  Demnd Regtm Ovrtm Subcn  Regtim Ovrtim Subcon Holdng Shortg Incres Decres
 Init    0     0     0     0
 Jan   500   700     0     0  || 70.00  0.00  0.00  3.00  10.00  0.00  0.00
 Feb   600   700     0     0  || 70.00  0.00  0.00  3.00  10.00  0.00  0.00
 Mar   600   700     0     0  || 70.00  0.00  0.00  3.00  10.00  0.00  0.00
 Apr   700   700     0     0  || 70.00  0.00  0.00  3.00  10.00  0.00  0.00
 May   700   700     0     0  || 70.00  0.00  0.00  3.00  10.00  0.00  0.00
 Jun   800   700     0     0  || 70.00  0.00  0.00  3.00  10.00  0.00  0.00
 Jul   900   700     0     0  || 70.00  0.00  0.00  3.00  10.00  0.00  0.00
 Aug   900   700     0     0  || 70.00  0.00  0.00  3.00  10.00  0.00  0.00
 Sep   800   700     0     0  || 70.00  0.00  0.00  3.00  10.00  0.00  0.00
 Oct   700   700     0     0  || 70.00  0.00  0.00  3.00  10.00  0.00  0.00
 Nov   600   700     0     0  || 70.00  0.00  0.00  3.00  10.00  0.00  0.00

 F1=Help F2=New  F3=Load F4=Main F5=Util F6=Quit F7=Save F9=Prnt F10=Run    Esc
 Press space bar to toggle overtime/subcontracting precedence or RETURN for menu
```

SCREEN 12.2

The production plan requires two screens. Most of the plan is shown in Screen 12.3. The units produced, held, and short appear on the right of the double bar. Paging down will show the total costs at the bottom.

```
┌═ Data file:wgsp1 ═══════════ Aggregate Planning ═══════════ Solution ═┐
│ Number of time periods (1-99) 12                                      │
│ ┌───────────────────────────────────────────────────────────────────┐ │
│ │ METHOD->  Smooth production (let inventory vary)                   │ │
│ │ SHORTAGES:Backorders - Carry shortages from period to period      │ │
│ │ All pds-->    700     0      0   $70.0  $0.00  $0.00  $3.00  $10.0  $0.00  $0.00 │ │
│ │               CAPACITIES                  U N I T S                │ │
│ │ Pd  Demnd Regtm Ovrtm Subcn  Regtim Ovrtim Subcon Holdng Shortg Incres Decres │ │
│ │ Init    0     0     0     0                                        │ │
│ │ Jan   500   700     0     0    700      0      0    200     0     0      0 │ │
│ │ Feb   600   700     0     0    700      0      0    300     0     0      0 │ │
│ │ Mar   600   700     0     0    700      0      0    400     0     0      0 │ │
│ │ Apr   700   700     0     0    700      0      0    400     0     0      0 │ │
│ │ May   700   700     0     0    700      0      0    400     0     0      0 │ │
│ │ Jun   800   700     0     0    700      0      0    300     0     0      0 │ │
│ │ Jul   900   700     0     0    700      0      0    100     0     0      0 │ │
│ │ Aug   900   700     0     0    700      0      0      0   100     0      0 │ │
│ │ Sep   800   700     0     0    700      0      0      0   200     0      0 │ │
│ │ Oct   700   700     0     0    700      0      0      0   200     0      0 │ │
│ │ Nov   600   700     0     0    700      0      0      0   100     0      0 │ │
│ └───────────────────────────────────────────────────────────────────┘ │
│ F3=Summary          F9-Print        ↑  ↓ PageUP, PageDOWN, Home, End      Esc │
│ Use direction keys to scroll through the answers; F9 or P to print; Esc to end │
└───────────────────────────────────────────────────────────────────────┘
```

───────────────── SCREEN 12.3 ─────────────────

A summary screen contains the cost totals.

```
┌═ Data file:wgsp1 ═══════════ Aggregate Planning ═══════════ Solution ═┐
│ Number of time periods (1-99) 12                                      │
│ ┌───────────────────────────────────────────────────────────────────┐ │
│ │                         SUMMARY TABLE                              │ │
│ │   TYPE        UNITS         COST      Total cost =   $600300.00    │ │
│ │   Regtim      8400     $588000.00                                  │ │
│ │   Ovrtim         0          $0.00                                  │ │
│ │   Subcon         0          $0.00                                  │ │
│ │   Holdng      2100       $6300.00                                  │ │
│ │   Shortg       600       $6000.00                                  │ │
│ │   Incres         0          $0.00                                  │ │
│ │   Decres         0          $0.00                                  │ │
│ │                                            F9=Print    Esc         │ │
│ └───────────────────────────────────────────────────────────────────┘ │
│ Press <Esc> key to edit data or highlighted key or function key for options │
└───────────────────────────────────────────────────────────────────────┘
```

───────────────── SCREEN 12.4 ─────────────────

2. Holmes-Shuttle Ford sold the following numbers of cars last year.

Month	Escort	Taurus	T-Bird
September	24	26	12
October	20	21	10
November	17	18	9
December	15	16	8
January	15	15	8
February	16	15	8
March	18	17	9
April	20	18	10
May	20	20	10
June	21	22	9
July	22	22	10
August	23	24	11
	231	234	114

In the current model year, sales after three months are as follows.

Car	Sales
Escort	63
Taurus	68
T-Bird	35

The dealership had been ordering based on the previous year's sales, but Ford requires them to supply order figures for the remainder of the production year at this time (December 1) so it may adjust its production figures. Using the percentage done method, how should the schedule for Holmes-Shuttle be revised?

Solution

Calculate the percentage done for each month.

Month	Escort	Taurus	T-Bird	Aggregate Monthly Demand	Aggregate Monthly Percentage	Percentage Done
September	24	26	12	62	.107	.107
October	20	21	10	51	.088	.195
November	17	18	9	44	.076	.271
December	15	16	8	39	.067	.338
January	15	15	8	38	.066	.404
February	16	15	8	39	.067	.471
March	18	17	9	44	.076	.547
April	20	18	10	48	.083	.630
May	20	20	10	50	.086	.716
June	21	22	9	52	.090	.806
July	22	22	10	54	.093	.899
August	23	24	11	58	.101	1.000
				579	1.000	

Sales thus far (to November 30) have been 166 cars (63 + 68 + 35). From the preceding calculations, this should be 27.1 percent of the sales for the year. We can use this figure to compute the revised sales estimates for the entire year.

$$\text{Escort} = \frac{63}{.271} = 232$$

$$\text{Taurus} = \frac{68}{.271} = 251$$

$$\text{T-Bird} = \frac{35}{.271} = 129$$

QUESTIONS

1. How does aggregate planning fit in with the overall planning activities of the organization?

2. How are aggregate planning and capacity planning linked?

3. What types of decisions are made under the heading of aggregate planning?

4. What are the objectives and the trade-offs in the aggregate planning problem?

5. Explain the process of aggregation.

6. Discuss the following statement and its implications for production planning: The only thing known for sure about demand forecasts is that they will be wrong!

7. How does the aggregate planner modify and control capacities to achieve his or her goals?

8. How do costs influence production planning decisions? Which costs are most relevant?

9. What is the turnover ratio? How can it be improved?

10. What is meant by saying that inventory "balances" the production plan?

11. What is a pure strategy? Provide a few examples.

12. Describe mixed strategies and provide a few examples.

13. How would a negative inventory be interpreted?

14. How does the just-in-time approach affect the use of inventory in the planning process?

15. You are a production foreman who has just been informed that higher management will approve a just-in-time inventory policy, beginning in two weeks. Why are you afraid of this?

16. What is disaggregation?

PROBLEMS

1. Butler Inc. manufactures toy soldiers. The demands for the next four quarters follow.

Quarter	Demand (in sets)
1	80,000
2	60,000
3	100,000
4	120,000

plan I: 90,000; 90,000;
90,000; 90,000
plan II: 80,000; 60,000;
100,000; 120,000

Butler has no current inventory of soldier sets. Develop two production plans using pure strategies. What are the strengths and weaknesses of each of the two plans?

2. Heidi Ski Company produces skis and other related equipment, which are sold worldwide. The forecasted demands for the next four quarters are as follows.

Quarter	Demand (in pairs of skis)
Fall	72,000
Winter	87,000
Spring	53,000
Summer	48,000

plan I: 65,000; 65,000;
65,000; 65,000
plan II: 72,000; 87,000;
53,000; 48,000

Heidi Ski Company currently has no inventory of skis. Develop two production plans using pure strategies. What are the advantages and disadvantages of each of these two plans? (Any demand that cannot be met in one period is met in the next.)

3. The demand for gallon containers of Clearshock chlorine for the next six months is as follows.

Month	Demand
April	1,800
May	2,600
June	2,900
July	2,500
August	2,700
September	400

April: 1,760; May: 2,630;
June: 2,860; July: 2,520;
Aug.: 2,470; Sept.: 360

Clearshock has a current (end of March) inventory of 300 containers. The company policy is to maintain an inventory at the end of each month that is 10 percent of the forecasted demand for the next month. Develop the six-month production plan that satisfies the company policy.

4. Demand and production levels for a twelve-month period are as follows.

Month	Demand	Production
July	80	90
August	50	90
September	70	90
October	90	90
November	100	90
December	80	90
January	110	90
February	120	90
March	100	90
April	70	90
May	90	90
June	80	90

There is no beginning inventory.

10; 50; 70; 70; 60; 70; 50;
20; 10; 30; 30; 40
no
40
pure

(a) What are the end-of-month inventory levels?
(b) Are there any shortages?
(c) What is the inventory level at the end of the planning period?
(d) Is this production schedule based on a pure strategy or a mixed strategy?

5. The following table shows a firm's demand and production levels for the next six months.

Month	Demand	Production
October	600	500
November	400	400
December	300	400
January	700	600
February	600	600
March	500	600

There is no beginning inventory.

(a) What are the end-of-month inventory levels?
(b) Are there any shortages?
(c) What is the inventory level at the end of the planning period?
(d) Is this production schedule based on a pure strategy or a mixed strategy?

−100; −100; 0; −100; −100; 0
yes
0
mixed

6. Use the data of Problem 5 for the following.

(a) Develop another production schedule. Use a pure strategy based on minimizing work force variations.
(b) Develop another production schedule. Use a pure strategy based on minimizing inventory and shortage levels.
(c) Develop another production schedule. Use a mixed strategy.

517; 517; 517; 517; 517; 517
600; 400; 300; 700; 600; 500
Several answers are possible.

7. For the data of Problem 5, assume that the work force variation cost is $3 per unit (for increases and decreases) the shortage cost is $10 per unit per period, and the inventory cost is $1.25 per unit per period. Compare the four production schedules developed in Problems 5 and 6 on a cost basis.

Problem 5 cost: $4,900; Problem 6a cost: $1,423.75; Problem 6b cost: $2,700; Problem 6c cost: several possible answers

8. After six months, the end-of-period inventories were as follows for the firm in Problem 5.

Month	Inventory
October	0
November	100
December	200
January	0
February	0
March	0

(a) Determine the production schedule that was used.
(b) Using the costs given in Problem 7, evaluate the schedule developed in part (a) on a cost basis.

600; 500; 400; 500; 600; 500
$1,875

9. The table shows the demand for the next twelve-month period for Fan Hall Inc.

Month	Demand	Month	Demand
May	790	November	730
June	640	December	860
July	580	January	730
August	430	February	630
September	540	March	570
October	620	April	680

produce to demand:
$3,960; produce 650 per
month: $3,240

Several answers are
possible.

948; 620; 558; 400; 562;
636; 752; 886; 704; 610;
558; 702; cost = $6,930

The cost of work force variation is $2 per unit for increases from the previous month and $4 per unit for decreases. Production in April was 650 units. The backorder (shortage) and inventory costs are $5 and $1 per unit per month, respectively. There is no initial inventory. Develop the two production schedules based on pure strategies and evaluate them on a cost basis.

10. Develop a production schedule for Fan Hall Inc. that is less costly than either of the two schedules developed in Problem 9.

11. Fan Hall Inc. (see Problem 9) is somewhat concerned about the accuracy of its forecasts. To be safe, the company is considering requiring that end-of-month inventory be 20 percent of the forecast for that month. Find the production schedule that satisfies this policy. How does the cost of this policy compare with the policies that were developed in Problems 9 and 10?

12. A certain firm's demands for the next three months are 800, 600, and 900 units, respectively. Production costs are $8 per item produced on regular time and $9.50 per item produced on overtime. Inventory holding cost is $1.25 per item per month, and no shortages are allowed. Model this as a transportation problem. Regular-time capacity is 700 units per month, and overtime capacity is 100 units per month.

See Instructor's Section.

See Instructor's Section.

See Instructor's Section.

13. Solve the model developed in Problem 12. What production schedule results?

14. Model the situation given in Problem 12 as a linear program.

15. Demands for two items over the next six months are as follows.

Month	Item A	Item B
February	120	210
March	170	180
April	140	190
May	130	240
June	120	220
July	130	200

600; 615; 590; 675; 620;
595 hr.

Labor hours required are 1.5 for item A and 2 for item B. Find the aggregate demand for each month.

Several answers are
possible.

16. Consider Problem 15. Inventory costs per period are $2.25 for item A and $3 for item B. For both items, overtime costs $10 per hour. No shortages are allowed. Design a production schedule based on the aggregation of the two items to minimize cost.

17. A state's highway department purchases salt monthly to spread on the roads during snow and ice storms. Average monthly usage is as follows.

Month	Salt Tonnage
December	50
January	60
February	75
March	30

167 tons

This year, salt requirements have been 45 tons and 40 tons for the first two months. What is the revised salt requirement for the four-month season?

COMPUTER CASE STUDY 12.1: CORNWELL GLASS

Cornwell Glass produces replacement automobile glass for all makes of cars. Cornwell has a sophisticated forecasting system that uses data from past years to find seasonal factors and long-term trends. Data from past weeks is used to find recent trends. Given in the following table are the forecasted demands for the coming year on a weekly basis.

Week		Demand	Week		Demand
April	15	1,829	November	4	1,864
	22	1,820		11	1,989
	29	1,887		18	2,098
May	6	1,958		25	2,244
	13	2,011	December	2	2,357
	20	2,063		9	2,368
	27	2,104		16	2,387
June	3	2,161		23	2,402
	10	2,258		30	2,418
	17	2,307	January	6	2,417
	24	2,389		13	2,324
July	1	2,434		20	2,204
	8	2,402		27	2,188
	15	2,385	February	3	2,168
	22	2,330		10	2,086
	29	2,323		17	1,954
August	5	2,317		24	1,877
	12	2,222	March	3	1,822
	19	2,134		10	1,803
	26	2,065		17	1,777
September	2	1,973		24	1,799
	9	1,912		31	1,803
	16	1,854	April	7	1,805
	23	1,763			
	30	1,699			
October	7	1,620			
	14	1,689			
	21	1,754			
	28	1,800			

Cornwell uses these forecasts for its production planning. Several types of glass are manufactured, so the demands are aggregated across products and measured in pounds.

It is obvious from the demands that there is a great deal of seasonality/cyclicality in the demand pattern. Cornwell will need to take this into account in developing a production plan for the coming year.

Cornwell must consider the costs involved with hiring or firing workers; using overtime; subcontracting; and holding inventory or running out of the product. The holding cost for glass is $.12 per pound per week. The company estimates that the cost of a late order is $20 per pound per week late.

Cornwell currently costs out each hire at $5.63 per pound (based on training costs and production rates per worker); each fire, at $15.73 per pound (based on unemployment compensation and loss of good will). The company currently has the capacity to manufacture 1,900 pounds of glass per week. This capacity cannot be exceeded under any plan. At most, 2,000 pounds can be subcontracted in a given week, and overtime is limited to 250 pounds per week. Glass that is manufactured during overtime costs $8 per pound more than glass that is manufactured during regular time. Glass that is subcontracted costs $2 more per pound than glass that is produced during overtime.

The current inventory is 73 units, and the current production is working at the capacity of 1,900 units. Cornwell has not been able to determine whether demands that are not met in the current month can be met later or whether these orders are lost. Find the production schedule that Cornwell should follow under the various assumptions and policies and detail the differences among these schedules.

REFERENCES

Buffa, E. S., and J. G. Mills. *Production-Inventory Systems: Planning and Control,* 3rd ed. Homewood, Ill.: Richard D. Irwin Inc., 1979.

Fogarty, D. W., J. H. Blackstone, and T. R. Hoffman. *Production and Inventory Management.* 2nd ed. Cincinnati: South-Western Publishing Company, 1991.

Freeland, J., and R. Landel. *Aggregate Production Planning: Text and Cases.* Reston, Virginia: Reston Publishing Company, 1984.

Fullmer, W. E. *Managing Production: The Adventure.* Boston: Allyn and Bacon, 1984.

Greene, J. H. *Production and Inventory Control: Systems and Decisions.* Rev. ed. Homewood, Ill.: Richard D. Irwin Inc., 1974.

McLeavey, D., and S. Narasimhan. *Production Planning and Inventory Control.* Boston: Allyn and Bacon, 1985.

Peterson, R., and E. A. Silver. *Decision Systems for Inventory Management and Production Planning.* 2nd ed. New York: John Wiley and Sons, 1985.

C H A P T E R

13

INVENTORY MANAGEMENT

■ **To explain the reasons for maintaining an inventory**
■ **To enumerate the costs incurred in an inventory system**
■ **To describe the cost trade-offs that are made due to inventory**
■ **To present the types of policies that are associated with operating inventory systems**
■ **To discuss the implementation of inventory systems**

INTRODUCTION

The topic of the previous chapter was intermediate-range production planning. One of the pure strategies presented in that chapter consisted of using inventory as a buffer for high demand. Also presented was the turnover ratio (sales/average inventory) as a measure of performance. Of course, the inventory discussed in the last chapter was finished goods inventory. This is only one of the types of inventory with which we are concerned. In addition to finished goods inventory, operations managers need to manage work-in-process, raw materials and/or component parts, and processing supplies. In this chapter and the next, we discuss the concepts of inventory management for these four types of inventories.

Our discussion in this chapter is, of course, from an operations management point of view. However, as we have stated in previous chapters, the inventory of finished goods is strongly related to the marketing function. In times of high inventory levels, a major control is to run marketing promotions to increase sales and lower the inventory level.

THE ROLE OF INVENTORY

anticipation of future demand

Inventory is a stock of goods that is maintained by a business in anticipation of some future demand. This demand could be for the product that the company manufactures or for supplies used in the transformation process. When a company has an optimistic outlook, carrying increased levels of inventory is justified due to the anticipated high demand. During pessimistic times, inventories must be reduced. Because it is more difficult to reduce inventories during weak economic times, it is the responsibility of marketing to inform top management that a downturn is beginning, so that inventories may be reduced before it is too late. For this reason, inventory levels are considered to be a major predictor of economic trends, as evidenced by their role in the government's index of leading economic indicators.

Inventory levels are related to expected demand levels for products or supplies. As a result, the marketing and salespeople in any organization will try to use their influence to increase levels of inventories. Their sales efforts can only be helped by increased levels of inventory, because the salespeople can promise delivery from stock, without requiring customers to wait long. By increasing inventory levels, their predictions of higher demand can be self-fulfilling. In general, production and operations people also like to have large inventories. High inventory levels make production planning easier (the discussion of production planning in Chapter 12 showed how inventories can be used to smooth production schedules). Larger inventories reduce the risk of lost production due to equipment failure or labor walkouts, too. It is no coincidence that mines and factories work at maximum overtime capacity just prior to a strike deadline. Management builds up inventories to sustain the organization through the strike. In a sense, the workers also build an inventory to sustain them through the strike; the workers' inventory is the extra income they earn from the overtime pay. **benefits of high inventories**

Although there are distinct advantages to maintaining high inventory levels for both marketing and operations, the finance department would like to see very low inventory levels because money tied up in inventory is not available for other uses. Inventory control is the mechanism through which a company can maintain enough inventory. How one determines what is "enough" inventory is the subject of most of this chapter. Excessive inventory levels place extra cost burdens on a business, raising the costs of its products and impairing its competitiveness in the marketplace. These costs are discussed in the next section. At the other extreme, insufficient inventory of finished products causes lost sales; insufficient inventory of raw materials causes production delays. **inventory ties up money**

role of inventory control

In the pure inventory situation, an item is purchased or produced, stored, and then either used in the process or sold. Retail and wholesale stores and distribution warehouses are obvious examples of pure inventory situations. The discussion in this chapter applies to these situations. It also applies to the stocking of office supplies, such as light bulbs, paper clips, and printer ribbons; the stocking of hospital supplies, such as film, medicine, and plasma; and the stocking of shop repair supplies, such as screws, fan belts, and circuit boards. Although the models in this chapter apply to both the production and the service settings, the next chapter (on materials requirements planning) will deal more directly with the production situation and will link the inventory needs to the needs of production scheduling. The major difference between the pure situation and the production situation is that the demand for one item in the production situation usually is highly dependent on the demand for a different item. In the pure situation, the demands for items are independent of one another. **pure inventory**

production marked by dependent inventory

In the pure inventory situation, there is little need to classify inventory because the models apply to each type of inventory. However, in the production environment, inventory usually is classified as one of four types.

- raw materials/component parts inventory
- in-process goods inventory
- finished goods inventory
- supplies and miscellaneous inventory

types of inventory

RAW MATERIALS/COMPONENT PARTS INVENTORY

The stock of goods from which the product of the company is made is the raw materials. The raw material does not include any material that supports production; it is limited to the material or component that actually becomes a part of the final product.

Output from many ranches is input to the international livestock market at Liniers, Argentina. (© Jean Guichard/Sygma)

The steel used for automobile production is a good example of a raw material. Keep in mind, however, that the raw material of one industry is usually the finished product of another. Higher-level (closer to the consumer) industries such as those that produce automobiles or refrigerators use steel as a raw material but, as Figure 13.1 shows, that same steel is a finished product to the steel industry (which is further removed from the consumer). Its raw materials are coke, limestone, and iron. At the lowest level, the iron ore company views the iron as its final product, and the iron ore that it mines as its raw material. The fact that one company's finished good is another company's raw material is critical. If the auto manufacturer is operating its inventory of steel efficiently, then the steel manufacturer can do likewise. (This is one of the major principles of just-in-time deliveries.) The illustration in Figure 13.1 is relevant, not only to inventory, but also to quality control. If the finished goods inspection at the lower level is done well, then the raw materials at the next level need less scrupulous inspection (and, therefore, fewer resources for inspection). We will discuss the inspection of raw materials and finished goods in a later chapter.

just-in-time

Teaching Suggestion 13.1: The Operations Chain. See the Instructor's Section for details.

IN-PROCESS GOODS INVENTORY

All of the materials that have been transformed from their raw materials state by some production process but are not yet final products are in-process goods. A foundry will have raw ingots of metal as its raw materials. All of the ingots that have started through the production process but have not yet completed that process are considered to be in-process inventory. Sometimes, what may appear to be a final product is still really

FIGURE 13.1 Relationship of raw materials and finished goods

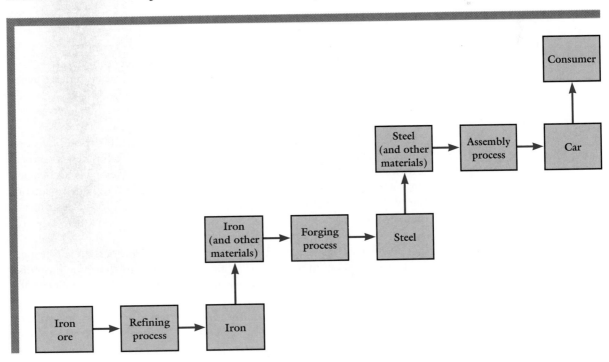

an in-process good if packaging is the final production step. It is in-process until it is in the form that can leave the plant. The problem of defining the desired levels of in-process inventory to be stocked can be viewed as a pure inventory situation at any point in the production cycle, although the pure inventory situation has no in-process inventory at all. (A retailer or a distributor does not transform the product.)

FINISHED GOODS INVENTORY

Finished goods inventory consists of all of the stock that is ready for sale. In a bottling plant, for example, the finished products are the bottles of beverage that are in their cartons or cases and are ready for shipment. In the pure inventory situation, there is no difference between raw material (purchased) and finished goods (sold). For this case, the term *inventory* suffices; no descriptive prefixes are needed.

SUPPLIES AND MISCELLANEOUS INVENTORY

Supplies and miscellaneous inventory are any items stocked by a company that do not become part of the final product but are needed in order for the company to function. The office supplies maintained by almost all businesses fall into this category. Some items, such as the oil needed to lubricate production equipment, also fall into this category, even though they are production related, because they are not part of the final product. Materials handling equipment in a warehouse is another example of miscellaneous inventory. In a slightly more abstract sense, backup electricity generation capacity, installed at most large plants, can be considered an inventory item (the inventory of power to run the plant), and so it, too, falls into this category.

INVENTORY COSTS

We have said that maintaining an inventory adds costs to any operation. In this section, we consider the sources of these costs and what factors should be considered when computing them. Consider the simple inventory situation of a new business.

> **Example 13.1**   A shoe salesman has just decided to open his own shoe store. However, he has very little money to invest and wants to start his business as soon as possible. His solution is to maintain no stock of shoes on hand. He opens his business by printing some advertisements; he operates out of his home. Whenever anyone wants a pair of shoes, the salesman orders them and delivers them to the customer in a few weeks. ∎

The salesman's idea has the advantage of eliminating inventories. However, people do not like to buy shoes in this way; they almost always want to try them on first. Although some "low overhead" businesses can do extremely well, especially catalog sales, the shoe business is not one of them.

major costs   For this example, we can identify both the major costs associated with maintaining inventory and the major cost of not having inventory. For the shoe salesman to open his own shoe store, he must stock a wide variety of shoes. To do this, he must borrow

An inventory of
finished goods
awaiting distribution.
(© Chris Morris/Black
Star)

(from a bank or from his own sources) a large sum of money. In order for the new
shoe store to make a profit (see the discussion of break-even analysis in Chapter 3),
the revenue from sales must cover the interest payments on the money borrowed to
purchase the shoes. The salesman also must buy or lease space (the store) to display
some of the inventory and to stock the remainder. So the major cost of inventory, the
inventory **holding costs,** results mostly from the capital invested and from the cost of
renting or leasing the space required for the inventory. It is quite common for a supermarket to have over $100,000 worth of stock and for a department store or a hospital
to have $1 million worth of stock, or more.

holding costs

    The contribution of each of the two costs just mentioned to the holding cost of
an item depends on the item in inventory. Diamonds, for example, are very capital
intensive and take up little space. However, due to the required security precautions,
the space they use may be expensive. In addition, there may be other costs that are
directly proportional to the amount of inventory. Two such costs are insurance and
taxes. Because of the wide variety of direct holding costs, most companies do not
conduct a detailed evaluation of the holding costs for each item. Instead, companies
often use a percentage of the value of an item, based on past financial records. From
an accounting viewpoint, only variable costs are included in the holding cost. Fixed
costs (those that are incurred regardless of the inventory level) are not considered. Let
us consider the computation of holding costs.

Teaching Suggestion 13.2:
Determining Holding
Costs. See the Instructor's
Section for details.

Example 13.2   Five items are stored in inventory at a warehouse that uses a holding cost percentage of 25 percent per year for each of the items. The costs of the items are as follows.

Item	Cost
1	$ 40
2	90
3	70
4	120
5	60

What holding cost should be used for each item?

Based on the fact that the policy of the company is to use a 25-percent annual holding cost, the annual holding cost is obtained by multiplying the cost of the item by .25.

Item	Purchase Cost × Holding Cost Percentage	Annual Holding Cost
1	$40 × .25	$10.00
2	$90 × .25	22.50
3	$70 × .25	17.50
4	$120 × .25	30.00
5	$60 × .25	15.00

shortage cost

At this point, it would still seem that the way to minimize inventory costs (and, thus, operating expenses) is to maintain no inventory, but as Example 13.1 showed, there is another inventory cost: the **shortage cost.** The shortage cost is more difficult to measure than the holding cost. The shortage cost is the cost of lost sales, the cost of customers that never return for future sales, and the cost relating to loss of good will. Because shortage costs are so difficult to estimate, many companies specify a **service level,** or percentage of shortages allowed, and then calculate the shortage cost implied by the tolerated service level. A higher service level (fewer shortages allowed) implies a higher shortage cost. Larger inventories are needed to minimize shortage costs. In Example 13.1, the service level was 0, because no shoes were available for sale.

fixed order cost

The final inventory cost is the **order cost.** This is the fixed cost associated with placing an order in the inventory system. When inventory is ordered, there is a cost associated with ordering, transporting, and receiving the items. This order cost is independent of the number of items ordered. In a production environment, the order cost can be thought of as the setup cost of rearranging equipment and personnel to produce the item.

unit cost

There is one further cost that, although only marginally related to inventory, already has been mentioned in this section. That is the **unit cost** of the inventory item. The unit cost was used to calculate the holding cost in Example 13.2. We shall see it used again later when quantity discounts are considered.

INVENTORY SYSTEMS

The inventory system is the set of procedures, or operating policies, on which the acquisition and maintenance of inventory is based. The two basic types of inventory systems are

Teaching Suggestion 13.3: Continuous vs. Periodic. See the Instructor's Section for details.

■ continuous review systems and
■ periodic review systems.

In the **continuous review system,** the level of inventory is monitored at all times. When the inventory level is low, a fixed quantity is ordered, as common sense would suggest. A reorder point, R, is calculated to determine how low inventory must be to trigger a new order. The fixed amount ordered, Q, is calculated also. Once Q and R have been determined, the policy (known as a Q, R policy) is complete. The company will order Q items whenever the inventory level drops to R. Because the same amount is ordered each time, continuous review systems also are known as **fixed order size systems** (FOSS), **economic order quantity** (EOQ) systems, or event-triggered systems. Although only a computerized inventory system can perform true continuous monitoring, in practice, it is not necessary to use a computer. We will speak further about implementation of continuous review systems in the last section of this chapter.

fixed quantity

The **periodic review system** takes a different approach. At fixed time intervals— say, weekly or monthly—the inventory level is checked and an order is placed. The size of the order is the amount required to bring the inventory level up to some predetermined full level and, therefore, will vary from period to period. Periodic review systems also are known as **fixed order interval systems** (FOIS), **economic order interval systems** (EOI), or time-triggered systems.

fixed time

Inventory systems also are classified by the assumptions made in their analysis. Two key assumptions are related to the

■ **replenishment rate** and the
■ allowance for **shortages.**

The replenishment rate may be either infinite or finite. Use of the infinite rate implies that all items ordered arrive at one time (instantaneous replenishment). This is the usual situation for supplies, materials, or components that are ordered from an outside vendor. Use of a finite replenishment rate implies that the items arrive at some rate over time, frequently a production rate. When an item is being produced internally rather than ordered from an outside supplier, it usually is replenished at a finite rate.

Shortages may be allowed, or not allowed, as a matter of policy. As we shall see later on, allowing no shortages is equivalent to assuming an infinite shortage cost. In such a case, the cost of a shortage is so high that none can be tolerated.

Additional assumptions are made about the demand pattern. In this chapter, the demand pattern is presented as constant over time. First, it will be viewed as being deterministic, or known with certainty. Later in the chapter, it will be viewed as being probabilistic. Discussion of the case where demand levels change according to the production plan is left for the next chapter.

demand assumptions

ABC SYSTEMS

Every manager who has responsibility for a number of activities soon realizes that he or she cannot give each of the activities complete attention. The successful manager

Teaching Suggestion 13.4:
Pareto Distribution. See
the Instructor's Section for
details.

gives more attention to those activities that require more control and less attention to those activities that require less control. The ability to identify the appropriate amount of control required for each activity is of utmost importance.

When a very great number of items are maintained in inventory, the inventory manager has this same problem: to identify which items require more attention and which items can be monitored less closely. If not all of the items can be modeled correctly due to time constraints, the manager needs to be able to identify the high-priority items. In this way, the most effort can be expended where it will have the greatest benefit.

To identify these high-priority items, many large inventory control systems classify all items in inventory according to what is termed an **ABC classification system.** Under such a system, the most important items are termed *A* items, the next most important group of items are termed *B* items, and the least important group of items are termed *C* items. Each class of items, as should be expected, is treated differently, with the A items subjected to the most complete inventory analysis.

a minority of items accounts for a majority of costs

The theory behind the ABC classification is that the majority of the capital invested in inventory is found in a minority of the items. It is this small minority of items (the A items) that warrant the most control. This situation is analogous to the distribution of wealth in the U.S. economy. As economists have noted, 5 percent of the population controls 50 percent of the wealth. For inventory items, it seems that about 70 percent to 80 percent of the capital is tied up in between 10 and 20 percent of the items. Then, 15 to 20 percent of the capital is invested in 30 or 35 percent of the items, and, finally, only 5 to 10 percent of the capital is invested in nearly 50 percent of the items. This situation is illustrated in Figure 13.2. Let us consider how the classification of items is performed.

Example 13.3   An investigation of the inventory levels at a large manufacturing plant yields the following information.

Item	Average Inventory	Value (in dollars per unit)
4016	400	3.75
5817	300	4.00
5816	120	2.50
4024	75	1.50
5809	60	1.75
4057	30	2.00
4001	20	1.15
5812	12	2.05
5819	8	1.80
5818	7	2.00
4050	6	3.00

How would the plant classify these items according to an ABC classification system?

First, two more columns of data must be prepared. Because the basis of the classification is the total dollar volume, this amount must be calculated. The second col-

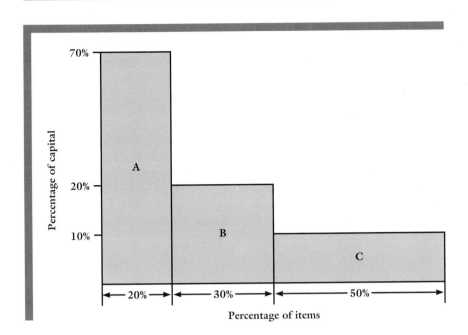

Transparency Master 13.1:
ABC Classification.

FIGURE 13.2 ABC classification scheme

umn, percent of total dollar volume, could be considered optional but is helpful in conducting operations on the items.

Item	Average Inventory	Value (in dollars per unit)	Average Dollar Volume	Percentage of Total Dollar Volume
4016	400	3.75	1,500.00	44.0
5817	300	4.00	1,200.00	36.0
5816	120	2.50	300.00	9.0
4024	75	1.50	112.50	3.3
5809	60	1.75	105.00	3.1
4057	30	2.00	60.00	1.8
4001	20	1.15	23.00	.7
5812	12	2.05	24.60	.7
5819	8	1.80	14.40	.4
5818	7	2.00	14.00	.4
4050	6	3.00	18.00	.5
			3,371.50	100.0

The plant might classify the items as follows.

A	B	C
4016	5816	4001
5817	4024	5812
	5809	5819
	4057	5818
		4050

Here, 18 percent (two of the eleven items) is made up of A items having 80 percent of the value, 36 percent (four of the eleven items) consists of B items having 17 percent of the value, and 46 percent (five of the eleven items) consists of C items having 3 percent of the value. ∎⌐

alternate ABC classifications

The preceding example raises some questions. *Is this the only classification?* Of course not. Item 4057 could easily be classified as a C item, and the resulting classification still would be correct; the classification has a subjective element. Very often, the average dollar volume column will show smoother changes, resulting in even less clear lines of separation into A, B, and C categories. *Is total dollar volume the only basis for the classification?* No; again, from a managerial viewpoint, it may be more useful to classify items by volume only. The company that provided the data for the previous example used average inventory to classify the items, which yielded the following classification.

A	B	C
4016	5816	4057
5817	4024	4001
	5809	5812
		5819
		5818
		4050

This time, 18 percent of the items have approximately 67 percent of the volume, 27 percent of the items have 25 percent of the volume, and 55 percent of the items have 8 percent of the volume.

There also are exceptions to the classifications. For example, the availability of a particular item may be critical to meeting production schedules. If this item is a low-volume (C) item, then it needs more control than the ABC classification would provide. The solution is either to redefine it as an A or B item, as appropriate, or just to flag it as a special case for treatment outside the scope of the ABC system.

CONTINUOUS REVIEW INVENTORY SYSTEMS

The models presented in this section are the Q, R models described previously. In this section, we present the procedure for calculating the order quantity, Q, for four similar models.

Model I: instantaneous replenishment, no shortages

Model II: gradual replenishment, no shortages

Model III: instantaneous replenishment, with shortages

Model IV: gradual replenishment, with shortages

The relationships between the two assumptions with the models are illustrated in Table 13.1. The first three models, as we shall see, are all special cases of the fourth. In the next section, we will discuss the computation of the reorder point, R. Our presentation of the four models begins with model I, the basic EOQ model. We then present a discussion of sensitivity analysis on this model, which is followed by a description of the case where quantity discounts are available as options to the standard prices.

TABLE 13.1 Assumptions and models

Shortages	Replenishment Rate	
	Infinite	Finite
No	Model I	Model II
Yes	Model III	Model IV

Finally, models II, III, and IV are presented as extensions of the basic model. The general points of the sensitivity and quantity discount discussions also hold for these extensions, although they are not explicitly repeated for each.

THE BASIC ECONOMIC ORDER QUANTITY (EOQ) SYSTEM

Inventory analysis is based on the calculation of the total inventory costs as a function of some unknown decision variable. In the basic EOQ system (model I), that variable is the size of the order quantity. Based on the total cost function, an optimal level for the decision variable can be found. The models presented in this section have been derived in this way, but they represent only a small percentage of the many different inventory situations that are encountered in practice.

Figure 13.3 shows the inventory level as a function of time. No shortages are allowed; each new order arrives just as the inventory level reaches 0. We assume that

FIGURE 13.3 Inventory as a function of time—sawtooth curve

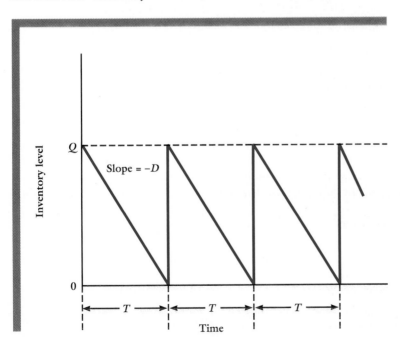

EOQ assumptions

demand is constant and is given by a rate of D. Because items are withdrawn from inventory, the slope of the inventory level curve is $-D$. The maximum inventory level is shown to be Q, because Q items arrive when the inventory level drops to 0.

cost trade-off

The cost trade-off in this model (there are no shortage costs) is made between the holding costs (variable costs) and the order costs (fixed costs). If large amounts are ordered each time—that is, if Q is large—the fixed costs are low, because fewer orders need to be placed. However, a larger order quantity results in more items held in inventory and, of course, higher holding costs. We wish to find the order quantity, $Q^\star$, that minimizes the sum of these two costs. To find $Q^\star$, we must develop the total cost equation. We let

D = annual demand (units/year);

P = purchase price (dollars/unit);

H = holding cost (dollars/unit-year);

S = order cost (dollars/order);

Q = order quantity (units/order); and

TC = total (annual) cost (dollars/year).

annual unit cost is independent of order quantity

Let us now consider each of these costs. The purchase cost per year is the price per unit times the number of units, or PD. Given P and D, the annual cost of purchasing units is constant, regardless of the quantity ordered. The yearly holding cost is the holding cost, H, times the average number in inventory. For the basic EOQ model (model I), the average inventory is $Q/2$ because the inventory varies at a constant rate from Q to 0 (see Figure 13.3). So the total holding cost per year is $HQ/2$. Similarly, the total ordering cost per year is the cost per order, S, times the number of orders per year. In terms of the order quantity, the number of orders per year is the yearly demand, D, divided by the size of each order, Q, or D/Q. So the annual order cost is SD/Q. Therefore, the total cost is

annual inventory cost

$$TC = PD + \frac{HQ}{2} + \frac{SD}{Q}.$$

Teaching Suggestion 13.5: Unit Costs. See the Instructor's Section for details.

In the absence of quantity discounts, the purchase cost, PD, is independent of the order quantity and can be omitted from consideration; that is, it can be treated as a sunk cost.

Let us consider an example that details the three types of costs.

Example 13.4 Warehouse Tire Distributors sells 4,800 tires per year. Tires are purchased at a price of $27 per tire in batches of 240 tires each. The holding cost is $2 per tire per year, and the ordering cost is $30 per order. What is the total inventory cost?

The average inventory is

$$\frac{Q}{2} = \frac{240}{2} = 120.$$

The number of orders per year is

$$\frac{D}{Q} = \frac{4,800}{240} = 20.$$

So the total cost is

$$TC = PD + \frac{HQ}{2} + \frac{SD}{Q} = (\$27 \times 4,800) + \frac{(\$2 \times 240)}{2} + \frac{(\$30 \times 4,800)}{240}$$
$$= \$129,600 + \$240 + \$600 = \$130,440.$$

■⌐

Notice that the cost for the units is $129,600. This figure is independent of the order size. Whether we place one order of size 4,800 or 4,800 orders of one tire each, the total cost for tires will be $129,600. Second, notice that because the number of orders is given by D/Q, the time between orders is given by Q/D. In our example, an order is placed every 1/20th of a year (approximately every 18 calendar days). Finally, note that the annual ordering costs ($600) are greater than the annual holding costs ($240). Typically, this is a sign that too many orders are being placed and that fewer but larger orders would be more cost efficient. We detail the individual costs presently.

We have developed a table for various values of the order quantity (see Table 13.2) and plotted these costs in Figure 13.4. As both the table and the figure show, as the order quantity increases, the holding cost increases and the setup cost decreases. In addition, the total cost is minimized at the point where the holding cost and setup cost are equal. Hence, the optimal order quantity, $Q^\star$, satisfies

holding cost = setup cost

$$\frac{HQ^\star}{2} = \frac{SD}{Q^\star},$$

TABLE 13.2 Inventory costs as a function of order quantity (based on Example 13.4)

(1) Order Quantity (Q)	(2) Annual Setup Cost (SD/Q)	(3) Annual Holding Cost (HQ/2)	(4) Inventory Cost [(2) + (3)]	(5) Annual Unit Cost (PD)	(6) Annual Total Cost [(4) + (5)]
50	2,880	50	2,930	129,600	132,530
100	1,440	100	1,540	129,600	131,140
150	960	150	1,110	129,600	130,710
200	720	200	920	129,600	130,520
250	576	250	826	129,600	130,426
300	480	300	780	129,600	130,380
350	411	350	761	129,600	130,361
400	360	400	760	129,600	130,360
450	320	450	770	129,600	130,370
500	288	500	788	129,600	130,388
550	262	550	812	129,600	130,412
600	240	600	840	129,600	130,440
650	222	650	872	129,600	130,472
700	206	700	906	129,600	130,506
750	192	750	942	129,600	130,542
800	180	800	980	129,600	130,580

Note: All costs in dollars

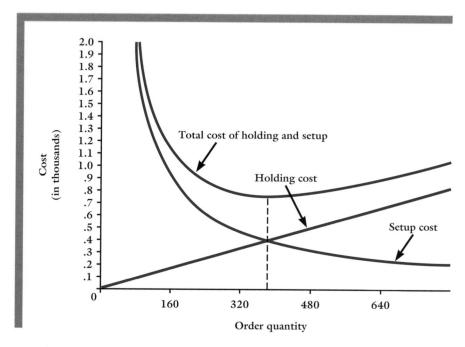

FIGURE 13.4 **Warehouse Tire Distributors: inventory costs as a function of order quantity (Example 13.4)**

or

the EOQ formula

$$Q^\star = \sqrt{\frac{2DS}{H}}.$$

(Technically, this formula results from taking the derivative of the total cost equation with respect to the order quantity, setting it to zero, and solving for Q. The remainder of the models are derived in the same way.)

Figure 13.5 shows the general cost curve. Notice that the total cost curve, which is the sum of holding costs and ordering costs plus the cost of the units, has a minimum point, $TC^\star$. The order quantity associated with this minimum cost $TC^\star$ is the economic order quantity (EOQ), $Q^\star$, as given earlier. Finding $Q^\star$ is the major decision required for setting up continuous review systems. For model I, $Q^\star$ will always be at the point where annual holding costs and annual setup (ordering) costs are equal, as the figure shows.

Let us consider the computation of the EOQ.

Example 13.5   The Aman Painting Company consumes 58 gallons of paint per day, at a price of $5 per gallon. Assuming that the company works 251 days per year, the annual consumption is 14,558 gallons. The holding cost is $4 per gallon per year, and the order cost is $22 per order. Compute the optimal order quantity and the total cost.

The first step is to find the EOQ. From the formula, we have

$$Q^* = \sqrt{\frac{2DS}{H}} = \sqrt{\frac{2 \times 14{,}558 \times 22}{4}} = 400 \text{ gallons per order (rounded off)}.$$

Each order placed is for 400 gallons of paint. The number of orders per year is D/Q, or about 36, so orders are placed about 3 times per month. The actual time between orders is Q/D, or .027 years. This means that an order is placed every 6.9 (working) days, based on the working year of 251 days.

The total cost is

$$TC = PD + \frac{HQ}{2} + \frac{SD}{Q}$$

$$= (\$5 \times 14{,}558) + \frac{(\$4 \times 400)}{2} + \frac{(\$22 \times 14{,}558)}{400}$$

$$= \$72{,}790 + \$800 + \$800.69$$

$$= \$74{,}390.69.$$

The holding cost and the ordering cost are essentially equal, as should be expected for the optimal order quantity.

Transparency Master 13.3: General Cost Curve.

FIGURE 13.5 **General total cost curve (model I)**

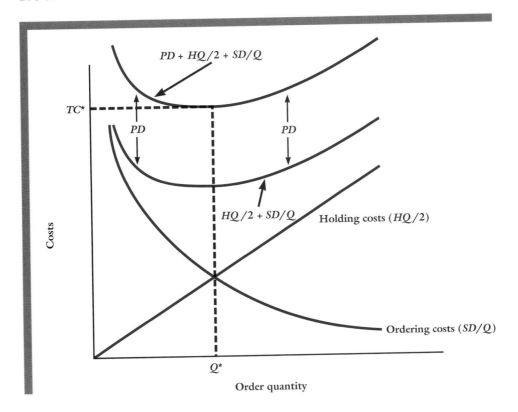

SENSITIVITY

One of the determining factors of the optimal order quantity is the demand. Although we have assumed that the demand is known, this is not typically the case. For this reason, we need to have some indication of how sensitive the costs are to the wrong order quantity being placed.

SENSITIVITY TO ORDER QUANTITY

In Table 13.3, we present the inventory costs for the Aman Painting Company. We exclude the unit costs because these are out of our control. Suppose that we make an ordering mistake and underorder by 50 percent. That is, suppose that we order 200 units at a time rather than 400 units. Thus, we see from the table that the cost will be $2,001 rather than $1,601. The ratio of costs is

$$\frac{\$2,001}{\$1,601} = 1.25.$$

Although we are making an ordering mistake of 50 percent, it is costing us only an additional 25 percent.

Now suppose that we overorder by 50 percent. The ratio of this cost to the optimal cost is

$$\frac{\$1,734}{\$1,601} = 1.083.$$

The 50 percent overorder only costs us an additional 8.3 percent. In fact, as shown in Figure 13.5, inventory systems are much more sensitive to ordering too little than to ordering too much; that is, the curve is flatter to the right of Q^* than to the left.

TABLE 13.3 Aman Painting Company: annual costs as a function of order quantity

(1) Order Quantity (Q)	(2) Annual Setup Cost (DS/Q)	(3) Annual Holding Cost (HQ/2)	(4) Inventory Cost [(2) + (3)]
50	6,406	100	6,506
100	3,203	200	3,403
150	2,135	300	2,435
200	1,601	400	2,001
250	1,281	500	1,781
300	1,068	600	1,668
350	915	700	1,615
400	801	800	1,601
450	712	900	1,612
500	641	1,000	1,641
550	582	1,100	1,682
600	534	1,200	1,734

Note: All costs in dollars

TABLE 13.4 Aman Painting Company: optimal annual cost as a function of setup cost

Setup Cost (S)	Optimal Order Quantity (Q*)	Optimal Inventory Cost $(DS/Q^*) + (HQ^*/2)$
2	121	483
4	171	683
6	209	836
8	241	965
10	270	1,079
12	296	1,182
14	319	1,277
16	341	1,365
18	362	1,448
20	382	1,526
22	400	1,601

Note: All costs in dollars

SENSITIVITY TO THE SETUP COST

In Table 13.4, we present the optimal order quantity and the optimal inventory cost for the data presented in Example 13.5, but we vary the setup cost. Suppose that we could invest in new equipment that will reduce the setup cost by slightly less than one half, or to $12 per order. This means that the order quantity can be reduced to 296. We will save holding costs because of the reduction in order size, and we will save setup costs because they will have been lowered. Then the annual inventory cost will be lowered to $1,182. This is a savings of $419 per year compared to $1,601. Thus, if the net present value savings exceed the cost of the investment that yields the savings, the new system should be purchased. This reduction in setup costs or setup times is a basic principle of the just-in-time (JIT) inventory philosophy.

relationship between setup costs and just-in-time

QUANTITY DISCOUNTS

A major assumption of the EOQ models is that the purchase price per unit is constant, regardless of the number of units that are purchased. As a result, the purchase price does not enter into the calculations for the optimal order quantity.

purchase price assumption

There are many instances, however, when this assumption is not valid. Most vendors, in attempting to keep their best customers happy, will provide inducements to large purchasers of their products. These inducements often are in the form of price discounts. To avoid any appearance of favoritism toward one customer over another, the discounts are formally incorporated in the vendor's published price structure and are available to all customers.

In addition to keeping good customers happy, there are other benefits to the producer who offers quantity discounts. Customers will place larger orders, which means that the company can have longer production runs with fewer costly setups. Furthermore, the demand estimate is more accurate with larger orders.

Teaching Suggestion 13.6: Discount Structure. See the Instructor's Section for details.

The formal price break scheme might appear as follows.

price schedule

Quantity Purchased	Price per Unit
1–39 units	$20.00
40 or more units	$17.50

In this case, if fewer than 40 units are purchased at one time, the cost is $20 per unit. But if 40 or more units are purchased, the cost is only $17.50 per unit. The price break, Q_d (for quantity discount), is 40. The **price break** is defined as the amount that must be purchased in order to take advantage of a lower price.

For some items, the price structure may include more than one price break. Consider the following extension of the previous example.

Quantity Purchased	Price per Unit
1–39 units	$20.00
40–59 units	17.50
60 or more units	16.00

This time, there are two price breaks—at 40 and at 60.

It seems logical that, if price breaks are available, the change in price should be considered when determining the optimal order quantity. However, we have seen that, regardless of the price, the total cost curve has a minimum point that determines the EOQ. Figure 13.6 illustrates the structure of this cost curve for the case of a single price break. The first thing to notice in this figure is that there are now two total cost curves, one for each price. Of course, there is really only one total cost curve in effect at any time, so the upper curve is in effect for order quantities that are less than Q_d,

FIGURE 13.6 Total cost curve for quantity discounts

Transparency Master 13.4: Quantity Discounts.

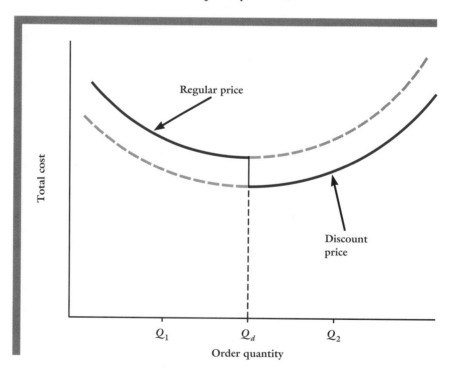

such as Q_1, and the lower curve is in effect for order quantities that are at or above Q_d, such as Q_2.

Because identifying the cost curve (price) that is in effect is very important, we use a solid line to show the actual total cost curve that is in effect for the different order quantities. As you can see, a customer purchasing Q_1 units must pay the regular price, while a customer purchasing Q_2 units receives a discount.

identify cost curve in effect

To determine the optimal order quantity for this quantity discount case, the key is still the EOQ, despite the fact that it fails to consider the price. Figure 13.7 shows the three cases that may occur. In case (a), the EOQ, Q^*, is large enough that it will take advantage of the lower cost for the item. Because Q^* minimizes the total costs other than price and also takes advantage of the lower (in this case, the lowest) price, Q^* must be the optimal order quantity. This is the simplest case. In cases (b) and (c), Q^* is less than Q_d, so the higher price is in effect at Q^*. These two cases identify the trade-off that must be made when a quantity discount is offered: If Q^* minimizes the ordering and holding costs and Q_d minimizes the purchasing costs, which should be the order quantity? The order quantity that yields the lower total cost should be selected and, by looking at the figure, Q_d is chosen in case (b) and Q^* is chosen in case (c).

The analysis of Figure 13.7 suggests a sequence of steps that can be followed to solve the problem of determining order quantity.

Step 1. Compute the EOQ using $Q^* = \sqrt{2DS/H}$.

Step 2. Compute the total cost for the EOQ and all price break points above the EOQ.

Step 3. Select the order quantity that yields the minimum total cost.

steps for quantity discount problem

The listed procedure solves the problem posed by quantity discounts, but you may be wondering why an order quantity greater than Q_d could not be a possible choice unless it is the EOQ. In parts (b) and (c) of Figure 13.7, the total cost rises past Q_d, so Q_d is the most that should be ordered. In part (a), the total cost decreases past Q_d to Q^*, which is why Q^* is given by the EOQ. The reason that no more than Q_d is desirable is that, as the order quantity increases past Q^*, the total inventory costs rise. At Q_d, the inventory costs are still rising (not optimal), but the decrease in purchase costs is larger than the deviation from the optimal inventory costs. At any point greater than Q_d, however, the inventory costs are higher still, while the purchase costs stay the same. So no further savings can be achieved past Q_d.

Let us consider an example that demonstrates the application of quantity discounts.

Example 13.6 Prince Electronics purchases videocassette recorders at $350 per VCR. The holding cost is $35 per unit per year, the ordering cost is $120 per order, and sales are steady at 400 per month. The company's supplier decides to offer price breaks for larger orders, resulting in the following price structure.

Quantity Purchased	Price per Unit
1–99 units	$350
100–199 units	325
200 or more units	300

Prince Electronics wishes to find the optimal order quantity and the minimum cost.

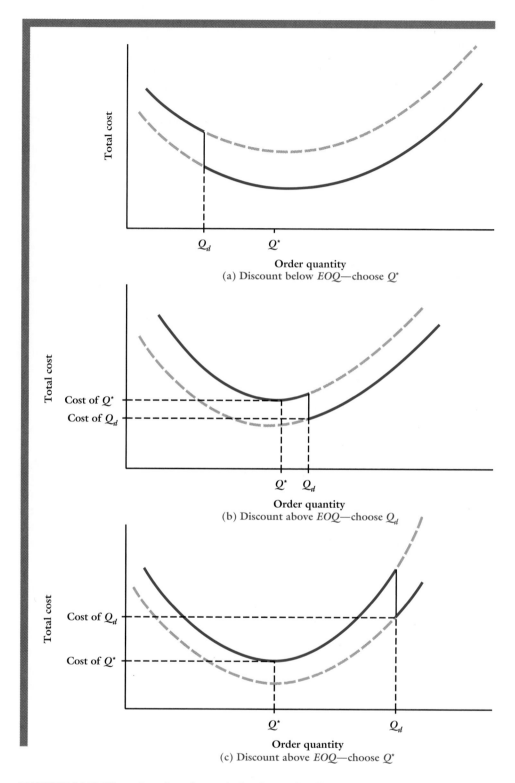

FIGURE 13.7   Three situations for analysis of quantity discounts

Step 1. $Q^* = \sqrt{\dfrac{2DS}{H}} = \sqrt{\dfrac{2 \times (400 \times 12) \times \$120}{\$35}} = 181.42,$

which we round to 181. (Notice that, because the holding cost is annual, the demand used in the formula must be annualized—that is, multiplied by 12.)

Step 2. There is a price break at 100, which is less than 181. There also is a price break at 200, which is greater than 181. Therefore, we have to consider the total cost of ordering 181 units versus the total cost of ordering 200 units. (We do not need to consider ordering 100 units, because this is below the EOQ.)

$$TC_{181} = (4,800 \times \$325) + \frac{(\$35 \times 181)}{2} + \frac{(\$120 \times 4,800)}{181}$$

$$= \$1,560,000 + \$3,168 + \$3,182 = \$1,566,350$$

We note that the difference between the holding cost ($3,168) and the setup cost ($3,182) is due to our rounding the EOQ from 181.41 to 181.

$$TC_{200} = (4,800 \times \$300) + \frac{(\$35 \times 200)}{2} + \frac{(\$120 \times 4,800)}{200}$$

$$= \$1,440,000 + \$3,500 + \$2,880 = \$1,446,380$$

Step 3. Order 200 units, because the total cost of ordering that quantity is less than the total cost that results from the use of Q^*. ■

The price paid for this order is $300 per unit. Notice that the comparison of ordering 181 units versus ordering 200 units is the same as case (b) in Figure 13.7. Had we compared ordering 100 units with ordering 181 units, the comparable scenario would have been case (a).

In the previous example, the holding cost was fixed at $35. As we indicated earlier in the chapter, the holding cost often is given as a percentage of the unit cost. If this is the case, then the economic order quantity changes when the price changes, and these changes must be taken into consideration when using quantity discounts. Consider the following example, where holding costs vary as a function of the price.

holding cost as percentage of unit cost

| **Example 13.7**   Prince Electronics has been using a $35 holding cost for an item priced at $350. In light of the discount the supplier is offering, Prince Electronics wishes to use a 10 percent holding cost rather than the fixed $35 holding cost. What is the optimal order quantity, and what is the optimal cost?

We begin by examining three different economic order quantities—one for each price. In the following formulas, notice that the holding cost is the only figure that changes.

$$Q_a^* = \sqrt{\frac{2(4,800 \times \$120)}{.10 \times \$350}} = \sqrt{\frac{2(4,800 \times \$120)}{35}} = 181$$

$$Q_b^* = \sqrt{\frac{2(4,800 \times \$120)}{.10 \times \$325}} = \sqrt{\frac{2(4,800 \times \$120)}{32.5}} = 188$$

$$Q_c^* = \sqrt{\frac{2(4,800 \times \$120)}{.10 \times \$300}} = \sqrt{\frac{2(4,800 \times \$120)}{30}} = 196$$

$Q_a{}^*$ is the optimal order quantity based on a price of \$350 per unit, because the holding cost is $.10 \times \$350 = 35$. However, $Q_a{}^* = 181$ and, at 181 units, the price is \$325, not \$350. This means that $Q_a{}^*$ does not make sense and can be discarded. $Q_b{}^*$ is based on a price of \$325 and, because this is the price if we order 188 units, $Q_b{}^*$ is a possible solution. $Q_c{}^*$ is based on a \$300 price, but because $Q_c{}^* = 196$, which generates a different price, $Q_c{}^*$ is not feasible. Thus, of the three EOQs, the only feasible one is 188. Therefore, we need to compare the total cost of ordering 188 units with the total cost of ordering 200 units.

$$TC_{188} = (4,800 \times \$325) + \frac{.10(\$325 \times 188)}{2} + \frac{(4,800 \times \$120)}{188}$$

$$= \$1,560,000 + \$3,055 + \$3,064 = \$1,566,119$$

$$TC_{200} = (4,800 \times \$300) + \frac{.10(\$300 \times 200)}{2} + \frac{(4,800 \times \$120)}{200}$$

$$= \$1,440,000 + \$3,000 + \$2,880 = \$1,445,880$$

Again, the answer is to order 200 units. (Notice that the cost is less than the cost in Example 13.6, because the holding cost has been reduced from \$35 to \$30.)   ∎

THE ECONOMIC PRODUCTION QUANTITY MODEL

finite replenishment rate

For our second model (model II), no shortages are allowed, as in the first model, but, unlike the first model, the replenishment rate is finite. Figure 13.8 shows how the inventory levels vary with time for this model. Because the finite replenishment rate usually implies a production rate, model II usually is referred to as an **economic production quantity model** (EPQ) or **economic lot size model** (ELS). Within the context of this discussion, however, the EPQ model is merely an extension of the EOQ model.

The total cost analysis for the EPQ model is exactly the same as for the EOQ model. Purchase (or production) costs plus holding costs plus ordering costs yield total costs. The purchase price is the same (PD), as is the ordering cost (SD/Q), because the number of units required and the number of orders per year are determined in the same manner.

The cost that changes is the annual holding cost, because the parameter that changes is the average inventory level. If the replenishment rate is p (units per day) and the demand rate (in units per day) is d (D divided by the number of days), the inventory level increases at a rate of $p - d$ units per day during production. The effect of using the inventory at the same time that replenishment is taking place is that the maximum inventory level will be less than Q (see Figure 13.8). Consequently, the

average inventory is less

average inventory level is less than it was in the EOQ model for the same Q. This should alert us to the fact that, given the same costs as in model I, the EPQ, Q^*, will be higher now.

Teaching Suggestion 13.7: Utilization. See the Instructor's Section for details.

From Figure 13.8, we know that $T = Q/d$ (in days). Furthermore, T_p is defined as the time required to produce Q units, or

production time per cycle

$$T_p = \frac{Q}{p}.$$

Transparency Master 13.5:
The EPQ Model.

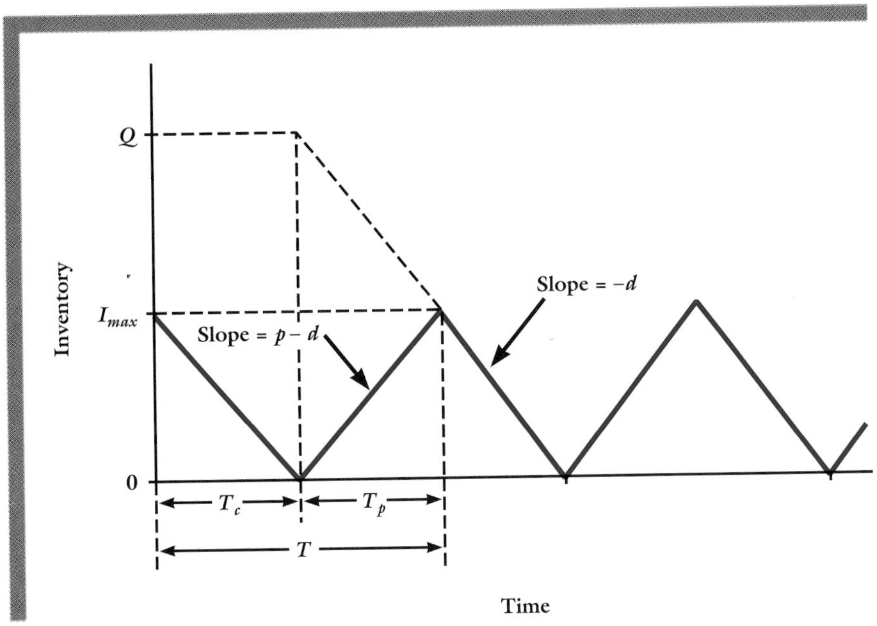

FIGURE 13.8 Sawtooth curve, model II

Also, we define T_c as the time when no production takes place. Because

$$T_c + T_p = T,$$

we have

$$T_c = T - T_p = \frac{Q}{d} - \frac{Q}{p} = \frac{pQ - dQ}{pd}.$$

Therefore,

$$T_c = \frac{Q}{d}\left(\frac{p - d}{p}\right).$$

The inventory required during the consumption period is I_{max} or $T_c \times d$.

$$I_{max} = d \times \frac{Q}{d}\left(\frac{p - d}{p}\right)$$

$$I_{max} = Q\left(\frac{p - d}{p}\right) \qquad \text{**maximum inventory**}$$

Because the inventory rises and falls at a constant rate, the average inventory is given by $I_{max}/2$. Therefore, the total cost equation is

EPQ total cost

$$TC = PD + \frac{HQ}{2}\left(\frac{p - d}{p}\right) + \frac{SD}{Q}.$$

Setting the holding and setup costs equal yields

$$\frac{HQ}{2}\left(\frac{p - d}{p}\right) = \frac{SD}{Q},$$

which in turn yields

the EPQ (ELS) formula

$$Q^\star = \sqrt{\frac{2DS}{H}} \times \sqrt{\frac{p}{p - d}}.$$

Example 13.8   Bala Aerospace Corporation can produce subcomponents at a rate of 300 per day, and it uses these subcomponents at a rate of 12,500 per year (of 250 working days). Holding costs are $2 per item per year, and ordering costs are $30 per order.

(a) What is the economic production quantity?
(b) How many production runs per year will be made?
(c) What will be the maximum inventory level?
(d) What percentage of time will the inventory system be operating in a pure consumption mode?

(a) $Q^\star = \sqrt{\dfrac{2DS}{H}} \times \sqrt{\dfrac{p}{p - d}} = \sqrt{\dfrac{2(12,500)(30)}{2}} \times \sqrt{\dfrac{300}{300 - 50}} = 671$

All entries in this equation are given explicitly, except for d, which is $12,500/250 = 50$.

(b) The number of production runs per year is

$$n = \frac{D}{Q} = \frac{12,500}{671} = 18.63.$$

(The length of time between production runs is $250/18.63 = 13.42$ working days.)

(c) $I_{max} = Q\left(\dfrac{p - d}{p}\right) = 559$

(d) $T_c = \dfrac{I_{max}}{d} = \dfrac{559}{50} = 11.18$ days in pure consumption mode

$T_p = \dfrac{Q}{p} = \dfrac{671}{300} = 2.24$ days in production mode in each cycle

$T = T_c + T_p = 11.18 + 2.24 = 13.42$ days per cycle

Note that this agrees with what was found in part (b). The percentage of time in pure consumption is

$$\frac{T_c}{T} = \frac{11.18}{13.42} = .833, \text{ or } 83.3 \text{ percent of the time.}$$ ∎

The EPQ model is a slightly more complex model than the EOQ model. As such, the EPQ model has a few additional considerations of concern to the inventory manager or planner. First, it has already been shown that the maximum inventory level for which planning must be done (design of sufficient shelf space, for example) is less than it was in the EOQ model. For the EOQ model, $I_{max} = Q$. In this model, the maximum inventory level is

$$I_{max} = Q\left(\frac{p-d}{p}\right).$$

When calculated directly from the costs (without calculating Q), it is

$$I_{max} = \sqrt{\frac{2DS}{H}} \times \sqrt{\frac{p-d}{p}}.$$

The second additional consideration of the EPQ model concerns the amount of time when production is occurring and the amount of time when the inventory system is operating in a pure consumption mode. This consideration is especially important when the production planner is dealing with more than one item, each of which has an EPQ to be produced and each of which shares some or all of the same production equipment and personnel. (Chapter 15 contains a discussion of this production scheduling problem.) Figure 13.8 shows these times as T_p and T_c. The time to produce one lot in the amount Q is

$$T_p = \frac{Q}{p},$$

or

$$T_p = \frac{I_{max}}{p-d}.$$

The time during which the inventory is decreasing (pure consumption) and machines are available for other items is

$$T_c = \frac{I_{max}}{d},$$

or

$$T_c = T - T_p = \frac{Q}{d} - \frac{Q}{p}.$$

Example 13.9 What happens when $p = d$? What happens when $p < d$? When the production rate equals the demand rate, it should be clear that no inventory level will ever build up and that the item must be produced at all times. There is no time when the system is in a state of pure consumption. From the formulas,

$$I_{max} = Q\left(\frac{p-d}{p}\right).$$

If $p - d = 0$, $I_{max} = 0$. Also,

$$T_c = \frac{Q}{d} - \frac{Q}{p}.$$

With $d = p$, $T_c = 0$. Finally,

$$Q^\star = \sqrt{\frac{2DS}{H}} \times \sqrt{\frac{p}{0}},$$

or $Q^\star$ = infinity (always produce).

Similarly, the case of $d > p$ is nonsensical. Production would fall farther and farther behind demand. The practical solution is to obtain additional sources of production. Because this solution relates more to production scheduling and capacity planning, our inventory analysis is limited to the practical case where $p > d$. ■|

Example 13.10   What is p in the EOQ model?

There is no value of p used anywhere in the equations of the EOQ model. However, the definition of this model is that it has an instantaneous replenishment, or an infinite rate of replenishment. Therefore, p must be infinity (∞). Using the formula for the EPQ for demonstration,

$$Q^\star = \sqrt{\frac{2DS}{H}} \times \sqrt{\frac{\infty}{\infty}} = \sqrt{\frac{2DS}{H}},$$

which is the EOQ for model I. Thus, model I is really just a special case of model II, with $p = \infty$. ■|

MODELS WITH SHORTAGES

MODEL III

In terms of the replenishment rate, model III is the same as model I; that is, an instantaneous replenishment is assumed. The difference is that shortages are allowed in model III, which means that a corresponding shortage cost must be provided. In the **backorders vs. lost sales** shortage situation in this model, the demand that cannot be satisfied is backordered, to be met after the next shipment arrives. This is very different from the case of lost sales, where the customer does not return, thereby reducing demand.

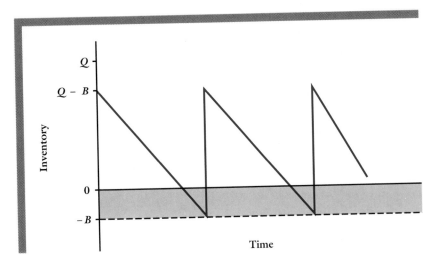

FIGURE 13.9 Sawtooth curve, model III

The inventory levels for model III are shown in Figure 13.9. Notice that the maximum shortage is B and that the maximum inventory is $Q - B$, which means that Figure 13.9 is the same as Figure 13.3, but with all inventory levels reduced by the amount B. Again, common sense should tell us that, because inventory levels and the associated holding costs will be lower than in model I, the order quantity can be increased and orders can be placed less often.

To analyze this situation, let us define the cost of a backorder per unit per year, G. This cost is defined in terms of units (dollars per item per year), which is similar to the definition of the inventory holding cost. Also, the total cost for this model is similar to the total cost for model I, with the addition of costs due to shortages.

$$TC = \text{purchase costs} + \text{holding costs} + \text{ordering costs} + \text{shortage costs}$$

There is no change in the purchase and the order costs. However, the holding cost changes due to the difference in the calculation of the average inventory level for this situation. The average inventory level is

$$\frac{(Q - B)^2}{2Q}.$$

Similarly, the average backorder position is

$$\frac{B^2}{2Q}.$$

Consequently, the total cost is

$$TC = PD + \frac{H(Q - B)^2}{2Q} + \frac{SD}{Q} + \frac{GB^2}{2Q}.$$

model III—total cost

Teaching Suggestion 13.8: Use of These Models. See the Instructor's Section for details.

To obtain the EOQ, we differentiate the total cost with respect both to Q and to B and solve two simultaneous equations, which yield

formula for EOQ with shortages

$$Q^\star = \sqrt{\frac{2DS}{H}} \times \sqrt{\frac{H + G}{G}}.$$

Because $H + G$ is more than G, the second square root is greater than 1, leading to the increased Q, which was expected.

The determination of the maximum number of demands outstanding, B, is

$$B^\star = \frac{HQ}{H + G}.$$

The maximum inventory level $(Q - B)$ has been given already. The length of the cycle, T, is Q/D, as it was previously. The extra concern with this model is the percentage of time that the company is out of stock. This is B/Q, or $H/(H + G)$.

If no shortages are allowed, the decision regarding percentage of time out of stock should be based on the presence of intolerably high shortage costs. However, this decision often is a political one within a company, so it should be recognized that $G = \infty$ leads to model I, where no shortages are allowed.

Example 13.11   The Aman Painting Company (see Example 13.5) estimates that it has a shortage cost of $10 per gallon per year. Recalculate the order quantity and the total cost.

$$Q^\star = \sqrt{\frac{2DS}{H}} \times \sqrt{\frac{H + G}{G}} = \sqrt{\frac{2 \times 14{,}558 \times 22}{4}} \times \sqrt{\frac{4 + 10}{10}} = 473$$

$$B^\star = Q\left(\frac{H}{H + G}\right) = 473 \times \left(\frac{4}{4 + 10}\right) = 135$$

$$I_{max} = Q - B = 473 - 135 = 338$$

$$TC = PD + \frac{H(Q - B)^2}{2Q} + \frac{SD}{Q} + \frac{GB^2}{2Q}$$

$$= [\$5 \times 14{,}558] + [\$4 \times (473 - 135)^2/(2 \times 473)]$$

$$+ \;[(\$22 \times 14{,}558)/473] + [\$10 \times (135)^2/(2 \times 473)]$$

$$= \$72{,}790 + \$483 + \$677 + \$193$$

$$= \$74{,}143$$

setup = holding + shortage

Notice that the setup cost ($677) is equal (taking the effects of rounding into consideration) to the sum of the holding and shortage costs ($483 + $193). This is always the case.   ∎⌐

MODEL IV

Model IV is the most general of the four models presented. In fact, models I, II, and III are all special cases of model IV, which allows shortages (finite shortage cost) and

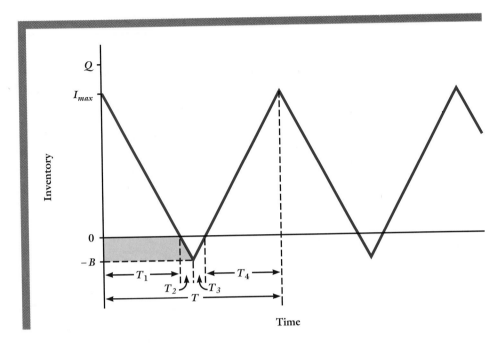

FIGURE 13.10 Sawtooth curve, model IV

has a finite rate of replenishment. In short, models II and III each generalized one assumption from model I, but model IV includes both generalizations simultaneously. The inventory levels over time for this model are shown in Figure 13.10. Results for this model appear in Table 13.5.

The cycle, T, was broken down into T_c and T_p for model II and into inventory and shortage times in model III. For this model, all four times are important. As shown in Figure 13.10,

$$T = T_c + T_p$$
$$= (T_1 + T_2) + (T_3 + T_4),$$

where

T_1 = time of pure consumption while there is inventory on hand;

T_2 = time of pure consumption while there is a shortage situation;

T_3 = time of producing while there is a shortage situation; and

T_4 = time of producing while there is inventory on hand.

These times can be calculated as follows.

$$T_1 = I_{max}/d$$
$$T_2 = B/d$$
$$T_3 = B/(p - d)$$
$$T_4 = I_{max}/(p - d)$$

TABLE 13.5 Summary of continuous review models

Model	Shortage Cost (G)	Rate of Production (P)	Optimal Order Quantity (Q*)
I	Infinite	Infinite	$\sqrt{\dfrac{2DS}{H}}$
II	Infinite	Finite	$\sqrt{\dfrac{2DS}{H}}\sqrt{\dfrac{p}{p-d}}$
III	Finite	Infinite	$\sqrt{\dfrac{2DS}{H}}\sqrt{\dfrac{H+G}{G}}$
IV	Finite	Finite	$\sqrt{\dfrac{2DS}{H}}\sqrt{\dfrac{H+G}{G}}\sqrt{\dfrac{p}{p-d}}$

D = demand rate (units/time)
d = daily demand rate (units/day)
H = holding cost (dollars/unit-time), where time must match demand
S = setup or fixed cost (dollars/order)
p = daily production rate (units/day)

Models III and IV are seldom used in practice. Shortages usually are handled by means of a specified service level because of the difficulty of obtaining an accurate estimate of the shortage cost. It would be wrong, however, to think that one avoids specifying a shortage cost by using the service level approach. As we will show later, the specification of a service level carries with it an implied shortage cost. The models are presented here to emphasize the link between the EOQ models and the service level approach to safety stocks, which is presented later. The models are presented here, instead of later in the chapter, to emphasize some of the many assumptions that can be built into an EOQ model and to show how these assumptions can be incorporated into the model. Table 13.5 summarizes the formulas for the four models.

REORDER POINTS

To this point, we have been concerned only with the order quantity—the Q in the Q, R policy. To complete the inventory policy, we must know when to reorder. This is specified by a **reorder point,** R. The reorder point depends on several factors. Among these are the lead time, the demand distribution, and the desire for safety stock.

LEAD TIMES

Denote by L the **lead time** in days between the time an order is placed and the time the units arrive. Figure 13.11 is the EOQ model with a lead time included. The order

Maximum Inventory Level (I_{max})	Maximum Backorders (B)	Cost (TC)
Q	None	$PD + \dfrac{DS}{Q} + \dfrac{HQ}{2}$
$Q\left(\dfrac{p-d}{p}\right)$	None	$PD + \dfrac{DS}{Q} + \dfrac{HQ}{2}\left(\dfrac{p-d}{p}\right)$
$Q\left(\dfrac{G}{H+G}\right)$	$Q\left(\dfrac{H}{H+G}\right)$	$PD + \dfrac{DS}{Q} + \dfrac{H(Q-B)^2}{2Q} + \dfrac{GB^2}{2Q}$
$\dfrac{Q\left(\dfrac{p-d}{p}\right)G}{H+G}$	$\dfrac{Q\left(\dfrac{p-d}{p}\right)H}{H+G}$	$PD + \dfrac{DS}{Q} + \dfrac{H\left[Q\left(\dfrac{p-d}{p}\right)-B\right]^2}{2Q\left(\dfrac{p-d}{p}\right)} + \dfrac{GB^2}{2Q\left(\dfrac{p-d}{p}\right)}$

P = unit price (dollars/unit)

G = shortage cost (dollars/unit-time), where time must match demand

Q = order quantity

B = maximum amount short

FIGURE 13.11 Basic EOQ model with lead time

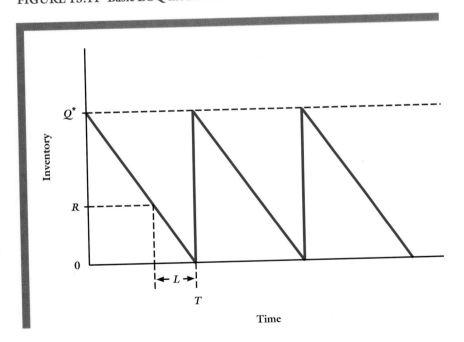

Transparency Master 13.6: Lead Times.

for Q^* units needs to be placed, not at T, but at L days before T if the order is to arrive when the inventory runs out at time T. Rather than express the reorder point in days, we express it in units. During the lead time, the daily demand rate is d. Therefore, at the lead time, the amount of inventory on hand should be Ld. We can now set the reorder point:

reorder point

$$R = Ld.$$

The following example demonstrates both the reorder point and the complete inventory policy.

Example 13.12 The MIS department of Jones Department Store uses diskettes at a rate of 4,000 per year (250 working days). The annual holding cost is $2 per diskette and the cost of placing an order is $10. It takes the vendor 5 days from the time the order is placed to deliver the diskettes. What is the complete inventory policy (amount to order and time to order)?

The complete policy is given by Q^* and R. The order quantity is

$$Q^* = \sqrt{\frac{2DS}{H}} = \sqrt{\frac{2(4,000)(10)}{2}} = 200.$$

The reorder point is given by Ld, where d is the daily demand rate. In this example, the daily demand rate is given by $d = 4,000/250 = 16$ diskettes per day. Therefore,

$$R = Ld = 5 \times 16 = 80.$$

Teaching Suggestion 13.9: Ease of Execution. See the Instructor's Section for details.

The complete Q, R policy is given as follows: Order 200 diskettes whenever the inventory level drops to 80 diskettes. ∎

SAFETY STOCK

demand assumption

The assumption of a known, constant demand rate is now dropped. We still assume that the demand rate does not change over time; that is, the *expected demand*, or the average, does not change. But we allow for the possibility of a variable rate of demand. A simple discussion will illustrate this point.

A family's drive from Philadelphia to New York is exactly 200 miles round trip. If their car gets 25 miles per gallon, how much gasoline is needed in the tank at the start of the trip?

Clearly, eight gallons should be in the tank. But the family's car does not always get 25 miles per gallon. The prudent action, therefore, is to make sure that, although an initial inventory of 8 gallons is required, there will be more than 8 gallons in the tank at the start of the trip.

Maintaining **safety stock** is similar to buying more gasoline than necessary; it is merely the formalization of common, everyday practice. Essentially, it amounts to a proper exercise of caution. People who have a nine o'clock appointment plan to arrive a little early in case of delays. In inventory, similarly cautious practice is used everywhere, even where the kind of formal inventory analysis presented in this chapter is not employed. The inventory manager decides how much is needed and orders that amount plus "a little extra," just in case. This "little extra" is the safety stock. In any situation where a risk is present, steps should be taken to reduce that risk.

Figure 13.12 shows the inventory levels over time with no safety stock and probabilistic demand. When demand during the lead time is greater than the expected demand, there are shortages. When demand is less than expected, the new order may arrive before inventory is depleted. If R is the median, then shortages will occur in half of the cycles—an intolerable state, unless shortage costs are low. This probability of a shortage, $P(s)$, is very important, because it will be used to help determine the optimal size of the safety stock. The complement of $P(s)$, of course, is the **service level,** the measure of reliability for the inventory system.

Teaching Suggestion 13.10: Definition of Service Level. See the Instructor's Section for details.

Figure 13.13 differs from Figure 13.12 only in that safety stock (SS) has been added. Notice that the inventory system operates in the same way, with or without the safety stock. The order quantity is the same, and the time cycle is the same. Only the service level and the reorder point change. Because there are fewer shortages, the service level improves. The reorder point is increased by the amount of the safety stock.

There is, of course, one additional nonoperational difference: the holding cost. The average inventory increases by the amount of the safety stock, SS, from $Q/2$ to $SS + Q/2$, because the safety stock is always on hand. It is this extra holding cost that is compared to the shortage cost to arrive at an optimal service level, as we shall see later. The reorder point also increases by the amount of the safety stock. As a result,

$$R = \text{expected lead time demand} + SS.$$

reorder point with safety stock

Let us look at the calculation of the safety stock for a few examples and how the size of the safety stock is related to the specified service level.

Example 13.13 During the past fifty lead times (the reason for the use of lead time demands will be explained in the next section) demands for a product have been as follows.

Demand	Frequency
2	1
3	5
4	15
5	17
6	8
7	3
8	$\dfrac{1}{50}$

What safety stock should be kept to achieve the indicated service level?

(a) 99 percent
(b) 95 percent
(c) 90 percent
(d) 50 percent
(e) 25 percent

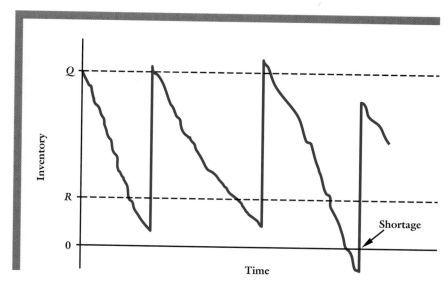

FIGURE 13.12   Probabilistic demand

The first step is to calculate the probability of meeting the demand given some reorder point. The real problem, from an operational viewpoint, is to determine the reorder point, because it has two components (the expected lead time demand and the safety stock) built into it. Obviously, the service level is 0 if our reorder point is 0 or 1, because at least two items will be required before the order arrives. Similarly, the service level for a reorder point of 8 is 1, or 100 percent, because the given probability

FIGURE 13.13   Probabilistic demand with safety stock

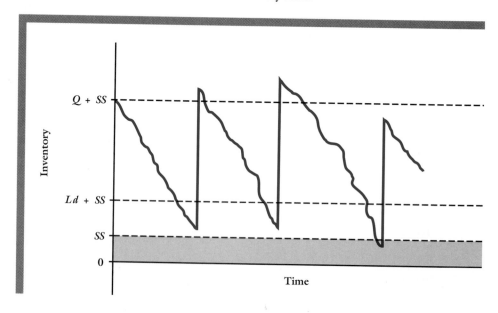

distribution says that there is never a lead time demand greater than 8. The service levels for each of the possible reorder points (from 2 to 8) are given in the following table.

Lead Time Demand (m)	Frequency	Probability	Service Level	Probability of Shortage [$P(D > m)$]
2	1	1/50 = .02	.02	.98
3	5	5/50 = .10	.12	.88
4	15	15/50 = .30	.42	.58
5	17	17/50 = .34	.76	.24
6	8	8/50 = .16	.92	.08
7	3	3/50 = .06	.98	.02
8	1	1/50 .02	1.00	0
	50	1.00		

use of discrete distribution

We can use the data in the preceding table to find the service levels.

(a) To achieve a service level of 99 percent, a reorder point of 8 is required. A reorder point of 7 yields a service level of 98 percent, which fails to meet the specification.

(b) A reorder point of 7 (SL = 98 percent) is needed to achieve the 95-percent service level.

(c) A reorder point of 6 (SL = 92 percent) is required to achieve the 90-percent target.

(d) A reorder point of 5 (SL = 76 percent) is required to achieve the 50-percent target.

(e) A reorder point of 4 (SL = 42 percent) is required to achieve the 25-percent target.

The safety stock has not been calculated yet. Each reorder point is the sum of the expected lead time demand and the safety stock. Therefore, it is necessary to calculate the expected lead time demand, $\overline{m}$.

$$\overline{m} = (.02 \times 2) + (.10 \times 3) + (.30 \times 4) + (.34 \times 5)$$
$$+ (.16 \times 6) + (.06 \times 7) + (.02 \times 8) = 4.78$$

Now we can compute the safety stocks.

(a) $SS = R - m = 8 - 4.78 = 3.22$ items
(b) $SS = 7 - 4.78 = 2.22$ items
(c) $SS = 6 - 4.78 = 1.22$ items
(d) $SS = 5 - 4.78 = .22$ items
(e) $SS = 4 - 4.78 = -.78$ items   ◼

A negative safety stock, as obtained in (e), is used if either the shortage cost is very low or the desired service level is very low. The negative safety stock is used to increase the probability of a shortage, just as the (positive) safety stock is used to increase the service level.

use of normal distribution

Example 13.14   Looking at the data from the previous example, an analyst decides (somewhat erroneously) that the lead time demand is normally distributed, with a mean of 5 and a standard deviation of 1. What are the safety stocks and reorder points for the 99-percent, 95-percent, 90-percent, 50-percent, and 25-percent service levels?

The size of the safety stock for the case of the normal distribution is

$$SS = z\sigma,$$

where σ is the standard deviation and z is the standard normal variate obtained from Appendix B2. For the various service levels, the safety stocks and reorder points are as follows.

SL	z	SS	R = m + SS
.99	2.33	2.33 × 1 = 2.33	5 + 2.33 = 7.33, or 8
.95	1.64	1.64	5 + 1.64 = 6.64, or 7
.90	1.28	1.28	5 + 1.28 = 6.28, or 7
.50	0	0	5 + 0 = 5
.25	− .67	− .67	5 + − .67 = 4.33, or 5

use 1-tailed normal distribution

OPTIMAL SERVICE LEVELS

A marginal analysis provides the basis for determining an optimal service level; that is, the point at which the additional holding cost is balanced by the reduced shortage cost is the optimal level of safety stock. If we start with a small safety stock, the expected shortage cost will be high. As the safety stock is increased in small increments, the point at which these costs are equal can be found.

The holding cost per cycle associated with one additional unit of safety stock is $H(Q/D)$, where H is the holding cost per unit per year. The shortage cost per cycle is the shortage cost per backorder per unit of time, G, times the probability of a shortage, $P(s)$. These two costs are equal when

$$H\left(\frac{Q}{D}\right) = P(s) \times G.$$

The optimal probability of a shortage, which balances holding and shortage costs, can be expressed as

$$P(s) = \frac{HQ}{GD},$$

and, of course, the optimal service level is $1 - P(s)$, or $1 - HQ/GD$.

Once this optimal service level is known, the entire inventory system based on probabilistic demand can be completed, according to the following procedure.

Step 1. Given the necessary parameters (demand, costs), determine the EOQ as if demand is not probabilistic; that is, use the expected demand.

$$Q^* = \sqrt{\frac{2DS}{H}}$$

Step 2. Calculate the optimal probability of a shortage.

$$P(s) = \frac{HQ^*}{GD}$$

Step 3. Determine the reorder point

$$R = \overline{m} + SS,$$

where $\overline{m}$ is the expected lead time demand and SS is the safety stock. For the normal case,

$$SS = z\sigma,$$

where z is obtained from the normal table (Appendix B2) based on the probability $P(s)$.

These three steps lead to the complete development of a Q, R system with safety stock.

Example 13.15 To continue with the problem described in the two previous examples, assume that the following costs apply:

D = 500 units per year;

H = $10 per unit per year;

S = $100 per order; and

G = $20 per unit backordered.

(a) Design the appropriate Q, R system.
(b) If there are 200 working days per year, what is the lead time?

(a) **Step 1.** $Q^* = \sqrt{\dfrac{(2)(500 \times 100)}{10}} = 100$

Step 2. $P(s) = \dfrac{10 \times 100}{20 \times 500} = .1$

The optimal service level is 90 percent $(1 - .1 = .9)$.

Step 3. This step was completed in Example 13.14 (SL = 90 percent).

$$R = \overline{m} + SS = 5 + 1.28 = 6.28, \text{ or } 7$$

Order 100 units whenever the inventory is down to 7 units.

(b) Daily demand is

$$\frac{500 \text{ units}}{200 \text{ days}} = 2.5 \text{ units per day.}$$

Lead time demand is given as 5. So the lead time is

$$\frac{5}{2.5} = 2 \text{ days.} \qquad \blacksquare$$

The question still remaining is why probabilistic analysis is applied only to the lead time demand when, in fact, all of the demand is probabilistic. This question can be answered by considering the workings of the Q, R system. It does not matter how long it takes to reduce the inventory to level R. A new order is not placed until that level is reached and it is certain that no shortages will be incurred prior to this time. The randomness of demand during this time only serves to change the cycle time, so that one order period may be longer or shorter than the next. As a result, the possibility of a shortage is present only during the lead time. Therefore, the probability of a shortage in any cycle is really just the probability of a shortage during the lead time. This, of course, is only a function of the reorder point, the expected demand during lead time, and the standard deviation of that demand.

shortage cost is difficult to estimate

In the analysis of most inventory systems, a shortage cost is difficult to estimate. Also, common practice is to specify target service levels without going through a formal analysis of inventory costs. This practice, it must be recognized, implies a shortage cost. Using the equation for the optimal service level, and solving for the shortage cost, the **implied shortage cost** is

$$G = \frac{HQ}{P(s) \times D}.$$

This implied shortage cost is useful in analyzing (as opposed to designing) inventory systems and policies. For example, the implied shortage cost can be calculated if a company specifies a service level of 95 percent, uses an order quantity of Q, and H and D are known. Once this calculation has been done, the implied shortage cost can be evaluated to see if it is reasonable. If the implied shortage cost for a doughnut, for example, is \$140 for each doughnut short for one year, based on a diner's ordering policy for doughnuts, then something is clearly wrong. Less safety stock should be kept (or less doughnuts ordered). Being short one additional doughnut cannot cost the diner \$140.

Example 13.16 What is the implied shortage cost with the 99-percent service level in Example 13.15? What is the implied shortage cost with the 50-percent service level? Are these costs reasonable in light of the estimated value of \$20?

$$SL = 99 \text{ percent: } G = \frac{HQ}{P(s) \times D} = \frac{10 \times 100}{.01 \times 500} = \$200 \text{ per unit}$$

$$SL = 50 \text{ percent: } G = \frac{10 \times 100}{.5 \times 500} = \$4 \text{ per unit}$$

Given the estimate of \$20, surely neither of these costs is reasonable. Notice how fast the cost increases as the service level approaches 100 percent. This shows that service levels can be too high to be justified on a cost basis. $\qquad \blacksquare$

THE SINGLE PERIOD MODEL

A common practice is purchasing an inventory item for one period only. For this practice, the assumption that inventory can be held from one period to the next is no longer valid. At the end of the period, the item is of little or no use. For example, a Sunday newspaper is of little use on Monday, and the bread that is fresh today cannot be sold as fresh tomorrow. Even though the market will buy bread every day and the newsstand will buy newspapers, these items have a shelf life of exactly one day. Each day, then, must be evaluated as a single period model. A single period model also can be used for the commodity that is available only once per season, such as farm products (available once per year) and clothing (available for separate seasons per year).

The major question is how much to purchase (or produce or plant), given that the entire amount for the period must be purchased (or produced or planted) at one time. The risks are those associated with buying too much or too little.

increased risks

For this model, we could look again at both the deterministic and the probabilistic cases. However, no analysis is required when the demand is known. If the store will sell exactly 80 loaves of bread today, it should buy exactly 80 loaves. If the car dealership will sell 75 cars this month, it should order 75 cars. These represent the trivial cases.

The practical situation, and the reason that this problem causes concern, is that the exact demand usually is not known in advance. If too much is purchased, there will be a loss due to the cost of the unsold goods. If the amount purchased is insufficient to satisfy demand, an opportunity cost is incurred due to the lost sales. There can be no backordering in the single period problem, so this opportunity cost is, essentially, the profit that could have been made on the sale.

The goal of the analysis is to find the point at which the expected shortage cost (shortage cost times probability of being short) is equal to the expected cost of excess goods. When these are equal, the order quantity is optimal. A simple example of a classic single period problem illustrates this concept.

goal of the analysis

Example 13.17   Jeremy Decker sells the Sunday paper on the same busy street corner each week. He purchases the papers for $.75 apiece and sells them for $1.25. Toward the end of his first year, Jeremy decides to evaluate the demand distribution for the paper and use this information to arrive at a constant order quantity. Until this time, his order policy had been to order for the next week whatever amount was sold the week before. The demand distribution is as follows.

Demand	Frequency	Probability
160	3	.06
161	7	.14
162	8	.16
163	10	.20
164	12	.24
165	8	.16
166	2	.04
	50	1.00

(a) How many papers should Jeremy order?

(b) Name two factors that bring this analysis into question.

(a) First, set up a table of profits that result from each combination of orders and demands. For example, if 160 are ordered, the profit is $80 ($.50 per paper), regardless of the demand. If 161 are ordered, the profit is $80.50 if demand is 161 or greater, but $79.25 if demand is only 160 (80 for the 160 sold minus $.75 for the unsold paper). The complete table, with total expected profit on the right, follows. Of course, order sizes greater than 166 or less than 160 need not be evaluated.

Teaching Suggestion
13.11: Decision Tables.
See the Instructor's Sec-
tion for details.

| Number of Papers Ordered | Demand (Probability) | | | | | | | Expected Profit |
	160 (.06)	161 (.14)	162 (.16)	163 (.20)	164 (.24)	165 (.16)	166 (.04)	
160	$80.00	$80.00	$80.00	$80.00	$80.00	$80.00	$80.00	$80.000
161	79.25	80.50	80.50	80.50	80.50	80.50	80.50	80.425
162	78.50	79.75	81.00	81.00	81.00	81.00	81.00	80.675
163	77.75	79.00	80.25	81.50	81.50	81.50	81.50	80.725
164	77.00	78.25	79.50	80.75	82.00	82.00	82.00	80.525
165	76.25	77.50	78.75	80.00	81.25	82.50	82.50	80.025
166	75.50	76.75	78.00	79.25	80.50	81.75	83.00	79.325

The maximum expected profit is $80.725, which results from the purchase of 163 papers. Bear in mind that a profit of $80.725 will never actually be realized. Actual profits in any given week will be one of the entries in the row of the table associated with the order of 163. Over the course of many weeks, the profits will average $80.725.

(b) The first assumption that has been made is that the demand distribution for the papers is constant throughout the year. This may or may not be true. Specific data analysis is required to confirm this assumption. This data analysis should be carried out in accordance with forecasting concepts and guidelines for using forecasts presented earlier in the text.

A second possible problem area concerns the appropriateness of the data collected. If the data accurately reflect demand each week, then this estimate is fine. However, one must be careful to avoid using actual sales for demand. Sales and demand are the same only if enough papers are available to satisfy demand. If Jeremy leaves the street corner once he has sold all of his papers, he is not aware of any further demand. ∎

sales vs. demand

The previous example was solved in a very laborious manner. Let us continue with the idea of balancing shortage costs and excess costs (using a marginal analysis). If the marginal profit is *MP*, then the expected shortage cost (lost profit) is

marginal analysis

$$p \times MP,$$

where p is the probability of selling an additional item. If *ML* is the cost per unit in excess (marginal loss), then the expected excess cost for a given order quantity is

$$(1 - p) \times ML.$$

Raleigh Cycle Company

Since its beginning as a 3-man frame shop in Nottingham, England in 1887, Raleigh Cycle has expanded its global operations to become one of the largest and best known bicycle manufacturers in the world. From easy riding and cruiser bicycles, to mountain bikes and the most radical racing machines, Raleigh is the standard against which other bicycles are judged. For 105 years Raleigh has successfully guided its own career by relying upon its self-imposed criterion of quality and innovation.

Raleigh is the first manufacturer to bring production of bicycles back to the United States while other bicycle companies have moved production out of the country. Their state of the art factory in Seattle, Washington is unlike any other.

To continually improve upon its own competitive performance, Raleigh stresses innovation in its strategic planning. Extensive research and in-depth testing of prototypes has resulted in such leading edge breakthroughs as Technium.
Realizing the limitations inherent in the adhesives typically used in manufacturing their product, Raleigh worked with suppliers from the aerospace industry to develop a unique product called "toughened" epoxy.
The resulting Technium (R) process is a breakthrough in traditional bicycle manufacturing and allows Raleigh to make a high quality, affordably priced bicycle. The medals won by the U. S. Cycling Team on Technium bicycles were proof of the technological challenge met by Raleigh.

(Photographs courtesy of Raleigh Cycle Company.)

Raleigh is better able to control the entire quality of its USA-made bicycles because each step of the manufacturing process can be monitored. This includes strict inspection of incoming parts, in-process inspections, and final product audits.

The first step in the process of construction is frame building. The frame is a critical component since its geometry determines a major portion of the ride and handling characteristics. Tubing, lugs, and stays are meticulously pressed together and thermally bonded for ultimate strength. While robotics have been judiciously brought into the manufacturing process, the majority of the work is still done by a work force known by Raleigh as its "craftspeople".

After bonding, each frame is checked for perfect alignment and detailing and then put through a thorough cleaning process.

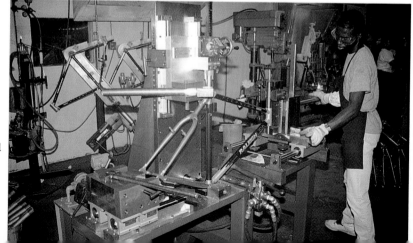

The next step is painting. Each frame receives hand applied primer, polyurethane color, graphics, and clearcoat as it progresses through this department. Each finished frameset undergoes a quality check as it leaves the paint department. From here, technicians install the headset, bottom bracket, fork, and cables. Wheel truing is done by special robots which guarantee that the wheels are perfectly trued when the bicycle leaves the facility.

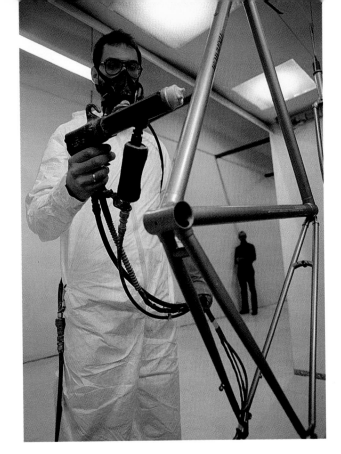

Each person in the Raleigh factory takes an inordinate amount of pride in what they do and everyone at Raleigh is responsible for quality. Manufacturing and industrial engineers supervise the process, interacting directly with the people guiding the parts of the frame together. The final quality check is performed by a highly trained, full-time employee.

Each completed bicycle is then carefully packed for shipment to the dealers. Dealer feedback goes directly to the source (the actual manufacturing people, not through a third or fourth party). The new Raleigh Technium USA-made mountain and racing bicycles are already in great demand in other countries like Switzerland, Germany, Italy, France, Canada, Australia, and South America.

By maintaining strict quality standards and daring to rely upon innovative techniques including space age adhesives, high technology componentry, and industrial robots, Raleigh has managed to become a leader in its field despite international competition. Long range plans now include new business relations with the former Soviet Union as well as expansion in the world market.

Equating the two costs and solving for p yields

$$p \times MP = (1 - p) \times ML$$

$$p = \frac{ML}{ML + MP}.$$

The additional unit should be purchased if

$$p \geq \frac{ML}{ML + MP}.$$

This is a logical result, because it implies that the purchaser should be willing to take larger risks if a higher profit margin is involved. If there is a salvage value for the unused item, it may be possible to recover some of the excess cost. This should be considered in the determination of ML.

Example 13.18   Use the results of the marginal analysis to determine Jeremy's optimal order quantity (using the data from Example 13.17).

To determine the expected costs, it is necessary to know the probability of selling the full amount, given the order size. This probability can be summarized in another column in the table of demand information. First, assume that 160 papers are ordered. From the demand distribution, it is clear that there is a 100 percent chance of selling all of these papers, because some amount between 160 and 166 will be the demand. Similarly, if 161 papers are purchased, the probability of selling them all is the probability that the demand will be greater than or equal to 161, or .94. The rest of the column can be filled in as follows.

Order	Probability of Demand ≥ Order
160	1.00
161	.94
162	.80
163	.64
164	.44
165	.20
166	.04

$ML = .75$, the cost of the papers (there is no salvage)

$MP = .50$, the sales price (1.25) minus the cost (.75), or the profit

The optimal probability is

$$p \geq \frac{ML}{ML + MP} = \frac{.75}{.75 + .50} = .60.$$

If the probability of selling the additional paper is .60 or greater, it should be purchased.

The probability of selling the 163rd paper is .64, which is greater than .60, so at least 163 papers should be purchased. The probability of selling the 164th paper is only .44, so Jeremy should purchase only 163 papers. ◼

IMPLEMENTATION

Now that we have seen a variety of procedures for determining optimal inventory policies, some thought must be given to how the inventory system is implemented. Only in the rare case of the start-up of a new plant in a very large company with sufficient staff personnel is a complete inventory system designed from scratch for implementation. In this rare case, the procedures presented in this chapter can be used without conflict.

EVOLUTION OF INVENTORY SYSTEMS

inventory systems need to change

In most companies, the inventory system grows and changes as the needs of the company change. When a small business is started, little formal inventory analysis is used. The entrepreneur usually can monitor inventory levels mentally for the few items carried. When inventories are small, the time and money required to perform the formal inventory analysis probably would outweigh the savings that would result from the analysis. The major use of inventory data at this stage of business development is for income tax purposes—businesses are required to report the value of inventory on hand at year end. We all know of local business people who put a lot of effort into taking year-end inventory but do little to monitor it formally during the rest of the year. A recommendation for the small business with a small inventory is to monitor its investment level in inventories periodically (once a year may be enough if the company is growing slowly) to see when inventory is becoming burdensome.

inventory tracking

Growth typically is accompanied by two inventory problems. First, keeping track of inventory levels in one's head becomes less desirable as more items are added to inventory. The usual practice is to start a formal record-keeping system to keep track of inventory. Most often, this system takes the form of a card file. The Japanese **Kanban** system (see Chapter 14) is a highly structured card-filing replenishment system (*Kanban* is the Japanese word for cards).

inventory analysis

The second inventory problem associated with a company's growth is this: As quantities in inventory grow, more space is required to do business and more capital is tied up in inventory. With escalating holding costs, some analysis needs to be performed on the ordering policies. For larger inventories, a simple EOQ analysis may lead to worthwhile savings. At some point certainly, a formal analysis of inventory policies will prove helpful, especially because many businesses give this area little attention.

The transition from seat-of-the-pants ordering policies and little or no record keeping to a formal inventory system that includes specific ordering policies and a formalized inventory record file is a difficult one for most companies to make. It is but one of the many sources of growing pains that emerging companies experience, especially those in fast-growing industries such as fast food or high technology. This transition requires the creation of new job functions to identify the costs (holding, shortage) associated with inventory and to implement the inventory analysis. The inventory record file also must be maintained by someone and, periodically, audited by someone. In addition, the transition requires more coordination between different company functions. If an EOQ is used, for example, the individual responsible for purchasing must coordinate orders with the individual who maintains the inventory records. The transition has an impact at a higher level, too, requiring company management to

---

APPLICATIONS OF P/OM

Spare Parts Inventory at PennDOT

The Pennsylvania Department of Transportation (PennDOT) recently decided to look into the possibility of reducing its spare parts inventory for road maintenance vehicles such as snowplows and graders. The initial inventory survey placed the value of the spare parts on hand at $50 million, which was considerably more than had been expected.

In the next stage of the analysis, the inventory was examined for obsolescence. Years of failing to control inventories had led to a situation in which PennDOT had many spare parts that were no longer needed, including, for example, spare engines for vehicles that

were no longer in the fleet. Inventory was reduced by $5 million after the obsolete parts were sold.

PennDOT ultimately purchased software to manage its spare parts inventory. The software checked for obsolescence, using this rule: Any part not used for six months, as identified by part number, should be eliminated from the spare parts inventory. There was a glitch, however: In October, the software indicated that all spare snowplow blades should be sold, as none had been used since March. Once this setup bug was eliminated, the program proved quite successful.

---

make specific policy statements that were not required previously. The best example of this is the specification (explicit or implicit) of service levels.

The next step in the evolution of the inventory system comes when a computerized record-keeping system is implemented. This step necessitates the involvement of data processing in the inventory system, requiring further interdepartmental coordination. The motivation for computerizing the system may be that growth has created so many new inventory items that the card system is no longer an adequate monitor. Very often, however, the motivation is to keep in line with the computerization of other company functions, such as payroll and billing. **computerized system**

Inventory record keeping and forecasting are very intimately related. Recall from Chapter 4 that operations management forecasting is based largely on predicting future sales from past sales. Past sales show up in the Management Information System as drops in the inventory level of finished goods. Companies that can tie the inventory records into the forecasting function will have timely, complete information. Toys "R" Us is such a company. The sales records from individual stores are tied in with both the inventory and forecasting, a distinct advantage when it comes to getting out in front of fads—and staying there.

No other major transitions occur during the life cycle of an inventory system unless a conversion is made to the just-in-time philosophy, which is discussed in the next chapter. The inventory system, however, does continue to change as the business changes. It is desirable to audit inventory policies and procedures periodically to ensure that they continue to meet current needs. **just-in-time**

This brings us to the last topic concerning the evolution of the inventory system. What can the newly hired analyst (perhaps the recent graduate) contribute upon entering an environment where the inventory system is already in place and functioning? Certainly no employer will wish for or agree to a complete change of the system. Change, if required, must be accomplished with tact, moderation, and caution. A starting point is to perform an analysis using many of the tools explained in this chapter on the functioning of the current system. The best advice is to start with a change that can be implemented with little trouble and to prepare a convincing case for this change. The effects of increasing or decreasing order sizes, taking advantage of quantity discount policies, or combining orders for different items are all logical and useful areas of investigation.

BIN POLICIES

In practice, the continuous review system often is implemented in a form known as the **two-bin system.** Most factories store items that can be stored in bulk form in bins that can be rolled from one point to another, or in bins that are part of the sophisticated materials handling systems connected by conveyors. The inventory is stored in two bins; when one is empty, another is ordered. In this case, the amount in the other bin is the reorder point, R, and the amount ordered, Q, is the amount in the incoming bin. If the bins are the same size, R must equal Q. To get around this, a bright yellow line usually is painted on each bin at a height that corresponds to the reorder level. When the worker sees the yellow line, it is time to order another bin. The beauty of this system is its simplicity. No time is spent counting or monitoring inventory levels, and the workers require no knowledge of inventory systems.

S U M M A R Y

Every business maintains inventories of some kind and incurs costs as a result. Inventory management involves controlling the levels of inventories to control these costs. The two primary types of inventory systems, systems of procedures to control inventory levels, are *continuous review (economic order quantity) systems* and *periodic review (economic order interval) systems.* With the continuous system, inventory levels are monitored continuously, and the proper order quantity is ordered each time the inventory level is reduced to a specified *reorder point.* With the periodic system, orders are placed at regular time intervals. Inventory systems are modeled in a variety of ways. The models make assumptions on *replenishment rate, shortages,* and price structure (quantity discounts). When, as is usual, probabilistic demand patterns are assumed, *safety stocks* are maintained. The size of the safety stock depends on the *service level* desired. One special model that is encountered often in practice is the *single period model,* which analyzes inventory stocks when purchases can be made for one time period only.

Inventory systems take on different forms, depending on the size and needs of the company. One simple way of implementing an EOQ system is to use a *two-bin policy.* An overall framework for classifying many items in an inventory system is to use the *ABC classification,* where items that are frequently used or that are very expensive receive the most attention from management.

KEY TERMS

holding cost

shortage cost

service level

order cost

unit cost

continuous review system

fixed order size system

economic order quantity

periodic review system

fixed order interval system

economic order interval systems

replenishment rate

shortages

ABC classification system

price break

economic production quantity model

economic lot size model

reorder point

lead time

safety stock

service level

implied shortage cost

Kanban

two-bin system

SOLVED PROBLEMS

1. R & J Auto Parts purchases 120,000 oil filters annually. An average of 400 filters per day are sold over the course of the year at R & J stores nationwide. If the annual holding cost is $.50 per filter, and the order cost is $75 per order, how many filters should be ordered at one time and how often will an order be placed? If the lead time for the filters is 4 days, what is the reorder point? Explain the resulting inventory policy.

Solution

First, we compute the order quantity.

$$Q^* = \sqrt{\frac{2DS}{H}}$$

$$= \sqrt{\frac{2(120,000)(75)}{.5}}$$

$$= 6,000 \text{ oil filters in each order}$$

Next, we compute the time between orders.

$$T = \frac{Q}{D} = \frac{6,000}{120,000}$$

$$= .05 \text{ years, or } .05 \times 300 \text{ days} = 15 \text{ days}$$

Alternatively, 6,000 filters in an order, used at a rate of 400 per day, will last

$$\frac{6,000}{400} = 15 \text{ days.}$$

The reorder point is

$$R = L \times d$$
$$= 4 \text{ days} \times 400/\text{day}$$
$$= 1,600.$$

The resulting inventory policy is to check the inventory level and order only if 1,600 or fewer filters remain. The size of the order is 6,000 filters.

Using AB:POM to Solve This Problem

Five inventory models are available in AB:POM. These models are the basic EOQ model (model I), the production order quantity model (model II), the backorder inventory model (model III), the production with backorders model (model IV), and the quantity discount model. Screen 13.1 shows the input and output for Solved Problem 1. The software does not compute the reorder point.

```
============================ Inventory =============== Solution =
  Economic Order Quantity (EOQ) Model (Model I)

==================== Chapter 13, Solved Problem 1 ====================
Demand rate(D)        120000.00 Optimal order quantity (Q*)      6000.00

Setup cost(S)             75.00 Maximum Inventory Level (Imax)   6000.00

Holding cost(H)            0.50

Unit cost                  0.00 Orders per period(year)            20.00

                                Inventory $$(Hold,Setup,Short)  $3,000.00

                                Unit costs (PD)                     $0.00

                                Total Cost                      $3,000.00




                                                   F9=Print     Esc
Press <Esc> key to edit data or highlighted key or function key for options
```

SCREEN 13.1

2. Lead time demand for Wilma's Widgets is normally distributed with a mean of 1,400 and a standard deviation of 200. In order to achieve a 95 percent service level, what should be the reorder point? How much of this is safety stock?

Solution

For a service level of 95 percent, the z value from the normal table is 1.64. The reorder point is

$$R = \overline{m} + z\sigma$$
$$= 1,400 + (1.64 \times 200)$$
$$= 1,728 \text{ widgets.}$$

The safety stock portion of this is

$$SS = z\sigma$$
$$= 1.64 \times 200$$
$$= 328 \text{ widgets.}$$

3. Chips Chocolate Chips sells fresh-baked cookies at the main terminal of the Tri-County Airport. Daily demand is distributed as follows.

Dozens Sold	Probability
24	.05
25	.10
26	.20
27	.25
28	.25
29	.10
30	.05

If the cookies cost $1.10 per dozen and sell for $2 per dozen, how many dozen cookies should be ordered for each day? There is no salvage value for day-old cookies.

Solution

The additional dozen cookies should be purchased if the probability of selling it is at least

$$p \geq \frac{ML}{ML + MP},$$

where ML = cost of not selling cookies (purchase cost), or $1.10, and MP = cost of running short (profit), or $.90. Thus,

$$p \geq \frac{1.10}{1.10 + .90} = \frac{1.10}{2.00} = .55.$$

The probability of selling each dozen is as follows.

Dozens Sold	Probability
24	1.00
25	.95
26	.85
27	.65
28	.40
29	.15
30	.05

There is a 65-percent chance of selling at least 27 dozen cookies, so 27 dozen should be ordered. The chance of selling additional cookies is too low to make investment in them worthwhile. (Refer to Chapter 3, Solved Problem 2, for another, longer approach to this problem.)

QUESTIONS

1. What is an inventory?

2. Name the different types of inventory.

3. Identify and explain the types of costs that are involved in an inventory system.

4. What is the difference between a continuous review and a periodic review inventory system?

5. What is the purpose of the ABC classification system?

6. What is the relationship of the economic order quantity to demand? to the holding cost? to the setup cost?

7. When quantity discounts are offered, why is it not necessary to check discount points that are below the EOQ or points above the EOQ that are not discount points?

8. Explain the following: All things being equal, the economic production quantity will be larger than the economic order quantity.

9. What is the relationship between shortages and service levels?

10. What is a safety stock and why is it necessary to maintain one?

11. Cite three products for which the single period model is appropriate.

12. How are inventory levels monitored in department stores?

PROBLEMS

1. Nicor maintains inventories of fourteen different items in its spare parts warehouse. The number used of each item over the last year was as follows.

Item	Number Used
1	123
2	154
3	19
4	54
5	114
6	63
7	29
8	32
9	35
10	72
11	4
12	166
13	2
14	118

A:12, 2; B:1, 14, 5, 10, 6, 4; C:9, 8, 7, 3, 11, 13 (*Note:* Other answers are possible.)

Classify these items using an ABC analysis.

2. Tricolor Industries distributes nineteen varieties of hardware components from its warehouse to local hardware stores. The demand and price for each of these components over the last year were as follows.

Item	Demand	Price (in $)
1	561	8.50
2	1,496	1.67
3	1,223	6.58
4	1,008	7.68
5	2,754	9.36
6	1,112	9.94
7	558	6.51
8	490	7.03
9	41	5.81
10	987	4.46
11	269	0.22
12	523	8.50
13	248	0.11
14	1,199	9.79
15	1,084	6.32
16	44	5.28
17	9	5.37
18	941	1.14
19	827	6.23

by volume—A:5, 2, 3, 14;
B:6, 15, 4, 10, 18, 19; C:1,
7, 12, 8, 11, 13, 16, 9, 17
by $ volume—A:5, 14, 6;
B:3, 4, 15, 19, 1; C:12, 10,
7, 8, 2, 18, 9, 16, 17,
13,11

Classify the hardware components using an ABC analysis.

3. Lucky Lady Supermarket sells 2,440 bottles of a sparkling cider per year. There is only one supplier, and this supplier offers only this one specialty product. The cost per order is $35, and the holding cost is $2 per bottle per year.

(a) How many bottles should be ordered?
(b) How often should the supermarket order the cider?
(c) What is the total cost?

292 bottles
8.4 times per year
$584 per year

4. The De Railleur Bicycle Company sells 400 bikes per *month*. De Railleur buys the seats for its bikes, and each order costs $50. The holding cost is $5 per seat per year.

(a) How many seats are in each order?
(b) How often should the seats be ordered?
(c) What is the total cost?

310 seats
15.5 times per year
$1,550 per year

5. Demand for gold corkscrews at Lafayette Gallery Department Store is 25 per month. The order cost is $25 per order, and the holding cost is $.50 per corkscrew per month. Lead time is 10 business days (assume 25 business days per month).

(a) What quantity should be ordered?
(b) What is the time between orders?
(c) What is the reorder point?

50 corkscrews
every 2 months
10 corkscrews

6. Ray James is a world-renowned poker player. Unfortunately for Ray, he is playing poker in the Holmesburg prison due to an auto-theft conviction. Fortunately for Ray, he is able to set up poker games at the right price. Each time Ray wishes to set up a game, he pays the prison guard $5. The prison poker players play for cigarettes, and Ray has a habit of 40 cigarettes per day. Because Ray does not like stale cigarettes, he figures that, by keeping cigarettes around, it costs $.01 per cigarette per day. How many cigarettes should Ray win at each poker game he sets up?

200 cigarettes

7. Panzer's Peanut Butter uses 100 peanuts per jar of peanut butter. The company can order peanuts from either the JC Peanut Company or Brother Bill's Peanut Company. Brother Bill sells at the price of 2 peanuts per penny, and JC sells at the price of 3 peanuts per penny. The procurement (setup) cost is $8 per order if the order is placed with Brother Bill. Dealing with JC involves four times more paperwork than dealing with Brother Bill, so the procurement cost is $32 per order if the order is placed with JC. Either way, the storage cost is $.01 to store 100 peanuts per week. The demand for peanut butter is 900 jars per week.

JC Peanut Company
every 2.67 weeks
$.36 per jar

order 1,800 jars

(a) From which peanut supplier should Panzer's order peanuts?
(b) What is the time between orders?
(c) What is the inventory cost, expressed per jar of peanut butter?
(d) If Panzer's warehouse can store only 180,000 peanuts, what should be the company's inventory policy?

8. Rudolph Manufacturing Company makes toy reindeer with noses that light up. The company operates its production facility 300 days per year. It produces 12,000 toy reindeer per year and has the capability of producing 100 nose lights per day. Setting up the nose light production costs $50 and takes 3 days. The cost of each nose light is $1. The holding cost is $.10 per light per year.

4,472 lights per run
$134.16 per year
$134.16 per year
$12,268.32 per year
2.68 runs per year
.373 years
$1.0224 per nose light
40 percent

(a) What is the optimal size of the production run?
(b) What is the average holding cost per year?
(c) What is the average setup cost per year?
(d) What is the total cost per year?
(e) What is the average number of production runs per year?
(f) What is the average time between production runs?
(g) What is the inventory cost per nose light?
(h) What percentage of the year is Rudolf producing nose lights?

9. Tasty-Host Baking Company is a new company specializing in canned baked goods. (The market is flooded with fresh and frozen baked goods.) Tasty-Host has a choice between making or buying the cans into which it will put its cakes. If it manufactures its own cans, the cost will be $.10 per can with a setup cost of $30 each time a production run begins. The company has the capability to produce 56,250 cans per week. Buying cans from a can supplier will cost $.15 per can, with a fixed cost of $7.50 per order. In either case, the cost of holding cans in inventory is $.03 per can per week. The anticipated demand for the cakes is approximately 50,000 per week. Should the company buy cans or manufacture its own cans?

manufacture its own cans

10. Findlandia Pharmaceutical Company makes implants for applying chemotherapy medication at a rate of 8,000 per year. The pumps for the implants are ordered from a supplier. The ordering cost is $50 per order, and the cost of keeping one pump in stock for one year is $2.

632.5 units
$632.50 per year
$632.50 per year

(a) What is the optimal order size?
(b) What is the average annual holding cost?
(c) What is the average annual setup cost?

Suppose the company would produce its own pumps. The production rate would be 12,000 pumps per year, and the production setup cost would be $50 per production run.

1,095 per run
$365.30 per year
producing the pumps

(d) What should be the size of the production run?
(e) What is the average annual setup cost?
(f) Which option—ordering the pumps from a supplier or producing the pumps—is less expensive, excluding unit costs?

11. Rocky Mountain Tire Center sells 20,000 tires of a particular type per year. The ordering cost for each order is $40, and the holding cost is 20 percent of the purchase price of the tires per year. The purchase price is $20 per tire if fewer than 500 tires are ordered, $18 per tire if more than 500 but fewer than 1,000 tires are ordered, and $17 per tire if 1,000 or more tires are ordered. How many tires should Rocky Mountain order each time it places an order?

1,000 tires

12. Chamberlain Supply Company sells pencils to the city school district. Yearly demand for pencils is 5,000 gross (1 gross = 144 pencils, or 12 dozen). The order cost is $11 per order, and the holding cost is $1 per gross per year. The purchase price is $8 per gross if less than 500 gross is ordered and $7.50 per gross if 500 gross or more is ordered. What should be the order quantity for pencils?

500 gross of pencils

13. Refer to Problem 5. The manager of Lafayette Gallery Department Store estimates that the shortage cost for gold corkscrews is $5 per corkscrew per month. How does this affect the manager's inventory policies?

The order quantity increases to 52.44 corkscrews.

14. For the data in Problem 7, assume that there is a shortage cost of $.01 per jar per week.

(a) Does this affect which supplier is chosen?
(b) How does it affect Panzer's inventory policies?
(c) What is the maximum size of Panzer's shortage?
(d) What percent of the time is Panzer's short?

no
raise Q to 3,394 jars
1,697 jars
50 percent

15. For the data in Problem 8, assume that there is a shortage cost of $.05 per nose light per year.

(a) What is the optimal size of a production run?
(b) What is the maximum inventory level?
(c) What is the maximum size of the shortage allowed?
(d) How long is each production run?
(e) What percentage of time is Rudolph out of nose lights in each cycle?

7,746 lights
1,550 lights
3,098 lights
77.46 days
67 percent

16. The lead time demand for microwave ovens is found to be distributed according to the following probability distribution.

Demand	Probability
7	.03
8	.07
9	.10
10	.70
11	.06
12	.04

(a) For a 95-percent service level, what should the reorder point be? What is the safety stock?
(b) If the service level is changed to 85 percent, what is the reorder point?

$R = 11$; $SS = 1.19$
$R = 10$

17. For the data in Problem 16, assume a shortage cost of $500 per unit. Find the optimal service level, reorder point, and safety stock. The monthly demand (assume a month of 25 working days) is 25 microwaves, the holding cost is $50 per unit per month, and the order quantity is 50. If the shortage cost were $200, how would this affect your answers?

service level = 80 percent; reorder point = 10; safety stock = .19; no effect on answers

18. For the data in Problem 16, what shortage costs are implied by the use of the

(a) 95-percent service level?
(b) 85-percent service level?

$20 per unit
$6.67 per unit

19. Staying with the situation presented in Problem 16, now assume that the lead time demand is distributed according to a normal distribution, with a mean of 10 and a standard deviation of .8.

(a) What should the reorder point be for a service level of 95 percent? What is the size of the safety stock?
(b) What would the reorder point be for a service level of 85 percent? What is the size of the safety stock?

$R = 11.31$; $SS = 1.31$

$R = 10.83$; $SS = .83$

20. What shortage cost is implied by the use of the 95-percent service level for the data in Problem 19?

(a) Compare your result here with that given by Problem 18.
(b) Is your answer independent of the probability distribution of demand?

$20 per unit
yes

$SL = .80; R = 10.672;$
$SS = .672;$ yes; $SL;$ costs
are same

21. For the data in Problem 19, find the optimal service level, reorder point, and safety stock, assuming a shortage cost of $500 per unit, a holding cost of $50 per unit-month, demand of 25 per month, and an order quantity of 50. Does part of the solution here match that given for Problem 17? Which part? Why?

22. The Huachuca Doughnut Shop bakes its doughnuts fresh daily. Any doughnuts not sold on the day they are baked are sold at half-price to an outlet store for day-old baked goods. The popular powdered doughnut costs $1 per dozen to make, and the selling price is $1.20 per dozen. The probability distribution for sales is as follows.

Sales (in dozens)	Probability
26	.1
27	.2
28	.4
29	.2
30	.1

28 dozen

How many dozen powdered doughnuts should be baked each day?

28 dozen

23. For the data in Problem 22, assume a normal distribution, with a mean of 28 and a standard deviation of .75. How many dozen powdered doughnuts should be baked each day?

24. The Carbon Steel Corporation is purchasing a new furnace for its aging Ferrite Hill plant. The manufacturer of the furnace sells spare compressor units for $800 each if purchased with the furnace. The retailer sells these compressors for $1,500. The probability distribution for failed compressor units is as follows.

Failures	Probability
0	.1
1	.3
2	.3
3	.2
4	.1

2 spares

How many spare compressors should be purchased with the furnace?

2 spares

25. For the data in Problem 24, how many compressors should be purchased with the furnace if the failures are normally distributed, with a mean of 2 and a standard deviation of .7?

COMPUTER CASE STUDY 13.1: ROCHESTER PAPER COMPANY

Jim Rhodes has recently been hired as the inventory manager at Rochester Paper Company. Rochester manufactures typing paper in assorted colors. The manufacturing process for each color is the same. The only difference is the length of the run for each color; these lengths vary due to the fact that demand varies for the different colors.

When Jim took the job at RPC, he examined the inventory systems and found that RPC was using a standard economic production model. At first, he was not sure what model was being used, because in going through the RPC records and computer programs, he found an assortment of names—among them, gradual replacement, production order quantity, economic production lot, gradual deliveries, EOQ with delivery, noninstantaneous delivery, economic run length, finite production rate, simultaneous production/consumption, economic manufacturing quantity, and, most often, economic production quantity. After satisfying himself that all systems were using the formula

$$Q^\star = \sqrt{\frac{2SD}{H}} \sqrt{\frac{p}{p-d}}$$

and that the same formula was being used for all products, he went about trying to determine the values for the demand rates (D), the setup costs (S), and the holding costs (H) being used.

The demand rates were easy to calculate. Jim found the total amount of paper that was manufactured last year for each color and assumed that demand would not change. The overall demands were as follows.

Color	Demand (in 000s of cases)
White	183,425
Yellow	87,178
Green	76,829
Blue	57,263

Accounting indicated to Jim that he should use a figure of 28 percent of the selling price of the case for the holding cost. The appropriate figures are given below.

Color	Price (per case)
White	$21.95
Yellow	29.95
Green	29.95
Blue	29.95

In order to determine the setup cost per order, Jim spoke with the shop foreman about the length of time needed to set up the run for each color and the number of people used to set up the machine. He determined that the setup cost was approximately $70 per run. This, in fact, agreed with the numbers that he found in the data.

Color	$Q^\star$	Inventory Cost per Year
White	2,568	$ 9,996.38
Yellow	1,328	9,192.66
Green	1,231	8,737.29
Blue	1,039	7,715.54
	Total	$35,641.87

Because Jim had heard so much about just-in-time and zero-inventory, he wanted to see if he could reduce some of the costs. After observing the machines being set up, he determined that adding one more employee to the setup cleaning process would mean much less time spent for the other employees moving from side to side around the equipment. The net effect of the increase by one employee would be a savings of manhours that would reduce the setup cost from $70 to $52. As machine cleaning would account for only about 20 percent of the new employee's time, he or she would be free to perform other tasks as well. At minimum wage, the new employee is estimated by the cost accountant to cost the company $12,840 per year, including benefits. Should the change be made in the method for setting up?

REFERENCES

Fogarty, D. W., J. H. Blackstone, and T. R. Hoffman. *Production and Inventory Management*. 2nd ed. Cincinnati: South-Western, 1991.

Hax, A. C., and D. Candea. *Production and Inventory Management*. Englewood Cliffs, N.J.: Prentice-Hall, 1984.

McLeavey, D. W., and S. L. Narasimhan. *Production Planning and Inventory Control*. Boston: Allyn and Bacon, 1985.

Reinfeld, N. V. *Handbook of Production and Inventory Control*. Englewood Cliffs, N.J.: Prentice-Hall, 1987.

Silver, E. A., and R. Peterson. *Decision Systems for Inventory Management and Production Planning*. 2nd ed. New York: John Wiley and Sons, 1985.

Tersine, R. J. *Principles of Inventory and Materials Management*. 3rd ed. New York: North-Holland, 1988.

MATERIALS REQUIREMENTS PLANNING AND JUST-IN-TIME

OBJECTIVES

- To explain the dependencies of items in inventories
- To present the just-in-time philosophy
- To illustrate the use of bills of materials
- To present the method for scheduling inventories, purchasing, and/or production using MRP
- To describe extensions of the MRP concepts that apply to the areas of capacity planning and business planning

INTRODUCTION

This chapter could be viewed as a second chapter on the subject of inventory. However, this viewpoint limits the uses of materials requirements planning (MRP), and just-in-time systems. We present just-in-time as a philosophy applicable to MRP and many other areas of operations.

Materials requirements are inventories required for some purpose. This purpose may be sales or something else, but in this chapter, the purpose is primarily production. Given that we are dealing with materials requirements for production, many would classify MRP as inventory analysis, making certain assumptions that differ from the assumptions made in the previous chapter. Most of this introductory section is devoted to explaining these different assumptions.

MRP sets inventory procedures and keeps track of inventory levels, but it also serves as a link between inventory, production, and purchasing. The term *requirements planning* implies that the inventory needs occur in response to production needs created by demands. Purchasing satisfies these inventory needs on a just-in-time basis when ordering additional stocks. MRP *coordinates* these activities, and this coordina-
production planning tion (see Figure 14.1) is its primary benefit. This is the reason that many consider MRP a production planning tool.

RELATIONSHIP BETWEEN INVENTORY AND PRODUCTION

assumptions In our previous inventory analyses, we assumed that the demand was constant over time and continuous. The models we presented also assumed that demand remained

644

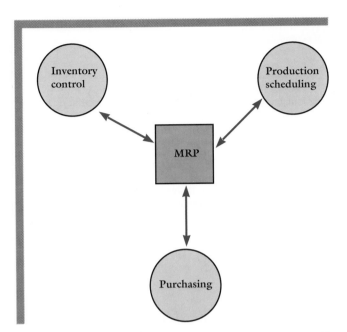

Transparency Master 14.1:
MRP as a Coordinator.

FIGURE 14.1 Materials requirements planning as a coordinator

constant forever. Our third and most critical assumption was that each item could be modeled, analyzed, and ordered in isolation from the others. Although these assumptions are useful in what we call the *pure inventory* situation and in some production settings, they do not hold true for large-scale production environments where complex products are manufactured or assembled.

When a complex product such as an airplane is assembled, the demand for each component, and for the airplane as well, may be intermittent or sporadic. For example, for a few days, large quantities of a certain kind of bolt may be used, but operations performed during subsequent time periods may not require this particular bolt. Although the part will be required again in future periods, logic dictates that a part should not be held in inventory when it is not needed for production.

To put it slightly differently, ideally a part should arrive just in time for production. This **time phasing** of orders for inventory in response to intermittent needs is the major distinguishing characteristic of the MRP approach. In fact, another name for MRP is *time-phased requirements planning*.

The classical inventory approach uses an EOQ to fill the inventory stock each time it gets low, which means that some levels of inventory are always maintained. This notion of a full level of inventory seems to be in opposition to the goal of reducing inventory levels. MRP is a **zero-based inventory system:** No inventories are maintained unless they are needed for current production. Many large companies have used this approach to reduce their overall levels of inventories and to achieve significant savings in their inventory costs. The inventory levels are reduced without risking delays in production schedules because the time phasing of inventory is linked to the production schedules. This is where MRP's coordination between purchasing, inventory management, and production scheduling is most evident.

intermittent needs

inventory is linked to production

APPLICATIONS OF P/OM

MRP at Uniform Tubes

Uniform Tubes is a major producer of specialty metal tubing. The company is set up as a job shop, making tubing only in response to customer orders. Much of the production scheduling and shop floor control, as well as the materials, is managed by a computerized MRP system.

In 1989, Uniform Tubes embarked on a major implementation of total quality management and statistical process control. As part of this program, the company began to study some of its support processes using control charts—one to monitor production efficiency and another to study inventory accuracy. Data for several years were needed because the relevant numbers were reported monthly.

The charts showed a dramatic improvement in both of these measures in the fall of 1987. It did not take long to find the cause of the process change in each case: Uniform Tubes had installed an MRP system the previous summer.

INDEPENDENT VERSUS DEPENDENT DEMAND ITEMS

A second characteristic of the demand for an item in a classical inventory model is that each item's *forecasted* demand level is not determined by the level of demand for any other items; that is, items in a classical inventory are **independent demand items.** Even in an MRP system, independent demand items must be forecasted. It is for a second, much larger group of items, the **dependent demand items,** that the MRP approach differs.

A complex production item may require hundreds or even thousands of stock items for its manufacture and assembly. If all of these items are independent demand items, then a very large set of forecasting jobs must be performed. However, assuming that the producer knows how to produce the end item and knows what parts go into it, only one forecast is required in actuality: that of the end item. The materials requirements for each of the many parts or components of the end item are not forecasted; instead, they are *calculated* from the end item forecast and the number of each component required for that end item.

component needs depend on end-item production

As a simple example, consider the manufacture of a chair. Each chair requires four legs, which is a known fact for this particular chair (and most chairs) regardless of the level of demand for the chair. If the forecast for chairs is that 400 will be sold next month, there is no need to obtain another forecast for the number of legs that will be required. This requirement can be calculated: Multiply the number of chairs needed (400) by the number of legs per chair (4) to yield the required number of legs for production next month (1,600). The demand for the legs is dependent on the demand for the chairs.

Although this is a trivial example used only to explain the relationship between the independent and the dependent demand items, it indicates how much effort can be saved in making forecasts for components of a more complex item, such as an automobile. There is one forecast for the automobile, and the calculations of the requirements for each of its many hundreds of parts are based on that forecast. The American Production and Inventory Control Society suggests that companies having about 4,000 or more total inventory items (across all product lines) use MRP.

In complex assembly, there are many subcomponents and the usage of the
subcomponents depends on the end-product production. (© T. Matsumoto/Sygma)

HISTORICAL PERSPECTIVE OF MRP

The MRP approach is quite simple: Order exactly what is needed at the time it is
needed. It would seem, then, that using MRP is tantamount to using one's common
sense. It follows that MRP has been around in some form as long as there has been
production. Yet MRP is viewed as a modern phenomenon. First implemented on a
large scale in the United States in the 1970s, MRP is still something of a novelty at
many of the largest companies in this country and is just now filtering down to many
smaller production plants.

We have stated that MRP is simple and that it is a modern development. We normally do not expect "the latest thing" to be characterized chiefly by its simplicity.
Usually, time *adds* layers of complexity, abstraction, and difficulty. There is another
sense in which MRP is an exception: Researchers in academia usually work with techniques for a period of years before the techniques are used in industry. MRP comes
from industry, with little or no involvement from academia. The first book on the
subject was written by an IBM employee (Orlicky) in the mid-1970s.

**MRP requires
computers**

Although MRP is simplistic, it requires the coordination of a great deal of information when an inventory system has many parts. Access and use of this information was impossible prior to the widespread availability of computers. Once the means of storing and accessing the information was available, MRP was a natural outgrowth of simpler inventory control and production planning systems. The first MRP systems were developed in the early 1960s (primarily at IBM) and were first adopted by the Japanese. The initial adoption of MRP in the United States was mostly a response to the threat of Japanese competition, but now U.S. companies are adopting MRP systems on their own merits—because of the cost and time savings that they can achieve.

In the 1950s, researchers were looking into inventory systems with varying levels of demand. The techniques that they developed, now incorporated into MRP systems, are the MRP lot sizing techniques explained in this chapter. Although these techniques follow historically in the line of approaches discussed in the previous chapter on inventory analysis, they have found their greatest application within the MRP environment.

JUST-IN-TIME

We have seen that MRP systems are useful in situations where there are varying demand levels over time and where there is a strong relationship between the demands for various components. However, the demand relationship has been characterized as one of *number* only. Given a level of end-item demand, we can calculate the number required of each component. From an inventory viewpoint, it is this number that is most significant. However, from an MRP viewpoint—or, more important, from a production scheduling viewpoint—the *timing* of these material needs is of equal or perhaps greater significance. The earlier discussion of time phasing alluded to this relationship but did not specify how MRP deals with it.

THE JUST-IN-TIME PHILOSOPHY

The just-in-time philosophy applied to MRP is that no inventory should be obtained until it is needed. When a need arises, the exact amount is ordered, and it is scheduled to arrive at the exact time that it is required. The order will arrive just in time for use. This just-in-time philosophy is the basis for all MRP schedules, and greatly reduces the inventories of companies that use MRP.

The just-in-time philosophy is applied beyond the limited focus of materials requirements as well. A company that adopts the just-in-time approach also produces on a just-in-time basis, avoiding holding the large stockpiles of finished goods that are found in many operations. Purchasing is another operation that often is managed on a just-in-time basis. The philosophy, once adopted, needs to be implemented and coordinated throughout the business. The companywide implementation of the just-in-time philosophy is initiated by a requirement in the master production schedule, which is derived from the primary source of demand, the orders customers give to sales or marketing personnel.

risk

The just-in-time philosophy carries with it certain risks: Orders may arrive late; orders may be incomplete; orders may be filled incorrectly. Any of these situations will force production to stop until the situation is corrected. Furthermore, all schedules for assemblies that follow in the production sequence will be violated, resulting eventually in the late delivery of the end item.

Increased risk is at the heart of the philosophy. The approach works because it exposes bottlenecks, quality problems, supply problems, and other problems by forcing the operation to run tighter and leaner. Once the problem areas are discovered, they can be corrected. The operation will run more efficiently over time because it is a continuous process improvement system.

continuous process improvement system

Traditionally, most U.S. companies build a safety stock into every process, allowing for a margin of error. The use of safety stock is sarcastically referred to as a "just-in-case approach": A safety stock is maintained just in case there is a problem with production. The users of the just-in-time approach would say that the traditional way of doing things covers up problems by hiding them behind the safety stocks. The problems are tolerated as "just part of the business," and the production process will not improve as long as the company perpetuates problems.

Teaching Suggestion 14.1: JIT Analogy. See the Instructor's Section for details.

Another advantage of the just-in-time approach is that it leads to reduced run sizes. The approach requires more efficient changeovers and setups, thereby reducing the run size. In turn, reduced run sizes generate smaller inventories. In a nutshell, this philosophy fosters an environment in which it will always be necessary to find better ways of working.

reduced run sizes

The just-in-time philosophy requires a reduction in the number of suppliers, the ultimate goal being the use of single sourcing for all purchased materials. Reducing the number of suppliers leads to easier logistics of shipping, easier coordination on the part of the purchasing department, and larger quantities for the supplier. In fact, suppliers come to be seen more as partners in production than as separate companies bound by short-term purchase orders.

single supplier

The just-in-time philosophy places a heavy emphasis on quality. Obviously, if no extra stocks are ordered, all of the material that arrives must be usable. The same is true if no extra time is allocated for production and no in-process or final product inventory is maintained. Unless all of the material produced meets customer specifications, the required quantities will not be attained. For this reason, just-in-time programs are compatible with total quality management (TQM) programs (see Chapter 16). In fact, JIT/TQM programs are now quite common.

Much of the JIT philosophy is motivated by its very broad definition of waste as anything other than the absolute minimum resources of material, time, machines, and manpower required to add value to the product. Viewed in this way, setup times are waste; machine imbalances leading to excess capacity are waste; inventory is waste; backlogs of work, inspection, and paperwork are waste; downtimes are waste; design changes are waste; late shipments are waste; and scrap is waste. The list could go on. If we focus on attacking waste—which, given the broad definition, should not be a terribly difficult task—we will be reducing the hidden problems and reducing the costs of all operations.

waste

There are five essential goals of a just-in-time system.

- *Total quality*—The entire planning and production cycle, from design to order scheduling to shipment of parts, must meet established quality standards.
- *Logistics*—The right amounts must be shipped and delivered at the right time. Too few or too late leads to delays; too many or too early also leads to inefficiencies (waste).
- *Quantities*—Production and order quantities should be as small as possible.

- *Total cost*—All partners in the customer–supplier chain must work together to lower end-product costs.
- *Supplier relationship*—Establishing long-term partnership relationships on the basis of trust is required to work together to achieve all of these goals.

The Japanese have had great success with this just-in-time approach, especially in their automotive industry. For this reason, U.S. auto companies all rushed to adopt it in the late 1970s and early 1980s, hoping to reduce their inventories and their production costs per car. Unfortunately, although the U.S. companies now consider their implementation of the approach to have been successful, the U.S. companies failed to match the inventory reduction of the Japanese companies. The culprit, it turned out, was (and is) industrial geography. The Japanese industry is highly centralized; because the distances from parts suppliers to assembly plants are small, variations in lead times can be reduced and Japanese automakers can count on just-in-time deliveries. The U.S. auto industry, on the other hand, is spread out and sometimes depends on parts produced in other countries and on other continents. This decentralization reduces the effectiveness of the just-in-time approach due to the increased risk described earlier.

Recognizing this problem, General Motors based the design of its Saturn plant on the tenets of the just-in-time system. The plant location decision was influenced greatly by the close proximity of suppliers and by commitments from suppliers to locate their new plants near the same site. Thus, use of the just-in-time approach affects location planning decisions. It also affects capacity planning, as we shall see later in this chapter. We also will see how it relates to distribution planning. The just-in-time approach requires management to pay very close attention to purchasing lead times (activities outside the plant once considered outside of management control) as well as to many details of coordination between separate functions and departments in the plants.

IMPLEMENTING JUST-IN-TIME

Just-in-time is currently a very popular management philosophy. The only guarantee that comes with just-in-time, however, is that any attempt to turn it on like a light switch will fail. Improper implementation of JIT could easily turn out to be disastrous.

Consider the production manager who is told that his company is going on just-in-time next week. An extreme position, one that views implementation of just-in-time in absolute terms, would be to wait until the last minute before starting production—so that the customer gets the order "just in time." But what if a problem occurs, making the production late? Employees do get sick, machines do break down, defects do get produced, raw materials may not be perfect. If a shipment of raw materials is late, production will shut down. Since just-in-time requires single sourcing, another concern is that the supplier will suffer a fire or other disaster or go out of business.

Unfortunately, the preceding are just a few of the problems that could cause our hypothetical production manager to need a little extra time. Therefore, just-in-time must be viewed as an ideal, not an absolute. Most new technology is either used (completely on) or not used (completely off). Just-in-time should be implemented gradually, and continuous efforts should be made to improve toward the ultimate goals (which, by the way, are almost certainly unattainable). For example, while few companies that implement JIT go to single sourcing, almost all eventually are able to reduce the number of suppliers by 80 or 90 percent.

A certain Pepsi bottling plant with which the authors of this text are familiar claims to have implemented JIT completely. Every hour, a truck brings a trailer loaded with aluminum cans to the plant. The cans are loaded directly from the trailer onto a conveyor, which takes them directly to the filling workstations. The cans are in and out of the plant in a very short time. No inventory is maintained. But is this really *just* in time? For one thing, each truck is scheduled to arrive about five minutes early, "just in case." Also, the trucks arrive every hour; wouldn't vans that arrive every five minutes be closer to the ideal of arriving just in time? To be sure, the Pepsi plant represents an excellent just-in-time implementation. Due consideration of the risks involved—not any inability or unwillingness to complete the task—prevents this plant, and others implementing JIT, from coming even closer to the ideal.

A company should begin by finding out how much raw material inventory is maintained by its operation today. If it is ten days, the company should find out why, and then work on eliminating some of the reasons for the ten-day inventory. It might prove possible to reduce the need to six days. The company can keep working this way until (if possible) none is required. The rule is always to eliminate the need, rather than to mandate the reduction.

One of the first areas to target in a just-in-time implementation is incoming shipments. The first step is to control their timing and quantities very closely. The next step is to work on the quality. With regard to quality, the goal is *shipping directly to stock* instead of shipping to the incoming inspection department. Incoming inspection should be eliminated or greatly reduced. The next step is to achieve tighter production scheduling. This will allow us to bypass stocks (we shouldn't need any) and ship directly to production, like the Pepsi plant mentioned previously. The goal here is summed up by the expression "Ship to WIP," where WIP is work-in-process.

INTEGRATION OF JUST-IN-TIME

Just-in-time is not an area of operations but, rather, a philosophy affecting all operations—in other words, every chapter topic in this text. For this reason, just-in-time has been integrated throughout the text. This section serves as a guide to linking just-in-time with the rest of the text.

The critical role of just-in-time was established in the first two chapters. It is clearly central to any claim of having a world-class operation for any organization.

The third chapter dealt with capacity. From the standpoint of JIT, extra capacity is viewed as waste, so capacities need to be reduced to their bare minima. But capacity also needs to be increased in terms of flexibility; that is, we must be able to reduce response times for a variety of products or services. The assumptions concerning cost–volume trade-offs are also brought into question by just-in-time.

Poor forecasts are a major deterrent to the successful implementation of just-in-time. Timely and accurate forecasting—the topic of Chapter 4—is required.

Many references to just-in-time are made in the chapters dealing with location, distribution, and layout—all of which affect movement of materials. There is no real link between JIT and waiting lines, but notice that the goals expressed in waiting line analysis (reducing waiting times and increasing system utilization) are similar to the goals expressed in this chapter.

Reliability is an essential, though as yet unmentioned element in a just-in-time program. The specific program required is aimed at preventive maintenance. The increased reliabilities resulting from this program improve just-in-time performance. Texas Gulf has instituted a "predictive maintenance" program; the company feels confident that it can predict the actual timing of failures and therefore take the best response actions.

Teaching Suggestion 14.2: Apparent Contradiction. See the Instructor's Section for details.

The chapters on production planning, inventory, and MRP are where just-in-time is most directly applied. You will find many references to JIT in these chapters. Just a word is needed on the apparent contradiction between just-in-time and EOQ (zero-based versus planned inventory levels). Just-in-time works by reducing the fixed costs that force us to keep inventory. These fixed costs appear in the numerator of the EOQ formula, showing quantitatively how much inventories can be reduced for a given reduction in costs. In the last chapter, we showed the sensitivity of the EOQ to the fixed costs.

We have already discussed the links between just-in-time and the final chapters. It is impossible to determine when materials are needed without improved scheduling of operations. The idea of continuous improvement presented as total quality management is very similar to the just-in-time philosophy of reducing the frequency of problems. Finally, quality control assures that all product is useful, thereby minimizing quantities, inspection times, and scrap.

MATERIALS REQUIREMENTS PLANNING: THE APPROACH

Materials requirements planning combines traditional inventory methods that stress quantity with the important element of time. Through time phasing, inventory requirements are expressed in terms of time in addition to quantity. Through MRP, the user is supplied with valuable information that was unavailable with older methods, such as

when customer demand and demand for component parts must be satisfied and whether such demand will be

questions answered by MRP

- spaced in time or
- all at once;

when existing stock will run out;

when replenishment orders should be sent out (order release); and

when the quantity ordered will arrive (order receipt).

The main objective of MRP in its standard form is to generate information that will initiate the correct order action—be it a release or a revision. It applies equally to purchase (external) orders and shop (internal) orders.

Given the demand for end items derived from forecasting methods at the discretion of the user, MRP converts gross inventory requirements into net requirements for each component by comparing gross requirements with supplies on hand. These net requirements are then time phased to ensure the timely release of an order that will fulfill future demand for that item or component with exactly the right quantity.

MRP INPUTS AND OUTPUTS

As we have seen, the MRP system is a commonsense computer-based approach to coordinating the purchasing and use of materials with the needs of complex production schedules. Because it is computer based, some discussion of the inputs and outputs is necessary for a complete understanding of how MRP works. The three major inputs are

- the master production schedule;
- the bill of materials; and
- the inventory record file.

Most of this section will deal with the inputs and their use. The outputs are the decisions resulting from the use of the MRP system. Specifically, these decisions are

- which parts to order;
- how many to order; and
- when to order.

The **master production schedule** is the controlling mechanism of the MRP system. In it, the needs for each end item are spelled out by scheduling period (daily, weekly, and so forth), or **time bucket.** The manager using an MRP system specifies the needs, and the system generates all of the production and purchasing schedules for each component and subcomponent of each end item.

controlling mechanism

We have stated that end item needs are forecasted. If the master production schedule is just a period-by-period listing of these forecasts for each end item, what is the role of the production scheduler? First, given the forecasts, there are many different production schedules that will meet the needs. We learned this in our discussion of aggregate planning and production scheduling. The production scheduler uses the MRP system as an analysis tool to quickly evaluate a variety of production scheduling options. For each master production schedule, the resulting timing and quantities of materials needs can be analyzed to help design a schedule that seems most appropriate in terms of ordering costs, equipment changeovers, and in general, ease of implementation.

How far into the future to schedule is very much dependent on circumstances. The confidence that we have in forecasts decreases as forecasts project farther into the future, so a given forecast may not be reliable enough to use as a basis for a master schedule. At a minimum, however, it is necessary that the master schedule go far enough into the future to cover the sum of the lead times necessary to produce the end item. If, for example, the end item requires that a sequence of five operations be performed, and these five operations require lead times of two, one, three, one, and two weeks, respectively, then a (cumulative) lead time of $2 + 1 + 3 + 1 + 2 = 9$ weeks is required for the end item. No production of this item could be added to the master schedule for less than nine weeks from the present time, because that schedule could not be met unless work had already begun.

The **bill of materials** is the means by which the end item needs are linked to the needs for the component items. As such, it also is the means by which the master production schedule acts as the controller for the system. For each end item, the bill of materials lists all of the materials required to produce that end item. This list includes all components, of course, but it also includes items required for production that do not become part of the end item, such as solder for welding, flocculents for refining processes, annealing bath ingredients, grease for lubrication, and dies for forming processes. The bill of materials used in an MRP system also provides additional information to link the items, including the specific place in the process where each item is needed and lead times for obtaining each item. This type of bill of materials is referred to as a "structured" bill of materials. Bills of materials are discussed in more detail in the next section, after which their use in MRP scheduling is presented.

The third input is the **inventory record file.** Recall the discussion of the evolution of an inventory system in Chapter 13. As inventory needs grow in size and complexity, the inventory record system evolves from one that is stored in the head of the responsible individual, to one that is stored in some form of card or paper file, and finally, to one that is stored in a computer data base. This computer data base is, essentially, the inventory record file required for MRP. Thus, the use of an MRP system is a logical next step in this progression of the inventory system. Clearly, the MRP system cannot determine how many of a particular part to order until it knows how many of that part it currently has on hand. The inventory record file provides this information for the MRP system.

The inputs are linked to the outputs by the MRP scheduling calculations, which are explained later. Briefly, the master production schedule specifies both the number and the time requirements for the end items. The bill of materials (there is one for each end item) is used to calculate the needs (again, in terms of number and time) for all components. The inventory record file is used to determine if the needs can be met from current stocks or if an order needs to be placed.

BILLS OF MATERIALS

The bill of materials (BOM) is a complete list of all parts that are required for the manufacture and/or assembly of an end item. Anyone who has ever purchased a product that comes disassembled has seen that a complete parts list comes with assembly instructions. This parts list is a bill of materials. A bill of materials for a backyard swing set may look like the one shown in Table 14.1.

If the only purpose in using this bill of materials is to check to see if all of the parts have been provided, then it is fine in its present form. To build any given number of swing sets, we can calculate the exact number of each part that will be required. For example, building four swing sets will require 48 (4 × 12 per set) of the 5/16" hex nuts. Similar calculations may be performed for each of the other parts.

structured bill of materials

For assembly, separate instructions on the use of the parts are required. However, the use of a structured bill of materials is helpful, independent of any instructions, in that it provides guidance as to which parts are used with which other parts and which parts are included in subassemblies prior to final assembly. The structured bill of materials attempts to show the materials needs within the context of the assembly procedure.

There are a variety of ways to represent a structured bill of materials. The best type in list form is called the **indented bill of materials.** For the swing set, the indented bill of materials might be as shown in Table 14.2.

Notice that the indented bill of materials provides a great deal of additional information. First, the subassemblies were not listed on our first bill of materials. They are listed in the indented bill of materials and are assigned their own part numbers, allowing for their possible storage in inventory. Second, for each subassembly, all parts

TABLE 14.1 Swing set bill of materials

Part Number	Part Description	Number Required
2044	1/4″ × 2″ bolt	6
2046	1/4″ × 2-1/4″ bolt	16
2048	1/4″ × 2-1/2″ bolt	8
1840	1/4″ lock washer	30
1940	1/4″ hex nut	30
1850	5/16″ lock washer	12
2058	5/16″ × 2-3/4″ bolt	8
1950	5/16″ hex nut	12
2052	5/16″ × 1-3/4″ bolt	4
5701	Seat hanger	4
5900	Bearing assembly	8
1740	1/4″ protective cap	38
1798	2″ cap	4
1750	5/16″ protective cap	12
6102	#1/0 chain	4
6101	Swing seat	2
5704	Ladder rung	13
6110	Ring assembly	2
5712	Anchor rod	4
4004	Ladder rail	2
4006	Top bar	2
4008	Leg	4
5705	Brace	4
6112	Chain and trapeze bar	1
5725	2″ straight assembly	4

Transparency Master 14.2: The Bill of Materials.

needed for that assembly are listed immediately after it in the indented form. Searching through a parts list for the appropriate part is not necessary. Third, some information that gives guidance as to the timing of the assembly operations and the materials needs is provided: The more a part number is indented, the closer that part is to the first stage of assembly.

The indented bill of materials also indicates that some parts needed for final assembly have just one or even no assembly operations required—for example, the anchor rod and the chain and trapeze bar require no assembly oprations, as evidenced by their alignment with the various completed subassemblies (where assembly results in the end item). Because these parts require little work prior to final assembly, the scheduling of their assembly operations is more flexible, as is the purchasing. Subassemblies such as the frame assembly, which require two or more levels of assembly operations, have little scheduling flexibility. So, in terms of our project scheduling discussion in Chapter 10, the indented bill of materials can help to identify, in some sense, the critical parts associated with the production of the swing set. Of course, our critical path analogy holds only if one swing set is to be assembled, but the scheduling concepts are similar in the production environment.

There is one piece of information that was easy to find on the first bill of materials that appears to be missing from the indented bill of materials: the total requirements

TABLE 14.2 Swing set indented bill of materials

Part Number	Part Description	Number Required		
1000	Swing set	1		
6110	Ring assembly		2	
5712	Anchor rod		4	
6112	Chain and trapeze bar		1	
1740	1/4″ protective cap		38	
1798	1″ protective cap		4	
1750	5/16″ protective cap		12	
6100	Swing assembly		2	
5701	Seat hanger			2
6102	#1/0 chain			2
6101	Swing seat			1
1010	Frame assembly	1		
1011	Ladder rail assembly		1	
5704	Ladder rung			3
4004	Ladder rail			2
2044	1/4″ × 2″ bolt			6
1840	1/4″ lock washer			6
1940	1/4″ hex nut			6
1012	Leg and top bar assembly		2	
4006	Top bar			1
5725	2″ straight assembly			2
5900	Bearing assembly			4
2052	5/16″ × 1-3/4″ bolt			2
1850	5/16″ lock washer			6
1950	5/16″ hex nut			6
2058	5/16″ × 2-3/4″ bolt			4
1018	Brace and ladder rung assembly			2
5704	Ladder rung			1
5705	Brace			1
2048	1/4″ × 2-1/2″ bolt			2
1840	1/4″ lock washer			2
1940	1/4″ hex nut			2
1013	Leg assembly			1
4008	Leg			2
5704	Ladder rung			3
2046	1/4″ × 2-1/4″ bolt			8
1840	1/4″ lock washer			8
1940	1/4″ hex nut			8

for each part. This information is given on the indented bill of materials, but it takes some searching and some calculation to determine it. For example, while the listing for the ladder rail (4004) says that 2 are required, which is correct, the listing for the top bar (4006) says that only 1 is required, which is not correct. This listing, in the indented form, means that 1 top bar is required per leg and top bar assembly. Because

2 top bar assemblies are required, the total requirement for top bars is 2. More complicated is the case of the ladder rungs (5704). This part is listed three times:

- under ladder rail assembly (1011), where 3 are needed;
- under leg assembly (1013), where 3 are needed per leg and top bar assembly (2 of these are needed) for a total of 6;
- under brace and ladder rung assembly (1018), where 2 are needed per leg and top bar assembly (2 of these are needed) for a total of 4.

Thus, assembling one swing set requires a total of 13 ladder rungs.

Which bill of materials is better? It depends on the use. For the purposes of MRP, the indented form is superior, because it links the material requirements to the needs and the timing of the production operations.

The actual form of the bill of materials used by MRP is not either of the two that we have seen thus far. MRP uses a pictorial form of the indented bill of materials, sometimes referred to as a **parts explosion.** The parts explosion is a structured bill of materials that starts with the end item node alone on the top level. This usually is called level zero and is reserved for end items for which the requirements are forecasted. The parts explosion branches out (or explodes) from this node, extending one branch for each part that will be required for that level of assembly. Items at this level (level one) are those listed on the first indent of the indented bill of materials. From each of these nodes, additional branches are extended in accordance with the material needs. Branches and nodes are developed until the entire sequence of assembly and material needs is represented in the diagram. The parts explosion for the swing set is shown in Figure 14.2. The numbers in parentheses to the right of each node indicate the lead time for acquiring (ordering, assembling, and so forth) that particular part. The circled number above each node indicates the number of that part required.

pictorial BOM

The parts explosion has the same deficiency as the indented bill of materials; that is, it does not readily provide total quantities required for specific parts. It is a little easier to perform these calculations using the parts explosion, however, because it is only necessary to follow the branches from level zero to the part of interest. At each level, multiply the needs by the number required at that level. For example, for each swing set, 16 of the $1/4" \times 2\text{-}1/4"$ bolts (2046) are required (1 for item 1000, 1 for item 1010, 2 for item 1012, 1 for item 1013, and 8 for item 2046, or $1 \times 1 \times 2 \times 1 \times 8 = 16$). The difficulty that remains is finding all of the places where any item is used. When a parts explosion has tens, hundreds, or even thousands of levels, it would be inefficient to search the entire diagram to find where each part number is required.

MRP gets around this difficulty through the use of **low-level coding.** The goal of low-level coding is to enable the user to identify every place where an item is required by searching only one level of the diagram. An additional benefit of this coding is that it labels each item by level (a level one item, level two item, and so forth). It is not possible to label all items in Figure 14.2 by level. It is clear that part 6110 is a level one item and 5705 is a level four item. These items appear on only one level. However, look at item 1940. It is used once on level three and twice on level four. Using low-level coding, we would not put an item on the level where it appears most, although this might seem logical until we tried to redraw the diagram. The rule is to redraw the diagram so that any item appearing on more than one level is put on the lowest level on which it appears—hence the name. Therefore, part 1940 is a level four item. Our sample parts explosion has been redrawn using low-level coding in Figure 14.3.

Teaching Suggestion 14.3:
Low-Level Coding. See the
Instructor's Section for
details.

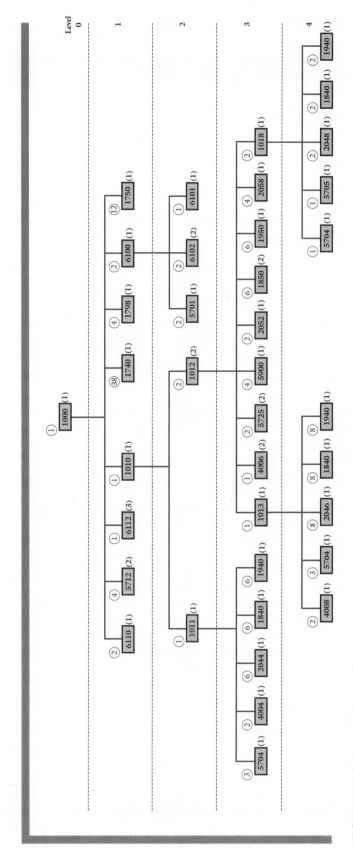

FIGURE 14.2 Parts explosion for swing set

Transparency Master 14.4:
The Parts Explosion.

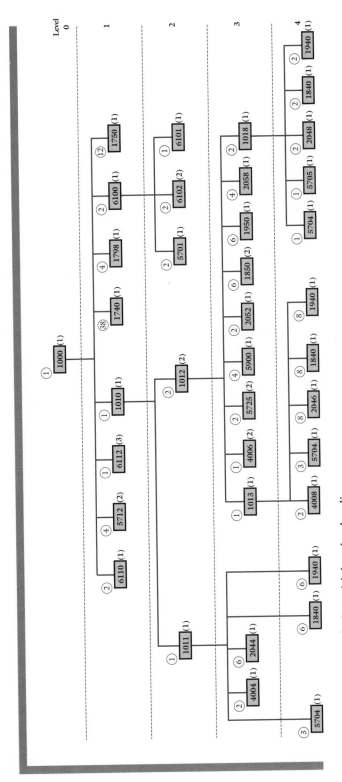

FIGURE 14.3 Parts explosion with low-level coding

USE OF THE MASTER PRODUCTION SCHEDULE IN MRP SCHEDULING

The master production schedule provides the needs for the level zero items over a planning horizon (number of planning periods). A master production schedule for our plant that assembles the swing sets could appear as follows.

	Week							
	1	2	3	4	5	6	7	8
Production	60	60	60	60	60	60	60	60

This master production schedule tells us that 60 swing sets will be required for each of the next eight weeks. Presumably, the number of swing sets to be produced after the eighth week is not known, or else we would want to use that information in our planning.

The preceding master production schedule has, as its major characteristic, a constant demand. Anyone looking at it may conclude that weeks 9, 10, 11, and so on will have a demand of 60 as well. Such a master production schedule fits into the inventory analysis for constant demand items that was presented in Chapter 13. However, that analysis did not consider the scheduling of many components simultaneously.

In the constant demand situation, the EOQ for the swing sets would be calculated. Then, the needs for each of the components could be calculated from the bill of materials. The timing of these needs also could be calculated from the bill of materials. In the more usual case, the demands are not constant, so the EOQ is not used. The example that follows explains the methodology by which the needs for each item are calculated.

methodology

> **Example 14.1**   Suppose that the only demand for the swing sets is the demand of 60 in week 8. How many 1/4" lock washers (item 1840) are needed, when are they needed, and when should they be ordered? Refer to Figure 14.3 for parts requirements and lead times.
>
> The master production schedule is as follows.

	Week							
	1	2	3	4	5	6	7	8
Demand	0	0	0	0	0	0	0	60

For every item in the bill of materials, an MRP scheduling table can be completed. The set of tables provides all of the information needed for ordering and using each of the components. Because we are only interested in item 1840, we will not develop all of the tables. However, we must develop more tables than just the one for item 1840.

The procedure is to develop a table for the level zero item first. This table shows when to order the level zero item. This order (or orders) creates a need (in a sense, it is another master schedule) for the level one items. We continue generating the tables until we reach item 1840.

In our bill of materials, we can trace item 1840 through the path

$$1000 \rightarrow 1010 \rightarrow 1011 \rightarrow 1840.$$

We find the 1840 item again by the path

$$1000 \rightarrow 1010 \rightarrow 1012 \rightarrow 1013 \rightarrow 1840$$

and a third time by the path

$$1000 \rightarrow 1010 \rightarrow 1012 \rightarrow 1018 \rightarrow 1840.$$

Consequently, we must develop tables for items 1000, 1010, 1011, 1012, 1013, and 1018—that is, for all the items on the paths to item 1840—before we can develop the table for item 1840.

The MRP table contains the following information for each time period:

- total requirement;
- on-hand inventory;
- net requirement;
- order receipt; and
- order release.

Thus, we will set up all of our tables as follows.

	Week							
	1	2	3	4	5	6	7	8
Total requirement								
On-hand inventory								
Net requirement								
Order receipt								
Order release								

The total requirement for the level zero item is taken directly from the master production schedule. This requirement is forecasted. For lower-level items, the total requirement is taken directly from the order release of the item(s) on the immediately higher level. This requirement is calculated. If 60 swing sets are ordered at week 7, then the total requirement for item 1010 (the level one item) is 60 in week 7. The calculation is not so simple for item 1840, as we shall see. This item has three higher-level items (1011, 1013, and 1018) from which it is derived. The orders for these three items must be added together to obtain the total requirement for item 1840. Other than for the level zero item, a need for an item can be generated only by a need for an item on the immediately higher level.

On-hand inventory is obtained from the inventory record file. It represents the number available for use at any given time. It is subtracted from the total requirement to obtain the net requirement, the amount to be ordered. In any table, the order

matching of needs with requirements

accounting for lead times

receipt row will be identical to the net requirement row. This is the amount that should be received. Because of this duplication, the order receipt row is sometimes omitted. We include it here primarily because it emphasizes the exact matching of needs with requirements and because a common practice is to include it.

The order release entry shows the amount ordered and the time at which the order is made. The amount ordered must, of course, match the amount received and the amount required listed in the two previous rows in the table. The lead time should be used to calculate the time of the order. Subtracting the lead time from the time when it is required to be on hand will produce the timing of the order. For example, an item that has a two-week lead time and is required in week 6, such as item 1012, should be ordered in week 4 (6 − 2). This procedure is called **lead time offsetting.**

The tables for calculating the needs for item 1840 are given in parts (a) through (g) of Table 14.3. We start with item 1000 (level zero) and assume that no on-hand inventories are available. This is the ideal assumption, because it implies that we carry inventory only at the time that it is being used. After the net requirement is calculated for the first period, the inventory on-hand for the next period, including any shipments that are due to arrive, is computed. A shipment is scheduled to arrive whenever the inventory on hand is insufficient to meet the demand. This situation is easy to identify because it is the only case where the net requirement is not zero.

All of the entries in each table are easily calculated from the total requirements for each part. The total requirements for part 1000 (the swing set) comes directly from the master production schedule. The order release is in week 7 because the lead time for this item is one week. Notice that an arrow has been drawn from this order down to the table for item 1010, generating the requirement for this item. This is the link between the tables; and such links always flow from the higher-level items to the lower-level components. (The arrows are not really needed, because the information they provide is obtained directly from the bill of materials. However, you might consider drawing them as a way of keeping track of things during the calculations.) The rest of the tables are completed in the same way. For item 1840 (see the last table), we have needs of twice the number of item 1018s and eight times the number of item 1013s, or 480 + 960 = 1,440, in week 3. There is also a need in week 5 for six times the number of 1011s, or 360.

The results for item 1840 are these:

- 1,440 are ordered in week 2 to be received in week 3;
- 360 are ordered in week 4 to be received in week 5.

Other orders are known as well:

- 240 of item 1018 are ordered in week 3;
- 120 of item 1013 are ordered in week 3;
- 120 of item 1012 are ordered in week 4;
- 60 of item 1011 are ordered in week 5;
- 60 of item 1010 are ordered in week 6;
- 60 of item 1000 are ordered in week 7.

All of these orders are required to ensure the timely completion (neither early nor late) of the 60 swing sets in week 8. The lead times can be viewed as either the time needed to assemble the subassembly or the time needed to wait for the parts to arrive (or some combination). ◼︎

TABLE 14.3 MRP tables (Example 14.1)

Item 1000

	Week 1	Week 2	Week 3	Week 4	Week 5	Week 6	Week 7	Week 8	
Total requirement	0	0	0	0	0	0	0	60	
On-hand inventory									
Net requirement								60	(a)
Order receipt								60	
Order release							60		

Item 1010

	Week 1	Week 2	Week 3	Week 4	Week 5	Week 6	Week 7	Week 8	
Total requirement							60		
On-hand inventory									
Net requirement							60		(b)
Order receipt							60		
Order release						60			

Item 1011

	Week 1	Week 2	Week 3	Week 4	Week 5	Week 6	Week 7	Week 8	
Total requirement						60			
On-hand inventory									
Net requirement						60			(c)
Order receipt						60			
Order release					60				

Item 1012

	Week 1	Week 2	Week 3	Week 4	Week 5	Week 6	Week 7	Week 8	
Total requirement						120			
On-hand inventory									
Net requirement						120			(d)
Order receipt						120			
Order release				120					

Item 1013

	Week 1	Week 2	Week 3	Week 4	Week 5	Week 6	Week 7	Week 8	
Total requirement				120					
On-hand inventory									
Net requirement				120					(e)
Order receipt				120					
Order release			120						

Item 1018

	Week 1	Week 2	Week 3	Week 4	Week 5	Week 6	Week 7	Week 8	
Total requirement				240					
On-hand inventory									
Net requirement				240					(f)
Order receipt				240					
Order release			240						

Item 1840

	Week 1	Week 2	Week 3	Week 4	Week 5	Week 6	Week 7	Week 8	
Total requirement			1,440		360				
On-hand inventory									
Net requirement			1,440		360				(g)
Order receipt			1,440		360				
Order release		1,440		360					

The calculations required for Example 14.1 are all quite simple. They also are quite tedious and time-consuming. Our example looked at only a small portion of the problem. We did not complete tables for most of the items. In reality, tables for all the items would need to be done. The result of this effort would be a much longer list of order releases and receipts to monitor. Consequently, as we have stated, MRP always is done on the computer in practice. The computer provides daily reports of orders to be received and released. There was one more significant simplification in the example: Swing sets were needed only in week 8. All of these orders are needed for only one end-item order. In reality, the swing sets would presumably be needed (in varying amounts) during most or all of the weeks. This would require adding more entries to each table, rather than creating more tables. However, the number of orders to be monitored would increase dramatically.

LOT SIZING

In Example 14.1, we determined that 1,440 lock washers (item 1840 in our bill of materials) are to be ordered during week 2, and 360 more are to be ordered during week 4. In this section, we discuss the merits of strictly following the "order what is needed when it is needed" philosophy of MRP versus ordering lot sizes based on some of the principles of the EOQ models presented in Chapter 13. With the MRP approach, we would place orders precisely as Example 14.1 determined. On the other hand, the lock washer is a tiny, low-cost part that is very inexpensive to store. Maybe we should buy all 1,800 of them at once. Consider the following example.

Example 14.2   The orders for part 1840 are as follows.

Week	Order
1	0
2	1,440
3	0
4	360

It costs $10 for each order placed. The holding cost for the lock washer is $.01 per unit per week. Compare the two ordering policies.

With MRP, the holding costs are zero, but the ordering costs are $20, because two orders are being placed.

For one order of 1,800 parts, the order cost is $10 and the holding cost for storing the 360 parts for two weeks is

$$(360 \text{ units} \times \$.01/\text{unit/week}) \times 2 \text{ weeks} = \$7.20.$$

This yields a total cost of $17.20, versus the $20 total cost incurred with MRP. Therefore, the two lots should be combined, and the order of 1,800 parts should be placed during week 2. ∎

Example 14.2 shows that a strict use of the MRP ordering policy may not be advantageous, but it does not specify how to select the best grouping of orders for any given situation. Four kinds of approaches have been taken to formalize lot sizing policies:

1. lot for lot;
2. EOQ;
3. optimization; and
4. heuristic.

MRP calls for the **lot-for-lot** approach. The orders are placed exactly as specified in the last row of the MRP tables. As we have seen, EOQ models are appropriate when there is a continuous and constant demand. Generally, there is not constant demand in an MRP system. However, in a complex MRP system, there may be a few components that exhibit this demand pattern. For these components, the EOQ should be used. Furthermore, for many items that are needed continuously (during each time period), demand is erratic—that is, it varies from one period to the next. Use of the EOQ for these systems, based on their average demand, can provide cost-effective lot sizes for purchasing.

The use of the EOQ is restrictive in that it does not allow variable-size lot sizes to be used. Recall, however, that the EOQ formulas were obtained by *optimizing* the selection of an order size by minimizing the inventory costs. The same thing can be done for the case of erratic demand patterns, but the procedure is much more complex. This procedure is known as Wagner-Whitin. Because this technique is outside the scope of this text, no details are provided here. Suffice it to say that this technique yields the best results, but that the computer time required (it is too laborious to do by hand) can be prohibitive. Most business schools (and AB:POM) have this method available on computer for student use. Try using it on some of the problems at the end of this chapter and compare your results with those of the other methods.

Because the optimization approach is too difficult to solve (even on a computer) for many problems of practical size, a variety of heuristic procedures have been developed. All of these attempt to equate ordering and holding costs. The one demonstrated here is the part period method, or part period balancing. This method calculates a **part period value** (*PPV*), which is simply the ordering cost divided by the holding cost.

equate ordering and holding costs

$$PPV = \frac{S}{H}$$

Defining a part period as the number of parts stored for one period, this *PPV* is the number of part periods that would be included in a lot when holding and ordering costs are in balance.

The part period method consists of four steps.

Step 1. Calculate the part period value using the formula

$$PPV = \frac{S}{H}.$$

This is the largest number of part periods that should be included in any individual order.

Step 2. Build the order, one period at a time, and calculate the actual part periods included. To calculate the actual part periods, multiply the number of parts times the number of periods that the parts must be held in inventory. The parts used in the first period are held for zero periods, so no part periods accrue. The parts used in the second period are held for one period, those used in the third period are held for two periods, and so forth.

Step 3. When more part periods have accrued than were calculated for the part period value, too many parts have been ordered. Order only up to the start of the period in which accrued part periods exceed *PPV*. For example, if including the needs of the fourth period results in the accumulation of too many part periods, then order for three periods only.

Step 4. An order is now developed. Since we know the size of the order and the number of periods it will last, we also know when the next order should be due to arrive. Go back to step 2 and build the next order in the same way, until all demands are satisfied by the orders.

The following example illustrates the use of the lot sizing approaches.

Teaching Suggestion 14.4: Planned Orders. See the Instructor's Section for details.

Example 14.3 The following MRP table shows the orders for item 1840 for the next six weeks.

Week	Order
1	400
2	1,200
3	800
4	360
5	500
6	1,000

Evaluate the three methods that can be done by hand and refer to Example 14.2 for costs. How many should be ordered, and when, based on the total cost?

Lot-for-lot method: The orders are as given. The total inventory cost is $60 (six orders times $10 per order). There is no holding cost.

EOQ method: The annual holding cost is given by $H = \$.52$/unit-year, because there are 52 weeks in a year and the weekly holding cost is $\$.01$, as stated in Example 14.2.

$D = 4,260$ parts in six weeks, or 710 per week, or 36,920 per year

$S = \$10$

To find the EOQ, use the formula $Q = \sqrt{2DS/H}$.

$$Q = \sqrt{\frac{(2)(36,920 \times 10)}{.52}} \simeq 1,200 \text{ per order}$$

So the orders are

1,200 in week 1 to cover 400 for week 1 and 800 for week 2;

1,200 in week 2 to cover 400 for week 2 and 800 for week 3;

1,200 in week 4 to cover 360 for week 4, 500 for week 5, and 340 for week 6; and

660 in week 6 to complete the requirements.

Teaching Suggestion 14.5: Last Order in EOQ. See the Instructor's Section for details.

The resulting cost is approximately $67.80, which is found as follows. The order cost is

$$4 \text{ orders} = \$10 \times 4 = \$40.$$

The holding cost is

800 from order 1 stored one week $= \$.01 \times 800 = \$8.00$,

800 from order 2 stored one week $= \$.01 \times 800 = \$8.00$,

500 from order 3 stored one week $= \$.01 \times 500 = \$5.00$, and

340 from order 3 stored two weeks $= (\$.01 \times 340) \times 2 = \$6.80$,

or approximately $27.80, yielding the total of $67.80.

Part period method:

$$PPV = \frac{\$10}{.01} = 1,000$$

Order Number 1. Ordering 400 results in zero part periods.

$$400 \text{ parts} \times 0 \text{ periods}$$

Ordering 1,600 results in 1,200 part periods.

$$1,200 \text{ parts} \times 1 \text{ period}$$

This is too many. Therefore, *order 400 during week 1.*

Order Number 2. Ordering 1,200 results in zero part periods.

$$1,200 \times 0 \text{ periods}$$

Ordering 2,000 results in 800 part periods.

$$(1,200 \times 0) + (800 \times 1 \text{ period})$$

Ordering 2,360 results in 1,520 part periods.

$$(1,200 \times 0) + (800 \times 1 \text{ period}) + (360 \times 2 \text{ periods})$$

This is too many. Therefore, *order 2,000 during week 2.*

Order Number 3. Ordering 360 results in zero part periods.

$$360 \times 0 \text{ periods}$$

Ordering 860 results in 500 part periods.

$$(360 \times 0) + (500 \times 1 \text{ period})$$

Ordering 1,860 results in 2,500 part periods.

$$360 \times 0 + 500 \times 1 + 1,000 \times 2$$

This is too many. Therefore, *order 860 during week 4.*

Order Number 4. *Order 1,000 during week 6.*

The cost of this policy is calculated as follows.

Ordering cost $= \$40$ (4 orders of $10 per order)

Holding cost $=$ (800 parts and 500 parts each held for one period) $=$ $8 + $5 = $13

Total cost $= \$53$

In summary, the three methods yield the following costs for this example.

- Lot for lot = $60.00
- EOQ = $67.80
- Part period = $53.00

The part period method performs best on this problem and, in general, performs very well.

EXTENSIONS OF MRP

The benefits of using MRP systems in complex manufacturing environments are now well recognized. By keeping track of large amounts of information and by coordinating the use of this information properly, we can more effectively monitor and control our inventories and our production schedules.

When a good idea (such as MRP) is adopted, we are inclined to use it and to enjoy its benefits—usually. MRP has had a somewhat frustrating affect on its users. The MRP user often finds that this system merely whets the appetite for bigger and better things. Given all of the things that MRP can do, why can't we use the same approach to control other activities in our business? In fact, we can: The MRP concept has been extended to accomplish this. Three of these extensions—BRP (or MRP II), CRP, and DRP—are discussed in this section.

BUSINESS REQUIREMENTS PLANNING (OR MRP II)

Figure 14.4 illustrates the flow of information in MRP. The master production schedule is provided, and then the bill of materials is used to generate orders for the purchasing and production control departments. Because this is the end of the line and nothing more is done with the information, MRP is referred to as an open loop system. In Figure 14.5, a feedback mechanism has been added to the master production schedule, allowing the analysis of the various production schedules. When an MRP system includes feedback mechanism, it is referred to as a closed loop system. The addition of the feedback mechanism is the most basic modification to MRP, and this more advanced system is known as MRP II.

MRP II facilitates production scheduling much better than MRP, which actually gives higher priority to materials management. Because of this, the "MRP" in MRP II stands for "manufacturing resources planning" to many companies. Other capabilities in a complete MRP II system may include distribution requirements planning, capacity requirements planning, and sales requirements planning. For obvious reasons, the complete system is known as **business requirements planning** (BRP) and addresses manufacturing and other concerns. Thus, BRP is more complete than MRP II. An essential element of the complete system is that the extensions of MRP are linked together in a common data base.

Figure 14.6 provides a comparison between a typical MRP system and the more complete MRP II system. Notice that MRP is still the heart of MRP II. MRP II, which takes on many forms, is just an extension of MRP.

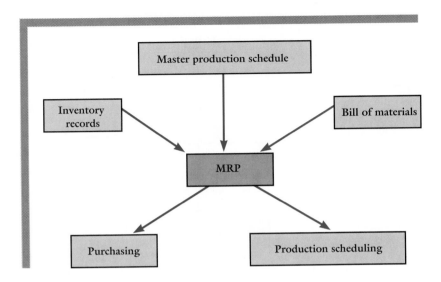

FIGURE 14.4 Open loop system

How far should MRP be extended? There is no clear answer to this question. Ideally, we would like a system that could control all aspects of a business for us. For a midsize company, this may be nearly, but not completely, attainable. For a large company, it probably is not even remotely attainable and may even be undesirable. It might, for example, force standardization of practices within a company whose strength comes from the independence of its smaller groups. How much an MRP system should be allowed to do depends on the desired balance between control and flexibility, between central planning and innovation.

FIGURE 14.5 Closed loop system

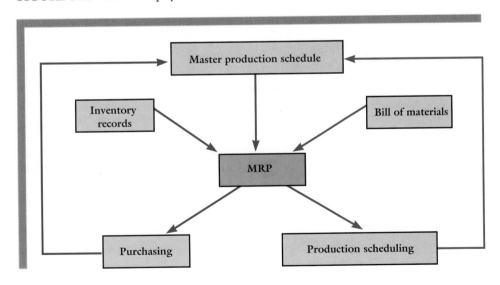

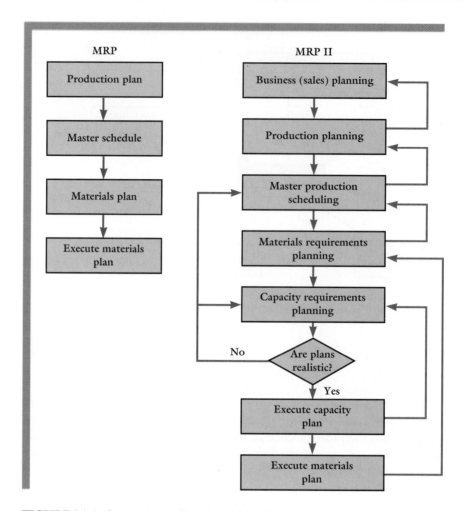

FIGURE 14.6 Comparison of MRP and MRP II

CAPACITY REQUIREMENTS PLANNING

The most basic closed loop system was presented in Figure 14.5. The provision of a feedback mechanism allows the system to be used more easily and more advantageously for production scheduling. However, although it allows for better testing of alternative production schedules, it never provides guidance concerning how or why these schedules should be changed. The addition of **capacity requirements planning** (CRP) in the feedback loop does provide this information. The diagram of this simple MRP II system is shown in Figure 14.7.

The capacity requirements planning system guides the production schedules in two ways. First, it evaluates all planned orders and production to determine if there is sufficient capacity to implement the schedule. If there is insufficient capacity, either additional capacity must be found or the master production schedule must be changed. Second, it calculates the utilization, or efficiency, of the various capacities for

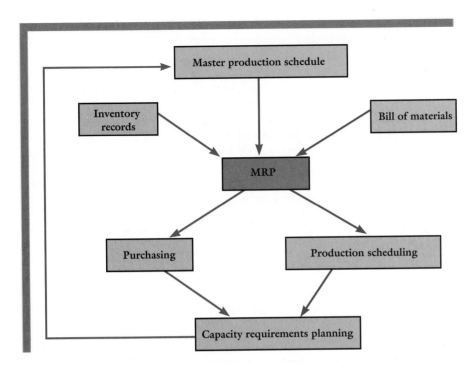

FIGURE 14.7 Closed loop system with capacity requirements planning

each component required. Low utilizations may indicate that a schedule change is in order. These utilizations, discussed in Chapter 3, often are drawn on load charts (Gantt charts) as a visual aid in the scheduling process.

It seems that the basic function of the capacity requirements planning system is to compare the capacity required (based on the orders derived from the MRP tables) to the capacity available. If the utilization is less than 100 percent, the schedule is feasible. If it is significantly less, then either there is too much capacity or some schedule changes should be made to better utilize the capacity. If the utilization is more than 100 percent, then there is insufficient capacity. Clearly, capacity requirements planning is a useful tool for some of the capacity design problems given in Chapter 3. Whereas Chapter 3 focused on long-range strategic capacity decisions, here we consider short-range capacity analysis.

There is another function of capacity requirements planning. The available capacity is not static. Rather, it is dynamic, depending on many scheduling factors. For example, in a factory, there may be three pieces of a particular type of equipment that correspond to some level of production capacity. If the MRP system has already scheduled two of these machines during one week, then the capacity available for additional production in that week is only the capacity of one machine (the third one). The following week, when all three are available, may be a better time to schedule additional production. In any case, the capacity changes over time as schedules change. Capacity may be increased through the use of additional shifts, overtime, or subcontracting (see Chapter 12). However, the capacities of each of these options must be monitored also, because they too change in response to conditions that may be outside the scope of the MRP system. Consequently, a major function of the capacity requirements planning system is to constantly update capacities to ensure that the utilizations are calculated correctly.

Using a capacity requirements planning system, we can help to decide the short-term levels of capacity, such as overtime used, transfers of workers, equipment assignment, work assignment, and subcontracting. These are all options for modifying capacity that can be chosen in the process of modifying or implementing the master schedule. If the schedule cannot be met, another option—as yet unmentioned—is informing the customer that delivery will be late. Depending on the circumstances (cost of increasing capacity versus loss associated with the late delivery), this may be the best alternative. Often, a salesperson will request that a capacity requirements analysis be done prior to committing the company to a delivery date for a customer. In this way, the MRP system is used to avoid conflict between the salesperson and the customer, as well as between the sales department and the production department within the company.

> **Example 14.4** Shamrock Beverages bottles soda at its plant on Fortieth Street. The master production schedule for two-liter bottles for the next five months is given below.

	Month				
	1	2	3	4	5
Number of bottles	100,000	125,000	100,000	175,000	150,000

Enough workers have been hired to produce 150,000 bottles per month, and there is enough equipment to produce 200,000 per month. Determine the utilizations for labor and equipment, and suggest any revisions to the master schedule.

First we calculate the labor utilization for each of the five months.

Month 1:

$$\frac{100,000}{150,000} = .67, \text{ or } 67 \text{ percent}$$

Month 2:

$$\frac{125,000}{150,000} = .83, \text{ or } 83 \text{ percent}$$

Month 3:

$$\frac{100,000}{150,000} = .67, \text{ or } 67 \text{ percent}$$

Month 4:

$$\frac{175,000}{150,000} = 1.17, \text{ or } 117 \text{ percent}$$

Month 5:

$$\frac{150,000}{150,000} = 1.00, \text{ or } 100 \text{ percent}$$

Next we calculate the equipment utilization for each of the five months.

Month 1:

$$\frac{100,000}{200,000} = .50, \text{ or } 50 \text{ percent}$$

Month 2:

$$\frac{125,000}{200,000} = .625, \text{ or } 62.5 \text{ percent}$$

Month 3:

$$\frac{100,000}{200,000} = .50, \text{ or } 50 \text{ percent}$$

Month 4:

$$\frac{175,000}{200,000} = .875, \text{ or } 87.5 \text{ percent}$$

Month 5:

$$\frac{150,000}{200,000} = .75, \text{ or } 75 \text{ percent}$$

The bottleneck is the labor capacity. Production in month 4 cannot be met. Because there is no spare capacity in month 5, any delay in month 4 shipments will result in additional delays to the shipments scheduled for month 5. Unless a drop in demand is forecasted for month 6 (which is outside of our planning horizon), delaying shipments is not the way to modify the schedule. Using overtime in month 4 to accommodate the extra 25,000 bottles is one possibility. If storage costs for one month are less than the additional cost of overtime, the schedule should be modified to produce these extra 25,000 bottles in month 3.

	Month				
	1	2	3	4	5
Number of bottles	100,000	125,000	125,000	150,000	150,000

DISTRIBUTION REQUIREMENTS PLANNING

As noted in Chapter 6, **distribution requirements planning** (DRP) focuses on the material needs (in terms of timing, quantity, and location) within the distribution net-

Teaching Suggestion 14.6:
Push System. See the
Instructor's Section for
details.

work. The purpose of the entire distribution function, as we have seen, is to meet these material needs in a timely and cost-effective manner. Therefore, DRP is central to the operation of the system. The standard DRP is a pull system; that is, orders are initiated, as required, at the lowest level of the distribution network. This is where the product is finally sold. The retail store initiates the order, which forces the product to be "pulled" through the network from the factory, through the various levels of distribution centers, to the store. This is the more traditional DRP system for two reasons. First, the traditional way of planning material needs has been to respond to the lowest-level needs (decentralized planning). So, in this sense, the pull system described here introduces better order and better planning into the process, without significantly changing operating strategy. Second, the approach is very similar to that of MRP. Many advanced MRP commercial software packages possess a DRP capability. Those DRP capabilities are always pull systems.

steps in pull system   The pull system works as follows.

> **Step 1.** Identify the needs at the lowest (closest to customer) level in the network.
>
> **Step 2.** Generate an order from the next higher level for the amount required.
>
> **Step 3.** Schedule it so that it arrives at the time when it is needed. (The order from the lower level creates a need at this next higher level.)
>
> **Step 4.** Return to step 2 to continue generating orders until the highest level (factory) is reached.

Three things should be noticed here.

1. There is no independent demand for material at any level except the first.
2. All other needs (demands) at higher levels are generated to meet specific needs at the first level. They are dependent on the first level.
3. The need of the first level "pulls" the material through the network.

Example 14.5   Consider the distribution network shown in Figure 14.8 for the Bounty Basket Supermarket chain. Bounty Basket runs a canning plant in Hometown to supply its six stores with canned vegetables. Three of the stores are supplied from a distribution warehouse in Kingston and the other three stores are supplied from a distribution warehouse in Plymouth.

The weekly demands for canned peas at each of the supermarkets, their current stock, and their order quantities are shown in the following tables.

Supplied from Kingston Warehouse

Location	Demand (cases/week)	Stock on Hand	Order Quantity
Southampton	6	10	14
Kingston	7	10	20
Exeter	4	9	17

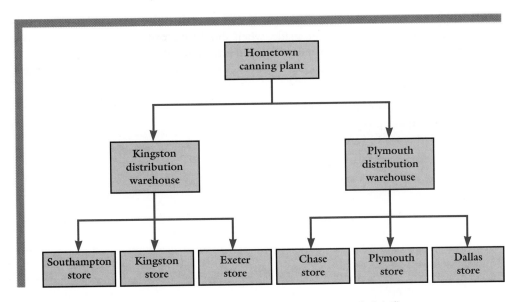

FIGURE 14.8 Network for Bounty Basket Supermarket (Example 14.5)

Supplied from Plymouth Warehouse

Location	Demand (cases/week)	Stock on Hand	Order Quantity
Chase	5	12	22
Plymouth	6	11	22
Dallas	9	15	30

There really are no direct customer demands at the distribution centers. The demands on the distribution centers are made in response to the direct customer demands made at the supermarkets. (The customers pull units out of the supermarkets, which in turn pull units from the distribution centers, which in turn pull units from the plants.) The order quantities and current stock at the distribution centers are as follows.

Location	Stock on Hand	Order Quantity
Kingston	37	35
Plymouth	52	55

The factory at Hometown currently has 100 cases of peas in stock ready for shipment. Each lot that it produces contains 120 cases.

Each time an order is placed, the amount ordered is the order quantity. We must assume that this quantity is selected to minimize costs of shipping and storing the peas.

What is required is the planning of shipments for the next seven weeks. Assume that each shipment has to be made one week before it is required and that the factory must plan its production one week before shipment. For the next seven weeks, how many shipments will need to be made, when should the orders be placed, and what are the quantities and destinations of these shipments?

For each location, it is necessary to track, in each of the seven weeks, four pieces of information—namely,

- projected gross requirements;
- projected inventory available;
- planned receipt of shipment; and
- planned order.

We begin by developing a table for the Southampton store.

					Week			
Southampton Store	0	1	2	3	4	5	6	7
Gross requirements		6	6	6	6	6	6	6
Available inventory	10	4	12	6	0	8	2	10
Planned receipt			14			14		14
Planned order		14			14		14	

First, we insert into the table the 6 cases of peas required each week and the 10 cases currently on hand. After inserting the known pieces of information, we fill in the rest of the table, beginning with week 1 and proceeding from week to week. It stands to reason that if 6 cases are used in the first week, then only 4 cases are left in stock (available inventory, week 1). Because these remaining 4 cases will not meet the demand for the second week (which, again, is 6 cases), an order for a shipment of 14 cases (the order quantity) must be scheduled to arrive during week 2 (planned receipt, week 2). Because the lead time is one week, the order is placed during week 1 from the Kingston distribution warehouse (planned order, week 1).

Now, the 4 cases in stock plus the 14 that arrive in week 2 yield a stock of 18 (this number is not entered), from which 6 are used. This leaves 12 cases in stock (available inventory, week 2). Six more cases are used in week 3, leaving 6 cases at the end of week 3, which will be used up in week 4. No inventory remains at the end of week 4, so another shipment of 14 cases must be ordered at this time (planned order, week 4). These 14 cases are received in week 5, when 6 cases are used, leaving 8 cases (available inventory, week 5). The rest of the table is completed in the same way.

Similarly, a table is developed for each of the remaining five supermarkets. All six tables are shown in Table 14.4.

The next step is to develop tables for each of the distribution warehouses, using the demands (planned shipments) generated by the supermarkets. As Figure 14.8 shows, the demands from the Southampton, Kingston, and Exeter supermarkets generate demands at the Kingston warehouse, and the demands from the Chase, Plymouth, and Dallas supermarkets generate demands at the Plymouth warehouse.

As an example, consider the Kingston warehouse, which supplies the Southampton, Kingston, and Exeter stores and which must satisfy the following demands.

TABLE 14.4 DRP tables for supermarkets (Example 14.5)

		Week						
Southampton Store	0	1	2	3	4	5	6	7
Gross requirements		6	6	6	6	6	6	6
Available inventory	10	4	12	6	0	8	2	10
Planned receipt			14			14		14
Planned order		14			14		14	

		Week						
Kingston Store	0	1	2	3	4	5	6	7
Gross requirements		7	7	7	7	7	7	7
Available inventory	10	3	16	9	2	15	8	1
Planned receipt			20			20		
Planned order		20			20			20*

		Week						
Exeter Store	0	1	2	3	4	5	6	7
Gross requirements		4	4	4	4	4	4	4
Available inventory	9	5	1	14	10	6	2	15
Planned receipt				17				17
Planned order			17				17	

		Week						
Chase Store	0	1	2	3	4	5	6	7
Gross requirements		5	5	5	5	5	5	5
Available inventory	12	7	2	19	14	9	4	21
Planned receipt				22				22
Planned order			22				22	

		Week						
Plymouth Store	0	1	2	3	4	5	6	7
Gross requirements		6	6	6	6	6	6	6
Available inventory	11	5	21	15	9	3	19	13
Planned receipt			22				22	
Planned order		22				22		

		Week						
Dallas Store	0	1	2	3	4	5	6	7
Gross requirements		9	9	9	9	9	9	9
Available inventory	15	6	27	18	9	0	21	12
Planned receipt			30				30	
Planned order		30				30		

* A shipment is planned here on the assumption that the demand will continue past week 7.

Week	Cases Shipped	Destination
1	14	Southampton
	20	Kingston
2	17	Exeter
3	—	
4	14	Southampton
	20	Kingston
5	—	
6	14	Southampton
	17	Exeter
7	20	Kingston

These demands are then inserted in a table.

Kingston Warehouse	Week							
	0	1	2	3	4	5	6	7
Gross requirements		34	17	0	34	0	31	20
Available inventory	37	3	21	21	22	22	26	6
Planned receipt			35		35		35	
Planned shipment		35		35		35		

Similarly, the demands for the Plymouth warehouse are used to develop its table.

Plymouth Warehouse	Week							
	0	1	2	3	4	5	6	7
Gross requirements		52	22	0	0	52	22	0
Available inventory	52	0	33	33	33	36	14	14
Planned receipt			55			55		
Planned shipment		55			55			

Finally, these demands at the warehouses create a need for production at the canning plant at Hometown. The canning plant must produce enough cases of peas to make the following shipments.

Week	Cases Shipped	Destination
1	90	35 to Kingston
		55 to Plymouth
3	35	All to Kingston
4	55	All to Plymouth
5	35	All to Kingston

We may now develop the table for the Hometown plant.

Hometown Plant		Week							
	0	1	2	3	4	5	6	7
Gross requirements		90	0	35	55	35	0	0
Available inventory	100	10	10	95	40	5	5	5
Planned shipping				120				
Planned production			120				(?)	(?)

Only one lot of 120 cases is produced, and it is produced during week 2. Production for weeks 6 and 7 cannot be decided until the demands beyond week 7 are known. The headings for the last two rows of this table have been changed to relate to the factory situation as opposed to the distribution or store situations. ∎

This completes the example problem. All of the questions are answered in the last two rows of each table. Twenty separate shipments are made in the seven-week planning horizon. We note that demands were constant for each of the six supermarkets. For example, the demand at Southampton was 6 cases each week. It should be obvious that demand will not necessarily be constant. If we forecast that the demands at Southampton will be 6, 5, 10, 3, 8, 4, 7, and 2 cases, respectively, in the next weeks, we simply use these numbers in the first row as our gross requirements.

IMPLEMENTATION OF MRP SYSTEMS

Once the appropriate system has been chosen, its implementation must be planned carefully. The cost and difficulty of implementation are easily underestimated. The programs that do succeed have several common ingredients, which we detail in this section. First, we note that unified support from upper management, financial and psychological, is an especially important asset; with such support, MRP is certain to be successful, even in the face of other problems.

FACTORS FOR SUCCESSFUL IMPLEMENTATION

We now examine several concerns that are critical when installing any MRP system.

THE IMPLEMENTATION TASK FORCE

A task force dedicated solely to the successful implementation of MRP is one such concern. The members of the task force usually are lower to middle managers of the departments that will be using the system. Other members that could be valuable to the team would have previous experience with implementation, have political clout in the company, or be from a department that will need to change its procedures to support MRP.

The responsibilities of the task force are extensive. While members may be able to perform the implementation in addition to performing their usual duties, performance appraisals from home departments may cause conflicts with task force objectives. The task force members may need to leave their regular positions for a period of one to two years. This would alleviate any conflicts of interest and allow the members to fully concentrate their efforts on attaining the goals of the implementation program. The departments from which the task force members come must be prepared for either possibility. They may need to redistribute duties, make temporary or permanent replacements, or work task force duties into the member's performance appraisal.

EDUCATING THE EMPLOYEES

The education of employees is the single most expensive, time-consuming, and important factor to the success of the system. Employees will be using the system, after all, and it is they who determine its integrity.

Before the system is in use, employees should be thoroughly indoctrinated in standard MRP principles. One sure way to accomplish this is to send middle managers to a series of seminars. Another, less extravagant approach, such as distributing written material and holding in-house seminars, may be just as effective.

most important factor

At least one person on the task force should be responsible for coordinating people and departments for educational purposes. The educational coordinator should be in contact with the vendor to take advantage of educational support. Many vendors will send specially trained instructors to the company to hold seminars for the users. Often, this service is included in the price of the system and should be exploited.

Each department must be eased into using this new tool. The reporting system may need to be changed entirely. Of course, employees will be working with the same information, but it will be rearranged. A department-wide inability to find the information necessary to do the job is the certain result of sudden, full implementation in an unprepared department.

A LITTLE AT A TIME

Ideally, MRP should not be implemented until the users are properly prepared, and it should be taken module by module then. Each module in itself usually can be divided into subsections that build on one another. It is important to take "small bites" that can be easily digested without causing a major setback to normal corporate operations. Business cannot stop because MRP is being implemented.

An additional expense, above and beyond the cost of the system and educational programs, must be considered. As our discussion of the learning curve effect in Chapter 9 showed, users will make mistakes and perform their duties more slowly than usual until they are familiar with the system.

TRANSITIONAL PROGRAMS

In-house programs that simulate module subsections will help smooth the transition from the old reporting system to that required by MRP. Such programs will familiarize users with the system and prevent costly on-line mistakes in real time. Usually, the vendor will help develop a custom-designed program, which is another reason to adopt a system with strong vendor support.

COMMON IMPLEMENTATION PROBLEMS

There are many problems that the implementation task force will encounter. Not everything can be foreseen, so the implementors must be prepared for the unexpected. Some problems, however, are encountered commonly by many user companies.

1. *Resistance to change.* In the implementation stage, resistance usually is found in the lower ranks, because MRP already has been accepted by upper management (or it would not have been purchased). However, there almost always is a minority of upper and middle managers who—out of ignorance, fear, stubbornness, or internal politics—will resist making a change. The workers on the production floor should be made dependent on the system for instructions and for credit for work in process.
2. *Protection of turf.* There is the possibility that harsh feelings could erupt between departments for control of MRP responsibilities. It is not always clear who would be the best supplier of required inputs. Production control, for instance, may want control of work in process, while the task force may want this responsibility to go to the shop-floor foremen.
3. *Systems modifications.* After implementation has begun, some needed modifications may suddenly become apparent. Because the system does run in the current environment, making modifications should not be impossible. With help from the vendor, most modifications can be developed in-house.

The time needed to implement an MRP system depends on a variety of factors, including the size of the company involved, the number of component items tracked, the number of end items, and the experience of the company with similar systems. A full year is a reasonable approximation, but many larger companies may require even more time. McNeil, the makers of Tylenol, implemented their MRP system over a two-year period. To ensure success, the important thing is to recognize that the MRP system should be implemented gradually, not suddenly. If the concerns mentioned in this section are taken seriously from the start and throughout the implementation period, the probability of a successful implementation is very high.

In summary, the special attention that successful implementation requires should be provided by following eight steps.

Step 1. Form a task force.

Step 2. Indoctrinate the task force.

Step 3. Coordinate people and departments.

Step 4. Assign input responsibilities to specific departments.

Step 5. Prepare each department for forthcoming changes.

Step 6. Give in-house seminars prior to and simultaneous with initial module implementation.

Step 7. Implement one module at a time in digestible subsections.

Step 8. Develop minor in-house modifications with the vendor, as needs arise.

SUMMARY

Materials requirements planning looks at inventory management for situations where demand is not continuous or constant over time, where many items are maintained in the same inventory system, and where many of the inventory items are linked directly to other items in the inventory. MRP also goes beyond the scope of inventory management to include production scheduling and purchasing considerations. The primary idea is to coordinate all activities so as to order exactly the amount required at exactly the time that it is needed. Although MRP requires only the simplest of calculations, the complex business systems to which it is applied require that a computer be used to implement MRP and manage the necessary information.

The MRP system consists of three basic components: the *master production schedule,* the *bill of materials,* and the *inventory record file.* The master production schedule specifies the needs for the end items; the bill of materials translates this schedule into needs for all component items; and the inventory record file keeps track of on-hand inventory for all items.

Extensions of MRP, which maintain MRP's philosophy and approach to the use of the information to facilitate production scheduling, include MRP II (a closed-loop system), *distribution requirements planning,* and *capacity requirements planning.*

Implementing an MRP system is very difficult in that it requires a company to change the way it does business. Most departments are affected, and they are required to coordinate their respective activities much more closely.

KEY TERMS

time phasing

zero-based inventory system

independent demand items

dependent demand items

just-in-time

master production schedule

time bucket

bill of materials

inventory record file

indented bill of materials

parts explosion

low-level coding

lead time offsetting

lot sizing

lot-for-lot

part period value

business requirements planning

capacity requirements planning

distribution requirements planning

1. The parts explosion diagram for product X is provided below. Convert the diagram to low-level coding and calculate the quantities of each component part required to produce 70 units of X.

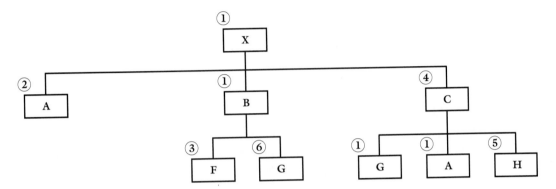

The following parts are on hand.

Component	Amount on Hand
X	0
A	10
B	20
C	10
F	10
G	20
H	50

Solution

The diagram with low-level coding is

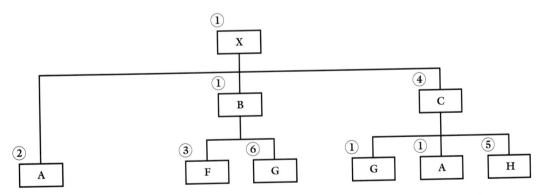

Now we present the calculations for the quantities required of each part.

Level	Component	Total Required	Amount on Hand	Net Required
0	X	70	0	70
1	B	70	20	50
2	F	150	10	140
2	C	280	10	270
3	A	140 + 270	10	400
3	G	300 + 270	20	550
3	H	1,350	50	1,300

Using AB:POM to Solve This Problem

The initial input for the MRP module consists of the number of lines in the bill of materials and the number of demand periods. Solved Problem 1 has nine lines and seven demand periods, as indicated in Screen 14.1. The bill of materials is converted to a list of components. The first column contains the name. If a component appears twice in the BOM, then it also appears twice in the MRP table. For example, component A is a component ("child") both of X and of C (its "parents"). The second column contains the level of the item. *Do not use low-level coding.* The level does increase by one when a component is a child. A component can be at two levels. For example, component A is a level one child of the finished good X at level zero and a

```
┌─ Data file:wgsp1 ════════ Materials Requirements Planning ═══════ Data Screen ═
│  Number of BOM lines (1-37) 9                      Number of demand periods (1-18)  7
├──────────────────────── Chapter 14, Solved Problem 1 ════════════
│  Item Lvl    ldtm #per    nhnd  Lot  pd1  pd2  pd3  pd4  pd5  pd6  pd7
│  X        0   1    1       0     0    0    0    0    0    0    0   70
│  A        1   1    2      10     0    0    0    0    0    0    0    0
│  B        1   1    1      20     0    0    0    0    0    0    0    0
│  F        2   1    3      10     0    0    0    0    0    0    0    0
│  G        2   1    6      20     0    0    0    0    0    0    0    0
│  C        1   1    4      10     0    0    0    0    0    0    0    0
│  G        2   1    1       0     0    0    0    0    0    0    0    0
│  A        2   1    1       0     0    0    0    0    0    0    0    0
│  H        2   1    5      50     0    0    0    0    0    0    0    0
│
│
│
│
│
│
│
│
└──────────────────────────────────────────────────────────────────
F1=Help F2=New  F3=Load F4=Main F5=Util F6=Quit F7=Save F9=Prnt F10=Run      Esc
Enter the label/name/id number for this component
```

SCREEN 14.1

level two child of the component C at level one. The next column is the lead time. In this example, all lead times are one week. The next column is the number of components needed for each assembly. The next column is the initial inventory at the start of the problem. The next column is the lot size. If the number is 0 or 1, lot-for-lot ordering is used; otherwise, the specified lot size is used. The remaining table contains either demands or scheduled receipts. Numbers in level zero items are treated as demands, whereas numbers in higher-level items are treated as shipments of the component that previously have been scheduled to arrive. For this example, the only demand is for 70 items in order to compute the component needs.

```
┌─ Data file:wgsp1 ════════ Materials Requirements Planning ═══════ Solution ─┐
│   Number of BOM lines (1-37) 9                  Number of demand periods (1-18)   7 │
└─────────────────────────────────────────────────────────────────────────────┘

┌───────────────────────────────────────────────────────────────────────────┐
│                                                                           │
│   Item X                                                                  │
│           Week 1 Week 2 Week 3 Week 4 Week 5 Week 6 Week 7                 │
│                                                                           │
│   TOT.REQ    0      0      0      0      0      0     70                    │
│                                                                           │
│   ON HAND    0      0      0      0      0      0      0                    │
│                                                                           │
│   ORD REC    0      0      0      0      0      0      0                    │
│                                                                           │
│   NET REQ    0      0      0      0      0      0     70                    │
│                                                                           │
│   ORD REL    0      0      0      0      0     70      0                    │
│                                                                           │
│                                                                           │
└───────────────────────────────────────────────────────────────────────────┘
  F1=Toggle item to display       F8= All items print            F9=Print    Esc
  Press <Esc> key to edit data or highlighted key or function key for options
```

SCREEN 14.2

There is one table of output generated for each part in the list. Screen 14.2 shows the output table for the finished good—item X. Pressing the **F1** key will toggle the item that is displayed. Pressing the **F9** key will print one item. Pressing the **F8** key will print all items, which is what we used to generate the following output table.

Item X	Week 1	Week 2	Week 3	Week 4	Week 5	Week 6	Week 7
TOT.REQ.	0	0	0	0	0	0	70
ON HAND	0	0	0	0	0	0	0
ORD REC.	0	0	0	0	0	0	0
NET REQ.	0	0	0	0	0	0	70
ORD REL.	0	0	0	0	0	70	0

Item A

	Week 1	Week 2	Week 3	Week 4	Week 5	Week 6	Week 7
TOT.REQ.	0	0	0	0	270	140	0
ON HAND	10	10	10	10	10	0	0
ORD REC.	0	0	0	0	0	0	0
NET REQ.	0	0	0	0	260	140	0
ORD REL.	0	0	0	260	140	0	0

Item B

	Week 1	Week 2	Week 3	Week 4	Week 5	Week 6	Week 7
TOT.REQ.	0	0	0	0	0	70	0
ON HAND	20	20	20	20	20	20	0
ORD REC.	0	0	0	0	0	0	0
NET REQ.	0	0	0	0	0	50	0
ORD REL.	0	0	0	0	50	0	0

Item F

	Week 1	Week 2	Week 3	Week 4	Week 5	Week 6	Week 7
TOT.REQ.	0	0	0	0	150	0	0
ON HAND	10	10	10	10	10	0	0
ORD REC.	0	0	0	0	0	0	0
NET REQ.	0	0	0	0	140	0	0
ORD REL.	0	0	0	140	0	0	0

Item G

	Week 1	Week 2	Week 3	Week 4	Week 5	Week 6	Week 7
TOT.REQ.	0	0	0	0	570	0	0
ON HAND	20	20	20	20	20	0	0
ORD REC.	0	0	0	0	0	0	0
NET REQ.	0	0	0	0	550	0	0
ORD REL.	0	0	0	550	0	0	0

Item C

	Week 1	Week 2	Week 3	Week 4	Week 5	Week 6	Week 7
TOT.REQ.	0	0	0	0	0	280	0
ON HAND	10	10	10	10	10	10	0
ORD REC.	0	0	0	0	0	0	0
NET REQ.	0	0	0	0	0	270	0
ORD REL.	0	0	0	0	270	0	0

Item H

	Week 1	Week 2	Week 3	Week 4	Week 5	Week 6	Week 7
TOT.REQ.	0	0	0	0	1350	0	0
ON HAND	50	50	50	50	50	0	0
ORD REC.	0	0	0	0	0	0	0
NET REQ.	0	0	0	0	1300	0	0
ORD REL.	0	0	0	1300	0	0	0

2. For the following parts explosion, develop the MRP scheduling tables required to develop the purchase orders for item E. The numbers in parentheses are the lead times for each item. Assume that there is no on-hand inventory. In week 6, 100 units of item A are required; 150 units of item A are required in week 7.

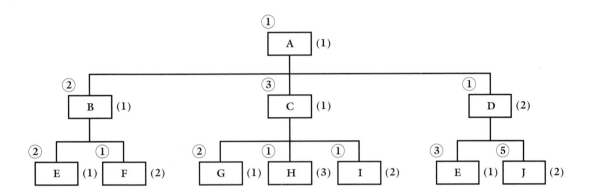

Solution

To generate the table for item E, tables first must be generated for items B and D. As items B and D each require that a table for item A be generated, we know that four tables need to be developed.

				Item A			
	Week 1	Week 2	Week 3	Week 4	Week 5	Week 6	Week 7
Total requirement						100	150
Inventory on hand							
Net requirement						100	150
Order receipt						100	150
Order release					100	150	

				Item B			
	Week 1	Week 2	Week 3	Week 4	Week 5	Week 6	Week 7
Total requirement					200	300	
Inventory on hand							
Net requirement					200	300	
Order receipt					200	300	
Order release				200	300		

Item D							
	Week 1	Week 2	Week 3	Week 4	Week 5	Week 6	Week 7
Total requirement					100	150	
Inventory on hand							
Net requirement					100	150	
Order receipt					100	150	
Order release			100	150			

Item E							
	Week 1	Week 2	Week 3	Week 4	Week 5	Week 6	Week 7
Total requirement			300	850*	600		
Inventory on hand							
Net requirement			300	850	600		
Order receipt			300	850	600		
Order release		300	850	600			

*850 includes 400 for B and 450 for D.

3. Silitek manufactures silicon computer chips, which it distributes through two distribution centers—one in San Francisco and the other in Hong Kong. Demands for the four quarters of the coming year and current inventories are as follows.

Distributor	Q_1	Q_2	Q_3	Q_4	Inventory on Hand
San Francisco	14,000	12,000	15,000	16,000	4,000
Hong Kong	19,000	18,000	23,000	28,000	5,000

Using a delivery lead time of one quarter, determine the shipments that need to be made using a pull system.

Solution

A shipping schedule table needs to be set up for each distribution center.

	Quarter				
San Francisco	0	1	2	3	4
Gross requirements		14,000	12,000	15,000	16,000
Available inventory	4,000	4,000			
Planned receipt		10,000	12,000	15,000	16,000
Planned order	10,000	12,000	15,000	16,000	

Hong Kong	Quarter				
	0	1	2	3	4
Gross requirements		19,000	18,000	23,000	28,000
Available inventory	5,000	5,000			
Planned receipt		14,000	18,000	23,000	28,000
Planned order	14,000	18,000	23,000	28,000	

Note that quarter 0 is really the fourth quarter of the current year.
The requirements from Silitek can now be calculated as follows.

Quarter	To San Francisco	To Hong Kong	Total Production
0	10,000	14,000	24,000
1	12,000	18,000	30,000
2	15,000	23,000	38,000
3	16,000	28,000	44,000

This production and shipping schedule includes no inventories maintained at any location, utilizing the efficient, but risky, just-in-time philosophy.

QUESTIONS

1. As an inventory management tool, how does MRP differ from the approach taken in the previous chapter?

2. Under what conditions is an MRP approach preferable to an EOQ approach? Under what conditions is the opposite true?

3. Why is MRP viewed as more than just an inventory system? What additional capabilities does it possess?

4. Relate the concepts of time phasing and just-in-time.

5. Does the use of just-in-time automatically lead to a zero-based inventory system?

6. Give three examples of situations where there are dependent demands.

7. Why does an intermittent demand require a different inventory approach from the EOQ?

8. Discuss the following statement: Just-in-time is a reckless course of action that allows a problem to occur when that problem could have been avoided.

9. Explain why the lot sizing discussed in this chapter applies both here and in the previous chapter. Under what assumptions do these techniques link the two chapters?

10. What is the advantage of using a "structured" bill of materials? Is there a disadvantage to using this type of parts list?

11. Describe the three major inputs to the MRP system.

12. Explain the role of the scheduler in creating the master schedule. What role do the forecasts play?

13. How can the critical path concept of project management apply in the MRP environment?

14. What is the purpose of low-level coding?

15. How is the idea of lead time offsetting used in developing the MRP tables?

16. Is MRP a pull system or a push system? Explain.

17. Discuss the following statement: The lot sizing discussion is inconsistent with the just-in-time focus of the chapter.

18. What is meant by an open loop system and by a closed loop system?

19. A large percentage of MRP programs either go unused after their implementation or fail to work up to their true capabilities. What accounts for this? What steps should be taken to increase the probability of a successful implementation?

PROBLEMS

See Instructor's Section.

1. Draw the parts explosion diagram for the following indented bill of materials.

Part	Number Required
A	1
B	2
E	3
F	1
G	6
C	1
H	4
B	2
E	3
F	1
G	6
D	4

2. Draw the parts explosion diagram for the following indented bill of materials.   See Instructor's Section.

Part	Number Required
760	1
770	3
722	4
733	2
774	1
775	5
776	2
788	4
789	2
777	2
788	2
789	4
775	5
776	2
788	4
789	2
777	2
788	2
789	4
785	2
791	7
801	4
802	3
790	8

3. Convert the following parts explosion diagram to an indented bill of materials.   See Instructor's Section.

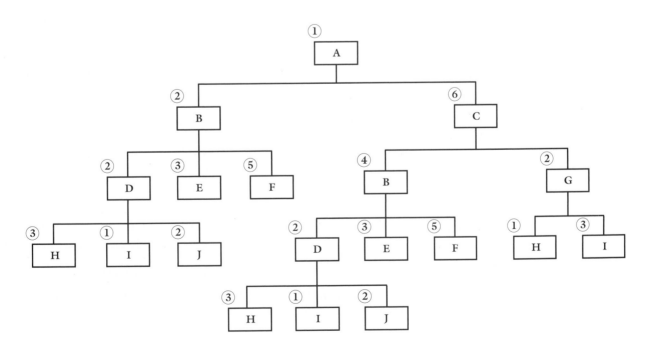

See Instructor's Section.

4. Convert the following parts explosion diagram to an indented bill of materials.

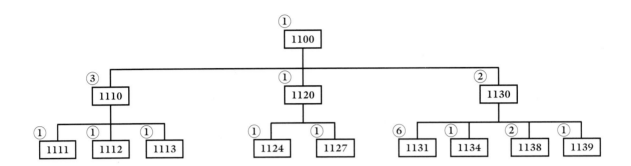

See Instructor's Section.
5. Refer to Problem 2. How many of each part are required to make 124 units of item 760?

See Instructor's Section.
6. Refer to Problem 3. How many of each part are required to make 517 units of item A?

See Instructor's Section.
7. Redraw the parts explosion shown in Problem 3 using low-level coding.

8. Apply low-level coding to the parts explosion diagram drawn for the indented bill of materials in Problem 1.

See Instructor's Section.

9. Use the following parts explosion for parts (a) and (b) below.

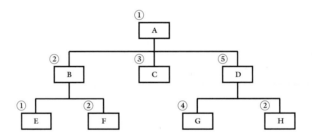

(a) Develop the MRP tables for the case where 120 units of item A are required in week 6 and all lead times are one week.

See Instructor's Section.
See Instructor's Section.
(b) List all of the planned purchase orders.

10. Suppose that the production schedule for item A in Problem 9 is given as follows.

	Week							
	1	2	3	4	5	6	7	8
Production	0	0	0	150	80	120	0	175

See Instructor's Section.
Generate the MRP tables and each planned order that will be required to meet this schedule.

11. Develop the MRP tables for each item in the parts explosion given in Problem 3 and list all planned purchase orders required to produce 70 units of item A in week 8. There is a one-week lead time for each item, except items D and H, which have lead times of two weeks.

See Instructor's Section.

12. Using the following master production schedule, repeat the procedure you followed in Problem 11.

	Week				
	8	9	10	11	12
Production	70	120	70	120	70

See Instructor's Section.

13. The planned requirements for part 7510 for the next ten weeks are as follows.

	Week									
	1	2	3	4	5	6	7	8	9	10
Order	460	120	370	410	180	350	220	540	410	500

Ordering costs are $20 per order, and holding costs are $.02 per week. Using the part period method, determine when the orders should be placed and how many should be included in each order.

week 1:950; week 4:940; week 7:760; week 9:910

14. The planned requirements for part A2 for the next eight weeks are as follows.

	Week							
	1	2	3	4	5	6	7	8
Order	170	0	210	30	0	180	210	20

Ordering costs are $50 per order, and holding costs are $.05 per week. Construct the set of planned purchase orders using the part period method.

week 1:410; week 6:410

15. Use an EOQ as an approximation to develop the orders for Problem 13. Compare the costs to those costs incurred by using the part period method. Do the same using a lot-for-lot method. Which sequence of orders provides the best results? Explain.

See Instructor's Section.

16. Use a cost comparison to decide which of the three lot sizing methods (lot for lot, EOQ, or part period) provides the best results for the data in Problem 14.

part period = $138

17. The production facility that produces item 7510 (see Problem 13) can produce only 400 units per week. What are the utilizations in each week? Is there sufficient capacity to meet the schedule as given in Problem 13? If not, modify the schedule to use the capacity more evenly. If item 7510 is a level three item, what effect will your changes have on the master production schedule?

weekly utilizations: 1.15, .3, .925, 1.025, .45, .875, .55, 1.35, 1.025, 1.25; not sufficient

18. Krephauser Brewery supplies beer to distribution centers in Munich and Dusseldorf. Demands, current inventory, and order quantities for Munich and Dusseldorf for the next four months are given in the following table. The delivery lead time is one month. Use a pull system (distribution requirements planning) to determine the shipments that need to be made.

Krephauser to Munich: 1,500 cases in weeks 2 and 3; Krephauser to Dusseldorf: 1,200 cases in weeks 1 and 2

		Month			Current	Order
Distributor	1	2	3	4	Inventory	Quantity
Munich	1,000	1,100	1,200	900	2,500	1,500
Dusseldorf	800	700	900	1,000	1,100	1,200

one additional shipment to Dusseldorf in week 3
See Instructor's Section.

Munich: 2; Dusseldorf: 3

quantity shipped (weeks in parentheses)—Atlanta: 200(0), 200(2), 200(3); center 1: none; center 2: 60(1), 60(3), 60(4); center 3: 60(2), 60(4), 60(5); center 4: 60(3), 60(4), 60(5)

19. Krephauser Brewery (see Problem 18) is considering reducing the sizes of the order quantities. (Perhaps they have been reading too many books on Japanese management.) Redo your solution to Problem 18 using an order quantity of 1,000 for both Munich and Dusseldorf.

(a) How many extra shipments are required with the lower order quantity?
(b) What is the average inventory at the distributors under each of the two plans?

20. In a JIT system, the order quantity would be allowed to vary, and the demand would be met exactly in each period. If Krephauser Brewery (see Problem 18) operates in this ideal fashion, what is the number of shipments?

21. The fastest selling item at FAD pharmacies is FAD soap. The four local centers in the Atlanta region will sell, over the next six weeks, the numbers of cases of soap shown in the following table.

Assuming a one-week delivery time, use the pull system to determine the shipments that need to be made in each week. The order quantity from central distribution to Atlanta is 200.

			Week				Order	Starting
Center	1	2	3	4	5	6	Quantity	Inventory
1	20	30	20	30	40	30	50	200
2	50	40	35	40	50	40	60	75
3	35	40	30	20	50	40	60	80
4	40	30	40	40	50	60	60	110

COMPUTER CASE STUDY 14.1: BRENNER MANUFACTURING

Brenner Manufacturing is a truck manufacturer that recently relocated from Pennsylvania to North Carolina. Prior to the move, the company faced decreased demand, increasing labor costs, and deteriorating management–labor relations. Management offered positions in North Carolina to the entire work force, and about half of the employees decided to make the move.

Prior to setting up the new operation, the new operations director instructed each of his subordinates to examine various aspects of the production process. The subordinates who had moved from Pennsylvania were already very familiar with the operations, but the new operations personnel needed to familiarize themselves with Brenner's policies.

One of the assistant plant managers, a newly minted MBA named Steve Mills, was assigned the task of examining the ordering policies for supplies used in production. He found that Brenner was using an EOQ policy for ordering cases of lubricating oil. Steve called the finance department and was told that for purposes of analysis the appropriate interest rate was 24 percent per year. Demand over the past three years was for 7,486 cases, or an average of 2,495 cases per year. At a cost of $6.32 per case, the cost of ordering the oil was estimated to be $83 per order. He used the numbers to find the EOQ:

$$EOQ = \sqrt{\frac{2DS}{H}}$$

$$= \sqrt{\frac{(2)\,(7{,}486/3)\,(83)}{(.24)(\$6.32)}}$$

$$= \sqrt{\frac{414{,}225.32}{1.5168}}$$

$$= \sqrt{273{,}091.58}$$

$$\approx 523,$$

which basically agreed with the fact that Brenner was ordering in lots of size 500.

Steve developed a table showing Brenner's oil usage for the past thirty-six months.

Month	Year 1989	1990	1991
January	345	379	368
February	28	32	4
March	417	489	423
April	52	50	48
May	0	4	15
June	379	433	382
July	288	267	306
August	76	83	84
September	221	244	218
October	34	32	38
November	322	354	333
December	227	259	252
Total	2,389	2,626	2,421

Grand total = 7,486

Steve was somewhat dismayed. In business school, he had been led to believe that the EOQ was appropriate when the demand was somewhat constant; the numbers he saw were far from constant. Furthermore, he had heard a great deal about just-in-time inventory and felt that perhaps the amount ordered each month should be the expected demand. Steve felt that a new policy should be implemented, but he wanted to test out his theory by experimenting with past data.

Would lot-for-lot ordering be better than the current EOQ policy? Would lot-for-lot ordering be the best possible policy? Is just-in-time a relevant notion for lot sizing?

REFERENCES

Deis, R. *Production and Inventory Management in the Technological Age.* Englewood Cliffs, N.J.: Prentice-Hall, 1983.

Lubben, R. *Just-in-Time Manufacturing.* New York: McGraw-Hill, 1988.

McLeavey, D. W., and S. L. Narasimhan. *Production Planning and Inventory Control.* Boston: Allyn and Bacon, 1985.

Orlicky, J. A. *Materials Requirements Planning.* New York: McGraw-Hill, 1975.

Plossl, G. W. *Production and Inventory Control: Principles and Techniques.* 2nd ed. Englewood Cliffs, N.J.: Prentice-Hall, 1985.

Tersine, R. J. *Principles of Inventory and Materials Management.* 3rd ed. New York: North Holland, 1988.

Vollman, T. E., W. L. Berry, and D. C. Whybark. *Manufacturing Planning and Control Systems.* 2nd ed. Homewood, Ill.: Irwin, 1988.

C H A P T E R

15

O U T L I N E

OPERATIONS SCHEDULING

- To explain general concepts of scheduling
- To relate scheduling to type of layout
- To demonstrate the goals and methods of machine scheduling
- To present concepts on sequencing and run length
- To develop the assignment model and related models

INTRODUCTION

To this point in the text, we have discussed both the aggregate plan and the master schedule. Both of these are schedules, but they are created to provide an overview or show the overall planning picture. Neither addresses the problem of scheduling the detailed processes required to carry out the plans on a daily basis. **Scheduling,** as discussed in this chapter, is the process by which the (medium-range) production plan is implemented. The master schedule, which indicates the quantity of each product to be manufactured, is transformed into a time table of when and where each activity must take place in order to meet the schedule. A general picture of the production–planning scheduling relationship is presented in Figure 15.1.

Typically, the scheduling process is broken down into five categories (see Figure 15.2).

- **routing:** determining *where* the work is to be done
- **scheduling:** determining *when* the work is to be done
- **dispatching:** issuing the order to begin work
- **control:** monitoring the process to determine that operations are running according to plan
- **expediting:** improving the completion time of a job

These activities occur on a daily basis outside of industry, although to a less formalized extent. For example, consider a family that is planning a vacation. First, there is the long-range plan of where they will visit. Then comes the routing (plane, train, or car) and scheduling (time and day of trip). On the day of the trip, the alarm rings (dispatching). A call to the airport confirms that the plane is leaving on time (control). If the family is running late, they forgo cleaning the house prior to leaving (expediting).

Of the five functions of routing, scheduling, dispatching, control, and expediting, the two key functions are routing and scheduling. In combination, these two functions dictate which process is loaded (routing) and when (scheduling), decisions that dictate both the personnel and material requirements for the firm. Although decisions regarding scheduling processes, personnel, and materials are highly interrelated, it is easiest to treat these decisions separately. The inventory materials scheduling has been discussed in Chapters 13 and 14. The scheduling topics are presented in this chapter both for production and for service applications.

Transparency Master 15.1:
Overview of Scheduling.

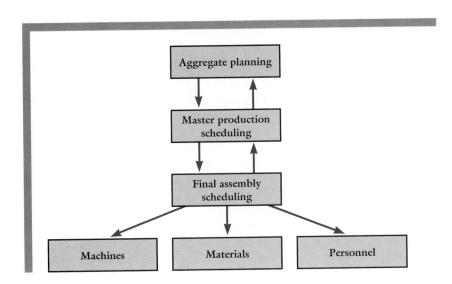

FIGURE 15.1 Overview of production scheduling

In previous chapters, different types of production processes and plant layouts have been discussed. In particular, the layouts have been classified as fixed position layout (project), process layout (job shop), or product layout (assembly line). Not surprisingly, these layouts each lead to different types of scheduling problems. The remainder of this chapter is organized accordingly, with the bulk of the chapter devoted to process layout, because this layout presents the most difficult short-term problems.

FIGURE 15.2 Production scheduling activities

Transparency Master 15.1:
Overview of Scheduling.

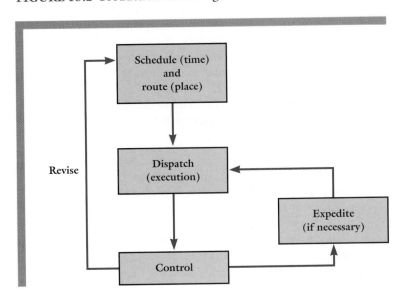

FIXED POSITION LAYOUT AND PROJECTS

Recall that fixed position layout implies that the transformation process occurs at a given (fixed) site. Examples previously mentioned were the construction of a road or dam or building. Of course, these examples are just a subset of a larger class, which we term *projects*. The major questions that arise during the scheduling of projects have been addressed in Chapter 10. One goal of scheduling projects is to find which of the tasks are critical in order to ensure that the project is completed as soon as possible. Of course, project scheduling requires that each of the tasks is begun at the proper time according to the order specified by the precedence graph.

Projects are not the only types of process with fixed position layouts. Some businesses consist of deliveries or repairs made at fixed positions. Examples of such processes are the delivery of products (newspapers, baked goods, and so forth) to stores, the delivery of furniture or appliances to homes, and home or office repair or installation (telephone installation, large appliance repair). In each case, one or more delivery persons or repairpersons must travel from fixed location to fixed location. We will discuss this type of problem in a later section of this chapter.

PROCESS LAYOUT/JOB SHOP SCHEDULING

Job shop scheduling is the process of scheduling jobs with different requirements that compete for similar equipment or personnel. For example, a student who needs to study for a final exam and also needs to write a term paper has a job shop scheduling problem in deciding which to do first. Job shop situations vary, but, in order to analyze job shop scheduling in general, the situations are classified according to several key characteristics.

The components of a job shop are detailed in Figure 15.3. Jobs arrive at the shop needing to be transformed by one or more processes. There are several different types of processes and different numbers of machines within each type of process. Different employees are available to staff the different processes. As you will see, one of the questions job shop scheduling must answer is which employee should be assigned to which process. The major question to be addressed, however, is this: When different jobs compete for the same process, which job should be performed first? Prior to answering this question, let us examine the job shop in more detail.

shop characteristics   The first step in job shop scheduling is characterizing the shop itself. There are two basic ways to characterize a job shop situation.

1. *Static or dynamic shop.* By a **static job shop,** we mean one in which all jobs that will ever enter the system are known. In a **dynamic job shop,** more jobs will arrive in the system during the time those currently in the system are being processed. Most job shop situations are dynamic. For example, consider an automobile service station. It is highly possible that, while the mechanic is tuning one of the five cars currently in the garage, a sixth (new) car will drive up needing a repair. As an example of a (relatively) static situation, consider the student who must study for an exam and write a term paper. If these are the only two assign-

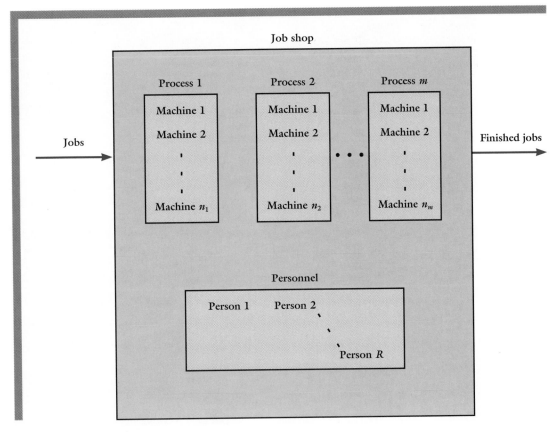

FIGURE 15.3   The job shop

Transparency Master 15.2:
The Job Shop.

ments in the only two courses the student is taking, then, presumably, there will
be no work in addition to studying for the final and writing the term paper.

2. *Facility layout.* Figure 15.4 presents different types of process layouts. The most
general layout has m different processes, each with a different number of
resources. See part (a) in the figure. In this example, we show a three-process
layout, where process 1 has three machines, process 2 has two machines, and
process 3 has four machines. We could be speaking of a manufacturer of kitchen
cabinets who has three saws (process 1), two sanders (process 2), and four pol-
ishers (process 3). The resources, in this case, are the machines. This general case
is the most difficult to analyze; therefore, much attention has been focused on
the three special cases indicated in Figure 15.4. The easiest situation, shown in
part (b), is where there is only one process and one machine in that process. An
example of this situation is a computer—more precisely, the central processing
unit (CPU) of a mainframe computer. Another special case is when there is only
one process, but several machines are available for that process. This situation is
shown in part (c) of Figure 15.4. An example of this situation is a gas station
with three repair bays. The last special case, indicated in part (d) of the figure, is

Teaching Suggestion 15.1:
Another Example. See the
Instructor's Section for
details.

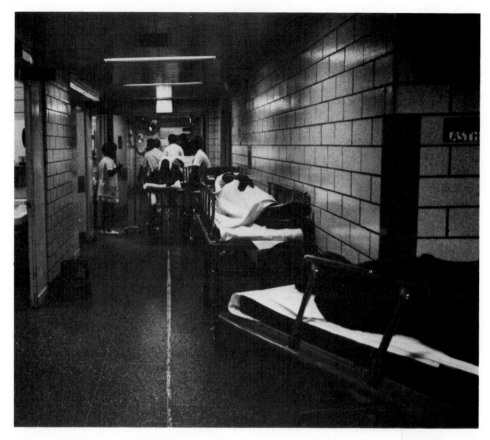

An emergency room—sequencing jobs in a process layout. (© Gilles Peress/Magnum Photos, Inc.)

that of *m* processes, each with exactly one machine. This last case occurs when the equipment is expensive and the company wishes to have only one of each type. Much hospital equipment would fit this description.

Implicit in our discussion of machines in the preceding examples is that there are enough operators in each shop for the machines. If this is not the case, then a problem arises: the assignment of personnel to machines. If the critical (scarce) resource is the personnel instead of the machine, the operators are used in the problem—not the machines.

We have indicated how to characterize the shop, but job shop scheduling also depends on certain characteristics of the jobs themselves.

job characteristics

1. *The flow pattern.* In some situations, all jobs follow the same pattern of flow through the system; in others, each job follows its own (specified) pattern. The first situation is termed a **flow shop** and is exemplified by woodworking, in which the flow might be sawing, followed by sanding, followed by finishing. In a flow shop, routing is not typically a problem. The second situation is termed a **randomly routed job shop** and is exemplified by student registration at a typical university. In Figure 15.5, we have indicated that the registration process consists of three steps. Student A might follow the steps in order, going from adviser

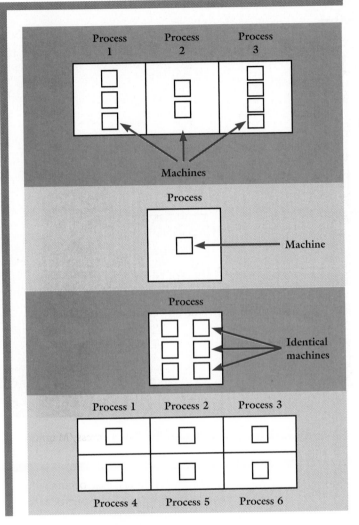

(a) General layout: m processes, n_i machines in process i

(b) One process, one machine

(c) One processes, multiple machines

(d) m processes, one machine each

FIGURE 15.4 Process layout types

Transparency Master 15.3: Process Layout Types.

to registrar to cashier. Student B might find that one of the courses is closed and, thus, return to the adviser, generating the following pattern:

> adviser $\rightarrow$ registar $\rightarrow$ adviser (different course) $\rightarrow$ registrar $\rightarrow$ cashier.

The randomly routed job shop is a more difficult shop to analyze than the flow shop. Furthermore, it requires that more information be maintained; that is, the likelihood of going from process i to process j must be known. For example, the university registration shop would be presented as in Figure 15.6, where the percentage of students going from process to process is indicated.

2. *Machine usage time.* In job shop scheduling, it is assumed that the length of time each job will require for each process is known beforehand. In fact, the scheduling is based on machine usage time. Furthermore, if machine usage times are not known, then, essentially, the problem is treated, not as a job shop scheduling

Transparency Master 15.4:
Randomly Routed Shops.

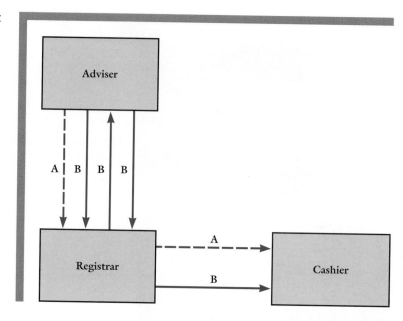

FIGURE 15.5   Randomly routed job shop: three-step university registration process

FIGURE 15.6   University registration with process-to-process flows

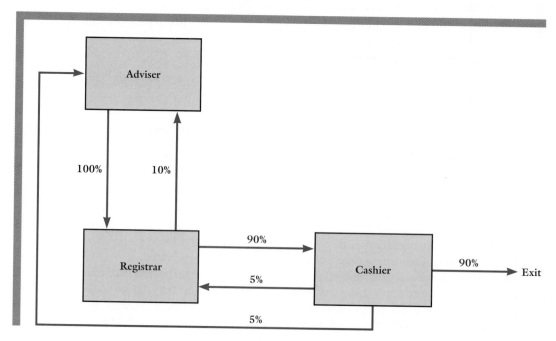

problem, but as a queueing problem (see Chapter 8). In most queueing models, the service times are unknown! (Averages are known.)

3. *Due dates.* In many situations, "due dates" are given for each job. We have enclosed the term in quotation marks because its meaning can vary. That is, the meaning of "due date" could be anything from a promise to a contractual obligation.

Obviously, the implications of breaking a promise are different from the implications of breaking a contract. In some contracts, the due date is fixed. In others, it is specified as a target, with penalties stated for late delivery and incentive payments offered for early delivery.

Given the shop characteristics and the job characteristics, all that remains to be done before actually scheduling is to discuss the criteria that will be used to evaluate and compare schedules. When we look at an individual job, we might measure performance on that particular job in one of several different ways. One measurement is the **job flow time,** which is defined as the length of time a job is in the shop, or

schedule evaluation criteria

Job flow time = time job is completed − time job enters shop.

flow time

Notice that we measure from the time that the job enters the shop, not when work starts on the job. A second measurement is simply answering, with a yes or a no, the question, Was the job completed on time (prior to its due date)? Alternatively, we might be more specific and measure the number of days that the job was late. These measurements refer to individual jobs, and we need to aggregate the job measures in order to set system measures. If due dates are not given, then only the flow time is relevant, because lateness measures do not apply. There are two important criteria for schedule evaluation. The first is termed *average flow time,* which is the average of the flow time of each job, calculated in order to determine the average length of time a job is in the shop. The second criterion is the length of time it takes to finish all of the jobs currently in the shop. This is termed *maximum flow time,* or **makespan.**

Teaching Suggestion 15.2: Flow Time Assumption. See the Instructor's Section for details.

If due dates are given, the two criteria of average flow time and maximum flow time still may be used. However, other criteria also come into play—namely, the number of jobs that are late, the average lateness, or the maximum lateness. Consider the following example.

Example 15.1 College Prose Painters (CPP) employs college students to paint houses during the summer. Currently, the company has six houses lined up for painting. CPP will paint one house at a time. The times are as follows.

Transparency Master 15.5: One-Machine Sequencing.

House	Painting Time (in days)	Due Date
A	9	22
B	7	17
C	3	16
D	4	13
E	8	16
F	6	9

The schedule that CPP is going to follow is FDCBEA. For this schedule, find the average flow time, maximum flow time, average lateness, and maximum lateness.

Gantt chart

The easiest way to analyze a schedule is to draw a scheduling graph, known as a Gantt chart (see Chapter 10), such as the one in Figure 15.7. In this figure, we have identified the individual jobs, the time at which processing begins for each job, and the time at which painting ends for each job. The end time is the flow time, because it is assumed that all jobs entered the shop at time 0 (because information to the contrary is not given).

We can put all of our information in tabular form.

Job	Flow Time (Completion Time)	Due Date	Late Days	Early Days
A	37	22	15	
B	20	17	3	
C	13	16		3
D	10	13		3
E	28	16	12	
F	6	9		3
	114		30	9

Thus, the average flow time is $114/6 = 19$ days. That is, the average time that it takes to complete each job is 19 days. The makespan is the maximum flow time, which is 37 days for job A. This is the time at which all jobs are completed and the machine (which, in this example, is the paint crew) is available for new jobs. The average late days is 30/6, or 5 days. Alternatively, because only three of the six jobs are late, we might say that the average late days is $30/3 = 10$ days for those jobs that are late. The maximum lateness is 15 days for job A.   ■⌐

Although the preceding table notes early jobs, this is not a criterion. While there may be penalties for being late, finishing a job early typically carries no reward. For example, completing a term paper after it is due may cause a reduction in grade, but completing the paper before it is due will not improve the grade (although the reward is peace of mind). The early times are considered only when incentives for early completion are written into the contract.

With the explanation of the job shop scheduling problem complete, let us look at approaches toward solving the problem. For the remainder of this section, we divide

FIGURE 15.7 Arbitrary schedule for College Prose Painters (Example 15.1)

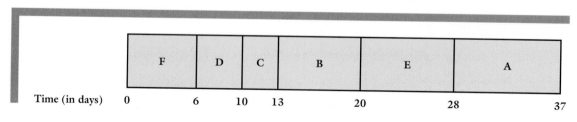

the job shops according to whether one machine, two machines, or more than two machines are used.

SEQUENCING JOBS ON ONE MACHINE

The one-machine problem can be given in a very straightforward manner. There are n jobs that need to be processed on one machine. Each job has a given processing time and may have a given due date. The n jobs are to be sequenced so that one of the decision criteria is optimized.

Notice that there are $n!$ ways in which the jobs can be sequenced. If n is small (let us say $n \leq 7$), then every sequence can be examined and evaluated according to the appropriate criteria. However, as n increases, the number of sequences gets too large for the explicit enumeration of each sequence. For example, $10! = 3,628,000$, while $20!$ is larger than 10^{21}. Therefore, we need a method for finding the best schedule that does not entail examining every possible sequence.

SHORTEST PROCESSING TIME

Let us begin by considering situations without due dates. In these cases, all criteria relating to lateness are irrelevant, which leaves the two criteria of average flow time and makespan. However, because there is only one machine, the schedule always is completed at the same time, regardless of the order in which the jobs are processed. This time is given by the sum of the processing times. For example, for the information given in Example 15.1, all schedules complete the last job after 37 days. This leaves us with only one important goal, which is to minimize the average flow time.

for one machine, schedule completion time does not depend on order

Fortunately, the goal of minimizing average flow time is easy to accomplish for the one-machine problem. The rule for minimizing average flow time is to schedule the jobs according to the **shortest processing time** (SPT). That is, the job that takes the least amount of time is scheduled first, the second shortest job is scheduled second, and so on, with the longest job being scheduled last. Consider the following.

SPT minimizes average flow time

> | **Example 15.2** Given the jobs in Example 15.1, find the sequence that mini-mizes the average flow time.
>
> The answer is to schedule according to the shortest processing time rule. So the optimal schedule is to paint the houses in the following order: C (3 days), D (4 days), F (6 days), B (7 days), E (8 days), and A (9 days). The schedule for this sequence is represented in Figure 15.8. From the figure, we see that the flow times are 3 (job C), 7 (job D), 13 (job F), 20 (job B), 28 (job E), and 37 (job A). The total flow time is the sum of these six flow times, or 108, which means that the average flow time is $108/6 = 18$ days. Of the $6! = 720$ possible sequences, none has an average flow time of less than 18 days. Also, notice that all the jobs are finished by 37 days, just as in the schedule in Example 15.1. As promised, all schedules for the one-machine problem finish at the same time. ■

The principle underlying the shortest processing time rule is that it is better to have long jobs wait for short jobs to finish rather than to have short jobs wait for long jobs to finish. The logic of this principle becomes exceedingly clear when one consid-

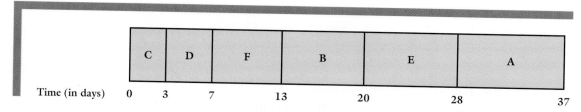

FIGURE 15.8 Shortest processing time schedule for College Prose Painters (Example 15.2)

Transparency Master 15.5:
One-Machine Sequencing.

ers a job with a duration of 1 minute and a job with a duration of 60 minutes. Practical application of the principle underlying the shortest processing time rule can be seen in most supermarkets in the form of express lines for shoppers with "10 items or less" or in banks with tellers devoted solely to certain types of transactions, such as deposits. As a final example, consider that the typical basis for deciding which job is run next on a computer is the time estimate of each job: The job with the lowest time estimate gets highest priority.

SPT minimizes average wait

There are two beneficial by-products of following the shortest processing time rule. The first is that it minimizes, not only the average flow time, but also the average waiting time, where the waiting time is the time a job must wait until its processing begins. The second useful by-product is that at least as many jobs are completed under the SPT schedule as any other schedule if processing is stopped before the end of the schedule. This is demonstrated in Figure 15.9. In this figure, we represent the two schedules already examined for the data of Example 15.1. Suppose that after 8 days there is a strike and no more work is done. Under the schedule FDCBEA, only job F is complete, while under the shortest processing time schedule of CDFBEA, two jobs (C and D) have been completed. Note that although we have used 8 days as the cutoff point in our example, the shortest processing time schedule will ensure at least as many jobs completed as any other schedule for any number of days.

A potential hazard associated with the use of the shortest processing time rule occurs in a dynamic job shop. For our house painters, assume that every 10 days (every two weeks) the schedule is updated based on all current jobs waiting to be done. If new jobs that take less time than jobs currently in the shop come in, the longer jobs

FIGURE 15.9 Day-by-day comparison of schedules for College Prose Painters

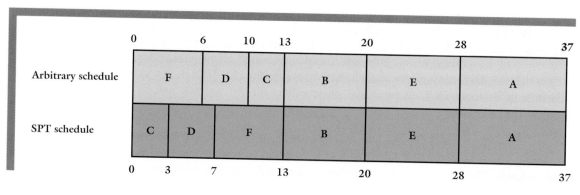

SPT pushes back long jobs

are put off indefinitely. As long as there is a house waiting to be painted that will require less than 9 days, house A will never be painted! Certainly, then, average flow time cannot be used as the sole criterion. Some adjustment to the SPT schedule must be made to be certain that long jobs are not put off forever. Alternatively, the due dates might be considered.

CONSIDERATION OF DUE DATES

To this point in our discussion of one-machine scheduling, we have not considered due dates. When due dates are considered, the shortest processing time rule might not be the most appropriate rule to follow. Consider, again, the case of our College Prose Painters (Example 15.1). Following the shortest processing time rule resulted in the schedule CDFBEA. Analyzing the schedule, we find the following.

Job	Processing Time	Flow Time	Due Date	Late Days	Tardy Days
C	3	3	16	−13	
D	4	7	13	−6	
F	6	13	9	4	4
B	7	20	17	3	3
E	8	28	16	12	12
A	9	37	22	15	15

We now provide two measures of "nontimeliness"—**lateness** and **tardiness.** We define lateness as the difference between the flow time and the due date:

$$\text{Lateness} = \text{flow time} - \text{due date}.$$

Lateness can be positive or negative. For example, job A is completed 15 days after it is due, so it is late by 15 days. On the other hand, job C is completed 13 days before it is due; hence, it is early by 13 days or, to put it a different way, late by −13 days.

As indicated earlier, the effects of being early differ from those of being late. For example, filing tax returns before the due date of April 15 causes no reward, but filing returns after the due date causes penalties. Therefore, typically, we do not consider early jobs as being worthy of note and do not want to allow lateness to be negative. Hence, if the job is done early—that is, before the due date—we define tardiness as nothing (0); however, if the job is late—that is, completed after the due date—we define tardiness as lateness. The tardy days for the schedule are given in the last column in the preceding table.

The jobs C, D, F, B, E, and A are late by −13, −6, 4, 3, 12, and 15 days, respectively. The average lateness is $(-13 - 6 + 4 + 3 + 12 + 15)/6 = 2.5$ days, while the maximum lateness is 15 days. The average tardiness is given by $(4 + 3 + 12 + 15)/6 = 8.5$ days, while the maximum tardiness is 15 days.

SPT minimizes average lateness

It turns out that the shortest processing time rule finds the schedule that has the least amount of average (or total) lateness. Notice that we said "lateness," not "tardiness." The shortest processing time rule does not necessarily minimize the maximum lateness, the maximum tardiness, the average tardiness, or the number of jobs that are tardy. For these criteria, we use other approaches, which are termed *priority rules.*

DUE DATE SCHEDULING

Teaching Suggestion 15.4: Due Date Scheduling. See the Instructor's Section for details.

It seems very reasonable that the first job we may want to perform is the one that is due first. We term this **due date scheduling,** or **earliest due date** (EDD). The earliest due date rule is this: Schedule the jobs by increasing order of due date. We can use EDD to find a schedule for our College Prose Painters example.

Job	Processing Time	Flow Time	Due Date	Late Days	Tardy Days
F	6	6	9	−3	
D	4	10	13	−3	
C	3	13	16	−3	
E	8	21	16	5	5
B	7	28	17	11	11
A	9	37	22	15	15

The average number of late days is $22/6 = 3.67$, which is worse than the number given by the schedule developed following the SPT rule; the average number of tardy days is $31/6 = 5.17$, which is better than the average given by the SPT schedule; and the maximum tardiness (and lateness) is 15, which is the same as that given by the SPT schedule. It turns out that due date scheduling always minimizes the maximum (worst) lateness or tardiness.

EDD minimizes the worst lateness

MINIMIZING THE NUMBER OF TARDY JOBS

If we extend the due date scheduling, we can find the schedule that has the fewest number of tardy jobs. Moore (1968) developed the following simple method for minimizing the number of tardy jobs.

Step 1. Order the jobs by due date (earliest to latest).

Step 2. Find the first job that is late. (If none are late, then stop; the current sequence is optimal.)

Step 3. Consider all jobs from the first job through the late job (found in step 2). Of those jobs, find the job with the longest processing time and move it to the end of the schedule. Do not consider this job again.

Step 4. Go back to step 2.

Let us try **Moore's method** on our College Prose Painters example.

Example 15.3   For the jobs listed in Example 15.1, find the sequence that minimizes the number of late jobs.

Step 1 is to schedule according to due dates, yielding the schedule FDCEBA. (Do not worry about ties.) The flow times and due dates are represented in part (a) of Figure 15.10. We see in the figure that the first late job is job E. Therefore, we find

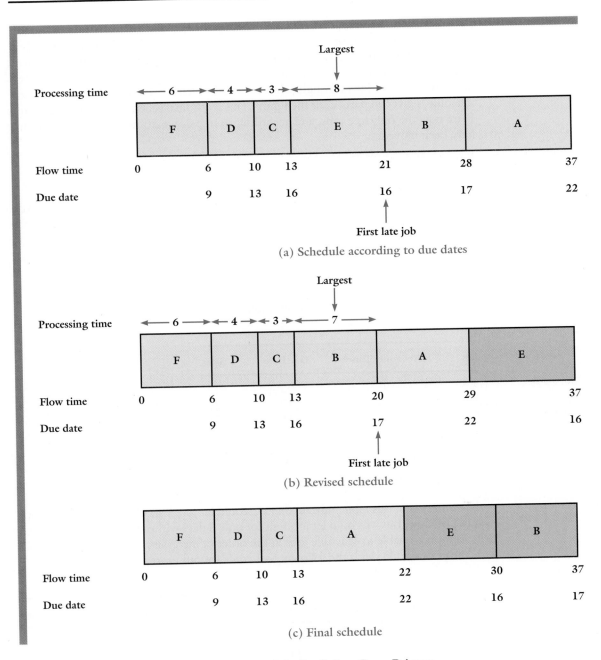

FIGURE 15.10 Minimizing the number of late jobs for College Prose Painters
(Example 15.3)

the job with the longest processing time among the jobs F, D, C, and E. This is job E, with a processing time of 8 days. We move job E to the end of the schedule and do not consider it again. We continue by returning to step 2. The new schedule is given in part (b) of Figure 15.10. The first late job in this schedule is job B. The longest processing time of jobs through job B is job B, which we move to the end. The new schedule is given in part (c) of the figure. This is the final schedule because jobs B and E are now the only late jobs, and according to step 3, we do not reconsider jobs that have been moved.   ■」

SLACK TIME RULE

Previously, we suggested that jobs should be scheduled by due date. Now we make a different argument, based on intuition. Let us consider the difference between when a job is due and how long the job takes. That is, let us define the **slack** for each job:

slack time

$$\text{Slack} = \text{due date} - \text{processing time}.$$

In our College Prose Painters example, we find the following.

Job	Processing Time	Due Date	Slack
A	9	22	13
B	7	17	10
C	3	16	13
D	4	13	9
E	8	16	8
F	6	9	3

The numbers in this table indicate that we could let job A sit idle for 13 days and still finish on time, but we could let job F sit for only 3 days without missing the due date. It seems reasonable to schedule jobs in the order of increasing slack time. Using slack as the priority rule yields the following schedule for our example.

Job	Processing Time	Flow Time	Due Date	Late Days	Tardy Days
F	6	6	9	−3	
E	8	14	16	−2	
D	4	18	13	5	5
B	7	25	17	8	8
A	9	34	22	12	12
C	3	37	16	21	21

The total for late days is 41 days, the total for tardy days is 46 days, and the maximum lateness or tardiness is 21 days. These are the worst numbers we have seen yet. It turns out that our intuition about slack is wrong, and, in fact, scheduling according to slack maximizes the minimum lateness (minimizes the maximum earliness). This is hardly a goal we would like to achieve, as seen in the examples (-3 for this schedule, -13 for CDFBEA).

SLACK TIME PER OPERATION

It is difficult to fight intuition, and the slack time rule is intuitively appealing. Suppose that in addition to knowing the number of days of processing for each job, we also know the number of operations each job requires. Then each operation represents a time when a job might be delayed. Therefore, slack is to be divided by the number of operations. We define **slack per operation** as follows:

$$\text{Slack per operation} = \frac{\text{due date} - \text{processing time}}{\text{number of operations}}.$$

slack per operation

We schedule the jobs according to increasing order of slack per operation. Suppose that our example has the following numbers of operations.

Job	Number of Operations
A	2
B	4
C	3
D	4
E	2
F	1

The slack time per operation rule yields the following.

Job	Slack	Operations	Slack per Operation
A	13	2	6.5
B	10	4	2.5
C	13	3	4.3
D	9	4	2.25
E	8	2	4
F	3	1	3

Hence, the schedule is given by DBFECA. This rule does not necessarily lead to a good schedule, but it appeals to us intuitively and accounts for jobs having different numbers of operations.

SEQUENCING JOBS ON TWO MACHINES

The extension of job shop scheduling techniques from one machine to two machines is not a trivial matter. In the one-machine problem, all schedules finish at the same time. However, this is not true in the two-machine problem. Because schedules finish

minimize the makespan

at different times, the usual goal is to find the schedule that finishes the soonest (minimizes the makespan). Consider the following example.

Teaching Suggestion 15.5:
Order Assumption of Two-
Machine Scheduling. See
the Instructor's Section for
details.

Example 15.4   Three jobs are to be processed on two machines. Each job must be performed first on machine 1 and then on machine 2. The processing times are given in the following table.

Job	Processing Time (in hours)	
	Machine 1	Machine 2
A	4	2
B	7	7
C	6	5

Transparency Master 15.6:
Two-Machine Scheduling.

Which schedule finishes sooner: ABC or CBA?

Again, the easiest way to examine the schedules is with a Gantt chart. For this example, bar charts for the two schedules are given in Figure 15.11. For each schedule, the loading of each job on each machine is presented on an hour-by-hour basis. As the figure indicates, the schedule ABC finishes after 23 hours, while the schedule CBA finishes one hour sooner, after 22 hours.   ■」

In the preceding example, note that under the schedule ABC, the flow times are 6 (job A), 18 (job B), and 23 (job C), for a total flow time of 47. Under the schedule CBA, however, the flow times are 11 (job C), 20 (job B), and 22 (job A), for a total flow time of 53. Hence, although the schedule ABC has a lower average flow time than the schedule CBA, the completion time of ABC is worse that that of CBA. You may be wondering which is more important for two machines, average flow time or maximum flow time (that is, schedule completion time).

The general rule is that completion of the schedule is of prime importance. The reason for this is that, although the preceding example presented a static problem, the situation typically is dynamic. That is, sometime during the operation of jobs A, B, and C, a new job will arrive for processing. Hence, the goal is to be as prepared as possible for new jobs by finishing the jobs currently in the system as soon as possible. This also maximizes utilization of capacity.

**maximize capacity
utilization**

The following simple method for finding the schedule that finishes the earliest is termed **Johnson's method** and was developed in the early 1950s.

Step 1. List the operation times for each job on each of the two machines (for *n* jobs, there will be 2*n* times).

Step 2. Find the shortest available operation time and the job that has this time.

Step 3. Schedule the job found in step 2 as soon as possible if its shortest processing time is on machine 1. Schedule the job found in step 2 as late as possible if its shortest processing time is on machine 2.

Step 4. Repeat steps 2 and 3 until all jobs are scheduled.

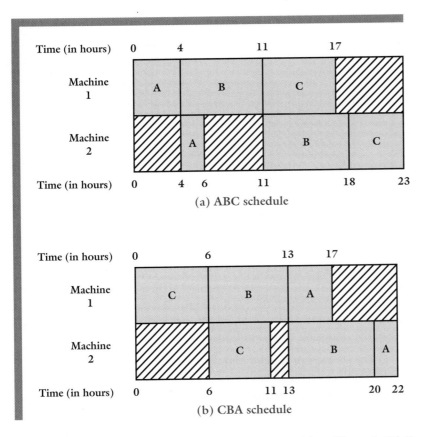

FIGURE 15.11 Comparison of schedules for two machines (Example 15.4)

Example 15.5   For the data given in Example 15.4, find the schedule that minimizes the makespan—that is, completes the last job the soonest.

Using Johnson's method, we find that 2 hours is the shortest processing time (for job A); because it occurs on machine 2, job A is scheduled last. The next shortest available time is 5 hours for job C (the 4 hours for job A is not available because job A is scheduled already). Because the 5 hours occur on machine 2, job C is scheduled as late as possible, which means it is next to last. Since only job B remains, the optimal schedule is BCA. The graph of this schedule is given in Figure 15.12. It can be seen that this schedule is completed after 21 days. None of the 3! possible sequences ends sooner than 21 days. ∎

SEQUENCING JOBS ON MORE THAN TWO MACHINES

For situations with more than two machines, the prime concern, again, is finding the schedule that finishes the soonest. Unfortunately, when there are more than two machines, there is no general method for finding such a schedule. (For information

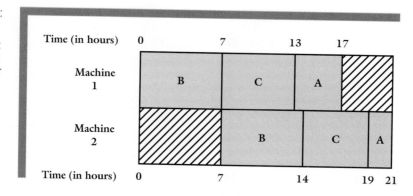

FIGURE 15.12 Johnson's method (Example 15.5)

about the various heuristic rules that have been developed, consult Woolsey and Swanson (1975), which is listed in the References section at the end of this chapter.) We mention one special case where the three-machine problem can be solved.

The three-machine problem can be solved using a modification of Johnson's method if either of the following two conditions is met.

Condition 1. The shortest processing time on machine 1 is longer than the longest processing time on machine 2.

Condition 2. The shortest processing time on machine 3 is longer than the longest processing time on machine 2.

Example 15.6   Does the following three-machine problem meet either of the stated conditions?

Job	Time on Machine 1	Time on Machine 2	Time on Machine 3
A	7	1	4
B	10	6	8
C	5	2	10
	(Shortest = 5)	(Longest = 6)	(Shortest = 4)

Neither condition is met. Hence, the problem is not directly solvable by modifying Johnson's method. ▪

Example 15.7   Does the following problem meet either condition for the use of a modified Johnson's method?

Job	Time on Machine 1	Time on Machine 2	Time on Machine 3
A	18	9	16
B	12	3	11
C	10	2	20
D	1	4	15
	(Shortest = 1)	(Longest = 9)	(Shortest = 11)

Since condition 2 is met, the problem can be solved using the three-machine John- **three-machine**
son's method. We must first generate a two-machine problem, where machine A con- **Johnson's method**
sists of the sum of processing times on the first two machines and machine B consists
of the sum of the processing times on the last two machines. Then we use Johnson's
method. For our example, we create the following new problem.

Job	Machine A	Machine B
A	18 + 9 = 27	9 + 16 = 25
B	12 + 3 = 15	3 + 11 = 14
C	10 + 2 = 12	2 + 20 = 22
D	1 + 4 = 5	4 + 15 = 19

Using Johnson's method on our new problem, we schedule job D in position 1, job
C in position 2, job B in position 4, and job A in position 3. The scheduling chart
appears in Figure 15.13. No schedule completes all jobs sooner than 67 days.   ∎

FIGURE 15.13 Three-machine scheduling (Example 15.7)

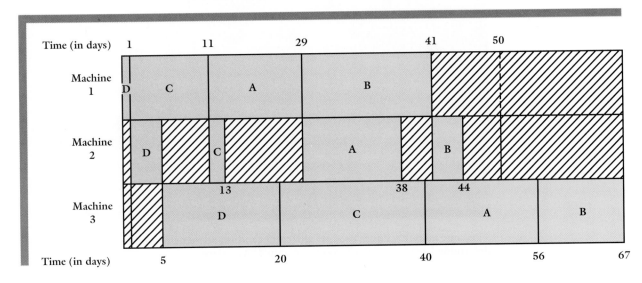

The same assembly line is used for different candies. Sequencing and run lengths must be determined. (© Sepp Seitz/Woodfin Camp & Associates)

PRODUCT LAYOUT

Several different types of scheduling problems may arise when assembly lines are in place. One problem, which we addressed in our discussion of layout (Chapter 7), is the trade-off to be made between the production rate (or cycle time) and the number of stations (laborers) required to achieve this cycle time. A second set of problems arises if one machine (or assembly line) is used for more than one product. Both of these problems are difficult to solve, yet they are encountered often.

PRODUCT SEQUENCING

There are two different **product sequencing** problems that we wish to examine. The first is to minimize setups, and the second is to decide on loadings and run sizes. Consider one machine that is used to produce chocolate, vanilla, and strawberry cupcakes. Typically, a machine used to produce different flavors (or colors) is cleaned between production runs of the different flavors (or colors). The cleaning time is a function of the flavor just produced and the flavor to be produced. In our three flavor example, the times might be given as follows.

minimizing setup times

	To		
From	Chocolate	Vanilla	Strawberry
Chocolate		100 minutes	120 minutes
Vanilla	20 minutes		10 minutes
Strawberry	80 minutes	60 minutes	

Now, there are different sequences that could be run. For example, the production schedule might be given as either of the following two sequences.

Sequence 1
chocolate→vanilla→strawberry→chocolate→vanilla · · ·

Sequence 2
chocolate→strawberry→vanilla→chocolate→strawberry · · ·

The following cleaning times are required for one complete cycle of sequence 1.

chocolate→vanilla	100 minutes
vanilla→strawberry	10 minutes
strawberry→chocolate	80 minutes

The total time for cleaning per cycle is 190 minutes.
We calculate the times for sequence 2 in the same manner.

chocolate→strawberry	120 minutes
strawberry→vanilla	60 minutes
vanilla→chocolate	20 minutes

The total cleaning time per cycle for sequence 2 is 200 minutes, which means that the sequence chocolate→vanilla→strawberry is preferred, because it requires less cleaning time. Although machine changeover is a production scheduling problem, we will examine it in greater detail later in this chapter because it directly relates to a particular service scheduling problem known as the traveling salesman problem.

different run lengths

A second decision that must be made when different jobs are performed on one machine is the length of the run of each product. Suppose that we know the weekly demands in our cupcake example.

Flavor	Demand (in cases/week)
Chocolate	1,000
Vanilla	800
Strawberry	400

One possibility is that the production schedule would read as follows.

Step	Task
1	Produce 500 cases of chocolate
2	Produce 400 cases of vanilla
3	Produce 200 cases of strawberry

This schedule would be run twice a week. However, there are other possible schedules, including the following.

Step	Task
1	Produce 500 cases of chocolate
2	Produce 400 cases of vanilla
3	Produce 400 cases of strawberry
4	Produce 500 cases of chocolate
5	Produce 400 cases of vanilla

This schedule would be run once per week. Several different factors need to be balanced. These include the inventory costs and machine changeover costs and times.

ECONOMIC RUN LENGTHS

If each product were considered by itself, the run size would be determined according to the economic run length as presented in Chapter 13 and given by

$$Q = \sqrt{\frac{2DS}{H}} \times \sqrt{\frac{p}{p-d}}.$$

Very difficult scheduling problems are encountered when this approach is used for multiple items, because it will not coordinate their individual run cycles. The complex methods for overcoming the problems are beyond the scope of this text. Instead, we consider some simple approaches for addressing run lengths.

RUNOUT TIME METHOD

Suppose that we have items that use the same machine or assembly line. Further suppose that the production run lengths are known for these items (perhaps determined by the preceding economic run length formula). The problem to be addressed is, In which order should the product be run on the facility? The **runout time method**

(ROT) bases the decision on the expected time of depletion for the inventory. For item i, this is given by

$$ROT = \frac{\text{current inventory of item } i}{\text{demand rate for item } i}.$$

runout time

Example 15.8   Table 15.1 contains a list of the three items (our cupcakes) that use the same assembly line. Included in the list are the current inventory and demand rates for each product. In which order should the products be produced?

The runout times appear in the last column of the table. We see that we will run out of vanilla in less than a week, we will run out of chocolate in one and one-half weeks, and we will run out of strawberry in two weeks. Hence, the schedule should be vanilla, followed by chocolate, followed by strawberry. ▪

If the lot sizes are fixed (perhaps by the economic run length), then problems may arise. Consider the following example.

Example 15.9   Columns (1) through (5) of Table 15.2 contain the characteristics of five products that are run on the same machine. In which order should the products be produced? Is there enough capacity to meet the demand if there are 80 machine hours available during the week?

In column (6) of Table 15.2, we have computed the runout time for the five products, and the order is given by EABDC. Our second concern, though, is with the capacity. Because the products are different, we need to compute an aggregate measure; this is production hours, which is shown in column (7). For each item, this measure is given as the product of the number of units in a lot times the number of hours per unit. The total production hours required, 86.25, are greater than the 80 hours that are available. ▪

AGGREGATE RUNOUT TIME METHOD

The difficulty encountered in Example 15.9 arose because of the fixed lot sizes. The **aggregate runout time method** (ART) presumes that the lot sizes do not need to be fixed. Essentially, we compute the time at which we will run out of all products (the

TABLE 15.1 Runout time determination (Example 15.8)

Item	Current Inventory	Demand (in cases per week)	Runout Time (in weeks)
Chocolate cupcakes	1,500	1,000	1.5
Vanilla cupcakes	600	800	.75
Strawberry cupcakes	800	400	2

TABLE 15.2 Production requirements (Example 15.9)

(1) Item	(2) Production Hours/Unit	(3) Lot Size	(4) Forecast for Week	(5) Current Inventory	(6) ROT [(5)/(4)]	(7) Production Hours [(3) × (2)]
A	.20	50	20	10	.50	10.00
B	.15	100	25	15	.60	15.00
C	.05	75	10	20	2.00	3.75
D	.10	200	50	40	.80	20.00
E	.25	150	30	10	.33	37.50
						86.25

aggregate runout time) and schedule around this time. Let us continue with our example.

In Table 15.3, the aggregate runout time is computed. The first steps are to transform both the demands and the current inventory from units to machine hours. Column (5) contains the inventory in machine hours (units × hours/unit) and column (6) contains the forecasted demand in machine hours (again, units × hours/unit). The aggregate runout time is given by

aggregate runout time

$$ART = \frac{\text{total machine hours available}}{\text{total machine hours required}}$$

$$= \frac{\text{machine hours in inventory} + \text{machine hours in production period}}{\text{machine hours required by forecast}}.$$

In our example, we have

$$ART = \frac{11.75 + 80}{20.75}$$

$$= 4.42 \text{ (rounded to the nearest hundredth)}.$$

TABLE 15.3 Aggregate runout time computation (Example 15.9)

(1) Item	(2) Production Hours/Unit	(3) Forecast for Week	(4) Current Inventory	(5) Inventory in Machine Hours [(4) × (2)]	(6) Forecast in Machine Hours [(3) × (2)]
A	.20	20	10	2.00	4.00
B	.15	25	15	2.25	3.75
C	.05	10	20	1.00	.50
D	.10	50	40	4.00	5.00
E	.25	30	10	2.50	7.50
				11.75	20.75

Assignment of several resources (trucks, crews, loaders) to several jobs (planes).
(© Herman J. Kokojan/Black Star)

Therefore, if we work for one week (80 machine hours), the current inventory and the inventory generated during the week will last for 4.42 weeks. We will base the lot sizes of each product on the *ART* of 4.42.

Table 15.4 contains our allocation of machine time. In column (5), we have generated the total number of units required for each product during the 4.42 weeks. This is simply the demand, as given in column (3), times the *ART*, as given in column (4). We subtract the current inventory—column (6)—from the gross requirements—column (5)—which generates the net requirements shown in column (7). By multiplying the unit requirements of column (7) by the hours per unit in column (2) we translate the net requirements to machine hours. Thus, the lot sizes are given in column (7), and the hours required are given in column (8). Notice that the total time required is the 80 hours available during the week.

We would implement this schedule. At the end of one week, we would revise the inventory and forecasts, find the new *ART*, and determine a new production schedule.

TABLE 15.4 Aggregate runout time schedule (Example 15.9)

(1) Item	(2) Production Hours/Unit	(3) Forecast for Week	(4) ART	(5) Gross Requirement [(3) × (4)]	(6) Current Inventory	(7) Net Requirement [(5) − (6)]	(8) Hours Required [(7) × (2)]
A	.20	20	4.421686	88.43	10	78.4337	15.68674
B	.15	25	4.421686	110.54	15	95.5422	14.33132
C	.05	10	4.421686	44.22	20	24.2169	1.21084
D	.10	50	4.421686	221.08	40	181.0843	18.10843
E	.25	30	4.421686	132.65	10	122.6506	30.66265
				596.9277			80

ASSIGNMENT-TYPE PROBLEMS

In this section, we look at special types of scheduling problems. The first type of problem is the **assignment problem,** in which we must assign n jobs to n machines, assigning only one job to a machine and using only one machine for each job. The cost of performing each job varies by machine, and the objective is to minimize the total cost. The assignment problem is simple to state and simple to solve. Following our discussion of the assignment problem in the next section, we present problems that are similar in nature to the assignment problem. These are the bottleneck assignment problem, which is an assignment problem (n jobs on n machines) but with the objective of minimizing the highest cost (the bottleneck or makespan), rather than the total cost; the traveling salesman problem, which is the problem of finding the shortest route that a salesman can travel in order to visit n locations; and the machine changeover problem, which is the problem of determining in which order jobs should be processed so as to minimize the total time required to set up the machine for each job.

THE ASSIGNMENT PROBLEM

one-to-one matching

In the assignment problem, n entities must be matched with n different entities. Examples of assignment problems include assigning workers to machines, jobs to machines, swimmers to a stroke type in a swimming medley, men to women in a dating service, salespersons to sales districts, teachers to classes, subcontractors to project tasks, and materials to factories. We explain the problem by means of the following example.

Example 15.10 Four programmers, Bob, Carol, Ted, and Alice, have the capability to write any of four programs, 1, 2, 3, or 4, that need to be completed. Although they have the capability as a group, their individual capabilities vary; the four programmers have strengths in different programming languages. Hence, the time required for each of the four programs is a function of the programmers, as Table 15.5 indicates. Each programmer is paid $10 per hour. The problem is to assign each pro-

Transparency Master 15.7:
The Assignment Problem.

TABLE 15.5 Programming time in hours
(Example 15.10)

Programmer	Program			
	1	2	3	4
Bob	80	120	125	140
Carol	20	115	145	60
Ted	40	100	85	45
Alice	65	35	25	75

grammer to a single program and complete all four programs in a minimum amount of total time, because the total programming cost is simply the total time multiplied by the wage rate of $10 per hour.

In general, for an $n \times n$ problem, there are $n!$ combinations of assignments. In this example, there are $4! = 24$ different ways to make the assignment. As with job shop sequencing, we can enumerate all of the solutions for small assignment problems such as this one and choose the one that is best. The solutions for the example are listed in Table 15.6. As is indicated in the table, the solution that takes the minimum time is to make the assignment as follows.

Programmer	Program	Time (in hours)
Bob	2	120
Carol	1	20
Ted	4	45
Alice	3	25

Of course, with twenty-four solutions, it is easy to examine each of them. However, $n!$ grows rather quickly, as we noted in our discussion of job shop scheduling. Therefore, it is imperative that we develop an efficient solution procedure for the assignment problem.

SOLUTION PROCEDURES

You have probably noticed the similarity (as discussed in Chapters 6 and 11) between the transportation problem and the assignment problem. In the transportation problem, suppliers are allocated to destinations. The only difference is that a supplier may provide goods to more than one destination point and a destination may be served by more than one supplier. Indeed, because this is the only difference, it follows that the assignment problem is simply a special case of the transportation problem, where the number of origins equals the number of destinations and where each supply and each demand is equal to one. Hence, the problem in Example 15.10 can be expressed as a transportation problem with the following cost matrix, with cost in hours.

assignment problem is a special case of transportation

TABLE 15.6 Enumeration of all solutions (Example 15.10)

	Programmer				
Bob	Carol	Ted	Alice	Times (in hours)	Total
1	2	3	4	80 + 115 + 85 + 75	355
1	2	4	3	80 + 115 + 45 + 25	265
1	3	2	4	80 + 145 + 100 + 75	310
1	3	4	2	80 + 145 + 45 + 35	305
1	4	2	3	80 + 60 + 100 + 25	265
1	4	3	2	80 + 60 + 85 + 35	260
2	1	3	4	120 + 20 + 85 + 75	300
2	1	4	3	120 + 20 + 45 + 25	210*
2	3	1	4	120 + 145 + 40 + 75	380
2	3	4	1	120 + 145 + 45 + 65	375
2	4	1	3	120 + 60 + 40 + 25	245
2	4	3	1	120 + 60 + 85 + 65	330
3	1	2	4	125 + 20 + 100 + 75	320
3	1	4	2	125 + 20 + 45 + 35	225
3	2	1	4	125 + 115 + 45 + 75	355
3	2	4	1	125 + 115 + 45 + 65	350
3	4	1	2	125 + 60 + 40 + 35	260
3	4	2	1	125 + 60 + 100 + 65	350
4	1	2	3	140 + 20 + 100 + 25	285
4	1	3	2	140 + 20 + 85 + 35	280
4	2	1	3	140 + 115 + 40 + 25	320
4	2	3	1	140 + 115 + 85 + 65	405
4	3	1	2	140 + 145 + 40 + 35	360
4	3	2	1	140 + 145 + 100 + 65	450

* Optimal solution

	Program				
Programmer	1	2	3	4	Supply
Bob	80	120	125	140	1
Carol	20	115	145	60	1
Ted	40	100	85	45	1
Alice	65	35	25	75	1
Demand	1	1	1	1	4

When the problem is expressed in this fashion, it is clear that one method of solution is to use the classical transportation algorithm.

assignment problem is a special case of linear programming

Now, because the assignment problem is a special case of the transportation problem and because the transportation problem is a special case of linear programming, it follows that the assignment problem is a special type of linear programming problem.

The linear programming formulation is as follows.

$$\text{Minimize } Z = \sum_{i=1}^{n} \sum_{j=1}^{n} c_{ij} x_{ij}$$

$$\text{Subject to } \sum_{j}^{n} = 1 \; x_{ij} = 1 \quad i = 1, 2, \ldots, n$$

$$\sum_{i}^{n} = 1 \; x_{ij} = 1 \quad j = 1, 2, \ldots, n,$$

where x_{ij} is interpreted as 1 if programmer i is assigned to program j and 0 if not, and c_{ij} is simply the cost of assigning programmer i to program j. Notice that the first set of constraints guarantees that each programmer (i) has exactly one program to write, and the second set of constraints guarantees that each program is written by exactly one programmer. Hence, linear programming (see Chapter 11) can be used to solve the assignment problem.

THE HUNGARIAN METHOD

Although we could use the linear programming or transportation methods to solve the problem, there is an even more efficient solution method, one that takes advantage of the fact that all "supplies" and "demands" are equal to one. The method is termed the **Hungarian method** because it was developed by the Hungarian mathematician D. Honig. The procedure is based on the following two properties of the problem.

> **Property 1.** Any constant may be added to or subtracted from a column or a row of the cost matrix of an assignment (or transportation) problem without changing the optimal assignment. (It will only change the cost of that assignment.)
>
> **Property 2.** If the cost matrix contains only nonnegative numbers, and if a solution exists with a total cost equal to zero, then this solution is optimal.

The solution procedure is as follows.   **solution procedure**

> **Step 1.** For each row, find the smallest number in the row and subtract this from every element in the row (generating a new cost matrix that, according to property 1, has the same solution as the original matrix).
>
> **Step 2.** For each column of the new matrix, find the smallest number in that column (which may be zero) and subtract this number from every number in that column (again generating a new cost matrix that has the same solution as the original matrix).
>
> **Step 3.** Attempt to find a solution with a total cost equal to zero.
>
> (a) Examine the matrix row by row. If no zeroes remain in a row, or if multiple zeroes remain in a row, skip the row. If there is exactly one zero in the row, circle the zero and draw a line through the *column*.
>
> (b) Examine the matrix column by column. If there is exactly one zero in the column, circle it and cross off the *row*. Otherwise, skip the column.
>
> (c) Repeat steps 3(a) and 3(b) until no more circles can be drawn around the zeroes.
>
> **Step 4.** If n zeroes are circled (and, hence, n lines are drawn), then stop,

Teaching Suggestion 15.7: Row/Column Order. See the Instructor's Section for details.

because, according to property 2, the problem is solved and the optimal solution is given by the circled zeroes.

Step 5. Find the smallest uncrossed number and generate a new table using steps 5(a)–5(c).

    (a) Subtract this number from every uncrossed number.
    (b) Add this number to every number crossed by two lines.
    (c) Copy all numbers crossed by one line.

Step 6. Go back to step 3.

Note that step 5 is equivalent to adding the smallest uncrossed number to every row with a line drawn through it and subtracting this number from every column without a line drawn through it. Hence, the revised matrix has the same solution as the original matrix, by property 1. Let us solve the problem in Example 15.10 using the Hungarian method.

We begin by drawing the original matrix without labeled rows or columns.

80	120	125	140
20	115	145	60
40	100	85	45
65	35	25	75

Step 1. We subtract 80 from row 1, 20 from row 2, 40 from row 3, and 25 from row 4.

0	40	45	60
0	95	125	40
0	60	45	5
40	10	0	50

Step 2. We subtract 0 from column 1, 10 from column 2, 0 from column 3, and 5 from column 4.

0	30	45	55
0	85	125	35
0	50	45	0
40	0	0	45

Step 3.

    (a) Row 1 has exactly one zero; therefore, we circle it and draw a line through column 1.

⓪	30	45	55
0	85	125	35
0	50	45	0
40	0	0	45

Row 2 has no zeroes (since one has been crossed off); therefore, we skip it. Row 3 has one zero; therefore, we circle it and draw a line through column 4.

⓪	30	45	55
0	85	125	35
0	50	45	⓪
40	0	0	45

Row 4 has multiple zeroes; therefore, we skip it.

(b) Column 2 has exactly one zero; therefore, we circle it and draw a line through the row.

⓪	30	45	55
0	85	125	35
0	50	45	⓪
40	⓪	0	45

Because no zeroes remain to be circled, we proceed to the next step.

Step 4. The number of circles (and lines) is three, and the goal is to have four. Hence, we continue.

Step 5. The smallest uncrossed number is 30, which we subtract from the six uncrossed numbers and add to the two numbers that are crossed by two lines.

0	0	15	55
0	55	95	35
0	20	15	0
70	0	0	75

We next return to step 3.

Step 3.

(a) Row 1 has multiple zeroes; therefore, we skip it. Row 2 has a single zero, so we circle it and cross off column 1. Row 3 has a single zero (column 1 is crossed off), so we circle it and cross off column 4. Row 4 has multiple zeroes, so we skip it.

0	0	15	55
⓪	55	95	35
0	20	15	⓪
70	0	0	75

(b) Column 3 has exactly one zero. We circle it and cross off row 4.

0	0	15	55
⓪	55	95	35
0	20	15	⓪
70	0	⓪	75

A zero still remains, so we return to step 3(a) again.

(c) Row 1 has one zero; therefore, we circle it and cross off column 2.

	Program			
Programmer	1	2	3	4
Bob	0	⓪	15	55
Carol	⓪	55	95	35
Ted	0	20	15	⓪
Alice	70	0	⓪	75

Step 4. The number of assignments (and lines) is four; hence, the problem is solved, and the solution is to use the pattern of circled zeroes. That is, assign Bob to program 2, Carol to program 1, Ted to program 4, and Alice to program 3. The times are found from the original table, which indicates a total time of $120 + 20 + 45 + 25 = 210$ hours. The solution is, of course, the same as the one identified previously by explicit enumeration.

SPECIAL CASES

MAXIMIZATION: In certain instances, it may be necessary to maximize total profit, rather than to minimize total cost. Consider the following.

> **Example 15.11**   Computer Dating Services (CDS) took applications from four men—Ned, Ted, Fred, and Zed—and from four women—Andi, Sandy, Randy, and Mandy. Based on an analysis of these applications, CDS then developed a compatibility matrix, which is given in Table 15.7. The ratings in the table are based on a scale of 0 to 100 percent and indicate the probability that the two persons who get matched will ultimately get married. Obviously, the higher the score, the better the match, which means that CDS needs to make the dates in a fashion that maximizes the total score. (The sum represents the expected number of marriages.)
>
>   If this were a minimization problem, we could begin immediately with the Hungarian method. As cost and profit differ only in sign (that is, cost $= -$ profit), we can easily convert the problem into a minimization of cost problem.

-30	-20	-10	-40
-70	-10	-60	-70
-40	-20	-50	-40
-60	-70	-30	-90

The first step is to find the smallest number in each row and to subtract this number from every number in that row. Hence, we subtract -40 from row 1, -70 from row 2, -50 from row 3, and -90 from row 4.

10	20	30	0
0	60	10	0
10	30	0	10
30	20	60	0

TABLE 15.7 CDS compatibility matrix (Example 15.11)

Male Applicants	Female Applicants			
	Andi	Sandy	Randy	Mandy
Ned	30	20	10	40
Ted	70	10	60	70
Fred	40	20	50	40
Zed	60	70	30	90

Now we can continue with step 2 of the Hungarian method. Before continuing, though, note that the two steps of changing the sign and then subtracting the smallest number are equivalent to a new step 1.

Step 1. For maximization, find the highest number in each row and subtract every number in the row from this highest number.

In other words, for a maximization problem, simply substitute the preceding step 1 for the original step 1 given for the minimization problem.

Step 2. We subtract 0 from column 1, 20 from column 2, and 0 from columns 3 and 4.

10	0	30	0
0	40	10	0
10	10	0	10
30	0	60	0

Step 3.

(a) We skip rows 1 and 2. In row 3, we circle the zero and draw a line through column 3. We skip row 4.

10	0	30	0
0	40	10	0
10	10	(0)	10
30	0	60	0

(b) In column 1, we circle the zero and draw a line through row 2.

10	0	30	0
(0)	40	10	0
10	10	(0)	10
30	0	60	0

We cannot do more circling because the remaining rows and columns either do not have zeroes or have multiple zeroes. In the solution to the problem in Example 15.10, this situation of multiple zeroes did not occur. This situation signifies that there is more than one solution with the same cost or profit. Therefore, at this point, we choose any zero, cross off its row or column, and continue with the method. Hence, in this example, we end up with one of the following two solutions. **alternate optimal solutions**

10	(0)	30	0
(0)	40	10	0
10	10	(0)	10
30	0	60	(0)

10	0	30	(0)
(0)	40	10	0
10	10	(0)	10
30	(0)	60	0

Both solutions are optimal, as indicated by the fact that the profit (see the original compatibility matrix in Table 15.7) of the first solution is given by

$$20 + 70 + 50 + 90 = 230,$$

and the profit of the second solution is given by

$$40 + 70 + 50 + 70 = 230.$$

■

CASES WITH UNEQUAL "ORIGINS" AND "DESTINATIONS"

The Hungarian method is founded on the notion that the problem is an $n \times n$ problem. In some cases, if two sets are to be matched, it may be that the sets are of unequal size. Consider the following example.

add dummy

> **Example 15.12**   Three jobs are to be performed, and each is to use one of the four available machines. Each machine is to process at most one job. The cost of performing each job on each machine is given in Table 15.8. Find which machine should be used for each job.

It is clear that one of the machines will perform no operations. In order to have a problem with an equal number of rows and columns, let us add a dummy row with no cost. Thus, the matrix we use to solve the problem is the 4×4 matrix, where the last row indicates a fictional job that will not take place.

Job	Machine			
	1	2	3	4
A	3	2	1	4
B	5	4	2	1
C	1	3	4	5
Dummy	0	0	0	0

After performing row subtractions, we can draw the new matrix.

2	1	0	3
4	3	1	0
0	2	3	4
0	0	0	0

As the smallest number in each column is 0, column subtractions are unnecessary, and the optimal solution is identified easily.

Machine	Job	Cost
1	C	1
2	None	
3	A	1
4	B	1

The total cost is equal to 3.

■

TABLE 15.8 Job–machine costs (Example 15.12)

Job	Machine			
	1	2	3	4
A	3	2	1	4
B	5	4	2	1
C	1	3	4	5

THE BOTTLENECK ASSIGNMENT PROBLEM

To this point, we have considered the assignment problem with an objective function of minimizing the total cost or maximizing the total profit. Often, however, the objective is somewhat different; the goal is to minimize the highest cost or maximize the smallest profit. Determining the highest cost and the smallest profit are termed **bottleneck assignment problems** for reasons that will be readily apparent.

Example 15.13 Reconsider the programmer/program problem of Example 15.10 in a slightly different light. Suppose that the four programs, when put together, form a system. Further suppose that the goal is not to minimize the cost of the system (as was done in Example 15.10), but to complete the system as soon as possible. Clearly, the system is not complete until the last task is finished, so the objective is to minimize the longest amount of time spent on any one program.

The solution to Example 15.10 (which is not necessarily the solution to this example because the objective has changed) was given in Table 15.6. The solution's programming times are 120, 20, 45, and 25 hours. Hence, the bottleneck value of this assignment is the highest number, which is 120. In this assignment, the bottleneck is Bob writing program 2 (see Table 15.5). If the bottleneck can be reduced, the optimal assignment will contain no time greater than or equal to 120 hours. Therefore, let us exclude from the table of times entries greater than or equal to 120 and solve this revised problem. Revising Table 15.5, the new problem reads as follows.

80	X	X	X
20	115	X	60
40	100	85	45
65	35	25	75

Notice that when an assignment cannot be made, we have written an X. Now we perform the row subtraction (step 1).

0	X	X	X
0	95	X	40
0	60	45	5
40	10	0	50

The next step is column subtraction, followed by executing step 3.

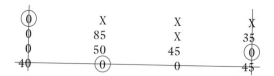

Step 5 (adding and subtracting 45) results in the following.

0	X	X	X
0	40	X	35
0	5	0	0
85	0	0	90

We must return to step 3.

After adding and subtracting 35, we can find the solution.

Returning to the original table of times (Table 15.5), we find the values to be 80, 35, 85, and 60. Hence, the bottleneck has been reduced from 120 hours to 85 hours.

In order to determine whether the bottleneck can be reduced even further, we eliminate all numbers greater than or equal to 85 from the original problem.

80	X	X	X
20	X	X	60
40	X	X	45
65	35	25	75

It is clear that this problem cannot be solved. (Columns 2 and 3 each require the use of row 4, which is not permitted.) Hence, no solution exists with a bottleneck of less than 85 hours, which means that the previous answer is the optimal solution.   ◼

In Example 15.13, we found the optimal solution. However, we note that at each *step,* it is only necessary to find *any* solution.

Let us now summarize the method for solving the bottleneck assignment problem.

Step 1. Find any assignment for the problem.

Step 2. If no assignment exists, stop—the previous assignment is optimal.

Step 3. Identify the bottleneck value.

Step 4. Generate a new problem by eliminating all entries in the table with a value equal to or greater than the bottleneck value.

Step 5. Go back to step 1.

Teaching Suggestion 15.8:
Bottleneck Method. See
the Instructor's Section for
details.

THE MACHINE CHANGEOVER PROBLEM

A common problem in many industries is scheduling different jobs on a single machine when the machine must be cleaned between jobs. Typical examples include the scheduling of products that vary in color or flavor, such as paint or ice cream. The **machine changeover problem** differs from a job shop scheduling problem in that the concern is not the processing times of the jobs themselves but, instead, the downtime of the machine while it is between jobs. Consider the following.

> **Example 15.14**   Flavor King is an ice cream producer specializing in only five flavors: chocolate, vanilla, strawberry, cherry, and banana. One machine is used to produce all flavors of the ice cream. Demand for the different flavors is equal, so each flavor is run in a batch of 100 gallons at a time. It is necessary to clean the machine between batches. The amount of time required to clean the machine depends on the old flavor and the new flavor. These times are given in Table 15.9. In which sequence should ice cream production be repeated in order to minimize the total cleaning time?
>
> Consider a specific sequence—say, chocolate → vanilla → strawberry → cherry → banana → chocolate → vanilla. . . . This sequence can be expressed in tabular form.

Old Flavor	New Flavor				
	Chocolate	Vanilla	Strawberry	Cherry	Banana
Chocolate		(200)	180	120	140
Vanilla	20		(40)	80	60
Strawberry	30	100		(10)	50
Cherry	40	110	20		(70)
Banana	(50)	70	30	40	

The circles indicate going from an old flavor to a new flavor. The total time is 200 + 40 + 10 + 70 + 50 = 370. Note that the sequence is cyclical; we go from banana

TABLE 15.9   Changeover times (in minutes) going from flavor to flavor (Example 15.14)

Old Flavor	New Flavor				
	Chocolate	Vanilla	Strawberry	Cherry	Banana
Chocolate		200	180	120	140
Vanilla	20		40	80	60
Strawberry	30	100		20	50
Cherry	40	110	20		70
Banana	50	70	30	40	

Transparency Master 15.8: Machine Changeover/Traveling Salesman.

to chocolate and begin the sequence again. Because of this cyclical property, we can always assume that any one of the flavors is the first one in the sequence to be produced.

The interesting fact about the preceding table is that the circles represent a solution to the assignment problem. Each old flavor has been assigned exactly one new flavor, and vice versa. Because the objective is the same as the objective of the assignment problem (namely, to minimize the total cost), one might conclude that the machine changeover problem is actually an assignment problem. Unfortunately, this is not the case, as evidenced by the following table, which is the optimal solution to the assignment problem but not to the changeover problem.

Old Flavor	New Flavor				
	Chocolate	Vanilla	Strawberry	Cherry	Banana
Chocolate		200	180	120	(140)
Vanilla	(20)		40	80	60
Strawberry	30	100		(10)	50
Cherry	40	110	(20)		70
Banana	50	(70)	30	40	

Applying this solution to the changeover problem would mean that there are two unrelated subsequences:

$$\text{chocolate} \rightarrow \text{banana} \rightarrow \text{vanilla} \rightarrow \text{chocolate}$$

and

$$\text{strawberry} \rightarrow \text{cherry} \rightarrow \text{strawberry}.$$

It is not possible to get from one subsequence to the other. In fact, because the first flavor can be fixed, there are $(n - 1)!$ solutions to the changeover problem, as opposed to the $n!$ solutions to the assignment problem. Thus, a solution to the changeover problem is a feasible solution for the assignment problem as well, but a solution to the assignment problem may or may not be a feasible solution for the changeover problem.

Although the difference between the two problems may appear minor, the changeover problem is considerably more difficult to solve than the assignment problem. In order to find the optimal solution to this problem, a method that may be employed is dynamic programming. However, because this method is complex, a heuristic solution method (that is, a rule of thumb) often is used to generate a good, although not necessarily optimal, solution. For this problem, the rule of thumb may be expressed as follows: The next flavor scheduled is the one that has yet to be scheduled and requires the least cleaning. (In general, this rule is termed the **next best strategy** or **greedy method.**) Using the times in Table 15.9 and starting with chocolate, this rule would generate the following table.

greedy method

APPLICATIONS OF P/OM

The Chinese Postman Problem

Many companies face the problem of determining what routes vehicles or people should take in order to cover the most territory with the least amount of travel. What routes should letter carriers use in order to deliver the mail? What routes should snow plows follow in order to clear the streets? What blocks should parking enforcement officers walk when giving out parking tickets? What routes should trash trucks follow to pick up all of the trash? What routes should street sweepers follow? Mathematically, this type of problem—termed the *Chinese postman problem*—is very difficult to solve. However, good solutions to this problem can save many dollars.

Consider the case of the Beersheva branch of Israel's major electric company, which wanted to make the job of meter reading more efficient. When the branch managers decided to minimize the number of people required to read the electric meters in the houses in one particular neighborhood, they set a precedent by applying the tools of operations management. Formerly, each person's route had been worked out by trial and error and intuition, with no help from mathematics. The whole job required twenty-four people, each reading meters in a section of the neighborhood in a five-hour shift.

By following a mathematical procedure, researchers managed to cover the neighborhood with 15 five-hour routes, a 40-percent reduction over the original 24 five-hour routes. Altogether, these routes involve a total of 4,338 minutes of walking time, of which only 41 minutes (less than 1 percent) is deadheading (repeating a block a second time).

Source: Introduction to Contemporary Mathematics, S. Garfunkel, ed. (New York: W. H. Freeman and Company, 1988), p. 17.

Step	From	Available Flavors	Easiest	Time
1	Chocolate	Vanilla, strawberry, cherry, banana	Cherry	120
2	Cherry	Vanilla, strawberry, banana	Strawberry	20
3	Strawberry	Vanilla, banana	Banana	50
4	Banana	Vanilla	Vanilla	70

The sequence generated is chocolate → cherry → strawberry → banana → vanilla → chocolate . . . , with a total cleaning time of $120 + 20 + 50 + 70 + 20 = 280$ minutes for every cycle (almost as good as the unattainable 260 minutes given by the assignment method). Again, we note that this sequence was easy to generate, but it is not necessarily optimal. However, this greedy method generally provides very good solutions, as it does in this example. ◼

THE TRAVELING SALESMAN PROBLEM

In the **traveling salesman problem** (we recognize the sexist language but bow to tradition here), a salesman begins at his home city and must visit $n - 1$ cities exactly one time and then return home. The objective is to minimize either the number of miles traveled or the cost or the time of the route. Obviously, all three measures are related. Although the name of the problem indicates only one application, any industry with a delivery or home repair service is confronted with the traveling salesman problem. Consider the following example.

> **Example 15.15**   Gregory's Department Store has a rug cleaning service. On Tuesday, Ralph the rug cleaner is scheduled to clean rugs at the homes of the Adamses, the Burnses, the Coneheads, the Dells, and the Evanses. After examining a map, Ralph has computed a table of driving times from each house to the others, including the origin at Gregory's. These times are presented in Table 15.10. Because the rug cleaning time is fixed, Ralph wishes to find the route that minimizes his driving time so that he can return to Gregory's as early as possible.
>
> As you may have noticed, this problem is identical to the machine changeover problem. The table is 6 × 6, yet there are 5! possible ways to schedule (visit) the five customers. Each customer must be visited exactly one time, so there must be exactly one entry circled in every row and one entry circled in every column. Again, dynamic programming can be used, but, as before, this is a rather complex solution method for this problem. Hence, a rule of thumb is used: Visit the nearest unvisited location. Using this rule, we generate the tour as follows.

Step	Current Location	Unvisited Houses	Nearest Unvisited House
1	Gregory's	Adamses, Burnses, Coneheads, Dells, Evanses	Dells
2	Dells	Adamses, Burnses, Coneheads, Evanses	Coneheads
3	Coneheads	Adamses, Burnses, Evanses	Burnses
4	Burnses	Adamses, Evanses	Evanses
5	Evanses	Adamses	Adamses

Teaching Suggestion 15.9: Multiple Traveling Salesman Problem. See the Instructor's Section for details.

The route generated is Gregory's to Dells to Coneheads to Burnses to Evanses to Adamses and back to Gregory's with a total driving time of $12 + 17 + 5 + 42 + 45$

Transparency Master 15.8: Machine Changeover/Traveling Salesman.

TABLE 15.10   Driving times in minutes (Example 15.15)

From	To					
	Gregory's	Adamses	Burnses	Coneheads	Dells	Evanses
Gregory's		56	70	83	12	55
Adamses	56		47	19	36	45
Burnses	70	47		5	26	42
Coneheads	83	19	5		17	37
Dells	12	36	26	17		21
Evanses	55	45	42	37	21	

+ 56 = 177 minutes. Again, this solution was easy to generate, but it may or may not be the best solution. ∎

SUMMARY

In this chapter, we have discussed many different aspects of *scheduling*. Scheduling problems vary according to the type of layout. With fixed position layouts, the problem is to schedule tasks so that they are done in the right order and on time. This was discussed in great detail in Chapter 10. With process layouts, the problem is to schedule different jobs on different machines. The general problem is termed *job shop scheduling*. We have examined special cases of job shop scheduling where all jobs follow the same flow. Scheduling for these cases is termed *flow shop scheduling*.

Flow shop scheduling can have many different criteria for determining a good schedule. Among these criteria are the *average flow time, makespan, tardiness,* and number of jobs late. For one-machine sequencing, different priority rules have been developed for scheduling. The best priority rule is the *shortest processing time rule* (*SPT*). This rule minimizes the average flow, minimizes the average lateness (not tardiness), and maximizes the number of jobs done at any given point in time. One major difficulty with SPT is that long jobs keep being put back in the schedule. A second difficulty is that SPT does not include due dates. Other priority rules for one-machine sequencing are *earliest due date (EDD), slack time, slack time per operation,* and *Moore's method*.

The scheduling of two or more machines differs from one-machine scheduling in that different schedules have different makespans. When scheduling for two machines (and sometimes for three), *Johnson's method* can be used to minimize the makespan.

Product layout leads to problems related to determining the sequence in which batches of products should be run on the same equipment. Some problems involve minimizing setup times, while others involve the *runout* of items.

Aside from scheduling, there is the problem of assigning workers to machines or jobs to machines to minimize cost. The *assignment problem* and its variations address these issues.

In Chapter 12, we discussed aggregate (medium-range) planning and how the medium-range plan will dictate inventory and scheduling problems. The inventory issues were discussed in Chapters 13 and 14, and the scheduling problems have been discussed in this chapter. The topics of these four chapters are highly interrelated.

KEY TERMS

scheduling	static job shop	makespan
routing	dynamic job shop	shortest processing time
dispatching	flow shop	lateness
control	randomly routed job shop	tardiness
expediting	job flow time	due date scheduling

earliest due date	runout time method	machine changeover
Moore's method	aggregate runout time method	next best strategy
slack		greedy method
slack per operation	assignment problem	traveling salesman problem
Johnson's method	Hungarian method	
product sequencing	bottleneck assignment	

S O L V E D
P R O B L E M S

1. Grassgrow Inc. is bidding on five different landscaping contracts. The director of contracts needs to review the five contracts. The following gives the (estimated) lengths of time it will take the contract director to review each contract and the time when each contract manager needs the contract.

Contract	Time to Review (in days)	Due (in days)
A	3	8
B	2	4
C	5	6
D	1	12
E	9	7

(a) For the shortest processing time schedule, find the average flow time, the number of jobs late, and the average days tardy.

(b) For the due date schedule, find the average flow time, the number of jobs late, and the average days tardy.

Solution

(a) We first need to find the shortest processing time schedule. This is given by taking the jobs in order of their performance times, from shortest to longest. In this problem, the SPT schedule is DBACE. We draw a Gantt chart in order to find the flow times.

	D	B	A	C	E

Flow time	0	1	3	6	11	20
Due date	0	12	4	8	6	7

From the Gantt chart, we see that the flow times are 1, 3, 6, 11, and 20 days, for a total flow time of 41 days, or an average flow time of $41/5 = 8.2$ days.

The Gantt chart also shows that jobs D, B, and A are done ahead of schedule and that jobs C and E are late by 5 and 13 days, respectively. The average tardiness is $(5 + 13)/2 = 9$ days; we divide by 2 because we only consider tardiness for those jobs that are tardy. Alternatively, we could divide by 5.

(b) The due date schedule is given by performing the jobs in the order in which they are due. In this case, that means the schedule is BCEAD. Again, we draw a Gantt chart.

	B	C	E	A	D

Flow time	0	2	7	16	19	20
Due date	0	4	6	7	8	12

From the Gantt chart, we see that the flow times are 2, 7, 16, 19, and 20 days, for a total of 64 days, or an average of $64/5 = 12.8$ days. We also see that only job B is on time and that the other four jobs are tardy by 1, 9, 11, and 8 days, for an average tardiness of $(1 + 9 + 11 + 8)/4 = 29/4 = 7.25$ days.

Using AB:POM to Solve This Problem

AB:POM can solve job shop sequencing problems for one or two machines. The initial input is the number of jobs and the number of machines. For one machine, eight priority rules can be selected.

The data and solution for Solved Problem 1 are given in Screen 15.1. Using the

```
┌─ Data file:wgsp1 ═══════════ Job Shop Sequencing ══════════ Solution ═┐
│   Number of jobs (1-99) 5                    Number of machines (1-2)  1 │
│                                                                          │
│ ┌══════════════════════ Chapter 15, Solved Problem 1 ═══════════════┐  │
│   SPT        mach. 1 Due Dat #OPNS              Order Flow tm       Tardy  │
│   A            3      8     0                   third     6           0    │
│   B            2      4     0                   second    3           0    │
│   C            5      6     0                   fourth    11          5    │
│   D            1     12     0                   first     1           0    │
│   E            9      7     0                   fifth     20          13   │
│   Today #             0                         TOTAL     41          18   │
│   Average # jobs in system =      2.05          AVERAGE   8.20        3.60 │
│   SEQUENCE                                                                 │
│   D,B,A,C,E                                                                │
│                                                                          │
│                                                                          │
│                                                                          │
│                                                                          │
│                                                        F9=Print    Esc   │
│  Press <Esc> key to edit data or highlighted key or function key for options │
└────────────────────────── SCREEN 15.1 ──────────────────────────┘
```

SPT rule, the sequence of jobs is given at the bottom left as DBACE. In addition, the "Order" column shows that A is third, B is second, and so on. The flow times for the job and the tardiness are shown. The total and average flow and tardiness are computed at the bottom of the column; the average number of jobs in the system is also presented. Note that the tardiness is averaged over all 5 jobs. ▬▬▬▬▬

2. The following table gives data for a two-machine problem where all jobs are first processed on machine A and then processed on machine B. Find the schedule that minimizes the makespan and then find this minimum makespan.

	Processing Time (in hours)	
Job	Machine A	Machine B
V	7	8
W	7	6
X	2	1
Y	5	9
Z	8	4

Solution

We begin by having an empty schedule with five slots in it.

Next, we find the shortest time in the table. This is 1, for job X on machine B. Because the time occurs on the second machine, we schedule job X as late as possible, which is in the last position.

The next shortest time (excluding job X) is 4, for job Z on machine B. We schedule job Z as late as possible, which is next to last.

The next shortest time (excluding jobs X and Z) is 5, for job Y on machine A. Because this occurs on the first machine, we schedule job Y as soon as possible, or first.

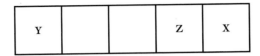

The next shortest time (among jobs V and W) is 6, for job W on machine B. Therefore, we place W after V.

Y	V	W	Z	X

In order to find the time, we need a Gantt chart with two bars—one for machine A and one for machine B. First, we will fill in the times for the first machine.

0	5	12	19	27	29
Y	V	W	Z	X	

Now we can add the second machine.

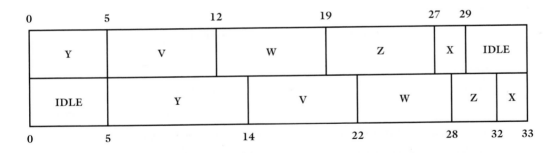

Using AB:POM to Solve This Problem

Solved Problem 2 is displayed in Screen 15.2. Johnson's method is used; the order is listed in an order column and at the bottom left. The makespan is listed below the problem.

```
┌─ Data file:wgsp2 ═══════════════ Job Shop Sequencing ════════════════ Solution ─┐
│   Number of jobs (1-99) 5                           Number of machines (1-2)  2  │
│ ┌═══════════════════════════════ Chapter 15, Solved Problem 2 ════════════════┐ │
│ │ Johnson   Mach A   Mach B    Order   Done 1   Done 2(flow time)             │ │
│ │ V            7        8      second     12        22                        │ │
│ │ W            7        6      third      19        28                        │ │
│ │ X            2        1      fifth      29        33                        │ │
│ │ Y            5        9      first       5        14                        │ │
│ │ Z            8        4      fourth     27        32                        │ │
│ │               Makespan (maximum flow time) = 33                            │ │
│ │                                                                            │ │
│ │ SEQUENCE                                                                   │ │
│ │ Y,V,W,Z,X                                                                  │ │
│ │                                                                            │ │
│ │                                                                            │ │
│ │                                                                            │ │
│ │                                                                            │ │
│ │                                                                            │ │
│ └────────────────────────────────────────────────────────────────────────────┘ │
│                                                         F9=Print      Esc        │
│   Press <Esc> key to edit data or highlighted key or function key for options    │
└──────────────────────────────── SCREEN 15.2 ────────────────────────────────────┘
```

QUESTIONS

1. Name and briefly explain the five categories of scheduling.

2. Give an example of these five categories as they apply to an activity of yours (such as schoolwork).

3. What scheduling problems are related to fixed position layout?

4. Explain the difference between a static and a dynamic job shop. Which is more common?

5. Explain the difference between a general job shop and a flow shop.

6. How does a queueing system compare with a job shop system?

7. What is a due date? Why was the term enclosed in quotation marks in the text?

8. Explain the following terms: flow time, makespan, lateness, tardiness.

9. What are the advantages and disadvantages of the shortest processing time rule?

10. Cite an example of a two-machine flow shop.

11. What is the runout time? the aggregate runout time?

12. What is the difference between the assignment problem and the bottleneck assignment problem?

13. What is the difference between the machine changeover problem and the traveling salesman problem?

PROBLEMS

1. UXB Air has six flights that all arrive in Philadelphia at 5:00 P.M. Unfortunately, UXB has only one crew to unload the baggage from each of the six flights. The following is a list of the average number of passengers per flight. Assume that each passenger has (on the average) 1.5 bags and that it takes (on the average) 4 seconds to unload each bag.

(a) In which order should the planes be unloaded to minimize the average unloading time for each plane (from the time of landing)?

(b) What is the minimum average unloading time for this schedule?

602; 405; 227; 312; 711; 822

20.7 minutes

Flight	Number of Passengers
602	20
227	60
405	40
822	210
711	130
312	70

2. The following table gives data on five jobs to be processed on one machine.

Job	Processing Time (in hours)	Due Date (in hours)
A	7	52
B	15	45
C	10	30
D	20	20
E	5	15

For each of the following methods, find the average flow time, maximum flow time, number of late jobs, average lateness, and average tardiness.

(a) SPT

(b) EDD

26.6 hours; 57 hours; 1; 5.8 hours early; 7.4 hours
34.4 hours; 57 hours; 4; 2 hours late; 4 hours

3. The following gives data on four jobs to be processed on one machine.

Job	Processing Time (in days)	Due Date (in days)
A	10	22
B	25	45
C	12	18
D	18	30

(a) What schedule minimizes the average flow time?

(b) What schedule minimizes the average lateness?

(c) What schedule minimizes the maximum tardiness?

ACDB
ACDB
CADB

4. The following table presents data on six jobs to be processed on one machine.

Job	Processing Time (in weeks)	Due Date (in weeks)	Number of Operations
A	2	3	3
B	4	8	1
C	3	12	2
D	6	11	1
E	8	16	4
F	1	4	2

Find the schedule using the method indicated.

FACBDE
AFBDCE
AFBDEC
AFEBCD
AFBCDE

(a) SPT
(b) EDD
(c) slack time
(d) slack time per operation
(e) Moore's method

5. Compurizon is a company that does computerized accounting. A client brings its weekly records to Compurizon. These records are first stored on a disk file; later, computations are performed and written on a tape file. Compurizon has only one disk unit and one tape unit. They both may be in use at the same time. One Friday at 3:00 P.M., six companies bring their weekly records to Compurizon and wait for the results. The average time it takes to process each company's records on the disk and tape units is given in the following table.

BEFCAD
5:30 P.M.

(a) In which order should the company records be processed in order to finish the six jobs as soon as possible?
(b) At what time will all processing end?

Company	Disk Time (in minutes)	Tape Time (in minutes)
Arca, Inc.	30	20
Bowa, Inc.	5	10
Cala, Inc.	25	30
Dupo, Inc.	40	5
Eror, Inc.	10	35
Fasto, Inc.	15	45

6. Captain Clark of the Philadelphia Police Department's vice squad has six busts on his list of things to do today. For each bust, he and his squad must first arrest the criminals and then book them at headquarters. The times for arrests and bookings of the six gangs are listed in the accompanying table.

Reno, What, River, Doog, Car, Bama

8:09 A.M.

(a) In what order should Captain Clark make the arrests so that he and his officers can go home as soon as possible?
(b) If the shift starts at midnight, at what time will his officers finish their tour of duty for the night?

Criminal Leader	Number in Gang	Time for Arrest (in minutes)	Time for Booking (in minutes)
Jim What	6	25	42
Frank Reno	2	16	28
Willie Doog	4	63	72
James Car	29	104	200
Al A. Bama	3	37	29
Moses River	8	52	81

7. At Smallville Hospital, sheets are washed and then dried. The sheets always return to the same unit they came from. At 9:00 A.M., sheets were waiting to be laundered from seven different units. The processing times vary because of the different number of sheets in each batch and the requirements of each unit. These times are given in the table. There is only one washer and one dryer.

Unit	Wash Time (in minutes)	Dry Time (in minutes)
A	40	50
B	60	30
C	100	80
D	20	10
E	110	90
F	50	40
G	120	100

(a) The laundry personnel wish to finish as soon as possible. In what order should the jobs be done?

(b) At what time will they finish?

(c) What is the average flow time per unit?

AGECFBD
5:50 P.M.
385.71 minutes

8. The University Duplicating Services prints and collates the work of famous faculty. The shop has only one duplicating machine and one collating machine. Of course, jobs must be printed before they are collated. Seven faculty members have left jobs to be processed. Processing times are given in the following table. Duplicating Services personnel like to leave as early as possible.

Faculty Member	Printing Time (in minutes)	Collating Time (in minutes)
A	40	50
B	10	30
C	100	80
D	20	10
E	110	60
F	50	40
G	120	100

BAGCEFD
4:10 P.M.
310 minutes

(a) In what order should the shop work the jobs?
(b) If they start at 8:00 A.M., what time will they finish?
(c) What is the average flow time of the seven jobs?

9. At the Federal Unemployment Office, six people are scheduled to arrive at 9:00 A.M. Processing requires two stages. The first is to gather information, and the second is to try to match each person with a job. There is one person to gather the information and one person to find jobs. (Due to governmental regulations, each of these two individuals can perform only the task assigned.) The following table gives processing times.

CGHTER
11:37 A.M.

(a) In which order should the unemployed be processed so that the two civil servants will be done as soon as possible?
(b) At what time will all processing be completed?

Unemployed	Processing Time (in minutes)	
	Information Gathering	Job Matching
Reese	8	4
Evans	21	12
Herbert	5	22
Thomas	14	46
Gordon	4	21
Charles	3	49

10. Drug tests are being administered to a group of athletes. Each athlete must pass through two processes, and the length of time spent at each process is a function of the individual's physical characteristics. Thus, the times will vary for each competitor. The two tests are performed sequentially—that is, test 1 is given, then test 2.

The following table gives the times to test some of the athletes.

Athlete	Test 1 (in minutes)	Test 2 (in minutes)
Anna	30	20
Boris	5	12
Colette	25	35
Doris	40	8
Elisha	10	45
Fritz	15	50

The testing is scheduled to begin at 8:00 P.M.

BEFCAD
10:55 P.M.

BEFCAD

(a) In what order should the tests be given so that the testing committee can go home as soon as possible?
(b) At what time will the testing committee finish?
(c) If only test 1 is given, in what order should the athletes be tested in order to minimize the average waiting time?

11. Curt's Custom Cabinet Shop has received three orders for cabinets. The length of time that it takes to complete the jobs and the profit per job are given in the following table. Curt can work on only one cabinet at a time. If the interest rate is 1 percent per month and payments are made at the time each cabinet is completed, in what order should Curt make the cabinets in order to maximize the present value of profits?

Cabinet	Time (in months)	Profit
A	6	$1,000
B	2	400
C	4	700

CBA

12. The following table provides data for a three-job, two-machine (#1, #2) problem.

Job	Machine Processing Time (in days) #1	#2	Due Date (in days)	Penalty per Day Late
A	3	2	5	10
B	6	8	14	2
C	5	7	12	8

(a) What schedule minimizes the makespan?   CBA
(b) What schedule minimizes total penalty costs? (Hint: Try all possible schedules.)   ACB
(c) What schedule minimizes the average completion time per job?   ACB

13. In order to process certain lab tests, two machines must be used. Machine 1 is used first, then machine 2. Different lab tests require different amounts of time on the two machines. The following table lists three tests that are to be performed, the times at which they were promised, and the estimated penalty for each hour the test results are late.

Test	Machine Processing Time (in hours) #1	#2	Promised	Penalty
A	4	2	5	5
B	6	8	14	4
C	5	7	12	3

(a) Which schedule minimizes total penalty costs?   ACB
(b) Which schedule minimizes the average flow time?   ACB
(c) Which schedule completes all jobs the soonest?   CBA

14. Data for a three-machine job shop appear in the following table. What schedule minimizes the makespan?

	Processing Time (in hours)		
Job	Machine 1	Machine 2	Machine 3
A	22	8	10
B	18	6	5
C	16	3	3
D	20	12	17
E	15	14	12

EDABC

15. Three jobs have come in for processing at the Custom-Finish shop. Each piece must be stripped, then sanded, and then varnished. The times for these tasks and the due dates are as follows.

	Processing Time (in days)			Due Date
Job	Strip	Sand	Varnish	(in days)
A	2	4	3	16
B	6	1	3	10
C	3	3	4	15

Consider only the schedules ABC, ACB, and BAC.

ACB   **(a)** Which schedule completes all jobs the soonest?
BAC   **(b)** Which schedule minimizes total tardy days?
ACB or BAC   **(c)** Which schedule minimizes the number of jobs tardy?
ABC or ACB   **(d)** Which schedule minimizes twice the total tardy days minus total early days?

16. The following table gives the changeover times in minutes required in going from one color to another in the production of crayons. Find the pattern that minimizes the changeover time per cycle.

	To		
From	Sky Blue (S)	Indigo (I)	Violet (V)
Sky Blue (S)		80	35
Indigo (I)	15		40
Violet (V)	55	60	

SVIS

17. The changeover times (in minutes) required in going from one product to another are given as follows. Use the greedy method to find the sequence and the minutes per cycle.

	To					
From	A	B	C	D	E	F
A		15	16	10	20	18
B	20		35	20	30	25
C	30	10		16	19	21
D	10	18	25		20	12
E	18	20	15	26		25
F	15	18	28	14	20	

ADFBECA; 115 minutes per cycle (*Note:* Other answers are possible.)

18. Alice Allen is a piano teacher who gives lessons to Bob, Carl, Don, and Ed on Monday nights. The following table contains Alice's driving times (in minutes) from house to house.

(a) In which order should she give the lessons? Use the greedy method.
(b) How much time does Alice spend driving each Monday?

ADBCEA
60 (*Note:* Other answers are possible.)

	To				
From	Alice	Bob	Carl	Don	Ed
Alice		25	30	15	20
Bob	25		10	5	15
Carl	30	10		20	10
Don	15	5	20		5
Ed	20	15	10	5	

19. The following table contains a list of four items that are produced on the same assembly line. According to the runout time method, in which order should the products be produced?

Item	Current Inventory	Demand (in units/week)
A	3,000	1,000
B	1,600	400
C	1,200	600
D	2,000	2,000

DCAB

20. The following table contains information on five items that share the same process.

Item	Production Time (hours/unit)	Lot Size	Forecast for Week	Current Inventory
A	.5	150	25	10
B	.2	200	40	35
C	.1	75	10	15
D	.3	100	20	10
E	.4	50	15	20

ADBEC
no

ART = 4.3134 weeks

(a) Schedule the items according to the runout time method.
(b) If 120 hours are available this week, is there enough capacity to meet the demand?

21. Schedule the jobs in Problem 20 using the aggregate runout time method.

22. Minimize the cost of assigning each of four workers to four machines.

	Machine			
Worker	W	X	Y	Z
A	25	30	15	20
B	25	10	5	15
C	30	10	25	10
D	20	15	10	5

A–W, B–Y, C–X, D–Z; $45

23. Minimize the cost of assigning each of four jobs to each of four workers.

	Worker			
Job	Al	Bill	Carl	Dean
1	400	600	500	450
2	500	900	600	700
3	300	800	400	400
4	450	850	500	650

1–Bill, 2–Al, 3–Dean, 4–Carl; $2,000

24. Minimize the cost of assigning each of six jobs to each of six machines.

	Machine					
Job	U	V	W	X	Y	Z
A	22	36	16	19	69	70
B	98	56	31	84	45	12
C	89	91	28	80	52	36
D	92	73	23	34	16	13
E	40	73	66	55	83	46
F	76	42	56	77	28	35

A–X, B–Z, C–W, D–Y, E–U, F–V; $157

25. Maximize the profit associated with assigning each of five consultants to each of five clients.

			Client		
Consultant	OSS	CIA	KGB	FBI	HMSS
Bond	78	66	98	24	74
Smart	47	69	47	44	41
Hoover	54	39	95	13	54
Smiley	26	31	72	62	79
Karlov	28	83	85	66	40

Bond–OSS, Smart–CIA, Hoover–KGB, Smiley–HMSS, Karlov–FBI; $387

26. Solve the following as a bottleneck minimization assignment problem.

	W	X	Y	Z
A	47	97	26	74
B	45	87	26	74
C	38	82	13	62
D	59	96	37	66

bottleneck = 82; A–Z, B–Y, C–X, D–W (*Note:* Other assignments are possible.)

27. Five engineers are to be assigned to five parts of a project (one engineer per part; one part per engineer). The following table indicates the number of days that any engineer would require for any part of the project. What assignment minimizes the project completion time?

			Part		
Engineer	1	2	3	4	5
Abrams	46	59	24	62	67
Barnes	47	56	32	55	70
Casey	44	52	19	61	60
Davis	47	59	17	64	73
Evans	43	65	20	60	75

bottleneck = 60; A–2; B–4; C–5; D–3; E–1 (*Note:* Other assignments are possible.)

28. The five engineers in Problem 27 are paid as follows.

Engineer	**Salary (in dollars/day)**
Abrams	900
Barnes	400
Casey	600
Davis	700
Evans	500

What assignment minimizes the total cost?

A–1, B–2, C–5, D–3, E–4

COMPUTER CASE STUDY 15.1: ACCOUNTFREE

Accountfree is a company that provides accounting services for small businesses. Small businesses drop off their payroll records weekly, biweekly, or monthly. Accountfree then processes the records and issues the checks. The following table shows the processing times and types for jobs dropped off by Accountfree clients on Friday, May 1.

Client	Processing Type	Time (in minutes)
AAA Repairs	Weekly	72
ABC Supplies	Monthly	26
Ben's Ice Cream	Weekly	28
Che's Lounge	Weekly	47
Darren's	Weekly	33
Ed's Travel	Biweekly	63
Ernie's Toy Store	Monthly	95
Fred's Fast Food	Monthly	87
Garrison's Glass	Weekly	15
Gunter's Guns	Weekly	32
Handyman Inc.	Weekly	24
Izenman Ads	Monthly	55
Jerry's Ice Cream	Weekly	33
Keystone Repairs	Weekly	31
Lifeblood Inc.	Weekly	25
Lisa's Bakery	Weekly	48
Living Well	Biweekly	42
Mork's Morticians	Weekly	43
New Life Vitamins	Weekly	64
Owens & Marshal	Monthly	42
Philly Cheesedogs	Weekly	24
Quick Tune	Weekly	14
Rockin' Robin	Weekly	74
Sam's Sporting Goods	Monthly	110
Swinging Starts	Weekly	13
Tetris Inc.	Weekly	18
Underworld Connections	Weekly	22
Varnish Removers	Weekly	23
Willie's Chocolates	Biweekly	64
XXX Inc.	Monthly	88
Yugo's Yugos	Weekly	8
Zen Book Store	Monthly	76
Ziegfried's Folly	Weekly	42
ZZZ Inc.	Weekly	36

When companies drop off their records on time, Accountfree typically manages to get the checks printed on time. However, Accountfree has occasionally run into scheduling difficulties. The company feels that examining what has happened in the past will provide some insight into how to deal with similar situations in the future.

Accountfree sets due dates according to the type of customer. For monthly customers, the due date is 9:00 A.M.; for biweekly customers, the due date is noon; and for weekly customers, the due date is 3:00 P.M. All of the processing will begin on the third shift (at midnight) on the day that the records are due.

Accountfree has been using a due date scheduling rule because this accords the highest priority to the monthly clients and the lowest priority to the weekly. If clients come in only once per month, there is less room for error (lateness) than if they use a weekly payroll. While Accountfree has been following this logic for the past decade, they want to determine whether or not this is the best scheduling rule. Using the data in the table, explore alternative scheduling possibilities for Accountfree.

REFERENCES

Hansen, P., and R. E. Wendell. "A Note on Airline Commuting," *Interfaces* 12, no. 1 (1982): 85–87.

Hesse, R., and G. Woolsey. *Applied Management Science.* Chicago: Science Research Associates, 1980.

Johnson, S. M. "Optimal and Three Stage Production Schedules with Set-up Times Included," *Naval Research Logistics Quarterly* 1 (1954): 61–68.

Lev, B., and H. J. Weiss. *Introduction to Mathematical Programming.* New York: North Holland, 1982.

Machol, R. E. *Elementary System Mathematics.* New York: McGraw-Hill, 1976.

McLeavey, D. W., and S. L. Narasimhan. *Production Planning and Inventory Control.* Boston: Allyn and Bacon, 1985.

Moore, J. M. "One Job, One Machine Sequencing Method for Minimizing the Number of Late Jobs," *Management Science* 15, no. 15 (September 1968): 102–109.

Smith, W. E. "Various Optimizers for Single Stage Production," *Naval Research Logistics Quarterly* 1 (1954): 61–68.

Woolsey, G. "An Essay on the Set-Up, Tear-Down Problem or on Being Clean, Being Profitable, or Both," *Interfaces* 12, no. 4 (August 1982): 11–13.

Woolsey, R. E. D., and H. S. Swanson. *Operations Research for Immediate Application: A Quick and Dirty Manual.* New York: Harper & Row, 1975.

PART FIVE

QUALITY

C H A P T E R

16

O U T L I N E

TOTAL QUALITY MANAGEMENT: THE DEMING APPROACH

■ **To present the Deming approach to total quality management**
■ **To describe the behavioral side of the quality program for management**
■ **To show how problem solving is a prerequisite for continuous quality improvement**
■ **To describe the statistical tools for quality improvement**

INTRODUCTION

In today's competitive business environment, quality is viewed as more than a function within operations. Quality has grown beyond the scope of operations. Today, quality is a competitive strategy, the basis for a complete management philosophy.

quality as a strategy

Our topic in this chapter is the quality-based management philosophy, which, while it goes beyond operations, emphasizes the importance of operations as the key to business success. The quality-based management philosophy employs a broad definition of quality: For example, profitability is a measure of quality, as are inventory levels. In fact, in this approach, every business performance measure can be viewed as a measure of quality. Therefore, we can view all of the tools presented up to this point in the text as being aimed at improving quality. The management philosophy presented in this chapter, then, provides a basis for integrating all of the chapters in this text into a cohesive framework.

Teaching Suggestion 16.1: TQM in Action. See the Instructor's Section for details.

The quality-based philosophy now being adopted throughout American industry is that of W. Edwards Deming and is termed **total quality management** (TQM). Deming introduced this philosophy in Japan over forty years ago. The subsequent resurgence of the Japanese economy is often attributed to the adoption by the Japanese of Deming's approach. Over the years, many variations of Deming's philosophy have been developed, but all are based on the central tenet of the Deming approach: instituting a culture of **continuous improvement.** The Crosby, Juran, and Taguchi approaches, to name just a few, all stress never-ending improvement through the use of statistical tools, participative management, and problem solving.

Actually, the Deming approach is much more than a philosophy. Unlike the zero defects programs of the 1960s, which demanded quality without providing the methods for achieving it, the Deming approach provides a wide array of necessary tools. Most of these tools are quantitative; that is, they rely heavily on the use of statistics. Taken together, these statistical tools constitute a program of **statistical process control** (SPC), the visible and measurable core of a Deming program. SPC improves many cost and productivity variables in addition to product quality.

every employee is involved

The implementation of a TQM program typically occurs in four phases. The first phase involves the creation of the proper cultural environment for instituting SPC. In this phase, every employee is trained in the TQM philosophy. The second phase

Deming and "Made in Japan"

Dr. W. Edwards Deming is one of the pioneers of statistical quality control. Until recently, his most receptive audiences were Japanese, not American. After World War II, Japanese industry lay in ruins. One of the tasks of the American occupation was to help Japan rebuild its shattered economy. Over the next thirty years, the phrase "made in Japan" was transformed from a stamp of inferior, cheaply made goods to a sign of quality respected the world over, just as Deming predicted would happen if the Japanese followed his advice.

> I told the Japanese that they would capture markets within five years the world over, that they would take their place alongside prosperous nations. They have done it. They have done it!

Deming's teaching of statistics is part of a broader management philosophy adopted by the Japanese—one that places an emphasis on people, quality, participative management, long-term thinking, and never-ending improvement. However, Deming is clearly a central figure in the astonishing turnaround of Japanese industry.

One measure of the debt owed to Deming by the Japanese: The most prestigious prize in Japanese industry is the Deming Prize, awarded each year to companies with outstanding records in quality and productivity.

Source: Against All Odds (New York: W.H. Freeman, 1988).

involves problem solving. Here, process studies and Pareto analysis are used. Again, every employee must be knowledgeable in the use of these tools and must be able to work on teams to investigate specific problems. The third phase involves the statistical process control itself. Again, there is a heavy emphasis on employee training. The fourth phase uses more advanced statistics to go beyond controlling a process to the actual design of optimal process parameter settings. Specifically, the fourth and last phase of the implementation process involves the statistical design of experiments through **Taguchi methods.** Taguchi methods focus the statistical analysis on the decisions that management will need to make in order to run complex processes in an optimal manner. In this phase, it is not advisable to train all employees. Only a small group of individuals acting as a resource group when the technique needs to be applied is required.

THE CULTURE OF TQM

We have stated that the first step in implementing a TQM program is the creation of the proper cultural environment. Putting the TQM culture into place very often involves changing the attitudes of management and employees toward teamwork and **participative management.** Management must change its focus and concentrate on the company's long-term prospects. The result: a company in which everyone is actively looking for continuous process improvement and in which problems, rather than being covered up, are brought to the fore so that they may be solved.

long-term focus

DEMING'S FOURTEEN POINTS

The key to successfully implementing a TQM program, then, is an initial stage of consensus-building among all employees. In other words, a TQM program is far more likely to succeed when employees buy into the central tenets of Deming's approach, of which there are fourteen.

1. Create constancy of purpose toward improvement of product and service with a plan to become competitive, stay in business, and provide jobs.
2. Adopt the new philosophy. We are in a new economic age. We can no longer live with commonly accepted levels of delays, mistakes, defective materials, and defective workmanship.
3. Cease dependence on mass inspection. Require, instead, statistical evidence that quality is built in to eliminate the need for inspection on a mass basis.

Teaching Suggestion 16.2: Price vs. Cost. See the Instructor's Section for details.

4. End the practice of awarding business on the basis of price tag. Instead, depend on meaningful measures of quality, along with price. Move toward a single supplier for any one item in order to develop a long-term relationship of loyalty and trust.
5. Improve constantly and forever the system of production and service to improve quality and productivity and, thus, to constantly decrease costs. The heart of this is finding problems and taking corrective action.
6. Institute modern training methods.
7. Institute a program of supervisor training conducive to a participative environment.
8. Drive out fear, so that everyone may work effectively for the company.
9. Break down organizational barriers. Encourage teamwork to foresee and to solve problems across departmental boundaries.
10. Eliminate arbitrary numerical goals, posters, and slogans that seek new levels of productivity without providing methods.
11. Eliminate numerical quotas.
12. Remove barriers that rob employees of their pride of workmanship.
13. Institute a vigorous program of education and retraining.
14. Create a structure within management that will push the prior thirteen points every day.

Teaching Suggestion 16.3: Industrial Revolution. See the Instructor's Section for details.

COMMENTS ON DEMING'S POINTS

reduce number of suppliers

Some of these points may require elaboration, because they seem to be at odds with common business practices. For example, Deming calls for reducing the number of suppliers, with **single sourcing** for each component purchased the ideal. The chief advantage of this recommendation is a reduction in product variation. This point is the basis for the **vendor certification** programs that are instituted at the second stage of a TQM implementation. Note that reducing product variation—and, therefore, the need for inspections—is consistent with the just-in-time inventory approach.

Deming's fifth point, continuously improving the system, is deceptively simple. It typically requires a complete cultural change. Most workers are encouraged to keep problems to themselves. Contrast this with the culture advocated by Deming—one in which workers are encouraged to bring up problems because only problems that have been brought to light can be solved.

bring problems to light

Deming recommends the elimination of goals, quotas, and employee evaluations. Such policies add fear to the work environment, and the absence of fear is critical to the open problem-solving culture desired. Additionally, such policies force employees to compete against each other; instead, policies should be implemented that foster a culture of teamwork. The true enemies, after all, are competing companies. Finally, goals and quotas retard the improvement process by defining what is good enough. Fixed goals are incompatible with the goal of never-ending improvement.

avoid fear

Although not recommended by Deming, a major contributing factor to the success of establishing the TQM culture is the use of problem-solving teams. Also called employee-involvement teams, quality-action teams, and **quality circles,** among other things, such groups provide an outlet for bringing up problems and emphasize the culture of cooperation that is desired. They also can have the advantage of working across departmental boundaries.

teams lead to success

Some people refer to Deming's fourteen "points" as "obligations" of management. This terminology clarifies management's role. Fundamental, lasting improvements in quality result from process changes, which only management has the authority to make. Asking employees to work better or harder has never been an effective strategy.

only management can improve processes

Since the culture is one that encourages more employee participation in problem solving and decision making, it will not work unless every employee is trained in it. Since this culture places most obligations squarely on management, employees respond positively to it and are receptive to its use. This reduces turnover and morale problems and, in addition to the other benefits mentioned previously, leads to a nicer place to work and a more competitive and profitable company.

employees respond positively to TQM

TOOLS FOR PROBLEM SOLVING

A culture of continuous improvement is synonymous with a problem-solving culture. It is not enough to make employees aware of the new philosophy; management must be the first to put it into practice, leading by example.

Any problem-solving procedure begins, obviously, with a problem. But where does the recognition of this problem come from? Problems are brought to light by control charts; by customers and inspectors; and by managers and workers. In the desired participative management scheme, it is best if workers call attention to a problem, but workers traditionally are not trained to *solve* problems. As those working closest to the problems, they must be trained to use basic problem-solving tools, especially the following:

- process analysis;
- brainstorming;
- cause-and-effect diagrams; and
- Pareto analysis.

Another problem-solving tool—working in teams—has already been discussed.

PROCESS ANALYSIS

standardize
procedures

Process analysis is essentially **methods analysis,** as discussed in Chapter 9. One goal of TQM is to reduce variation. One way to reduce variation is to standardize procedures. At most companies, three people doing the same job will have developed three different procedures with three different outputs.

Teaching Suggestion 16.4:
Peanut Butter and Jelly.
See the Instructor's Sec-
tion for details.

It will not be possible in TQM to improve any process until that process is fully understood. After the team has broken down the process into all of its component steps, possible causes for the problem can be identified at each step. Then possible solutions can be discussed and tested before being put into place.

A very simple process—one that culminates in an order for small tools—is depicted in Figure 16.1. After reviewing the process, the process is revised, as depicted in Figure 16.2. Notice that two key changes have been made between Figure 16.1 and 16.2:

process improvement
example

1. a layer of approval authority has been eliminated; and
2. the requisition and purchase order have been combined into one form.

The second step is typical; this kind of change has few, if any, drawbacks. In most cases, a great deal more care must be exercised when determining whether or not to eliminate layers of approval authority. For small tools, it is doubtful that the eliminated layer of approval authority was necessary. For, say, a commercial lending institution, dispensing with even one layer of approval authority could be very costly. Still, many companies have reduced output by placing unnecessary barriers in front of their workers. It is the job of management to trim this bureaucracy, enabling everyone to work better and faster. Process analysis exposes barriers so that they can be eliminated.

eliminate barriers

BRAINSTORMING

generate ideas

Another useful tool for the quality team is **brainstorming.** Brainstorming is an idea-generating approach that is used to find problems, causes of problems, causes of variation, ways to prevent problems, solutions to problems, or ways to implement these solutions. It can be viewed as a meeting in which those in attendance are encouraged to think of as many ideas as possible.

We can define brainstorming more formally, as a specific procedure that serves to foster creativity.

Step 1. On a piece of paper, each person makes a list of his or her ideas.

Step 2. Sitting in a circle to lessen dominance by any individual, each person takes a turn reading one idea at a time, starting at the top of his or her list.

Step 3. As the ideas are read, they are displayed so that everyone can see them.

Step 4. Participants skip ideas that have been read by someone else, proceeding to the next original idea on the list.

procedure for
brainstorming

Step 5. When all of the lists have been read, the leader asks the participants, in turn, if any new ideas have occurred to them. It is very likely that, upon seeing other people's ideas, group members will think of more ideas.

Step 6. The leader continues asking each person, in turn, if there are any more ideas until the group runs out of suggestions.

Step 7. Participants reflect on all of the ideas generated.

PROCESS FLOW

Name of Process _____REQUISITION - PURCHASING_____

Process Objectives _____TO REQUISITION FOR SMALL TOOLS_____

Symbol	Description
O	Requisition written by supervisor (one copy)
D	On supervisor's desk (awaiting messenger)
⇨	By messenger to superintendent's secretary
D	On secretary's desk (awaiting typing)
O	Requisition typed (original requisition copied)
⇨	By secretary to superintendent
D	On superintendent's desk (awaiting approval)
□	Examined and approved by superintendent
D	On superintendent's desk (awaiting messenger)
⇨	To purchasing department
D	On purchasing agent's desk (awaiting approval)
□	Examined and approved
D	On purchasing agent's desk (awaiting messenger)
⇨	To typist's desk
D	On typist's desk (awaiting typing of purchase order)
O	Purchase order typed
D	On typist's desk (awaiting transfer to main office)

○ **Operation**   ⇨ **Transportation**   □ **Inspection**   D **Delay**

▽ **Storage**   **R Rework**

FIGURE 16.1   Process prior to improvement

PROCESS FLOW

Name of Process _REQUISITION - PURCHASING_

Process Objectives _TO REQUISITION FOR SMALL TOOLS_

Symbol	Description
○	Purchase order written in triplicate by supervisor
D	On supervisor's desk (awaiting messenger)
⇒	By messenger to purchasing agent
D	On purchasing agent's desk (awaiting approval)
□	Examined and approved by purchasing agent
D	On purchasing agent's desk (awaiting transfer to main office)

○ **Operation** ⇒ **Transportation** □ **Inspection** D **Delay**

▽ **Storage** **R** **Rework**

FIGURE 16.2 Improved process

The new ideas developed at step 5 are the main reason for emphasizing that brainstorming is a group technique. Ideally, brainstorming has a synergistic effect; group members generate more ideas as a group than they would merely by aggregating their individual lists.

brainstorming is synergistic

Brainstorming can be viewed as having two phases: the idea-generation phase and idea-evaluation phase. Step 7 is the evaluation phase. If brainstorming is to be as successful as possible, evaluations or criticism of any idea should not be allowed during the idea-generation phase (steps 1–5). Such criticism could inhibit someone from suggesting an idea for fear that it may sound dumb. An idea that sounds dumb at first could end up, after careful thought, contributing to the solution.

lack of criticism leads to generation of ideas

There is also the possibility that a "dumb idea" may cause a good idea to click in someone else's head. For example, an automobile manufacturer is supposed to have asked the company that supplied its paints and coatings to help overcome problems the automaker was having in getting the coatings into small openings in car bodies. Two brainstorming teams were set up: one to investigate new coatings and another to look at new methods of applying the coatings. As the methods group was running out of ideas, someone suggested ants! Ants could run through the coatings and then into the small openings. Within minutes, someone else said, "Not ants, but amps!" This led to a series of patents for electroplating. The amount of truth in this story is less important than the point it makes.

CAUSE-AND-EFFECT DIAGRAM

The end product of brainstorming is a lengthy and disorganized list of ideas. The next tool we will examine is the cause-and-effect diagram. The cause-and-effect diagram—sometimes called the **Ishikawa diagram,** after one of the leading Japanese contributors to TQM—is used to classify and present the ideas from brainstorming in a manner more likely to lead to solving the problem at hand.

classify ideas from brainstorming

There are many ways to present this diagram. One is the risk diagram, or fault tree (see Figure 16.3), in which the problem under analysis is placed at the "root" of a tree. The major causes of the problem branch from the root, each successive branching becoming more specific in determining the cause. At the end, everything that can possibly go wrong has been listed and the likelihood of each can be considered. It is also possible to add extra layers. One such layer might show actions taken to prevent each cause from occurring. Another layer might list response actions to more effectively deal with each problem should it occur.

risk diagram

A more common form of the cause-and-effect diagram is the **fishbone diagram.** In a fishbone diagram, the problem is placed at the "head," a "spine" is drawn, and all the causes branch off the spine, as shown in Figure 16.4.

The problem with Figure 16.4 is that it fails to classify the causes in any way. In TQM, there are four primary causes of variation:

- manpower,
- methods,
- materials, and
- machines.

Teaching Suggestion 16.5: Coffee. See the Instructor's Section for details.

It is most common, then, to use these as four categories for classifying the causes shown in Figure 16.5. Other ways to classify the causes are by major cause areas (see

categories of causes

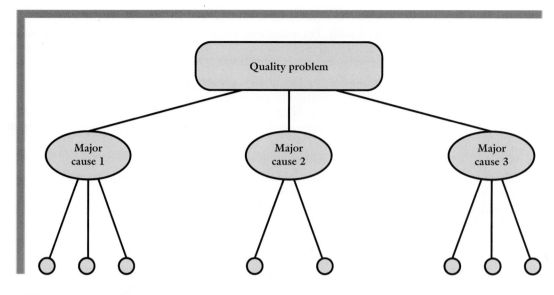

FIGURE 16.3   Fault tree

Figure 16.6), as was also done in the fault tree, or by sequence in the process (see Figure 16.7).

PARETO ANALYSIS

The final tool presented in this section is the Pareto analysis. Of the myriad things that can go wrong in a process, some—perhaps many—cannot be fixed or prevented due

FIGURE 16.4   Fishbone diagram listing causes

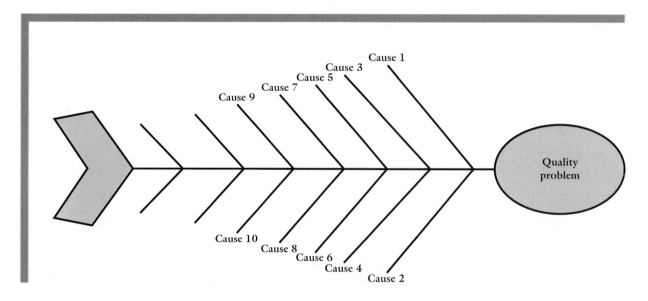

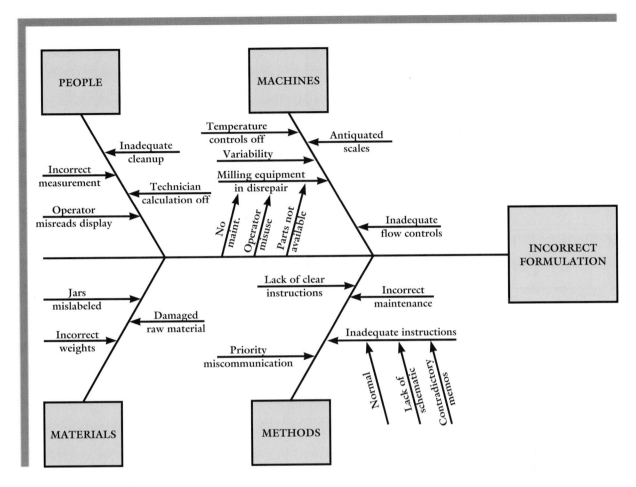

FIGURE 16.5 Fishbone diagram classified by four factors

to time and budget limitations. Pareto analysis helps to decide which problems are the most important to study.

The Pareto analysis is based on the Pareto distribution, which, in its original analysis, says that 5 percent of the people control 50 percent of the wealth, or that 20 percent control 80 percent of the wealth. The ABC classification system presented in Chapter 13 was a form of Pareto analysis. There, 5 percent of the part numbers in inventory accounted for 50 percent of the usage.

In TQM, where the focus is on problems, all of the problems identified during brainstorming or listed on the cause-and-effect diagram will not occur with equal frequency. It turns out that their rate of occurrence follows the Pareto distribution, most commonly stated in the form of the 20-80 rule:

Twenty percent of the potential causes will account for 80 percent of the actual occurrences.

20-80 rule

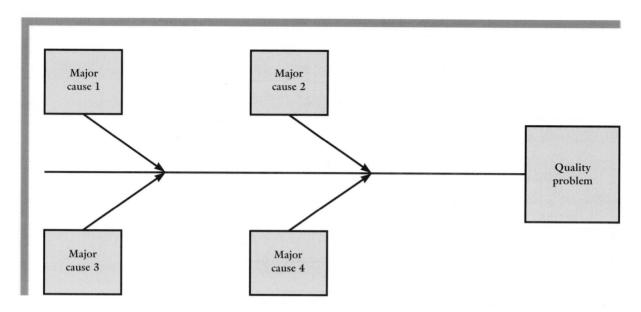

FIGURE 16.6 Fishbone diagram classified by major causes

A Pareto analysis consists of four steps.

Step 1. List all of the potential causes.

Step 2. Monitor the process for an appropriate time period to see how often each cause occurs.

Step 3. Rank the causes from greatest to least importance.

Step 4. Draw the Pareto chart, a bar chart showing frequency of occurrence.

A **Pareto chart** is shown in Figure 16.8. It should be obvious that inadequate parts—represented by the tallest bar—is the problem most urgently in need of a solution.

long-term procedure for solving problems

The Pareto chart goes beyond selecting the one problem to concentrate on in the near term. The sequence of problems on the chart provides a longer-term basis for planning process improvements, an orderly scheme for the eventual solution of all the problems.

STATISTICAL PROCESS CONTROL: MONITORING A PROCESS

The tools we have presented to this point are part of any good problem-solving methodology. However, such tools are more useful in service industries and for administrative applications than in manufacturing operations. Issues related more directly to product quality in manufacturing require more emphasis on different tools—primarily those associated with statistical process control.

Many statistical tools are used in statistical process control, but the **control chart** is the most useful and the best known. We preface our discussion of the control chart with a look at some related statistical tools, because an understanding of the statistical fundamentals on which the control charts are based is essential to interpreting the charts correctly.

major tool of TQM

BASIC STATISTICAL TOOLS

The most basic statistical tool used to study processes is the **histogram,** which is simply a bar chart that shows frequency (see Figure 16.9). From the histogram, it is possible to identify the shape (distribution) of the data and to estimate its central tendency (average) and variation (range). These are the three primary descriptors used to characterize data.

histogram analyzes data

Another frequently used statistical tool is the correlation diagram, or **scattergram** (see Figure 16.10 on page 774). The purpose of this tool is to determine if a relationship exists between two process parameters. Beyond the existence of a relationship, the slope of the line shows the actual effect that one variable has on the other, and the correlation coefficient indicates the strength (and usefulness) of that relationship. If a strong relationship exists, one variable can be measured to predict the second, or one variable (input to process) can be varied to control the desired output of the process—that is, the second variable.

scattergram identifies correlations

In terms of statistical knowledge, familiarity with only one shape (or distribution) is needed to understand control charts. This is the bell-shaped curve, or normal distribution, that naturally results from many types of data (see Figure 16.11 on page 775).

FIGURE 16.7 Cause-and-effect diagram on the process

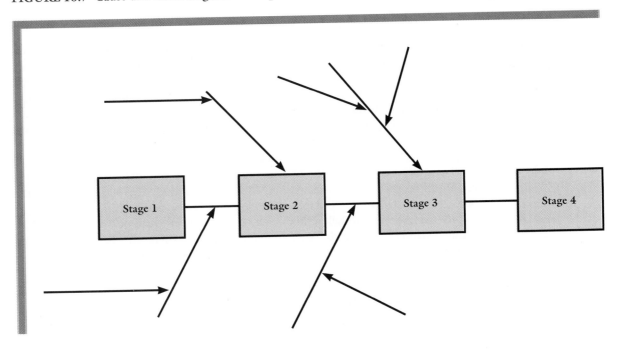

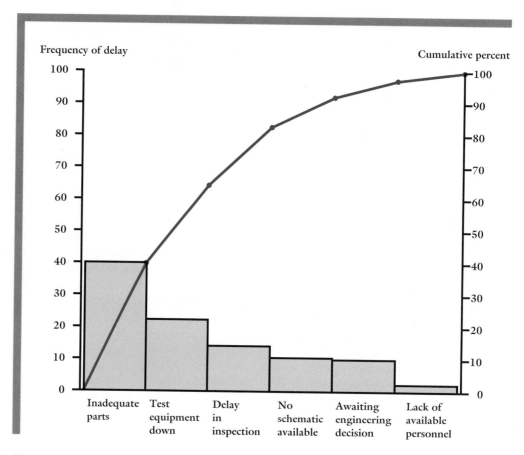

FIGURE 16.8 Pareto chart

Of the statistics that can be used to measure central tendency, only one, the average, is needed for purposes of control charts. Either of two statistics, the range or the standard deviation, can be used to characterize the variation of the data. The range, which is the difference between the highest and lowest readings, is used for the control chart. The standard deviation, which can be viewed as the average amount by which each reading misses the process average, is used for the capability study, which we will discuss later. Every bell curve can be described in terms of its average ($\bar{x}$ in Figure 16.11) and its standard deviation (σ in Figure 16.11).

description of the normal curve

For every bell curve, wide or narrow, for practical purposes we use 3 standard deviations on each side of the average. As shown in Figure 16.11, two-thirds of the outcomes will fall within 1 standard deviation in either direction from the average. Ninety-five percent will fall within 2 standard deviations. All but 3 in 1,000 will be within 3 standard deviations. We note that this pattern will result when a series of data is plotted; single readings can occur randomly anywhere within the bell.

NORMAL VERSUS ABNORMAL VARIATION

operational use of variation

We move now toward a more operational definition of variation. Since individual readings can fall randomly (by luck) anywhere within the resulting bell, there is no need to adjust a process when it provides a reading that is off target but within the bell. In fact, we should not be running processes for which the resulting bell has not been identified because there is no basis for action without it! Once we have the bell, any single reading that falls within its 3 standard deviation range is considered to result from **normal variation.** No action is required for such a reading. A failure to understand the last point has caused many companies to overreact to the variation that is part of every process.

Abnormal variation describes a situation in which a point falls outside of the bell. In this case, the process is not running as it should and needs to be adjusted. More important, the cause of the **abnormal variation** needs to be investigated so that corrective action can be taken and preventive measures can be put into place.

When a process shows only normal variation, it is operating in control. When abnormal variation appears, the process is out of control. We note that no value judgment is made in our use of the term *control.* A process that is in control is not necessarily good; it is merely stable, or predictable. A process operating in control may be **out of control can be good**

FIGURE 16.9 Histogram

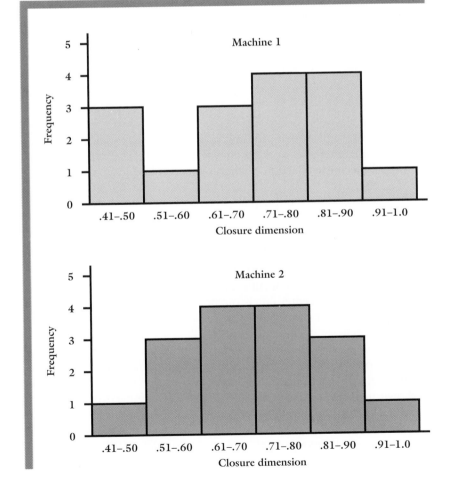

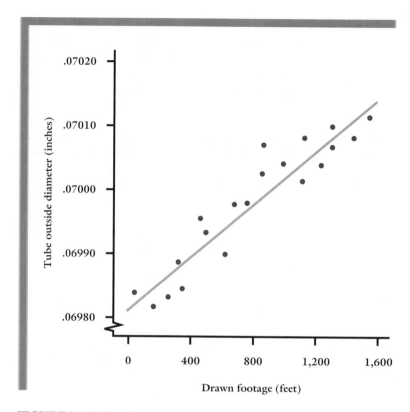

FIGURE 16.10   Scattergram

control charts lead to a
course of action

predictably bad. Likewise, a plant that produces no defects for a month is almost certainly out of control; the process is working unexpectedly well. The statistical notion of control provides for a course of action whenever data is collected from a process.

CONTROL CHARTS

The purpose of a control chart, such as the one in Figure 16.12, is to provide a statistical means for determining whether a particular reading is the result of normal or abnormal variation. A control chart contains three lines: the upper and lower control limits and the center line. The center line is the process average (not necessarily the target) and the upper and lower control limits are set to the 3 standard deviation limits of the normal bell curve, as shown in Figure 16.13.

charts track both central tendency and variation

There are many types of control charts. Some of these are demonstrated in more detail in the next chapter. Variables charts are used to track numerical measurements. The classic control chart is really a combination of two charts, the $\overline{X}$-charts and the R-charts, as shown in Figure 16.14 (see page 778). Both are needed to track the process average and the process variation simultaneously. For this chart, four or five measurements are taken whenever the process is checked, and the average from this group and the range from the group are plotted on the chart.

It is not always possible to obtain a group of measurements. Sometimes, only one measurement is available. This is especially true of process parameters (pressure or temperature), administrative processes (accounts receivable, inventory accuracy, production volumes), and liquid or gaseous product from continuous flow or batch processes. The chart used for this type of process is the **individuals chart,** which also tracks the process average and variation.

The *p*-chart (or the *np*-chart) is designed to monitor the process for pass–fail, or attributes, data. The *p*-chart usually monitors the percent defective, though it can be used to monitor any percent occurrence. More data are required for this type of chart, but the data are usually easier to obtain. Figure 16.15 (see page 779) shows a *p*-chart. If the sample sizes are held constant, the *p*-chart is usually replaced by the *np*-chart, where number defective, a simpler measure, is plotted instead of the percentage.

np-chart is easier

CAPABILITY ANALYSIS

Once it can be demonstrated that a process has stabilized, or is in control, a capability analysis can be performed. Specifications, which are never used in control charts, are

FIGURE 16.11   Normal curve

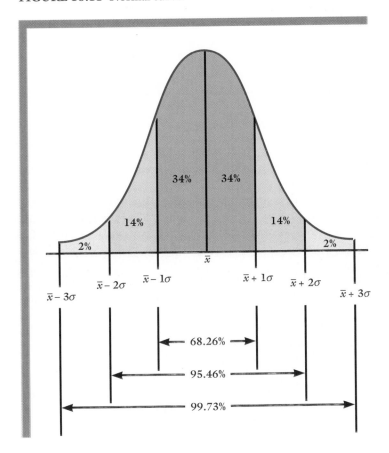

Transparency Master 16.3: Normal Curve.

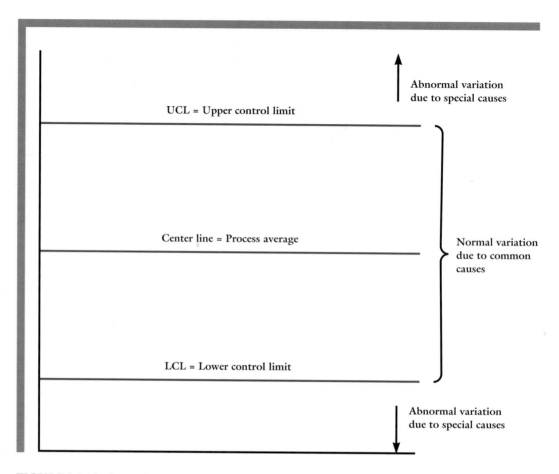

FIGURE 16.12 Control chart

the cornerstone of capability analysis. Capability is the measure that evaluates whether or not a process is meeting specifications.

The most common index used to identify a process capability is the C_{pk} **index.** The C_{pk} index tells how well the process is designed compared to the specifications. Figure 16.16 on page 780 shows three situations that can be translated into a C_{pk} index. In part (a), the larger standard deviation leads to a wider bell curve, which fails to fit within the specification.

calculating C_{pk}

The C_{pk} index can be defined pictorially as the number of bells that will fit inside the specification limits. In part (a), two-thirds of the bell shown fits inside these limits, so the C_{pk} is .67. The C_{pk} index also can be expressed as one-third of the number of standard deviations between the process average and the nearer specification limit. In part (a), there are 2 standard deviations from the average to either limit, again leading to the C_{pk} of .67. Roughly, this translates into a 5-percent defective rate.

C_{pk}-percent defective relationships

Parts (b) and (c) show the effects of reducing variation. In part (b), the variation has been reduced by one-third—in other words, the standard deviation has been reduced from 3 to 2—leaving 3 standard deviations within the specifications. The bell curve now fits perfectly inside the limits for a C_{pk} of 1.0. In many industries, a process meeting this target is considered minimally acceptable. (Its defect rate is 3 in 1,000.)

A more desirable target for the C_{pk} on any process is 1.33, as shown in part (c), where the product falls within 75 percent of the specification range, and the defect rate is only 6 in 100,000. From part (a) to part (c), the inconsistency of the process has been cut in half, but the defect rate has been reduced a thousand times—clear proof that the way to improve any process, or any business, is to focus on consistency, on reducing variation.

Finally, part (d) shows the case where the process is not centered between the specifications. Here, the C_{pk} index looks only at one specification limit, the closer one. Consequently, even though the process is designed to have the same variation as in part (b), its C_{pk} is only .67, as in part (a). This index measures, not only the variation designed into a process, but also how the process is being run. In the case of part (d), it could meet the defect rate of part (b) if set up properly, but its defect rate is almost 2.5 percent as currently being run.

INTERPRETING CONTROL CHARTS

The last statistical concept for monitoring a process is the interpretation of the control charts. Since each worker should be monitoring his or her own charts, training workers to interpret the charts is essential. There is more to interpreting a control chart than

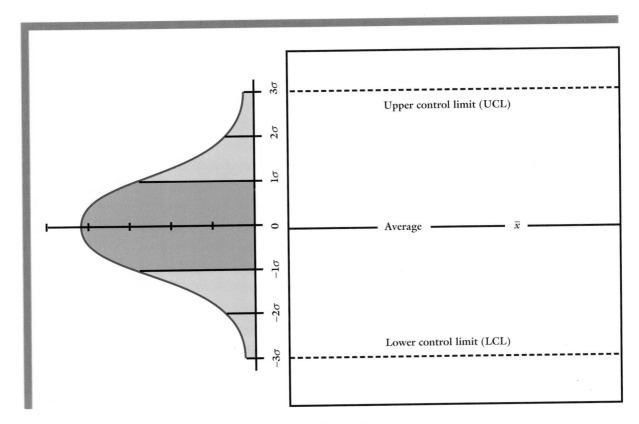

FIGURE 16.13 Relationship between control limits and normal curve

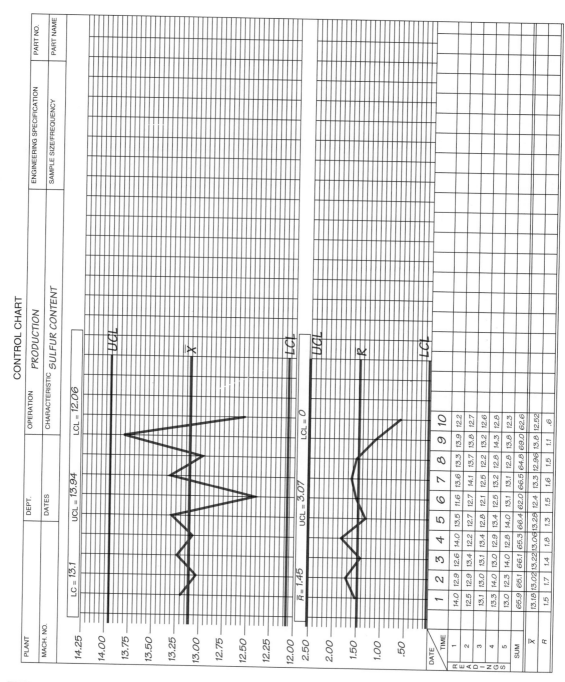

FIGURE 16.14 Variable control chart (X and R)

Transparency Master 16.4:
Sample Control Chart.

CONTROL CHART FOR ATTRIBUTE DATA

PLANT		PART NUMBER AND NAME

DEPARTMENT	OPERATION NUMBER AND NAME	
	REBLENDING	

Avg = 5.83   UCL = .0769   LCL = .0397

	Sample (n)	1524	1275	1821	1496	1213	1371	1248	1123	1517	1488	2052	1696										
Discrepancies	Number (np.c)	70	53	32	91	32	55	69	67	159	94	105	37										
	Proportion (p.u)	4.59	4.16	7.25	6.08	2.64	4.01	5.53	5.97	10.48	6.32	5.12	2.18										
	Date	8/11	8/12	8/13	8/14	8/15	8/16	8/17	8/18	8/19	8/20	8/21	8/22										

ANY CHANGE IN PEOPLE, MATERIALS, EQUIPMENT, METHODS OR ENVIRONMENT SHOULD BE NOTED. THESE NOTES WILL HELP YOU TO TAKE CORRECTIVE OR PROCESS IMPROVEMENT ACTION WHEN SIGNALED BY THE CONTROL CHART.

DATE	TIME	COMMENTS
		(Over)

FIGURE 16.15 Attribute control chart (p-chart)

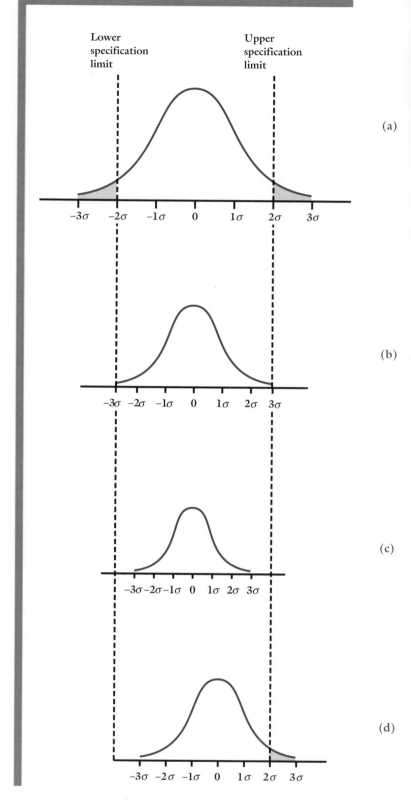

FIGURE 16.16 Capability analysis

merely checking to see whether or not the points fall within the limits, as was implied previously. Of course, any point that falls outside the limits indicates that the process is out of control, but points within the limits also can indicate this condition.

It is necessary to understand that, within the limits, the points should also demonstrate a normal pattern, or the bell curve. The implications of the last statement are several.

- Most points should fall near the center line—two-thirds within one standard deviation.
- A few points should fall near the control limits—approximately 5 percent in the third standard deviation.
- Points should balance on both sides of the center line.
- Points should cross the center line frequently.
- Points should show a random pattern within the limits. There should be no shifts, trends, cycles, or clustering of points.

Most companies use only a few specific rules to guide the operators in their responses to the data they collect. The most common of these call for stopping and adjusting the process whenever one or more of the following events occurs.

- One point falls outside of the control limits.
- Two out of any three consecutive points fall outside of warning limits placed at the 2-sigma line.
- Seven consecutive points fall above or below the center line (indicating a shift) or seven consecutive points are increasing or decreasing (indicating a trend).

DESIGN OF EXPERIMENTS: OPTIMIZING PROCESS PARAMETERS

Statistical process control brings about improvements in a process indirectly. The statistical tool that has a more direct impact is the **design of experiments,** or, as we have already discussed, the Taguchi methods. Taguchi methods address both the design of optimal process specifications and the design of optimal process parameters.

DESIGN OF PROCESS SPECIFICATIONS

When the quality of a product fails to meet some target, there is a loss to society imparted by that product after it is shipped. At the same time, there is some gain to society from having the product (its value) and even some gain (especially to the manufacturer) for an allowance to deviate from the quality target. For this reason, tolerances are granted, leading to specification limits. Taguchi suggests that the optimal amount of tolerance is a break-even point at which the loss to society is equal to the gain achieved by allowing that amount of deviation. Beyond this point, the product creates a net loss to society and is not an acceptable product. Within the tolerance, there is a net gain, so the product is desirable. The detailed equations that prescribe how to calculate specification limits are beyond the scope of this text.

Teaching Suggestion 16.6: Weight Control. See the Instructor's Section for details.

normal control chart patterns

rules for action

loss to society

on-line and off-line
control

Taguchi differentiates between on-line quality control and off-line quality control. Most companies use on-line quality control, which involves the use of the control charts and related tools described in the previous section. Off-line quality control involves the use of design of experiments to optimize process and product design. Together with the quality function deployment, which incorporates customer service activities, these two areas of quality control are termed **quality engineering.**

OPTIMIZING PROCESS PARAMETERS

learning about process
relationships

The design of experiments allows for the evaluation of the effects of each of the process inputs on the desired process output (product characteristic). It also allows us to study the correlations between the inputs. Through the use of this approach, those control parameters having the most effect on the product can be identified and their effects can be quantified. The result is a process that is better understood by those who run it, a process designed to yield product with minimum variation, and a process for which adjustments have been thoroughly analyzed and prescribed prior to their being needed in response to some problem.

A complete design of experiments to achieve the goals just described requires a large amount of data—data that can be expensive to gather. For example, assume that we have a simple package-sealing operation that is governed by four inputs (factors)—pressure applied, temperature, moisture content of the cardboard, and viscosity of the glue—each of which can be set at only two levels, high and low. To completely analyze all situations, sixteen combinations (2^4) of input settings would have to be examined. After the first run, it would be necessary to modify each of the four factors (resulting in four more runs), each combination of two factors (resulting in six more runs), each combination of three factors (resulting in four more runs), and, finally, all four factors together.

full-factorial analysis

Statistically, the above approach, known as the full-factorial analysis, is necessary to find all interactions and to model the process completely. The operational goal is somewhat simpler—to set up the process optimally and to control it effectively. The concern is primarily with the main effects, those found by varying one factor at a time and testing each factor with all combinations of the other factors. This is especially true in that the higher-order interactions are difficult to interrupt or control in the working environment.

Taguchi approach
minimizes testing
required

As a result, Taguchi recommends using a special subset of the full-factorial analysis known as the **orthogonal array.** In terms of the testing saved, consider a slightly more complex process—one with seven factors at two levels each. The full-factorial array would require 128 runs (2^7), while the orthogonal array would require only 8. In addition to the requirement of much less testing, the orthogonal array provides an average response over a number of runs, as opposed to one result for each treatment combination. It also provides for a direct comparison of the levels for any factor.

Teaching Suggestion 16.7:
Full-Factorial Array. See
the Instructor's Section for
details.

The conclusion from running a set of experiments based on the orthogonal array is an optimized set of input parameters under which the process should be run. Beyond this, it is possible to calculate the average output that will result from the optimal or any other set of process parameters. Confirmation runs can then be conducted to check the reproducibility of the results.

In a Taguchi analysis, the best set of parameters is not necessarily the one that leads to the target value. Instead, it is based also on the variability of the result with respect to the inputs. Thus, the result is a robust set of parameters; specifically, it is the one that will be hurt the least if any of the input parameters shift by some amount—that is, the one most likely to produce good product.

rules for action

COMMON MISTAKES IN IMPLEMENTING TQM

The introduction of a TQM/SPC system is not always successful. An awareness of the many common mistakes that lead to failure or that slow down the success of the program often goes a long way toward helping a company avoid failure. The majority of failures result from managerial or behavioral mistakes; the rest are categorized as operational or statistical mistakes.

MANAGERIAL MISTAKES

Most problems on the managerial side result from a lack of top management support. A TQM/SPC program needs to be pushed from the top down and constantly tested from the bottom up. Lack of management support assumes various forms. For example, it is management's responsibility to maintain a constancy of purpose; problem solving is impossible when management's priorities are constantly changing. A lack of patience or need for instant gratification will likewise doom a TQM/SPC program. Sometimes, management does not fully understand how to implement a necessary change, relying on tentative objectives while searching for a case study to follow for firm objectives. No case study will be an exact fit for a particular company's needs, however; each situation requires its own set of objectives. In some cases, management tries to legislate TQM/SPC. Such attempts to force improvement on the system will not work—in large part because they encourage the perception that TQM/SPC is yet another soon-to-be discredited management approach. Management must change its style before the rest of the organization can be expected to respond.

success takes time

There will always be bias when management evaluates the company's culture, usually resulting in an overly optimistic view of the quality of the environment. Failure to actively address this at all levels will shut off the flow of ideas and the problem-solving activities. In the chain of command—and there still must be one—it only takes one individual or one level to ruin the system. Most often, this occurs at the supervisor level, because supervisors have a tendency to manage by fear. After all, this is what they learned from *their* supervisors. Bias can be even more dangerous, however, if it occurs at higher levels in the organization.

Finally, there is the tendency by management to take shortcuts, especially with employee training. Workers typically can be taught how to fill in control charts in less than four hours; it takes far longer to ground workers in the overall philosophy and to provide them with the statistical knowledge they need to understand and interpret the charts. Since computers can be used to complete the control charts, managers often use automation as the excuse for failing to train workers properly. Another common shortcut is dispensing with problem-solving teams. Many managers view them as unproductive, a waste of time—especially when it is already the responsibility of individuals who are already in place to solve problems. Bypassing the problem-solving teams leaves standing many of the barriers that the TQM/SPC program is intended to knock down.

In summary, there seem to be four keys to the success of the TQM/SPC program:

- management commitment;
- a long-term view;
- use of statistical techniques in which all employees are trained; and
- use of problem-solving teams.

TECHNICAL MISTAKES

Operational or statistical mistakes are far greater in number than managerial mistakes but have far less serious consequences. We discuss three technical mistakes in this section.

statistical vs. operational concerns

All control charts assume a normal distribution. The individuals chart, by plotting single measurements—that is, by failing to group the data—fails to guarantee that this assumption is true. Therefore, the individuals data needs to be grouped. In industries having continuous flow or batch processes, such as the pharmaceutical, oil, or chemical industries, each group of four or five consecutive readings is combined into one point on the chart. This is statistically correct, but it is not operationally correct. Data may be collected every hour, for example, but a point is put on the chart every four hours. In this way, data is collected at times when no control action will be taken, losing the real-time control that is so important to the process. The correct approach is to take a moving average in which the most recent hourly readings are averaged each hour and the resulting point is plotted on the chart.

measure the appropriate variation

Another problem is a lack of understanding about what is actually being charted and how it relates to the process being monitored. There are two sources of variation in addition to the random variation assumed in the control chart: variation due to trends and variation due to cycling. These must be filtered out prior to using the charts. Within the random variation itself, different parts of the process may be contributing to the variation. Thus, we must ensure that the variation *measured* focuses on the part of the process that has been selected for improvement. We must answer three simple questions before starting a control chart:

- What variation needs to be controlled?
- How can this variation be measured?
- Can it be controlled?

The recalculation of the control limits also causes problems. New limits are often calculated daily or weekly—whenever enough data become available to perform the calculation. When this is done, the long-term perspective is lost. Short-term control is also affected, because changes in the process are hidden by the new limits. In fact, a change in the limits could very well indicate a process change. The point is that the same control limits should be maintained for a long time on any single process. Even after process improvements have been made, limits should be modified only after

- statistical proof of the change has been collected and
- the cause of the change is clearly identified and understood.

SUMMARY

Clearly, TQM is a valuable philosophy for managing any business. Deming's fourteen points provide the foundation for the TQM program, which has four essential elements: the philosophy and culture of *continuous improvement*, the tools of problem solving, the statistical tools for monitoring and control, and the statistical *design of experiments* for optimizing the process. A key ingredient of the TQM culture is *participative management*, which means that all employees are constantly looking to bring problems to light so that the problems can be solved. The *quality circle* is a useful vehicle for identifying and solving problems. Other problem-solving tools include the *methods analysis* of the process; *brainstorming*; cause-and-effect diagrams such as the *Ishikawa* or *fishbone* diagram; and the *Pareto chart*. Particularly in manufacturing operations, *statistical process control* is an important part of the problem-solving process. The primary tool of SPC is the *control chart,* which differentiates between *normal* and *abnormal variation*. Related tools are the *histogram*, which displays central tendency and variation; the *scattergram*, which demonstrates relationships; and the capability index, or C_{pk} *index*, which illustrates performance against specifications. *Design of experiments* is a statistical tool that sets process specifications and process operating parameters.

TQM programs are not always implemented successfully. Their failure can usually be attributed either to certain managerial or behavioral mistakes or to operational or statistical mistakes.

KEY TERMS

total quality management	methods analysis	normal variation
continuous improvement	brainstorming	abnormal variation
statistical process control	Ishikawa diagram	individuals chart
Taguchi methods	fishbone diagram	C_{pk} index
participative management	Pareto chart	design of experiments
single sourcing	control chart	quality engineering
vendor certification	histogram	orthogonal array
quality circles	scattergram	

QUESTIONS

1. Relate Deming's fourteen points to other topics presented in previous chapters.

2. Which three of Deming's fourteen points do you feel are most critical to the success of a TQM program?

3. How would implementing a TQM program affect the rate of purchasing?

4. Why is it important to reduce the number of suppliers?

5. How does fear in the classroom inhibit learning?

6. What is the purpose of using a Pareto chart for a given problem?

7. Discuss the role of the management–employee culture in a problem-solving situation.

8. What are the two types of variation?

9. How should an employee respond to abnormal variation?

10. Who is responsible for reducing normal variation?

11. How should an employee respond to normal variation?

12. Name three types of control charts.

13. How does a control chart enable us to decide whether the variation is normal or abnormal?

14. What is the purpose of using design of experiments?

15. What is the basis for setting specifications according to Taguchi?

REFERENCES

Crosby, P. *Quality Is Free*. New York: McGraw-Hill, 1979.

Deming, W. E. *Out of Crisis*. Cambridge, Mass.: MIT Center for Advanced Engineering Study, 1981.

Goldratt, E., and J. Cox. *The Goal*. Croton-on-Hudson, N.Y.: North River Press, 1986.

Ishikawa, K. *Guide to Quality Control*. White Plains, N.Y.: UNI-PUB, 1984.

———. *What Is Total Quality Control? The Japanese Way*. Englewood Cliffs, N.J.: Prentice-Hall, 1985.

Juran, J. M., and F. Gryna. *Quality Planning and Analysis*. New York: McGraw-Hill, 1980.

Krantz, K. T. "How Velcro Got Hooked on Quality," *Harvard Business Review* 89, no. 5 (September/October 1989).

Ross, P. J. *Taguchi Techniques for Quality Engineering*. Milwaukee: Quality Press, 1988.

Schonberger, R. J. *World Class Manufacturing: The Lessons of Simplicity Applied*. New York: Free Press, 1986.

Walton, Mary. *The Deming Management Method*. New York: Perigee Books, 1986.

C H A P T E R

17

O U T L I N E

QUALITY CONTROL

- To impart an understanding of the role of quality control in operations
- To explain the use of inspection as a procedure within a quality program
- To emphasize that quality is designed and built into the operation and that inspection can verify, but not instill, quality
- To illustrate the use of two commonly used techniques of statistical quality control: acceptance sampling and control charts

INTRODUCTION

When a craftsperson creates a product, he or she obtains raw material and the required tools, checks them to be sure that they are satisfactory, and begins work. Much of the checking of the material is done as the material is used. At each step of the production process, the craftsperson makes sure that the work is good before proceeding to the next step. When the product is complete, it is carefully checked again to be sure that it is perfect and, if the product is to serve some function, that it works properly.

The Industrial Revolution introduced machinery that accomplished production at much greater speed and at much less cost than before, and it eventually led to a high degree of automation in production. Although the automation helped to make goods more plentiful and to raise the standard of living in our society, there were problems associated with this mode of production. A major problem was how to control the quality of the goods produced in this manner. The mechanized production replaced the work of the craftsperson in many ways, but it failed to constantly inspect the product. The quality control function is aimed at correcting this problem.

A craftsperson merges the inspection function with the production function. To understand how the inspection function is incorporated into an automated production environment, it is necessary to look at the timing of and the motivation for the inspections done by the craftsperson. The craftsperson inspects

Teaching Suggestion 17.1: The Operations System. See the Instructor's Section for details.

areas of inspection

Teaching Suggestion 17.2: The Operations Chain. See the Instructor's Section for details.

- raw materials,
- equipment,
- in-process goods, and
- finished products.

Raw materials inspection is done as the materials are received. The method of inspection and the criteria for acceptance (labeling the material as "good") must be specified by contract if the materials are produced by an outside supplier. Procedures and criteria to do this are discussed later in this chapter. If the materials are produced within the same company, similar procedures are followed.

The reason that materials inspection is specified by contract with an outside supplier should be clear: A company will pay for the material only if it meets the company's acceptance criteria. It is not so clear, however, why the same inspection procedures should be followed when the material is obtained from internal sources, where no payment is involved. Internally produced material is inspected for the same reason that equipment and in-process goods are inspected. If the company's only interest is to determine whether the products are satisfactory, then it need inspect only finished goods in addition to purchased goods. However, the goal of quality management is, not only to make judgments concerning the quality of the product/service, but also *to enable the producer to take the necessary steps to improve quality throughout the operation.* Quality management accomplishes these goals by providing information concerning the causes of low quality in addition to indicating its presence. Inspections of in-house goods, in-process goods, and the production equipment are made to provide this information.

goals of quality management

The terms *quality management,* **quality control,** and **quality assurance** often are used interchangeably. Regardless of the term used within any business, this function is directly responsible for the continual evaluation of the effectiveness of the total quality system. The elements of this **total quality control** (TQC) system, outlined in the ANSI/ASQC Standard Z–1.15 (available from the American Society for Quality Control), are

- policy, planning, and administration;
- product design and design change control;
- control of purchased material;
- production quality control;
- user contact and field performance;
- corrective action; and
- employee selection, training, and motivation.

ANSI—the American National Standards Institute—has recently adopted the international quality standard, ISO 9000.

The overall quality function is referred to as *quality management.* Within this function, there are two managerial responsibilities: *control* and *assurance.* Quality control includes all steps that management can take to increase the quality of the *areas directly under its control,* including the quality of the product design, in-process inspections, training programs, quality circles, employee award programs, and even employee drug-testing programs. Quality assurance encourages higher quality production in *areas outside of management control.* The most obvious quality assurance function is the inspection of incoming goods and finished goods. Neither of these inspections, however, controls the quality of the operation directly. They merely "assure" that accepted or shipped items are satisfactory, independent of the process. Other, less obvious quality assurance functions include programs publicizing the names of the top-quality suppliers, contractual penalties for delivering poor quality material, and inspection of the outgoing product. This inspection of the outgoing product can be considered to be within the direct control of management, but the usual view is that it is too late for management control after the product is complete. Thus, the assurance function is applied prior to delivery.

quality of vendors

In the 1920s, the concept of **control charts** was developed at Western Electric. The control chart uses inspections conducted on in-process goods during production to identify any change in quality and to help assign a cause to that change. Although many variations of the control chart have since been developed, it remains a widely used tool throughout industry for controlling quality. The development of control charts is considered to be the beginning of the modern practice of quality control. It also is the foundation of the techniques known collectively as *statistical process control*.

The other major development in the initial stage of modern quality control practice was **acceptance sampling,** which is the primary tool used in quality assurance. Developed at Bell Labs in the late 1920s, the practice introduced the idea that decisions could be made on a quantity of products from a given production process without inspecting every product. Only a sample, selected randomly, needs to be inspected, assuming that all the products come from the same population (same batch of raw material, same production environment, and so on). As will be shown later in this chapter, acceptance sampling is merely an application of statistical hypothesis testing. Acceptance sampling is used for raw material and finished goods inspections.

maximize quality, minimize inspection costs

Taken together, control charts and acceptance sampling are known as **statistical quality control.** The aim of statistical quality control is to maximize quality while minimizing inspection costs. The trade-off between these two goals must always be considered in a production (or purchasing) environment. Statistical quality control was used extensively in World War II and the U.S. military has been a leader in its application ever since. The Japanese have applied it most effectively in private industry, helping them to overtake many U.S. products in terms of quality, thus providing the recent impetus for U.S. firms to emphasize it as well. We introduce the field of statistical quality control in our later sections on acceptance sampling and process control.

In the modern production environment, automation is taking over much of the inspection function. Optical scanners can "see" much of what the craftsperson sees. More sophisticated inspection techniques, such as ultrasonic, holographic, or eddy current inspection, allow automated inspection systems to "see" *more* than the craftsperson by "looking" inside the product. The human element cannot be replaced entirely, but the use of computer-aided manufacturing and inspection systems has helped to achieve the highest quality that has ever been attained in a high-volume production environment. In a sense, the eventual goal is to come full circle — to arrive at a point where the producer of a part (the machine) also can inspect it to the same (or better) degree of detail as the craftsperson.

inspection is reactive

Inspection is not the only tool of quality control. It may be an important tool, but it can be done only after a manufacturing task has been completed. Consequently, it is a reactive tool of management. It will identify poor workmanship, but if the low quality is due to human error, inspection does nothing to prevent the error from occurring again. Corrective action must be taken to avoid the reoccurrence.

An effective manager of operations designs every component of the operation with quality in mind. Even in the research and development phase, product design must aim toward a product that can be inspected easily, can be repaired easily, and is made of the appropriate materials. Job design, as we discussed in Chapter 9, must place each worker in a situation where the job can be done, not only quickly, but also well. Workstation design should incorporate the elements of human factors so that each worker will be alerted promptly to quality deviations and will be able to perform his or her tasks without overload. Finally, it must be clear to all involved in operations that quality has the same priority as meeting production schedules and that every person plays a key role in maintaining a high level of quality. One method for involving all workers is the implementation of **quality circles,** which have been used extensively in Japan and are now gaining more widespread use in the United States. Quality circles have been very successful in raising quality awareness among workers, thereby raising the quality of products produced.

In many production plants, an adversarial relationship develops between production managers and quality managers. The production manager is judged (to some extent) by the quantity of goods produced. If quality standards slip, it is up to the quality manager to stop production and take corrective action or to have poor products reworked or scrapped. A similar relationship can develop between the production worker and the inspector. Good management practice (in terms of the organizational behavior or personnel management) will prevent these adversarial relationships from developing. Furthermore, not only can the development of these relationships be prevented, but these individuals can be convinced that mutual cooperation will help both production and quality and that these functions are not as distinct as they may seem on the company's organizational charts.

CURRENT TRENDS TOWARD QUALITY

As emphasized in Chapters 2 and 16, a great deal has been written in recent years about the higher quality of Japanese goods. Although the Japanese have set the trend in using modern approaches to quality control, in many cases, the approaches used are not Japanese in origin. U.S. management claims to use the same approaches. If there is a difference between the approaches of Japanese and U.S. managements toward quality, it is one of emphasis. U.S. managers talk about quality, while the Japanese really do something about it every day. We now briefly describe three aspects of quality management that are used by Japanese manufacturers.

Japanese attitude

EVALUATION OF QUALITY PLANS: THE QUALITY AUDIT

For higher-level managers, there is little time to be concerned with the details of product design, process control, or inspection plans and procedures. Yet upper management needs to be able to evaluate the performance of the company with respect to quality, just as it needs to evaluate production rates or profit margins. For this reason, every firm must have an established set of quality control procedures, outlined in a formal quality control plan. This plan should outline the policies and objectives related to quality, in addition to the detailed procedures.

the quality plan

Teaching Suggestion 17.3: The Quality Plan and Audit. See the Instructor's Section for details.

The quality plan must detail the progression from raw material to final product, specifying the procedures employed at each step that ensure that the product is of high quality. It also must include a system of reviews to ensure that the plan truly is aimed at achieving the company's quality objectives. Finally, it must prescribe a system of audits to ensure that the plan is being followed and to measure its effectiveness.

The **quality audit** was first implemented in Japan in the early 1960s; it is now used extensively in the United States as well. However, in Japan, the audit done has a broader scope than in the United States, where the business implications of the quality function often are excluded. An excellent guide to developing quality plans and quality audits can be found in *Quality and Reliability Assurance Handbook H50*, under the title, "Evaluation of a Contractor's Quality Program." This guide should be used with MIL-STD-9858A, *Quality Program Requirements*. Both guides are available from the U.S. Government Publications and Printing Office.

Quality audits can be done internally by company personnel, or they can be done externally, also by company personnel but at a vendor's facility. Most often, however, an independent consultant whose specialty is quality control is brought in to conduct this audit. This practice is analogous to the required practice of independent audits of financial records by accountants. An important feature of all quality audits is that they are scheduled in advance, not in response to some crisis. They also must be legitimized by clear authorization from company management.

the product audit

A more specific audit, most often part of the larger quality audit, is the product audit. This audit compares actual performance with the service needs of the consumer. It should be carried out in each stage of the product life cycle, from R&D and product design to final manufacturing.

QUALITY MOTIVATION: QUALITY CIRCLES

Modern quality management emphasizes the view that quality is designed and built into a product, not inspected into it. Yet we devote almost the entire chapter to inspection procedures that seem to be aimed at achieving the latter goal. The reason for this coverage is that there are specific inspection procedures that can be implemented effectively. The means for motivating the work force to produce quality, however, are less clear. Such means were addressed in the previous chapter on total quality management.

However, we would be remiss if our discussion of quality control failed to mention the specific development that is the most outstanding development in quality control in the last two decades: the quality circle. Although it relates to areas of management outside of operations management, the quality circle is the best means available today for meeting the goal of designing quality into a product.

The quality circle, as is true of many recent advances in quality control, was first implemented in Japan. However, at the same time that quality circles were being implemented in Japan, many U.S. companies were striving to motivate workers to produce quality through the use of "zero defects" programs. The quality circle concept is of broader scope than these programs, but it includes most of the characteristics of the zero defects programs.

workers know tasks best

The idea behind quality circles is that no person in the organization knows a production task better than the individual worker who actually performs that task. Every worker is frustrated, in some way, by the work environment, which seems to prevent the worker from doing the job as well as it should be done. The quality circle is a formal group of individuals (both workers and managers) who meet to discuss and, hopefully, overcome these problems.

voluntary participation

A company begins a quality circle by offering to provide the work force with training in quality analysis and in participating in quality circles. The quality circle is strictly a voluntary group, but experience shows that about half of the work force participates. The circle meets on company time at scheduled intervals to discuss possible projects that could lead to improvements in quality. After the projects have been selected, the circle studies them and is involved with their implementation. Of course, many of the projects proposed by quality circles also relate to productivity.

In the first decade of their use in Japan, the number of projects was on the order of five million, and each project resulted in savings of thousands of dollars. The effect of quality circles has been widely felt in Japan.

A similar approach, aimed at shifting the burden of quality from the inspector to the worker, is the Saratov system, used in the Soviet Union. Others are the Polish *Dobra Robota* (good work) and the German *Ohne Fehler* (without defects) systems.

FIRST AND LAST SAMPLING

As we detailed in Chapter 15, one assembly line may be used to produce different products. Unfortunately, a changeover in product may cause problems at the beginning of production of the new unit. The Japanese pay close attention to the first item that comes off the assembly line. If there are problems with the first item, there will be problems with later items.

Similarly, rather than taking random samples of different items, some Japanese firms also inspect the last item produced in a lot. The quality of this last item gives a good indication of the quality of the preceding items.

This approach is most useful for automated production. Random sampling is used to avoid the problem that arises when workers know which part will be inspected. They always do a better job on that part. With automated production, this problem does not arise, and first and last sampling is appropriate.

THE INSPECTION PROCESS

Although quality is designed and worked into a product—not inspected into it—the primary day-to-day tasks of quality control personnel revolve around the inspections of work produced. For this reason, it is necessary for the operations manager to be familiar with the details of and alternatives to the inspections performed. Specifically, the operations manager must make decisions concerning what to inspect for, how to inspect, and how often to perform the inspection. **major decisions**

DESTRUCTIVE VERSUS NONDESTRUCTIVE TESTING

One classification of the types of inspections identifies each inspection procedure as either destructive or nondestructive. **Destructive testing,** as shown in Example 17.1, precludes the object being tested from being sold; products that undergo **nondestructive testing** can be sold later.

Example 17.1 Aluminum cans are being produced in a plant for sales to a soup company. One quality characteristic of the can that is a measure of its acceptability is its strength. Actually, it is decided that there are two measures of strength that must be inspected. First, the can must be strong enough to support other cans (or some reasonable weight that must be agreed upon in advance) that may be stored on top of it. Second, the can must be able to support pressure from its sides (again, a quantification of the strength must be given). How can these characteristics of the cans be checked and how often should the inspection be performed?

A destructive test—testing textile samples for fiber strength. (© Michal Heron/Woodfin Camp & Associates)

One procedure to inspect the cans is to place each can in a fixture that will gradually exert more force on its top until it collapses. The fixture can be calibrated to measure the pressure required to accomplish this. The same procedure can then be applied to the sides of each can.

As for how often to perform the inspection, this is a question best left for later in the chapter. However, one thing should be clear in this example: If the first test is performed on every can, there will be no cans left to sell. In fact, there will be no cans to subject to the second test. ∎

An example of a nondestructive test on the cans in Example 17.1 is inspecting the size of each can. If diameter is the dimension to be inspected, measuring this diameter does not preclude a can from being sold.

ATTRIBUTES AND VARIABLES INSPECTION

Example 17.1 also included another classification of inspection procedures: **inspection for attributes** versus **inspection for variables.** The inspection that was done in the example does not merely provide information concerning whether the can is good; it provides an exact measurement of the strength of the can. This is a variables inspection. The variable is strength, and the inspection goes beyond a reading of good or bad to determine just how good or how bad the can is. With a variables inspection, a probability distribution (such as the normal or lognormal distribution) can be used to make judgments concerning the strength characteristics of the cans.

variables: exact measurement

An inspection by attributes merely determines whether or not the can meets the required specifications. Instead of determining the actual strength of the can, what is determined is whether the strength of the can is greater or less than the desired strength. The attributes inspection for the strength characteristics of the can in Example 17.1 subjects the can to a weight that corresponds to the minimum acceptable strength of the can. If the can supports the weight (does not show any signs of bending or collapsing), it passes; if not, it fails. The probability distribution most often associated with the attributes inspection is the binomial distribution. There is, however, a trade-off to consider when deciding which type of inspection to use. Although it provides less information per inspection, the inspection by attributes is less expensive than variables inspection, thereby allowing for the testing of more parts on the same inspection budget.

attributes: good or bad

CHOOSING THE CHARACTERISTICS TO INSPECT

Another major decision regarding the inspection function is which characteristics to inspect. For example, the thickness of its walls is one characteristic of a can. However, it probably is not a characteristic that one would wish to inspect. The strength test has already indicated that the walls of the can are of sufficient thickness to prevent crushing. Also, a thickness inspection most probably has been performed on the sheet metal from which the can was formed.

In addition to the two compressive strengths discussed previously, there is a third strength characteristic, which has not been inspected. This is the tensile strength, or the ability of the can to withstand pressures from within. It is assumed here that the can will contain nothing that will create such pressure, so no inspection is done for this characteristic. Bear in mind, however, that the decision to perform this inspection is dependent on the contents of the can. If the can contained a carbonated beverage, the possibility of a buildup in pressure would necessitate inspection for tensile strength.

The dimensions of the can (height and diameter) also should be inspected, either by variables or attributes inspection. For the diameter, the specification might be set as 3.000 inches $\pm$ .005 inches. The required variables inspection measures the actual diameter with a micrometer or a similar measuring device. An optical scanner could accomplish this task, too.

The attributes inspection for the diameter is easier to perform than the variables inspection, but its design is less obvious to those who have not worked in a quality control setting. Two attributes inspections are required: one to see if the diameter is too small (less than 2.995 inches) and one to see if it is too large (greater than 3.005 inches). For the first test, a plug gauge (a solid cylinder) of diameter equal to 2.995 inches is inserted into the can. If it fits, the can passes. If it does not fit, the can is rejected as being too small. For the larger dimension, a ring gauge (a circle with the center open) of diameter 3.005 inches is placed over the can. If it fits, the can passes. If it does not, the can is rejected as being too large. Similar inspections are designed for the height characteristics.

The can is a rather simple example; it has few characteristics that can be defective. More complex products, possibly assembled from many components, present more difficult inspection decisions. The product designer provides every specification on the design drawings. Many quality control departments feel that every dimension on those drawings must be inspected. Often, this is a waste of resources. Recall that *the ultimate purpose of inspection is not to measure conformance to the specification, but to measure quality.* Only the characteristics that affect the manufacture, use, or appeal of the product need to be inspected. In addition, a dimension of the component may be inspected so that it need not be inspected again on the final product. Another situation where multiple inspections could be avoided is where one part must fit inside another. The part fitting inside must be checked to see if it is too small, but not to see if it is too large, because it will not fit inside the other part if it is too large. These are just a few examples of the concerns related to the design of an inspection plan for a product. In each case, the ultimate decision depends on the production environment; the cost of detecting a defective part later in the production process rather than earlier; and company philosophy.

defining quality

You may have noticed that a definition of quality is conspicuously missing from this chapter. The discussion just completed indicates a major reason why it is unwise to define quality. The definition changes based on the perception of the individual providing the judgment or using the product or service. As a general rule, quality should be defined for each product or service in accordance with the end use of that product or service. The only inspections required are the ones that measure performance in achieving that end use.

AUTOMATED INSPECTION DESIGN

Thus far, the discussions on inspection have all applied to automated inspection as well as manual inspection. A few types of automated inspection, such as optical scanners, ultrasonic inspection, or eddy current inspection, have been mentioned. Other types are X-ray and holographic inspections, but various kinds of optical scanners are the most widely used types of automated inspection.

The key concept requiring a special section of the text for automated inspection relates to the design of the test station. An automated inspection must fit into the materials handling system of conveyors in a special way. This required concept of design is known as the **fail-safe concept.**

After parts pass through an inspection station, the easiest flow design is to allow the good parts (hopefully, the majority) to continue along the same track and to knock the bad parts into a chute or conveyor leading to a reject bin. Many times, the flow of a part is controlled by a gate that opens or closes depending on the result of the inspection. However, what if the mechanism that diverts a bad part to the reject bin fails to operate properly? If this happens, bad parts will be mixed with the good ones, and the quality control function will have failed.

fail-safe design

Applying the fail-safe concept, the diverting mechanism must operate in order to accept a part. If this mechanism fails, all parts will be rejected. That there is no production will be noticed quickly and corrected. The parts in the reject bin (most of which probably are good in this case) can be reinspected. In this way, no bad parts are allowed through because it takes a positive action to accept a part.

ACCEPTANCE SAMPLING

To this point, our discussion has centered on how to decide whether a single item is acceptable. Generally, products are grouped into production lots, each lot identified in some manner so that any problems can be traced back to the time and place of production. This is how companies know which lots to recall when a problem is identified. Examples of such recalls are the Tylenol contaminations and the fake Ortho birth control pills in the mid-1980s.

production lots

In this section, the discussion concerning whether a lot (rather than an individual unit) is acceptable is discussed. As mentioned previously, a purchase contract for raw material will contain, not only the specifications to be met, but also provisions for acceptance testing to be done prior to payment. Each inspection that will be performed, as well as how many from each lot of a given size will be inspected and the number of defectives that will be allowed, if any, must be in the contract (even the best lots might have some defective units).

The obvious way to determine whether or not the lot is acceptable is to inspect each item in that lot. Then the acceptable items can be used and the unacceptable items can be discarded, reworked, or returned, depending on economic and contractual factors. This is the most accurate way to determine the quality of each lot, but it also is the most expensive. However, it cannot be assumed that even this method of

acceptance by lot

A sampling inspection—examining a milk sample for cream content and purity in a plant near Madison, Wisconsin. (© Roger Malloch/Magnum Photos, Inc.)

inspection error

acceptance testing will catch all of the defective items. Inspection error, whether human or mechanical, is always present. In addition, as previously mentioned, this method is impractical if testing is destructive.

Inspecting each item, commonly referred to as **100-percent inspection,** is not used in the majority of cases. However, the trend toward the use of more automated test equipment has resulted in a greater use of 100-percent inspection. Another, more important criterion for choosing 100-percent inspection is consumer safety. An automobile, for example, will not function properly if the ignition fails to work, but this is not critical to the safety of the driver. Brake failure is another matter; brake systems require 100-percent inspection.

Teaching Suggestion 17.4: 100-Percent Inspection. See the Instructor's Section for details.

When 100-percent inspection is not required, acceptance sampling is often used. With acceptance sampling, only a small percentage, or sample, of the items are chosen (randomly) from the lot for testing. Based on the results for the sample, the entire lot is accepted or rejected.

entire lot is accepted or rejected

The use of 100-percent inspection determines the quality for each lot; acceptance sampling does not. *The purpose of acceptance sampling is to determine a course of action, not to estimate lot quality.* The course of action is either to accept or to reject the entire lot. Acceptance sampling is a procedure that, on average, will yield a specified level of quality when applied to a series of production lots.

disposition of bad lots

The disposition of a lot that is accepted is clear: It is used for its intended purpose. The disposition of a lot that is rejected is a more difficult consideration. The obvious action is to return the lot to the producer, and most sampling plans assume that this is done. However, returning the lot can be very expensive. An option is to accept the lot, but pay a lower price for it. Another reason to keep the lot is that the material may be required for production; if the lot is returned, production will stop due to lack of raw material. In this case, an option is to do a 100-percent screening of the lot, pay only for the good items, and use these good items for production. Purchasing contracts must specify who pays for any return shipping, additional inspections, and so forth. The government has formalized another disposition option: accept on waiver. With this option, the government can accept a lot that has failed its sampling test with appropriate justification. A formal material review board meets to decide the disposition of each failed lot.

THE SAMPLING PLAN

One danger involved in the use of acceptance sampling is that the sample chosen for inspection can be good even when the lot is not. Because the decision to accept or reject the lot is based on a relatively small sample from that lot, this danger will always be present. In quality control, this is known as the **consumer's risk.** Specifically, the consumer's risk is the probability that such an error will be made.

Teaching Suggestion 17.5: Consumer's Risk. See the Instructor's Section for details.

If the consumer is to accept this risk in order to take advantage of sampling, then it is only fair that the producer also accept the risk that the opposite error will be made. This risk relates to the probability that the sample is bad, although the lot actually is good, and it is referred to as the **producer's risk.** Of course, whenever a lot is rejected, the producer is convinced that this error has occurred—it must be an unlucky coincidence that the small sample selected happens to include all of the defectives from the large lot!

risks of sampling

The quality control manager is responsible for the development of the **sampling plan.** In a sampling plan, n items are chosen from the lot of size N, and a cutoff value, or critical value, c, is defined that stipulates whether or not the test has been passed. For example, an attributes sampling plan of $n = 10$, $c = 2$ means that ten items are inspected and, if two or less are defective, the lot is accepted. The design of all sampling plans incorporates the consumer's risk and the producer's risk.

The following are among several types of acceptance sampling plans that have been developed.

1. attributes sampling plans for

   - fraction defective
   - defects per unit

2. variables sampling plans for

   - process mean
   - process variability
   - both mean and variability

types of sampling plans

For attributes testing, recall that each item inspected is classified either as defective or as nondefective. When this type of inspection is used, the usual sampling plan tests for the number, or fraction, of items that are defective. This is a fraction defective attributes sampling plan. In certain circumstances, however, an item is not considered to be defective simply because it has one defect. A roll of cloth, for example, can tolerate a number of defects per roll without being considered defective. A plan that inspects for defects per unit is another attributes plan, based on the use of the Poisson, instead of the binomial, probability distribution.

When variables inspection is used, a variables sampling plan is selected. The plan can test for the mean, the variability, or both. (These same considerations will arise again later in the chapter, when control charts are discussed.) Because a variables inspection provides more detailed information than an attributes inspection, the variables plan generally uses a smaller sample size. This partially offsets the increased inspection cost.

Within each type of sampling plan, there are various sampling procedures, including

- single sampling plans;
- double sampling plans;
- multiple sampling plans; and
- sequential sampling plans.

sampling procedures

The plans that will be covered in this text are the attributes plan for fraction defective and the variables plan for the process mean. These are the most commonly used plans, and they provide a framework for the development of acceptance sampling plans in general. Only single sampling procedures are presented here. Any text devoted to the subject of quality control, including those referenced at the conclusion of this chapter, will provide information on the other plans and procedures.

Statistical hypothesis testing is the basis of acceptance sampling. Fortunately, however, one need not be an expert in statistics. Because virtually every plan that could be needed in any situation has been tabulated in published tables of sampling plans, what is required is that one be able to discuss a sampling plan in terms of the hypotheses that it desires to test.

The hypothesis that must be tested is that the lot is of some good quality, known as the **acceptable quality level** (AQL). The sampling plan tests this hypothesis against an alternative hypothesis that the lot is of marginally acceptable quality, known as the **lot tolerance percent defective** (LTPD). The acceptable quality level is the quality level that should be accepted most of the time. More specifically, the percentage of time that a lot having quality equal to the acceptable quality level will be *rejected* is equal to the producer's risk, α. This is a type I error. Similarly, the lot tolerance percent defective is the level of quality that should be rejected most of the time. The probability that a lot having this quality is *accepted* is the consumer's risk, β. This is a type II error. The probabilities for correct and incorrect decisions are summarized in Table 17.1. Standard values of $\alpha = .05$ and $\beta = .10$ are used for most of the published tables of sampling plans.

ATTRIBUTES SAMPLING PLAN

For attributes sampling plans, the acceptable quality level, lot tolerance percent defective, producer's risk, and consumer's risk must be specified. To develop the sampling plan, the values of n and c must be found. We will use Table 17.2 to calculate n and c according to the following procedure.

Step 1. Compute the ratio LTPD/AQL.

Step 2. Find the entry that is closest to this ratio in the LTPD/AQL column.

Step 3. Set the critical value, c, equal to the corresponding entry in the same row in the first column.

Step 4. Set the sample size, n, equal to the corresponding entry in the third column, divided by the AQL. (Alternatively, the entry in the fourth column divided by the LTPD can be used.)

The following example illustrates the use of this procedure.

> **Example 17.2**   Reconsider the production of aluminum cans in Example 17.1. The height of the can is a characteristic that has been mentioned as requiring inspec-

TABLE 17.1 Acceptance testing outcomes and probabilities

Decision	Lot	
	Satisfactory	Unsatisfactory
Accept lot (Sample passes)	Correct decision $1 - \alpha$	Type II error β
Reject lot (Sample fails)	Type I error α	Correct decision $1 - \beta$

Transparency Master 17.2:
Determining Sampling
Plans.

TABLE 17.2 Parameters to define attributes sampling plans
$(\alpha = .05, \beta = .10)$

(1) c	(2) LTPD/AQL	(3) $(AQL)n_\alpha$	(4) $(LTPD)n_\beta$
0	45.10	.051	2.30
1	10.96	.355	3.89
2	6.50	.818	5.32
3	4.89	1.366	6.68
4	4.06	1.970	7.99
5	3.55	2.613	9.28
6	3.21	3.285	10.53
7	2.96	3.981	11.77
8	2.77	4.695	12.99
9	2.62	5.425	14.21
10	2.50	6.169	15.41

Source: A. J. Duncan, *Quality Control and Industrial Statistics,* 5th ed. (Homewood, Ill.: Richard O. Irwin, 1986), p. 172. Copyright 1986. Reprinted by permission.

tion. The desired quality is no more than 1-percent defective (that is, the AQL = 1%). The minimum tolerable quality is 4-percent defective (that is, the LTPD = 4%). The values of α and β are .05 and .10, respectively. Develop an attributes sampling plan.

Notice first that the actual height of the can—that is, its measurement in inches—does not need to be mentioned here. Although the height must be known in order for the inspection to be set up, the sampling plan only needs to determine how many from the sample fail to meet the specification.

Step 1. The ratio of the LTPD/AQL is $.04/.01 = 4$.

Step 2. The nearest entry in column (2) is 4.06.

Step 3. This entry occurs in the row $c = 4$.

Step 4. The value in this row in column (3) is 1.970, which means that

$$n = 1.970/.01 = 197.$$

The sampling plan is given by $n = 197$, $c = 4$. In other words, inspect 197 cans and accept the entire lot if the number of defects is 4 or less. ∎

We note that it is highly unlikely that α and β will be met exactly. For the sampling plan found in Example 17.2 ($n = 197$, $c = 4$), $\alpha = .05$ and $\beta = .102$. If it is required to hold α within its specification—that is, if α must be at or below .05, but β can vary—then column (3) should be used. If it is required to hold β within its specification—that is, if β must be at or below .10, but α can vary—then column (4) should be used. Using the fourth column, $n = 7.99/.04 = 200$. The resulting plan is $n = 200$, $c = 4$. Under this plan, the producer will have a more difficult task of having its lots accepted ($\alpha > .05$) because more are tested (200 > 197) and no additional defectives are allowed (4 in each case). Under this plan, $\alpha = .052$ and $\beta = .095$.

If it is required that both α and β be less than or equal to their specifications, then step 2 will consist of finding the first entry less than or equal to the computed ratio rather than finding the nearest entry.

The similarity of the two plans obtained from the preceding example is a result of our using a rather large sample size. For example, if the values of the AQL and the LTPD were .01 and .10, respectively, then a smaller sample size would be required to detect this larger difference between the AQL and the LTPD. The value of c resulting in this case is 1 (from Table 17.2) and the size of n is 39 if β is held at .10, but only 36 if α is held at .05. The table can target either α or β, not both simultaneously. As the values of AQL and LTPD get closer, it is more difficult to make an accurate decision on a lot, so more data (a larger n) are needed. A larger sample size also is required for attributes inspection, because less information is obtained from each item inspected.

assumption of large lot size

The size of the lot, N, has not been used in any of the calculations done here. Table 17.2 assumes that the lot is large. That is, it is assumed to be large enough, relative to the sample size, that it can be considered to be infinite. As the lot size decreases, the sample becomes a more accurate predictor of the lot quality, thereby reducing the error probabilities, α and β. If, for example, the sample of 200 in Example 17.2 is taken from a lot of size 200, then there is no chance of error and $\alpha = 0$ and $\beta = 0$. This, of course, is 100-percent inspection.

VARIABLES SAMPLING PLAN

The design of a variables sampling plan for the mean is the only variables sampling plan we present. However, it is indicative of the way that all variables sampling plans are designed. For the can described in Example 17.1, a variables plan for the strength characteristic is required. The first step is to determine the probability distribution for strength by testing an introductory sample or by using data from past records. This must be done even if the sampling plan is to be taken from the published tables, because different tables have been developed for different probability distributions. Different tests exist to determine the probability distribution for a set of data, but the simplest is to draw a histogram. Because we are testing for the mean, the primary parameter needed is the standard deviation.

The histogram for the cans is shown in Figure 17.1. It seems to possess the bell-shaped characteristics of the normal distribution, so the sampling plan should be based on the use of that distribution. Most of the published tables do use the normal distribution.

To set up the sampling plan, we must specify two parameters that are analogous to the AQL and LTPD. These are μ_0 and μ_1, which refer to some variable mean. In the case of the cans, this variable is strength. The minimum desired strength, which is analogous to the AQL, is μ_0. The barely acceptable strength, which is analogous to the LTPD, is μ_1. Assume also that α and β are specified. In this case, the lot should be rejected if $\overline{X}$, the average strength of the sample, is less than c, the cutoff strength or critical value to be specified in the plan.

$$\sigma_{\bar{x}}^2 = \frac{\sigma_x^2}{n}$$

To completely describe the sampling plan, it is necessary only to find n, the number to test, and c, the minimum average strength required of the sample. If X, the strength of each can, is distributed normally with mean μ and variance σ^2, then the average strength of the sample, $\overline{X}$, also is distributed normally with mean μ. But the variance of $\overline{X}$ is σ^2/n. This relationship between the sample variance and the population variance is also used for designing the control charts in the next section.

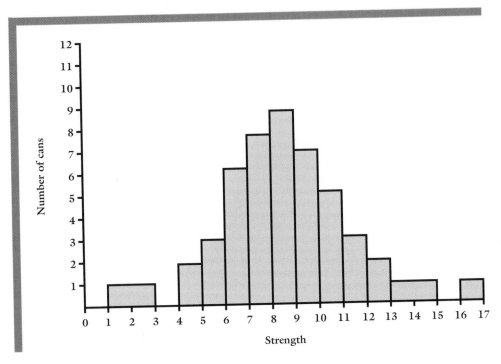

FIGURE 17.1 Histogram from inspection of fifty cans

It can be very easy to compute n and c for a variable sampling plan for the mean, but the computation depends on whether the variable has a one-sided or two-sided specification. In our example, we have specified a minimum strength. This is a one-sided specification. In other cases, such as measuring pollutants, we might specify a maximum for a variable. In yet other cases, such as temperature, we might present both a minimum and a maximum for the variable (two-sided). The appropriate equations for n and c in the one-sided case are as follows.

Teaching Suggestion 17.6: Standard Deviation of Sample Mean. See the Instructor's Section for details.

$$n = \frac{(z_{1-\alpha} - z_\beta)^2 \sigma^2}{(\mu_1 - \mu_0)^2}$$

$c = \mu_0 - z_{1-\alpha}\sigma/\sqrt{n}$ for the one-sided minimum

$c = \mu_0 + z_{1-\alpha}\sigma/\sqrt{n}$ for the one-sided maximum

one-tailed sampling plans

The equations for the two-sided case are not presented due to their increased complexity. We continue with our measurements on the cans in the following example.

Example 17.3   The strength of the can in Example 17.1 must be such that any can having a strength of 10 pounds per square inch will have a 95-percent chance of being accepted. A can having a strength of 8 pounds per square inch should be accepted only 10 percent of the time. The standard deviation, σ, of the cans is 4. Develop the sampling plan for this case.

The specifications are $\mu_0 = 10$, $\mu_1 = 8$, $\alpha = .05$, and $\beta = .10$. Using the equations for n and c, we find

$$n = \frac{[1.64 - (-1.28)]^2 \times (4)^2}{(10 - 8)^2} = 34.1$$

and

$$c = 10 - (1.64 \times 4)/\sqrt{34.1} = 10 - 1.12 = 8.88.$$

The required sampling plan calls for testing 34 cans and accepting the lot if the average strength is 8.88 pounds per square inch or greater.   ■⌋

OPERATING CHARACTERISTIC CURVES

An **operating characteristic** (OC) **curve** is associated with every sampling plan. The OC curve is a graph of the probability of acceptance, P_a, for a lot as a function of the process percent defective. The extreme values on this graph are already known. It should be obvious that if there are no defectives, $P_a = 1$ (all lots accepted) and that if all units are defective, $P_a = 0$ (no lots accepted). After our discussion of acceptance sampling, we also know that at the acceptable quality level, $P_a = 1 - \alpha$ and that at the lot tolerance percent defective, $P_a = \beta$. The complete OC curve provides information about the probability of lot acceptance for lots having any defect rate.

at AQL, $P_a = 1 - \alpha$
at LTPD, $P_a = \beta$

Figure 17.2 shows a typical OC curve for an AQL of .02 and an LTPD of .10 ($\alpha = .05$, $\beta = .10$). The curve starts at a P_a of 1.0 and is relatively flat toward the AQL. It drops at an increasing rate, and then starts to level off again toward the LTPD,

FIGURE 17.2 OC curve (AQL = .02, LTPD = .10, α = .05, β = .10)

Transparency Master 17.3: The Operating Characteristic Curve.

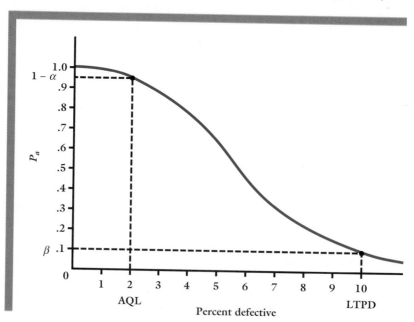

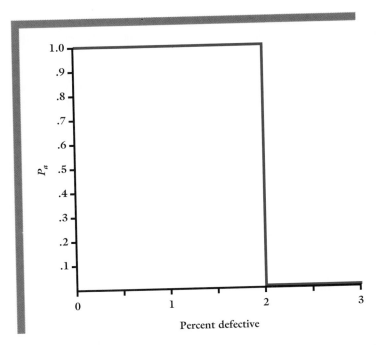

FIGURE 17.3 OC curve of 100-percent inspection (2-percent cutoff)

finally approaching 0 as the percent defective gets large. Of primary interest is just how fast the curve drops.

Ideally, the drop should be as shown in Figure 17.3, which depicts the case of 100-percent inspection. The P_a is 1.0 up to the allowable fraction defective, and drops to 0 instantaneously at this same point. Notice that only one point is needed (the cutoff) to define this curve. Two points—the AQL and the LTPD—as well as the sample size are needed to define the OC curve in Figure 17.2. This is the usual case.

The calculation of points on the OC curve is beyond the scope of this text. The operations manager will not be calculating OC curves, but he or she will be responsible for reading and analyzing them, most often from the published tables. Although two sampling plans can match up for α and β (the extremes of the curve), it is only after review of the entire OC curve that the choice between sampling plans should be made.

Once an OC curve has been developed, it is read in a straightforward manner. The **reading the OC curve** height of the curve (the y-axis value) is the probability that a lot having the percent defective shown on the x-axis will be accepted. As should be expected, the curve is always decreasing. As the percent defective in any lot increases, the probability that the lot will be accepted decreases.

AVERAGE OUTGOING QUALITY

Suppose that we are performing 100-percent inspection, as indicated by the OC curve in Figure 17.3. In this case, our cutoff of 2-percent defective represents a maximum percentage of defectives that are in any lot. That is, the lots that pass will have between 0 and 2 percent defective. Thus, the average percentage of defective items that are shipped (or accepted) will be between 0 and 2 percent (depending on the distribution of the percent defective). We term this percentage the **average outgoing quality** (AOQ).

Because we are sampling, our OC curve appears not as in Figure 17.3, but as in Figure 17.2. The sampling plan does not reject all lots with too many defectives; rather, it accepts lots with probabilities as given by the OC curve. Therefore, the average outgoing quality is given by

average outgoing quality

$$AOQ = \frac{pP_a(p) \times (N - n)}{N},$$

where

$$p = \text{the percent defective in the lot;}$$
$$P_a(p) = \text{the probability of accepting a lot that has a percentage defective}$$
$$\text{given by } p;$$
$$N = \text{the lot size; and}$$
$$n = \text{the sample size.}$$

If the lot size is very large ($N = \infty$), then

$$AOQ = pP_a(p).$$

Notice that the average outgoing quality is a function of the percent defective in a lot. This is illustrated in Figure 17.4. The figure shows that the AOQ begins at 0 when there are 0-percent defective and increases as the percent defective increases, as should be expected. What might at first glance be unexpected is that, at some point, the AOQ improves (decreases) as the quality worsens. The reason for this improvement in the AOQ is that as quality worsens, more bad lots are discovered and not shipped. This illustrates a key point: It is easy to identify very good or very bad lots because they will be so obvious. The difficult task is identifying lots of marginal quality.

Our main interest with the average outgoing quality is the worst case—that is, the highest point on the curve. This is termed the **average outgoing quality limit** (AOQL). The average outgoing quality limit represents the maximum percentage of defectives, on average, that will leave the plant under this sampling plan. For the preceding case of 100-percent inspection, the AOQL is 2 percent. In general, it is given by the peak of the AOQ curve, as shown in Figure 17.4.

PUBLISHED TABLES OF SAMPLING PLANS

Because the design of sampling plans virtually always is done using published tables of plans, it is important to be familiar with the tables that are available. The standards of the Department of Defense (military standards) and the Dodge-Romig tables are the most popular. The MIL-STDs are based on an acceptable quality level, analogous to using the third column of Table 17.2. Various plans are presented for each AQL and if the β value is of significance, one can select the most appropriate plan from an analysis of the OC curves provided. The Dodge-Romig tables are based on lot tolerance percent defective, so the β is fixed and the α varies for the various plans presented.

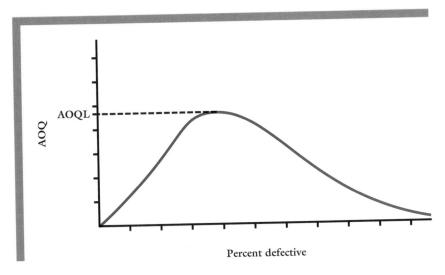

FIGURE 17.4 AOQ as a function of percent defective

Table 17.3 shows a few of the most widely used tables. MIL-STD-105D contains sampling plans and OC curves for single, double, and multiple sampling. It also provides for reduced and tightened inspection procedures. It is to be used only for attribute plans. The Dodge-Romig tables for attribute plans differ mainly in their basis (LTPD versus AQL) and in their assumption that the process average is known in advance. The Japanese equivalent is Japanese Industrial Standard Z–9015.

The major standard for variables inspection is MIL-STD-414. It is set up in a manner very similar to MIL-STD-105D, so that anyone familiar with 105D should be able to learn to use it. It is more complex than 105D, because variables inspection is more complex. The best-known alternative standard for variables plans is Defense Standard 05–30/1 (British).

For continuous sampling (when sampling is done automatically on the production line at regular intervals), MIL-STD-1235 provides the basis for most sampling plans.

MIL-STD-105D contains many tables, two of which are reproduced here. Table 17.4 converts lot size to sample size, and Table 17.5 provides the acceptance number for each AQL. In Table 17.4, general inspection level II is most commonly used for normal inspection.

Example 17.4 The cans in the previous examples are produced in lots of 8,000 cans each. An AQL of 1 percent is desired. What sampling plan should be chosen according to MIL-STD-105, level II?

In Table 17.4, the sample size code letter for 8,000 cans is L, using the general inspection level II, normal inspection. Going to Table 17.5, row L, the sample size, n, is 200 and the acceptance number, c, in the 1-percent column is 5. ◾

MIL-STD-105D is more lenient than Table 17.2 in this case (see Example 17.2). Actually, α is better than 5 percent at an AQL of 1 percent. This results, in part, from a different definition of AQL used by the MIL-STD.

TABLE 17.3   Published sampling plans

Name of Plan	Type of Sampling	Type of Application	Key Features
MIL-STD-105D	Single, double, and multiple	General application whether or not rejected lots can be 100-percent inspected	Maintains average quality at a specified level or better. Aims to minimize rejection of good lots. Also provides single-sampling plans for fixed consumer risks and average quality levels in the long run. Tables and mechanics of operation are simplified to minimize training required.
Dodge-Romig	Single and double	General application where rejected lots can be 100-percent inspected	One type of plan has a consumer's risk of .10 of accepting bad quality. A second type of plan limits the average quality level in the long run. Protection is provided with minimum inspection per lot.
Chain sampling	Single and two stage	Particularly useful when inspection involves destructive or costly tests	Aims to minimize sample sizes without a large risk of rejection of good lots. Occurrence of a single defective does not necessarily cause rejection.
Bayesian plans (discovery sampling)	Generally single	General application where probability of occurrence of defective lots can be estimated *a priori*	Smaller sample size required as compared with standard attribute schemes.
Skip-lot sampling plans	Single	Particularly useful when indicated quality level is high and inspection involves costly or destructive tests	Aims to minimize inspection with adequate protection against major degradation in quality.
H107	Continuous single level	General application when production is truly continuous and inspection is nondestructive	Although plans are indexed by AQL, plans actually limit the average quality in the long run.
H106	Continuous multilevel	Same as for H107	Plans limit the average quality in the long run.
Cumulative sum	Continuous single level	General application when production is truly continuous and there is no restriction on the nature of inspection	Plans limit the average quality in the long run but in a sense different from limits of H107 and H106.

Source: J. M. Juran, *Quality Control Handbook.* Copyright © 1974, McGraw-Hill, p. 24–19, reprinted by permission.

TABLE 17.4 Table for sample sizes, MIL-STD-105D

Lot or Batch Size	Special Inspection Levels				General Inspection Levels		
	S–1	S–2	S–3	S–4	I	II	III
2–8	A	A	A	A	A	A	B
9–15	A	A	A	A	A	B	C
16–25	A	A	B	B	B	C	D
26–50	A	B	B	C	C	D	E
51–90	B	B	C	C	C	E	F
91–150	B	B	C	D	D	F	G
151–280	B	C	D	E	E	G	H
281–500	B	C	D	E	F	H	J
501–1,200	C	C	E	F	G	J	K
1,201–3,200	C	D	E	G	H	K	L
3,201–10,000	C	D	F	G	J	L	M
10,001–35,000	C	D	F	H	K	M	N
35,001–150,000	D	E	G	J	L	N	P
150,001–500,000	D	E	G	J	M	P	Q
500,001 and over	D	E	H	K	N	Q	R

DOUBLE SAMPLING PLANS

For an example of how a double sampling plan works, consider the following plan for our example situation, as obtained from MIL-STD-105D (not presented here).

Step 1. Select a first sample with $n = 125$.

Step 2. If 2 or less are defective, accept lot.

Step 3. If 5 or more are defective, reject lot.

Step 4. If 3 or 4 are defective, select a second sample of size 125.

Step 5. If there are now 6 or less defective (from the 250) then the lot is acceptable; otherwise, reject the lot.

This double sampling plan is calculated to match the OC curve of the single sampling plan $n = 200$, $c = 5$. Again, although we provide no tables or formulas for developing double sampling plans, it is important to understand how such plans are used.

A double sampling plan has two advantages. First, it provides a psychological **two advantages** advantage in that it gives the manufacturer a second chance. Recall that the manufacturer will be convinced that the sample is bad and that the lot is good, so this second chance responds to that notion without relaxing α and β.

The second advantage is that it provides an economic incentive to exceed the desired level of quality by choosing a smaller sample on the first try than is used for the single sampling plan (125 versus 200). If the quality is very good, the lot may pass on the first try, thus cutting down on inspection costs. Of course, inspection costs also are saved if quality is very bad—that is, if the lot fails on first sample—but there is r.o economic incentive in this direction. The cost of rejected lots far exceeds the savings in inspection costs.

TABLE 17.5 Table for single sampling plans, MIL-STD-105D

Acceptable Quality Levels (normal inspection)

Sample size code letter	Sample size	0.010		0.015		0.025		0.040		0.065		0.10		0.15		0.25		0.40		0.65		1.0		1.5		2.5		4.0		6.5		10		15		25		40		65		100		150		250		400		650		1000	
		Ac	Re	Ac	Re	Ac	Re	Ac	Re	Ac	Re	Ac	Re	Ac	Re	Ac	Re	Ac	Re	Ac	Re	Ac	Re	Ac	Re	Ac	Re	Ac	Re	Ac	Re	Ac	Re	Ac	Re	Ac	Re	Ac	Re	Ac	Re	Ac	Re	Ac	Re	Ac	Re	Ac	Re	Ac	Re
A	2																													→		0	1	1	2	2	3	3	4	5	6	7	8	10	11	14	15	21	22	30	31
B	3																											→		0	1	1	2	2	3	3	4	5	6	7	8	10	11	14	15	21	22	30	31	44	45
C	5																							→		0	1	1	2	2	3	3	4	5	6	7	8	10	11	14	15	21	22	30	31	44	45	↑	
D	8																					→		0	1	1	2	2	3	3	4	5	6	7	8	10	11	14	15	21	22	30	31	44	45	↑			
E	13																			→		0	1	1	2	2	3	3	4	5	6	7	8	10	11	14	15	21	22	30	31	44	45	↑					
F	20																	→		0	1	1	2	2	3	3	4	5	6	7	8	10	11	14	15	21	22	30	31	44	45	↑							
G	32															→		0	1	1	2	2	3	3	4	5	6	7	8	10	11	14	15	21	22	30	31	44	45	↑									
H	50													→		0	1	1	2	2	3	3	4	5	6	7	8	10	11	14	15	21	22	30	31	44	45	↑											
J	80											→		0	1	1	2	2	3	3	4	5	6	7	8	10	11	14	15	21	22	30	31	44	45	↑													
K	125									→		0	1	1	2	2	3	3	4	5	6	7	8	10	11	14	15	21	22	30	31	44	45	↑															
L	200							→		0	1	1	2	2	3	3	4	5	6	7	8	10	11	14	15	21	22	30	31	44	45	↑																	
M	315					→		0	1	1	2	2	3	3	4	5	6	7	8	10	11	14	15	21	22	30	31	44	45	↑																			
N	500				→		0	1	1	2	2	3	3	4	5	6	7	8	10	11	14	15	21	22	30	31	44	45	↑																					
P	800			→		0	1	1	2	2	3	3	4	5	6	7	8	10	11	14	15	21	22	30	31	44	45	↑																							
Q	1250	→		0	1	1	2	2	3	3	4	5	6	7	8	10	11	14	15	21	22	30	31	44	45	↑																									
R	2000	0	1	1	2	2	3	3	4	5	6	7	8	10	11	14	15	21	22	30	31	44	45	↑																												

→ = Use first sampling plan below arrow. If sample size equals, or exceeds, lot or batch size, do 100-percent inspection.

↑ = Use first sampling plan above arrow.

Ac = Acceptance number

Re = Rejection number

AVERAGE SAMPLE NUMBER CURVE

Associated with each sampling plan is a curve representing the *average number inspected* versus the percent defective in the lot. An **average sample number** (ASN) curve is shown in Figure 17.5. Notice that more inspection needs to be done when the process defective is between the AQL and the LTPD. As was the case with the AOQ, this is the area where making a correct judgment on the lot is difficult. Less inspection is required when the lot is either very good or very bad. Of course, the ASN curve for a single sampling plan is flat, because the same number is sampled from each lot. Therefore, the ASN curve is used only for double (or multiple or sequential) sampling.

PROCESS CONTROL

Acceptance sampling is a major and desirable function of quality control, but it only leads to a determination about whether the product should be accepted or rejected. Also desirable is being able to apply a quality control function during production itself to control the quality of the production process. As noted in Chapter 16, the control chart is the tool used for this purpose. Control charts are used for the inspection of finished parts as well as during in-process inspection. **control charts**

The major purpose of the control chart is *to detect changes in a production process.* **major purpose** A process is "in control" as long as no change is detected. When it goes "out of control," production must stop until the assignable cause is found and corrected. A process can be out of control if an improvement in quality is detected as well as if a deterioration of quality occurs. Production is not stopped if quality improves, but an investigation into the assignable cause should be conducted anyway. In this way, the gain in quality can be carried over to other production processes.

FIGURE 17.5 ASN curve

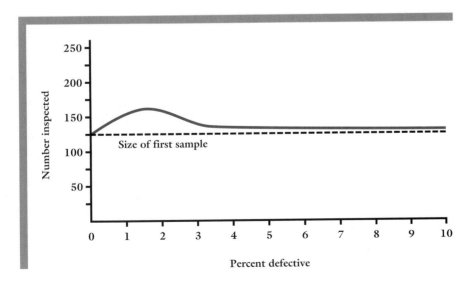

Checking quality during production—in-process inspection at General Motors. (© Gerd Ludwig/Woodfin Camp & Associates)

two types of control charts

Just as there are two kinds of acceptance sampling, there are two types of control charts: charts for attributes and charts for variables. The major chart for attributes is the chart on fraction defective. To control a variables inspection, such as a dimension, two charts are desirable. Of course, the process mean must be controlled, which is done using an $\overline{X}$-chart. However, the process variability also must be controlled, because consistency is a major factor in control. An **R-chart,** to control the range of samples, is used most often for this purpose. A more complete list of control charts is found in Table 17.6. Only the **p-charts,** $\overline{X}$-charts, and R-charts will be demonstrated here. Details concerning the other charts listed in Table 17.6 can be found in any quality control text.

All of the control charts work in the same manner. The chart actually is a graph; each sample that is tested is an entry. The horizontal axis represents the sample number or time, and the vertical axis represents the variable of interest (p, $\overline{X}$, R, and so on).

TABLE 17.6 List of control charts

(a) Attributes	Use
p-chart	Fraction defective
np-chart	Number of defectives
U-chart	Defects per unit
c-chart	Defects per sample

(b) Variables	Use
$\overline{X}$-chart	Process mean
σ-chart	Process standard deviation
R-chart	Sample range
Cu-sum chart	Cumulative sums

Figure 17.6 shows a sample p-chart. Notice that there are only three lines on this chart. Knowing where to draw these lines is all that is required to design a control chart.

The middle line of the three, known appropriately enough as the **center line** (CL), is the process average. It is not necessarily the desired average, but it should be the actual average, because the purpose of the chart is to identify changes in the process rather than adherence to a specification. This process average usually is found from analysis of data from the recent past (recent production lots). Having said how the CL should be found, we note that, in practice, the desired average (the specification on the drawing) is used very often.

FIGURE 17.6 Sample p-chart

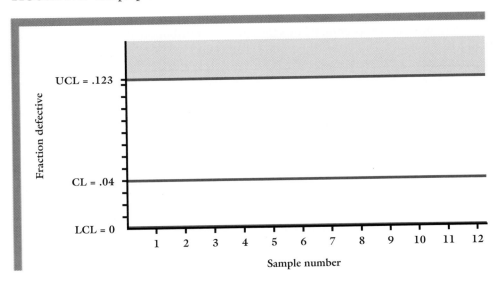

control limits

The remaining two lines are called the **lower control limit** (LCL) and **upper control limit** (UCL). These lines are positioned so that any sample falling outside of them represents a shift in the process and signals that production should be shut down. They can be set to confidence intervals (95-percent or 99-percent limits), but the more common practice is to use 3σ limits. This practice assumes that about three out of a thousand samples should fall outside of these limits, even when the process is working well. Very often, an additional set of lines, 2σ limits, also are used as warning lines. Sometimes, the occurrence of two samples outside of these warning lines is cause for shutting down the line. The examples presented here all use 3σ limits.

A primary reason for the widespread use of control charts is their simplicity of application. Once a chart has been designed, it is displayed on a wall or some other suitable location at an inspection station on the production line. At regular intervals, a sample is taken from production and tested. The result of the inspection is plotted with an X on the chart. The analysis required is to observe if the X is inside or outside of the control limits.

In addition to noting whether the reading is within the control limits, any trend indicated is observed. Figure 17.7 illustrates three different trends and what they mean. In practice, a run of seven consecutive points typically is used to identify a process that is out of control. These seven points may be increasing, decreasing, above the mean, or below the mean, as shown in Figure 17.7. Additional rules that may be used were discussed in Chapter 16.

p-CHARTS

The first step in designing a chart to control the process fraction defective is to determine the center line. This can be calculated from past data or, if no past history is available, from a large sample tested at the start. If a large number of items, N, are tested and X are defective, the process fraction defective is

mean percent defective

$$p = \frac{X}{N}.$$

Because attributes inspection follows the binomial distribution, the standard deviation of p is

sample percent defective standard deviation

$$s_p = \sqrt{\frac{p(1 - p)}{n}},$$

where n is the size of each sample to be tested. Therefore, using 3σ limits,

$$\text{CL} = p,$$

$$\text{UCL} = p + 3\sqrt{\frac{p(1 - p)}{n}}, \text{ and}$$

$$\text{LCL} = p - 3\sqrt{\frac{p(1 - p)}{n}}.$$

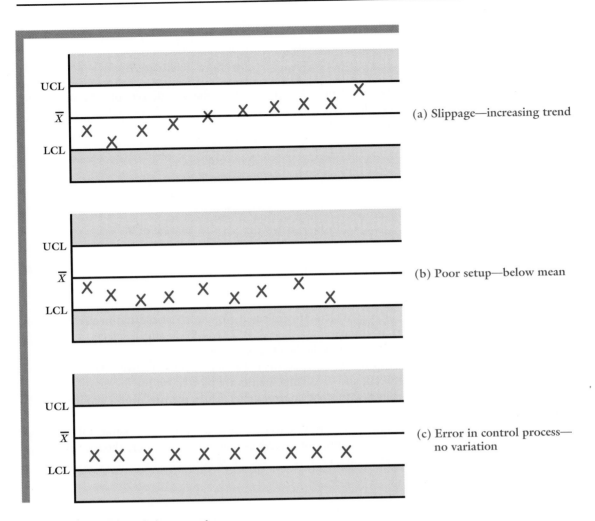

FIGURE 17.7 Control chart trends

If the calculated value of the LCL is negative, then the LCL is zero, because the fraction defective cannot be below zero. For p-charts, the UCL is of major concern, because exceeding this limit brings the quality of the product into question. Before presenting some examples, we note that all sample sizes must be identical. That is, every control chart is designed for one specific sample size.

all sample sizes must be identical

> **Example 17.5** Samples of 50 units are selected from a production line for inspection every hour. The line produces 250 units per hour, and records show that 400 defectives were found in 100-percent inspection of last week's production (40 hours). Design the p-chart for this production line.
>
> To calculate the center line, p, we must first determine the number in the sample.

$$250 \text{ parts/hour} \times 40 \text{ hours/week} = 10,000 \text{ parts}$$

The fraction defective, then, is

$$p = \frac{400}{10,000} = .04, \text{ or 4 percent.}$$

The control limits are calculated next, based on the sample size of 50 units. Again, using the 3σ control limits,

$$UCL = .04 + 3\sqrt{\frac{.04 \times .96}{50}} = .123$$

and

$$LCL = .04 - 3\sqrt{\frac{.04 \times .96}{50}} = -.043, \text{ or 0.}$$

This is the chart that was shown in Figure 17.6. ▪

Example 17.6   As data are collected for the chart created in the preceding example, the first 10 samples have 2, 4, 3, 0, 2, 1, 4, 3, 5, and 1 defects, respectively. Plot these points on the chart. Is the process in control?

Each number of defectives is converted to a percent defective: .04, .08, .06, .0, .04, .02, .08, .06, .10, and .02. These points are plotted on the control chart shown in Figure 17.8. All fall within the control limits. Thus, the process is in control. ▪

All managers should design systems that are as foolproof as possible. Observe that it is easier to count the number of defectives than it is to calculate the fraction defec-

FIGURE 17.8 Points plotted on p-chart (Example 17.6)

Transparency Master 17.6: Sample p-Chart and np-Chart.

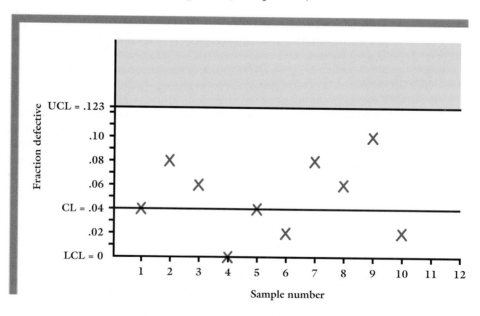

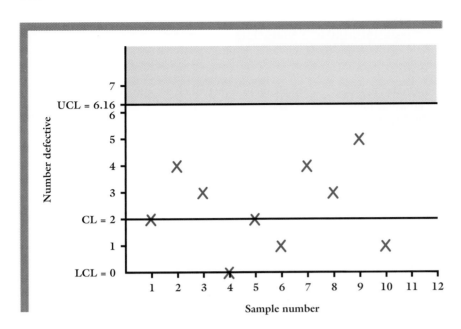

Transparency Master 17.6:
Sample *p*-Chart and
np-Chart.

FIGURE 17.9 Number defective plotted on *np*-chart

tive. Therefore, the chart in the previous example can be recalculated so that only the number of defectives need to be plotted, as shown in Figure 17.9. This is a special case of a *p*-chart, known as an *np*-chart.

Teaching Suggestion 17.7:
Interpretation. See the
Instructor's Section for
details.

$$CL = np = 50 \times .04 = 2$$
$$UCL = np + 3\sqrt{np(1 - p)} = 6.16$$
$$LCL = np - 3\sqrt{np(1 - p)} = -2.16, \text{ or } 0$$

$\overline{X}$-CHARTS, *R*-CHARTS

The variable charts are used in the same manner as the *p*-charts. When the standard deviation of the process is known, the equations are almost identical. If each sample has a mean $\overline{X}$, then the average of all samples (the average of the averages) is called $\overline{\overline{X}}$. So, using 3σ limits,

$$CL = \overline{\overline{X}},$$
$$UCL = \overline{\overline{X}} + 3\sigma_{\overline{X}}, \text{ and}$$
$$LCL = \overline{\overline{X}} - 3\sigma_{\overline{X}}.$$

As before, $\sigma_{\overline{X}} = \sigma_X/\sqrt{n}$. The resulting $\overline{X}$-chart is used to control the process mean; a σ-chart can be used for the control of the process variability.

The usual case, however, is that the variance is not known. In this case, the range, *R*, is used instead of σ, because the range is very easy to calculate. It is merely the

---

APPLICATIONS OF P/OM

Process Control at Frito-Lay

Making potato chips is a carefully controlled process. Actually, it's several processes, all involving human labor and complex machinery. So, how do potato chip manufacturers know when and where they have a problem? In the past, the Frito-Lay company would inspect the product at the end of the process, but that's a little late to find out that something's wrong. There are better ways, including sampling, which allows the manufacturer to check on the process as it's happening. Frito-Lay reduced variability by 50 percent since implementing its statistical process control.

Every fifteen minutes, three batches of Ruffles are sampled for salt content. The batches are ground up, weighed, and placed in an electronic salt meter. The sample mean is plotted on a control chart. Frito-Lay workers know that the process has to be adjusted if any of the following occur.

- One point is out of control (greater than 3 standard deviations from the mean).
- Two of three points are more than 2 standard deviations on the same side of the mean.
- Four of five points are more than 1 standard deviation on the same side of the mean.
- There is a run of eight points on the same side of the mean.

Source: Against All Odds (New York: W.H. Freeman, 1988).

difference between the largest and smallest reading in each sample. The range is not as easy to use in statistical formulas, but tables of coefficients have been developed for its use in developing $\overline{X}$-charts and R-charts. A small portion of these tables is reproduced in Table 17.7. Using Table 17.7, we can define the control limits for the $\overline{X}$-chart.

$$\text{UCL} = \overline{\overline{X}} + A_2\overline{R}$$
$$\text{LCL} = \overline{\overline{X}} - A_2\overline{R}$$

The control limits for the R-chart are as follows.

$$\text{LCL} = D_3\overline{R}$$
$$\text{UCL} = D_4\overline{R}$$

Example 17.7   From the production line, 25 samples of 5 cans each have been selected and tested. $\overline{X}$ is found for each of the 25 samples, and $\overline{\overline{X}} = 18.5$. Similarly, the range for each sample is found, resulting in an $\overline{R}$ of .458. Design the $\overline{X}$-chart and R-chart for this situation.

Teaching Suggestion 17.8: Weight Control. See the Instructor's Section for details.

For the $\overline{X}$-chart, the center line is

$$\overline{\overline{X}} = 18.5,$$

and the control limits are

$$\text{UCL} = 18.5 + (.577 \times .458) = 18.764$$

TABLE 17.7 Factors for $\overline{X}$-charts and R-charts (3σ limits)

Number of Observations in Subgroup	Factor for $\overline{X}$-Chart A_2	Factors for R-Chart	
		Lower Limit D_3	Upper Limit D_4
2	1.880	0	3.267
3	1.023	0	2.575
4	0.729	0	2.282
5	0.577	0	2.115
6	0.483	0	2.004
7	0.419	0.076	1.924
8	0.373	0.136	1.864
9	0.337	0.184	1.816
10	0.308	0.223	1.777
11	0.285	0.256	1.744
12	0.266	0.284	1.716
13	0.249	0.308	1.692
14	0.235	0.329	1.671
15	0.223	0.348	1.652
16	0.212	0.364	1.636
17	0.203	0.379	1.621
18	0.194	0.392	1.608
19	0.187	0.404	1.596
20	0.180	0.414	1.586
21	0.173	0.425	1.575
22	0.167	0.434	1.566
23	0.162	0.443	1.557
24	0.157	0.452	1.548
25	0.153	0.459	1.541

Source: A. J. Duncan, *Quality Control and Industrial Statistics,* 5th ed. (Homewood, Ill.: Richard O. Irwin, 1986), p. 1,025. Copyright 1986. Reprinted by permission.

and

$$\text{LCL} = 18.5 - (.577 \times .458) = 18.236.$$

For the R-chart the center line is

$$\overline{R} = .458,$$

and the control limits are

$$\text{UCL} = .458 \times 2.115 = .969$$

and

$$\text{LCL} = .458 \times 0 = 0.$$

These control charts are shown in Figures 17.10 and 17.11.

Transparency Master 17.7: Sample $\overline{X}$-Chart and R-Chart.

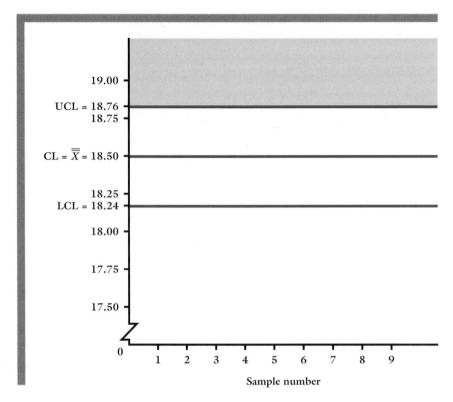

FIGURE 17.10 $\overline{X}$-chart (Example 17.7)

QUALITY COSTS

There are a number of major costs that must be considered when determining an economic level of sampling inspection. Primary among these are the costs of inspection (for labor and equipment). These inspection costs add to the cost of the product and if they are a significant part of the product cost, they may result in overpricing, thereby contributing to reduced sales.

Because too much inspection can price a product out of its market, a desired level of quality must be attained for a given market. Higher quality will cost more, and there is a point at which consumers will not pay for the higher quality. Thus, there is a diminishing return on each inspection performed for increased quality.

appraisal costs

There are other costs in addition to inspection costs that are incurred by using techniques to increase the level of quality. These include the costs of testing incoming material, periodically testing material in storage, maintaining the accuracy of testing equipment (calibration), and the materials or services (dyes, films, electricity, lubricants) used for inspection. In addition to these quality appraisal costs, there are pre-

prevention costs

vention costs. These include planning, training, reporting, data acquisition, and analysis costs.

To determine the optimal level of inspection (or the associated optimal quality level), it is necessary to balance the costs of increasing quality with the costs associated

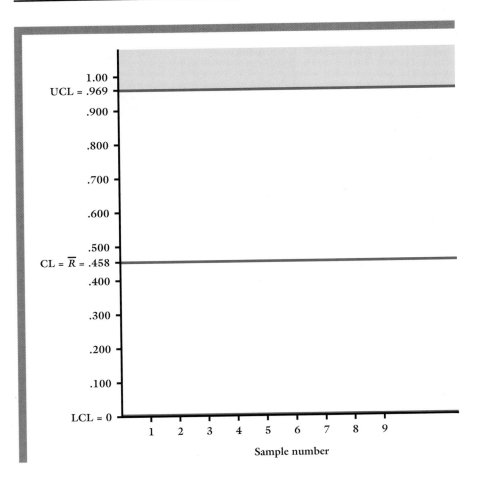

Transparency Master 17.7:
Sample $\bar{X}$-Chart and
R-Chart.

FIGURE 17.11 R-chart (Example 17.7)

with poor quality; that is, it is necessary to determine the benefits of higher quality. The costs associated with poor quality are considered to be failure costs and include **failure costs** the costs of production downtime, reworking material, material scrapped due to defective workmanship, shipping returned lots, and the additional inspection required for returned lots. Less apparent, but present nevertheless, is the cost of lost sales associated with dissatisfied customers.

Figure 17.12 shows the trade-off between these costs. Unfortunately, there is no simple way to calculate these costs and find an optimal quality level. Because the term *optimal quality level* implies that one need no longer worry about improving quality after reaching this level, we can view Figure 17.12 in a different way. The region of the total cost curve associated with the decreasing quality costs (to the left of optimal) is one of low quality and is referred to as the *zone of improvement*. At this level of quality, failure costs are too high and more inspection is warranted. The region around optimality is a *zone of indifference*, where the emphasis is shifted from inspections to control. Finally, the region to the right of optimal is known as the *zone of perfectionism*.

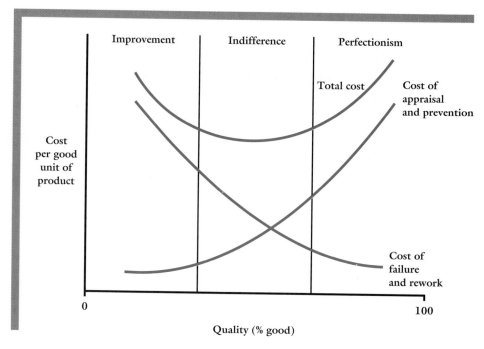

FIGURE 17.12 Quality costs

In this zone, inspection should be reduced and emphasis should be placed on prevention studies.

SUMMARY

Quality is the product that every company, whether manufacturing or service oriented, hopes to sell. Specific operations that have proven to yield significant improvements in quality include assurance plans (sampling and acceptance testing) and process control plans (*control charts*). The basis for all these operations is the inspection operation. What to inspect for, how to inspect it, and how often to inspect it are the key decisions to be made. Additional concerns and functions related to quality are the evaluation and control of quality costs and the development of the quality plan. This quality plan outlines the company's broad objectives and policies relating to quality and details the procedures to ensure conformance to the policies. The *quality audit* provides upper management with the necessary feedback on quality performance. Finally, reliance on inspection to assure quality has lessened and more companies are now making individual workers more responsible for and more aware of the quality of their work. A variety of approaches aimed at improving workers' contributions to quality control have been used successfully around the world, but the most successful is the *quality circle*, which originated in Japan.

KEY TERMS

quality control

quality assurance

total quality control

control charts

acceptance sampling

statistical quality control

quality circle

quality audit

destructive testing

nondestructive testing

inspection for attributes

inspection for variables

fail-safe concept

100-percent inspection

consumer's risk

producer's risk

sampling plan

acceptable quality level

lot tolerance percent defective

operating characteristic curve

average outgoing quality

average outgoing quality limit

average sample number

$\overline{X}$-chart

R-chart

p-chart

center line

lower control limit

upper control limit

SOLVED PROBLEMS

1. National Express Air Delivery Service promises customers that any package picked up prior to 3:00 P.M. on any given day will be delivered by 10:00 A.M. on the next morning. The company has hired a consultant to verify its claim of having the highest quality service. The consultant defines quality as the percentage of on-time deliveries, with the desired level being 99 percent and a minimum tolerable level being 95 percent. The consultant decides to check a random sample of package deliveries to test if these levels are being achieved. For a producer's risk of .05 and a consumer's risk of .10, develop the sampling plan for this situation. Be sure to hold the producer's risk to .05.

Solution

Using Table 17.2, an AQL of .01, and an LTPD of .05,

$$\text{LTPD/AQL} = .05/.01 = 5.$$

The closest value to 5 in the table is 4.89, corresponding to $c = 3$. Holding α to .05, the sample size, n, is found from

$$\text{AQL } n_\alpha = 1.366$$

$$n = 1.366/.01 = 136.6, \text{ or } 137.$$

The sampling plan is

$$n = 137, c = 3.$$

Using AB:POM to Solve This Problem

The quality control module consists of five models. The model to determine a sampling plan is shown in Screen 17.1. The input consists of the AQL and the LTPD and toggles for α and β. The solution is shown on the right side of the screen.

```
╔════════════════ Quality Control ═══════════════ Solution ═╗
║ ┌─────────────────────────────────────────────────────────┐ ║
║ │                                                         │ ║
║ └─────────────────────────────────────────────────────────┘ ║
║ ┌═══════════════ Chapter 17, Solved Problem 1 ═══════════┐ ║
║      Attributes sampling -determine the plan              ║
║                                                           ║
║   AQL    .0100            The sample size    (n) = 137    ║
║                                                           ║
║   LTPD   .0500            The critical value (c) = 3      ║
║                                                           ║
║   α      .05                                              ║
║                                                           ║
║   β      .10                                              ║
║                                                           ║
║                                                           ║
║                                                           ║
║                                                           ║
║                                                           ║
║ └─────────────────────────────────────────────────────────┘ ║
║                                                           ║
║ F2=Error analysis/OC Curve              F9=Print    Esc   ║
║ Press <Esc> key to edit data or highlighted key or function key for options ║
╚═══════════════════════════════════════════════════════════╝
```

SCREEN 17.1

2. In the previous problem, the consultant told National Express that it was failing to meet its on-time delivery criteria. The company protested that deliveries arriving between 10:00 and 10:15 were counting too heavily against it. The consultant suggested using a variables plan to check the company's contention that only 5 percent would arrive after 10:15 and that 90 percent would arrive by 9:30 as an alternate way of expressing their quality. Further analysis showed that delivery time has a standard deviation of 10 minutes. Develop the variables sampling plan.

Solution

$$\mu_0 = 9{:}30 \qquad \mu_1 = 10{:}15$$

$$n = \frac{(Z_{1-\alpha} - Z_\beta)^2 \times \sigma^2}{(\mu_1 - \mu_0)^2} = \frac{(1.64 + 1.28)^2 \times 20^2}{(45 \text{ minutes})^2}$$

$$= 1.68$$

Therefore, we sample 2 items.

$$c = 9{:}30 + 1.64(20)/\sqrt{2} = 9{:}30 + 23.19 \text{ minutes.}$$

The number sampled should be 2, and the mean delivery time must be prior to 9:53.

Note that the equation for c is the equation for the one-sided maximum. This is due to the fact that in this example, the μ_0 is the lower (sooner) time as opposed to the higher number (strength) in Example 17.3.

Using AB:POM to Solve This Problem

Solved Problem 2 determines the plan for attributes sampling, as shown in Screen 17.2. Note that times have been converted to decimal numbers.

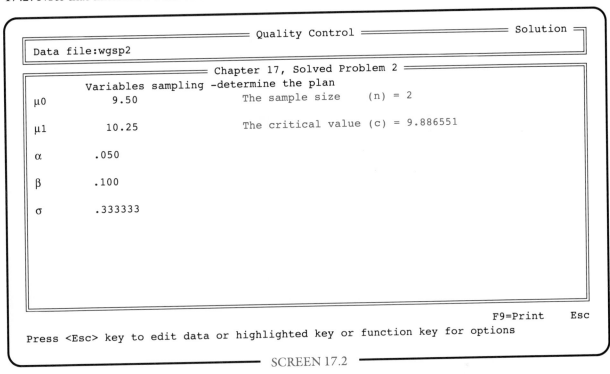

```
════════════════════════ Quality Control ════════════════ Solution ═
 ┌─────────────────────────────────────────────────────────────────┐
 │ Data file:wgsp2                                                   │
 └─────────────────────────────────────────────────────────────────┘
 ┌──────────────────────── Chapter 17, Solved Problem 2 ═══════════┐
 │        Variables sampling -determine the plan                     │
 │  μ0         9.50              The sample size    (n) = 2          │
 │                                                                   │
 │  μ1        10.25              The critical value (c) = 9.886551   │
 │                                                                   │
 │  α          .050                                                  │
 │                                                                   │
 │  β          .100                                                  │
 │                                                                   │
 │  σ          .333333                                               │
 │                                                                   │
 │                                                                   │
 │                                                                   │
 └──────────────────────────────────────────────────┤F9=Print  Esc├─┘
  Press <Esc> key to edit data or highlighted key or function key for options
```

SCREEN 17.2

3. Using the variables sampling plan, National Express has proven that its on-time record is as good as advertised. The final portion of the consulting project is to set up a plan for monitoring the company's record in order that it may control delivery times and be able to react early and quickly should it ever begin to deviate from its schedule. Set up an $\overline{X}$-chart and R-chart to monitor the company's mean delivery time and the range of delivery times. Samples of 10 deliveries from each day of the past month show a mean time of 9:30 A.M. for deliveries and an average range of 35 minutes.

Solution

We must first determine the control limits for the $\overline{X}$-chart with a center line of 9:30.

$$\text{UCL} = \overline{\overline{X}} + A_2\overline{R} \text{ (value for } A_2 \text{ found in Table 17.7)}$$
$$= 9{:}30 + (.308 \times 35 \text{ minutes})$$
$$= 9{:}30 + 10.78 \text{ minutes}$$
$$= 9{:}41$$

$$LCL = \overline{\overline{X}} - A_2\overline{R}$$
$$= 9{:}30 - 10.78 \text{ minutes}$$
$$= 9{:}19$$

The range chart is set up with a center line of 35 minutes and the following control limits.

$$LCL = D_3 \overline{R}$$
$$= .223 \times 35 \text{ minutes}$$
$$= 7.805 \text{ minutes}$$

$$UCL = D_4\overline{R}$$
$$= 1.777 \times 35 \text{ minutes}$$
$$= 62.195 \text{ minutes}$$

Using AB:POM to Solve This Problem

AB:POM can also compute control chart limits. In Screen 17.3, we have entered Solved Problem 3. Notice that the times are entered as decimals rather than times—that is, 9:30 becomes 9.50 and 35 minutes is $35/60 = .583$. The output shows an upper control limit of 9.68, which is 9:41, and a lower control limit of 9.32, which is 9:19. Similarly, when converted from decimal to clock time, the output for the range limits agree with the 7.805 and 62.195 minutes found in Solved Problem 3.

```
======================= Quality Control ======================= Solution =
 Number of samples (1-36) 1                      Sample size (n) (2-25)   10
======================= Chapter 17, Solved Problem 3 =======================
 Sample        Center        Sample
 number        line          Range
    1              9.50       0.583
                             Xbar          Range
 Upper Control Limit   9.679564         1.036
 Center Line ( ave )       9.50         0.583
 Lower Control Limit   9.320436         0.1300




                                                      F9=Print    Esc
 Press <Esc> key to edit data or highlighted key or function key for options
```

SCREEN 17.3

QUESTIONS

1. In light of the fact that quality is a subjective measure, how then can we define quality for any single product or service?

2. "Quality cannot be inspected into a product." Explain this statement and its significance in the design of a quality program.

3. Discuss the adversarial relationship between the production manager and the quality manager.

4. Describe the four inspection areas and what quality control tools might be used in each case.

5. List the seven elements of a total quality control system.

6. What are the differences between quality control and quality assurance?

7. Of the seven elements of a total quality control system, which fit our definition of quality control and which fit our definition of quality assurance?

8. How might the philosophy behind the ABC analysis, presented earlier with regard to the management of inventories, be applied to the quality environment?

9. Most companies have outside auditors conduct a financial audit. Why do so few companies do a quality audit?

10. What would be the effect on the workings of a quality circle if a manager attended all of the meetings?

11. Discuss the concept of first and last sampling.

12. Compare and contrast destructive versus nondestructive testing. Give two examples of each of these types of tests that might be done in industry.

13. What characteristics of a product need to be inspected? Why are some product characteristics inspected while others are not?

14. Inspections should, as a general rule, be performed as early as possible in the production process. Why is this so?

15. What is the difference between attributes inspection and variables inspection?

16. What is an OC curve?

17. What two risks are present when acceptance sampling is used?

18. What is the purpose of acceptance sampling?

19. What are the advantages of using a double sampling plan?

20. Why does the average sample number and/or the average outgoing quality improve when quality gets very bad?

21. Can a production process be labeled as "out of control" because it is too good? Explain.

22. In a control chart, what would be the effect on the control limits if the sample size varied from one sample to the next?

PROBLEMS

1. H & R Auditors has been asked to perform an audit on the customer records for a broker-age firm that processes thousands of customer transactions each day. H & R will use an AQL of 1 percent and an LTPD of 3 percent. Using $\alpha = .05$ and $\beta = .10$, design the appropriate sampling plan. (Hold α fixed.)

$n = 398, c = 7$

2. Consumer Advocates, Inc. checks products for proper labeling with regard to the amount of product in the container. A problem has come to their attention concerning Citrus City Orange Juice. They wish to purchase some of the product to evaluate whether or not the complaints are justified. They decide that the maximum acceptable percentage of underfilled containers is 2 percent and they would tolerate no more than 5 percent. They want a sampling plan that will not accuse Citrus City falsely more than 5 percent of the time and not fail to recognize the problem (if it exists) more than 10 percent of the time. How many containers should be purchased and how many of them are allowed to be short?

$n = 308, c = 10$

3. Joe Carter has recently been assigned the responsibility for quality control at his company. Joe has found that the company is using a sampling plan with $n = 100$ and $c = 7$, but he is unable to find out why these numbers are used. If $\alpha = .05$ and $\beta = .10$, determine the AQL and the LTPD.

AQL = 4%; LTPD = 12%

AQL = 3.3%; LTPD = 10.5%

4. Joe Carter (see Problem 3) is happy with the sample size of 100, but wants to reduce the acceptance number to 6. What effect does this have on the AQL and the LTPD?

5. PennSylvania produces light bulbs and sells them with a claim that they will last, on average, for 1,200 hours of use. In fact, the production process produces bulbs that have a life that is distributed normally, with a standard deviation of 200 hours. Design a sampling plan that will only accept an average life of 1,200 hours no more than 5 percent of the time and that will accept an average of 1,300 hours at least 97.5 percent of the time ($\alpha = .025, \beta = .05$).

$n = 52, c = 1{,}246$ hours

6. Suppose that PennSylvania (see Problem 5) decides to sample 100 bulbs from each lot. How does this affect the critical value (c)?

$c = 1{,}261$ hours

$\alpha = .1; \beta = .2$

7. Determine α and β from the following OC curve for a particular sampling plan.

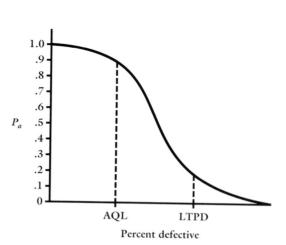

Percent defective

8. Given an AQL of .01 and an LTPD of .04, draw an OC curve for an α of .03 and a β of .14.

See Instructor's Section.

9. Which of the following OC curves, both based on an n of 100, has the larger critical value?

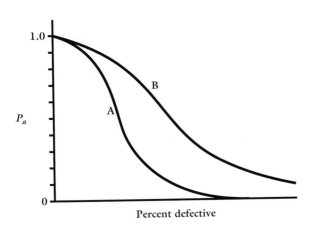

Percent defective

curve B

10. An OC curve is given below for the sampling plan used for bolts that are produced in very large lots.

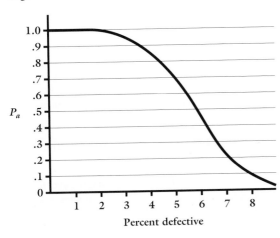

Percent defective

What is the average outgoing quality at 3 percent? at 6 percent?

.0285; .0270

11. Draw the average outgoing quality curve for the bolts produced in the previous problem and find the AOQL. Use the points 0, .01, .02, . . . , .08.

See Instructor's Section for curve; AOQL = 3.5% at $p = .05$.

12. Window glass is cut to specifications and shipped in lots of 100 panes. Suppose that the sample size is 13 panes and that the following table gives the probability of accepting lots as a function of the percent defective. Draw the average outgoing quality curve and find the AOQL.

Percent Defective	P_a
.00	1.00
.01	0.98
.02	0.95
.03	0.90
.04	0.75
.05	0.40
.06	0.15
.07	0.10

See Instructor's Section for curve; AOQL is around 2.6% at $p = .04$.

$n = 315, c = 7$

13. Use MIL-STD-105 to develop a sampling plan for a lot size of 12,000 to achieve an AQL of 1 percent.

14. Suppose that there have been problems with the process in the previous problem. It has been suggested that a tighter inspection system be put into place. Use general inspection level III from MIL-STD-105 to develop the new sampling plan for the window glass.

$n = 500, c = 10$

UCL $= .104$; CL $= .02$; LCL $= 0$

15. Samples of 25 units are taken every half hour. The average percent defective is 2 percent. Construct the 3σ p-chart.

UCL $= .05$; CL $= .013$; LCL $= 0$

16. Over the past month 17,000 parts have been inspected, 221 of which were found to be defective. Construct a 1.96σ (95-percent confidence) p-chart for a sample size of 36 parts.

17. Given below are the results of inspection of samples taken over the past 10 days. Sample size is 100.

Day	Defective
1	7
2	6
3	6
4	9
5	5
6	6
7	0
8	8
9	9
10	1

UCL $= .126$; CL $= .057$; LCL $= 0$

(a) Construct a 3σ p-chart using this information.
(b) If the number of defectives on the next three days are 12, 5, and 13, is the process in control?

no

UCL $= 14.05$ oz.; CL $= 14$ oz.; LCL $= 13.95$ oz.

18. Boxes of Krispy Flakes are produced to contain 14 ounces, with a standard deviation of .1 ounce. Set up the 3σ $\bar{X}$-chart for a sample size of 36 boxes.

19. Desk tops are cut to a target dimension of 3 feet by 5 feet. From past data, the averages have been right on target for both length and width. The average range from samples of $n = 5$ for width has been 2.4 inches, while the average range for the length has been 6 inches. Construct the 3σ $\bar{X}$-charts and the 3σ R-charts for each dimension.

See Instructor's Section.

20. Artillery shells (155 mm) are produced in a forging process, the diameter of the shell is a critical factor that must be controlled. From sample sizes of 10 shells produced each day, the mean and the range of this diameter have been as follows.

Day	Mean	Range
1	156.9	4.2
2	153.2	4.6
3	153.6	4.1
4	155.5	5.0
5	156.6	4.5

$\bar{X}$-chart: UCL $= 156.54$ mm; CL $= 155.16$ mm; LCL $= 153.78$ mm
R-chart: UCL $= 7.96$ mm; CL $= 4.48$ mm; LCL $= 1$mm

Construct the 3σ $\bar{X}$-chart and the 3σ R-chart for this dimension.

COMPUTER CASE STUDY 17.1: GREEN RIVER CHEMICAL COMPANY

Green River Chemical Company has had complaints from its customers regarding the sulfate content of its product. Every customer allows some sulfate content, but theoretically there should be none. The usual customer specification is 90 parts per million (PPM) sulfate.

The quality control department at Green River feels that there is no problem with sulfate content, which has been averaging just over 50 PPM. The production department estimates that a substantial investment would be required to lower the amount of this contaminant in the product. These two departments, after consulting with the marketing department and customers, suggest that a control chart be set up to monitor sulfate content. Five samples will be tested per day and plotted as one point on the chart.

Use the data in Table 17.8 to set up the control limits. Then, after the limits are in place for this process, use Table 17.9 to determine whether or not the process remains in control for the week of April 6–10.

TABLE 17.8 Original Green River Chemical Company data

Date		Sample 1	2	3	4	5	$\overline{X}$	R
March	2	57	54	62	45	36	50.8	26
	3	56	54	47	42	62	52.2	20
	4	40	70	58	45	44	51.4	30
	5	52	58	40	52	46	49.6	18
	6	57	42	52	58	59	53.6	17
	9	62	49	42	33	55	48.2	29
	10	40	39	49	59	48	47.0	20
	11	64	50	42	57	50	52.6	22
	12	58	53	52	48	50	52.2	10
	13	60	50	41	41	50	48.4	19
	16	52	47	48	58	40	49.0	18
	17	55	40	56	49	45	49.0	16
	18	47	48	50	50	48	48.6	3
	19	50	50	49	51	51	50.2	2
	20	51	50	51	51	62	53.0	12
	23	51	50	49	50	50	50.0	2
	24	45	47	70	46	36	48.8	34
	25	50	35	48	39	47	43.8	15
	26	55	70	50	30	51	51.2	40
	27	49	38	64	36	47	46.8	28
	30	59	62	40	54	64	55.8	24
	31	36	33	49	48	56	44.4	23
April	1	50	67	53	43	40	50.6	27
	2	44	52	46	47	44	46.6	8
	3	70	45	50	47	41	50.6	29

TABLE 17.9 Data for week of April 6–10

Date	Sample				
	1	2	3	4	5
April 6	63	49	50	45	53
7	57	70	45	52	61
8	45	38	46	54	52
9	48	52	39	57	61
10	45	53	48	46	66

Does the process remain in control? Does the data for the month of March appear to be in control?

REFERENCES

Besterfield, D. H. *Quality Control*. Englewood Cliffs, N.J.: Prentice-Hall, 1986.

Crosby, P. B. *Quality Is Free*. New York: Mentor, 1979.

Deming, W. Edwards. *Quality, Productivity and Competitive Position*. Cambridge, Mass.: MIT Press, 1982.

Diprimio, A. *Quality Assurance in Service Organizations*. Radnor, Penn.: Chilton Book Company, 1987.

Duncan, A. J. *Quality Control and Industrial Statistics*. 5th ed. Homewood, Ill.: Irwin, 1986.

Gitlow, H. S., and S. J. Gitlow. *The Deming Guide to Quality and Competitive Position*. Englewood Cliffs, N.J.: Prentice-Hall, 1987.

Juran, J. M. *Quality Control Handbook*. New York: McGraw-Hill, 1974.

Juran, J. M., and F. M. Gryna. *Quality Planning and Analysis*. New York: McGraw-Hill, 1980.

Montgomery, D. C. *Introduction to Statistical Quality Control*. New York: John Wiley and Sons, 1985.

Rosander, A. C. *Applications of Quality Control in the Service Industries*. New York: Marcel Dekker Inc., 1985.

Sinha, M. N., and W. O. Willborn. *The Management of Quality Assurance*. New York: John Wiley and Sons, 1985.

APPENDIXES

A P P E N D I X
A

CAPITAL
INVESTMENT

- To explain the time value of money
- To demonstrate the use of present value in assessing the cost (in today's dollars) of an investment
- To present the means for analyzing capital investment alternatives
- To show the effect of taxes (and depreciation) on investments
- To present common examples of the complete investment analysis

INTRODUCTION

financial decisions

Many of the decisions faced by an operations manager involve the investment of capital. Typically, several options may be available for accomplishing the same task. For example, a hospital operations manager may need to choose between investing money in new laundry facilities or contracting laundry to a private service. An airline's operations manager may be faced with a choice between two types of aircraft. The operations manager of a bank may need to decide between an automated teller machine and a drive-in window. A production supervisor may need to choose between buying or leasing a delivery vehicle. Although cost will not be the only criterion for making these decisions, it obviously is one of the most important. Even though understanding the details of capital investment involves familiarity with concepts from the fields of finance and accounting, operations managers must be able to identify the dollar effects of their decisions. Furthermore, it is imperative that finance managers understand the effects of financial decisions on operations.

As indicated by the examples just given, our main concern is with medium- to long-term capital investments. In Chapter 3, the decision-making tools that were introduced did not specifically take into account the length of time of the investment, which is what we address here. It will be necessary to begin each analysis by identifying the expenditures and/or revenues (cash flow) that result from each alternative. Because this will represent a flow of money over periods of time (months, years), it will be necessary to include the time value of money in the decision-making process.

In the next section, we define the time value of money. Then we define the decision-making criteria that are based on the time value of money. Later, tax and depreciation are introduced, because taxes represent an outflow of funds that is offset by the purchase (and depreciation) of equipment or services.

TIME VALUE OF MONEY

Teaching Suggestion A.1: Reality: Student Perceptions. See the Instructor's Section for details.

Given a choice between receiving a gift of $100 today or the same gift one year from today, most sane people would choose to receive the gift today. Thus, a dollar is not always a dollar; its worth depends on when it is received or paid. This is the **time value**

of money. The value of money changes over time for three reasons: interest, inflation, and risk. In our example, the lucky recipient could put the money in a savings account and earn $6 in interest for the year. At the end of the year, the recipient would have $106, which would be preferable to the alternative of receiving $100 then. Alternatively, the recipient could spend the $100 and, due to inflation, could purchase more today than one year from today. Lastly, the recipient might feel that "a bird in the hand is worth two in the bush" and prefer to grab the $100 today, rather than risk not being able to get this same amount of money in one year.

Our concern here is with the first consideration—namely, interest. Discussions of inflation and risk are left to textbooks in other disciplines. Essentially, there are two concepts to consider in relation to the time value of money. These are the future amounts that one dollar today will yield, or the **future value,** and the **present value** of one dollar when it is received or paid in the future. Both concepts are founded on the notion of **compound interest.**

COMPOUND INTEREST

The time horizons of the various alternatives that must be compared may be different. It is necessary for decision makers to be able to compare, for example, the "value" of a machine that is expected to last three years against the "value" of a machine that is expected to last five years. The analysis begins with the concept of compound interest. Consider the following example, which demonstrates the compounding process.

Example A.1   Gyro Electric Company (GEC) has invested $10,000 in a sevenyear savings certificate. The interest rate is fixed at 10 percent per year, and interest is compounded annually. What is the value of the certificate when it matures at the end of seven years?

This problem is very simple. The interest after one year is 10 percent of $10,000, or $1,000. Thus, after one year, the certificate is worth $10,000 + $1,000 = $11,000. The interest during the second year is 10 percent of $11,000, or $1,100. Thus, after two years, the certificate is worth $11,000 + $1,100 = $12,100. The interest during the third year is 10 percent of $12,100, or $1,210, so the certificate is worth $12,100 + $1,210 = $13,310 after the third year. The remaining computations are summarized in Table A.1, where it can be seen that, in seven years, the value of the certificate is nearly double its original value. ■

The implication of Example A.1 is that GEC is indifferent as to whether it receives $10,000 today that will be invested in a 10-percent, seven-year certificate or $19,448 seven years from today. Alternatively, seven years from today, $19,488 may be equal in worth to only $10,000 in today's money (presuming that the interest rate remains fixed at 10 percent per year).

The general formula for finding the future amount of money that a sum will compound to is

$$FV = PV(1 + i)^n,$$

TABLE A.1 Interest computations for savings certificate (Example A.1)

Year	Beginning Amount	Interest 10% × Beginning Amount	Ending Amount
1	$10,000	$1,000	$11,000
2	11,000	1,100	12,100
3	12,100	1,210	13,310
4	13,310	1,331	14,641
5	14,641	1,464	16,105
6	16,105	1,611	17,716
7	17,716	1,772	19,488

where

FV (future value) of a single payment is the amount of money that will be available in the future;

PV (present value) of a single payment is the amount of money invested today;

n is the number of interest periods; and

i is the interest rate per period.

Applying the formula to our example, in which PV = $10,000, i = 10%, and n = 7, we have

$$FV = \$10,000(1 + .10)^7 = \$10,000(1.9488) = \$19,488.$$

Teaching Suggestion A.2:
Effects of Compounding.
See the Instructor's Section for details.

In order to make computations easier, the values $(1 + i)^n$ are presented in Table A.2. The values $(1 + i)^n$ are termed the **compound value of a single payment** ($CVSP$) and indicate what one dollar will grow to when compounded for n periods at interest rate i; that is,

compound value factor of a single payment

$$CVSP(i, n) = (1 + i)^n.$$

To find the future value (FV), we simply multiply the present value (PV) by the appropriate factor found in the table. For example, assume $5,000 is invested at 12-percent interest for four years. From the compound interest table, we see that $(1 + .12)^4$ is equal to 1.574 (row 4, column 12%), which means that the $5,000 grows to $5,000 × 1.574 = $7,870.

The relationship between the future value, the interest rate, and time can be expressed graphically. Figure A.1 demonstrates the value of money over time for selected interest rates. Curves could be drawn for any interest rate, but we have chosen 0 percent, 10 percent, 15 percent, and 20 percent. The figure graphs how one dollar grows in value over time. As the interest rate increases, so does the value of the money. Similarly, the longer the period of time, the greater the value of the money. If the initial amount is PV, then the future amount is simply the compound value of one dollar ($CVSP$) multiplied by the present amount (PV).

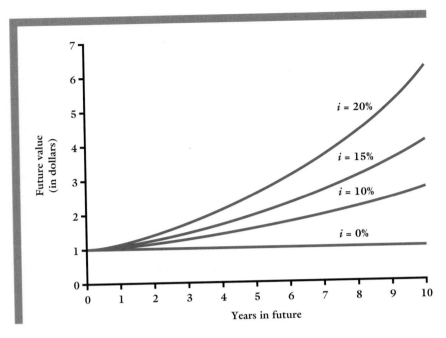

FIGURE A.1 Future value of one dollar (n years in future at interest rate i)

PRESENT VALUE

We have indicated that the value of money changes over time and that the relationship of money to time can be viewed through the compound interest process. There is an alternative way to express this relationship. Because money in the future is worth less than the same amount today, we can **discount** the money and find its present value. That is, given some amount of money, FV, received n years in the future, how much money would we need to invest today, PV, at interest rate i, in order to end up with the future amount, FV?

Since the formula for compounding is given as

$$FV = PV(1 + i)^n,$$

it must be true that

$$PV = \frac{FV}{(1 + i)^n}.$$

present value

To put it another way, the present value (PV) is the future amount (FV) multiplied by the factor $1/(1 + i)^n$. Hence, to find the present value given the future sums, this formula can be used as shown in the following example.

Example A.2 Four years from today, a payment of $7,000 is to be made. The interest rate is 12 percent. Find the present value (in today's dollars).

TABLE A.2 Compound value factors

Number of Years	.01	.02	.03	.04	.05	.06	.07	.08	.09	.10	.11	.12	.13
1	1.010	1.020	1.030	1.040	1.050	1.060	1.070	1.080	1.090	1.100	1.110	1.120	1.130
2	1.020	1.040	1.061	1.082	1.103	1.124	1.145	1.166	1.188	1.210	1.232	1.254	1.277
3	1.030	1.061	1.093	1.125	1.158	1.191	1.225	1.260	1.295	1.331	1.368	1.405	1.443
4	1.041	1.082	1.126	1.170	1.216	1.262	1.311	1.360	1.412	1.464	1.518	1.574	1.630
5	1.051	1.104	1.159	1.217	1.276	1.338	1.403	1.469	1.539	1.611	1.685	1.762	1.842
6	1.062	1.126	1.194	1.265	1.340	1.419	1.501	1.587	1.677	1.772	1.870	1.974	2.082
7	1.072	1.149	1.230	1.316	1.407	1.504	1.606	1.714	1.828	1.949	2.076	2.211	2.353
8	1.083	1.172	1.267	1.369	1.477	1.594	1.718	1.851	1.993	2.144	2.305	2.476	2.658
9	1.094	1.195	1.305	1.423	1.551	1.689	1.838	1.999	2.172	2.358	2.558	2.773	3.004
10	1.105	1.219	1.344	1.480	1.629	1.791	1.967	2.159	2.367	2.594	2.839	3.106	3.395
11	1.116	1.243	1.384	1.539	1.710	1.898	2.105	2.332	2.580	2.853	3.152	3.479	3.836
12	1.127	1.268	1.426	1.601	1.796	2.012	2.252	2.518	2.813	3.138	3.498	3.896	4.335
13	1.138	1.294	1.469	1.665	1.886	2.133	2.410	2.720	3.066	3.452	3.883	4.363	4.898
14	1.149	1.319	1.513	1.732	1.980	2.261	2.579	2.937	3.342	3.797	4.310	4.887	5.535
15	1.161	1.346	1.558	1.801	2.079	2.397	2.759	3.172	3.642	4.177	4.785	5.474	6.254
16	1.173	1.373	1.605	1.873	2.183	2.540	2.952	3.426	3.970	4.595	5.311	6.130	7.067
17	1.184	1.400	1.653	1.948	2.292	2.693	3.159	3.700	4.328	5.054	5.895	6.866	7.986
18	1.196	1.428	1.702	2.026	2.407	2.854	3.380	3.996	4.717	5.560	6.544	7.690	9.024
19	1.208	1.457	1.754	2.107	2.527	3.026	3.617	4.316	5.142	6.116	7.263	8.613	10.197
20	1.220	1.486	1.806	2.191	2.653	3.207	3.870	4.661	5.604	6.727	8.062	9.646	11.523
21	1.232	1.516	1.860	2.279	2.786	3.400	4.141	5.034	6.109	7.400	8.949	10.804	13.021
22	1.245	1.546	1.916	2.370	2.925	3.604	4.430	5.437	6.659	8.140	9.934	12.100	14.714
23	1.257	1.577	1.974	2.465	3.072	3.820	4.741	5.871	7.258	8.954	11.026	13.552	16.627
24	1.270	1.608	2.033	2.563	3.225	4.049	5.072	6.341	7.911	9.850	12.239	15.179	18.788
25	1.282	1.641	2.094	2.666	3.386	4.292	5.427	6.848	8.623	10.835	13.585	17.000	21.231
26	1.295	1.673	2.157	2.772	3.556	4.549	5.807	7.396	9.399	11.918	15.080	19.040	23.991
27	1.308	1.707	2.221	2.883	3.733	4.822	6.214	7.988	10.245	13.110	16.739	21.325	27.109
28	1.321	1.741	2.288	2.999	3.920	5.112	6.649	8.627	11.167	14.421	18.580	23.884	30.633
29	1.335	1.776	2.357	3.119	4.116	5.418	7.114	9.317	12.172	15.863	20.624	26.750	34.616
30	1.348	1.811	2.427	3.243	4.322	5.743	7.612	10.063	13.268	17.449	22.892	29.960	39.116
31	1.361	1.848	2.500	3.373	4.538	6.088	8.145	10.868	14.462	19.194	25.410	33.555	44.201
32	1.375	1.885	2.575	3.508	4.765	6.453	8.715	11.737	15.763	21.114	28.206	37.582	49.947
33	1.389	1.922	2.652	3.648	5.003	6.841	9.325	12.676	17.182	23.225	31.308	42.092	56.440
34	1.403	1.961	2.732	3.794	5.253	7.251	9.978	13.690	18.728	25.548	34.752	47.143	63.777
35	1.417	2.000	2.814	3.946	5.516	7.686	10.677	14.785	20.414	28.102	38.575	52.800	72.069
36	1.431	2.040	2.898	4.104	5.792	8.147	11.424	15.968	22.251	30.913	42.818	59.136	81.437

Number of Years						Interest Rate						
	.14	.15	.16	.17	.18	.19	.20	.21	.22	.23	.24	.25
1	1.140	1.150	1.160	1.170	1.180	1.190	1.200	1.210	1.220	1.230	1.240	1.250
2	1.300	1.323	1.346	1.369	1.392	1.416	1.440	1.464	1.488	1.513	1.538	1.563
3	1.482	1.521	1.561	1.602	1.643	1.685	1.728	1.772	1.816	1.861	1.907	1.953
4	1.689	1.749	1.811	1.874	1.939	2.005	2.074	2.144	2.215	2.289	2.364	2.441
5	1.925	2.011	2.100	2.192	2.288	2.386	2.488	2.594	2.703	2.815	2.932	3.052
6	2.195	2.313	2.436	2.565	2.700	2.840	2.986	3.138	3.297	3.463	3.635	3.815
7	2.502	2.660	2.826	3.001	3.185	3.379	3.583	3.797	4.023	4.259	4.508	4.768
8	2.853	3.059	3.278	3.511	3.759	4.021	4.300	4.595	4.908	5.239	5.590	5.960
9	3.252	3.518	3.803	4.108	4.435	4.785	5.160	5.560	5.987	6.444	6.931	7.451
10	3.707	4.046	4.411	4.807	5.234	5.695	6.192	6.727	7.305	7.926	8.594	9.313
11	4.226	4.652	5.117	5.624	6.176	6.777	7.430	8.140	8.912	9.749	10.657	11.642
12	4.818	5.350	5.936	6.580	7.288	8.064	8.916	9.850	10.872	11.991	13.215	14.552
13	5.492	6.153	6.886	7.699	8.599	9.596	10.699	11.918	13.264	14.749	16.386	18.190
14	6.261	7.076	7.988	9.007	10.147	11.420	12.839	14.421	16.182	18.141	20.319	22.737
15	7.138	8.137	9.266	10.539	11.974	13.590	15.407	17.449	19.742	22.314	25.196	28.422
16	8.137	9.358	10.748	12.330	14.129	16.172	18.488	21.114	24.086	27.446	31.243	35.527
17	9.276	10.761	12.468	14.426	16.672	19.244	22.186	25.548	29.384	33.759	38.741	44.409
18	10.575	12.375	14.463	16.879	19.673	22.901	26.623	30.913	35.849	41.523	48.039	55.511
19	12.056	14.232	16.777	19.748	23.214	27.252	31.948	37.404	43.736	51.074	59.568	69.389
20	13.743	16.367	19.461	23.106	27.393	32.429	38.338	45.259	53.358	62.821	73.864	86.736
21	15.668	18.822	22.574	27.034	32.324	38.591	46.005	54.764	65.096	77.269	91.592	108.420
22	17.861	21.645	26.186	31.629	38.142	45.923	55.206	66.264	79.418	95.041	113.574	135.525
23	20.362	24.891	30.376	37.006	45.008	54.649	66.247	80.180	96.889	116.901	140.831	169.407
24	23.212	28.625	35.236	43.297	53.109	65.032	79.497	97.017	118.205	143.788	174.631	211.758
25	26.462	32.919	40.874	50.658	62.669	77.388	95.396	117.391	144.210	176.859	216.542	264.698
26	30.167	37.857	47.414	59.270	73.949	92.092	114.475	142.043	175.936	217.537	268.512	330.872
27	34.390	43.535	55.000	69.345	87.260	109.589	137.371	171.872	214.642	267.570	332.955	413.590
28	39.204	50.066	63.800	81.134	102.967	130.411	164.845	207.965	261.864	329.112	412.864	516.988
29	44.693	57.575	74.009	94.927	121.501	155.189	197.814	251.638	319.474	404.807	511.952	646.235
30	50.950	66.212	85.850	111.065	143.371	184.675	237.376	304.482	389.758	497.913	634.820	807.794
31	58.083	76.144	99.586	129.946	169.177	219.764	284.852	368.423	475.505	612.433	787.177	1009.742
32	66.215	87.565	115.520	152.036	199.629	261.519	341.822	445.792	580.116	753.292	976.099	1262.177
33	75.485	100.700	134.003	177.883	235.563	311.207	410.186	539.408	707.741	926.550	1210.363	1577.722
34	86.053	115.805	155.443	208.123	277.964	370.337	492.224	652.683	863.444	1139.656	1500.850	1972.152
35	98.100	133.176	180.314	243.503	327.997	440.701	590.668	789.747	1053.402	1401.777	1861.054	2465.190
36	111.834	153.152	209.164	284.899	387.037	524.434	708.802	955.594	1285.150	1724.186	2307.707	3081.488

$$PV = \frac{\$7,000}{(1 + .12)^4} = \frac{\$7,000}{1.574} = \$4,447$$

The present value is simply the amount of money needed today in order to end up with the given future value n periods in the future when the interest rate is i. Again, to make computations easier, Table A.3 contains the **present value of a single payment** ($PVSP$) factors, or discount factors for one dollar given by the formula

present value of a single payment

$$PVSP(i, n) = \frac{1}{(1 + i)^n}.$$

Figure A.2 shows the discount process over time at 0-percent, 10-percent, 15-percent, and 20-percent interest rates. The present value is seen to be decreasing over time; the farther into the future that money is received, the less we need now to compound to that sum. Also, the present value decreases more quickly as the interest rate increases—in other words, the higher the interest rate, the less money needed to compound to the sum. As with compound interest, the present value of an amount FV is simply the present value of one dollar ($PVSP$) times the amount FV.

There are two additional properties of compounding and discounting that are useful to know. The first is that the relationship between the compound value factors and the present value factors is reciprocal. The present value single payment ($PVSP$) factor and the future (compound) value single payment factor ($CVSP$) are related as follows:

$$PVSP(i, n) = \frac{1}{CVSP(i, n)}$$

FIGURE A.2 Present value of one dollar (n years in future at interest rate i)

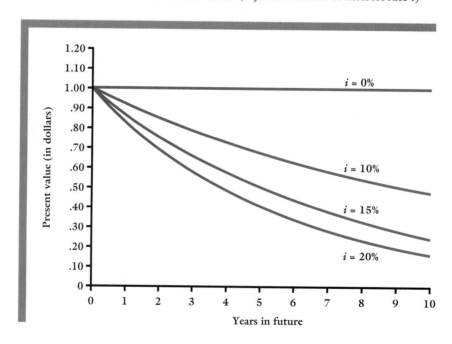

and

$$CVSP(i, n) = \frac{1}{PVSP(i, n)}.$$

For example, since the compound value factor of one dollar at 10-percent interest over three years is given in Table A.2 as 1.331, it follows that the present value factor for one dollar at 10-percent interest over three years is given by

$$PVSP(10\%, 3 \text{ years}) = \frac{1}{1.331} = .751.$$

This can be verified in Table A.3.

The second property is that the compound value factor for n years can be computed as the product of the compound value for n_1 years times the compound factor value for n_2 years provided that $n = n_1 + n_2$. For example, we can compute $CVSP$ ($i = 10\%$, $n = 4$ years) as **time periods not in table**

$$CVSP(10\%, 4) = CVSP(10\%, 3) \times CVSP(10\%, 1)$$

or

$$CVSP(10\%, 4) = CVSP(10\%, 2) \times CVSP(10\%, 2)$$

Take some time to verify this. The usefulness of this property should be apparent: It allows the computation of compound value factors when n is not in the table.

Because present value factors are reciprocals of future value factors, it follows that the same property applies to present value factors. So, if $n = n_1 + n_2$, then

$$PVSP(i, n) = PVSP(i, n_1) \times PVSP(i, n_2).$$

ANNUITIES

Our discussion to this point has focused on single payments. However, we ultimately need to evaluate a flow of payments or receipts. Often, the flow of money paid or received each period is the same. This typically is true in the case of a lease or repayment of a loan. When the cash flow is identical in each period (and the interest rate remains fixed) the flow is termed an **annuity.** More precisely, we define an n-year annuity as an amount of money paid (or received) at the *end* of each year for n years at a specific interest rate. For example, a six-year annuity of $5,000 means that a total of $30,000 will be paid in six equal installments beginning in one year. The following example presents an analysis of an annuity.

Example A.3 Cedars Hospital contracts its laundry operations at a cost of $30,000 per year. Payments on the hospital's three-year contract are made at the end of each year. The hospital would like to know the present value cost of the contract. The interest rate is 17 percent.

The cash flow appears on page 846.

TABLE A.3 Present value factors

Number of Years	.01	.02	.03	.04	.05	.06	.07	.08	.09	.10	.11	.12	.13
1	.990	.980	.971	.962	.952	.943	.935	.926	.917	.909	.901	.893	.885
2	.980	.961	.943	.925	.907	.890	.873	.857	.842	.826	.812	.797	.783
3	.971	.942	.915	.889	.864	.840	.816	.794	.772	.751	.731	.712	.693
4	.961	.924	.888	.855	.823	.792	.763	.735	.708	.683	.659	.636	.613
5	.951	.906	.863	.822	.784	.747	.713	.681	.650	.621	.593	.567	.543
6	.942	.888	.837	.790	.746	.705	.666	.630	.596	.564	.535	.507	.480
7	.933	.871	.813	.760	.711	.665	.623	.583	.547	.513	.482	.452	.425
8	.923	.853	.789	.731	.677	.627	.582	.540	.502	.467	.434	.404	.376
9	.914	.837	.766	.703	.645	.592	.544	.500	.460	.424	.391	.361	.333
10	.905	.820	.744	.676	.614	.558	.508	.463	.422	.386	.352	.322	.295
11	.896	.804	.722	.650	.585	.527	.475	.429	.388	.350	.317	.287	.261
12	.887	.788	.701	.625	.557	.497	.444	.397	.356	.319	.286	.257	.231
13	.879	.773	.681	.601	.530	.469	.415	.368	.326	.290	.258	.229	.204
14	.870	.758	.661	.577	.505	.442	.388	.340	.299	.263	.232	.205	.181
15	.861	.743	.642	.555	.481	.417	.362	.315	.275	.239	.209	.183	.160
16	.853	.728	.623	.534	.458	.394	.339	.292	.252	.218	.188	.163	.141
17	.844	.714	.605	.513	.436	.371	.317	.270	.231	.198	.170	.146	.125
18	.836	.700	.587	.494	.416	.350	.296	.250	.212	.180	.153	.130	.111
19	.828	.686	.570	.475	.396	.331	.277	.232	.194	.164	.138	.116	.098
20	.820	.673	.554	.456	.377	.312	.258	.215	.178	.149	.124	.104	.087
21	.811	.660	.538	.439	.359	.294	.242	.199	.164	.135	.112	.093	.077
22	.803	.647	.522	.422	.342	.278	.226	.184	.150	.123	.101	.083	.068
23	.795	.634	.507	.406	.326	.262	.211	.170	.138	.112	.091	.074	.060
24	.788	.622	.492	.390	.310	.247	.197	.158	.126	.102	.082	.066	.053
25	.780	.610	.478	.375	.295	.233	.184	.146	.116	.092	.074	.059	.047
26	.772	.598	.464	.361	.281	.220	.172	.135	.106	.084	.066	.053	.042
27	.764	.586	.450	.347	.268	.207	.161	.125	.098	.076	.060	.047	.037
28	.757	.574	.437	.333	.255	.196	.150	.116	.090	.069	.054	.042	.033
29	.749	.563	.424	.321	.243	.185	.141	.107	.082	.063	.048	.037	.029
30	.742	.552	.412	.308	.231	.174	.131	.099	.075	.057	.044	.033	.026
31	.735	.541	.400	.296	.220	.164	.123	.092	.069	.052	.039	.030	.023
32	.727	.531	.388	.285	.210	.155	.115	.085	.063	.047	.035	.027	.020
33	.720	.520	.377	.274	.200	.146	.107	.079	.058	.043	.032	.024	.018
34	.713	.510	.366	.264	.190	.138	.100	.073	.053	.039	.029	.021	.016
35	.706	.500	.355	.253	.181	.130	.094	.068	.049	.036	.026	.019	.014
36	.699	.490	.345	.244	.173	.123	.088	.063	.045	.032	.023	.017	.012

Number of Years	Interest Rate											
	.14	.15	.16	.17	.18	.19	.20	.21	.22	.23	.24	.25
1	.877	.870	.862	.855	.847	.840	.833	.826	.820	.813	.806	.800
2	.769	.756	.743	.731	.718	.706	.694	.683	.672	.661	.650	.640
3	.675	.658	.641	.624	.609	.593	.579	.564	.551	.537	.524	.512
4	.592	.572	.552	.534	.516	.499	.482	.467	.451	.437	.423	.410
5	.519	.497	.476	.456	.437	.419	.402	.386	.370	.355	.341	.328
6	.456	.432	.410	.390	.370	.352	.335	.319	.303	.289	.275	.262
7	.400	.376	.354	.333	.314	.296	.279	.263	.249	.235	.222	.210
8	.351	.327	.305	.285	.266	.249	.233	.218	.204	.191	.179	.168
9	.308	.284	.263	.243	.225	.209	.194	.180	.167	.155	.144	.134
10	.270	.247	.227	.208	.191	.176	.162	.149	.137	.126	.116	.107
11	.237	.215	.195	.178	.162	.148	.135	.123	.112	.103	.094	.086
12	.208	.187	.168	.152	.137	.124	.112	.102	.092	.083	.076	.069
13	.182	.163	.145	.130	.116	.104	.093	.084	.075	.068	.061	.055
14	.160	.141	.125	.111	.099	.088	.078	.069	.062	.055	.049	.044
15	.140	.123	.108	.095	.084	.074	.065	.057	.051	.045	.040	.035
16	.123	.107	.093	.081	.071	.062	.054	.047	.042	.036	.032	.028
17	.108	.093	.080	.069	.060	.052	.045	.039	.034	.030	.026	.023
18	.095	.081	.069	.059	.051	.044	.038	.032	.028	.024	.021	.018
19	.083	.070	.060	.051	.043	.037	.031	.027	.023	.020	.017	.014
20	.073	.061	.051	.043	.037	.031	.026	.022	.019	.016	.014	.012
21	.064	.053	.044	.037	.031	.026	.022	.018	.015	.013	.011	.009
22	.056	.046	.038	.032	.026	.022	.018	.015	.013	.011	.009	.007
23	.049	.040	.033	.027	.022	.018	.015	.012	.010	.009	.007	.006
24	.043	.035	.028	.023	.019	.015	.013	.010	.008	.007	.006	.005
25	.038	.030	.024	.020	.016	.013	.010	.009	.007	.006	.005	.004
26	.033	.026	.021	.017	.014	.011	.009	.007	.006	.005	.004	.003
27	.029	.023	.018	.014	.011	.009	.007	.006	.005	.004	.003	.002
28	.026	.020	.016	.012	.010	.008	.006	.005	.004	.003	.002	.002
29	.022	.017	.014	.011	.008	.006	.005	.004	.003	.002	.002	.002
30	.020	.015	.012	.009	.007	.005	.004	.003	.003	.002	.002	.001
31	.017	.013	.010	.008	.006	.005	.004	.003	.002	.002	.001	.001
32	.015	.011	.009	.007	.005	.004	.003	.002	.002	.001	.001	.001
33	.013	.010	.007	.006	.004	.003	.002	.002	.001	.001	.001	.001
34	.012	.009	.006	.005	.004	.003	.002	.002	.001	.001	.001	.001
35	.010	.008	.006	.004	.003	.002	.002	.001	.001	.001	.001	.000
36	.009	.007	.005	.004	.003	.002	.001	.001	.001	.001	.000	.000

End of Year	Payment	PVSP (17%, n) (Table A.3)	Present Value of Payment
1	$30,000	.855	$25,650
2	30,000	.731	21,930
3	30,000	.624	18,720
		Total 2.210	$66,300

Thus, the total amount required today in order to pay the contract would not be $90,000; instead, it would be $66,300. ◾

Rather than finding the present value for each year and then adding these values, as was done in the preceding example, it is possible to simply use Table A.4, which contains the present value of an annuity of one dollar for n periods with an interest rate i, which is denoted by $PVA(i, n)$. For the example, the number in this table (row 3, column 17%) is 2.210; hence, the present value of the annuity is the payment amount times the annuity factor, or $30,000(2.210) = $66,300. Notice that the numbers in the annuity table (Table A.4) are simply the sums of the first n terms of the numbers in the single payment table (Table A.3). For example, at 17-percent interest, 2.210 = .855 + .731 + .624. If A is the payment of an n-year annuity, then its present value, PV, is given by

Teaching Suggestion A.3: Closed-Form Annuity Formula. See the Instructor's Section for details.

$$PV = A\left[\frac{1}{(1 + i)^1} + \frac{1}{(1 + i)^2} + \cdots \frac{1}{(1 + i)^n}\right].$$

The term in brackets in the preceding equation gives the present value of an annuity of one dollar for n years at interest rate i, which we denote by $PVA(i, n)$. The next example indicates how to use the annuity table.

Teaching Suggestion A.4: Annuity Timing. See the Instructor's Section for details.

Example A.4   New furniture has been installed in the main lobby of Merion University. The furniture will last eight years and during this time, maintenance (mostly cleaning) will be contracted at $3,000 per year. The current rate of interest is 18 percent. What is the present value of the expenditures for cleaning the furniture?

This represents an eight-year annuity at 18 percent annual interest and, from Table A.4, we find that the present value factor is 4.078. Hence, the total present value of the cleaning costs is 4.078($3,000) = $12,234. Notice that using the annuity factor implies that the first maintenance payment is made at the end of the first year. ◾

Armed with an understanding of the time value of money—more specifically, the present value of money—we now are prepared to analyze capital investments.

INVESTMENT ANALYSIS

Often, we will have several means to accomplish the same task. For example, we can buy equipment or we can lease it. Also, we can choose from among different types of equipment. Each option will involve a different amount of money to be paid or received in each year. The amount of money we receive or disburse in each year is termed the **cash flow.** It is desirable for us to have methods for evaluating our options financially. We emphasize, though, that the final decision is not based solely on financial data. Our methods of ranking here are primarily predicated on the present value of the cash flow; however, in our section on payback, we offer one widely used measure that does not discount the cash flow.

NET PRESENT VALUE

In this section, we present the most basic measure of investment analysis: **net present value** *(NPV).* Net present value will form the foundation for the two measures that follow—namely, equivalent annual cost and internal rate of return.

basic measure of investment analysis

Net present value is defined as the total of the present values of the cash flow. One simply takes the present value of each amount (cost or revenue) in the cash flow and sums these numbers. We actually have computed net present value already (see Example A.3), but we demonstrate the analysis more fully in the next example.

Example A.5   Xpress Inc. is considering the purchase of a new delivery vehicle and would like to decide which of two models to buy. The data are given in the following table. Notice that the GM van would be used for five years, while the Ford van would be used for four years. Of course, the fact that the vans last for a different number of years means that we will have to be careful when comparing their costs. The cost of money is assumed to be 20 percent. Find the net present value cost for each of the two vans.

	GM	Ford
Initial cost (purchase price)	$17,000	$15,000
Operating expenses		
Year 1	$800	$1,000
Year 2	$900	$1,000
Year 3	$1,000	$1,000
Year 4	$1,100	$1,000
Year 5	$1,200	
Salvage value	$3,000	$2,000

In order to aid in the decision of which of the two vehicles should be chosen, for each van we must compute the net present value of the total cost of the van—that is, purchase price *plus* operating expenses *less* salvage. The computations are given in Table A.5. Each item in the cash flow is multiplied by the appropriate present value of a single payment factor. The salvage is negative because this is a cost analysis and the salvage is an inflow.   ∎

Notice that the computations for the Ford can actually be done more easily because the maintenance cost is an annuity. The computation is given on page 850.

TABLE A.4   Present value of annuity factors

Number of Years	.01	.02	.03	.04	.05	.06	.07	.08	.09	.10	.11	.12	.13
1	.990	.980	.971	.962	.952	.943	.935	.926	.917	.909	.901	.893	.885
2	1.970	1.942	1.913	1.886	1.859	1.833	1.808	1.783	1.759	1.736	1.713	1.690	1.668
3	2.941	2.884	2.829	2.775	2.723	2.673	2.624	2.577	2.531	2.487	2.444	2.402	2.361
4	3.902	3.808	3.717	3.630	3.546	3.465	3.387	3.312	3.240	3.170	3.102	3.037	2.974
5	4.853	4.713	4.580	4.452	4.329	4.212	4.100	3.993	3.890	3.791	3.696	3.605	3.517
6	5.795	5.601	5.417	5.242	5.076	4.917	4.767	4.623	4.486	4.355	4.231	4.111	3.998
7	6.728	6.472	6.230	6.002	5.786	5.582	5.389	5.206	5.033	4.868	4.712	4.564	4.423
8	7.652	7.325	7.020	6.733	6.463	6.210	5.971	5.747	5.535	5.335	5.146	4.968	4.799
9	8.566	8.162	7.786	7.435	7.108	6.802	6.515	6.247	5.995	5.759	5.537	5.328	5.132
10	9.471	8.983	8.530	8.111	7.722	7.360	7.024	6.710	6.418	6.145	5.889	5.650	5.426
11	10.368	9.787	9.253	8.760	8.306	7.887	7.499	7.139	6.805	6.495	6.207	5.938	5.687
12	11.255	10.575	9.954	9.385	8.863	8.384	7.943	7.536	7.161	6.814	6.492	6.194	5.918
13	12.134	11.348	10.635	9.986	9.394	8.853	8.358	7.904	7.487	7.103	6.750	6.424	6.122
14	13.004	12.106	11.296	10.563	9.899	9.295	8.745	8.244	7.786	7.367	6.982	6.628	6.302
15	13.865	12.849	11.938	11.118	10.380	9.712	9.108	8.559	8.061	7.606	7.191	6.811	6.462
16	14.718	13.578	12.561	11.652	10.838	10.106	9.447	8.851	8.313	7.824	7.379	6.974	6.604
17	15.562	14.292	13.166	12.166	11.274	10.477	9.763	9.122	8.544	8.022	7.549	7.120	6.729
18	16.398	14.992	13.754	12.659	11.690	10.828	10.059	9.372	8.756	8.201	7.702	7.250	6.840
19	17.226	15.678	14.324	13.134	12.085	11.158	10.336	9.604	8.950	8.365	7.839	7.366	6.938
20	18.046	16.351	14.877	13.590	12.462	11.470	10.594	9.818	9.129	8.514	7.963	7.469	7.025
21	18.857	17.011	15.415	14.029	12.821	11.764	10.836	10.017	9.292	8.649	8.075	7.562	7.102
22	19.660	17.658	15.937	14.451	13.163	12.042	11.061	10.201	9.442	8.772	8.176	7.645	7.170
23	20.456	18.292	16.444	14.857	13.489	12.303	11.272	10.371	9.580	8.883	8.266	7.718	7.230
24	21.243	18.914	16.936	15.247	13.799	12.550	11.469	10.529	9.707	8.985	8.348	7.784	7.283
25	22.023	19.523	17.413	15.622	14.094	12.783	11.654	10.675	9.823	9.077	8.422	7.843	7.330
26	22.795	20.121	17.877	15.983	14.375	13.003	11.826	10.810	9.929	9.161	8.488	7.896	7.372
27	23.560	20.707	18.327	16.330	14.643	13.211	11.987	10.935	10.027	9.237	8.548	7.943	7.409
28	24.316	21.281	18.764	16.663	14.898	13.406	12.137	11.051	10.116	9.307	8.602	7.984	7.441
29	25.066	21.844	19.188	16.984	15.141	13.591	12.278	11.158	10.198	9.370	8.650	8.022	7.470
30	25.808	22.396	19.600	17.292	15.372	13.765	12.409	11.258	10.274	9.427	8.694	8.055	7.496
31	26.542	22.938	20.000	17.588	15.593	13.929	12.532	11.350	10.343	9.479	8.733	8.085	7.518
32	27.270	23.468	20.389	17.874	15.803	14.084	12.647	11.435	10.406	9.526	8.769	8.112	7.538
33	27.990	23.989	20.766	18.148	16.003	14.230	12.754	11.514	10.464	9.569	8.801	8.135	7.556
34	28.703	24.499	21.132	18.411	16.193	14.368	12.854	11.587	10.518	9.609	8.829	8.157	7.572
35	29.409	24.999	21.487	18.665	16.374	14.498	12.948	11.655	10.567	9.644	8.855	8.176	7.586
36	30.108	25.489	21.832	18.908	16.547	14.621	13.035	11.717	10.612	9.677	8.879	8.192	7.598

Number of Years	Interest Rate											
	.14	.15	.16	.17	.18	.19	.20	.21	.22	.23	.24	.25
1	.877	.870	.862	.855	.847	.840	.833	.826	.820	.813	.806	.800
2	1.647	1.626	1.605	1.585	1.566	1.547	1.528	1.509	1.492	1.474	1.457	1.440
3	2.322	2.283	2.246	2.210	2.174	2.140	2.106	2.074	2.042	2.011	1.981	1.952
4	2.914	2.855	2.798	2.743	2.690	2.639	2.589	2.540	2.494	2.448	2.404	2.362
5	3.433	3.352	3.274	3.199	3.127	3.058	2.991	2.926	2.864	2.803	2.745	2.689
6	3.889	3.784	3.685	3.589	3.498	3.410	3.326	3.245	3.167	3.092	3.020	2.951
7	4.288	4.160	4.039	3.922	3.812	3.706	3.605	3.508	3.416	3.327	3.242	3.161
8	4.639	4.487	4.344	4.207	4.078	3.954	3.837	3.726	3.619	3.518	3.421	3.329
9	4.946	4.772	4.607	4.451	4.303	4.163	4.031	3.905	3.786	3.673	3.566	3.463
10	5.216	5.019	4.833	4.659	4.494	4.339	4.192	4.054	3.923	3.799	3.682	3.571
11	5.453	5.234	5.029	4.836	4.656	4.486	4.327	4.177	4.035	3.902	3.776	3.656
12	5.660	5.421	5.197	4.988	4.793	4.611	4.439	4.278	4.127	3.985	3.851	3.725
13	5.842	5.583	5.342	5.118	4.910	4.715	4.533	4.362	4.203	4.053	3.912	3.780
14	6.002	5.724	5.468	5.229	5.008	4.802	4.611	4.432	4.265	4.108	3.962	3.824
15	6.142	5.847	5.575	5.324	5.092	4.876	4.675	4.489	4.315	4.153	4.001	3.859
16	6.265	5.954	5.668	5.405	5.162	4.938	4.730	4.536	4.357	4.189	4.033	3.887
17	6.373	6.047	5.749	5.475	5.222	4.990	4.775	4.576	4.391	4.219	4.059	3.910
18	6.467	6.128	5.818	5.534	5.273	5.033	4.812	4.608	4.419	4.243	4.080	3.928
19	6.550	6.198	5.877	5.584	5.316	5.070	4.843	4.635	4.442	4.263	4.097	3.942
20	6.623	6.259	5.929	5.628	5.353	5.101	4.870	4.657	4.460	4.279	4.110	3.954
21	6.687	6.312	5.973	5.665	5.384	5.127	4.891	4.675	4.476	4.292	4.121	3.963
22	6.743	6.359	6.011	5.696	5.410	5.149	4.909	4.690	4.488	4.302	4.130	3.970
23	6.792	6.399	6.044	5.723	5.432	5.167	4.925	4.703	4.499	4.311	4.137	3.976
24	6.835	6.434	6.073	5.746	5.451	5.182	4.937	4.713	4.507	4.318	4.143	3.981
25	6.873	6.464	6.097	5.766	5.467	5.195	4.948	4.721	4.514	4.323	4.147	3.985
26	6.906	6.491	6.118	5.783	5.480	5.206	4.956	4.728	4.520	4.328	4.151	3.988
27	6.935	6.514	6.136	5.798	5.492	5.215	4.964	4.734	4.524	4.332	4.154	3.990
28	6.961	6.534	6.152	5.810	5.502	5.223	4.970	4.739	4.528	4.335	4.157	3.992
29	6.983	6.551	6.166	5.820	5.510	5.229	4.975	4.743	4.531	4.337	4.159	3.994
30	7.003	6.566	6.177	5.829	5.517	5.235	4.979	4.746	4.534	4.339	4.160	3.995
31	7.020	6.579	6.187	5.837	5.523	5.239	4.982	4.749	4.536	4.341	4.161	3.996
32	7.035	6.591	6.196	5.844	5.528	5.243	4.985	4.751	4.538	4.342	4.162	3.997
33	7.048	6.600	6.203	5.849	5.532	5.246	4.988	4.753	4.539	4.343	4.163	3.997
34	7.060	6.609	6.210	5.854	5.536	5.249	4.990	4.755	4.540	4.344	4.164	3.998
35	7.070	6.617	6.215	5.858	5.539	5.251	4.992	4.756	4.541	4.345	4.164	3.998
36	7.079	6.623	6.220	5.862	5.541	5.253	4.993	4.757	4.542	4.345	4.165	3.999

TABLE A.5 Xpress Inc.: net present value analyses (Example A.5)

GM van

Year	Payment	Present Value Factor for a Single Payment @ 20% interest	Present Value Cost (rounded to nearest dollar)
0	$17,000	1.000	$17,000
1	800	.833	666
2	900	.694	625
3	1,000	.579	579
4	1,100	.482	530
5	1,200	.402	482

	Subtotal	$19,882
	Less salvage ($3,000)(.402)	− 1,206
	Total (net present value)	$18,676

Ford van

Year	Payment	Present Value Factor for a Single Payment @ 20% interest	Present Value Cost (rounded to nearest dollar)
0	$15,000	1.000	$15,000
1	1,000	.833	833
2	1,000	.694	694
3	1,000	.579	579
4	1,000	.482	482

	Subtotal	$17,588
	Less salvage ($2,000)(.482)	− 964
	Total (net present value)	$16,624

Year 0 cost	$15,000
Maintenance [4 years at 20% = $PVA(20\%, 4) \times \$1,000$ = $2.589 \times \$1,000$]	+ 2,589
Subtotal	$17,589
Salvage ($2,000 \times .482$)	− 964
Total (NPV)	$16,625

(The one-dollar difference between the two computations is due to a rounding off error.)

The analysis indicates that the Ford van is less expensive than the GM van. However, we caution against making statements such as, "Xpress should buy the Ford because it is less expensive" for several reasons. First, we again note that the lifetimes of the two vans differ. We expect the GM van to be more expensive because it should last longer. Second, all of the costs in the analysis that occur after year 0—that is, the maintenance costs and salvage value—represent estimates (forecasts). These numbers are not known. It could be that neither van will last even two years, let alone have the salvage value used in the example. Net present value, or any other financial technique, is merely one tool for use in the overall decision-making process.

EQUIVALENT ANNUAL COST

As indicated in our discussion of Example A.5, one of the difficulties with net present value analysis is that it will be a very biased technique if the choice is between investments with unequal lifetimes. Therefore, we now look toward methods that will annualize the cost. Two such methods are **equivalent annual cost** and **internal rate of return.** Both are based on the net present value.   **investments with unequal lifetimes**

Equivalent annual cost *(EAC)* is the annualized net present value given by

$$EAC = \frac{\text{net present value}}{\text{present value of } n\text{-year annuity at rate } i} = \frac{NPV}{PVA(i, n)},$$

where n is the investment lifetime.

The reason for using equivalent annual cost is best seen by turning the formula around, yielding

$$EAC \times PVA(i, n) = NPV.$$

If the cost were given by the equivalent annual cost rather than by the actual cash flow, then the net present value would be the same as the net present value of the actual cash flow. Let us continue with our analysis of Xpress Inc.

Example A.6   Find the equivalent annual cost for the GM and Ford vans (see data presented in Example A.5).

For the GM van we have

$$EAC = \frac{\$18{,}676}{2.991} = \$6{,}244,$$

and for the Ford van we have

$$EAC = \frac{\$16{,}625}{2.589} = \$6{,}421.$$

Hence, on an annual basis, the Ford is more expensive!   ■

Notice that if the costs for the GM van had been $6,244 per year for five years, rather than the cash flow given in the example, the net present value would be $6,244(2.991) = $18,676, as given by the actual cash flow. In other words, $6,244 per year for five years is equivalent to the cash flow given in the example for the GM vehicle when the interest rate is 20 percent. Similarly, $6,421 per year for four years is equivalent to the cash flow given for the Ford if the interest rate is 20 percent.

We note that there is another way to interpret the GM equivalent annual cost. We could say that we are indifferent between purchasing the GM van or leasing it for five years at an annual cost of $6,244 (paid at the *end* of each year).

INTERNAL RATE OF RETURN

The internal rate of return (IRR) measures investments in a fashion similar to equivalent annual cost in the sense that we can compare investments with unequal life spans. Internal rate of return is defined as the interest rate that yields a net present value of zero dollars. Essentially, we are looking for the interest rate that makes the net present value of future savings equal to the initial cost. Typically, a firm's top management or financial executives determine a cutoff value and if the IRR is at least as large as the cutoff value, the investment will be made. The computation of the IRR is simple when the cash flow is an annuity. Otherwise, the computation is by trial and error. We begin with an example using an annuity.

Example A.7 Mitlick Trucking is considering paying $50,000 for a new fuel-efficient tractor. The tractor is expected to last five years and to have no salvage value after that time. The tractor will save $15,000 per year in fuel costs over the five years. Mitlick will invest in the tractor only if the IRR is 20 percent or more. Should Mitlick buy the tractor?

The internal rate of return is the interest rate such that total net present value = 0. Hence, we wish to find the interest rate that allows for

$$\$50,000 - \$15,000 \times PVA(i, 5 \text{ years}) = 0.$$

In other words, the five-year present value factor must be given by $50,000/$15,000 = 3.33. Examining Table A.4 in row 5 (because $n = 5$ years), we find that, at 15 percent, the PVA is equal to 3.352; at 16 percent, the PVA is equal to 3.274. Hence, the internal rate of return is somewhere between 15 percent and 16 percent (and is closer to 15 percent), and Mitlick should not purchase the tractor. (Note that we could interpolate to get a more exact answer for the IRR.) ∎

If the cash flow is not represented by an annuity, then, as mentioned before, the only way to determine the internal rate of return is through trial and error, which we demonstrate in the next example.

Example A.8 U.S. Tin Company is purchasing a new computerized packaging machine for $27,230. The savings in years one through three are estimated to be $15,000, $10,000, and $5,000, respectively. After three years, the machine will be sold (as scrap) for $5,000. Find the internal rate of return.

trial and error

We begin the trial-and-error process by using a 20-percent interest rate. (The choice of 20 percent is arbitrary.) The following table gives the net present value of costs.

Year	Savings	20% Present Value Factor for a Single Payment	Present Value Savings (at 20%)
1	$15,000	.833	$12,495
2	10,000	.694	6,940
3	10,000 ($5,000 in savings and $5,000 in salvage)	.579	5,790
		Subtotal	$25,225
		Less initial cost	− 27,230
		Total (*NPV*)	−$ 2,005

Since − $2,005 represents a negative net present value, the trial internal rate of return chosen (20 percent) must be too high. We now try 10 percent.

Year	Savings	10% Present Value Factor for a Single Payment	Present Value Savings (at 10%)
1	$15,000	.909	$13,635
2	10,000	.826	8,260
3	10,000	.751	7,510
		Subtotal	$29,405
		Less initial cost	− 27,230
		Total (*NPV*)	$ 2,175

We are not getting closer. The positive $2,175 net present value indicates that the savings are larger than the cost, hence the internal rate of return must be better than (greater than) 10 percent. Let us try one final guess—12 percent.

Year	Savings	12% Present Value Factor for a Single Payment	Present Value Cost
1	$15,000	.893	$12,140
2	10,000	.797	7,970
3	10,000	.712	7,120
		Subtotal	$27,230
		Less initial cost	− 27,230
		Total (*NPV*)	$ 0

Since the net present value of the investment is zero, the internal rate of return is given by 12 percent. ∎

LOAN PAYMENTS

There is an intimate relationship between the internal rate of return and the payments to be made on a loan when the loan payments are equal. The relationship is that the present value of the payment flow must equal the amount of the loan. In order to compute the payment on a loan, we use the following formula:

loan payments

$$\text{Payment} = \frac{\text{amount of loan}}{PVA(i, n)},$$

where i is the interest rate on the loan and n is the number of payments.

Example A.9   Henry Patrick has taken a loan for $20,000 to be repaid in twelve monthly payments. The interest rate is 1 percent per month. How much is each payment?

Using the formula just presented and finding PVA (1%, 12) from Table A.4, it follows that

$$\text{Payment} = \frac{\$20,000}{11.255} = \$1,777 \text{ per month.} \quad \blacksquare$$

Now consider the reverse process. That is, a bank loans Henry Patrick $20,000 and receives in return $1,777 per month for 12 months. Find the internal rate of return. Following the procedure used earlier, we find that the present value annuity factor must equal

$$PVA = \frac{\$20,000}{\$1,777} = 11.255.$$

Looking at row 12 of Table A.4, we find that the factor is 11.255 at $i = 1\%$. Hence, the internal rate of return is 1 percent. In other words, what the borrower terms "interest rate" is, in fact, an internal rate of return to the bank. The only difference is that interest is paid and internal rate of return is received.

PAYBACK

The last measurement of investments to be considered is one that does *not* consider the time value of money. It is termed **payback** and is defined as the length of time required for a cash flow to turn positive—that is, the length of time required to recoup the original investment. Of course, from the perspective of payback, the shorter the length of time to recover an investment, the better the investment.

Example A.10   Find the payback for Mitlick's investment (see data given in Example A.7).

The cash flow (savings) is given by $15,000 per year, and the initial cost is $50,000. Hence, the payback period is given by $50,000/$15,000 = 3.33 years. $\blacksquare$

Payback is widely used; choosing the investment that will be recovered the soonest obviously has tremendous appeal. After the payback period, all returns are profits. Therefore, payback maximizes the short-term return on investment in equipment. If a firm is undecided among several small investments, payback periods are simple to calculate and will be useful decision-making tools. However, if a choice is between a small and a large investment, payback usually will indicate the smaller investment. For example, based solely on payback, one would invest in equipment that has a three-year payback rather than a new plant, which has a ten-year payback. The difficulty with this approach is that, many times, the returns on the investment that has a longer payback period are considerably higher (as was its initial cost). Furthermore, these returns will continue for a longer period of time. In the past, short-term investments by U.S. manufacturers have led to antiquated plants. Changes in the tax code with respect to depreciation were made for the express purpose of reducing the payback period for large investments.

myopic management

DEPRECIATION AND TAXES

Money spent on an asset used in a business is tax deductible. Unfortunately, the cost cannot be deducted from income as a lump sum when spent, but, instead, must be depreciated. That is, the cost must be spread over a number of years. There are different depreciation methods, but all require knowledge of the original cost of the asset, the estimated lifetime of the equipment, which we denote by n, and the estimated salvage value of the equipment. Regardless of the method chosen, the total depreciation is given by

Total depreciation = cost − salvage value.

We note that tax laws are constantly changing. Therefore, it would be unwise to rely on our presentation of depreciation methods without consulting an accountant.

STRAIGHT-LINE DEPRECIATION

The easiest method of depreciation to compute is the **straight-line depreciation** *(SLD)* method. When this method is used, an equal amount is depreciated each year. The total depreciation is the original cost less the salvage value, so the yearly amount of depreciation is given by

$$SLD = \frac{cost - salvage}{lifetime}.$$

straight-line depreciation

Example A.11 An X-ray machine that costs $15,000 will be sold after eight years for $3,000. Find the annual depreciation using the straight-line method.

The depreciation expense for each of the eight years is given by

$$SLD = \frac{\$15,000 - \$3,000}{8} = \frac{\$12,000}{8} = \$1,500$$

Notice that when using straight-line depreciation, the depreciation expense is an annuity. This is not true of the two methods that we present next. Because these two methods push the depreciation from later years to earlier years, we term them **accelerated depreciation methods.**

SUM OF YEARS' DIGITS DEPRECIATION

A second depreciation method is the **sum of years' digits** (SYD) method. The process begins by listing the years over the lifetime and adding them up to generate the sum. In Example A.11, $n = 8$, so $SUM = 1 + 2 + \cdots + 8 = 36$. Now, in year one, we depreciate n/SUM times the total depreciation, in year two, we depreciate $(n - 1)/SUM$ of the total depreciation, and so on. For the X-ray example, the depreciation for the eight years is given as follows.

Year	Sum of Years' Digit Fraction	Depreciation Fraction × $12,000
1	8/36	$ 2,666.67
2	7/36	2,333.33
3	6/36	2,000.00
4	5/36	1,666.67
5	4/36	1,333.33
6	3/36	1,000.00
7	2/36	666.67
8	1/36	333.33
36	36/36 = 1	$12,000.00

We say that the depreciation is accelerated, because there is more depreciation in the first year when the sum of years' digits method is used than there is when the straight-line depreciation method is used. The total depreciation for either method is the same ($12,000 in our X-ray example). However, the present value under sum of years' digits depreciation is larger than the present value under straight-line depreciation, because the depreciation has been pushed closer to year one.

DECLINING BALANCE DEPRECIATION

The final method we consider is termed **declining balance depreciation** (DBD). This method is somewhat different than the others in that the book value of the asset is reduced each year by a certain percentage and then the depreciation is computed. For example, declining balances at 20 percent means that the depreciation expense should be computed as 20 percent of the book value for each year. For the X-ray machine example, the depreciation is computed as follows.

Year	Book Value at Beginning of Year	20% Declining Balance Depreciation	Book Value at End of Year
1	$15,000	$3,000	$12,000
2	12,000	2,400	9,600
3	9,000	1,920	7,680
4	7,680	1,536	6,144
5	6,144	1,229	4,915
6	4,915	983	3,932
7	3,932	786	3,145
8	3,145	145*	3,000

*Because the book value of the asset should not be reduced below the expected salvage value, the depreciation expense in the last year is not 20 percent of $3,145, but $3,145 − $3,000 = $145.

At this point, we have introduced all of the factors needed to analyze the cash flows resulting from investment in production assets. Let us now put these factors together in some final examples that will give a complete picture of the steps involved in the analysis.

EXAMPLES OF INVESTMENT ANALYSIS

In this section, we present several different examples of investment analysis. Of course, the foundation for each analysis is the computation of the net present value. The general formula for computing the savings after taxes in a particular year is

Savings after taxes = savings after expenses − tax rate(savings − tax deductions).

Alternatively, it follows that

Savings after taxes = savings after expenses − savings × tax rate
+ tax rate × tax deductions.

Teaching Suggestion A.5: Different Approaches. See the Instructor's Section for details.

Either formula may be used and, in either case, tax deductions consist of all expenses that can be written off, including maintenance costs, operating costs, depreciation, and interest costs. After we compute the savings after taxes, we find the net present value by totaling the present value of savings after taxes for each year, subtracting the initial investment, and adding the present value of the salvage value. In the event that the analysis is a cost analysis rather than a savings (profit) analysis, we simply change the signs (from plus to minus and vice versa). We begin with an example in which taxes and depreciation are incorporated and the cash flow is an annuity.

Example A.12   Typing Operations Inc. (Typo) is investing $3,500 in order to purchase new word processing equipment. The yearly maintenance costs will be $400. The new equipment is expected to reduce the amount of overtime occurring, thus reducing costs by $2,000 per year. At the end of four years, it will be sold for $1,500.

If Typo uses the straight-line method of depreciation and the tax rate is 30 percent, find the net present value of the cash flow using a 12-percent interest rate.

The first step is to determine taxable income. The total depreciation is given by cost − salvage value = $3,500 − $1,500 = $2,000. Thus, the annual depreciation is $2,000/4 years = $500 per year. The tax is paid on the $2,000 additional income due to the savings, minus $400 in maintenance expenses and minus $500 in depreciation, or $1,100. Because the tax rate is 30 percent, the annual taxes are .3($1,100) = $330. Thus, we compute Typo's annual savings after taxes as follows.

savings	$2,000
expenses	− 400
additional taxes	− 330
	$1,270

(Notice that the depreciation is not deducted from the savings after taxes.) The present value of a four-year annuity of $1,270 at 12-percent interest is given by $1,270(3.037) = $3,857. The present value of the salvage of $1,500 after four years is given by $1,500(.636) = $954. The *NPV* of the cash flow, then, is $3,857 + $954 − $3,500 = $1,311. This indicates that the investment on new typing equipment returns more than 12 percent. ◾

When the cash flow is not an annuity, the considerations in the analysis are the same, but they must be performed on a year-by-year basis. Typically, this means a table must be created to perform the analysis. We do this in the next example.

Example A.13 Consider the Typo data again. Find the net present value using an interest rate of 14 percent and the sum of years' digits method of depreciation.

This time, the annual income after taxes is not an annuity, because the depreciations varies each year. Computations similar to those done in Example A.12 must be performed, but on a year-by-year basis. The computations are presented in Table A.6. Columns (1), (2), and (3) contain the year, the annual savings of $2,000, and the additional maintenance expenses of $400 per year, respectively. We again begin with the computation of the depreciation. Because we are using the sum of years' digits method, first we find that the *SUM* = 1 + 2 + 3 + 4 = 10, and then, in column (4), we depreciate the different percentages of the total depreciation of $2,000. As before, we next compute the taxable income, which, as shown in column (5), is the savings less the expenses less the depreciation. The tax, given in column (7), is 30 percent of the taxable income, and the savings after taxes, given in column (8), is the savings less the additional expenses less the tax. In column (9), we multiply the income after taxes by the present value factors for single payments in order to arrive at the present value of the savings in column (10). This totals $3,729, to which we add the present value of the salvage, yielding $4,617. Finally, we subtract the original investment, which yields a net present value of $1,117. The implication is that the internal rate of return of the investment is at least 14 percent. ◾

Oftentimes, a company will borrow money to make an investment in equipment. Let us consider a net present value analysis for such a situation.

TABLE A.6 Typo net present value analysis (Example A.13)

(1) Year	(2) Savings	(3) Additional Expenses	(4) Depreciaton	(5) Taxable Income [(2) − (3) − (4)]
1	$2,000	$400	$(4/10)($2,000) = \$\ \ 800$	$2,000 − $400 − $800 = \$\ \ 800$
2	2,000	400	$(3/10)($2,000) = \$\ \ 600$	$2,000 − $400 − $600 = $1,000
3	2,000	400	$(2/10)($2,000) = \$\ \ 400$	$2,000 − $400 − $600 = $1,200
4	2,000	400	$(1/10)($2,000) = \$\ \ 200$	$2,000 − $400 − $200 = $1,400
			$2,000	

(6) Year	(7) Tax [.3 × (5)]	(8) Savings After Taxes [(2) − (3) − (7)]	(9) Present Value Factors $PSVP(14\%, n)$	(10) Present Value of Savings [(8) × (9)]
1	.3($\ \ $800) = $240	$2,000 − $400 − $240 = $1,360	.877	$1,193
2	.3($1,000) = $300	$2,000 − $400 − $300 = $1,300	.769	1,000
3	.3($1,200) = $360	$2,000 − $400 − $360 = $1,240	.675	837
4	.3($1,400) = $420	$2,000 − $400 − $420 = $1,180	.592	699
				$3,729

Total present value of savings $3,729
Total salvage [$1,500(.592)]   +   888
Subtotal $4,617
Investment   − 3,500
Total (*NPV* at 14%) $1,117

Example A.14   Suppose that Typo borrows the $3,500 from a bank and pays it back in four equal payments. If the interest rate is 16 percent, what is the net present value of the cash flow using straight-line depreciation? (Use a 16-percent interest rate for the analysis as well as for the loan.)

Because the interest is tax deductible and will vary each year, the annual cash flow is not an annuity. The first step is to determine the loan payments.

$$\text{Payment} = \frac{\text{amount of loan}}{PVA(16\%, 4 \text{ years})} = \frac{\$3,500}{2.798} = \$1,251/\text{year}$$

Now the analysis may begin. It is presented in Table A.7. This time, our analysis begins with the loan. Throughout year one, $3,500 is owed. As shown in column (4), the interest on this after one year is .16($3,500) = $560. Because $1,251 is repaid at the end of year one, the balance on the loan after year one, as shown in column (5), is $3,500 (starting balance) + $560 (interest) − $1,251 (payment) = $2,809. This becomes the starting balance for year two, which means that the interest in year two is .16($2,809) = $449. Continuing in this fashion, we complete columns (4) and (5). Notice that the difference between the $1,251 payment and the interest in column (4) is the amount of the principal that is repaid each year. From the table, we see that the total loan payment is $5,004, and the total interest is $1,502, which means that

TABLE A.7 Typo net present value analysis of loan (Example A.14)

(1) Year	(2) Savings	(3) Loan Payment	(4) Loan Interest (.16 × Balance)	(5) Loan Balance [Previous Balance + (4) − (3)]	(6) Additional Expenses
1	$2,000	$1,251	$ 560	$3,500 + $560 − $1,251 = $2,809	$400
2	2,000	1,251	449	$2,809 + $449 − $1,251 = $2,007	400
3	2,000	1,251	321	$2,007 + $321 − $1,251 = $1,077	400
4	2,000	1,251	172	$1,077 + $172 − $1,251 = $ −2*	500
		$5,004	$1,502		

(7) Year	(8) Straight-Line Depreciation	(9) Deductions [(4) + (6) + (8)]	(10) Taxable Income [(2) − (9)]	(11) Tax [.3 × (10)]
1	$500	$560 + $400 + $500 = $1,460	$2,000 − $1,460 = $540	.3($540) = $162
2	500	$449 + $400 + $500 = $1,349	$2,000 − $1,349 = $651	.3($651) = $195
3	500	$321 + $400 + $500 = $1,221	$2,000 − $1,221 = $779	.3($779) = $234
4	500	$172 + $400 + $500 = $1,072	$2,000 − $1,072 = $928	.3($928) = $278

(12) Year	(13) Income After Taxes [(2) − (3) − (6) − (11)]	(14) Present Value Factor [$PVSP(16\%, n)$]	(15) Present Value of Income [(13) × (14)]
1	$2,000 − $1,251 − $400 − $162 = $187	.862	$161
2	$2,000 − $1,251 − $400 − $195 = $154	.743	114
3	$2,000 − $1,251 − $400 − $234 = $115	.641	74
4	$2,000 − $1,251 − $400 − $278 = $ 71	.552	39
			$388

Total present value of income $ 388
Salvage [$1,500(.552)] +   828
Total (*NPV* at 16%) $1,216

*Difference due to rounding off

the principal is $5,004 − $1,502 = $3,502 (there is a $2 round-off difference). Column (9) contains the total amount that is deducted each year and is given by the interest plus the expenses plus the depreciation. The taxable income, given in column (10), is the savings of $2,000 less the deductions, while the tax, given in column (11), is 30 percent of this amount. As shown in column (13), the income after taxes consists of the savings less the loan payment less the expenses less the taxes. We multiply each annual savings by the present value of a single payment and total in order to arrive at the present value total of $388, to which we add the present value of the salvage, yielding an *NPV* of $1,216. Notice that we do not subtract $3,500, because this money was not paid at the beginning but was included in the loan payments. ▪ꟷ

Consider one last example. A common problem in operations is deciding between buying a piece of equipment and renting a piece of equipment. The following example performs an analysis of such a decision.

Example A.15 An unofficial group of unscrupulous "boosters" of a certain university's athletic program decides that the university's star athletes should each be given free use of an automobile for the duration of their college careers. The boosters can rent cars from United Car Loan (UCL) or buy cars from U.S. Car. Given below are the costs involved with each option. It is safe to assume a five-year lifetime for the cars because athletes typically are in school for five years. Also, the costs are written off on the alumni's business tax returns. The tax rate is 40 percent. Sum of years' digits depreciation is used. If the interest rate is 16 percent, should the boosters use UCL or U.S. Car?

Lease from UCL
Leasing cost: $1,000/year

Buy from U.S. Car
Purchase price: $8,000
Salvage value: $3,000
Maintenance cost: $250/year

In Table A.8, we present the leasing cost analysis. Although the lease is an annuity because it occurs at the beginning of the year, we have listed the cash flow on an annual basis. Column (2) contains the $1,000 cost. Because this cost is deductible, the boosters pay 40-percent less in taxes than if they do not lease. This $400 tax advantage is listed in column (3), and the net cost of $600 is given in column (4). After multiplying by the present value factors in column (5), we find the present value costs on an annual basis, which, as shown in column (6), total $2,279.

There is an easier way to arrive at this number. The net present value of a five-year annuity of $600 at 16-percent interest is $PVA(16\%, 5) \times 600 = 3.274(\$600) = \$1,964.40$. This would be the cost if payments occurred at the end of each year. Since payments occur at the beginning of each year, they are worth more by one year's interest. Thus, we *compound* the $1,964 by 16 percent and find that

$$\$1,964 \times CVSP(16\%, 1) = \$1,964(1.16) = \$2,279.$$

This agrees with our answer. An annuity paid or received at the beginning of a year rather than at the end of the year is called an **annuity due,** and its present value can be computed as

$$PVA(\text{annuity due}) = PVA(i, n) \times (1 + i).$$

present value annuity due

TABLE A.8 UCL lease costs (Example A.15)

(1) Year	(2) Lease	(3) 40% Tax Advantage [.4 × (2)]	(4) Lease Cost After Taxes [(2) − (3)]	(5) Present Value Factors [$PVSP(16\%, n)$]	(6) Present Value of Lease After Taxes [(4) × (5)]
0	$1,000	$400	$600	1.000	$ 600
1	1,000	400	600	.862	517
2	1,000	400	600	.743	446
3	1,000	400	600	.641	385
4	1,000	400	600	.552	331
					$2,279

TABLE A.9 U.S. Car purchase costs (Example A.15)

(1) Year	(2) Maintenance	(3) Depreciation	(4) Deductible [(2) + (3)]	(5) Tax Advantage [.4 × (4)]
1	$250	$1,667	$1,917	$766.80
2	250	1,333	1,583	633.20
3	250	1,000	1,250	500.00
4	250	667	917	366.80
5	250	333	583	233.20
		$5,000		

(6) Year	(7) Net Cost After Taxes [(2) − (5)]	(8) Present Value Factor $PSVP(16\%, n)$	(9) Present Value of Cost After Taxes [(7) × (8)]
1	− $516.80	.862	− $445.48
2	− 383.20	.743	− 284.72
3	− 250.00	.641	− 160.25
4	− 116.80	.552	− 64.47
5	16.80	.476	8.00
		Total *NPV* annual costs	− $910.92

Purchase price	$8,000.00
NPV annual costs	− 910.92
Subtotal	$7,089.08
Salvage ($3,000 × .476)	− 1,428.00
Total (*NPV* of all costs)	$5,661.08

Table A.9 contains the analysis for purchasing the vehicle. Maintenance, shown in column (2), and depreciation, shown in column (3), are deductible. The tax advantage of the deduction shown in column (4) is given in column (5). The net cost is the maintenance less the tax advantage and is given in column (7). Notice that during these years, the net cost is negative, meaning that the benefit of deduction outweighs the maintenance cost. The present values are computed in column (9) and total − $910.92. This means that the cost is actually a profit. The bottom of the table completes the computations by including the original purchase cost and salvage cost. The net present value of all costs is $5,661.08. ∎

SUMMARY

In this discussion, we have examined the application of financial techniques to operations management problems. We have presented the major concept (taken from finance) that the value of money changes over time as a function of the interest rate. The primary tool for analysis is the amount of money one needs today in order to accrue one dollar in *n* years at a given interest rate. This is called the *present value of a single payment,* or discount factor, and is founded on the everyday concept of compound interest.

Discount factors enable us to develop the net present value of a cash flow, and we can use the net present value to compare different alternatives facing a decision maker. In order to be able to make meaningful comparisons between investments with different lifetimes, we use either *equivalent annual cost* or *internal rate of return.* One additional criterion that does not discount the cash flow is *payback,* which is the length of time an investment requires before it returns the original investment.

Expenses incurred in business are tax deductible, which means that analysis must include the effect of taxes. Furthermore, capital equipment expenses are depreciated (rather than deducted) in the year in which they occur, and we have considered different types of depreciation. Constantly changing tax laws necessitate consultation with an accountant regarding depreciation methods.

One final word of caution: The financial techniques that we have presented are to be considered as *aids* in decision making; they do not actually make the decision. Many other considerations, such as reliability, service, and support, must be taken into account during the decision-making process.

KEY TERMS

time value of money	annuity	sum of years' digits
future value	cash flow	declining balance depreciation
present value	net present value	annuity due
compound interest	equivalent annual cost	
compound value of a single payment	internal rate of return	
discount	payback	
present value of a single payment	straight-line depreciation	
	accelerated depreciation	

SOLVED PROBLEMS

1. KH Appliance Manufacturers is considering the modernization of its major appliance plant. The costs of modernizing would be $1.2 million. It is expected that the modernization would save $200,000 per year in operating costs over the next fifteen years. KH will only make this investment if the internal rate of return is at least 18 percent. Should KH modernize?

Solution

This problem has an annuity as the return. Therefore, finding the internal rate of return is a simple procedure. We begin by finding the annuity factor.

$$\text{Annuity factor} = \text{investment/return}$$
$$= \$1,200,000/\$200,000 = 6$$

Next, we go to the annuity table and look in the row for fifteen years for an entry close to 6. From Table A.4, we find that the nearest entry in the row for fifteen years is 6.142, which is at an interest rate of 14 percent. Therefore, the investment should not be made, because it yields less than the required 18 percent.

2. Direct Market Zones (DMZ) is a sales company that uses an automated system to place its telephone sales calls. DMZ is considering the purchase of new equipment and is trying to decide between purchasing a computer or leasing a computer. Lease costs would be $2,000 per year, and maintenance would be provided by the leasing company. The purchase cost would be $4,500, and there would be maintenance expenses of $600 per year. Which choice should DMZ make if the interest rate is 16 percent, the tax rate is 33 percent, the depreciation method is straight-line depreciation, and the time horizon is five years?

Solution

Let us begin with the lease analysis. Since the annual cost is $2,000, over five years, the cost would be $2,000 times the *PVA* factor, which, from Table A.4, is 3.274. The total is 3.274 × $2,000, or $6,548. Due to taxes, the net cost after taxes is 67 percent of this, or $4,365.

Now consider the purchase cost, using the following information.

Years	Costs	Depreciation	Tax Benefit	Net Cost After Tax
1–5	$600	$900	$500	$100

The net cost after taxes is $100 per year. The total after-tax cost is $100 times the annuity factor, or $327. Thus, the total cost is $327 + $4,500 = $4,827. Therefore, leasing is preferred.

3. Consider again the data presented in Solved Problem 2. Which choice should DMZ make if the sum of years' digits method of depreciation is used?

Solution

The leasing costs are the same. The only difference is the purchase option. Because the sum of years' digits method does not yield an annuity, we must create one line for each year and include the depreciation and the present value factor.

Year	Costs	Depreciation	Tax Benefit	Net Cost After Tax	PV Factor	PV of Cost
1	$600	$4,500 × 5/15 = $1,500	$700	−$100	.862	−$ 86.20
2	600	$4,500 × 4/15 = 1,200	600	0	.743	0.00
3	600	$4,500 × 3/15 = 900	500	100	.641	64.10
4	600	$4,500 × 2/15 = 600	400	200	.552	110.40
5	600	$4,500 × 1/15 = 300	300	300	.476	142.80
		$4,500			3.274	$231.10

The total after-tax cost is $231.10 using the sum of years' digits method (as opposed to $327 when the straight-line method was used). The total purchase cost is $4,500 + $231 = $4,731, which is still more than the lease cost.

QUESTIONS

1. What is meant by the term *cash flow*?

2. Why is it necessary to know cash flows when evaluating investments?

3. What should the analyst do when comparing two investments with different lifetimes, and why?

4. Since depreciation is neither an outflow nor an inflow of cash, why is it necessary to consider it in the analysis?

5. In your own words, what does the term *internal rate of return* mean?

6. What is the relationship of equivalent annual cost and loan payments?

7. Discuss the advantages and disadvantages of present value methods and payback.

8. Explain what is meant by equivalent annual cost, why it is needed, and when it is used.

9. Compare the following methods: straight-line depreciation, sum of years' digits depreciation, and declining balance depreciation. How does the use of a certain depreciation method change the present value of a cash flow?

10. The examples in this chapter show the value of money changing over time by the use of an interest rate. What other two factors cause the value of money to change?

11. Describe the benefits of leasing over buying. What are the benefits of buying over leasing? In what industries would leasing be a better alternative, and why (give an intuitive answer)?

PROBLEMS

1. Rentco Real Estate has just purchased an empty lot for $15,000. The value of the lot will increase at an estimated rate of 15 percent per year. What will be the value of the lot after

(a) four years? $26,235
(b) eight years? $45,885

2. Use the information given in Problem 1 to answer the following.

(a) How long will it take for Rentco Real Estate to double its investment? 5 years
(b) Now suppose the interest rate is 10 percent. How long will it take Rentco Real Estate to double its investment? 7 years

3. Paul Easthead has signed an agreement to purchase a new warehouse for his company three years from today for $100,000. If the interest rate is 18 percent, how much money should be put away today in order to pay for the purchase in three years? $60,864

4. Dave Senior is a high school student who is undecided on the value of a college education. Tuition at his state university is $2,200 per year. If, rather than paying tuition, Dave puts

$10,494

$2,200 each year for four years into an investment that earns 12 percent annually, how much money will he have after four years?

5. Consolidated Tractors (ConTras) has just signed a ten-year lease agreement with a computer company. ConTras will pay $17,000 per year at the beginning of each of the ten years. The interest rate is 10 percent per year. What is the present value of the ten payments?

$114,912

6. A state lottery commission is attempting to decide between two lottery payoff mechanisms. One is to pay a lottery winner a flat sum of one million dollars. The other is to give the lottery winner $100,000 per year at the *beginning* of each year for twenty-five years. The lottery commission does not know the cost of money but is certain that interest is between 6 percent and 10 percent. From the commission's point of view, which of the two alternatives is better if the interest rate is

flat sum
flat sum
$100,000 per year

(a) 6 percent?
(b) 8 percent?
(c) 10 percent?

7. Find the internal rate of return for the following piece of equipment, which costs $11,800.

Year	Savings
1	$5,000
2	$5,000
3	$5,000

13 percent

8. Find the internal rate of return for the following piece of equipment, which costs $11,800.

Year	Savings
1	$7,000
2	$5,000
3	$3,000

15.2 percent

9. Harry Stottle has borrowed $8,658 from a bank at 8-percent annual interest. He is going to pay back the loan over five years, with equal payments at the end of each of the five years.

$2,168
$2,182

(a) What is his annual payment?
(b) What is the total amount of interest he pays?

$3,985

10. A company has taken a loan for $20,000, which it will repay in ten equal annual payments. The interest rate is 15 percent. How much is each annual payment?

15 percent

11. A company is investing $20,000 per new employee in a training session. The company estimates that each employee will be more productive and save the company $3,985 per year. (Employees usually stay with the company for ten years.) What is the internal rate of return of the training program?

$3,985 per year

12. A company has bought a machine in order to reduce production costs. The net present value of all factors involved (purchase cost, salvage, savings, taxes, maintenance, and so forth) is $20,000 over the ten-year useful life of the machine. If the interest rate is 15 percent, what is the equivalent annual savings of the new machine?

$2,000 per year
$3,200; $2,400; $1,600;
$800
$2,000; $1,600; $1,280;
$3,120

13. Gym Corporation bought a $10,000 trampoline that has an economic life of four years and a salvage value of $2,000 at the end of the four years. Find the amount of depreciation in each year using the following depreciation methods.

(a) straight-line depreciation
(b) sum of years' digits depreciation
(c) declining balance depreciation (with a rate of 20 percent)

14. A company purchased a furnace for $12,000. The furnace will last for six years and will then be sold as scrap metal for $3,000. The company is in the 35-percent tax bracket. Find both the depreciation and the tax savings due to depreciation in each of the six years using the following depreciation methods.

(a) straight-line depreciation
(b) sum of years' digits depreciation
(c) declining balance depreciation (with a rate of 15 percent)

depreciation: $1,500 per year; total tax savings: $3,150
See Instructor's Section.
See Instructor's Section.

15. Consumer Management Corporation has a choice of three investments—A, B, and C. The following table gives the cost of each investment as well as the cash flows for each investment.

	A	B	C
Cost	$10,000	$12,000	$15,000
Income			
Year 1	4,000	10,000	6,000
Year 2	3,000	5,000	6,000
Year 3	6,000	3,000	6,000
Year 4	1,000	3,000	6,000
Year 5	7,000	3,000	6,000

(a) Which investment is "best" based on the payback criterion?
(b) Which investment is "best" based on the net present value criteria, if the cost of money is 9 percent?

B
C

16. Answer the following questions for each of the three investments presented in Problem 15.

(a) What is the equivalent annual income?
(b) Is the internal rate of return at least as high as 30 percent?

A: $1,563; B: $1,996; C: $2,141
A < 30%; B > 30%;
C < 30%

17. Joshua Marsten has taken a loan of $400,000 in order to purchase a building in Philadelphia to use as headquarters when he campaigns for mayor of that city. The loan is to be paid back in five equal annual payments, and the interest rate is 16 percent per year.

(a) What is the total amount of interest paid by Marsten?
(b) If Marsten plans on selling the building for $100,000 at the end of five years, how much depreciation can be written off in each of the five years using the sum of years' digits method?
(c) If Marsten is in the 30-percent tax bracket and writes off the interest and depreciation calculated in parts (a) and (b), what is his net present value expenditure for the building?

$210,875
$100,000; $80,000; $60,000; $40,000; $20,000

$190,509

18. The legal firm of Red, White, and Blue (RWB) is undecided on whether to buy or lease a new vehicle in which to chase ambulances. RWB can purchase a new car for $11,000. Maintenance and insurance costs would run $600 per year over the eight years they would keep the car. After eight years, the car would be sold for $1,000. Using an interest rate of 14 percent, find the annual lease payment that would be equivalent to the purchase costs, assuming that the lease payment is made

(a) at the end of each year.
(b) at the beginning of each year.

$2,895 per year
$2,539 per year

(*Note:* There are no taxes to be considered.)

19. Solve Problem 18 when the tax rate is 25 percent, using the following depreciation methods.

$11,286.46
$11,069.26

(a) straight-line depreciation
(b) sum of years' digits depreciation

20. PRICO, a private company, is negotiating with a university regarding the construction of its new arena. PRICO wishes to pay for the $500,000 construction and, in return, get a percentage of each ticket sold over the next five years. PRICO would own the building for these five years but would then give the building to the university. If PRICO uses straight-line depreciation, pays taxes at a rate of 40 percent, and the revenues to PRICO are as given in the following table, what is the net present value (after taxes) of all building-related expenditures using an interest rate of 12 percent?

$167,272

Year	Anticipated PRICO Revenues
1	$100,000
2	$150,000
3	$300,000
4	$350,000
5	$400,000

23 percent

21. What is the internal rate of return to PRICO (see Problem 20)?

22. Joe Student has borrowed $1,000 from a bank at 16-percent interest to be paid off in four years. He is going to use this money, plus $2,500 of his own money, to buy a video game machine to install in his house. His yearly operating costs will be $80 and his expected income will be $1,700 annually (all $1,700 will be from his friends and neighbors). At the end of four years, he will sell the machine for $1,500. If he uses sum of years' digits depreciation and the tax rate is 30 percent, will he earn a 20-percent return on his $2,500 investment?

yes

REFERENCES

Black, S. B., and G. A. Hurt. *Foundations of Financial Management.* 3rd ed. Homewood, Ill.: Richard D. Irwin, 1984.

Brigham, E. F. *Financial Management: Theory and Practice.* 4th ed. Hinsdale, Ill.: Dryden Press, 1985.

Eskew, R. K., and D. L. Jensen. *Financial Accounting.* 2nd ed. New York: Random House, 1986.

Schall, L. D., and C. W. Haley. *Introduction to Financial Management.* 4th ed. New York: McGraw-Hill, 1986.

Skousen, K., F. Langenderfer, and S. W. Albrecht. *Financial Accounting.* 3rd ed. New York: Worth, 1986.

Weston, J. F., and E. F. Brigham. *Essentials of Managerial Finance.* 7th ed. Hinsdale, Ill.: Dryden Press, 1985.

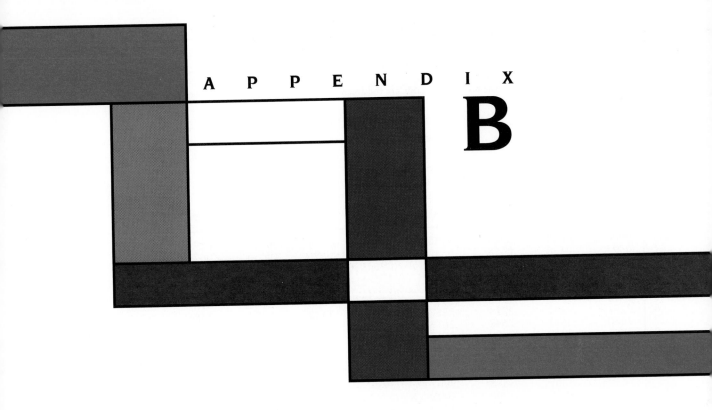

NORMAL DISTRIBUTION TABLES

APPENDIX B1   Normal probabilities: areas of the standard normal distribution

The values in the body of the table are the areas between the mean and z standard deviations.

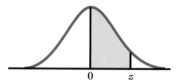

z	.00	.01	.02	.03	.04	.05	.06	.07	.08	.09
.0	.0000	.0040	.0080	.0120	.0160	.0199	.0239	.0279	.0319	.0359
.1	.0398	.0438	.0478	.0517	.0557	.0596	.0636	.0675	.0714	.0753
.2	.0793	.0832	.0871	.0910	.0948	.0987	.1026	.1064	.1103	.1141
.3	.1179	.1217	.1255	.1293	.1331	.1368	.1406	.1443	.1480	.1517
.4	.1554	.1591	.1628	.1664	.1700	.1736	.1772	.1808	.1844	.1879
.5	.1915	.1950	.1985	.2019	.2054	.2088	.2123	.2157	.2190	.2224
.6	.2257	.2291	.2324	.2357	.2389	.2422	.2454	.2486	.2517	.2549
.7	.2580	.2611	.2642	.2673	.2703	.2734	.2764	.2793	.2823	.2852
.8	.2881	.2910	.2939	.2967	.2995	.3023	.3051	.3078	.3106	.3133
.9	.3159	.3186	.3212	.3238	.3264	.3289	.3315	.3340	.3365	.3389
1.0	.3413	.3438	.3461	.3485	.3508	.3531	.3554	.3577	.3599	.3621
1.1	.3643	.3665	.3686	.3708	.3729	.3749	.3770	.3790	.3810	.3830
1.2	.3849	.3869	.3888	.3907	.3925	.3944	.3962	.3980	.3997	.4015
1.3	.4032	.4049	.4066	.4082	.4099	.4115	.4131	.4147	.4162	.4177
1.4	.4192	.4207	.4222	.4236	.4251	.4265	.4279	.4292	.4306	.4319
1.5	.4332	.4345	.4357	.4370	.4382	.4394	.4406	.4418	.4429	.4441
1.6	.4452	.4463	.4474	.4484	.4495	.4505	.4515	.4525	.4535	.4545
1.7	.4554	.4564	.4573	.4582	.4591	.4599	.4608	.4616	.4625	.4633
1.8	.4641	.4649	.4656	.4664	.4671	.4678	.4686	.4693	.4699	.4706
1.9	.4713	.4719	.4726	.4732	.4738	.4744	.4750	.4756	.4761	.4767
2.0	.4772	.4778	.4783	.4788	.4793	.4798	.4803	.4808	.4812	.4817
2.1	.4821	.4826	.4830	.4834	.4838	.4842	.4846	.4850	.4854	.4857
2.2	.4861	.4864	.4868	.4871	.4875	.4878	.4881	.4884	.4887	.4890
2.3	.4893	.4896	.4898	.4901	.4904	.4906	.4909	.4911	.4913	.4916
2.4	.4918	.4920	.4922	.4925	.4927	.4929	.4931	.4932	.4934	.4936
2.5	.4938	.4940	.4941	.4943	.4945	.4946	.4948	.4949	.4951	.4952
2.6	.4953	.4955	.4956	.4957	.4959	.4960	.4961	.4962	.4963	.4964
2.7	.4965	.4966	.4967	.4968	.4969	.4970	.4971	.4972	.4973	.4974
2.8	.4974	.4975	.4976	.4977	.4977	.4978	.4979	.4979	.4980	.4981
2.9	.4981	.4982	.4982	.4983	.4984	.4984	.4985	.4985	.4986	.4986
3.0	.4987	.4987	.4987	.4988	.4988	.4989	.4989	.4989	.4990	.4990
3.1	.4990	.4991	.4991	.4991	.4992	.4992	.4992	.4992	.4993	.4993
3.2	.4993	.4993	.4994	.4994	.4994	.4994	.4994	.4995	.4995	.4995
3.3	.4995	.4995	.4995	.4996	.4996	.4996	.4996	.4996	.4996	.4997
3.4	.4997	.4997	.4997	.4997	.4997	.4997	.4997	.4997	.4997	.4998
3.5	.4998	.4998	.4998	.4998	.4998	.4998	.4998	.4998	.4998	.4998
3.6	.4998	.4998	.4999	.4999	.4999	.4999	.4999	.4999	.4999	.4999

Note: For example, if we want to find the area under the standard normal curve between $z = 0$ and $z = 1.96$, we find the $z = 1.9$ row and .06 column (for $z = 1.90 + .06 = 1.96$) and read .4750 at the intersection.

Source: Adapted from Billingsley et al., *Statistical Inference for Management and Economics,* Third Edition. Copyright 1986 © by Allyn and Bacon, Inc. Reprinted by permission.

APPENDIX B2 Normal probabilities: areas of the standard normal distribution

The values in the body of the table are the areas between $-\infty$ and z.

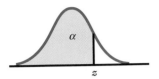

z	.00	.01	.02	.03	.04	.05	.06	.07	.08	.09
.0	.5000	.5040	.5080	.5120	.5160	.5199	.5239	.5279	.5319	.5359
.1	.5398	.5438	.5478	.5517	.5557	.5596	.5636	.5675	.5714	.5753
.2	.5793	.5832	.5871	.5910	.5948	.5987	.6026	.6064	.6103	.6141
.3	.6179	.6217	.6255	.6293	.6331	.6368	.6406	.6443	.6480	.6517
.4	.6554	.6591	.6628	.6664	.6700	.6736	.6772	.6808	.6844	.6879
.5	.6915	.6950	.6985	.7019	.7054	.7088	.7123	.7157	.7190	.7224
.6	.7257	.7291	.7324	.7357	.7389	.7422	.7454	.7486	.7517	.7549
.7	.7580	.7611	.7642	.7673	.7704	.7734	.7764	.7794	.7823	.7852
.8	.7881	.7910	.7939	.7967	.7995	.8023	.8051	.8078	.8106	.8133
.9	.8159	.8186	.8212	.8238	.8264	.8289	.8315	.8340	.8365	.8389
1.0	.8413	.8438	.8461	.8485	.8508	.8531	.8554	.8577	.8599	.8621
1.1	.8643	.8665	.8686	.8708	.8729	.8749	.8770	.8790	.8810	.8830
1.2	.8849	.8869	.8888	.8907	.8925	.8944	.8962	.8980	.8997	.9015
1.3	.9032	.9049	.9066	.9082	.9099	.9115	.9131	.9147	.9162	.9177
1.4	.9192	.9207	.9222	.9236	.9251	.9265	.9279	.9292	.9306	.9319
1.5	.9332	.9345	.9357	.9370	.9382	.9394	.9406	.9418	.9429	.9441
1.6	.9452	.9463	.9474	.9484	.9495	.9505	.9515	.9525	.9535	.9545
1.7	.9554	.9564	.9573	.9582	.9591	.9599	.9608	.9616	.9625	.9633
1.8	.9641	.9649	.9656	.9664	.9671	.9678	.9686	.9693	.9699	.9706
1.9	.9713	.9719	.9726	.9732	.9738	.9744	.9750	.9756	.9761	.9767
2.0	.9772	.9778	.9783	.9788	.9793	.9798	.9803	.9808	.9812	.9817
2.1	.9821	.9826	.9830	.9834	.9838	.9842	.9846	.9850	.9854	.9857
2.2	.9861	.9864	.9868	.9871	.9875	.9878	.9881	.9884	.9887	.9890
2.3	.9893	.9896	.9898	.9901	.9904	.9906	.9909	.9911	.9913	.9916
2.4	.9918	.9920	.9922	.9925	.9927	.9929	.9931	.9932	.9934	.9936
2.5	.9938	.9940	.9941	.9943	.9945	.9946	.9948	.9949	.9951	.9952
2.6	.9953	.9955	.9956	.9957	.9959	.9960	.9961	.9962	.9963	.9964
2.7	.9965	.9966	.9967	.9968	.9969	.9970	.9971	.9972	.9973	.9974
2.8	.9974	.9975	.9976	.9977	.9977	.9978	.9979	.9979	.9980	.9981
2.9	.9981	.9982	.9982	.9983	.9984	.9984	.9985	.9985	.9986	.9986
3.0	.9987	.9987	.9987	.9988	.9988	.9989	.9989	.9989	.9990	.9990
3.1	.9990	.9991	.9991	.9991	.9992	.9992	.9992	.9992	.9993	.9993
3.2	.9993	.9993	.9994	.9994	.9994	.9994	.9994	.9995	.9995	.9995
3.3	.9995	.9995	.9995	.9996	.9996	.9996	.9996	.9996	.9996	.9997
3.4	.9997	.9997	.9997	.9997	.9997	.9997	.9997	.9997	.9997	.9998
3.5	.9998	.9998	.9998	.9998	.9998	.9998	.9998	.9998	.9998	.9999
3.6	.9998	.9998	.9999	.9999	.9999	.9999	.9999	.9999	.9999	.9999

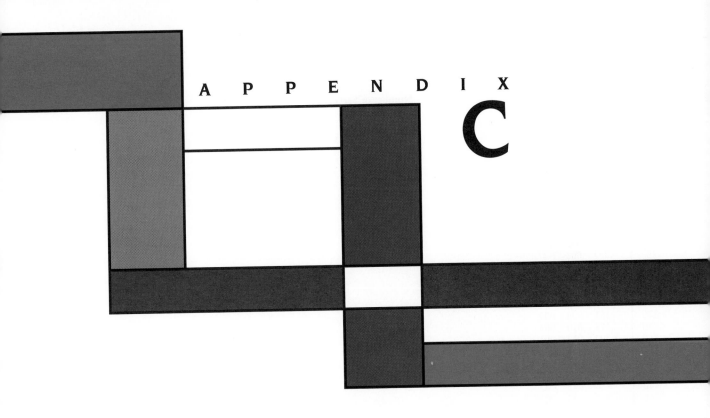

QUEUEING TABLES

APPENDIX C1 *M/M/s* queue: expected number of customers waiting in the queue, L_q

$\dfrac{\lambda}{\mu}$	Number of Servers (Channels)																			
	1	2	3	4	5	6	7	8	9	10	11	12	13	14	15	16	17	18	19	20
.020																				
.040	.002																			
.060	.004																			
.080	.007																			
.100	.011																			
.120	.016																			
.140	.023	.001																		
.160	.030	.001																		
.180	.040	.001																		
.200	.050	.002																		
.220	.062	.003																		
.240	.076	.004																		
.260	.091	.004																		
.280	.109	.006																		
.300	.129	.007																		
.320	.151	.008	.001																	
.340	.175	.010	.001																	
.360	.202	.012	.001																	
.380	.233	.014	.001																	
.400	.267	.017	.001																	
.420	.304	.019	.002																	
.440	.346	.022	.002																	
.460	.392	.026	.002																	
.480	.443	.029	.003																	
.500	.500	.033	.003																	
.520	.563	.038	.004																	
.540	.634	.042	.004																	
.560	.713	.048	.005																	
.580	.801	.053	.005	.001																
.600	.900	.059	.006	.001																
.620	1.012	.066	.007	.001																
.640	1.138	.073	.008	.001																
.660	1.281	.081	.009	.001																
.680	1.445	.089	.010	.001																
.700	1.633	.098	.011	.001																
.720	1.851	.107	.013	.001																
.740	2.106	.117	.014	.002																
.760	2.407	.128	.015	.002																
.780	2.765	.140	.017	.002																
.800	3.200	.152	.019	.002																
.820	3.736	.166	.021	.003																
.840	4.410	.180	.023	.003																
.860	5.283	.195	.025	.003																
.880	6.453	.211	.027	.004																
.900	8.100	.229	.030	.004	.001															
.920	10.580	.247	.033	.005	.001															
.940	14.727	.267	.036	.005	.001															
.960	23.040	.287	.039	.006	.001															
.980	48.020	.310	.042	.006	.001															
1.000		.333	.045	.007	.001															
1.200		.675	.094	.016	.003															

APPENDIX C1 (Continued)

Number of Servers (Channels)

λ/μ	1	2	3	4	5	6	7	8	9	10	11	12	13	14	15	16	17	18	19	20
1.400		1.345	.177	.032	.006	.001														
1.600		2.844	.313	.060	.012	.002														
1.800		7.674	.532	.105	.023	.005	.001													
2.000			.889	.174	.040	.009	.002													
2.200			1.491	.277	.066	.016	.004	.001												
2.400			2.589	.431	.105	.027	.007	.002												
2.600			4.933	.658	.161	.043	.011	.003	.001											
2.800			12.273	1.000	.241	.066	.018	.005	.001											
3.000				1.528	.354	.099	.028	.008	.002											
3.200				2.386	.513	.145	.043	.012	.003	.001										
3.400				3.906	.737	.209	.063	.019	.005	.001										
3.600				7.090	1.055	.295	.091	.028	.008	.002	.001									
3.800				16.937	1.519	.412	.129	.041	.013	.004	.001									
4.000					2.216	.570	.180	.059	.019	.006	.002									
4.200					3.327	.784	.248	.083	.027	.009	.003	.001								
4.400					5.268	1.078	.337	.114	.039	.013	.004	.001								
4.600					9.289	1.487	.453	.156	.054	.018	.006	.002	.001							
4.800					21.641	2.071	.607	.209	.074	.026	.009	.003	.001							
5.000						2.938	.810	.279	.101	.036	.013	.004	.001							
5.200						4.301	1.081	.368	.135	.049	.018	.006	.002	.001						
5.400						6.661	1.444	.483	.178	.066	.024	.009	.003	.001						
5.600						11.519	1.944	.631	.233	.088	.033	.012	.004	.001						
5.800						26.373	2.648	.823	.303	.116	.044	.017	.006	.002	.001					
6.000							3.683	1.071	.392	.152	.059	.022	.008	.003	.001					
6.200							5.298	1.397	.504	.197	.078	.030	.011	.004	.001					
6.400							8.077	1.831	.645	.253	.101	.040	.015	.006	.002	.001				
6.600							13.770	2.420	.825	.322	.130	.052	.021	.008	.003	.001				
6.800							31.127	3.245	1.054	.409	.167	.068	.027	.011	.004	.001				
7.000								4.447	1.347	.517	.212	.088	.036	.014	.005	.002	.001			
7.200								6.314	1.729	.652	.268	.112	.046	.019	.007	.003	.001			
7.400								9.511	2.233	.820	.337	.142	.060	.025	.010	.004	.001	.001		
7.600								16.039	2.912	1.031	.421	.179	.076	.032	.013	.005	.002	.001		
7.800								35.898	3.856	1.298	.525	.224	.097	.041	.017	.007	.003	.001		
8.000									5.227	1.637	.653	.280	.122	.052	.022	.009	.004	.001		
8.200									7.344	2.074	.811	.347	.152	.066	.028	.012	.005	.002	.001	
8.400									10.960	2.647	1.006	.429	.189	.084	.036	.015	.006	.002	.001	
8.600									18.323	3.417	1.249	.529	.234	.104	.046	.020	.008	.003	.001	
8.800									40.683	4.481	1.553	.650	.289	.130	.058	.025	.011	.004	.002	.001
9.000										6.019	1.937	.798	.354	.161	.072	.032	.014	.006	.002	.001
9.200										8.387	2.430	.979	.434	.198	.090	.040	.018	.008	.003	.001
9.400										12.420	3.073	1.201	.529	.242	.111	.050	.022	.010	.004	.002
9.600										20.618	3.932	1.475	.644	.295	.137	.063	.028	.012	.005	.002
9.800										45.480	5.116	1.817	.783	.359	.167	.078	.035	.016	.007	.003

APPENDIX C2   *M/M/1* queue with a limited queue/system size: probability that the system is empty

$\frac{\lambda}{\mu}$	1	2	3	4	5	6	7	8	9	10	11	12	13	14	15	16	17	18	19	20
.02	.980	.980	.980	.980	.980	.980	.980	.980	.980	.980	.980	.980	.980	.980	.980	.980	.980	.980	.980	.980
.04	.962	.960	.960	.960	.960	.960	.960	.960	.960	.960	.960	.960	.960	.960	.960	.960	.960	.960	.960	.960
.06	.943	.940	.940	.940	.940	.940	.940	.940	.940	.940	.940	.940	.940	.940	.940	.940	.940	.940	.940	.940
.08	.926	.920	.920	.920	.920	.920	.920	.920	.920	.920	.920	.920	.920	.920	.920	.920	.920	.920	.920	.920
.10	.909	.901	.900	.900	.900	.900	.900	.900	.900	.900	.900	.900	.900	.900	.900	.900	.900	.900	.900	.900
.12	.893	.882	.880	.880	.880	.880	.880	.880	.880	.880	.880	.880	.880	.880	.880	.880	.880	.880	.880	.880
.14	.877	.862	.860	.860	.860	.860	.860	.860	.860	.860	.860	.860	.860	.860	.860	.860	.860	.860	.860	.860
.16	.862	.843	.841	.840	.840	.840	.840	.840	.840	.840	.840	.840	.840	.840	.840	.840	.840	.840	.840	.840
.18	.847	.825	.821	.820	.820	.820	.820	.820	.820	.820	.820	.820	.820	.820	.820	.820	.820	.820	.820	.820
.20	.833	.806	.801	.800	.800	.800	.800	.800	.800	.800	.800	.800	.800	.800	.800	.800	.800	.800	.800	.820
.22	.820	.788	.782	.780	.780	.780	.780	.780	.780	.780	.780	.780	.780	.780	.780	.780	.780	.780	.780	.800
.24	.806	.771	.763	.761	.760	.760	.760	.760	.760	.760	.760	.760	.760	.760	.760	.760	.760	.760	.760	.780
.26	.794	.753	.743	.741	.740	.740	.740	.740	.740	.740	.740	.740	.740	.740	.740	.740	.740	.740	.760	.760
.28	.781	.736	.724	.721	.720	.720	.720	.720	.720	.720	.720	.720	.720	.720	.720	.720	.720	.720	.740	.740
.30	.769	.719	.706	.702	.701	.700	.700	.700	.700	.700	.700	.700	.700	.700	.700	.700	.700	.700	.720	.720
.32	.758	.703	.687	.682	.681	.680	.680	.680	.680	.680	.680	.680	.680	.680	.680	.680	.680	.680	.680	.680
.34	.746	.687	.669	.663	.661	.660	.660	.660	.660	.660	.660	.660	.660	.660	.660	.660	.660	.660	.660	.660
.36	.735	.671	.651	.644	.641	.641	.640	.640	.640	.640	.640	.640	.640	.640	.640	.640	.640	.640	.660	.660
.38	.725	.656	.633	.625	.622	.621	.620	.620	.620	.620	.620	.620	.620	.620	.620	.620	.620	.620	.640	.640
.40	.714	.641	.616	.606	.602	.601	.600	.600	.600	.600	.600	.600	.600	.600	.600	.600	.600	.600	.600	.600
.42	.704	.626	.599	.588	.583	.581	.581	.580	.580	.580	.580	.580	.580	.580	.580	.580	.580	.580	.580	.580
.44	.694	.612	.582	.569	.564	.562	.561	.560	.560	.560	.560	.560	.560	.560	.560	.560	.560	.560	.580	.580
.46	.685	.598	.565	.551	.545	.542	.541	.540	.540	.540	.540	.540	.540	.540	.540	.540	.540	.540	.540	.540
.48	.676	.585	.549	.534	.526	.523	.521	.521	.520	.520	.520	.520	.520	.520	.520	.520	.520	.520	.540	.540
.50	.667	.571	.533	.516	.508	.504	.502	.501	.500	.500	.500	.500	.500	.500	.500	.500	.500	.500	.520	.520
.52	.658	.559	.518	.499	.490	.485	.483	.481	.481	.480	.480	.480	.480	.480	.480	.480	.480	.480	.500	.500
.54	.649	.546	.503	.482	.472	.466	.463	.462	.461	.461	.460	.460	.460	.460	.460	.460	.460	.460	.480	.480
.56	.641	.534	.488	.466	.454	.448	.444	.442	.441	.441	.440	.440	.440	.440	.440	.440	.440	.440	.460	.460
.58	.633	.522	.474	.450	.437	.429	.425	.423	.422	.421	.421	.420	.420	.420	.420	.420	.420	.420	.420	.420
.60	.625	.510	.460	.434	.420	.412	.407	.404	.402	.401	.401	.401	.400	.400	.400	.400	.400	.400	.400	.400
.62	.617	.499	.446	.418	.403	.394	.388	.385	.383	.382	.381	.381	.380	.380	.380	.380	.380	.380	.380	.380
.64	.610	.488	.433	.403	.387	.377	.370	.367	.364	.363	.362	.361	.361	.360	.360	.360	.360	.360	.380	.380
.66	.602	.477	.420	.389	.371	.360	.353	.348	.345	.344	.342	.342	.341	.341	.340	.340	.340	.340	.360	.360
.68	.595	.467	.407	.374	.355	.343	.335	.330	.327	.325	.323	.322	.321	.321	.320	.320	.320	.320	.340	.340
.70	.588	.457	.395	.361	.340	.327	.318	.313	.309	.306	.304	.303	.302	.301	.301	.301	.300	.300	.300	.300
.72	.581	.447	.383	.347	.325	.311	.302	.295	.291	.288	.286	.284	.283	.282	.281	.281	.281	.281	.280	.280
.74	.575	.437	.371	.334	.311	.296	.286	.279	.273	.270	.267	.265	.264	.263	.262	.262	.261	.261	.261	.260
.76	.568	.428	.360	.322	.297	.281	.270	.262	.256	.252	.249	.247	.245	.244	.243	.242	.242	.241	.241	.260
.78	.562	.419	.349	.309	.284	.267	.255	.246	.240	.235	.232	.229	.227	.225	.224	.223	.223	.222	.222	.241
.80	.556	.410	.339	.297	.271	.253	.240	.231	.224	.219	.215	.212	.209	.207	.206	.205	.204	.203	.202	.221
.82	.549	.401	.329	.286	.259	.240	.226	.216	.209	.203	.198	.195	.192	.190	.188	.186	.185	.184	.183	.183
.84	.543	.393	.319	.275	.247	.227	.213	.202	.194	.188	.183	.179	.175	.173	.170	.169	.167	.166	.165	.164
.86	.538	.385	.309	.264	.235	.215	.200	.189	.180	.173	.167	.163	.159	.156	.154	.152	.150	.148	.147	.146
.88	.532	.377	.300	.254	.224	.203	.187	.176	.166	.159	.153	.148	.144	.141	.138	.135	.133	.132	.130	.129
.90	.526	.369	.291	.244	.213	.192	.176	.163	.154	.146	.139	.134	.130	.126	.123	.120	.118	.116	.114	.112
.92	.521	.361	.282	.235	.203	.181	.164	.152	.141	.133	.127	.121	.116	.112	.109	.106	.103	.101	.099	.097
.94	.515	.354	.274	.225	.193	.171	.154	.141	.130	.122	.114	.109	.104	.099	.095	.092	.089	.087	.085	.082
.96	.510	.347	.266	.217	.184	.161	.144	.130	.119	.111	.103	.097	.092	.087	.083	.080	.077	.074	.072	.069
.98	.505	.340	.258	.208	.175	.152	.134	.120	.109	.100	.093	.087	.081	.077	.072	.069	.066	.063	.072	.069
1.00	.500	.333	.250	.200	.167	.143	.125	.111	.100	.091	.083	.077	.071	.067	.063	.059	.056	.053	.050	.048
1.20	.455	.275	.186	.134	.101	.077	.061	.048	.039	.031	.025	.021	.017	.014	.011	.009	.008	.006	.005	.004
1.40	.417	.229	.141	.091	.061	.042	.029	.020	.014	.010	.007	.005	.004	.003	.002	.001	.001	.001	.000	.000

APPENDIX C2 (Continued)

$\dfrac{\lambda}{\mu}$	Maximum System Size, C																			
	1	2	3	4	5	6	7	8	9	10	11	12	13	14	15	16	17	18	19	20
1.60	.385	.194	.108	.063	.038	.023	.014	.009	.006	.003	.002	.001	.001	.001	.000	.000	.000	.000	.000	.000
1.80	.357	.166	.084	.045	.024	.013	.007	.004	.002	.001	.001	.000	.000	.000	.000	.000	.000	.000	.000	.000
2.00	.333	.143	.067	.032	.016	.008	.004	.002	.001	.000	.000	.000	.000	.000	.000	.000	.000	.000	.000	.000
2.20	.313	.124	.054	.024	.011	.005	.002	.001	.000	.000	.000	.000	.000	.000	.000	.000	.000	.000	.000	.000
2.40	.294	.109	.044	.018	.007	.003	.001	.001	.000	.000	.000	.000	.000	.000	.000	.000	.000	.000	.000	.000
2.60	.278	.097	.036	.014	.005	.002	.001	.000	.000	.000	.000	.000	.000	.000	.000	.000	.000	.000	.000	.000
2.80	.263	.086	.030	.011	.004	.001	.000	.000	.000	.000	.000	.000	.000	.000	.000	.000	.000	.000	.000	.000
3.00	.250	.077	.025	.008	.003	.001	.000	.000	.000	.000	.000	.000	.000	.000	.000	.000	.000	.000	.000	.000
3.20	.238	.069	.021	.007	.002	.001	.000	.000	.000	.000	.000	.000	.000	.000	.000	.000	.000	.000	.000	.000
3.40	.227	.063	.018	.005	.002	.000	.000	.000	.000	.000	.000	.000	.000	.000	.000	.000	.000	.000	.000	.000
3.60	.217	.057	.016	.004	.001	.000	.000	.000	.000	.000	.000	.000	.000	.000	.000	.000	.000	.000	.000	.000
3.80	.208	.052	.013	.004	.001	.000	.000	.000	.000	.000	.000	.000	.000	.000	.000	.000	.000	.000	.000	.000
4.00	.200	.048	.012	.003	.001	.000	.000	.000	.000	.000	.000	.000	.000	.000	.000	.000	.000	.000	.000	.000
4.20	.192	.044	.010	.002	.001	.000	.000	.000	.000	.000	.000	.000	.000	.000	.000	.000	.000	.000	.000	.000
4.40	.185	.040	.009	.002	.000	.000	.000	.000	.000	.000	.000	.000	.000	.000	.000	.000	.000	.000	.000	.000
4.60	.179	.037	.008	.002	.000	.000	.000	.000	.000	.000	.000	.000	.000	.000	.000	.000	.000	.000	.000	.000
4.80	.172	.035	.007	.001	.000	.000	.000	.000	.000	.000	.000	.000	.000	.000	.000	.000	.000	.000	.000	.000
5.00	.167	.032	.006	.001	.000	.000	.000	.000	.000	.000	.000	.000	.000	.000	.000	.000	.000	.000	.000	.000
5.20	.161	.030	.006	.001	.000	.000	.000	.000	.000	.000	.000	.000	.000	.000	.000	.000	.000	.000	.000	.000
5.40	.156	.028	.005	.001	.000	.000	.000	.000	.000	.000	.000	.000	.000	.000	.000	.000	.000	.000	.000	.000
5.60	.152	.026	.005	.001	.000	.000	.000	.000	.000	.000	.000	.000	.000	.000	.000	.000	.000	.000	.000	.000
5.80	.147	.025	.004	.001	.000	.000	.000	.000	.000	.000	.000	.000	.000	.000	.000	.000	.000	.000	.000	.000
6.00	.143	.023	.004	.001	.000	.000	.000	.000	.000	.000	.000	.000	.000	.000	.000	.000	.000	.000	.000	.000
6.20	.139	.022	.004	.001	.000	.000	.000	.000	.000	.000	.000	.000	.000	.000	.000	.000	.000	.000	.000	.000
6.40	.135	.021	.003	.001	.000	.000	.000	.000	.000	.000	.000	.000	.000	.000	.000	.000	.000	.000	.000	.000
6.60	.132	.020	.003	.000	.000	.000	.000	.000	.000	.000	.000	.000	.000	.000	.000	.000	.000	.000	.000	.000
6.80	.128	.019	.003	.000	.000	.000	.000	.000	.000	.000	.000	.000	.000	.000	.000	.000	.000	.000	.000	.000
7.00	.125	.018	.002	.000	.000	.000	.000	.000	.000	.000	.000	.000	.000	.000	.000	.000	.000	.000	.000	.000
7.20	.122	.017	.002	.000	.000	.000	.000	.000	.000	.000	.000	.000	.000	.000	.000	.000	.000	.000	.000	.000
7.40	.119	.016	.002	.000	.000	.000	.000	.000	.000	.000	.000	.000	.000	.000	.000	.000	.000	.000	.000	.000
7.60	.116	.015	.002	.000	.000	.000	.000	.000	.000	.000	.000	.000	.000	.000	.000	.000	.000	.000	.000	.000
7.80	.114	.014	.002	.000	.000	.000	.000	.000	.000	.000	.000	.000	.000	.000	.000	.000	.000	.000	.000	.000
8.00	.111	.014	.002	.000	.000	.000	.000	.000	.000	.000	.000	.000	.000	.000	.000	.000	.000	.000	.000	.000
8.20	.109	.013	.002	.000	.000	.000	.000	.000	.000	.000	.000	.000	.000	.000	.000	.000	.000	.000	.000	.000
8.40	.106	.013	.001	.000	.000	.000	.000	.000	.000	.000	.000	.000	.000	.000	.000	.000	.000	.000	.000	.000
8.60	.104	.012	.001	.000	.000	.000	.000	.000	.000	.000	.000	.000	.000	.000	.000	.000	.000	.000	.000	.000
8.80	.102	.011	.001	.000	.000	.000	.000	.000	.000	.000	.000	.000	.000	.000	.000	.000	.000	.000	.000	.000
9.00	.100	.011	.001	.000	.000	.000	.000	.000	.000	.000	.000	.000	.000	.000	.000	.000	.000	.000	.000	.000
9.20	.098	.011	.001	.000	.000	.000	.000	.000	.000	.000	.000	.000	.000	.000	.000	.000	.000	.000	.000	.000
9.40	.096	.010	.001	.000	.000	.000	.000	.000	.000	.000	.000	.000	.000	.000	.000	.000	.000	.000	.000	.000
9.60	.094	.010	.001	.000	.000	.000	.000	.000	.000	.000	.000	.000	.000	.000	.000	.000	.000	.000	.000	.000
9.80	.093	.009	.001	.000	.000	.000	.000	.000	.000	.000	.000	.000	.000	.000	.000	.000	.000	.000	.000	.000
10.00	.091	.009	.001	.000	.000	.000	.000	.000	.000	.000	.000	.000	.000	.000	.000	.000	.000	.000	.000	.000
20.00	.048	.002	.000	.000	.000	.000	.000	.000	.000	.000	.000	.000	.000	.000	.000	.000	.000	.000	.000	.000
30.00	.032	.001	.000	.000	.000	.000	.000	.000	.000	.000	.000	.000	.000	.000	.000	.000	.000	.000	.000	.000
40.00	.024	.001	.000	.000	.000	.000	.000	.000	.000	.000	.000	.000	.000	.000	.000	.000	.000	.000	.000	.000
50.00	.020	.000	.000	.000	.000	.000	.000	.000	.000	.000	.000	.000	.000	.000	.000	.000	.000	.000	.000	.000
60.00	.016	.000	.000	.000	.000	.000	.000	.000	.000	.000	.000	.000	.000	.000	.000	.000	.000	.000	.000	.000
70.00	.014	.000	.000	.000	.000	.000	.000	.000	.000	.000	.000	.000	.000	.000	.000	.000	.000	.000	.000	.000
80.00	.012	.000	.000	.000	.000	.000	.000	.000	.000	.000	.000	.000	.000	.000	.000	.000	.000	.000	.000	.000
90.00	.011	.000	.000	.000	.000	.000	.000	.000	.000	.000	.000	.000	.000	.000	.000	.000	.000	.000	.000	.000
100.00	.010	.000	.000	.000	.000	.000	.000	.000	.000	.000	.000	.000	.000	.000	.000	.000	.000	.000	.000	.000

APPENDIX C3 *M/M/1* queue with a limited queue/system size: probability that the system is full

$\dfrac{\lambda}{\mu}$	\multicolumn{20}{c}{Maximum System Size, C}

$\dfrac{\lambda}{\mu}$	1	2	3	4	5	6	7	8	9	10	11	12	13	14	15	16	17	18	19	20
.02	.020	.000	.000	.000	.000	.000	.000	.000	.000	.000	.000	.000	.000	.000	.000	.000	.000	.000	.000	.000
.04	.038	.002	.000	.000	.000	.000	.000	.000	.000	.000	.000	.000	.000	.000	.000	.000	.000	.000	.000	.000
.06	.057	.003	.000	.000	.000	.000	.000	.000	.000	.000	.000	.000	.000	.000	.000	.000	.000	.000	.000	.000
.08	.074	.006	.000	.000	.000	.000	.000	.000	.000	.000	.000	.000	.000	.000	.000	.000	.000	.000	.000	.000
.10	.091	.009	.001	.000	.000	.000	.000	.000	.000	.000	.000	.000	.000	.000	.000	.000	.000	.000	.000	.000
.12	.107	.013	.002	.000	.000	.000	.000	.000	.000	.000	.000	.000	.000	.000	.000	.000	.000	.000	.000	.000
.14	.123	.017	.002	.000	.000	.000	.000	.000	.000	.000	.000	.000	.000	.000	.000	.000	.000	.000	.000	.000
.16	.138	.022	.003	.001	.000	.000	.000	.000	.000	.000	.000	.000	.000	.000	.000	.000	.000	.000	.000	.000
.18	.153	.027	.005	.001	.000	.000	.000	.000	.000	.000	.000	.000	.000	.000	.000	.000	.000	.000	.000	.000
.20	.167	.032	.006	.001	.000	.000	.000	.000	.000	.000	.000	.000	.000	.000	.000	.000	.000	.000	.000	.000
.22	.180	.038	.008	.002	.000	.000	.000	.000	.000	.000	.000	.000	.000	.000	.000	.000	.000	.000	.000	.000
.24	.194	.044	.011	.003	.001	.000	.000	.000	.000	.000	.000	.000	.000	.000	.000	.000	.000	.000	.000	.000
.26	.206	.051	.013	.003	.001	.000	.000	.000	.000	.000	.000	.000	.000	.000	.000	.000	.000	.000	.000	.000
.28	.219	.058	.016	.004	.001	.000	.000	.000	.000	.000	.000	.000	.000	.000	.000	.000	.000	.000	.000	.000
.30	.231	.065	.019	.006	.002	.001	.000	.000	.000	.000	.000	.000	.000	.000	.000	.000	.000	.000	.000	.000
.32	.242	.072	.023	.007	.002	.001	.000	.000	.000	.000	.000	.000	.000	.000	.000	.000	.000	.000	.000	.000
.34	.254	.079	.026	.009	.003	.001	.000	.000	.000	.000	.000	.000	.000	.000	.000	.000	.000	.000	.000	.000
.36	.265	.087	.030	.011	.004	.001	.001	.000	.000	.000	.000	.000	.000	.000	.000	.000	.000	.000	.000	.000
.38	.275	.095	.035	.013	.005	.002	.001	.000	.000	.000	.000	.000	.000	.000	.000	.000	.000	.000	.000	.000
.40	.286	.103	.039	.016	.006	.002	.001	.000	.000	.000	.000	.000	.000	.000	.000	.000	.000	.000	.000	.000
.42	.296	.110	.044	.018	.008	.003	.001	.001	.000	.000	.000	.000	.000	.000	.000	.000	.000	.000	.000	.000
.44	.306	.119	.050	.021	.009	.004	.002	.001	.000	.000	.000	.000	.000	.000	.000	.000	.000	.000	.000	.000
.46	.315	.127	.055	.025	.011	.005	.002	.001	.000	.000	.000	.000	.000	.000	.000	.000	.000	.000	.000	.000
.48	.324	.135	.061	.028	.013	.006	.003	.001	.001	.000	.000	.000	.000	.000	.000	.000	.000	.000	.000	.000
.50	.333	.143	.067	.032	.016	.008	.004	.002	.001	.000	.000	.000	.000	.000	.000	.000	.000	.000	.000	.000
.52	.342	.151	.073	.036	.019	.010	.005	.003	.001	.001	.000	.000	.000	.000	.000	.000	.000	.000	.000	.000
.54	.351	.159	.079	.041	.022	.012	.006	.003	.002	.001	.001	.000	.000	.000	.000	.000	.000	.000	.000	.000
.56	.359	.167	.086	.046	.025	.014	.008	.004	.002	.001	.001	.000	.000	.000	.000	.000	.000	.000	.000	.000
.58	.367	.176	.092	.051	.029	.016	.009	.005	.003	.002	.001	.001	.000	.000	.000	.000	.000	.000	.000	.000
.60	.375	.184	.099	.056	.033	.019	.011	.007	.004	.002	.001	.001	.001	.000	.000	.000	.000	.000	.000	.000
.62	.383	.192	.106	.062	.037	.022	.014	.008	.005	.003	.002	.001	.001	.001	.000	.000	.000	.000	.000	.000
.64	.390	.200	.113	.068	.042	.026	.016	.010	.007	.004	.003	.002	.001	.001	.000	.000	.000	.000	.000	.000
.66	.398	.208	.121	.074	.046	.030	.019	.013	.008	.005	.004	.002	.002	.001	.001	.000	.000	.000	.000	.000
.68	.405	.216	.128	.080	.052	.034	.023	.015	.010	.007	.005	.003	.002	.001	.001	.001	.000	.000	.000	.000
.70	.412	.224	.135	.087	.057	.038	.026	.018	.012	.009	.006	.004	.003	.002	.001	.001	.001	.000	.000	.000
.72	.419	.232	.143	.093	.063	.043	.030	.021	.015	.011	.008	.006	.004	.003	.002	.001	.001	.001	.001	.000
.74	.425	.239	.150	.100	.069	.049	.035	.025	.018	.013	.010	.007	.005	.004	.003	.002	.002	.001	.001	.001
.76	.432	.247	.158	.107	.075	.054	.040	.029	.022	.016	.012	.009	.007	.005	.004	.003	.002	.002	.001	.001
.78	.438	.255	.166	.114	.082	.060	.045	.034	.026	.020	.015	.012	.009	.007	.005	.004	.003	.003	.002	.002
.80	.444	.262	.173	.122	.089	.066	.050	.039	.030	.023	.018	.015	.012	.009	.007	.006	.005	.004	.003	.002
.82	.451	.270	.181	.129	.096	.073	.056	.044	.035	.028	.022	.018	.015	.012	.010	.008	.006	.005	.004	.003
.84	.457	.277	.189	.137	.103	.080	.063	.050	.040	.033	.027	.022	.018	.015	.012	.010	.009	.007	.006	.005
.86	.462	.285	.197	.145	.111	.087	.070	.056	.046	.038	.032	.027	.022	.019	.016	.014	.012	.010	.008	.007
.88	.468	.292	.204	.152	.118	.094	.077	.063	.053	.044	.037	.032	.027	.023	.020	.018	.015	.013	.011	.010
.90	.474	.299	.212	.160	.126	.102	.084	.070	.059	.051	.044	.038	.033	.029	.025	.022	.020	.017	.015	.014
.92	.479	.306	.220	.168	.134	.110	.092	.078	.067	.058	.051	.044	.039	.035	.031	.028	.025	.022	.020	.018
.94	.485	.313	.227	.176	.142	.118	.100	.086	.075	.065	.058	.052	.046	.042	.038	.034	.031	.028	.026	.024
.96	.490	.320	.235	.184	.150	.126	.108	.094	.083	.074	.066	.060	.054	.049	.045	.042	.038	.036	.033	.031
.98	.495	.327	.242	.192	.158	.134	.116	.102	.091	.082	.074	.068	.062	.058	.053	.050	.047	.044	.041	.039
1.00	.500	.333	.250	.200	.167	.143	.125	.111	.100	.091	.083	.077	.071	.067	.063	.059	.056	.053	.050	.048
1.20	.545	.396	.322	.279	.251	.231	.217	.207	.199	.193	.188	.184	.181	.178	.176	.175	.173	.172	.171	.170
1.40	.583	.450	.386	.351	.329	.316	.306	.300	.296	.293	.291	.289	.288	.288	.287	.287	.286	.286	.286	.286

APPENDIX C3 (Continued)

$\frac{\lambda}{\mu}$	Maximum System Size, C																			
	1	2	3	4	5	6	7	8	9	10	11	12	13	14	15	16	17	18	19	20
1.60	.615	.496	.443	.415	.399	.390	.384	.381	.378	.377	.376	.376	.376	.375	.375	.375	.375	.375	.375	.375
1.80	.643	.536	.491	.469	.458	.452	.449	.447	.446	.445	.445	.445	.445	.445	.444	.444	.444	.444	.444	.444
2.00	.667	.571	.533	.516	.508	.504	.502	.501	.500	.500	.500	.500	.500	.500	.500	.500	.500	.500	.500	.500
2.20	.688	.602	.570	.556	.550	.548	.546	.546	.546	.545	.545	.545	.545	.545	.545	.545	.545	.545	.545	.545
2.40	.706	.629	.601	.591	.586	.585	.584	.584	.583	.583	.583	.583	.583	.583	.583	.583	.583	.583	.583	.583
2.60	.722	.653	.629	.621	.617	.616	.616	.615	.615	.615	.615	.615	.615	.615	.615	.615	.615	.615	.615	.615
2.80	.737	.674	.653	.647	.644	.643	.643	.643	.643	.643	.643	.643	.643	.643	.643	.643	.643	.643	.643	.643
3.00	.750	.692	.675	.669	.668	.667	.667	.667	.667	.667	.667	.667	.667	.667	.667	.667	.667	.667	.667	.667
3.20	.762	.709	.694	.690	.688	.688	.688	.688	.688	.688	.688	.688	.688	.688	.688	.688	.688	.688	.688	.688
3.40	.773	.724	.711	.707	.706	.706	.706	.706	.706	.706	.706	.706	.706	.706	.706	.706	.706	.706	.706	.706
3.60	.783	.738	.727	.723	.723	.722	.722	.722	.722	.722	.722	.722	.702	.722	.722	.722	.722	.722	.722	.722
3.80	.792	.751	.740	.738	.737	.737	.737	.737	.737	.737	.737	.737	.737	.737	.737	.737	.737	.737	.737	.737
4.00	.800	.762	.753	.751	.750	.750	.750	.750	.750	.750	.750	.750	.750	.750	.750	.750	.750	.750	.750	.750
4.20	.808	.772	.764	.762	.762	.762	.762	.762	.762	.762	.762	.762	.762	.762	.762	.762	.762	.762	.762	.762
4.40	.815	.782	.775	.773	.773	.773	.773	.773	.773	.773	.773	.773	.773	.773	.773	.773	.773	.773	.773	.773
4.60	.821	.791	.784	.783	.783	.783	.783	.783	.783	.783	.783	.783	.783	.783	.783	.783	.783	.783	.783	.783
4.80	.828	.799	.793	.792	.792	.792	.792	.792	.792	.792	.792	.792	.792	.792	.792	.792	.792	.792	.792	.792
5.00	.833	.806	.801	.800	.800	.800	.800	.800	.800	.800	.800	.800	.800	.800	.800	.800	.800	.800	.800	.800
5.20	.839	.813	.809	.808	.808	.808	.808	.808	.808	.808	.808	.808	.808	.808	.808	.808	.808	.808	.808	.808
5.40	.844	.820	.816	.815	.815	.815	.815	.815	.815	.815	.815	.815	.815	.815	.815	.815	.815	.815	.815	.815
5.60	.848	.826	.822	.822	.821	.821	.821	.821	.821	.821	.821	.821	.821	.821	.821	.821	.821	.821	.821	.821
5.80	.853	.832	.828	.828	.828	.828	.828	.828	.828	.828	.828	.828	.828	.828	.828	.828	.828	.828	.828	.828
6.00	.857	.837	.834	.833	.833	.833	.833	.833	.833	.833	.833	.833	.833	.833	.833	.833	.833	.833	.833	.833
6.20	.861	.842	.839	.839	.839	.839	.839	.839	.839	.839	.839	.839	.839	.839	.839	.839	.839	.839	.839	.839
6.40	.865	.847	.844	.844	.844	.844	.844	.844	.844	.844	.844	.844	.844	.844	.844	.844	.844	.844	.844	.844
6.60	.868	.851	.849	.849	.848	.848	.848	.848	.848	.848	.848	.848	.848	.848	.848	.848	.848	.848	.848	.848
6.80	.872	.856	.853	.853	.853	.853	.853	.853	.853	.853	.853	.853	.853	.853	.853	.853	.853	.853	.853	.853
7.00	.875	.860	.858	.857	.857	.857	.857	.857	.857	.857	.857	.857	.857	.857	.857	.857	.857	.857	.857	.857
7.20	.878	.863	.861	.861	.861	.861	.861	.861	.861	.861	.861	.861	.861	.861	.861	.861	.861	.861	.861	.861
7.40	.881	.867	.865	.865	.865	.865	.865	.865	.865	.865	.865	.865	.865	.865	.865	.865	.865	.865	.865	.865
7.60	.884	.870	.869	.868	.868	.868	.868	.868	.868	.868	.868	.868	.868	.868	.868	.868	.868	.868	.868	.868
7.80	.886	.874	.872	.872	.872	.872	.872	.872	.872	.872	.872	.872	.872	.872	.872	.872	.872	.872	.872	.872
8.00	.889	.877	.875	.875	.875	.875	.875	.875	.875	.875	.875	.875	.875	.875	.875	.875	.875	.875	.875	.875
8.20	.891	.880	.878	.878	.878	.878	.878	.878	.878	.878	.878	.878	.878	.878	.878	.878	.878	.878	.878	.878
8.40	.894	.882	.881	.881	.881	.881	.881	.881	.881	.881	.881	.881	.881	.881	.881	.881	.881	.881	.881	.881
8.60	.896	.885	.884	.884	.884	.884	.884	.884	.884	.884	.884	.884	.884	.884	.884	.884	.884	.884	.884	.884
8.80	.898	.888	.887	.886	.886	.886	.886	.886	.886	.886	.886	.886	.886	.886	.886	.886	.886	.886	.886	.886
9.00	.900	.890	.889	.889	.889	.889	.889	.889	.889	.889	.889	.889	.889	.889	.889	.889	.889	.889	.889	.889
9.20	.902	.892	.891	.891	.891	.891	.891	.891	.891	.891	.891	.891	.891	.891	.891	.891	.891	.891	.891	.891
9.40	.904	.895	.894	.894	.894	.894	.894	.894	.894	.894	.894	.894	.894	.894	.894	.894	.894	.894	.894	.894
9.60	.906	.897	.896	.896	.896	.896	.896	.896	.896	.896	.896	.896	.896	.896	.896	.896	.896	.896	.896	.896
9.80	.907	.899	.898	.898	.898	.898	.898	.898	.898	.898	.898	.898	.898	.898	.898	.898	.898	.898	.898	.898
10.00	.909	.901	.900	.900	.900	.900	.900	.900	.900	.900	.900	.900	.900	.900	.900	.900	.900	.900	.900	.900
20.00	.952	.950	.950	.950	.950	.950	.950	.950	.950	.950	.950	.950	.950	.950	.950	.950	.950	.950	.950	.950
30.00	.968	.967	.967	.967	.967	.967	.967	.967	.967	.967	.967	.967	.967	.967	.967	.967	.967	.967	.967	.967
40.00	.976	.975	.975	.975	.975	.975	.975	.975	.975	.975	.975	.975	.975	.975	.975	.975	.975	.975	.975	.975
50.00	.980	.980	.980	.980	.980	.980	.980	.980	.980	.980	.980	.980	.980	.980	.980	.980	.980	.980	.980	.980
60.00	.984	.983	.983	.983	.983	.983	.983	.983	.983	.983	.983	.983	.983	.983	.983	.983	.983	.983	.983	.983
70.00	.986	.986	.986	.986	.986	.986	.986	.986	.986	.986	.986	.986	.986	.986	.986	.986	.986	.986	.986	.986
80.00	.988	.988	.988	.988	.988	.988	.988	.988	.988	.988	.988	.988	.988	.988	.988	.988	.988	.988	.988	.988
90.00	.989	.989	.989	.989	.989	.989	.989	.989	.989	.989	.989	.989	.989	.989	.989	.989	.989	.989	.989	.989
100.00	.990	.990	.990	.990	.990	.990	.990	.990	.990	.990	.990	.990	.990	.990	.990	.990	.990	.990	.990	.990

APPENDIX C4 *M/M/1* queue with a limited queue/system size: average number of customers in the system, *L*

$\frac{\lambda}{\mu}$	1	2	3	4	5	6	7	8	9	10	11	12	13	14	15	16	17
.02	.020	.020	.020	.020	.020	.020	.020	.020	.020	.020	.020	.020	.020	.020	.020	.020	.020
.04	.038	.041	.042	.042	.042	.042	.042	.042	.042	.042	.042	.042	.042	.042	.042	.042	.042
.06	.057	.063	.064	.064	.064	.064	.064	.064	.064	.064	.064	.064	.064	.064	.064	.064	.064
.08	.074	.085	.087	.087	.087	.087	.087	.087	.087	.087	.087	.087	.087	.087	.087	.087	.087
.10	.091	.108	.111	.111	.111	.111	.111	.111	.111	.111	.111	.111	.111	.111	.111	.111	.111
.12	.107	.131	.136	.136	.136	.136	.136	.136	.136	.136	.136	.136	.136	.136	.136	.136	.136
.14	.123	.155	.161	.163	.163	.163	.163	.163	.163	.163	.163	.163	.163	.163	.163	.163	.163
.16	.138	.178	.188	.190	.190	.190	.190	.190	.190	.190	.190	.190	.190	.190	.190	.190	.190
.18	.153	.202	.215	.219	.219	.219	.220	.220	.220	.220	.220	.220	.220	.220	.220	.220	.220
.20	.167	.226	.244	.248	.250	.250	.250	.250	.250	.250	.250	.250	.250	.250	.250	.250	.250
.22	.180	.250	.273	.279	.281	.282	.282	.282	.282	.282	.282	.282	.282	.282	.282	.282	.282
.24	.194	.274	.302	.312	.315	.315	.316	.316	.316	.316	.316	.316	.316	.316	.316	.316	.316
.26	.206	.298	.333	.345	.349	.351	.351	.351	.351	.351	.351	.351	.351	.351	.351	.351	.351
.28	.219	.322	.364	.380	.386	.388	.389	.389	.389	.389	.389	.389	.389	.389	.389	.389	.389
.30	.231	.345	.396	.416	.424	.427	.428	.428	.428	.429	.429	.429	.429	.429	.429	.429	.429
.32	.242	.369	.428	.454	.464	.468	.470	.470	.470	.471	.471	.471	.471	.471	.471	.471	.471
.34	.254	.392	.461	.492	.506	.511	.514	.515	.515	.515	.515	.515	.515	.515	.515	.515	.515
.36	.265	.416	.494	.532	.549	.557	.560	.562	.562	.562	.562	.562	.562	.562	.562	.562	.562
.38	.275	.439	.528	.573	.595	.605	.609	.611	.612	.613	.613	.613	.613	.613	.613	.613	.613
.40	.286	.462	.562	.615	.642	.655	.661	.664	.666	.666	.666	.667	.667	.667	.667	.667	.667
.42	.296	.484	.596	.658	.691	.708	.716	.720	.722	.723	.724	.724	.724	.724	.724	.724	.724
.44	.306	.506	.630	.702	.742	.763	.774	.780	.783	.784	.785	.785	.786	.786	.786	.786	.786
.46	.315	.528	.664	.747	.794	.821	.836	.844	.848	.850	.851	.851	.852	.852	.852	.852	.852
.48	.324	.550	.699	.792	.849	.882	.900	.911	.917	.920	.921	.922	.923	.923	.923	.923	.923
.50	.333	.571	.733	.839	.905	.945	.969	.982	.990	.995	.997	.998	.999	1.000	1.000	1.000	1.000
.52	.342	.592	.768	.886	.962	1.011	1.040	1.058	1.069	1.075	1.079	1.081	1.082	1.083	1.083	1.083	1.083
.54	.351	.613	.802	.933	1.021	1.079	1.116	1.139	1.153	1.161	1.167	1.170	1.171	1.172	1.173	1.173	1.174
.56	.359	.634	.836	.981	1.082	1.150	1.195	1.224	1.242	1.254	1.261	1.266	1.269	1.270	1.271	1.272	1.272
.58	.367	.654	.871	1.030	1.144	1.223	1.277	1.314	1.338	1.353	1.364	1.370	1.374	1.377	1.378	1.379	1.380
.60	.375	.673	.904	1.078	1.206	1.298	1.363	1.408	1.439	1.460	1.474	1.483	1.489	1.493	1.495	1.497	1.498
.62	.383	.693	.938	1.127	1.270	1.376	1.453	1.508	1.547	1.574	1.593	1.606	1.614	1.620	1.624	1.627	1.628
.64	.390	.712	.971	1.176	1.335	1.456	1.546	1.613	1.661	1.696	1.721	1.738	1.751	1.759	1.765	1.769	1.772
.66	.398	.731	1.004	1.225	1.401	1.537	1.642	1.722	1.782	1.826	1.859	1.882	1.899	1.912	1.920	1.927	1.931
.68	.405	.749	1.037	1.274	1.467	1.620	1.742	1.836	1.909	1.965	2.007	2.038	2.061	2.079	2.091	2.101	2.108
.70	.412	.767	1.069	1.323	1.533	1.705	1.844	1.955	2.043	2.111	2.165	2.206	2.238	2.262	2.280	2.294	2.304
.72	.419	.785	1.101	1.372	1.600	1.791	1.949	2.078	2.182	2.267	2.334	2.387	2.429	2.462	2.488	2.507	2.523
.74	.425	.802	1.133	1.420	1.667	1.878	2.056	2.205	2.328	2.430	2.514	2.581	2.636	2.680	2.716	2.744	2.766
.76	.432	.819	1.164	1.468	1.734	1.966	2.165	2.335	2.480	2.602	2.704	2.789	2.860	2.918	2.966	3.005	3.037
.78	.438	.836	1.195	1.516	1.802	2.054	2.275	2.469	2.636	2.781	2.904	3.010	3.100	3.176	3.239	3.293	3.338
.80	.444	.852	1.225	1.563	1.868	2.142	2.387	2.605	2.797	2.966	3.115	3.244	3.356	3.453	3.537	3.608	3.670
.82	.451	.869	1.255	1.610	1.935	2.231	2.500	2.743	2.962	3.158	3.334	3.490	3.628	3.750	3.858	3.952	4.035
.84	.457	.884	1.284	1.656	2.001	2.320	2.613	2.883	3.130	3.356	3.561	3.746	3.915	4.066	4.203	4.325	4.434
.86	.462	.900	1.313	1.701	2.066	2.408	2.727	3.024	3.301	3.557	3.794	4.013	4.215	4.400	4.569	4.725	4.866
.88	.468	.915	1.341	1.746	2.131	2.495	2.840	3.166	3.473	3.762	4.034	4.288	4.526	4.749	4.957	5.150	5.330
.90	.474	.930	1.369	1.790	2.195	2.582	2.953	3.308	3.647	3.969	4.277	4.569	4.847	5.111	5.361	5.597	5.821
.92	.479	.944	1.396	1.834	2.258	2.668	3.066	3.449	3.820	4.178	4.523	4.855	5.175	5.483	5.779	6.063	6.336
.94	.485	.959	1.423	1.876	2.320	2.753	3.176	3.590	3.993	4.386	4.769	5.143	5.507	5.861	6.206	6.542	6.868
.96	.490	.973	1.449	1.918	2.381	2.837	3.286	3.728	4.164	4.593	5.015	5.431	5.840	6.243	6.639	7.028	7.411
.98	.495	.987	1.475	1.960	2.441	2.919	3.394	3.865	4.333	4.798	5.259	5.717	6.172	6.623	7.071	7.516	7.957
1.00	.500	1.000	1.500	2.000	2.500	3.000	3.500	4.000	4.500	5.000	5.500	6.000	6.500	7.000	7.500	8.000	8.500
1.20	.545	1.121	1.726	2.359	3.021	3.710	4.424	5.164	5.926	6.711	7.516	8.340	9.183	10.041	10.915	11.802	12.702
1.40	.583	1.220	1.908	2.642	3.419	4.234	5.081	5.958	6.858	7.779	8.715	9.666	10.627	11.597	12.574	13.556	14.542

APPENDIX C4 (Continued)

$\dfrac{\lambda}{\mu}$	1	2	3	4	5	6	7	8	9	10	11	12	13	14	15	16	17
								Maximum System Size, C									
1.60	.615	1.302	2.054	2.860	3.714	4.604	5.524	6.466	7.425	8.396	9.376	10.362	11.353	12.346	13.342	14.339	15.337
1.80	.643	1.371	2.171	3.029	3.932	4.866	5.823	6.796	7.778	8.767	9.760	10.756	11.754	12.752	13.751	14.751	15.750
2.00	.667	1.429	2.267	3.161	4.095	5.055	6.031	7.018	8.010	9.005	10.003	11.002	12.001	13.000	14.000	15.000	16.000
2.20	.688	1.478	2.345	3.266	4.220	5.195	6.181	7.174	8.170	9.169	10.168	11.167	12.167	13.167	14.167	15.167	16.167
2.40	.706	1.520	2.410	3.349	4.317	5.301	6.293	7.289	8.287	9.286	10.286	11.286	12.286	13.286	14.286	15.286	16.286
2.60	.722	1.556	2.464	3.417	4.394	5.384	6.379	7.377	8.376	9.375	10.375	11.375	12.375	13.375	14.375	15.375	16.375
2.80	.737	1.588	2.511	3.474	4.457	5.450	6.447	7.445	8.445	9.445	10.444	11.444	12.444	13.444	14.444	15.444	16.444
3.00	.750	1.615	2.550	3.521	4.508	5.503	6.501	7.500	8.500	9.500	10.500	11.500	12.500	13.500	14.500	15.500	16.500
3.20	.762	1.640	2.584	3.560	4.551	5.547	6.546	7.546	8.546	9.545	10.545	11.545	12.545	13.545	14.545	15.545	16.545
3.40	.773	1.662	2.613	3.594	4.587	5.585	6.584	7.583	8.583	9.583	10.583	11.583	12.583	13.583	14.583	15.583	16.583
3.60	.783	1.681	2.639	3.624	4.618	5.616	6.616	7.615	8.615	9.615	10.615	11.615	12.615	13.615	14.615	15.615	16.615
3.80	.792	1.699	2.662	3.649	4.645	5.643	6.643	7.643	8.643	9.643	10.643	11.643	12.643	13.643	14.643	15.643	16.643
4.00	.800	1.714	2.682	3.672	4.668	5.667	6.667	7.667	8.667	9.667	10.667	11.667	12.667	13.667	14.667	15.667	16.667
4.20	.808	1.729	2.700	3.691	4.689	5.688	6.688	7.688	8.688	9.688	10.688	11.688	12.688	13.688	14.688	15.688	16.688
4.40	.815	1.742	2.717	3.709	4.707	5.706	6.706	7.706	8.706	9.706	10.706	11.706	12.706	13.706	14.706	15.706	16.706
4.60	.821	1.753	2.731	3.725	4.723	5.722	6.722	7.722	8.722	9.722	10.722	11.722	12.722	13.722	14.722	15.722	16.722
4.80	.828	1.764	2.744	3.739	4.737	5.737	6.737	7.737	8.737	9.737	10.737	11.737	12.737	13.737	14.737	15.737	16.737
5.00	.833	1.774	2.756	3.752	4.750	5.750	6.750	7.750	8.750	9.750	10.750	11.750	12.750	13.750	14.750	15.750	16.750
5.20	.839	1.783	2.767	3.763	4.762	5.762	6.762	7.762	8.762	9.762	10.762	11.762	12.762	13.762	14.762	15.762	16.762
5.40	.844	1.792	2.777	3.774	4.773	5.773	6.773	7.773	8.773	9.773	10.773	11.773	12.773	13.773	14.773	15.773	16.773
5.60	.848	1.800	2.787	3.784	4.783	5.783	6.783	7.783	8.783	9.783	10.783	11.783	12.783	13.783	14.783	15.783	16.783
5.80	.853	1.807	2.795	3.792	4.792	5.792	6.792	7.792	8.792	9.792	10.792	11.792	12.792	13.792	14.792	15.792	16.792
6.00	.857	1.814	2.803	3.801	4.800	5.800	6.800	7.800	8.800	9.800	10.800	11.800	12.800	13.800	14.800	15.800	16.800
6.20	.861	1.820	2.810	3.808	4.808	5.808	6.808	7.808	8.808	9.808	10.808	11.808	12.808	13.808	14.808	15.808	16.808
6.40	.865	1.826	2.817	3.815	4.815	5.815	6.815	7.815	8.815	9.815	10.815	11.815	12.815	13.815	14.815	15.815	16.815
6.60	.868	1.832	2.824	3.822	4.822	5.821	6.821	7.821	8.821	9.821	10.821	11.821	12.821	13.821	14.821	15.821	16.821
6.80	.872	1.837	2.829	3.828	4.828	5.828	6.828	7.828	8.828	9.828	10.828	11.828	12.828	13.828	14.828	15.828	16.828
7.00	.875	1.842	2.835	3.834	4.833	5.833	6.833	7.833	8.833	9.833	10.833	11.833	12.833	13.833	14.833	15.833	16.833
7.20	.878	1.847	2.840	3.839	4.839	5.839	6.839	7.839	8.839	9.839	10.839	11.839	12.839	13.839	14.839	15.839	16.839
7.40	.881	1.851	2.845	3.844	4.844	5.844	6.844	7.844	8.844	9.844	10.844	11.844	12.844	13.844	14.844	15.844	16.844
7.60	.884	1.855	2.850	3.849	4.849	5.848	6.848	7.848	8.848	9.848	10.848	11.848	12.848	13.848	14.848	15.848	16.848
7.80	.886	1.859	2.854	3.853	4.853	5.853	6.853	7.853	8.853	9.853	10.853	11.853	12.853	13.853	14.853	15.853	16.853
8.00	.889	1.863	2.858	3.857	4.857	5.857	6.857	7.857	8.857	9.857	10.857	11.857	12.857	13.857	14.857	15.857	16.857
8.20	.891	1.867	2.862	3.861	4.861	5.861	6.861	7.861	8.861	9.861	10.861	11.861	12.861	13.861	14.861	15.861	16.861
8.40	.894	1.870	2.866	3.865	4.865	5.865	6.865	7.865	8.865	9.865	10.865	11.865	12.865	13.865	14.865	15.865	16.865
8.60	.896	1.873	2.869	3.869	4.868	5.868	6.868	7.868	8.868	9.868	10.868	11.868	12.868	13.868	14.868	15.868	16.868
8.80	.898	1.876	2.872	3.872	4.872	5.872	6.872	7.872	8.872	9.872	10.872	11.872	12.872	13.872	14.872	15.872	16.872
9.00	.900	1.879	2.876	3.875	4.875	5.875	6.875	7.875	8.875	9.875	10.875	11.875	12.875	13.875	14.875	15.875	16.875
9.20	.902	1.882	2.879	3.878	4.878	5.878	6.878	7.878	8.878	9.878	10.878	11.878	12.878	13.878	14.878	15.878	16.878
9.40	.904	1.885	2.881	3.881	4.881	5.881	6.881	7.881	8.881	9.881	10.881	11.881	12.881	13.881	14.881	15.881	16.881
9.60	.906	1.887	2.884	3.884	4.884	5.884	6.884	7.884	8.884	9.884	10.884	11.884	12.884	13.884	14.884	15.884	16.884
9.80	.907	1.890	2.887	3.886	4.886	5.886	6.886	7.886	8.886	9.886	10.886	11.886	12.886	13.886	14.886	15.886	16.886
10.00	.909	1.892	2.889	3.889	4.889	5.889	6.889	7.889	8.889	9.889	10.889	11.889	12.889	13.889	14.889	15.889	16.889
20.00	.952	1.948	2.947	3.947	4.947	5.947	6.947	7.947	8.947	9.947	10.947	11.947	12.947	13.947	14.947	15.947	16.947
30.00	.968	1.966	2.966	3.966	4.966	5.966	6.966	7.966	8.966	9.966	10.966	11.966	12.966	13.966	14.966	15.966	16.966
40.00	.976	1.974	2.974	3.974	4.974	5.974	6.974	7.974	8.974	9.974	10.974	11.974	12.974	13.974	14.974	15.974	16.974
50.00	.980	1.980	2.980	3.980	4.980	5.980	6.980	7.980	8.980	9.980	10.980	11.980	12.980	13.980	14.980	15.980	16.980
60.00	.984	1.983	2.983	3.983	4.983	5.983	6.983	7.983	8.983	9.983	10.983	11.983	12.983	13.983	14.983	15.983	16.983
70.00	.986	1.986	2.986	3.986	4.986	5.986	6.986	7.986	8.986	9.986	10.986	11.986	12.986	13.986	14.986	15.986	16.986
80.00	.988	1.987	2.987	3.987	4.987	5.987	6.987	7.987	8.987	9.987	10.987	11.987	12.987	13.987	14.987	15.987	16.987
90.00	.989	1.989	2.989	3.989	4.989	5.989	6.989	7.989	8.989	9.989	10.989	11.989	12.989	13.989	14.989	15.989	16.989
100.00	.990	1.990	2.990	3.990	4.990	5.990	6.990	7.990	8.990	9.990	10.990	11.990	12.990	13.990	14.990	15.990	16.990

APPENDIX C5   *M/M/1* queue with a finite population: expected number of customers in the system, *L*

$\frac{\lambda}{\mu}$	1	2	3	4	5	6	7	8	9	10	11	12	13	14	15	16	17	18	19	20
.02	.02	.04	.06	.08	.11	.13	.15	.18	.21	.24	.27	.30	.33	.36	.40	.44	.47	.52	.56	.60
.04	.04	.08	.12	.17	.22	.28	.34	.41	.48	.56	.65	.74	.85	.96	1.09	1.24	1.40	1.57	1.77	2.00
.06	.06	.12	.19	.27	.35	.45	.56	.68	.83	.99	1.17	1.38	1.63	1.91	2.23	2.60	3.02	3.50	4.04	4.64
.08	.07	.16	.25	.36	.49	.64	.81	1.01	1.25	1.52	1.85	2.23	2.67	3.18	3.76	4.41	5.14	5.93	6.77	7.67
.10	.09	.20	.32	.47	.64	.85	1.09	1.38	1.73	2.15	2.63	3.20	3.84	4.57	5.36	6.22	7.13	8.07	9.04	10.02
.12	.11	.23	.39	.57	.79	1.06	1.39	1.78	2.25	2.81	3.45	4.18	4.98	5.85	6.77	7.72	8.69	9.68	10.67	11.67
.14	.12	.27	.45	.68	.95	1.29	1.70	2.19	2.78	3.46	4.23	5.07	5.97	6.92	7.88	8.87	9.86	10.86	11.86	12.86
.16	.14	.31	.52	.78	1.11	1.51	2.01	2.60	3.29	4.07	4.93	5.84	6.79	7.77	8.76	9.75	10.75	11.75	12.75	13.75
.18	.15	.34	.58	.89	1.27	1.74	2.31	2.99	3.76	4.61	5.53	6.48	7.46	8.45	9.45	10.45	11.44	12.44	13.44	14.44
.20	.17	.38	.65	.99	1.42	1.96	2.60	3.35	4.19	5.09	6.04	7.02	8.01	9.00	10.00	11.00	12.00	13.00	14.00	15.00
.22	.18	.41	.71	1.09	1.58	2.17	2.88	3.68	4.57	5.50	6.48	7.46	8.46	9.46	10.45	11.45	12.45	13.45	14.45	15.45
.24	.19	.45	.77	1.19	1.72	2.37	3.13	3.98	4.90	5.86	6.84	7.84	8.83	9.83	10.83	11.83	12.83	13.83	14.83	15.83
.26	.21	.48	.83	1.29	1.87	2.56	3.37	4.25	5.20	6.17	7.16	8.16	9.15	10.15	11.15	12.15	13.15	14.15	15.15	16.15
.28	.22	.51	.89	1.38	2.00	2.74	3.58	4.50	5.45	6.44	7.43	8.43	9.43	10.43	11.43	12.43	13.43	14.43	15.43	16.43
.30	.23	.54	.95	1.48	2.13	2.91	3.78	4.71	5.68	6.67	7.67	8.67	9.67	10.67	11.67	12.67	13.67	14.67	15.67	16.67
.32	.24	.57	1.00	1.56	2.25	3.06	3.96	4.91	5.89	6.88	7.88	8.88	9.88	10.88	11.88	12.88	13.88	14.87	15.87	16.87
.34	.25	.60	1.06	1.65	2.37	3.20	4.12	5.08	6.07	7.06	8.06	9.06	10.06	11.06	12.06	13.06	14.06	15.06	16.06	17.06
.36	.26	.63	1.11	1.73	2.48	3.34	4.27	5.24	6.23	7.22	8.22	9.22	10.22	11.22	12.22	13.22	14.22	15.22	16.22	17.22
.38	.28	.65	1.16	1.80	2.58	3.46	4.40	5.38	6.37	7.37	8.37	9.37	10.37	11.37	12.37	13.37	14.37	15.37	16.37	17.37
.40	.29	.68	1.21	1.87	2.67	3.57	4.52	5.51	6.50	7.50	8.50	9.50	10.50	11.50	12.50	13.50	14.50	15.50	16.50	17.50
.42	.30	.70	1.25	1.94	2.76	3.68	4.64	5.62	6.62	7.62	8.62	9.62	10.62	11.62	12.62	13.62	14.62	15.62	16.62	17.62
.44	.31	.73	1.30	2.01	2.85	3.77	4.74	5.73	6.73	7.73	8.73	9.73	10.73	11.73	12.73	13.73	14.73	15.73	16.73	17.73
.46	.32	.75	1.34	2.07	2.93	3.86	4.84	5.83	6.83	7.83	8.83	9.83	10.83	11.83	12.83	13.83	14.83	15.83	16.83	17.83
.48	.32	.78	1.38	2.13	3.00	3.95	4.93	5.92	6.92	7.92	8.92	9.92	10.92	11.92	12.92	13.92	14.92	15.92	16.92	17.92
.50	.33	.80	1.42	2.19	3.07	4.02	5.01	6.00	7.00	8.00	9.00	10.00	11.00	12.00	13.00	14.00	15.00	16.00	17.00	18.00
.52	.34	.82	1.46	2.24	3.14	4.10	5.08	6.08	7.08	8.08	9.08	10.08	11.08	12.08	13.08	14.08	15.08	16.08	17.08	18.08
.54	.35	.84	1.50	2.30	3.20	4.16	5.15	6.15	7.15	8.15	9.15	10.15	11.15	12.15	13.15	14.15	15.15	16.15	17.15	18.15
.56	.36	.86	1.53	2.35	3.26	4.23	5.22	6.22	7.21	8.21	9.21	10.21	11.21	12.21	13.21	14.21	15.21	16.21	17.21	18.21
.58	.37	.88	1.57	2.39	3.32	4.29	5.28	6.28	7.28	8.28	9.28	10.28	11.28	12.28	13.28	14.28	15.28	16.28	17.28	18.28
.60	.37	.90	1.60	2.44	3.37	4.34	5.34	6.33	7.33	8.33	9.33	10.33	11.33	12.33	13.33	14.33	15.33	16.33	17.33	18.33
.62	.38	.92	1.63	2.48	3.42	4.39	5.39	6.39	7.39	8.39	9.39	10.39	11.39	12.39	13.39	14.39	15.39	16.39	17.39	18.39
.64	.39	.94	1.66	2.52	3.46	4.44	5.44	6.44	7.44	8.44	9.44	10.44	11.44	12.44	13.44	14.44	15.44	16.44	17.44	18.44
.66	.40	.96	1.69	2.56	3.51	4.49	5.49	6.49	7.48	8.48	9.48	10.48	11.48	12.48	13.48	14.48	15.48	16.48	17.48	18.48
.68	.40	.98	1.72	2.60	3.55	4.53	5.53	6.53	7.53	8.53	9.53	10.53	11.53	12.53	13.53	14.53	15.53	16.53	17.53	18.53
.70	.41	.99	1.75	2.63	3.59	4.58	5.57	6.57	7.57	8.57	9.57	10.57	11.57	12.57	13.57	14.57	15.57	16.57	17.57	18.57
.72	.42	1.01	1.77	2.67	3.63	4.61	5.61	6.61	7.61	8.61	9.61	10.61	11.61	12.61	13.61	14.61	15.61	16.61	17.61	18.61
.74	.43	1.03	1.80	2.70	3.66	4.65	5.65	6.65	7.65	8.65	9.65	10.65	11.65	12.65	13.65	14.65	15.65	16.65	17.65	18.65
.76	.43	1.04	1.82	2.73	3.70	4.69	5.68	6.68	7.68	8.68	9.68	10.68	11.68	12.68	13.68	14.68	15.68	16.68	17.68	18.68
.78	.44	1.06	1.85	2.76	3.73	4.72	5.72	6.72	7.72	8.72	9.72	10.72	11.72	12.72	13.72	14.72	15.72	16.72	17.72	18.72
.80	.44	1.07	1.87	2.79	3.76	4.75	5.75	6.75	7.75	8.75	9.75	10.75	11.75	12.75	13.75	14.75	15.75	16.75	17.75	18.75
.82	.45	1.09	1.89	2.81	3.79	4.78	5.78	6.78	7.78	8.78	9.78	10.78	11.78	12.78	13.78	14.78	15.78	16.78	17.78	18.78
.84	.46	1.10	1.91	2.84	3.82	4.81	5.81	6.81	7.81	8.81	9.81	10.81	11.81	12.81	13.81	14.81	15.81	16.81	17.81	18.81
.86	.46	1.11	1.94	2.87	3.84	4.84	5.84	6.84	7.84	8.84	9.84	10.84	11.84	12.84	13.84	14.84	15.84	16.84	17.84	18.84
.88	.47	1.13	1.96	2.89	3.87	4.86	5.86	6.86	7.86	8.86	9.86	10.86	11.86	12.86	13.86	14.86	15.86	16.86	17.86	18.86
.90	.47	1.14	1.97	2.91	3.89	4.89	5.89	6.89	7.89	8.89	9.89	10.89	11.89	12.89	13.89	14.89	15.89	16.89	17.89	18.89
.92	.48	1.15	1.99	2.93	3.92	4.91	5.91	6.91	7.91	8.91	9.91	10.91	11.91	12.91	13.91	14.91	15.91	16.91	17.91	18.91
.94	.48	1.17	2.01	2.96	3.94	4.94	5.94	6.94	7.94	8.94	9.94	10.94	11.94	12.94	13.94	14.94	15.94	16.94	17.94	18.94
.96	.49	1.18	2.03	2.98	3.96	4.96	5.96	6.96	7.96	8.96	9.96	10.96	11.96	12.96	13.96	14.96	15.96	16.96	17.96	18.96
.98	.49	1.19	2.05	3.00	3.98	4.98	5.98	6.98	7.98	8.98	9.98	10.98	11.98	12.98	13.98	14.98	15.98	16.98	17.98	18.98
1.00	.50	1.20	2.06	3.02	4.00	5.00	6.00	7.00	8.00	9.00	10.00	11.00	12.00	13.00	14.00	15.00	16.00	17.00	18.00	19.00
1.20	.55	1.30	2.20	3.17	4.17	5.17	6.17	7.17	8.17	9.17	10.17	11.17	12.17	13.17	14.17	15.17	16.17	17.17	18.17	19.17
1.40	.58	1.38	2.31	3.29	4.29	5.29	6.29	7.29	8.29	9.29	10.29	11.29	12.29	13.29	14.29	15.29	16.29	17.29	18.29	19.29

APPENDIX C5 (Continued)

$\frac{\lambda}{\mu}$	Population Size, N																			
	1	2	3	4	5	6	7	8	9	10	11	12	13	14	15	16	17	18	19	20
1.60	.62	1.44	2.39	3.38	4.38	5.38	6.38	7.38	8.38	9.38	10.38	11.38	12.38	13.38	14.38	15.38	16.38	17.38	18.38	19.38
1.80	.64	1.49	2.45	3.45	4.44	5.44	6.44	7.44	8.44	9.44	10.44	11.44	12.44	13.44	14.44	15.44	16.44	17.44	18.44	19.44
2.00	.67	1.54	2.51	3.50	4.50	5.50	6.50	7.50	8.50	9.50	10.50	11.50	12.50	13.50	14.50	15.50	16.50	17.50	18.50	19.50
2.20	.69	1.58	2.55	3.55	4.55	5.55	6.55	7.55	8.55	9.55	10.55	11.55	12.55	13.55	14.55	15.55	16.55	17.55	18.55	19.55
2.40	.71	1.61	2.59	3.58	4.58	5.58	6.58	7.58	8.58	9.58	10.58	11.58	12.58	13.58	14.58	15.58	16.58	17.58	18.58	19.58
2.60	.72	1.63	2.62	3.62	4.62	5.62	6.62	7.62	8.62	9.62	10.62	11.62	12.62	13.62	14.62	15.62	16.62	17.62	18.62	19.62
2.80	.74	1.66	2.64	3.64	4.64	5.64	6.64	7.64	8.64	9.64	10.64	11.64	12.64	13.64	14.64	15.64	16.64	17.64	18.64	19.64
3.00	.75	1.68	2.67	3.67	4.67	5.67	6.67	7.67	8.67	9.67	10.67	11.67	12.67	13.67	14.67	15.67	16.67	17.67	18.67	19.67
3.20	.76	1.70	2.69	3.69	4.69	5.69	6.69	7.69	8.69	9.69	10.69	11.69	12.69	13.69	14.69	15.69	16.69	17.69	18.69	19.69
3.40	.77	1.72	2.71	3.71	4.71	5.71	6.71	7.71	8.71	9.71	10.71	11.71	12.71	13.71	14.71	15.71	16.71	17.71	18.71	19.71
3.60	.78	1.73	2.72	3.72	4.72	5.72	6.72	7.72	8.72	9.72	10.72	11.72	12.72	13.72	14.72	15.72	16.72	17.72	18.72	19.72
3.80	.79	1.74	2.74	3.74	4.74	5.74	6.74	7.74	8.74	9.74	10.74	11.74	12.74	13.74	14.74	15.74	16.74	17.74	18.74	19.74
4.00	.80	1.76	2.75	3.75	4.75	5.75	6.75	7.75	8.75	9.75	10.75	11.75	12.75	13.75	14.75	15.75	16.75	17.75	18.75	19.75
4.20	.81	1.77	2.76	3.76	4.76	5.76	6.76	7.76	8.76	9.76	10.76	11.76	12.76	13.76	14.76	15.76	16.76	17.76	18.76	19.76
4.40	.81	1.78	2.77	3.77	4.77	5.77	6.77	7.77	8.77	9.77	10.77	11.77	12.77	13.77	14.77	15.77	16.77	17.77	18.77	19.77
4.60	.82	1.79	2.78	3.78	4.78	5.78	6.78	7.78	8.78	9.78	10.78	11.78	12.78	13.78	14.78	15.78	16.78	17.78	18.78	19.78
4.80	.83	1.80	2.79	3.79	4.79	5.79	6.79	7.79	8.79	9.79	10.79	11.79	12.79	13.79	14.79	15.79	16.79	17.79	18.79	19.79
5.00	.83	1.80	2.80	3.80	4.80	5.80	6.80	7.80	8.80	9.80	10.80	11.80	12.80	13.80	14.80	15.80	16.80	17.80	18.80	19.80
5.20	.84	1.81	2.81	3.81	4.81	5.81	6.81	7.81	8.81	9.81	10.81	11.81	12.81	13.81	14.81	15.81	16.81	17.81	18.81	19.81
5.40	.84	1.82	2.81	3.81	4.81	5.81	6.81	7.81	8.81	9.81	10.81	11.81	12.81	13.81	14.81	15.81	16.81	17.81	18.81	19.81
5.60	.85	1.82	2.82	3.82	4.82	5.82	6.82	7.82	8.82	9.82	10.82	11.82	12.82	13.82	14.82	15.82	16.82	17.82	18.82	19.82
5.80	.85	1.83	2.83	3.83	4.83	5.83	6.83	7.83	8.83	9.83	10.83	11.83	12.83	13.83	14.83	15.83	16.83	17.83	18.83	19.83
6.00	.86	1.84	2.83	3.83	4.83	5.83	6.83	7.83	8.83	9.83	10.83	11.83	12.83	13.83	14.83	15.83	16.83	17.83	18.83	19.83
6.20	.86	1.84	2.84	3.84	4.84	5.84	6.84	7.84	8.84	9.84	10.84	11.84	12.84	13.84	14.84	15.84	16.84	17.84	18.84	19.84
6.40	.86	1.85	2.84	3.84	4.84	5.84	6.84	7.84	8.84	9.84	10.84	11.84	12.84	13.84	14.84	15.84	16.84	17.84	18.84	19.84
6.60	.87	1.85	2.85	3.85	4.85	5.85	6.85	7.85	8.85	9.85	10.85	11.85	12.85	13.85	14.85	15.85	16.85	17.85	18.85	19.85
6.80	.87	1.85	2.85	3.85	4.85	5.85	6.85	7.85	8.85	9.85	10.85	11.85	12.85	13.85	14.85	15.85	16.85	17.85	18.85	19.85
7.00	.88	1.86	2.86	3.86	4.86	5.86	6.86	7.86	8.86	9.86	10.86	11.86	12.86	13.86	14.86	15.86	16.86	17.86	18.86	19.86
7.20	.88	1.86	2.86	3.86	4.86	5.86	6.86	7.86	8.86	9.86	10.86	11.86	12.86	13.86	14.86	15.86	16.86	17.86	18.86	19.86
7.40	.88	1.87	2.86	3.86	4.86	5.86	6.86	7.86	8.86	9.86	10.86	11.86	12.86	13.86	14.86	15.86	16.86	17.86	18.86	19.86
7.60	.88	1.87	2.87	3.87	4.87	5.87	6.87	7.87	8.87	9.87	10.87	11.87	12.87	13.87	14.87	15.87	16.87	17.87	18.87	19.87
7.80	.89	1.87	2.87	3.87	4.87	5.87	6.87	7.87	8.87	9.87	10.87	11.87	12.87	13.87	14.87	15.87	16.87	17.87	18.87	19.87
8.00	.89	1.88	2.88	3.88	4.88	5.88	6.88	7.88	8.88	9.88	10.88	11.88	12.88	13.88	14.88	15.88	16.88	17.88	18.88	19.88
8.20	.89	1.88	2.88	3.88	4.88	5.88	6.88	7.88	8.88	9.88	10.88	11.88	12.88	13.88	14.88	15.88	16.88	17.88	18.88	19.88
8.40	.89	1.88	2.88	3.88	4.88	5.88	6.88	7.88	8.88	9.88	10.88	11.88	12.88	13.88	14.88	15.88	16.88	17.88	18.88	19.88
8.60	.90	1.88	2.88	3.88	4.88	5.88	6.88	7.88	8.88	9.88	10.88	11.88	12.88	13.88	14.88	15.88	16.88	17.88	18.88	19.88
8.80	.90	1.89	2.89	3.89	4.89	5.89	6.89	7.89	8.89	9.89	10.89	11.89	12.89	13.89	14.89	15.89	16.89	17.89	18.89	19.89
9.00	.90	1.89	2.89	3.89	4.89	5.89	6.89	7.89	8.89	9.89	10.89	11.89	12.89	13.89	14.89	15.89	16.89	17.89	18.89	19.89
9.20	.90	1.89	2.89	3.89	4.89	5.89	6.89	7.89	8.89	9.89	10.89	11.89	12.89	13.89	14.89	15.89	16.89	17.89	18.89	19.89
9.40	.90	1.89	2.89	3.89	4.89	5.89	6.89	7.89	8.89	9.89	10.89	11.89	12.89	13.89	14.89	15.89	16.89	17.89	18.89	19.89
9.60	.91	1.90	2.90	3.90	4.90	5.90	6.90	7.90	8.90	9.90	10.90	11.90	12.90	13.90	14.90	15.90	16.90	17.90	18.90	19.90
9.80	.91	1.90	2.90	3.90	4.90	5.90	6.90	7.90	8.90	9.90	10.90	11.90	12.90	13.90	14.90	15.90	16.90	17.90	18.90	19.90
10.00	.91	1.90	2.90	3.90	4.90	5.90	6.90	7.90	8.90	9.90	10.90	11.90	12.90	13.90	14.90	15.90	16.90	17.90	18.90	19.90
20.00	.95	1.95	2.95	3.95	4.95	5.95	6.95	7.95	8.95	9.95	10.95	11.95	12.95	13.95	14.95	15.95	16.95	17.95	18.95	19.95
30.00	.97	1.97	2.97	3.97	4.97	5.97	6.97	7.97	8.97	9.97	10.97	11.97	12.97	13.97	14.97	15.97	16.97	17.97	18.97	19.97
40.00	.98	1.98	2.98	3.98	4.98	5.98	6.98	7.98	8.98	9.98	10.98	11.98	12.98	13.98	14.98	15.98	16.98	17.98	18.98	19.98
50.00	.98	1.98	2.98	3.98	4.98	5.98	6.98	7.98	8.98	9.98	10.98	11.98	12.98	13.98	14.98	15.98	16.98	17.98	18.98	19.98
60.00	.98	1.98	2.98	3.98	4.98	5.98	6.98	7.98	8.98	9.98	10.98	11.98	12.98	13.98	14.98	15.98	16.98	17.98	18.98	19.98
70.00	.99	1.99	2.99	3.99	4.99	5.99	6.99	7.99	8.99	9.99	10.99	11.99	12.99	13.99	14.99	15.99	16.99	17.99	18.99	19.99
80.00	.99	1.99	2.99	3.99	4.99	5.99	6.99	7.99	8.99	9.99	10.99	11.99	12.99	13.99	14.99	15.99	16.99	17.99	18.99	19.99
90.00	.99	1.99	2.99	3.99	4.99	5.99	6.99	7.99	8.99	9.99	10.99	11.99	12.99	13.99	14.99	15.99	16.99	17.99	18.99	19.99
100.00	.99	1.99	2.99	3.99	4.99	5.99	6.99	7.99	8.99	9.99	10.99	11.99	12.99	13.99	14.99	15.99	16.99	17.99	18.99	19.99

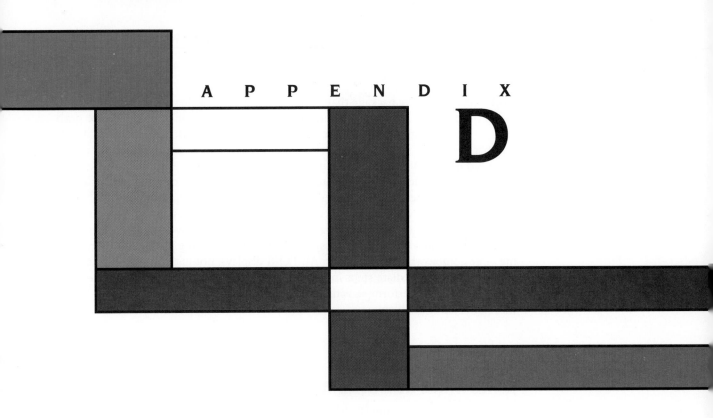

INSTRUCTIONS FOR USING THE AB:POM SOFTWARE

INTRODUCTION

AB:POM is a software package that has been designed to facilitate a better understanding of production/operations management. The software can be used to solve problems or to check answers that have been found by hand. AB:POM contains a large number of models, which means that most of the homework problems in the text can be solved using AB:POM. Specific models and applications of AB:POM can be found in the Solved Problems section located toward the end of most chapters. In this appendix, we describe the general features of the software.

We encourage you to read this appendix while sitting at a personal computer; we have written it as if you were. With a minimal investment of time in learning the basics of AB:POM, you will have a very easy-to-use means for solving problems or for checking your homework. In many cases, AB:POM displays, not just the answer to a problem, but the intermediate steps in its solution as well. In addition, the software gives you the ability to perform sensitivity analysis on these problems or to solve bigger, more interesting problems.

HARDWARE REQUIREMENTS

AB:POM will work on any IBM PC, XT, AT, PS/2, or compatible machine. The programs themselves require less than 256K of available memory. Newer machines—and most older machines—have at least this much memory, but don't forget that DOS and memory resident programs (such as Sidekick) reduce the amount of available memory. You can determine the amount of available memory with the DOS program CHKDSK.

The system has two 5.25-inch diskettes or one 3.5-inch diskette. It is possible to run the 5.25-inch diskette system with only one disk drive, but a second drive will eliminate the need for swapping diskettes. (If you have a 5.25-inch disk drive, a second drive will usually be available.) The programs also can be loaded onto a hard disk and run from there.

The software has no special monitor requirements. However, while all messages, output, and data will appear on any monitor, the display is best on a color monitor. This is because different colors are used for different items. For example, red or bright white is used for error messages. (As you will discover later, colors can be customized.)

AB:POM can take advantage of high-resolution monitors (EGA or VGA) by displaying 43 or 50 lines on the screen rather than the standard 25 lines. In some cases, this enables you to solve larger problems, as problem size in AB:POM is sometimes a function of the number of lines on the screen. To determine if you have a high-resolution monitor, try starting the program as if you did. If you do not have a high-resolution monitor, AB:POM will issue a message to that effect and continue operating.

A printer is not required to run AB:POM. Of course, if you want a hard copy (printout), it is necessary to have a printer attached. No special features, characters, installation or printer are required. It is possible to print the learning curve and linear programming graphs by running the DOS program GRAPHICS.EXE prior to starting up AB:POM and then pressing the **Prt Scn** key.

NOTE: AB:POM will run under DOS 2.10 or higher. See the note in the section entitled "Normal Startup" for details about one minor complication when running under a DOS below DOS 3.00.

GETTING STARTED

Regardless of the configuration of your system, you should begin by making a backup copy of AB:POM. Because AB:POM is not copy-protected, it is very easy to copy with the DOS **copy *.*** or **diskcopy** command.

NORMAL STARTUP

In order to run AB:POM, simply follow the procedure below. The description that follows assumes that you have a standard one– or two–disk drive system and are not using a hard drive.

1. Insert a DOS diskette into drive a: (usually the top drive or the left drive).

2. Turn on the computer.

3. When the A> prompt appears on the screen, insert the AB:POM-1 diskette into drive a:. If you have a second disk drive, insert the AB:POM-2 diskette into drive b:.

4. Type **pom** with any options (described in the following section).

If you have trouble starting, try typing **go** (with any options) rather than **pom.**

NOTE: If you use a version of DOS under DOS 3.00, a prompt will appear after you have typed **pom.** The machine will ask you to input the run-time module path.

In order to run the system, you must type a backslash (\) or the drive name in which AB:POM-1 is running (usually drive a:). When AB:POM-1 is in drive a:, the proper response to the prompt is to type **a:** and then press **Return** or **Enter.**

Notice that the third character is a backslash, not a slash. On some machines, the backslash is not required. Alternatively, it is possible to begin the program by typing **path = ** prior to typing **pom.** The file GO.BAT will do this for you.

OPENING SCREEN

When you start the program normally by typing (**pom**), the opening screen will appear as in Screen D.1 (without the shadows). Let's take a look at some of the noteworthy information found in Screen D.1.

VERSION NUMBER: One important piece of information is the version number of the software. In Screen D.1, the version is 3.20. (This book has been designed around version 3.20.) However, there may be improvements to the software *after* this book

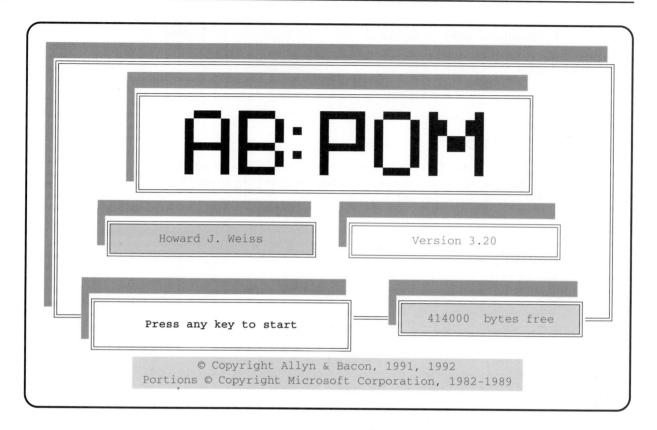

SCREEN D.1 Opening screen

has been finished, in which case the version number will be different (probably version 3.21). If the version number on the screen is not 3.20, you should check the AB:POM diskette to see if it contains a README file. In fact, you should check this file anyway to see if the information has been added to the disk after the production of the book.

STARTING KEY: The opening display screen also contains the instructions for starting. The instruction reads "Press any key to start." Most of the time, you will not need to read the display screen, and you will simply press any key to get started. (As explained in the next section, you may bypass the second display screen by pressing **m, 1,** or **2** at this point.)

COLOR SELECTION SCREEN

If you do not press **1, 2,** or **m,** the second screen will appear as in Screen D.2. This screen allows you to select the type of display that is best suited to your monitor and to your tastes. If you have a single-color (monochrome) screen, you should press **m.** If you have a color monitor, you can press **m, 1,** or **2.** Displays 1 and 2 in Screen D.2 are in color; display 2 has a colored background and shadowing.

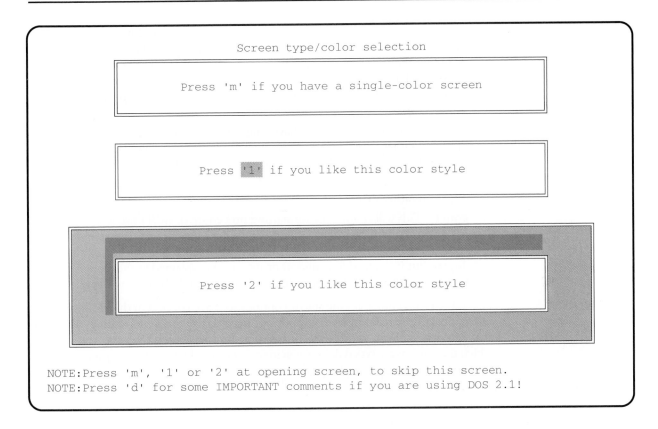

```
                    Screen type/color selection

          Press 'm' if you have a single-color screen


          Press  1  if you like this color style



                Press '2' if you like this color style



   NOTE:Press 'm', '1' or '2' at opening screen, to skip this screen.
   NOTE:Press 'd' for some IMPORTANT comments if you are using DOS 2.1!
```

SCREEN D.2 Color selection screen

STARTUP OPTIONS

As you know, after booting the computer, you must type **pom** to get the AB:POM system started. There are some useful options that can be included when you start the program, which we now explain.

> **pom m, pom 1,** or **pom 2**   This option allows you to select the display you prefer when you start the program, bypassing the color selection screen.
>
> **pom u**   If you start the program with this command, the program will use your custom color setup (created with the color option utility, described later).
>
> **pom *x***   Use this option to change the name of the data disk drive. The *x* stands for **a, b, c, d,** or **e** and represents the drive on which data is to be stored. Without this option, the program will store data on the drive from which it is started. With or without the drive option, the drive can be changed as many times as you like during program execution (as will be explained in a later section). If you start the program with more than one letter of **a, b, c, d, e,** the program will use the last letter. For example, **pom abc** will have the program store and load data files from drive c:, while **pom bca** will use drive a:. You can start the program from any drive or directory, provided that a path is supplied. For example, sup-

pose you have a data diskette in drive a: and AB:POM-1 in drive b:. If you use the DOS command PATH = b:, the program will start and the data will be stored on the a: drive if you type **pom** at the A> prompt. This option is exceedingly useful if you have a hard drive. If the program is in a subdirectory and a path is set to that subdirectory, the program can be started from any drive or subdirectory.

pom h   Use this option if you have a high-resolution monitor and want 43 lines displayed rather than 25 lines. This also will allow you to solve larger problems in some instances, since problem size sometimes is dictated by the screen.

pom v   Use this option if you have a high-resolution monitor and want 50 lines displayed rather than 25 lines.

pom f   This will change the formatting procedure of AB:POM. Typically, AB:POM allows nine spaces for numbers and decimal points. If this option is chosen, the number of places after the decimal is fixed. This makes for a neater display, but it can lead to roundoff problems. As explained in the section on formatting at the end of this appendix, this option should be used with great care.

Table D.1 summarizes the startup options we have covered in this section. Before moving on to the main menu, however, we need to note two more things about the startup options. First, more than one option can be chosen. Second, the order in which the options are typed does not matter. For example, **pom mc** (or **pom cm**) starts the program using a monochrome monitor and storing and accessing data on drive c:.

THE MAIN MENU

After color selection, the main menu will appear, as in Screen D.3. The menu has twenty options—a HELP option, eighteen POM modules (listed in chapter order), and an EXIT option. Details about each option may be found in the appropriate chapter in the text.

In general, we have tried to make menu use as easy as possible for you. There are two ways to access an option on the main menu (and similar menus).

TABLE D.1 Startup option summary

Code	Meaning
m	Monochrome (for use with single-color monitors)
1	Color display 1
2	Color display 2
u	User-defined colors
h	43 lines available on the screen
v	50 lines available on the screen
f	Fixed number of digits after the decimal
a, b, c, d, or **e**	Drive on which to store data

```
╔══════════════════════════════════════════════════════════════╗
║                        ═ Main menu ═                           ║
║                                                                ║
║                                                                ║
║   Help                           CPM/PERT Project Scheduling   ║
║   Decision and Breakeven Analysis   Linear Programming         ║
║   Forecasting                    Aggregate Planning            ║
║   Plant Location                 Inventory                     ║
║   Transportation                 Material Requirements Planning║
║   Operations Layout              Sizing, Lot                   ║
║   Balancing, Assembly line       Job Shop Sequencing           ║
║   Waiting Line Models            Assignment                    ║
║   Experience (learning) Curves   Quality Control               ║
║   Reliability                    Exit to DOS                   ║
║                                                                ║
║                                                                ║
║          Select menu option by highlighted letter or          ║
║        point with arrow keys and then press RETURN key         ║
╚══════════════════════════════════════════════════════════════╝
```

SCREEN D.3 Main menu screen

- Type the highlighted letter of the option you want. This highlighted letter is almost always the first letter.
- Point and shoot. Use the arrow keys on the keypad to change the highlighted option (point); when the highlighted option is the one you want, press **Return** or **Enter** (shoot).

For example, suppose we wish to use the transportation method, (see Screen D.3). We either type **t** (or **T**) or use the arrow keys to move the highlighted cell and then press the **Return** key when the transportation module is highlighted.

Typically, after the module is chosen, a message that indicates the module being loaded will flash on the screen.

THE MODULE SUBMENU SCREEN

The module submenu will appear after the module has been chosen. A sample submenu for CPM/PERT project scheduling is presented in Screen D.4.

SUBMENU OPTIONS

Each submenu will have the following six options, which can be selected by typing the highlighted (first) letter or the corresponding function key.

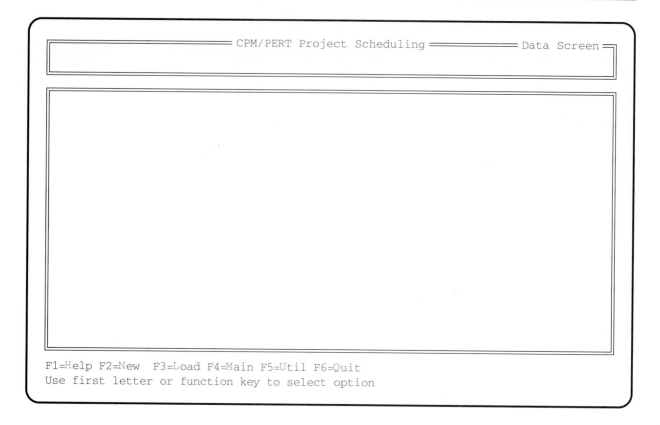

```
╔════════════════ CPM/PERT Project Scheduling ══════════ Data Screen ═╗
║                                                                     ║
║                                                                     ║
║                                                                     ║
║                                                                     ║
║                                                                     ║
║                                                                     ║
║                                                                     ║
║                                                                     ║
║                                                                     ║
║                                                                     ║
║                                                                     ║
║                                                                     ║
║                                                                     ║
║                                                                     ║
║                                                                     ║
║                                                                     ║
╚═════════════════════════════════════════════════════════════════════╝
F1=Help F2=New  F3=Load F4=Main F5=Util F6=Quit
Use first letter or function key to select option
```

SCREEN D.4 Module submenu screen

HELP (**F1**)

This option will present a brief description of the module, the data required for input, the output results, and the available options. It is worthwhile to look at this screen at least one time in order to be certain that there are no unsuspected differences between your assumptions and the assumptions of the program. The same help screen can also be accessed from the data screen, where it is perhaps more useful, because you will then be looking at the data to which the help screen is referring. You can examine the help screen at any time; the screen appears instantaneously and takes little time to read.

CREATE A NEW DATA SET (**F2**)

This will be a frequently chosen option. After the create option is chosen, one of three types of screens will appear, depending on the module. For some modules (decision and break-even analysis, forecasting, plant location, project scheduling, and quality control), a model submenu will appear, indicating that different programs are available within the broad context of the module. An example of this type of submenu is presented in Screen D.5, which tells us that in the project scheduling module, four programs are available. The desired choice is made in the usual way—by using the first letter or point and shoot. After selecting a model, it will be possible to give the problem a title.

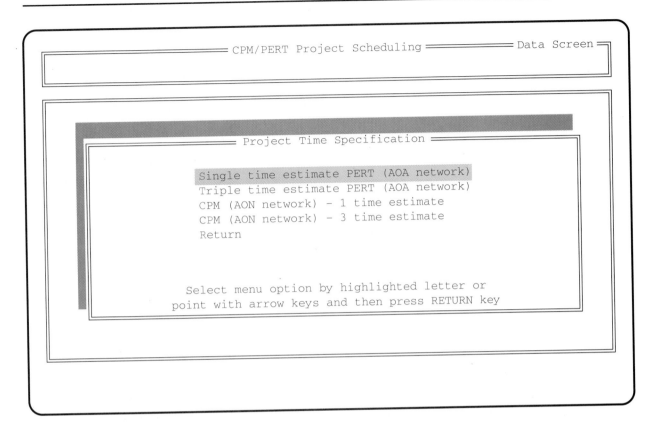

SCREEN D.5 Sample submodel menu screen

The second type of screen is a setup screen, as shown in Screen D.6. For many modules, the program must set the dimensions. That is, to set up the problem, the number of rows, the number of columns, or both must be given. In Screen D.6, we have indicated that a table will be set up for six activities (rows). After pressing **Return,** we will be placed in the data screen, which will be described later.

In some of the programs, the program storage is allocated at this point for the dimensions that were just set. It is possible that your machine will not have sufficient storage, as indicated by an error message. If you get an error message, you probably do not want to try solving such a large problem. However, you do have a couple of other options: use a different machine or check the storage on the machine by using the CHKDSK command in DOS.

The last possibility after choosing the create option is that the data screen will be displayed immediately. This happens for several of the options where no dimensioning is necessary.

LOAD A DATA SET FROM THE DISK (**F3**)

If you have previously stored data on a disk, it is possible to load the data into memory. If you choose the load data option, a screen similar to Screen D.7 will appear. The screen will contain the name of the drive, the name of the subdirectory (if there is one), and a list of the available files. In Screen D.7, the two files on drive c: in subdi-

```
┌──────────────────────────────────────────────────────────────────────────┐
│  ┌────────────────── CPM/PERT Project Scheduling ═══════════ Data Screen ┐ │
│  │ Number of activities (1-99)      6                                     │ │
│  └───────────────────────────────────────────────────────────────────────┘ │
│  ┌───────────────────────────────────────────────────────────────────────┐ │
│  │                                                                       │ │
│  │                                                                       │ │
│  │                                                                       │ │
│  │                                                                       │ │
│  │                                                                       │ │
│  │                                                                       │ │
│  │                                                                       │ │
│  │                                                                       │ │
│  │                                                                       │ │
│  │                                                                       │ │
│  │                                                                       │ │
│  │                                                                       │ │
│  └───────────────────────────────────────────────────────────────────────┘ │
│  Enter an integer between 1 and 99                                          │
│                                                                             │
└──────────────────────────────────────────────────────────────────────────┘
```

SCREEN D.6 Setup screen

rectory \BC7 are listed. To load a file, simply type its name and then press **Return.** Standard DOS file names *without* extensions are legal. In other words, you may type in up to eight characters, but a period is illegal. You may preface the file name with a drive letter (with its colon). Examples of legal file names are **sample, test, b:sample, problem1.** It does not matter whether you use uppercase or lowercase characters. DOS treats all characters as uppercase. You may type them as uppercase, lowercase, or mixed. The following are examples of illegal file names.

sample.1p   The program will not allow you to type the period.

abcdefghij   The name is too long; the program will issue an error message.

lpt1   This is a reserved DOS word.

It is possible at this point to change the drive from which data files are loaded (and also to which data files are stored). In order to use this option, press the **F1** key. A screen similar to Screen D.8 will appear. The desired drive can be chosen by using the regular menu selection options. Note that it is not possible to change directories when on this screen. (To do this, you must use the utility option described later.) In the event that there is a problem with the drive or file, an error message to that effect will appear.

After the file is loaded, you will be placed in the data screen and can edit the data, the topic of a later section.

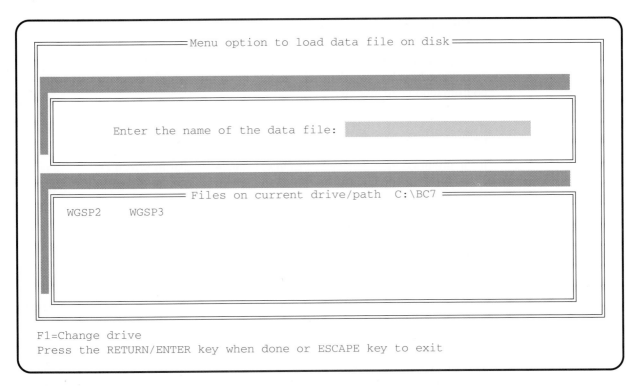

SCREEN D.7 Load data screen

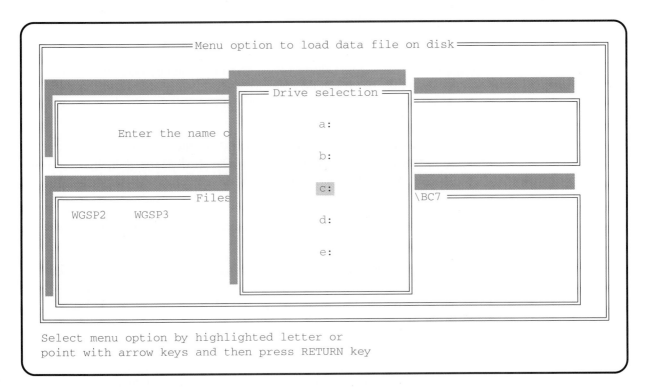

SCREEN D.8 Drive selection screen

RETURN TO THE MAIN MENU (**F4**)

The next option on the submenu list in Screen D.4 is to return to the main menu. This option is not necessary if all of your problems come from the same module. However, if you have homework problems from more than one chapter, this is one way to go from module to module.

UTILITIES (**F5**)

If the utilities option is chosen, a submenu similar to that in Screen D.9 will appear. The submenu options are again chosen in the normal fashion.

CUSTOMIZE COLORS: The first option allows you to create a custom color file. If this option is chosen, you will see a screen similar to Screen D.10. The colors of thirteen different items can be changed (in the usual way). For example, to change the color of the boxes in AB:POM, keep pressing **b** until you are satisfied with the color. The colors of the two boxes on the screen change each time you press **b.**

If you have a monochrome monitor, it may take eight presses of a button in order for the shades to change. Be patient.

After you have made all of the desired color changes, you have a few additional choices to make. For example, you must decide whether or not you want to keep a permanent file of these colors; if you do want to save these colors, select the save colors option. (Once saved, these colors can be used by starting the program with **pom u.**) If you plan to use these colors one time only, select the quit option. If you want to cancel the changes and revert to the colors that you started the program with, pick the restore initial colors option.

SHELL TO DOS: This option allows you to go to DOS and execute DOS commands without having to restart AB:POM.

NOTE: This option should not be used by inexperienced PC users. Experienced users, however, will find this option useful for tasks such as changing directories. If you shell to DOS, type **exit** to return to AB:POM (or any other system).

DELETE A FILE: This option can be used to delete (erase) files from your diskette. If you choose this option, a list of your files for the module currently in use will appear, along with a prompt asking you for the name of the file you wish to delete. To erase a file, simply type the file name. This option should be used if you have trouble saving files because your diskette has gotten full. Obviously, an option that erases files should be used with great care.

PRINT TO DISK FILE OR PRINTER TOGGLE SWITCH: It is possible to send the output to a file rather than to the printer. If this option is chosen, the program will request a name for the output file. All output will be sent to the file named until this option is toggled back to the printer. It is possible to use an extension (file.ext) for this file name.

```
============================ Utilities ============================

                          Customize colors

                          Shell to DOS

                          Delete a file

                          Print to disk file

                          Toggle fix format on

                          Error beeps/sound off

                          Function key display off

                          Lines per screen(25,43,50)

                          Return to data screen


                Select menu option by highlighted letter or
                point with arrow keys and then press RETURN key
```

SCREEN D.9 Utilities/options screen

```
========================= Customize colors =========================

        Main text/data              Input data foreground
        Letter highlight            Reverse video-first letter
        Titles                      Boxes
        Instructions/messages       Background
        Answers                     Menu background
        Function key bar            Restore initial colors
        Data/solution label         Save colors to disk
        Input data background       Quit color customization
                Select menu option by highlighted letter or
                point with arrow keys and then press RETURN key


Function key bar
Instructions/messages

=================== Sample data solution screen ======= Data/solution label =

    Main text/data                      Answers
    Main text/data                      Answers
    Main text/data                      Answers
```

SCREEN D.10 Color customization screen

TOGGLE FIX FORMAT ON: For most of the modules, you can fix the number of decimal places displayed on output by setting on the toggle for fixed number of places. This option must be used with care. (We demonstrate this option later in this section.)

ERROR BEEPS/SOUND OFF: Use this toggle to turn off or on the beep that alerts you when an error has occurred.

FUNCTION KEY DISPLAY OFF/ON: Use this toggle to turn off or on the function key display on the last row of the data screen. The function keys will work even when they are not displayed.

EXIT (**F6**)

The last option on the submenu screen is the exit option. This is the option to choose when you have completed all of your work. The exit option will return control to DOS. If you wish to return to AB:POM from DOS after selecting this option, you must restart the system in the usual manner—by typing **pom** with any desired options.

> NOTE: If DOS is not on your diskette, the computer will issue a message stating that COMMAND.COM is missing. If you wish to continue working, you must insert a DOS diskette; otherwise, you can simply turn the machine off.

THE DATA SCREEN

We have already identified two of the three types of screens that will appear—the module submenu and the setup screen. The third type of screen is the data screen. On some modules, the data screen will appear after the new data option has been chosen or after a file has been loaded. On other modules, you must set up the data screen according to the aforementioned procedures. In either case, you ultimately will get to the data screen.

A sample data screen for an assembly line balancing example appears in Screen D.11. Screen D.11 contains eight pieces of information.

1. *Title.* The title appears in the top row of the larger—that is, the second—box. The default name is the name of the module, but this can be changed. (See the discussion of **F8**.)
2. *Screen identifier.* The identifier appears on the right-hand side of the top row. This identifier distinguishes a data screen from an answer screen. The latter is identified by the word *solution,* which appears in the upper right-hand corner.
3. *Function key definitions.* These definitions give a four-letter code that appears in the next-to-last row and describes what the function key will do.
4. *Instruction.* The bottom row functions as an instruction/help line for the data screen, briefly explaining what to do.
5. *Data.* The data occupy the interior of the box.

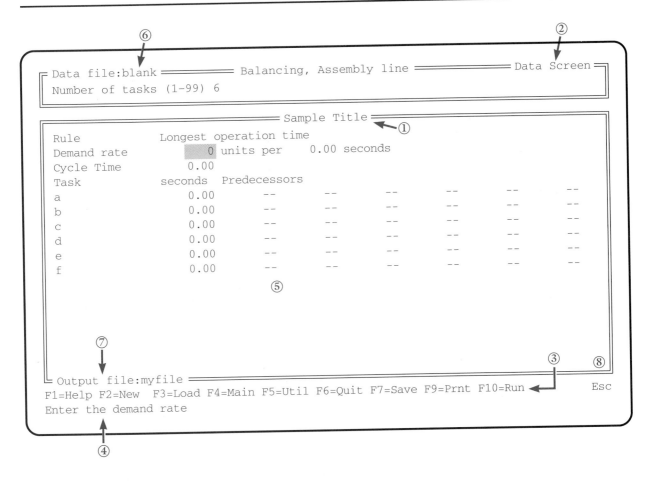

SCREEN D.11 Data screen

6. *Data file name.* If a data file has been loaded or saved, the upper left corner of the screen will contain the name of the file. This name is erased whenever a new data set is created.

7. *Printer file name.* If you have chosen the option of printing to a file rather than the printer, the name of the file is displayed at the bottom left corner of the data screen, as shown in Screen D.11. Otherwise, nothing is displayed there.

8. *Format message.* If you started the program with the **f** option, the lower right-hand corner of the screen will display a message to that effect. This is not the case for Screen D.11; for an example, see Screen D.13.

ENTERING AND EDITING DATA

The data can be edited after a new data set has been created using option 2 or after an existing data set has been loaded using option 3. Each data screen is set up as a spread sheet. The spacing in the spread sheet is determined by the program. Depending on the number of rows, the spread sheet will be either single-spaced or double-spaced.

TABLE D.2 Cursor movement keys summary

Key	Function
Home	Move to the top left corner of the spread sheet.
↑	Move up one row. On some screens, the highlighted cell will wrap around to the bottom if you are at the top row. On others, if you are at the top of the screen and try to go up, you will be beeped.
PgUp	Move to the top of the current column. If you are at the top of a column and try to move up, you will be notified.
←	Move left one cell. On some screens, the highlighted cell will wrap around to the far right column if you are in the far left column. On others, you will be beeped if you try to move left from the far left column.
→	Move right one cell. On some screens, the highlighted cell will wrap around to the far left column if you are in the far right column. On others, you will be beeped if you try to move right from the far right column.
End	Move to the bottom right corner of the spread sheet.
↓	Move down one row. On some screens, the cursor will wrap around to the top if you are on the bottom row. On others, you will be beeped if you try to move down from the bottom row.
PgDn	Move to the bottom of the current column. If you are at the bottom and try to page down, you will be beeped.
Tab	Move to the far right column or, on problems that require more than one screen (linear programming, transportation, assignment), move right one screen.
Shift-Tab	Move to the far left column or move left one screen's worth.
Return	Place the new entry into the data set and move forward one cell. (In many cases, forward is across, though in some cases forward is down.)

Each entry has a row and column position. To navigate through the spread sheet, use the cursor movement keys, as described in Table D.2.

For each highlighted cell, the bottom line of the screen tells what is to be done. You will be instructed to enter one of three types of data—character data (names), numeric data, or options to be toggled.

CHARACTER DATA AND NUMERICAL DATA

When entering names and numbers, simply type the name or number and then press one of the direction keys from Table D.2 or a function key. If you make a mistake while editing, there are two other direction keys to consider: **Back Space** and **Del,** both of which will delete the last character typed.

A beep indicates that you have typed an illegal key while entering data. One of the following messages will appear.

- Typing a character when a number is required.
- Trying to enter a number larger than permitted.
- Trying to enter a name longer than permitted.
- Trying to enter more digits after the decimal than permitted.
- Trying to enter a character that is not permitted for this entry.

NOTE: The format of numerical displays is handled by the program. Furthermore, any number less than .00001 is displayed as 0.

TOGGLE ENTRIES

As mentioned previously, you will not always be entering data. Some entries are toggled—that is, the allowable entries have been preset. For example, in the assembly line balancing example shown in Screen D.11 the time unit can be toggled. You can change seconds to minutes to hours and back to seconds again by moving the cursor to the top cell of the column with zeros and pressing the space bar three times. The time unit will change each time the space bar is pressed. So, when the desired unit appears, simply go on to the next cell. Alternatively, you can call up a menu of all available options by pressing the **Enter** key.

While you are editing the data, the function keys shown on the bottom row of the data screen are available. Table D.3 tells what each function key does. Notice that function keys **F1** through **F6** correspond exactly to the menu options from the submenu. We now explain the four options we have not discussed.

SAVE (**F7**)

This option is similar to the load a data file option. When you choose this option, a screen will appear with the names of your data files, and you will be asked for the name under which to save the data.

If you give the file the name of an existing file, you will be warned about replacing the existing file. The existing file will be replaced by the more recent one if you press **y** (or **Y**) or **Return.** After entering the name, press **Return** to save the data. As before, it is possible to change the drive by using the **F1** key option. It also is possible to use the shell option in the set utilities option from the data screen to change the drive or the directory.

TITL (**F8**)

When you press **F8,** the top line of the data requests that you enter a new title. You will be permitted to enter a title up to thirty-seven characters in length. The title is entered in the usual manner and will appear at the top of the data after **Return,** a direction key, or a function key is pressed.

TABLE D.3 Function key summary

Function key	Abbreviation	Meaning
F1	Help	Help
F2	New	Create a new data set
F3	Load	Load a data set from disk
F4	Main	Return to the main menu
F5	Util	Utilities
F6	Exit	Exit AB:POM and exit to DOS
F7	Save	Save a data file to disk
F8	Titl	Change the title on the top line
F9	Prnt	Print the screen on a line printer
F10	Run	Solve the problem

PRNT (**F9**)

This option will print the contents of the data or solution screen. The bottom lines and the outside box will not be printed. (It is possible to have everything printed character for character; use **Shift-PrtScn.**) The program prints to the LPT1 file, the standard printer file. If your printer is not attached to LPT1 (if, for example, you have a serial printer), you need to use the DOS MODE statement to redirect the output to the appropriate place; see your DOS manual for instructions. In one or two cases (most notably, linear programming and MRP) the output will not be exactly as it appears on screen. Changes have been made to fit more than one screen's worth of data onto the printer.

If you have used the utility option, you can print to a file. Later, you can use a word processor to edit this file. In most cases, one of two things will happen if you press F9 and your computer is not attached to a printer or your printer is not turned on: Either you will get an error message or the program will think that it is printing when it is not—which is harmless. It is also possible that the printer will keep trying to print every thirty seconds or so. You can stop this by pressing the **Esc** key.

RUN (**F10**)

After you have entered all of the data, you can press **F10** to solve the problem. Answers will appear either in addition to the data or in place of the data. In either case, the function key bar at the bottom of the screen will change. In all modules, **F9** will be available to print the solution. In some modules, additional function keys for displaying more information will be defined. These definitions appear in the chapters for those modules. After viewing or printing the solution, press any key to return to the data screen.

FORMATS FOR DATA

All of the formats for the data are determined by the program. In general, the maximum value that can be input for a number is determined by the width of the field in which the number appears. For example, the largest possible number in a field with six spaces is 999,999. The field width also determines the number of places after the decimal. In most cases, this will not pose a problem. However, as Screen D.12 shows, there will be occasions when the number of places after the decimal varies within a column, even though the screen would appear more orderly if there were no variation.

There is a way to bring more order to the screens. Compare Screen D.13 with Screen D.12. The orderly columns in Screen D.13 resulted from starting the program with the **f** option. There is a trade-off involved in the use of this option: In order to have neat columns, we must express the data in round numbers. For example, the standard deviation of .5 in Screen D.12 becomes 1 in Screen D.13. In many cases, rounding poses no problem, but we advise you to use the **f** option with great care.

SYSTEM ERROR MESSAGES

In this section, we define the system errors that you may encounter. Some system errors occur only at the beginning of the program (startup errors); others may occur at any time.

```
┌─ Data file:wgsp3 ═════════ CPM/PERT Project Scheduling ═══════════ Solution ═┐
│  Number of activities (1-99) 9                                               │
└──────────────────────────────────────────────────────────────────────────────┘

  ═══════════════════════════════ Chapter 10, Solved Problem 3 ═══════════════════
   Project completion time =  66.33334   Project standard deviation = 2.44949
  StartEnd  Opt. LikelPess.
  Node Node Time Time Time     Time     ES      EF      LS      LF   slack  sd ( σ)
      1    2   12   15   18      15       0      15       0      15       0      1
      2    3   19   27   31  26.333      15  41.333      15  41.333       0      2
      2    4   13   14   16  14.167      15  29.167  32.833      47  17.833    0.5  ←
      3    5   14   17   20      17  41.333  58.333  41.333  58.333       0      1
      3    6   10   15   20      15  41.333  56.333      48      63  6.6667 1.6667
      4    6   15   16   17      16  29.167  45.167      47      63  17.833 .33333
      5    6    0    0    0       0  58.333  58.333      63      63  4.6667      0
      5    7    8    8    8       8  58.333  66.333  58.333  66.333       0      0
      6    7    1    3    7  3.3333  58.333  61.667      63  66.333  4.6667      1


                                                              F9=Print    Esc
  Press <Esc> key to edit data or highlighted key or function key for options
```

SCREEN D.12 Sample output: normal format

STARTUP ERRORS

INPUT RUN TIME MODULE: The appropriate response to this message is the name of the disk drive that contains the ABRUNLIB.EXE file—typically, **a:** or \.

ERROR 1.1: If you start the program with the **u** option (user-defined color file), the program expects to find the file COLOR.POM on the diskette from which AB:POM is started. COLOR.POM may not be on your diskette if you have never created a startup file. You also may get this message if there is something wrong with COLOR.POM (perhaps because you have been playing with it outside of the AB:POM environment). Lastly, this message will appear if you try to restore colors (utility option 5, suboption 13) and never had this file to begin with. Note that whenever this error occurs, the program uses colors (rather than monochrome) as its default. Therefore, if you have a monochrome monitor, you either need to reset the colors using utility option 5 or start over.

ERROR 1.2: This error message tells you that you used the **h** option when you started AB:POM even though you do not have a high-resolution monitor. The program will simply treat everything as a standard 25-line monitor.

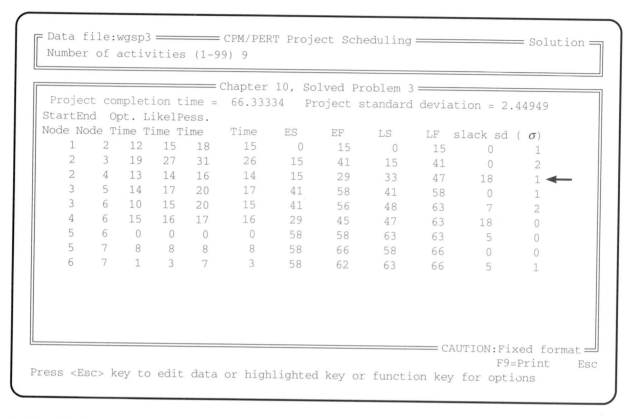

```
┌─ Data file:wgsp3 ════════════ CPM/PERT Project Scheduling ══════════════ Solution ─┐
│  Number of activities (1-99) 9                                                      │
└────────────────────────────────────────────────────────────────────────────────────┘

┌═══════════════════════════════ Chapter 10, Solved Problem 3 ═══════════════════════┐
│  Project completion time =  66.33334   Project standard deviation = 2.44949         │
│ StartEnd  Opt. LikelPess.                                                           │
│ Node Node Time Time Time    Time     ES     EF     LS     LF   slack sd ( σ)         │
│    1    2   12   15   18      15       0     15      0     15       0      1          │
│    2    3   19   27   31      26      15     41     15     41       0      2          │
│    2    4   13   14   16      14      15     29     33     47      18      1  ←        │
│    3    5   14   17   20      17      41     58     41     58       0      1          │
│    3    6   10   15   20      15      41     56     48     63       7      2          │
│    4    6   15   16   17      16      29     45     47     63      18      0          │
│    5    6    0    0    0       0      58     58     63     63       5      0          │
│    5    7    8    8    8       8      58     66     58     66       0      0          │
│    6    7    1    3    7       3      58     62     63     66       5      1          │
│                                                                                     │
│                                              ════════════════ CAUTION:Fixed format ═│
│                                                               F9=Print      Esc      │
│  Press <Esc> key to edit data or highlighted key or function key for options        │
└─────────────────────────────────────────────────────────────────────────────────────┘
```

SCREEN D.13   Sample output: fixed format

SYSTEM ERRORS OCCURRING DURING MODULE EXECUTION

ERROR 1.3: Some modules have different allowable problem sizes for high-resolution monitors. If you create a large data set with the **h** option, you must use the **h** option to read it if it is larger than the maximum allowable problem size under normal conditions.

ERROR 1.4: Your machine is not large enough to solve this problem. Some modules—namely, linear programming, transportation, and assignment—need more storage when they execute a problem.

ERROR 1.5: You are trying to load a file that does not exist. (You probably have typed the name incorrectly.)

ERROR 1.6: The program is having trouble getting a file or disk drive. (Have you left the drive door open? Is there a write-protect on your diskette?)

ERROR 1.7: The diskette is write-protected. Either remove the tab or, on a 3.5-inch diskette, change the write protect key.

ERROR 1.8: Disk full. Either delete files from the diskette or use a new diskette.

ANSWERS TO SELECTED ODD-NUMBERED PROBLEMS

CHAPTER 3

1. 96 cars per day
3. (a) 54 million forms per year
   (b) 56 percent
5. 5.48 employees
7. .00796 houses per dollar
9. 1,100 units
11. 1.17 percent
13. 100 inches (20 inches per year)
15. (b) BEP(typewriter, computer) = 1,000,000 pages; BEP(typewriter, typesetter) = 1,250,000 pages (irrelevant); BEP(typesetter, computer) = 1,500,000 pages
17. (a) 10,000 cases
    (b) $9,700,000
    (c) 100,000 cases
19. (b) BEP(city vs. near) = 13,333 jobs; BEP(city vs. far) = 12,500 jobs (irrelevant); BEP(near vs. far) = 12,000 jobs
21. EV(overtime) = 6.8
23. Use part-time help; EV(part-time) = 47.5.
25. $p = .4$
27. (a) maximin = $2 at 10 glasses
    (b) maximax = $8 at 40 glasses
29. (a) minimax = 6,000 at 200 pints
    (b) minimin = 3,000 at 100 pints
31. (a) 2 spares
    (b) 4 spares
    (c) 0 spares
33. B; $630.75
35. Marktech should lease the smaller office and then expand if demand becomes higher.

CHAPTER 4

1. bias = 2.8; SE = 7.16; MAD = 6
3. vice-president of operations
5. 2.667 inches
7. (a) 374.33 pints
   (b) 412.9148 pints
9. 2.74 inches
11. (a) 372.9 pints
    (b) 411.51 pints
13. 2.33 inches
15. (a) 374.26 pints
    (b) 436 pints
17. 105 accidents
19. (a) 234 closings
    (b) SE = 5.657
21. (a) 3,200
    (b) 3,675
    (c) 3,270
    (d) 3,880

23. year 11: 140.3748 students; year 12: 138.8828 students; year 13: 135.8988 students; year 14: 115.7568 students; year 15: 153.0568 students
25. (a) $Y = 21.748 - 1,080X$
    (b) The trend coefficient ($-1,080$) is negative, but sales are increasing.
    (c) Use two separate regressions or multiple regression.
29. (a) $Y = 87.714 + 1.7857X$
    (c) Monday: 129.95; Tuesday: 117.74; Wednesday: 105.61; Thursday: 117.11; Friday: 128.55
31. (a) 2.3538, 2.5424, 2.3023, 5.0526, .6585, $-.8936, -.5294, .4186$
    (b) Process seems to be back in control.
33. $Y = 14,742 + (1,613 \times \text{year}); +10,602$ if spring/summer, $-10,602$ if fall/winter

CHAPTER 5

1. BEP = 33,333 units
3. Sam should locate in the city.
5. New York; Philadelphia violates the discordance level.
7. site C
9. (a) 3700 block; 566 block-trips
   (b) 3016 block; 10,974 block-trips
11. between 10W and 15E and between 10S and 30N
13. 96.75°, 36.25°
15. (a) St. Louis
    (b) Dallas

CHAPTER 6

1. 384 pharmacies; arborescent
3. complex network
7. at least 200,000 tons
9. A–W: 160; A–X: 60; B–X: 60; B–Y: 200; B–Z: 40; C–Z: 190; C–Dummy: 245; total cost = $116,160
11. Memphis–Dallas: 300; Memphis–Denver: 400; Minneapolis–Denver: 100; Minneapolis–Detroit: 500; Miami–Dallas: 300; total cost = $23,000
13. X–A: 5; X–B: 12; X–C: 15; Y–A: 2; Y–D: 18; Z–A: 20; total cost = $1,506
15. A–F: 5; A–G: 5; B–D: 3; B–E: 15; C–D: 12; C–F: 5; total profit = $2,005
17. Austin–Dallas: 35; Austin–Ft. Worth: 65; Beaumont–El Paso: 70; Beaumont–Houston: 10; Corpus Christi–Dallas: 15; Corpus Christi–Galveston: 55; Corpus Christi–Houston: 80; total cost = $13,375
19. *Philadelphia*.
    LA–Denver: 150; New Orleans–Denver: 225; Philadelphia–Pittsburgh: 200; Philadelphia–St. Louis: 100; Philadelphia–Denver: 25; Philadelphia–Dummy: 25; total cost = $43,000 (*Note:* An alternative solution exists.)

Seattle.
LA–St. Louis: 75; LA–Denver: 50; LA–Dummy: 25; New Orleans–Pittsburgh: 200; New Orleans–St. Louis: 25; Seattle–Denver: 350; total cost = $36,125

CHAPTER 7

1. (a) 30 seconds per unit
   (b) 4 stations
5. (a) 5 minutes
   (b) 4 stations
   (d) 80 percent
7. (b) 3,000 units per week
   (c) 24 seconds per unit
   (e) 84.67 percent
9. (a) room 1: secretary; room 2: duplication; room 3: coffee; room 4: vice president (*Note:* Other solutions exist.)
   (b) 1,880 trip-feet
11. B–C–D–A–F–E or A–D–F–E–B–C

CHAPTER 8

1. (a) .9 customers
   (b) 1.5 customers
   (c) 18 minutes
   (d) 30 minutes
   (e) 60 percent
3. (a) .604 cars
   (b) 1.254 cars
   (c) 2.79 minutes
   (d) 5.79 minutes
   (e) 35 percent
5. (a) .889 shoppers
   (b) 5.776 minutes
   (c) 66.7 percent
7. (a) 1.533 phone lines
   (b) 5.7 percent
9. 8(a): .25 persons; 8(b): .75 persons; 8(c): 2.5 minutes; 8(d): 7.5 minutes
11. (a) 2.79 pages
   (b) 3.57 pages
   (c) .5712 hours
   (d) 22 percent
   (e) (a): 5.25 pages; (b): 6.11 pages; (c): .888 hours; (d): 14 percent
   (f) (a): .14 pages; (b): .921 pages; (c): .0184 hours; (d): 61 percent
13. current: $13.32 per hour; option 1: $8.33 per hour; option 2: $9 per hour
15. 6 servers

CHAPTER 9

1. .9667
3. .931
5. .998
7. .9668
9. $n = 17$
11. (a) 2.14 minutes
    (b) 2.033 minutes
    (c) 2.114 minutes
13. 81.6 percent
15. 384 observations
17. (a) $p = .11667$
    (b) 11.67% ± 2.4%
19. between 36 and 37 minutes

CHAPTER 10

1. (a) A: 0; B: 0; C: 4; D: 10; E: 0; F: 7; G: 14; H: 21
   (b) 30 days
   (c) days 1–12
   (d) A–C–D–G–H
3. (a) A–B–D–E–G–H–I–J;34 months
   (b) A–B–D–E–G–H–I–J;34 months
   (c) C: 10; F: 1; all others: 0
5. (a) A–B–E–G;21 days
   (b) no
7. (a) A–C–F–H–J
   (b) 31 days
   (c) B: 6; D: 7; E: 3; G: 8; I: 8; all others: 0
9. A: 15, 1.33; B: 32, 2.33; C: 18, 0; D: 13.17, 1.83; E: 18.17, .5; F: 19, 1
11. (a) 23 days
    (b) .1746
    (c) .337
15. 13 days
17. (a) 15
    (b) 4
    (c) 17 (by trial and error)
    (d) 24 (by trial and error)

CHAPTER 11

1. Maximize $Z = 600H + 1,000B$
   Subject to $\quad 40H + 30B \le 2,400$ (chips)
   $\qquad\qquad\quad 2H + 3B \le 200$ (labor)
   $\qquad\qquad\qquad H, B \ge 0$

3. Minimize $Z = .25C + .22G$
Subject to $\quad 80C + 60G \geq 100$ (vitamin A)
$\quad\quad\quad\quad 20C + 40G \geq 100$ (vitamin B)
$\quad\quad\quad\quad 70C + 30G \geq 100$ (vitamin C)
$\quad\quad\quad\quad\quad\quad C, G \geq 0$
5. Maximize $Z = 200C + 250R$
Subject to $\quad 3C + 4R \leq 36,000$ (wood)
$\quad\quad\quad\quad 5C + 4R \leq 50,000$ (square feet)
$\quad\quad\quad\quad\quad\quad C, R \geq 0$
11. $H = 0; B = 66.67; Z = \$66,667$
13. $C = .4545; G = 2.27; Z = .613635$
15. $x = 1.33; y = 3.33; Z = 25.33$
17. $x = 0; y = 7.5; Z = 30$
19. $x = 16.67; y = 0; Z = 100$
or $x = 9.09; y = 22.72;$
$Z = 100$
21. $x = 16.43; y = 29.29; Z = 545$

CHAPTER 12

1. plan I: 90,000; 90,000; 90,000; 90,000
plan II: 80,000; 60,000; 100,000; 120,000
3. April: 1,760; May: 2,630; June: 2,860; July: 2,520;
Aug.: 2,470; Sept.: 360
5. **(a)** $-100; -100; 0; -100; -100; 0$
(b) yes
(c) 0
(d) mixed
7. cost of 5: $4,900; cost of 6(a): $1,423.75; cost of
6(b): $2,700; cost of 6(c): several answers possible
9. produce to demand: $3,960; produce 650 per
month: $3,240
11. 948; 620; 558; 400; 562; 636; 752; 886; 704; 610;
558; 702 (Cost of this plan is $6,930.)
15. 600; 615; 590; 675; 620; 595 (hours)
17. 167 tons

CHAPTER 13

1. A: 12, 2; B: 1, 14, 5, 10, 6, 4; C: 9, 8, 7, 3, 11, 13
(*Note:* Other answers are possible.)
3. **(a)** 292 bottles
(b) 8.4 times per year
(c) $584 per year
5. **(a)** 50 corkscrews
(b) 2 months
(c) 10 corkscrews
7. **(a)** JC Peanut Company
(b) 2.67 weeks
(c) $.36 per jar
(d) order 1,800 jars

9. manufacture its own cans
11. 1,000 tires
13. The order quantity increases to 52.44 corkscrews.
15. **(a)** 7,746 lights
(b) 1,550 lights
(c) 3,098 lights
(d) 77.46 days
(e) 67 percent
17. service level: 80 percent; reorder point: 10; safety
stock: .19; no effect on answers
19. **(a)** $R = 11.31; SS = 1.31$
(b) $R = 10.83; SS = .83$
21. $SL = .80; R = 10.672; SS = .672$
23. 28 dozen
25. 2 spares

CHAPTER 14

3. A $\quad\quad\quad\quad\quad\quad\quad\quad$ 1
$\quad$ B $\quad\quad\quad\quad\quad\quad\quad\quad$ 2
$\quad\quad$ D $\quad\quad\quad\quad\quad\quad\quad$ 2
$\quad\quad\quad$ H $\quad\quad\quad\quad\quad\quad$ 3
$\quad\quad\quad$ I $\quad\quad\quad\quad\quad\quad\quad$ 1
$\quad\quad\quad$ J $\quad\quad\quad\quad\quad\quad\quad$ 2
$\quad\quad$ E $\quad\quad\quad\quad\quad\quad\quad$ 3
$\quad\quad$ F $\quad\quad\quad\quad\quad\quad\quad$ 5
$\quad$ C $\quad\quad\quad\quad\quad\quad\quad\quad$ 6
$\quad$ B $\quad\quad\quad\quad\quad\quad\quad\quad$ 4
$\quad\quad$ D $\quad\quad\quad\quad\quad\quad\quad$ 2
$\quad\quad\quad$ H $\quad\quad\quad\quad\quad\quad$ 3
$\quad\quad\quad$ I $\quad\quad\quad\quad\quad\quad\quad$ 1
$\quad\quad\quad$ J $\quad\quad\quad\quad\quad\quad\quad$ 2
$\quad\quad$ E $\quad\quad\quad\quad\quad\quad\quad$ 3
$\quad\quad$ F $\quad\quad\quad\quad\quad\quad\quad$ 5
$\quad$ G $\quad\quad\quad\quad\quad\quad\quad\quad$ 2
$\quad\quad$ H $\quad\quad\quad\quad\quad\quad\quad$ 1
$\quad\quad$ I $\quad\quad\quad\quad\quad\quad\quad\quad$ 3
5. 760: 124; 770: 372; 775: 2,480; 785: 248; 722:
1,488; 776: 4,960; 777: 4,960; 791: 1,736; 790:
1,984; 733: 2,976; 774: 1,488; 788: 29,760; 789:
29,760; 801: 6,944; 802: 5,208
9. **(b)** (week in parentheses)—A: 120(5); B: 240(4);
C: 360(4); D: 600(4); E: 240(3); F: 480(3);
G: 2,400(3); H: 1,200(3)
11. order releases (week in parentheses)—A: 70(7);
B: 1,680(5), 140(6); C: 420(6); D: 3,360(3),
280(4); E: 5,040(4), 420(5); F: 8,400(4), 700(5);
G: 840(5); H: 10,080(1), 840(2), 840(3);
I: 3,360(2), 280(3), 2,520(4); J: 6,720(1), 560(2)
13. week 1: 950; week 4: 940; week 7: 760; week 9: 910
15. week 1: 844; week 3: 844; week 6: 844; week 8: 844;
week 10: 184;

part period cost = \$135.60; lot-for-lot cost = \$200; EOQ cost = \$179.36

17. weekly utilizations: 1.15; .3; .925; 1.025; .45; .875; .55; 1.35; 1.025; 1.25; not sufficient
19. (a) one additional shipment to Dusseldorf

CHAPTER 15

1. (a) 602; 405; 227; 312; 711; 822
   (b) 20.7 minutes
3. (a) ACDB
   (b) ACDB
   (c) CADB
5. (a) BEFCAD
   (b) 5:30 P.M.
7. (a) AGECFBD
   (b) 5:50 P.M.
   (c) 385.71 minutes
9. (a) CGHTER
   (b) 11:37 A.M.
11. CBA
13. (a) ACB
    (b) ACB
    (c) CBA
15. (a) ACB
    (b) BAC
    (c) ACB or BAC
    (d) ABC or ACB
17. ADFBECA; 115 minutes per cycle (*Note:* Other answers are possible.)
19. DCAB
21. $ART = 4.3134$ weeks
23. 1–Bill, 2–Al, 3–Dean, 4–Carl; \$2,000
25. Bond–OSS, Smart–CIA, Hoover–KGB, Smiley–HMSS, Karlov–FBI; \$387
27. bottleneck = 60; several optimal assignments

CHAPTER 17

1. $n = 398, c = 7$
3. AQL = .04, LTPD = .12
5. $n = 52, c = 1,246$ hours
7. $\alpha = .1; \beta = .2$
9. curve B
11. AOQL = 3.5% at $p = .05$
13. $n = 315, c = 7$
15. UCL = .104; CL = .02; LCL = 0
17. (a) UCL = .126; CL = .057; LCL = 0
    (b) no
19. $\overline{X}$-chart for width: UCL = 37.4 in., CL = 36 in., LCL = 34.6 in.; R-chart for width: UCL = 5.076 in., CL = 2.4 in., LCL = 0 in.; $\overline{X}$-chart for height: UCL = 63.5 in., CL = 60 in., LCL = 56.5 in.; R-chart for height: UCL = 12.7 in., CL = 6 in., LCL = 0 in.

APPENDIX A

1. (a) \$26,235
   (b) \$45,885
3. \$60,864
5. \$114,912
7. 13 percent
9. (a) \$2,168
   (b) \$2,182
11. 15 percent
13. (a) \$2,000 per year
    (b) \$3,200; \$2,400; \$1,600; \$800
    (c) \$2,000; \$1,600; \$1,280; \$3,120
15. (a) B
    (b) C
17. (a) \$210,875
    (b) \$100,000; \$80,000; \$60,000; \$40,000; \$20,000
    (c) \$190,509
19. (a) \$11,286.46
    (b) \$11,069.26
21. 23 percent

INDEX